The Cambridge Hand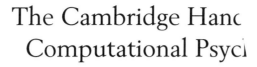 Computational Psyc

This book is a definitive reference source for the growing, increasingly important, and inter-disciplinary field of computational cognitive modeling, that is, computational psychology. It combines breadth of coverage with definitive statements by leading scientists in this field. Research in computational cognitive modeling (or, simply, computational psychology) explores the essence of cognition and various cognitive functionalities through developing detailed, process-based understanding by specifying computational mechanisms, structures, and processes. Given the complexity of the human mind and its manifestation in behavioral flexibility, process-based computational models may be necessary to explicate and elucidate the intricate details of the mind. The key to understanding cognitive processes is often in fine details. Computational models provide algorithmic specificity: detailed, exactly specified, and carefully thought-out steps, arranged in precise yet flexible sequences. These models provide both conceptual clarity and precision at the same time. This book substantiates this approach through overviews and many examples.

Ron Sun is professor of cognitive science at Rensselaer Polytechnic Institute. A well-known researcher in the field of cognitive science, Sun explores the fundamental structure of the human mind and aims for the synthesis of many interesting intellectual ideas into one coherent model of cognition. The goal is to form a generic cognitive architecture that captures a variety of cognitive processes in a unified way and, thus, to provide unified explanations for a wide range of cognitive data. To do so, for the last two decades, he has been advocating the use of hybrid connectionist-symbolic systems in developing cognitive models, and he has been developing theories of human skill learning and human everyday reasoning as the centerpieces of the cognitive architecture.

The Cambridge Handbook of Computational Psychology

Edited by

RON SUN

Rensselaer Polytechnic Institute

CAMBRIDGE UNIVERSITY PRESS
Cambridge, New York, Melbourne, Madrid, Cape Town, Singapore, São Paulo, Delhi

Cambridge University Press
32 Avenue of the Americas, New York, NY 10013-2473, USA

www.cambridge.org
Information on this title: www.cambridge.org/9780521674102

First published 2008

Printed in the United States of America

A catalog record for this publication is available from the British Library.

Library of Congress Cataloging in Publication Data

The Cambridge handbook of computational psychology / [edited by] Ron Sun.
    p. cm.
Includes bibliographical references and index.
ISBN 978-0-521-85741-3 (hardback) – ISBN 978-0-521-67410-2 (pbk.)
1. Cognition.   2. Cognitive science.   3. Philosophy of mind.   I. Sun, Ron, 1960–
II. Title: Handbook of computational psychology.
BF311.C36   2008
153.01′13–dc22   2007026278

ISBN   978-0-521-85741-3 hardback
ISBN   978-0-521-67410-2 paperback

Contents

Preface   *page* vii
List of Contributors   ix

PART I: INTRODUCTION   1

1 Introduction to Computational Cognitive Modeling   3
   Ron Sun

PART II: COGNITIVE MODELING PARADIGMS   21

2 Connectionist Models of Cognition   23
   Michael S. C. Thomas and James L. McClelland

3 Bayesian Models of Cognition   59
   Thomas L. Griffiths, Charles Kemp, and Joshua B. Tenenbaum

4 Dynamical Systems Approaches to Cognition   101
   Gregor Schöner

5 Declarative/Logic-Based Cognitive Modeling   127
   Selmer Bringsjord

6 Constraints in Cognitive Architectures   170
   Niels A. Taatgen and John R. Anderson

**PART III: COMPUTATIONAL MODELING OF VARIOUS COGNITIVE
FUNCTIONALITIES AND DOMAINS**   187

7 Computational Models of Episodic Memory   189
   Kenneth A. Norman, Greg Detre, and Sean M. Polyn

8   Computational Models of Semantic Memory   226
    Timothy T. Rogers

9   Models of Categorization   267
    John K. Kruschke

10 Micro-Process Models of Decision Making   302
    Jerome R. Busemeyer and Joseph G. Johnson

11 Models of Inductive Reasoning   322
    Evan Heit

12 Mental Logic, Mental Models, and Simulations of Human Deductive Reasoning   339
    Philip N. Johnson-Laird and Yingrui Yang

13 Computational Models of Skill Acquisition   359
    Stellan Ohlsson

14 Computational Models of Implicit Learning   396
    Axel Cleeremans and Zoltán Dienes

15 Computational Models of Attention and Cognitive Control   422
    Nicola De Pisapia, Grega Repovš, and Todd S. Braver

16 Computational Models of Developmental Psychology   451
    Thomas R. Shultz and Sylvain Sirois

17 Computational Models of Psycholinguistics   477
    Nick Chater and Morten H. Christiansen

18 Computational Models in Personality and Social Psychology   505
    Stephen J. Read and Brian M. Monroe

19 Cognitive Social Simulation   530
    Ron Sun

20 Models of Scientific Explanation   549
    Paul Thagard and Abninder Litt

21 Cognitive Modeling for Cognitive Engineering   565
    Wayne D. Gray

22 Models of Animal Learning and Their Relations to Human Learning   589
    Francisco J. López and David R. Shanks

23 Computational Modeling of Visual Information Processing   612
    Pawan Sinha and Benjamin J. Balas

24 Models of Motor Control   635
    Ferdinando A. Mussa-Ivaldi and Sara A. Solla

PART IV: CONCLUDING REMARKS   665

25 An Evaluation of Computational Modeling in Cognitive Science   667
    Margaret A. Boden

26 Putting the Pieces Together Again   684
    Aaron Sloman

Index   711

Preface

The goal of the *Cambridge Handbook of Computational Psychology* is to provide a definitive reference source for the rapidly growing, increasingly important, and strongly interdisciplinary field of computational cognitive modeling – that is, computational (and theoretical) psychology. It is part of the *Cambridge Handbook in Psychology* series.

This volume combines the breadth of coverage of the field with the authoritative statements by leading scientists in this discipline. It should thus appeal to researchers and advanced students working in this research field, as well as to researchers and advanced students working in cognitive science (in general), philosophy, experimental psychology, linguistics, anthropology, neuroscience, and artificial intelligence. For example, it could serve as a textbook for a course in a cognitive science program or, more generally, in social and behavioral sciences programs. This book could also be used by social science researchers, education researchers, intelligent systems engineers, and psychology and education software developers.

Models in cognitive science are often roughly divided into computational, mathematical, or verbal-conceptual models. Although each of these types of models has its role to play, in this volume, we are mainly concerned with computational modeling. The reason for this emphasis is that, at least at present, computational modeling appears to be the most promising approach in many ways and offers the flexibility and the expressive power that no other approaches can match. (Mathematical models may be viewed somehow as a subset of computational models, as they may lead readily to computational implementations.) A computational model may often be viewed as a theory of the phenomena it aims to capture and may be highly intellectually enlightening in this way.

Each chapter in this volume introduces and explains basic concepts, techniques, and findings for a major topic area within the realm of computational cognitive modeling (e.g., computational models and theories of a particular cognitive domain or functionality); sketches its history; assesses its successes and failures; and evaluates the directions of current and future research. This handbook thus provides quick overviews for experts in each topic area and also for researchers in allied topic areas. However, equally important, the book provides an introduction to the field of computational cognitive modeling (computational psychology). It discusses the methodologies of computational cognitive modeling and justifies its use in cognitive science. It introduces influential approaches, describing in detail these approaches and providing ample examples. Thus, this volume provides an entry point into the field for the next generation of researchers by supplying a text for courses for graduate students and upper-level undergraduate students and for self-study.

I would like to thank all the contributing authors. Many of them not only contributed chapters, but also participated in mutual reviews of draft chapters, thus helping to ensure the quality of this book.

I would like to thank all the reviewers of the chapters. The external reviewers include: Edward Wasserman, Gert Westermann, Frank Ritter, Robert Wray, Robert French, Roger Levy, Jeff Schrager, Michael J. Frank, Sam Gilbert, Kostas Arkoudas, Brad Love, Emo Todorov, Russ Burnett, Chris Schunn, Ernest Davis, Robert West, Paul Bello, Michael Schoelles, Robert Port, Mike Byrne, John Spencer, David Peebles, Robert Jacobs, and Maximilian Riesenhuber. The internal reviewers include: Thomas Shultz, David Shank, Paul Thagard, Aaron Sloman, Stellan Ohlsson, Tim Rogers, Stephen Read, Evan Heit, Nick Chater, and Ken Norman.

I would also like to thank the members of the advisory board, who contributed suggestions that made the volume more comprehensive and more interesting. The members of the advisory board include: Thomas Shultz, Wayne Gray, and Jay McClelland.

Finally, I would like to thank Phil Laughlin for inviting me to put together this volume. It has been a pleasure working with Eric Schwartz, Phil Laughlin, Armi Macaballug, Peggy Rote, and others at Cambridge University Press in the process of developing this book.

Ron Sun
Troy, New York

List of Contributors

JOHN R. ANDERSON
Department of Psychology
Carnegie Mellon University
5000 Forbes Avenue
Pittsburgh, PA 15213, USA
ja+@cmu.edu
http://act-r.psy.cmu.edu/people/ja/

BENJAMIN J. BALAS
Department of Brain and Cognitive
    Sciences
Massachusetts Institute of Technology
Cambridge, MA 02139, USA
bjbalas@mit.edu
http://web.mit.edu/bcs/bjbalas/www/

MARGARET A. BODEN
Centre for Cognitive Science, School of
    Science and Technology
University of Sussex
Brighton BN1 9QH, UK
m.a.boden@sussex.ac.uk
http://www.informatics.sussex.ac.uk/
    users/maggieb

TODD S. BRAVER
Department of Psychology

Washington University
St. Louis, MO 63139, USA
tbraver@wustl.edu
http://ccpweb.wustl.edu/braver.html

SELMER BRINGSJORD
Department of Cognitive Science and
    Department of Computer Science
Rensselaer Polytechnic Institute
Troy, NY 12180, USA
brings@rpi.edu
http://www.rpi.edu/~brings

JEROME R. BUSEMEYER
Department of Psychological and Brain
    Sciences
Indiana University
Bloomington, IN 47405, USA
jbusemey@indiana.edu
http://mypage.iu.edu/~jbusemey/
    home.html

NICK CHATER
Department of Psychology
University College London
Gower Street
London, WC1E 6BT, UK

n.chater@ucl.ac.uk
http://www.psychol.ucl.ac.uk/people/
    profiles/chater_nick.htm

MORTEN H. CHRISTIANSEN
Department of Psychology
Cornell University
Ithaca, NY 14853, USA
mhc27@cornell.edu
http://cnl.psych.cornell.edu/people/
    morten.html

AXEL CLEEREMANS
Department of Psychology
Université Libre de Bruxelles
50 avenue F. D. Roosevelt CP191,
    B1050
Bruxelles, Belgium
axcleer@ulb.ac.be
http://srsc.ulb.ac.be/axcWWW/
    axc.html

GREG DETRE
Department of Psychology
Princeton University
Green Hall, Washington Road
Princeton, NJ 08540, USA
gdetre@princeton.edu
http://compmem.princeton.edu

ZOLTÁN DIENES
Department of Psychology
University of Sussex
Brighton, East Sussex BN1 9RH, UK
dienes@sussex.ac.uk
http://www.lifesci.sussex.ac.uk/home/
    Zoltan_Dienes/

WAYNE D. GRAY
Cognitive Science Department
Rensselaer Polytechnic Institute
Troy, NY 12180, USA
grayw@rpi.edu
http://www.rpi.edu/~grayw

THOMAS L. GRIFFITHS
Department of Psychology
University of California, Berkeley
Berkeley, CA 94720, USA
tom_griffiths@berkeley.edu
http://cocosci.berkeley.edu/tom/

EVAN HEIT
Department of Psychology
University of California, Merced
Merced, CA 95344, USA
eheit@ucmerced.edu
http://faculty.ucmerced.edu/eheit/
    index.html

JOSEPH G. JOHNSON
Department of Psychology
Miami University
Oxford, OH 45056, USA
johnsojg@muohio.edu
http://www.users.muohio.edu/johnsojg/

PHILIP N. JOHNSON-LAIRD
Psychology Department
Princeton University
Princeton, NJ 08540, USA
phil@princeton.edu
https://weblamp.princeton.edu/~psych/
    psychology/research/johnson_laird

CHARLES KEMP
Department of Brain and Cognitive
    Sciences
Massachusetts Institute of Technology
Cambridge, MA 02139, USA
ckemp@mit.edu
http://www.mit.edu/~ckemp/

JOHN K. KRUSCHKE
Department of Psychological and Brain
    Sciences
Indiana University
1101 East 10th Street
Bloomington, IN 47405, USA
kruschke@indiana.edu
http://www.indiana.edu/~kruschke/

ABNINDER LITT
Cheriton School of Computer Science
University of Waterloo
Waterloo, ON N2L3G1, Canada
alitt@uwaterloo.ca
http://www.student.cs.uwaterloo.ca/~alitt/

FRANCISCO J. LÓPEZ
Departamento de Psicologia Basica
Universidad de Malaga
Campus de Teatinos

Malaga, Spain
frjlopez@uma.es

JAMES L. MCCLELLAND
Department of Psychology and Center
    for Mind, Brain and Computation
Stanford University
344 Jordan Hall, Bldg 420, 450 Serra
    Mall
Stanford, CA 94305, USA
jlm@psych.stanford.edu
http://www-psych.stanford.edu/~jlm/

BRIAN M. MONROE
Department of Psychology
University of Southern California
Los Angeles, CA 90089, USA
monroe@usc.edu
http://psychology.usc.edu/Monroe.php

FERDINANDO A. MUSSA-IVALDI
Department of Physiology
Northwestern University
Chicago, IL 60611, USA
sandro@northwestern.edu
http://www.northwestern.edu/nuin/fac/
    mussa-ivaldi.htm

KENNETH A. NORMAN
Department of Psychology
Princeton University
Green Hall, Washington Road
Princeton, NJ 08540, USA
knorman@princeton.edu
http://compmem.princeton.edu

STELLAN OHLSSON
Department of Psychology
University of Illinois at Chicago
1007 West Harrison Street
Chicago, IL 60607, USA
stellan@uic.edu
http://www.uic.edu/depts/psch/
    ohlson-1.html

NICOLA DE PISAPIA
Department of Psychology
Washington University
St. Louis, MO 63139, USA
ndepisap@artsci.wustl.edu
http://www.artsci.wustl.edu/~ndepisap

SEAN M. POLYN
Department of Psychology
University of Pennsylvania
3401 Walnut Street
Philadelphia, PA 19104, USA
polyn@psych.upenn.edu
http://polyn.com/struct/researchindex.html

STEPHEN J. READ
Department of Psychology
University of Southern California
Los Angeles, CA 90089, USA
read@usc.edu
http://www-rcf.usc.edu/~read/

GREGA REPOVŠ
Department of Psychology
Washington University
St. Louis, MO 63139, USA
grepovs@artsci.wustl.edu
http://iac.wustl.edu/~grepovs

TIMOTHY T. ROGERS
Department of Psychology
524 WJ Brogden Hall
University of Wisconsin-Madison
Madison, WI 53706, USA
ttrogers@wisc.edu
http://psych.wisc.edu/Rogers/

GREGOR SCHÖNER
Institut für Neuroinformatik
Ruhr-Universität Bochum
44780 Bochum, Germany
gregor.schoener@neuroinformatik.ruhr-
    uni-bochum.de
http://www.neuroinformatik.rub.de/thbio/
    members/profil/Schoener/index.html

DAVID R. SHANKS
Department of Psychology
University College London
Gower Street
London WC1E 6BT, UK
d.shanks@ucl.ac.uk
http://www.psychol.ucl.ac.uk/david.shanks/
    Shanks.html

THOMAS R. SHULTZ
Department of Psychology and School
    of Computer Science

McGill University
1205 Penfield Avenue
Montreal, Quebec H3A 1B1, Canada
thomas.shultz@mcgill.ca
http://www.psych.mcgill.ca/perpg/fac/
    shultz/personal/default.htm

PAWAN SINHA
Department of Brain and Cognitive
    Sciences
Massachusetts Institute of Technology
Cambridge, MA 02139, USA
psinha@mit.edu
http://web.mit.edu/bcs/sinha/
    home.html

SYLVAIN SIROIS
School of Psychological Sciences
University of Manchester
Oxford Road
Manchester, M13 9PL, UK
sylvain.sirois@manchester.ac.uk
http://www.psych-sci.manchester
    .ac.uk/staff/SylvainSirois

AARON SLOMAN
School of Computer Science
University of Birmingham
Birmingham B15 2TT, UK
a.sloman@cs.bham.ac.uk
http://www.cs.bham.ac.uk/~axs/

SARA A. SOLLA
Department of Physiology
Northwestern University
Chicago, IL 60611, USA
solla@northwestern.edu
http://dept-www.physio.northwestern.edu/
    Secondlevel/Solla.html

RON SUN
Cognitive Science Department
Rensselaer Polytechnic Institute

Troy, NY 12180, USA
rsun@rpi.edu
http://www.cogsci.rpi.edu/~rsun

NIELS A. TAATGEN
Department of Psychology
Carnegie Mellon University
5000 Forbes Avenue
Pittsburgh, PA 15213, USA
taatgen@cmu.edu
http://www.ai.rug.nl/~niels

JOSHUA B. TENENBAUM
Department of Brain and Cognitive
    Sciences
Massachusetts Institute of Technology
Cambridge, MA 02139, USA
jbt@mit.edu
http://web.mit.edu/cocosci/josh.html

PAUL THAGARD
Philosophy Department
University of Waterloo
Waterloo, ON N2L3G1, Canada
pthagard@uwaterloo.ca
http://cogsci.uwaterloo.ca

MICHAEL S. C. THOMAS
Developmental Neurocognition
    Laboratory, School of Psychology
Birkbeck College, University of London
Malet Street
London WC1E 7HX, UK
m.thomas@bbk.ac.uk
http://www.bbk.ac.uk/psyc/staff/academic/
    mthomas

YINGRUI YANG
Cognitive Science Department
Rensselaer Polytechnic Institute
Troy, NY 12180, USA
yangyri@rpi.edu
http://www.cogsci.rpi.edu/

Part I

INTRODUCTION

This part provides a general introduction to the field of computational psychology and an overview of the book. It discusses the general methodology of computational cognitive modeling, and justifies its use in cognitive science and beyond.

CHAPTER 1

Introduction to Computational Cognitive Modeling

Ron Sun

Instead going straight into dealing with specific approaches, issues, and domains of computational cognitive modeling, it is appropriate to first take some time to explore a few general questions that lie at the very core of cognitive science and computational cognitive modeling. What is computational cognitive modeling? What exactly can it contribute to cognitive science? What has it contributed thus far? Where is it going? Answering such questions may sound overly defensive to the insiders of computational cognitive modeling and may even seem so to some other cognitive scientists, but they are very much needed in a volume like this because they lie at the very foundation of this field. Many insiders and outsiders alike would like to take a balanced and rational look at these questions without indulging in excessive cheerleading, which, as one would expect, happens sometimes among computational modeling enthusiasts.

However, given the large number of issues involved and the complexity of these issues, only a cursory discussion is possible in this introductory chapter. One may thus view this chapter as a set of pointers to the existing literature rather than a full-scale discussion.

1. What Is Computational Cognitive Modeling?

Research in computational cognitive modeling, or simply computational psychology, explores the essence of cognition (including motivation, emotion, perception, etc.) and various cognitive functionalities through developing detailed, process-based understanding by specifying corresponding computational models (in a broad sense) of representations, mechanisms, and processes. It embodies descriptions of cognition in computer algorithms and programs, based on computer science (Turing, 1950); that is, it imputes computational processes (in a broad sense) onto cognitive functions, and thereby it produces runnable computational models. Detailed simulations are then conducted based on the computational models (see, e.g., Newell, 1990; Rumelhart et al., 1986; Sun, 2002). Right from the beginning of the formal establishment of cognitive science around the late 1970s, computational modeling has been a mainstay of cognitive science.[1]

In general, models in cognitive science may be roughly categorized into computational, mathematical, or verbal-conceptual models (see, e.g., Bechtel & Graham, 1998). Computational models present process details using algorithmic descriptions. Mathematical models present relationships between variables using mathematical equations. Verbal-conceptual models describe entities, relations, and processes in rather informal natural languages. Each model, regardless of its genre, might as well be viewed as a *theory* of whatever phenomena it purports to capture (as argued before by, e.g., Newell, 1990; Sun, 2005).

Although each of these types of models has its role to play, the discussion in this volume is mainly concerned with computational modeling, including models based on computational cognitive architectures. The reason for this emphasis is that, at least at present, computational modeling (in a broad sense) appears to be the most promising approach in many respects, and it offers the flexibility and expressive power that no other approach can match, as it provides a variety of modeling techniques and methodologies, and supports practical applications of cognitive theories (Pew & Mavor, 1998). In this regard, note that mathematical models may be viewed as a subset of computational models, as normally they can readily lead to computational implementations (although some of them may be sketchy and lack process details).

Computational models are mostly process-based theories, that is, they are mostly directed at answering the question of how human performance comes about; by what psychological mechanisms, processes,

and knowledge structures; and in what ways exactly. In this regard, note that it is also possible to formulate theories of the same phenomena through so-called product theories, which provide an accurate functional account of the phenomena but do not commit to a particular psychological mechanism or process (Vicente & Wang, 1998). Product theories may also be called blackbox theories or input-output theories. Product theories do not make predictions about processes (even though they may constrain processes). Thus, product theories can be evaluated mainly by product measures. Process theories, in contrast, can be evaluated by using process measures when they are available and relevant (which are, relatively speaking, rare), such as eye movement and duration of pause in serial recall, or by using product measures, such as recall accuracy, recall speed, and so on. Evaluation of process theories using the latter type of measures can only be indirect, because process theories have to generate an output given an input based on the processes postulated by the theories (Vicente & Wang, 1998). Depending on the amount of process details specified, a computational model may lie somewhere along the continuum from pure product theories to pure process theories.

There can be several different senses of "modeling" in this regard, as discussed in Sun and Ling (1998). The match of a model with human cognition may be, for example, qualitative (i.e., nonnumerical and relative) or quantitative (i.e., numerical and exact). There may even be looser "matches" based on abstracting general ideas from observations of human behaviors and then developing them into computational models. Although different senses of modeling or matching human behaviors have been used, the overall goal remains the same, which is to understand cognition (human cognition in particular) in a detailed (process-oriented) way.

This approach of utilizing computational cognitive models for understanding human cognition is relatively new. Although earlier precursors might be identified, the major

---

1 The roots of cognitive science can, of course, be traced back to much earlier times. For example, Newell and Simon's early work in the 1960s and 1970s has been seminal (see, e.g., Newell & Simon, 1976). The work of Miller, Galanter, and Pribram (1960) has also been highly influential. See Chapter 25 in this volume for a more complete historical perspective (see also Boden, 2006).

developments of computational cognitive modeling have occurred since the 1960s. Computational cognitive modeling has since been nurtured by the Annual Conferences of the Cognitive Science Society (which began in the late 1970s), by the International Conferences on Cognitive Modeling (which began in the 1990s), as well as by the journals *Cognitive Science* (which began in the late 1970s), *Cognitive Systems Research* (which began in the 1990s), and so on.

From Schank and Abelson (1977) to Minsky (1981), a variety of influential symbolic "cognitive" models were proposed in artificial intelligence. They were usually broad and capable of a significant amount of information processing. However, they were usually not rigorously matched against human data. Therefore, it was hard to establish the cognitive validity of many of these models. Psychologists have also been proposing computational cognitive models, which are usually narrower and more specific. They were usually more rigorously evaluated in relation to human data. (An early example is Anderson's HAM (Anderson 1983)). Many such models were inspired by symbolic AI work at that time (Newell & Simon, 1976).

The resurgence of neural network models in the 1980s brought another type of model into prominence in this field (see, e.g., Rumelhart et al., 1986; Grossberg, 1982). Instead of symbolic models that rely on a variety of complex data structures that store highly structured pieces of knowledge (such as Schank's scripts or Minsky's frames), simple, uniform, and often massively parallel numerical computation was used in these neural network models (Rumelhart et al., 1986). Many of these models were meant to be rigorous models of human cognitive processes, and they were often evaluated in relation to human data in a quantitative way (but see Massaro, 1988).

Hybrid models that combine the strengths of neural networks and symbolic models emerged in the early 1990s (see, e.g., Sun & Bookman, 1994). Such models could be used to model a wider variety of cognitive phenomena because of their more diverse and thus more expressive representations (but see Regier, 2003, regarding constraints on models). They have been used to tackle a broad range of cognitive data, often (though not always) in a rigorous and quantitative way (see, e.g., Sun & Bookman, 1994; Sun, 1994; Anderson & Lebiere, 1998; Sun, 2002).

For overviews of some currently existing software, tools, models, and systems for computational cognitive modeling, see the following Web sites:

http://www.cogsci.rpi.edu/~rsun/arch.html
http://books.nap.edu/openbook.php?isbn= 0309060966
http://www.isle.org/symposia/cogarch/archabs.html.

The following Web sites for specific software, cognitive models, or cognitive architectures (e.g., Soar, ACT-R, and CLARION) may also be useful:

http://psych.colorado.edu/~oreilly/PDP++ /PDP++.html
http://www.cogsci.rpi.edu/~rsun/clarion.html
http://act-r.psy.cmu.edu/
http://sitemaker.umich.edu/soar/home
http://www.eecs.umich.edu/~kieras/epic.html.

2. What Is Computational Cognitive Modeling Good For?

There are reasons to believe that the goal of understanding the human mind strictly from observations of human behavior is ultimately untenable, except for small and limited task domains. The rise and fall of behaviorism is a case in point. This point may also be argued on the basis of analogy with physical sciences (see Sun, Coward & Zenzen, 2005). The key point is that the processes and mechanisms of the mind cannot be understood purely on the basis of behavioral experiments, with tests that inevitably amount to probing only relatively superficial features of human behavior, which are further obscured by individual/group differences and contextual factors. It would be extremely hard to understand the human mind in this way, just like it would be extremely hard to understand a complex computer system purely on the basis of testing its behavior, if we do not have any a priori ideas about the nature, inner working, and theoretical underpinnings of that system (Sun, 2005). For a simple example, in any experiment involving the human mind, there is a very large number of parameters that could influence the results, and these parameters are either measured or left to chance. Given the large number of parameters, many have to be left to chance. The selection of which parameters to control and which to leave to chance is a decision made by the experimenter. This decision is made on the basis of which parameters the experimenter thinks are important. Therefore, clearly, theoretical development needs to go hand in hand with experimental tests of human behavior.

Given the complexity of the human mind and its manifestation in behavioral flexibility, complex process-based theories, that is, computational models (in the broad sense of the term) are necessary to explicate the intricate details of the human mind. Without such complex process-based theories, experimentation may be blind – leading to the accumulation of a vast amount of data without any apparent purpose or any apparent hope of arriving at a succinct, precise, and meaningful understanding. It is true that even pure experimentalists may often be guided by their intuitive theories in designing experiments and in generating their hypotheses. It is reasonable to say, therefore, that they are in practice not completely blind. However, without detailed theories, most of the details of an intuitive (or verbal-conceptual) theory are left out of consideration, and the intuitive theory may thus be somehow vacuous or internally inconsistent, or otherwise invalid. These problems of an intuitive theory may not be discovered until a detailed model is developed (Sun, Coward, & Zenzen, 2005; Sun, 2005).

There are many reasons to believe that the key to understanding cognitive processes is often in the fine details, which only computational modeling can bring out (Newell, 1990; Sun, 2005). Computational models provide algorithmic specificity: detailed, exactly specified, and carefully thought-out steps, arranged in precise and yet flexible sequences. Therefore, they provide both conceptual clarity and precision. As related by Hintzman (1990), "The common strategy of trying to reason backward from behavior to underlying processes (analysis) has drawbacks that become painfully apparent to those who work with simulation models (synthesis). To have one's hunches about how a simple combination of processes will behave repeatedly dashed by one's own computer program is a humbling experience that no experimental psychologist should miss" (p. 111).

One viewpoint concerning the theoretical status of computational modeling and simulation is that they, including those based on cognitive architectures, should not be taken as theories. A simulation/model is a generator of phenomena and data. Thus, it is a theory-building tool. Hintzman (1990) gave a positive assessment of the role of simulation/model in theory building: "a simple working system that displays some properties of human memory may suggest other properties that no one ever thought of testing for, may offer novel explanations for known phenomena, and may provide insight into which modifications that next generation of models should include" (p. 111). That is, computational models are useful media for thought experiments and hypothesis generation. In particular, one may use simulations for exploring various possibilities regarding details of a cognitive process. Thus, a simulation/model may serve as a theory-building tool for developing future theories. A related view is that computational modeling and simulation are suitable for facilitating the precise instantiation of a preexisting verbal-conceptual theory (e.g., through exploring various possible details in instantiating the theory) and consequently the careful evaluation of the theory against data. A radically different position (e.g., Newell, 1990; Sun, 2005) is that a simulation/model may provide a theory. It is not the case that a simulation/model is limited to being built on top of an existing theory, being applied for the sake of generating data, being applied for the sake of validating an existing theory, or being applied for the sake of building a future theory. To the contrary, according to this view, a simulation/model may be a theory by itself. In philosophy of science, constructive empiricism (van Fraasen, 1980) may make a sensible philosophical foundation for computational cognitive modeling, consistent with the view of models as theories (Sun, 2005).

Computational models may be necessary for understanding a system as complex and as internally diverse as the human mind. Pure mathematics, developed to describe the physical universe, may not be sufficient for understanding a system as different and as complex as the human mind (cf. Luce, 1995; Coombs et al., 1970). Compared with scientific theories developed in other disciplines (e.g., in physics), computational cognitive modeling may be mathematically less elegant – but the point is that the human mind itself is likely to be less mathematically elegant compared with the physical universe (see, e.g., Minsky, 1985) and therefore an alternative form of theorizing is called for, a form that is more complex, more diverse, and more algorithmic in nature. Computational cognitive models provide a viable way of specifying complex and detailed theories of cognition. Consequently, they may provide detailed interpretations and insights that no other experimental or theoretical approach can provide.

In particular, a cognitive architecture denotes a comprehensive, domain-generic computational cognitive model, capturing the essential structures, mechanisms, and processes of cognition. It is used for broad, multiple-level, multiple-domain analysis of cognition (Sun, 2004; Sun, Coward, & Zenzen, 2005, Sun, 2005, 2007). It deals with componential processes of cognition in a structurally and mechanistically well defined way (Sun, 2004). Its function is to provide an essential framework to facilitate more detailed modeling and under-

standing of various components and processes of the mind. A cognitive architecture is useful because it provides a comprehensive initial framework for further exploration of many different cognitive domains and functionalities. The initial assumptions may be based on either available scientific data (e.g., psychological or biological data), philosophical thoughts and arguments, or ad hoc working hypotheses (including computationally inspired such hypotheses). A cognitive architecture helps to narrow down possibilities, provides scaffolding structures, and embodies fundamental theoretical postulates. The value of cognitive architectures has been argued many times before; see, for example, Newell (1990), Anderson and Lebiere (1998), Sun (2002), Anderson and Lebiere (2003), Sun (2004), Sun, Coward, and Zenzen (2005), and Sun (2005, 2007).[2]

As we all know, science in general often progresses from understanding to prediction and then to prescription (or control). Computational cognitive modeling potentially may contribute to all of these three phases of science. For instance, through process-based simulation, computational modeling may reveal dynamic aspects of cognition, which may not be revealed otherwise, and allows a detailed look at constituting elements and their interactions on the fly during performance. In turn, such understanding may lead to hypotheses concerning hitherto undiscovered or unknown aspects of cognition and may lead to predictions regarding cognition. The ability to make reasonably accurate predictions about cognition can further allow prescriptions or control, for example, by choosing appropriate environmental conditions for certain tasks or by choosing appropriate mental types for certain tasks or environmental conditions.

In summary, the utility and the value of computational cognitive modeling (including cognitive architectures) can be

---

2 For information about different existing cognitive architectures, see, for example, http://www.cogsci.rpi.edu/~rsun/arch.html. See also Sun (2006) for information on three major cognitive architectures.

**Table 1.1: A traditional
hierarchy of levels (Marr, 1982)**

Level	Object of analysis
1	Computation
2	Algorithms
3	Implementations

argued in many different ways (see Newell, 1990; Sun, 2002; Anderson & Lebiere, 2003). These models in their totality are clearly more than just simulation tools or programming languages of some sorts. They are theoretically pertinent because they represent theories in a unique and indispensable way. Cognitive architectures, for example, are broad theories of cognition in fact.

3. Multiple Levels of Computational Cognitive Modeling

A strategic decision that one has to make with respect to cognitive science is the level of analysis (i.e., level of abstraction) at which one models cognitive agents. Computational cognitive modeling can vary in terms of level of process details and granularity of input and output, and may be carried out at multiple levels. Let us look into this issue of multiple levels of computational cognitive modeling, drawing on the work of Sun, Coward, and Zenzen (2005).

Traditional theories of multilevel analysis hold that there are various levels each of which involves a different amount of computational details (e.g., Marr, 1982). In Marr's theory, first, there is the *computational theory* level, in which one is supposed to determine proper computation to be performed, its goals, and the logic of the strategies by which the computation is to be carried out. Second, there is the *representation and algorithm* level, in which one is supposed to be concerned with carrying out the computational theory determined at the first level and, in particular, the representation for the input and the output, and the algorithm for the transformation from the

input to the output. The third level is the *hardware implementation* level, in which one is supposed to physically realize the representation and algorithms determined at the second level. According to Marr, these three levels are only loosely coupled; that is, they are relatively independent. Thus, there are usually a wide array of choices at each level, independent of the other two. Some phenomena may be explained at only one or two levels. Marr (1982) emphasized the "critical" importance of formulation at the level of computational theory, that is, the level at which the goals and purposes of a cognitive process are specified and internal and external constraints that make the process possible are worked out and related to each other and to the goals of computation. His reason was that the nature of computation depended more on the computational problems to be solved than on the way the solutions were to be implemented. In his own words, "an algorithm is likely to be understood more readily by understanding the nature of the problem being solved than by examining the mechanism (and the hardware) in which it is embodied" (p. 27). Thus, he preferred a top-down approach – from a more abstract level to a more detailed level. See Table 1.1 for the three levels. It often appears that Marr's theory centered too much on the relatively minor differences in computational abstractions (e.g., algorithms, programs, and implementations; see Sun, Coward, & Zenzen, 2005; Dayan, 2003; Dawson, 2002). It also appears that his theory represented an oversimplification of biological reality (e.g., ignoring the species-specific or motivation-relevant representations of the environment and the close relationship between low-level implementations and high-level computation) and as a result represented an over-rationalization of cognition.

Another variant is Newell and Simon's three-level theory. Newell and Simon (1976) proposed the following three levels: (1) the knowledge level, in which why cognitive agents do certain things is explained by appealing to their goals and their knowledge, and by showing rational

Table 1.2: Another hierarchy of four levels (Sun, Coward, & Zenzen, 2005)

Level	Object of analysis	Type of analysis	Computational model
1	Inter-agent processes	Social/cultural	Collections of agents
2	Agents	Psychological	Individual agents
3	Intra-agent processes	Componential	Modular construction of agents
4	Substrates	Physiological	Biological realization of modules

connections between them; (2) the symbol level, in which the knowledge and goals are encoded by symbolic structures, and the manipulation of these structures implements their connections; and (3) the physical level, in which the symbol structures and their manipulations are realized in some physical form. (Sometimes, this three-level organization was referred to as "the classical cognitive architecture" (Newell, 1990).) The point being emphasized here was very close to Marr's view: What is important is the analysis at the knowledge level and then at the symbol level, that is, identifying the task and designing symbol structures and symbol manipulation procedures suitable for it. Once this analysis (at these two levels) is worked out, the analysis can be implemented in any available physical means.

In contrast, according to Sun, Coward, and Zenzen (2005), the differences (borrowed from computer programming) among "computation," algorithms, programs, and hardware realizations, and their variations, as have been the focus in Marr's (1982) and Newell and Simon's (1976) level theories, are relatively insignificant. This is because, first of all, the differences among them are usually small and subtle, compared with the differences among the processes to be modeled (that is, the differences among the sociological vs. the psychological vs. the intra-agent, etc.). Second, these different computational constructs are in reality closely tangled (especially in the biological world): One cannot specify algorithms without at least some considerations of possible implementations, and what is to be considered "computation" (i.e., what can be computed) relies on algorithms, especially

the notion of algorithmic complexity, and so on. Therefore, one often has to consider computation, algorithms, and implementation together somehow (especially in relation to cognition). Third, according to Sun, Coward, and Zenzen (2005), the separation of these computational details failed to produce any major useful insight in relation to cognition, but instead produced theoretical baggage. A reorientation toward a systematic examination of *phenomena*, instead of tools one uses for modeling them, is thus a step in the right direction.

The viewpoint of Sun, Coward, and Zenzen (2005) focused attention on the very phenomena to be studied and on their scopes, scales, degrees of abstractness, and so on. Thus, the differences among levels of analysis can be roughly cast as the differences among disciplines, from the most macroscopic to the most microscopic. These levels of analysis include the sociological level, psychological level, componential level, and physiological level. See Table 1.2 for these levels. Different levels of modeling may be established in exact correspondence with different levels of analysis.

First, there is the sociological level, which includes collective behavior of agents (Durkheim, 1895), inter-agent processes (Vygotsky, 1986), and sociocultural processes, as well as interaction between agents and their (physical and sociocultural) environments. Only recently, the field of cognitive science has come to grips with the fact that cognition is, at least in part, a social/cultural process (Lave, 1988; Vygotsky, 1986; Sun, 2006). To ignore the sociocultural process is to ignore a major underlying determinant of individual cognition. The lack of understanding of sociological processes may result in the lack of understanding of some major structures and constraints in cognition. Thus, any understanding of individual cognition can only be partial and incomplete when sociocultural processes are ignored or downplayed.[3]

The second level is the psychological level, which covers individual behaviors, beliefs, knowledge, concepts, and skills (as well as motivation, emotion, perception, and so on). In relation to the sociological level, one can investigate the relationship of individual beliefs, knowledge, concepts, and skills with those of the society and the culture, and the processes of change of these beliefs, knowledge, concepts, and skills, independent of or in relation to those of the society and the culture. At this level, one can examine human behavioral data and compare them with models and with insights from the sociological level and further details from the lower levels.

The third level is the componential level. In computational cognitive modeling, the computational process of an agent is mostly specified in terms of *components* of the agent, that is, in terms of intra-agent processes. Thus, at this level, one may specify a cognitive architecture and components therein. In the process of analysis, one specifies essential computational processes of each component as well as essential connections among various components. Thus, analysis of capacity (functional analysis) and analysis of components (structural analysis) become one and the same at this level. However, at this level, unlike at the psychological level, work is more along the line of structural analysis than functional analysis (whereas the psychological level is mostly concerned with functional analysis). At this level, one models cognitive agents in terms of components, with the theoretical language of a particular paradigm, for example, symbolic computation or connectionist networks, or their combinations (Sun

& Bookman, 1994); that is, one imputes a computational process onto a cognitive function. Ideas and data from the psychological level – the psychological constraints from above, which bear on the division of components and possible implementations of components, are among the most important considerations. This level may also incorporate biological/physiological observations regarding plausible divisions and implementations; that is, it can incorporate ideas from the next level down – the physiological level, which offers the biological constraints. This level results in cognitive *mechanisms*, although they are usually computational and abstract, compared with physiological-level specifications of details.

Although this level is essentially in terms of intra-agent processes, computational models developed therein may also be used to model processes at higher levels, including the interaction at a sociological level where multiple individuals are involved. This can be accomplished, for example, by examining interactions of multiple copies of individual agents (Sun, 2006).

The lowest level of analysis is the physiological level, that is, the biological substrate, or biological implementation, of computation (Dayan, 2003). This level is the focus of a range of disciplines, including physiology, biology, computational neuroscience, cognitive neuroscience, and so on. Although biological substrates are not among our major concerns here, they may nevertheless provide valuable input as to what kind of computation is likely employed and what a plausible architecture (at a higher level) should be like. The main utility of this level is to facilitate analysis at higher levels, that is, to use low-level information to narrow down, at higher levels, choices in selecting computational architectures and choices in implementing componential computation.

Although computational cognitive modeling is often limited to within a particular level at a time (inter-agent, agent, intra-agent, or substrate), this need not always be the case: Cross-level analysis and modeling could be intellectually highly enlightening

---

3 See Sun (2001, 2006) for a more detailed argument of the relevance of sociocultural processes to cognition and vice versa.

and might be essential to the progress of computational cognitive modeling in the future (Sun, Coward, & Zenzen, 2005; Dayan, 2003). These levels described earlier do interact with each other (e.g., constraining each other) and may not be easily isolated and tackled alone. Moreover, their respective territories are often intermingled, without clear-cut boundaries.

For instance, the cross-level link between the psychological and the neurophysiological level has been emphasized in recent years (in the form of cognitive neuroscience; see, e.g., LeDoux, 1992; Damasio, 1994; Milner & Goodale, 1995). For example, Wilson et al. (2000) presented a model of human subjects perceiving the orientation of the head of another person. They accounted for the empirical findings from psychological experiments with a model based on a population code of neurons in the visual cortex, and thus the underlying neural structures were used to explain a psychological phenomenon at a higher level. For another instance of cross-level research, the psychological and the social level may also be crossed in many ways to generate new insights into social phenomena on the basis of cognitive processes (e.g., Boyer & Ramble, 2001; Sun, 2006) and, conversely, to generate insights into cognitive phenomena on the basis of sociocultural processes (e.g., Hutchins, 1995; Nisbett et al., 2001). In all of these cases, shifting appropriately between levels when needed is a critical part of the work.

Beyond cross-level analysis, there may be "mixed-level" analysis (Sun, Coward, Zenzen, 2005). The idea of mixed-level analysis may be illustrated by the research at the boundaries of quantum mechanics. In deriving theories, physicists often start working in a purely classical language that ignores quantum probabilities, wave functions, and so forth, and subsequently overlay quantum concepts on a classical framework (Greene, 1999; Coward & Sun, 2004). The very same idea applies to mixing cognitive modeling and social simulation as well. One may start with purely social descriptions but then substitute cognitive principles and cog-

nitive process details for simpler descriptions of agents (e.g., Sun & Naveh, 2004). Relatedly, there has also been strong interplay between psychological models and neurophysiological models – for example, going from psychological descriptions to neurobiological details.

Note that Rasmussen (1986) proposed something similar to the view described above on levels. His hierarchy was a more general framework but had a number of constraining properties (see also Vicente & Wang 1998): (1) all levels deal with the same system, with each level providing a different description of the system; (2) each level has its own terms, concepts, and principles; (3) the selection of levels may be dependent on the observer's purpose, knowledge, and interest; (4) the description at any level may serve as constraints on the operation of lower levels, whereas changes at a higher level may be specified by the effects of the lower levels; (5) by moving up the hierarchy, one understands more the significance of some process details with regard to the purpose of the system; by moving down the hierarchy, one understands more how the system functions in terms of the process details; and (6) there is also a means–ends relationship between levels in a hierarchy.

Note also Ohlsson and Jewett's (1997) and Langley's (1999) idea of abstract cognitive model, which is relevant here as well. To guard against overinterpretation of empirical evidence and to avoid the (usually large) gaps between evidence and full-blown computational models, Ohlsson and Jewett (1997) proposed "abstract computational models," which were relatively abstract models that were designed to test a particular (high-level) hypothesis without taking a stand on all the (lower-level) details of a cognitive architecture. Similar ideas were also expressed by Langley (1999), who argued that the source of explanatory power of a model often lay at a higher level of abstraction.

In summary, there have been various proposals regarding multiple levels of computational cognitive modeling. Although details vary, the notion of multiple levels of cognitive modeling appears to be useful. It can be expected to be of importance for the further development of this field.

4. Success Stories of the Past

There have been quite a few success stories of computational cognitive modeling, in a practical or a theoretical sense. They include, among many others:

- the various models of developmental psychology, including the connec tionist models of verb past-tense learning and the controversies stemming from such models;
- the tutoring systems based on the ACT-R cognitive architecture; and
- the model of implicit and explicit learning based on the CLARION cognitive architecture.

For instance, computational models of child development have been successful in accounting for, and in explaining, fine-grained developmental proccsses. In terms of widespread impact and associated theoretical interests and controversies, computational models of verb past-tense learning may be ranked as being at the top of all computational cognitive models (see, e.g., Rumelhart et al., 1986).

Theoretically, successful development models have clarified a number of major issues. In developmental psychology, there is the dichotomy contrasting knowledge that the child acquires through interacting with the environment (nurture) with knowledge of phylogenic origin (nature). It was argued that mechanisms of gene expression and brain development did not allow for the detailed specification of neural networks in the brain as required by the nativist (nature) position. It has been argued that a more plausible role for innate knowledge is at the level of architectures and timing of development (see Chapter 16 in this volume). In this regard, neural network models have provided new ways of thinking about innateness. That is, instead of asking whether or not something is innate, one should ask how evolution constrains the emergence of a brain function during individual development. This kind of theorizing has benefited from the use of neural networks (as detailed in Chapter 16).

Developmental psychologists have also been debating the distinction between learning and development. A static neural network can only learn what is within its representational power. Thus, when static neural networks are used, it is assumed that the ultimate brain network topology has already been developed (even if initial weights are random). However, this assumption implies representational innateness, which has been argued to be implausible. An alternative is to use constructive neural network models that form their network topology as a result of their experience. Using constructive learning models also resolves the "paradox of development": It was argued that if learning was done by proposing and testing hypotheses, it was not possible to learn anything that could not already be represented. This argument becomes irrelevant in light of constructive learning models where learning mechanisms that construct representations are separate from the representation of domain-specific knowledge. A constructive model builds representational power that it did not previously possess. Thus, computational modeling suggests that development is functionally distinct from learning (as argued in Chapter 16).

Similarly, as another example, an interpretation of a broad range of skill learning data (including those from the implicit learning literature) was proposed based on the CLARION cognitive architecture (see Sun, Slusarz, & Terry, 2005; and Sun, 2002; see also Chapter 6 in this volume concerning cognitive architectures). At a theoretical level, this work explicates the interaction between implicit and explicit cognitive processes in skill learning, in contrast to the tendency of studying each type in isolation. It highlights the interaction between the two types of processes and its various effects on learning (including the so-called synergy effects; see Sun, 2002). At an empirical level, a model centered on such an interaction constructed based on CLARION was used to account for data in a variety of task domains: process control tasks, artificial grammar learning tasks, and serial reaction time tasks, as well as some much more complex task domains (such as Tower of Hanoi and Minefield Navigation). The model was able to explain data in these task domains, shedding light on some apparently contradictory findings (including some findings once considered as casting doubt on the theoretical status of implicit learning). Based on the data and the match between the CLARION architecture and the data, this work argues for an integrated theory/model of skill learning that takes into account both implicit and explicit processes, as the match pointed to the usefulness of incorporating both explicit and implicit processes in theorizing about cognition (Sun, Slusarz, & Terry, 2005). Moreover, it argues for a bottom-up approach (first learning implicit knowledge and then explicit knowledge on its basis) in an integrated theory/model of skill learning, which was radically different from the then-existing models (see Sun, 2002; see also Chapter 13 in this volume). So, in this case, the application of the computational cognitive architecture CLARION to the skill learning data helped to achieve a level of theoretical integration and explanation beyond the previous theorizing (Sun, Slusarz, & Terry, 2005; Sun, 2002). For yet another example of using cognitive architectures to provide theoretical interpretation and integration, see Meyer and Kieras (1997).

As a final example, a number of interesting tutoring systems have been constructed on the basis of the ACT-R cognitive architecture (Koedinger et al., 1997; see also Chapter 6 in this volume). These tutoring systems were based on the analysis of the task units that were necessary to achieve competence in a number of domains of mathematics and computer programming. These units were represented as production rules. A typical course involved on the order of 500 production rules. On the assumption that learning in these domains involved the acquisition of such production rules, it was possible to diagnose whether students had acquired such production rules and provide instructions to remedy any difficulties they might have with specific rules. This led to the design of tutoring systems that ran production rule models in parallel with a student and attempted to interpret the student behavior in terms of these rules. Such systems tried to find some sequence of production rules that produced the behavior exhibited by a student. The model-tracing process allowed the interpretation of student behavior, and in turn the interpretation controlled the tutorial interactions. Thus, such tutoring systems were predicated on the validity of the cognitive model and the validity of the attributions that the model-tracing process made about student learning. There have been a few assessments that established to some extent the effectiveness of these systems. The tutoring systems have been used to deliver instructions to more than 100,000 students thus far. They demonstrated the practical usefulness of computational cognitive modeling. Other examples of practical applications of computational cognitive modeling may be found in Pew and Mavor (1998), and many in the area of human-computer interaction.

5. Directions for the Future

Many accounts of the history and the current state of the art of computational cognitive modeling in different areas will be provided by the subsequent chapters in this volume. At this point, however, it may be worthwhile to speculate a little about future developments of computational cognitive modeling.

First, some have claimed that grand scientific theorizing has become a thing of the past. What remains to be done is filling in details and refining some minor points. Fortunately, many cognitive scientists believe otherwise. Indeed, many of them are pursuing integrative principles that attempt to explain data in multiple domains and in multiple functionalities (Anderson & Lebiere, 1998; Sun, 2002). In cognitive science, as in many other scientific fields, significant advances may be made through discovering (hypothesizing and confirming) deep-level principles that unify superficial explanations across multiple domains, in a way somewhat analogous to Einstein's theory that unified electromagnetic and gravitational forces, or String Theory, which aims to provide even further unifications (Green, 1999). Such theories are what cognitive science needs, currently and in the foreseeable future.

Integrative computational cognitive modeling may serve in the future as an antidote to the increasing specialization of scientific research. In particular, cognitive architectures are clearly going against the trend of increasing specialization, and thus constitute an especially effective tool in this regard. Cognitive scientists are currently actively pursuing such approaches and, hopefully, will be increasingly doing so in the future. In many ways, the trend of overspecialization is harmful, and thus the reversal of this trend by the means of computational cognitive modeling is a logical (and necessary) next step toward advancing cognitive science (Sun et al., 1999).

Second, although the importance of being able to reproduce the nuances of empirical data from specific psychological experiments is evident, broad functionality is also important (Newell, 1990). The human mind needs to deal with the full cycle that includes all of the followings: transducing signals, processing them, storing them, representing them, manipulating them, and generating motor actions based on them. In computational cognitive modeling, there is clearly a need to develop generic models of cognition that are capable of a wide range of cognitive functionalities, to avoid the myopia often resulting from narrowly scoped research (e.g., in psychology). In particular, cognitive architectures may incorporate all of the following cognitive functionalities: perception, categorization and concepts, memory, decision making, reasoning, planning, problem solving, motor control, learning, metacognition, motivation, emotion, and language and communication, among others. In the past, this issue often did not get the attention it deserved in cognitive science (Newell, 1990), and it remains a major challenge for cognitive science.

However, it should be clearly recognized that overgenerality, beyond what is minimally necessary, is always a danger in computational cognitive modeling and in developing cognitive architectures (Sun, 2007). It is highly desirable to come up with a well-constrained cognitive model with as few parameters as possible while accounting for as large a variety of empirical observations and phenomena as possible (Regier, 2003). This may be attempted by adopting a broad perspective – philosophical, psychological, and biological, as well as computational – and by adopting a multilevel framework going from sociological to psychological, to componential, and to physiological levels, as discussed before (and as argued in more detail in Sun, Coward, & Zenzen, 2005). Although some techniques have been developed to accomplish this, more work is needed (see, e.g., Sun & Ling, 1998; Regier, 2003; Sun, 2007).

Third, in integrative computational cognitive modeling, especially in developing cognitive architectures with a broad range of functionalities, it is important to keep in mind a broad set of desiderata. For example, in Anderson and Lebiere (2003), a set of desiderata proposed by Newell (1990) was used to evaluate a cognitive architecture versus conventional connectionist models. These desiderata include flexible behavior, real-time performance, adaptive behavior, vast knowledge base, dynamic behavior, knowledge integration, natural language, learning, development, evolution, and brain realization (see Newell 1990 for detailed explanations). In Sun (2004), another, broader set of desiderata was proposed and used to evaluate a larger set of cognitive architectures. These desiderata include ecological realism, bioevolutionary realism, cognitive realism, and many others (see Sun, 2004, for details). The advantages of coming up with and applying these sets of desiderata in computational cognitive modeling include: (1) avoiding overly narrow models and (2) avoiding missing important functionalities. We can reasonably expect that this issue will provide impetus for further research in the field of computational cognitive modeling in the future.

Fourth, the validation of process details of computational cognitive models has been a difficult, but extremely important, issue (Pew & Mavor, 1998). This is especially true for cognitive architectures, which often involve a great deal of intricate details that are almost impossible to disentangle. This issue needs to be better addressed in the future. There have been too many instances in the past of research communities rushing into some particular model or some particular approach toward modeling cognition and human intelligence without knowing exactly how much of the approach or the model was veridical or even useful. Theoretical (including mathematical) analysis often lagged behind. Thus, often without sufficient effort at validation and theoretical analysis, claims were boldly made about the promise of a certain model or a certain approach. Unfortunately, we have seen quite a few setbacks in the history of cognitive science as a result of this cavalier attitude toward the science of cognition. As in any other scientific field, painstakingly detailed work needs to be carried out in cognitive science before sweeping claims can be made. Not only is empirical validation necessary, theoretical analysis, including detailed mathematical and computational analysis, is also necessary to better understand models and modeling approaches before committing a large amount of resource (cf. Roberts & Pashler, 2000). In particular, sources of explanatory power need to be identified and analyzed (as called for in Sun & Ling, 1998). The issue of validation should be an important factor in directing future research in the field of computational cognitive modeling.

Related to that, the "design" space of computational cognitive models needs to be more fully explored (as pointed out in Sun & Ling, 1998; and Sloman & Chrisley, 2005). While we explore the behavioral space, in the sense of identifying the range and variations of human behavior, we also need to ex-plore the design space (that is, all the possibilities for constructing computational models) that maps onto the behavioral space, so that we may gain a better understanding of the possibilities and the limitations of modeling methodologies, and thereby open up new avenues for better capturing cognitive processes. This is especially important for cognitive architectures, which are complex and in which many design decisions need to be made, often without the benefit of a clear understanding of their full implications in computational or behavioral terms. More systematic exploration of the design space of cognitive models is thus necessary. Future research in this field should increasingly address this issue (Sloman & Chrisley, 2005).

Computational cognitive models may find both finer and broader applications, that is, both at lower levels and at higher levels, in the future. For example, some cognitive models found applications in large-scale simulations at a social and organizational level. For another example, some other cognitive models found applications in interpreting not only psychological data but also neuroimaging data (at a biological/ physiological level). A review commissioned by the National Research Council found that computational cognitive modeling had progressed to a degree that had made them useful in a number of application domains (Pew & Mavor, 1998). Another review (Ritter et al., 2003) pointed to similar conclusions. Both reviews provided interesting examples of applications of computational cognitive modeling. Inevitably, this issue will provide impetus for future research, not only in applied areas of computational cognitive modeling, but also in theoretical areas of computational cognitive modeling.

In particular, cognitive modeling may be profitably applied to social simulation. An important recent development in the social sciences has been agent-based social simulation.[4] So far, however, the two fields of

---

4 This approach consists of instantiating a population of agents, allowing the agents to run, and observing the interactions among them.

social simulation and cognitive modeling have been developed largely separately from each other (with some exceptions). Most of the work in social simulation assumed rudimentary cognition on the part of the agents. As has been argued before (e.g., Sun & Naveh, 2004; Sun, 2001, 2006; Zerubavel, 1997), social processes ultimately rest on the decisions of individuals, and thus understanding the mechanisms of individual cognition can lead to better theories of social processes. At the same time, by integrating social simulation and cognitive modeling, we may arrive at a better understanding of individual cognition. By modeling cognitive agents in a social context (as in cognitive social simulation), we may learn more about how sociocultural processes influence individual cognition. (See Chapter 19 in this volume regarding cognitive social simulation.)

Cross-level and mixed-level work integrating the psychological and the neurophysiological level, as discussed before, will certainly be an important direction for future research. Increasingly, researchers are exploring constraints from both psychological and neurobiological data. In so doing, the hope is that more realistic and better constrained computational cognitive models may be developed. (see, e.g., Chapter 7 in this volume for some such models.)

Finally, will this field eventually become a full-fledged discipline – computational psychology? This is an interesting but difficult issue. There are a number of open questions in this regard. For example, how independent can this field be from closely allied fields such as experimental psychology (and cognitive psychology in particular)? What will the relationship be between data generation and modeling? How useful or illuminating can this field be in shedding new light on cognition per se (as opposed to leading up to building intelligent systems)? And so on and so forth. These are the questions that will determine the future status of this field. So far, the answers to these questions are by no means clear-cut. They will have to be worked out in the future through the collective effort of the researchers of this field.

6. About This Book

The present volume, the *Cambridge Handbook of Computational Psychology*, is part of the *Cambridge Handbook in Psychology* series. This volume is aimed to be a definitive reference source for the growing field of computational cognitive modeling. Written by leading experts in various areas of this field, it is meant to combine breadth of coverage with depth of critical details.

This volume aims to appeal to researchers and advanced students in the computational cognitive modeling community, as well as to researchers and advanced students in cognitive science (in general), philosophy, experimental psychology, linguistics, cognitive anthropology, neuroscience, artificial intelligence, and so on. For example, it could serve well as a textbook for courses in social, cognitive, and behavioral sciences programs. In addition, this volume might also be useful to social sciences researchers, education researchers, intelligent systems engineers, psychology and education software developers, and so on.

Although this field draws on many humanity and social sciences disciplines and on computer science, the core of the approach is based on psychology, and this is a constant focus in this volume. At the same time, this volume is also distinguished by its incorporation of one contemporary theme in scientific research: how technology (namely computing technology) affects our understanding of the subject matter – cognition and its associated issues.

This volume contains 26 chapters, organized into 4 parts. The first part (containing the present chapter) provides a general introduction to the field of computational cognitive modeling. The second part, Cognitive Modeling Paradigms, introduces the reader to broadly influential approaches in cognitive modeling. These chapters have been written by some of those influential scholars who helped to define the field. The third part, Computational Modeling of Various Cognitive Functionalities and Domains, describes a range of computational modeling efforts that researchers in this field have undertaken regarding major cognitive functionalities and domains. The interdisciplinary combination of cognitive modeling, experimental psychology, linguistics, artificial intelligence, and software engineering in this field has required researchers to develop a novel set of research methodologies. This part surveys and explains computational modeling research, in terms of detailed computational mechanisms and processes, on memory, concepts, learning, reasoning, decision making, skills, vision, motor control, language, development, scientific explanation, social interaction, and so on. It contains case studies of projects, as well as details of significant models, in the computational cognitive modeling field. These chapters have been written by some of the best experts in these areas. The final part, Concluding Remarks, explores a range of issues associated with computational cognitive modeling and cognitive architectures, and provides some perspectives, evaluations, and assessments.

Although the goal has been to be as comprehensive as possible, the coverage of this volume is, by necessity, selective. The selectivity is made necessary by the length limitation, as well as by the amount of activities in various topic areas – areas with large amounts of scholarly activities need to be covered, inevitably at the cost of less active areas. Given the wide-ranging and often fast-paced research activities in computational cognitive modeling, it has never been hard to find interesting topics to include, but some less active topics had to be sacrificed.

As research in this field has developed at an exciting pace in recent years, the field is ready for an up-to-date reference to the best and latest work. What has been missing in this field is a true handbook. Such a handbook should bring together top researchers to work on chapters each of which summarizes and explains the basic concepts, techniques, and findings of a major topic area, sketching its history, assessing its successes and failures, and outlining the directions in which it is going. A handbook should also provide quick overviews for experts as well as provide an entry point into the field

for the next generation of researchers. The present volume has indeed been conceived with these broad and ambitious goals in mind.

7. Conclusions

It is clear that highly significant progress has been made in recent decades in advancing research on computational cognitive modeling (i.e., computational psychology). However, it appears that there is still a long way to go before we fully understand the computational processes of the human mind.

Many examples of computational cognitive modeling are presented in this volume. However, it is necessary to explore and study more fully various possibilities in computational cognitive modeling to further advance the state of the art in understanding the human mind through computational means. In particular, it would be necessary to build integrative cognitive models with a wide variety of functionalities, that is, to build cognitive architectures so that they can exhibit and explain the full range of human behaviors (as discussed earlier). Many challenges and issues need to be addressed, including those stemming from designing cognitive architectures, from validation of cognitive models, and from the applications of cognitive models to various domains.

It should be reasonable to expect that the field of computational cognitive modeling will have a profound impact on cognitive science, as well as on other related fields, such as linguistics, philosophy, experimental psychology, and artificial intelligence, both in terms of better understanding cognition and in terms of developing better (more intelligent) computational systems. As such, it should be considered a crucial field of scientific research, lying at the intersection of a number of other important fields. Through the collective effort of this research community, significant advances can be achieved, especially in better understanding the human mind.

Acknowledgments

This work was carried out while the author was supported in part by ARI grants DASW01-00-K-0012 and W74V8H-05-K-0002 (to Ron Sun and Bob Mathews). Thanks are due to Aaron Sloman and Frank Ritter for their comments on the draft.

References

Anderson, J. R. (1983). *The architecture of cognition.* Cambridge, MA: Harvard University Press.

Anderson, J. R., & Lebiere, C. (1998). *The atomic components of thought.* Mahwah, NJ: Lawrence Erlbaum.

Anderson, J. R., & Lebiere, C. (2003). The Newell Test for a theory of cognition. *Behavioral and Brain Sciences, 26,* 587–640.

Bechtel, W., & Graham, G. (Eds.). (1998). *A companion to cognitive science.* Cambridge, UK: Blackwell.

Boden, M. (2006). *Mind as machine: A history of cognitive science.* Oxford, UK: Oxford University Press.

Boyer, P., & Ramble, C. (2001). Congitive templates for religious concepts: Cross-cultural evidence for recall of counter-intuitive representations. *Cognitive Scicence, 25,* 535–564.

Coombs, C., Dawes, R., & Tversky, A. (1970). *Mathematical psychology.* Englewood Cliffs, NJ: Prentice Hall.

Coward, L., & Sun, R. (2004). Criteria for an effective theory of consciousness and some preliminary attempts. *Consciousness and cognition, 13,* 268–301.

Damasio, A. (1994). *Descartes' error: Emotion, reason and the human brain.* New York: Grosset/Putnam.

Dawson, M. (2002). Computer modeling of cognition: Levels of analysis. In L. Nadel (Ed.), *Encyclopedia of cognitive science* (pp. 635–638). London: Macmillan.

Dayan, P. (2003). Levels of analysis in neural modeling. In L. Nadel (Ed.), *Encyclopedia of cognitive science.* London: Macmillan.

Durkheim, W. (1895/1962). *The rules of the sociological method.* Glencoe, IL: Free Press.

Greene, G. (1999). *The elegant universe.* New York: Norton.

Grossberg, S. (1982). *Studies of mind and brain: Neural principles of learning, perception, development, cognition, and motor control.* Norwell, MA: Kluwer Academic Publishers.

Hintzman, D. (1990). Human learning and memory: Connections and dissociations. In *Annual review of psychology* (vol. 41, pp. 109–139). Palo Alto, CA: Annual Reviews.

Hutchins, E. (1995). How a cockpit remembers its speeds. *Cognitive Science, 19,* 265–288.

Koedinger K., Anderson, J. R., Hadley, W. H., & Mark, M. (1997). Intelligent tutoring goes to school in the big city. *International Journal of Artificial Intelligence in Education, 8,* 30–43.

Langley, P. (1999). Concrete and abstract models of category learning. In *Proceedings of the 21st Annual Conference of the Cognitive Science Society.* Mahwah, NJ: Lawrence Erlbaum.

Lave, J. (1988). *Cognition in practice.* Cambridge, UK: Cambridge University Press.

LeDoux, J.(1992). Brain mechanisms of emotion and emotional learning. *Current Opinion in Neurobiology, 2*(2), 191–197.

Luce, R. D. (1995). Four tensions concerning mathematical modeling in psychology. *Annual Review of Psychology, 46,* 1–26.

Marr, D. (1982). *Vision.* Cambridge, MA: MIT Press.

Massaro, D. (1988). Some criticisms of connectionist models of human performance. *Journal of Memory and Language, 27,* 213–234.

Meyer, D., & Kieras, D. (1997). A computational theory of executive cognitive processes and human multiple-task performance: Part 1, basic mechanisms. *Psychological Review, 104*(1), 3–65.

Miller, G., Galanter, E., & Pribram, K. (1960). *Plans and the structure of behavior.* New York: Holt, Rinehart, and Winston.

Milner, D., & Goodale, N. (1995). *The visual brain in action.* New York: Oxford University Press.

Minsky, M. (1981). A framework for representing knowledge. In J. Haugeland (Ed.), *Mind design* (pp. 95–128). Cambridge, MA: MIT Press.

Minsky, M. (1985). *The society of mind.* New York: Simon and Schuster.

Newell, A. (1990). *Unified theories of cognition.* Cambridge, MA: Harvard University Press.

Newell, A., & Simon, H. (1976). Computer science as empirical inquiry: Symbols and search. *Communication of ACM, 19,* 113–126.

Nisbett, R., Peng, K. Choi, I., & Norenzayan, A. (2001). Culture and systems of thought: Holistic versus analytic cognition. *Psychological Review, 108*(2), 291–310.

Ohlsson S., & Jewett, J. (1997). Simulation models and the power law of learning. In *Proceedings of the 19th Annual Conference of the Cognitive Science Society*. Mahwah, NJ: Lawrence Erlbaum.

Pew, R. W., & Mavor, A. S. (Eds). (1998). *Modeling human and organizational Behavior: Application to military simulations*. Washington, DC: National Academy Press.

Rasmussen, J. (1986). *Information processing and human-machine interaction: An approach to cognitive engineering*. Amsterdam: North-Holland.

Regier, T. (2003). Constraining computational models of cognition. In L. Nadel (Ed.), *Encyclopedia of cognitive science* (pp. 611–615). London: Macmillan.

Ritter, F. E., Shadbolt, N., Elliman, D., Young, R., Gobet, F., & Baxter, G. (2003). *Techniques for modeling human performance in synthetic environments: A supplementary review*. Dayton, OH: Human Systems Information Analysis Center, Wright-Patterson Air Force Base.

Roberts, S., & Pashler, H. (2000). How persuasive is a good fit? A comment on theory testing. *Psychological Review*, 107(2), 358–367.

Rumelhart, D., McClelland J., & the PDP Research Group. (1986). *Parallel distributed processing: Explorations in the microstructures of cognition*. Cambridge, MA: MIT Press.

Schank, R., & Abelson, R. (1977). *Scripts, plans, goals, and understanding: An inquiry into human knowledge structures*. Hillsdale, NJ: Lawrence Erlbaum.

Sloman, A., & Chrisley, R. (2005). More things than are dreamt of in your biology: Information processing in biologically-inspired robots. *Cognitive Systems Research*, 6(2), 145–174.

Sun, R. (1994). *Integrating rules and connectionism for robust commonsense reasoning*. New York: John Wiley.

Sun, R. (2001). Cognitive science meets multi-agent systems: A prolegomenon. *Philosophical Psychology*, 14(1), 5–28.

Sun, R. (2002). *Duality of the mind*. Mahwah, NJ: Lawrence Erlbaum.

Sun, R. (2004). Desiderata for cognitive architectures. *Philosophical Psychology*, 17(3), 341–373.

Sun, R. (2005). *Theoretical status of computational cognitive modeling*. Troy, NY: Technical report, Cognitive Science Department, Rensselaer Polytechnic Institute.

Sun, R. (Ed.). (2006). *Cognition and multi-agent interaction: From cognitive modeling to social simulation*. New York: Cambridge University Press.

Sun, R. (2007). The importance of cognitive architectures: An analysis based on CLARION. *Journal of Experimental and Theoretical Artificial Intelligence*, 19(2), 159–193.

Sun, R., & Bookman, L. (Eds.). (1994). *Computational architectures integrating Neural and symbolic processes*. Boston, MA: Kluwer Academic Publishers.

Sun, R., Coward, A., & Zenzen, M. (2005). On levels of cognitive modeling. *Philosophical Psychology*, 18(5), 613–637.

Sun, R., Honavar, V., & Oden, G. (1999). Integration of cognitive systems across disciplinary boundaries. *Cognitive Systems Research*, 1(1), 1–3.

Sun, R., & Ling, C. (1998). Computational cognitive modeling, the source of power and other related issues. *AI Magazine*, 19(2), 113–120.

Sun, R., & Naveh, I. (2004). Simulating organizational decision-making using a cognitively realistic agent model. *Journal of Artificial Societies and Social Simulation*, 7(3). June, 2004, http://jasss.soc.surrey.ac.uk/7/3/5.html

Sun, R., Slusarz, P., & Terry, C. (2005). The interaction of the explicit and the implicit in skill learning: A dual-process approach. *Psychological Review*, 112(1). 159–192.

Turing, A. M. (1950). Computing machinery and intelligence. *Mind*, 59(236), 433–460.

van Fraasen, B. (1980). *The scientific image*. Oxford, UK: Oxford University Press.

Vicente, K., & Wang, J. (1998). An ecological theory of expertise effects in memory recall. *Psychological Review*, 105(1), 33–57.

Vygotsky, L. (1986). *Mind in society*. Hillsdale, NJ: Lawrence Erlbaum Associates.

Wilson, H., Wilkinson, F., Lin, L., & Castilo, M. (2000). Perception of head orientation. *Vision Research*, 10, 459–472.

Zerubavel, E. (1997). *Social mindscape: An invitation to cognitive sociology*. Cambridge, MA: Harvard University Press.

Part II

COGNITIVE MODELING PARADIGMS

The chapters in Part II introduce the reader to broadly influential and foundational approaches to computational cognitive modeling. Each of these chapters describes in detail one particular approach and provides examples of its use in computational cognitive modeling.

CHAPTER 2

Connectionist Models of Cognition

Michael S. C. Thomas and James L. McClelland

1. Introduction

In this chapter, computer models of cognition that have focused on the use of neural networks are reviewed. These architectures were inspired by research into how computation works in the brain and subsequent work has produced models of cognition with a distinctive flavor. Processing is characterized by patterns of activation across simple processing units connected together into complex networks. Knowledge is stored in the strength of the connections between units. It is for this reason that this approach to understanding cognition has gained the name of *connectionism*.

2. Background

Over the last twenty years, connectionist modeling has formed an influential approach to the computational study of cognition. It is distinguished by its appeal to principles of neural computation to inspire the primitives that are included in its cognitive level models. Also known as artificial neural network (ANN) or parallel distributed processing (PDP) models, connectionism has been applied to a diverse range of cognitive abilities, including models of memory, attention, perception, action, language, concept formation, and reasoning (see, e.g., Houghton, 2005). Although many of these models seek to capture adult function, connectionism places an emphasis on learning internal representations. This has led to an increasing focus on developmental phenomena and the origins of knowledge. Although, at its heart, connectionism comprises a set of computational formalisms, it has spurred vigorous theoretical debate regarding the nature of cognition. Some theorists have reacted by dismissing connectionism as mere implementation of preexisting verbal theories of cognition, whereas others have viewed it as a candidate to replace the Classical Computational Theory of Mind and as carrying profound implications for the way human knowledge is acquired and represented; still others have viewed connectionism as a subclass of statistical models involved in universal function approximation and data clustering.

This chapter begins by placing connectionism in its historical context, leading up to its formalization in Rumelhart and McClelland's two-volume *Parallel Distributed Processing* (1986), written in combination with members of the Parallel Distributed Processing Research Group. Then, three important early models that illustrate some of the key properties of connectionist systems are discussed, as well as how the novel theoretical contributions of these models arose from their key computational properties. These three models are the Interactive Activation model of letter recognition (McClelland & Rumelhart, 1981; Rumelhart and McClelland, 1982), Rumelhart and McClelland's (1986) model of the acquisition of the English past tense, and Elman's (1991) simple recurrent network for finding structure in time. Finally, the chapter considers how twenty-five years of connectionist modeling has influenced wider theories of cognition.

2.1. *Historical Context*

Connectionist models draw inspiration from the notion that the information-processing properties of neural systems should influence our theories of cognition. The possible role of neurons in generating the mind was first considered not long after the existence of the nerve cell was accepted in the latter half of the nineteenth century (Aizawa, 2004). Early neural network theorizing can therefore be found in some of the associationist theories of mental processes prevalent at the time (e.g., Freud, 1895; James, 1890; Meynert, 1884; Spencer, 1872). However, this line of theorizing was quelled when Lashley presented data appearing to show that the performance of the brain degraded gracefully depending only on the quantity of damage. This argued against the specific involvement of neurons in particular cognitive processes (see, e.g., Lashley, 1929).

In the 1930s and 1940s, there was a resurgence of interest in using mathematical techniques to characterize the behavior of networks of nerve cells (e.g., Rashevksy, 1935). This culminated in the work of Mc-Culloch and Pitts (1943) who characterized the function of simple networks of binary threshold neurons in terms of logical operations. In his 1949 book *The Organization of Behavior*, Donald Hebb proposed a cell assembly theory of cognition, including the idea that specific synaptic changes might underlie psychological principles of learning. A decade later, Rosenblatt (1958, 1962) formulated a learning rule for two-layered neural networks, demonstrating mathematically that the *perceptron convergence rule* could adjust the weights connecting an input layer and an output layer of simple neurons to allow the network to associate arbitrary binary patterns. With this rule, learning converged on the set of connection values necessary to acquire any two-layer-computable function relating a set of input-output patterns. Unfortunately, Minsky and Papert (1969, 1988) demonstrated that the set of two-layer computable functions was somewhat limited – that is, these simple artificial neural networks were not particularly powerful devices. While more computationally powerful networks could be described, there was no algorithm to learn the connection weights of these systems. Such networks required the postulation of additional internal, or "hidden," processing units, which could adopt intermediate representational states in the mapping between input and output patterns. An algorithm (backpropagation) able to learn these states was discovered independently several times. A key paper by Rumelhart, Hinton, and Williams (1986) demonstrated the usefulness of networks trained using backpropagation for addressing key computational and cognitive challenges facing neural networks.

In the 1970s, serial processing and the Von Neumann computer metaphor dominated cognitive psychology. Nevertheless, a number of researchers continued to work on the computational properties of neural systems. Some of the key themes identified by these researchers included the role of competition in processing and learning (e.g., Grossberg, 1976; Kohonen, 1984), the properties of distributed representations (e.g., Anderson, 1977; Hinton & Anderson, 1981), and the possibility of

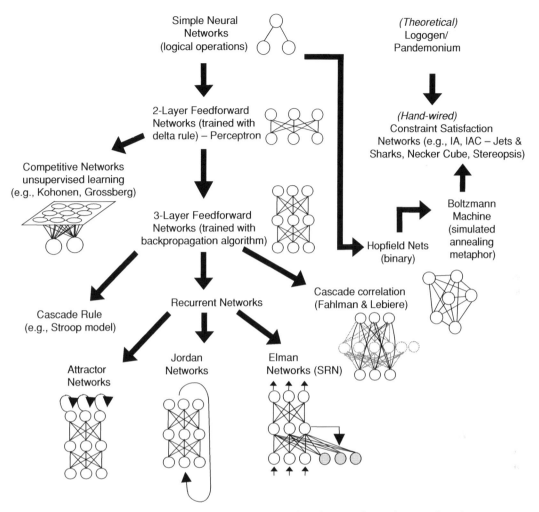

Figure 2.1. A simplified schematic showing the historical evolution of neural network architectures. Simple binary networks (McCulloch & Pitts, 1943) are followed by two-layer feedforward networks (perceptrons; Rosenblatt, 1958). Three subtypes then emerge: three-layer feedforward networks (Rumelhart & McClelland, 1986), competitive or self-organizing networks (e.g., Grossberg, 1976; Kohonen, 1984), and interactive networks (Hopfield, 1982; Hinton & Sejnowksi, 1986). Adaptive interactive networks have precursors in detector theories of perception (Logogen: Morton, 1969; Pandemonium: Selfridge, 1959) and in handwired interactive models (interactive activation: McClelland & Rumelhart, 1981; interactive activation and competition: McClelland, 1981; Stereopsis: Marr & Poggio, 1976; Necker cube: Feldman, 1981, Rumelhart et al., 1986). Feedforward pattern associators have produced multiple subtypes: for capturing temporally extended activation states, cascade networks in which states monotonically asymptote (e.g., Cohen, Dunbar, & McClelland, 1990), and attractor networks in which states cycle into stable configurations (e.g., Plaut & McClelland, 1993); for processing sequential information, recurrent networks (Jordan, 1986; Elman, 1991); and for systems that alter their structure as part of learning, constructivist networks (e.g., cascade correlation: Fahlman & Lebiere, 1990; Shultz, 2003). SRN = simple recurrent network.

content addressable memory in networks with attractor states, formalized using the mathematics of statistical physics (Hopfield, 1982). A fuller characterization of the many historical influences in the development of connectionism can be found in Rumelhart and McClelland (1986, Chapter 1), Bechtel and Abrahamsen (1991), McLeod, Plunkett, and Rolls (1998), and O'Reilly and Munakata (2000). Figure 2.1 depicts a selective schematic of this history and demonstrates the multiple types of neural network systems that have latterly come to be used in building models of cognition. Although diverse, they are unified on the one hand by the proposal that cognition comprises processes of constraint satisfaction, energy minimization, and pattern recognition, and on the other hand that adaptive processes construct the microstructure of these systems, primarily by adjusting the strengths of connections among the neuron-like processing units involved in a computation.

2.2. Key Properties of Connectionist Models

Connectionism starts with the following inspiration from neural systems: Computations will be carried out by a set of simple processing units operating in parallel and affecting each others' activation states via a network of weighted connections. Rumelhart, Hinton, and McClelland (1986) identified seven key features that would define a general framework for connectionist processing.

The first feature is the set of processing units u_i. In a cognitive model, these may be intended to represent individual concepts (such as letters or words), or they may simply be abstract elements over which meaningful patterns can be defined. Processing units are often distinguished into input, output, and hidden units. In associative networks, input and output units have states that are defined by the task being modeled (at least during training), whereas hidden units are free parameters whose states may be determined as necessary by the learning algorithm.

The second feature is a state of activation (a) at a given time (t). The state of a set of units is usually represented by a vector of real numbers $a(t)$. These may be binary or continuous numbers, bounded or unbounded. A frequent assumption is that the activation level of simple processing units will vary continuously between the values 0 and 1.

The third feature is a pattern of connectivity. The strength of the connection between any two units will determine the extent to which the activation state of one unit can affect the activation state of another unit at a subsequent time point. The strength of the connections between unit i and unit j can be represented by a matrix W of weight values w_{ij}. Multiple matrices may be specified for a given network if there are connections of different types. For example, one matrix may specify excitatory connections between units and a second may specify inhibitory connections. Potentially, the weight matrix allows every unit to be connected to every other unit in the network. Typically, units are arranged into layers (e.g., input, hidden, output), and layers of units are fully connected to each other. For example, in a three-layer feedforward architecture where activation passes in a single direction from input to output, the input layer would be fully connected to the hidden layer and the hidden layer would be fully connected to the output layer.

The fourth feature is a rule for propagating activation states throughout the network. This rule takes the vector $a(t)$ of output values for the processing units sending activation and combines it with the connectivity matrix W to produce a summed or net input into each receiving unit. The net input to a receiving unit is produced by multiplying the vector and matrix together, so that

$$net_i = W \times a(t) = \sum_j w_{ij} a_j. \qquad (2.1)$$

The fifth feature is an activation rule to specify how the net inputs to a given unit are combined to produce its new activation state. The function F derives the new activation state

$$a_i(t+1) = F(net_i(t)). \qquad (2.2)$$

For example, F might be a threshold so that the unit becomes active only if the net input exceeds a given value. Other possibilities include linear, Gaussian, and sigmoid functions, depending on the network type. Sigmoid is perhaps the most common, operating as a smoothed threshold function that is also differentiable. It is often important that the activation function be differentiable because learning seeks to improve a performance metric that is assessed via the activation state whereas learning itself can only operate on the connection weights. The effect of weight changes on the performance metric therefore depends to some extent on the activation function. The learning algorithm encodes this fact by including the derivative of that function (see the following discussion).

The sixth key feature of connectionist models is the algorithm for modifying the patterns of connectivity as a function of experience. Virtually all learning rules for PDP models can be considered a variant of the Hebbian learning rule (Hebb, 1949). The essential idea is that a weight between two units should be altered in proportion to the units' correlated activity. For example, if a unit u_i receives input from another unit u_j, then if both are highly active, the weight w_{ij} from u_j to u_i should be strengthened. In its simplest version, the rule is

$$\Delta w_{ij} = \eta \, a_i a_j \qquad (2.3)$$

where η is the constant of proportionality known as the learning rate. Where an external target activation $t_i(t)$ is available for a unit i at time t, this algorithm is modified by replacing a_i with a term depicting the disparity of unit u_i's current activation state $a_i(t)$ from its desired activation state $t_i(t)$ at time t, so forming the delta rule:

$$\Delta w_{ij} = \eta \, (t_i(t) - a_i(t)) a_j. \qquad (2.4)$$

However, when hidden units are included in networks, no target activation is available for these internal parameters. The weights to such units may be modified by variants of the Hebbian learning algorithm (e.g., Contrastive Hebbian; Hinton, 1989; see Xie & Seung, 2003) or by the backpropagation of error signals from the output layer.

Backpropagation makes it possible to determine, for each connection weight in the network, what effect a change in its value would have on the overall network error. The policy for changing the strengths of connections is simply to adjust each weight in the direction (up or down) that would tend to reduce the error, and change it by an amount proportional to the size of the effect the adjustment will have. If there are multiple layers of hidden units remote from the output layer, this process can be followed iteratively: First, error derivatives are computed for the hidden layer nearest the output layer; from these, derivatives are computed for the next deepest layer into the network, and so forth. On this basis, the backpropagation algorithm serves to modify the pattern of weights in powerful multilayer networks. It alters the weights to each deeper layer of units in such a way as to reduce the error on the output units (see Rumelhart, Hinton, et al., 1986, for the derivation). We can formulate the weight change algorithm by analogy to the delta rule shown in equation 2.4. For each deeper layer in the network, we modify the central term that represents the disparity between the actual and target activation of the units. Assuming u_i, u_h, and u_o are input, hidden, and output units in a three-layer feedforward network, the algorithm for changing the weight from hidden to output unit is:

$$\Delta w_{oh} = \eta \, (t_o - a_o) \, F'(net_o) \, a_h \qquad (2.5)$$

where $F'(net)$ is the derivative of the activation function of the units (e.g., for the sigmoid activation function, $F'(net_o) = a_o(1 - a_o)$). The term $(t_o - a_o)$ is proportional to the negative of the partial derivative of the network's overall error with respect to the activation of the output unit, where the error E is given by $E = \sum_o (t_o - a_o)^2$. In this and the following equations, time t has been omitted for clarity.

The derived error term for a unit at the hidden layer is a product of three components: the derivative of the hidden unit's activation function multiplied by the sum across all the connections from that hidden unit to the output later of the error term on each output unit weighted by the derivative of the output unit's activation function $(t_o - a_o) F'(net_o)$ multiplied by the weight connecting the hidden unit to the output unit:

$$F'(net_h) \sum_o (t_o - a_o) F'(net_o) w_{oh}. \quad (2.6)$$

The algorithm for changing the weights from the input to the hidden layer is therefore:

$$\Delta w_{hi} = \eta \, F'(net_h) \sum_o (t_o - a_o)$$
$$\times F'(net_o) w_{oh} \, a_i. \quad (2.7)$$

It is interesting that the previous computation can be construed as a backward pass through the network, similar in spirit to the forward pass that computes activations. This is because it involves propagation of signals across weighted connections, this time from the output layer back toward the input. The backward pass, however, involves the propagation of error derivatives rather than activations.

It should be emphasized that a very wide range of variants and extensions of Hebbian and error-correcting algorithms have been introduced in the connectionist learning literature. Most importantly, several variants of backpropagation have been developed for training recurrent networks (Williams & Zipser, 1995); and several algorithms (including the Contrastive Hebbian Learning algorithm and O'Reilly's 1998 LEABRA algorithm) have addressed some of the concerns that have been raised regarding the biological plausibility of backpropagation construed in its most literal form (O'Reilly & Munakata, 2000).

The last general feature of connectionist networks is a representation of the environment with respect to the system. This is assumed to consist of a set of externally provided events or a function for generating such events. An event may be a single pattern, such as a visual input; an ensemble of related patterns, such as the spelling

of a word and its corresponding sound or meaning; or a sequence of inputs, such as the words in a sentence. A number of policies have been used for specifying the order of presentation of the patterns. These range from sweeping through the full set to random sampling with replacement. The selection of patterns to present may vary over the course of training but is often fixed. Where a target output is linked to each input, this is usually assumed to be simultaneously available. Two points are of note in the translation between PDP network and cognitive model. First, a representational scheme must be defined to map between the cognitive domain of interest and a set of vectors depicting the relevant informational states or mappings for that domain. Second, in many cases, connectionist models are addressed to aspects of higher-level cognition, where it is assumed that the information of relevance is more abstract than sensory or motor codes. This has meant that the models often leave out details of the transduction of sensory and motor signals, using input and output representations that are already somewhat abstract. We hold the view that the same principles at work in higher-level cognition are also at work in perceptual and motor systems, and indeed there is also considerable connectionist work addressing issues of perception and action, although these will not be the focus of the present chapter.

2.3. Neural Plausibility

It is a historical fact that most connectionist modelers have drawn their inspiration from the computational properties of neural systems. However, it has become a point of controversy whether these "brain-like" systems are indeed neurally plausible. If they are not, should they instead be viewed as a class of statistical function approximators? And if so, shouldn't the ability of these models to simulate patterns of human behavior be assessed in the context of the large number of free parameters they contain (e.g., in the weight matrix; Green, 1998)?

Neural plausibility should not be the primary focus for a consideration of connectionism. The advantage of connectionism, according to its proponents, is that it provides *better theories of cognition*. Nevertheless, we will deal briefly with this issue because it pertains to the origins of connectionist cognitive theory. In this area, two sorts of criticism have been leveled at connectionist models. The first is to maintain that many connectionist models either include properties that are not neurally plausible or omit other properties that neural systems appear to have. Some connectionist researchers have responded to this first criticism by endeavoring to show how features of connectionist systems might in fact be realized in the neural machinery of the brain. For example, the backward propagation of error across the same connections that carry activation signals is generally viewed as biologically implausible. However, a number of authors have shown that the difference between activations computed using standard feedforward connections and those computed using standard return connections can be used to derive the crucial error derivatives required by backpropagation (Hinton & McClelland, 1988; O'Reilly, 1996). It is widely held that connections run bidirectionally in the brain, as required for this scheme to work. Under this view, backpropagation may be shorthand for a Hebbian-based algorithm that uses bidirectional connections to spread error signals throughout a network (Xie & Seung, 2003).

Other connectionist researchers have responded to the first criticism by stressing the cognitive nature of current connectionist models. Most of the work in developmental neuroscience addresses behavior at levels no higher than cellular and local networks, whereas cognitive models must make contact with the human behavior studied in psychology. Some simplification is therefore warranted, with neural plausibility compromised under the working assumption that the simplified models share the same flavor of computation as actual neural systems. Connectionist models have succeeded in stimulating a great deal of progress in cognitive theory – and have sometimes generated radically different proposals to the previously prevailing symbolic theory – just given the set of basic computational features outlined in the preceding section.

The second type of criticism leveled at connectionism questions why, as Davies (2005) puts it, connectionist models should be reckoned any more plausible as putative descriptions of cognitive processes just because they are "brain-like." Under this view, there is independence between levels of description because a given cognitive level theory might be implemented in multiple ways in different hardware. Therefore, the details of the hardware (in this case, the brain) need not concern the cognitive theory. This functionalist approach, most clearly stated in Marr's three levels of description (computational, algorithmic, and implementational; see Marr, 1982) has been repeatedly challenged (see, e.g., Rumelhart & McClelland, 1985; Mareschal et al., 2007). The challenge to Marr goes as follows. Although, according to computational theory, there may be a principled independence between a computer program and the particular substrate on which it is implemented, in practical terms, different sorts of computation are easier or harder to implement on a given substrate. Because computations have to be delivered in real time as the individual reacts with his or her environment, in the first instance, cognitive level theories should be constrained by the computational primitives that are most easily implemented on the available hardware; human cognition should be shaped by the processes that work best in the brain.

The relation of connectionist models to symbolic models has also proved controversial. A full consideration of this issue is beyond the scope of the current chapter. Suffice to say that because the connectionist approach now includes a diverse family of models, there is no single answer to this question. Smolensky (1988) argued that connectionist models exist at a lower (but still cognitive) level of description than symbolic cognitive theories, a level that he called the *subsymbolic*. Connectionist models have sometimes been put forward as a way to implement symbolic production systems on neural architectures (e.g., Touretzky & Hinton, 1988). At other times, connectionist researchers have argued that their models represent a qualitatively different form of computation: Whereas under certain circumstances, connectionist models might produce behavior approximating symbolic processes, it is held that human behavior, too, only approximates the characteristics of symbolic systems rather than directly implementing them. Furthermore, connectionist systems incorporate additional properties characteristic of human cognition, such as content-addressable memory, context-sensitive processing, and graceful degradation under damage or noise. Under this view, symbolic theories are approximate descriptions rather than actual characterizations of human cognition. Connectionist theories should replace them both because they capture subtle differences between human behavior and symbolic characterizations, and because they provide a specification of the underlying causal mechanisms (van Gelder, 1991).

This strong position has prompted criticisms that in their current form, connectionist models are insufficiently powerful to account for certain aspects of human cognition – in particular, those areas best characterized by symbolic, syntactically driven computations (Fodor & Pylyshyn, 1988; Marcus, 2001). Again, however, the characterization of human cognition in such terms is highly controversial; close scrutiny of relevant aspects of language – the ground on which the dispute has largely been focused – lends support to the view that the systematicity assumed by proponents of symbolic approaches is overstated and that the actual characteristics of language are well matched to the characteristics of connectionist systems (Bybee & McClelland, 2005; McClelland et al., 2003). In the end, it may be difficult to make principled distinctions between symbolic and connectionist models. At a fine scale, one might argue that two units in a network represent variables, and the connection between them specifies a symbolic rule linking these variables. One might also argue that a production system in which rules are allowed to fire probabilistically and

in parallel begins to approximate a connectionist system.

2.4. The Relationship between Connectionist Models and Bayesian Inference

Since the early 1980s, it has been apparent that there are strong links between the calculations carried out in connectionist models and key elements of Bayesian calculations (see Chapter 3 in this volume on Bayesian models of cognition). The state of the early literature on this point was reviewed in McClelland (1998). There it was noted, first of all, that units can be viewed as playing the role of probabilistic hypotheses; that weights and biases play the role of conditional probability relations between hypotheses and prior probabilities, respectively; and that if connection weights and biases have the correct values, the logistic activation function sets the activation of a unit to its posterior probability given the evidence represented on its inputs.

A second and more important observation is that, in stochastic neural networks (Boltzmann machines and Continuous Diffusion Networks; Hinton & Sejnowski, 1986; Movellan & McClelland, 1993), a network's state over all of its units can represent a constellation of hypotheses about an input, and (if the weights and the biases are set correctly) that the probability of finding the network in a particular state is monotonically related to the probability that the state is the correct interpretation of the input. The exact nature of the relation depends on a parameter called temperature; if set to one, the probability that the network will be found in a particular state exactly matches its posterior probability. When temperature is gradually reduced to zero, the network will end up in the most probable state, thus performing optimal perceptual inference (Hinton & Sejnowski, 1983). It is also known that backpropagation can learn weights that allow Bayes-optimal estimation of outputs given inputs (MacKay, 1992) and that the Boltzmann machine learning algorithm (Ackley, Hinton, & Sejnowski, 1985; Movellan & McClelland,

1993) can learn to produce correct conditional distributions of outputs given inputs. The algorithm is slow but there has been recent progress producing substantial speedups that achieve outstanding performance on benchmark data sets (Hinton & Salakhutdinov, 2006).

3. Three Illustrative Models

In this section, we outline three of the landmark models in the emergence of connectionist theories of cognition. The models serve to illustrate the key principles of connectionism and demonstrate how these principles are relevant to explaining behavior in ways that were different from other prior approaches. The contribution of these models was twofold: they were better suited than alternative approaches to capturing the actual characteristics of human cognition, usually on the basis of their context sensitive processing properties; and compared to existing accounts, they offered a sharper set of tools to drive theoretical progress and to stimulate empirical data collection. Each of these models significantly advanced its field.

3.1. *An Interactive Activation Model of Context Effects in Letter Perception (McClelland & Rumelhart, 1981, Rumelhart & McClelland, 1982)*

The interactive activation model of letter perception illustrates two interrelated ideas. The first is that connectionist models naturally capture a graded constraint satisfaction process in which the influences of many different types of information are simultaneously integrated in determining, for example, the identity of a letter in a word. The second idea is that the computation of a perceptual representation of the current input (in this case, a word) involves the simultaneous and mutual influence of representations at *multiple levels of abstraction* – this is a core idea of parallel distributed processing.

The interactive activation model addressed a puzzle in word recognition. By

the late 1970s, it had long been known that people were better at recognizing letters presented in words than letters presented in random letter sequences. Reicher (1969) demonstrated that this was not the result of tending to guess letters that would make letter strings into words. He presented target letters in words, in unpronounceable nonwords, or on their own. The stimuli were then followed by a pattern mask, after which participants were presented with a forced choice between two letters in a given position. Importantly, both alternatives were equally plausible. Thus, the participant might be presented with WOOD and asked whether the third letter was O or R. As expected, forced-choice performance was more accurate for letters in words than for letters in nonwords or letters presented on their own. Moreover, the benefit of surrounding context was also conferred by pronounceable pseudowords (e.g., recognizing the P in SPET) compared with random letter strings, suggesting that subjects were able to bring to bear rules regarding the orthographic legality of letter strings during recognition.

Rumelhart and McClelland (Rumelhart & McClelland, 1981; Rumelhart & McClelland, 1982) took the contextual advantage of words and pseudowords on letter recognition to indicate the operation of *top-down* processing. Previous theories had put forward the idea that letter and word recognition might be construed in terms of detectors that collect evidence consistent with the presence of their assigned letter or word in the input (Morton, 1969; Selfridge, 1959). Influenced by these theories, Rumelhart and McClelland built a computational simulation in which the perception of letters resulted from excitatory and inhibitory interactions of detectors for visual features. Importantly, the detectors were organized into different layers for letter features, letters and words, and detectors could influence each other both in a bottom-up and a top-down manner.

Figure 2.2 illustrates the structure of the Interactive Activation (IA) model, both at the macro level (left) and for a small section of the model at a finer level (right).

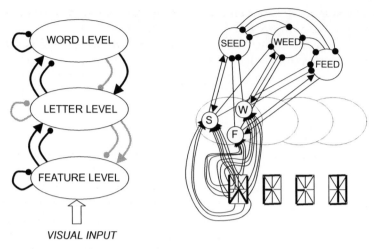

VISUAL INPUT

Figure 2.2. Interactive Activation model of context effects in letter recognition (McClelland & Rumelhart, 1981, 1982). Pointed arrows are excitatory connections, circular headed arrows are inhibitory connections. *Left*: macro view (connections in gray were set to zero in implemented model). *Right*: micro view for the connections from the feature level to the first letter position for the letters S, W, and F (only excitatory connections shown) and from the first letter position to the word units SEED, WEED, and FEED (all connections shown).

The explicit motivation for the structure of the IA was neural: "[We] have adopted the approach of formulating the model in terms similar to the way in which such a process might actually be carried out in a neural or neural-like system" (McClelland & Rumelhart, 1981, p. 387). There were three main assumptions of the IA model: (1) Perceptual processing takes place in a system in which there are several levels of processing, each of which forms a representation of the input at a different level of abstraction; (2) visual perception involves parallel processing, both of the four letters in each word and of all levels of abstraction simultaneously; and (3) perception is an interactive process in which conceptually driven and data driven processing provide multiple, simultaneously acting constraints that combine to determine what is perceived.

The activation states of the system were simulated by a sequence of discrete time steps. Each unit combined its activation on the previous time step, its excitatory influences, its inhibitory influences, and a decay factor to determine its activation on the next

time step. Connectivity was set at unitary values and along the following principles. In each layer, mutually exclusive alternatives should inhibit each other. Each unit in a layer excited all units with which it was consistent and inhibited all those with which it was inconsistent in the layer immediately above. Thus, in Figure 2.2, the first-position W letter unit has an excitatory connection to the WEED word unit but an inhibitory connection to the SEED and FEED word units. Similarly, a unit excited all units with which it was consistent and inhibited all those with which it was inconsistent in the layer immediately below. However, in the final implementation, top-down word-to-letter inhibition and within-layer letter-to-letter inhibition were set to zero (gray arrows, Figure 2.2).

The model was constructed to recognize letters in four-letter strings. The full set of possible letters was duplicated for each letter position, and a set of 1,179 word units was created to represent the corpus of four-letter words. Word units were given base rate activation states at the beginning of processing to reflect their different frequencies.

A trial began by clamping the feature units to the appropriate states to represent a letter string and then observing the dynamic change in activation through the network. Conditions were included to allow the simulation of stimulus masking and degraded stimulus quality. Finally, a probabilistic response mechanism was added to generate responses from the letter level, based on the relative activation states of the letter pool in each position.

The model successfully captured the greater accuracy of letter detection for letters appearing in words and pseudowords compared with random strings or in isolation. Moreover, it simulated a variety of empirical findings on the effect of masking and stimulus quality, and of changing the timing of the availability of context. The results on the contextual effects of pseudowords are particularly interesting, because the model only contains word units and letter units and has no explicit representation of orthographic rules. Let us say on a given trial, the subject is required to recognize the second letter in the string SPET. In this case, the string will produce bottom-up excitation of the word units for SPAT, SPIT, and SPOT, which each share three letters. In turn, the word units will propagate top-down activation, reinforcing activation of the letter P and so facilitating its recognition. Were this letter to be presented in the string XPQJ, no word units could offer similar top-down activation, hence the relative facilitation of the pseudoword. Interestingly, although these top-down "gang" effects produced facilitation of letters contained in orthographically legal nonword strings, the model demonstrated that they also produced facilitation in orthographically illegal, unpronounceable letter strings, such as SPCT. Here, the same gang of SPAT, SPIT, and SPOT produce top-down support. Rumelhart and McClelland (1982) reported empirical support for this novel prediction. Therefore, although the model behaved *as if it contained orthographic rules influencing recognition*, it did not in fact do so because continued contextual facilitation could be demonstrated for strings that had

gang support but violated the orthographic rules.

There are two specific points to note regarding the IA model. First, this early connectionist model was not adaptive – connectivity was set by hand. Although the model's behavior was shaped by the statistical properties of the language it processed, these properties were built into the structure of the system in terms of the frequency of occurrence of letters and letter combinations in the words. Second, the idea of bottom-up excitation followed by competition among mutually exclusive possibilities is a strategy familiar in Bayesian approaches to cognition. In that sense, the IA bears similarity to more recent probability theory based approaches to perception (see Chapter 3 in this volume).

3.1.1. WHAT HAPPENED NEXT?

Subsequent work saw the principles of the IA model extended to the recognition of spoken words (the TRACE model: McClelland & Elman, 1986) and more recently to bilingual speakers, where two languages must be incorporated in a single representational system (see Thomas & van Heuven, 2005, for review). The architecture was applied to other domains where multiple constraints were thought to operate during perception, for example, in face recognition (Burton, Bruce, & Johnston, 1990). Within language, more complex architectures have tried to recast the principles of the IA model in developmental settings, such as Plaut and Kello's (1999) model of the emergence of phonology from the interplay of speech comprehension and production.

The more general lesson to draw from the interactive activation model is the demonstration of multiple influences (feature, letter, and word-level knowledge) working simultaneously and in parallel to shape the response of the system, as well as the somewhat surprising finding that a massively parallel constraint satisfaction process of this form can appear to behave as if it contains rules (in this case, orthographic) when no such rules are included in the processing structure. At the time, the model brought into question whether it was necessary to postulate rules as processing structures to explain regularities in human behavior. This skepticism was brought into sharper focus by our next example.

3.2. *On Learning the Past Tense of English Verbs (Rumelhart & McClelland, 1986)*

Rumelhart and McClelland's (1986) model of English past tense formation marked the real emergence of the PDP framework. Where the IA model used localist coding, the past tense model employed distributed coding. Where the IA model had handwired connection weights, the past tense model learned its weights via repeated exposure to a problem domain. However, the models share two common themes. Once more, the behavior of the past tense model will be driven by the statistics of the problem domain, albeit these will be carved into the model by training rather than sculpted by the modelers. Perhaps more importantly, we see a return to the idea that a connectionist system can exhibit rule-following behavior without containing rules as causal processing structures; but in this case, the rule-following behavior will be the product of learning and will accommodate a proportion of exception patterns that do not follow the general rule. The key point that the past tense model illustrates is how (approximate) conformity to the regularities of language – and even a tendency to produce new regular forms (e.g., regularizations like "thinked" or past tenses for novel verbs like "wugged") – can arise in a connectionist network without an explicit representation of a linguistic rule.

The English past tense is characterized by a predominant regularity in which the majority of verbs form their past tenses by the addition of one of three allomorphs of the "-ed" suffix to the base stem (walk/ walked, end/ended, chase/chased). However, there is a small but significant group of verbs that form their past tense in different ways, including changing internal vowels (swim/ swam), changing word final consonants (build/built), changing both internal vowels

and final consonants (think/ thought), and an arbitrary relation of stem to past tense (go/went), as well as verbs that have a past tense form identical to the stem (hit/hit). These so-called irregular verbs often come in small groups sharing a family resemblance (sleep/slept, creep/crept, leap/leapt) and usually have high token frequencies (see Pinker, 1999, for further details).

During the acquisition of the English past tense, children show a characteristic U-shaped developmental profile at different times for individual irregular verbs. Initially, they use the correct past tense of a small number of high-frequency regular and irregular verbs. Later, they sometimes produce "overregularized" past tense forms for a small fraction of their irregular verbs (e.g., thinked; Marcus et al., 1992), along with other, less frequent errors (Xu & Pinker, 1995). They are also able to extend the past tense "rule" to novel verbs (e.g., wug-wugged). Finally, in older children, performance approaches ceiling on both regular and irregular verbs (Berko, 1958; Ervin, 1964; Kuczaj, 1977).

In the early 1980s, it was held that this pattern of behavior represented the operation of two developmental mechanisms (Pinker, 1984). One of these was symbolic and served to learn the regular past tense rule, whereas the other was associative and served to learn the exceptions to the rule. The extended phase of overregularization errors corresponded to difficulties in integrating the two mechanisms, specifically, a failure of the associative mechanism to block the function of the symbolic mechanism. That the child comes to the language acquisition situation armed with these two mechanisms (one of them full of blank rules) was an a priori commitment of the developmental theory.

By contrast, Rumelhart and McClelland (1986) proposed that a single network that does not distinguish between regular and irregular past tenses is sufficient to learn past tense formation. The architecture of their model is shown in Figure 2.3. A phoneme-based representation of the verb root was recoded into a more distributed, coarser

Phonological representation of past tense

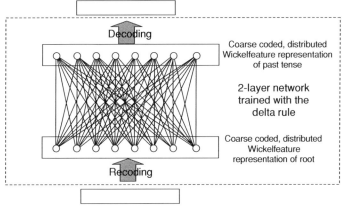

Figure 2.3. Two-layer network for learning the mapping between the verb roots and past tense forms of English verbs (Rumelhart & McClelland, 1986). Phonological representations of verbs are initially encoded into a coarse, distributed "Wickelfeature" representation. Past tenses are decoded from the Wickelfeature representation back to the phonological form. Later connectionist models replaced the dotted area with a three-layer feedforward backpropagation network (e.g., Plunkett & Marchman, 1991, 1993).

(more blurred) format, which they called "Wickelfeatures." The stated aim of this recoding was to produce a representation that (a) permitted differentiation of all of the root forms of English and their past tenses, and (b) provided a natural basis for generalizations to emerge about what aspects of a present tense correspond to what aspects of a past tense. This format involved representing verbs over 460 processing units. A two-layer network was used to associate the Wickelfeature representations of the verb root and past tense form. A final decoding network was then used to derive the closest phoneme-based rendition of the past tense form and reveal the model's response (the decoding part of the model was somewhat restricted by computer processing limitations of the machines available at the time).

The connection weights in the two-layer network were initially randomized. The model was then trained in three phases, in each case using the delta rule to update the connection weights after each verb root/past tense pair was presented (see Section 2.2, and Equation 4). In Phase 1, the network was trained on ten high-frequency verbs, two regular and eight irregular, in line with the greater proportion of irregular verbs among the most frequent verbs in English. Phase 1 lasted for ten presentations of the full training set (or "epochs"). In Phase 2, the network was trained on 410 medium frequency verbs, 334 regular and 76 irregular, for a further 190 epochs. In Phase 3, no further training took place, but 86 lower-frequency verbs were presented to the network to test its ability to generalize its knowledge of the past tense domain to novel verbs.

There were four key results for this model. First, it succeeded in learning both regular and irregular past tense mappings in a single network that made no reference to the distinction between regular and irregular verbs. Second, it captured the overall pattern of faster acquisition for regular verbs than irregular verbs, a predominant feature of children's past tense acquisition. Third, the model captured the U-shaped profile of development: an early phase of accurate performance on a small set of regular and irregular verbs, followed by a phase of over-regularization of the irregular forms, and finally recovery for the irregular verbs and performance approaching ceiling on both verb types. Fourth, when the model was presented with the low-frequency verbs on which it had not been trained, it was able to generalize the past tense rule to a substantial proportion of them, as if it had indeed learned a rule. Additionally, the model captured more fine-grained developmental patterns for subsets of regular and irregular verbs, and generated several novel predictions.

Rumelhart and McClelland explained the generalization abilities of the network in terms of the *superpositional* memory of the two-layer network. All the associations between the distributed encodings of verb root and past tense forms must be stored across the single matrix of connection weights. As a result, similar patterns blend into one another and reinforce each other. Generalization is contingent on the similarity of verbs at input. Were the verbs to be presented using an orthogonal, localist scheme (e.g., 420 units, 1 per verb), then there would be no similarity between the verbs, no blending of mappings, no generalization, and therefore no regularization of novel verbs. As the authors state, "It is the statistical relationships among the base forms themselves that determine the pattern of responding. The network merely reflects the statistics of the featural representations of the verb forms" (Rumelhart & McClelland, 1986, p. 267). Based on the model's successful simulation of the profile of language development in this domain and, compared with the dual mechanism model, its more parsimonious a priori commitments, Rumelhart and McClelland viewed their work on past tense morphology as a step toward a revised understanding of language knowledge, language acquisition, and linguistic information processing in general.

The past tense model stimulated a great deal of subsequent debate, not least because of its profound implications for the-

ories of language development (no rules!). The model was initially subjected to concentrated criticism. Some of this was overstated – for instance, the use of domain-general learning *principles* (such as distributed representation, parallel processing, and the delta rule) to acquire the past tense in a single network was interpreted as a claim that all of language acquisition could be captured by the operation of a single domain-general learning *mechanism*. Such an absurd claim could be summarily dismissed. As it stood, the model made no such claim: Its generality was in the processing principles. The model itself represented a domain-specific system dedicated to learning a small part of language. Nevertheless, a number of the criticisms were more telling: The Wickelfeature representational format was not psycholinguistically realistic; the generalization performance of the model was relatively poor; the U-shaped developmental profile appeared to be a result of abrupt changes in the composition of the training set; and the actual response of the model was hard to discern because of problems in decoding the Wickelfeature output into a phoneme string (Pinker & Prince, 1988).

The criticisms and following rejoinders were interesting in a number of ways. First, there was a stark contrast between the precise, computationally implemented connectionist model of past tense formation and the verbally specified dual-mechanism theory (e.g., Marcus et al., 1992). The implementation made simplifications but was readily evaluated against quantitative behavioral evidence; it made predictions and it could be falsified. The verbal theory by contrast was vague – it was hard to know how or whether it would work or exactly what behaviors it predicted (see Thomas, Forrester, & Richardson, 2006, for discussion). Therefore, it could only be evaluated on loose qualitative grounds. Second, the model stimulated a great deal of new multidisciplinary research in the area. Today, inflectional morphology (of which past tense is a part) is one of the most studied aspects of language processing in children, in adults, in second language learners, in adults with acquired brain damage, in children and adults with neurogenetic disorders, and in children with language impairments, using psycholinguistic methods, event-related potential measures of brain activity, functional magnetic resonance imaging, and behavioral genetics. This rush of science illustrates the essential role of computational modeling in driving forward theories of human cognition. Third, further modifications and improvements to the past tense model have highlighted how researchers go about the difficult task of understanding which parts of their model represent the key theoretical claims and which are implementational details. Simplification is inherent in modeling, but successful modeling relies on making the *right* simplifications to focus on the process of interest. For example, in subsequent models, (1) the Wickelfeature representation was replaced by more plausible phonemic representations based on articulatory features; (2) the recoding/two-layer network/decoding component of the network (the dotted rectangle in Figure 2.3) that was trained with the delta rule was replaced by a three-layer feedforward network trained with the backpropagation algorithm; and the (3) U-shaped developmental profile was demonstrated in connectionist networks trained with a smoothly growing training set of verbs or even with a fixed set of verbs (see, e.g., Plunkett & Marchman, 1991, 1993, 1996).

3.2.1. WHAT HAPPENED NEXT?
The English past tense model prompted further work within inflectional morphology in other languages (e.g., pluralization in German: Goebel & Indefrey, 2000; pluralization in Arabic: Plunkett & Nakisa, 1997), as well as models that explored the possible causes of deficits in acquired and developmental disorders, such as aphasia, Specific Language Impairment and Williams syndrome (e.g., Hoeffner & McClelland, 1993; Joanisse & Seidenberg, 1999; Thomas & Karmiloff-Smith, 2003b; Thomas, 2005). The idea that rule-following behavior could emerge in a developing system that also had to accommodate exceptions to the rules was

also successfully pursued via connectionist modeling in the domain of reading (e.g., Plaut, et al., 1996). This led to work that also considered various forms of acquired and developmental dyslexia.

For the past tense itself, there remains much interest in the topic as a crucible to test theories of language development. However, in some senses the debate between connectionist and dual-mechanism accounts has ground to a halt. There is much evidence from child development, adult cognitive neuropsychology, developmental neuropsychology, and functional brain imaging to suggest partial dissociations between performance on regular and irregular inflection under various conditions. Both connectionist and dual-mechanism models have been modified: the connectionist model to include the influence of lexical-semantics as well as verb root phonology in driving the production of the past tense form (Joanisse & Seidenberg, 1999; Thomas & Karmiloff-Smith, 2003b); the dual-mechanism model to suppose that regular verbs might also be stored in the associative mechanism, thereby introducing partial redundancy of function (Pinker, 1999). Both approaches now accept that performance on regular and irregular past tenses partly indexes different things – in the connectionist account, different underlying knowledge, in the dual-mechanism account, different underlying processes. In the connectionist theory, performance on regular verbs indexes reliance on knowledge about phonological regularities, whereas performance on irregular verbs indexes reliance on lexical-semantic knowledge. In the dual-mechanism theory, performance on regular verbs indexes a dedicated symbolic processing mechanism implementing the regular rule, whereas performance on irregular verbs indexes an associative memory device storing information about the past tense forms of specific verbs. Both approaches claim to account for the available empirical evidence. However, to date, the dual-mechanism account remains unimplemented, so its claim is weaker.

How does one distinguish between two theories that (a) both claim to explain the data but (b) contain different representational assumptions? Putting aside the different level of detail of the two theories, the answer is that it depends on one's preference for consistency with other disciplines. The dual-mechanism theory declares consistency with linguistics – if rules are required to characterize other aspects of language performance (such as syntax), then one might as well include them in a model of past tense formation. The connectionist theory declares consistency with neuroscience – if the language system is going to be implemented in the brain, then one might as well employ a computational formulism based on how neural networks function.

Finally, we return to the more general connectionist principle illustrated by the past tense model. So long as there are regularities in the statistical structure of a problem domain, a massively parallel constraint satisfaction system can learn these regularities and extend them to novel situations. Moreover, as with humans, the behavior of the system is flexible and context sensitive – it can accommodate regularities and exceptions within a single processing structure.

3.3. *Finding Structure in Time (Elman, 1990)*

In this section, the notion of the simple recurrent network and its application to language are introduced. As with past tense, the key point of the model will be to show how conformity to regularities of language can arise without an explicit representation of a linguistic rule. Moreover, the following simulations will demonstrate how learning can lead to the discovery of useful internal representations that capture conceptual and linguistic structure on the basis of the co-occurrences of words in sentences.

The IA model exemplified connectionism's commitment to parallelism: All of the letters of the word presented to the network were recognized in parallel, and processing occurred simultaneously at different levels of abstraction. But not all processing can be carried out in this way. Some human behaviors intrinsically revolve around temporal sequences. Language, action planning, goal-directed behavior, and reasoning about causality are examples of domains that rely on events occurring in sequences. How has connectionism addressed the processing of temporally unfolding events? One solution was offered in the TRACE model of spoken word recognition (McClelland & Elman, 1986), where a word was specified as a sequence of phonemes. In that case, the architecture of the system was duplicated for each time-slice and the duplicates wired together. This allowed constraints to operate over items in the sequence to influence recognition. In other models, a related approach was used to convert a temporally extended representation into a spatially extended one. For example, in the past tense model, all the phonemes of a verb were presented across the input layer. This could be viewed as a sequence if one assumed that the representation of the first phoneme represents time slice t, the representation of the second phoneme represents time slice $t + 1$, and so on. As part of a comprehension system, this approach assumes a buffer that can take sequences and convert them to a spatial vector. However, this solution is fairly limited, as it necessarily pre-commits to the size of the sequences that can be processed at once (i.e., the size of the input layer).

Elman (1990, 1991) offered an alternative and more flexible approach to processing sequences, proposing an architecture that has been extremely influential and much used since. Elman drew on the work of Jordan (1986) who had proposed a model that could learn to associate a "plan" (i.e., a single input vector) with a series of "actions" (i.e., a sequence of output vectors). Jordan's model contained recurrent connections permitting the hidden units to "see" the network's previous output (via a set of "state" input units that are given a copy of the previous output). The facility for the network to shape its next output according to its previous response constitutes a kind of memory. Elman's innovation was to build a recurrent facility into the internal units of the network, allowing it to compute statistical relationships across sequences of inputs

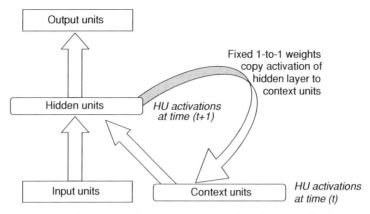

Figure 2.4. Elman's simple recurrent network architecture for finding structure in time (Elman, 1991, 1993). Connections between input and hidden, context and hidden, and hidden and output layers are trainable. Sequences are applied to the network element by element in discrete time steps; the context layer contains a copy of the hidden unit (HU) activations on the previous time step transmitted by fixed, 1-to-1 connections.

and outputs. To achieve this, first time is discretized into a number of slices. On time step t, an input is presented to the network and causes a pattern of activation on hidden and output layers. On time step $t + 1$, the next input in the sequence of events is presented to the network. However, crucially, a copy of the activation of the hidden units on time step t is transmitted to a set of internal "context" units. This activation vector is also fed to the hidden units on time step $t + 1$. Figure 2.4 shows the architecture, known as the *simple recurrent network* (SRN). It is usually trained with the backpropagation algorithm (see Section 2.3) as a multi-layer feedforward network, ignoring the origin of the information on the context layer.

Each input to the SRN is therefore processed in the context of what came before, but in a way subtly more powerful than the Jordan network. The input at $t + 1$ is processed in the context of the activity produced on the hidden units by the input at time t. Now consider the next time step. The input at time $t + 2$ will be processed along with activity from the context layer that is shaped by *two* influences:

(the input at $t + 1$ (shaped by the input at t)).

The input at time $t + 3$ will be processed along with activity from the context layer that is shaped by *three* influences:

(the input at $t + 2$ (shaped by the input at $t + 1$ (shaped by the input at t))).

The recursive flavor of the information contained in the context layer means that each new input is processed in the context of the *full history* of previous inputs. This permits the network to learn statistical relationships across sequences of inputs or, in other words, to find structure in time.

In his original 1990 article, Elman demonstrated the powerful properties of the SRN with two examples. In the first, the network was presented with a sequence of letters made up of concatenated words, for example:

MANYYEARSAGOABOYANDGIRLLIV-EDBYTHESEATHEYPLAYEDHAPPILY

Each letter was represented by a distributed binary code over five input units. The network was trained to predict the next letter in the sentence for 200 sentences constructed from a lexicon of fifteen words. There were 1,270 words and 4,963 letters. Because each word appeared in many sentences, the network was not particularly successful at predicting the next letter when it got to the end of each word, but within a word it was able to predict the sequences of letters. Using the accuracy of prediction as a measure, one could therefore identify which sequences in the letter string were words: They were the sequences of good prediction bounded by high prediction errors. The ability to extract words was of course subject to the ambiguities inherent in the training set (e.g., for *the* and *they*, there is ambiguity after the third letter). Elman suggested that if the letter strings are taken to be analogous to the speech sounds available to the infant, the SRN demonstrates a possible mechanism to extract words from the continuous stream of sound that is present in infant-directed speech. Elman's work has contributed to the increasing interest in the statistical learning abilities of young children in language and cognitive development (see, e.g., Saffran, Newport, & Aslin, 1996).

In the second example, Elman (1990) created a set of 10,000 sentences by combining a lexicon of 29 words and a set of short sentence frames (noun + [transitive] verb + noun; noun + [intransitive] verb). There was a separate input and output unit for each word, and the SRN was trained to predict the next word in the sentence. During training, the network's output came to approximate the transitional probabilities between the words in the sentences, that is, it could predict the next word in the sentences as much as this was possible. Following the first noun, the verb units would be more active as the possible next word, and verbs that tended to be associated with this particular noun would be more active than those that did not. At this point, Elman examined the similarity structure of the internal representations to discover how the network was achieving its prediction ability. He found that the internal representations were sensitive to the difference between nouns and verbs, and within verbs, to the difference between transitive and intransitive verbs. Moreover, the network was also sensitive to a range of semantic distinctions:

Not only were the internal states induced by nouns split into animate and inanimate, but the pattern for "woman" was most similar to "girl," and that for "man" was most similar to "boy." The network had learned to structure its internal representations according to a mix of syntactic and semantic information because these information states were the best way to predict how sentences would unfold. Elman concluded that the representations induced by connectionist networks need not be flat but could include hierarchical encodings of category structure.

Based on his finding, Elman also argued that the SRN was able to induce representations of entities that varied according to their context of use. This contrasts with classical symbolic representations that retain their identity regardless of the combinations into which they are put, a property called "compositionality." This claim is perhaps better illustrated by a second article Elman (1993) published two years later, called "Learning and Development in Neural Networks: The importance of Starting Small." In this later article, Elman explored whether rule-based mechanisms are required to explain certain aspects of language performance, such as syntax. He focused on "long-range dependencies," which are links between words that depend only on their syntactic relationship in the sentence and, importantly, not on their separation in a sequence of words. For example, in English, the subject and main verb of a sentence must agree in number. If the noun is singular, so must be the verb; if the noun is plural, so must be the verb. Thus, in the sentence "The *boy chases* the cat," *boy* and *chases* must both be singular. But this is also true in the sentence "The *boy* whom the boys chase *chases* the cat." In the second sentence, the subject and verb are further apart in the sequence of words but their relationship is the same; moreover, the words are now separated by plural tokens of the same lexical items. Rule-based representations of syntax were thought to be necessary to encode these long-distance relationships because, through the recursive nature of syntax, the words that have to agree in a sentence can be arbitrarily far apart.

(a) (b)

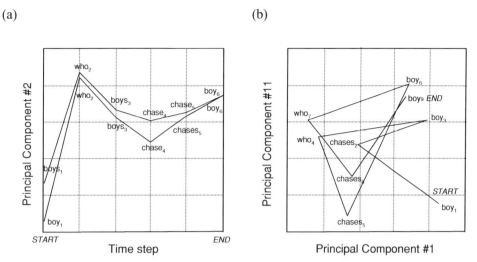

Figure 2.5. Trajectory of internal activation states as the simple recurrent network (SRN) processes sentences (Elman, 1993). The data show positions according to the dimensions of a principal components analysis (PCA) carried out on hidden unit activations for the whole training set. Words are indexed by their position in the sequence but represent activation of the same input unit for each word. (a) PCA values for the second principal component as the SRN processes two sentences, "*Boy who boys chase chases boy*" or "*Boys who boys chase chase boy;*" (b) PCA values for the first and eleventh principal components as the SRN processes "*Boy chases boy who chases boy who chases boy.*"

Using an SRN trained on the same prediction task as that previously outlined but now with more complex sentences, Elman (1993) demonstrated that the network was able to learn these long-range dependencies even across the separation of multiple phrases. If *boy* was the subject of the sentence, when the network came to predict the main verb *chase* as the next word, it predicted that it should be in the singular. The method by which the network achieved this ability is of particular interest. Once more, Elman explored the similarity structure in the hidden unit representations, using principal component analyses to identify the salient dimensions of similarity across which activation states were varying. This enabled him to reduce the high dimensionality of the internal states (150 hidden units were used) to a manageable number to visualize processing. Elman was then able to plot the *trajectories* of activation as the network altered its internal state in response to each subsequent input. Figure 2.5 depicts these trajectories as the network processes differ-

ent multi-phrase sentences, plotted with reference to particular dimensions of principal component space. This figure demonstrates that the network adopted similar states in response to particular lexical items (e.g., tokens of *boy*, *who*, *chases*), but that it modified the pattern slightly according to the grammatical status of the word. In Figure 2.5a, the second principal component appears to encode singularity/plurality. Figure 2.5b traces the network's state as it processes two embedded relative clauses containing iterations of the same words. Each clause exhibits a related but slightly shifted triangular trajectory to encode its role in the syntactic structure.

The importance of this model is that it prompts a different way to understand the processing of sentences. Previously, one would view symbols as possessing fixed identities and as being bound into particular grammatical roles via a syntactic construction. In the connectionist system, sentences are represented by trajectories through activation space in which the activation pattern for each word is subtly shifted according to the context of its usage. The implication is that the property of compositionality at the heart of the classical symbolic computational approach may not be necessary to process language.

Elman (1993) also used this model to investigate a possible advantage to learning that could be gained by initially restricting the complexity of the training set. At the start of training, the network had its memory reset (its context layer wiped) after every third or fourth word. This window was then increased in stages up to six to seven words across training. The manipulation was intended to capture maturational changes in working memory in children. Elman (1993) reported that *starting small* enhanced learning by allowing the network to build simpler internal representations that were later useful for unpacking the structure of more complex sentences (see Rohde & Plaut, 1999, for discussion and further simulations). This idea resonated with developmental psychologists in its demonstration of the way in which learning and maturation might interact in constructing cognition. It is an idea that could turn out to be a key principle in the organization of cognitive development (Elman et al., 1996).

3.3.1. WHAT HAPPENED NEXT?

Elman's simulations with the SRN and the prediction task produced striking results. The ability of the network to induce structured representations containing grammatical and semantic information from word sequences prompted the view that associative statistical learning mechanisms might play a much more central role in language acquisition. This innovation was especially welcome given that symbolic theories of sentence processing do not offer a ready account of language development. Indeed, they are largely identified with the nativist view that little in syntax develops. However, one limitation of the prior simulations is that the prediction task does not learn any categorizations over the input set. Although the simulations demonstrate that information important for language comprehension and

production can be induced from word sequences, neither task is actually performed. The learned distinction between nouns and verbs apparent in the hidden unit representations is tied up with carrying out the prediction task. But to perform comprehension, for example, the SRN would need to learn categorizations from the word sequences, such as deciding which noun was the agent and which noun was the patient in a sentence, regardless of whether the sentence was presented in the active ("the dog chases the cat") or passive voice ("the cat is chased by the dog"). These types of computations are more complex and the network's solutions typically more impenetrable. Although SRNs have borne the promise of an inherently developmental connectionist theory of parsing, progress on a full model has been slow (see Christiansen & Chater, 2001; and chapter 17 of this volume). Parsing is a complex problem – it is not even clear what the output should be for a model of sentence comprehension. Should it be some intermediate depiction of agent–patient role assignments, some compound representation of roles and semantics, or a constantly updating mental model that processes each sentence in the context of the emerging discourse? Connectionist models of parsing await greater constraints from psycholinguistic evidence.

Nevertheless, some interesting preliminary findings have emerged. For example, some of the grammatical sentences that the SRN finds the hardest to predict are also the sentences that humans find the hardest to understand (e.g., center embedded structures like "the mouse the cat the dog bit chased ate the cheese") (Weckerly & Elman, 1992). These are sequences that place maximal load on encoding information in the network's internal recurrent loop, suggesting that recurrence may be a key computational primitive in language processing. Moreover, when the prediction task is replaced by a comprehension task (such as predicting the agent/patient status of the nouns in the sentence), the results are again suggestive. Rather than building a syntactic structure for the whole sentence as a symbolic parser might, the network focuses on the predictability of lexical cues for identifying various syntactic structures (consistent with Bates and MacWhinney's [1989] Competition model of language development. The salience of lexical cues that each syntactic structure exploits and the processing load that each structure places on the recurrent loop makes them differentially vulnerable under damage. Here, neuropsychological findings from language breakdown and developmental language disorders have tended to follow the predictions of the connectionist account in the relative impairments that each syntactic construction should show (Dick et al., 2001; 2004; Thomas & Redington, 2004).

For more recent work and discussion of the use of SRNs in syntax processing, see Mayberry, Crocker, and Knoeferle (2005), Miikkulainen and Mayberry (1999), Morris, Cottrell, and Elman (2000), Rohde (2002), and Sharkey, Sharkey, and Jackson (2000). Lastly, the impact of SRNs has not been restricted to language. These models have been usefully applied to other areas of cognition where sequential information is important. For example, Botvinick and Plaut (2004) have shown how this architecture can capture the control of routine sequences of actions without the need for schema hierarchies, and Cleeremans and Dienes (chapter 14 in this volume) show how SRNs have been applied to implicit learning.

In sum, then, Elman's work demonstrates how simple connectionist architectures can learn statistical regularities over temporal sequences. These systems may indeed be sufficient to produce many of the behaviors that linguists have described with grammatical rules. However, in the connectionist system, the underlying primitives are context-sensitive representations of words and trajectories of activation through recurrent circuits.

4. Related Models

Before considering the wider impact of connectionism on theories of cognition, we should note a number of other related approaches.

4.1. *Cascade-Correlation and Incremental Neural Network Algorithms*

Backpropagation networks specify input and output representations, whereas in self-organizing networks, only the inputs are specified. These networks therefore include some number of internal processing units whose activation states are determined by the learning algorithm. The number of internal units and their organization (e.g., into layers) plays an important role in determining the complexity of the problems or categories that the network can learn. In pattern associator networks, too few units and the network will fail to learn; in self-organizing networks, too few output units and the network will fail to provide good discrimination between the categories in the training set. How does the modeler select in advance the appropriate number of internal units? Indeed, for a cognitive model, should this be a decision that the modeler gets to make?

For pattern associator networks, the cascade correlation algorithm (Fahlman & Lebiere, 1990) addresses this problem by starting with a network that has no hidden units and then adding in these resources during learning as it becomes necessary to carry on improving on the task. New hidden units are added with weights from the input layer tailored so that the unit's activation correlates with network error, that is, the new unit responds to parts of the problem on which the network is currently doing poorly. New hidden units can also take input from existing hidden units, thereby creating detectors for higher order features in the problem space.

The cascade correlation algorithm has been widely used for studying cognitive development (Mareschal & Shultz, 1996; Shultz, 2003; Westermann, 1998), for example, in simulating children's performance in Piagetian reasoning tasks (see Section 5.2). The algorithm makes links with the *constructivist* approach to development (Quartz, 1993; Quartz & Sejnowski, 1997), which argues that increases in the complexity of children's cognitive abilities are best explained by the recruitment of additional neurocomputational resources with age and experience. Related models that also use this "incremental" approach to building network architectures can be found in the work of Carpenter and Grossberg (Adaptive Resonance Theory; e.g., Carpenter & Grossberg, 1987a, 1987b) and in the work of Love and colleagues (e.g., Love, Medin, & Gureckis, 2004).

4.2. *Mixture-of-Experts-Models*

The preceding sections assume that only a single architecture is available to learn each problem. However, it may be that multiple architectures are available to learn a given problem, each with different computational properties. Which architecture will end up learning the problem? Moreover, what if a cognitive domain can be broken down into different parts, for example, in the way that the English past tense problem comprises regular and irregular verbs – could different computational components end up learning the different parts of the problem? The mixture-of-experts approach considers ways in which learning could take place in just such a system with multiple components available (Jacobs et al., 1991). In these models, functionally specialized structures can emerge as a result of learning, in the circumstance where the computational properties of the different components happen to line up with the demands presented by different parts of the problem domain (so-called *structure-function correspondences*).

During learning, mixture-of-experts algorithms typically permit the multiple components to compete with each other to deliver the correct output for each input pattern. The best performer is then assigned the pattern and allowed to learn it. The involvement of each component during functioning is controlled by a gating mechanism. Mixture-of-experts models are one of several approaches that seek to explain the origin of functionally specialized processing components in the cognitive system (see Elman et al., 1996; Jacobs, 1999; Thomas &

Richardson, 2006, for discussion). An example of the application of mixture of experts can be found in a developmental model of face and object recognition, where different "expert" mechanisms come to specialize in processing visual inputs that correspond to faces and those that correspond to objects (Dailey & Cottrell, 1999). The emergence of this functional specialization can be demonstrated by damaging each expert in turn and showing a double dissociation between face and object recognition in the two components of the model (see Section 5.3). Similarly, Thomas and Karmiloff-Smith 2002a showed how a mixture-of-experts model of English past tense could produce emergent specialization of separate mechanisms to regular and irregular verbs, respectively (see also Westermann, 1998, for related work with a constructivist network).

4.3. *Hybrid Models*

The success of mixture-of-experts models suggests that when two or more components are combined within a model, it can be advantageous for the computational properties of the components to differ. Where the properties of the components are radically different, for example, involving the combination of symbolic (rule-based) and connectionist (associative, similarity-based) architectures, the models are sometimes referred to as "hybrid." The use of hybrid models is inspired by the observation that some aspects of human cognition seem better described by rules (e.g., syntax, reasoning), whereas some seem better described by similarity (e.g., perception, memory). We have previously encountered the debate between symbolic and connectionist approaches (see Section 2.3) and the proposal that connectionist architectures may serve to implement symbolic processes (e.g., Touretzky & Hinton, 1988). The hybrid systems approach takes the alternative view that connectionist and symbolic processing principles should be combined within the same model, taking advantage of the strengths of each computational formalism. A discussion of this approach can be found in

Sun (2002a, 2002b). Example models include CONSYDERR (Sun, 1995), CLARION (Sun & Peterson, 1998), and ACT-R (Anderson & Lebiere, 1998).

An alternative to a truly hybrid approach is to develop a multi-part connectionist architecture that has components that employ different representational formats. Such a system may be described as having "heterogeneous" computational components. For example, in a purely connectionist system, one component might employ distributed representations that permit different degrees of similarity between activation patterns, whereas a second component employs localist representations in which there is no similarity between different representations. Behavior is then driven by the interplay between two associative components that employ different similarity structures. One example of a heterogeneous, multiple-component architecture is the complementary learning systems model of McClelland, McNaughton, and O'Reilly (1995), which employs localist representations to encode individual episodic memories but distributed representations to encode general semantic memories. Heterogeneous developmental models may offer new ways to conceive of the acquisition of concepts. For example, the cognitive domain of number may be viewed as heterogeneous in the sense that it combines three systems: the similarity-based representations of quantity, the localist representations of number facts (such as the order of number labels in counting), and a system for object individuation. Carey and Sarnecka (2006) argue that a heterogeneous multiple component system of this nature could acquire the concept of positive integers even though such a concept could not be acquired by any single component of the system on its own.

4.4. *Bayesian Graphical Models*

The use of Bayesian methods of inference in graphical models, including causal graphical models, has recently been embraced by a number of cognitive scientists (Chater, Tenenbaum, & Yuille, 2006; Gopnik et al., 2004; see Chapter 3 in this volume). This approach stresses how it may be possible to combine prior knowledge in the form of a set of explicit alternative graph structures and constraints on the complexity of such structures with Bayesian methods of inference to select the best type of representation of a particular data set (e.g., lists of facts about many different animals); and within that, to select the best specific instantiation of a representation of that type (Tenenbaum, Griffiths, & Kemp, 2006). These models are useful contributions to our understanding, particularly because they allow explicit exploration of the role of prior knowledge in the selection of a representation of the structure present in each data set. It should be recognized, however, that such models are offered as characterizations of learning at Marr's (1982) "Computational Level" and as such they do not specify the representations and processes that are actually employed when people learn. However, these models do present a challenge for the connectionist research focused on answering such questions. Specifically, the work provides a benchmark against which connectionist approaches might be tested for their success in learning to represent the structure from a data set and in using such a structure to make inferences consistent with optimal performance according to a Bayesian approach within a graphical model framework. More substantively, the work raises questions about whether or not optimization depends on the explicit representation of alternative structured representations or whether an approximation to such structured representations can arise without their prespecification. For an initial examination of these issues as they arise in the context of causal inference, see McClelland and Thompson (2007).

5. Connectionist Influences on Cognitive Theory

Connectionism offers an *explanation* of human cognition because instances of behavior in particular cognitive domains can be explained with respect to set of general principles (parallel distributed processing) and the conditions of the specific domains. However, from the accumulation of successful models, it is also possible to discern a wider influence of connectionism on the nature of theorizing about cognition, and this is perhaps a truer reflection of its impact. How has connectionism made us think differently about cognition?

5.1. *Knowledge Versus Processing*

One area where connectionism has changed the basic nature of theorizing is memory. According to the old model of memory based on the classical computational metaphor, the information in long-term memory (e.g., on the hard disk) has to be moved into working memory (the central processing unit, or CPU) for it to be operated on, and the long-term memories are laid down via a domain-general buffer of short-term memory (random access memory, or RAM). In this type of system, it is relatively easy to shift informational content between different systems, back and forth between central processing and short and long-term stores. Computation is predicated on variables: the same binary string can readily be instantiated in different memory registers or encoded onto a permanent medium.

By contrast, knowledge is hard to move about in connectionist networks because it is encoded in the weights. For example, in the past-tense model, knowledge of the past tense rule "add -ed" is distributed across the weight matrix of the connections between input and output layers. The difficulty in portability of knowledge is inherent in the principles of connectionism – Hebbian learning alters connection strengths to reinforce desirable activation states in connected units, tying knowledge to structure. If we start from the premise that knowledge will be very difficult to move about in our information processing system, what kind of cognitive architecture do we end up with? There are four main themes.

First, we need to distinguish between two different ways in which knowledge can be encoded: *active* and *latent* representa-tions (Munakata & McClelland, 2003). Latent knowledge corresponds to the information stored in the connection weights from accumulated experience. By contrast, active knowledge is information contained in the current activation states of the system. Clearly, the two are related because the activation states are constrained by the connection weights. But, particularly in recurrent networks, there can be subtle differences. Active states contain a trace of recent events (how things are at the moment), whereas latent knowledge represents a history of experience (how things tend to be). Differences in the ability to maintain the active states (e.g., in the strength of recurrent circuits) can produce errors in behavior where the system lapses into more typical ways of behaving (Munakata, 1998; Morton & Munakata, 2002).

Second, if information does need to be moved around the system, for example, from a more instance-based (episodic) system to a more general (semantic) system, this will require special structures and special (potentially time-consuming) processes. Thus McClelland, McNaughton, and O'Reilly (1995) proposed a dialogue between separate stores in the hippocampus and neocortex to gradually transfer knowledge from episodic to semantic memory. French, Ans, and Rousset (2001) proposed a special method to transfer knowledge between two memory systems: internally generated noise produces "pseudopatterns" from one system that contain the central tendencies of its knowledge; the second memory system is then trained with this extracted knowledge to effect the transfer. Chapters 7 and 8 in the current volume offer a wider consideration of models of episodic and semantic memory, respectively.

Third, information will be processed in the same substrate where it is stored. Therefore, long-term memories will be active structures and will perform computations on content. An external strategic control system plays the role of differentially activating the knowledge in this long-term system that is relevant to the current context. In anatomical terms, this distinction broadly corresponds to frontal/anterior (strategic control) and posterior (long-term) cortex. The design means, somewhat counterintuitively, that the control system has no content. Rather, the control system contains placeholders that serve to activate different regions of the long-term system. The control system may contain plans (sequences of placeholders). It may be involved in learning abstract concepts (using a placeholder to temporarily coactivate previously unrelated portions of long-term knowledge while Hebbian learning builds a new association between them), but it does not contain content in the sense of a domain-general working memory. The study of frontal systems then becomes an exploration of the activation dynamics of these placeholders and their involvement in learning (see, e.g., work by Davelaar & Usher, 2002; Haarmann & Usher, 2001; O'Reilly, Braver, & Cohen, 1999; Usher & McClelland, 2001).

Similarly, connectionist research has explored how activity in the control system can be used to modulate the efficiency of processing elsewhere in the system, for instance, to implemented selective attention. For example, Cohen et al., (1990) demonstrated how task units could be used to differentially modulate word-naming and color-naming processing channels in a model of the color-word Stroop task. In this model, latent knowledge interacted with the operation of task control, so that it was harder to selectively attend to color-naming and ignore information from the more practiced word-naming channel than vice versa. This work was later extended to demonstrate how deficits in the strategic control system (prefrontal cortex) could lead to problems in selective attention in disorders such as schizophrenia (Cohen & Servan-Schreiber, 1992). Chapter 15 in this volume contains a wider consideration of computational models of attention and cognitive control.

Lastly, the connectionist perspective on memory alters how we conceive of *domain generality* in processing systems. It is unlikely that there are any domain-general processing systems that serve as a "Jack-of-all-trades," that is, that can move between

representing the content of multiple domains. However, there may be domain-general systems that are involved in modulating many disparate processes without taking on the content of those systems, what we might call a system with "a finger in every pie." Meanwhile, short-term or working memory (as exemplified by the active representations contained in the recurrent loop of a network) is likely to exist as a devolved panoply of discrete systems, each with its own content-specific loop. For example, research in the neuropsychology of language now tends to support the existence of separate working memories for phonological, semantic, and syntactic information (see MacDonald & Christiansen, 2002, for a discussion of these arguments).

5.2. *Cognitive Development*

A key feature of PDP models is the use of a learning algorithm for modifying the patterns of connectivity as a function of experience. Compared with symbolic, rule-based computational models, this has made them a more sympathetic formalism for studying cognitive development (Elman et al., 1996). The combination of domain-general processing principles, domain-specific architectural constraints, and structured training environments has enabled connectionist models to give accounts of a range of developmental phenomena. These include infant category development, language acquisition and reasoning in children (see Mareschal & Thomas, 2007, for a recent review and chapter 16 in this volume).

Connectionism has become aligned with a resurgence of interest in statistical learning and a more careful consideration of the information available in the child's environment that may feed his or her cognitive development. One central debate revolves around how children can become "cleverer" as they get older, appearing to progress through qualitatively different stages of reasoning. Connectionist modeling of the development of children's reasoning was able to demonstrate that continuous incremental changes in the weight matrix driven by algorithms such as backpropagation can result in nonlinear changes in surface behavior, suggesting that the stages apparent in behavior may not necessarily be reflected in changes in the underlying mechanism (e.g., McClelland, 1989). Other connectionists have argued that algorithms able to supplement the computational resources of the network as part of learning may also provide an explanation for the emergence of more complex forms of behavior with age (e.g., cascade correlation; see Shultz, 2003).

The key contribution of connectionist models in the area of developmental psychology has been to specify detailed, implemented models of transition mechanisms that demonstrate how the child can move between producing different patterns of behavior. This was a crucial addition to a field that has accumulated vast amounts of empirical data cataloging what children are able to do at different ages. The specification of mechanism is also important to counter some strongly empiricist views that simply identifying statistical information in the environment suffices as an explanation of development; instead, it is necessary to show how a mechanism could use this statistical information to acquire some cognitive capacity. Moreover, when connectionist models are applied to development, it often becomes apparent that passive statistical structure is not the key factor; rather, the relevant statistics are in the transformation of the statistical structure of the environment to the output or the behavior that is relevant to the child, thereby appealing to notions like the regularity, consistency, and frequency of input-output mappings.

Recent connectionist approaches to development have begun to explore how the computational formalisms may change our understanding of the nature of the knowledge that children acquire. For example, Mareschal et al. (2007) argue that many mental representations of knowledge are partial (i.e., capture only some task-relevant dimensions); the existence of explicit language may blind us to the fact that there could be a limited role for truly abstract knowledge in the normal operation of the cognitive system (see Westermann et al., 2007). Current work also explores the computational basis of critical or sensitive periods in development, uncovering the mechanisms by which the ability to learn appears to reduce with age (e.g., McClelland et al., 1999; Thomas & Johnson, 2006).

5.3. *The Study of Acquired Disorders in Cognitive Neuropsychology*

Traditional cognitive neuropsychology of the 1980s was predicated on the assumption of underlying modular structure, that is, that the cognitive system comprises a set of independently functioning components. Patterns of selective cognitive impairment after acquired brain damage could then be used to construct models of normal cognitive function. The traditional models comprised box-and-arrow diagrams that sketched out rough versions of cognitive architecture, informed both by the patterns of possible selective deficit (which bits can fail independently) and by a task analysis of what the cognitive system probably has to do.

In the initial formulation of cognitive neuropsychology, caution was advised in attempting to infer cognitive architecture from behavioral deficits, since a given pattern of deficits might be consistent with a number of underlying architectures (Shallice, 1988). It is in this capacity that connectionist models have been extremely useful. They have both forced more detailed specification of proposed cognitive models via implementation and also permitted assessment of the range of deficits that can be generated by damaging these models in various ways. For example, models of reading have demonstrated that the ability to decode written words into spoken words and recover their meanings can be learned in a connectionist network; and when this network is damaged by, say, lesioning connection weights or removing hidden units, various patterns of acquired dyslexia can be simulated (e.g., Plaut et al., 1996; Plaut & Shallice, 1993). Connectionist models of acquired deficits have grown to be an influential aspect of cognitive neuropsychology and have been applied to domains such as language, memory, semantics, and vision (see Cohen, Johnstone, & Plunkett, 2000, for examples).

Several ideas have gained their first or clearest grounding via connectionist modeling. One of these ideas is that patterns of breakdown can arise from the statistics of the problem space (i.e., the mapping between input and output) rather than from structural distinctions in the processing system. In particular, connectionist models have shed light on a principal inferential tool of cognitive neuropsychology, the *double dissociation*. The line of reasoning argues that if in one patient, ability A can be lost while ability B is intact, and in a second patient, ability B can be lost while ability A is intact, then the two abilities might be generated by independent underlying mechanisms. In a connectionist model of category-specific impairments of semantic memory, Devlin et al. (1997) demonstrated that a single undifferentiated network trained to produce two behaviors could show a double dissociation between them simply as a consequence of different levels of damage. This can arise because the mappings associated with the two behaviors lead them to have different sensitivity to damage. For a small level of damage, performance on A may fall off quickly, whereas performance on B declines more slowly; for a high level of damage, A may be more robust than B. The reverse pattern of relative deficits implies nothing about structure.

Connectionist researchers have often set out to demonstrate that, more generally, double dissociation methodology is a flawed form of inference, on the grounds that such dissociations arise relatively easily from parallel distributed architectures where function is spread across the whole mechanism (e.g., Plunkett & Bandelow, 2006; Juola & Plunkett, 2000). However, on the whole, when connectionist models show robust double dissociations between two behaviors (for equivalent levels of damage applied to various parts of the network and over many replications), it does tend to be because different internal processing structures (units

or layers or weights) or different parts of the input layer or different parts of the output layer are differentially important for driving the two behaviors – that is, there is specialization of function. Connectionism models of breakdown have, therefore, tended to support the traditional inferences. Crucially, however, connectionist models have greatly improved our understanding of what modularity might look like in a neurocomputational system: a partial rather than an absolute property; a property that is the consequence of a developmental process where emergent specialization is driven by *structure-function correspondences* (the ability of certain parts of a computational structure to learn certain kinds of computation better than other kinds; see Section 4.2); and a property that must now be complemented by concepts such as division of labor, degeneracy, interactivity, and redundancy (see Thomas & Karmiloff-Smith, 2002a; Thomas et al., 2006, for discussion).

5.4. *The Origins of Individual Variability and Developmental Disorders*

In addition to their role in studying acquired disorders, the fact that many connectionist models learn their cognitive abilities makes them an ideal framework within which to study *developmental disorders*, such as autism, dyslexia, and specific language impairment (Joanisse & Seidenberg, 2003; Mareschal et al., 2007; Thomas & Karmiloff-Smith, 2002b, 2003a, 2005). Where models of normal cognitive development seek to study the "average" child, models of atypical development explore how developmental profiles may be disrupted. Connectionist models contain a number of constraints (architecture, activation dynamics, input and output representations, learning algorithm, training regimen) that determine the efficiency and outcome of learning. Manipulations to these constraints produce candidate explanations for impairments found in developmental disorders or for the impairments caused by exposure to atypical environments, such as in cases of deprivation.

In the 1980s and 1990s, many theories of developmental deficits employed the same explanatory framework as adult cognitive neuropsychology. There was a search for specific developmental deficits or dissociations, which were then explained in terms of the failure of individual modules to development. However, as Karmiloff-Smith (1998) and Bishop (1997) pointed out, most of the developmental deficits were actually being explained with reference to nondevelopmental, static, and sometimes adult models of normal cognitive structure. Karmiloff-Smith (1998) argued that the causes of developmental deficits of a genetic origin will lie in changes to low-level neurocomputational properties that only exert their influence on cognition via an extended atypical developmental process (see also Elman et al., 1996). Connectionist models provide the ideal forum to explore the thesis that an understanding of the constraints on the developmental process is essential for generating accounts of developmental deficits.

The study of atypical variability also prompts a consideration of what causes variability *within the normal range*, otherwise known as individual differences or intelligence. Are differences in intelligence caused by variation in the same computational parameters that can cause disorders? Are some developmental disorders just the extreme lower end of the normal distribution or are they qualitatively different conditions? What computational parameter settings are able to produce above-average performance or giftedness? Connectionism has begun to take advantage of the accumulated body of models of normal development to consider the wider question of cognitive variation in parameterized computational models (Thomas & Karmiloff-Smith, 2003a).

5.5. *Future Directions*

The preceding sections indicate the range and depth of influence of connectionism on contemporary theories of cognition. Where will connectionism go next? Necessarily, connectionism began with simple models of individual cognitive processes, focusing on those domains of particular theoretical interest. This piecemeal approach generated explanations of individual cognitive abilities using bespoke networks, each containing its own predetermined representations and architecture. In the future, one avenue to pursue is how these models fit together in the larger cognitive system – for example, to explain how the past tense network described in Section 3.2 might link up with the sentence processing model described in Section 3.3 to process past tenses as they arise in sentences. A further issue is to address the developmental origin of the architectures that are postulated. What processes specify the parts of the cognitive system to perform the various functions and how do these subsystems talk to each other, both across development and in the adult state? Improvements in computational power will aid more complex modeling endeavors. Nevertheless, it is worth bearing in mind that increasing complexity creates a tension with the primary goals of modeling – simplification and understanding. It is essential that we understand why more complicated models function as they do or they will merely become interesting artifacts (see Elman, 2005; Thomas, 2004, for further discussion).

In terms of its relation with other disciplines, a number of future influences on connectionism are discernible. Connectionism will be affected by the increasing appeal to *Bayesian probability theory* in human reasoning. In Bayesian theory, new data are used to update existing estimates of the most likely model of the world. Work has already begun to relate connectionist and Bayesian accounts, for example, in the domain of causal reasoning in children (McClelland & Thompson, 2007). In some cases, connectionism may offer alternative explanations of the same behavior; in others it may be viewed as an implementation of a Bayesian account (see Section 3.1). Connectionism will continue to have a close relation to *neuroscience*, perhaps seeking to build more neural constraints into its computational assumptions (O'Reilly & Munakata, 2000). Many of the new findings in cognitive neuroscience are influenced by *functional brain imaging techniques*. It will be important, therefore, for connectionism to make contact with these data, either via systems-level modeling of the interaction between subnetworks in task performance or in exploring the implications of the subtraction methodology as a tool for assessing the behavior of distributed interactive systems. The increasing influence of brain imaging foregrounds the relation of cognition to the neural substrate; it depends on how seriously one takes the neural plausibility of connectionist models as to whether an increased focus on the substrate will have particular implications for connectionism over and above any other theory of cognition.

Connectionist approaches to individual differences and developmental disorders suggest that this modeling approach has more to offer in considering the computational causes of variability. Research in *behavioral genetics* argues that a significant proportion of behavioral variability is genetic in origin (Bishop, 2006; Plomin, Owen & McGuffin, 1994). However, the neurodevelopmental mechanisms by which genes produce such variation are largely unknown. Although connectionist cognitive models are not neural, the fact that they incorporate neurally inspired properties may allow them to build links between behavior (where variability is measured) and the substrate on which genetic effects act. In the future, connectionism may therefore help to rectify a major shortcoming in our attempts to understand the relation of the human genome to human behavior – the omission of cognition from current explanations.

6. Conclusions

In this chapter, we have considered the contribution of connectionist modeling to our understanding of cognition. Connectionism was placed in the historical context of nineteenth-century associative theories of mental processes and twentieth-century attempts to understand the computations carried out by networks of neurons. The key properties of connectionist networks were then reviewed, and particular emphasis was placed on the use of learning to build the microstructure of these models. The core connectionist themes include the following: (1) that processing is simultaneously influenced by multiple sources of information at different levels of abstraction, operating via soft constraint satisfaction; (2) that representations are spread across multiple simple processing units operating in parallel; (3) that representations are graded, context-sensitive, and the emergent product of adaptive processes; and (4) that computation is similarity-based and driven by the statistical structure of problem domains, but it can nevertheless produce rule-following behavior. We illustrated the connectionist approach via three landmarks models, the Interactive Activation model of letter perception (McClelland & Rumelhart, 1981), the past tense model (Rumelhart & McClelland, 1986), and simple recurrent networks for finding structure in time (Elman, 1990). Apart from its body of successful individual models, connectionist theory has had a widespread influence on cognitive theorizing, and this influence was illustrated by considering connectionist contributions to our understanding of memory, cognitive development, acquired cognitive impairments, and developmental deficits. Finally, we peeked into the future of connectionism, arguing that its relationships with other fields in the cognitive sciences are likely to guide its future contribution to understanding the mechanistic basis of thought.

Acknowledgments

This work was supported by British Academy Grant SG–40400 and UK Medical Research Council Grant G0300188 to Michael Thomas, and National Institute of Mental Health Centre Grant P50 MH64445, James L. McClelland, Director.

References

Ackley, D. H., Hinton, G. E., & Sejnowski, T. J. (1985). A learning algorithm for Boltzmann machines. *Cognitive Science, 9,* 147–169.

Aizawa, K. (2004). History of connectionism. In C. Eliasmith (Ed.), *Dictionary of philosophy of mind*. Retrieved October 4, 2006, from http://philosophy.uwaterloo.ca/MindDict/connectionismhistory.html.

Anderson, J. A. (1977). Neural models with cognitive implications. In D. LaBerge & S. J. Samuels (Eds.), *Basic processes in reading perception and comprehension* (pp. 27–90). Hillsdale, NJ: Lawrence Erlbaum.

Anderson, J., & Lebiere, C. (1998). *The atomic components of thought*. Mahwah, NJ: Lawrence Erlbaum Associates.

Bates, E., & MacWhinney, B. (1989). Functionalism and the competition model. In B. MacWhinney & E. Bates (Eds.), *The crosslinguistic study of language processing* (pp. 3–37). New York: Cambridge University Press.

Bechtel, W., & Abrahamsen, A. (1991). *Connectionism and the mind*. Oxford, UK: Blackwell.

Berko, J. (1958). The child's learning of English morphology. *Word, 14*, 150–177.

Bishop, D. V. M. (1997). Cognitive neuropsychology and developmental disorders: Uncomfortable bedfellows. *Quarterly Journal of Experimental Psychology, 50A*, 899–923.

Bishop, D. V. M. (2006). Developmental cognitive genetics: How psychology can inform genetics and vice versa. *Quarterly Journal of Experimental Psychology, 59*(7), 1153–1168.

Botvinick, M., & Plaut, D. C. (2004). Doing without schema hierarchies: A recurrent connectionist approach to normal and impaired routine sequential action. *Psychological Review, 111*, 395–429.

Burton, A. M., Bruce, V., & Johnston, R. A. (1990). Understanding face recognition with an interactive activation model. *British Journal of Psychology, 81*, 361–380.

Bybee, J., & McClelland, J. L. (2005). Alternatives to the combinatorial paradigm of linguistic theory based on domain general principles of human cognition. *The Linguistic Review, 22*(2–4), 381–410.

Carey, S., & Sarnecka, B. W. (2006). The development of human conceptual representations: A case study. In Y. Munakata & M. H. Johnson (Eds.), *Processes of change in brain and cognitive development: Attention and performance XXI*, (pp. 473–496). Oxford, UK: Oxford University Press.

Carpenter, G. A., & Grossberg, S. (1987a). ART2: Self-organization of stable category recognition codes for analog input patterns. *Applied Optics, 26*, 4919–4930.

Carpenter, G. A., & Grossberg, S. (1987b). A massively parallel architecture for a self-organizing neural pattern recognition machine. *Computer Vision, Graphics and Image Processing, 37*, 54–115.

Chater, N., Tenenbaum, J. B., & Yuille, A. (2006). Probabilistic models of cognition: Conceptual foundations. *Trends in Cognitive Sciences 10*(7), 287–291.

Christiansen, M. H., & Chater, N. (2001). *Connectionist psycholinguistics*. Westport, CT: Ablex.

Cohen, G., Johnstone, R. A., & Plunkett, K. (2000). *Exploring cognition: damaged brains and neural networks*. Hove, Sussex, UK: Psychology Press.

Cohen, J. D., Dunbar, K., & McClelland, J. L. (1990). On the control of automatic processes: A parallel distributed processing account of the Stroop effect. *Psychological Review, 97*, 332–361.

Cohen, J. D., & Servan-Schreiber, D. (1992). Context, cortex, and dopamine: A connectionist approach to behavior and biology in schizophrenia. *Psychological Review, 99*, 45–77.

Dailey, M. N., & Cottrell, G. W. (1999). Organization of face and object recognition in modular neural networks. *Neural Networks, 12*, 1053–1074.

Davelaar, E. J., & Usher, M. (2003). An activation-based theory of immediate item memory. In J. A. Bullinaria, & W. Lowe (Eds.), *Proceedings of the Seventh Neural Computation and Psychology Workshop: Connectionist models of cognition and perception* (pp. 118–130). Singapore: World Scientific.

Davies, M. (2005). Cognitive science. In F. Jackson & M. Smith (Eds.), *The Oxford handbook of contemporary philosophy* (pp. 358–394). Oxford, UK: Oxford University Press.

Devlin, J., Gonnerman, L., Andersen, E., & Seidenberg, M. S. (1997). Category specific semantic deficits in focal and widespread brain damage: A computational account. *Journal of Cognitive Neuroscience, 10*, 77–94.

Dick, F., Bates, E., Wulfeck, B., Aydelott, J., Dronkers, N., & Gernsbacher, M. A. (2001). Language deficits, localization, and grammar: Evidence for a distributive model of language breakdown in aphasic patients and neurologically intact individuals. *Psychological Review, 108*(3), 759–788.

Dick, F., Wulfeck, B., Krupa-Kwiatkowski, M., & Bates, E. (2004). The development of complex sentence interpretation in typically developing children compared with children with specific language impairments or early unilateral focal lesions. *Developmental Science*, 7(3), 360–377.

Elman, J. L. (1990). Finding structure in time. *Cognitive Science, 14,* 179–211.

Elman, J. L. (1991). Distributed representations, simple recurrent networks, and grammatical structure. *Machine Learning, 7,* 195–224.

Elman, J. L. (1993). Learning and development in neural networks: The importance of starting small. *Cognition, 48,* 71–99.

Elman, J. L. (2005). Connectionist models of cognitive development: Where next? *Trends in Cognitive Sciences, 9,* 111–117.

Elman, J. L., Bates, E. A., Johnson, M. H., Karmiloff-Smith, A., Parisi, D., & Plunkett, K. (1996). *Rethinking innateness: A connectionist perspective on development.* Cambridge, MA: MIT Press.

Ervin, S. M. (1964). Imitation and structural change in children's language. In E. H. Lenneberg (Ed.), *New directions in the study of language* (pp. 163–189). Cambridge, MA: MIT Press.

Fahlman, S., & Lebiere, C. (1990). The cascade correlation learning architecture. In D. Touretzky (Ed.), *Advances in neural information processing 2* (pp. 524–532). Los Altos, CA: Morgan Kauffman.

Feldman, J. A. (1981). A connectionist model of visual memory. In G. E. Hinton & J. A. Anderson (Eds.), *Parallel models of associative memory* (pp. 49–81). Hillsdale, NJ: Hawrence Erlbaum.

Fodor, J. A., & Pylyshyn, Z. W. (1988). Connectionism and cognitive architecture: A critical analysis. *Cognition, 78,* 3–71.

French, R. M., Ans, B., & Rousset, S. (2001). Pseudopatterns and dual-network memory models: Advantages and shortcomings. In R. French & J. Sougné (Eds.), *Connectionist models of learning, development and evolution* (pp. 13–22). London: Springer.

Freud, S. (1895). Project for a scientific psychology. In J. Strachey (Ed.), *The standard edition of the complete psychological works of Sigmund Freud* (pp. 283–360). London: The Hogarth Press and the Institute of Psycho-Analysis.

Goebel, R., & Indefrey, P. (2000). A recurrent network with short-term memory capacity learning the German –s plural. In P. Broeder & J. Murre (Eds.), *Models of language acquisition: Inductive and deductive approaches* (pp. 177–

200). Oxford, UK: Oxford University Press.

Gopnik, A., Glymour, C., Sobel, D. M., Schulz, L. E., Kushnir, T., & Danks, D. (2004). A theory of causal learning in children: Causal maps and bayes nets. *Psychological Review, 111*(1): 3–32.

Green, D. C. (1998). Are connectionist models theories of cognition? *Psycoloquy, 9*(4).

Grossberg, S. (1976). Adaptive pattern classification and universal recoding: Parallel development and coding of neural feature detectors. *Biological Cybernetics, 23,* 121–134.

Haarmann, H., & Usher, M. (2001). Maintenance of semantic information in capacity limited item short-term memory. *Psychonomic Bulletin & Review, 8,* 568–578.

Hebb, D. O. (1949). *The organization of behavior: A neuropsychological approach.* New York: John Wiley & Sons.

Hinton, G. E. (1989). Deterministic Boltzmann learning performs steepest descent in weight-space. *Neural Computation, 1,* 143–150.

Hinton, G. E., & Anderson, J. A. (1981). *Parallel models of associative memory.* Hillsdale, NJ: Lawrence Erlbaum.

Hinton, G. E., & McClelland, J. L. (1988). Learning representations by recirculation. In D. Z. Anderson (Ed.), *Neural Information Processing Systems, 1987* (pp. 358–366). New York: American Institute of Physics.

Hinton, G. E., & Salakhutdinov, R. R. (2006). Reducing the dimensionality of data with neural networks. *Science, 313*(5786), 504–507.

Hinton, G. E., & Sejnowski, T. J. (1983). Optimal perceptual inference. In *Proceedings of the IEEE Conference on Computer Vision and Pattern Recognition* (pp. 448–453). Washington, DC.

Hinton, G. E., & Sejnowksi, T. (1986). Learning and relearning in Boltzmann machines. In D. Rumelhart & J. McClelland (Eds.), *Parallel distributed processing, Vol. 1* (pp. 282–317). Cambridge, MA: MIT Press.

Hoeffner, J. H., & McClelland, J. L. (1993). Can a perceptual processing deficit explain the impairment of inflectional morphology in developmental dysphasia? A computational investigation. In E. V. Clark (Ed.), *Proceedings of the 25th Child language research forum* (pp. 38–49). Stanford, CA: Center for the Study of Language and Information.

Hopfield, J. J. (1982). Neural networks and physical systems with emergent collective computational abilities. *Proceedings of the National Academy of Science USA, 79,* 2554–2558.

Houghton, G. (2005). *Connectionist models in cognitive psychology*. Hove, Sussex, UK: Psychology Press.

Jacobs, R. A. (1999). Computational studies of the development of functionally specialized neural modules. *Trends in Cognitive Sciences*, 3, 31–38.

Jacobs, R. A., Jordan, M. I., Nowlan, S. J., & Hinton, G. E. (1991). Adaptive mixtures of local experts. *Neural Computation*, 3, 79–87.

James, W. (1890). *Principles of psychology*. New York: Holt.

Joanisse, M. F., & Seidenberg, M. S. (1999). Impairments in verb morphology following brain injury: A connectionist model. *Proceedings of the National Academy of Science USA*, 96, 7592–7597.

Joanisse, M. F., & Seidenberg, M. S. (2003). Phonology and syntax in specific language impairment: Evidence from a connectionist model. *Brain and Language*, 86, 40–56.

Jordan, M. I. (1986). Attractor dynamics and parallelism in a connectionist sequential machine. In *Proceedings of the Eight Annual Conference of Cognitive Science Society* (pp. 531–546). Hillsdale, NJ: Lawrence Erlbaum.

Juola, P., & Plunkett, K. (2000). Why double dissociations don't mean much. In G. Cohen, R. A. Johnston, & K. Plunkett (Eds.), *Exploring cognition: Damaged brains and neural networks: Readings in cognitive neuropsychology and connectionist modelling* (pp. 319–327). Hove, Sussex, UK: Psychology Press.

Karmiloff-Smith, A. (1998). Development itself is the key to understanding developmental disorders. *Trends in Cognitive Sciences*, 2, 389–398.

Kohonen, T. (1984). *Self-organization and associative memory*. Berlin: Springer-Verlag.

Kuczaj, S. A. (1977). The acquisition of regular and irregular past tense forms. *Journal of Verbal Learning and Verbal Behavior*, 16, 589–600.

Lashley, K. S. (1929). *Brain mechanisms and intelligence: A quantitative study of injuries to the brain*. New York: Dover.

Love, B. C., Medin, D. L., & Gureckis, T. M. (2004). SUSTAIN: A network model of category learning. *Psychological Review*, 111, 309–332.

MacDonald, M. C., & Christiansen, M. H. (2002). Reassessing working memory: A comment on Just & Carpenter (1992) and Waters & Caplan (1996). *Psychological Review*, 109, 35–54.

MacKay, D. J. (1992). A practical Bayesian framework for backpropagation networks. *Neural Computation*, 4, 448–472.

Marcus, G. F. (2001). *The algebraic mind: Integrating connectionism and cognitive science*. Cambridge, MA: MIT Press

Marcus, G., Pinker, S., Ullman, M., Hollander, J., Rosen, T. & Xu, F. (1992). Overregularisation in language acquisition. *Monographs of the Society for Research in Child Development*, 57 (Serial No. 228).

Mareschal, D., Johnson, M., Sirios, S., Spratling, M., Thomas, M. S. C., & Westermann, G. (2007). *Neuroconstructivism: How the brain constructs cognition*. Oxford, UK: Oxford University Press.

Mareschal, D., & Shultz, T. R. (1996). Generative connectionist architectures and constructivist cognitive development. *Cognitive Development*, 11, 571–605.

Mareschal, D., & Thomas, M. S. C. (2007). Computational modeling in developmental psychology. *IEEE Transactions on Evolutionary Computation*, 11(2), 137–150.

Marr, D. (1982). *Vision*. San Francisco: W. H. Freeman.

Marr, D., & Poggio, T. (1976). Cooperative computation of stereo disparity. *Science*, 194, 283–287.

Mayberry, M. R., Crocker, M., & Knoeferle, P. (2005). A Connectionist Model of Sentence Comprehension in Visual Worlds. In: *Proceedings of the 27th Annual Conference of the Cognitive Science Society*, (COGSCI-05, Streas, Italy), Mahwah, NJ: Erlbaum.

McClelland, J. L. (1981). Retrieving general and specific information from stored knowledge of specifics. In *Proceedings of the Third Annual Meeting of the Cognitive Science Society* (pp. 170–172). Hillsdale, NJ: Lawrence Erlbaum Associates.

McClelland, J. L. (1989). Parallel distributed processing: Implications for cognition and development. In M. G. M. Morris (Ed.), *Parallel distributed processing, implications for psychology and neurobiology* (pp. 8–45). Oxford, UK: Clarendon Press.

McClelland, J. L. (1998). Connectionist models and Bayesian inference. In M. Oaksford & N. Chater (Eds.), *Rational models of cognition* (pp. 21–53). Oxford, UK: Oxford University Press.

McClelland, J. L., & Elman, J. L. (1986). The Trace model of speech perception. *Cognitive Psychology*, 18, 1–86.

McClelland, J. L., McNaughton, B. L., & O'Reilly, R. C. (1995). Why there are complementary learning systems in the hippocampus and neocortex: Insights from the successes and failures of connectionist models of learning and memory. *Psychological Review, 102,* 419–457.

McClelland, J. L., Plaut, D. C., Gotts, S. J., & Maia, T. V. (2003). Developing a domain-general framework for cognition: What is the best approach? Commentary on a target article by Anderson and Lebiere. *Behavioral and Brain Sciences, 22,* 611–614.

McClelland, J. L., & Rumelhart, D. E. (1981). An interactive activation model of context effects in letter perception: Part 1. An account of basic findings. *Psychological Review, 88*(5), 375–405.

McClelland, J. L., Rumelhart, D. E., & the PDP Research Group (1986). *Parallel distributed processing: Explorations in the microstructure of cognition, Vol. 2: Psychological and biological models* (pp. 2–4). Cambridge, MA: MIT Press.

McClelland, J. L., Thomas, A. G., McCandliss, B. D., & Fiez, J. A. (1999). Understanding failures of learning: Hebbian learning, competition for representation space, and some preliminary data. In J. A. Reggia, E. Ruppin, & D. Glanzman (Eds.), *Disorders of brain, behavior, and cognition: The neurocomputational perspective* (pp. 75–80). Oxford, UK: Elsevier.

McClelland, J. L., & Thompson, R. M. (2007). Using domain-general principles to explain children's causal reasoning abilities. *Developmental Science, 10,* 333–356.

McCulloch, W. S., & Pitts, W. (1943). A logical calculus of ideas immanent in nervous activity. *Bulletin of Mathematical Biophysics, 5,* 115–133. (Reprinted in Anderson J., & Rosenfield E. (1988). Neurocomputing: Foundations of research) Cambridge, MA: MIT Press.

McLeod, P., Plunkett, K., & Rolls, E. T. (1998). *Introduction to connectionist modelling of cognitive processes.* Oxford, UK: Oxford University Press

Meynert, T. (1884). *Psychiatry: A clinical treatise on diseases of the forebrain. Part I. The anatomy, physiology and chemistry of the brain* (B. Sachs, Trans.). New York: G.P. Putnam's Sons.

Miikkulainen, R., & Mayberry, M. R. (1999). Disambiguation and grammar as emergent soft constraints. In B. MacWhinney (Ed.), *Emergence of language* (pp. 153–176). Hillsdale, NJ: Lawrence Erlbaum.

Minsky, M., & Papert, S. (1969). *Perceptrons: An introduction to computational geometry.* Cambridge, MA: MIT Press.

Minsky, M. L., & Papert, S. (1988). *Perceptrons: An introduction to computational geomety.* Cambridge, MA: MIT Press.

Morris, W., Cottrell, G., & Elman, J. (2000). A connectionist simulation of the empirical acquisition of grammatical relations. In S. Wermter & R. Sun (Eds.), *Hybrid neural systems* (pp. 175–193). Heidelberg: Springer Verlag.

Morton, J. (1969). Interaction of information in word recognition. *Psychological Review, 76,* 165–178.

Morton, J. B., & Munakata, Y. (2002). Active versus latent representations: A neural network model of perseveration, dissociation, and decalage in childhood. *Developmental Psychobiology, 40,* 255–265.

Movellan, J. R., & McClelland, J. L. (1993). Learning continuous probability distributions with symmetric diffusion networks. *Cognitive Science, 17,* 463–496.

Munakata, Y. (1998). Infant perseveration and implications for object permanence theories: A PDP model of the AB task. *Developmental Science, 1,* 161–184.

Munakata, Y., & McClelland, J. L. (2003). Connectionist models of development. *Developmental Science, 6,* 413–429.

O'Reilly, R. C. (1996). Biologically plausible error-driven learning using local activation differences: The generalized recirculation algorithm. *Neural Compuation, 8*(5), 895–938.

O'Reilly, R. C. (1998). Six principles for biologically-based computational models of cortical cognition. *Trends in Cognitive Sciences, 2,* 455–462.

O'Reilly, R. C., Braver, T. S., & Cohen, J. D. (1999). A biologically based computational model of working memory. In A. Miyake & P. Shah (Eds.), *Models of working memory: Mechanisms of active maintenance and executive control* (pp. 375–411). New York: Cambridge University Press.

O'Reilly, R. C., & Munakata, Y. (2000). *Computational explorations in cognitive neuroscience: Understanding the mind by simulating the brain.* Cambridge, MA: MIT Press.

Pinker, S. (1984). *Language learnability and language development.* Cambridge, MA: Harvard University Press.

Pinker, S. (1999). *Words and rules.* London: Weidenfeld & Nicolson.

Pinker, S., & Prince, A. (1988). On language and connectionism: Analysis of a parallel distributed processing model of language acquisition. *Cognition, 28,* 73–193.

Plaut, D. C., & Kello, C. T. (1999). The emergence of phonology from the interplay of speech comprehension and production: A distributed connectionist approach. In B. MacWhinney (Ed.), *The emergence of language* (pp. 381–415). Mahwah, NJ: Lawrence Erlbaum.

Plaut, D., & McClelland, J. L. (1993). Generalization with componential attractors: Word and nonword reading in an attractor network. In *Proceedings of the Fifteenth Annual Conference of the Cognitive Science Society* (pp. 824–829). Hillsdale, NJ: Lawrence Erlbaum.

Plaut, D. C., McClelland, J. L., Seidenberg, M. S., & Patterson, K. E. (1996). Understanding normal and impaired word reading: Computational principles in quasi-regular domains. *Psychological Review, 103,* 56–115.

Plaut, D. C., & Shallice, T. (1993). Deep dyslexia: A case study of connectionist neuropsychology. *Cognitive Neuropsychology, 10,* 377–500.

Plomin, R., Owen, M. J., & McGuffin, P. (1994). The genetic basis of complex human behaviors. *Science, 264,* 1733–1739.

Plunkett, K., & Bandelow, S. (2006). Stochastic approaches to understanding dissociations in inflectional morphology. *Brain and Language, 98,* 194–209.

Plunkett, K., & Marchman, V. (1991). U-shaped learning and frequency effects in a multi-layered perceptron: Implications for child language acquisition. *Cognition, 38,* 1–60.

Plunkett, K., & Marchman, V. (1993). From rote learning to system building: acquiring verb morphology in children and connectionist nets. *Cognition, 48,* 21–69.

Plunkett, K., & Marchman, V. (1996). Learning from a connectionist model of the English past tense. *Cognition, 61,* 299–308.

Plunkett, K., & Nakisa, R. (1997). A connectionist model of the Arabic plural system. *Language and Cognitive Processes, 12,* 807–836.

Quartz, S. R. (1993). Neural networks, nativism, and the plausibility of constructivism. *Cognition, 48,* 223–242.

Quartz, S. R. & Sejnowski, T. J. (1997). The neural basis of cognitive development: A constructivist manifesto. *Behavioral and Brain Sciences, 20,* 537–596.

Rashevsky, N. (1935). Outline of a physico-mathematical theory of the brain. *Journal of General Psychology, 13,* 82–112.

Reicher, G. M. (1969). Perceptual recognition as a function of meaningfulness of stimulus material. *Journal of Experimental Psychology, 81,* 274–280.

Rohde, D. L. T. (2002). *A connectionist model of sentence comprehension and production.* Unpublished doctoral dissertation, Carnegie Mellon University, Pittsburgh, PA.

Rohde, D. L. T., & Plaut, D. C. (1999). Language acquisition in the absence of explicit negative evidence: How important is starting small? *Cognition, 72,* 67–109.

Rosenblatt, F. (1958). The perceptron: A probabilistic model for information storage and organization in the brain. *Psychological Review, 65,* 386–408.

Rosenblatt, F. (1962). *Principles of neurodynamics: Perceptrons and the theory of brain mechanisms.* Washington, DC: Spartan Books.

Rumelhart, D. E., & McClelland, J. L. (1982). An interactive activation model of context effects in letter perception: Part 2. The contextual enhancement effect and some tests and extensions of the model. *Psychological Review, 89,* 60–94.

Rumelhart, D. E., Hinton, G. E., & McClelland, J. L. (1986). A general framework for parallel distributed processing. In D. E. Rumelhart, J. L. McClelland, & the PDP Research Group, *Parallel distributed processing: Explorations in the microstructure of congnition. Volume 1: Foundations* (pp. 45–76). Cambridge, MA: MIT Press.

Rumelhart, D. E., & McClelland, J. L. (1985). Levels indeed! *Journal of Experimental Psychology General, 114*(2), 193–197.

Rumelhart, D. E., & McClelland, J. L. (1986). On learning the past tense of English verbs. In J. L. McClelland, D. E. Rumelhart & the PDP Research Group (Eds.), *Parallel distributed processing: Explorations in the microstructure of cognition, Vol. 2: Psychological and biological models* (pp. 216–271). Cambridge, MA: MIT Press.

Rumelhart, D. E., Hinton, G. E., & Williams, R. J. (1986). Learning internal representations by error propagation. In D. E. Rumelhart, J. L. McClelland and The PDP Research Group, *Parallel distributed processing: Explorations in the microstructure of cognition. Volume 1: Foundations* (pp. 318–362). Cambridge, MA: MIT Press.

Rumelhart, D. E., McClelland, J. L., & the PDP Research Group (1986). *Parallel distributed processing: Explorations in the microstructure of cognition, Vol. 1: Foundations* (p. 2-4). Cambridge, MA: MIT Press.

Rumelhart, D. E., Smolensky, P., McClelland, J. L., & Hinton, G. E. (1986). Schemata and sequential thought processes in PDP models. In J. L. McClelland & D. E. Rumelhart (Eds.), *Parallel distributed processing, Vol. 2* (pp. 7–57). Cambridge, MA: MIT Press.

Saffran, J. R., Newport, E. L., & Aslin, R. N. (1996). Word segmentation: The role of distributional cues. *Journal of Memory and Language, 35,* 606–621.

Selfridge, O. G. (1959). Pandemonium: A paradigm for learning. In D. V. Blane, & A. M. Uttley (Eds.). *Proceedings of the Symposium on Mechanisation of Thought Processes* (pp. 511–529). London: HMSO.

Shallice, T. (1988). *From neuropsychology to mental structure.* Cambridge, UK: Cambridge University Press.

Sharkey, N., Sharkey, A., & Jackson, S. (2000). Are SRNs sufficient for modelling language acquisition. In P. Broeder & J. Murre (Eds.), *Models of language acquisition: Inductive and deductive approaches* (pp. 33–54). Oxford, UK: Oxford University Press.

Shultz, T. R. (2003). *Computational developmental psychology.* Cambridge, MA: MIT Press.

Smolensky, P. (1988). On the proper treatment of connectionism. *Behavioral and Brain Sciences, 11,* 1–74.

Spencer, H. (1872). *Principles of psychology* (3rd ed.). London: Longman, Brown, Green, & Longmans.

Sun, R. (1995). Robust reasoning: Integrating rule-based and similarity-based reasoning. *Artificial Intelligence, 75,* 241–295.

Sun, R. (2002a). Hybrid connectionist symbolic systems. In M. Arbib (Ed.), *Handbook of brain theories and neural networks* (2nd ed.), (pp. 543–547). Cambridge, MA: MIT Press.

Sun, R. (2002b). Hybrid systems and connectionist implementationalism. In L. Nadel, D. Chalmers, P. Culicover, R. Goldstone, & B. French (Eds.), *Encyclopedia of Cognitive Science* (pp. 697–703). London: Macmillan.

Sun, R., & Peterson, T. (1998). Autonomous learning of sequential tasks: Experiments and analyses. *IEEE Transactions on Neural Networks, 9*(6), 1217–1234.

Tenenbaum, J. B., Griffiths, T. L., & Kemp, C. (2006). Theory-based Bayesian models of inductive learning and reasoning. *Trends in Cognitive Sciences 10*(7), 309–318.

Thomas, M. S. C. (2004). The state of connectionism in 2004. *Parallaxis, 8,* 43–61.

Thomas, M. S. C. (2005). Characterising compensation. *Cortex, 41*(3), 434–442.

Thomas, M. S. C., Forrester, N. A., & Richardson, F. M. (2006). What is modularity good for? In R. Sun & N. Miyake (Eds.). *Proceedings of the 28th Annual Conference of the Cognitive Science Society* (pp. 2240–2245). Vancouver, Canada: Cognitive Science Society.

Thomas, M. S. C., & Johnson, M. H. (2006). The computational modelling of sensitive periods. *Developmental Psychobiology, 48*(4), 337–344.

Thomas, M. S. C., & Karmiloff-Smith, A. (2002a). Are developmental disorders like cases of adult brain damage? Implications from connectionist modelling. *Behavioral and Brain Sciences, 25*(6), 727–788.

Thomas, M. S. C., & Karmiloff-Smith, A. (2002b). Modelling typical and atypical cognitive development. In U. Goswami (Ed.), *Handbook of childhood development* (pp. 575–599). Oxford, UK: Blackwells.

Thomas, M. S. C., & Karmiloff-Smith, A. (2003a). Connectionist models of development, developmental disorders and individual differences. In R. J. Sternberg, J. Lautrey, & T. Lubart (Eds.), *Models of intelligence: International perspectives* (pp. 133–150). Washington, DC: American Psychological Association.

Thomas, M. S. C., & Karmiloff-Smith, A. (2003b). Modeling language acquisition in atypical phenotypes. *Psychological Review, 110*(4), 647–682.

Thomas, M. S. C., & Karmiloff-Smith, A. (2005). Can developmental disorders reveal the component parts of the human language faculty? *Language Learning and Development, 1*(1), 65–92.

Thomas, M. S. C., & Redington, M. (2004). Modelling atypical syntax processing. In W. Sakas (Ed.), *Proceedings of the first workshop on psycho-computational models of human language acquisition at the 20th International Conference on Computational Linguistics* (pp. 85–92).

Thomas, M. S. C., & Richardson, F. (2006). Atypical representational change: Conditions for the emergence of atypical modularity. In

Y. Munakata & M. H. Johnson (Eds.), *Processes of change in brain and cognitive development: Attention and Performance XXI*, (pp. 315–347). Oxford, UK: Oxford University Press.

Thomas, M. S. C., & van Heuven, W. (2005). Computational models of bilingual comprehension. In J. F. Kroll & A. M. B. De Groot (Eds.), *Handbook of bilingualism: Psycholinguistic approaches* (pp. 202–225). Oxford, UK: Oxford University Press.

Touretzky, D. S., & Hinton, G. E. (1988). A distributed connectionist production system. *Cognitive Science, 12*, 423–466.

Usher, M., & McClelland, J. L. (2001). On the time course of perceptual choice: The leaky competing accumulator model. *Psychological Review, 108*, 550–592.

van Gelder, T. (1991). Classical questions, radical answers: Connectionism and the structure of mental representations. In T. Horgan & J. Tienson (Eds.), *Connectionism and the philosophy of mind.* (pp. 355–381). Dordrecht: Kluwer Academic.

Weckerly, J., & Elman, J. L. (1992). A PDP approach to processing center-embedded sentences. In *Proceedings of the Fourteenth Annual Conference of the Cognitive Science Society.* Hillsdale, NJ: Lawrence Erlbaum.

Westermann, G. (1998). Emergent modularity and U-shaped learning in a constructivist neural network learning the English past tense. In *Proceedings of the 20th Annual Conference of the Cognitive Science Society* (pp. 1130–1135). Hillsdale, NJ: Lawrence Erlbaum.

Westermann, G., Mareschal, D., Johnson, M. H., Sirois, S., Spratling, M. W., & Thomas, M. S. C. (2007). Neuroconstructivism. *Developmental Science, 10*, 75–83.

Williams, R. J., & Zipser, D. (1995). *Gradient-based learning algorithms for recurrent networks and their computational complexity.* In Y. Chauvin & D. E. Rumelhart (Eds.), *Backpropagation: Theory, architectures and applications.* Hillsdale, NJ: Lawrence Erlbaum.

Xie, X., & Seung, H. S. (2003). Equivalence of backpropagation and contrastive Hebbian learning in a layered network. *Neural Computation, 15*, 441–454.

Xu, F., & Pinker, S. (1995). Weird past tense forms. *Journal of Child Language, 22*, 531–556.

CHAPTER 3

Bayesian Models of Cognition

Thomas L. Griffiths, Charles Kemp,
and Joshua B. Tenenbaum

1. Introduction

For over 200 years, philosophers and mathematicians have been using probability theory to describe human cognition. Although the theory of probabilities was first developed as a means of analyzing games of chance, it quickly took on a larger and deeper significance as a formal account of how rational agents should reason in situations of uncertainty (Gigerenzer et al., 1989; Hacking, 1975). The goal of this chapter is to illustrate the kinds of computational models of cognition that we can build if we assume that human learning and inference approximately follow the principles of Bayesian probabilistic inference and to explain some of the mathematical ideas and techniques underlying those models.

Bayesian models are becoming increasingly prominent across a broad spectrum of the cognitive sciences. Just in the last few years, Bayesian models have addressed animal learning (Courville, Daw, & Touretzky, 2006), human inductive learning and generalization (Tenenbaum, Griffiths, & Kemp, 2006), visual scene perception (Yuille & Kersten, 2006), motor control (Kording & Wolpert, 2006), semantic memory (Steyvers, Griffiths, & Dennis, 2006), language processing and acquisition (Chater & Manning, 2006; Xu & Tenenbaum, 2007), symbolic reasoning (Oaksford & Chater, 2001), causal learning and inference (Steyvers et al., 2003; Griffiths & Tenenbaum, 2005, 2007a), and social cognition (Baker, Tenenbaum, & Saxe, 2007), among other topics. Behind these different research programs is a shared sense of which are the most compelling computational questions that we can ask about the human mind. To us, the big question is this: How does the human mind go beyond the data of experience? In other words, how does the mind build rich, abstract, veridical models of the world given only the sparse and noisy data that we observe through our senses? This is by no means the only computationally interesting aspect of cognition that we can study, but it is surely one of the most central and also one of the most challenging. It is a version of the classic problem of induction, which is as old as recorded Western thought and is the source of many deep problems and debates in modern philosophy of knowledge and philosophy of science. It is also at the heart of the difficulty in building machines with anything resembling human-like intelligence.

The Bayesian framework for probabilistic inference provides a general approach to understanding how problems of induction can be solved in principle and perhaps how they might be solved in the human mind. Let us give a few examples. Vision researchers are interested in how the mind infers the intrinsic properties of a object (e.g., its color or shape) as well as its role in a visual scene (e.g., its spatial relation to other objects or its trajectory of motion). These features are severely underdetermined by the available image data. For instance, the spectrum of light wavelengths reflected from an object's surface into the observer's eye is a product of two unknown spectra: the surface's color spectrum and the spectrum of the light illuminating the scene. Solving the problem of "color constancy" – inferring the object's color given only the light reflected from it, under any conditions of illumination – is akin to solving the equation $y = a \times b$ for a given y, without knowing b. No deductive or certain inference is possible. At best, we can make a reasonable guess, based on some expectations about which values of a and b are more likely a priori. This inference can be formalized in a Bayesian framework (Brainard & Freeman, 1997), and it can be solved reasonably well given prior probability distributions for natural surface reflectances and illumination spectra.

The problems of core interest in other areas of cognitive science may seem very different from the problem of color constancy in vision, and they are different in important ways, but they are also deeply similar. For instance, language researchers want to understand how people recognize words so quickly and so accurately from noisy speech, how we parse a sequence of words into a hierarchical representation of the utterance's syntactic phrase structure, or how a child infers the rules of grammar – an infinite generative system – from observing only a finite and rather limited set of grammatical sentences, mixed with more than a few incomplete or ungrammatical utterances. In each of these cases, the available data severely underconstrain the inferences that people make, and the best the mind can do is to make a good guess, guided – from a Bayesian standpoint – by prior probabilities about which world structures are most likely a priori. Knowledge of a language – its lexicon, its syntax, and its pragmatic tendencies of use – provides probabilistic constraints and preferences on which words are most likely to be heard in a given context or which syntactic parse trees a listener should consider in processing a sequence of spoken words. More abstract knowledge, in a sense, what linguists have referred to as "universal grammar" (Chomsky, 1988), can generate priors on possible rules of grammar that guide a child in solving the problem of induction in language acquisition. Chater and Manning (2006) survey Bayesian models of language from this perspective.

The focus of this chapter will be on problems in higher-level cognition: inferring causal structure from patterns of statistical correlation, learning about categories and hidden properties of objects, and learning the meanings of words. This focus is partly a pragmatic choice, as these topics are the subject of our own research and hence we know them best. But there are also deeper reasons for this choice. Learning about causal relations, category structures, or the properties or names of objects are problems that are very close to the classic problems of induction that have been much discussed and puzzled over in the Western philosophical tradition. Showing how Bayesian methods can apply to these problems thus illustrates clearly their importance in understanding phenomena of induction more generally. These are also cases where the important mathematical principles and techniques of Bayesian statistics can be applied in a relatively straightforward way. They thus provide an ideal training ground for readers new to Bayesian modeling.

Beyond their value as a general framework for solving problems of induction,

Bayesian approaches can make several contributions to the enterprise of modeling human cognition. First, they provide a link between human cognition and the normative prescriptions of a theory of rational inductive inference. This connection eliminates many of the degrees of freedom from a cognitive model: Baycsian principles dictate how rational agents should update their beliefs in light of new data, based on a set of assumptions about the nature of the problem at hand and the prior knowledge possessed by the agents. Bayesian models are typically formulated at Marr's (1982) level of "computational theory," rather than the algorithmic or process level that characterizes more traditional cognitive modeling paradigms, as described in other chapters of this volume: connectionist networks (see Chapter 2), exemplar-based models (see Chapter 9), production systems and other cognitive architectures (see Chapter 6), or dynamical systems (see Chapter 4). Algorithmic or process accounts may be more satisfying in mechanistic terms, but they may also require assumptions about human processing mechanisms that are no longer needed when we assume that cognition is an approximately optimal response to the uncertainty and structure present in natural tasks and environments (Anderson, 1990). Finding effective computational models of human cognition then becomes a process of considering how best to characterize the computational problems that people face and the logic by which those computations can be carried out (Marr, 1982).

This focus implies certain limits on the phenomena that are valuable to study within a Bayesian paradigm. Some phenomena will surely be more satisfying to address at an algorithmic or neurocomputational level. For example, that a certain behavior takes people an average of 450 milliseconds to produce, measured from the onset of a visual stimulus, or that this reaction time increases when the stimulus is moved to a different part of the visual field or decreases when the same information content is presented auditorily, are not facts that a rational computational theory is likely to predict. Moreover,

not all computational-level models of cognition may have a place for Bayesian analysis. Only problems of inductive inference, or problems that contain an inductive component, are naturally expressed in Bayesian terms. Deductive reasoning, planning, or problem solving, for instance, are not traditionally thought of in this way. However, Bayesian principles are increasingly coming to be seen as relevant to many cognitive capacities, even those not traditionally seen in statistical terms (Anderson, 1990; Oaksford & Chater, 2001), because of the need for people to make inherently underconstrained inferences from impoverished data in an uncertain world.

A second key contribution of probabilistic models of cognition is the opportunity for greater communication with other fields studying computational principles of learning and inference. These connections make it a uniquely exciting time to be exploring probabilistic models of the mind. The fields of statistics, machine learning, and artificial intelligence have recently developed powerful tools for defining and working with complex probabilistic models that go far beyond the simple scenarios studied in classical probability theory; we present a taste of both the simplest models and more complex frameworks here. The more complex methods can support multiple hierarchically organized layers of inference, structured representations of abstract knowledge, and approximate methods of evaluation that can be applied efficiently to data sets with many thousands of entities. For the first time, we now have practical methods for developing computational models of human cognition that are based on sound probabilistic principles and that can also capture something of the richncss and complexity of everyday thinking, reasoning, and learning.

We can also exploit fertile analogies between specific learning and inference problems in the study of human cognition and in these other disciplines to develop new cognitive models or new tools for working with existing models. We discuss some of these relationships in this chapter, but there are many other cases. For example, prototype and exemplar models of categorization (Reed, 1972; Medin & Schaffer, 1978; Nosofsky, 1986) can both be seen as rational solutions to a standard classification task in statistical pattern recognition: An object is generated from one of several probability distributions (or "categories") over the space of possible objects, and the goal is to infer which distribution is most likely to have generated that object (Duda, Hart, & Stork, 2000). In rational probabilistic terms, these methods differ only in how these category-specific probability distributions are represented and estimated (Ashby & Alfonso-Reese, 1995; Nosofsky, 1998).

Finally, probabilistic models can be used to advance and perhaps resolve some of the great theoretical debates that divide traditional approaches to cognitive science. The history of computational models of cognition exhibits an enduring tension between models that emphasize symbolic representations and deductive inference, such as first-order logic or phrase structure grammars, and models that emphasize continuous representations and statistical learning, such as connectionist networks or other associative systems. Probabilistic models can be defined with either symbolic or continuous representations, or hybrids of both, and help to illustrate how statistical learning can be combined with symbolic structure. More generally, we think that the most promising routes to understanding human intelligence in computational terms will involve deep interactions between these two traditionally opposing approaches, with sophisticated statistical inference machinery operating over structured symbolic knowledge representations. Contemporary probabilistic methods give us the first general-purpose set of tools for building such structured statistical models, and we will see several simple examples of these models in this chapter.

The tension between symbols and statistics is perhaps only exceeded by the tension between accounts that focus on the importance of innate, domain-specific knowledge in explaining human cognition and accounts that focus on domain-general learning mechanisms. Again, probabilistic models provide a middle ground where both approaches can productively meet, and they suggest various routes to resolving the tensions between these approaches by combining the important insights of both. Probabilistic models highlight the role of prior knowledge in accounting for how people learn as much as they do from limited observed data and provide a framework for explaining precisely how prior knowledge interacts with data in guiding generalization and action. They also provide a tool for exploring the kinds of knowledge that people bring to learning and reasoning tasks, allowing us to work forwards from rational analyses of tasks and environments to predictions about behavior and to work backwards from subjects' observed behavior to viable assumptions about the knowledge they could bring to the task. Crucially, these models do not require that the prior knowledge be innate. Bayesian inference in hierarchical probabilistic models can explain how abstract prior knowledge may itself be learned from data and then put to use to guide learning in subsequent tasks and new environments.

This chapter discusses both the basic principles that underlie Bayesian models of cognition and several advanced techniques for probabilistic modeling and inference that have come out of recent work in computer science and statistics. The first step is to summarize the logic of Bayesian inference, which is at the heart of many probabilistic models. A discussion is then provided of three recent innovations that make it easier to define and use probabilistic models of complex domains: graphical models, hierarchical Bayesian models, and Markov chain Monte Carlo. The central ideas behind each of these techniques is illustrated by considering a detailed cognitive modeling application, drawn from causal learning, property induction, and language modeling, respectively.

2. The Basics of Bayesian Inference

Many aspects of cognition can be formulated as solutions to problems of induction. Given some observed data about the world, the mind draws conclusions about the underlying process or structure that gave rise to these data and then uses that knowledge to make predictive judgments about new cases. Bayesian inference is a rational engine for solving such problems within a probabilistic framework and consequently is the heart of most probabilistic models of cognition.

2.1. *Bayes' Rule*

Bayesian inference grows out of a simple formula known as *Bayes' rule* (Bayes, 1763/1958). When stated in terms of abstract random variables, Bayes' rule is no more than an elementary result of probability theory. Assume we have two random variables, A and B.[1] One of the principles of probability theory (sometimes called the *chain rule*) allows us to write the *joint probability* of these two variables taking on particular values a and b, $P(a, b)$, as the product of the *conditional probability* that A will take on value a given B takes on value b, $P(a \mid b)$, and the *marginal probability* that B takes on value b, $P(b)$. Thus, we have

$$P(a, b) = P(a \mid b)P(b). \quad (3.1)$$

There was nothing special about the choice of A rather than B in factorizing the joint probability in this way, so we can also write

$$P(a, b) = P(b \mid a)P(a). \quad (3.2)$$

It follows from Equations 3.1 and 3.2 that $P(a \mid b)P(b) = P(b \mid a)P(a)$, which can be rearranged to give

$$P(b \mid a) = \frac{P(a \mid b)P(b)}{P(a)}. \quad (3.3)$$

1 We will use uppercase letters to indicate random variables and matching lowercase variables to indicate the values those variables take on. When defining probability distributions, the random variables will remain implicit. For example, $P(a)$ refers to the probability that the variable A takes on the value a, which could also be written $P(A = a)$. We will write joint probabilities in the form $P(a, b)$. Other notations for joint probabilities include $P(a\&b)$ and $P(a \cap b)$.

This expression is Bayes' rule, which indicates how we can compute the conditional probability of b given a from the conditional probability of a given b.

Although Equation 3.3 seems relatively innocuous, Bayes' rule gets its strength, and its notoriety, when we make some assumptions about the variables we are considering and the meaning of probability. Assume that we have an agent who is attempting to infer the process that was responsible for generating some data, d. Let h be a hypothesis about this process. We will assume that the agent uses probabilities to represent degrees of belief in h and various alternative hypotheses h'. Let $P(h)$ indicate the probability that the agent ascribes to h being the true generating process, prior to (or independent of) seeing the data d. This quantity is known as the *prior probability*. How should that agent change his or her beliefs in light of the evidence provided by d? To answer this question, we need a procedure for computing the *posterior probability*, $P(h \mid d)$, or the degree of belief in h conditioned on the observation of d.

Bayes' rule provides just such a procedure, if we treat both the hypotheses that agents entertain and the data that they observe as random variables, so that the rules of probabilistic inference can be applied to relate them. Replacing a with d and b with h in Equation 3.3 gives

$$P(h \mid d) = \frac{P(d \mid h)P(h)}{P(d)}, \quad (3.4)$$

the form in which Bayes' rule is most commonly presented in analyses of learning or induction. The posterior probability is proportional to the product of the prior probability and another term $P(d \mid h)$, the probability of the data given the hypothesis, commonly known as the *likelihood*. Likelihoods are the critical bridge from priors to posteriors, reweighting each hypothesis by how well it predicts the observed data.

In addition to telling us how to compute with conditional probabilities, probability theory allows us to compute the probability distribution associated with a single variable (known as the *marginal probability*) by summing over other variables in a joint distribution: for example, $P(b) = \sum_a P(a, b)$. This is known as *marginalization*. Using this principle, we can rewrite Equation 3.4 as

$$P(h \mid d) = \frac{P(d \mid h)P(h)}{\sum_{h' \in \mathcal{H}} P(d \mid h')P(h')}, \quad (3.5)$$

where $\mathcal{H}$ is the set of all hypotheses considered by the agent, sometimes referred to as the *hypothesis space*. This formulation of Bayes' rule makes it clear that the posterior probability of h is directly proportional to the product of its prior probability and likelihood, relative to the sum of these same scores – products of priors and likelihoods – for all alternative hypotheses under consideration. The sum in the denominator of Equation 3.5 ensures that the resulting posterior probabilities are normalized to sum to one.

A simple example may help to illustrate the interaction between priors and likelihoods in determining posterior probabilities. Consider three possible medical conditions that could be posited to explain why a friend is coughing (the observed data d): $h_1 = $ "cold," $h_2 = $ "lung cancer," $h_3 = $ "stomach flu." The first hypothesis seems intuitively to be the best of the three, for reasons that Bayes' rule makes clear. The probability of coughing given that one has lung cancer, $P(d \mid h_2)$, is high, but the prior probability of having lung cancer, $P(h_2)$, is low. Hence, the posterior probability of lung cancer, $P(h_2 \mid d)$, is low, because it is proportional to the product of these two terms. Conversely, the prior probability of having stomach flu, $P(h_3)$, is relatively high (as medical conditions go), but its likelihood, $P(d \mid h_3)$, the probability of coughing given that one has stomach flu, is relatively low. So again, the posterior probability of stomach flu, $P(h_3 \mid d)$, will be relatively low. Only for hypothesis h_1 are both the prior $P(h_1)$ and the likelihood $P(d \mid h_1)$ relatively high: Colds are fairly common medical conditions, and coughing is a symptom frequently found in people who have colds. Hence, the posterior probability $P(h_1 \mid d)$ of having a cold given that one is coughing is substantially higher than the posteriors for the competing alternative hypotheses – each of which is less likely for a different sort of reason.

2.2. *Comparing Hypotheses*

The mathematics of Bayesian inference is most easily introduced in the context of comparing two simple hypotheses. For example, imagine that you are told that a box contains two coins: one that produces heads 50% of the time and one that produces heads 90% of the time. You choose a coin, and then flip it ten times, producing the sequence HHHHHHHHHH. Which coin did you pick? How would your beliefs change if you had obtained HHTHTHTTHT instead?

To formalize this problem in Bayesian terms, we need to identify the hypothesis space, $\mathcal{H}$, the prior probability of each hypothesis, $P(h)$, and the probability of the data under each hypothesis, $P(d \mid h)$. We have two coins, and thus two hypotheses. If we use θ to denote the probability that a coin produces heads, then h_0 is the hypothesis that $\theta = 0.5$, and h_1 is the hypothesis that $\theta = 0.9$. Because we have no reason to believe that one coin is more likely to be picked than the other, it is reasonable to assume equal prior probabilities: $P(h_0) = P(h_1) = 0.5$. The probability of a particular sequence of coin flips containing N_H heads and N_T tails being generated by a coin that produces heads with probability θ is

$$P(d \mid \theta) = \theta^{N_H}(1 - \theta)^{N_T}. \quad (3.6)$$

Formally, this expression follows from assuming that each flip is drawn independently from a Bernoulli distribution with parameter θ; less formally, that heads occurs with probability θ and tails with probability $1 - \theta$ on each flip. The likelihoods associated with h_0 and h_1 can thus be obtained by substituting the appropriate value of θ into Equation 3.6.

We can take the priors and likelihoods defined in the previous paragraph and plug them directly into Equation 3.5 to compute the posterior probabilities for both hypotheses, $P(h_0 \mid d)$ and $P(h_1 \mid d)$. However, when we have just two hypotheses, it is often easier to work with the *posterior odds*, or the ratio of these two posterior probabilities. The posterior odds in favor of h_1 is

$$\frac{P(h_1 \mid d)}{P(h_0 \mid d)} = \frac{P(d \mid h_1)}{P(d \mid h_0)} \frac{P(h_1)}{P(h_0)}, \quad (3.7)$$

where we have used the fact that the denominator of Equation 3.4 or 3.5 is constant over all hypotheses. The first and second terms on the right-hand side are called the *likelihood ratio* and the *prior odds*, respectively. We can use Equation 3.7 (and the priors and likelihoods defined previously) to compute the posterior odds of our two hypotheses for any observed sequence of heads and tails: For the sequence HHHHHHHHHH, the odds are approximately 357:1 in favor of h_1; for the sequence HHTHTHTTHT, approximately 165:1 in favor of h_0.

The form of Equation 3.7 helps to clarify how prior knowledge and new data are combined in Bayesian inference. The two terms on the right-hand side each express the influence of one of these factors: The prior odds are determined entirely by the prior beliefs of the agent, whereas the likelihood ratio expresses how these odds should be modified in light of the data d. This relationship is made even more transparent if we examine the expression for the log posterior odds,

$$\log \frac{P(h_1 \mid d)}{P(h_0 \mid d)} = \log \frac{P(d \mid h_1)}{P(d \mid h_0)} + \log \frac{P(h_1)}{P(h_0)}$$

$$(3.8)$$

in which the extent to which one should favor h_1 over h_0 reduces to an additive combination of a term reflecting prior beliefs (the log prior odds) and a term reflecting the contribution of the data (the log likelihood ratio). Based on this decomposition, the log likelihood ratio in favor of h_1 is often used as a measure of the evidence that d provides for h_1.

2.3. *Parameter Estimation*

The analysis outlined earlier for two simple hypotheses generalizes naturally to any finite set, although posterior odds may be less useful when there are multiple alternatives to be considered. Bayesian inference can also be applied in contexts where there are (uncountably) infinitely many hypotheses to evaluate – a situation that arises often. For example, instead of choosing between just two possible values for the probability θ that a coin produces heads, we could consider any real value of θ between 0 and 1. What, then, should we infer about the value of θ from a sequence such as HHHHHHHHHH?

Under one classical approach, inferring θ is treated as a problem of estimating a fixed parameter of a probabilistic model, to which the standard solution is *maximum-likelihood* estimation (see, e.g., Rice, 1995). Maximum-likelihood estimation is simple and often sensible, but can also be problematic, particularly as a way to think about human inference. Our coin-flipping example illustrates some of these problems. The maximum-likelihood estimate of θ is the value $\hat{\theta}$ that maximizes the probability of the data as given in Equation 3.6. It is straightforward to show that $\hat{\theta} = \frac{N_H}{N_H + N_T}$, which gives $\hat{\theta} = 1.0$ for the sequence HHHHHHHHHH.

It should be immediately clear that the single value of θ, which maximizes the probability of the data, might not provide the best basis for making predictions about future data. Inferring that θ is exactly 1 after seeing the sequence HHHHHHHHHH implies that we should predict that the coin will never produce tails. This might seem reasonable after observing a long sequence consisting solely of heads, but the same conclusion follows for an all-heads sequence of *any* length (because N_T is always 0, so $\frac{N_H}{N_H + N_T}$ is always 1). Would you really predict that a coin would produce only heads after seeing it produce a head on just one or two flips?

A second problem with maximum-likelihood estimation is that it does not take into account other knowledge that we might have about θ. This is largely by design: maximum-likelihood estimation and other classical statistical techniques have historically been promoted as "objective" procedures that do not require prior probabilities, which were seen as inherently and irremediably subjective. Although such a goal of objectivity might be desirable in certain scientific contexts, cognitive agents typically do have access to relevant and powerful prior knowledge, and they use that knowledge to make stronger inferences from sparse and ambiguous data than could be rationally supported by the data alone. For example, given the sequence HHH produced by flipping an apparently normal, randomly chosen coin, many people would say that the coin's probability of producing heads is nonetheless around 0.5, perhaps because we have strong prior expectations that most coins are nearly fair.

Both of these problems are addressed by a Bayesian approach to inferring θ. If we assume that θ is a random variable, then we can apply Bayes' rule to obtain

$$p(\theta \mid d) = \frac{P(d \mid \theta)p(\theta)}{P(d)}, \tag{3.9}$$

where

$$P(d) = \int_0^1 P(d \mid \theta)p(\theta) \, d\theta. \tag{3.10}$$

The key difference from Bayesian inference with finitely many hypotheses is that our beliefs about the hypotheses (both priors and posteriors) are now characterized by *probability densities* (notated by a lowercase "p") rather than probabilities strictly speaking, and the sum over hypotheses becomes an integral.

The posterior distribution over θ contains more information than a single point estimate: It indicates not just which values of θ are probable, but also how much uncertainty there is about those values. Collapsing this distribution down to a single number discards information, so Bayesians prefer to maintain distributions wherever possible (this attitude is similar to Marr's [1982, p. 106] "principle of least commitment"). However, there are two methods that are commonly used to obtain a point estimate from a posterior distribution. The first method is *maximum a posteriori*

(MAP) estimation: choosing the value of θ that maximizes the posterior probability, as given by Equation 3.9. The second method is computing the *posterior mean* of the quantity in question: a weighted average of all possible values of the quantity, where the weights are given by the posterior distribution. For example, the posterior mean value of the coin weight θ is computed as follows:

$$\bar{\theta} = \int_0^1 \theta \, p(\theta \mid d) \, d\theta. \tag{3.11}$$

In the case of coin flipping, the posterior mean also corresponds to the *posterior predictive distribution*: the probability that the next toss of the coin will produce heads, given the observed sequence of previous flips.

Different choices of the prior, $p(\theta)$, will lead to different inferences about the value of θ. A first step might be to assume a *uniform* prior over θ, with $p(\theta)$ being equal for all values of θ between 0 and 1 (more formally, $p(\theta) = 1$ for $\theta \in [0, 1]$). With this choice of $p(\theta)$ and the Bernoulli likelihood from Equation 3.6, Equation 3.9 becomes

$$p(\theta) = \frac{\theta^{N_H}(1 - \theta)^{N_T}}{\int_0^1 \theta^{N_H}(1 - \theta)^{N_T} d\theta} \tag{3.12}$$

where the denominator is just the integral from Equation 3.10. Using a little calculus to compute this integral, the posterior distribution over θ produced by a sequence d with N_H heads and N_T tails is

$$p(\theta \mid d) = \frac{(N_H + N_T + 1)!}{N_H! \, N_T!} \theta^{N_H}(1 - \theta)^{N_T}. \tag{3.13}$$

This is actually a distribution of a well-known form: a beta distribution with parameters $N_H + 1$ and $N_T + 1$, denoted Beta($N_H + 1$, $N_T + 1$) (e.g., Pitman, 1993). Using this prior, the MAP estimate for θ is the same as the maximum-likelihood estimate, $\frac{N_H}{N_H + N_T}$, but the posterior mean is slightly different, $\frac{N_H + 1}{N_H + N_T + 2}$. Thus, the posterior mean is sensitive to the consideration that we might not want to put as much evidential weight on seeing a single head as on a sequence of ten heads in a row: On seeing a single head, the posterior mean predicts that the next toss will produce a head with probability $\frac{2}{3}$, whereas a sequence of ten heads leads to the prediction that the next toss will produce a head with probability $\frac{11}{12}$.

We can also use priors that encode stronger beliefs about the value of θ. For example, we can take a Beta($V_H + 1$, $V_T + 1$) distribution for $p(\theta)$, where V_H and V_T are positive integers. This distribution gives

$$p(\theta) = \frac{(V_H + V_T + 1)!}{V_H! V_T!} \theta^{V_H} (1 - \theta)^{V_T}$$

$$(3.14)$$

having a mean at $\frac{V_H+1}{V_H+V_T+2}$, and gradually becoming more concentrated around that mean as $V_H + V_T$ becomes large. For instance, taking $V_H = V_T = 1,000$ would give a distribution that strongly favors values of θ close to 0.5. Using such a prior with the Bernoulli likelihood from Equation 3.6 and applying the same kind of calculations as described earlier, we obtain the posterior distribution

$$p(\theta \mid d) = \frac{(N_H + N_T + V_H + V_T + 1)!}{(N_H + V_H)! \, (N_T + V_T)!}$$

$$\times \, \theta^{N_H + V_H} (1 - \theta)^{N_T + V_T}, \quad (3.15)$$

which is Beta($N_H + V_H + 1$, $N_T + V_T + 1$). Under this posterior distribution, the MAP estimate of θ is $\frac{N_H + V_H}{N_H + N_T + V_H + V_T}$, and the posterior mean is $\frac{N_H + V_H + 1}{N_H + N_T + V_H + V_T + 2}$. Thus, if $V_H = V_T = 1,000$, seeing a sequence of ten heads in a row would induce a posterior distribution over θ with a mean of $\frac{1,011}{2,012} \approx 0.5025$. In this case, the observed data matter hardly at all. A prior that is much weaker but still biased towards approximately fair coins might take $V_H = V_T = 5$. Then an observation of ten heads in a row would lead to a posterior mean of $\frac{16}{22} \approx .727$, significantly tilted toward heads but still closer to a fair coin than the observed data would suggest on their own. We can say that such a prior

acts to "smooth" or "regularize" the observed data, damping out what might be misleading fluctuations when the data are far from the learner's initial expectations. On a larger scale, these principles of Bayesian parameter estimation with informative "smoothing" priors have been applied to a number of cognitively interesting machine-learning problems, such as Bayesian learning in neural networks (Mackay, 2003).

Our analysis of coin flipping with informative priors has two features of more general interest. First, the prior and posterior are specified using distributions of the same form (both being beta distributions). Second, the parameters of the prior, V_H and V_T, act as "virtual examples" of heads and tails, which are simply pooled with the real examples tallied in N_H and N_T to produce the posterior, as if both the real and virtual examples had been observed in the same data set. These two properties are not accidental: They are characteristic of a class of priors called *conjugate priors* (e.g., Bernardo & Smith, 1994). The likelihood determines whether a conjugate prior exists for a given problem and the form that the prior will take. The results we have given in this section exploit the fact that the beta distribution is the conjugate prior for the Bernoulli or binomial likelihood (Equation 3.6) – the uniform distribution on [0, 1] is also a beta distribution, being Beta(1, 1). Conjugate priors exist for many of the distributions commonly used in probabilistic models, such as Gaussian, Poisson, and multinomial distributions, and greatly simplify many Bayesian calculations. Using conjugate priors, posterior distributions can be computed analytically, and the interpretation of the prior as contributing virtual examples is intuitive.

Although conjugate priors are elegant and practical to work with, there are also important forms of prior knowledge that they cannot express. For example, they can capture the notion of smoothness in simple linear predictive systems but not in more complex nonlinear predictors, such as multilayer neural networks. Crucially, for modelers interested in higher-level cognition, conjugate priors cannot capture knowledge that the causal process generating the observed data could take on one of several qualitatively different forms. Still, they can sometimes be used to address questions of selecting models of different complexity, as we do in the next section, when the different models under consideration have the same qualitative form. A major area of current research in Bayesian statistics and machine learning focuses on building more complex models that maintain the benefits of working with conjugate priors, building on the techniques for model selection that we discuss next (e.g., Neal, 1992, 1998; Blei et al., 2004; Griffiths & Ghahramani, 2005).

2.4. Model Selection

Whether there were a finite number or not, the hypotheses that we have considered so far were relatively homogeneous, each offering a single value for the parameter θ characterizing our coin. However, many problems require comparing hypotheses that differ in their complexity. For example, the problem of inferring whether a coin is fair or biased based on an observed sequence of heads and tails requires comparing a hypothesis that gives a single value for θ – if the coin is fair, then $\theta = 0.5$ – with a hypothesis that allows θ to take on any value between 0 and 1.

Using observed data to choose between two probabilistic models that differ in their complexity is often called the problem of *model selection* (Myung & Pitt, 1997; Myung, Forster, & Browne, 2000). One familiar statistical approach to this problem is via hypothesis testing, but this approach is often complex and counterintuitive. In contrast, the Bayesian approach to model selection is a seamless application of the methods discussed so far. Hypotheses that differ in their complexity can be compared directly using Bayes' rule, once they are reduced to probability distributions over the observable data (see Kass & Raftery, 1995).

To illustrate this principle, assume that we have two hypotheses: h_0 is the hypothesis that $\theta = 0.5$, and h_1 is the hypothesis that θ takes a value drawn from a uni-

form distribution on $[0, 1]$. If we have no a priori reason to favor one hypothesis over the other, we can take $P(h_0) = P(h_1) = 0.5$. The probability of the data under h_0 is straightforward to compute, using Equation 3.6, giving $P(d \mid h_0) = 0.5^{N_H + N_T}$. But how should we compute the likelihood of the data under h_1, which does not make a commitment to a single value of θ?

The solution to this problem is to compute the marginal probability of the data under h_1. As discussed earlier given a joint distribution over a set of variables, we can always sum out variables until we obtain a distribution over just the variables that interest us. In this case, we define the joint distribution over d and θ given h_1, and then integrate over θ to obtain

$$P(d \mid h_1) = \int_0^1 P(d \mid \theta, h_1) p(\theta \mid h_1) \, d\theta$$

(3.16)

where $p(\theta \mid h_1)$ is the distribution over θ assumed under h_1 – in this case, a uniform distribution over $[0, 1]$. This does not require any new concepts – it is exactly the same kind of computation as we needed to perform to compute the denominator for the posterior distribution over θ (Equation 3.10). Performing this computation, we obtain $P(d \mid h_1) = \frac{N_H! \, N_T!}{(N_H + N_T + 1)!}$, where again the fact that we have a conjugate prior provides us with a neat analytic result. Having computed this likelihood, we can apply Bayes' rule just as we did for two simple hypotheses. Figure 3.1a shows how the log posterior odds in favor of h_1 change as N_H and N_T vary for sequences of length 10.

The ease with which hypotheses differing in complexity can be compared using Bayes' rule conceals the fact that this is actually a very challenging problem. Complex hypotheses have more degrees of freedom that can be adapted to the data and can thus always be made to fit the data better than simple hypotheses. For example, for any sequence of heads and tails, we can always find a value of θ that would give higher probability to that sequence than

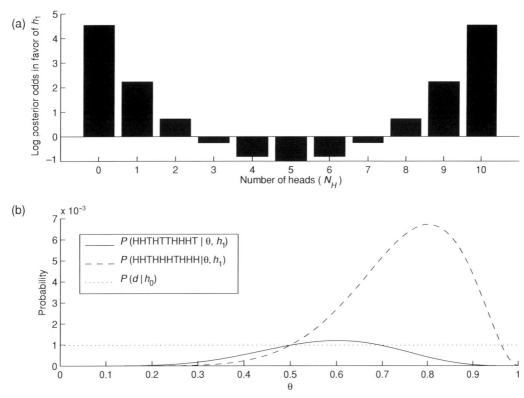

Figure 3.1. Comparing hypotheses about the weight of a coin. (a) The vertical axis shows log posterior odds in favor of h_1, the hypothesis that the probability of heads (θ) is drawn from a uniform distribution on [0, 1], over h_0, the hypothesis that the probability of heads is 0.5. The horizontal axis shows the number of heads, N_H, in a sequence of 10 flips. As N_H deviates from 5, the posterior odds in favor of h_1 increase. (b) The posterior odds shown in (a) are computed by averaging over the values of θ with respect to the prior, $p(\theta)$, which in this case is the uniform distribution on [0, 1]. This averaging takes into account the fact that hypotheses with greater flexibility – such as the free-ranging θ parameter in h_1 – can produce both better and worse predictions, implementing an automatic "Bayesian Occam's razor." The solid line shows the probability of the sequence HHTHTTHHHT for different values of θ, whereas the dotted line is the probability of any sequence of length 10 under h_0 (equivalent to $\theta = 0.5$). Although there are some values of θ that result in a higher probability for the sequence, on average, the greater flexibility of h_1 results in lower probabilities. Consequently, h_0 is favored over h_1 (this sequence has $N_H = 6$). In contrast, a wide range of values of θ result in higher probability for for the sequence HHTHHHHTHHH, as shown by the dashed line. Consequently, h_1 is favored over h_0 (this sequence has $N_H = 8$). Reproduced with permission from Griffiths and Yuille (2006).

does the hypothesis that $\theta = 0.5$. It seems like a complex hypothesis would thus have an inherent unfair advantage over a simple hypothesis. The Bayesian solution to the problem of comparing hypotheses that differ in their complexity takes this into account. More degrees of freedom provide the opportunity to find a better fit to the data, but this greater flexibility also makes a worse

fit possible. For example, for d consisting of the sequence HHTHTTHHHT, $P(d \mid \theta, h_1)$ is greater than $P(d \mid h_0)$ for $\theta \in (0.5, 0.694]$, but is less than $P(d \mid h_0)$ outside that range. Marginalizing over θ averages these gains and losses: A more complex hypothesis will be favored only if its greater complexity consistently provides a better account of the data. To phrase this principle another way, a Bayesian learner judges the fit of a parameterized model not by how well it fits using the *best* parameter values, but by how well it fits using *randomly selected* parameters, where the parameters are drawn from a prior specified by the model ($p(\theta \mid h_1)$ in Equation 3.16) (Ghahramani, 2004). This penalization of more complex models is known as the "Bayesian Occam's razor" (Jeffreys & Berger, 1992; Mackay, 2003), and is illustrated in Figure 3.1b.

2.5. *Summary*

Bayesian inference stipulates how rational learners should update their beliefs in the light of evidence. The principles behind Bayesian inference can be applied whenever we are making inferences from data, whether the hypotheses involved are discrete or continuous, or have one or more unspecified free parameters. However, developing probabilistic models that can capture the richness and complexity of human cognition requires going beyond these basic ideas. The remainder of the chapter summarizes several recent tools that have been developed in computer science and statistics for defining and using complex probabilistic models, and provides examples of how they can be used in modeling human cognition.

3. Graphical Models

The previous discussion of Bayesian inference was formulated in the language of "hypotheses" and "data." However, the principles of Bayesian inference, and the idea of using probabilistic models, extend to much richer settings. In its most general form, a probabilistic model simply defines the joint distribution for a system of random variables. Representing and computing with these joint distributions becomes challenging as the number of variables grows, and their properties can be difficult to understand. Graphical models provide an efficient and intuitive framework for working with high-dimensional probability distributions, which is applicable when these distributions can be viewed as the product of smaller components defined over local subsets of variables.

A graphical model associates a probability distribution with a graph. The nodes of the graph represent the variables on which the distribution is defined, the edges between the nodes reflect their probabilistic dependencies, and a set of functions relating nodes and their neighbors in the graph are used to define a joint distribution over all of the variables based on those dependencies. There are two kinds of graphical models, differing in the nature of the edges that connect the nodes. If the edges simply indicate a dependency between variables, without specifying a direction, then the result is an *undirected graphical model*. Undirected graphical models have long been used in statistical physics, and many probabilistic neural network models, such as Boltzmann machines (Ackley, Hinton, & Sejnowski, 1985), can be interpreted as models of this kind. If the edges indicate the direction of a dependency, the result is a *directed graphical model*. Our focus here will be on directed graphical models, which are also known as Bayesian networks or Bayes nets (Pearl, 1988). Bayesian networks can often be given a causal interpretation, where an edge between two nodes indicates that one node is a direct cause of the other, which makes them particularly appealing for modeling higher-level cognition.

3.1. *Bayesian Networks*

A Bayesian network represents the probabilistic dependencies relating a set of variables. If an edge exists from node A to node B, then A is referred to as a "parent" of B, and B is a "child" of A. This genealogical relation is often extended to identify the "ancestors" and "descendants" of a node. The directed graph used in a Bayesian network has one node for each random variable in the associated probability distribution and is constrained to be *acyclic*: One can never return to the same node by following a sequence of directed edges. The edges express the probabilistic dependencies between the variables in a fashion consistent with the *Markov condition*: Conditioned on its parents, each variable is independent of all other variables except its descendants (Pearl, 1988; Spirtes, Glymour, & Schienes, 1993). As a consequence of the Markov condition, any Bayesian network specifies a canonical factorization of a full joint probability distribution into the product of local conditional distributions, one for each variable conditioned on its parents. That is, for a set of variables $X_1, X_2, \ldots, X_N$, we can write $P(x_1, x_2, \ldots, x_N) = \prod_i P(x_i \mid \mathrm{Pa}(X_i))$ where $\mathrm{Pa}(X_i)$ is the set of parents of X_i.

Bayesian networks provide an intuitive representation for the structure of many probabilistic models. For example, in the previous section, we discussed the problem of estimating the weight of a coin, θ. One detail that we left implicit in that discussion was the assumption that successive coin flips are independent, given a value for θ. This conditional independence assumption is expressed in the graphical model shown in Figure 3.2a, where $x_1, x_2, \ldots, x_N$ are the outcomes (heads or tails) of N successive tosses. Applying the Markov condition, this structure represents the probability distribution

$$P(x_1, x_2, \ldots, x_N, \theta) = p(\theta) \prod_{i=1}^{N} P(x_i \mid \theta)$$

(3.17)

in which the x_i are independent given the value of θ. Other dependency structures are possible. For example, the flips could be generated in a Markov chain, a sequence of random variables in which each variable is independent of all of its predecessors given the variable that immediately precedes it (e.g., Norris, 1997). Using a Markov chain structure, we could represent a hypothesis space of coins that are particularly biased toward alternating or maintaining their last outcomes, letting the parameter θ be the probability that the outcome x_i takes the same value as x_{i-1} (and assuming that x_1 is heads with probability 0.5). This distribution would corre-

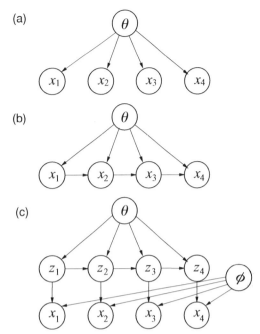

Figure 3.2. Graphical models showing different kinds of processes that could generate a sequence of coin flips. (a) Independent flips, with parameters θ determining the probability of heads. (b) A Markov chain, where the probability of heads depends on the result of the previous flip. Here, the parameters θ define the probability of heads after a head and after a tail. (c) A hidden Markov model, in which the probability of heads depends on a latent state variable z_i. Transitions between values of the latent state are set by parameters θ, whereas other parameters ϕ determine the probability of heads for each value of the latent state. This kind of model is commonly used in computational linguistics, where the x_i might be the sequence of words in a document and the z_i the syntactic classes from which they are generated.

spond to the graphical model shown in Figure 3.2b. Applying the Markov condition, this structure represents the probability distribution

$$P(x_1, x_2, \ldots, x_N, \theta)$$
$$= p(\theta)P(x_1) \prod_{i=2}^{N} P(x_i \mid x_{i-1}\theta), \quad (3.18)$$

in which each x_i depends only on x_{i-1}, given θ. More elaborate structures are also possible: any directed acyclic graph on $x_1, x_2, \ldots, x_N$ and θ corresponds to a valid set of assumptions about the dependencies among these variables.

When introducing the basic ideas behind Bayesian inference, we emphasized the fact that hypotheses correspond to different assumptions about the process that could have generated some observed data. Bayesian networks help to make this idea transparent. Every Bayesian network indicates a sequence of steps that one could follow to generate samples from the joint distribution over the random variables in the network. First, one samples the values of all variables with no parents in the graph. Then, one samples the variables with parents taking known values, one after another. For example, in the structure shown in Figure 3.2b, we would sample θ from the distribution $p(\theta)$, then sample x_1 from the distribution $P(x_1 \mid \theta)$, then successively sample x_i from $P(x_i \mid x_{i-1}, \theta)$ for $i = 2, \ldots, N$. A set of probabilistic steps that can be followed to generate the values of a set of random variables is known as a *generative model*, and the directed graph associated with a probability distribution provides an intuitive representation for the steps that are involved in such a model.

For the generative models represented by Figure 3.2a or 3.2b, we have assumed that all variables except θ are observed in each sample from the model, or each data point. More generally, generative models can include a number of steps that make reference to unobserved or *latent* variables. Introducing latent variables can lead to apparently complicated dependency structures among the observable variables. For example, in the graphical model shown in Figure 3.2c, a sequence of latent variables $z_1, z_2, \ldots, z_N$ influences the probability that each respective coin flip in a sequence $x_1, x_2, \ldots, x_N$ comes up heads (in conjunction with a set of parameters ϕ). The latent variables form a Markov chain, with the value of z_i depending only on the value of z_{i-1} (in conjunction with the parameters θ). This model, called a *hidden Markov model*, is widely used in computational linguistics, where z_i might be the syntactic class (such as noun or verb) of a word, θ encodes the probability that a word of one class will appear after another (capturing simple syntactic constraints on the structure of sentences), and ϕ encodes the probability that each word will be generated from a particular syntactic class (e.g., Charniak, 1993; Jurafsky & Martin, 2000; Manning & Schütze, 1999). The dependencies among the latent variables induce dependencies among the observed variables – in the case of language, the constraints on transitions between syntactic classes impose constraints on which words can follow one another.

3.2. Representing Probability Distributions over Propositions

The treatment of graphical models in the previous section – as representations of the dependency structure among variables in generative models for data – follows their standard uses in the fields of statistics and machine learning. Graphical models can take on a different interpretation in artificial intelligence, when the variables of interest represent the truth value of certain propositions (Russell & Norvig, 2002). For example, imagine that a friend of yours claims to possess psychic powers, in particular, the power of psychokinesis. He proposes to demonstrate these powers by flipping a coin and influencing the outcome to produce heads. You suggest that a better test might be to see if he can levitate a pencil because the coin producing heads could also be explained by some kind of sleight of hand, such as substituting a two-headed coin. We can express all possible outcomes of the proposed tests, as well as their causes, using the binary random variables X_1, X_2, X_3, and X_4 to represent (respectively) the truth of the coin being flipped and producing heads, the pencil levitating, your friend having psychic powers, and the use of a two-headed coin. Any set of beliefs about these outcomes can be encoded in a joint probability distribution, $P(x_1, x_2, x_3, x_4)$. For example, the probability that the coin comes up heads ($x_1 = 1$) should be higher if your

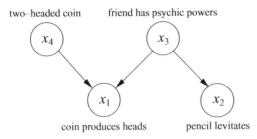

two-headed coin   friend has psychic powers

x_4 x_3

x_1 x_2

coin produces heads   pencil levitates

Figure 3.3. Directed graphical model (Bayesian network) showing the dependencies among variables in the "psychic friend" example discussed in the text. Reproduced with permission from Griffiths and Yuille (2006).

friend actually does have psychic powers ($x_3 = 1$). Figure 3.3 shows a Bayesian network expressing a possible pattern of dependencies among these variables. For example, X_1 and X_2 are assumed to be independent given X_3, indicating that once it was known whether or not your friend was psychic, the outcomes of the coin flip and the levitation experiments would be completely unrelated. By the Markov condition, we can write $P(x_1, x_2, x_3, x_4) = P(x_1 \mid x_3, x_4) P(x_2 \mid x_3) P(x_3) P(x_4)$.

In addition to clarifying the dependency structure of a set of random variables, Bayesian networks provide an efficient way to represent and compute with probability distributions. In general, a joint probability distribution on N binary variables requires $2^N - 1$ numbers to specify (one for each set of joint values taken by the variables, minus one because of the constraint that probability distributions sum to 1). In the case of the psychic friend example, where there are four variables, this would be $2^4 - 1 = 15$ numbers. However, the factorization of the joint distribution over these variables allows us to use fewer numbers in specifying the distribution over these four variables. We only need one number for each variable conditioned on each possible set of values its parents can take, or $2^{|Pa(X_i)|}$ numbers for each variable X_i (where $\mid Pa(X_i) \mid$ is the size of the parent set of X_i). For our "psychic friend" network, this adds up to 8 numbers rather than 15, because X_3 and X_4 have no parents (contributing one number each),

X_2 has one parent (contributing two numbers), and X_1 has two parents (contributing four numbers). Recognizing the structure in this probability distribution can also greatly simplify the computations we want to perform. When variables are independent or conditionally independent of others, it reduces the number of terms that appear in sums over subsets of variables necessary to compute marginal beliefs about a variable or conditional beliefs about a variable given the values of one or more other variables. A variety of algorithms have been developed to perform these probabilistic inferences efficiently on complex models, by recognizing and exploiting conditional independence structures in Bayesian networks (Pearl, 1988; Mackay, 2003). These algorithms form the heart of many modern artificial intelligence systems, making it possible to reason efficiently under uncertainty (Korb & Nicholson, 2003; Russell & Norvig, 2002).

3.3. Causal Graphical Models

In a standard Bayesian network, edges between variables indicate only statistical dependencies between them. However, recent work has explored the consequences of augmenting directed graphical models with a stronger assumption about the relationships indicated by edges: that they indicate direct causal relationships (Pearl, 2000; Spirtes et al., 1993). This assumption allows causal graphical models to represent not just the probabilities of events that one might observe, but also the probabilities of events that one can produce through intervening on a system. The inferential implications of an event can differ strongly, depending on whether it was observed passively or under conditions of intervention. For example, observing that nothing happens when your friend attempts to levitate a pencil would provide evidence against his claim of having psychic powers; but secretly intervening to hold the pencil down while your friend attempts to levitate it would make the pencil's nonlevitation unsurprising and uninformative about his powers.

In causal graphical models, the consequences of intervening on a particular variable can be assessed by removing all incoming edges to that variable and performing probabilistic inference in the resulting "mutilated" model (Pearl, 2000). This procedure produces results that align with our intuitions in the psychic powers example: Intervening on X_2 breaks its connection with X_3, rendering the two variables independent. As a consequence, X_2 cannot provide evidence about the value of X_3. Several recent papers have investigated whether people are sensitive to the consequences of intervention, generally finding that people differentiate between observational and interventional evidence appropriately (Hagmayer et al., in press; Lagnado & Sloman, 2004; Steyvers et al., 2003). Introductions to causal graphical models that consider applications to human cognition are provided by Glymour (2001) and Sloman (2005).

The prospect of using graphical models to express the probabilistic consequences of causal relationships has led researchers in several fields to ask whether these models could serve as the basis for learning causal relationships from data. Every introductory class in statistics teaches that "correlation does not imply causation," but the opposite is true: Patterns of causation do imply patterns of correlation. A Bayesian learner should thus be able to work backward from observed patterns of correlation (or statistical dependency) to make probabilistic inferences about the underlying causal structures likely to have generated those observed data. We can use the same basic principles of Bayesian inference developed in the previous section, where now the data are samples from an unknown causal graphical model and the hypotheses to be evaluated are different candidate graphical models. For technical introductions to the methods and challenges of learning causal graphical models, see Heckerman (1998) and Glymour and Cooper (1999).

As in the previous section, it is valuable to distinguish between the problems of parameter estimation and model selection. In the context of causal learning, model selec-

Table 3.1: Contingency table representation used in elemental causal induction

	Effect present (e^+)	Effect absent (e^-)
Cause present (c^+)	$N(e^+, c^+)$	$N(e^-, c^+)$
Cause absent (c^-)	$N(e^+, c^-)$	$N(e^-, c^-)$

tion becomes the problem of determining the graph structure of the causal model – which causal relationships exist – and parameter estimation becomes the problem of determining the strength and polarity of the causal relations specified by a given graph structure. We will illustrate the differences between these two aspects of causal learning and how graphical models can be brought into contact with empirical data on human causal learning, with a task that has been extensively studied in the cognitive psychology literature: judging the status of a single causal relationship between two variables based on contingency data.

3.4. *Example: Causal Induction from Contingency Data*

Much psychological research on causal induction has focused on this simple causal learning problem: given a candidate cause, C, and a candidate effect, E, people are asked to give a numerical rating assessing the degree to which C causes E.[2] We refer to tasks of this sort as "elemental causal induction" tasks. The exact wording of the judgment question varies and until recently was not the subject of much attention, although as we will see later, it is potentially quite important. Most studies present information corresponding to the entries in a 2 × 2 contingency table, as in Table 3.1. People are given information about the frequency

---

2 As elsewhere in this chapter, we will represent variables such as C, E with capital letters and their instantiations with lowercase letters, with c^+, e^+ indicating that the cause or effect is present and c^-, e^- indicating that the cause or effect is absent.

with which the effect occurs in the presence and absence of the cause, represented by the numbers $N(e^+, c^+)$, $N(e^-, c^-)$, and so forth. In a standard example, C might be injecting a chemical into a mouse and E the expression of a particular gene. $N(e^+, c^+)$ would be the number of injected mice expressing the gene, whereas $N(e^-, c^-)$ would be the number of uninjected mice not expressing the gene.

The leading psychological models of elemental causal induction are measures of association that can be computed from simple combinations of the frequencies in Table 3.1. A classic model first suggested by Jenkins and Ward (1965) asserts that the degree of causation is best measured by the quantity

$$
\Delta P = \frac{N(e^+, c^+)}{N(e^+, c^+) + N(e^-, c^+)}
$$
$$
- \frac{N(e^+, c^-)}{N(e^+, c^-) + N(e^-, c^-)}
$$
$$
= P(e^+ \mid c^+) - P(e^+ \mid c^-), \quad (3.19)
$$

where $P(e^+ \mid c^+)$ is the empirical conditional probability of the effect given the presence of the cause, estimated from the contingency table counts $N(\cdot)$. ΔP thus reflects the change in the probability of the effect occurring as a consequence of the occurrence of the cause. More recently, Cheng (1997) has suggested that people's judgments are better captured by a measure called "causal power,"

$$
\text{power} = \frac{\Delta P}{1 - P(e^+ \mid c^-)}, \quad (3.20)
$$

which takes ΔP as a component, but predicts that ΔP will have a greater effect when $P(e^+ \mid c^-)$ is large.

Several experiments have been conducted with the aim of evaluating ΔP and causal power as models of human jugments. In one such study, Buehner and Cheng (1997, Experiment 1B; this experiment also appears in Buehner, Cheng, & Clifford, 2003) asked people to evaluate causal relationships for

15 sets of contingencies expressing all possible combinations of $P(e^+ \mid c^-)$ and ΔP in increments of 0.25. The results of this experiment are shown in Figure 3.4, together with the predictions of ΔP and causal power. As can be seen from the figure, both ΔP and causal power capture some of the trends in the data, producing correlations of $r = 0.89$ and $r = 0.88$, respectively. However, because the trends predicted by the two models are essentially orthogonal, neither model provides a complete account of the data.[3]

ΔP and causal power seem to capture some important elements of human causal induction, but miss others. We can gain some insight into the assumptions behind these models, and identify some possible alternative models, by considering the computational problem behind causal induction using the tools of causal graphical models and Bayesian inference. The task of elemental causal induction can be seen as trying to infer which causal graphical model best characterizes the relationship between the variables C and E. Figure 3.5 shows two possible causal structures relating C, E, and another variable B, which summarizes the influence of all of the other "background" causes of E (which are assumed to be constantly present). The problem of learning which causal graphical model is correct has two aspects: inferring the right causal structure, a problem of model selection, and determining the right parameters assuming a particular structure, a problem of parameter estimation.

To formulate the problems of model selection and parameter estimation more precisely, we need to make some further assumptions about the nature of the causal graphical models shown in Figure 3.5. In particular, we need to define the form of the conditional probability distribution $P(E \mid B, C)$ for the different structures, often called the *parameterization* of the graphs. Sometimes, the parameterization is

---

3 See Griffiths and Tenenbaum (2005) for the details of how these correlations were evaluated, using a power-law transformation to allow for nonlinearities in participants' judgment scales.

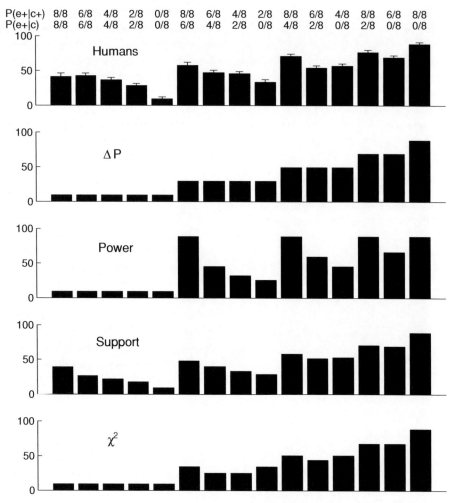

Figure 3.4. Predictions of models compared with the performance of human participants from Buehner and Cheng (1997, Experiment 1B). Numbers along the top of the figure show stimulus contingencies; error bars indicate one standard error. P(e+ | c+) and P(e+ | c−) indicate probability of the effect in the presence and absence of the cause, respectively. ΔP, power, support, and χ^2 are four models of causal judgements. Reproduced with permission from Griffiths and Tenenbaum (2005).

trivial – for example, C and E are independent in Graph 0, so we just need to specify $P_0(E \mid B)$, where the subscript indicates that this probability is associated with Graph 0. This can be done using a single numerical parameter w_0, which provides the probability that the effect will be present in the presence of the background cause, $P_0(e^+ \mid b^+; w_0) = w_0$. However, when a node has multiple parents, there are many different ways in which the functional relationship between causes and

effects could be defined. For example, in Graph 1, we need to account for how the causes B and C interact in producing the effect E.

A simple and widely used parameterization for Bayesian networks of binary variables is the noisy-OR distribution (Pearl, 1988). The noisy-OR can be given a natural interpretation in terms of causal relations between multiple causes and a single joint effect. For Graph 1, these assumptions are that B and C are both generative causes,

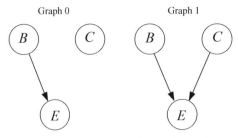

Figure 3.5. Directed graphs involving three variables, B, C, E, relevant to elemental causal induction. B represents background variables, C a potential causal variable, and E the effect of interest. Graph 1 is assumed in computing ΔP and causal power. Computing causal support involves comparing the structure of Graph 1 to that of Graph 0 in which C and E are independent. Reproduced with permission from Griffiths and Tenenbaum (2005).

increasing the probability of the effect; that the probability of E in the presence of just B is w_0, and in the presence of just C is w_1; and that, when both B and C are present, they have independent opportunities to produce the effect. This parameterization can be represented in a compact mathematical form as

$$P_1(e^+ \mid b, c; w_0, w_1)$$
$$= 1 - (1 - w_0)^b(1 - w_1)^c, \qquad (3.21)$$

where w_0, w_1 are parameters associated with the strength of B, C respectively. The variable c is 1 if the cause is present (c^+) or 0 if the cause if is absent (c^-), and likewise for the variable b with the background cause. This expression gives w_0 for the probability of E in the presence of B alone, and $w_0 + w_1 - w_0 w_1$ for the probability of E in the presence of both B and C. This parameterization is called a noisy-OR because if w_0 and w_1 are both 1, Equation 3.21 reduces to the logical OR function: The effect occurs if and only if B or C are present, or both. With w_0 and w_1 in the range $[0, 1]$, the noisy-OR softens this function but preserves its essentially disjunctive interaction: The effect occurs if and only if B causes it (which happens with probability w_0) or C causes it (which happens with probability w_1), or both.

An alternative to the noisy-OR might be a linear parameterization of Graph 1, asserting that the probability of E occurring is a linear function of B and C. This corresponds to assuming that the presence of a cause simply increases the probability of an effect by a constant amount, regardless of any other causes that might be present. There is no distinction between generative and preventive causes. The result is

$$P_1(e^+ \mid b, c; w_0, w_1) = w_0 \cdot b + w_1 \cdot c.$$
$$(3.22)$$

This parameterization requires that we constrain $w_0 + w_1$ to lie between 0 and 1 to ensure that Equation 3.22 results in a legal probability distribution. Because of this dependence between parameters that seem intuitively like they should be independent, such a linear parameterization is not normally used in Bayesian networks. However, it is relevant for understanding models of human causal induction.

Given a particular causal graph structure and a particular parameterization – for example, Graph 1 parameterized with a noisy-OR function – inferring the strength parameters that best characterize the causal relationships in that model is straightforward. We can use any of the parameter-estimation methods discussed in the previous section (such as maximum-likelihood or MAP estimation) to find the values of the parameters (w_0 and w_1 in Graph 1) that best fit a set of observed contingencies. Tenenbaum and Griffiths (2001; Griffiths & Tenenbaum, 2005) showed that the two psychological models of causal induction introduced above – ΔP and causal power – both correspond to maximum-likelihood estimates of the causal strength parameter w_1, but under different assumptions about the parameterization of Graph 1. ΔP results from assuming the linear parameterization, whereas causal power results from assuming the noisy-OR.

This view of ΔP and causal power helps to reveal their underlying similarities and differences: They are similar in being maximum-likelihood estimates of the strength parameter describing a causal relationship, but differ in the assumptions that they make about the form of that relationship. This analysis also suggests another class of models of causal induction that has not until recently been explored: models of learning causal graph structure or causal model selection rather than parameter estimation. Recalling our discussion of model selection, we can express the evidence that a set of contingencies d provide in favor of the existence of a causal relationship (i.e., Graph 1 over Graph 0) as the log-likelihood ratio in favor of Graph 1. Terming this quantity "causal support," we have

$$\text{support} = \log \frac{P(d \mid \text{Graph 1})}{P(d \mid \text{Graph 0})} \qquad (3.23)$$

where $P(d \mid \text{Graph 1})$ and $P(d \mid \text{Graph 0})$ are computed by integrating over the parameters associated with the different structures

$$P(d \mid \text{Graph 1})$$
$$= \int_0^1 \int_0^1 P_1(d \mid w_0, w_1, \text{Graph 1})$$
$$\times P(w_0, w_1 \mid \text{Graph 1})\, dw_0\, dw_1$$
$$(3.24)$$

$$P(d \mid \text{Graph 0}) = \int_0^1 P_0(d \mid w_0, \text{Graph 0})$$
$$\times P(w_0 \mid \text{Graph 0})\, dw_0. \qquad (3.25)$$

Tenenbaum and Griffiths (2001; Griffiths & Tenenbaum, 2005) proposed this model and specifically assumed a noisy-OR parameterization for Graph 1 and uniform priors on w_0 and w_1. Equation 3.25 is identical to Equation 3.16 and has an analytic solution. Evaluating Equation 3.24 is more of a challenge, but one that we will return to later in this chapter when we discuss Monte Carlo methods for approximate probabilistic inference.

The results of computing causal support for the stimuli used by Buehner and Cheng (1997) are shown in Figure 3.4. Causal support provides an excellent fit to these

data, with $r = 0.97$. The model captures the trends predicted by both ΔP and causal power, as well as trends that are predicted by neither model. These results suggest that when people evaluate contingency, they may be taking into account the evidence that those data provide for a causal relationship as well as the strength of the relationship they suggest. The figure also shows the predictions obtained by applying the χ^2 measure to these data, a standard hypothesis-testing method of assessing the evidence for a relationship (and a common ingredient in non-Bayesian approaches to structure learning, e.g. Spirtes et al., 1993). These predictions miss several important trends in the human data, suggesting that the ability to assert expectations about the nature of a causal relationship that go beyond mere dependency (such as the assumption of a noisy-OR parameterization) is contributing to the success of this model. Causal support predicts human judgments on several other datasets that are problematic for ΔP and causal power, and also accommodates causal learning based on the rate at which events occur (see Griffiths & Tenenbaum, 2005, for more details).

The Bayesian approach to causal induction can be extended to cover a variety of more complex cases, including learning in larger causal networks (Steyvers et al., 2003), learning about dynamic causal relationships in physical systems (Tenenbaum & Griffiths, 2003), choosing which interventions to perform in the aid of causal learning (Steyvers et al., 2003), learning about hidden causes (Griffiths, Baraff, & Tenenbaum, 2004), distinguishing hidden common causes from mere coincidences (Griffiths & Tenenbaum, 2007a), and online learning from sequentially presented data (Danks, Griffiths, & Tenenbaum, 2003).

Modeling learning in these more complex cases often requires us to work with stronger and more structured prior distributions than were needed earlier to explain elemental causal induction. This prior knowledge can be usefully described in terms of intuitive domain theories (Carey, 1985; Wellman & Gelman, 1992; Gopnik & Meltzoff, 1997), systems of abstract concepts and principles that specify the kinds of entities that can exist in a domain, their properties and possible states, and the kinds of causal relations that can exist between them. We have begun to explore how these abstract causal theories can be formalized as probabilistic generators for hypothesis spaces of causal graphical models, using probabilistic forms of generative grammars, predicate logic, or other structured representations (Griffiths, 2005; Griffiths & Tenenbaum, 2007b; Mansinghka et al., 2006; Tenenbaum et al., 2006; Tenenbaum, Griffiths, & Niyogi, 2007; Tenenbaum & Niyogi, 2003). Given observations of causal events relating a set of objects, these probabilistic theories generate the relevant variables for representing those events, a constrained space of possible causal graphs over those variables, and the allowable parameterizations for those graphs. They also generate a prior distribution over this hypothesis space of candidate causal models, which provides the basis for Bayesian causal learning in the spirit of the methods described previously.

We see it as an advantage of the Bayesian approach that it forces modelers to make clear their assumptions about the form and content of learners' prior knowledge. The framework lets us test these assumptions empirically and study how they vary across different settings by specifying a rational mapping from prior knowledge to learners' behavior in any given task. It may also seem unsatisfying, though, by passing on the hardest questions of learning to whatever mechanism is responsible for establishing learners' prior knowledge. This is the problem we address in the next section, using the techniques of hierarchical Bayesian models.

4. Hierarchical Bayesian Models

The predictions of a Bayesian model can often depend critically on the prior distribution that it uses. The early coin flipping examples provided a simple and clear case of the effects of priors. If a coin is tossed once and comes up heads, then a learner who began with a uniform prior on the bias of the coin should predict that the next toss will produce heads with probability $\frac{2}{3}$. If the learner began instead with the belief that the coin is likely to be fair, she should predict that the next toss will produce heads with probability close to $\frac{1}{2}$.

Within statistics, Bayesian approaches have at times been criticized for necessarily requiring some form of prior knowledge. It is often said that good statistical analyses should "let the data speak for themselves," hence the motivation for maximum-likelihood estimation and other classical statistical methods that do not require a prior to be specified. Cognitive models, however, will usually aim for the opposite goal. Most human inferences are guided by background knowledge, and cognitive models should formalize this knowledge and show how it can be used for induction. From this perspective, the prior distribution used by a Bayesian model is critical because an appropriate prior can capture the background knowledge that humans bring to a given inductive problem. As mentioned in the previous section, prior distributions can capture many kinds of knowledge: priors for causal reasoning, for example, may incorporate theories of folk physics or knowledge about the powers and liabilities of different ontological kinds.

Because background knowledge plays a central role in many human inferences, it is important to ask how this knowledge might be acquired. In a Bayesian framework, the acquisition of background knowledge can be modeled as the acquisition of a prior distribution. We have already seen one piece of evidence that prior distributions can be learned: Given two competing models, each of which uses a different prior distribution, Bayesian model selection can be used to choose between them. Here, we provide a more comprehensive treatment of the problem of learning prior distribution and show how this problem can be addressed using hierarchical Bayesian models (Good, 1980; Gelman et al., 1995). Although we will focus on just two applications, the hierarchical Bayesian approach has been applied to

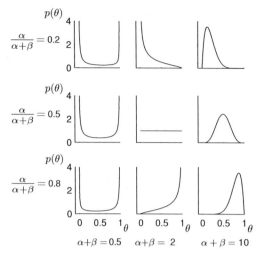

Figure 3.6. The beta distribution serves as a prior on the bias θ of a coin. The mean of the distribution is $\frac{\alpha}{\alpha+\beta}$, and the shape of the distribution depends on $\alpha + \beta$. Reproduced with permission from Kemp, Perfors, and Tenenbaum (2007).

several other cognitive problems (Lee, 2006; Tenenbaum et al., 2006; Mansinghka et al., 2006), and many additional examples of hierarchical models can be found in the statistical literature (Gelman et al., 1995; Goldstein, 2003).

Consider first the case where the prior distribution to be learned has known form but unknown parameters. For example, suppose that the prior distribution on the bias of a coin is Beta(α, β), where the parameters α and β are unknown. We previously considered cases where the parameters α and β were positive integers, but in general these parameters can be positive real numbers.[4] As with integer-valued parameters, the mean of the beta distribution is $\frac{\alpha}{\alpha+\beta}$, and $\alpha + \beta$ determines the shape of the distribution. The distribution is tightly peaked around its mean when $\alpha + \beta$ is large, flat

---

4 The general form of the beta distribution is

$$p(\theta) = \frac{\Gamma(\alpha + \beta)}{\Gamma(\alpha)\Gamma(\beta)} \theta^{\alpha-1}(1 - \theta)^{\beta-1} \qquad (3.26)$$

where $\Gamma(\alpha) = \int_0^\infty x^{\alpha-1} e^{-x}\, dx$ is the generalized factorial function (also known as the *gamma function*), with $\Gamma(n) = (n - 1)!$ for any integer argument n and smoothly interpolating between the factorials for real-valued arguments (e.g., Boas, 1983).

when $\alpha = \beta = 1$, and U-shaped when $\alpha + \beta$ is small (Figure 3.6). Observing the coin being tossed provides some information about the values of α and β, and a learner who begins with prior distributions on the values of these parameters can update these distributions as each new coin toss is observed. The prior distributions on α and β may be defined in terms of one or more hyperparameters. The hierarchical model in Figure 3.7a uses three levels, where the hyperparameter at the top level (λ) is fixed. In principle, however, we can develop hierarchical models with any number of levels – we can can continue adding hyperparameters and priors on these hyperparameters until we reach a level where we are willing to assume that the hyperparameters are fixed in advance.

At first, the upper levels in hierarchical models like Figure 3.7a might seem too abstract to be of much practical use. Yet

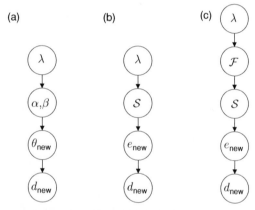

Figure 3.7. Three hierarchical Bayesian models. (a) A model for inferring θ_{new}, the bias of a coin. d_{new} specifies the number of heads and tails observed when the coin is tossed. θ_{new} is drawn from a beta distribution with parameters α and β. The prior distribution on these parameters has a single hyperparameter, λ. (b) A model for inferring e_{new}, the extension of a novel property. d_{new} is a sparsely observed version of e_{new}, and e_{new} is assumed to be drawn from a prior distribution induced by structured representation S. The hyperparameter λ specifies a prior distribution over a hypothesis space of structured representations. (c) A model that can discover the form $\mathcal{F}$ of the structure S. The hyperparameter λ now specifies a prior distribution over a hypothesis space of structural forms.

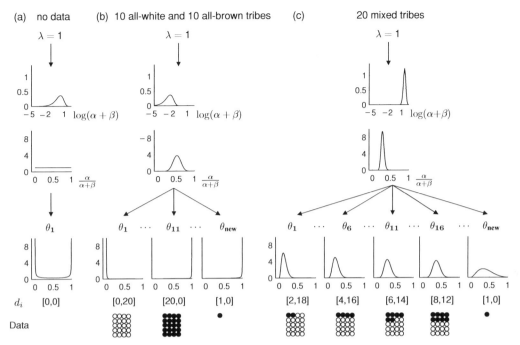

Figure 3.8. Inferences about the distribution of features within tribes. (a) Prior distributions on θ, $\log(\alpha + \beta)$ and $\frac{\alpha}{\alpha+\beta}$. (b) Posterior distributions after observing 10 all-white tribes and 10 all-brown tribes. (c) Posterior distributions after observing 20 tribes. Black circles indicate obese indiviuals and the rate of obesity varies among tribes. Reproduced with permission from Kemp, Perfors, and Tenenbaum (2007).

these upper levels play a critical role – they allow knowledge to be shared across contexts that are related but distinct. In our coin-tossing example, these contexts correspond to observations of many different coins, each of which has a bias sampled from the same prior distribution Beta(α, β). It is possible to learn something about α and β by tossing a single coin, but the best way to learn about α and β is probably to experiment with many different coins. If most coins tend to come up heads about half the time, we might infer that α and β are both large and are close to each other in size. Suppose, however, that we are working in a factory that produces trick coins for magicians. If 80% of coins come up heads almost always, and the remainder come up tails almost always, we might infer that α and β are both very small and that $\frac{\alpha}{\alpha+\beta} \approx 0.8$.

More formally, suppose that we have observed many coins being tossed and that d_i is the tally of heads and tails produced by the ith coin. The ith coin has bias θ_i, and each bias θ_i is sampled from a beta distribu-

tion with parameters α and β. The hierarchical model in Figure 3.8 captures these assumptions and is known by statisticians as a beta-binomial model (Gelman et al., 1995). To learn about the prior distribution Beta(α, β) we must formalize our expectations about the values of α and β. We will assume that the mean of the beta distribution $\frac{\alpha}{\alpha+\beta}$ is uniformly drawn from the interval $[0, 1]$ and that the sum of the parameters $\alpha + \beta$ is drawn from an exponential distribution with hyperparameter λ. Given the hierarchical model in Figure 3.8, inferences about any of the θ_i can be made by integrating out α and β:

$$p(\theta_i \mid d_1, d_2, \ldots, d_n)$$

$$= \int p(\theta_i \mid \alpha, \beta, d_i)$$

$$\times \, p(\alpha, \beta \mid d_1, d_2, \ldots, d_n) d\alpha d\beta \quad (3.27)$$

and this integral can be approximated using the Markov chain Monte Carlo methods described in the next section (see also Kemp, Perfors, & Tenenbaum, 2007).

4.1. *Example: Learning about Feature Variability*

Humans acquire many kinds of knowledge about categories and their features. Some kinds of knowledge are relatively concrete. For instance, children learn that balls tend to be round and that televisions tend to be box-shaped. Other kinds of knowledge are more abstract and represent discoveries about categories in general. For instance, 30-month-old children display a *shape bias*: They appear to know that the objects in any given category tend to have the same shape, even if they differ along other dimensions, such as color and texture (Heibeck & Markman, 1987; Smith et al., 2002). The shape bias is one example of abstract knowledge about feature variability, and Kemp et al. (2007) have argued that knowledge of this sort can be acquired by hierarchical Bayesian models.

A task carried out by Nisbett et al., (1983) shows how knowledge about feature variability can support inductive inferences from very sparse data. These researchers asked participants to imagine that they were exploring an island in the Southeastern Pacific, that they had encountered a single member of the Barratos tribe, and that this individual was brown and obese. Based on this single example, participants concluded that most Barratos were brown, but gave a much lower estimate of the proportion of obese Barratos. These inferences can be explained by the beliefs that skin color is a feature that is consistent within tribes and that obesity tends to vary within tribes and the model in Figure 3.8 can explain how these beliefs might be acquired.

Kemp et al. (2007) describe a model that can reason simultaneously about multiple features, but for simplicity we will consider skin color and obesity separately. Consider first the case where θ_i represents the proportion of brown-skinned individuals within tribe i, and suppose that we have observed 20 members from each of 20 tribes. Half the tribes are brown and the other half are white, but all of the individuals in a given tribe have the same skin color. Given these observations, the posterior distribution on $\alpha + \beta$ indicates that $\alpha + \beta$ is likely to be small (Figure 3.8b). Recall that small values of $\alpha + \beta$ imply that most of the θ_i will be close to 0 or close to 1 (Figure 3.6): in other words, that skin color tends to be homogeneous within tribes. Learning that $\alpha + \beta$ is small allows the model to make strong predictions about a sparsely observed new tribe: Having observed a single brown-skinned member of a new tribe, the posterior distribution on θ_{new} indicates that most members of the tribe are likely to be brown (Figure 3.8b). Note that the posterior distribution on θ_{new} is almost as sharply peaked as the posterior distribution on θ_{11}: The model has realized that observing one member of a new tribe is almost as informative as observing twenty members of that tribe.

Consider now the case where θ_i represents the proportion of obese individuals within tribe i. Suppose that obesity is a feature that varies within tribes: a quarter of the twenty tribes observed have an obesity rate of 10% and the remaining three quarters have rates of 20%, 30%, and 40% respectively (Figure 3.8c). Given these observations, the posterior distributions on $\alpha + \beta$ and $\frac{\alpha}{\alpha+\beta}$ (Figure 3.8c) indicate that obesity varies within tribes ($\alpha + \beta$ is high) and that the base rate of obesity is around 25% ($\frac{\alpha}{\alpha+\beta}$ is around 0.25). Again, we can use these posterior distributions to make predictions about a new tribe, but now the model requires many observations before it concludes that most members of the new tribe are obese. Unlike the case in Figure 3.8b, the model has learned that a single observation of a new tribe is not very informative, and the distribution on θ_{new} is now similar to the average of the θ values for all previously observed tribes.

In Figures 3.8b and 3.8c, a hierarchical model is used to simultaneously learn about high-level knowledge (α and β) and low-level knowledge (the values of θ_i). Any hierarchical model, however, can be used for several different purposes. If α and β are fixed in advance, the model supports top-down learning: Knowledge about α and β can guide inferences about the θ_i. If the θ_i are fixed in advance, the model supports bottom-up learning, and the θ_i can guide inferences about α and β. The ability to support top-down and bottom-up inferences is a strength of the hierarchical approach, but simultaneous learning at multiple levels of abstraction is often required to account for human inferences. Note, for example, that judgments about the Barratos depend critically on learning at two levels: Learning at the level of θ is needed to incorporate the observation that the new tribe has at least one obese, brown-skinned member, and learning at the level of α and β is needed to discover that skin-color is homogeneous within tribes but that obesity is not.

4.2. *Example: Property Induction*

We have just seen that hierarchical Bayesian models can explain how the parameters of a prior distribution might be learned. Prior knowledge in human cognition, however, is often better characterized using more structured representations. Here, we present a simple case study that shows how a hierarchical Bayesian model can acquire structured prior knowledge.

Structured prior knowledge plays a role in many inductive inferences, but we will consider the problem of property induction. In a typical task of this sort, learners find out that one or more members of a domain have a novel property and decide how to extend the property to the remaining members of the domain. For instance, given that gorillas carry enzyme X132, how likely is it that chimps also carry this enzyme? (Rips, 1975; Osherson et al., 1990). For our purposes, inductive problems like these are interesting because they rely on relatively rich prior knowledge and because this prior knowledge often appears to be learned. For example, humans learn at some stage that gorillas are more closely related to chimps than to squirrels, and taxonomic knowledge of this sort guides inferences about novel anatomical and physiological properties.

The problem of property induction can be formalized as an inference about the extension of a novel property (Kemp & Tenenbaum, 2003). Suppose that we are working with a finite set of animal species. Let e_{new} be a binary vector that represents the true extension of the novel property (Figures 3.7 and 3.9). For example, the element in e_{new} that corresponds to gorillas will be 1 (represented as a black circle in Figure 3.9) if gorillas have the novel property and 0 otherwise. Let d_{new} be a partially observed version of extension e_{new} (Figure 3.9). We are interested in the posterior distribution on e_{new} given the sparse observations in d_{new}. Using Bayes' rule, this distribution can be written as

$$P(e_{new}|d_{new}, \mathcal{S}) = \frac{P(d_{new}|e_{new})P(e_{new}|\mathcal{S})}{P(d_{new}|\mathcal{S})}$$

$$(3.28)$$

where $\mathcal{S}$ captures the structured prior knowledge that is relevant to the novel property. The first term in the numerator, $P(d_{new} \mid e_{new})$, depends on the process by which the observations in d_{new} were sampled from the true extension e_{new}. We will assume for simplicity that the entries in d_{new} are sampled at random from the vector e_{new}. The denominator can be computed by summing over all possible values of e_{new}:

$$P(d_{new} \mid \mathcal{S}) = \sum_{e_{new}} P(d_{new} \mid e_{new})P(e_{new} \mid \mathcal{S}).$$

$$(3.29)$$

For reasoning about anatomy, physiology, and other sorts of generic biological properties (e.g., "has enzyme X132"), the prior $P(e_{new} \mid \mathcal{S})$ will typically capture knowledge about taxonomic relationships between biological species. For instance, it seems plausible a priori that gorillas and chimps are the only familiar animals that carry a certain enzyme, but less probable that this enzyme will only be found in gorillas and squirrels.

Prior knowledge about taxonomic relationships between living kinds can be captured using a tree-structured representation

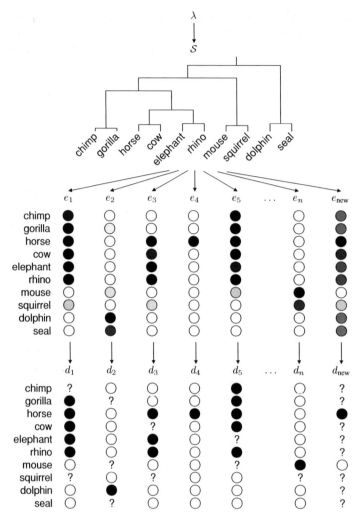

Figure 3.9. Learning a tree-structured prior for property induction. Given a collection of sparsely observed properties d_i (a black circle indicates that a species has a given property), we can compute a posterior distribution on structure S and posterior distributions on each extension e_i. Because the distribution over S is difficult to display, we show a single tree with high posterior probability. Because each distribution on e_i is difficult to display, we show instead the posterior probability that each species has each property (dark circles indicate probabilities close to 1).

like the taxonomy shown in Figure 3.9. We will therefore assume that the structured prior knowledge S takes the form of a tree and define a prior distribution $P(e_{new} \mid S)$ using a stochastic process over this tree. The stochastic process assigns some prior probability to all possible extensions, but the most likely extensions are those that are smooth with respect to tree S. An extension is smooth if nearby species in the tree tend to have the same status – either both have the novel property or neither does. One example of a stochastic process that tends to generate properties smoothly over the tree is a mutation process, inspired by biological evolution: The property is randomly chosen to be on or off at the root of the tree, and then has some small probability of switching state at each point of each branch of the tree (Huelsenbeck & Ronquist, 2001; Kemp, Perfors, & Tenenbaum, 2004).

For inferences about generic biological properties, the problem of acquiring prior knowledge has now been reduced to the problem of finding an appropriate tree S. Human learners acquire taxonomic representations in part by observing properties of entities: noticing, for example, that gorillas and chimps have many properties in common and should probably appear nearby in a taxonomic structure. This learning process can be formalized using the hierarchical Bayesian model in Figure 3.9. We assume that a learner has partially observed the extensions of n properties and that these observations are collected in vectors labeled d_1 through d_n. The true extensions e_i of these properties are generated from the same tree-based prior that is assumed to generate e_{new}, the extension of the novel property. Learning the taxonomy now amounts to making inferences about the tree S that is most likely to have generated all of these partially observed properties. Again, we see that a hierarchical formulation allows information to be shared across related contexts. Here, information about n partially observed properties is used to influence the prior distribution for inferences about e_{new}. To complete the hierarchical model in Figure 3.9 it is necessary to specify a prior distribution on trees S. For simplicity, we can use a uniform distribution over tree topologies and an exponential distribution with parameter λ over the branch lengths.

Inferences about e_{new} can now be made by integrating out the underlying tree S:

$$P(e_{new} \mid d_1, \ldots, d_n, d_{new})$$

$$= \int P(e_{new} \mid d_{new}, S)$$

$$\times p(S \mid d_1, \ldots, d_n, d_{new}) \, dS \quad (3.30)$$

where $P(e_{new} \mid d_{new}, S)$ is defined in Equation 3.28. This integral can be approximated by using Markov chain Monte Carlo methods of the kind discussed in the next section to draw a sample of trees from the distribu-

tion $p(S \mid d_1, \ldots, d_n, d_{new})$ (Huelsenbeck & Ronquist, 2001). If preferred, a single tree with high posterior probability can be identified, and this tree can be used to make predictions about the extension of the novel property. Kemp et al. (2004) follow this second strategy and show that a single tree is sufficient to accurately predict human inferences about the extensions of novel biological properties.

The model in Figures 3.7b and 3.9 assumes that the extensions e_i are generated over some true but unknown tree S. Tree structures may be useful for capturing taxonomic relationships between biological species, but different kinds of structured representations, such as chains, rings, or sets of clusters, are useful in other settings. Understanding which kind of representation is best for a given context is sometimes thought to rely on innate knowledge. Atran (1998), for example, argues that the tendency to organize living kinds into tree structures reflects an innately determined cognitive module. The hierarchical Bayesian approach challenges the inevitability of this conclusion by showing how a model might discover which kind of representation is best for a given data set. We can create such a model by adding an additional level to the model in Figure 3.7b. Suppose that variable $\mathcal{F}$ indicates whether S is a tree, a chain, a ring, or an instance of some other structural form. Given a prior distribution over a hypothesis space of possible forms, the model in Figure 3.7c can simultaneously discover the form $\mathcal{F}$ and the instance of that form S that best account for a set of observed properties. Kemp et al. (2004) formally define a model of this sort, and show that it chooses appropriate representations for several domains. For example, the model chooses a tree-structured representation given information about animals and their properties, but chooses a linear representation (the liberal–conservative spectrum) when supplied with information about the voting patterns of Supreme Court judges.

The models in Figure 3.7b and 3.7c demonstrate that the hierarchical Bayesian approach can account for the acquisition of structured prior knowledge. Many domains of human knowledge, however, are organized into representations that are richer and more sophisticated than the examples we have considered. The hierarchical Bayesian approach provides a framework that can help to explore the use and acquisition of richer prior knowledge, such as the intuitive causal theories we described at the end of Section 3. For instance, Mansinghka et al. (2006) describe a two-level hierarchical model in which the lower level represents a space of causal graphical models, whereas the higher level specifies a simple abstract theory: it assumes that the variables in the graph come in one or more classes, with the prior probability of causal relations between them depending on these classes. The model can then be used to infer the number of classes, which variables are in which classes, and the probability of causal links existing between classes directly from data, at the same time as it learns the specific causal relations that hold between individual pairs of variables. Given data from a causal network that embodies some such regularity, the model of Mansinghka et al. (2006) infers the correct network structure from many fewer examples than would be required under a generic uniform prior because it can exploit the constraint of a learned theory of the network's abstract structure. Although the theories that can be learned using our best hierarchical Bayesian models are still quite simple, these frameworks provide a promising foundation for future work and an illustration of how structured knowledge representations and sophisticated statistical inference can interact productively in cognitive modeling.

5. Markov Chain Monte Carlo

The probability distributions one has to evaluate in applying Bayesian inference can quickly become very complicated, particularly when using hierarchical Bayesian models. Graphical models provide some tools for speeding up probabilistic inference, but these tools tend to work best when most variables are directly dependent on a relatively small number of other variables. Other methods are needed to work with large probability distributions that exhibit complex interdependencies among variables. In general, ideal Bayesian computations can only be approximated for these complex models, and many methods for approximate Bayesian inference and learning have been developed (Bishop, 2006; Mackay, 2003). This section introduces the Markov chain Monte Carlo approach, a general-purpose toolkit for inferring the values of latent variables, estimating parameters, and learning model structure, which can work with a very wide range of probabilistic models. The main drawback of this approach is that it can be slow, but given sufficient time, it can yield accurate inferences for models that cannot be handled by other means.

The basic idea behind Monte Carlo methods is to represent a probability distribution by a set of samples from that distribution. Those samples provide an idea of which values have high probability (because high-probability values are more likely to be produced as samples) and can be used in place of the distribution itself when performing various computations. When working with Bayesian models of cognition, we are typically interested in understanding the posterior distribution over a parameterized model, such as a causal network with its causal strength parameters, or over a class of models, such as the space of all causal network structures on a set of variables or all taxonomic tree structures on a set of objects. Samples from the posterior distribution can be useful in discovering the best parameter values for a model or the best models in a model class and for estimating how concentrated the posterior is on those best hypotheses (i.e., how confident a learner should be in those hypotheses).

Sampling can also be used to approximate averages over the posterior distribution. For example, in computing the posterior probability of a parameterized model given data, it is necessary to compute the model's marginal likelihood or the average probability of the data over all parameter settings of the model (as in Equation 3.16 for determining whether we have a fair or weighted coin). Averaging over all parameter settings is also necessary for ideal Bayesian prediction about future data points (as in computing the posterior predictive distribution for a weighted coin, Equation 3.11). Finally, we could be interested in averaging over a space of model structures, making predictions about model features that are likely to hold regardless of which structure is correct. For example, we could estimate how likely it is that one variable A causes variable B in a complex causal network of unknown structure by computing the probability that a link $A \rightarrow B$ exists in a high-probability sample from the posterior over network structures (Friedman & Koller, 2000).

Monte Carlo methods were originally developed primarily for approximating these sophisticated averages, that is, approximating a sum over all of the values taken on by a random variable with a sum over a random sample of those values. Assume that we want to evaluate the average (also called the *expected value*) of a function $f(\mathbf{x})$ over a probability distribution $p(\mathbf{x})$ defined on a set of k random variables taking on values $\mathbf{x} = (x_1, x_2, \ldots, x_k)$. This can be done by taking the integral of $f(\mathbf{x})$ over all value of $\mathbf{x}$, weighted by their probability $p(\mathbf{x})$. Monte Carlo provides an alternative, relying on the law of large numbers to justify the approximation

$$\int f(\mathbf{x}) p(\mathbf{x}) \, d\mathbf{x} \approx \frac{1}{m} \sum_{i=1}^{m} f(\mathbf{x}^{(i)}) \quad (3.31)$$

where the $\mathbf{x}^{(i)}$ are a set of m samples from the distribution $p(\mathbf{x})$. The accuracy of this approximation increases as m increases.

To show how the Monte Carlo approach to approximate numerical integration is useful for evaluating Bayesian models, recall our model of causal structure-learning known as causal support. To compute the evidence that a set of contingencies d provides in favor of a causal relationship, we

needed to evaluate the integral

$$P(d \mid \text{Graph 1})$$
$$= \int_0^1 \int_0^1 P_1(d \mid w_0, w_1, \text{Graph 1})$$
$$\times P(w_0, w_1 \mid \text{Graph 1}) \, dw_0 \, dw_1$$
$$(3.32)$$

where $P_1(d \mid w_0, w_1, \text{Graph 1})$ is derived from the noisy-OR parameterization and $P(w_0, w_1 \mid \text{Graph 1})$ is assumed to be uniform over all values of w_0 and w_1 between 0 and 1. If we view $P_1(d \mid w_0, w_1, \text{Graph 1})$ simply as a function of w_0 and w_1, it is clear that we can approximate this integral using Monte Carlo. The analogue of Equation 3.31 is

$$P(d \mid \text{Graph 1})$$
$$\approx \frac{1}{m} \sum_{i=1}^{m} P_1\left(d \mid w_0^{(i)}, w_1^{(i)}, \text{Graph 1}\right) (3.33)$$

where the $w_0^{(i)}$ and $w_1^{(i)}$ are a set of m samples from the distribution $P(w_0, w_1 \mid \text{Graph 1})$. A version of this simple approximation was used to compute the values of causal support shown in Figure 3.4 (for details, see Griffiths & Tenenbaum, 2005).

One limitation of classical Monte Carlo methods is that it is not easy to automatically generate samples from most probability distributions. There are a number of ways to address this problem, including methods such as rejection sampling and importance sampling (see, e.g., Neal, 1993). One of the most flexible methods for generating samples from a probability distribution is Markov chain Monte Carlo (MCMC), which can be used to construct samplers for arbitrary probability distributions, even if the normalizing constants of those distributions are unknown. MCMC algorithms were originally developed to solve problems in statistical physics (Metropolis et al., 1953), and are now widely used across physics, statistics, machine learning, and related fields (e.g., Newman & Barkema, 1999;

Gilks, Richardson, & Spiegelhalter, 1996; Mackay, 2003; Neal, 1993).

As the name suggests, MCMC is based on the theory of Markov chains – sequences of random variables in which each variable is conditionally independent of all previous variables given its immediate predecessor (as in Figure 3.2b). The probability that a variable in a Markov chain takes on a particular value conditioned on the value of the preceding variable is determined by the *transition kernel* for that Markov chain. One well-known property of Markov chains is their tendency to converge to a *stationary distribution*: As the length of a Markov chain increases, the probability that a variable in that chain takes on a particular value converges to a fixed quantity determined by the choice of transition kernel. If we sample from the Markov chain by picking some initial value and then repeatedly sampling from the distribution specified by the transition kernel, we will ultimately generate samples from the stationary distribution.

In MCMC, a Markov chain is constructed such that its stationary distribution is the distribution from which we want to generate samples. If the target distribution is $p(\mathbf{x})$, then the Markov chain would be defined on sequences of values of $\mathbf{x}$. The transition kernel $K(\mathbf{x}^{(i+1)} \mid \mathbf{x}^{(i)})$ gives the probability of moving from state $\mathbf{x}^{(i)}$ to state $\mathbf{x}^{(i+1)}$. For the stationary distribution of the Markov chain to be the target distribution $p(\mathbf{x})$, the transition kernel must be chosen so that $p(\mathbf{x})$ is invariant to the kernel. Mathematically, this is expressed by the condition

$$p(\mathbf{x}^{(i+1)}) = \sum_{\mathbf{x}^{(i)}} p(\mathbf{x}^{(i)}) K(\mathbf{x}^{(i+1)} \mid \mathbf{x}^{(i)}).$$

$$(3.34)$$

If this is the case, once the probability that the chain is in a particular state is equal to $p(\mathbf{x})$, it will continue to be equal to $p(\mathbf{x})$, hence the term "stationary distribution." Once the chain converges to its stationary distribution, averaging a function $f(\mathbf{x})$ over the values of $\mathbf{x}^{(i)}$ will approximate the average of that function over the probability distribution $p(\mathbf{x})$.

Fortunately, there is a simple procedure that can be used to construct a transition kernel that will satisfy Equation 3.34 for any choice of $p(\mathbf{x})$, known as the *Metropolis-Hastings algorithm* (Hastings, 1970; Metropolis et al., 1953). The basic idea is to define $K(\mathbf{x}^{(i+1)} \mid \mathbf{x}^{(i)})$ as the result of two probabilistic steps. The first step uses an arbitrary *proposal distribution*, $q(\mathbf{x}^* \mid \mathbf{x}^{(i)})$, to generate a proposed value $\mathbf{x}^*$ for $\mathbf{x}^{(i+1)}$. The second step is to decide whether to accept this proposal. This is done by computing the *acceptance probability*, $A(\mathbf{x}^* \mid \mathbf{x}^{(i)})$, defined to be

$$A(\mathbf{x}^* \mid \mathbf{x}^{(i)}) = \min \left[\frac{p(\mathbf{x}^*)q(\mathbf{x}^{(i)} \mid \mathbf{x}^*)}{p(\mathbf{x}^{(i)})q(\mathbf{x}^* \mid \mathbf{x}^{(i)})}, 1 \right].$$

$$(3.35)$$

If a random number generated from a uniform distribution over $[0, 1]$ is less than $A(\mathbf{x}^* \mid \mathbf{x}^{(i)})$, the proposed value $\mathbf{x}^*$ is accepted as the value of $\mathbf{x}^{(i+1)}$. Otherwise, the Markov chain remains at its previous value, and $\mathbf{x}^{(i+1)} = \mathbf{x}^{(i)}$. An illustration of the use of the Metropolis-Hastings algorithm to generate samples from a Gaussian distribution (which is generally easy to sample from, but convenient to work with in this case) appears in Figure 3.10.

One advantage of the Metropolis-Hastings algorithm is that it requires only limited knowledge of the probability distribution $p(\mathbf{x})$. Inspection of Equation 3.35 reveals that, in fact, the Metropolis-Hastings algorithm can be applied even if we only know some quantity proportional to $p(\mathbf{x})$ because only the ratio of these quantities affects the algorithm. If we can sample from distributions related to $p(\mathbf{x})$, we can use other MCMC methods. In particular, if we are able to sample from the conditional probability distribution for each variable in a set given the remaining variables, $p(x_j \mid x_1, \ldots, x_{j-1}, x_{j+1}, \ldots, x_n)$, we can use another popular algorithm, *Gibbs sampling* (Geman & Geman, 1984; Gilks et al., 1996), which is known in statistical physics as the heatbath algorithm (Newman & Barkema,

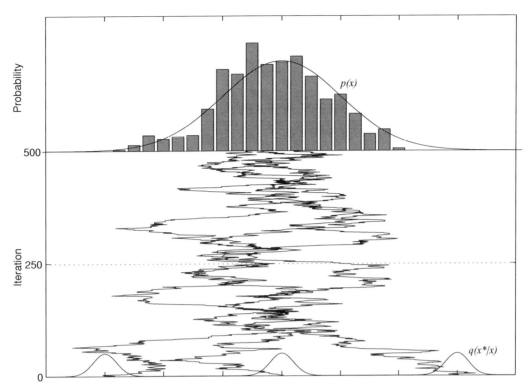

Figure 3.10. The Metropolis-Hastings algorithm. The solid lines shown in the bottom part of the figure are three sequences of values sampled from a Markov chain. Each chain began at a different location in the space, but used the same transition kernel. The transition kernel was constructed using the procedure described in the text for the Metropolis-Hastings algorithm: The proposal distribution, $q(x^* \mid x)$, was a Gaussian distribution with mean x and standard deviation 0.2 (shown centered on the starting value for each chain at the bottom of the figure), and the acceptance probabilities were computed by taking $p(x)$ to be Gaussian with mean 0 and standard deviation 1 (plotted with a solid line in the top part of the figure). This guarantees that the stationary distribution associated with the transition kernel is $p(x)$. Thus, regardless of the initial value of each chain, the probability that the chain takes on a particular value will converge to $p(x)$ as the number of iterations increases. In this case, all three chains move to explore a similar part of the space after around 100 iterations. The histogram in the top part of the figure shows the proportion of time the three chains spend visiting each part in the space after 250 iterations (marked with the dotted line), which closely approximates $p(x)$. Samples from the Markov chains can thus be used similarly to samples from $p(x)$.

1999). The Gibbs sampler for a target distribution $p(\mathbf{x})$ is the Markov chain defined by drawing each x_j from the conditional distribution $p(x_j \mid x_1, \ldots, x_{j-1}, x_{j+1}, \ldots, x_k)$.

Markov chain Monte Carlo can be a good way to obtain samples from probability distributions that would otherwise be difficult to compute with, including the posterior distributions associated with complex probabilistic models. To illustrate how MCMC can be applied in the context of a Bayesian model of cognition, we will show how Gibbs sampling can be used to extract a statistical representation of the meanings of words from a collection of text documents.

5.1. Example: Inferring Topics from Text

Several computational models have been proposed to account for the large-scale structure of semantic memory, including semantic networks (e.g., Collins & Loftus, 1975; Collins & Quillian, 1969) and semantic spaces (e.g., Landauer & Dumais, 1997;

Lund & Burgess, 1996). These approaches embody different assumptions about the way that words are represented. In semantic networks, words are nodes in a graph where edges indicate semantic relationships, as shown in Figure 3.11a. In semantic space models, words are represented as points in high-dimensional space, where the distance between two words reflects the extent to which they are semantically related, as shown in Figure 3.11b.

Probabilistic models provide an opportunity to explore alternative representations for the meaning of words. One such representation is exploited in topic models, in which words are represented in terms of the set of topics to which they belong (Blei, Ng, & Jordan, 2003; Hofmann, 1999; Griffiths & Steyvers, 2004). Each topic is a probability distribution over words, and the content of the topic is reflected in the words to which it assigns high probability. For example, high probabilities for WOODS and STREAM would suggest a topic refers to the countryside, whereas high probabilities for FEDERAL and RESERVE would suggest a topic refers to finance. Each word will have a probability under each of these different topics, as shown in Figure 3.11c. For example, MEADOW has a relatively high probability under the countryside topic, but a low probability under the finance topic, similar to WOODS and STREAM.

Representing word meanings using probabilistic topics makes it possible to use Bayesian inference to answer some of the critical problems that arise in processing language. In particular, we can make inferences about which semantically related concepts are likely to arise in the context of an observed set of words or sentences to facilitate subsequent processing. Let z denote the dominant topic in a particular context and w_1 and w_2 be two words that arise in that context. The semantic content of these words is encoded through a set of probability distributions that identify their probability under different topics: If there are T topics, then these are the distributions $P(w \mid z)$ for $z = \{1, \ldots, T\}$. Given w_1, we can infer

which topic z was likely to have produced it by using Bayes' rule,

$$P(z \mid w_1) = \frac{P(w_1 \mid z)P(z)}{\sum_{z'=1}^{T} P(w_1 \mid z')P(z')} \quad (3.36)$$

where $P(z)$ is a prior distribution over topics. Having computed this distribution over topics, we can make a prediction about future words by summing over the possible topics,

$$P(w_2 \mid w_1) = \sum_{z=1}^{T} P(w_2 \mid z)P(z \mid w_1).$$

$$(3.37)$$

A topic-based representation can also be used to disambiguate words: If BANK occurs in the context of STREAM, it is more likely that it was generated from the bucolic topic than the topic associated with finance.

Probabilistic topic models are an interesting alternative to traditional approaches to semantic representation, and in many cases, actually provide better predictions of human behavior (Griffiths & Steyvers, 2003; Griffiths, Steyvers, & Tenenbaum, 2007). However, one critical question in using this kind of representation is which topics should be used. Fortunately, work in machine learning and information retrieval has provided an answer to this question. As with popular semantic space models (Landauer & Dumais, 1997; Lund & Burgess, 1996), the representation of a set of words in terms of topics can be inferred automatically from the text contained in large document collections. The key to this process is viewing topic models as generative models for documents, making it possible to use standard methods of Bayesian statistics to identify a set of topics that are likely to have generated an observed collection of documents. Figure 3.12 shows a sample of topics inferred from the TASA corpus (Landauer & Dumais, 1997), a collection of passages excerpted from educational texts used in curricula from the first year of school to the first year of college.

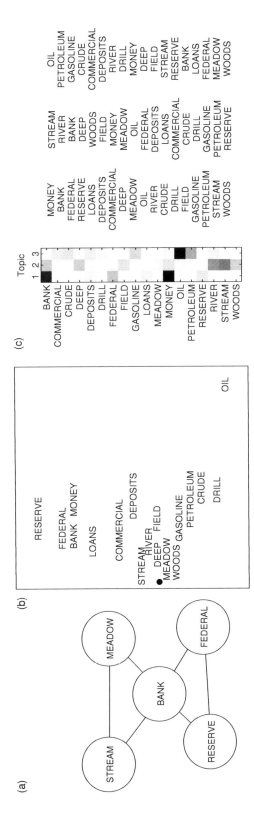

Figure 3.11. Approaches to semantic representation. (a) In a semantic network, words are represented as nodes, and edges indicate semantic relationships. (b) In a semantic space, words are represented as points, and proximity indicates semantic association. These are the first two dimensions of a solution produced by Latent Semantic Analysis (Landauer & Dumais, 1997). The black dot is the origin. (c) In the topic model, words are represented as belonging to a set of probabilistic topics. The matrix shown on the left indicates the probability of each word under each of three topics. The three columns on the right show the words that appear in those topics, ordered from highest to lowest probability. Reproduced with permission from Griffiths, Steyvers, and Tenenbaum (2007).

PRINTING	**PLAY**	TEAM	JUDGE	HYPOTHESIS	STUDY	**CLASS**	ENGINE
PAPER	PLAYS	GAME	TRIAL	EXPERIMENT	**TEST**	MARX	FUEL
PRINT	STAGE	BASKETBALL	**COURT**	SCIENTIFIC	STUDYING	ECONOMIC	ENGINES
PRINTED	AUDIENCE	PLAYERS	CASE	OBSERVATIONS	HOMEWORK	CAPITALISM	STEAM
TYPE	THEATER	PLAYER	JURY	SCIENTISTS	NEED	CAPITALIST	GASOLINE
PROCESS	ACTORS	**PLAY**	ACCUSED	EXPERIMENTS	**CLASS**	SOCIALIST	AIR
INK	DRAMA	PLAYING	GUILTY	SCIENTIST	MATH	SOCIETY	**POWER**
PRESS	SHAKESPEARE	SOCCER	DEFENDANT	EXPERIMENTAL	TRY	SYSTEM	COMBUSTION
IMAGE	ACTOR	PLAYED	JUSTICE	**TEST**	**POWER**	RULING	DIESEL
PRINTER	THEATRE	BALL	**EVIDENCE**	METHOD	TEACHER	SOCIALISM	EXHAUST
PRINTS	PLAYWRIGHT	TEAMS	WITNESSES	HYPOTHESES	WRITE	HISTORY	MIXTURE
PRINTERS	PERFORMANCE	BASKET	CRIME	TESTED	PLAN	POLITICAL	GASES
COPY	DRAMATIC	FOOTBALL	LAWYER	**EVIDENCE**	ARITHMETIC	SOCIAL	CARBURETOR
COPIES	COSTUMES	SCORE	WITNESS	BASED	ASSIGNMENT	STRUGGLE	GAS
FORM	COMEDY	**COURT**	ATTORNEY	OBSERVATION	PLACE	REVOLUTION	COMPRESSION
OFFSET	TRAGEDY	GAMES	HEARING	SCIENCE	STUDIED	WORKING	JET
GRAPHIC	**CHARACTERS**	TRY	INNOCENT	FACTS	CAREFULLY	PRODUCTION	BURNING
SURFACE	SCENES	COACH	DEFENSE	DATA	DECIDE	CLASSES	AUTOMOBILE
PRODUCED	OPERA	GYM	CHARGE	RESULTS	IMPORTANT	BOURGEOIS	STROKE
CHARACTERS	PERFORMED	SHOT	CRIMINAL	EXPLANATION	NOTEBOOK		INTERNAL

Figure 3.12. A sample of topics from a 1,700 topic solution derived from the Touchstone Applied Science Associates corpus. Each column contains the twenty highest probability words in a single topic, as indicated by $P(w \mid z)$. Words in boldface occur in different senses in neighboring topics, illustrating how the model deals with polysemy and homonymy. These topics were discovered in a completely unsupervised fashion, using just word-document co-occurrence frequencies. Reproduced with permission from Griffiths, Steyvers, and Tenenbaum (2007).

We can specify a generative model for documents by assuming that each document is a mixture of topics, with each word in that document being drawn from a particular topic and the topics varying in probability across documents. For any particular document, we write the probability of a word w in that document as

$$P(w) = \sum_{z=1}^{T} P(w \mid z) P(z), \qquad (3.38)$$

where $P(w \mid z)$ is the probability of word w under topic z, which remains constant across all documents, and $P(z)$ is the probability of topic j in this document. We can summarize these probabilities with two sets of parameters, taking $\phi_w^{(z)}$ to indicate $P(w \mid z)$ and $\theta_z^{(d)}$ to indicate $P(z)$ in a particular document d. The procedure for generating a collection of documents is then straightforward. First, we generate a set of topics, sampling $\phi^{(z)}$ from some prior distribution $p(\phi)$. Then, for each document d, we generate the weights of those topics, sampling $\theta^{(d)}$ from a distribution $p(\theta)$. Assuming that we know in advance how many words will appear in the document, we then generate those words in turn. A topic z is chosen for each word that will be in the document by sampling from the distribution over topics implied by $\theta^{(d)}$. Finally, the identity of the word w is determined by sampling from the distri-

bution over words $\phi^{(z)}$ associated with that topic.

To complete the specification of our generative model, we need to specify distributions for ϕ and θ so that we can make inferences about these parameters from a corpus of documents. As in the case of coin flipping, calculations can be simplified by using a conjugate prior. Both ϕ and θ are arbitrary distributions over a finite set of outcomes, or *multinomial distributions*, and the conjugate prior for the multinomial distribution is the Dirichlet distribution. Just as the multinomial distribution is a multivariate generalization of the Bernoulli distribution we used in the coin flipping example, the Dirichlet distribution is a multivariate generalization of the beta distribution. We assume that the number of "virtual examples" of instances of each topic appearing in each document is set by a parameter α and likewise use a parameter β to represent the number of instances of each word in each topic. Figure 3.13 shows a graphical model depicting the dependencies among these variables. This model, known as Latent Dirichlet Allocation, was introduced in machine learning by Blei, Ng, and Jordan (2003).

We extract a set of topics from a collection of documents in a completely unsupervised fashion, using Bayesian inference. Because the Dirichlet priors are conjugate to the multinomial distributions ϕ and θ, we can compute the joint distribution $P(\mathbf{w}, \mathbf{z})$

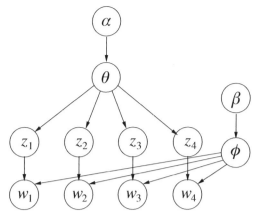

Figure 3.13. Graphical model for Latent Dirichlet Allocation (Blei, Ng, & Jordan, 2003). The distribution over words given topics, ϕ, and the distribution over topics in a document, θ, are generated from Dirichlet distributions with parameters β and α, respectively. Each word in the document is generated by first choosing a topic z_i from θ, and then choosing a word according to $\phi^{(z_i)}$.

where $(\mathbf{w}) = (w_1, \ldots, w_n)$ are the words in the documents and $\mathbf{z} = (z_1, \ldots, z_n)$ are their topic assignments, by integrating out ϕ and θ, just as we did in the model selection example earlier (Equation 3.16). We can then ask questions about the posterior distribution over $\mathbf{z}$ given $\mathbf{w}$, given by Bayes' rule:

$$P(\mathbf{z} \mid \mathbf{w}) = \frac{P(\mathbf{w}, \mathbf{z})}{\sum_{\mathbf{z}} P(\mathbf{w}, \mathbf{z})}. \qquad (3.39)$$

Because the sum in the denominator is intractable, having T^n terms, we are forced to evaluate this posterior using MCMC. In this case, we use Gibbs sampling to investigate the posterior distribution over assignments of words to topics, $\mathbf{z}$.

The Gibbs sampling algorithm consists of choosing an initial assignment of words to topics (e.g., choosing a topic uniformly at random for each word) and then sampling the assignment of each word z_i from the conditional distribution $P(z_i \mid \mathbf{z}_{-i}, \mathbf{w})$. Each iteration of the algorithm is thus a probabilistic shuffling of the assignments of words to topics. This procedure is illustrated in Figure 3.14. The figure shows the results of ap-

plying the algorithm (using just three topics) to a small portion of the TASA corpus. This portion features thirty documents that use the word MONEY, thirty documents that use the word OIL, and thirty documents that use the word RIVER. The vocabulary is restricted to eighteen words, and the entries indicate the frequency with which the 731 tokens of those words appeared in the ninety documents. Each word token in the corpus, w_i, has a topic assignment, z_i, at each iteration of the sampling procedure. In the figure, we focus on the tokens of three words: MONEY, BANK, and STREAM. Each word token is initially assigned a topic at random, and each iteration of MCMC results in a new set of assignments of tokens to topics. After a few iterations, the topic assignments begin to reflect the different usage patterns of MONEY and STREAM, with tokens of these words ending up in different topics, and the multiple senses of BANK.

The details behind this particular Gibbs sampling algorithm are given in Griffiths and Steyvers (2004), where the algorithm is used to analyze the topics that appear in a large database of scientific documents. The conditional distribution for z_i that is used in the algorithm can be derived using an argument similar to our derivation of the posterior predictive distribution in coin flipping, giving

$$P(z_i \mid \mathbf{z}_{-i}, \mathbf{w}) \propto \frac{n_{-i,z_i}^{(w_i)} + \beta}{n_{-i,z_i}^{(\cdot)} + W\beta} \frac{n_{-i,z_i}^{(d_i)} + \alpha}{n_{-i,\cdot}^{(d_i)} + T\alpha}$$

$$(3.40)$$

where $\mathbf{z}_{-i}$ is the assignment of all z_k such that $k \neq i$, and $n_{-i,z_i}^{(w_i)}$ is the number of words assigned to topic z_i that are the same as w_i, $n_{-i,z_i}^{(\cdot)}$ is the total number of words assigned to topic z_i, $n_{-i,z_i}^{(d_i)}$ is the number of words from document d_i assigned to topic z_i, and $n_{-i,\cdot}^{(d_i)}$ is the total number of words in document d_i, all not counting the assignment of the current word w_i. The two terms in this expression have intuitive interpretations, being the posterior predictive distributions on words within a topic and topics within

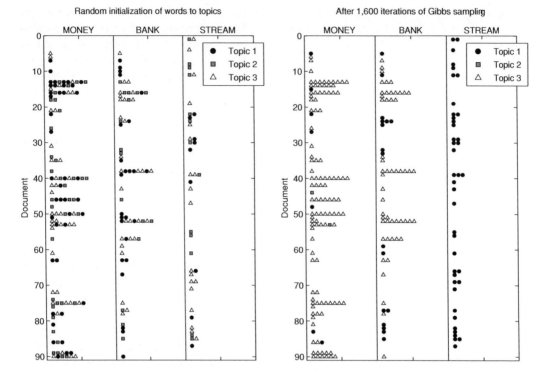

Figure 3.14. Illustration of the Gibbs sampling algorithm for learning topics. Each word token w_i appearing in the corpus has a topic assignment, z_i. The figure shows the assignments of all tokens of three types – MONEY, BANK, and STREAM – before and after running the algorithm. Each marker corresponds to a single token appearing in a particular document, and shape and color indicates assignment: Topic 1 is a black circle, topic 2 is a gray square, and topic 3 is a white triangle. Before running the algorithm, assignments are relatively random, as shown in the left panel. After running the algorithm, tokens of MONEY are almost exclusively assigned to topic 3, tokens of STREAM are almost exclusively assigned to topic 1, and tokens of BANK are assigned to whichever of topic 1 and topic 3 seems to dominate a given document. The algorithm consists of iteratively choosing an assignment for each token, using a probability distribution over tokens that guarantees convergence to the posterior distribution over assignments. Reproduced with permission from Griffiths, Steyvers, and Tenenbaum (2007).

a document given the current assignments $\mathbf{z}_{-i}$, respectively. The result of the MCMC algorithm is a set of samples from $P(\mathbf{z} \mid \mathbf{w})$, reflecting the posterior distribution over topic assignments given a collection of documents. A single sample can be used to evaluate the topics that appear in a corpus, as shown in Figure 3.12, or the assignments of words to topics, as shown in Figure 3.14. We can also compute quantities such as the strength of association between words (given by Equation 3.37) by averaging over many samples.[5]

5 When computing quantities such as $P(w_2 \mid w_1)$, as given by Equation 3.37, we need a way of finding the parameters ϕ that characterize the distribution

Although other inference algorithms exist that can be used with this generative model (e.g., Blei et al., 2003; Minka & Lafferty, 2002), the Gibbs sampler is an extremely simple (and reasonably efficient) way to investigate the consequences of using

over words associated with each topic. This can be done using ideas similar to those applied in our coin flipping example: for each sample of $\mathbf{z}$ we can estimate ϕ as

$$\hat{\phi}_z^{(w)} = \frac{n_z^{(w)} + \beta}{n_z^{(\cdot)} + W\beta} \tag{3.41}$$

which is the posterior predictive distribution over new words w for topic z conditioned on $\mathbf{w}$ and $\mathbf{z}$.

topics to represent semantic relationships between words. Griffiths and Steyvers (2002, 2003) suggested that topic models might provide an alternative to traditional approaches to semantic representation and showed that they can provide better predictions of human word association data than Latent Semantic Analysis (LSA) (Landauer & Dumais, 1997). Topic models can also be applied to a range of other tasks that draw on semantic association, such as semantic priming and sentence comprehension (Griffiths et al., 2007).

The key advantage that topic models have over semantic space models is postulating a more structured representation – different topics can capture different senses of words, allowing the model to deal with polysemy and homonymy in a way that is automatic and transparent. For instance, similarity in semantic space models must obey a version of the triangle inequality for distances: If there is high similarity between words w_1 and w_2, and between words w_2 and w_3, then w_1 and w_3 must be at least fairly similar. But word associations often violate this rule. For instance, ASTEROID is highly associated with BELT, and BELT is highly associated with BUCKLE, but ASTEROID and BUCKLE have little association. LSA thus has trouble representing these associations. Out of approximately 4,500 words in a large-scale set of word association norms (Nelson, McEvoy, & Schreiber, 1998), LSA judges that BELT is the thirteenth most similar word to ASTEROID, that BUCKLE is the second most similar word to BELT, and consequently BUCKLE is the forty-first most similar word to ASTEROID – more similar than TAIL, IMPACT, or SHOWER. In contrast, using topics makes it possible to represent these associations faithfully, because BELT belongs to multiple topics, one highly associated with ASTEROID but not BUCKLE and another highly associated with BUCKLE but not ASTEROID.

The relative success of topic models in modeling semantic similarity is thus an instance of the capacity for probabilistic models to combine structured representations with statistical learning – a theme that has run through all of the examples we have considered in this chapter. The same capacity makes it easy to extend these models to capture other aspects of language. As generative models, topic models can be modified to incorporate richer semantic representations such as hierarchies (Blei et al., 2004), as well as rudimentary syntax (Griffiths et al., 2005), and extensions of the MCMC algorithm described in this section make it possible to sample from the posterior distributions induced by these models.

6. Conclusion

The aim of this chapter has been to survey the conceptual and mathematical foundations of Bayesian models of cognition and to introduce several advanced techniques that are driving state-of-the-art research. There has been space to discuss only a few specific and rather simple cognitive models based on these ideas, but much more can be found in the current literature referenced in the introduction. These Bayesian models of cognition represent just one side of a larger movement that seeks to understand intelligence in terms of rational probabilistic inference. Related ideas are providing new paradigms for the study of neural coding and computation (Doya et al., 2007), children's cognitive development (Gopnik & Tenenbaum, 2007), machine learning (Bishop, 2006), and artificial intelligence (Russell & Norvig, 2002).

We hope that this chapter conveys some sense of what all this excitement is about. Bayesian models give us ways to approach deep questions of human cognition that have not been previously amenable to rigorous formal study. How can human minds make predictions and generalizations from such limited data and so often be correct? How can structured representations of abstract knowledge constrain and guide sophisticated statistical inferences from sparse data? What specific forms of knowledge support human inductive inference across different domains and tasks? How can these structured knowledge representations themselves be acquired from experience? And how can the necessary computations be carried out or approximated tractably for complex models that might approach the scale of interesting chunks of human cognition? We are still far from having good answers to these questions, but as this chapter shows, we are beginning to see what answers might look like and to have the tools needed to start building them.

Acknowledgments

This chapter is based in part on tutorials given by the authors at the Annual Meeting of the Cognitive Science Society in 2004 and 2006, and on portions of a tutorial on probabilistic inference written by Thomas L. Griffiths and Alan Yuille that appeared as an online supplement to the special issue of *Trends in Cognitive Sciences* on "Probabilistic Models of Cognition" (Volume 10, Issue 7). We thank the participants in those tutorials and the special issue for their feedback on this material. The writing of this chapter was supported in part by grants from the James S. McDonnell Foundation Causal Learning Research Collaborative, the DARPA BICA program (JBT), the National Science Foundation (TLG), the Air Force Office of Scientific Research (JBT, TLG), the William Asbjornsen Albert fellowship (CK), and the Paul E. Newton Career Development Chair (JBT).

References

Ackley, D. H., Hinton, G. E., & Sejnowski, T. J. (1985). A learning algorithm for Boltzmann machines. *Cognitive Science, 9,* 147–169.

Anderson, J. R. (1990). *The adaptive character of thought.* Hillsdale, NJ: Lawrence Erlbaum.

Ashby, F. G., & Alfonso-Reese, L. A. (1995). Categorization as probability density estimation. *Journal of Mathematical Psychology, 39,* 216–233.

Atran, S. (1998). Folk biology and the anthropology of science: Cognitive universals and cultural particulars. *Behavioral and Brain Sciences, 21,* 547–609.

Baker, C. L., Tenenbaum, J. B., & Saxe, R. R. (2007). Goal inference as inverse planning. In D. S. McNamara & J. G. Trafton (Eds.), *Proceedings of the 29th Annual Meeting of the Cognitive Science Society* (pp. 779–784). Austin, TX: Cognitive Science Society

Bayes, T. (1763/1958). Studies in the history of probability and statistics: IX. Thomas Bayes's essay towards solving a problem in the doctrine of chances. *Biometrika, 45,* 296–315.

Bernardo, J. M., & Smith, A. F. M. (1994). *Bayesian theory.* New York: Wiley.

Bishop, C. M. (2006). *Pattern recognition and machine learning.* New York: Springer.

Blei, D., Griffiths, T., Jordan, M., & Tenenbaum, J. (2004). Hierarchical topic models and the nested Chinese restaurant process. In S. Thrun, L. K. Saul & B. Schölkopt (Eds.), *Advances in Neural Information Processing Systems 16* (pp. 17–24). Cambridge, MA: MIT Press.

Blei, D. M., Ng, A. Y., & Jordan, M. I. (2003). Latent Dirichlet Allocation. *Journal of Machine Learning Research, 3,* 993–1022.

Boas, M. L. (1983). *Mathematical methods in the physical sciences* (2nd ed.). New York: Wiley.

Brainard, D. H., & Freeman, W. T. (1997). Bayesian color constancy. *Journal of the Optical Society of America A, 14,* 1393–1411.

Buehner, M., & Cheng, P. W. (1997). Causal induction: The Power PC theory versus the Rescorla-Wagner theory. In M. Shafto & P. Langley (Eds.), *Proceedings of the 19th Annual Conference of the Cognitive Science Society* (pp. 55–61). Hillsdale, NJ: Lawrence Erlbaum.

Buehner, M. J., Cheng, P. W., & Clifford, D. (2003). From covariation to causation: A test of the assumption of causal power. *Journal of Experimental Psychology: Learning, Memory, and Cognition, 29,* 1119–1140.

Carey, S. (1985). *Conceptual change in childhood.* Cambridge, MA: MIT Press.

Charniak, E. (1993). *Statistical language learning.* Cambridge, MA: MIT Press.

Chater, N., & Manning, C. D. (2006). Probabilistic models of language processing and acquisition. *Trends in Cognitive Sciences, 10,* 335–344.

Cheng, P. (1997). From covariation to causation: A causal power theory. *Psychological Review, 104,* 367–405.

Chomsky, N. (1988). *Language and problems of knowledge: The Managua lectures.* Cambridge, MA: MIT Press.

Collins, A. M., & Loftus, E. F. (1975). A spreading activation theory of semantic processing. *Psychological Review, 82,* 407–428.

Collins, A. M., & Quillian, M. R. (1969). Retrieval time from semantic memory. *Journal of Verbal Learning and Verbal Behaviour, 8,* 240–247.

Courville, A. C., Daw, N. D., & Touretzky, D. S. (2006). Bayesian theories of conditioning in a changing world. *Trends in Cognitive Sciences, 10,* 294–300.

Danks, D., Griffiths, T. L., & Tenenbaum, J. B. (2003). Dynamical causal learning. In S. Becker, S. Thrun, & K. Obermayer (Eds.), *Advances Neural Information Processing Systems 15* (pp. 67–74). Cambridge, MA: MIT Press.

Doya, K., Ishii, S., Pouget, A., & Rao, R. P. N. (Eds.). (2007). *The Bayesian brain: Probabilistic approaches to neural coding.* Cambridge, MA: MIT Press.

Duda, R. O., Hart, P. E., & Stork, D. G. (2000). *Pattern classification.* New York: Wiley.

Friedman, N., & Koller, D. (2000). Being Bayesian about network structure. In *Proceedings of the 16th Annual Conference on Uncertainty in AI* (pp. 201–210). San Francisco, CA: Morgan Kaufmann.

Gelman, A., Carlin, J. B., Stern, H. S., & Rubin, D. B. (1995). *Bayesian data analysis.* New York: Chapman & Hall.

Geman, S., & Geman, D. (1984). Stochastic relaxation, Gibbs distributions, and the Bayesian restoration of images. *IEEE Transactions on Pattern Analysis and Machine Intelligence, 6,* 721–741.

Ghahramani, Z. (2004). Unsupervised learning. In O. Bousquet, G. Raetsch, & U. von Luxburg (Eds.), *Advanced lectures on machine learning* (pp. 72–122). Berlin: Springer-Verlag.

Gigerenzer, G., Swijtink, Z., Porter, T., Daston, L., Beatty, J., & Kruger, L. (1989). *The empire of chance.* Cambridge, UK: Cambridge University Press.

Gilks, W., Richardson, S., & Spiegelhalter, D. J. (Eds.). (1996). *Markov chain Monte Carlo in practice.* Suffolk, UK: Chapman and Hall.

Glymour, C. (2001). *The mind's arrows: Bayes nets and graphical causal models in psychology.* Cambridge, MA: MIT Press.

Glymour, C., & Cooper, G. (1999). *Computation, causation, and discovery.* Cambridge, MA: MIT Press.

Goldstein, H. (2003). *Multilevel statistical models* (3rd ed.). London: Hodder Arnold.

Good, I. J. (1980). Some history of the hierarchical Bayesian methodology. In J. M. Bernardo, M. H. DeGroot, D. V. Lindley, & A. F. M. Smith (Eds.), *Bayesian statistics* (pp. 489–519). Valencia, Spain: Valencia University Press.

Gopnik, A., & Meltzoff, A. N. (1997). *Words, thoughts, and theories.* Cambridge, MA: MIT Press.

Gopnik, A., & Tenenbaum, J. B. (2007). Bayesian networks, Bayesian learning, and cognitive development. *Developmental Science, 10,* 281–287.

Griffiths, T. L. (2005). *Causes, coincidences, and theories.* Unpublished doctoral dissertation, Stanford University, Stanford, CA.

Griffiths, T. L., Baraff, E. R., & Tenenbaum, J. B. (2004). Using physical theories to infer hidden causal structure. In K. Forbus, D. Gentner, & T. Regier (Eds.), *Proceedings of the 26th Annual Meeting of the Cognitive Science Society* (pp. 446–451). Mahwah, NJ: Lawrence, Erlbaum.

Griffiths, T. L., & Ghahramani, Z. (2005). *Infinite latent feature models and the Indian buffet process* (Tech. Rep. No. 2005-001). London, UK: Gatsby Computational Neuroscience Unit.

Griffiths, T. L., & Steyvers, M. (2002). A probabilistic approach to semantic representation. In W. D. Gray & C. Schunn (Eds.), *Proceedings of the Twenty-Fourth Annual Conference of the Cognitive Science Society* (pp. 381–386). Hillsdale, NJ: Lawrence Erlbaum.

Griffiths, T. L., & Steyvers, M. (2003). Prediction and semantic association. In S. Becker, S. Thrun, & K. Obermayer (Eds.), *Neural information processing systems 15* (pp. 11–18). Cambridge, MA: MIT Press.

Griffiths, T. L., & Steyvers, M. (2004). Finding scientific topics. *Proceedings of the National Academy of Science, 101,* 5228–5235.

Griffiths, T. L., Steyvers, M., Blei, D. M., & Tenenbaum, J. B. (2005). Integrating topics and syntax. In L. K. Saul, Y. Weiss, & L. Bottou (Eds.), *Advances in Neural Information Processing Systems 17* (pp. 537–544). Cambridge, MA: MIT Press.

Griffiths, T. L., Steyvers, M., & Tenenbaum, J. B. (2007). Topics in semantic association. *Psychological Review, 114,* 211–244.

Griffiths, T. L., & Tenenbaum, J. B. (2005). Structure and strength in causal induction. *Cognitive Psychology, 51,* 354–384.

Griffiths, T. L., & Tenenbaum, J. B. (2007a). From mere coincidences to meaningful discoveries. *Cognition, 103,* 180–226.

Griffiths, T. L., & Tenenbaum, J. B. (2007b). Two proposals for causal grammars. In A. Gopnik & L. Schulz (Eds.), *Causal learning: Psychology, philosophy, and computation* (pp. 323–345). Oxford, UK: Oxford University Press.

Hacking, I. (1975). *The emergence of probability.* Cambridge, UK: Cambridge University Press.

Hagmayer, Y., Sloman, S. A., Lagnado, D. A., & Waldmann, M. R. (in press). Causal reasoning through intervention. In A. Gopnik & L. Schulz (Eds.), *Causal learning: Psychology, philosophy, and computation.* (pp. 323–345). Oxford, UK: Oxford University Press.

Hastings, W. K. (1970). Monte Carlo methods using Markov chains and their applications. *Biometrika, 57,* 97–109.

Heckerman, D. (1998). A tutorial on learning with Bayesian networks. In M. I. Jordan (Ed.), *Learning in graphical models* (pp. 301–354). Cambridge, MA: MIT Press.

Heibeck, T., & Markman, E. (1987). Word learning in children: An examination of fast mapping. *Child Development, 58,* 1021–1024.

Hofmann, T. (1999). Probablistic latent semantic indexing. In *Proceedings of the Twenty-Second Annual International SIGIR Conference* (pp. 50–57). New York: ACM Press.

Huelsenbeck, J. P., & Ronquist, F. (2001). MR-BAYES: Bayesian inference of phylogenetic trees. *Bioinformatics, 17*(8), 754–755.

Jeffreys, W. H., & Berger, J. O. (1992). Ockham's razor and Bayesian analysis. *American Scientist, 80*(1), 64–72.

Jenkins, H. M., & Ward, W. C. (1965). Judgment of contingency between responses and outcomes. *Psychological Monographs, 79.*

Jurafsky, D., & Martin, J. H. (2000). *Speech and language processing.* Upper Saddle River, NJ: Prentice Hall.

Kass, R. E., & Raftery, A. E. (1995). Bayes factors. *Journal of the American Statistical Association, 90,* 773–795.

Kemp, C., Perfors, A., & Tenenbaum, J. B. (2004). Learning domain structures. In R. Alterman & D. Kirsh (Eds.), *Proceedings of the 26th Annual Conference of the Cognitive Science Society* (pp. 658–683). Hillsdale, NJ: Lawrence Erlbaum.

Kemp, C., Perfors, A., & Tenenbaum, J. B. (2007). Learning overhypotheses with hierarchical bayesian models. *Developmental Science, 10,* 307–321.

Kemp, C., & Tenenbaum, J. B. (2003). Theory-based induction. In *Proceedings of the Twenty-Fifth Annual Conference of the Cognitive Science Society.*

Korb, K., & Nicholson, A. (2003). *Bayesian artificial intelligence.* Boca Raton, FL: Chapman and Hall/CRC.

Kording, K. P., & Wolpert, D. M. (2006). Bayesian decision theory in sensorimotor control. *Trends in Cognitive Sciences, 10,* 319–326.

Lagnado, D., & Sloman, S. A. (2004). The advantage of timely intervention. *Journal of Experimental Psychology: Learning, Memory, and Cognition, 30,* 856–876.

Landauer, T. K., & Dumais, S. T. (1997). A solution to Plato's problem: the Latent Semantic Analysis theory of acquisition, induction, and representation of knowledge. *Psychological Review, 104,* 211–240.

Lee, M. D. (2006). A hierarchical Bayesian model of human decision-making on an optimal stopping problem. *Cognitive Science, 30,* 555–580.

Lund, K., & Burgess, C. (1996). Producing high-dimensional semantic spaces from lexical cooccurrence. *Behavior Research Methods, Instrumentation, and Computers, 28,* 203–208.

Mackay, D. J. C. (2003). *Information theory, inference, and learning algorithms.* Cambridge, UK: Cambridge University Press.

Manning, C., & Schütze, H. (1999). *Foundations of statistical natural language processing.* Cambridge, MA: MIT Press.

Mansinghka, V. K., Kemp, C., Tenenbaum, J. B., & Griffiths, T. L. (2006). Structured priors for structure learning. In R. Dechter & T. S. Richardson (Eds.), *Proceedings of the 22nd Conference on Uncertainty in Artificial Intelligence (UAI)* Arlington, VA: ANAI Press.

Marr, D. (1982). *Vision.* San Francisco, CA: W. H. Freeman.

Medin, D. L., & Schaffer, M. M. (1978). Context theory of classification learning. *Psychological Review, 85,* 207–238.

Metropolis, A. W., Rosenbluth, A. W., Rosenbluth, M. N., Teller, A. H., & Teller, E. (1953). Equations of state calculations by fast computing machines. *Journal of Chemical Physics, 21,* 1087–1092.

Minka, T., & Lafferty, J. (2002). Expectation-Propagation for the generative aspect model. In A. Darwiche & N. Frichman (Eds.), *Proceedings of the 18th Conference on Uncertainty in Artificial Intelligence (UAI)* (pp. 352–359). San Francisco, CA: Morgan Kaufmann.

Myung, I. J., Forster, M. R., & Browne, M. W. (2000). Model selection [Special issue]. *Journal of Mathematical Psychology, 44*.

Myung, I. J., & Pitt, M. A. (1997). Applying Occam's razor in modeling cognition: A Bayesian approach. *Psychonomic Bulletin and Review, 4*, 79–95.

Neal, R. M. (1992). Connectionist learning of belief networks. *Artificial Intelligence, 56*, 71–113.

Neal, R. M. (1993). *Probabilistic inference using Markov chain Monte Carlo methods* (Tech. Rep. No. CRG-TR-93-1). Toronto, Canada: University of Toronto.

Neal, R. M. (1998). *Markov chain sampling methods for Dirichlet process mixture models* (Tech. Rep. No. 9815). Toronto, Canada: Department of Statistics, University of Toronto.

Nelson, D. L., McEvoy, C. L., & Schreiber, T. A. (1998). *The University of South Florida word association, rhyme, and word fragment norms.* Retrieved month, day, year, from http://w3.usf.edu/FreeAssociation/

Newman, M. E. J., & Barkema, G. T. (1999). *Monte carlo methods in statistical physics.* Oxford, UK: Clarendon Press.

Nisbett, R. E., Krantz, D. H., Jepson, C., & Kunda, Z. (1983). The use of statistical heuristics in everyday inductive reasoning. *Psychological Review, 90*(4), 339–363.

Norris, J. R. (1997). *Markov chains.* Cambridge, UK: Cambridge University Press.

Nosofsky, R. M. (1986). Attention, similarity, and the identification-categorization relationship. *Journal of Experimental Psychology: General, 115*, 39–57.

Nosofsky, R. M. (1998). Optimal performance and exemplar models of classification. In M. Oaksford & N. Chater (Eds.), *Rational models of cognition* (pp. 218–247). Oxford, UK: Oxford University Press.

Oaksford, M., & Chater, N. (2001). The probabilistic approach to human reasoning. *Trends in Cognitive Sciences, 5*, 349–357.

Osherson, D. N., Smith, E. E., Wilkie, O., Lopez, A., & Shafir, E. (1990). Category-based induction. *Psychological Review, 97*(2), 185–200.

Pearl, J. (1988). *Probabilistic reasoning in intelligent systems.* San Francisco, CA: Morgan Kaufmann.

Pearl, J. (2000). *Causality: Models, reasoning and inference.* Cambridge, UK: Cambridge University Press.

Pitman, J. (1993). *Probability.* New York: Springer-Verlag.

Reed, S. K. (1972). Pattern recognition and categorization. *Cognitive Psychology, 3*, 393–407.

Rice, J. A. (1995). *Mathematical statistics and data analysis* (2nd ed.). Belmont, CA: Duxbury.

Rips, L. J. (1975). Inductive judgments about natural categories. *Journal of Verbal Learning and Verbal Behavior, 14*, 665–681.

Russell, S. J., & Norvig, P. (2002). *Artificial intelligence: A modern approach* (2nd ed.). Englewood Cliffs, NJ: Prentice Hall.

Sloman, S. (2005). *Causal models: How people think about the world and its alternatives.* Oxford, UK: Oxford University Press.

Smith, L. B., Jones, S. S., Landau, B., Gershkoff-Stowe, L., & Samuelson, L. (2002). Object name learning provides on-the-job training for attention. *Psychological Science, 13*(1), 13–19.

Spirtes, P., Glymour, C., & Schienes, R. (1993). *Causation prediction and search.* New York: Springer-Verlag.

Steyvers, M., Griffiths, T. L., & Dennis, S. (2006). Probabilistic inference in human semantic memory. *Trends in Cognitive Sciences, 10*, 327–334.

Steyvers, M., Tenenbaum, J. B., Wagenmakers, E. J., & Blum, B. (2003). Inferring causal networks from observations and interventions. *Cognitive Science, 27*, 453–489.

Tenenbaum, J. B., & Griffiths, T. L. (2001). Structure learning in human causal induction. In T. Leen, T. Dieterich, & V. Tresp (Eds.), *Advances in neural information processing systems 13* (pp. 59–65). Cambridge, MA: MIT Press.

Tenenbaum, J. B., & Griffiths, T. L. (2003). Theory-based causal induction. In S. Becker, S. Thrun, & K. Obermayer (Eds.), *Advances in neural information processing systems 15* (pp. 35–42). Cambridge, MA: MIT Press.

Tenenbaum, J. B., Griffiths, T. L., & Kemp, C. (2006). Theory-based Bayesian models of inductive learning and reasoning. *Trends in Cognitive Science, 10*, 309–318.

Tenenbaum, J. B., Griffiths, T. L., & Niyogi, S. (2007). Intuitive theories as grammars for causal inference. In A. Gopnik & L. Schulz (Eds.), *Causal learning: Psychology, philosophy, and computation* (pp. 301–322). Oxford, UK: Oxford University Press.

Tenenbaum, J. B., & Niyogi, S. (2003). Learning causal laws. In R. Alterman & D. Kirsh (Eds.), *Proceedings of the 25th Annual Meeting of the Cognitive Science Society* (pp. 1152–1157). Hillsdale, NJ: Erlbaum.

Wellman, H. M., & Gelman, S. A. (1992). Cognitive development: Foundational theories of core domains. *Annual Review of Psychology, 43,* 337–375.

Xu, F., & Tenenbaum, J. B. (2007). Word learning as Bayesian inference. *Psychological Review, 114,* 245–272.

Yuille, A., & Kersten, D. (2006). Vision as Bayesian inference: analysis by synthesis? *Trends in Cognitive Sciences, 10,* 301–308.

CHAPTER 4

Dynamical Systems Approaches to Cognition

Gregor Schöner

1. Introduction

Think of a little boy playing in the playground, climbing up on ladders, balancing on beams, jumping, running, catching other kids. Or think of a girl who prepares to draw a picture, finding and setting up her painting utensils, dipping the brush in water, carefully wiping it off, whipping up the water paint of the selected color with small circular movements, the brush just touching the pad of paint. When she actually paints, she makes a sequence of brush strokes to sketch a house. Clearly, both scenes involve lots of cognition. The ongoing, complex behaviors of the two children are certainly not simple reflexes, nor fixed action patterns elicited by key stimuli, nor strictly dictated by stimulus–response relationships. Hallmarks of cognition are visible: selection, sequence generation, working memory. And yet, what makes these daily life activities most intriguing is how seamlessly the fine and gross motor control is tuned to the environment; how sensory information is actively sought by looking around, searching, establishing reference; and how seam-lessly the flow of activities moves forward. No artificial system has ever achieved even remotely comparable behavior. Although computer programs may play chess at grand master level, their ability to generate smooth flows of motor actions in natural environments remains extremely limited.

Clearly, cognition takes place when organisms with bodies and sensory systems are situated in structured environments, to which they bring their individual behavioral history and to which they quickly adjust. There is a strong theoretical tension in cognitive science about the extent to which cognition can be studied while abstracting from embodiment, situatedness and the structure of the nervous systems that control cognitive processes in organisms. This chapter argues that in making such abstractions, important concepts are missed, including most importantly the concepts of stability and instability.

The embodied view of cognition emphasizes the close link of cognition to the sensory and motor surfaces and the structured environments in which these are immersed. The dynamical systems approach to cognition is the theoretical framework within which this embodied view of cognition can be formalized. This chapter reviews the core concepts of the dynamical systems approach and illustrates them through a set of experimentally accessible examples. Particular attention will be given to how cognition can be understood in terms that are compatible with principles of neural function, most prominently, with the space–time continuity of neural processes.

2. Embodiment, Situatedness, and Dynamical Systems

Cognition is embodied in the obvious sense that natural cognitive systems are housed in a physical and physiological body, and that cognitive processes take place within the organism's nervous system. Cognition is situated in the similarly obvious sense that this body acts in a specific, structured environment from which it receives sensory information and on which it may have an effect. Body and nervous system are adapted to natural environments on many time scales, from evolution to development and learning. Any individual organism brings its particular history of behavior and stimulation to any situation in which cognition is acted out.

In another sense, embodiment is a scientific stance, in which researchers aim to understand cognition in ways that do not neglect the linkage between cognitive processes and the sensory and motor surfaces, do not neglect the structured environments in which cognition takes place, are mindful of the potential role of individual experience in cognition, and are careful when abstracting from the concrete neuronal processes that are the basis for the behavior of organisms.

Taking that stance does not prevent researchers from building artificial cognitive systems or from constructing abstract mathematical models of cognitive processes. But in each case, the potential link to a body, to an environment, and to a stream of behavior must be considered. Whether the theoretical constructs employed are compatible with organizational principles of the nervous system must be examined. Models of cognition that take the embodied stance must be process models that can capture, at least as a matter of principle, the unfolding in time of cognition and the associated sensory and motor processes.

Often, building a robotic demonstration of a process model is a useful test of the extent to which the principles of embodiment have been respected. Many classical production system modelers of cognition for instance, face serious, sometimes insurmountable problems when they try to feed their systems from real sensors in the real world and let their systems control real bodies. The limited success of the artificial intelligence approach to autonomous robotics reflects these difficulties (Brooks, 1991).

Dynamical systems theory provides the language in which the embodied and situated stance can be developed into a scientific theory of cognition. To examine this claim, we need to clarify what dynamical systems theory refers to. There is, of course, the field of mathematics that concerns itself with dynamical systems (Perko, 1991). The mathematical concepts capture the property of many natural systems in which a sufficiently rich characterization of the present state of the system enables prediction of future states. Scientific theories based on this mathematical framework have been extraordinarily successful in physics and many branches of science connected to physics. In each case, this required forming scientific concepts based on the mathematical framework, concepts that had to prove their power by capturing laws of nature, properties, and constraints of systems. The mathematics alone did not do that job. By analogy, developing an understanding of cognition within the mathematical framework of dynamical systems requires that concepts are defined that bring the mathematics to bear on the subject matter.

One level at which this has been done with considerable success is that of metaphor. Dynamical systems as a metaphor promote thinking about underlying "forces" (vector-fields), from which the observed pattern or behavior emerges. The solutions of nonlinear dynamical systems may change qualitatively, even as the underlying vector-fields change only in a graded way. This fact may serve as a metaphor for how qualitatively distinct states or events may emerge from continuous processes, for how there may be multiple possible causes for the emergence of such qualities, and for how all contributions to a system may matter, not only the ones most specifically linked to the new quality. This image dates back, perhaps, to the notion of the Gestalt field in Gestalt psychology (Köhler, 1920/1939) and has been a source of fresh thinking in developmental psychology (Thelen & Smith, 1994). The strongest impact of dynamical systems as a metaphor may be in heuristics, that is, as a source of new questions and new view points.

This chapter, however, reviews efforts to form concepts based on the mathematical theory of dynamical systems into a rigorous scientific approach toward cognition that embraces the embodied and situated stance. The argument will be laid out that the concepts of attractor states with their stability properties, the loss of stability when such states go through bifurcations, and the emergence of new attractor states from instabilities are necessary ingredients of an account of embodied and situated cognition. No physical realization of cognition is possible without addressing the problems to which these concepts provide solutions. Not covered in this review is recent discussion about dynamical systems and embodiment within philosophy (see, for instance, Van Gelder, 1998; Juarrero, 1999; Keijzer, 2001).

3. Dynamical Systems Thinking: Uniquely Instantiated Dynamics

Control systems provide an interesting metaphor for the notion that meaningful function may emerge from simple, embodied mechanisms. A highly illustrative example comes from the orientation behaviors of the common house fly (Reichardt & Poggio,

1976; Poggio & Reichardt, 1976). Flies orient toward moving objects, which they chase as part of their mating behavior. Detailed analysis revealed that the circuitry underlying this behavior forms a simple controller: A motion detection system fed by luminance changes on the fly's facet eye drives the flight motor, generating an amount of torque that is a function of where on the sensory surface motion was detected. If the speck of motion is detected on the right, a torque to the right is generated. If the speck is detected on the left, a torque to the left is generated. The level of torque passes through zero when the speck is right ahead. The torque changes the flight direction of the fly, which in turn changes the location on the facet eye at which the moving stimulus is detected. Given the aerodynamics of flies, the torque and its on-line updating generate an orientation behavior, in which the insect orients its flight into the direction in which a moving stimulus is detected.

That meaningful behavior emerges as a stable state, an attractor, from the neural circuitry linking the sensory surface to the flight motor, which together with the physics of flight establish a dynamical system (Figure 4.1). In the lab, the behavior can be elicited by imposing a motion signal on the fly's facet eye. In the fly's natural environment, the sensory signal typically comes from other flies. In fact, the system is tuned such that pursuit of another fly works amazingly well, probably the outcome of evolutionary optimization.

There is an irony in the scientific history of this analysis. Reichardt and colleagues (Reichardt & Poggio, 1976; Poggio & Reichardt, 1976) had opened the loop by fixing the fly to a torque meter, so that the amount of torque generated by the flight motor could measured. This was done as a function of the location in the visual array, at which a moving stimulus was presented. From the measured torque, these authors predicted the closed loop behavior. Measuring closed loop behavior still required fixing the fly to the torque meter, but now the visual surround was moved as a function of the measured torque to imitate natural

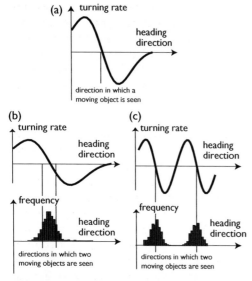

Figure 4.1. Schematic illustration of how the dynamics of heading direction accounts for how flies select and orient to visual targets. (a) The torque exerted by the fly's flight motor generates a turning rate, which is a function of the fly's heading direction relative to a visual target, an object that makes small oscillatory movements around the indicated position. This dependence effectively defines a dynamics of heading direction, which has an attractor (zero-crossing with negative slope) at the direction in which the target lies. (b) When two objects are metrically close (see the two vertical lines) they generate a fused attractor. Over time, the fly's average heading lies between the two targets. (c) When two objects are metrically far (vertical lines), a bistable dynamics results. The fly switches randomly between the two heading directions, generating a bimodal histogram (bottom) of flying directions over time.

flight. When imperfections of this early form of virtual reality were removed, researchers found that the prediction did not hold up (Heisenberg & Wolf, 1988). Apparently, the fly's simple nervous system computes an expected visual motion from its own motor commands (reafference) and treats detected visual motion matching that prediction differently than extraneous motion signals related to movement of an object relative to the fly. So even this very simple control system provides hints that uncovering the dynamics from which behavior emerges re-

quires more than an input-output analysis in open loop.

Even so, there is no explicit representation of the speck in motion, nor reasoning about goals and plans to reach those goals. The behavior emerges when a neural system linked to the sensory and motor surfaces is immersed in an environment to which it is adapted. The complete system, including neural network and coupling through the body and environment, can be understood as a dynamical system. Its attractor solution is the emergent behavior. Although in some abstract sense one could say that the neurons controlling the flight motor "estimate" the direction in which the target lies, their firing does not "re-present" this value because the estimate is implicit in the control circuitry driving the flight system and cannot be forwarded to be used in any other context.

Some have argued that such emergence of a behavior from a closed control could form the core of a potential dynamical systems refoundation of cognition (van Gelder & Port, 1995). But is control already a form of cognition? Would that not imply that every heater with a thermostat is already a cognitive system? One dimension along which systems maybe be distinguished is flexibility. One could argue that the threshold of cognition has not been reached as long as an emergent behavior is uniquely determined by sensory inputs. By contrast, when a control system makes decisions, selects among a range of inputs, and generates behavior based on its own inner state, then this might represent the most elementary form of cognition. That implies a form of flexibility, in which the emergent outcome is no longer dictated by the sensed outer world but is instead, at least to some minimal extent, based on choices generated from within the system.

The flight control system of house flies is capable of such flexibility. When confronted with several patches of visual motion on its facet eye, the fly selects one of the patches and directs its flight in pursuit of that visual object (Poggio & Reichardt, 1976). This capacity to select emerges from the control dynamics. Superposing the torque patterns generated by each motion patch, two attractors emerge (Fig. 4.1c). One of these is selected depending on the initial orientation and on chance. When the two patches are close to each other, the two attractors merge, and the fly flies in an averaged direction (as shown in Fig. 4.1b).

This example illustrates ideas that generalize well beyond the framework of control theory. A summary of the principles of a dynamic approach to behavioral patterns can be formulated as follows (Schöner & Kelso, 1988a). (1) Patterns of behavior are characterized by inner states, which determine the persistence of the patterns over time and under changing conditions. A state can be characterized by variables with specific values corresponding to specific states. States and associated variables are not limited to those of sensorimotor loops. State variables may originate, for instance, from within the neural networks that control behavior. (2) The evolution in time of these state variables is generated by neural networks linked to sensory and motor surfaces that can be modeled as dynamical systems. Many factors may contribute to the effective dynamics of such systems, including the physical dynamics and material properties of the body and of the environment. Sensory inputs, including internal sensory feedback, also act as forces on this dynamics. (3) Asymptotically stable states structure the solutions of this dynamical system. Over the long run, only attractor solutions are robust and likely to be observed. The nervous system is extensively interconnected, so that for any particular circuit and any particular pattern, other connections act effectively as perturbations, as do variable sensory inputs and the complex and temporally variable natural environment. (4) As a corollary, only when states are released from stability does behavioral flexibility arise. Release from stability takes the form of instabilities (bifurcations) in which the restoring forces around an attractor become too weak to resist change. New solutions may be reached or even created from instabilities. The full complexity of behavior may ultimately be generated from the complex structure of stable dynam-

ical states and their instabilities in a nonlinear, strongly interlinked dynamical system.

As an illustration of these principles, consider the coordination of rhythmic movement, a domain in which dynamical systems ideas have been developed and evaluated in detail (Schöner & Kelso, 1988a; Kelso, 1995). Patterns of coordination underlying such behaviors as the gaits of locomotion, speech articulatory movements, or the playing of a musical instrument can be characterized through measures of the relative timing of components, such as the relative phase, ϕ. Their evolution reflects the coupling between the neural networks that control the components (Grossberg, Pribe, & Cohen, 1997) as well as, in some instances, mechanical coupling (Turvey, 1990). The temporal evolution and stability of the coordination patterns can be described by an effective dynamical system governing the measures of relative timing, which can be modeled as a relative phase dynamics (Schöner, Haken, & Kelso, 1986). Stable states (attractors) of the dynamics correspond to stable patterns of coordination. The coordination of homologous limbs, for instance, occurs generally in two symmetric patterns, the limbs either moving in-phase or in phase alternation ("anti-phase"). These patterns stay invariant under a variety of conditions, including changes in the frequency of the rhythmic movement. Their stability does not stay invariant, however. The anti-phase pattern of coordination typically becomes less stable at higher movement frequencies. This manifests itself in associated changes of stability measures, such as an increase in the amount of fluctuation of relative phase and an increase in the amount of time needed to recover from a perturbation of the coordination pattern (Schöner et al., 1986). Stability is thus an essential property of coordination patterns. Without stability, patterns do not persist. In fact, at sufficiently high movement frequencies, an involuntary switch out of the anti-phase into an in-phase pattern of coordination occurs. An understanding of coordination thus requires more than an account of the information processing needed to compute the pattern. It also requires an account for how the pattern is reached from all kinds of perturbed states. In dynamical systems thinking, both the specification of the state and the mechanisms for its stabilization emerge from the same underlying dynamical system.

Are stability properties perhaps generated at a lower level of control, whereas relative timing per se is planned at a more abstract, disembodied level? Information processing models of timing have invoked "clocks" that generate time signals representing more or less complex patterns of coordination, which are then handed down to a "motor" system that handles the control (Vorberg & Wing, 1996). A first response is that the clocks themselves must have stability properties if they are to account for coordination, and this makes them dynamical systems as well (Schöner, 2002). Abstracting from the dynamic, embodied properties of timing means, however, missing out on important constraints for higher cognitive function. How people switch intentionally from one pattern of coordination to another, for instance, is constrained by stability (Scholz, Kelso, & Schöner, 1988). First, switching from a more stable to a less stable pattern takes longer than vice versa. Second, the intention to switch to a pattern increases that pattern's stability so that it is possible to switch to a pattern that is unstable under less specific intentional constraints. The experimental results were quantitatively accounted for by a model in which the intention to switch to a coordination pattern is a force in the coordination dynamics that increases the stability of the intended pattern (Schöner & Kelso, 1988b). Another study had participants learn a new pattern of coordination that initially was not in the behavioral repertoire (Schöner, Zanone, & Kelso, 1992). The process of learning amounted to increasing the stability of the target pattern. That the underlying coordination dynamics was changed could be shown when participants were asked at different points during their training to produce patterns of coordination near the target pattern. Before learning performance was biased toward the in-

trinsic patterns of in-phase and anti-phase. After learning a new bias toward the learned pattern was observable. The bias could be attributed to the underlying dynamics of relative timing, which changed during learning, with new forces stabilizing the learned pattern (Schöner et al., 1992). Related work established that perceived or memorized constraints for relative timing could likewise be understood as contributions to the dynamics of coordination (Schöner & Kelso, 1988c).

The picture that emerges from this exemplary system is that movement coordination emerges as stable states from a nonlinear, potentially multistable dynamics, realized by neural networks coupled to the body in a structured environment. Cognitive aspects of motor control, such as intentional movement goals, motor memory, or skill learning, are all mediated through this dynamics of coordination. Its graded change may lead to both graded and categorical change of movement behavior.

Beyond motor control, nonlinear dynamics has been invoked as a general framework for cognition, in which the concept of representation is unneeded (van Gelder & Port, 1995). This has been viewed as a strength by some, as a weakness by others (Markman & Dietrich, 2000). Extending dynamical systems ideas beyond motor control, we run into a conceptual limitation, however. Take the coordination of rhythmic movement we just discussed, for example. What value does relative phase have when the movement is stopped? When movement is restarted, does the coordination system start up at the last value that relative phase had? Describing the state of a motor system by a variable such as relative phase requires that variable to have a unique value at all times. That value must evolve continuously in time, cannot jump, cannot split into two values, or disappear and have no value. The dynamical system description of coordination by relative phase is thus "uniquely instantiated."

For another example, consider the biomechanics of the human arm, which has a well-defined physical state at all times, characterized by the spatial positions of its segments or the ensemble of its joint angles. That physical state changes only continuously, that is, the arm obviously does not disappear in one position and reappear at another. The biomechanics of the arm are characterized by the equations of motion, a set of differential equations for the joint angles that generate continuous joint angle trajectories. The variables in this dynamical description are uniquely instantiated. Every joint angle has exactly one value at each time, and that value changes continuously in time.

Now think about planning a movement. A movement plan may exist before a movement is initiated. This is revealed by the movement starting out in the direction of the target, by the latency between a movement command and the initiation of the movement being shorter when the movement goal is known ahead of time, or by observing specific neuronal activity prior to movement initiative. A movement plan may be described in the same terms as the state of the arm, for example, as a desired configuration of the joint angles. But are those variables uniquely instantiated? After having made a movement, is the movement plan still around? When a new movement is prepared, do the joint angle variables containing the planned arm configuration evolve continuously from the values of the previous movement plan to the required new values? Clearly, that does not make sense. In a first approximation, the preparation of a new movement does not depend on the previous motor act. Also, early during movement planning, movement parameters may have multiple values (Ghez et al., 1997; Wilimzig, Schneider, & Schöner, 2006).

Is it possible that the planning of movements does not fall into the domain of dynamical systems thinking? The answer is no, because there are clear indications of dynamics at the level of movement preparation (Erlhagen & Schöner, 2002). Movement plans evolve continuously in time (Ghez et al., 1997) and are updated at any time during movement preparation when sensory information changes (Goodale, Pélisson, & Prablanc, 1986). The neural substrate reflects both neuronal properties (Georgopoulos et al., 1989; Scott, 2004).

Similarly, perception has signatures both of dynamics and of a lack of unique instantiation. That percepts cannot be described by uniquely instantiated variables is intuitive. When we watch a slide show, each slide induces a new percept. It does not seem to make sense to say that the new percept induced by the next slide emerges from the percept of what was on the previous slide by continuous transformation. Evidence for a new percept, depending on what has just previously been perceived, comes, however, from multistable stimuli. The motion quartet (Hock, Kelso, & Schöner, 1993) is a particularly clear example, illustrated in Figure 4.2. Spots at the four corners of an imaginary rectangle have luminance levels above background. Two spots lying on one diagonal are much brighter, the two spots on the other diagonal are only a little bit brighter than background. If the two diagonals switch from frame to frame, then one of two motion patterns is clearly seen: Either the bright spots move horizontally (panel c) or vertically (panel d), but never both at the same time. Different stimulus geometries favor either perceptual outcome: Flat rectangles (panel e) generate predominantly vertical motion percepts, tall rectangles (panel f) generate predominantly horizontal motion percepts. When the stimulus geometry is changed continuously in time, the perceptual state tends to persist, leading to perceptual hysteresis (panel g). This is a very robust finding, immune to intentional or semantic influences and to eye movements, and not caused by response bias Hock et al., 2005). Hysteresis is evidence for continuity of the underlying perceptual state and supports a dynamical systems account for perception (Hock, Schöner, & Giese, 2003).

When, on the other hand, the perception of motion is briefly interrupted while the stimulus series is presented, hysteresis is abolished (Hock & Ploeger, 2006; Nichols, Hock, & Schöner, 2006). A sophisticated way of demonstrating that fact employs the background relative luminance contrast

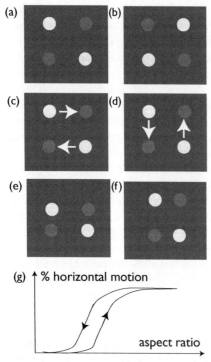

(g) ↑ % horizontal motion

aspect ratio

Figure 4.2. The two frames (a and b) of the motion quartet stimulus and its two possible percepts, horizontal (c) and vertical (d) motion, indicated by white arrows. Motion is seen from locations at which luminance decreases to locations at which luminance increases. If the stimulus is periodically repeated, the direction of motion is inverted on subsequent frame changes, but the pattern of horizontal versus vertical tends to persist. Low aspect ratios (e) favor vertical, high aspect ratios (f) favor horizontal motion. When the aspect ratio is continuously varied from frame to frame (g), the initially established motion direction tends to persist, leading to hysteresis, the dependence of perceptual outcome on the direction of stimulus change (arrows).

(BRLC; see Figure 4.3). This is the amount of change in luminance from frame to frame in relation to how much the spots' average luminance is above background. A BRLC of 2 (panel a) provides the strongest motion signal. This is when the change of luminance goes all the way down to background luminance. BRLCs below two have considerable contrast in both frames, but more contrast in one frame than in the other. Near a BRLC of zero (panel b), there is hardly any lumi-

nance change between frames. When BRLC is varied, the probability of motion being perceived varies between these limit cases (panel c); Hock, Gilroy, & Harnett, 2002). (This transition from nonmotion to motion perception is likewise hysteretic, a fact we shall return to later.) At intermediate levels of BRLC, motion perception is bistable: Sometimes, motion will be perceived, sometimes not. Thus, if during a stimulus series that changes the geometry from, say, flat to tall, the BRLC level is abruptly lowered for just a single frame, then on a certain percentage of trials, the perception of motion will stop altogether, whereas on the other trials, motion will continue to be perceived through the perturbation. Hock and Ploeger (2006) found that hysteresis was abolished on those trials, on which motion had stopped, but not on those on which motion had continued. Thus, whether or not the direction of motion is preserved over

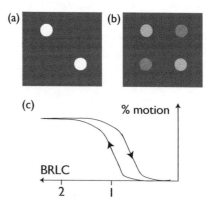

(c) % motion ↑

BRLC
← 2   1

Figure 4.3. The background relative luminance contrast (BRLC) is the amount luminance changes from frame to frame divided by the distance between average luminance and background. (a) A BRLC of two means luminance changes between a high level and background. (b) A small BRLC means luminance changes little from frame to frame, so that all locations in the motion quartet have similar contrast relative to background in both frames (c). The probability of perceiving motion increases with increasing BRLC. The transition between motion and nonmotion shows hysteresis, that is, depends on the direction of BRLC change (arrows).

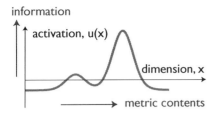

Figure 4.4. Activation fields are defined over the metric space, x, relative to which information is being represented, for example, space, feature, or movement parameters. Activation, u, itself encodes the amount of information about specific values, for example, the readiness to activate a specified action or the certainty of a sensory estimate.

time depends on whether or not motion remained active.

The continuity captured by the dynamical variables of uniquely instantiated descriptions is thus not sufficient to move from motor control toward movement planning or to perception. What is missing is a dynamic representation of the presence or absence of plans or percepts. The classical concept of activation can play that role (Spencer & Schöner, 2003).

4. Dynamical Field Theory

4.1. *Activation Fields*

To represent metric information in terms of dynamical state variables, we need two dimensions (Figure 4.4). One is the metric dimension along which information is specified. Each location in the field corresponds to a particular value along the metric dimension. For each such value, the activation level of the field spans the second dimension that encodes a measure of the amount of information about that value.

For a sensory representation, the first dimension may entail parameters whose values must be estimated from sensory information. Such parameters may be, for instance, the location in visual space of a stimulus, perceptual features such as orientation, spatial frequency, and pitch, or even relatively high-level parameters, such as the

estimation of the pose of a visual object. The body scheme is another example, which may involve estimating joint angles from proprioceptive information. For such sensory representations, low levels of activation at a particular field location indicate that the value of the represented dimension associated with that location is not a likely estimate. High levels of activation mark field locations that contribute substantially to the current estimate of sensory information.

For motor representations, metric dimensions may be spanned by movement parameters like movement direction or movement extent, level of force, or movement time. Low levels of activation at a field location indicate that the associated movement is not a likely movement plan. High levels of activation indicate that the movement represented at that location is close to being initiated, and activation from that field site will be handed down to the motor control system.

In this picture, localized peaks of activation are units of representation. The location of the peaks in the field encodes metric information about the underlying dimension. The activation level of the peaks is the strength of representation, which may variably encode the certainty of an estimate, the closeness to execution of a plan, or the physical intensity of a stimulus. A flat distribution of activation, by contrast, represents the absence of specific information.

The limit case of uniquely instantiated dynamics is modeled whenever a single positive peak moves continuously along the metric dimension. Its motion may be described by an instantiated dynamics in which the peak location is the dynamical state variable, whose time course is generated through an ordinary dynamical system. By contrast, in the more general conception of a dynamic field, it is the activation level at each field location that acts as state variable. Thus, dynamic fields are infinite dimensional dynamical systems, and activation levels rather than peak locations evolve continuously in time. Peaks may be suppressed and created. For instance, harking back to the problem of coordination, a peak over the dimension "relative phase" would indicate that relative phase has a well-defined value. If the movement is stopped, that peak decays. When movement resumes, a peak could be generated at a new location, so that relative phase could start up at a new value. Similarly, peaks of activation in a dynamic field defined over the direction and location of perceived motion signify the perception of a particular movement pattern. When the peaks decay (e.g., because BRLC was lowered), the motion percept is lost. When the stimulus is restored in strength, peaks may come up at new locations, restoring the percept of motion but potentially in a new direction.

4.2. *Field Dynamics*

The dynamical system from which the temporal evolution of activation fields is generated is constrained by the postulate that localized peaks of activation are stable objects, or, in mathematical terms, fixed point attractors. Such a field dynamics has the generic form

$$\tau \dot{u}(x, t) = -u(x, t) + \text{resting level}$$
$$+ \text{ input} + \text{interaction} \quad (4.1)$$

where $u(x, t)$ is the activation field defined over the metric dimension, x, and time, t. The first three terms define an input-driven regime, in which attractor solutions have the form $u(x, t) = \text{resting level} + \text{input}$. The rate of relaxation is determined by the time scale parameter, τ. The interaction stabilizes localized peaks of activation against decay by local excitatory interaction and against diffusion by global inhibitory interaction (Figure 4.5). In Amari's formulation (Amari, 1977) the mathematical form is specified as

$$\tau \dot{u}(x, t) = -u(x, t) + h + S(x, t)$$
$$+ \int dx' w(x - x') \sigma(u(x', t)).$$
$$(4.2)$$

Here, $h < 0$ is a constant resting level, $S(x, t)$ is spatially and temporally variable input function, $w(\Delta x)$ is an interaction ker-

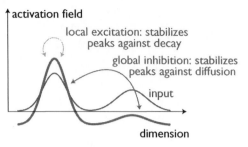

Figure 4.5. Local excitatory interaction helps sustain localized peaks of activation, whereas long-range inhibitory interaction prevents diffusion of peaks and stabilizes against competing inputs.

nel, and $\sigma(u)$ is a sigmoidal nonlinear threshold function (Figure 4.6). The interaction term collects input from all those field sites, x', at which activation is sufficiently large. The interaction kernel determines if inputs from those sites are positive, driving up activation (excitatory), or negative, driving down activation (inhibitory). Excitatory input from nearby location and inhibitory

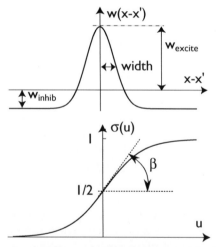

Figure 4.6. The interaction kernel, $w(\Delta x)$, in Amari's neural field dynamics depends only on the distance, Δx, between the field locations as illustrated on top. The kernel depicted here is excitatory only over small distances, whereas over larger distances, inhibitory interaction dominates. Only sufficiently activated field sites contribute to interaction. This is modeled by sigmoidal threshold functions, such as the one illustrated on bottom, $\sigma(u) = 1/(1 + \exp(-\beta u))$.

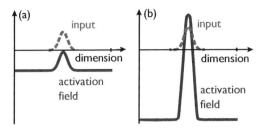

Figure 4.7. The dynamic activation field (solid line) in response to input distributions (dashed line). (a) Localized input is applied to the activation field that is initially at the negative resting level. This induces a subthreshold peak, which does not yet engage interaction. (b) When input is slightly increased, excitatory interaction pulls the activation peak up, which in turn inhibits the field elsewhere.

input from all field locations generically stabilize localized peaks of activation. For this class of dynamics, detailed analytical results provide a framework for the inverse dynamics task facing the modeler, determining a dynamical system that has the appropriate attractor solutions.

A literature on neuronally more realistic or detailed models includes multilayer field dynamics (in which excitation and inhibition are separated, as in real neuronal systems; Wilson & Cowan, 1972) and models of spiking neurons (Gerstner & Kistler, 2002). The qualitative dynamics of the generic Amari formulation are shared features of this entire class of neuronal dynamics, however. In particular, two functionally relevant kinds of attractor solutions arise. The input-driven attractor is a largely subthreshold pattern of activation in which the contribution of the neuronal interaction is negligible (Figure 4.7a). Self-excited attractors, by contrast, are localized patterns of activation with levels sufficient to engage neuronal interaction (Figure 4.7b). In this state, local excitatory interaction lifts activation within the peak beyond levels induced by input, whereas global inhibitory interaction suppresses levels elsewhere below the levels justified by the resting level or inputs.

That these two kinds of attractors are qualitatively different states can be seen from the fact that there is a dynamical instability separating them, the detection insta-

bility (see Bicho, Mallet, & Schöner, 2000, for discussion). This instability can be observed, for instance, if the amplitude of a single localized input is increased. Below a critical point, this leads to a subthreshold input-driven solution (Figure 4.7a). When input strength reaches a threshold, this solution becomes unstable and disappears. The system relaxes to a peaked solution, which coexists bistably with the (input-driven solution. As a result, the detection decision is stabilized against small changes of input: When the input level drops again, the peak is sustained within a range of input strengths. This leads to hysteresis, that is, dependence of the observed state on the direction of change.

Next to detection decisions, selection among multiple inputs is another elementary form of cognition. This function emerges from a second instability, illustrated in Figure 4.8. When inputs are sufficiently strong and metrically close, the detection instability leads to a peak positioned over an averaged location. For broad input distributions, averaging may occur in the input stream, although the excitatory interaction may bring about averaging even when input is bimodal (as in Figure 4.8a). When the metric distance between inputs is larger, however, the dynamic field is bistable, instead. A single peak emerges from the detection decision, localized either at one or at

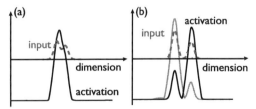

Figure 4.8. (a) The dynamic activation field (solid line) may generate a peak at an averaged position in response to bimodal input (dashed line) when the input peaks are within the range of excitatory interaction. (b) At larger distance, inhibitory interaction dominates, and the field dynamics becomes bistable: Either a peak positioned over one input mode may be generated (black solid line) or a peak positioned over the other (gray solid line), but not both at the same time.

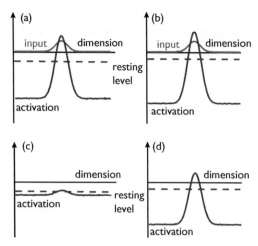

Figure 4.9. In the left column, a self-stabilized activation peak generated in response to a localized input is only stable while that input is present (a). When the input is removed (c), the peak decays to a subthreshold distribution. In the right column, the input-induced peak (b) is sustained when input is removed (d). The difference between the two columns is the slightly larger resting level (dashed horizontal lines) on the right.

the other location of input. Asymmetries in input, fluctuations, or prior activation history may favor one over the other state, but competition prevents simultaneous activation at both locations.

When activation levels are sufficiently high in the field, many locations have activation levels above threshold and contribute to interaction. This may enable the dynamic field to sustain a peak of activation, even when the localized input that first generated the peak (through a detection instability) is removed (Figure 4.9). Sustained activation of localized peaks of activation provides a neural mechanism for metric working memory (Schutte, Spencer, & Schöner, 2003). Metric information about past stimulation is thus preserved over much longer time scales than the dynamic time scale of individual neurons or field sites (Amit, 1994).

This is true, of course, only to the extent to which there are not other localized inputs that would attract sustained peaks. Such inputs may be small enough to not be able to push the dynamic field through the

detection instability. Even so, they may induce drift of sustained peaks (Schutte et al., 2003; Spencer et al., 2007). Relatedly, small inputs may be sufficient to trap peaks that are induced by broad or even homogenous inputs to the field, which push the field broadly through a detection instability. This may lead to categorical representations of metrically graded inputs (Spencer, Simmering, & Schutte, 2006).

Instabilities may amplify small differences. A peak of activation can be induced, for instance, by providing a homogeneous boost to the field. Where the peak comes up then depends on small subthreshold patterns of localized input or any other inhomogeneities in the field. Such inhomogeneities may arise because input connections have slightly different strengths as a result of Hebbian strengthening of those inputs that have successfully induced peaks. Another simple form of learning is the laying down of a memory trace at those field sites at which peaks have been generated. In either case, the history of activation may influence ongoing decision making. This is illustrated in the following section by showing how habits may be formed and how the behavioral history biases decisions.

4.3. *Behavioral Signatures of Dynamic Fields*

How may dynamic fields, their instabilities, and their functional modes help understand the emergence of elementary forms of cognition? We will answer this question in the context of a few exemplary case studies and show, at the same time, how behavioral signatures of the neural field dynamics may provide evidence for the Dynamical Field Theory (DFT) account of cognition.

Most psychophysics makes use of detection decisions in one form or another. Are these decisions related to the detection instability of DFT (Figure 4.7)? Hock, Kogan, and Espinoza (1997) observed that a psychophysical detection decision was self-stabilizing when the perceptual alternative to a detection was perceptually clear. They asked participants to indicate whether they saw apparent motion or flicker between two spots of changing luminance. The parameter they varied was the BRLC discussed earlier (Figure 4.3). Changing BRLC continuously in time led to perceptual hysteresis, the initially established percept persisting into the regime, in which both motion and nonmotion percepts were possible (illustrated schematically in Figure 4.3c). The authors argued that perception is always based on the activation of ensembles of neurons. Within such ensembles, interaction supports self-stabilization of patterns of activation, and this could account for the observed stabilization of the detection decision in the manner of the detection instability (Figure 4.7). In a follow-up study, Hock et al. (2004) exposed participants to motion stimuli of constant BRLC within the bistable region for a variable amount of time. They asked participants to report when percepts switched from motion to nonmotion and vice versa. The resultant switching rates revealed that the switching probability increased over time both for switches to motion as well as for switches to nonmotion perception. This would typically be interpreted in terms of selective adaptation, indicating that both the motion and the nonmotion percepts are embodied by neural populations that build up inhibition while they are activated. (See Hock et al., 2003, for how adaptation relates to dynamical systems ideas in perception.)

Thus, even though the mean behavior may be perfectly well described in the classical threshold manner, psychophysical detection decisions may involve the stabilization of decisions through a bistable regime around threshold. The decisions underlying selection are less commonly studied, in part, because tasks in which the stimulus does not uniquely specify the required choice tend to be fragile experimentally (e.g., by being subject to cognitive penetration, response strategies, and response bias). The gaze control system frequently performs selection decisions and is relatively immune to these problems. Our gaze is reoriented to new visual targets at a high rate of approximately three times a second. Selecting the next visual target is thus one of the most basic sensorimotor decision problems solved by the human central nervous systems. Empirically, a transition is observed from averaging for visual targets that can be fovealized simultaneously to selection when targets are metrically too far from each other for that to be possible (van Ottes, Gisbergen, & Eggermont, 1984). DFT has provided an account for this transition that captures a range of experimental details (Kopecz & Schöner, 1995; Trappenberg et al., 2001). The most recent addition to that range is an account for the time course of selection, with fast saccades tending more toward averaging than slow saccades, because the competitive inhibition required for selection needs more time to become effective (Wilimzig et al., 2006).

Development offers another, wonderful window into the study of selection. Infants are not at risk of adopting dodgy cognitive schemes when confronted with a range of choices and no stimulus that disambiguates the selection. Instead, they select movement targets reliably, such as in the classical paradigm of Jean Piaget (Piaget, 1954) in which two locations, A and B, are perceptually marked on a box. In the classical version, a toy is hidden at the A location, covered by a lid, and after a delay, the box is pushed toward the infant, who reaches for the A lid and may also retrieve the toy. After four to six such A trials, the toy is hidden at the B location. If a delay continues to be imposed, young infants below about 12 months of age are likely to make the A-not-B error, that is, they persevere and reach to the A location rather than the cued B location. Older infants do not make the perseverative error, nor do young infants when the delay is short. Smith et al. (1999) have demonstrated that a toyless version works just as well: The cue consists of waving the A or the B lid and attracting the infant's attention to the corresponding location. Thus, sensorimotor decision making is a critical component of this paradigm.

In the dynamic field account of perseverative reaching (Thelen et al., 2001; Schöner & Dineva, 2006; Dineva & Schöner, 2007), an

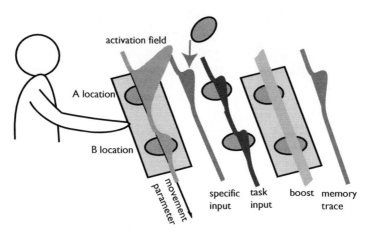

Figure 4.10. A Dynamical Field Theory model of perseverative reaching in Piaget's A not B paradigm represents the planned movement by an activation field defined over a movement parameter. A peak over the A location (here at the left-most lid) represents a reach to A. The dynamic activation field evolves under the influence of specific input (attracting attention to the A location by waving the lid), task input (the two visibly distinct lids), boost (the box with lids is pushed toward the infant), and the memory trace left by earlier reaches to A.

activation field represents the range of possible reaching movements, described parametrically, for instance, by the direction of end-effector movement in space (Figure 4.10). A suprathreshold activation peak centered over the direction in which either of the two lids are located represents an intention to move the hand in the corresponding direction. Various forms of input drive the generation of such a peak. The two locations are perceptually marked by the lids, so both associated directions receive permanent "task" input representing the layout of the reaching space. The cuing action that attracts the infant's attention to one of the two locations generates transient "specific" input to the cued location only. Finally, when the box is pushed into the reaching space of the infant, all reaching locations on the box receive a homogeneous "boost" input. On later trials, an accumulated "memory trace" of previous activation patterns also acts as input, preactivating the locations to which earlier reaches were directed.

The mathematical model that formalizes this account is reviewed in the Appendix. Figure 4.11 illustrates the temporal evolu-

tion of the field and the memory trace over the course of an "A not B" experiment. On the initial A trials, the specific input generates some activation at the cued A location, which decays again during the delay. When the boost is applied after the delay, this pushes the field through the detection instability, generating a peak at the A location. The small remnant activation advantage of A over B left over from the specific input is sufficient to bias the decision in favor of A. The peak at A signifies a reach to A and a memory trace is laid down at that location. This memory trace preactivates the field near A on subsequent trials, further biasing the selection toward the A location. The memory trace thus represents the motor habit formed during A trials.

The memory trace is sufficiently strong to tip the balance on the first B trial in favor of the A location. In that trial, the specific cue provided input to the B location, but the remnant activation after the delay is not strong enough to overcome the bias to A induced by the memory trace. Generally, when the delay is sufficiently long and when sufficiently many reaches to A have

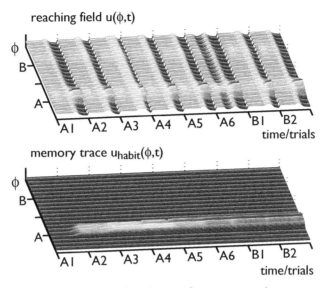

Figure 4.11. Temporal evolution of activation in the reaching field (top) and the associated memory trace (bottom) during the time course of an A not B experiment performed on the Dynamical Field Theory model. Six A trials are followed by two B trials. In each trial, a specific cue is presented at A or B, inducing activation at the associated locations (small bumps in the middle of each trial in the top graph). During the ensuing delay, these activations decay. When the boost arrives (ridges along the ϕ-axis in top graph, a peak is induced at the location with most remaining activation. This peak generates a memory trace (bottom), which biases peak generation on B trials. In these simulations, the model perseverates by generating peaks at the A location on B trials.

built enough of a memory trace at A, the bias to A generates a perseverative reach.

Figure 4.12 shows how the behavioral history in an individual run of the experiment matters. In this instance, a fluctuation leads to the generation of a peak at the B location during an A trial. Such a reach to B on an A trial is called a spontaneous error. It leaves a memory trace at B and weakens the trace at A, predicting increased probability of a spontaneous error being observed again and, in particular, a reduced probability of perseverative reaching. Both are true in the experiment (Dineva & Schöner, 2007).

Why do older infants reach correctly? In the DFT account, this is due to a subtle shift in dynamic regime. Older infants are closer to the cooperative regime, that is, the regime

in which activation peaks are sustained in the absence of localized input (right column in Figure 4.9). This may arise because their overall level of activation is higher or because of characteristic changes in neuronal interaction (Schutte et al., 2003). They are thus capable of generating a sustained peak of activation when the specific cue is given and thus stabilize the reaching decision toward B during the delay against competing input from the memory trace at A.

In fact, whether or not people are capable of stabilizing decisions against competing influences depends on a variety of contextual factors. Toddlers and even 4-year-olds display perseverative errors, for instance, when toys are hidden in a sandbox (Spencer, Smith, & Thelen, 2001). After the toy is hidden, the sand is smoothed over

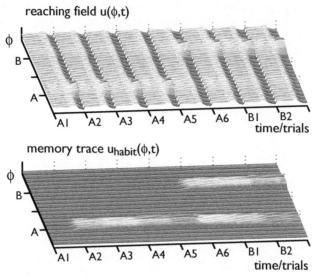

reaching field u(φ,t)

memory trace u_habit(φ,t)

Figure 4.12. Another simulation run for the Dynamical Field Theory model of perseverative reaching. In this simulation, a fluctuation in activation leads to a spontaneous error on the fifth A trial: The field generates a peak at the B location rather than at the A location. This leads to a a memory trace being laid down at B and the memory trace at A being weakened. As a result, a second spontaneous error occurs, and the model responds correctly on the B trials.

and no perceptual marker of the reaching location is left. On B trials after the delay, these children search for the toy in the sand at a location that is metrically attracted to the A location by as much as half the distance between A and B. In DFT, this metric bias comes from sustained peaks drifting during the delay, attracted by the memory trace input laid down during the A trials .

John Spencer and colleagues have extended this picture into the domain of spatial working memory (Spencer & Hund, 2002; Hund & Spencer, 2003; Spencer & Hund, 2003). They had children of various ages and adults point to a location on a featureless surface, at which variable amounts of time earlier a marker had been displayed. By varying the delay between presentation of the location and its probe, these researchers have been able to directly observe the drift of metric spatial memory. Drift occurs in the direction of locations previously held in spatial working memory and

away from any visual landmarks. Older children and adults drift less and more slowly. Here is a set of behavioral data that uncovers direct behavior signatures of the underlying neural picture of self-stabilized neural activation patterns storing metric information (Schutte et al., 2003)!

5. Discussion

5.1. *Is the Dynamical Systems Approach Embodied and Situated?*

Given the abstract mathematics behind the dynamical systems approach, it is legitimate to ask whether the approach does, in fact, embrace the theoretical stance of embodiment and situatedness as announced. Does the dynamical systems approach take seriously the link of cognitive processes to sensory and motor processes? Does it take into account the embedding of cognition within structured environments as well as within the behavioral history of an organism? The more general issue is *autonomy*, that is, the continuous flow of experience under both the action of the individual and the time-varying sensory information about a changing environment. Cognition in naturalistic settings is based on such autonomy. We humans move seamlessly from decision to decision, generating action on our own time frame, only exceptionally reacting to stimuli, more typically actively controlling sensory flow. We update action plans as new sensory information arises. When we are interrupted, the last state of our cognitive processes continues to be available when we resume an action. Thus, cognitive processing is never really off-line.

Dynamical systems thinking is all about autonomy. The theoretical concept of stability, at the core of dynamical systems thinking, is key to understanding autonomy. Only if stability is warranted may cognitive processes be linked to on-line sensory input. Linking cognitive processes to motor systems that act in the real world requires control-theoretic stability. This includes the need to stabilize decisions against fluctuating sensory input and internal neuronal interaction long enough to physically act out what was decided. Conversely, in a system that is open to sensory input and that stabilizes decisions, the release from stability is required to bring about behavioral change. In fact, instabilities are crucial for understanding how the discrete behavioral events may emerge that structure the continuous flow of experience.

By applying dynamical systems concepts at multiple time scales, it is possible to understand how behavioral history as well as the history of stimulation matter. The accumulation of behavioral history is the basis of learning and adaptation. Individual differences may be preserved over time as differences in experience condition further differences in behavior.

Even so, one may ask whether the link of cognitive processes to the sensory and motor surfaces is really always required. Are classical information-processing accounts and many connectionist models not legitimately simplifying analysis by neglecting those links? Such simplification may, however, hide serious problems in the interface between the abstract information processing model and the sensory and motor processes through which cognition is realized. When, for instance, input units in a neural network are assumed to encode objects or symbols, this hides nontrivial processing, including segmentation, classification, and estimation of object parameters. Similarly, if a neuron encodes a motor output, this may hide the nontrivial processes, of control in realtime, including reactions to unforeseen perturbations of the effector system.

One qualitative form of demonstration and exploration of such issues hidden in the interfaces of cognitive models with the real world is to implement the models on physical robotic platforms. A robotic implementation requires complete specification of the entire path from the sensory surface to the cognitive model as well as on to the motor control system. Robotic function may require particular environmental conditions (e.g., uncluttered perceptual scenes), which expose hidden assumptions about simplifications and abstractions that may or may not limit the explanatory power of the cognitive model.

Dynamical systems thinking has been tested extensively with robotic implementations. In fact, an entire approach to robotic behavior has been developed based on dynamical systems thinking (Schöner, Dose, & Engels, 1995). Implementations have sometimes used very simple sensory systems and simple motor control strategies that did not include a detailed model of the plant (Bicho & Schöner, 1997). On the other hand, more complex systems with more highly developed cognitive processes have also been demonstrated (Bergener et al., 1999). The conceptual framework includes DFT employed to endow robots with representations (Engels & Schöner, 1995; Bicho et al., 2000; Erlhagen & Bicho, 2006; Faubel & Schöner, 2006). By generating complex behavioral sequences from attractor dynamics that undergo instabilities, these implementations have demonstrated how autonomy emerges in dynamical systems architectures (Steinhage & Schöner, 1998; Althaus & Christensen, 2003).

Is dynamical systems thinking primarily limited to the sensorimotor domain? Historically, dynamical system thinking arose from work on movement coordination, and this review reflected that history. This history sets dynamical systems thinking apart from both the classical information processing approaches and connectionism and is reflected in the relationship between dynamical systems thinking and the embodied and situated conception of cognition. Much of the recent development of the dynamical systems approach, however, moves well beyond the sensorimotor domain. This newer work was only briefly touched, referring to accounts for working memory, category formation, and object recognition, for instance. DFT has been critical to the extension of dynamical systems thinking beyond the sensorimotor domain. In fact, through DFT, the concept of representation could be integrated into dynamical systems thinking (Spencer & Schöner, 2003). The DFT framework gives the concept of representation a very concrete, embodied sense. For instance, self-stabilized peaks induced by sensory information "re-present" that sensory information even when it is no longer available at the sensory surface. Similarly, self-stabilized peaks are "re-presentations" of motor decisions when they stabilize these decisions while they are not (yet) acted out. The strongly interacting neuronal dynamics of DFT are thus capable of achieving the two qualities that define representations: First, they enable the coupling to the sensory and motor surfaces through which representations establish and maintain links to the outside world. Second, they stabilize these representations, which thus continue to be effective even when no longer linked to sensory or motor systems. This is a sense of representation close to that invoked by the neuroscientist Joaquín Fuster (2005) as a universal feature of the cerebral cortex.

5.2. Is the Dynamical Systems Approach Neurally Based?

The second component of the embodied stance requires accounts to be consistent with principles of neural function. Do the abstract mathematical concepts of the dynamical systems approach live up to this requirement?

Biophysically, neurons really are, of course, little dynamical systems (Wilson, 1999). The historical origin of the concept of dynamic neural fields comes from biophysical models of cortical activation dynamics (Wilson & Cowan, 1972, 1973; Amari, 1977). The insight that cognitive function is best described in terms of neural dynamics is probably due to Grossberg (1980).

On this basis, the two branches of dynamics systems thinking reviewed in this chapter may be roughly mapped onto two forms of neuronal coding. In rate coding, different levels of firing rate are assumed to represent different states of a sensor or effector system. This form of coding is typical at the periphery of the nervous system. Motor neurons, for instance, bring about different levels of force production in muscles when active at different rates. Interestingly, even in these simplest cases, the actual physical state of the associated muscle–joint system depends on the resistance encountered and on local reflex loops requiring a proper dynamical understanding of the embodied and situated system (Latash, 1993). The uniquely instantiated dynamical systems approach generalizes the rate code principle to include forms of instability from which qualitatively new neural functions may emerge as the neuronal dynamics change gradually. Even invertebrate nervous systems, in which rate coding is the prevalent form of neural representation (Bullock, Orkand, & Grinnell, 1977), provide examples of such instabilities. In these systems, neurons may switch allegiance among different patterns of neuronal activity that are responsible for different elementary behaviors. When sufficiently large populations of neurons switch, a macroscopic change of behavior may result, for instance, a switch to another pattern of coordinated activity in Central Pattern Generators (Nusbaum & Beenhakker, 2002).

The other form of neuronal representation is based on the space code principle, which states that what a neuron represents is determined by its position within the neuronal network. The firing rate then merely expresses how strongly the information represented by each neuron contributes. The space code principle is typically assumed to be prevalent in the central nervous system of vertebrates. In vertebrate nervous systems, space coding is postulated for cortex but also such subcortical structures as the thalamus, colliculus, or the hippocampus. Dynamic neuronal fields are direct abstractions of neuronal representations based on the space coding principle.

The concept of a dynamic neuronal field adds two assumptions to the space code principle. First, dynamic fields postulate a topology, in which neurons representing metrically similar contents interact excitatorily, whereas inhibitory interaction relates neurons across the represented metric dimension. This principle is consistent with the existence of topographic maps, in which neighborhood relationships on the sensory or motor surface are preserved in neuronal representation. Within such maps, local excitatory interaction is typically observed (Douglas & Martin, 2004). The overlapping patterns of input activation together with local excitatory interaction justify the continuous description of neuronal patterns of activation on which DFT is based.

A topographical layout of functional maps is not the only way in which this basic assumption of DFT can be realized. Population coding is a more general way for dynamical fields to be realized (Jancke et al., 1999; Erlhagen et al., 1999). The conception of population coding is based on the observation that cortical and subcortical neurons typically have broadly overlapping tuning functions, so that for any given perceptual or motor state, many neurons are active (Georgopoulos, Schwartz, & Kettner, 1986). This is true of most cortical maps, but also of brain structures without

apparent topographical order such as the motor and premotor cortices with respect to movement parameters such as the direction of end-effector motion or the spatial direction of end-effector force (Georgopoulos et al., 1992). In some instances, researchers were able to show that interaction is excitatory among neurons coding for metrically similar values of movement parameters (Georgopoulos, Taira, & Lukashin, 1993). A systematic mapping of neuronal population coding onto dynamic fields can be based on the concept of Distributions of Population Activation, in which not only the most active neurons and their preferred stimulus or motor state are taken into account, but the entire distribution of activation is interpreted (Erlhagen, Bastian, Jancke, Riehle, & Schöner, 1999; Bastian, Schöner, & Riehle, 2003).

Dynamic field theory makes the second major assumption that under some circumstances neuronal interaction can be dominant in the sense that activation patterns are not necessarily dictated by afferent input but may be stabilized by interaction from "within" a neuronal representation. Neuroanatomically, the vast majority of neuronal connections are not part of a unidirectional feed-forward path from the sensory to the motor surfaces (Braitenberg & Schüz, 1991). This fact speaks in favor of the assumption that interaction may be dominant. There is still not much general understanding of the strength and effectiveness of neuronal interaction compared with neuronal input from the sensory surfaces. This may in large part be a consequence of the methodological bias toward input-output characterizations, for which we have a large ensemble of powerful techniques available. By contrast, the identification of strong forms of neuronal interaction is comparatively more difficult and methodologically not systematized.

Does any structure in the brain "read" population codes or cortical maps? In other words, could one ignore the structure of neuronal representations built on the space code principle and instead study cognition at a "higher" level, at which symbols and their manipulation might be directly represented? Although there have been theoretical analyses of how population codes may be "read" (Seung & Sompolinsky, 1993; Denève, Latham, & Pouget, 1999), it is difficult logically to answer this question. What one can say is that a transformation into a different coding regime for higher brain function is unnecessary and not justified by any data. Furthermore, it is easy to conceive of dynamical principles that govern neuronal function all the way through to the effector systems. In this view, stable patterns of neuronal activation ultimately steer the periphery into dynamical states, from which behavior emerges, without any need to ever abstract from the space-time contiguous processes that embody cognition.

All this having been said, the dynamical systems approaches sketched here do remain at a certain level of abstraction. More detailed neuronal realism may entail taking into account the spiking nature of neuronal interaction, cellular processes both at the level of activation dynamics and their modification by processes of learning and adaptation. What is the right level of abstraction for an understanding of neuronal function? This question may be difficult to answer in general. It is useful to keep in mind, however, that all answers to this question are subject to critical assessment. If one assumes primacy of the micro level, then the flight toward the microscopic would find no end. Why wouldn't molecular or even atomic levels of description be privileged over cellular descriptions, for instance?

So what are the arguments in favor of the particular neural level of description at which our dynamical systems approach is so effective? The answer lies within the embodied stance: It is mass action in the nervous system that is correlated with those motor and sensory parameters to which cognition is sensitive. Neural activity of populations of neurons in various parts of the central nervous system modulate their temporal evolution with the demands of cognitive tasks. The time courses of population activation are predictive of behavioral events (Shadlen & Newsome, 2001; Schall, 2001; Bastian et al., 2003), and the metrics of distributions of population activation are predictive of the metrics of behavioral responses (Cisek & Kalaska, 2005). Similar arguments can be made for the instantiated dynamical systems approach (Schöner & Kelso, 1988a).

The level of description of DFT makes explicitly the assumption that the temporal discreteness of neuronal spiking is unrelated to cognitive and behavioral events. Such events must therefore be understood as emerging from an underlying temporally continuous process. Analogously, the assumption is made that the discrete nature of neurons is unrelated to any cognitive or behavioral discreteness. In particular, the formation of discrete cognitive categories is understood as emerging from an underlying continuum of neuronal representation.

5.3. What Kind of Account Does Dynamical Systems Thinking Generate?

If all practical difficulties were removed, what would an ultimate dynamical systems account of cognition look like? It is easier to say what it would not look like. It would not look like the ultimate information-processing model of cognition, with all cognitive processing units listed and their pathways of information exchange identified. Nor would it be like the ultimate connectionist network model, the layers of which would encode all existing neural representations and the network topology of which would reflect the neuronal architecture.

In fact, in dynamical systems thinking, the conceptual interaction with experiment, proposing new questions and new measures, has been more important than the models that resulted. In that sense, dynamical systems thinking is primarily aimed at developing a generative theoretical language that facilitates the uncovery of regularities in nervous systems. Models are tools to test concepts both for internal consistency and, through quantitative theory-experiment relationships, for consistency with nature. Models are not by themselves the main goal of a dynamical systems approach to cognition.

This emphasis on concepts over models is fostered by a central property of dynamical systems, sometimes designated as *emergence*. Attractors in a dynamical system emerge when the conditions are right (when parameters have particular values). The dynamical system relaxes to a new attractor when the history is right, so that the initial condition puts the system in a position from which the attractor is reached. Both may occur in response to changes that are not specific to the newly realized attractor. For instance, a change of resting level in a dynamic field may lead to the attractor state, in which a localized peak is sustained in the absence of localized input. The resting level does not specify any particular location for a peak, nor that a peak must be generated. But everything else being equal, a peak may persist stably only when the resting level is sufficiently large. That attractor is the basis of such cognitive functions as working memory or sensorimotor decision making. These capacities may thus emerge from a neural field dynamics in the here and now, in response to inputs or global changes. These capacities are not enclosed in a particular module that sits somewhere in the brain, waiting to be invoked. Instead, the same neuronal dynamics may under some circumstances have the cognitive functions of working memory and decision making and, under other circumstances, lose these functions. Any individual contribution to the neuronal dynamics is thus *multifunctional*.

Conversely, there are multiple ways a new stable state may emerge as well as disappear again (*multicausality*). There is quite possibly no single parameter that is strictly necessary or is always sufficient for a given cognitive function to emerge. Even a complete understanding of the dynamics of the neural cognitive system is not by itself sufficient to predict all possible ways cognition may unfold when an organism is immersed in a new and rich environment. When processes of adaptation and learning incorporate parts of the environment and of experience into the system, the resultant complexity may become inextricable (Rosen, 2005).

Dynamical systems thinking is in that sense open ended. It is not aimed, even in principle, at an ultimate model, which would include process models of all cognitive, sensory, and motor capacities of the human. Instead, it is aimed at understanding constraints for learning and development, for how individual differences may manifest themselves in different contexts, how individual learning and developmental histories may lead to the same function. So although we may never be able to predict how a child moves about in the playground, which swing or slide she will select, we may very well understand how progress in her motor skills may improve her spatial orientation or how perceptual experience with a set of objects will impact on what she pays attention to when naming a new object.

Appendix: Dynamical Field Theory of Perseverative Reaching

The dynamic field theory of perseverative reaching has its roots in a metaphorical dynamical systems account of Piaget's A not B error (Thelen & Smith, 1994). A first formalization into a mathematical model was reported in (Thelen et al., 2001). Conceptual errors in that earlier account were corrected by Evelina Dineva, and it is her model that I review here (Schöner & Dineva, 2006; Dineva & Schöner, 2007).

A dynamical activation field is defined over the space of movement directions, ϕ, of the infant's hand. This is the "reaching" field, $u(\phi, t)$. Its dynamics has the form of an interactive neuronal field (Amari, 1977) receiving a set of inputs:

$$\tau \dot{u}(\phi, t) = -u(\phi, t) + h$$
$$+ \int d\phi' w(\phi - \phi') \sigma(u(\phi', t))$$
$$+ S_{\text{task}}(\phi) + S_{\text{spec}}(\phi, t)$$
$$+ S_{\text{boost}}(t) + u_{\text{habit}}(\phi, t).$$

$$(4.3)$$

Here, $\tau\dot{u}(\phi, t) = -u(\phi, t) + h$ sets the activation field up as a dynamical system with resting state $u(\phi) = h < 0$, a homogenous stationary stable state in the absence of input and interaction, to which the field relaxes on the time scale, τ. Interaction consists of input from other field locations, ϕ', which is excitatory or inhibitory, depending on the interaction kernel

$$w(\phi - \phi') = w_{\text{excitatory}}$$
$$\exp\left[-(\phi - \phi')^2/2\Delta\right] - w_{\text{inhibitory}}.$$
$$(4.4)$$

For sufficiently close field locations ($|\phi - \phi'| < \Delta$), the intra-field connectivity is predominantly excitatory ($w_{\text{excitatory}} > w_{\text{inhibitory}}$), for larger distances it is inhibitory. Only sites, ϕ', with sufficiently positive levels of activation contribute to interaction, as controlled by the nonlinear sigmoidal function

$$\sigma(u) = \frac{1}{1 + \exp(-\beta u)} \qquad (4.5)$$

whose parameter, β, controls how nonlinear the interaction term is.

The input functions, $S_{\text{task}}(\phi)$, $S_{\text{spec}}(\phi, t)$, and $S_{\text{boost}}(t)$ model the experimental scenario. The task input, S_{task}, captures the visual layout of the workspace and is modeled as a sum of two gaussians centered over the two movement directions, in which the two locations, A and B, lie. The specific input, $S_{\text{spec}}(\phi, t)$, captures the experimenter's effort to attract attention to the A location on A trials and to the B location on B trials. It is modeled as a gaussian centered on the corresponding location that is nonzero only during the time interval during which the experimenter performs this stimulation. The boost, $S_{\text{boost}}(t)$, captures the effect of pushing the box with the two lids into the reaching space of the infant. It is modeled as a positive constant present only during the time interval when the box is in reaching space.

Finally, the formation of a habit of reaching is modeled by a second dynamical activation field, $u_{\text{habit}}(\phi, t)$, which evolves over a longer time scale, τ_{habit}, and forms a memory trace of locations in the reaching field, $u(\phi, t)$, at which sufficient levels of activation have been generated. The dynamics of this memory trace is modeled as follows:

$$\tau_{\text{habit}}\, \dot{u}_{\text{habit}}(\phi, t)$$
$$= [-u_{\text{habit}}(\phi, t) + c_{\text{habit}}\sigma(u(\phi, t))]$$
$$\times \Theta\left(\int d\phi' \Theta(u(\phi', t))\right). \qquad (4.6)$$

The last term turns the memory trace mechanism off if there is no positive activity anywhere in the reaching field. This makes use of the step function, $\Theta(u) = 1$ if $u > 0$ and $\Theta(u) = 0$ while $u \leq 0$. Thus, during epochs in which there is no activation in the reaching field, the memory trace remains unchanged. This captures the observation that inter-trial intervals do not seem to matter much in the A not B paradigm. In fact, perseverative tendencies persist through considerable delays.

When an activation peak has been induced in the reaching field, then the memory trace mechanism leads to increase of the memory trace in locations on which the peak is centered, whereas activation elsewhere in the memory trace decays toward zero. Thus, a dynamical balance emerges between different locations at which peaks are induced in different trials. The constant, c_{habit}, determines the amplitude of the memory trace. In Dineva's implementation of this dynamics, a memory trace is laid down only during the interval when the box is in the reaching space (that is, while the boosting input is present). At the end of a trial, the peak in the reaching field is deleted, and the field starts the next trial from its resting state (Figures 4.11 and 4.12).

Neuronal activity in the nervous system has a stochastic component. To account for fluctuations in activation, which make the outcome of reaching decisions nondeterministic, the model contains stochastic forces. The generic model for such forces is additive gaussian white noise. This noise may be spatially uncorrelated at different field sites or also be correlated, modeling stochastic input distributed by input kernels.

To simulate DFT models, the equations must be numerically solved on a computer using standard numerical procedures (Kloeden & Platen, 1999). Simulating the experimental paradigm typically requires programming the time courses of sensory inputs that describe the experience in such paradigms. Under some circumstances, this may include the need for sensor and motor models, in which the sensory consequences of a motor act driven from the DFT model is also taken into account (Steinhage & Schöner, 1998).

References

Althaus, P., & Christensen, H. I. (2003). Smooth task switching through behaviour competition. *Robotics and Autonomous Systems, 44,* 241–249.

Amari, S. (1977). Dynamics of pattern formation in lateral-inhibition type neural fields. *Biological Cybernetics, 27,* 77–87.

Amit, D. J. (1994). The hebbian paradigm reintegrated: Local reverberations as internal representations. *Behavioral and Brain Sciences, 18*(4), 617–626.

Bastian, A., Schöner, G., & Riehle, A.(2003). Preshaping and continuous evolution of motor cortical representations during movement preparation. *European Journal of Neuroscience, 18,* 2047–2058.

Bergener, T., Bruckhoff, C., Dahm, P., Janssen, H., Joublin, F., Menzner, R., et al. (1999). Complex behavior by means of dynamical systems for an anthropomorphic robot. *Neural Networks, 12*(7), 1087–1099.

Bicho, E., Mallet, P., & Schöner, G. (2000). Target representation on an autonomous vehicle with low-level sensors. *The International Journal of Robotics Research, 19,* 424–447.

Bicho, E., & Schöner, G. (1997). The dynamic approach to autonomous robotics demonstrated on a low-level vehicle platform. *Robotics and Autonomous Systems, 21,* 23–35.

Braitenberg, V., & Schüz, A. (1991). *Anatomy of the cortex.* Berlin: Springer Verlag.

Brooks, R. A. (1991). New approches to robotics. *Science, 253,* 1227–1232.

Bullock, T. H., Orkand, R., & Grinnell, A. (1977). *Introduction to nervous systems.* San Francisco: W.H. Freeman.

Cisek, P., & Kalaska, J. F. (2005). Neural correlates of reaching decisions in dorsal premotor cortex: Specification of multiple direction choices and final selection of action. *Neuron, 3*(45), 801–814.

Denève, S., Latham, P., & Pouget, A. (1999). Reading population codes: A neural implementation of ideal observers. *Nature Neuroscience, 2*(8), 740–745.

Dineva, E., & Schöner, G. (2007). Behavioral history matters: A dynamic field account of spontaneous and perseverative errors in infant reaching. Manuscript submitted for publication.

Douglas, R. J., & Martin, K. A. C. (2004). Neural circuits of the neocortex. *Annual Review of Neuroscience, 27,* 419–451.

Engels, C., & Schöner, G. (1995). Dynamic fields endow behavior-based robots with representations. *Robotics and Autonomous Systems, 14,* 55–77.

Erlhagen, W., Bastian, A., Jancke, D., Riehle, A., & Schöner, G. (1999). The distribution of neuronal population activation (DPA) as a tool to study interaction and integration in cortical representations. *Journal of Neuroscience Methods, 94,* 53–66.

Erlhagen, W., & Bicho, E. (2006). The dynamic neural field approach to cognitive robotics—part of the 3rd neuro-it and neuroengineering summer school tutorial series. *Journal of Neural Engineering, 3*(3), R36–R54.

Erlhagen, W., & Schöner, G. (2002). Dynamic field theory of movement preparation. *Psychological Review, 109,* 545–572.

Faubel, C., & Schöner, G. (2006). Fast learning to recognize objects: Dynamic fields in label-feature space. In *Proceedings of the Fifth International Conference on Development and Learning ICDL 2006.* Bloomington: Indiana University.

Fuster, J. M. (2005). *Cortex and mind—Unifying cognition.* New York: Oxford University Press.

Georgopoulos, A. P., Ashe, J., Smyrnis, N., & Taira, M. (1992). The motor cortex and the coding of force. *Science, 245,* 1692–1695.

Georgopoulos, A. P., Lurito, J. T., Petrides, M., Schwartz, A. B., & Massey, J. T. (1989). Mental rotation of the neural population vector. *Science, 243,* 1627-1630. (Reprinted in

Kelnser, K. L., Koshland, D. E., Jr. (Eds.), *Molecules to models*, AAAS, 1989.)

Georgopoulos, A. P., Schwartz, A. B., & Kettner, R. E. (1986). Neural population coding of movement direction. *Science, 233*, 1416–1419.

Georgopoulos, A. P., Taira, M., & Lukashin, A. (1993). Cognitive neurophysiology of the motor cortex. *Science, 260*(5104), 47–52. (Comment in Science 1994 Mar 4; 263:1295–1297)

Gerstner, W., & Kistler, W. M. (2002). *Spiking neuron models: Single neurons, populations, plasticity*. Cambridge, UK: Cambridge University Press.

Ghez, C., Favilla, M., Ghilardi, M. F., Gordon, J., Bermejo, R., & Pullman, S. (1997). Discrete and continuous planning of hand movements and isometric force trajectories. *Experimental Brain Research, 115*, 217–233.

Goodale, M. A., Pélisson, D., & Prablanc, C. (1986). Large adjustments in visually guided reaching do not depend on vision of the hand or perception of target displacement. *Nature, 320*, 748–750.

Grossberg, S. (1980). Biological competition: Decision rules, pattern formation, and oscillations. *Proceedings of the National Academy of Sciences (USA), 77*, 2338–2342.

Grossberg, S., Pribe, C., & Cohen, M. A. (1997). Neural control of interlimb oscillations. I. Human bimanual coordination. *Biological Cybernetics, 77*, 131–140.

Heisenberg, M., & Wolf, R. (1988). Reafferent control of optomotor yaw torque in drosophilia melanogaster. *Journal of Comparative Physiology, 163*, 373–388.

Hock, H. S., Bukowski, L., Nichols, D. F., Huisman, A., & Rivera, M. (2005). Dynamical vs. judgemental comparison: Hysteresis effects in motion perception. *Spatial Vision, 18*(3), 317–335.

Hock, H. S., Gilroy, L., & Harnett, G. (2002). Counter-changing luminance: A nonfourier, nonattentional basis for the perception of single-element apparent motion. *Journal of Experimental Psychology: Human Perception and Performance, 28*(1), 93–112.

Hock, H. S., Kelso, J. A. S., & Schöner, G. (1993). Perceptual stability in the perceptual organization of apparent motion patterns. *Journal of Experimental Psychology: Human Perception and Performance, 19*, 63–80.

Hock, H. S., Kogan, K., & Espinoza, J. K. (1997). Dynamic, state-dependent thresholds for the perception of single-element apparent motion: Bistability from local cooperativity. *Perception & Pschophysics, 59*, 1077–1088.

Hock, H. S., Nichols, D. F., & Espinoza, J. (2004). When motion is not perceived: Evidence from adaptation and dynamical stability. *Spatial Vision, 17*(3), 235–248.

Hock, H. S., & Ploeger, A. (2006). Linking dynamical perceptual decisions at different levels of description in motion pattern formation: Psychophysics. *Perception & Psychophysics, 68*(3), 505–514.

Hock, H. S., Schöner, G., & Giese, M. A. (2003). The dynamical foundations of motion pattern formation: Stability, selective adaptation, and perceptual continuity. *Perception & Psychophysics, 65*, 429–457.

Hund, A. M., & Spencer, J. P. (2003). Developmental changes in the relative weighting of geometric and experience-dependent location cues. *Journal of Cognition and Development, 4*(1), 3–38.

Jancke, D., Erlhagen, W., Dinse, H. R., Akhavan, A. C., Giese, M., Steinhage, A. (1999). Parametric population representation of retinal location: Neuronal interaction dynamics in cat primary visual cortex. *Journal of Neuroscience, 19*, 9016–9028.

Juarrero, A. (1999). *Dynamics in action: Intentional behavior as a complex system*. Cambridge, MA: MIT Press.

Keijzer, F. A. (2001). *Representation and behavior*. Cambridge, MA: MIT Press.

Kelso, J. A. S. (1995). *Dynamic patterns: The self-organization of brain and behavior*. Cambridge, MA: MIT Press.

Kloeden, P. E., & Platen, E. (1999). *The numerical solution of stochastic differential equations* (2nd ed.). Berlin: Springer-Verlag.

Köhler, W. (1920/1939). *Physical gestalten*. London: Routledge & Kegan. (Reprinted in W.D. Ellis (Ed.), *A source book of gestalt psychology*.

Kopecz, K., & Schöner, G. (1995). Saccadic motor planning by integrating visual information and pre-information on neural, dynamic fields. *Biological Cybernetics, 73*, 49–60.

Latash, M. (1993). *Control of human movement*. Champaign, IL: Human Kinetics.

Markman, A. B., & Dietrich, E. (2000). In defense of representation. *Cognitive Psychology, 40*, 138–171.

Nichols, D. F., Hock, H. S., & Schöner, G. (2006). Linking dynamical perceptual decisions at different levels of description in motion pattern formation: Computational simulations. *Perception & Psychophysics*, *68*(3), 515–533.

Nusbaum, M. P., & Beenhakker, M. P. (2002). A small-systems approach to motor pattern generation. *Nature*, *417*, 434–450.

Perko, L. (1991). *Differential equations and dynamical systems*. Berlin: Springer Verlag.

Piaget, J. (1954). *The construction of reality in the child*. New York: Basic Books.

Poggio, T., & Reichardt, W. (1976). Visual control of orientation behaviour in the fly. *Quarterly Reviews of Biophysics*, *9*, 377–438.

Reichardt, W., & Poggio, T. (1976). Visual control of orientation behaviour in the fly: I. A quantitative analysis. *Quarterly Reviews in Biophysics*, *9*, 311–375.

Rosen, R. (2005). *Life itself: A comprehensive inquiry into the nature, origin, and fabrication of life*. New York: Columbia University Press.

Schall, J. D. (2001). Neural basis of deciding, choosing and action. *Nature Reviews Neuroscience*, *2*, 33–42.

Scholz, J. P., Kelso, J. A. S., & Schöner, G. (1988). Dynamics governs switching among patterns of coordinations in biological movement. *Physics Letters*, *A134*, 8–12.

Schöner, G. (2002). Timing, clocks, and dynamical systems. *Brain and Cognition*, *48*, 31–51.

Schöner, G., & Dineva, E. (2006). Dynamic instabilities as mechanisms for emergence. *Developmental Science*, *10*, 69–74.

Schöner, G., Dose, M., & Engels, C. (1995). Dynamics of behavior: Theory and applications for autonomous robot architectures. *Robotics and Autonomous Systems*, *16*, 213–245.

Schöner, G., Haken, H., & Kelso, J. A. S. (1986). A stochastic theory of phase transitions in human hand movement. *Biological Cybernetics*, *53*, 247–257.

Schöner, G., & Kelso, J. A. S. (1988a). Dynamic pattern generation in behavioral and neural systems. *Science*, *239*, 1513–1520.

Schöner, G., & Kelso, J. A. S. (1988b). A dynamic theory of behavioral change. *Journal of Theoretical Biology*, *135*, 501–524.

Schöner, G., & Kelso, J. A. S. (1988c). Synergetic theory of environmentally-specified and learned patterns of movement coordination: I. Relative phase dynamics. *Biological Cybernetics*, *58*, 71–80.

Schöner, G., Zanone, P. G., & Kelso, J. A. S. (1992). Learning as change of coordination dynamics: Theory and experiment. *Journal of Motor Behavior*, *24*, 29–48.

Schutte, A. R., & Spencer, J. P. (2002). Generalizing the Dynamic Field Theory of the A-not-B error beyond infancy: Three-year-olds' delay- and experience-dependent location memory biases. *Child Development*, *73*, 377–404.

Schutte, A. R., Spencer, J. P., & Schöner, G. (2003). Testing the dynamic field theory: Working memory for locations becomes more spatially precise over development. *Child Development*, *74*, 1393–1417.

Scott, S. H. (2004). Optimal feedback control and the neural basis of volitional motor control. *Nature Reviews Neuroscience*, *5*, 534–546.

Seung, H. S., & Sompolinsky, H. (1993). Simple models for reading neuronal population codes. *Proceedings of the National Academy of Science (U.S.A.)*, *90*, 10749–10753.

Shadlen, M. N., & Newsome, W. T. (2001). Neural basis of a perceptual decision in the parietal cortex (area LIP) of the rhesus monkey. *Journal of Neurophysiology*, *86*, 1916–1936.

Smith, L. B., Thelen, E., Titzer, R., & McLin, D. (1999). Knowing in the context of acting: The task dynamics of the a-not-b error. *Psychological Review*, *106*(2), 235–260.

Spencer, J. P., & Hund, A. M. (2002). Prototypes and particulars: Geometric and experience-dependent spatial categories. *Journal of Experimental Psychology: General*, *XX*(1), 16–37.

Spencer, J. P., & Hund, A. M. (2003). Developmental continuity in the processes that underlie spatial recall. *Cognitive Psychology*, *47*, 432–480.

Spencer, J. P., & Schöner, G. (2003). Bridging the representational gap in the dynamical systems approach to development. *Developmental Science*, *6*, 392–412.

Spencer, J. P., Simmering, V. R., & Schutte, A. R. (2006). Toward a formal theory of flexible spatial behavior: Geometric category biases generalize across pointing and verbal response types. *Journal of Experimental Psychology: Human Perception and Performance*, *32*(2), 473–490.

Spencer, J. P., Simmering, V. R., Schutte, A. R., & Schöner, G. (2007). What does theoretical neuroscience have to offer the study of behavioral development? Insights from a dynamic field theory of spatial cognition. In J. Plumert & J. P. Spencer (Eds.), *The emerging spatial mind* (pp. 320–361). New York: Oxford University Press.

Spencer, J. P., Smith, L. B., & Thelen, E. (2001). Tests of a dynamic systems account of the a-not-b error: The influence of prior experience on the spatial memory abilities of 2-year-olds. *Child Development, 72*(5), 1327–1346.

Steinhage, A., & Schöner, G. (1998). Dynamical systems for the behavioral organization of autonomous robot navigation. In M. G. T. Schenker P. S. (Ed.), *Sensor fusion and decentralized control in robotic systems: Proceedings of SPIE* (Vol. 3523, p. 169–180). Boston, MA: SPIE Publishing.

Thelen, E., Schöner, G., Scheier, C., & Smith, L. (2001). The dynamics of embodiment: A field theory of infant perseverative reaching. *Brain and Behavioral Sciences, 24*, 1–33.

Thelen, E., & Smith, L. B. (1994). *A dynamic systems approach to the development of cognition and action.* Cambridge, MA: MIT Press.

Trappenberg, T. P., Dorris, M. C., Munoz, D. P., & Klein, R. M. (2001). A model of saccade initiation based on the competitive integration of exogenous and endogenous signals in the superior colliculus. *Journal of Cognitive Neuroscience, 13*(2), 256–271.

Turvey, M. T. (1990). Coordination. *American Psychologist, 45*(8), 938–953.

van Gelder, T., & Port, R. F. (1995). It's about time: An overview of the dynamical approach to cognition. In R. F. Port & T. van Gelder (Eds.), *Mind as motion: Explorations in the dynamics of cognition.* Cambridge, MA: MIT Press.

van Gelder, T. (1998). The dynamical hypothesis in cognitive science. *Brain and Behavioral Sciences, 21*, 615–665.

van Ottes, F. P., Gisbergen, J. A. M., & Eggermont, J. J. (1984). Metrics of saccade responses to visual double stimuli: Two different modes. *Vision Research, 24*, 1169–1179.

Vorberg, D., & Wing, A. (1996). Modeling variability and dependence in timing. In H. Heuer & S. W. Keele (Eds.), *Handbook of perception and action* (Vol. 2, pp. 181–262). London: Academic Press.

Wilimzig, C., Schneider, S., & Schöner, G. (2006). The time course of saccadic decision making: Dynamic field theory. *Neural Networks, 19*, 1059–1074.

Wilson, H. R. (1999). *Spikes, decisions, and actions: Dynamical foundations of neurosciences.* New York: Oxford University Press.

Wilson, H. R., & Cowan, J. D. (1972). Excitatory and inhibitory interactions in localized populations of model neurons. *Biophysical Journal, 12*, 1–24.

Wilson, H. R., & Cowan, J. D. (1973). A mathematical theory of the functional dynamics of cortical and thalamic nervous tissue. *Kybernetik, 13*, 55–80.

CHAPTER 5

Declarative/Logic-Based Cognitive Modeling

Selmer Bringsjord

1. Introduction

1.1. *What Is Logic-Based Computational Cognitive Modeling?*

This chapter is a systematization of a particular approach to modeling the mind: *declarative* computational cognitive modeling. (In light of the fact that if an agent knows p, p must be a proposition or declarative statement, sometimes the term "knowledge-based" is used in place of "declarative." Some writers use the term "symbolic.") The basic units of such modeling are declarative, or propositional: They are formal objects associated with those particular sentences or expressions in natural languages (like English, German, Chinese) that are declarative statements (as opposed to expressions in the imperative or inquisitive mode) taking values such as TRUE, FALSE, UNKNOWN, and PROBABLE (sometimes to particular numerical degrees). The basic process over such units is inference, which may be deductive, inductive, probabilistic, abductive, or analogical. Because the basic units of declarative computational cognitive modeling are declar-

ative, a hallmark of declarative computational cognitive modeling is a top-down, rather than bottom-up, approach. As Brachman and Levesque (2004) put it, when speaking of declarative computational cognitive modeling within the field of artificial intelligence (AI):

> *It is at the very core of a radical idea about how to understand intelligence: instead of trying to understand or build brains from the* bottom *up,* we try to understand or *build intelligent behavior from the* top down. *In particular, we ask what an agent would need to know in order to behave intelligently, and what computational mechanisms could allow this knowledge to be made available to the agent as required.* (p. iv)

The top-down approach is unavoidable, because, as reflected in relevant formalisms commonly associated with bottom-up approaches (e.g., artificial neural networks), the basic units in bottom-up processing are numerical, not declarative. The systematization of declarative computational cognitive modeling, the overarching purpose of the present chapter, is achieved by using formal logic; hence, declarative computational cognitive modeling, from the formal perspective, becomes *logic-based* computational cognitive modeling (LCCM).

Logic-based computational cognitive modeling is an interdisciplinary field that cuts across cognitive modeling based on certain cognitive architectures (such as ACT-R, Soar, CLARION, Polyscheme, etc.), logic itself, and computational psychology of reasoning. In addition, LCCM has a sister field in logic-based human-level artificial intelligence (AI), and, being computational, it inevitably draws heavily from computer science, which is itself, as has been explained (e.g., in Halpern et al., 2001), based on formal logic. Specifically, and unsurprisingly, the declarative programming paradigm is naturally associated with declarative computational cognitive modeling.

1.2. *Level of Description of LCCM*

This chapter is pitched at a level of description having nothing to do with supporting one group of practitioners in computational cognitive modeling over another or one paradigm for computational cognitive modeling over another, or one particular cognitive architecture or model over others. Logic-based computational cognitive modeling as set out herein, is not a description of the day-to-day *practice* of all cognitive modelers operating under the umbrella of declarative computational cognitive modeling. Such practice is heterogeneous. Logic-based computational cognitive modeling is a formal framework, one directly analogous to what enabled the systematization of mathematics provided by many decades of formal exposition in books authored by Bourbaki[1] –

exposition that shows that discovery and confirmation in mathematics consists, fundamentally, in the derivation and use of theorems all extractable from a small set of axioms (e.g., the Zermelo-Fraenkel axioms for set theory). The parallel in the present chapter is that all declarative computational cognitive modeling is fundamentally the use of logical systems and logic-based computer programs to model the human mind. In contemporary declarative computational cognitive modeling, one researcher may in daily practice use production rules, another first-order logic, another graphs to record probability distributions across declarative statements, another semantic models, and yet another semantic networks, but they are all united by the fact that the structures and processes they produce are all and only parameterized instantiations of the formal structures explicated in this chapter.

Furthermore, the purpose of this chapter is not to introduce a new competitor to extant, mature computational cognitive architectures, such as Soar (Rosenbloom, Laird & Newell, 1993), ACT-R (Anderson 1993; Anderson & Lebiere, 1998; Anderson, & Lebiere, 2003), CLARION (Sun, 2002), ICARUS (Langley et al., 1991), SNePS (Shapiro & Rapaport, 1987), and Polyscheme Cassimatis, 2002; Cassimatis et al., 2004), nor to declarative computational simulations of parts of human cognition, such as PSYCOP (Rips, 1994), and programs written by Johnson-Laird and others to simulate various aspects of so-called mental models-based reasoning (a review is provided in Bucciarelli & Johnson-Laird, 1999). These systems are all pitched at a level well above LCCM; they can all be derived from LCCM. The formal umbrella used for the systematization herein is to offer a way to understand and rationalize *all* computational cognitive architectures that are declarative, that is, that are, at least in part, rule-based, explicitly logic-based, predicate-and-argument-based, propositional, and production-rule-based. The ancient roots of this kind of work date back to Aristotle.

---

1 A group allonym for the mathematicians who authored a collection of eight painstakingly rigorous, detailed books showing that all the publishable results of classical mathematics can in fact be expressed as derivations from axiomatic set theory using the logical system known as first-order logic, which is $\mathcal{L}_1$ in the family $\mathcal{F}$ of systems introduced and explained in the present chapter. The starting place in the Bourbaki oeuvre is Bourbaki (2004).

The formal foundations of declarative computational cognitive modeling are straight-forward: They rest only on a generalization of (a) the concept of *logical system*, used in mathematical logic; and (b) the notions of reasoning and computing in such systems, by way of logic-based computer programs. A computational simulation of some human cognition amounts to the execution of such a program in the context of certain selected parameters, where these parameters determine which logical system is operative. All of this will be explained in due course.

1.3. *The Ancient Roots of LCCM*

Declarative computational cognitive modeling is the oldest paradigm for modeling the mind. As shown in the standard timelines on such matters, over 300 years B.C., and hence many centuries before the arrival of probability theory and artificial neural networks, logic and logic alone was being used to model and predict human cognition. For example, consider the following argument:

(1) All professors are pusillanimous people.
(2) All pusillanimous people are proud.
∴ (3) All professors are proud.

The symbol ∴, often read as "therefore," says that statement (3) can be logically inferred from statements (1) and (2); or in other words that if statements (1) and (2) are true, then (3) must be true as well. Is that so? The odds are exceedingly good that you will see the answer is "Yes." The cognition that consists in your assimilating this argument, declaring it valid, and – were you requested to do so – providing a proof to justify your response, was modeled and predicted by Aristotle.[2] To use today's well-understood concept, which will soon turn out to be central to the present chapter, Aristotle's modeling

was expressed in a primitive *logical system*. This system was the theory of the syllogism, according to which the schema

(1*) All As are Bs.
(2*) All Bs are Cs.
∴ (3*) All As are Cs.

is deductively valid, no matter what classes are denoted by A, B, and C. According to Aristotle, if you were now to be presented with an instantiation of this schema different from the one given about professors (e.g., if A = pigeons, B = pongid, C = smart) you would respond that it, too, is a valid inference (and you would of course be correct again). The noteworthy thing about your response in the second case is that you will grasp the logical validity of the inference in question, despite the fact that, necessarily, no pigeons are pongid. In other words, Aristotle discovered that certain context-independent structures describe and predict human thinking: You do not assent to the second argument because you know the *meaning* of "pigeon" and "pongid," but rather because you grasp that the abstract structure of the argument is what makes it a valid inference. Because computation was in its infancy 300 B.C., and the concept of a general-purpose programmable computer would have to wait until logic made enough progress to give birth to it, it was far from clear to Aristotle how the schemas in his logical system were computational, but in essence, he had indeed presented a series of parameterized functions for computing the composite function from triples of formulas in the formal language he invented to the set {VALID, INVALID}. If the function is s, then because the formulas are of four types, namely,

English	Abbreviation
All As are Bs.	All AB
No As are Bs.	No AB
Some As are Bs.	I AB
Some As are non-Bs.	O $A\bar{B}$

one can say that s returns VALID on the triple (All AB, All BC, All AC), with substitutions for A – C. For another example, notice that

2 Aristotle's work on logic, including the theory of the syllogism, can be found in his *Organon*, the collection of his logical treatises. This collection, and Aristotle's other main writings, are available in McKeon (1941).

s returns VALID on the triple (I *AB*, All *BC*, I *AC*). Later, an INVALID triple will turn out to be relevant to modern-day research in psychology of reasoning (Section 3.1.4).

Today, using modern experimental design and statistical analysis for the behavioral sciences, a large amount of data has been accumulated in support of large parts of Aristotle's model (e.g., see Newstead & Evans, 1995). However, there are two serious problems with the theory of the syllogism. These two problems are in fact the main drivers that have brought LCCM to the level of maturity it enjoys today, and explaining the solution to them forms the heart of the present chapter. They are:

Problem 1: Some humans do not reason in normatively correct fashion. Tied to the ancient theory at hand, some human subjects fail to reason in conformity to valid syllogisms (i.e., to *s*), and in fact sometimes reason in conformity to provably *in*valid syllogisms. Aristotle, and his successors in the LCCM paradigm all the way up to and including Piaget (who held that in the course of normal development humans would acquire a capacity to think not only in accordance with the theory of the syllogism, but with the more expressive, powerful modern logical system known as first-order logic [Inhelder & Piaget, 1958]), failed to realize this. The realization came when, in the twentieth century A.D., Wason and Johnson-Laird showed that normatively correct thinking is in surprisingly short supply among humans (see, e.g., Wason, 1966), as can be seen when clever stimuli are devised and presented. (Such stimuli are visited later, in Section 3.1.4. They are syllogisms that, by *s*, are classified as INVALID, and yet many humans report that they are VALID.)

Problem 2: The theory of the syllogism was agreed by the relevant thinkers, even at the time of Aristotle, to be at best a model of only a smidgeon of the parts of human cognition that are obvious targets for declarative modeling (e.g., the specification of proofs, as routinely carried out by mathematicians). The specific evidence that gave rise to this agreement consisted of the brute fact that only a tiny part of Euclid's seminal logical and mathematical reasoning, published in his *Elements*, could be modeled as syllogistic reasoning (Glymour, 1992). Today, courtesy of modern logic, LCCM can model all that Euclid did – and more, as shall be seen.

1.4. LCCM's Sister Discipline: Logic-Based Human-Level AI

Artificial intelligence is the field devoted to building intelligent agents that map percepts (perceived information about the agent's environment) to actions that cause changes in the agent's environment, in the service of goals desired by the agent (Russell & Norvig, 2002). This definition is consistent with attempts to build agents having no more intelligence than, say, an insect. (Some famous AI engineers have in fact strived to build robotic insects. Brooks, 1991, is an example.) *Human-level* AI is AI focused not on insects, but on intelligent agents capable of human-level behavior. Recently, a recrudescence of this form of AI has begun, as a number of writings confirm (e.g., see Cassimatis, 2006; Nilsson, 1995; Nilsson, 2005; Brooks et al., 1999). Of the authors just cited, Nilsson avowedly pursues logic-based human-level AI, whereas Brooks avowedly does not; Cassimatis straddles both camps.

How are LCCM and human-level logic-based AI related? The encapsulated answer is straightforward: The two fields are largely based on the same formalisms, both exploit the power of general-purpose programmable computing machines to process symbolic data, but LCCM targets computational simulations of human cognition, whereas human-level logic-based AI, strives to build beings that, at least behaviorally speaking, can pass for humans. Although it is conceivable that both fields might well be on the same exact path (one that leads to building a computational system indistinguishable from a human), LCCM insists that the engineered system, at some suitably selected level of description, operates as a human does. Human-level AI would be content with artifacts that *seem* human, but "under the hood" really are not. As to shared formalisms, interested readers are directed to treatments of logic-based AI that introduce the relevant technical material (summarized, e.g., in Bringsjord & Ferrucci, 1998a; Bringsjord & Ferrucci, 1998b; Nilsson, 1991). The present chapter provides more modern, systematic, and comprehensive treatment of the underlying formal content than provided in these publications.

1.5. *Different Levels of Description*

This chapter is based on an ecumenical conception of what it is to computationally model human thinking, particularly human reasoning over declarative content. (Because of space constraints, the exposition herein leaves aside psychology of decision making, despite the fact this discipline is highly declarative, as revealed by the fact that seminal experiments in the field present subjects with declarative statements to be reasoned over in order for decisions to be expressed. For exemplars, see the experiments carried out by Kahneman and Tversky (2000) to establish the so-called framing effect.) To explain, consider the structure of the kind of experiments traditionally used in psychology of reasoning.[3] Let S be some stimulus in some experiment involving a person (subject) P, and specifically assume that S is constituted by a list L of declarative statements, a query (or "stem," to use the argot of psychometrics) Q, and possibly a single declarative statement D to which Q refers. (If there is no D in S, then Q is simply: "What logically follows from L?") The last ingredient is simply a request for a justifica-

tion. For example, one might present to P a stimulus such as the following:

> Consider L. $Q =$ Does the following proposition logically follow from L? D. Please provide a justification for your answer.

Now suppose that P gives a verdict ("Yes" or "No") and provides justification J. To achieve a computational simulation of P in this context, given the inclusive orientation of this chapter, it suffices to produce a computer program that takes in S, produces the relevant verdict (e.g., the verdict given by the vast majority of subjects, the normatively correct verdict, etc.), and gives a proof or argument that matches the justification given. (This is not easy to do, because humans often give justifications, especially when erroneous, that depart considerably from established machine reasoning patterns.) The proof or argument itself, in the logic-based paradigm, constitutes the algorithm for transforming the stimulus in question into the output. Put in a way connected to traditional accounts of levels of description found in cognitive science, logic-based computational cognitive models are intended to be successful at Marr's (1982) *algorithmic* level, or Pylyshyn's (1984) *symbolic* level. In addition, please note that it is perfectly acceptable that justification be articulated by subjects on the basis of introspection, as long as established empirical techniques are used, such as verbal protocol analysis (Ericsson & Simon, 1984). In the sequel, when a series of specific puzzles are considered as stimuli (in Section 3.1), in the interests of space, and consistent with the formal orientation of the present chapter, details concerning the normatively correct and incorrect justifications typically provided by subjects are suppressed.

1.6. *Brief Overview of the Three Challenges*

In general, scientific fields and subfields are devoted to addressing various challenges and problems. Whereas, say, physics can be

---

3 For prominent use of this structure in psychology of reasoning, one can read nearly any experiment-based work in that field. For an example of the structure in action, on a topic that bears directly on the present chapter, see for example, Johnson-Laird et al. (2000).

explained in terms of its meeting certain challenges to model physical phenomena, logic-based computational cognitive modeling can be explained in terms of its meeting challenges to model certain cognitive phenomena. Three challenges in the cognitive realm are discussed in this chapter, with emphasis falling on the first. They are:

- (C1): Human reasoning, although in its primitive forms, uncovered and charted through decades of research in psychology of reasoning and psychology of decision making, and, in its more mature forms, through advances in the closely connected fields of logic, formal philosophy, mathematics, (parts of) economics, and computer science (the so-called *formal sciences*), has for the most part not been modeled and computationally simulated in declarative computational cognitive modeling, as evidenced, for example, by what has been modeled in the declarative computational cognitive architectures associated with LCCM.

- (C2): Although a number of computational cognitive architectures have been developed in the striving for Newell's (Newell, 1973; Newell, 1990) original dream of providing a unified computational account of human cognition, the core underlying mechanisms that they each individually offer (e.g., production rules, representation and reasoning in the propositional or predicate calculus, Bayesian networks, artificial neural networks) seem to be insufficiently powerful for the task, for either of two reasons: Either the core mechanism, although logic-based, is insufficiently expressive to model the kind of sophisticated human reasoning referred to in C1 (as happens, e.g., if the core mechanism for representation and reasoning is at the level of the propositional calculus or first-order logic, both of which are quite elementary relative to the full space of logical systems); or the core mechanism, by its very nature, cannot directly model the high-level human reasoning referred to in (C1) (as happens in the case of neural networks and other nondeclarative mechanisms). What is needed is a core mechanism that is *transparently* able to range from high-level reasoning and meta-reasoning down to perception of, and action on, the external environment. This mech-

anism would constitute the comprehensive "logico-mathematical language" Sun (2002) has said is missing in computational cognitive modeling.

- (C3): The languages that most computational cognitive architectures (whether declarative or not) use for writing simulations do not have a clear and precise syntax and semantics, and the field of computational cognitive modeling is (with a few exceptions) bereft of theorems that could guide and inform the field. (Of course, some computational cognitive modelers may not want to be guided by theorems, as those in computer science and physics are. This issue is addressed later.) This adds another degree of vagueness to a field that is already quite nebulous by the standards of established, rigorous, theorem-based sciences (such as physics, [parts of] economics, computer science, mathematics, and logic itself). By contrast, models in LCCM are not only fully declarative, but their meaning is mathematically precise by virtue of the formal syntax and semantics that is part and parcel of the logical systems on which they are based.

1.7. *Structure of the Chapter*

In Section 2, the context for logic-based computational cognitive modeling is set by taking note of the overarching goal of this field: the computational modeling of human personhood. In Section 3, the three challenges (C1) to (C3) are described in more detail. In Section 4, the logico-mathematical foundation for LCCM is presented: a straightforward generalization of the concept of a logical system, as used in mathematical logic. As is explained (Section 4.1), depending on what aspect of human cognition is to be modeled and simulated, the appropriate logical system is selected. As to computation, that is handled by logic-based computer programs. Once the cognitive modeler has selected the appropriate logical system, a logic-based program relative to that selection is written and, of course, executed. The execution produces a computational simulation of the cognition under scrutiny. Using the logico-mathematical foundation for logic-based computational cognitive modeling,

Section 5 explains how LCCM addresses the three aforementioned challenges. In Section 6, the future and limitations of computational cognitive modeling are briefly discussed in the context of what has been presented in this chapter. The chapter ends with a brief conclusion.

2. The Goal of Computational Cognitive Modeling/LCCM

The goal of computational cognitive modeling (and by immediate implication, the goal of declarative computational cognitive modeling and systematization thereof in LCCM) is to understand the kind of cognition distinctive of human persons by modeling this cognition in information processing systems.

Clearly, given this goal, no computational cognitive model is provided by merely noting the particular DNA structure of humans. When it is said that x is human just in case x has a particular genetic code, the perspective is not that of computational cognitive modeling. Likewise, our minds are not modeled by charting the physiology of our brains. (After all, computational cognitive modeling is committed to the dogma that simulations can be produced in silicon-based substrates, not carbon-based ones.) Rather, computational cognitive modelers are asking what it means to be a human being, from the *psychological*, and indeed specifically the *cognitive*, perspective. That is, the question is: What does it mean to be a human *person*? For ambitious AI, LCCM's sister field, the centrality of personhood is plain in the relevant literature. For example, here is the more than two-decade-old objective for AI announced by Charniak and McDermott (1985): "The ultimate goal of AI, which we are very far from achieving, is to build a person, or, more humbly, an animal" (p. 7).

One generic account of human personhood has been proposed, defended, and employed by Bringsjord (1997, 2000) This account is a fairly standard one; for example, it generally coincides with one given by Dennett (1978) and by others as well, for example, Chisholm (1978). In addition, this account is in line with the capacities covered, chapter by chapter and topic by topic, in surveys of cognitive psychology (e.g., see Goldstein, 2005; Ashcraft, 1994). The account in question holds that x is a person provided that x has the *capacity*

1. to "will," to make choices and decisions, set plans and projects – autonomously;
2. for subjective consciousness: for experiencing pain and sorrow and happiness, and a thousand other emotions – love, passion, gratitude, and so on;
3. for *self*-consciousness for being aware of his/her states of mind, inclinations, and preferences, and for grasping the concept of himself/herself;
4. to communicate through a language;
5. to know things and believe things, to believe things about what others believe (second-order beliefs), and to believe things about what others believe about one's beliefs (third-order beliefs), and so on;
6. to desire not only particular objects and events, but also changes in his or her character;
7. to reason (for example, in the fashion exhibited in the writing and reading/studying of this very chapter).

Given this list, which is indeed psychologically, not physiologically, oriented, computational cognitive modeling and LCCM are fields devoted to capturing these seven capacities in computation. This position on the ultimate objective of LCCM and computational cognitive modeling meshes seamlessly with a recent account of what computational cognitive modeling is shooting for given by Anderson and Lebiere (2003), who, instead of defining personhood, give an operational equivalent of this definition by describing "Newell's Program," an attempt to build computational simulations of human-level intelligence, where that intelligence is cashed out in the form of a list of abilities that correspond to those on the list just given. For example, part of Newell's Program is to build a computational simulation of natural-language communication at the normal, adult level. This is attribute 4 on the previous list. As Anderson and Lebiere (2003) concede, computational cognitive modeling (whether or not logic-based) is finding it rather difficult to mechanically simulate this attribute.

Attribute 4 is not the only sticking point. An even more challenging problem is attribute 2, subjective consciousness, the representation of which in third-person machine terms remains elusive (Yang & Bringsjord, 2003; Bringsjord, 1998; Bringsjord, 2001; Bringsjord, 1995; Bringsjord, 1999).

In this chapter, the emphasis is on attribute 7. Some of the other attributes are ones LCCM can apparently handle, as shown elsewhere. For example, the simulation of attribute 5 in accordance with the LCCM paradigm would seem attainable in light of the fact that this attribute, from the standpoint of AI, has been partially attained via the formalization and implementation given in Arkoudas and Bringsjord (2005).

3. Three Challenges Facing Computational Cognitive Modeling

In this section, a more detailed account of the three aforementioned challenges is provided.

3.1. *Challenge 1: Computational Cognitive Modeling Data from Psychology of Reasoning*

At least for the most part, computational cognitive architectures have not been designed in the light of what psychology of reasoning has taught us over many decades of empirical research, stretching back to Piaget. In addition, whereas computer science and AI have been driven by the powerful use of logic (Halpern et al., 2001), which is the science of reasoning, computational cognitive modeling, whether or not of the declarative type, has largely ignored powerful human reasoning. (Notice that it is said: *powerful* human reasoning. Such reasoning is normatively correct, and sometimes produces sig-

nificant, publication-worthy results. When the reasoning in question is everyday reasoning, it should be noted that Sun's (2002) CLARION cognitive architecture, discussed later, has been used to model significant parts of human reasoning.) For example, there is no denying that although computer science has produced software capable of discovering nontrivial proofs, no such thing can be accomplished by any computational cognitive architecture.

The first challenge (C1) is now expressed as a series of desiderata that any acceptable computational cognitive architecture would need to satisfy. Some of these desiderata come in the form of specific puzzles (selected across a range of human reasoning) expressed in accordance with the experimental structure set out in Section 1, where the challenge is to model the cognition (both normatively correct and incorrect) catalyzed by the attempt to solve these puzzles. The section ends with answers to two questions that will occur to a number of readers having some familiarity with psychology of reasoning and computational cognitive modeling.

3.1.1. DESIDERATUM #1: MODELING SYSTEM 1 VERSUS SYSTEM 2 COGNITION

In a wide-ranging article in *Behavioral and Brain Sciences* that draws on empirical data accumulated over more than half a century, Stanovich and West (2000) explain that there are two dichotomous systems for thinking at play in the human mind: what they call System 1 and System 2. Reasoning performed on the basis of System 1 thinking is bound to concrete contexts and is prone to error; reasoning on the basis of System 2 cognition "abstracts complex situations into canonical representations that are stripped of context" (Stanovich & West, 2000, p. 662), and when such reasoning is mastered, the human is armed with powerful techniques that can be used to handle the increasingly abstract challenges of the modern, symbol-driven marketplace. But before considering these challenges, it is wise to get a better handle on System 1 versus System 2 reasoning.

Psychologists have devised many tasks to illuminate the distinction between System 1 and System 2 (without always realizing, it must be granted, that that was what they were doing). One such problem is the Wason Selection Task (Wason, 1966), which runs as follows. Suppose that you are dealt four cards out of a larger deck, where each card in the deck has a digit from 1 to 9 on one side and a capital Roman letter on the other. Here is what appears to you when the four cards are dealt out on a table in front of you:

$$\boxed{E} \quad \boxed{K} \quad \boxed{4} \quad \boxed{7}$$

Now, your task is to pick just the card or cards you would turn over to try your best at determining whether the following rule is true:

(R$_1$) If a card has a vowel on one side, then it has an even number on the other side.

Less than 5% of the educated adult population can solve this problem (but, predictably, trained mathematicians and logicians are rarely fooled). This result has been repeatedly replicated over the past 15 years, with subjects ranging from seventh-grade students to illustrious members of the Academy (see Bringsjord, Bringsjord & Noel, 1998). About 30% of subjects do turn over the E card, but that isn't enough: The 7 card must be turned over as well. The reason is as follows. The rule in question is a so-called *conditional*, that is, a proposition having an if-then form, which is often symbolized as $\phi \rightarrow \psi$, where the Greek letters are variables ranging over formulas from some logical system in the family $\mathcal{F}$, introduced later. As the truth-tables routinely taught to young pre-twelfth-grade math students make clear (e.g., see Chapter 1 of Bumby et al., 1995), a conditional is false if and only if its antecedent, ϕ, is true, whereas its consequent, ψ, is false; it is true in the remaining three permutations. So, if the E card has an odd number on the other side, (R$_1$) is overthrown. However, if

the 7 card has a vowel on the other side, this, too, would be a case sufficient to refute (R$_1$). The other cards are entirely irrelevant, and flipping them serves no purpose whatsoever.

This is the abstract, context-independent version of the task. But now let's see what happens when some System 1 context-*dependent* reasoning is triggered in you, for there is incontrovertible evidence that *if the task in question is concretized*, System 1 reasoning can get the job done (Ashcraft, 1994). For example, suppose one changes rule (R$_1$) to this rule:

(R$_2$) If an envelope is sealed for mailing, it must carry a 20-cent stamp on it.

And now suppose one presents four envelopes to you (keeping in mind that these envelopes, like our cards, have a front and back, only one side of which will be visible if the envelopes are "dealt" out onto a table in front of you), namely,

| sealed envelope |
| unsealed envelope |
| env. w/ 20 cent stamp |
| env. w/ 15 cent stamp |

Suppose as well that you are told something analogous to what subjects were told in the abstract version of the task, namely, that they should turn over just those envelopes needed to check whether (R$_2$) is being followed. Suddenly, the results are quite different: Most subjects choose the sealed envelope (to see if it has a 20-cent stamp on the other side), *and* this time they choose the envelope with the 15-cent stamp (to see if it is sealed for mailing!). Such is the power of domain *dependent* reasoning flowing from System 1.

The challenge to logic-based computational cognitive modeling will be to model *both* types of human reasoning. This challenge will be met if both normatively correct and incorrect responses to the stimuli (puzzles) used in psychology of reasoning are modeled. Prior research that can be plausibly viewed as setting out and tackling aspects of both System 1 and System 2 cognition is hard to find. One exception, to some degree, is Sun's (2002) exploration of implicit versus explicit cognition, discussed later (Section 4.2.3).

3.1.2. DESIDERATUM #2: MODELING MENTAL LOGIC-BASED, MENTAL MODELS-BASED, AND MENTAL METALOGIC-BASED REASONING

There is another idea the data in psychology of reasoning implies: Although sometimes (logically untrained *and* trained) humans reason by explicitly manipulating linguistic entities (e.g., formulas, as when humans construct line-by-line linguistic proofs in proof construction environments, like Barwise and Etchemendy's (1999) Fitch; natural deduction of this linguistic variety is explained in Section 4.1), they also sometimes reason by imagining and manipulating "mental models," nonlinguistic entities capturing possible situations, *and* they sometimes reason in a fashion that involves both mental logic, mental models, and meta-reasoning over the structures posited in these two theories. This meta-reasoning uses rules of inference that at once range over formulas *and* mental models, and are rules that cannot be independently modeled in simulations based either exclusively on mental logic theory or exclusively on mental models theory.

The first kind of reasoning is explained, explored, and defended by proponents of the theory known as *mental logic* (Rips, 1994; Braine, 1990; Yang, Braine, & O'Brien, 1998; Braine, 1998b; Braine, 1998a). Mental logic has its roots in Piaget, who held (at least at one point) that humans naturally acquire the ability to reason at the level of the proof theory of first-order logic (Inhelder & Piaget, 1958; Bringsjord et al., 1998). Quintessential cases of this kind of reasoning include giving a proof that from, say, "If Gooker is a sequaat, then Peeves is a rooloy" and "Gooker is a sequaat" one can infer "Peeves is a rooloy" by the rule (*modus ponens*, or, to use the term introduced later, *conditional elimination*):

$$\frac{\text{If } \phi \text{ then } \psi, \phi}{\psi}.$$

Note that with respect to arguments such as these, it would seem rather odd to say that those who produce them have a mental model of anything. They seem to be working just from the surface-level pattern of the linguistic expressions in question. In fact, that is the justification they customarily give when confronted by stimuli of this sort.

The second type of reasoning has been discovered, explained, and defended by Johnson-Laird (1983), who characterizes mental models in their contribution to the present volume like this:

> *The theory of mental models postulates that when individuals understand discourse, they construct models of the possibilities consistent with the discourse. Each mental model represents a possibility. A frequent misunderstanding is that mental models are images. In fact, they are more akin to three-dimensional models of the world of the sort that underlie the phenomena of mental rotation [as introduced, e.g., by Metzler & Shepard, 1982] (see Chapter 12).*

The third sort of reasoning is explained and explored in a theory known as *mental meta-logic* (Yang & Bringsjord, in press; Rinella, Bringsjord, & Yang, 2001; Yang & Bringsjord, 2001; Yang & Bringsjord, 2006). According to mental meta-logic, human reasoners, both trained and untrained, often reason in ways that, at once, invoke representations and inference of the sort posited in mental logic *and* mental models, and also meta-inferential rules that manipulate these rules and these models.

Desideratum #2 is that both LCCM and computational cognitive modeling should provide the machinery for mechanizing human reasoning in all three of these modes. The remaining desiderata each consist in the need to model human reasoning stimulated by a particular puzzle. Each of these puzzles, note, conforms exactly to the structure of experiments set out in Section 1. Each of the variables (L, Q, D, etc.) in this structure can be directly instantiated by the specifics in each of the puzzles. Note, as well, that the puzzles are selected so as to ensure that the modeling of human reasoning in question will entail that the first two desiderata are satisfied.

3.1.3. DESIDERATUM #3: PUZZLE 1: THE KING-ACE PUZZLE

The third desideratum is to model human reasoning triggered by the following puzzle, a slight variant[4] of a puzzle introduced by Johnson-Laird (1997):

Assume that the following is true:

"If there is a king in the hand, then there is an ace in the hand," or "If there is not a king in the hand, then there is an ace in the hand," – but not both of these if–thens are true.

What can you infer from this assumption? Please provide a careful justification for your answer.

Subjects (logically untrained) almost invariably respond with: "That there is an ace in the hand." This response is incorrect. In point of fact, what one can infer is that there is *not* an ace in the hand. Later, all readers will see exactly why this is the correct answer. The challenge to computational cognitive modeling and LCCM in the case of this second desideratum is to provide a mechanical simulation of both the normatively correct and normatively incorrect responses to this puzzle and the justification for those responses.

3.1.4. DESIDERATUM #4: PUZZLE 2: THE WINE-DRINKER PUZZLE

Now let us consider an interesting puzzle devised by Johnson-Laird and Savary (1995) that relates directly to Aristotle's theory of the syllogism:

Suppose:

- All the Frenchmen in the restaurant are gourmets.

4 The variation arises from disambiguating Johnson-Laird's "*s* or else *s'*" as "either *s* or *s'*, but not both."

- Some of the gourmets are wine-drinkers.

Does it follow that some of the Frenchmen are wine-drinkers? Please provide a careful justification for your answer.

The vast majority of (logically untrained) subjects respond in the affirmative. Yet, the correct answer is "No." Some subjects (some of whom are logically untrained, but the vast majority of which have had significant formal training) respond in the negative *and* offer a disproof, that is, a proof that "Frenchmen are wine-drinkers" does *not* follow from the two suppositions. The disproof includes an example (following standard terminology in mathematical logic, a *countermodel*) in which the premises are true but the conclusion false and the point that such an example establishes a negative answer to the wine-drinker query. The requirement to be met by both computational cognitive modeling and LCCM is that computational simulations of both types of responses be provided.

3.1.5. DESIDERATUM #5 PUZZLE 3: THE WISE MAN PUZZLE

Now to the next puzzle:

Suppose there are three wise men who are told by their king that at least one of them has a white spot on his forehead; actually, all three have white spots on their foreheads. You are to assume that each wise man can see the others' foreheads but not his own, and thus each knows whether the others have white spots. Suppose you are told that the first wise man says, "I do not know whether I have a white spot," and that the second wise man then says, "I also do not know whether I have a white spot." Now consider the following questions:

(1) Does the third wise man now know whether or not he has a white spot?
(2) If so, what does he know, that he has one or doesn't have one?
(3) And, if so, that is, if the third wise man does know one way or the other, provide a detailed account (showing all work, all notes, etc.; use

scrap paper as necessary) of the reasoning that produces his knowledge.

In the case of this puzzle, only the challenge of modeling the (or at least *a*) normatively correct response will be explicitly considered.

3.1.6. DESIDERATUM #6 PUZZLE 4: INFINITARY DEMORGAN

Here is the next puzzle:

Consider a disjunction as big as the natural numbers, that is,

$$\phi_1 \vee \phi_2 \vee \phi_3 \vee \ldots \vee \phi_n, \phi_{n+1} \vee \ldots \quad (5.1)$$

Suppose that (5.1) is true. Now suppose you also know that

$$\phi_{4,599,223,811} \quad (5.2)$$

is false. What can you now conclude must be the case from (5.1) and (5.2)? Why?

As in the puzzle that immediately precedes this one, only concern for modeling the normatively correct answer will be present herein, which of course is that from (5.1) and (5.2), it can be immediately deduced that

$$\phi_1 \vee \phi_2 \vee \ldots \vee \phi_{4,599,223,810} \vee \phi_{4,599,223,812}$$

$$\vee \phi_{4,599,223,813} \vee \ldots$$

3.2. *Challenge 2: Unify Cognition via a Comprehensive Theoretical Language*

The original dream of the founders of the field of computational cognitive modeling (a dream shared by the founders of modern-day AI) was to provide a core unifying representation scheme, and mechanical processes over this scheme, so as to cover all of human cognition. In the case of Soar and ACT-R, the core representation and process are intended to be essentially the same: chaining in a production system. Other computational cognitive architectures include different core processes. For example, in CLARION, core processing includes a sub-declarative dimension, carried out in artificial neural networks.

The second problem LCCM addresses is that the core processes at the heart of these and other in-progress cognitive architectures certainly don't *seem* well-suited to range across the entire gamut of human cognition. For example, although one can certainly imagine rapid-fire processing of production rules to cover simple rule-based thinking, it is difficult to imagine formalizing, for example, Gödel's declarative cognition in discovering and specifying his famous incompleteness results in the form of production rules. As the attempt to meet the first challenge will reveal later (see Section 4.2.1), much of cognition that seems to call for declarative modeling, specifically calls for logical systems much more expressive than those at the level of production rules. As will be seen, logical systems at the level of merely the propositional and predicate calculi (i.e., the logical systems $\mathcal{L}_{PC}$ and $\mathcal{L}_I$, respectively) suffice to formalize production rules and systems.

To sum up, one can view C2 as the search for the "unified theoretical language" Sun correctly says is rather hard to come by:

[I]t is admittedly highly desirable to develop a single, completely unified theoretical language, as a means of expressing fundamental theories of the mind and its various manifestations, components, and phenomena. In place of the classical formalism – symbolic computation, we would certainly like to see a new logico-mathematical formalism that is (1) more analyzable (e.g., in the form of mathematical entities, as opposed to computer programs, which are notoriously difficult to analyze), (2) more inclusive (for example, being able to include both symbols and numeric values, and both serial and parallel processing), and (3) properly constrained (that is, being able to express exactly what needs to be expressed). However, thus far, there is no such a single unified formalism in sight. (Sun, 2002, p. 248)

LCCM, as defined herein, would seem to be the formalism Sun is looking for. On Sun's three points: (1) LCCM is in fact *fully* analyzable, and its programs are transparently so because they are in the declarative mode and are themselves well-defined logico-mathematical objects (more about this when the third challenge (C3) is shown to be met by LCCM). (2) LCCM, in virtue of logics infused with strength factors (e.g., see Section 4.2.3) and probabilities, and of the fact that logic is ideally suited to parallelism (e.g., see Shapiro, 1987), is fully inclusive. (3) The expressibility of LCCM is unparalleled: There is no competitor able to directly and easily express the declarative knowledge in the puzzles in the desiderata composing (C1).

3.3. *Challenge 3: Computational Cognitive Meodeling Suffers from a Lack of Mathematical Maturity*

In computational cognitive modeling, a cognitive model is a computational simulation produced by executing code written in some cognitive architecture. Computational cognitive modeling is thus clearly intimately related to computer science, which centrally involves algorithms, programs that are tokens of those algorithms, and the execution of these programs to produce computation. But given this clear connection between computational cognitive modeling and computer science, it is at least somewhat surprising that although the latter is today so rigorous as to be considered by many to be in large part a subfield of formal logic (Halpern et al., 2001), which is theorem-based, computational cognitive modeling apparently counts nary a theorem among that which it has produced over the course of decades. Part of the root cause of this state of affairs is that the *meaning* of code written in computational cognitive modeling is often somewhat mysterious. Of course, one might retort that because code written in some computational cognitive architecture can be, and indeed sometimes is, written in some established programming language (L_{PL}) having a formal semantics, the meaning of a model can simply be identified with the meaning of the program P written in this L_{PL} (e.g., L_{PL} could be Common Lisp). Unfortunately, the meaning of a computational model obviously must be *cognitive*. It is crucial that the meaning of a model relates to the goal of computational cognitive

modeling, which is to model human cognition at the symbolic level (as, again, Marr [1982] and Pylyshyn [1984] would put it), and thereby advance the science of cognition.

This challenge is met by LCCM, as will be seen. Programs written in declarative form have an exact meaning, and that meaning accords with the categories that are constitutive of human cognition for the simple reason that the declarative level is preserved in the relevant programs. Furthermore, the machinery that yields this precision in turn yields the result that logic-based computational cognitive modeling can be guided by theorems. This result, and the desirability thereof, are discussed later.

4. Logic-Based Computational Cognitive Modeling

4.1. *Logical Systems*

Logic-based computational cognitive modeling is based on a generalized form of the concept of *logical system* as defined rather narrowly in mathematical logic, where this concept stands at the heart of Lindström's Theorems (for details, see Ebbinghaus, Flum, & Thomas, 1994).[5] For LCCM, the generalized form of a logical system $\mathcal{L}$ is composed of the following six parameterized elements:

1. An object-level alphabet A, partitioned into those symbols that are invariant across the use of $\mathcal{L}$ for particular applications and those that are included by the human for particular uses. The former are called *fixed* symbols and the latter *application* symbols.

2. A grammar $\mathcal{G}$ that yields well-formed expressions (usually called *formulas*) L^A from A.

3. An argument theory $\vdash^M_X$ (called a *proof theory* when the reasoning in question is deductive in nature) that specifies

---

5 In a word, these theorems express the fact that logics more expressive than first-order logic necessarily lose certain attributes that first-order logic possesses. It should be pointed out that there are a *number* of different *narrow* accounts of *logical system*; e.g., see Gabbay (1994).

correct (relative to the system $\mathcal{L}$) inference from one or more expressions to one or more expressions. The superscript is a placeholder for the *mode* of inference: deductive, abductive, inductive, probabilistic, and analogical. The subscript is a placeholder for *particular* inferential mechanisms. For example, in Aristotle's theory of the syllogism, visited at the beginning of the chapter, the first two declarative statements in a valid syllogism deductively imply the third. Where D is used to indicate the deductive mode of inference, and *Syll* the particular deductive scheme introduced by Aristotle, we can write

$$\{\text{All } AB, \text{All } BC\} \vdash^{D}_{Syll} \text{All } AC$$

to indicate that any declarative statement of the form All AC can be deductively inferred (in this context) in Aristotle's syllogistic system. The space of deductive (D) mechanisms include various forms of deduction well beyond what Aristotle long ago devised (e.g., resolution, sequent calculus, Fitch-style natural deduction; they are explained later). Other modes of inference include: probabilistic inference in Bayesian frameworks, inductive inference, and nonmonotonic or defeasible inference.

4. An *argument semantics* that specifies the meaning of inferences allowed by $\vdash^{M}_{x}$, which makes possible a mechanical verification of the correctness of arguments.
5. A *formula semantics* that assigns a meaning to members of L^A given announcements about what the application symbols are. The values traditionally include such things as TRUE, FALSE, INDETERMINATE, PROBABLE, and numbers in some continuum (e.g., 0 to 1, as in the case of probability theory).
6. A meta-theory that defines meta-mathematical attributes over the previous five components and includes proofs that the attributes are or are not possessed. Examples of such attributes include soundness (inference in the argument theory from some subset Φ of L^A

to ϕ, where $\phi \in L^A$, implies that if all of Φ are true, ϕ must be as well) and completeness (if ϕ is true whenever Φ is, then there is a way to infer ϕ from Φ).

The family $\mathcal{F}$ of logical systems populated by the setting of parameters in the sextet just given is infinite, and includes zero-, first-, and higher-order extensional logics (in Hilbert style, or sequent style, or natural deduction Fitch style, etc.); modal logics (including temporal, epistemic, deontic logics, etc.); propositional dynamic logics; Hoare-Floyd logics for reasoning about imperative programs; inductive logics that subsume probability theory; abductive logics; strength-factor-based and probabilistic logics; nonmonotonic logics, and many, many others. Because all of classical mathematics, outside formal logic, is derivable from merely a small proper subset of these systems (with some specific axioms), the machinery of LCCM is enormous. Of necessity, this scope must be strategically limited in the present chapter.

Accordingly, it is now explained how four logical systems (the first two of which are elementary) are based on particular instantiations of five of the six elements. In addition, two additional clusters of logical systems, nonmonotonic logical systems and probabilistic logical systems, are briefly discussed after the quartet of logical systems is presented.

The first logical system is $\mathcal{L}_{PC}$, known as the propositional calculus. The second, more powerful logical system is $\mathcal{L}_I$, known as the "predicate calculus," or "first-order logic," or sometimes just "FOL." Every comprehensive introductory cognitive science or AI textbook provides an introduction to these two simple, limited systems and makes it clear how they are used to engineer intelligent systems (e.g., see Russell & Norvig, 2002). In addition, coverage of FOL is often included in surveys of cognitive science (e.g., see Stillings et al., 1995). Surveys of cognitive psychology, although rarely presenting FOL, often give encapsulated presentations of $\mathcal{L}_{PC}$ (e.g., see Ashcraft, 1994). Unfortunately, it is usually the case that when these two logical systems are described, the reader is not told that this pair is but an infinitesimally small speck in the family $\mathcal{F}$.

In both both $\mathcal{L}_{PC}$ and $\mathcal{L}_I$, reasoning is deductive in nature. The third logical system introduced is a particular propositional modal logic, $\mathcal{L}_{KT}$, designed to allow modeling of possibility, necessity, belief, and knowledge. The fourth logical system is based on the simplest infinitary logic: $\mathcal{L}\omega_1\omega$.

4.1.1. THE ALPHABET AND GRAMMAR OF $\mathcal{L}_{PC}$

The alphabet for propositional logic is simply an infinite list $p_1, p_2, \ldots, p_n, p_{n+1}, \ldots$ of propositional variables (according to tradition p_1 is p, p_2 is q, and p_3 is r), and the five familiar truth-functional connectives $\neg, \rightarrow, \leftrightarrow, \wedge, \vee$. The connectives can at least provisionally be read, respectively, as "not," "implies" (or "if-then"), "if and only if," "and," and "or." In cognitive science and AI, it is often convenient to use propositional variables as mnemonics that help one remember what they are intended to represent. For an example, recall Puzzle 1. Instead of representing "There is an ace in the hand" as p_i, for some $i \in \mathbf{N} = \{0, 1, 2, \ldots\}$, it would no doubt be useful to represent this proposition as A, and this representation is employed later. Now, the grammar for propositional logic is composed of the following three rules.

1. Every propositional variable p_i is a well-formed formula (wff).
2. If ϕ is a wff, then so is $\neg\phi$.
3. If ϕ and ψ are wffs, then so is $(\phi \star \psi)$, where $\star$ is one of $\wedge, \vee, \rightarrow, \leftrightarrow$. (We allow outermost parentheses to be dropped.)

This implies, for example, that $p \rightarrow (q \wedge r)$ is a wff, whereas $\rightarrow q$ is not. To represent the declarative sentence "If there is an ace in the hand, then there is a king in the hand," we can use $A \rightarrow K$.

4.1.2. AN ARGUMENT (PROOF) THEORY FOR $\mathcal{L}_{PC}$

A number of proof theories are possible, including ones that are descriptive and normatively incorrect (as in the proof theory provided in Rips, 1994) and ones that are normatively correct. The former are based

on the latter, and hence the presentation now proceeds to a normatively correct system, specifically an elegant Fitch-style system of natural deduction, F, fully explained by Barwise and Etchemendy (1999). (Such systems are commonly referred to simply as "natural" systems.) In F, each of the truth-functional connective has a pair of corresponding inference rules, one for introducing the connective and one for eliminating the connective. Proofs in F proceed in sequence line by line, each line number incremented by 1. Each line not only includes a line number, but also a formula (the one deduced at this line) and, in the rightmost column, a rule cited in justification for the deduction. The vertical ellipsis

$$\vdots$$

is used to indicate the possible presence of 0 or more lines in the proof.

Here is the rule for eliminating a conjunction:

$$
\begin{array}{c|cc}
\vdots & \vdots & \vdots \\
k & \phi \wedge \psi & \\
\vdots & & \vdots \\
m & \phi & k \wedge \text{Elim} \\
\vdots & \vdots & \vdots
\end{array}
$$

Intuitively, this rule says that if at line k in some derivation you have somehow obtained a conjunction $\phi \wedge \psi$, then at a subsequent line m, one can infer to either of the conjuncts alone. Now here is the rule that allows a conjunction to be introduced; intuitively, it formalizes the fact that if two propositions are independently the case, it follows that the conjunction of these two propositions is also true.

$$
\begin{array}{c|cc}
\vdots & \vdots & \vdots \\
k & \phi & \\
\vdots & \vdots & \vdots \\
l & \psi & \\
\vdots & & \vdots \\
m & \phi \wedge \psi & k, l \wedge \text{Intro} \\
\vdots & \vdots & \vdots
\end{array}
$$

A key rule in F is *supposition*, according to which you are allowed to assume any wff at any point in a derivation. The catch is that you must signal your use of supposition by setting it off typographically. Here is the template for supposition:

$$
\begin{array}{c|c}
\vdots & \vdots \quad \vdots \\
k & \underline{\phi} \quad \text{supposition} \\
\vdots & \vdots \quad \vdots
\end{array}
$$

Often, a derivation will be used to establish that from some set Φ of propositional formulas a particular formula ϕ can be derived. In such a case, Φ will be given as suppositions (or, as it is sometimes said, *givens*), and the challenge will be to derive ϕ from these suppositions. To say that ϕ can be derived from a set of formulas Φ in F we follow the notation introduced above and write

$$\Phi \vdash_F^D \phi.$$

When it is clear from context which system the deduction is to take place in, the subscript on $\vdash$ can be omitted. Here is a proof that puts to use the rules presented previously and establishes that $\{(p \wedge q) \wedge r\} \vdash_F^D q$:

$$
\begin{array}{c|ll}
1 & (p \wedge q) \wedge r & \text{given} \\
2 & (p \wedge q) & 1 \wedge \text{Elim} \\
3 & q & 2 \wedge \text{Elim}
\end{array}
$$

Now here is a slightly more complicated rule, one for introducing a conditional. It basically says that if you can carry out a subderivation in which you suppose ϕ and derive ψ you are entitled to close this subderivation and infer to the conditional $\phi \to \psi$.

$$
\begin{array}{c|c}
\vdots & \vdots \\
k & \quad \underline{\phi} \quad \text{supposition} \\
\vdots & \quad \vdots \\
m & \quad \psi \\
\vdots & \vdots \\
n & \phi \to \psi \qquad k-m \to \text{Intro}
\end{array}
$$

As stated previously, in a Fitch-style system of natural deduction, the rules come in pairs. Here is the rule in F for eliminating conditionals:

$$
\begin{array}{c|ll}
k & \phi \to \psi & \\
\vdots & \vdots & \vdots \\
l & \phi & \\
\vdots & \vdots & \vdots \\
m & \psi & k, l \to \text{Elim}
\end{array}
$$

Here is the rule for introducing $\vee$:

$$
\begin{array}{c|ll}
\vdots & \vdots & \vdots \\
k & \phi & \\
\vdots & \vdots & \vdots \\
m & \phi \vee \phi & k \vee \text{Intro} \\
\vdots & \vdots & \vdots
\end{array}
$$

And here is the rather more elaborate rule for eliminating a disjunction:

$$
\begin{array}{c|cl}
\vdots & \vdots & \\
k & \phi \vee \psi & \\
\vdots & \vdots & \\
l & \quad \underline{\phi} \quad \text{supposition} \\
\vdots & \quad \vdots \\
m & \quad \chi \\
\vdots & \vdots \\
n & \quad \underline{\psi} \quad \text{supposition} \\
\vdots & \quad \vdots \\
o & \quad \chi \\
\vdots & \vdots \\
p & \chi & k, l-m, n-o \vee \text{Elim}
\end{array}
$$

The rule $\vee$ Elim is also known as *constructive dilemma*. The core intuition behind this rule is that if one knows that either ϕ or ψ is true, and if one can show that χ can be proved from ϕ alone and ψ alone, then χ follows from the disjunction.

Next is a very powerful rule corresponding to *proof by contradiction* (sometimes called *indirect proof* or *reductio ad absurdum*). Notice that in F this rule is $\neg Intro$.

Figure 5.1. A proof of *modus tollens* in $\mathcal{F}$, constructed in HYPERPROOF.

$$
\begin{array}{c|l}
\vdots \;\;\big|\;\; \vdots & \\
k \;\;\;\big|\;\; \phi \underline{\qquad} & \text{supposition} \\
\vdots \;\;\;\big|\;\; \vdots & \\
m \;\;\;\big|\;\; \psi \wedge \neg\psi & \\
\vdots \;\;\;\big|\;\; \vdots & \\
n \;\;\big|\;\; \neg\phi & k - m \;\neg\; \text{Intro}
\end{array}
$$

Sometimes, a natural deduction system can be a little obnoxious because by insisting that inference rules come exclusively in the form of pairs for each truth-functional connective, it leaves out certain rules that are exceedingly useful. Two examples are *modus tollens* and DeMorgan's Laws. The former rule allows one to infer $\neg\phi$ from $\phi \to \psi$ and $\neg\psi$. This rule can be established through a proof in F, as is shown in Figure 5.1. This figure shows a screenshot of the completed proof as constructed in the HYPERPROOF proof construction environment, which accompanies the book by the same name authored by Barwise & Etchemendy (1994).[6] The core of this proof is *reductio ad absurdum*, or $\neg$ Intro. DeMorgan's Laws for propositional logic sanction moving from a formula of the form $\neg(\phi \wedge \psi)$ to one of the form $\neg\phi \vee \neg\psi$, and vice versa. The laws also allow an inference from a formula of the form $\neg(\phi \vee \psi)$ to one of the form $\neg\phi \wedge \neg\psi$, and vice versa. When, in constructing a proof in F, one wants to use *modus tollens* or DeMorgan's Laws, or any number of other timesaving rules, one can make the inference in question, using the rule of *tautological consequence* as a justification. This rule, abbreviated as TAUT CON in HYPERPROOF, is designed to allow the human proof constructor a way to declare that a given inference is obvious, and could with more work be fully specified using only the rules of F. HYPERPROOF responds with a check to indicate that an attempted inference is in fact correct. As can be seen in Figure 5.2, HYPERPROOF approves of our use of TAUT CON, which, again, corresponds in this case not just to DeMorgan's Law in the first two occurrences of this rule, but to the useful inference of $\phi \wedge \neg\psi$ from $\neg(\phi \to \psi)$.

This section ends with two more key concepts. A formula provable from the null set is said to be a *theorem*, and where ϕ is such a formula, customary notation is

$$\vdash^{D}_{X} \phi$$

to express such a fact, where of course the variable X would be instantiated to the particular deductive calculus in question. Here are two examples that the reader should pause to verify in his or her own mind: $\vdash^{D}_{F} (p \wedge q) \to q; \vdash^{D}_{F} (p \wedge \neg p) \to r$. It is said that a set Φ of formulas is *syntactically consistent* if and only if it is not the case that a contradiction $\phi \wedge \neg\phi$ can be derived from Φ.

4.1.3. FORMAL SEMANTICS FOR $\mathcal{L}_{PC}$

The precise meaning of the five truth-functional connectives of the propositional calculus is given via truth-tables, which tell us what the value of a statement is, given the truth-values of its components. The simplest truth-table is that for negation, which informs us, unsurprisingly, that if ϕ is

---

6 For data on the power of HYPERPROOF to help teach logic, see Rinella et al. (2001) and Bringsjord et al. (1998).

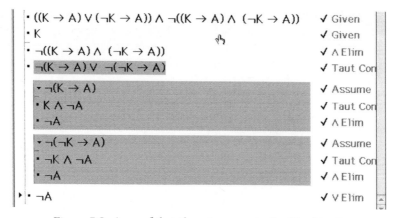

Figure 5.2. A proof that there is no ace in the Hand in $\mathcal{F}$.

T (= TRUE) then $\neg\phi$ is F (= FALSE; see first row below double lines), and if ϕ is F then $\neg\phi$ is T (second row).

ϕ	$\neg\phi$
T	F
F	T

Here are the remaining truth-tables.

ϕ	ψ	$\phi \wedge \psi$	ϕ	ψ	$\phi \vee \psi$
T	T	T	T	T	T
T	F	F	T	F	T
F	T	F	F	T	T
F	F	F	F	F	F

ϕ	ψ	$\phi \rightarrow \psi$	ϕ	ψ	$\phi \leftrightarrow \psi$
T	T	T	T	T	T
T	F	F	T	F	F
F	T	T	F	T	F
F	F	T	F	F	T

Notice that the truth-table for disjunction says that when both disjuncts are true, the entire disjunction is true. This is called *inclusive* disjunction. In *exclusive* disjunction, it is one disjunct or another, but not both. This distinction becomes particularly important if one is attempting to symbolize parts of English (or any other *natural language*). It would not do to represent the sentence "George will either win or lose" as:

$$W \vee L,$$

because under the English meaning there is no way both possibilities can be true,

whereas by the meaning of $\vee$ it would be possible that W and L are *both* true. (As we shall soon see, inclusive versus exclusive disjunction is a key distinction in cracking the King-Ace Puzzle.) One could use $\vee_x$ to denote *exclusive disjunction*, which can be defined through the following truth-table.

ϕ	ψ	$\phi \vee_x \psi$
T	T	F
T	F	T
F	T	T
F	F	F

Before concluding this section, it is worth mentioning another issue involving the meaning of English sentences and their corresponding symbolizations in propositional logic: the issue of the "oddity" of *material conditionals* (formulas of the form $\phi \rightarrow \psi$). Consider the following English sentence: If the moon is made of green cheese, then Dan Quayle will be the next President of the United States. Is this sentence true? If you were to ask "the man on the street," the answer would likely be "Of course not!" or perhaps you would hear: "This isn't even a meaningful sentence; you're speaking nonsense." These responses are quite at odds with the undeniable fact that when represented in the propositional calculus, the sentence turns out true. Why? The sentence is naturally represented as

$$G \rightarrow Q.$$

Because G is false, the truth-table for $\rightarrow$ classifies the conditional as true. Results such as these have encouraged some to devise better (but much more complicated) accounts of the "if-then's" seen in natural languages (e.g., see Goble, 2001a). In fact, a substantial subspace within the space $\mathcal{F}$ of logical systems includes those devoted to just formalizing conditionals (Nute, 1984). These accounts will be beyond the purview of this chapter, however. No such search will be embarked upon, so readers must for now be content with the conditional as defined by the customary truth-table for $\rightarrow$ presented earlier.

Given a truth-value assignment v (i.e., an assignment of T or F to each propositional variable p_i), one can say that v "makes true" or "models" or "satisfies" a given formula ϕ; this is standardly written

$$v \models \phi.$$

A formula such that there is some model that satisfies it is said to be *satisfiable*. A formula that cannot be true on any model (e.g., $p \wedge \neg p$) is said to be *unsatisfiable*. Some formulas are true on all models. For example, the formula $((p \vee q) \wedge \neg q) \rightarrow p$ is in this category. Such formulas are said to be *valid* and are sometimes referred to as *validities*. To indicate that a formula ϕ is valid we write

$$\models \phi.$$

Another important semantic notion is *consequence*. An individual formula ϕ is said to be a consequence of a set Φ of formulas provided that all the truth-value assignments on which all of Φ are true is also one on which ϕ is true; this is customarily written

$$\Phi \models \phi.$$

The final concept in the semantic component of the propositional calculus is the concept of consistency once again: We say that a set Φ of formulas is *semantically consistent* if and only if there is a truth-value assignment

on which all of Φ are true. As a check of understanding, the readers may want to satisfy themselves that the conjunction of formulas taken from a semantically consistent set must be satisfiable.

4.1.4. SOME META-THEORETICAL RESULTS FOR $\mathcal{L}_{PC}$

This section describes some key meta-theory for the propositional calculus. In general, meta-theory would deploy logical and mathematical techniques to answer such questions as whether or not provability implies consequence and whether or not the reverse holds. When the first direction holds, a logical system is said to be *sound*, and this fact can be expressed in the notation that has now been introduced as

$$\text{If } \Phi \vdash \phi \text{ then } \Phi \models \phi.$$

Roughly put, a logical system is sound if it is guaranteed that true formulas can only yield (through proofs) true formulas; one cannot pass from the true to the false. When the "other direction" is true of a system, it is said to be *complete*; in the notation now available, this is expressed by

$$\text{If } \Phi \models \phi \text{ then } \Phi \vdash \phi.$$

The propositional calculus is both provably sound and complete. One consequence of this is that all theorems in the propositional calculus are valid, and all validities are theorems. This last fact is expressed more formally as:

$$\models \phi \text{ if and only if } \vdash \phi.$$

4.1.5. THE ALPHABET AND GRAMMAR OF $\mathcal{L}_I$

For $\mathcal{L}_I$, our alphabet will now be augmented to include

- $=$
  - the identity or equality symbol
- variables $x, y, \ldots$
  - like variables in elementary algebra,

except they can range of anything, not just numbers

- constants $c_1, c_2, \ldots$
  - you can think of these as proper names for objects
- relation symbols $R, G, \ldots$
  - used to denote properties, e.g., W for *being a wine-drinker*
- functors $f_1, f_2, \ldots$
  - used to refer to functions
- quantifiers $\exists, \forall$
  - the first (existential) quantifier says that "there exists at least one ...," the second (universal) quantifier that "for all ..."
- truth-functional connectives ($\neg, \vee, \wedge, \rightarrow, \leftrightarrow$)
  - now familiar to you, same as in the propositional calculus

Predictable *formation rules* are introduced to allow one to represent propositions like those seen earlier in Puzzle 2. In the interests of space, the grammar in question is omitted, and the reader is simply shown "in action" the kind of formulas that can be produced by this grammar. You will recall that these three propositions are relevant to Puzzle 2:

1. All the Frenchmen in the restaurant are gourmets.
2. Some of the gourmets are wine-drinkers.
3. Some of the Frenchmen in the restaurant are wine-drinkers.

With these rules, we can now represent the first of these propositions as

$$\forall x(Fx \rightarrow Gx),$$

which says that for every thing x, if it has property F (is a Frenchman), then it has property G (is a gourmet). The second of the two propositions becomes

$$\exists x(Gx \wedge Wx),$$

and the third is represented as

$$\exists x(Fx \wedge Wx).$$

4.1.6. ARGUMENT (PROOF) THEORY OF $\mathcal{L}_I$

As in propositional logic, sets of formulas (say Φ), given certain *rules of inference*, can be used to prove individual formulas (say ϕ); such a situation is expressed by meta-expressions having exactly the same form as those introduced previously, for example, $\Phi \vdash^D_X \phi$, where of course X will be instantiated to a particular deductive calculus. The rules of inference for FOL in such systems as F include those we saw for the propositional level and new ones: two corresponding to the existential quantifier $\exists$ and two corresponding to the universal quantifier $\forall$. For example, one of the rules associated with $\forall$ says, intuitively, that if you know that everything has a certain property, then any particular thing a has that property. This rule, known as *universal elimination* or just $\forall$Elim (or, sometimes, *universal instantiation*, $\forall$I) allows one to move from some formula $\forall x\phi$ to a formula with $\forall x$ dropped, and the variable x in ϕ replaced with the constant of choice. For example, from "All Frenchman in the room are wine-drinkers," that is, again,

$$\forall x(Fx \rightarrow Wx),$$

one can infer by $\forall$ Elim that, where a names some particular object,

$$Fa \rightarrow Wa,$$

and if one happens to know that in fact Fa, one could then infer by familiar propositional reasoning that Ra. The rule $\forall$ Elim in $\mathcal{F}$, when set out more carefully, is

$$
\begin{array}{c|ll}
k & \forall x\phi & \\
\vdots & \vdots \quad\quad \vdots & \\
l & \phi(\frac{a}{x}) & k\,\forall\,\text{Elim}
\end{array}
$$

where $\phi(\frac{a}{x})$ denotes the result of replacing occurrences of x in ϕ with a.

4.1.7. SEMANTICS OF $\mathcal{L}_I$

First-order logic includes a semantic side that systematically provides meaning (i.e., truth or falsity) for formulas. Unfortunately, the formal semantics of FOL is more tricky than the truth-table-based scheme sufficient for the propositional level. The central concept is that FOL formulas are said to be true (or false) on *interpretations*; that some formula ϕ is true on an interpretation is often written as $\mathcal{I} \models \phi$. (This is often read, "$\mathcal{I}$ satisfies, or models, ϕ.") For example, the formula $\forall x \exists y Gyx$ might mean, on the standard interpretation for arithmetic, that for every natural number n, there is a natural number m such that $m > n$. In this case, the *domain* is the set of natural numbers, that is, **N**, and G symbolizes "greater than." Much more could of course be said about the formal semantics (or *model theory*) for FOL, but this is an advanced topic beyond the scope of the present, brief treatment. For a fuller but still-succinct discussion using the traditional notation of model theory, see Ebbinghaus et al. (1994). The scope of the present discussion does allow the reader to appreciate that FOL, like the propositional calculus, is both sound and complete; proofs can be found in Ebbinghaus et al. (1994). This fact entails a proposition that will prove useful momentarily: that if ϕ is not a consequence of Φ, then ϕ cannot be proved from Φ. In the notation introduced earlier, this is expressed as:

$$\Phi \not\models \phi \text{ then } \Phi \not\vdash \phi.$$

4.1.8. ALPHABET AND GRAMMAR FOR $\mathcal{L}_{KT}$

This logical system $\mathcal{L}_{KT}$ adds the modal operators $\square$ and $\lozenge$ to the grammatical machinery of $\mathcal{L}_{PC}$, with subscripts on these operators to refer to agents. Because the concern here is with what agents believe and know (i.e., with what is called epistemic or doxastic logic; an overview is provided in (Goble, 2001), the focus is on the box, and therefore, $\square_\alpha$ is rewritten as $\mathbf{K}_\alpha$. So, to represent that "Wise man A knows he doesn't have a white spot on his forehead," one can write $\mathbf{K}_A(\neg \text{White}(A))$. Here is the grammar for $\mathcal{L}_{KT}$.

1. All ordinary wffs are wffs.
2. If ϕ is a closed wff and α is a constant, then $\square_\alpha \phi$ is a wff. Because the concern in the wise man puzzle is with **doxastic**

matters, that is, matters involving believing and knowing, one says that $\mathbf{B}_\alpha \phi$ is a wff, or, if one is concerned with "knows" rather than "believes," that $\mathbf{K}_\alpha \phi$ is a wff.
3. If ϕ and ψ are wffs, then so are any strings that can be constructed from ϕ and ψ by the usual propositional connectives (e.g., $\rightarrow, \wedge, \ldots$).

4.1.9. SEMANTICS FOR $\mathcal{L}_{KT}$

The formal semantics for $\mathcal{L}_{KT}$ can be achieved via three steps. The cornerstone of these steps is the concept of a *possible world*. Intuitively, the idea, which goes back to Hintikka (1962) and can arguably be traced back as far as Aristotle's treatment of the logic of knowledge and belief in his *De Sophisiticis Elenchis* and in his *Prior* and *Posterior Analytics* (McKeon, 1941), is that some agent α knows some declarative statement (= some proposition) ϕ provided that, in all possible worlds compatible with what α knows, it is the case that ϕ. The compatibility between worlds can be regimented by way of an *accessibility relation* between them. Here are the three steps:

1. Associate with each interpretation (which now includes a set, A, of agents) a **possible world**.
2. Establish a relation – the **accessibility relation** – $k \subseteq A \times W \times W$ where W denotes the set of all possible worlds.
3. Now it is said that $\mathbf{K}_\alpha \phi$ is true in some possible world w_i if ϕ is true in every world w_j such that $< \alpha, w_i, w_j > \in k$. We write this as $\models_{w_i} \mathbf{K}_\alpha \phi$.

For a full, modern treatment of epistemic logic in connection with computationally modeling the mind (from the standpoint of AI), see Fagin et al. (2004).

4.1.10. THE SIMPLEST INFINITARY LOGICAL SYSTEM: $\mathcal{L}\omega_1 \omega$

Because $\mathcal{L}_I$ is so limited (most interesting mathematical statements cannot be expressed in FOL; e.g., the concept of finitude, central to mathematics, probably cannot be expressed in FOL), logicians have studied infinitary logics, including simple, complete ones like $\mathcal{L}_{\omega_1\omega}$, the definition of which is now provided.

The basic idea behind $\mathcal{L}_{\omega_1\omega}$ is straightforward. This logical system allows for infinite disjunctions and conjunctions, where these disjunctions and conjunctions are no longer than the size of the set of natural numbers (let's use ω to denote the size of the set of natural numbers).[7] This fundamental idea is effortlessly regimented: First, one simply adds to the customary alphabet for FOL the symbols $\bigvee$ and $\bigwedge$. To the ordinary formation rules for building grammatically correct first-order formulas, one then adds

- If Φ is a set of well-formed formulas $\{\phi_1, \phi_2, \ldots\}$ no larger than ω, then $\bigvee \Phi\, (\bigwedge \Phi)$ is also a well-formed formula, viz., the disjunction (conjunction) of the formulas in Φ.

The conditions under which an infinite formula is true is fixed by extending the notion of truth in ordinary FOL:

- A possibly infinite disjunction, $\bigvee \Phi$, is true on an interpretation $\mathcal{I}$ (written $\mathcal{I} \models \bigvee \Phi$) if and only if there is a formula ϕ in Φ which is true on $\mathcal{I}$.
- A possibly infinite conjunction, $\bigwedge \Phi$, is true on an interpretation $\mathcal{I}$ (written $\mathcal{I} \models \bigwedge \Phi$) if and only if every formula ϕ in Φ is true on $\mathcal{I}$.

Proofs (= derivations) in $\mathcal{L}_{\omega_1\omega}$ can, as the relevant literature states, be "infinitely long" (Ebbinghaus, Flum, & Thomas, 1984). This is because in addition to classical cornerstones like *modus ponens* covered previously,

from $\phi \to \psi$ and ϕ infer to ψ,

$\mathcal{L}_{\omega_1\omega}$ allows rules of inference like

7 This chapter, as stated at the outset, is aimed at an audience assumed to have familiarity with elementary logic. So this is not the place to intorduce readers into the world of cardinal numbers. Hence, the size implications of the subscripts in $\mathcal{L}_{\omega_1\omega}$ and other related niceties, such as the precise meaning of ω, are left to the side. For a comprehensive array of the possibilities arising from varying the subscripts, see Dickmann (1975).

from $\phi \to \psi$ for all $\psi \in \Phi$,

infer to $\phi \to \bigwedge \Psi$.

This rule says that if in a derivation you have an infinite list of if–thens (i.e., formulas of the form $\phi \to \psi$) where each consequent (ψ) in each if–then is an element of some infinite set Φ, then you can infer to an if–then whose consequent is the infinite conjunction obtained by conjoining all the elements of Φ. It may be worth pausing to create a picture of the sort of derivation that is here permitted. Suppose that Γ is an infinite set of the same size as $\mathbf{N}$, the natural numbers. So Γ is $\{\gamma_1, \gamma_2, \ldots, \gamma_n, \gamma_{n+1}, \gamma_{n+2}, \ldots\}$. Then here is one possible picture of an infinite derivation:

$$
\begin{array}{l}
\phi \to \gamma_1 \\
\phi \to \gamma_2 \\
\phi \to \gamma_3 \\
\vdots \\
\phi \to \gamma_n \\
\phi \to \gamma_{n+1} \\
\vdots \\
\hline
\phi \to \gamma_1 \wedge \gamma_2 \wedge \ldots \wedge \gamma_n \wedge \gamma_{n+1} \wedge \gamma_{n+2} \cdots
\end{array}
$$

It should be clear from this that derivations in $\mathcal{L}_{\omega_1\omega}$ can indeed be infinitely long.

4.1.11. NONMONOTONIC LOGICAL SYSTEMS

Deductive reasoning is monotonic. That is, if ϕ can be deduced from some knowledge base Φ of formulas (written, recall, $\Phi \vdash^D_x \phi$), then for any formula $\psi \notin \Phi$, it remains true that $\Phi \cup \{\psi\} \vdash^D_x \phi$. In other words, when the reasoning in question is deductive, new knowledge never invalidates prior reasoning. More formally, where Φ is some set of formulas, the closure of this set under standard deduction (i.e., the set of all formulas that can be deduced from Φ), denoted by $\Phi^\vdash$, is guaranteed to be a subset of $(\Phi \cup \Psi)^\vdash$ for all sets of formulas Ψ. This is not how real life works, at least when it comes to humans; this is easy to see. Suppose that at present, Jones knows that his house is still standing as he sits in it, typing. If, later in the day, while away from his home and working at his office, he learns that a vicious tornado passed over the town in which his house is located, he has new information that probably leads him to at least suspend judgment as to whether or not his house still stands. Or to take the much-used example from AI, if Smith knows that Tweety is a bird, he will probably deduce that Tweety can fly on the strength of a general principle saying that birds can fly. But if he learns that Tweety is a penguin, the situation must be revised: That Tweety can fly should now not be in Smith's knowledge base. Nonmonotonic reasoning is the form of reasoning designed to model, formally, this kind of *defeasible* inference.

There are many different logic-based approaches that have been designed to model defeasible reasoning, and each one is associated with a group of logical systems, as such systems have been defined previously. Such systems include: default logic, circumscription, argument-based defeasible reasoning, and so on. (The *locus classicus* of a survey can be found in Genesereth and Nilsson (1987). An excellent survey is also provided in the *Stanford Encyclopedia of Philosophy*.[8]) In the limited space available in the present chapter, the wisest course is to briefly explain one of these approaches. Argument-based defeasible reasoning is selected because it seems to accord best with what humans actually do as they adjust their knowledge through time.[9]

Let us return to the tornado example. What is the argument that Jones might give to support his belief that his house still stands, while he sits within it, typing? There are many possibilities, one respectable one is what can be labeled "Argument 1," where

the indirect indexical refers of course to Jones:

(1) I perceive that my house is still standing.
(2) If I perceive ϕ, ϕ holds.
∴ (3) My house is still standing.

The second premise is a principle that seems a bit risky, perhaps. No doubt there should be some caveats included within it: that when the perception in question occurs, Jones is not under the influence of drugs, not insane, and so on. But to ease exposition, let us leave aside such clauses. So, on the strength of this argument, we assume that Jones' knowledge base includes (3), at time t_1.

Later on, as we have said, he finds himself working in his office, away from home. A tornado passes over his building. Jones quickly queries his Web browser once the roar and rumble die down, and learns from the National Weather Service this very same tornado has touched down somewhere in the town T in which Jones' house is located. At this point (t_2, assume), if Jones were pressed to articulate his current position on (3) and his reasoning for that position, and he had sufficient time and patience to comply, he might offer something like this (Argument 2):

(4) A tornado has just (i.e., at some time between t_1 and t_2) touched down in T, and destroyed some houses there.
(5) My house is located in T.
(6) I have no evidence that my house was *not* struck to smithereens by a tornado that recently passed through the town in which my house is located.
(7) If a tornado has just destroyed some houses in (arbitrary) town T', and house h is located in T, and one has no evidence that h is not among the houses destroyed by the tornado, then one ought not to believe that h was not destroyed.
∴ (8) I ought not to believe that my house is still standing. [I ought not to believe (3).]

8 At http://plato.stanford.edu/entries/logic-ai.
9 From a purely formal perspective, the simplest way to achieve nonmonotonicity is to use the so-called *closed world assumption* (CWA), according to which, given a set Φ of initially believed declarative statements, what an agent believes after applying the CWA to the set is not only what can be deduced from Φ, but also the negation of every formula that *cannot* be deduced. It is easy to verify that it does not always hold that CWA(Φ) $\subset$ CWA($\Phi \cup \Psi$), for all sets Ψ, i.e., monotonicity does not hold.

Assuming that Jones meets all of his "epistemic obligations" (in other words, assuming that he is rational), he will not believe (3) at t_2. Therefore, at this time, (3) will not be in his knowledge base. (If a cognitive system s does not believe ϕ, it follows immediately that s doesn't know ϕ.) The nonmonotonicity should be clear.

The challenge is to devise formalisms and mechanisms that model this kind of mental activity through time. The argument-based approach to nonmonotonic reasoning does this. Although the details of the approach must be left to outside reading (see Pollock 1992, 2001), it should be easy enough to see that the main point is to allow one argument to shoot down another (and one argument to shoot down an argument that shoots down an argument, which revives the original, etc.), and to keep a running tab on which propositions should be believed at any particular time. Argument 2 previously discussed rather obviously shoots down Argument 1; this is the situation at t_2. Should Jones then learn that only two houses in town T were leveled, and that they are both located on a street other than his own, Argument 2 would be defeated by a third argument, because this third argument would overthrow (6). With Argument 2 defeated, (3) would be reinstated, and be back in Jones' knowledge base. Clearly, this ebb and flow in argument-versus-argument activity is far more than just straight deductive reasoning.

4.1.12. PROBABILISTIC LOGICAL SYSTEMS

Although, as we have seen, declarative/logic-based computational cognitive modeling was being pursued in earnest more than 2,300 years ago, probability theory is only about 200 years old; it emerged from technical philosophy and logic (Glymour, 1992; Skyrms, 1999). Kolmogorov's axioms, namely,

1. All probabilities fall between 0 and 1, that is, $\forall p (0 \leq P(p) \leq 1)$,
2. Valid (in the traditional logic-based sense explained earlier in the present chapter) propositions have a probability of 1; unsatisfiable (in the traditional logic-based sense explained earlier) propositions have a probability of 0, and
3. $P(p \vee q) = P(p) + P(q) - P(p \wedge q)$

are simple formulas from a simple logical system, but modern probability theory can be derived from them in straightforward fashion.

The reader may wonder where probabilistic *inference* enters the picture, because traditional deduction is not used for inference in probability theory. Probabilistic inference consists in computing, from observed evidence expressed in terms of probability theory, posterior probabilities of propositions of interest. In the relevant class of logical systems, the symbol to be used is $\vdash_X^{Prob}$, where X would be the particular way of computing over prior distributions to support relevant posterior formulas. Recently, the assignment to X has received much interest, because some strikingly efficient ways of representing and computing over distributions have arrived because of the use of graph-theoretic structures, but the expressiveness of probability theory is ultimately bounded by the logical system with which it is associated, and the two systems in question (the propositional calculus and FOL, both of course introduced earlier as $\mathcal{L}_{PC}$ and $\mathcal{L}_I$, respectively) are rather inexpressive, from the mathematical point of view afforded by $\mathcal{F}$. In fact, extending probability theory to the first-order case is a very recent achievement, and things are not settled (Russell & Norvig, 2002).

Because another chapter in the present handbook covers probabilistic computational cognitive modeling (see Chapter 3 in this volume), no more is said about such logical systems here. The interested reader is also directed to Skyrms (1999), Russell and Norvig (2002), Bringsjord (in-press) for additional coverage of probabilisitc formalisms and modeling.

4.2. *Sample Declarative Modeling in Conformity to LCCM*

Though the purpose of this chapter is to present logic-based computational cognitive modeling itself and to show it at work directly, it is appropriate to present a few examples of declarative computational cognitive modeling and to see how this kind of modeling is formalized by LCCM. Three such examples will be provided.

4.2.1. PRODUCTION RULE-BASED MODELING

Much computational cognitive modeling is based on production rules. For example, Soar, ACT-R, and EPAM are based on such rules, and, accordingly, are often called *production systems*. But what is a production rule? In a seminal article dealing with the relationship between logic and production rule-based modeling, Eisenstadt & Simon (1997) tell said that

> *A production [rule] can be represented in the form* C → A, *where the* C *represents a set of conditions, which are knowledge elements, either stored in memory or derived from current stimuli; and the* A *represents a set of actions, that either alter internal symbol structures or initiate more responses, or both.* (p. 368)

Given the technical content shared with the reader earlier, what should come to mind when seeing "C → A" is a conditional in $\mathcal{L}_I$ (or even, in some simple cases, in $\mathcal{L}_{PC}$), and in point of fact, this logical system does provide a precise formalization of activity in collections of interconnected production rules. In any case, where A is performed, the declarative content C is satisfied, and there exists a mechanical sequence of deductive inference (a proof) that produces C as a conclusion, and indeed a proof that produces a declarative representation of A as a conclusion.[10]

Let us consider an example to make this clearer; the example parallels one given, for different purposes, by Eisenstadt and Simon (1997). Three consequences result from a dog chasing a cat, where this event consists in the instantiation of **Chasing(x,y)**, **Dog(x)**, and **Cat(y)**. The consequences are certain actions, denoted, respectively, by **Consequence1(x)**, **Consequence2(y)**, and a general consequence **Consequence3**; the third consequence, Eisenstadt and Simon tell us, consists in the cat knocking over a bowl. The idea is that if instantiations of the three conditions appear in memory, that is, that if **Chasing(a,b)**, **Dog(a)**, **Cat(b)** are in memory, the production is executed and the consequences ensue.

Where

$$Happens(Consequence1(x))$$
$$\wedge\ Happens(Consequence2(y))$$
$$\wedge\ Happens(Consequence3))$$

expresses in $\mathcal{L}_I$ that the three consequences do in fact transpire, this proposition combined with the following four formulae allows any standard automated prover (ATP) to instantly prove exactly what is desired.

1. $\forall x \forall y((Chasing(x, y) \wedge Dog(x) \wedge Cat(y)) \rightarrow$

   $(Happens(Consequence1(x))$
   $\wedge\ Happens(Consequence2(y))$
   $\wedge\ Happens(Consequence3))))$

2. $Chasing(a, b)$
3. $Dog(a)$
4. $Cat(b)$

As we shall see, ATPs stand to logic-based computer programming as, say, built-in functions like addition stand to an

---

10 More generally, the production rules used to specify the operation of a Turing machine (in some formalizations of these machines, such rules are used), and executions of these rules, can be entirely al-gorithmically replaced with deduction over these rules expressed exclusively in $\mathcal{L}_I$. A readable proof of this is found in Boolos and Jeffrey (1989). Going from the abstract and mathematical to the concrete, any production rule-based activity in an *implemented* system (such as Soar), can be directly matched by the corresponding execution of a program in the general space $P_{\mathcal{L}_{PC}}$ of such program (see the following coverage of logic-based computer programs).

established programming language like Common Lisp (Steele, 1984; which happens to be long associated with computational cognitive modeling and AI).[11] In Lisp, (+ 4 5), when executed, returns 9. Likewise, a standard ATP, on given the five previous formulas, and a request to prove whether the second consequence obtains, brings the correct answer back immeditately. For example, here is a proof instantly returned by the well-known and long-established ATP known as Otter (Wos et al., 1992), once the five formulas are asserted, and the query is issued.

```
---------------- PROOF ----------------
2 [] -Chasing(x,y)| -Dog(x)|
   -Cat(y)|Happens(consequence2(y)).
4 [] -Happens(consequence2(b)).
5 [] Dog(a).
6 [] Cat(b).
7 [] Chasing(a,b).
9 [hyper,7,2,5,6] Happens
   (consequence2(b)).
10 [binary,9.1,4.1] F.
------------ end of proof -------------
```

This particular proof uses a mode of deductive inference called *resolution*, a mode that, using the notation introduced earlier, can be labeled $\vdash_{res}^{D}$. The core rule of inference in resolution is simply that from $\phi \lor \psi$ and $\neg\phi$ it can be inferred that ψ. In this inference, it can be accurately said that ϕ and $\neg\phi$ "cancel each other out," leaving ϕ. The careful reader can see this "cancellation" at work in the inference at the line containing hyper and in the inference at the line containing binary.

It is important to know that although all that is represented in a production system, and all processes over those representations, corresponds, formally speaking, to representation and reasoning in simple logical systems, the converse does not hold. The reason for this is simply that some declarative information exceeds the particular structure for expressing declarative information available in the production paradigm. Whereas every production rule maps directly to a particular formula in some logical system and every firing of production rules maps directly to a machine-generated proof, many formulas in many logical systems exceed the expressive power of production rules and systems. This is without question true for an entire subclass; infinitary logical systems are in this category. Even the smallest infinitary logical system ($\mathcal{L}_{\omega_1\omega}$, visited earlier) allows for declarative statements that exceed production rules. Even more mundane declarative statements, although easily expressed by particular formulas in particular logical systems, at the very least, pose an extreme challenge to production systems. For example, although ϕ = "Everyone loves anyone who loves at least three distinct people" is trivially mapped to a formula in $\mathcal{L}_I$,[12] it is impossible to devise one production rule to correspond directly to this declarative statement. Things get even harder when expressivity must increase. For example, operators can range over ϕ as when, in quantified epistemic logic ($\mathcal{L}_{QKT}$), we say such things as that Jones believes that Smith believes ϕ.

4.2.2. RIPS' PSYCOP AND JOHNSON-LAIRD-WRITTEN MODELS

Rips (1994) describes a system (PSYCOP) designed to model normatively incorrect human reasoning at the level of the propositional calculus (i.e., at the level of $\mathcal{L}_{PC}$), and to some degree (if for no other reason than that PSYCOP includes normatively correct deductive rules of inference), normatively correct reasoning at this level as well. This means that PSYCOP is couched in terms of the logical system $\mathcal{L}_{PC}$, discussed previously (from which it follows that whatever declarative statement(s) $\mathcal{L}_{PC}$ cannot express, PSYCOP cannot express).

PSYCOP reflects the driving dogma of the aforementioned theory of human reasoning known as *mental logic* – the dogma

---

11 For cognoscenti to see that the analogy between these built-in functions and ATPs holds firmly, it must be stipulated that calls like $\Phi \vdash^M \phi$? include an interval of time n beyond which the machine's deliberation will not be allowed to pass.

12 In $\mathcal{L}_I$ it is simply $\forall x \forall y((\exists z_1 \exists z_2 \exists z_3 (z_1 \neq z_2 \land z_2 \neq \land z_1 \neq z_3 \land Lyz_1 \land Lyz_2 \land Lyz_3)) \to Lxy)$.

being that (logically untrained) human reasoners reason by following rules of inference similar to those used in the argument theory of $\mathcal{L}_{PC}$. For example, although the inference rule mentioned in a moment is absent from the system, *modus ponens* is in it, as are a number of other rules. (PSYCOP and its underpinnings are critiqued in Chapter 12 in this volume.) It is important to note that PSYCOP is not an architecture designed to computationally model all of human cognition. In fact, PSYCOP cannot be used to model the human reasoning triggered by the puzzle-based desiderata listed earlier. This is so because PSYCOP is insufficiently expressive (e.g., it has no modal operators like those in $\mathcal{L}_{KT}$, and they are needed for WMP, as we shall soon see; nor does PSYCOP even have first-order models of $\mathcal{L}_I$), and it does not allow trivial normatively correct inferences that good deductive reasoners make all the time. For example, in PSYCOP, you cannot infer from the falsity of (where ϕ and ψ are wffs of $\mathcal{L}_{PC}$) "If ϕ, then ψ" to the falsity of ψ, but that is an inference that even logically untrained reasoners do sometimes make. For example, they sometimes say, when faced with such declarative sentences as:

> It is false that: If the cat is not on the mat, then Jones is away.

that if the if–then is false, the "if part" (= the antecedent) must be true whereas the "then part" (= the consequent) is not, which immediately implies here that Jones is not away.

Interestingly enough, Rips explicitly considers the possibility of a "deduction-based" cognitive architecture (in Chapter 8, "The Role of Deduction in Thought," in Rips, 1994). This possibility corresponds to a proper subset of what is realized by LCCM. Rips has in mind only a particular simple extensional logic as the core of this possibility (namely, $\mathcal{L}_{PC}$), whereas LCCM is based on the literally infinitely broader concept of the family $\mathcal{F}$ of logical systems; on not just deduction, but other forms of reasoning as well (e.g., induction, abduction, nonmono-

tonic reasoning, etc.); and on a dedicated programing paradigm tailor-made for implementing such systems.

Now, what about Johnson-Laird's (1983) mental models theory and specifically some computer programs that implement it? Does this work also fall under LCCM? Because Johnson-Laird's work is declarative, it does fall under LCCM.

Mental models theory has been, at least in part, implemented in the form of various computer programs (see Chapter 12 in this volume), but none of these programs constitute across-the-board computational cognitive models of the human cognizer. Instead, the reasons offered as to why such programs have been written include the standard (but very compelling) ones, such as that the computer implementation of a psychological theory can reveal ambiguities and inconsistencies in that theory. However, the programs in question fall under LCCM. After all, these are programs that produce models in the logic-based sense and then reason over these models in accordance with rules naturally expressed in logic. At the level of $\mathcal{L}_{PC}$, mental models in mental models theory correspond to rows in truth-tables that yield TRUE for the formula and where only the true literals in those rows are included (a literal is either some p_i, or $\neg p_i$). For example, the mental models corresponding to "The Yankees will win and the Red Sox will lose," assuming a symbolization of $Y \wedge R$ for this English sentence, yields one mental model:

$$Y \quad R.$$

In the case of disjunction, such as "Either the Yankees will win the World Series, or the Red Sox will," the models would be three in number, namely,

$$Y$$
$$R$$
$$Y \quad R.$$

Because in mental models theory a conclusion is necessary if it holds in all the models of the premises, some deductively valid inferences, such as "The Yankees will win" follows from "The Yankees will win and the Red Sox will lose," should be made by logically untrained subjects. This is a normatively correct inference. (However, standard normatively correct justifications are not available on Johnson-Laird's theory. This is so because standard justifications are proofs of the sort seen in formal logic and mathematics.) What about normatively *incorrect* reasoning? Clearly, such reasoning will frequently occur, according to the theory. Think back to the formal structure of experiments as set out at the beginning of this chapter (Section 1.5). Suppose the human reasoner assimilates premises in the list L yielding the mental models in a set S. The reasoner will declare a purported conclusion D to follow if $D \in S$, and such membership can obviously hold independent of formally valid inference.

4.2.3. RULE-BASED, SIMILARITY-BASED, AND COMMONSENSE REASONING IN LCCM

The CLARION cognitive architecture models human declarative reasoning in some very interesting nonlogic-based ways. For example, CLARION models two apparently distinct forms of (simple) reasoning detected in the logically untrained. Although the distinction between these two forms cannot be modeled through naive use of FOL $(= \mathcal{L}_I)$ because both forms of reasoning are declarative, it is easy to model the distinction using the full arsenal of LCCM, that is, using logical systems in the space $\mathcal{F}$ that are more expressive than $\mathcal{L}_I$. This is now shown.

The two forms of reasoning in question are what Sun and Zhang (2006) call "rule-based reasoning" (RBR) and "similarity-based reasoning" (SBR). To look more closely at the situation, one can turn to the specific stimuli on which Sun and Zhang focus, which are taken from Sloman (1998). Stimuli consisted of pairs of arguments. Some pairs are said to be in the form of "premise specificity," as for instance in this pair:

All flowers are susceptible to thrips
  ⇒ All roses are susceptible to thrips.
All plants are susceptible to thrips
  ⇒ All roses are susceptible to thrips.

Other pairs are in the form of what is called "inclusion similarity." Examples include:

All plants contain bryophytes.
  ⇒ All flowers contain bryophytes.
All plants contain bryophytes.
  ⇒ All mosses contain bryophytes.

Subjects were directed to pick the stronger argument from each pair. In response, the vast majority of subjects, for both types of pairs, selected as stronger the "more similar argument," as Sun and Zhang (2006) put it. By this they mean that the vast majority of subjects chose, from each pair, the argument whose subjects are intuitively regarded to be more similar. For example, the assumption is that roses are more similar to flowers than they are to plants.

> *It should be apparent that if only RBR (e.g., based on logics) was used, then similarity should not have made a difference, because the conclusion category was contained in the premise category, and thus both arguments in each pair should have been equally, perfectly strong. Therefore, the data suggested that SBR (as distinct from RBR or logics capturing category inclusion relations) was involved to a significant extent. (Sun & Zhang, 2006, p. 172)*

Of course, by RBR, Sun and Zhang here mean "barebone" RBR, which involves only category inclusion relations.

Sun and Zhang proceed to show that CLARION can be used to model the distinction between RBR and SBR. Although that modeling is impressive, the point relevant to the present chapter is that the RBR-is-distinct-from-SBR phenomenon, because it is declarative, can also be modeled in the LCCM approach because this approach is based on $\mathcal{F}$, the infinite family of logical systems, not on a particular logic. Sun and Zhang, in the parenthetical in the previous quote, indicate that RBR is "based on logics." The use of the plural here is wise, for it would be exceedingly peculiar for any proponent of LCCM to maintain that human reasoning, let alone human cognition, can be modeled by a *particular* logic. This would be even more peculiar than maintaining that in modeling various phenomena, mathematicians and physicists can restrict themselves to only one specific branch of mathematics for the purposes of modeling. (The tensor calculus is a thing of beauty when it comes to relativity, but of what good is it in, say, doing axiomatic set theory?) Following logical systems introduced by Chisholm (1966, 1977, 1987), and Pollock (1974), one can assign strength factors (note: not probabilities; strength factors) to nondeductive inferential links, as in fact has been done in the LCCM-based Slate interactive reasoning system (Bringsjord et al., 2007).[13] In Slate, these factors include, in descending strength, **certain** (4), **evident** (3), **beyond reasonable doubt** (2), **probable** (1), and **counterbalanced** (0), and then the negative counterparts to the first four of these (yielding, in the numerical shorthand, -1, -2, -3, and -4). These strength factors can be associated with knowledge about the similarity of the subjects involved in such arguments as those studied by Sloman, Sun, and Zhang. Given, then, a pair such as

All flowers are susceptible to thrips
  $\Rightarrow_2$ All roses are susceptible to thrips.
All plants are susceptible to thrips
  $\Rightarrow_1$ All roses are susceptible to thrips.

and a straightforward selection algorithm for strength of argument that works by simply selecting the argument whose inferential link is associated with a higher number, LCCM has no trouble modeling the phenomenon in question (i.e., the distinction between barebone RBR and SBR is formally captured). Moreover, because the cognitive plausibility of such strength factors inheres in the fact that the average subject assigns a higher strength factor to the

hidden premise (so that, e.g., "All roses are flowers" is epistemically stronger than "All roses are plants"), LCCM would allow us to model human reasoning that leads subjects to prefer the more similar pairs in the *nonenthymematic* versions of Sloman's arguments.

The reach of LCCM can be shown to formalize not just RBR and SBR, but the overall phenomenon of *commonsense reasoning*, as this phenomenon is characterized by Sun (1995). Sun points out that commonsense reasoning, although not strictly speaking definable, can be taken to include

> *informal kinds of reasoning in everyday life regarding mundane issues, where speed is oftentimes more critical than accuracy. The study of commonsense reasoning as envisaged here is neither about the study of a particular domain, nor about idiosyncratic reasoning in any particular domain. It deals with commonsense reasoning patterns; that is, the recurrent, domain-independent basic forms of reasoning that are applicable across a wide range of domains. (Sun, 1995, p. 242)*

Sun then goes on to show that such reasoning, insofar as a particular set of eleven examples can be taken as exemplars of this reasoning, can be modeled in the CON-SYDERR architecture. Although obviously there is insufficient space to show here how LCCM can also model commonsense reasoning characterized in this ostensive way, it can be indicated how such modeling would run.

The first of the eleven examples, all of which are taken from Collins and Michalski (1989) and Collins (1978), is as follows:

> Q: *Do you think they might grow rice in Florida?*
> A: *Yeah. I guess they could, if there were an adequate fresh water supply, certainly a nice, big, warm, flat area.*

About this example, Sun writes:

> *There is a rule in this example: if a place is big, warm, flat, and has an adequate fresh water supply, then it is a rice-growing area. The person answering the question deduced an uncertain conclusion based*

---

13 Information about Slate and a for-teaching version of the system itself can be obtained at http://www.cogsci.rpi.edu/research/rair.

(1)	$\forall x((Place(x) \land Big(x) \land Warm(x) \land Flat(x) \land Water(x)) \to GrowRice(x))$	premise
(2)	$Place(fl) \land Big(fl) \land Warm(fl) \land Flat(fl)$	premise
(3)	$Water(x)$	probable
(4)	$Place(fl) \land Big(fl) \land Warm(fl) \land Flat(fl) \land Water(fl)$	from (2), (3) BY $\land$I
(5)	$Place(fl) \land Big(fl) \land Warm(fl) \land Flat(fl) \land Water(fl)) \to GrowRice(fl)$	from (1) BY $\forall$E
$\therefore$ (6)	$GrowRice(fl)$	from (5), (6) by $\to$Elim

on partial knowledge, although a piece of crucial information (i.e., the presence of fresh water) is absent. Sun, 1995, p. 244)

One interesting aspect of this example is that the subject not only answers the question in the affirmative, but also sketches a justification. (Recall that the structure of experiments designed to uncover the nature of reasoning and decision making are assumed herein to request justifications. See Section 1.5.) The response is an enthymematic deductive argument easily expressed in $\mathcal{L}_I$, under the parameter $\vdash^D_F$ defined earlier in the chapter (with obvious meanings for the predicate letters), as shown in the box above.

Of course, although (4) follows deductively from $\{(1), (2), (3)\}$ using the rules of natural deduction introduced earlier (as shown in the proof immediately preceding), (3) is only probable, which means that, overall, the strength of the argument for (6) is itself probable.

There are other formal niceties that would be included in a full exposition, but the point should be clear: Commonsense reasoning, as a declarative phenomenon, that is, as reasoning over declarative statements, can, from the formal point of view, be modeled in an illuminating way by LCCM. The subject in this case has given an answer, and a justification, whose formal essence can be expressed with the machinery of LCCM. All of the remaining ten examples in Sun (1995) can be modeled in LCCM as well. Moreover, although it is not shown herein, using the concrete computational techniques covered in the next section, logic-based computer programs can be

written and executed to produce rapid, real-time simulations of the commonsense reasoning in question. Finally, whatever empirical data might be associated with human commonsense reasoning (e.g., response time for answer to be produced and justification to be articulated) can be formally expressed in the framework of LCCM.

4.3. Logic-Based Computer Programming

None of the foregoing has much value unless a program can be written which, when executed, produces a computational simulation of some cognition. After all, the subject being rationalized in this chapter is a particular paradigm for computational cognitive modeling, and computation is by definition the movement through time of a computer; now and in the foreseeable future, such movement is invariably caused and regulated by the creation (manual or automatic, or a hybrid of the two) and execution of computer programs. Given this, an obvious question is: With what programing paradigm, and languages within it, is LCCM naturally associated? Just as a generalization of the concept of *logical system* from mathematical logic was used to arrive at the family $\mathcal{F}$ of logical systems for LCCM, programs in logic-based computational cognitive modeling are written in declarative programming languages from a family $\mathcal{P}$ composed of languages that are generalizations of the long-established concept of a *logic program* in computer science. For each system S in $\mathcal{F}$, there is a corresponding programming language P_S in $\mathcal{P}$. In the interests of space, the focus here will be on $P_{\mathcal{L}_{PC}}$ and $P_{\mathcal{L}_I}$, in which programs are written based on the computation of the two central relations in $\mathcal{L}_{PC}$ and $\mathcal{L}_I$, namely, $\vdash_X^D$ and $\models$, both defined earlier. Fortunately, there are many well-established programming environments for writing programs based on the computing of these relations. For example, $\vdash_{Res}^D$ is computed by Vampire (Voronkov 1995) and Otter (Wos 1996, Wos, Overbeek, e. Lusk & Boyle 1992), $\vdash_F^D$ by Oscar (Pollock 1989, Pollock 1995), Athena and NDL (Arkoudas 2000, Bringsjord, Arkoudas & Bello 2006), among other such systems. As to $\models$, a number of mature, readily available systems now compute this relation as well, for example, Hyperproof (Barwise & Etchemendy 1994), and Paradox and Mace (Claessen & Sorensson 2003) at the level of $\mathcal{L}_I$, and at the level of $\mathcal{L}_{PC}$, many SAT solvers (e.g., see Kautz & Selman 1999).

5. Meeting the Challenges

It is time now to turn to showing how the problems composing (C1) can be solved in LCCM in a manner that matches the human normatively incorrect and normatively correct responses returned after the relevant stimuli are presented. Recall, yet again, the ecumenical experimental structure to which declarative/LCCM must conform (Section 1.5).

5.1. *Meeting the Challenge of Mechanizing Human Reasoning*

Let us begin by reviewing the desiderata under (C1): Desideratum 1 is modeling both System 1 and System 2. Desideratum 2 is modeling reasoning that is emphasized by the three theories. Desiderata 3 through 6 consist of the sequence of four puzzles: King-Ace, Wine-Drinker, Wise Man, and Infinitary DeMorgan. Now, how can it be shown that LCCM can meet the six requirements? By providing the following six demonstrations:

D1 a normatively correct solution to King-Ace can be modeled by LCCM;

D2 a normatively *in*correct, mental logic-based response to King-Ace can be modeled by LCCM;

D3 a normatively correct mental meta-logic-based solution to Wine-Drinker can be modeled by LCCM;

D4 a normatively incorrect mental models-based response to Wine-Drinker can be modeled by LCCM;

D5 a normatively correct solution to Wise Man can be modeled by LCCM.

D6 a normatively correct solution to Infinitary DeMorgan can be modeled by LCCM.

Once these things are demonstrated by elementary deduction, all desiderata are satisfied. These demonstrations, recall, are to be carried out at the "algorithmic" level in Marr's (1982) tripartite scheme, or, equivalently, the "symbolic" in Pylyshyn's (1984) corresponding three-level view of the computational modeling of cognition. Using Marr's language, that means that what is sought is a representation for the input and output, and the algorithm for the transformation from the former to the latter. The algorithm for transformation corresponds directly to the argument or proof provided. (Recall that what the algorithms in question are was provided in Section 4.3, when logic-based computer programming was defined. The programming is based directly on arguments or proofs returned by subjects.)

5.1.1. DESIDERATUM #1
A normatively correct solution to Puzzle 1 that follows what human cognizers do when succeeding on the puzzle is easy to construct in LCCM, with the logical system in question set to $\mathcal{L}_{PC}$. In a recent experiment (to test hypotheses outside the scope of the present chapter), forty subjects were given Puzzle 1. The subjects were divided into two groups, one that was given a paper-and-pencil version of Puzzle 1 and one that was given an electronic version encoded in our Slate system. In both cases, a justification for the given answer was requested. A number

of subjects did, in fact, answer correctly *and* give a normatively correct justification, that is, a proof in a particular deductive calculus, namely, the calculus F defined earlier. Figure 5.2 shows a proof in $\mathcal{F}$, constructed in HYPERPROOF, that follows the reasoning given by some students in proving that in Puzzle 1 one can correctly conclude $\neg A$. It is important to note that there are an unlimited number of deductive calculi that could be used to a proof establishing the correct answer "There is not an ace in the hand." The normative correct solution provided here is a direct match to the justification given by human subjects. For many examples of such normatively correct solutions produced by human subjects, see Rinella et al. (2001).

5.1.2. DESIDERATUM #2

The same experiment as mentioned in the previous section, combined with a number of predecessors relevantly like it, have enabled us to acquire an archive of "justifications" in support of A. The vast majority of these express reasoning that is in fact formally valid reasoning in conformity with mental logic theory – but in this reasoning, the declarative information is incorrectly represented. How does the reasoning run, specifically? It is perfectly straightforward; here is a sample:

> We know that if there's a king in the hand, then there's an ace in the hand. And we know that if there isn't a king in the hand, then there is an ace in the hand. But there are only two possibilities here. Either there is a king in the hand, or there isn't. But both of these possibilities let us conclude that there is an ace in the hand.

Obviously, such reasoning accords well with mental logic, and a simulation of this reasoning in the LCCM approach is trivial. One need only write a program $P_{\mathcal{L}_{PC}}$ such that, when evaluated, the reasoning quoted earlier is produced. Here's a simple NDL deduction that does the trick:

```
// The signature for this simple example
// (normatively incorrect
// deductive reasoning given in response to
// the king-ace puzzle)
// contains two propositional variables,
```

```
// A and K:
Relations A:0, K:0.

// One asserts the conjunction consisting of
// the claim that if there's
// a king in the hand, then there's an ace in
// the hand, and the claim
// that if there isn't a king in the hand then
// there's an ace in the hand.
assert ((K ==> A) & (~K ==> A))

// Either there's a king in the hand, or there
// isn't:
assert K \/ ~K

// And now for the argument, which mechanizes
// the idea that no
// matter which if-then one goes with, in
// either case one can
// show that there is an ace in the hand.
left-and ((K ==> A) & (~K ==> A));
right-and ((K ==> A) & (~K ==> A));
cases K \/ ~K, K ==> A, ~K ==> A
```

When evaluated, this returns a theorem exactly in line with what the normatively incorrect reasoning is supposed to produce, namely,

Theorem: A

Once again, note that it is not just that the desired answer is produced. The structure of the justification directly models what is given by human subjects who fall prey to the puzzle.

5.1.3. DESIDERATUM #3

How does $\mathcal{L}_I$ allow us to solve Puzzle 2? Recall yet again the three relevant statements, in English:

1. All the Frenchmen in the restaurant are gourmets.
2. Some of the gourmets are wine-drinkers.
3. Some of the Frenchmen in the restaurant are wine, drinkers.

The simplest solution to the puzzle is to note that one can find an interpretation $\mathcal{I}$ (in the logical system $\mathcal{L}_I$) in which the first two statements are true, but the third is not. This will show that the third is not a deductive consequence of the first two, from which it will immediately follow that the third cannot be proved from the first two. Here is

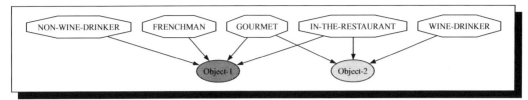

Figure 5.3. Visual countermodel in wine-drinker puzzle (provided by Andrew Shilliday and Joshua Taylor).

an interpretation that fits the bill: First, assume that everyone we are talking about is in the restaurant. Now, suppose that Alvin is a wine-drinker and a gourmet, and not a Frenchman. Bertrand is a Frenchman and a gourmet, but not a wine-drinker. No one else, in this imaginary scenario, exists. In this situation, all Frenchmen are gourmets, and there exists someone who is a wine-drinker and a gourmet. This ensures that both the first two statements are true. But it is *not* true that there exists someone who is both a Frenchman and a wine-drinker. This means that the third proposition is false; more generally, it means that the third is not a consequence of the first two, which in turn means that (using the list of the three just given)

$$\{(1), (2)\} \vdash (3),$$

and the full solution is accomplished. Please note that logic-based programming at the level of $\mathcal{L}_I$ allows for countermodels to be produced, and they can be rendered in visual form to be more quickly grasped. Figure 5.3 shows such a countermodel relevant to the present case, produced by the aforementioned Paradox system (Claessen & Sorensson, 2003), and translated and visually displayed by the Slate system (Bringsjord et al., 2007). For studies in which subjects respond to stimuli like the Wine Drinker in normatively correct fashion, see (Bringsjord et al., 1998; Rinella et al., 2001).

5.1.4. DESIDERATUM #4
This is easy to model in LCCM, as follows. First, most subjects who succumb to this

problem see not the list of English sentences as written, but rather

1. All the Frenchmen in the restaurant are gourmets.
2. All of the gourmets are wine-drinkers.
3. There are some Frenchman.
4. Some of the Frenchmen in the restaurant are wine-drinkers.

The deduction of the last of these from the first three in a natural calculus is straightforward. Here is an NDL deduction that, once evaluated, produces exactly the human-produced output (i.e., exactly (exists x (Frenchmen(x) & Winedrinker(x))), by exactly the human-produced reasoning:

```
// There are three obvious relations to declare:
Relations Frenchman:1, Gourmet:1, Winedrinker:1.

assert (forall x (Frenchman(x) ==> Gourmet(x)))
// The first proposition is asserted.

assert (forall x (Gourmet(x) ==> Winedrinker(x)))
// The second proposition is asserted.

assert (exists x Frenchman(x))
// There are some Frenchmen.

// Now for the reasoning corresponding to the
// normatively incorrect response.
// The reasoning itself, note, is formally valid.
pick-witness z for (exists x Frenchman(x))
// An arbitrary individual z is picked
// to facilitate the reasoning.
  begin specialize (forall x (Frenchman(x) ==>
// Gourmet(x))) with z;
  specialize (forall x (Gourmet(x) ==>
// Winedrinker(x))) with z;
    assume Frenchman(z)
      begin
        modus-ponens Frenchman(z) ==> Gourmet(z),
        // Frenchman(z);
        modus-ponens Gourmet(z) ==> Winedrinker(z),
        // Gourmet(z)
      end;
  modus-ponens Frenchman(z) ==> Winedrinker(z),
  // Frenchman(z);
  both Frenchman(z), Winedrinker(z);
  ex-generalize (exists x Frenchman(x) &
  // Winedrinker(x)) from z
end
```

5.1.5. DESIDERATUM #5

To ease exposition, the solution is restricted to the two-wise-men version. In this version, the key information consists in these three facts:

1. A knows that if A doesn't have a white spot, B will know that A doesn't have a white spot.
2. A knows that B knows that either A or B has a white spot.
3. A knows that B doesn't know whether or not B has a white spot.

Next, here are some key axioms and rules of inference:

K $\Box(\phi \Rightarrow \psi) \Rightarrow (\Box\phi \Rightarrow \Box\psi)$
T $\Box\phi \Rightarrow \phi$
LO ("logical omniscience") From $\phi \vdash^*$ ψ and $K_\alpha\phi$ infer $K_\alpha\psi$

We are now positioned to appreciate a traditional-style proof in $\mathcal{L}_{KT}$ that solves this problem and which is the direct correlate given by (the few) subjects who, when WMP is given, provide a normatively correct justification:

1. $K_A(\neg White(A) \Rightarrow K_B(\neg White(A)))$
2. $K_A(K_B(\neg White(A) \Rightarrow White(B)))$
3. $K_A(\neg K_B(White(B)))$
4. $\neg White(A) \Rightarrow K_B(\neg White(A))$ 1, T
5. $K_B(\neg White(A) \Rightarrow White(B))$ 2, T
6. $K_B\neg(White(A)) \Rightarrow K_B(White(B))$ 5, K
7. $\neg White(A) \Rightarrow K_B(White(B))$ 4, 6
8. $\neg K_B(White(B)) \Rightarrow White(A)$ 7
9. $K_A(\neg K_B(White(B)) \Rightarrow White(A))$ 4–8, 1, LO
10. $K_A(\neg K_B(White(B))) \Rightarrow K_A(White(A))$ 9, K
11. $K_A(White(A))$ 3, 10

To see how this can be rendered in computational form, implemented, and efficiently run in a logic-based computer program, see Arkoudas and Bringsjord (2005).

5.1.6. DESIDERATUM #6

Given the reach of LCCM through $\mathcal{L}_{\omega_1\omega}$, this puzzle is easy to solve. The disjunction

in question can be denoted by $\bigvee \Phi$. We then simply invoke the infinitary analogue to the inference rule known as disjunctive syllogism, which sanctions deducing ψ from the two formulas $\phi \vee \psi$ and $\neg\phi$. The analogue is

$$\text{from } \bigvee \Phi, \text{ where } \phi \in \Phi, \text{ and } \neg\phi,$$

$$\text{infer to } \bigvee \Phi - \{\phi\}.$$

5.2. *Meeting the Perception/Action Challenge*

(C2) can be solved if LCCM can *transparently* model, on the strength of the core mechanical processes given by the families $\mathcal{F}$ and $\mathcal{P}$, the range of high-level cognition all the way down to nondeliberative interaction with the environment, or what, following contemporary terminology, can be called *external perception and action*.[14] In Sun's (2002) words, discussed earlier, one can meet challenge (C2) if $\mathcal{F}$ and $\mathcal{P}$ constitute the unifying logico-mathematical language he says is sorely missing.

It has been shown above that LCCM can model high-level reasoning. If it can be shown that LCCM can meet the perception-and-action challenge, large steps will have been taken toward showing that (C2) can be met by LCCM.[15]

Of course, there is a general feeling afloat that logic is unacceptably slow. Can LCCM handle rapid, nondeliberative perception and action in an exchange with

---

14 The term "external" is used because human persons do routinely engage in introspection (perceive internal things) and do carry out all sorts of mental (= internal) actions.
15 Astute readers may wonder about learning. Note that the notion that logic is inappropriate for modeling learning, which because of limited space is not discussed in earnest herein, has certainly evaporated. This is so for two reasons. The first is that logic-based machine learning techniques are now well established (for a nice survey, see Russell & Norvig, 2002). The second reason is that machine learning by reading, which has never been pursued in AI or cognitive science, is now a funded enterprise – and is logic-based. For example, see the start of Project Halo (Friedland et al., 2004), and logic-based machine reading research sponsored by the U.S. government (e.g., see Bringsjord et al., 2007).

the physical environment? For example, can logic be used to model a human making his or her way through a rapid-fire first-person shooter computer game? In this section, it is explained why this challenge (a) may be beside the point of modeling human personhood, (b) needs to be distinguished from so-called *transduction*, and (c) can be met in at least two logic-based ways, one of which has already been successfully pursued to some degree and one of which would be based on *visual* logic, an area of growing and great future importance to LCCM.

5.2.1. IS PERCEPTION AND ACTION BESIDE THE POINT?

Note that nondeliberative, external perception and action are not part of the definition of human personhood given earlier in the chapter (Section 2). The reason for that is well known: In general, it seems entirely possible for us to *be* persons over a stretch of time during which no external perception and action occurs.[16] There is no reason why Smith cannot spend three hours in a sensory deprivation tank, during which time he cracks a math problem or writes a story in his head, or does any number of intellectual tasks. Moreover, it certainly seems mathematically possible that human persons could be brains in vats, having no exchange with the environment of the type that is supposed to be a challenge to LCCM (Bringsjord & Zenzen, 1991). Nonetheless, it is charitably assumed that LCCM is challenged with having to model external perception and action. An explanation that this challenge can apparently be met is now provided.

5.2.2. SEPARATING OUT TRANSDUCTION

It is important to distinguish between perception and action, and transduction. Transduction is the process by which data hitting sensors is transformed into information that can processed by an agent and by which information processed by an agent

is transformed into data emitted by effectors. Transduction is a purely physics- and engineering-relevant process having nothing to do with cognition. In other words, transduction is a process peripheral to human cognition. The quickest way to see this is to note that the transducers we currently have can be replaced with others, whereas the prereplacement and postreplacement persons remain numerically identical despite this replacement. If you go blind, and doctors replace your eyes with artificial cameras, it is still you who thanks the surgeons after the procedure has brought your sight back. It's *your* sight they have brought back, after all. (The overall picture just described is articulated in the context of human-level logic-based AI in Nilsson (1991). The picture transfers directly to the specific case of human persons.)

The assumption is made that for LCCM, information from the environment is cast as expressions in some logical system from $\mathcal{F}$, and the challenge is to process those expressions with sufficient speed and accuracy to match human performance. This can be accomplished in one of two ways. The first way is briefly described in the next section. The second way is still experimental and on the very frontier of LCCM and human-level logic-based AI, and will not be discussed here.[17]

5.2.3. AN EVENT CALCULUS WITH ATPS

Although logic has been criticized as too slow for real-time perception-and-action-heavy computation, as one might see in the computational modeling of a human playing first-person shooter game (as opposed to a strategy game, which for obvious reasons, fits nicely with the paradigm of LCCM), it has been shown that computation produced by the execution of programs in $P_{\mathcal{L}_I}$ is now so fast that it can enable the real-time behavior of a mobile robot

---

16 *Internal* perception and action is another story: In a sensory deprivation tank, one can perceive all sorts of mathematical objects (e.g.), and can take all kinds of mental actions.

17 In the second way, information from the environment is not transduced into traditional linguistic logics, but is rather left in visual form and represented in visual logics. For a discussion of visual logic, in the context of the study of the mind from a computational perspective, see Bringsjord (in press).

Figure 5.4. The wumpus world game. In the wumpus world, a robot must navigate a work in matrix form, where cells in the grid may contain pits or a monster (the Wumpus). The robot must shoot and kill the Wumpus, and retrieve the gold.

simulating human behavior in a robust environment. This has been shown by having a logic-based mobile robot successfully navigate the wumpus world game, a staple in AI (Brijgsjord et al., 2005), and a game that humans have long played (see Figures 5.4 and 5.5). This work parallels work done in John McCarthy's (logic-based) AI lab that

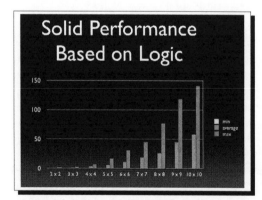

Figure 5.5. Performance of a RASCALS-powered robot in the wumpus world. This graph shows the time (in seconds) it takes the logic-powered robot to succeed in the wumpus world, as a function of the size of the world (i.e., the size of the grid). The speed is really quite remarkable. Engineering was carried out by Matt Daigle.

has shown it to be possible to control a real robot, operating in a realistic office environment in real time (Amir & Maynard-Reid, 2001; Amir & Maynard-Reid, 2000; Amir & Maynard-Reid, 1999).[18] In this approach, a calculus is used to represent time and change. Usually the calculus is the situation calculus, but the event calculus can also be used; both are summarized in Russell and Norvig (2002). It is important to know that such work is far from peripheral and tentative: Logic-based AI is starting to reveal that even in the area of perception and action, the speed demands can be met via well-established techniques that are part of the standard toolkit for the field, as seen by such textbooks as *Knowledge in Action* (Reiter, 2001).

5.3. *Meeting the Rigor Challenge*

This section briefly explains why every computational model produced in accordance with LCCM has a precise meaning, which allows LCCM to be theorem-guided. Space does not permit a sampling of relevant theorems to be canvassed in any detail, but a few are cited at the end of this section. For example, how to determine whether two different logic-based programs P and P' have the same meaning is explained.

Let P_L be a logic-based computer program from the space $\mathcal{P}$. It follows immediately by definitions given earlier that this program conforms to what has been called the *argument semantics* for the logical system L in $\mathcal{F}$. That is, every inference made when P_L is executed has a precise mechanical meaning in terms of the effect this inference has on the knowledge base associated with this program. (This has been seen firsthand by the reader earlier, in the sample logic-based computer programs that have been provided.) This meaning perfectly coincides with corresponding inferences made when reasoning is carried out in the logical system L using a particular mode of inference and a particular calculus. To make this clear, consider the precise

18 This research can be found online at: http://www.formal.stanford.edu/eyal/lsa.

meaning (albeit in English) of one of the key inferences used in logic-based computer programs; that inference is `cases`, as used, for example, in

```
cases K \/ ~K, K ==> A, ~K ==> A.
```

The meaning of this inference is that, assuming that the knowledge base contains the three formulas in question (the disjunction `K \/ K` and the two conditionals `K ==> A` and `K ==> A`), its application will add the formula `A` to the knowledge base. This is the kind of meaning that is regimented through the *argument semantics* element in the six elements that are needed for each logical system; recall Section 4.1. For every inference form, there is likewise a definition of this sort that fixes the meaning of that inference. As a result, any sequence of inferences has an absolutely clear meaning. Because every logic-based computer program is nothing more than the specification of a sequence of inferences, the meaning of the operation of a logic-based program is likewise entirely clear.

But what about the meaning of the formulas that are involved *in* the inferences? Here, too, precision is guaranteed. This is so because each and every formula appearing in a logic-based program is given a precise meaning via the formal semantics of the logical system that the formula is expressed in. As to why this is so, you have only to look back at the formula semantics for $\mathcal{L}_I$, given previously. One can determine, for every formula in every logic-based computer program, what the meaning of this formula is because one has on hand an interpretation specifying the formal meaning of all the elements in the signature of every program. Look back to any of the sample logic-based programs given earlier and note the declarations of relations (and sometimes constants) at the begining of the file. One has on hand an interpretation $\mathcal{I}$ telling us what these relations and constants mean. This pattern holds not just for programs written under $\mathcal{L}_I$ (i.e., programs from $P_{\mathcal{L}_I}$), but for any logical system in the family $\mathcal{F}$. In short, although in declarative computational cognitive modeling it may happen that a declarative state-

ment ϕ is employed, in the formalization of such modeling in LCCM, the machinery must be in place for mechanically determining the meaning of ϕ.

Given the logico-mathematical precision of LCCM, declarative computational cognitive modeling can, thankfully, be guided by theorems. Of course, theorem guidance is not something that can be counted on to be met with universal acclaim. There may well be those of the heterodox view that guidance by the light of mathematics is unwanted. However, there can be no denying the *effectiveness* of mathematics in not only describing, but predicting, the natural world, whether that description and prediction is pitched at the level of the "algorithmic" (like formal economics, computer science, and computational cognitive modeling), or at the lower levels at which physics and chemistry operate (as has been famously pointed out in the twentieth century; e.g., see Wigner, 1960; Hamming, 1980). To the extent that computational cognitive modeling takes the cognition distinctive of human persons to be natural phenomena that ought not only be carefully described, but predicted as well, theorem guidance would certainly be a welcome development; and in the case of at least declarative computational cognitive modeling, this development is achieved by virtue of LCCM.

There is not sufficient space to give some interesting theorems, but it should be pointed out that many such theorems can now be proved in connection with the earlier discussion. For example, one can prove without much effort that simulations (i.e., computational cognitive models) in LCCM produced by programs at the level of $\mathcal{L}_{KT}$ will never go into infinite loops (assuming no syntactic bugs). On the other hand, because $\mathcal{L}_I$ is only semi-decidable (the theorems are in any decent textbook on intermediate mathematical logic, e.g., see Boolos & Jeffrey, 1989), simulations in LCCM produced by programs at the level of this logical system can enter infinite loops, and explicit timeout catches must be included for all but very simple programs. For a more general example, note that given the foregoing, it is now known exactly when two logic-based computer programs $P_{\mathcal{L}}$ and $P'_{\mathcal{L}}$ have the same meaning under some interpretation $\mathcal{I}$: This equivalence holds provided that (1) both programs, given declarative input Φ (declarative sentences expressed as formulas in logical system $\mathcal{L}$), once executed, produce the very same theorems as output; and (2), the formulas in Φ, as well as those used in the execution of the two programs, have the same meaning under $\mathcal{I}$.

6. Limitations and the Future

What can be said about the future of computational cognitive modeling and in particular declarative/LCCM? The future of any field is notoriously difficult to predict. Nonetheless, present-day deficiencies in computational cognitive modeling, and specifically in LCCM, clearly point the way toward what cognitive modelers will in the future attempt to do. So, in a limited sense, the future can be predicted, as follows.

What are the deficiencies? First, although Turing (1950) predicted over half a century ago that by now we would be able to engineer machines linguistically indistinguishable from us (i.e., machines able to pass his so-called Turing Test), the fact of the matter is that, today, a bright toddler's conversational reach still exceeds that of any and all computers on our planet. This situation parallels the sad state of computational cognitive modeling when it comes to language: No robust computational cognitive models of human-level communication (attribute 4 in the list of capacities constitutive of personhood, given in Section 2) exist. Even Anderson (2003) concedes that the linguistic side of computational cognitive modeling has stalled and that in this regard, "Newell's Program" has not yet succeeded. There are those (e.g., Moravec, 1999) who hold that, relatively soon, person-level communication will be mechanized. Unfortunately, such writers are confident because of the continuous increase in processing speed produced by Moore's Law, but raw process-

ing speed is not the problem (as explained in Bringsjord, 2000): The challenge, from the standpoint of computational cognitive modeling, is to discover the information-processing procedures that enable human persons to communicate in natural languages. However fast the hardware, it does little good unless there are procedures to run on it. It can therefore be said with confidence that computational cognitive modeling will in the future see sustained work in the area of language-based communication. Breakthroughs are waiting to be made in this area.

What are the implications of this specifically for declarative/LCCM? At the dawn of AI in the United States, when AI was what is today called human-level AI, and for at least three decades thereafter, the dream was to capture natural languages like English, German, and Norwegian completely in first-order logic (= in $\mathcal{L}_I$; e.g., see the FOL-based Charniak & McDermott, 1985). Unfortunately, this specific logic-based approach has not succeeded. In fact, some originally logic-based experts in computational language processing have turned their backs on logic, in favor of purely statistical approaches. Charniak is an example. In 1985, his *Introduction to Artificial Intelligence* gave a unified presentation of AI, including natural language processing. This unification was achieved via first-order logic (= $\mathcal{L}_I$), which runs throughout the book and binds things together. But Charniak abandoned logic in favor of purely statistical approaches (Charniak, 1993).

To this point, despite the richness of the families $\mathcal{F}$ and $\mathcal{P}$, natural language has resisted attempts to model it in logico-computational terms. However, it seems clear that some traction has taken hold in the attempt to model *fragments* of natural language in formal logic (e.g., see Fuchs, Schwertel, & Schwitter, 1999), and this direction is certain to see more investment and at least some progress. Only time will tell if this research and development will be able to scale up to all of natural language.

A second present-day deficiency in computational cognitive modeling is subjective consciousness. Although some forms of consciousness have been modeled (e.g., see Sun, 1999), there are today no simulations of *subjective* consciousness (attribute 2 in the list of capacities constitutive of personhood). As was pointed out in Section 2, no one has a third-person account of what it is to (say) experience the taste of deep, dark chocolate or what it is to *be* you (Bringsjord, 1998). Absent such an account, mechanization – indeed, taking just initial steps toward some mechanization – is rather difficult. Given the importance of consciousness in human cognition (after all, the reason humans seek to continue to live is to continue to have conscious experiences), there is little doubt that in the future, computational cognitive modeling will be marked by a persistent attempt to express consciousness in computation. Again, breakthroughs are waiting to be made.

The present chapter has emphasized human reasoning, as the reader well knows by now. But only reasoning in connection with specific puzzles has been considered. What about the future of attempts to computationally simulate *robust* human reasoning within the declarative/logic-based paradigm? Here, it would seem that two prudent predictions can be made, given the current state of the art and severe limitations seen within it.

As to trends, there is a growing desire to engineer simulations not only of the sort of relatively simple reasoning required to solve the puzzles analyzed earlier, but of the sort of real-life reasoning seen in the proofs of historic theorems. Gödel's incompleteness theorems are in this category, and recently, some attempts have been made to build computational simulations of the reasoning involved (Sieg & Field, 2005; Quaife, 1988; Shankar, 1994). In the future, researchers will increasingly attempt to construct computational simulations of the production of such theorems, where the starting point involves only some basic knowledge. In other words, the attempt will be made to simulate the human ability to invent or create from scratch, rather than to simply process predefined representations. Declarative/LCCM,

as the present chapter shows, can provide impressive simulations when the declarative content is provided ahead of time. But what about the process of *generating* such content in the first place? This, currently, is a serious limitation, and it points toward a future in which much effort will be expended to surmount it.

7. Conclusion

This chapter has explained LCCM as a formal rationalization of declarative computational cognitive modeling. It has also presented the attempt to build computational simulations of all, or at least large portions of, human cognition, on the basis, fundamentally, of logic and logic alone, where logic here denotes the sense of logical system explained previously and the infinite family $\mathcal{F}$ of such systems. The absence of unified theory of cognition has been famously bemoaned rather long ago by Newell (1973). Although such complaints are generally regarded to be compelling, even to this day, it must be admitted that they are not sensitive to the fact that, in other fields more mature and (at least hitherto) more rigorous (e.g., physics) than computational cognitive modeling, unification is regarded to be of little or no value by many, if not most, researchers in these fields. There may be no grand synthesis between quantum mechanics and special relativity, but that does not stop physics from advancing year by year, and the benefits of that advance, from medical imaging to space exploration, are myriad. To put the point another way, *if* one ought to pursue declarative computational models of all of human cognition in a unified fashion, LCCM provides a rigorous route for the pursuit. But the antecedent of this conditional has not been established in the present chapter.

Acknowledgments

I am indebted to a number of anonymous referees, and to Ron Sun, for insightful comments, objections, and suggestions. Special thanks are due to Konstantine Arkoudas for myriad suggestions and for implemented systems that help make declarative computational cognitive modeling a concrete, rigorous reality.

References

Amir, E., & Maynard-Reid, P. (1999). Logic-based subsumption architecture. In *Proceedings of the Sixteenth International Joint Conference on Artificial Intelligence* (pp. 147–152). San Francisco, CA: Morgan Kaufmann.

Amir, E., & Maynard-Reid, P. (2000). Logic-based subsumption architecture: Empirical evaluation. In *Proceedings of the AAAI Fall Symposium on Parallel Architectures for Cognition*.

Amir, E., & Maynard-Reid, P. (2001). LiSA: A robot driven by logical subsumption. In *Proceedings of the Fifth Symposium on the Logical Formalization of Commonsense Reasoning*. http://cs.nyu.edu/faculty/davise/commonsense01.

Anderson, J., & Lebiere, C. (2003). The newell test for a theory of cognition. *Behavioral and Brain Sciences, 26*, 587–640.

Anderson, J. R. (1993). *Rules of mind*. Hillsdale, NJ: Lawrence Erlbaum.

Anderson, J. R., & Lebiere, C. (1998). *The atomic components of thought*. Mahwah, NJ: Lawrence Erlbaum.

Arkoudas, K. (2000). *Denotational proof languages*. PhD thesis, MIT.

Arkoudas, K., & Bringsjord, S. (2005). Metareasoning for multi-agent epistemic logics. In *Fifth International Conference on Computational Logic In Multi-Agent Systems* (CLIMA 2004), (Vol. 3487 (pp. 111–125). New York: Springer-Verlag.

Ashcraft, M. (1994). *Human memory and cognition*. New York: HarperCollins.

Barwise, J., & Etchemendy, J. (1994). *Hyperproof*. Stanford, CA: CSLI.

Barwise, J., & Etchemendy, J. (1999). *Language, proof, and logic*. New York: Seven Bridges.

Boolos, G. S., & Jeffrey, R. C. (1989). *Computability and logic*. Cambridge, UK: Cambridge University Press.

Bourbaki, N. (2004). *Elements of mathematics: theory of sets*. New York: Verlag. (Original work published 1939.)

Brachman, R. J., & Levesque, H. J. (2004). *Knowledge representation and reasoning*. San Francisco, CA: Morgan Kaufmann/Elsevier.

Braine, M. (1998a). How to investigate mental logic and the syntax of thought. In M. Braine & P. O'Brien (eds.), *Mental logic* (pp. 45–61). Mahwah, NJ: Lawrence Erlbaum.

Braine, M. (1998b). Steps toward a mental predicate-logic. In M. Braine & D. O'Brien (Eds.), *Mental logic* (pp. 273–331). Mahwah, NJ: Lawrence Erlbaum Associates.

Braine, M. D. S. (1990). On the relation between the natural logic of reasoning and standard logic. *Psychological Review, 85*, 1–21.

Bringsjord, S. (1995). In defense of impenetrable zombies. *Journal of Consciousness Studies, 2*(4), 348–351.

Bringsjord, S. (1997). *Abortion: A dialogue*. Indianapolis, IN: Hackett.

Bringsjord, S. (1998). Chess is too easy. *Technology Review, 101*(2), 23–28.

Bringsjord, S. (1999). The zombie attack on the computational conception of mind. *Philosophy and Phenomenological Research, 59.1*, 41–69.

Bringsjord, S. (2000). A contrarian future for minds and machines. *Chronicle of Higher Education* p. B5. Reprinted in *The Education Digest, 66.6*: 31–33.

Bringsjord, S. (2001). Is it possible to build dramatically compelling interactive digital entertainment (in the form, e.g., of computer games)? *Game Studies 1*(1). http://www.gamestudies.org.

Bringsjord, S. (in press). Artificial intelligence. In E. Zalta (ed.), *The stanford encyclopedia of philosophy*. Palo Alto, CA: CLSI. http://plato.stanford.edu.

Bringsjord, S., Arkoudas, K., & Bello, P. (2006). Toward a general logicist methodology for engineering ethically correct robots. *IEEE Intelligent Systems 21*(4), 38–44.

Bringsjord, S., Arkoudas, K., Clark, M., Shilliday, A., Taylor, J., Schimanski, B., et al. (2007). Reporting on some logic-based machine reading research. In O. Etzioni (Ed.), *Proceedings of the 2007 AAAI Spring Symposium: Machine Reading (SS–07–06)* (pp. 23–28). Menlo Park, CA: AAAI Press.

Bringsjord, S., Bringsjord, E., & Noel, R. (1998). In defense of logical minds. In *Proceedings of the 20th Annual Conference of the Cognitive Science Society* (pp. 173–178). Mahwah, NJ: Lawrence Erlbaum.

Bringsjord, S., & Ferrucci, D. (1998a). Logic and artificial intelligence: Divorced, still married, separated . . . ? *Minds and Machines, 8,* 273–308.

Bringsjord, S., & Ferrucci, D. (1998b). Reply to Thayse and Glymour on logic and artificial intelligence. *Minds and Machines, 8,* 313–315.

Bringsjord, S., Khemlani, S., Arkoudas, K., McEvoy, C., Destefano, M., & Daigle, M. (2005). Advanced synthetic characters, evil, and E. In M. Al-Akaidi & A. E. Rhalibi (Eds.), *6th International Conference on Intelligent Games and Simulation* (pp. 31–39). Ghent-Zwijnaarde, Belgium: European Simulation Society.

Bringsjord, S., & Zenzen, M. (1991). In defense of hyper-logicist AI. In *IJCAI 91* (pp. 1066–1072). Mountain View, CA: Morgan Kaufman.

Brooks, R. (1991). Intelligence without representation. *Artificial Intelligence, 47,* 139–159.

Brooks, R. A., Breazeal, C., Marjanovic, M., Scassellati, B., & Williamson, M. M. (1999). The cog project: Building a humanoid robot *Lecture Notes in Computer Science, 1562,* 52–87.

Bucciarelli, M., & Johnson-Laird, P. (1999). Strategies in syllogistic reasoning. *Cognitive Science, 23,* 247–303.

Bumby, D., Klutch, R., Collins, D., & Egbers, E. (1995). *Integrated mathematics course 1.* New York: Glencoe/McGraw-Hill.

Cassimatis, N. (2002). A Polyscheme: *A cognitive architecture for integrating multiple representation and inference schemes,* Unpublished doctoral dissertation, Massachusetts Institute of Technology, Cambridge, MA.

Cassimatis, N. (2006). Cognitive substrate for human-level intelligence. *AI Magazine, 27*(2), 71–82.

Cassimatis, N., Trafton, J., Schultz, A., & Bugajska, M. (2004). Integrating cognition, perception and action through mental simulation in robots. In C. Schilenoff & M. Uschold (Eds.), *Proceedings of the 2004 AAAI Spring Symposium on Knowledge Representation and Ontology for Autonomous Systems* (pp. 1-8). Menlo Park, CA: AAAI.

Charniak, E. (1993). *Statistical language learning.* Cambridge, MA: MIT Press.

Charniak, E., & McDermott, D. (1985). *Introduction to artificial intelligence.* Reading, MA: Addison-Wesley.

Chisholm, R. (1966). *Theory of knowledge.* Englewood Cliffs, NJ: Prentice Hall.

Chisholm, R. (1977). *Theory of knowledge* (2nd ed.). Englewood Cliffs, NJ: Prentice Hall.

Chisholm, R. (1978). Is there a mind-body problem? *Philosophic Exchange, 2,* 25–32.

Chisholm, R. (1987). *Theory of knowledge* (3rd ed.). Englewood Cliffs, NJ: Prentice Hall.

Claessen, K., & Sorensson, N. (2003). New techniques that improve Mace-style model finding. In *Model computation: Principles, algorithms, applications (Cade-19 Workshop).* Miami, Florida.

Collins, A. (1978). Fragments of a theory of human plausible reasoning. In D. Waltz (Ed.), *Theoretical issues in natural language processing II* (pp. 194–201). Urbana: University of Illinois Press.

Collins, A., & Michalski, R. (1989). The logic of plausible reasoning: A core theory. *Cognitive Science, 82,* 1–49.

Dennett, D. (1978). Conditions of personhood. In *Brainstorms: Philosophical essays on mind and psychology.* (pp. 267–285). Montgomery, VT: Bradford Books.

Dickmann, M. A. (1975). *Large infinitary languages.* The Netherlands: North-Holland, Amsterdam.

Ebbinghaus, H. D., Flum, J., & Thomas, W. (1984). *Mathematical logic.* New York: Springer-Verlag.

Ebbinghaus, H. D., Flum, J., & Thomas, W. (1994). *Mathematical logic* (2nd ed.) New York: Springer-Verlag.

Eisenstadt, S., & Simon, H. (1997). *Logic and thought: Minds and Machines, 7*(3), 365–385.

Ericsson, K. A., & Simon, H. (1984). *Protocol analysis: Verbal reports as data.* Cambridge, MA: MIT Press.

Fagin, R., Halpern, J., Moses, Y., & Vardi, M. (2004). *Reasoning about knowledge.* Cambridge, MA: MIT Press.

Friedland, N., Allen, P., Matthews, G., Witbrock, M., Baxter, D., Curtis, J., et al. (2004). Project halo: Towards a digital aristotle. *AI Magazine, 25*(4).

Fuchs, N. E., Schwertel, U., & Schwitter, R. (1999). *Attempto controlled English (ACE) language manual* (Version 3.0, Technical Report 99.03). Zurich, Switzerland: Department of Computer Science, University of Zurich.

Gabbay, D. (Ed.). (1994). *What is a logical system?* Oxford, UK: Clarendon Press.

Genesereth, M., & Nilsson, N. (1987). *Logical foundations of artificial intelligence.* Los Altos, CA: Morgan Kaufmann.

Glymour, C. (1992). *Thinking things through*. Cambridge, MA: MIT Press.

Goble, L. (Ed.). (2001). *The Blackwell guide to philosophical logic*. Oxford, UK: Blackwell Publishers.

Goldstein, E. B. (2005). *Cognitive psychology: Connecting mind, research, and everyday experience*. Belmont, CA: Wadsworth.

Halpern, J., Harper, R., Immerman, N., Kolaitis, P., Vardi, M., & Vianu, V. (2001). On the unusual effectiveness of logic in computer science. *The Bulletin of Symbolic Logic, 7*(2), 213–236.

Hamming, R. (1980). The unreasonable effectiveness of mathematics. *The American Mathematical Monthly, 87*, 81–90.

Hintikka, J. (1962). *Knowledge and belief: An introduction to the logic of the two notions*. Ithaca, NY: Cornell University Press.

Inhelder, B., & Piaget, J. (1958). *The growth of logical thinking from childhood to adolescence*. New York: Basic Books.

Johnson-Laird, P. (1997). Rules and illusions: A criticial study of Rips's *The psychology of proof*. *Minds and machines, 7*(3), 387–407.

Johnson-Laird, P. N. (1983). *Mental models*. Cambridge, MA: Harvard University Press.

Johnson-Laird, P. N., Legrenzi, P., Girotto, V., & Legrenzi, M. S. (2000). Illusions in reasoning about consistency. *Science, 288*, 531–532.

Johnson-Laird, P., & Savary, F. (1995). How to make the impossible seem probable. In M. Gaskell & W. Marslen-Wilson (Eds.), *Proceedings of the 17th Annual Conference of the Cognitive Science Society* (pp. 381–384). Hillsdale, NJ: Lawrence Erlbaum.

Kahneman, D., & Tversky, A. (Eds.). (2000). *Choices, values, and frames*. Cambridge, UK: Cambridge University Press.

Kautz, H., & Selman B. (1999). Unifying SAT-based and graph-based planning. In J. Minker, (Ed.), *Workshop on Logic-Based Artificial Intelligence*, Washington, DC, June 14–16, 1999, Computer Science Department, University of Maryland. http://citeseer.ist.psu.edu/kautz99unifying.html.

Langley, P., McKusick, K. B., Allen, J. A., Iba, W., & Thompson, K. (1991). A design for the icarus architecture. *SIGART Bulletin, 2*(4), 104–109.

Marr, D. (1982). *Vision: A computational approach*. San Francisco, CA: Freeman and Company.

McKeon, R. (Ed.). (1941). *The basic works of aristotle*. New York: Random House.

Metzler, J., & Shepard, R. (1982). Transformational studies of the internal representations of three-dimensional objects. In R. Shepard & L. Cooper (Eds.), *Mental images and their transformations* (pp. 25–71). Cambridge, MA: MIT Press.

Moravec, H. (1999), *Robot: Mere machine to transcendant mind*. Oxford, UK: Oxford University Press.

Newell, A. (1973). You can't play 20 questions with nature and win: Projective comments on the papers of this symposium. In W. Chase (Ed.), *Visual Information Processing* (pp. 283–308). New York: Academic Press.

Newell, A. (1990). *Unified theories of cognition*. Cambridge, MA: Harvard University Press.

Newstead, S. E., & Evans, J. S. T. (Eds.). (1995). *Perspectives on thinking and reasoning*. Englewood Cliffs, NJ: Lawrence Erlbaum.

Nilsson, N. (1991). Logic and Artificial Intelligence. *Artificial Intelligence, 47*, 31–56.

Nilsson, N. (1995). Eye on the prize. *AI Magazine, 16*(2), 9–16.

Nilsson, N. (2005). Human-level artificial intelligence? Be serious! *AI Magazine, 26*(4), 68–75.

Nute, D. (1984). Conditional logic. In D. Gabay & F. Guenthner (Eds.), *Handbook of Philosophical Logic Volume II: Extensions of Classical Logic* (pp. 387–439). Dordrecht, The Netherlands: D. Reidel.

Pollock, J. (1974). *Knowledge and justification*. Princeton, NJ: Princeton University Press.

Pollock, J. (1989). *How to build a person: A prolegomenon*. Cambridge, MA: MIT Press.

Pollock, J. (1995). *Cognitive carpentry: A blueprint for how to build a person*. Cambridge, MA: MIT Press.

Pollock, J. (2001). Defasible reasoning with variable degrees of justification. *Artificial Intelligence, 133*, 233–282.

Pollock, J. L. (1992). How to reason defeasibly. *Artificial Intelligence, 57*(1), 1–42.

Pylyshyn, Z. (1984). *Computation and cognition*. Cambridge, MA: MIT Press.

Quaife, A. (1988). Automated proofs of löb's theorem and gödel's two incompleteness theorems. *Journal of Automated Reasoning, 4*, 219–231.

Reiter, R. (2001). *Knowledge in action: Logical foundations for specifying and implementing dynamical systems*. Cambridge, MA: MIT Press.

Rinella, K., Bringsjord, S., & Yang, Y. (2001). Efficacious logic instruction: People are not irremediably poor deductive reasoners. In J. D.

Moore & K. Stenning (Eds.), *Proceedings of the Twenty-Third Annual Conference of the Cognitive Science Society* (pp. 851–856). Mahwah, NJ: Lawrence Erlbaum.

Rips, L. (1994). *The psychology of proof.* Cambridge, MA: MIT Press.

Rosenbloom, P., Laird, J., & Newell, A. (Eds.). (1993). *The Soar papers: Research on integrated intelligence.* Cambridge, MA: MIT Press.

Russell, S., & Norvig, P. (2002). *Artificial intelligence: A modern approach.* Upper Saddle River, NJ: Prentice Hall.

Shankar, N. (1994). *Metamathematics, machines, and Gödel's proof.* Cambridge, UK: Cambridge University Press.

Shapiro, E. (Ed.). (1987). *Concurrent prolog: Collected papers* (vols. 1–2). Cambridge, MA: MIT Press.

Shapiro, S., & Rapaport, W. (1987). SNePS considered as a fully intensional propositional semantic network. In N. Cercone & G. McCalla (Eds.), *The knowledge frontier: Essays in the representation of knowledge* (pp. 262–315). New York: Springer-Verlag.

Sieg, W., & Field, C. (2005). Automated search for gödel's proofs. *Annals of Pure and Applied Logic, 133,* 319–338.

Skyrms, B. (1999). *Choice and chance: An introduction to inductive logic.* Belmont, CA: Wadsworth.

Sloman, S. (1998). Category inference is not a tree: The myth of inheritance hierarchies. *Cognitive Psychology, 35,* 1–33.

Stanovich, K. E., & West, R. F. (2000). Individual differences in reasoning: Implications for the rationality debate. *Behavioral and Brain Sciences, 23*(5), 645–665.

Steele, G. (1984). *Common LISP, second edition: The language.* Woburn, MA: Digital Press.

Stillings, N., Weisler, S., Chase, C., Feinstein, M., Garfield, J., & Rissland, E., (1995). *Cognitive science.* Cambridge, MA: MIT Press.

Sun, R. (1995). Robust reasoning: Integrating rule-based and similarity-based reasoning. *Artificial Intelligence, 75,* 241–295.

Sun, R. (1999). Accounting for the computational basis of consciousness: A connectionist approach. *Consciousness and Cognition, 8,* 529–565.

Sun, R. (2002). *Duality of the Mind.* Mahwah, NJ: Lawrence Erlbaum.

Sun, R., & Zhang, X. (2006). Accounting for a variety of reasoning data within a cognitive architecture. *Journal of Experimental and Theoretical Artificial Intelligence, 18*(2), 157–168.

Turing, A. (1950). Computing machinery and intelligence. *Mind, 59*(236), 433–460.

Voronkov, A. (1995). The anatomy of vampire: Implementing bottom-up procedures with code trees. *Journal of Automated Reasoning 15*(2).

Wason, P. (1966). Reasoning. In Brian Foss (Ed.), *New horizons in psychology.* Hammondsworth, UK: Penguin.

Wigner, E. (1960). The unreasonable effectiveness of mathematics in the natural sciences. In *Communications in pure and applied mathematics* (pp. 1–14)., New York: John Wiley and Sons.

Wos, L. (1996). *The automation of reasoning: An experimenter's notebook with* OTTER *Tutorial,* San Diego, CA: Academic Press.

Wos, L., Overbeek, R., Lusk, E., & Boyle, J. (1992). *Automated reasoning: Introduction and applications.* New York: McGraw-Hill.

Yang, Y., Braine, M., & O'Brien, D. (1998). Some empirical justification of one predicate-logic model. In M. Braine & D. O'Brien (Eds.), *Mental logic* (pp. 333–365). Mahwah, NJ: Lawrence Erlbaum.

Yang, Y., & Bringsjord, S. (2001). Mental metalogic: A new paradigm for psychology of reasoning. In *Proceedings of the Third International Conference on Cognitive Science (ICCS 2001)* (pp. 199–204). Hefei, China: Press of the University of Science and Technology of China.

Yang, Y., & Bringsjord, S. (2003). Newell's program, like Hilbert's, is dead; let's move on. *Behavioral and Brain Sciences, 26*(5), 627.

Yang, Y., & Bringsjord, S. (2006). The mental possible worlds mechanism and the lobster problem: An analysis of a complex GRE logical reasoning task. *Journal of Experimental and Theoretical Artificial Intelligence, 18*(2), 157–168.

Yang, Y., & Bringsjord, S. (in press). *Mental metalogic: A new, unifying theory of human and machine reasoning.* Mahway, NJ: Erlbaum.

CHAPTER 6

Constraints in Cognitive Architectures

Niels A. Taatgen and John R. Anderson

1. Introduction

When Turing wrote his famous paper in which he asked whether machines can think and how that could be tested (Turing, 1950), he set out the goal of creating an intelligent machine whose intelligence was indistinguishable from human intelligence. Turing's earlier work (Turing, 1936) proved that the basic digital computer's potential is as great as any conceivable computational device, suggesting that it was only a matter of time before a computer could be developed that was as intelligent as a human. The exponential growth in power did not, however, turn out to make computers more intelligent, leading to a divergence into modern artificial intelligence and the smaller field of cognitive modeling. In modern artificial intelligence, the main goal is to create intelligent programs, with the human intelligence aspect only as a source of inspiration, whereas cognitive modeling has taken the opposite route of focusing on faithfully modeling human intelligence, but not being really interested in creating intelligent programs.

Cognitive architectures are on the one hand echoes of the original goal of creating an intelligent machine faithful to human intelligence and on the other hand attempts at theoretical unification in the field of cognitive psychology.[1] These two aspects imply a duality between functionality and theory. Cognitive architectures should offer functionality, that is, representations and cognitive mechanisms to produce intelligent behavior. More choices in representation and mechanisms offer a larger toolbox to create a model for a certain phenomenon. But cognitive architectures should also be theories. A theory offers only a single and not multiple explanations for a phenomenon. From the theory perspective, having many representations and mechanisms is not a good idea because it increases the probability that many models can fit the same data. Functionality and theory are therefore generally conflicting goals, and different architectures strike a different balance between them.

---

1 Note that we will restrict our discussion to cognitive architectures that have the goal to model psychological phenomena.

There are even cognitive architectures that primarily focus on the functionality aspect and have no or few theoretical claims (e.g., COGENT; Cooper & Fox, 1998).

The term cognitive architecture is an analogy of the term computer architecture (Newell, 1990; see also the discussion in Chapter 1 in this volume). A computer architecture serves as a flexible basis for a programmer to create any program. Similarly, a cognitive architecture allows modelers to create simulation models of human cognition. A model specifies the initial set of knowledge for the architecture to work with. For example, a model of multicolumn addition might consist of a set of simple addition facts and a set of production rules that specify that you have to start in the right column, how to handle carries, and so forth. The classical method of finding this set of knowledge is through task analysis: a careful study of the necessary knowledge and the control structure associated with it. The knowledge specified in the task analysis is then fed into the architecture, which can subsequently make predictions about various aspects of human performance, including reaction times, errors, choices made, eye movements, and functional magnetic resonance imaging (fMRI).

A problem of cognitive models is that it is not easy to assess their validity. One might assume that a model that produces the same behavior as people do is a valid model. However, several different models might produce the same behavior, in which case a different criterion is needed to determine which model is best. Unfortunately, there is no quantitative measure for model validity, but most cognitive modelers agree that the following qualitative factors contribute to the validity of a model:

- *A good model should have as few free parameters as possible.* Many cognitive architectures have free parameters that can be given arbitrary values by the modeler. Because free parameters enable the modeler to manipulate the outcome of the model, increasing the number of free parameters diminishes the model's predictive power (Roberts & Pashler, 2000)
- *A model should not only describe behavior, but should also predict it.* Cognitive models are often made after the experimental data have been gathered and analyzed. A model with high validity should be able to predict performance.
- *A model should learn its own task-specific knowledge.* Building knowledge into a model increases its specificity and may decrease its validity.

As discussed earlier, many current models use task analysis to specify the knowledge that an expert would need to do the task. This violates the validity criterion that a model should acquire task-specific knowledge on its own. Moreover, basing a model on a task analysis of expert performance means that the model is of an expert user whereas the typical user may not have mastered the task being modeled. Useful predictions and a complete understanding of the task requires that models are built starting at the level of a novice and gradually proceeding to become experts in the same way people do. In other words, many applications require building models that not only perform as humans do, but that also learn as human do.

2. Overview of Cognitive Architectures

To discuss the current state of cognitive architectures, we will briefly characterize four prime examples in this section, then examine areas of cognitive modeling, and discuss what constraints the various architectures offer in that area.

2.1. *Soar*

The Soar (States, Operators, And Reasoning) architecture, developed by Laird, Newell, and Rosenbloom (1987; Newell, 1990), is a descendant of the General Problem Solver (GPS), developed by Newell and Simon (1963). Human intelligence, according to the Soar theory, is an approximation of a knowledge system. Newell defines a knowledge system as follows (Newell, 1990):

> A knowledge system is embedded in an external environment, with which it interacts by a set of possible actions. The behavior of the system is the sequence of actions taken in the environment over time. The system has goals about how the environment should be. Internally, the system processes a medium, called knowledge. Its body of knowledge is about its environment, its goals, its actions, and the relations between them. It has a single law of behavior: the system takes actions to attain its goals, using all the knowledge that it has. (p. 50)

According to this definition, the single important aspect of intelligence is the fact that a system uses all available knowledge. Errors due to lack of knowledge are not failures of intelligence, but errors due to a failure in using available knowledge. Both human cognition and the Soar architecture are approximations of an ideal intelligent knowledge system. As a consequence, properties of human cognition that are not directly related to the knowledge system are not central to Soar.

The Soar theory views all intelligent behavior as a form of problem solving. The basis for a knowledge system is the problem-space computational model, a framework for problem solving in which a search process tries to accomplish a goal state through a series of operators. In Soar, all tasks are represented by problem spaces. Performing a certain task corresponds to reaching the goal in a certain problem space. To be able to find the goal in a problem space, knowledge is needed about possible operators, about consequences of operators, and about how to choose between operators if there is more than one available. If a problem (an *impasse* in Soar terms) arises due to the fact that certain knowledge is lacking, resolving this impasse automatically becomes the new goal. This new goal becomes a subgoal of the original goal, which means that once the subgoal is achieved, control is returned to the main goal. The subgoal has its own problem space,

state, and possible set of operators. Whenever the subgoal has been achieved, it passes its results to the main goal, thereby resolving the impasse. Learning is keyed to the subgoaling process: Whenever a subgoal has been achieved, new knowledge is added to the knowledge base to prevent the impasse that produced the subgoal from occurring again. If an impasse occurs because the consequences of an operator are unknown, and in the subgoal these consequences are subsequently found, knowledge is added to Soar's memory about the consequences of that operator. Because Soar can also use external input as part of its impasse resolution process, new knowledge can be incorporated into the learned rules.

Characteristic for Soar is that it is a purely symbolic architecture in which all knowledge is made explicit. Instead of attaching utility or activation to knowledge, it has explicit knowledge about its knowledge. This makes Soar a very constrained architecture in the sense that the only means to model a phenomenon are a single long-term memory, a single learning mechanism, and only symbolic representations. Despite the theoretical advantages of such a constrained theory, current developments in Soar seek to extend the architecture to achieve new functional goals, with more long-term memory systems, subsymbolic mechanisms, and a module to model the effects of emotion on the cognitive system (Nason & Laird, 2004; Marinier & Laird, 2004).

2.2. *ACT-R*

The ACT-R (Adaptive Control of Thought, Rational) theory (Anderson et al., 2004) rests on three important components: *rational analysis* (Anderson, 1990), the distinction between *procedural* and *declarative* memory (Anderson, 1976), and a *modular structure* in which components communicate through *buffers*. According to rational analysis, each component of the cognitive architecture is optimized with respect to demands from the environment, given its computational limitations. If we want to know how a particular aspect of the architecture should function, we first have to look at how this aspect can function as optimally as possible in the environment. Anderson (1990) relates this optimality claim to evolution. An example of this principle is the way choice is implemented in ACT-R. Whenever there is a choice between what strategy to use or what memory element to retrieve, ACT-R will take the one that has the highest utility, which is the choice that has the lowest expected cost while having the highest expected probability of succeeding. This is different from Soar's approach, which would involve finding knowledge to decide between strategies.

The principle of rational analysis can also be applied to task knowledge. Although evolution shapes the architecture, learning shapes knowledge and possibly part of the knowledge acquisition process. Instead of only being focused on acquiring knowledge per se, learning processes should also aim at finding the right representation. This may imply that learning processes have to attempt several different ways to represent knowledge, so that the optimal one can be selected. For example, in a model of the past tense (Taatgen & Anderson, 2002), the model had to choose between an irregular and a regular solution to inflect a word. It chose the more efficient irregular solution for the high-frequency words, because storing the exception is worth the efficiency gain. For low-frequency words, having an efficient exception does not pay off, so the model selected the more economic regular solution.

The second ACT-R foundation is the distinction between *declarative* and *procedural* knowledge. ACT-R has a separate procedural and declarative memory, each of which has their own representation and learning mechanisms. Procedural memory stores productions that can directly act on the current situation. Each of these productions maintains a *utility* value to keep track of its past success. Declarative memory is more passive: Knowledge in it has to be requested explicitly to be accessed. Elements in declarative memory have an *activation* value to track their past use that can model,

among other things, forgetting. Declarative memory also incorporates the function of working memory, making it unnecessary to have a separate working memory. Because ACT-R uses activation and utility values in addition to purely symbolic representations, it is called a hybrid architecture.

The third, and also most recent, foundation of ACT-R is its modular structure. The production system, which forms the core of the architecture, cannot arbitrarily access any information it wants, but has to communicate with other systems through a buffer interface. For example, if the visual module attends new information, it places the encoded information in the visual buffer, after which this information can be accessed by production rules. Although this restricts the power of a single production rule, it does allow each module to do its own processing in parallel with other modules.

Both Soar and ACT-R claim to be based on the principles of rationality, although they define rationality differently. In Soar, rationality means making optimal use of the available knowledge to attain the goal, whereas in ACT-R rationality means optimal adaptation to the environment. Not using all the knowledge available is irrational in Soar, although it may be rational in ACT-R if the costs of using all knowledge are too high. On the other hand, ACT-R takes into account the fact that its knowledge may be inaccurate, so additional exploration is rational. Soar will explore only when there is a lack of knowledge, but has, contrary to ACT-R, some built-in strategies to do so.

2.3. *EPIC*

Although most cognitive architectures start from the perspective of central cognition, the EPIC (Executive-Process Interactive Control) architecture (Meyer & Kieras, 1997) stresses the importance of peripheral cognition as a factor that determines task performance. In addition to a cognitive processor with its associated memory systems, EPIC provides a set of detailed perceptual and motor processors. The perceptual modules are capable of processing stimuli from simulated sensory organs, sending their outputs to working memory. They operate asynchronously, and the time required to process an input depends on the modality, intensity, and discriminability of the stimulus. The time requirements of the perceptual modules, as well as other modules, are based on fixed equations, like Fitts' law, and serve as a main source of constraints.

EPIC's cognitive processor is a parallel matcher: In each cycle, which takes 50 ms, production rules are matched to the contents of working memory. Each rule that matches is allowed to fire, so there is no conflict resolution. It is up to the modeler to prevent this parallel firing scheme from doing the wrong thing. Whereas both Soar and ACT-R have a production firing system that involves both parallel and serial aspects, EPIC has a pure parallel system of central cognition. As a consequence, EPIC predicts that serial aspects of behavior are mainly due to communication between central and peripheral processors and structural limitations of sense organs and muscles. An important aspect of EPIC's modular structure is the fact that all processors can work in parallel. Once the cognitive processor has issued a command to the ocular motor processor to direct attention to a spot, it does not have to wait until the visual processor has processed a new image. Instead, it can do something else. In a dual-task setting the cognitive processor may use this extra time to do processing on the secondary task. EPIC can represent multiple goals in a non-hierarchical fashion, and these goals can be worked on in parallel, provided they do not need the same peripheral resources. If they do, as is the case in experiments where participants have to perform multiple tasks simultaneously, executive processes are needed to coordinate which of the goals belonging to the tasks may access which peripheral processors. Because EPIC's executive processes are implemented by production rules, they do not form a separate part of the system. This makes EPIC very flexible, but it also means that EPIC's theory of central cognition is rather weak, in the sense of having few constraints as a theory, as opposed to a very strong theory of peripheral cognition.

EPIC is mainly focused on expert behavior and presently has no theory of how knowledge is learned. As we will see all the other architectures have picked up EPIC's peripheral modules, but try to have a constrained central cognitive system as well.

2.4. CLARION

The CLARION architecture (Connectionist Learning with Adaptive Rule Induction Online; Sun, 2003; Sun, Slusarz, & Terry, 2005; Sun, Merrill, & Peterson, 2001) has as its main architectural assumption that there is a structural division between explicit cognition and implicit cognition. As a consequence, the architecture has two subsystems, the top and the bottom level, each with their own representations and processes. Furthermore, each of the two levels is subdivided into two systems: action-centered and non-action-centered. This latter distinction roughly corresponds to procedural and declarative, respectively: The action-centered system can directly influence action, whereas the non-action-centered system can only do so indirectly. Learning can be bottom-up, in which case knowledge is first acquired implicitly and serves as a basis for later explicit learning, or top-down, in which case knowledge is acquired explicitly, and implicit learning follows later. A final central assumption of CLARION is that when there is no explicit knowledge available a priori, learning will be bottom-up. Many, but not all, of CLARION's representations use neural networks. In that sense, it is more a true hybrid architecture than ACT-R in having truly connectionist and symbolist characteristics.

The central theory of CLARION is that behavior is a product of interacting implicit (bottom-up) and explicit (top-down) processes, further modulated by a motivational subsystem (which holds, among others, the system's goals) and a meta-cognitive subsystem. The explicit action-centered system has a rule system in which rules map the perceived state onto actions. The implicit action-centered system assigns quality measures to state/action pairs. The final choice of an action is a combination of the values assigned to each action by the explicit and the implicit system. Each of the two systems has its own learning mechanisms: The implicit system uses a combination of reinforcement learning and backpropagation to improve its assessment of state/action pairs based on rewards, whereas the explicit system uses a rule-extraction mechanism that uses extraction, generalization, and specialization to generate new rules. Apart from these two subsystems, each of the other subsystems of CLARION uses their own mechanisms and representations.

3. Constraints on Modeling

As pointed out earlier, in each architecture, there is a tension between functional and theory goals. From the functional perspective, there is a pressure to add features, mechanisms, and systems to the architecture to capture more phenomena. From the theory perspective, there is a pressure to simplify representations and mechanisms, and to remove features that are not strictly necessary from the architecture. The goal of this pressure on simplicity is to keep the possible space of models for a particular phenomenon as small as possible. If an architecture allows many different models of the same phenomenon, there is no a priori method to select the right one. In this section we review how architectures can help constrain the space of possible models. We examine a number of topics that can serve as constraints on modeling and discuss how four architectures offer solutions to help modeling in that topic area. A summary can be found in Table 6.1. Note that not all architectures address all topic areas, so for example, EPIC does not constrain learning because it presently has no theory of learning.

3.1. *Working Memory Capacity*

One of the findings that established cognitive psychology as a field was Miller's experiment in which he found that people can only retain a limited number of unrelated new items in memory (Miller, 1956). This phe-

nomenon quickly became associated with short-term memory and later working memory. More generally, the function of working memory is to maintain a representation of the current task environment. What Miller's and subsequent experiments showed was that the capacity to maintain this representation is limited.

A naive model of working memory is to have a system with a limited number of slots (e.g. the seven suggested by Miller, 1956) that can be used to temporarily store items. Once you run out of slots, items have to be tossed out. Although such a model is an almost direct implementation of the phenomenon on which it is based, it does not work very well as a component in an architecture. Miller's task is about completely unrelated items, but as soon as knowledge *is* related, which is the case in almost any natural situation, the slot-model no longer holds.

A good theory of working-memory capacity can be a powerful source of constraint in a cognitive architecture because it rules out models that can interrelate unrealistically large sets of active knowledge. Although working memory is traditionally viewed from the perspective of *capacity*, a resource that can run out, another perspective is to consider working memory as a *cognitive function*. In the functional approach, limited working memory is not a hindrance, but the ability to separate relevant from irrelevant information. It allows the rest of the cognitive system to act on information that is relevant instead of irrelevant.

3.1.1. CAPACITY LIMITATIONS IN SOAR
An example of a functional approach of working memory is Soar (Young & Lewis, 1999). Young and Lewis explain working memory limitations in terms of what the current set of skills can do in limited time. For example, consider the following three sentences:

1. *The defendant examined the courtroom.*
2. *The defendant examined by the jury was upset.*
3. *The evidence examined by the jury was suspicious.*

Table 6.1: Overview on how architectures constrain aspects of information processing

Process	Architecture	Constraint	Reference
Working memory			
	Soar	Limitations of working memory arise on functional grounds, usually due to lack of reasoning procedures to properly process information.	Young & Lewis (1999).
	ACT-R	Limitations of working memory arise from decay and interference in declarative memory. Individual differences are explained by differences in spreading activation.	Lovett, Reder, & Lebiere (1999).
	CLARION	Limitations of working memory are enforced by a separate working memory with decay (as well as by functional limitations).	Sun & Zhang (2004).
Cognitive performance			
	Soar	A decision cycle in Soar takes 50 ms, although many production rules may fire in parallel leading to the decision.	Newell (1990).
	ACT-R	A production rule takes 50 ms to fire, no parallel firing is allowed. A rule is limited to inspecting the current contents of the perceptual and memory-retrieval systems and initiating motor action and memory-retrieval requests.	Anderson et al. (2004).
	EPIC	Production rules take 50 ms to fire, but parallel firing of rules is allowed.	Meyer & Kieras (1997).
	CLARION	Performance is produced by an implicit (parallel) and explicit (serial) reasoning system that both have an action-centered and a non-action-centered subsystem.	Sun (2003).
Perceptual and motor systems			
	EPIC	Perceptual and motor modules are based on timing from the Model Human Processor (Card, Moran, & Newell, 1983). Modules operate asynchronously alongside central cognition.	Kieras & Meyer (1997).
	ACT-R; Soar; CLARION	Use modules adapted from EPIC.	Byrne & Anderson (2001), Chong (1999), Sun (2003).
Learning			
	Soar	Learning is keyed to so-called impasses, where a subgoal is needed to resolve a choice problem in the main goal.	Newell (1990).
	ACT-R	Learning is based on rational analysis in which knowledge is added and maintained in memory on the basis of expected use and utility.	Anderson et al. (2004).
	CLARION	Learning is a combination of explicit rule extraction/refinement and implicit reinforcement learning.	Sun, Slusarz, & Terry (2005).
Neuroscience			
	ACT-R	Components in ACT-R are mapped onto areas in the brain, producing predictions of fMRI activity.	Anderson (2005).
	CLARION	Uses brain-inspired neural networks as components in the architecture	Sun (2003).

Assuming people read these sentences one word at a time from left to right, the word *examined* is ambiguous in sentences 1 and 2 because they can either be the main verb or the starting verb of a relative clause, but not in sentence 3 because the word *evidence* is inanimate. Just and Carpenter (1992) found that people differ in how they handle sentence 3 and attribute this to working memory capacity: High capacity individuals are able to keep the information that evidence is inanimate in working memory, disambiguating the sentences, whereas low-capacity individuals do not hold that information in memory, forcing them to disambiguate the sentence later, as in sentence 2. Lewis (1996), however, presented a different account of the individual differences based on a Soar model of natural language comprehension. In sentence 3 after reading *examined*, Soar will propose two operators to update the current comprehension of the sentence, one corresponding to each interpretation of the sentence. This will create an impasse, which Soar will try to resolve in a new problem space. Although the Soar model has the knowledge to solve this problem, it takes time, and given the time pressure, the model can revert to selecting the normally preferred disambiguation of interpreting a verb as the main verb, which means it will run into trouble later in the sentence. In this model, the individual differences are not explained by a limit in capacity of working memory as such, because the fact that *evidence* is animate is perfectly available in working memory, but by a limitation of the available knowledge to actually do something with that fact in the given problem context.

3.1.2. CAPACITY LIMITATIONS IN ACT-R

Similarly to Soar, ACT-R has no system that directly corresponds to the notion of working memory capacity. Indeed, ACT-R does not even have a working memory as such. Instead, the function of working memory is tied to several of ACT-R's systems. ACT-R's current task context is maintained in the set of buffers. A buffer is a means for the central production system to correspond to the various modules in the system. For example, there is a visual buffer to hold the representation of the currently attended item in the visual field, there is a retrieval buffer to hold the last item retrieved from declarative memory, and there is a goal item that holds the current goal context. Each of these buffers has a capacity of a single item and is constrained by its function (i.e., vision, manual, retrieval, etc.).

Although the buffers together are the main means of holding the current context, the system that is mainly associated with the notion of working memory capacity is declarative memory. Any new item that enters the system is eventually stored in declarative memory. If the task is to memorize a string of numbers, each of the numbers is stored in memory as separate item that is linked to the other numbers (Anderson & Matessa, 1997). To recall the string of numbers, each of the items must be retrieved successfully. However, as the string of numbers becomes longer, interference and decay in declarative memory decrease the probability that recall is successful, producing the phenomenon of a limited working memory capacity.

Although ACT-R's explanation seems to be closer to a capacity explanation, in the root of the theory the explanation is functional. The purpose of activation in declarative memory is not to model forgetting, but to rank knowledge in order of potential relevance. Knowledge receives a high activation due to frequent past use or a high correlation with the current context because that makes it more available and distinguishable from irrelevant knowledge. From that perspective, working memory capacity is the ability to increase the signal-to-noise ratio in declarative memory, and individuals who are good at increasing this ratio have a high working memory capacity (Lovett, Reder, & Lebiere, 1999).

3.2. *Cognitive Performance*

How powerful is the hum
tem? According to, for e
(1989), the human rea

powerful than a Turing Machine, making it possible for humans to solve problems that are computationally intractable. The challenge for cognitive architectures is, however, not to make the computing machinery more powerful, but to put constraints on the power that is already there, without constraining it so much that it cannot perform certain tasks that humans can perform.

3.2.1. THE SERIAL BOTTLENECK

A recurrent topic of debate in the psychology of human perception and performance is whether there is a central bottleneck in human cognition (Pashler, 1994; Schumacher et al., 2001). In terms of cognitive architectures, the debate is centered between ACT-R and EPIC. In ACT-R, the central production system can only fire one rule at a time. Although each rule firing only takes 50 ms, it limits the number of cognitive steps that can be taken. In EPIC, the central rule system can fire any number of rules in parallel. EPIC can therefore naturally explain dual-tasking experiments in which participants achieve perfect time-sharing. An example of such an experiment is by Schumacher et al. (2001). In that experiment, participants were given a visual stimulus and a tone at the same time. They had to respond to the visual stimulus by pressing a key and to the tone by saying a word. Given sufficient training, participants were eventually able to do the two tasks perfectly in parallel, meaning that their reaction times on each task were the same in the dual-task and in the single-task situation.

For ACT-R, dual-tasking experiments are a challenge. Nevertheless, Byrne and Anderson (2001) constructed a model that was able to perfectly share time between the models, and Taatgen, Anderson, and Byrne made models that can learn the perfect time-sharing that captured not only the eventual performance but also the learning trajectory toward this final performance (Taatgen, 2005; Anderson, Taatgen, & Byrne, 2005). In the ACT-R models, the key to perfect dual-tasking is the fact that most of time consumed in these tasks is needed for either perception or motor actions, especially

when the task is highly trained. The occasional central action is needed to shift attention or to select a response. In the highly trained cases, each of these actions only take a single production rule of 50 ms. Unless the response selection for both tasks has to happen at exactly the same moment (which is unlikely given noise in the perceptual processes), the costs of dual-tasking are very low or absent.

An interesting aspect of the central bottleneck is the way the discussion plays out. With a serial bottleneck, ACT-R has the more constrained theory, because it is always possible to do things serially in EPIC, but one cannot do them in parallel in ACT-R. ACT-R principally has the ability to predict circumstances in which the serial bottleneck constrains performance, whereas EPIC poses no constraints at all. For EPIC to prove its point, it needs to identify a phenomenon or task where ACT-R's serial rule system just does not have the time to do everything that needs to be done. Even when such a phenomenon would be found, it would only prove that ACT-R is wrong and not necessarily that EPIC is right. This example shows that a more constrained architecture almost automatically gains the scientific upper ground, despite (or, as Popper, 1962, would say, because of) the fact that it makes itself vulnerable to refutation.

3.2.2. HIDDEN COMPUTATIONAL POWER

The simplicity of production rules can be deceptive. If production rules can match arbitrary patterns, it is possible to write production rules in which matching a condition is an NP-complete problem (Tambe, Newell, & Rosenbloom, 1990). Production rules in Soar have that nature, and this is why Soar needs a powerful rule-matching algorithm (Rete; see Forgy, 1982). Although powerful rules offer a great deal of flexibility, they underconstrain what can be done in a single production-matching cycle. To counter this, Soar modelers try to refrain from writing rules that use the full Rete power. In CLARION (Sun, 2003), on the other hand, the rule system (the explicit, action-centered system) may be implemented in a neural network. Given the localist nature of neural networks, there is no hidden computational power, producing a more constrained system. ACT-R also has a constrained production system: It can only match items in its buffers. This implies that it cannot match arbitrary patterns in declarative memory, but can only retrieve items one at a time. A complex match of information might therefore takes up multiple retrieval steps, and is in no way a fail-safe process. ACT-R's performance system may eventually prove to be too restrictive, preventing it from fulfilling all functional goals.

3.3. *Perceptual and Motor Systems*

Perceptual and motor systems are potentially a strong source of constraint, because the perceptual and motor actions can be registered more precisely in experiments than cognitive actions, and because the psychophysical literature offers precise predictions about the timing of these actions. The EPIC architecture (Meyer & Kieras, 1997) is based on this premise.

The perceptual-motor modules in EPIC can handle only a single action at a time, and each of these actions takes a certain amount of time. Although a module can do only one thing at a time, expert behavior on a task is exemplified by skillful interleaving of perceptual, cognitive, and motor actions. EPIC's modules incorporate mathematical models of the time it takes to complete operations that are based on empirical data. The knowledge of the model is represented using production rules.

An example of how perceptual and motor constraints can inform a model is menu search (Hornof & Kieras, 1997). The task was to find a label in a pull-down menu as quickly as possible. Perhaps the simplest model of such a task is the serial-search model in which the user first attends to the top item on the list and compares it to the label being searched for. If the item does not match the target, the next item on the list is checked; otherwise, the search is terminated. An EPIC model based on this naive serial-search strategy grossly overes-

timates actual search time (obtained with human subjects), except when the target is in the first position to be searched. For example, if the menu item is in position 10, the serial-search model predicts that finding the item takes 4 seconds, whereas participants only need approximately 1.6 seconds.

Hornof and Kieras (1997) propose an alternative model, the overlapping search model that exploits the parallelism of the cognitive system. Instead of waiting for the cognitive system to finish deciding whether or not the requested label is found; the eye moves on to the next item in the list while the first item is still being evaluated. Such a strategy results in the situation that the eye has to move back to a previous item in the list once it has been decided that the item has been found; but this is a small price to pay for the speed-up this parallelism produces. Parallelism is allowed in EPIC as long as perceptual-motor modules do one thing at a time. In practice, the most influential constraint is posed by the duration of actions. For example, in the serial-search model, the parameter that influences the search time could, in theory, be changed to make this (incorrect) model match the data. EPIC precludes this from occurring because an eye-movement takes a certain amount of time, as does a decision as to whether the label is correct or not, such that the data can only be explained if these actions occur in parallel.

The menu-search example shows that although the perceptual and motor systems in EPIC provide strong constraints, central cognition is underconstrained in the sense that it allows both correct and incorrect models of menu search. EPIC's perceptual and motor modules, however, have proved to be so powerful as constraints that all the other architectures (ACT-R, Soar, and CLARION) have copied them.

3.4. *Learning*

As we mentioned in the introduction, a desirable feature of a model is that it learns its own knowledge. In the classical modeling paradigm, the only constraints placed on the knowledge come from the architecture and task analysis, and this usually leaves the knowledge specification partly up to the whim of the modeler. A more constrained approach is to have a model that learns its own knowledge. A weak variant of this type of modeling is to supply the model with some initial method that becomes faster through learning. For example, in an ACT-R model of alphabet-arithmetic (Anderson & Lebiere, 1998), the task is to verify additions using letters and numbers, like $G + 3 = J$. The model's initial strategy is to find the answer through a counting process. But because it stores its answers, the model gradually accumulates addition facts in declarative memory, allowing it to give a direct answer instead of having to count. Although the model learns the new addition facts, it already starts out with the production rules that can count and with the production rules that attempt retrieval of initially nonexisting addition facts.

3.4.1. LEARNING FROM DIRECT INSTRUCTION

A more ambitious approach is to have a model that learns all of its own task-specific knowledge through either instruction or feedback. An example in Soar of such a system is Instructo-Soar (Huffman & Laird, 1995). Instructo-Soar can learn to carry out commands in natural language. If it does not know how to perform a certain command, it will ask for an instruction. A sample dialog from Huffman and Laird (1995) is as follows (Soar's questions are in italics):

Push the green button.
  That's a new one. How do I do that?
  Move to the grey table.
  Ok. What next?
  Move above the green button.
    How do I do that?
    Move the arm up.
    Oh, I see! What next?
  Move down.
  Ok, What next?
  The operator is finished. (p. 273)

In this example, Soar receives instructions on how to push a green button. The indentation represents the structure of the problem solving, with each level of indentation an impasse that has to be resolved. Soar's learning mechanism will learn new rules to resolve similar cases in the future. For example, after this exchange, Soar will know how to move above things and how to push buttons. One of the challenges is to make the right generalization: Instead of learning how to push buttons, another generalization might have been a procedure to push green things. To make the right generalization, Soar used background knowledge to reason out that green is not a relevant attribute for pushing things. An alternative to knowledge-based generalization is CLARION's bottom-up generalization, in which associations between state, action, and success are first gathered by the implicit learning process. These bottom-up associations then gradually inform the rule-extraction mechanism to make the right generalization. So instead of making inferences about colors and buttons CLARION would rather induce out of experiences that colors do not matter but buttons do.

3.4.2. INTERPRETING INSTRUCTIONS STORED IN MEMORY

Instead of direct instruction, a model can also be taught what to do by memorizing an initial set of instructions. Several ACT-R models are based on this paradigm (Taatgen & Lee, 2003; Anderson et al., 2004; Taatgen, 2005). The idea is that the system first reads instructions that it then stores in declarative memory. When the task is performed, these instructions are retrieved from memory and carried out by production rules. These production rules are not specific for the task, but rather represent general skills, like pushing buttons, finding things on the screen, comparing items, and so forth. The declarative instructions string the general skills together to produce task-specific behavior. The cycle of retrieving and interpreting instructions from memory can explain many aspects of novice behavior. Performance is slow because the process of retrieving an instruction from memory is a time-consuming process during which the system cannot do much else. It is serial because only one instruction is active at the same time, making it impossible to do two steps in parallel. It is prone to errors, because instructions may have been forgotten, requiring the model to reconstruct them through a time-consuming problem-solving process. It also puts heavy demands on working memory capacity: Both instructions and temporary information have to be stored and retrieved from declarative memory, making it the main bottleneck of novice processing. Because declarative memory is the bottleneck, it is almost impossible to do other tasks in parallel that also make demands on declarative memory.

Novice behavior is gradually transformed into expert behavior through a knowledge compilation process (*production compilation*, Taatgen & Anderson, 2002). Production compilation combines two existing rules into one new rule, while substituting any memory retrieval in between those rules into the new rule. If the memory retrieval in between the two rules is an instruction, this instruction is effectively encoded into the newly learned rule, creating a production rule that is specific to the task. Production learning in ACT-R therefore gradually transforms task-specific declarative knowledge and general production rules into task-specific production rules. These newly learned rules exhibit many characteristics of expert behavior. They are no longer tied to a linear sequence of instructions, so they can be used out of sequence whenever they apply, allowing parallel performance and increased flexibility for carrying out a task (Taatgen, 2005).

Although models that learn from instructions cannot yet directly parse natural language, they do offer more constrained models than models that are given expert knowledge right away. Not all the expert models that can be encoded using production rules are learnable, and those that are not can therefore be ruled out. In addition to that, the fact that the model learns its knowledge offers the opportunity to match predictions about the learning trajectory to human data. This means that some expert models that are learnable in the sense that the knowledge could be produced by the mechanisms in the architecture can still be ruled out because their learning trajectory does not match the human data.

3.4.3. FROM IMPLICIT TO EXPLICIT LEARNING

One other way for a model to obtain its knowledge is by discovering regularities in the environment. Although many classical models of discovery focus on explicit discovery processes, many modern models start from the assumption that knowledge is often learned implicitly. In, for example, the sugar factory experiment by Berry and Broadbent (1984), participants have to decide how many workers they should send into the factory each day to achieve some target output. The output depends not only on the number of workers, but also on the production of the previous day. Although participants in the experiment generally do not explicitly discover the relationship, they do get better at adjusting the number of workers in the course of the experiment. This and similar experiments suggest that there is some unconscious component to learning, implicit learning, that improves our performance without awareness. Several models have been proposed to capture this effect. An ACT-R model by Wallach (Taatgen & Wallach, 2002) stores examples of input-output relations in declarative memory and retrieves the example that has the highest activation and similarity to the current situation. This model never gains explicit knowledge of the relationships in the task, but achieves better performance by learning a representative set of examples.

Sun et al. (2005) have modeled an extension to the original experiment, in which participants were explicitly taught particular input-output pairs in some conditions, or were given simple heuristic rules. In the control, no-explicit-training version of the model, the implicit level of CLARION was solely responsible for picking up the regularities in the task. In the instructed version of the model, the explicitly given instructions were represented in CLARION's explicit memory, driving the implicit learning processes together with experience. The explicit instructions provided a performance boost in the data, which was successfully captured by the model.

3.5. *Constraints from Neuroscience*

Human cognition is implemented in the brain. This fact can offer additional sources of constraint in a cognitive architecture. The architecture of the brain offers two levels of constraints: at the level of individual neurons and their interconnections, and at the level of global brain structures.

3.5.1. CONSTRAINTS AT THE LEVEL OF INDIVIDUAL BRAIN CELLS

The actual substrate of cognition is an interconnected network of neurons. Whether or not this is a significant source of constraint is open to debate. One view is that brain cells implement some virtual architecture and that the characteristics of brain cells are irrelevant for an understanding of cognition (e.g., Newell, 1990). A more moderate version of this point of view is adapted by the ACT-R architecture (Anderson & Lebiere, 2003). In that view, the main level of abstraction to study cognition is higher than the level of brain cells. However, Lebiere has implemented a neural network version of ACT-R that is functionally identical to the regular implementation. Nevertheless, this model proved to supply some additional restrictions on the architectures, for example, the restriction that declarative memory can only retrieve one item at a time.

CLARION (Sun, 2003) takes the point of view that elements and mechanisms that resemble neurons are an important source of constraint on the architecture. Many of CLARION's subsystems are composed from neural networks. This offers additional constraints, because neural networks are less easy to "program" than symbolic models. CLARION is still a hybrid architecture, with both symbolic and subsymbolic aspects. One can go even further and design an architecture completely built out of neural network components. Leabra (O'Reilly & Munakata, 2000) is an example of such an architecture. The challenge with an architecture built out of simulated neurons is that it has to deal with a number computational problems that are trivial to partly symbolic architectures. A first problem is the *binding problem*, the problem of how the cognitive systems group features together, like associating a filler with a role or a value with a variable or attribute (Fodor & Pylyshyn, 1988). Given the large number of possible combinations of attributes and values, it is not feasible that each combination already has a prewired connection that can be activated, so some other means must be found to temporarily connect concepts together. A second problem is called *catastrophic interference* (McCloskey & Cohen, 1989), which refers to the fact that many networks unlearn previously learned knowledge when new knowledge is presented. A third problem is *serial behavior*. Although networks perform particularly well with respect to massively parallel performance, it is much harder to let them do steps that have to be performed in a certain serial order. The three problems might seem to be an argument against neural network architectures, but they may turn out to be the opposite, because overcoming these problems will offer new constraints on the architecture. In fact, for each of the three problems, solutions have been proposed. One of the solutions of the binding problem is Smolensky's (1990) tensor product system. There are several solutions to the catastrophic interference problem, for example McClelland, McNaughton, and O'Reilly's (1995) solution to have a slow (cortical) and fast (hippocampal) learning system, now implemented in the Leabra (O'Reilly & Munakata, 2000) system. Serial behavior can be achieved partially by recurrent networks (e.g., Elman, 1990), although not with the full flexibility that symbolic systems offer. A neural network cognitive architecture that would offer solutions to each of these problems could make a very strong theory (Sun, 2003).

3.5.2. CONSTRAINTS AT THE GLOBAL BRAIN ARCHITECTURE LEVEL

Recent advances in brain imaging have allowed neuroscientists to build increasingly finer-grained theories of what the functions of various regions in the brain are and how these regions are interconnected. The result is a map of interconnected, functionally labeled regions. What brain imaging does not provide is the actual processing in these regions. Cognitive architectures can provide processing theories constrained by the processing map of the brain. ACT-R (Anderson, 2005; Anderson et al., 2004) has mapped its buffers and production system onto brain regions and is capable of making predictions of brain activity on the basis of a cognitive model. For example, in a study in which children had to learn to solve algebra equations, the ACT-R model predicted how activity in several brain areas would differ with problem difficulty and the effects of learning (Anderson, 2005).

4. Conclusions

The viewpoint of cognitive constraint is different from the perspective of how much functionality an architecture can provide, as expressed by, for example, Anderson and Lebiere (2003). Anderson and Lebiere have elaborated Newell's (1990) list of constraints that are mainly (but not all) functional goals (e.g., use natural language). Although both functionality and strength as a theory are important for a cognitive architecture, modelers tend to focus on functionality, and the critics tend to focus on theory strength. One symptom of the fact that cognitive architectures are still relatively weak theories is that few predictions are made, as opposed to fitting a model onto data after the experiment has been done (but see Salvucci & Macuga, 2002, and Taatgen, van Rijn, & Anderson, 2007, for examples of successful predictive research). A research culture in which modelers would routinely model their experiment *before* they would conduct the experiment would create a much better research environment, one in which confirmed predictions would be evidence for theory strength and in which failed predictions would be great opportunities to strengthen the theory. For this research strategy to work, it is necessary that architectures limit the number of possible models for a particular phenomenon. Alternatively, attempts could be made to rank the possible space of models with the goal of identifying the most plausible one based on nonarchitectural criteria. Chater and Vitányi (2003) argue, following a long tradition in science in general, that the most simple explanation should be preferred. More specific in the architecture context, Taatgen (2007) argues that if there is a choice between multiple models, the model with the most simple control structure should be preferred.

This is also the great promise for the field: As architectures become stronger theories, they can go beyond modeling small experimental tasks and provide a synergy that can lead to the more ambitious functional goals to make cognitive architectures truly intelligent systems.

References

Anderson, J. R. (1976). *Language, memory and thought*. Mahwah, NJ: Lawrence Erlbaum.

Anderson, J. R. (1990). *The adaptive character of thought*. Mahwah, NJ: Lawrence Erlbaum.

Anderson, J. R. (2005). Human symbol manipulation within an integrated cognitive architecture. *Cognitive Science, 29*(3), 313–341.

Anderson, J. R., Bothell, D., Byrne, M. D., Douglass, S., Lebiere, C., & Qin, Y. (2004). An integrated theory of mind. *Psychological Review, 111*(4), 1036–1060.

Anderson, J. R., & Lebiere, C. L. (1998). *The atomic components of thought*. Mahwah, NJ: Lawrence Erlbaum.

Anderson, J. R., & Lebiere, C. L. (2003). The Newell test for a theory of cognition. *Behavioral & Brain Sciences, 26*, 587–637.

Anderson, J. R., & Matessa, M. P. (1997). A production system theory of serial memory. *Psychological Review, 104*, 728–748.

Anderson, J. R., Taatgen, N. A., & Byrne, M. D. (2005). Learning to achieve perfect time sharing: Architectural implications of Hazeltine, Teague, & Ivry (2002). *Journal of Experimental Psychology: Human Perception and Performance, 31*(4), 749–761.

Berry, D. C., & Broadbent, D. E. (1984). On the relationship between task performance and associated verbalizable knowledge. *The Quarterly Journal of Experimental Psychology, 36A,* 209–231.

Byrne, M. D., & Anderson, J. R. (2001). Serial modules in parallel: The psychological refractory period and perfect time-sharing. *Psychological Review, 108,* 847–869.

Card, S. K., Moran, T. P., & Newell, A. (1983). *The psychology of human-computer interaction.* Hillsdale, NJ: Lawrence Erlbaum.

Chater, N., & Vitányi, P. (2003). Simplicity: A unifying principle in cognitive science? *Trends in Cognitive Sciences, 7*(1), 19–22.

Chong, R. S. (1999). *Modeling dual-task performance improvement: Casting executive process knowledge acquisition as strategy refinement.* Unpublished doctoral dissertation, University of Michigan.

Cooper, R., & Fox, J. (1998). COGENT: A visual design environment for cognitive modelling. *Behavior Research Methods, Instruments, & Computers, 30,* 553–564.

Elman, J. L. (1990). Finding structure in time. *Cognitive Science, 14,* 179–211.

Fodor, J. A., & Pylyshyn, Z. W. (1988). Connectionism and cognitive architecture: A critical analysis. *Cognition, 28,* 3–71.

Forgy, C. L. (1982). Rete: A fast algorithm for the many object pattern match problem. *Artificial Intelligence, 19,* 17–37.

Hornof, A. J., & Kieras, D. E. (1997). Cognitive modeling reveals menu search is both random and systematic. In *Proceedings of CHI-97* (pp. 107–114). New York: Association for Computing Machinery.

Huffman, S. B., & Laird, J. E. (1995). Flexibly instructable agents. *Journal of Artificial Intelligence Research, 3,* 271–324.

Just, M. A., & Carpenter, P. A. (1992). A Capacity theory of comprehension: Individual differences in working memory. *Psychological Review, 99,* 122–149.

Kieras, O. E., & Meyer, D. E. (1997). A computational theory of executive cognitive process and multiple-task performance: Part 1. *Psychological Review, 104*(1), 3–65.

Laird, J. E., Newell, A., & Rosenbloom, P. S. (1987). SOAR: An architecture for general intelligence. *Artificial Intelligence, 33,* 1–64.

Lewis, R. L. (1996). Interference in short-term memory: The magical number two (or three)

in sentence processing. *Journal of Psycholinguistic Research, 25,* 9–115.

Lovett, M. C., Reder, L. M., & Lebiere, C. (1999). Modeling working memory in a unified architecture: An ACT-R perspective. In A. Miyake & P. Shah (Eds.), *Models of working memory* (pp. 135–182). Cambridge, UK: Cambridge University Press.

Marinier, R. P., & Laird, J. E. (2004). Toward a comprehensive computational model of emotions and feelings. In *Proceedings of the Sixth International Conference on Cognitive Modeling* (pp. 172–177). Mahwah, NJ: Lawrance Erlbaum.

McClelland, J. L., McNaughton, B. L., & O'Reilly, R. C. (1995). Why there are complementary learning systems in the hippocampus and neocortex: Insights from the successes and failures of connectionist models of learning and memory. *Psychological Review, 102,* 419–457.

McCloskey, M., & Cohen, N. J. (1989). Catastrophic interference in connectionist networks: The sequential learning problem. In G. H. Bower (Ed.), *The psychology of learning and motivation, vol. 24* (pp. 109–164). San Diego, CA: Academic Press.

Meyer, D. E., & Kieras, D. E. (1997). A computational theory of executive cognitive processes and multiple-task performance. Part 1. Basic mechanisms *Psychological Review, 104,* 2–65.

Miller, G. A. (1956). The magic number seven, plus or minus two: Some limits on our capacity for processing information. *Psychological Review, 63,* 81–97.

Nason, S., & Laird, J. E. (2004). Soar-RL: Integrating reinforcement learning with Soar. In *Proceedings of the Sixth International Conference on Cognitive Modeling* (pp. 208–213). Mahwah, NJ: Lawrence Erlbaum.

Newell, A. (1990). *Unified theories of cognition.* Cambridge, MA: Harvard University Press.

Newell, A., & Simon, H. A. (1963). GPS, a program that simulates human thought. In E. A. Feigenbaum & J. Feldman (Eds.), *Computers and thought* (pp. 279–293). New York: McGraw-Hill.

O'Reilly, R. C., & Munakata, Y. (2000). *Computational explorations in cognitive neuroscience.* Cambridge, MA: MIT Press.

Pashler, H. (1994). Dual-task interference in simple tasks: Data and theory. *Psychological Bulletin, 116,* 220–244.

Penrose, R. (1989). *The emperor's new mind.* Oxford, UK: Oxford University Press.

Popper, K. R. (1962). *Conjectures and refutations: The growth of scientific knowledge.* New York: Basic Books.

Roberts, S., & Pashler, H. (2000). How persuasive is a good fit? A comment on theory testing. *Psychological Review, 107,* 358–367.

Salvucci, D. D., & Macuga, K. L. (2002). Predicting the effects of cellular-phone dialing on driver performance. *Cognitive Systems Research, 3,* 95–102.

Schumacher, E. H., Seymour, T. L., Glass, J. M., Fencsik, D. E., Lauber, E. J., Kieras, D. E., et al. (2001). Virtually perfect time sharing in dual-task performance: Uncorking the central cognitive bottleneck. *Psychological Science, 12*(2), 101–108.

Smolensky, P. (1990). Tensor product variable binding and the representation of symbolic structures in connectionist networks. *Artificial Intelligence, 46,* 159–216.

Sun, R. (2003). A tutorial on Clarion. Technical report. Cognitive Science Department, Rensselaer Polytechnic Institute. Retrieved December 6, 2005, from http://www.cogsci. rpi. edu/~rsun/ sun.tutorial.pdf.

Sun, R., Merrill, E., & Peterson, T. (2001). From implicit skills to explicit knowledge: A bottom-up model of skill learning. *Cognitive Science, 25*(2), 203–244.

Sun, R., Slusarz, P., & Terry, C. (2005). The interaction of the explicit and the implicit in skill learning: A dual-process approach. *Psychological Review, 112*(1), 159–192.

Sun, R., & Zhang, X. (2004). Top-down versus bottom-up learning in cognitive skill acquisition. *Cognitive Systems Research, 5*(1), 63–89.

Taatgen, N. A. (2005). Modeling parallelizationand speed improvement in skill acquisition: From dual tasks to complex dynamic skills. *Cognitive Science, 29,* 421–455.

Taatgen, N. A. (2007). The minimal control principle. In W. Gray (Ed.), *Integrated models of cognitive systems* (pp. 368–379). Oxford, UK: Oxford University Press.

Taatgen, N. A., & Anderson, J. R. (2002). Why do children learn to say "broke"? A model of learning the past tense without feedback, *Cognition, 86*(2), 123–155.

Taatgen, N. A., & Lee, F. J. (2003). Production compilation: A simple mechanism to model complex skill acquisition. *Human Factors, 45*(1), 61–76.

Taatgen, N. A., van Rijn, D. H., & Anderson, J. R. (2007). An integrated theory of prospective time interval estimation: the role of cognition, attention and learning. *Psychological Review, 114*(3), 577–598.

Taatgen, N. A., & Wallach, D. (2002). Whether skill acquisition is rule or instance based is determined by the structure of the task. *Cognitive Science Quarterly, 2*(2), 163–204.

Tambe, M., Newell, A., & Rosenbloom, P. S. (1990). The problem of expensive chunks and its solution by restricting expressiveness. *Machine Learning, 5,* 299–348.

Turing, A. (1936). On computable numbers, with an application to the Entscheidungsproblem. *Proceedings of the London Mathematical Society,* 2nd series, 42, 230–265.

Turing A. (1950). Computing machinery and intelligence. *Mind, 59,* 433–460.

Young, R. M., & Lewis, R. L. (1999). The Soar cognitive architecture and human working memory. In A. Miyake & P. Shah (Eds.), *Models of working memory* (pp. 224–256). Cambridge, UK: Cambridge University Press.

Part III

COMPUTATIONAL MODELING OF VARIOUS COGNITIVE FUNCTIONALITIES AND DOMAINS

Computational cognitive modeling has been applied to a wide range of task domains and cognitive functionalities. This part of the book addresses computational modeling of many such domains and functionalities.

The chapters in this part describe various computational modeling efforts that researchers in this field have undertaken concerning major cognitive functionalities and domains.

They survey and explain modeling research on memory, concepts, learning, reasoning, decision making, vision, motor control, language, development, scientific ecplanation, social interaction, and so on, in terms of detailed computational mechanisms and processes. The computational models covered here shed new light on corresponding cognitive phenomena and data.

CHAPTER 7

Computational Models of Episodic Memory

Kenneth A. Norman, Greg Detre, and Sean M. Polyn

1. Introduction

The term *episodic memory* refers to the ability to recall previously experienced events and to recognize things as having been encountered previously. Over the past several decades, research on the neural basis of episodic memory has increasingly come to focus on three structures:

- The hippocampus supports recall of specific details from previously experienced events (for neuroimaging evidence, see, e.g., Davachi, Mitchell, & Wagner, 2003; Dobbins et al., 2003; Eldridge et al., 2000; Ranganath et al., 2003; for a review of relevant lesion data, see Aggleton & Brown, 1999).
- Perirhinal cortex computes a scalar *familiarity signal* that discriminates between studied and nonstudied items (for neuroimaging evidence, see, e.g., Brozinsky et al., 2005; Gonsalves et al., 2005; Henson et al., 2003; for neurophysiological evidence, see, e.g., Li, Miller, & Desimone, 1993; Xiang & Brown, 1998; for evidence that perirhinal cortex can

support near-normal levels of familiarity-based recognition on its own, after focal hippocampal damage, see, e.g., Fortin Wright, & Eichenbaum, 2004; Yonelinas et al., 2002; but see, e.g., Manns et al., 2003, for an opposing viewpoint).

- Prefrontal cortex plays a critical role in *memory targeting*: In situations where the bottom-up retrieval cue is not sufficiently specific to trigger activation of memory traces in the medial temporal lobe, prefrontal cortex acts to flesh out the retrieval cue by actively maintaining additional information that specifies the to-be-retrieved episode (for reviews of how prefrontal cortex contributes to episodic memory, see Fletcher & Henson, 2001; Schacter, 1987; Shimamura, 1994; Simons & Spiers, 2003).

Although there is general agreement about the roles of these three structures, there is less agreement about how (mechanistically) these structures enact the roles specified previously. This chapter reviews two kinds of models: biologically based models that are meant to address how the

al structures mentioned previously conte to recognition and recall, and ab-
t models that try to describe the mental
algorithms that support recognition and recall judgments, without specifically addressing how these algorithms might be implemented in the brain.

1.1. *Weight-Based Versus Activation-Based Memory Mechanisms*

Within the realm of biologically based
episodic memory models, one can make a
distinction between *weight-based* and *activation-based* memory mechanisms (O'Reilly
& Munakata, 2000). Weight-based memory mechanisms support recognition and recall by making lasting changes to synaptic
weights at study. Activation-based memory
mechanisms support recognition and recall
of an item by actively maintaining the pattern of neural activity elicited by the item
during the study phase. Activation-based
memory mechanisms can support recognition and recall after short delays. However,
the ability to recognize and recall stimuli after longer delays depends on changes
to synaptic weights. This chapter primarily
focuses on weight-based memory mechanisms, although Section 4 discusses interactions between weight-based and activation-
based memory mechanisms.

1.2. *Outline*

Section 2 of this chapter provides an
overview of biological models of episodic
memory, with a special focus on the
Complementary Learning Systems model
(McClelland, McNaughton, & O'Reilly,
1995; Norman & O'Reilly, 2003). Section 3
reviews abstract models of episodic memory. Section 4 discusses how both abstract
and biological models have been extended
to address *temporal context memory*: our ability to focus retrieval on a particular time
period, to the exclusion of others. This section starts by describing the abstract Temporal Context Model (TCM) developed by
Howard and Kahana (2002). The remainder

of Section 4 discusses how temporal context memory can be instantiated in neural
systems.

2. Biologically Based Models of Episodic Memory

The first part of this section reviews the
Complementary Learning Systems (CLS)
model (McClelland et al., 1995) and how
it has been applied to understanding hippocampal and neocortical contributions to
episodic memory (Norman & O'Reilly,
2003). Section 2.2 discusses some alternative views of how neocortex contributes to
episodic memory.

2.1. *The CLS Model*

The CLS model incorporates several widely
held ideas about the division of labor between hippocampus and neocortex that
have been developed over many years by
many different researchers (e.g., Aggleton
& Brown, 1999; Becker, 2005; Burgess
& O'Keefe, 1996; Eichenbaum, Otto, &
Cohen, 1994; Grossberg, 1976; Hasselmo
& Wyble, 1997; Marr, 1971; McNaughton
& Morris, 1987; Moll & Miikkulainen, 1997;
O'Keefe & Nadel, 1978; Rolls, 1989; Scoville & Milner, 1957; Sherry & Schacter,
1987; Squire, 1992; Sutherland & Rudy,
1989; Teyler & Discenna, 1986; Treves &
Rolls, 1994; Wu, Baxter, & Levy, 1996;
Yonelinas, 2002). According to the CLS
model, neocortex forms the substrate of
our internal model of the structure of the
environment. In contrast, hippocampus is
specialized for rapidly and automatically
memorizing patterns of cortical activity, so
they can be recalled later (based on partial cues). The model posits that neocortex
learns incrementally; each training trial results in relatively small adaptive changes in
synaptic weights. These small changes allow cortex to gradually adjust its internal
model of the environment in response to
new information. The other key property of
neocortex (according to the model) is that

it assigns similar (overlapping) representations to similar stimuli. Use of overlapping representations allows cortex to represent the shared structure of events and therefore makes it possible for cortex to generalize to novel stimuli based on their similarity to previously experienced stimuli. In contrast, the model posits that hippocampus assigns distinct, *pattern-separated* representations to stimuli, regardless of their similarity. This property allows hippocampus to rapidly memorize arbitrary patterns of cortical activity without suffering unacceptably high (catastrophic) levels of interference.

2.1.1. APPLYING CLS TO EPISODIC MEMORY

CLS was originally formulated as a set of high-level principles for understanding hippocampal and cortical contributions to memory. More recently, Norman and O'Reilly (2003) implemented hippocampal and cortical networks that adhere to CLS principles and used the models to simulate episodic memory data. Learning was implemented in these simulations using a simple Hebbian rule, called *instar learning* by Grossberg (1976) and *Conditional Principal Components Analysis (CPCA) Hebbian learning* by O'Reilly and Munakata (2000):

$$\Delta w_{ij} = \epsilon y_j(x_i - w_{ij}). \qquad (7.1)$$

In this equation, x_i is the activation of sending unit i, y_j is the activation of receiving unit j, w_{ij} is the strength of the connection between i and j, and ϵ is the learning rate parameter. This rule has the effect of strengthening connections between active sending and receiving neurons, and weakening connections between active receiving neurons and inactive sending neurons.

In both the hippocampal and cortical networks, to-be-memorized items are represented by patterns of excitatory activity that are distributed across multiple units (simulated neurons) in the network. Excitatory activity spreads from unit to unit via positive-valued synaptic weights. The overall level of excitatory activity in the network is controlled by a *feedback inhibition* mechanism that samples the amount of excitatory activity in a particular subregion of the model and sends back a proportional amount of inhibition (O'Reilly & Munakata, 2000).

The CLS model instantiates the idea (mentioned in the Introduction) that hippocampus contributes to recognition memory by *recalling* specific studied details and that cortex contributes to recognition by computing a scalar *familiarity* signal. In this respect, the CLS model belongs to a long tradition of *dual-process* theories of recognition memory that posit conjoint contributions of recall and familiarity to recognition performance (see Yonelinas, 2002, for a review of dual-process theories). The next two sections provide an overview of the CLS hippocampal and cortical networks, and how they have been applied to episodic memory data. For additional details regarding the CLS model (equations and key model parameters), see the Appendix; also, a working, documented version of the CLS model can be downloaded from http://compmem.princeton.edu/.

2.1.2. CLS MODEL OF HIPPOCAMPAL RECALL

The job of the CLS hippocampal model is to memorize patterns of activity in entorhinal cortex (EC), the neocortical region that serves as an interface between hippocampus and the rest of neocortex, so these patterns can be retrieved later in response to partial cues. The architecture of the model (shown in Figure 7.1) reflects a broad consensus regarding key anatomical and physiological characteristics of different hippocampal subregions (Squire, Shimamura, & Amaral, 1989) and how these subregions contribute to the overall goal of memorizing cortical patterns. Although the fine-grained details of other hippocampal models may differ slightly from the CLS model, the "big picture" story (reviewed later) is remarkably consistent across models (Becker, 2005; Meeter, Murre, & Talamini, 2004; Hasselmo & Wyble, 1997; Rolls, 1989).

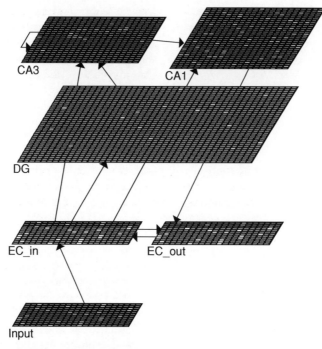

Figure 7.1. Diagram of the Complementary Learning Systems hippocampal network. The hippocampal network links input patterns in entorhinal cortex (EC) to relatively nonoverlapping (pattern separated) sets of units in region CA3. The dentate gyrus (DG) serves to facilitate pattern separation in region CA3. Recurrent connections in CA3 bind together all of the units involved in representing a particular EC pattern; the CA3 representation is linked back to EC via region CA1. Learning in the CA3 recurrent connections, and in projections linking EC to CA3 and CA3 to CA1, makes it possible to recall entire stored EC patterns based on partial cues.

In the brain, EC is split into two layers, a superficial layer that primarily sends input into the hippocampus and a deep layer that primarily receives output from the hippocampus (Witter et al., 2000); in the model, these layers are referred to as EC_in and EC_out. The part of the model corresponding to the hippocampus proper is subdivided into different layers, corresponding to different anatomical subregions of the hippocampus. At encoding, the hippocampal model binds together sets of co-occurring neocortical features (corresponding to a particular episode) by linking co-active units in EC_in to a cluster of units in region CA3. These CA3 units serve as the hippocampal representation of the episode.

In addition to strengthening feedforward connections between EC_in and CA3, recurrent connections between active CA3 units are also strengthened. To allow for recall, active CA3 units are linked back to the original pattern of cortical activity via region CA1. Like CA3, region CA1 also contains a representation of the input pattern. However, unlike the CA3 representation, the CA1 representation is *invertible* – if an item's representation is activated in CA1, well-established connections between CA1 and EC_out allow activity to spread back to the item's representation in EC_out. Thus, CA1 serves to translate between sparse representations in CA3 and more overlapping representations in EC (for more discussion of this issue, see McClelland & Goddard, 1996, and O'Reilly, Norman, & McClelland, 1998).

The projections described earlier are updated using the CPCA Hebbian learning rule during the study phase of the experiment (except for connections between EC and CA1, which are pretrained to form an invertible mapping). At test, when a partial version of a stored EC pattern is presented to the hippocampal model, the model is capable of reactivating the entire CA3 pattern corresponding to that item because of learning (in feedforward and recurrent connections) that occurred at study. Activation then spreads from the item's CA3 representation back to the item's EC representation (via CA1). In this manner, the hippocampal model manages to retrieve a complete version of the EC pattern in response to a partial cue. This process is typically referred to as *pattern completion*.

To minimize interference between episodes, the hippocampal model has a built-in bias to assign relatively nonoverlapping (pattern-separated) CA3 representations to different episodes. Pattern separation occurs because of strong feedback inhibition in CA3, which leads to sparse representations: In the hippocampal model, only the top 4% of units in CA3 (ranked in terms of excitatory input) are active for any given input pattern. The fact that CA3 units are hard to activate reduces the odds that a given unit will be active for any two input patterns, thereby leading to pattern separation.

Pattern separation in CA3 is greatly facilitated by the dentate gyrus (DG). Like CA3, the DG also receives a projection from EC_in. The DG has even sparser representations than CA3 and has a very strong projection to CA3 (the mossy fiber pathway). In effect, the DG can be viewed as selecting a (nearly) unique representation for each stimulus and then forcing that representation onto CA3 via the mossy fiber pathways (see O'Reilly & McClelland, 1994, for a much more detailed treatment of pattern separation in the hippocampus and the role of the DG in facilitating pattern separation). Recently, Becker (2005) has argued that neurogenesis in DG plays a key role in fostering pattern separation: Inserting new neurons and connections into DG ensures that, if two similar patterns are fed into DG on different occasions, they will elicit distinct patterns of DG activity (because the DG connectivity matrix is different on the first vs. second occasion).

To apply the hippocampal model to recognition, Norman and O'Reilly (2003) compared the test cue (presented on the EC_in layer) to the pattern of retrieved information (activated over the EC_out layer). When recalled information matches the test cue, this constitutes evidence that the item was studied; conversely, mismatch between recalled information and the test cue constitutes evidence that the test cue was not studied (e.g., study "rats"; test "rat"; if the hippocampal model recalls that "rats"-plural was studied, not "rat"-singular, this can serve as grounds for rejection of "rat").

2.1.2.1. *Optimizing the Dynamics of the Hippocampal Model.* As discussed by O'Reilly and McClelland (1994), the greatest computational challenge faced by the hippocampal model is dealing with the inherent trade-off between pattern separation and pattern completion. Pattern separation reduces the extent to which storing a new memory trace damages other, previously stored memory traces. However, this tendency to assign distinct hippocampal representations to similar EC inputs can interfere with pattern completion at retrieval: It is very uncommon for retrieval cues to *exactly* match stored patterns; if there is a mismatch between the retrieval cue and the to-be-recalled trace, pattern-separation mechanisms might cause the cue to activate a different set of CA3 units than the original memory trace (so retrieval will not occur). Hasselmo and colleagues (e.g., Hasselmo, 1995; Hasselmo & Wyble, 1997; Hasselmo, Wyble, & Wallenstein, 1996) have also pointed out that pattern completion can interfere with pattern separation: If, during storage of a new memory, the hippocampus recalls related memories such that both old and new memories are simultaneously active at encoding, these memories will become even more tightly associated (due to Hebbian learning between co-active neurons) and thus run the risk of blending together.

To counteract these problems, Hasselmo and others have argued that the hippocampus has an *encoding mode*, where the functional connectivity of the hippocampus is optimized for storage of new memories, and a *retrieval mode*, where the functional connectivity of the hippocampus is optimized for retrieval of stored memory traces that match the current input.

Two of the most prominent optimizations discussed by Hasselmo are:

- The strength of CA3 recurrents should be larger during retrieval mode than encoding mode. Increasing the strength of recurrent connections facilitates pattern completion.
- During encoding mode, the primary influence on CA1 activity should be the current input pattern in EC. During retrieval mode, the primary influence on CA1 activity should be the retrieved ("completed") pattern in CA3.

For discussion of these optimizations as well as others (relating to adjustments in hippocampal learning rates) see Hasselmo et al. (1996).[1]

Hasselmo originally proposed that mode-setting was accomplished by varying the concentration of the neuromodulatory chemical acetylcholine (ACh). Hasselmo and Wyble (1997) present a computational model of this process. According to this model, presenting a novel pattern to the hippocampus activates the basal forebrain, which (in turn) releases ACh into the hippocampus, triggering encoding mode (see Meeter et al., 2004, for a similar model).

---

1 Yet another optimization, not discussed by Hasselmo, would be to reduce the influence of the DG on CA3 at retrieval. As mentioned earlier, the DG's primary function in the CLS model is to foster pattern separation. Thus, reducing the influence of the DG at retrieval should reduce pattern separation and, through this, boost pattern completion (see Becker, 2005, for additional discussion of this point).

For physiological evidence that ACh triggers the key properties of encoding mode (as listed previously), see Hasselmo and Schnell (1994) and Hasselmo, Schnell, and Barkai (1995).

More recently, Hasselmo and Fehlau (2001) have argued that ACh cannot be the only mechanism of mode-setting in the hippocampus, because the temporal dynamics of ACh release are too slow (on the order of seconds) – by the time that ACh is released, the to-be-encoded stimulus may already be gone. Hasselmo and Fehlau (2001) argue that, in order to support more responsive mode-setting, the ACh-based mechanism discussed previously is supplemented by another mechanism that leverages hippocampal theta oscillations (rhythmic changes in the local field potential, at approximately 4–8 Hz in humans). Specifically, they argue that oscillatory changes in the concentration of the neurotransmitter gamma-aminotrityric acid (GABA) cause the hippocampus to flip back and forth between encoding and retrieval modes several times per second – as such, each stimulus is processed (several times) both as a new stimulus to be encoded and as a "reminder" to retrieve other stimuli. Hasselmo, Bodelon, and Wyble (2002) present a detailed computational model of this theta-based mode setting; for physiological evidence in support of this model, see Wyble, Linster, and Hasselmo (2000).

In its current form, the CLS hippocampal model only incorporates a very crude version of mode-setting (such that EC is the primary influence on CA1 during study of new items, and CA3 is the primary influence on CA1 during retrieval). Incorporating the other mode-related optimizations mentioned earlier (e.g., varying the strength of CA3 recurrents to facilitate encoding vs. retrieval) should greatly improve the efficacy of the CLS hippocampal model.

2.1.3. CLS MODEL OF CORTICAL FAMILIARITY

The CLS cortical model consists of an input layer (corresponding to lower regions of the cortical hierarchy), which projects in a

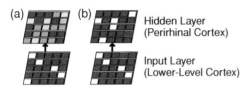

Figure 7.2. Illustration of the sharpening of hidden (perirhinal) layer activity patterns in a miniature version of the Complementary Learning Systems cortical model: (a) shows the network prior to sharpening; perirhinal activity (more active = lighter color) is relatively undifferentiated; (b) shows the network after Conditional Principal Components Analysis Hebbian learning and inhibitory competition produce sharpening; a subset of the perirhinal units are strongly active, whereas the remainder are inhibited.

feedforward fashion to a hidden layer (corresponding to perirhinal cortex). As mentioned earlier, the main function of cortex is to extract statistical regularities in the environment; the two-layer CLS cortical network (where "perirhinal" hidden units compete to encode regularities that are present in the input layer) is meant to capture this idea in the simplest possible fashion.

Because the cortical model uses a small learning rate, it is not capable of pattern completion following limited exposure to a stimulus. However, it is possible to extract a scalar signal from the cortical model that reflects stimulus familiarity: In the cortical model, as items are presented repeatedly, their representations in the upper (perirhinal) layer become *sharper*: Novel stimuli weakly activate a large number of perirhinal units, whereas previously presented stimuli strongly activate a relatively small number of units. Sharpening occurs in the model because Hebbian learning specifically tunes some perirhinal units to represent the stimulus. When a stimulus is first presented, some perirhinal units, by chance, will respond more strongly to the stimulus than other units. These "winning" units get tuned by CPCA Hebbian learning to respond even more strongly to the item the next time it is presented; this increased response triggers an increase in feedback inhibition to

units in the layer, resulting in decreased activation of the "losing" units. This latter property (whereby some initially responsive units drop out of the stimulus representation as it is repeated) is broadly consistent with the neurophysiological finding that some perirhinal neurons show decreased responding as a function of stimulus familiarity (e.g., Xiang & Brown, 1998; Li et al., 1993); see Section 2.2 (Alternative Models of Perirhinal Familiarity), for additional discussion of single-cell-recording data from perirhinal cortex. Figure 7.2 illustrates this sharpening dynamic.[2] In the Norman and O'Reilly (2003) article, cortical familiarity was operationalized by reading out the activation of the k winning units in the perirhinal layer (where k is a model parameter that defines the maximum number of units that are allowed to be strongly active at once), although other methods of operationalizing familiarity are possible.

Because there is more overlap between representations in the cortical model versus the hippocampal model, the familiarity signal generated by the cortical model has very different operating characteristics than the recall signal generated by the hippocampal model: In contrast to hippocampal recall, which only occurs when the test cue is very similar to a specific studied item, the cortical familiarity signal tracks – in a graded fashion – the amount of overlap between the test cue and the full set of studied items. This sensitivity to "global match" is one of the most critical psychological properties of the familiarity signal (for behavioral evidence that familiarity tracks global match, see, e.g., Brainerd & Reyna, 1998; Criss & Shiffrin, 2004; Koutstaal, Schacter, & Jackson, 1999; Shiffrin, Huber, & Marinelli, 1995; see also Section 3 for discussion of how abstract models implement a "global match" familiarity process).

Importantly, although the Norman and O'Reilly (2003) model focuses on the

2 For additional discussion of how competitive learning can lead to sharpening, see, e.g., Grossberg, 1986, Section 23, and Grossberg & Stone, 1986, Section 16.

contribution of perirhinal cortex to familiarity discrimination, the CLS framework is entirely compatible with other theories that have emphasized the role of perirhinal cortex in representing high-level conjunctions of object features (e.g., Barense et al., 2005; Bussey & Saksida, 2002; Bussey, Saksida, & Murray, 2002). The CLS cortical network performs competitive learning of object features in exactly the manner specified by these other models; the "sharpening" dynamic described earlier (which permits familiarity discrimination) is a byproduct of this feature extraction process. Another important point is that, according to the CLS model, perirhinal cortex works just like the rest of cortex. Its special role in familiarity discrimination (and learning of high-level object conjunctions) is attributable to its position at the top of the cortical hierarchy, which allows it to associate a wider range of features and also allows it to respond differentially to novel combinations of these features (when discriminating between old and new items on a recognition test). For additional discussion of this point, see Norman and O'Reilly (2003).

2.1.4. REPRESENTATIVE PREDICTION FROM THE CLS MODEL

Norman and O'Reilly (2003) showed how, taken together, the hippocampal network and cortical network can explain a wide range of behavioral findings from recognition and recall list-learning experiments. Furthermore, because the CLS model maps clearly onto the brain, it is possible to use the model to address neuroscientific data in addition to (purely) behavioral data. Here, we discuss a representative model prediction, relating to how target-lure similarity and recognition test format should interact with hippocampal damage.

The CLS model predicts that cortex and hippocampus can both support good recognition performance when lures are not closely related to studied items. However, when lures are closely related to studied items, hippocampally-based recognition performance should be higher than cortically based recognition performance, because of the hippocampus' ability to assign distinct representations to similar stimuli and its ability to reject lures when they trigger recall that mismatches the test cue. The model also predicts that effects of target-lure similarity should interact with test format. Most recognition tests use a yes-no (YN) format, where test items are presented one at a time, and subjects are asked to label them as old or new. The model predicts that cortex should perform very poorly on YN tests with related lures (because the distributions of familiarity scores associated with studied items and related lures overlap strongly). However, the model predicts that cortex should perform much better when given a *forced choice* between studied items and corresponding related lures (e.g., "rat" and "rats" are presented simultaneously, and subjects have to choose which item was studied). In this situation, the model predicts that the mean difference in familiarity between the studied item and the related lure will be small, but the studied item should reliably be slightly more familiar than the corresponding related lure (thereby allowing for correct responding; see Hintzman, 1988 for additional discussion of this idea). Taken together, these predictions imply that patients with hippocampal damage should perform very poorly on YN tests with related lures. However, the same patients should show relatively spared performance on tests with unrelated lures or when they are given a forced choice between targets and corresponding related lures (because cortex can pick up the slack in both cases). Holdstock et al. (2002) and Mayes et al. (2001) tested these predictions in a patient with focal hippocampal damage and obtained the predicted pattern of results; for additional evidence in support of these predictions, see also Westerberg et al. (2006).

2.1.5. MEMORY DECISION MAKING: A CHALLENGE FOR RECOGNITION MEMORY MODELS

There is one major way in which the CLS model is presently underspecified, namely, in how to combine the contributions of hippocampal recall and cortical familiarity when making recognition decisions. This problem is shared by all dual-process recognition memory models, not just CLS. Norman and O'Reilly (2003) treat recognition decision making as a "black box" that is external to the network model itself (i.e., the decision process is not itself simulated by a neural network). This raises two issues. First, at an abstract level, what algorithm should be implemented by the black box? Second, how could this algorithm be implemented in network form? In their combined cortico-hippocampal simulations, Norman and O'Reilly (2003) used a simple rule in which test items were called "old" if hippocampal recall exceeded a certain value, otherwise, the decision was made based on familiarity (Jacoby, Yonelinas, & Jennings, 1997). This reflects the common assumption that recall is more diagnostic than familiarity. However, the diagnosticity of both recall and familiarity varies from situation to situation. For example, Norman and O'Reilly (2003) discuss how recall of unusual features is more diagnostic than recall of common features. Also, familiarity is less diagnostic when lures are highly similar to studied items versus when lures are less similar to studied items. Ideally, the decision-making algorithm would be able to dynamically weight the evidence provided by recall of a particular feature (relative to familiarity) based on its diagnosticity.

However, even if subjects manage to successfully compute the diagnosticity of each process, there are many reasons why (in a particular situation) subjects might deviate from this diagnosticity-based weighting. For example, several studies have found that dual-task demands hurt recall-based responding more than familiarity-based responding (e.g., Gruppuso, Lindsay, & Kelley, 1997), suggesting that recall-based responding places stronger demands on cognitive resources than familiarity-based responding. If recall-based responding is generally more demanding than familiarity-based responding, this could cause subjects to underattend to recall (even when it is useful). Furthermore, the reward structure of the task will interact with decision weights

(e.g., if the task places a high premium on avoiding false alarms, subjects might attend relatively more to recall; see Malmberg & Xu, 2007, for additional discussion of how subjects weight recall vs. familiarity).

Finally, in constructing a model of memory decision making, it is important to factor in more dynamical aspects of the decision making process. In recent years, models of memory decision making have started to shift away from simple signal-detection accounts (where a cutoff is applied to a static memory strength value), toward models that accumulate evidence across time (see Chapter 10 in this volume). Although these dynamical "evidence-accumulation" models are more complex than models based on signal-detection theory (in the sense that they have more parameters), several researchers have demonstrated that evidence-accumulation models can be implemented using relatively simple neural network architectures (e.g., Usher & McClelland, 2001). As such, the shift to dynamical decision-making models may actually make it easier to construct a neural network model of memory decision-making processes. Overall, incorporating a more accurate model of the decision-making process (in terms of how recall and familiarity are weighted, in terms of temporal dynamics, and in terms of how this process is instantiated in the brain) should greatly increase the predictive utility of extant recognition memory models.

2.2. Alternative Models of Perirhinal Familiarity

Although (as mentioned earlier) the basic tenets of the CLS hippocampal model are relatively uncontroversial, there is much less agreement about whether the CLS cortical model adequately accounts for perirhinal contributions to recognition memory. Recently, the CLS cortical model was criticized by Bogacz and Brown (2003) on the grounds that it has inadequate storage capacity. Bogacz and Brown showed that, when input patterns are correlated with one another, the model's capacity for familiarity discrimination (operationalized as the number of studied stimuli that the network can distinguish from nonstudied stimuli with 99% accuracy) barely increases as a function of network size; because of this, the model's capacity (even in a "brain-sized" network) falls far short of the documented capacity of human recognition memory (e.g., Standing, 1973).

These capacity problems can be traced back to the CPCA Hebbian learning algorithm used by Norman and O'Reilly (2003). As discussed by Norman, Newman, and Perotte (2005), CPCA Hebbian learning is insufficiently judicious in how it adjusts synaptic strengths: It strengthens synapses between co-active units, even if the target memory is already strong enough to support recall, and it weakens synapses between active receiving units and all sending units that are inactive at the end of the trial, even if these units did not actively compete with recall of the target memory. As a result of this problem, CPCA Hebbian learning ends up overrepresenting features that are common to all items in the stimulus set and underrepresenting features that are specific to individual items. Insofar as recognition depends on memory for item-specific features (common features are, by definition, useless for recognition because they are shared by both studied items and lures), this tendency for CPCA Hebbian leaning to underrepresent item-specific features results in poor recognition discrimination. In their article, Bogacz and Brown (2003) also discuss a Hebbian familiarity discrimination model developed by Sohal and Hasselmo (2000). This model operates according to slightly different principles than the CLS cortical model, but it shares the same basic problem (overfocusing on common features) and thus performs poorly with correlated input patterns.

Given these capacity concerns, it is worth exploring how well other, recently developed models of perirhinal familiarity discrimination can address these capacity issues, as well as extant neurophysiological and psychological data on perirhinal contributions to recognition memory. Three

alternative models are discussed here: a model developed by Bogacz and Brown (2003) that uses anti-Hebbian learning to simulate decreased responding to familiar stimuli; a model developed by Meeter, Myers, and Gluck (2005) that shows decreased responding to familiar stimuli because of context-driven adaptation effects; and a model developed by Norman, Newman, Detre, and Polyn (2006) that probes the strength of memories by oscillating the amount of feedback inhibition.

2.2.1. THE ANTI-HEBBIAN MODEL

In contrast to the CLS familiarity model, in which familiarity discrimination was a byproduct of Hebbian feature extraction, the anti-Hebbian model proposed by Bogacz and Brown (2003) posits that separate neural populations in perirhinal cortex are involved in representing stimulus features (on the one hand) versus familiarity discrimination (on the other). Bogacz and Brown argue that neurons involved in familiarity discrimination use an anti-Hebbian learning rule, which weakens the weights from active presynaptic neurons to active postsynaptic neurons and increases the weights from inactive presynaptic neurons. This anti-Hebbian rule causes neurons that initially respond to a stimulus to respond less on subsequent presentations of that stimulus.

The primary advantage of the anti-Hebbian model over the CLS model is improved capacity. Whereas Hebbian learning ends up overrepresenting common features and underrepresenting unique features (resulting in poor overall capacity), anti-Hebbian learning biases the network to ignore common features and to represent what is distinctive or unusual about individual patterns. Bogacz and Brown (2003) present a mathematical analysis showing that the anti-Hebbian model's capacity for familiarity discrimination (given correlated input patterns) is orders of magnitude higher than the capacity of a model trained with Hebbian learning.

With regard to neurophysiological data: There are several salient differences in the predictions made by the anti-Hebbian model versus the CLS cortical model. A foundational assumption of the Bogacz and Brown (2003) model is that neurons showing steady, above-baseline firing versus decreased firing (as a function of stimulus repetition) belong to distinct neural populations: The former group (showing steady responding) is involved in representing stimulus features, whereas the latter group is involved in familiarity discrimination. This view implies that it should be impossible to find a neuron that shows steady responding to some stimuli and decreased responding to other stimuli. In contrast, the CLS cortical model posits that neurons that show steady (above-baseline) or increased firing to a given stimulus are the neurons that won the competition to represent this stimulus, and neurons that show decreased firing are the neurons that lost the competition to represent this stimulus. Furthermore, different neurons will win (vs. lose) the competition for different stimuli. Thus, contrary to the predictions of the Bogacz and Brown (2003) model, it should be possible to find a neuron that shows steady (or increased) responding to one stimulus (because it won the competition to represent that stimulus) and decreased responding to another stimulus (because it lost the competition to represent that stimulus). More data need to be collected to test these predictions.

2.2.2. THE MEETER, MYERS, & GLUCK MODEL

The Meeter et al. (2005) model uses the same basic Hebbian learning architecture as Norman and O'Reilly (2003), with two critical changes. First, they added a neural adaptation mechanism (such that units become harder to activate after a period of sustained activation). Second, they are more explicit in considering how context is represented in the input patterns. According to the Meeter et al. (2005) model, if an item is presented in a particular context (e.g., in a particular room, on a particular computer screen, in a particular font), then the units activated by the item become linked to the units activated by contextual features. As a result of this item-context link-

age, whenever the subject is in that context (and, consequently, context-sensitive neurons are firing), the linked item units will receive a small amount of activation. Over time, this low-level input from contextual features will lead to adaptation in the linked item units, thereby making them less likely to fire to subsequent repetitions of that item. In the Meeter et al. (2005) model, "context" is operationalized as a set of input units that receive constant (above-zero) excitation throughout the experiment; apart from this fact, context features function identically to units that represent the features of individual items.

This model has several attractive properties with regard to explaining data on single-unit activity in perirhinal cortex. It can account for the basic decrease in the neural response triggered by familiar versus novel stimuli. Moreover, it provides an elegant explanation of why some perirhinal neurons do not show decreased responding with stimulus repetition. Contrary to the Bogacz and Brown (2003) idea that neurons showing decreased versus steady responding come from separate populations (with distinct learning rules), the Meeter et al. (2005) model explains this difference in terms of a simple difference in context-sensitivity. Specifically, according to the Meeter et al. (2005) model, neurons that receive input from a large number of contextual features will show decreased responding to repeated stimuli (insofar as these contextual inputs will cause the neuron to be tonically active, leading to adaptation), whereas neurons that are relatively insensitive to contextual features will not show decreased responding.

The most salient prediction of the Meeter model is that familiarity should be highly context-sensitive: Insofar as the strengthened context-item association formed at study is what causes adaptation, changing context between study and test should eliminate adaptation and thus eliminate the decrement in responding to previously studied stimuli. This prediction has not yet been tested. With regard to capacity, the Meeter et al. (2005) model uses the same Hebbian learning mechanism as the CLS model, so the same capacity issues that were raised by Bogacz and Brown (2003) (with regard to the CLS model) also apply here.

2.2.3. THE OSCILLATING LEARNING ALGORITHM

In response to the aforementioned problems with CPCA Hebbian learning, Norman et al. (2006; see also Norman et al., 2005) developed a new learning algorithm that (like CPCA Hebbian learning) does feature extraction, but (unlike CPCA Hebbian learning) is more judicious in how it adjusts synapses: It selectively strengthens weak parts of target memories (vs. parts that are already strong) and selectively punishes strong competitors. The algorithm memorizes patterns in the following manner:

- First, the to-be-learned (target) pattern is imposed on the network (via external inputs).
- Second, the algorithm identifies weak parts of the target memory by raising feedback inhibition above baseline. This increase can be viewed as a "stress test" on the target memory. If a target unit is receiving relatively little collateral support from other target units, such that its net input is just above threshold, raising inhibition will trigger a decrease in the activation of that unit. The algorithm then acts to strengthen units that drop out when inhibition is raised, by increasing connections coming into these units units from active senders.
- Third, the algorithm identifies competing memories (non-target memories receiving strong input) by lowering feedback inhibition below baseline. Effectively, lowering inhibition lowers the threshold amount of excitation needed for a unit to become active. If a non-target unit is just below threshold (i.e., it is receiving strong input, but not quite enough to become active) lowering inhibition will cause that unit to become active. The algorithm then acts to weaken units that pop up when inhibition is lowered, by weakening connections coming into these units from active senders.

Weight change in the model is accomplished via the well-established Contrastive Hebbian Learning (CHL) equation (Ackley, Hinton, & Sejnowski, 1985; Hinton, 1989; Hinton & Sejnowski, 1986; Movellan, 1990). CHL learning involves contrasting a more desirable state of network activity (called the *plus* state) with a less desirable state of network activity (called the *minus* state). The CHL equation adjusts network weights to strengthen the more desirable state of network activity (so it is more likely to occur in the future) and weaken the less desirable state of network activity (so it is less likely to occur in the future).

$$\Delta w_{ij} = \epsilon \left((X_i^+ Y_j^+) - (X_i^- Y_j^-) \right) \qquad (7.2)$$

In this Equation, X_i is the activation of the presynaptic (sending) unit, Y_j is the activation of the postsynaptic (receiving) unit. The $^+$ and $^-$ superscripts refer to plus-state and minus-state activity, respectively. Δw_{ij} is the change in weight between the sending and receiving units, and ϵ is the learning rate parameter.

Changes in the strength of feedback inhibition have the effect of creating two kinds of "minus" states: Raising inhibition creates patterns that have too little activation (because target units drop out), and lowering inhibition creates patterns that have too much activation (because strong competitor units pop up). As inhibition is oscillated, the CHL equation is applied to states of network activation, with the normal-inhibition pattern serving as the plus state and the high-inhibition and low-inhibition patterns serving as minus states (Norman et al., 2006).

Because strengthening is limited to weak target features, the oscillating algorithm avoids the problem of "overstrengthening of common features" that plagues Hebbian learning. Also, the oscillating algorithm's ability to selectively punish competitors helps to prevent similar memories from collapsing into one another: Whenever memories start to blend together, they also start to compete with one another at retrieval, and the competitor-punishment mechanism pushes them apart.[3] Norman, Newman, Detre, and Polyn (2006) discuss how the oscillating algorithm may be implemented in the brain by neural theta oscillations (insofar as these oscillations involve regular changes in the strength of neural inhibition and are present in both cortex and the hippocampus).

Recently, Norman et al. (2005) explored the oscillating algorithm's ability to do familiarity discrimination. These simulations used a simple two-layer network: Patterns were presented to the lower part of the network (the *input-output* layer). The upper part of the network (the *hidden* layer) was allowed to self-organize according to the dictates of the learning algorithm. Every unit in the input-output layer was connected to every input-output unit (including itself) and to every hidden unit via modifiable, symmetric weights. A familiarity signal can be extracted from this network by looking at how activation changes when inhibition is raised above its baseline value: Weak (unfamiliar) memories show a larger decrease in activation than strong (familiar) memories. Norman et al. (2005) tested the network's ability to discriminate between 100 studied and 100 nonstudied patterns, where the average pairwise overlap between any two patterns (studied or nonstudied) was 41%. After 10 study presentations, discrimination accuracy was effectively at ceiling (99%). In this same situation, the performance of the Norman and O'Reilly (2003) CLS familiarity model (trained with CPCA Hebbian learning) was close to chance. This finding shows that the oscillating algorithm can show good familiarity discrimination in exactly the kind of situation (i.e., high correlation between patterns) where the CLS familiarity model performs poorly. Although

Norman et al. (2005) have not yet carried out the requisite mathematical analyses, it is quite possible that the oscillating algorithm's capacity for supporting familiarity-based discrimination, in a brain-sized network, will be large enough to account for the vast capacity of human familiarity discrimination.

3. Abstract Models of Recognition and Recall

In addition to the biologically based models discussed previously, there is a rich tradition of researchers building more abstract computational models of episodic memory. Although there is considerable diversity within the realm of abstract memory models, most of the abstract models that are currently being developed share a common set of properties: At study, memory traces are placed separately in a long-term store; because of this "separate storage" postulate, acquiring new memory traces does not affect the integrity of previously stored memory traces. At test, the model computes the match between the test cue and all of the items stored in memory. This item-by-item match information can be summed across all items to compute a "global match" familiarity signal. Some abstract models that conform to this overall structure are Search of Associative Memory model (SAM; Gillund & Shiffrin, 1984; Mensink & Raaijmakers, 1988; Raaijmakers & Shiffrin, 1981), the Retrieving Efficiently from Memory model (REM; Malmberg, Holden, & Shiffrin, 2004; Shiffrin & Steyvers, 1997), MINERVA 2 model (Hintzman, 1988), and the Noisy Exemplar model (NEMO; Kahana & Sekuler, 2002). Some notable exceptions to this general rule include the Theory of Distributed Associated Memory model (TODAM; Murdock, 1993) and the Matrix model (Humphreys, Bain, & Pike, 1989), which store memory traces in a composite fashion (instead of storing them separately).

One of the most important properties of global matching models is that the match

---

3 Importantly, unlike the CLS hippocampal model described earlier (which automatically enacts pattern separation, regardless of similarity), the oscillating algorithm is only concerned that memories observe a minimum separation from one another. So long as this constraint is met, memories in the cortical network simulated here are free to overlap according to their similarity (thereby allowing the network to enact similarity-based generalization).

computation weights multiple matches to a single trace more highly than the same total number of matches, spread out across multiple memory traces (e.g., a test cue that matches two features of one item yields a higher familiarity signal than a test cue that matches one feature of each of two items); see Clark and Gronlund (1996) for additional discussion of this point. Among other things, this property gives global matching models the ability to perform *associative recognition* (i.e., to discriminate pairs of stimuli that were studied together vs. stimuli that were studied separately).

Different models achieve this sensitivity to conjunctions in different ways. For example, in MINERVA 2, memory traces are vectors where each element is 1 (indicating that a feature is present), -1 (indicating that the feature is absent), and 0 (indicating that the feature is unknown). To compute global match, MINERVA 2 first computes the match between the test cue and each trace i stored in memory. Match is operationalized as the cue-trace dot product, divided by the number of features contributing to the dot product:

$$S_i = \frac{\sum_{j=1}^{N} P_j T_{i,j}}{N_i}.$$

(7.3)

S_i is the match value, P_j is the value of feature j in the cue, $T_{i,j}$ is the value of feature j in trace i, N is the number of features, and N_i is the number of features where either the cue or trace is nonzero.

Next, MINERVA 2 cubes each of these individual match scores to compute an "activation" value A_i for each trace.

$$A_i = S_i^3.$$

(7.4)

Finally, these activation values are summed together across the M traces in memory to yield an "echo intensity" (global match) score I:

$$I = \sum_{i=1}^{M} A_i.$$

(7.5)

MINERVA 2 shows sensitivity to conjunctions because matches spread across multiple stored traces are combined in an additive fashion, but (because of the cube rule) multiple matches to a single trace are combined in a positively accelerated fashion. For example, consider the difference between two traces with match values S_i of .5, versus one trace with a match value S_i of 1.0. Because of the cube rule, the total match value I in the former case is $.5^3 + .5^3 = .25$ whereas in the latter case, $I = 1.0^3 = 1.0$.

The NEMO model (Kahana & Sekuler, 2002) achieves sensitivity to conjunctions in a similar fashion: First, NEMO computes a vector distance $d(i, j)$ between the cue and the memory trace (note: small distance = high similarity). Next, the distance value is passed through an exponential function, which – like the cube function – has the effect of emphasizing close matches (i.e., small distances) relative to weaker matches (i.e., large distances):

$$\eta(i, j) = e^{-\tau d(i, j)}.$$

(7.6)

In this equation, $\eta(i, j)$ is the adjusted similarity score, and τ is a model parameter that determines the steepness of the generalization curve (i.e., how close a match has to be to contribute strongly to the overall "summed similarity" score).

In abstract models, the same "match" rule that is used to compute the global-match familiarity signal is also used when simulating recall, although the specific way in which the match rule is used during recall differs from model to model. For example, MINERVA 2 simulates recall by computing a weighted sum C of all of the items i stored in memory, where each item is weighted by its match to the test cue. The jth element of C is given by:

$$C_j = \sum_{i=1}^{M} A_i T_{i,j}.$$

(7.7)

In contrast, models like SAM and REM use the individual match scores to determine which (single) memory trace will be "sampled" for recall (see Section 3.1).

Collectively, abstract models have been very successful in explaining behavioral recall and recognition data from normal subjects (see Clark & Gronlund, 1996, and Raaijmakers, 2005; Raaijmakers & Shiffrin, 2002, for reviews).[4] The remaining part of this section is structured as follows: Section 3.1 presents a detailed description of the Shiffrin and Steyvers (1997) REM model. REM is highlighted because, of all of the models mentioned earlier, it is the model that is being developed and applied most actively and because it has the most principled mathematical foundation. Section 3.2 describes important differences between "separate storage" abstract models (e.g., REM) and biological models with regard to their predictions about the mechanisms of interference (i.e., does studying new items degrade previously stored memory traces). Finally, whereas most abstract models try to explain recognition memory data solely in terms of the "global match" familiarity mechanism (and not recall), Section 3.3 reviews two recently developed *dual-process* abstract models that address contributions of both recall and familiarity to recognition performance.

3.1. *The REM Model of Recognition and Recall*

The Shiffrin and Steyvers (1997) REM model is the most recent iteration of a line of models that date back to the Raaijmakers and Shiffrin (1981) SAM model. One of the main differences between REM and previous models like SAM and MINERVA 2 is that REM implements a principled Bayesian calculation of the likelihood that the cue "matches" (i.e., corresponds to

the same item as) a particular stored memory trace, whereas the match calculation was not defined in Bayesian terms in previous models (Raaijmakers & Shiffrin, 2002; for another example of a model that takes this Bayesian approach, see McClelland & Chappell, 1998; for additional discussion of Bayesian modeling, see Chapter 3 in this volume). The following REM equations were adapted from Shiffrin and Steyvers (1997), Xu and Malmberg (2007), and Malmberg and Shiffrin (2005).

In REM, items are vectors of features whose values, V, are geometrically distributed integers. Specifically, the probability of a particular feature being assigned a particular value is given by

$$P[V = j] = (1 - g)^{j-1} g \qquad (7.8)$$

where g is the geometric distribution parameter (with a value between 0 and 1). The primary consequence of feature values being distributed geometrically (according to Equation 7.8) is that high feature values are less common than low feature values.

When an item is studied, the features of that item are copied into an episodic trace for that item. The probability of storing a particular feature in an episodic trace is denoted by u^*. The probability of encoding that feature correctly (given that it has been stored) is denoted by c. If the feature is encoded incorrectly, a new value for that feature is randomly drawn from the geometric distribution. A zero value means that no value is stored for the feature.

At test, the retrieval cue is compared with each trace, and (for each trace j) the model calculates the likelihood λ_j that the cue and the trace match (i.e., they correspond to the same item):

$$\lambda_j = (1 - c)^{n_{jq}}$$
$$\times \prod_{i=1}^{\infty} \left[\frac{c + (1 - c) g (1 - g)^{i-1}}{g (1 - g)^{i-1}} \right]^{n_{ijm}}$$
$$(7.9)$$

---

4 In principle, abstract models can be used to account for data from memory-impaired populations as well as normal populations (by finding a set of parameter changes that lead to the desired pattern of memory deficits) but, in practice, few studies have taken this approach. Some notable exceptions include Malmberg, Zeelenberg, and Shiffrin (2004) and Howard, Kahana, and Wingfield (2006).

where n_{jq} is the number of nonzero features in the jth memory trace that mismatch the cue (regardless of value) and n_{ijm} is the number of nonzero features in the jth memory trace that match the cue and have value i. Equation 7.9 was derived by computing two different probabilities:

- The probability of obtaining the observed pattern of matching and mismatching features, assuming that the cue and trace correspond to the same item, and
- The probability of obtaining the observed pattern of matching and mismatching features, assuming that the cue and trace correspond to different items.

The likelihood value λ_j is computed by dividing the former probability by the latter. Shiffrin and Steyvers (1997), Appendix A, contains a detailed derivation of Equation 7.9.

The same core "match" calculation is used for both recognition and recall in REM. The model is applied to recognition by computing

$$\Phi = \frac{1}{n} \sum_{j=1}^{n} \lambda_j. \tag{7.10}$$

Mathematically, Φ corresponds to the overall odds that the item is old (vs. new). If the Φ exceeds a preset criterion (typically the criterion is set to $\Phi > 1.0$, indicating that the item is more likely to be old than new) then the item is called "old." The fact that the effects of individual matches (and mismatches) are combined *multiplicatively* within individual traces (Equation 7.9) and *additively* across traces (Equation 7.10) serves the same function as the "cube rule" in MINERVA 2 and the exponential function in NEMO, that is, it ensures that multiple matches to a single trace have a larger effect on Φ than the same number of feature matches, spread across multiple traces.

Recall in REM (like recall in SAM; Raaijmakers & Shiffrin, 1981) has both a *sampling* component (which picks a single trace out from the memory store) and a *recovery* component (which determines whether the

sampled memory trace is retrieved successfully). Sampling is done with replacement. The probability of sampling memory trace I_j, given the retrieval cue Q is as follows:

$$P(I_j | Q) = \frac{\lambda_j^\gamma}{\sum \lambda_k^\gamma} \tag{7.11}$$

λ_j is the match value (described earlier) for trace I_j, and γ is a scaling parameter. The denominator is the sum of the scaled likelihood ratios across the activated memory traces. Once an item is sampled, the probability that the trace will be recovered and output, $P(R)$, is given by

$$P(R) = \rho_r^\tau \tag{7.12}$$

where ρ_r is the proportion of correctly stored item features in that trace and τ is a scaling parameter. Thus, in REM, well-encoded items are more likely to be recovered than poorly encoded items.

3.1.1. REPRESENTATIVE REM RESULTS

Researchers have demonstrated that REM can explain a wide range of episodic memory findings. For example, Shiffrin and Steyvers (1997) demonstrated that the "global match" familiarity mechanism described previously can account for the word frequency mirror effect: the finding that subjects make more false alarms to high-frequency (HF) lures versus low-frequency (LF) lures and that subjects make more correct "old" responses to low-frequency targets versus high-frequency targets (e.g., Glanzer et al., 1993). REM's account of word frequency effects is based on the idea that LF words have more unusual features than HF words; specifically, REM can fit the observed pattern of word frequency effects by using a slightly lower value of the geometric distribution parameter g when generating LF items, which results in these items having slightly higher (and thus more unusual) feature values (see Equation 7.8). The fact that LF items have unusual features has two implications. First, it means that LF lures are not likely to spuriously match stored memory traces – this explains why there are fewer LF false alarms than HF false alarms. Second, it means that, when LF cues do match stored traces, this is strong evidence that the item was studied (because matches to unusual features are unlikely to occur due to chance); as such, LF targets tend to trigger high likelihood (λ) values, which explains why the hit rate is higher for LF targets than HF targets.

One implication of this account is that, if one could engineer a situation where the (unusual) features of LF lures match stored memory traces as often as the (more common) features of HF lures, subjects will show a higher false alarm rate for LF lures than HF lures (the reverse of the normal pattern). This prediction was tested and confirmed by Malmberg, Holden et al. (2004), who induced a high rate of "spurious match" for LF lures by using lures that were highly similar to studied items (e.g., study "yachts," test with "yacht").

3.2. Differences in How Models Explain Interference

One important difference between "separate storage" abstract models like REM and biological models like CLS relates to sources of interference. In REM, memory traces are stored in a noninterfering fashion, and interference arises at test (whenever the test cue matches memory traces other than the target memory trace).[5] For example, SAM and REM predict that strengthening some list items (by presenting them repeatedly) will impair recall of nonstrengthened items by increasing the odds that the strengthened items will be sampled instead of nonstrengthened items (Malmberg & Shiffrin, 2005). Effectively, the model's ability to sample these nonstrengthened

items is *blocked* by sampling of the strengthened items.

Biological models, like abstract models, posit that interference can occur at test (due to competition between the target memory and non-target memories). However, in contrast to models like REM, biological models also posit that interference can occur at study: Insofar as learning in biological models involves both strengthening and weakening of synapses, adjusting synapses to store one memory could end up weakening other memories that also rely on those synapses. This trace weakening process is sometimes referred to as *structural interference* (Murnane & Shiffrin, 1991) or *unlearning* (e.g., Melton & Irwin, 1940).

Models like SAM and REM have focused on interference at test, as opposed to structural interference at study, for two reasons:

- The first reason is parsimony: Models that rely entirely on interference at test can account for a very wide range of forgetting data. In particular, Mensink and Raaijmakers (1988) showed that a variant of the SAM model can account for several phenomena that were previously attributed to unlearning (e.g., retroactive interference in AB-AC interference paradigms; Barnes & Underwood, 1959).
- The second reason is that it is unclear how to instantiate structural interference properly within a separate-storage framework. For example, in REM, structural interference would presumably involve deletion of features from episodic traces, but it is unclear which features to delete. Biologically based neural network models fare better in this regard, insofar as these models incorporate synaptic learning rules that explicitly specify how to adjust synaptic strengths (upward or downward) as a function of presynaptic and postsynaptic activity.

The most important open issue with regard to modeling interference and forgetting is whether there are any results in the literature that can only be explained by positing trace-weakening mechanisms. Michael

---

5 Within the realm of abstract models positing interference-at-test, there is some controversy about whether interference arises from spurious matches to other items on the study list, as opposed to spurious matches to memory traces from outside the experimental context; see Dennis and Humphreys (2001) and Criss and Shiffrin (2004) for contrasting perspectives on this issue.

Anderson has argued that certain findings in the *retrieval-induced forgetting* literature may meet this criterion (see M. C. Anderson, 2003, for a review). In retrieval-induced forgetting experiments, subjects study a list of items, and then a subset of the studied items are strengthened during a second "practice" phase. Anderson and others have found that manipulations that affect the degree of retrieval competition during the practice phase (e.g., whether subjects are given a well-specified cue or a poorly specified cue; M. C. Anderson, Bjork, & Bjork, 2000) can affect the extent to which nonpracticed items are forgotten, without affecting the extent to which practiced items are strengthened. M. C. Anderson (2003) explains these results in terms of the idea that (1) *competitors are weakened* during memory retrieval, and (2) the degree of weakening is proportional to the degree of competition.[6] Anderson also points out that simple "blocking" accounts of forgetting may have difficulty explaining the observed pattern of results (increased forgetting without increased strengthening): According to these blocking accounts, forgetting of nonstrengthened items is a direct consequence of strengthened items being recalled in place of nonstrengthened items; as such, practice manipulations that lead to the same amount of strengthening should lead to the same amount of forgetting. At this point, it is unclear whether separate-storage models like REM (which are considerably more sophisticated than the simple blocking theories described by Anderson, 2003) can account for the retrieval-induced forgetting results described here.

3.3. *Abstract Models and Dual-Process Theories*

Abstract models have traditionally taken a single-process approach to recognition,

whereby they try to explain recognition performance exclusively in terms of the global match familiarity process (without positing that recall of specific details contributes to recognition). As with the structural-interference issue previously described, the main reason that abstract models have taken this approach is parsimony: The single-process approach has been extremely successful in accounting for recognition data; hence, there is no need to complicate the model by positing that recall contributes routinely to recognition judgments. However, more recently, Malmberg, Holden et al. (2004) and Xu and Malmberg (2007) have identified some data patterns (from paradigms that use lures that are closely related to studied items) that can not be fully explained using the REM familiarity process. Specifically, studies using related lures (e.g., switched-plurality lures: study "rats," test "rat") have found that increasing the number of study presentations of "rats" increases hits, but does not reliably increase false recognition of similar lures like "rat." Dual-process models can explain this result in terms of the idea that increased study of "rats" increases the familiarity of "rat" (which tends to boost false recognition), but it also increases the odds that subjects will recall that they studied "rats," not "rat" (Hintzman, Curran, & Oppy, 1992). Malmberg, Holden et al. (2004) showed that the REM global match process cannot simultaneously generate an increase in hit rates, coupled with no change (or a decrease) in false alarm rates to similar lures (see Xu & Malmberg, 2007, for a similar finding, using an associative recognition paradigm).

In response to this issue, Malmberg, Holden et al. (2004) developed a dual-process REM model of recognition, which incorporates both the REM "global match" familiarity judgment and the REM recall process described earlier. This model operates in the following manner. First, stimulus familiarity is computed (using Equation 7.9). If familiarity is below a threshold value, the item is called "new." If familiarity is above the threshold value, the recall

---

6 See Norman, Newman, and Detre (2007), for a neural network model of retrieval-induced forgetting that instantiates these ideas about competitor-weakening; the model uses the oscillating learning algorithm described earlier to strengthen the practiced item and weaken competitors.

process is engaged. The model samples a single memory trace and attempts to recover the contents of that trace. If recovery succeeds and the recovered item matches the test cue, the item is called "old." If recovery succeeds and the recovered item mismatches the test cue (e.g., the model recalls "rats" but the test cue is "rat"), the item is called "new." If the recovery process fails, the model guesses "old" with probability γ.[7] The addition of this extra recall process allows the model to accommodate the combination of increasing hits and no increase in false alarms to similar lures.

3.3.1. THE SOURCE OF ACTIVATION CONFUSION MODEL

Reder's Source of Activation Confusion (SAC) model (e.g., Reder et al., 2000) takes a different approach to simulating contributions of recall and familiarity to recognition memory. In the SAC model, items are represented as nodes in a network; episodic memory traces are represented as special nodes that are linked both to the item and to a node representing the experimental context. Activation is allowed to spread at test; the degree of spreading activation coming out of a node is a function of the node's activation and also the number of connections coming out of the node (the more connections, the less activation that spreads per connection; for discussion of empirical evidence that supports this "fan effect" assumption, see Anderson & Reder, 1999; see also Anderson & Lebiere, 1998, for discussion of another model that incorporates this assumption). In SAC, familiarity is a function of the activation of the item node itself, whereas recall is a function of the activation of the episodic node that was created when the item was studied.

Reder et al. (2000) demonstrated that the SAC model can account for word frequency mirror effects. According to SAC, the false alarm portion of the mirror effect (false alarms to HF lures > false alarms to LF lures) is due to familiarity, and the hit-rate portion of the mirror effect (hit rate for LF targets > hit rate for HF targets) is due to recall (for similar views, see Hirshman et al., 2002; Joordens & Hockley, 2000). In SAC, the fact that HF lures have been presented more often than LF lures (prior to the experiment) gives them a higher baseline level of activation, and – through this – a higher level of familiarity. The fact that LF targets are linked to fewer pre-experimental contexts than HF targets, and thus have a smaller "fan factor," means that activity can spread more efficiently to the "episodic node" associated with the study event (leading to a higher hit rate for LF items).

Reder et al. (2000) argue that this dual-process account of mirror effects is preferable to the REM account insofar as it models frequency differences in terms of actual differences in the number of preexperimental presentations, instead of the idea (used by REM) that LF words have more unusual features than HF words. However, it remains to be seen whether the Reder et al. (2000) model provides a better overall account of word frequency effects than REM (in terms of model fit and in terms of novel, validated predictions).

4. Context, Free Recall, and Active Maintenance

Up to this point, this chapter has discussed accounts of how the memory system responds to a particular cue, but it has not yet touched on how the memory system behaves when external cues are less well specified, and subjects have to generate their own cues to target a particular memory (or set of memories). Take the scenario of trying to remember where you left your keys. The most common advice in this situation is to reinstate your mental context as a means of prompting recall – if you succeed in remembering what you were doing and what you were thinking earlier in the day, this

---

7 To accommodate the idea that subjects rely more on recall in some situations than others (see Section 2.1.5), the dual-process version of REM includes an extra model parameter (a) that scales the probability of using recall on a given trial.

will boost the probability of recalling where you left the keys. This idea of reinstating mental context plays a key role in theories of strategic memory search. Multiple laboratory paradigms have been developed to examine this process of strategic memory search. The most commonly used paradigm is *free recall*, where subjects are given a word list and are then asked to retrieve the studied word list in any order. Section 4.1 describes an abstract modeling framework, the Temporal Context Model (TCM; Howard & Kahana, 2002) that has proved to be very useful in understanding how we selectively retrieve memories from a particular temporal context in free recall experiments. Section 4.2 discusses methods for implementing TCM dynamics in biologically based neural network models.

4.1. *The Temporal Context Model*

TCM is the most recent in a long succession of models that use a *drifting mental context* to explain memory targeting (e.g., Estes, 1955; Mensink & Raaijmakers, 1988). The basic idea behind these models is that the subject's inner mental context (comprised of the constellation of thoughts that are active at a particular moment) changes gradually over time. Mensink and Raaijmakers (1988) instantiate this idea in terms of a binary context vector, where each element of this context vector is updated (with some probability) on each time step; the higher the probability of updating, the faster the context vector drifts over time. During the study phase of a memory experiment, items are associated with the state of the context vector (at the time of presentation). At test, the recall process is initiated by cuing with the current state of the context vector, which (in turn) triggers retrieval of items that were associated with these contextual elements at study.

The main difference between TCM and previous contextual-drift models like Mensink and Raaijmakers (1988) is that, in TCM, context does not drift randomly. Rather, contextual updating is driven by the features of the items being studied. More precisely, the state of the context vector at time i, $\mathbf{t}_i$, is given by:

$$\mathbf{t}_i = \rho_i \mathbf{t}_{i-1} + \beta \mathbf{t}_i^{IN} \qquad (7.13)$$

where β is a free parameter that determines the rate of contextual drift, ρ_i is chosen at each time step such that $\mathbf{t}_i$ is always of unit length, and $\mathbf{t}_i^{IN}$ corresponds to "preexperimental context" associated with the item being studied at time i (i.e., an amalgamation of all of the contexts in which that item has previously appeared). The key thing to note is that preexperimental context is different for each item; thus, adding $\mathbf{t}_i^{IN}$ to the context vector has the effect of injecting specific information about the just-studied item into the context vector.

The most current version of TCM (Howard, Kahana, & Wingfield, 2006) posits that, on a given time step, the current item is associated with active contextual features, and then the context vector is updated according to Equation 7.13. Thus, the item studied at time i ends up being associated with the state of the context vector that was computed on time step $i - 1$. At test, the free recall process is initiated by cuing with the current state of the context vector. As in SAM, items are sampled according to how well the context cue matches the context associated with the stored item (see Howard & Kahana, 2002, for a more detailed description of how item-context associations are formed at study and how items are sampled at test). If the item studied at time i is sampled at time step r, the context is updated according to the following equations:

$$\mathbf{t}_r = \rho_i \mathbf{t}_{r-1} + \beta \mathbf{t}_r^{IN} \qquad (7.14)$$

where $\mathbf{t}_r^{IN}$ (the information injected into the context vector) is given by:

$$\mathbf{t}_r^{IN} = \alpha_O \mathbf{t}_i^{IN} + \alpha_N \mathbf{t}_{i-1} + \eta \mathbf{n}_r. \qquad (7.15)$$

In Equation 7.15, $\mathbf{t}_i^{IN}$ is the preexperimental context associated with item i, $\mathbf{t}_{i-1}$ is the contextual information that was associated with item i at study, and $\mathbf{n}_r$ is a noise term. α_O, α_N, and η are scaling parameters. Thus, the context-updating operation associated with recalling item i has much in common with the context-updating operation associated with studying item i. In both cases, context is updated by injecting $\mathbf{t}_i^{IN}$ (item-specific information relating to item i). The main difference, apart from the noise term, is that context is also updated with $\mathbf{t}_{i-1}$, the state of the context vector at the time the (just-retrieved) item was studied. This latter updating operation can be construed as "mentally jumping back in time" to the moment when the (just-retrieved) item was studied. As discussed later, the two kinds of updating mentioned here ($\mathbf{t}_i^{IN}$ vs. $\mathbf{t}_{i-1}$) have distinct effects on recall transition probabilities. Once the context vector is updated, it is used to cue for additional items, which leads to additional updating of the context vector, and so on.

4.1.1. HOW TCM ACCOUNTS FOR RECALL DATA

Contextual drift models (in general) and TCM (in particular) can account for a wide range of free recall findings; some representative findings are discussed in this section. As one example, contextual drift models provide an elegant account of the *long-term recency effect* in free recall. Circa 1970, it was believed that recency effects (better recall of items from the end of the list) were attributable to the fact that recently presented items were still being held in a short-term memory buffer. As such, manipulations that disrupt this buffer (e.g., a distraction-filled retention interval) should sharply reduce recency effects. However, Bjork and Whitten (1974) and other studies have since demonstrated that recency effects can still be observed after a distraction-filled delay. Bjork and Whitten showed that the key determinant of recency is the *ratio* of the time elapsed since study of item A to the time elapsed since study of item B; the smaller this ratio is (indicating that A was presented relatively more recently than B), the bet-

ter A will be recalled relative to B (Glenberg et al., 1980). This can be explained by contextual drift models in the following manner:

- Because of contextual drift, the current test context (being used as a cue) matches the context associated with recently presented items more than the context associated with less recently presented items.
- Because recall is a competitive process, recall of a particular trace is a function of the match between the cue and that trace, relative to other cue-trace match values. Increasing the recency of item A (relative to item B) increases the extent to which the test cue matches the A-context versus the B-context, thereby boosting recall of A relative to B.

Critically, to explain recency effects, the rate of drift cannot be too fast. If, for example, all of the contextual elements changed on every trial, then recently presented items would not have any more "contextual match" than less recently presented items. Put another way, at least some contextual elements need to persist long enough to span the gap between recently presented studied items and the time of test.

In their 2002 article, Howard & Kahana also showed that TCM can account for detailed patterns of transition data in free recall: Given that the Nth item from the study list was just recalled, what are the odds that the next item recalled will be the N+1st item, N-1st item, N+2nd item, and so on? Kahana (1996) plotted this conditional response probability (CRP) curve (see also Howard & Kahana, 1999). A representative CRP curve is shown in Figure 7.3.

There are two major findings to highlight. First, items that are studied in nearby serial positions in the study list tend to be recalled close together at test (Kahana, 1996, calls this regularity the *lag-recency* effect). This holds true even if filled distractor intervals are inserted between items at study, making it unlikely that these contiguity effects are due to subjects rehearsing contiguous items

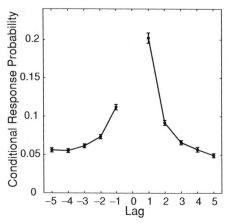

Figure 7.3. Conditional response probability (CRP) curve, showing the probability of recalling an item studied at serial position $i + lag$ immediately after recall of an item studied at serial position. This particular CRP curve was created by averaging together the CRP curves from multiple studies; see the caption of Figure 1A in Howard et al. (2007) for more details. (Figure courtesy of Marc Howard.)

together in short-term memory. This basic regularity can be explained in terms of the idea that, when subjects retrieve an item, they retrieve contextual features associated with that item, and then they use these retrieved contextual features to cue for more items. Insofar as items studied close in time to one another have similar context vectors, cuing with contextual information from time t will facilitate recall of other items studied in (temporal) proximity to time t.

Howard and Kahana (2002) point out retrieved context from the study phase ($\mathbf{t}_{i-1}$ from Equation 7.15) is a temporally symmetric cue: Assuming a steady rate of "contextual drift," the context active at one point in time should match the context from the preceding time step just as well as it matches the context from the following time step. However, as clearly shown in Figure 7.3, the CRP curve is asymmetric: Subjects are more likely to recall in the forward direction than the backward direction. This can be explained in terms of the idea that $\mathbf{t}_i^{IN}$ (the item-specific information that is injected into the context vector when item i is

studied and when it is retrieved at test) is an asymmetric cue: This information is present in the context vector for items that were studied after the retrieved item, but not for items that were studied before the retrieved item. Thus, cuing with this item-specific information at test biases recall in the forward direction.

4.2. *TCM in the Brain*

Importantly, TCM is not meant to stand on its own as a full-fledged model. Rather, it provides an abstract blueprint for how models can account for serial-position and transition data in free recall. Given this blueprint, a key challenge for computational models of episodic memory is to determine how these dynamics could be implemented in a neural network.

The next part of this section shows how neural network architectures that are capable of *active maintenance* can serve as the "context vector" in models of long-term memory. Traditionally, active maintenance networks have been used to model performance in short-term (working) memory tasks (e.g., Botvinick & Plaut, 2006; Usher & Cohen, 1999). A synthesis is proposed whereby active maintenance systems serve a dual role: They directly support performance on short-term memory tasks, and they also serve to contextualize episodic memory (via associations that are formed at study between the representation of the item being studied and other representations that are currently being maintained in active memory). Finally, the roles of different brain systems in implementing TCM dynamics are discussed, with a particular focus on prefrontal cortex and entorhinal cortex.

4.2.1. ARCHITECTURES FOR ACTIVE MAINTENANCE

The previous discussion of TCM, indicates that the context vector should have the following properties:

- When an item is studied, the context vector should be updated with information relating to that item.

- Information in the context vector needs to persist across multiple items and possibly longer (but not indefinitely). This persistent activity creates the "drift" dynamic whereby recently presented items match the current context more than less-recently presented items.

In the following paragraphs, two network architectures are described that meet these criteria. Both models were originally developed to account for working memory data (e.g., recall of items from a short-term buffer). The same active maintenance mechanisms that allow these models to support working memory performance also imbue the models with the requisite context-vector properties (i.e., item-specific updating and slow drift over time).

4.2.1.1. *The Usher and Cohen (1999) Localist Attractor Network.* In this network, when an item is presented, it triggers activation in the corresponding unit of the attractor network, which is then sustained (via a self-connection in that unit) over an extended period of time. Multiple units can be active at once, so the state of the network at any one time reflects contributions from multiple recently presented items. The total amount of network activity is limited by inhibitory connections between the units. Because of these inhibitory interactions, activating a new unit in the buffer reduces the activation of other units in the buffer, eventually causing them to drop out entirely. This dynamic causes the overall state of the buffer to drift over time.

4.2.1.2. *The O'Reilly and Frank (2006) Prefrontal Network.* Recently, O'Reilly and Frank (2006; see also Frank, Loughry, and O'Reilly 2001) developed a network architecture for active maintenance that is based explicitly on the neural architecture of prefrontal cortex (PFC). The network consists of multiple *stripes* (separate subregions of PFC; Levitt et al., 1993; Pucak et al., 1996), each of which is capable of actively maintaining (via bistable neuronal activity; Durstewitz, Kelc, & Gunturkun, 1999; Durstewitz, Seamans, & Sejnowski, 2000; Fellous, Wang, & Lisman, 1998) information about recently presented stimuli. Each PFC stripe has a corresponding region of the basal ganglia that controls when information should be gated into or out of that stripe. When a given stimulus is presented, information about that stimulus will be gated into some number of stripes and then actively maintained (possibly overwriting information about other stimuli that was previously being maintained in those stripes). At any given moment, the state of the PFC network will reflect a combination of influences from multiple recently presented items.

The previous list is not meant to be exhaustive. On the contrary, almost any network that is capable of maintaining information pertaining to multiple, recently presented items has the requisite properties to serve as the context vector.[8]

4.2.2. INTEGRATING ACTIVE MAINTENANCE AND LONG-TERM MEMORY

To date, only one model has been developed that uses an active maintenance network to contextualize long-term memory. This model (constructed by Polyn, Norman, & Cohen, 2003) is discussed in the next section, along with another free recall model presented by Davelaar et al. (2005). The Davelaar et al. (2005) model does not meet the TCM criteria in its current form, but it can easily be modified to meet these criteria.

4.2.2.1. *The Polyn, Norman, and Cohen (2003) Model.* This model merges the CLS cortical network and hippocampal network with a simplified variant of the O'Reilly and Frank (2006) PFC model. The "posterior cortex" part of the network (which has an architecture similar to the CLS cortical model described earlier) represents the item currently being presented; the PFC network actively maintains features from multiple,

---

8 One other architecture worth mentioning in this regard is the simple recurrent network (SRN; Elman, 1991). See Botvinick and Plaut (2006) for a discussion of how SRNs can be used to model short-term recall data, and see Howard and Kahana (2002) for discussion of how SRNs can instantiate the TCM contextual drift dynamic. For additional discussion of models of active maintenance, see Chapter 15 in this volume.

recently presented items; and the hippocampal model binds information in posterior cortex to the actively maintained PFC pattern. In this manner, the pattern of activity in PFC (at the moment that an item is studied) serves to contextualize that item representation. When an episodic memory (consisting of an item representation in posterior cortex and the associated PFC "context" representation) is retrieved at test, the current PFC representation is updated in two ways: The retrieved PFC pattern from the study phase is loaded directly into PFC, and the retrieved item representation is used to update PFC (in the exact same way that item information is used to update PFC at study). These two types of updating correspond directly to the two types of context-updating used by TCM (as described earlier). Polyn et al. (2003) showed that the model can account for data on recall transitions and other findings (see also Polyn, 2005), but the model is still in an early phase of development.

4.2.2.2. *The Davelaar et al. (2005) Free Recall Model.* The goal of the Davelaar et al. (2005) article was to address data showing that recall from a short-term buffer and recall from long-term memory both contribute to free recall (e.g., the finding from Carlesimo et al., 1996, that amnesics show intact recall of the last few list items on an immediate recall test, but not on a delayed recall test; presumably, this occurs because amnesics can rely on their intact short-term buffer given immediate testing but not delayed testing; see Davelaar et al., 2005, for a list of other relevant phenomena). To model the contributions of short-term memory, the Davelaar et al. (2005) model includes a variant of the Usher and Cohen (1999) localist attractor network described earlier. However, instead of using states of this localist attractor network to contextualize long-term recall, the Davelaar et al. (2005) model contextualizes recall using a separate, specialized context layer that operationalizes contextual drift as a one-dimensional random walk. States of the randomly drifting context vector are episodically associated with simultaneously active states of the localist

attractor network. At retrieval, items are directly read out from the localist attractor network (to model short-term recall), then the context vector is allowed to randomly drift (as it did at study), cuing – as it drifts – episodic recall of items that were associated with the currently active context state. The context-updating mechanism used by Davelaar et al. (2005) constitutes a step backward from TCM: Because context-updating is random, as opposed to being driven by item-specific information (as in TCM), the Davelaar et al. (2005) model fails to provide a principled account of some findings (e.g., the forward asymmetry in the conditional response probability curve) that are explained very naturally by TCM.[9]

According to the "dual role" hypothesis outlined in this section, it seems possible that one could improve the fit of the Davelaar et al. (2005) model to the data and simultaneously simplify the model, by eliminating the (randomly drifting) context vector, and using the information maintained in the short-term memory buffer to contextualize long-term item memory. However, additional simulation work is required to assess whether this simplified model can account for all of the findings described in the Davelaar et al. (2005) article as well as the lag-recency findings described by Howard and Kahana (2002).[10] One major challenge will be accounting for effects of distracting mental activity on recall. Several studies have obtained recency and lag-recency effects in *continuous distractor* paradigms, where an involving secondary task (e.g., mental arithmetic) is interposed between study trials (e.g., Howard & Kahana, 1999). These findings suggest that the temporal continuity of the context vector is preserved in the face of distraction. However, there have been numerous demonstrations that distracting

---

9 To account for the forward asymmetry in the CRP curve, Davelaar et al. (2005) add an extra parameter to their model that directly imposes a forward bias on the contextual random walk.

10 These ideas about integrating models of short-term and long-term memory were spurred by discussions at the 3rd Annual Context and Memory Symposium in March 2005, in Philadelphia, PA.

activity can reduce recall of items from short-term (active) memory to near-floor levels (e.g., Peterson & Peterson, 1959). To simultaneously explain these findings, models of the sort being discussed here (i.e., positing that the context vector and short-term memory buffer are coextensive) would have to posit that distraction degrades actively maintained representations, so they no longer support explicit recovery of items from short-term memory. However, so long as distraction does not completely eradicate the contents of active memory (i.e., so long as there is still some carry-over of activity from previously studied items) the pattern of activity in active memory should still be able to serve as a drifting context vector that supports long-term recency and lag-recency effects.[11]

4.2.3. RELEVANT BRAIN STRUCTURES

As of now, there is still extensive debate in the literature regarding which brain regions contribute most strongly to the context vector. Given the well-accepted role of PFC in active maintenance/working memory (based on neurophysiological findings in animals, human imaging studies, and human lesion studies showing that patients with PFC damage are selectively impaired in tests that tap memory for context, e.g., free recall and recency judgments; see Shimamura, 1994), it stands to reason that PFC would play an especially important role in establishing the kinds of contextual drift required by the TCM model. Furthermore, anatomical studies have established that there are several pathways connecting PFC and the hippocampus (see, e.g., Ferino, Thierry, & Glowinski, 1987; Goldman-Rakic, Selemon, & Schwartz, 1984; Jay & Witter, 1991; Morris, Pandya, & Petrides, 1999; Russchen, Amaral, & Price, 1987). Many of these pathways feed into the EC before projecting into the hippocampus proper. These pathways would allow the hippocampus to bind actively maintained information in PFC (serv-

ing as a context vector) with bottom-up activity in posterior cortex (corresponding to the currently presented stimulus).

For these reasons, the Polyn et al. (2003) model makes an explicit commitment to the idea that PFC is driving contextual drift. However, not all recently developed models have committed to this idea. The most prominent contrary view comes from Howard et al. (2005), who have argued that EC has *intrinsic maintenance properties* that allow it to serve as the TCM context vector (regardless of the input that it receives from PFC). Howard et al. (2005) cite evidence from Egorov et al. (2002), showing that layer V of EC shows persistent neural activity in the absence of bottom-up stimulation and thus can serve as a "neural integrator" that combines information from several recently presented stimuli. In summary, both the Polyn et al. (2003) model and the Howard et al. (2005) model posit that EC is involved in representing temporal context, but for different reasons: According to Polyn et al. (2003), EC is important because it serves as a conduit between PFC and the hippocampus, whereas Howard et al. (2005) posit that EC is important because of its intrinsic capability for active maintenance. At this point, the most plausible view is that both accounts are correct.[12]

5. Conclusions

Looking back on the past several decades, modelers have made tremendous strides toward understanding the mechanisms underlying episodic memory. As discussed in Section 3, abstract modelers have derived mathematically principled accounts of some of the most puzzling phenomena in episodic memory (e.g., how stimulus repetition

---

11 For additional discussion of the role of context in short-term and long-term recall, see Burgess and Hitch (2005).

12 The previous discussion has focused on how PFC and EC contribute to *temporal targeting* (i.e., selective retrieval of items from a particular temporal context). For a model of how PFC contributes to *semantic targeting* (i.e., organizing recall such that semantically similar items are recalled together), see Becker and Lim (2003).

affects false recognition of similar lures). There is an emerging consensus between biological and abstract models that both recall and familiarity can contribute to recognition memory (although the factors that determine *how much* recall contributes in a given situation need to be described in more detail). Another point of agreement between abstract and biological models is that interference between memory traces at retrieval can cause forgetting. One remaining issue is whether *structural interference* occurs between memory traces during learning (i.e., does acquiring new memories cause weakening of existing traces), and – if it occurs – how it affects behavioral memory performance. Biological models typically are subject to structural interference, but abstract models that store memory traces separately (e.g., REM) do not suffer from structural interference.

Although abstract models of episodic memory have been around for quite a while, modelers have only recently started to apply biologically based models to detailed patterns of episodic memory data. The combined influence of behavioral and neural constraints has led to rapid evolution of these biologically based models:

- As discussed in Section 2.1, there is now widespread agreement among modelers regarding how the hippocampus supports completion of missing pieces of previously stored cortical patterns and how pattern-separation mechanisms in the hippocampus allow it to rapidly memorize patterns without suffering catastrophic interference. One of the largest remaining challenges is understanding how the hippocampus manages to flip between "modes" where pattern separation predominates (to facilitate encoding) and modes where pattern completion predominates (to facilitate retrieval).
- With regard to modeling perirhinal contributions to familiarity-based recognition, as discussed in Section 2.2, some models of perirhinal familiarity (e.g., the CLS cortical model) can be ruled out based on capacity concerns. However, there are several other models with no obvious capacity problems that can fit basic aspects of extant neurophysiological data (e.g., decreased firing of some perirhinal neurons with stimulus repetition). More simulation work needs to be done, and additional neurophysiological and behavioral experiments need to be run (e.g., looking at the context-dependence of familiarity) to assess the detailed fit of these remaining models to experimental data on familiarity-based recognition.
- Finally, as discussed in Section 4, modelers have started to explore the idea that the pattern of actively maintained information in prefrontal cortex can serve as a drifting context vector. This actively maintained information is fed into entorhinal cortex (which may have intrinsic maintenance properties of its own), where it is bound together (by the hippocampus) with information pertaining to the currently presented item. This dynamic allows neural models to mimic the functioning of abstract contextual-drift models like TCM (Howard & Kahana, 2002), which (in turn) should allow the models to explain detailed patterns of recency and lag-recency data from free recall experiments.

The next challenge for biologically based models is to assemble these pieces into a unified theory. Even though there is general agreement about how this "unified theory" should be structured, there are an enormous number of critical details that need to be filled in. Some of these missing details were mentioned in the chapter (e.g., decision-making mechanisms for recognition memory) but there are innumerable other details that were not explicitly mentioned (e.g., what rules govern when information is gated into and out of active memory; see O'Reilly & Frank, 2006). In the process of working out these details, it will almost certainly become necessary to consider the contributions of other brain structures (e.g., the basal ganglia) that were not discussed at length in this chapter. Also, the models discussed in this chapter contain major simplifications. In particular, most of the models discussed here use rate-coded neurons (instead of spiking neurons) and static input patterns (instead of temporal sequences). Achieving a complete understanding of episodic memory will almost certainly require consideration of spiking neurons, spike-time-dependent learning rules, and sequence memory (for contrasting perspectives on how these factors interact, see Mehta, Lee, & Wilson, 2002, and Jensen & Lisman, 2005).

Any model that combines hippocampal, perirhinal, and prefrontal networks is going to be complex. The main factor that makes this complexity manageable is the sheer number of constraints that can be applied to biologically based models: In addition to constraints arising from behavioral data, we have discussed neuroanatomical constraints (e.g., regarding the connectivity of hippocampal subregions), neurophysiological constraints (e.g., how individual peririhinal neurons are affected by stimulus familiarity), neuropsychological constraints (e.g., how hippocampal lesions affect discrimination of studied items and similar lures), and functional constraints (e.g., ensuring that models of familiarity discrimination have adequate capacity when they are given a "brain-sized" number of neurons). In the future, neuroimaging data will also serve as an important source of model constraints (see, e.g., Deco, Rolls, & Horwitz, 2004, and Sohn et al., 2005, for examples of how models can be used to address neuroimaging data).

Another important factor with biological models is the models' ability to create crosstalk between different types of constraints. For example, adjusting the model to better fit neurophysiological data may alter the behavioral predictions generated by the model, and adjusting the model to fit both the neurophysiological data and the behavioral data may alter the overall capacity of the network for storing patterns. Even though there may be multiple, qualitatively different ways to explain these different types of findings in isolation, it seems unlikely that there will also be multiple different ways to explain all of these different types of findings taken together.

Finally, insofar as the brain systems involved in episodic memory also contribute to other forms of learning, it should be possible to use data from these other domains to constrain the episodic memory models discussed in this chapter. In particular, as mentioned in Section 2, the cortical network involved in familiarity discrimination also plays a key role in extracting the statistical structure of the environment and thus should contribute strongly to semantic memory (see Chapter 8 in this volume), categorization (see Chapter 9 in this volume), and forms of implicit learning (see Chapter 14 in this volume). Raaijmakers and Shiffrin (2002) discuss how it is possible to apply REM to implicit memory and semantic memory data. Also, several researchers have argued that the hippocampus plays a key role in training up semantic memory by playing back new information to cortex in an "off-line" fashion (e.g., during sleep); for models of this consolidation process, see Alvarez and Squire (1994) and Meeter and Murre (in press).

Medial temporal lobe structures involved in episodic memory have also been implicated in simple incremental learning tasks that have been used in animals and humans (e.g., discrimination learning and conditioning). For a discussion of ways in which the CLS model can be applied to discrimination learning and conditioning, see O'Reilly and Rudy (2001); see also Gluck, Meeter, and Myers (2003) and Meeter et al. (2005) for additional discussion of convergences between episodic memory, discrimination learning, and conditioning. Lastly, the hippocampus and surrounding cortical structures play a key role in spatial learning; for a discussion of models that relate spatial learning and episodic memory, see Burgess et al. (2001).

In summary, episodic memory modeling has a long tradition of trying to build comprehensive models that can simultaneously account for multiple recall and recognition findings. So long as future modeling work carries on with this tradition, and modelers continue to apply all available constraints to theory development, we should continue to see steady progress toward a complete, mechanistic account of how the brain stores and retrieves episodic memories.

Appendix: CLS Model Details

This appendix (adapted from Appendix A and Appendix B of Norman & O'Reilly, 2003) describes the computational details of the Norman and O'Reilly CLS model simulations. See Norman and O'Reilly (2003) for additional details and references.

Pseudocode

The pseudocode for the algorithm is given here, showing exactly how the pieces of the algorithm described in more detail in the subsequent sections fit together. The algorithm is identical to the Leabra algorithm described in O'Reilly and Munakata (2000; O'Reilly, 1998), except the error driven-learning component of the Leabra algorithm was not used here.

Outer loop: Iterate over events (trials) within an epoch. For each event, let the pattern of network activity settle across multiple cycles (time steps) of updating:

1. At start of settling, for all units:
   (a) Initialize all state variables (activation, V_m etc).
   (b) Apply external patterns.
2. During each cycle of settling, for all non-clamped units:
   (a) Compute excitatory net input ($g_e(t)$ or η_j, Equation 7.18).
   (b) Compute k-Winners-Take-All inhibition for each layer, based on g_i^{Θ} (Equation 7.21):

   i. Sort units into two groups based on g_i^{Θ}: top k and remaining $k + 1$ to n.
   ii. Set inhib conductance g_i between g_k^{Θ} and g_{k+1}^{Θ} (Equation 7.20).
   (c) Compute point-neuron activation combining excitatory input and inhibition (Equation 7.16).
3. Update the weights (based on linear current weight values), for all connections:
   (a) Compute Hebbian weight changes (Equation 7.22).
   (b) Increment the weights and apply contrast-enhancement (Equation 7.24).

Point Neuron Activation Function

Leabra uses a *point neuron* activation function that models the electrophysiological properties of real neurons, while simplifying their geometry to a single point.

The membrane potential V_m is updated as a function of ionic conductances g with reversal (driving) potentials E as follows:

$$\frac{dV_m(t)}{dt} = \tau \sum_c g_c(t)\overline{g_c}(E_c - V_m(t))$$

$$(7.16)$$

with 3 channels (c) corresponding to: e, excitatory input; l, leak current; and i, inhibitory input. Following electrophysiological convention, the overall conductance is decomposed into a time-varying component, $g_c(t)$, computed as a function of the dynamic state of the network and a constant, $\overline{g_c}$, that controls the relative influence of the different conductances. The equilibrium potential can be written in a simplified form by setting the excitatory driving potential (E_e) to 1 and the leak and inhibitory driving potentials (E_l and E_i) of 0:

$$V_m^{\infty} = \frac{g_e\overline{g_e}}{g_e\overline{g_e} + g_l\overline{g_l} + g_i\overline{g_i}},$$

$$(7.17)$$

which shows that the neuron is computing a balance between excitation and the opposing forces of leak and inhibition.

The excitatory net input/conductance $g_e(t)$ or η_j is computed as the proportion of open excitatory channels as a function of sending activations times the weight values:

$$\eta_j = g_e(t) = \frac{1}{\alpha} \langle x_i w_{ij} \rangle = \frac{1}{\alpha} \left(\frac{1}{n} \sum_i x_i w_{ij} \right),$$

(7.18)

where α is a normalizing term based on the expected average activity of the sending units, and n is the total number of sending units.

The inhibitory conductance is computed via the k-Winners-Take-All (kWTA) function described in the next section, and leak is a constant.

Activation communicated to other cells (y_j) is a thresholded (Θ) sigmoidal function of the membrane potential with gain parameter γ:

$$y_j(t) = \frac{\gamma [V_m(t) - \Theta]_+}{(\gamma [V_m(t) - \Theta]_+ + 1)}$$

(7.19)

where $[x]_+$ is a threshold function that returns 0 if $x < 0$ and x if $x > 0$. This sharply thresholded function is convolved with a Gaussian noise kernel ($\sigma = .005$), which reflects the intrinsic processing noise of biological neurons.

k-Winners-Take-All Inhibition

The CLS model uses a kWTA function to achieve sparse distributed representations (c.f., Minai & Levy, 1994). A uniform level of inhibitory current for all units in the layer is computed as follows:

$$g_i = g_{k+1}^\Theta + q(g_k^\Theta - g_{k+1}^\Theta)$$

(7.20)

where $0 < q < 1$ is a parameter for setting the inhibition between the upper bound of g_k^Θ and the lower bound of g_{k+1}^Θ. These boundary inhibition values are computed as a function of the level of inhibition necessary to keep a unit right at threshold:

$$g_i^\Theta = \frac{g_e^* \bar{g}_e (E_e - \Theta) + g_l \bar{g}_l (E_l - \Theta)}{\Theta - E_i} \quad (7.21)$$

where g_e^* is the excitatory net input.

In the basic version of the kWTA function used here, g_k^Θ and g_{k+1}^Θ are set to the threshold inhibition values for the kth and $k + 1^{st}$ most excited units, respectively. Thus, inhibition is placed exactly to allow k units to be above threshold and the remainder below threshold. For this version, the q parameter is set to .25, allowing the kth unit to be sufficiently above the inhibitory threshold.

Hebbian Learning

The simplest form of Hebbian learning adjusts the weights in proportion to the product of the sending (x_i) and receiving (y_j) unit activations: $\Delta w_{ij} = x_i y_j$. The weight vector is dominated by the principal eigenvector of the pairwise correlation matrix of the input, but it also grows without bound. Leabra uses essentially the same learning rule used in competitive learning or mixtures-of-Gaussians (Grossberg, 1976; Nowlan, 1990; Rumelhart & Zipser, 1986), which can be seen as a variant of the Oja normalization (Oja, 1982):

$$\Delta_{hebb} w_{ij} = x_i y_j - y_j w_{ij} = y_j (x_i - w_{ij})$$

(7.22)

Rumelhart and Zipser (1986) and O'Reilly and Munakata (2000) showed that, when activations are interpreted as probabilities, this equation converges on the conditional probability that the sender is active given that the receiver is active.

To renormalize Hebbian learning for sparse input activations, Equation 7.22 can be rewritten as follows:

$$\Delta w_{ij} = \epsilon [y_j x_i (m - w_{ij})$$
$$+ y_j (1 - x_i)(0 - w_{ij})] \quad (7.23)$$

where an m value of 1 gives Equation 7.22, whereas a larger value can ensure that the weight value between uncorrelated but

Table A7.1: Sizes of different subregions and their activity levels in the model

Area	Units	Activity (pct)[a]
EC	240	10.0
DG	1600	1.0
CA3	480	4.0
CA1	640	10.0

[a] pct = percent.

sparsely active units is around .5. In these simulations, $m = \frac{.5}{\alpha_m}$ and $\alpha_m = .5 - q_m(.5 - \alpha)$, where α is the sending layer's expected activation level, and q_m (called savg_cor in the simulator) is the extent to which this sending layer's average activation is fully corrected for ($q_m = 1$ gives full correction, and $q_m = 0$ yields no correction).

Weight Contrast Enhancement

One limitation of the Hebbian learning algorithm is that the weights linearly reflect the strength of the conditional probability. This linearity can limit the network's ability to focus on only the strongest correlations, while ignoring weaker ones. To remedy this limitation, a contrast enhancement function is used that magnifies the stronger weights and shrinks the smaller ones in a parametric, continuous fashion. This contrast enhancement is achieved by passing the linear weight values computed by the learning rule through a sigmoidal nonlinearity of the following form:

$$\hat{w}_{ij} = \frac{1}{1 + \left(\frac{w_{ij}}{\theta(1-w_{ij})}\right)^{-\gamma}} \qquad (7.24)$$

where $\hat{w}_{ij}$ is the contrast-enhanced weight value, and the sigmoidal function is parameterized by an offset θ and a gain γ (standard default values of 1.25 and 6, respectively, are used here).

Note that contrast-enhanced weight values $\hat{w}_{ij}$ are used for activation propagation, but weight adjustments are applied to the linear weight values w_{ij}.

Cortical and Hippocampal Model Details

The cortical model is comprised of a 240-unit input layer (with 10% activity) that projects (in a feedforward fashion) to a "perirhinal" layer with 10% activity. Each perirhinal unit receives connections from 25% of the input units. The number of units in the perirhinal layer was set to 1,920 in some simulations and 240 in other simulations.

Regarding the hippocampal model, Table A7.1 shows the sizes of different hippocampal subregions and their activity levels in the model. These activity levels are enforced by setting appropriate k parameters in the Leabra kWTA inhibition function. As discussed in the main text, activity is much more sparse in DG and CA3 than in EC.

Table A7.2 shows the properties of the four modifiable projections in the hippocampal model. For each simulated participant, connection weights in these projections are set to values randomly sampled from a uniform distribution with mean and variance (range) as specified in the table. The "scale" factor listed in the table shows

Table A7.2: Properties of modifiable projections in the hippocampal model: Mean initial weight strength, variance (Var) of the Initial weight distribution, Scaling of this projection relative to other projections, and percent connectivity (Con)

Projection	Mean	Var	Scale	% Con
EC to DG, CA3 (perforant path)	.5	.25	1	25
DG to CA3 (mossy fiber)	.9	.01	25	4
CA3 recurrent	.5	.25	1	100
CA3 to CA1 (Schaffer)	.5	.25	1	100

how influential this projection is, relative to other projections coming into the layer, and "percent connectivity" specifies the percentage of units in the sending layer that are connected to each unit in the receiving layer. Relative to the perforant path, the mossy fiber pathway is sparse (i.e., each CA3 neuron receives a much smaller number of mossy fiber synapses than perforant path synapses) and strong (i.e., a given mossy fiber synapse has a much larger impact on CA3 unit activation than a given perforant path synapse). The CA3 recurrents and the Schaffer collaterals projecting from CA3 to CA1 are relatively diffuse, so that each CA3 neuron and each CA1 neuron receive a large number of inputs sampled from the entire CA3 population.

The connections linking EC_in to CA1 and from CA1 to EC_out are not modified in the course of the simulated memory experiment. Rather, these connections are pretrained to form an invertible mapping, whereby the CA1 representation resulting from a given EC_in pattern is capable of recreating that same pattern on EC_out. CA1 is arranged into eight columns (consisting of 80 units apiece); each column receives input from three slots in EC_in and projects back to the corresponding three slots in EC_out. See O'Reilly and Rudy (2001) for a discussion of why CA1 is structured in columns.

Lastly, the model incorporates the claim, set forth by Michael Hasselmo and colleagues, that the hippocampus has two functional "modes": an *encoding mode*, where CA1 activity is primarily driven by EC_in, and a *retrieval mode*, where CA1 activity is primarily driven by stored memory traces in CA3 (e.g., Hasselmo & Wyble, 1997). To instantiate this hypothesis, the scaling factor for the EC_in to CA1 projection was set to a large value (6) at study, and the scaling factor was set to zero at test.

References

Ackley, D. H., Hinton, G. E., & Sejnowski, T. J. (1985). A learning algorithm for Boltzmann machines. *Cognitive Science, 9,* 147–169.

Aggleton, J. P., & Brown, M. W. (1999). Episodic memory, amnesia, and the hippocampal-anterior thalamic axis. *Behavioral and Brain Sciences, 22,* 425–490.

Alvarez, P., & Squire, L. R. (1994). Memory consolidation and the medial temporal lobe: A simple network model. *Proceedings of the National Academy of Sciences, USA, 91,* 7041–7045.

Anderson, J. R., & Lebiere, C. (1998). *The atomic components of thought.* Mahwah, NJ: Lawrence Erlbaum.

Anderson, J. R., & Reder, L. M. (1999). The fan effect: New results and new theories. *Journal of Experimental Psychology: General, 128,* 186.

Anderson, M. C. (2003). Rethinking interference theory: Executive control and the mechanisms of forgetting. *Journal of Memory and Language, 49,* 415–445.

Anderson, M. C., Bjork, E. L., & Bjork, R. A. (2000). Retrieval-induced forgetting: Evidence for a recall-specific mechanism. *Memory & Cognition, 28,* 522.

Barense, M. D., Bussey, T. J., Lee, A. C., Rogers, T. T., Davies, R. R., Saksida, L. M., et al. (2005). Functional specialization in the human medial temporal lobe. *Journal of Neuroscience, 25*(44), 10239–10246.

Barnes, J. M., & Underwood, B. J. (1959). Fate of first-list associations in transfer theory. *Journal of Experimental Psychology, 58,* 97–105.

Becker, S. (2005). A computational principle for hippocampal learning and neurogenesis. *Hippocampus, 15*(6), 722–738.

Becker, S., & Lim, J. (2003). A computational model of prefrontal control in free recall: Strategic memory use in the california verbal learning task. *Journal of Cognitive Neuroscience, 15,* 821–832.

Bjork, R. A., & Whitten, W. B. (1974). Recency-sensitive retrieval processes in long-term free recall. *Cognitive Psychology, 6,* 173–189.

Bogacz, R., & Brown, M. W. (2003). Comparison of computational models of familiarity discrimination in the perirhinal cortex. *Hippocampus, 13,* 494–524.

Botvinick, M., & Plaut, D. C. (2006). Short-term memory for serial order: A recurrent neural network model. *Psychological Review, 113,* 201–233.

Brainerd, C. J., & Reyna, V. F. (1998). When things that were never experienced are easier to "remember" than things that were. *Psychological Science, 9,* 484.

Brozinsky, C. J., Yonelinas, A. P., Kroll, N. E., & Ranganath, C. (2005). Lag-sensitive repetition suppression effects in the anterior parahippocampal gyrus. *Hippocampus, 15,* 557–561.

Burgess, N., Becker, S., King, J. A., & O'Keefe, J. (2001). Memory for events and their spatial context: Models and experiments. *Philosophical Transactions of the Royal Society of London. Series B, Biological Sciences, 356*(1413), 1493–503.

Burgess, N., & Hitch, G. (2005). Computational models of working memory: Putting long-term memory into context. *Trends in Cognitive Sciences, 9*(11), 535–41.

Burgess, N., & O'Keefe, J. (1996). Neuronal computations underlying the firing of place cells and their role in navigation. *Hippocampus, 6,* 749–762.

Bussey, T. J., & Saksida, L. M. (2002). The organisation of visual object representations: A connectionist model of effects of lesions in perirhinal cortex. *European Journal of Neuroscience, 15,* 355–364.

Bussey, T. J., Saksida, L. M., & Murray, E. A. (2002). The role of perirhinal cortex in memory and perception: Conjunctive representations for object identification. In M. P. Witter & F. G. Waterlood (Eds.), *The parahippocampal region: Organisation and role in cognitive functions* (pp. 239–254). New York: Oxford.

Carlesimo, G. A., Marfia, G. A., Loasses, A., & Caltagirone, C. (1996). Recency effect in anterograde amnesia: Evidence for distinct memory stores underlying enhanced retrieval of terminal items in immediate and delayed recall paradigms. *Neuropsychologia, 34*(3), 177–184.

Clark, S. E., & Gronlund, S. D. (1996). Global matching models of recognition memory: How the models match the data. *Psychonomic Bulletin and Review, 3,* 37–60.

Criss, A. H., & Shiffrin, R. M. (2004). Context noise and item noise jointly determine recognition memory: A comment on Dennis and Humphreys (2001). *Psychological Review, 111,* 800–807.

Davachi, L., Mitchell, J. P., & Wagner, A. D. (2003). Multiple routes to memory: Distinct medial temporal processes build item and source memories. *Proceedings of the National Academy of Sciences, 100,* 2157–2162.

Davelaar, E. J., Goshen-Gottstein, Y., Ashkenazi, A., Haarmann, H. J., & Usher, M. (2005). The demise of short-term memory revisited: Empirical and computational investigations of recency effects. *Psychological Review, 112,* 3–42.

Deco, G., Rolls, E. T., & Horwitz, B. (2004). "What" and "where" in visual working memory: A computational neurodynamical perspective. *Journal of Cognitive Neuroscience, 16*(4), 683–701.

Dennis, S., & Humphreys, M. S. (2001). A context noise model of episodic word recognition. *Psychological Review, 108,* 452–477.

Dobbins, I. G., Rice, H. J., Wagner, A. D., & Schacter, D. L. (2003). Memory orientation and success: Separate neurocognitive components underlying episodic recognition. *Neuropsychologia, 41,* 318–333.

Durstewitz, D., Kelc, M., & Gunturkun, O. (1999). A neurocomputational theory of the dopaminergic modulation of working memory functions. *Journal of Neuroscience, 19,* 2807.

Durstewitz, D., Seamans, J. K., & Sejnowski, T. J. (2000). Dopamine-mediated stabilization of delay-period activity in a network model of prefrontal cortex. *Journal of Neurophysiology, 83,* 1733.

Egorov, A. V., Hamam, B. N., Fransen, E., Hasselmo, M. E., & Alonso, A. A. (2002). Graded persistent activity in entorhinal cortex neurons. *Nature, 420,* 173–178.

Eichenbaum, H., H., Otto, T., & Cohen, N. J. (1994). Two functional components of the hippocampal memory system. *Behavioral and Brain Sciences, 17*(3), 449–518.

Eldridge, L. L., Knowlton, B. J., Furmanski, C. S., Bookheimer, S. Y., & Engel, S. A. (2000). Remembering episodes: A selective role for the hippocampus during retrieval. *Nature Neuroscience, 3,* 1149–1152.

Elman, J. L. (1991). Distributed representations, simple recurrent networks, and grammatical structure. *Machine Learning, 7,* 195–225.

Estes, W. K. (1955). Statistical theory of distributional phenomena in learning. *Psychological Review, 62,* 369–377.

Fellous, J. M., Wang, X. J., & Lisman, J. E. (1998). A role for NMDA-receptor channels in working memory. *Nature Neuroscience, 1,* 273–275.

Ferino, F., Thierry, A. M., & Glowinski, J. (1987). Anatomical and electrophysiological evidence for a direct projection from ammon's horn to the medial prefrontal cortex in the rat. *Experimental Brain Research, 65,* 421–426.

Fletcher, P. C., & Henson, R. N. (2001). Frontal lobes and human memory: Insights from functional neuroimaging. *Brain, 124*(5), 849–881.

Fortin, N. J., Wright, S. P., & Eichenbaum, H. B. (2004). Recollection-like memory retrieval in rats is dependent on the hippocampus. *Nature*, *431*, 188–191.

Frank, M. J., Loughry, B., & O'Reilly, R. C. (2001). Interactions between the frontal cortex and basal ganglia in working memory: A computational model. *Cognitive, Affective, and Behavioral Neuroscience*, *1*, 137–160.

Gillund, G., & Shiffrin, R. M. (1984). A retrieval model for both recognition and recall. *Psychological Review*, *91*, 1–67.

Glanzer, M., Adams, J. K., Iverson, G. J., & Kim, K. (1993). The regularities of recognition memory. *Psychological Review*, *100*, 546–567.

Glenberg, A. M., Bradley, M. M., Stevenson, J. A., Kraus, T. A., Tkachuk, M. J., Gretz, A. L., et al. (1980). A two-process account of long-term serial position effects. *Journal of Experimental Psychology: Learning, Memory, and Cognition*, *6*, 355–369.

Gluck, M. A., Meeter, M., & Myers, C. E. (2003). Computational models of the hippocampal region: Linking incremental learning and episodic memory. *Trends in Cognitive Sciences*, *7*(6), 269-276.

Goldman-Rakic, P. S., Selemon, L. D., & Schwartz, M. L. (1984). Dual pathways connecting the dorsolateral prefrontal cortex with the hippocampal formation and parahippocampal cortex in the rhesus monkey. *Neuroscience*, *12*, 719–743.

Gonsalves, B. D., Kahn, I., Curran, T., Norman, K. A., & Wagner, A. D. (2005). Memory strength and repetition suppression: Multimodal imaging of medial temporal contributions to recognition. *Neuron*, *47*, 751–761.

Grossberg, S. (1976). Adaptive pattern classification and universal recoding I: Parallel development and coding of neural feature detectors. *Biological Cybernetics*, *23*, 121–134.

Grossberg, S. (1986). The adaptive self-organization of serial order in behavior: Speech, language, and motor control. In E. C. Schwab & H. C. Nusbaum (Eds.), *Pattern recognition in humans and machines. Volume I: Speech perception* (pp. 187–294). New York: Academic Press.

Grossberg, S., & Stone, G. (1986). Neural dynamics of word recognition and recall: Attentional priming, learning, and resonance. *Psychological Review*, *93*, 46–74.

Gruppuso, V., Lindsay, D. S., & Kelley, C. M. (1997). The process-dissociation procedure and similarity: Defining and estimating recollection and familiarity in recognition memory. *Journal of Experimental Psychology: Learning, Memory, and Cognition*, *23*, 259.

Hasselmo, M. E. (1995). Neuromodulation and cortical function: Modeling the physiological basis of behavior. *Behavioural Brain Research*, *67*, 1–27.

Hasselmo, M. E., Bodelon, C., & Wyble, B. P. (2002). A proposed function for hippocampal theta rhythm: Separate phases of encoding and retrieval enhance reversal of prior learning. *Neural Computation*, *14*, 793–818.

Hasselmo, M. E., & Fehlau, B. P. (2001). Differences in time course of ACh and GABA modulation of excitatory synaptic potentials in slices of rat hippocampus. *Journal of Neurophysiology*, *86*(4), 1792–1802.

Hasselmo, M. E., & Schnell, E. (1994). Laminar selectivity of the cholinergic suppression of synaptic transmission in rat hippocampal region CA1: computational modeling and brain slice physiology. *Journal of Neuroscience*, *14*(6), 3898–3914.

Hasselmo, M. E., Schnell, E., & Barkai, E. (1995). Dynamics of learning and recall at excitatory recurrent synapses and cholinergic modulation in rat hippocampal region CA3. *Journal of Neuroscience*, *15*(7 Pt. 2), 5249–5262.

Hasselmo, M. E., & Wyble, B. (1997). Free recall and recognition in a network model of the hippocampus: Simulating effects of scopolamine on human memory function. *Behavioural Brain Research*, *89*, 1–34.

Hasselmo, M. E., Wyble, B., & Wallenstein, G. V. (1996). Encoding and retrieval of episodic memories: Role of cholinergic and GABAergic modulation in the hippocampus. *Hippocampus*, *6*, 693–708.

Henson, R. N. A., Cansino, S., Herron, J. E., Robb, W. G., & Rugg, M. D. (2003). A familiarity signal in human anterior medial temporal cortex? *Hippocampus*, *13*, 301–304.

Hinton, G. E. (1989). Deterministic Boltzmann learning performs steepest descent in weight-space. *Neural Computation*, *1*, 143–150.

Hinton, G. E., & Sejnowski, T. J. (1986). Learning and relearning in Boltzmann machines. In D. E. Rumelhart, J. L. McClelland, & PDP Research Group (Eds.), *Parallel distributed processing. Volume 1: Foundations* (pp. 282–317). Cambridge, MA: MIT Press.

Hintzman, D. L. (1988). Judgments of frequency and recognition memory in a multiple-trace memory model. *Psychological Review, 95*, 528–551.

Hintzman, D. L., Curran, T., & Oppy, B. (1992). Effects of similiarity and repetition on memory: Registration without learning. *Journal of Experimental Psychology: Learning, Memory, and Cognition, 18*, 667–680.

Hirshman, E., Fisher, J., Henthorn, T., Arndt, J., & Passannante, A. (2002). Midazolam amnesia and dual-process models of the word-frequency mirror effect. *Journal of Memory and Language, 47*, 499–516.

Holdstock, J. S., Mayes, A. R., Roberts, N., Cezayirli, E., Isaac, C. L., O'Reilly, R. C. et al. (2002). Under what conditions is recognition spared relative to recall after selective hippocampal damage in humans? *Hippocampus, 12*, 341–351.

Howard, M. W., Addis, K. M., Jing, B., & Kahana, M. J. (2007). Semantic structure and episodic memory. In T. Landauer, D. McNamara, S. Dennis, & W. Kintsch (Eds.), *Handbook of Latent Semantic Analysis* (pp. 121–141). Mahwah, NJ: Lawrence Erlbaum.

Howard, M. W., Fotedar, M. S., Datey, A. V., & Hasselmo, M. E. (2005). The temporal context model in spatial navigation and relational learning: Toward a common explanation of medial temporal lobe function across domains. *Psychological Review, 112*, 75–116.

Howard, M. W., & Kahana, M. J. (1999). Contextual variability and serial position effects in free recall. *Journal of Experimental Psychology: Learning, Memory, and Cognition, 25*, 923.

Howard, M. W., & Kahana, M. J. (2002). A distributed representation of temporal context. *Journal of Mathematical Psychology, 46*, 269–299.

Howard, M. W., Kahana, M. J., & Wingfield, A. (2006). Aging and contextual binding: Modeling recency and lag-recency effects with the temporal context model. *Psychonomic Bulletin and Review, 13*, 439–445.

Humphreys, M. S., Bain, J. D., & Pike, R. (1989). Different ways to cue a coherent memory system: A theory for episodic, semantic, and procedural tasks. *Psychological Review, 96*, 208–233.

Jacoby, L. L., Yonelinas, A. P., & Jennings, J. M. (1997). The relation between conscious and unconscious (automatic) influences: A declaration of independence. In J. D. Cohen & J. W. Schooler (Eds.), *Scientific approaches to consciousness* (pp. 13–47). Mahway, NJ: Lawrence Erlbaum.

Jay, T. M., & Witter, M. P. (1991). Distribution of hippocampal CA1 and subicular efferents in the prefrontal cortex of the rat studied by means of anterograde transport of phaseolus vulgaris-leucoagglutinin. *The Journal of Comparative Neurology, 313*, 574–586.

Jensen, O., & Lisman, J. E. (2005). Hippocampal sequence-encoding driven by a cortical multi-item working memory buffer. *Trends in Neurosciences, 28*(2), 67–72.

Joordens, S., & Hockley, W. E. (2000). Recollection and familiarity through the looking glass: When old does not mirror new. *Journal of Experimental Psychology: Learning, Memory, and Cognition, 26*, 1534.

Kahana, M. J. (1996). Associative retrieval processes in free recall. *Memory and Cognition, 24*, 103–109.

Kahana, M. J., & Sekuler, R. (2002). Recognizing spatial patterns: A noisy exemplar approach. *Vision Research, 42*, 2177–2192.

Koutstaal, W., Schacter, D. L., & Jackson, E. M. (1999). Perceptually based false recognition of novel objects in amnesia: Effects of category size and similarity to category prototypes. *Cognitive Neuropsychology, 16*, 317.

Levitt, J. B., Lewis, D. A., Yoshioka, T., & Lund, J. S. (1993). Topography of pyramidal neuron intrinsic connections in macaque monkey prefrontal cortex (areas 9 & 46). *Journal of Comparative Neurology, 338*, 360–376.

Li, L., Miller, E. K., & Desimone, R. (1993). The representation of stimulus familiarity in anterior inferior temporal cortex. *Journal of Neurophysiology, 69*, 1918–1929.

Malmberg, K. J., Holden, J. E., & Shiffrin, R. M. (2004). Modeling the effects of repetitions, similarity, and normative word frequency on old-new recognition and judgments of frequency. *Journal of Experimental Psychology: Learning, Memory, and Cognition, 30*(2), 319–331.

Malmberg, K. J., & Shiffrin, R. M. (2005). The "one-shot" hypothesis for context storage. *Journal of Experimental Psychology: Learning, Memory, and Cognition, 31*(2), 322–336.

Malmberg, K. J., & Xu, J. (2007). On the flexibility and fallibility of associative memory. *Memory and Cognition, 35*, 545–556.

Malmberg, K. J., Zeelenberg, R., & Shiffrin, R. M. (2004). Turning up the noise or turning down the volume? On the nature of the impairment of episodic recognition memory by midazolam. *Journal of Experimental Psychology. Learning, Memory, and Cognition, 30*(2), 540–549.

Manns, J. R., Hopkins, R. O., Reed, J. M., Kitchener, E. G., & Squire, L. R. (2003). Recognition memory and the human hippocampus. *Neuron, 37*, 171–180.

Marr, D. (1971). Simple memory: A theory for archicortex. *Philosophical Transactions of the Royal Society (London) B, 262*, 23–81.

Mayes, A. R., Isaac, C. L., Downes, J. J., Holdstock, J. S., Hunkin, N. M., Montaldi, D. et al. (2001). Memory for single items, word pairs, and temporal order in a patient with selective hippocampal lesions. *Cognitive Neuropsychology, 18*, 97–123.

McClelland, J. L., & Chappell, M. (1998). Familiarity breeds differentiation: A subjective-likelihood approach to the effects of experience in recognition memory. *Psychological Review, 105*, 724.

McClelland, J. L., & Goddard, N. H. (1996). Considerations arising from a complementary learning systems perspective on hippocampus and neocortex. *Hippocampus, 6*, 654–665.

McClelland, J. L., McNaughton, B. L., & O'Reilly, R. C. (1995). Why there are complementary learning systems in the hippocampus and neocortex: Insights from the successes and failures of connectionist models of learning and memory. *Psychological Review, 102*, 419–457.

McNaughton, B. L., & Morris, R. G. M. (1987). Hippocampal synaptic enhancement and information storage within a distributed memory system. *Trends in Neurosciences, 10*(10), 408–415.

Meeter, M., & Murre, J. (in press). Tracelink: A model of amnesia and consolidation. *Cognitive Neuropsychology*.

Meeter, M., Murre, J., & Talamini, L. M. (2004). Mode shifting between storage and recall based on novelty detection in oscillating hippocampal circuits. *Hippocampus, 14*, 722–741.

Meeter, M., Myers, C. E., & Gluck, M. A. (2005). Integrating incremental learning and episodic memory models of the hippocampal region. *Psychological Review, 112*, 560–85.

Mehta, M. R., Lee, A. K., & Wilson, M. A. (2002). Role of experience and oscillations in transforming a rate code into a temporal code. *Nature, 416*, 741–745.

Melton, A. W., & Irwin, J. M. (1940). The influence of degree of interpolated learning on retroactive inhibition and the overt transfer of specific responses. *American Journal of Psychology, 3*, 173–203.

Mensink, G., & Raaijmakers, J. G. (1988). A model for interference and forgetting. *Psychological Review, 95*, 434–455.

Minai, A. A., & Levy, W. B. (1994). Setting the activity level in sparse random networks [Letter]. *Neural Computation, 6*, 85–99.

Moll, M., & Miikkulainen, R. (1997). Convergence-zone episodic memory: Analysis and simulations. *Neural Networks, 10*, 1017–1036.

Morris, R., Pandya, D. N., & Petrides, M. (1999). Fiber system linking the mid-dorsolateral frontal cortex with the retrosplenial/presubicular region in the rhesus monkey. *The Journal of Comparative Neurology, 407*, 183–192.

Movellan, J. R. (1990). Contrastive Hebbian learning in the continuous Hopfield model. In D. S. Tourtezky, G. E. Hinton, & T. J. Sejnowski (Eds.), *Proceedings of the 1990 connectionist models summer school* (pp. 10–17). San Mateo, CA: Morgan Kaufmann.

Murdock, B. B. (1993). TODAM2: A model for the storage and retrieval of item, associative, and serial-order information. *Psychological Review, 100*, 183–203.

Murnane, K., & Shiffrin, R. (1991). Interference and the representation of events in memory. *Journal of Experimental Psychology: Learning, Memory, and Cognition, 17*, 855–874.

Norman, K. A., Newman, E. L., & Detre, G. J. (2007). A neural network model of retrieval-induced forgetting. *Psychological Review, 114*, 887–953.

Norman, K. A., Newman, E. L., Detre, G. J., & Polyn, S. M. (2006). How inhibitory oscillations can train neural networks and punish competitors. *Neural Computation, 18*, 1577–1610.

Norman, K. A., Newman, E. L., & Perotte, A. J. (2005). Methods for reducing interference in the complementary learning systems model: Oscillating inhibition and autonomous memory rehearsal. *Neural Networks, 18*, 1212–1228.

Norman, K. A., & O'Reilly, R. C. (2003). Modeling hippocampal and neocortical contributions to recognition memory: A complementary-learning-systems approach. *Psychological Review, 104*, 611–646.

Nowlan, S. J. (1990). Maximum likelihood competitive learning. In D. S. Touretzky (Ed.), *Advances in neural information processing systems, 2* (pp. 574–582). San Mateo, CA: Morgan Kaufmann.

Oja, E. (1982). A simplified neuron model as a principal component analyzer. *Journal of Mathematical Biology, 15*, 267–273.

O'Keefe, J., & Nadel, L. (1978). *The hippocampus as a cognitive map.* Oxford, UK: Oxford University Press.

O'Reilly, R. C. (1998). Six principles for biologically-based computational models of cortical cognition. *Trends in Cognitive Sciences, 2*(11), 455–462.

O'Reilly, R. C., & Frank, M. J. (2006). Making working memory work: A computational model of learning in the frontal cortex and basal ganglia. *Neural Computation, 18*, 283–328.

O'Reilly, R. C., & McClelland, J. L. (1994). Hippocampal conjunctive encoding, storage, and recall: Avoiding a tradeoff. *Hippocampus, 4*(6), 661–682.

O'Reilly, R. C., & Munakata, Y. (2000). *Computational explorations in cognitive neuroscience: Understanding the mind by simulating the brain.* Cambridge, MA: MIT Press.

O'Reilly, R. C., Norman, K. A., & McClelland, J. L. (1998). A hippocampal model of recognition memory. In M. I. Jordan, M. J. Kearns, & S. A. Solla (Eds.), *Advances in neural information processing systems 10* (pp. 73–79). Cambridge, MA: MIT Press.

O'Reilly, R. C., & Rudy, J. W. (2001). Conjunctive representations in learning and memory: Principles of cortical and hippocampal function. *Psychological Review, 108*, 311–345.

Peterson, L. R., & Peterson, M. R. (1959). Short-term retention of individual verbal items. *Journal of Experimental Psychology, 58*, 193–198.

Polyn, S. M. (2005). *Neuroimaging, behavioral, and computational investigations of memory targeting.* Unpublished doctoral dissertation, Princeton University, Princeton, NJ.

Polyn, S. M., Norman, K. A., & Cohen, J. D. (2003, April). *Modeling prefrontal and medial temporal contributions to episodic memory.* Paper Presented at the 10th Annual Meeting of the Cognitive Neuroscience Society, New York, NY.

Pucak, M. L., Levitt, J. B., Lund, J. S., & Lewis, D. A. (1996). Patterns of intrinsic and associational circuitry in monkey prefrontal cortex. *Journal of Comparative Neurology, 376*, 614–630.

Raaijmakers, J. G. W. (2005). Modeling implicit and explicit memory. In C. Izawa & N. Ohta (Eds.), *Human learning and memory: Advances in theory and application* (pp. 85–105). Mahwah, NJ: Lawrence, Erlbaum.

Raaijmakers, J. G. W., & Shiffrin, R. M. (1981). Search of associative memory. *Psychological Review, 88*, 93–134.

Raaijmakers, J. G. W., & Shiffrin, R. M. (2002). Models of memory. In H. Pashler & D. Medin (Eds.), *Stevens' handbook of experimental psychology, Third edition, Volume 2: Memory and cognitive processes* (pp. 43–76). New York: John Wiley and Sons.

Ranganath, C., Yonelinas, A. P., Cohen, M. X., Dy, C. J., Tom, S., & D'Esposito, M. (2003). Dissociable correlates for familiarity and recollection within the medial temporal lobes. *Neuropsychologia, 42*, 2–13.

Reder, L. M., Nhouyvanisvong, A., Schunn, C. D., Ayers, M. S., Angstadt, P., & Hiraki, K. A. (2000). A mechanistic account of the mirror effect for word frequency: A computational model of remember-know judgments in a continuous recognition paradigm. *Journal of Experimental Psychology: Learning, Memory, and Cognition, 26*, 294–320.

Rolls, E. T. (1989). Functions of neuronal networks in the hippocampus and neocortex in memory. In J. H. Byrne & W. O. Berry (Eds.), *Neural models of plasticity: Experimental and theoretical approaches* (pp. 240–265). San Diego, CA: Academic Press.

Rumelhart, D. E., & Zipser, D. (1986). Feature discovery by competitive learning. In D. E. Rumelhart, J. L. McClelland, & PDP Research Group (Eds.), *Parallel distributed processing. Volume 1: Foundations* (pp. 151–193). Cambridge, MA: MIT Press.

Russchen, F. T., Amaral, D. G., & Price, J. L. (1987). The afferent input to the magnocellular division of the mediodorsal thalamic nucleus in the monkey, macaca fascicularis. *The Journal of Comparative Neuroanatomy, 256*, 175–210.

Schacter, D. L. (1987). Memory, amnesia, and frontal lobe dysfunction. *Psychobiology, 15*, 21–36.

Scoville, W. B., & Milner, B. (1957). Loss of recent memory after bilateral hippocampal lesions. *Journal of Neurology, Neurosurgery, and Psychiatry, 20*, 11–21.

Sherry, D. F., & Schacter, D. L. (1987). The evolution of multiple memory systems. *Psychological Review, 94*(4), 439–454.

Shiffrin, R. M., Huber, D. E., & Marinelli, K. (1995). Effects of category length and strength on familiarity in recognition. *Journal of Experimental Psychology: Learning, Memory and Cognition, 21*, 267–287.

Shiffrin, R. M., & Steyvers, M. (1997). A model for recognition memory: REM – retrieving effectively from memory. *Psychonomic Bulletin and Review, 4*, 145–166.

Shimamura, A. P. (1994). Memory and frontal lobe function. In M. S. Gazzaniga (Ed.), *The cognitive neurosciences* (pp. 803–815). Cambridge, MA: MIT Press.

Simons, J. S., & Spiers, H. J. (2003). Prefrontal and medial temporal lobe interactions in long-term memory. *Nature Reviews Neuroscience, 4*(8), 637–648.

Sohal, V. S., & Hasselmo, M. E. (2000). A model for experience-dependent changes in the responses of inferotemporal neurons. *Network : Computation in Neural Systems, 11*, 169.

Sohn, M. H., Goode, A., Stenger, V. A., Jung, K. J., Carter, C. S., & Anderson, J. R. (2005). An information-processing model of three cortical regions: evidence in episodic memory retrieval. *Neuroimage, 25*(1), 21–33.

Squire, L. R. (1992). Memory and the hippocampus: A synthesis from findings with rats, monkeys, and humans. *Psychological Review, 99*, 195–231.

Squire, L. R., Shimamura, A. P., & Amaral, D. G. (1989). Memory and the hippocampus. In J. H. Byrne & W. O. Berry (Eds.), *Neural models of plasticity: Experimental and theoretical approaches* (pp. 208–239). San Diego, CA: Academic Press.

Standing, L. (1973). Learning 10,000 pictures. *Quarterly Journal of Experimental Psychology, 25*, 207–222.

Sutherland, R. J., & Rudy, J. W. (1989). Configural association theory: The role of the hippocampal formation in learning, memory, and amnesia. *Psychobiology, 17*(2), 129–144.

Teyler, T. J., & Discenna, P. (1986). The hippocampal memory indexing theory. *Behavioral Neuroscience, 100*, 147–154.

Treves, A., & Rolls, E. T. (1994). A computational analysis of the role of the hippocampus in memory. *Hippocampus, 4*, 374–392.

Usher, M., & Cohen, J. D. (1999). Short-term memory and selection processes in a frontal-lobe model. In D. Heinke, G. W. Humphries, & A. Olsen (Eds.), *Connectionist models in cognitive neuroscience* (pp. 78–91). London: Springer-Verlag.

Usher, M., & McClelland, J. L. (2001). The time course of perceptual choice: The leaky, competing accumulator model. *Psychological Review, 108*, 550–592.

Westerberg, C. E., Paller, K. A., Weintraub, S., Mesulam, M. M., Holdstock, J., Mayes, A., et al. (2006). When memory does not fail: Familiarity-based recognition in mild cognitive impairment and Alzheimer's disease. *Neuropsychology, 20*, 193–205.

Witter, M. P., Wouterlood, F. G., Naber, P. A., & Van Haeften, T. (2000). Anatomical organization of the parahippocampal-hippocampal network. *Ann. N. Y. Acad. Sci., 911*, 1–24.

Wu, X., Baxter, R. A., & Levy, W. B. (1996). Context codes and the effect of noisy learning on a simplified hippocampal CA3 model. *Biological Cybernetics, 74*, 159–165.

Wyble, B. P., Linster, C., & Hasselmo, M. E. (2000). Size of CA1-evoked synaptic potentials is related to theta rhythm phase in rat hippocampus. *Journal of Neurophysiology, 83*(4), 2138–2144.

Xiang, J. Z., & Brown, M. W. (1998). Differential encoding of novelty, familiarity, and recency in regions of the anterior temporal lobe. *Neuropharmacology, 37*, 657–676.

Xu, J., & Malmberg, K. J. (2007). Modeling the effects of verbal- and non-verbal pair strength on associative recognition. *Memory and Cognition, 35*, 526–544.

Yonelinas, A. P. (2002). The nature of recollection and familiarity: A review of 30 years of research. *Journal of Memory and Language, 46*, 441–517.

Yonelinas, A. P., Kroll, N. E., Quamme, J. R., Lazzara, M. M., Sauve, M. J., Widaman, K. F., et al. (2002). Effects of extensive temporal lobe damage or mild hypoxia on recollection and familiarity. *Nature Neuroscience, 5*(11), 1236–1241.

CHAPTER 8

Computational Models of Semantic Memory

Timothy T. Rogers

1. Introduction

Consider the predicament of a young infant recently arrived in the world and trying to make sense of it. She has some resources at her disposal: sensory information about her environment, the ability to act on it, and in most cases, a surrounding linguistic environment, family, and culture that can help to teach her what she needs to know. Nevertheless, the task is daunting. Suppose on one occasion that daddy gestures out the window and says, "Look, a bunny!" To what is he referring? The field of green? The tall structures dotting the horizon? The brownish object streaking rapidly along the ground? Later in the evening, mommy repeats the word, this time gesturing toward a white contour in a picture book – it is not moving, it is not brown, it is two-dimensional. At bedtime big brother says, "Here's your bunny," this time handing her a soft pink fuzzy object. What on earth could they all be talking about!

And yet, before she turns 10, she will know that the word "bunny" refers to a particular animal with long ears and a fluffy little tail, and what's more, she will know that bunnies have blood and bones inside; that they can reproduce, grow, and die; that they can feel pain and get hungry; that they are warm to the touch; that they live in holes in the ground; and that some people believe it brings good luck to wear a bunny-foot on a chain. When she gets a new bunny rabbit as a pet, she will be able to infer that all of these things are true, even though she has never before encountered this *particular* bunny; and when she brings her new pet to show-and-tell, she will be able to communicate all of these facts to her classmates simply by talking. And this knowledge about bunny rabbits constitutes a tiny fraction of the general factual world-knowledge she will have accumulated. Understanding the basis of these human abilities – to recognize, comprehend, and make inferences about objects and events in the world, and to comprehend and produce statements about them – is the goal of research in semantic memory.

Semantic memory is memory for meanings. In some disciplines (e.g., linguistics), the word *semantics* refers exclusively to the meanings of words and sentences. In cognitive science, however, the term typically encompasses knowledge of any kind of meaning, linguistic or nonlinguistic, including knowledge about the meanings of words, sentences, objects, and events, as well as general facts (Tulving, 1972). Accordingly, the terms "semantic memory" and "conceptual knowledge" are often used interchangeably in the literature. Semantic memory is usually differentiated from episodic memory (long-term declarative memory for particular episodes that are firmly rooted in a particular time and place; see Chapter 7 in this volume), procedural memory (long-term nondeclarative memory for well-learned action sequences; see Chapters 13 and 14 in this volume), and working memory (short-term memory for retention and manipulation of task-relevant information; see Chapter 15 in this volume).

Semantic abilities are central to a broad swath of cognitive science, including language comprehension and production, object recognition, categorization, induction and inference, and reasoning. Each of these topics constitutes a domain of study in its own right, and many are covered in other chapters in this Handbook (see Chapter 9 on concepts and categorization, Chapter 11 on induction and inference, and Chapter 3 on Bayesian models). This chapter focuses on three principal questions motivating research in semantic memory: How do we come to know which items and events in the environment should be treated as "the same kind of thing" for purposes of communication, action, and induction; how do we learn to map language onto these kinds; and how are these cognitive abilities subserved by neural processes?

These questions have, of course, been the subject of philosophical inquiry for centuries, but the application of computational methods has considerably advanced our understanding of the cognitive and neural bases of semantic abilities. Indeed, semantic memory was the target of some of the earliest computer simulation work in cognitive science, and much contemporary research in the domain can be fruitfully viewed as a re-

action to these early ideas. The next section of the chapter thus provides a brief overview of two theoretical frameworks that first came to prominence in the 1970s: *spreading activation* theories based on Collins and Quillian's (1969) influential computer model, and *prototype* theories deriving from the work of Eleanor Rosch (Rosch, 1978; Rosch & Mervis, 1975) and others. A consideration of the strengths and limitations of these basic ideas will highlight the most pressing questions guiding current research in semantic memory. The remaining sections then follow three parallel strands of modeling research that are beginning to offer leverage on this issues. Section 3 traces developments spurred by Hinton's (1981) Parallel Distributed Processing (PDP) model of semantics, culminating in the general approach to semantic cognition recently laid out by Rogers and McClelland (2004). Section 4 addresses how sensitivity to temporal structure in language and experience can shape conceptual representations, following a thread of research that begins with Elman's (1990) seminal work and culminates in Latent Semantic Analysis (LSA) and related approaches (Burgess & Lund, 1997; Landauer & Dumais, 1997; Steyvers, Griffiths, & Dennis, 2006). Section 5 considers models targeted at understanding the neural basis of semantic abilities.

2. Hierarchies and Prototypes

One of the earliest implemented computer models in cognitive science was the hierarchical spreading-activation model of semantic memory described by Collins and Quillian (1969). The model was predicated on the notion that semantic memory consists of a vast set of stored simple propositions (e.g., "cats have fur," "canaries can sing," and so on). Under the rules of logical inference, such a system of propositions can support new deductive inferences via the syllogism; for instance, given the propositions "Socrates is a man" and "all men are mortal," it is possible to infer that Socrates is mortal without requiring storage of a third proposition. Collins and Quillian's model effectively used the syllogism as a basis for organizing propositional knowledge in memory. In their model, concepts (mental representations of categories) are stored as nodes in a network, and predicates (specifying relationships between concepts) are stored as labeled links between nodes. Simple propositional beliefs are represented by linking two nodes with a particular predicate. For example, the belief that a robin is a kind of bird is represented by connecting the nodes *robin* and *bird* with a predicate that specifies class-inclusion (an ISA link, as in "a robin *is a* bird"); whereas the belief that birds can fly is represented by connecting the nodes *bird* and *fly* with a link labeled *can*, and so on.

The authors observed that, if concepts at different levels of specificity were linked with ISA predicates, the system could provide an economical means of knowledge storage and generalization. For instance, the knowledge that a canary is a kind of bird is represented by connecting the node for *canary* to the node for *bird* with an ISA link; knowledge that birds are animals is stored by connecting the *bird* node to the *animal* node, and so on. To make inferences about the properties of a given concept such as *canary*, the model first retrieves all of the predicates stored directly with the corresponding node (e.g., *can sing*); but the search process then moves upward along the ISA links and searches properties at the next node, so that the predicates attached to more inclusive concepts also get attributed to the probe concept. For *canary*, activation first searches the *bird* node, supporting the inference that the canary can fly, and then the *animal* node, supporting the inference that the canary can move.

In addition to economy of storage, this system provided a simple mechanism of knowledge generalization; for example, to store the fact that all birds have a spleen, it is sufficient to create a node for *spleen* and connect it to the *bird* node with a link labeled *has*. The retrieval process will then ensure that *has a spleen* generalizes to all of the individual bird concepts residing

beneath the *bird* node in the hierarchy. Similarly, if the system is "told" that there is something called a "Xxyzzyx" that is a kind of bird, it can store this information by creating a new node for *Xxyzzyx* and attaching it to the *bird* node. The retrieval mechanism will then ensure that all properties true of birds are attributed to the Xxyzzyx.

Early empirical assessments of the model appeared to lend some support to the notion that concepts were organized hierarchically in memory. Specifically, Collins and Quillian (1969) showed that the time taken to verify the truth of written propositions varied linearly with the number of nodes traversed in the hierarchy. Participants were fastest to verify propositions like "a canary can sing," which required searching a single node (i.e., *canary*), and slower to verify propositions like "a canary has skin," which required searching three nodes in series (first *canary*, then *bird*, then *animal*). Later studies, however, seriously challenged the model as originally formulated, showing for instance that property- and category-verification times vary systematically with the prototypicality of the item probed, so that participants are faster to decide that a robin (a typical bird) has feathers than that a penguin (an atypical bird) has feathers. Because the nodes in the network were cast as noncompositional primitives, there was no way to represent "typicality" in the original model, and no process that would permit typicality to influence judgment speed. Moreover, the influence of typicality on property decision times was sufficiently strong as to produce results that directly contradicted the Collins and Quillian model. For example, participants were faster to decide that a chicken is an animal than that it is a bird, even though *chicken* and *bird* must be closer together in the hierarchy (Rips, Shoben, & Smith, 1973).

These and other challenges led Collins and Loftus (1975) to elaborate the framework. Instead of a search process that begins at the bottom of the hierarchy and moves upward through class-inclusion links, the authors proposed a search mechanism by which the "activation" of a probe concept such as *canary* would "spread out" along all outgoing links, activating other nodes related to the probe, which in turn could pass activation via their own links. In this *spreading activation* framework, the strict hierarchical organization of the original model was abandoned, so that direct links could be established between any pair of concepts; and the authors further suggested that links between concept nodes could vary in their "strength," that is, the speed with which the spreading activation process could move from one node to the next. On this account, people are faster to retrieve the properties of typical items because these are more strongly connected to more general concepts than are less typical items; and the system can rapidly determine that a chicken is an animal by storing a direct link between the corresponding nodes, rather than having to "deduce" that this is true by allowing activation to spread to *animal* via *bird*. These elaborations were, however, purchased at the cost of computational simplicity. One appeal of the original model was its specification of a search process in sufficient detail that it could be programmed on a computer. This precision and simplicity depended on the strict hierarchical organization of concepts proposed by Collins and Quillian (1969). When all nodes can potentially be connected via links of varying strengths, it is not clear how to limit the search process – the spread of activation through the network – so as to retrieve only those properties true of the probe concept. For instance, if the proposition "all bikes have wheels" is stored by linking the nodes for *bike* and *wheel*, and the proposition "all wheels are round" is stored by linking *wheel* and *round*, how does the network avoid activating the predicate *is round* when probed with the concept *bike*?

A second limitation of the spreading-activation theory is that it was not clear how the propositional information encoded in the network should be "linked" to perceptual and motor systems. Spreading-activation theories seem intuitive when they are applied to purely propositional knowledge, that is, when the nodes in the network

are understood as corresponding to individual words, and the links to individual predicates, so that the entire system of knowledge may be accurately characterized as a system of propositions. Under such a scheme, there are few questions about which concepts – which nodes and links – should inhabit the network. Very simply, each node and link corresponds to a word in the language, so that the contents of the network are determined by the lexicon, and the structure of the network represents beliefs that can be explicitly stated by propositions (e.g., "all birds have feathers"). And such a representational scheme seems most plausible when considering experiments of the kind conducted by Collins and Quillian (1969), where participants must make judgments about the truth of written propositions. When the stimuli to be comprehended are perceptual representations of objects, things get more complicated, because it is less clear which nodes in the network should be "activated" by a given stimulus. A particular dog might belong equally to the classes collie, dog, pet, animal, and living thing, so which of these nodes should a visual depiction of the dog activate? More generally, it is unclear in propositional spreading-activation models how the nodes and links of the network relate to or communicate with the sensory and motor systems that provide input to and code output from the semantic system.

2.1. *Prototype and Similarity-Based Approaches*

Around the same time, there was intensive research focusing directly on the question of how objects are categorized for purposes of naming and induction (see Chapter 9 on concepts and categorization and Chapter 11 on induction and inference in this volume). Throughout the 1950s and 1960s, researchers appear to have assumed that membership in everyday categories could be determined with reference to necessary and sufficient criteria (Bruner, Goodnow, & Austin, 1956). Studies of category learning thus focused on understanding how people come to know which of an item's properties are necessary and sufficient for membership in some category, and such studies typically employed simple stimuli with well-defined properties organized into artificial categories according to some rule. For instance, participants might be shown a series of stimuli varying in shape, color, and size, arbitrarily grouped by the experimenter into categories on the basis of one or more of these dimensions. The participant's goal was to determine the rule governing which items would fall into which categories, and the aim of the research was to determine which strategies participants employed to determine the rule, which kinds of rules were easy or difficult to learn, how easily participants could switch from one rule to another, and so on.

In the early 1970s, Rosch (Rosch & Mervis, 1975; Rosch, Simpson, & Miller, 1976), citing Wittgenstein (1953), observed that most everyday categories are not, in fact, defined by necessary and sufficient criteria and that, instead, members of categories were best understood as sharing a set of family resemblances. For instance, most dogs tend to be hairy, four-legged friendly domesticated animals, even though none of these properties constitutes necessary or sufficient grounds for concluding that something is a dog. Rosch further showed that the cognitive processes by which we categorize and make inferences about names and properties of objects appear to be influenced by family resemblance relationships (Mervis & Rosch, 1981; Rosch, 1978; Rosch et al., 1976). For instance:

1. Members of a given category can vary considerably in their typicality or representativeness, and members of a given language community show remarkable consistency in their judgments of typicality. For instance, people reliably judge robins to be good examples of the category *bird*, but judge penguins to be relatively poor examples.
2. Judgments of typicality appear to reflect the attribute structure of the environment. Items judged to be good or typical members have many properties in common with other category members and

few distinguishing properties, whereas the reverse is true for items judged to be atypical.
3. Category typicality influences the speed and accuracy with which objects can be named and categorized: As previously mentioned, people are generally faster and more accurate to name and to categorize typical items than atypical items.

From these and other observations, Rosch proposed that semantic/conceptual knowledge about properties of common objects is stored in a set of *category prototypes*, that is, summary representations of categories that specify the properties most likely to be observed in category members. To retrieve information about a visually presented stimulus, the item is categorized by comparing its observed properties to those of stored category prototypes. The item is assigned to the prototype with the best match, and any properties stored with the matching prototype (including, for instance, its name, as well as other characteristics that may not be directly apparent in the stimulus itself) are then attributed to the object. On this view, category membership depends on similarity to a stored prototype and is therefore graded rather than all-or-nothing. People are faster to recognize typical category members because, by definition, they share more properties with their category prototype, so that the matching process completes more rapidly.

Rosch herself never proposed a computational implementation of prototype theory (Rosch, 1978). Her ideas did, however, spur a considerable volume of research into the computational mechanisms of categorization, which are the topic of another chapter (see Chapter 9 in this volume). For current purposes, it is sufficient to note that the *similarity-based* models deriving from Rosch's approach offer a quite different explanation of human semantic cognition than do spreading-activation theories. Specifically, generalization and induction occur as a consequence of similarity-based activation of stored representations in memory and not through a process of implicit deduction over stored propositions; representations in memory are not linked together in a propositional processing hierarchy or network; and items are treated as "the same kind of thing" when they activate the same prototype or similar sets of instance traces and not because they connect to the same node in a processing hierarchy.

The two approaches have complementary strengths and weaknesses. Spreading activation models, because they propose that category representations are organized within a processing hierarchy, are economical and provide an explicit mechanism for induction across categories at different levels of specificity. They do not, however, offer much insight into the basis of graded category membership, typicality effects, and so on. Similarity-based theories provide intuitive accounts of such phenomena, but raise questions about the representation of concepts at different levels of specificity. Consider, for instance, the knowledge that both dogs and cats have eyes, DNA, the ability to move, and so on. In spreading-activation theories, such information can be stored just once with the *animal* representation and then retrieved for particular individual animals through the spreading activation process. In similarity-based theories, it is not clear where such information resides. If it is stored separately with each category or instance representation, this raises questions of economy and capacity. On the other hand, if separate prototypes are stored for categories at different levels of specificity – one each for *animal*, *bird* and *penguin*, say – it is not clear whether or how these different levels of representation constrain each other. If, for example, the *bird* prototype contains the attribute *can fly* but the *penguin* representation contains the attribute *cannot fly*, how does the system "know" which attribution to make?

2.2. Challenges for Current Theories

It may seem that such issues are best resolved through some combination of spreading-activation and similarity-based approaches, and indeed Rosch (Rosch et al., 1976) and others (Jolicoeur, Gluck, & Kosslyn, 1984) do not seem to view the two frameworks as incompatible. Theoretical developments in semantic cognition have not, however, tended to move in this direction, partly because of serious critical reactions to similarity-based approaches raised in the 1980s that continue to shape research today. Five core issues arising from this criticism are summarized in the following section; the remainder of this chapter will consider how computational models offer insight as to how to resolve these issues.

2.2.1. CATEGORY COHERENCE

Some sets of items seem to form "good" or natural groupings, whereas others do not (Murphy & Medin, 1985). For instance, the category *dog* encompasses a variety of items that seem intuitively to "go together" or to cohere, whereas a category such as *grue* – things that are currently blue but will turn green after the year 2010 – does not. Moreover, the category *dog* supports induction; if you learn that a particular dog, say Lassie, has a certain kind of protein in her blood, you are likely to conclude that all or most other dogs have the same protein in their blood. Categories like *grue* do not support induction. What makes some categories, like *dog*, coherent and useful for induction, and other perfectly well-defined sets of items incoherent and useless? Put differently, how does the semantic system "know" for which groupings of items it should form a category representation – a prototype or a node in the network – and which not? One possibility is that the system stores a category representation for each word (or at least each noun) in the lexicon; but this solution just pushes the question a step back: Why should the language include a word for the concept *dog* but not for the concept *grue*? Any theory suggesting that semantic abilities depend on a mediating categorization process without specifying how the system "knows" which category representations should be created has, in some sense, assumed what it is trying to explain.

2.2.2. FEATURE SELECTION

Similarity-based models propose that retrieval of semantic information depends on the degree of similarity between a probe stimulus and a set of stored representations. Any such assessment must specify which probe features or characteristics "count" toward the measure of similarity and how different features are weighted in the determination. As Murphy and Medin (1985) have noted, a zebra and a barber pole might be categorized as "the same kind of thing" if the property *has stripes* were given sufficient weight.

It is an empirical fact that people do selectively weight different properties in semantic tasks. In the first of many such experiments, Landau, Smith, and Jones (1988) showed children a variety of blocks varying in shape, size, and texture. After labeling one of the blocks by pointing at it and saying, "See this, this is a dax," the authors asked children if they could find another "dax." Children could have used any of the salient features to generalize the new word; but the majority of children selected another object of a similar shape, largely ignoring its size and texture. Thus, the authors proposed that children are subject to a "shape bias" when learning new words, that is, they assume that the word encompasses items with similar shapes or, equivalently, they weight shape heavily when constructing a representation of the word's meaning.

Moreover, although some properties are undoubtedly inherently more salient than others, this cannot be the sole explanation of such biases because people will selectively weight the very same properties differently for items in different conceptual domains. For instance, Jones, Smith, and Landau (1991) have shown that the shape-bias can be attenuated simply by sticking a pair of eyes on the various blocks. Specifically, children were much more likely to use common texture as a basis for generalizing a new name when the blocks had eyes than when they did not, suggesting that they believe texture to be more "important" for categorizing animals (most of which have eyes)

than nonanimals. Such domain-specific attribute weighting poses an interesting puzzle for similarity-based models: One cannot compute similarity to stored representations and thus cannot categorize without knowing how different attributes should be weighted; but one cannot know which weightings to use until the item has been categorized, because different weightings are used for different kinds of things (Gelman & Williams, 1998).

2.2.3. CONTEXT SENSITIVITY

Of the many things one knows about a common object such as a piano, only a small subset is ever important or relevant in any given situation. For instance, if you have arrived at a friend's house to help her move, the most important fact about the piano is that it is heavy; if, however, you have come to audition for a band, the most important fact is that it makes music. That is, the semantic information that "comes to mind" in any given situation depends on the context. Meanings of words are also sensitive to both linguistic context and to real-world context; for instance, the referent of the phrase "Check out my hog" may be completely different depending on whether one is speaking to a farmer or a biker. Contextual influences on semantic task performance have been robustly documented in a very wide variety of tasks (Yeh & Barsalou, 2006), yet the implications of such context-sensitivity seem not to have penetrated many models of semantics (though see Medin & Shaffer, 1978). Both spreading-activation models and prototype theories specify how individual concepts may be represented and activated, but an implicit assumption of such models is that contextual information is effectively discarded – neither approach specifies, for instance, what would differ in the retrieval process when one moves a piano as opposed to playing it. The default assumption seems to be that the very same representation (node or prototype) would be activated in both cases, and it is not clear how different information would come to the fore in the two situations.

2.2.4. ABSTRACT CONCEPTS

What are the "properties" of concepts like *justice*, or *alive*, or *beautiful* that would allow one to construct prototypes of these categories or to connect them together with simple predicates in a spreading-activation network? Such questions may seem beyond the grasp of contemporary theories of semantic memory, which predominantly focus on knowledge about concrete objects with directly observable characteristics; but in fact the same questions are pressing even for such theories. The reason is that the properties often invoked as being critical for representing concrete concepts are frequently quite abstract in and of themselves. Consider, for instance, the properties important for the concept *animal*, which might include self-initiated movement and action-at-a-distance (Mandler, 2000), contingent movement (Johnson, 2000), goal-directedness (Csibra et al., 1999), and "biological" patterns of motion (Bertenthal, 1993), among other things. It is difficult to see how these might be directly available through perceptual mechanisms. For instance, different instances of self-initiated movement may be perceptually quite different – birds flap and glide, rabbits hop, snakes slither, people walk, and so on. To recognize that these different patterns of motion all have something important in common – "self-initiatedness," say – is to synthesize from them what is effectively an *abstract* feature. Even relatively concrete properties, such as having legs or a face, seem less and less concrete the more one considers the range of variability in the actual appearance of the legs or faces on, say, birds, dogs, fish, and insects. So a relatively concrete concept such as *animal* depends on the specification of properties that can be relatively abstract. Similarly, the most important properties for many manmade objects are often functions, which are also difficult or impossible to define with reference to purely perceptual characteristics. A hammer and a screwdriver, for example, have similar functions – they are used to fasten things together – and for this reason may be considered similar kinds of things, despite having quite different shapes and demanding quite different kinds of praxis. In general, theories of semantic memory must explain how people become sensitive to such abstract regularities and are able to use them to constrain property generalization. The suggestion that such regularities are directly apparent in the environment is not transparently true for many such properties.

2.2.5. REPRESENTING MULTIPLE OBJECTS, RELATIONSHIPS, AND EVENTS

Finally, it should be clear that both spreading-activation and similarity-based theories are targeted predominantly at explaining knowledge about individual concepts, corresponding roughly to the meanings of single words. But semantic abilities extend considerably beyond knowledge about the meanings of individual words and objects: They encompass knowledge about events and situations (e.g., how to order in a restaurant) as well as knowledge about various relationships between and within individual objects, including associative relationships (e.g., hammers are used with nails) and causal relationships among object properties (e.g., having hollow bones causes a bird to be light), and between objects (e.g., having a certain scent causes the flower to attract bees). In many cases, the single object's meaning seems to rely on its relationships to these other objects; for instance, it makes no sense to conceive of the hammer as a "decontextualized pounder" (Wilson & Keil, 2000); rather, the hammer's meaning depends partly on the fact that it is used specifically to pound nails, usually with the intent of attaching two separate objects. Without some account of how multiple objects and their relationships to one another combine to form representations of events and scenes, it is difficult to understand how such knowledge arises even for the meanings of single words and objects.

2.3. *Summary*

Two different computational frameworks informed research in semantic memory throughout the 1970s and 1980s: spreading activation models and prototype (and other similarity-based) theories. These two frameworks still form the theoretical background to much empirical research in cognitive psychology and are the most likely to be covered in cognitive psychology textbooks. And both approaches continue to foster ongoing research, especially in the domains of categorization (Smith, 2002; Zaki & Nosofsky, 2004) and in artificial intelligence (Crestani, 1997), and aspects of lexical processing and speech production (Bodner & Masson, 2003; Dell, 1986). These frameworks raise challenging questions, however, about the computational basis of human semantic abilities, specifically:

1. Why do some sets of items form more "coherent" categories than others, and how does the semantic system "know" which category representations to form?
2. Why are some properties more "important" for governing semantic generalization and induction than others, and how does the system "know" which properties are important for which concepts?
3. How is context represented, and how does it work to constrain which information "comes to mind" in a given situation?
4. How are abstract concepts and properties acquired?
5. How can the system combine multiple concepts together to represent events, scenes, and relationships among objects?

Some of these questions have been addressed, with varying degrees of success, by computational modeling efforts that fall outside the scope of this chapter because they mostly pertain to domains addressed by other chapters in this volume. Much of this work is specifically focused on understanding categorization phenomena. Anderson's Rational model of categorization (Anderson, 1991) provides an explanation of how a categorization-based semantic system can "decide" which category representations should be created in memory. Models proposed by Kruschke (1992) and Nosofsky (1986) provide hypotheses about how certain feature dimensions are selectively weighted when making categorization judgments; and the "context" models of categorization (Medin & Shaffer, 1978; Nosofsky, 1984) provide some suggestions as to how different kinds of information about a given concept may be retrieved in different situations or contexts. As previously noted, computational models focused on these questions are discussed at length in other chapters in this volume, specifically, Chapter 9 on categorization and concepts, Chapter 11 on induction and inference, and Chapter 3 on Bayesian approaches to cognition. The work discussed in the following Sections 3 through 5 will follow three threads of research in semantic cognition that derive from the Parallel Distributed Processing (PDP) approach to cognition.

3. Distributed Semantic Models

3.1. *Hinton's (1981) Distributed Model*

The first important thread begins with Hinton's (1981) proposal for storing propositional knowledge (of the kind described in a Quillian-like semantic network) in a PDP network. As in most information-processing frameworks, PDP models typically have "inputs" that respond to direct stimulation from the environment, and "outputs" that correspond to potential actions or behaviors. In such models, information is represented as a pattern of activation across a pool of simple, neuron-like processing units, and information processing involves the flow of activation within and between such pools by means of weighted, synapse-like connections. The activation of any given unit depends on the sum of the activations of the *sending units* from which it receives inputs, multiplied by the value of the intermediating weights. This *net input* is then transformed to an *activation value* according to some transfer function (often a logistic

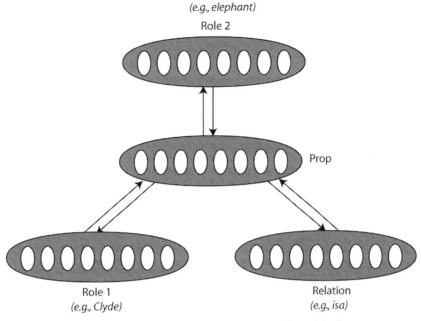

Figure 8.1. The architecture of Hinton's (1981) seminal model of semantic memory.

function bounded at 0 and 1). A network's ability to complete some input-output mapping depends on the values of the intermediating weights; in this sense, a network's "knowledge" is often said to be "stored" in the weights. To store new information in a network, it is not necessary to add new architectural elements; instead, the weights in the existing network must be adjusted to accommodate the new information. So learning in a connectionist framework does not involve the addition of new data structures, prototypes, or propositions, but instead involves the adjustment of connection weights to promote some new mapping between input and output (see Chapter 2 on connectionist approaches in this volume).

Hinton (1981) was interested in showing how a body of propositional information might be stored in such a network, without any explicit proposition-like data structures in the system. The architecture of his model, shown in Figure 8.1, reflects the structure of a simple proposition of the form Item-Relation-Attribute; there is a single bank of neuron-like processing units for each part

of the proposition. Different fillers for each slot are represented as different patterns of activation across the corresponding pool of units. For example, the representation of the proposition *Clyde is gray* would correspond to one pattern of activity across each of the three groups of units: one for *Clyde*, one for *is*, and one for *gray*.

All three banks send and receive weighted connections to a fourth layer (labeled *Prop* in the illustration). When a pattern of activation is applied across the three input layers, Prop units compute their inputs as the sum of the activations across input units weighted by the magnitude of the interconnecting weights. Each input thus produces a pattern of activity across the Prop units, which in turn send new signals back to the *Item, Relation* and *Attribute* units. These then update their states accordingly in reaction to the new inputs. The process iterates until the unit states stop changing, at which point the network is said to have *settled* into a steady state. Hinton demonstrated that individual propositions could be stored in the network by adjusting the interconnecting weights to make the patterns representing the proposition stable. To achieve this, Hinton trained the model with a variant of the *delta-rule learning algorithm*, which is explained in detail in Chapter 2 of this volume. After training, each stored proposition would be represented in the network by a unique pattern of activity across the Prop units, which simultaneously activated and received support from the input patterns.

This early model had several interesting properties and implications. First, it was capable of completing stored propositions when given two of its terms as inputs. For example, when provided with the inputs *Clyde* and *is*, the network settled into a steady state in which the pattern representing the correct completion of the proposition (*gray*) was observed across the Attribute units. Second, several such propositions could be stored in the network, in the same finite set of weights. Thus, in contrast to spreading-activation and similarity-based models, new information could be stored in memory without adding representational elements to the system. Third, when appropriate representations were chosen, the network provided a natural mechanism for generalization. If related objects (such as various individual elephants) were represented by overlapping patterns of activity across the Item units, they would contribute similar inputs to the Prop units. Thus, the entire network would tend to settle into an appropriate steady state (corresponding to the most similar stored proposition) when given a novel input that overlapped with familiar, stored patterns. For example, if the network had stored the proposition *Clyde is gray* and was then given the inputs *Elmer is* in the Item and Relation units, it would settle to a state in which the pattern corresponding to *gray* was observed across Attribute units, provided that the representations of *Clyde* and *Elmer* were sufficiently similar. Thus, the model exhibited the two characteristics most fundamental to both spreading-activation and prototype theories: an economical means of storing information and a mechanism for generalizing stored information to new stimuli.

The model also offered some leverage on two of the questions posed earlier from our consideration of prototype and spreading-activation theories. Specifically, the first question – how does the system "know" for which categories it should create representations – becomes moot in this framework. There are no discrete category representations in Hinton's model. Individual items – which in spreading activation theories would correspond to individual nodes and in prototype theories to individual category prototypes – are represented as distributed patterns of activity across the same set of processing units. The same is true of different predicates, different attributes, and full propositions: All are represented as distributed patterns across processing elements. Generalization is governed, not by a categorization process nor by the search of an explicit processing hierarchy, but by the similarities captured by these various distributed representations. This scheme does not address the important question of category coherence – why some sets of items form good categories that support induction, whereas others do not – but it no longer requires an answer to the question of which categories are stored in memory and which not.

Second, Hinton pointed out that, when many propositions are stored in the network, neither the Item nor the Relation inputs alone are sufficient to uniquely determine a correct pattern of activation in the Attribute units. For instance, suppose the model has stored the following propositions about Clyde the Elephant and Frank the Flamingo:

1. Clyde is gray
2. Frank is pink
3. Clyde has a trunk
4. Frank has a beak.

Here, the output generated by a given item (Clyde or Frank) depends on the particular relation, *is* or *has*, with which it occurs. Similarly, the response generated for a given relation depends on which item is being probed. Both the Item and Relation representations provide constraints on the ultimate interpretation of the inputs into which the network settles (the Prop representation), and jointly these determine the completion of the proposition. Put differently, the model generates different internal representations and hence different outputs for the very same item depending on the *context* in which the item is encountered. This early model thus provides some tools for understanding influences of context on semantic representation and processing.

Hinton's model also raised many questions, of course. Most obviously, the model's capacity to learn without interference and to generalize appropriately depends entirely on the particular patterns of activity chosen to represent various items, relations, and attributes. Hinton simply hand-selected certain patterns to illustrate the appeal of the basic framework. How are appropriate internal representations acquired under this framework?

3.2. *The Rumelhart Model*

This question was explicitly addressed by Rumelhart (Rumelhart, 1990; Rumelhart & Todd, 1993), who showed how the same propositional content stored in the Collins and Quillian (1969) hierarchical model can be learned by a simple connectionist network trained with backpropagation (see Chapter 2 on connectionist models in this volume for a detailed explanation of the backpropagation learning algorithm). An adaptation of Rumelhart's model is shown in Figure 8.2; it can be viewed as a feedforward instantiation of a model similar to Hinton's, in which the network is provided with the Item and Relation terms of a simple proposition as input and must generate all appropriate completions of the proposition as output.

The model consists of a series of nonlinear processing units, organized into layers, and connected in a feedforward manner, as shown in Figure 8.2. Patterns are presented by activating one unit in each of the Item and Relation layers, and allowing activation to spread forward through the network, mod-

ulated by the connection weights. To update a unit, its net input is first calculated by summing the activation of each unit from which it receives a connection multiplied by the value of the connection weight, that is:

$$net_j = \sum_i a_i w_{ij}$$

where net_j is the net input of the receiving unit j, i indexes units sending connections to j, a indicates activation of each sending unit, and w_{ij} indicates the value of the weight projecting from sending unit i to receiving unit j. The net input is then transformed to an activation a according to the logistic function, which bounds activation at 0 and 1:

$$a = \frac{1}{1 + e^{-net}}$$

To find an appropriate set of weights, the model is trained with the backpropagation learning algorithm (Rumelhart, Hinton, & Williams, 1986). First, an Item and Relation are presented to the network by setting the activations of the corresponding input units to 1 and all other inputs to 0, and activation is propagated forward to the output units, with each unit computing its net input and activation according to the previous equations. The observed output states are then compared to the desired or *target* values, and the difference is converted to a measure of error. In this case, the error is the sum over output units of the squared difference between the actual output activations and the target values:

$$err_p = \sum_i (a_{pi} - t_{pi})^2$$

where err_p indicates the total error for a given pattern p, i indexes each output unit, a indicates the activation of each output unit given the input pattern for p, and t indicates the target value for each output unit for pattern p. The partial derivative of this error with respect to each weight in the network is computed in a backward pass, and each weight is adjusted by a small amount

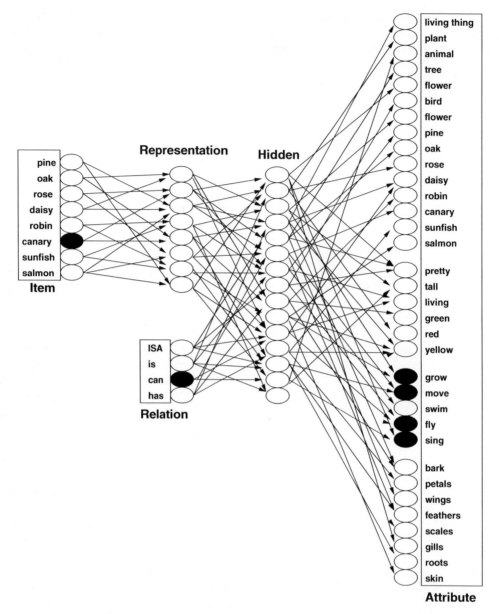

Figure 8.2. Rumelhart's (1990; Rumelhart and Todd, 1993) model, subsequently used as the basis for Rogers and McClelland's (2004) theory of semantic memory. Reprinted with permission from Rogers and McClelland (2004), *Semantic cognition: A parallel distributed processing approach*, Figure 2.2, p. 56, Cambridge, MA: MIT Press.

to reduce the error (see Chapter 2 in this volume on connectionist models for further information on the backpropagation learning rule).

Although the model's inputs are localist, each individual Item unit projects to all of the units in the layer labeled Representation. The activation of a single item in the model's input, then, generates a distributed pattern of activity across these units. The weights connecting item and representation units evolve during learning, so the pattern of activity generated across the Representations units for a given item is a learned internal representation of the item. Although the model's input and target states are constrained to locally represent particular items, attributes, and relations, the learning process allows it to derive distributed internal representations that do not have this localist character.

In the case of the Rumelhart network, for reasons elaborated later, the learned representations turn out to capture the semantic similarity relations that exist among the items in the network's training environment. These learned similarity relations provided a basis for generalization and property inheritance, just as did the assigned similarities in Hinton's (1981) model. For instance, after the model had learned about the eight items shown in Figure 8.2, the authors could teach the model a single fact about a new item – say, that a sparrow is a kind of bird – and then could query the model about other properties of the sparrow.[1] To learn that the new item (the sparrow) is a kind of bird, the model must represent it with a pattern of activation similar to the previously learned robin and canary, because these are the only items to which the label "bird" applies. Consequently, the model tends to attribute to the sparrow other properties common to both the robin and the canary: It "infers" that the sparrow can move and fly but cannot swim; has feathers, wings, and skin but not roots or gills; and so on. That is, the key function of semantic memory that, in Hinton's (1981) model, was achieved by hand-crafted

representations – generalization of previously learned information to new items – was accomplished in Rumelhart's model by internal representations that were "discovered" by the backpropagation learning rule.

3.3. *Feature Weighting and Category Coherence*

Rogers and McClelland (2004) have suggested that Rumelhart's model provides a simple theoretical framework for explaining many of the important phenomena motivating current research in semantic cognition. On this construal, the two input layers of the model represent a perceived object and a context provided by other information available together with the perceived object. For instance, the situation may be one in which a young child is looking at a robin on a branch of a tree and, as a cat approaches, sees it suddenly fly away. The object and the situation together provide a context in which it would be possible for an experienced observer to anticipate that the robin will fly away, and the observation that it does would provide input allowing a less experienced observer to develop such an anticipation. That is, an object and a situation afford the basis for implicit predictions (which may initially be null or weak), and observed events then provide the basis for adjusting the connection weights underlying these predictions, thereby allowing the experience to drive change in both underlying representations and predictions of observable outcomes. The range of contexts in which the child might encounter an object may vary widely: the child may observe the object and what others are doing with it (picking it up, eating it, using it to sweep the floor, etc.). Some encounters may involve watching what an object does in different situations; others may involve naming and other kinds of linguistic interactions. Semantic/conceptual abilities arise from the learning that occurs across many such situations, as the system comes to make increasingly accurate predictions about the consequences of observing different kinds of items in different situations and contexts.

---

1 In a more realistic model, the representation of a novel item would be achieved by recurrent connections projecting back from the attribute units toward the representation units; such a model is discussed in the final section of this chapter. To simulate this recurrent process in the feed-forward model shown in Figure 8.2, Rumelhart used a technique called backpropagation-to-activation: Beginning with a neutral pattern of activation across Representation units, activation was propagated forward to the outputs. Error was computed on *just* the "bird" output unit, and the derivative of this error was calculated, without changing any weights, in a backward pass. The activations of the Representation units were then adjusted to reduce the error on the "bird" unit. That is, the model adapted its internal representations by changing activations on the Representation units until it found a pattern that strongly activated the "bird" output unit. This pattern thus constitutes a representation of the novel item given just the information that it is a bird.

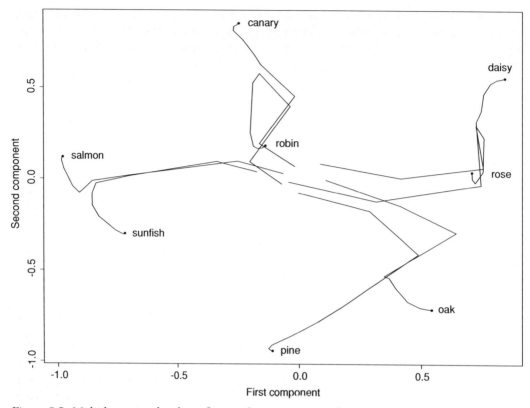

Figure 8.3. Multidimensional scaling of internal representations for 8 items at 10 equally spaced intervals during training of the Rumelhart model. The labeled end points indicate the similarities among the representations at the end of learning, whereas the lines trace the trajectory of these representations throughout learning. Reprinted with permission from Rogers and McClelland (2004), *Semantic cognition: A parallel distributed processing approach*, Figure 3.3, p. 89, Cambridge, MA: MIT Press.

The Rumelhart model provides a simplified implementation of this view of semantic abilities: The presentation of an "object" corresponds to the activation of the appropriate pattern of activity over the input units; the context can be represented via the activation of an appropriate pattern over the context units; the child's expectations about the outcome of the event may be equated with the model's outputs; and the presentation of the actual observed outcome is analogous to the presentation of the target for the output units in the network.

The authors suggested that this framework is appealing partly because it provides answers to some of the puzzling questions about the acquisition of semantic knowledge discussed previously. To show this, Rogers and McClelland (2004) trained a variant of the model shown in Figure 8.2 and investigated its behavior at several different points during the learning process.

The first important observation was that model's internal representations underwent a "coarse-to-fine" process of differentiation, such that items from broadly different semantic domains (the plants and animals) were differentiated earliest in learning; whereas closely related items (e.g., the rose and daisy) were differentiated latest. Figure 8.3 shows a multidimensional scaling of the internal representations generated by the model across the Representation layer for all eight items at ten different points during training. The lines trace the trajectory of each item throughout learning in the two-dimensional compression of the representation state space. The labeled end points represent the final learned internal representations after 1,500 epochs of training. These end points recapitulate the semantic similarity relations among the eight items: The robin and canary are quite similar, for instance, and both are more similar to the two fish than they are to the four plants. The lines tracing the developmental trajectory leading to these end points show that the eight items, initially bunched together in the middle of the space, soon divide into two clusters (plant or animal) based on animacy. Within these clusters, there is little differentiation of items. Next, the global categories split into smaller intermediate clusters (e.g., birds and fish) with little differentiation of the individual items within each cluster, and finally, the individual items are pulled apart. In short, the network's representations appear to differentiate in relatively discrete stages, first completing differentiation at the most general level before progressing to successively more fine-grained levels of differentiation.

The basis for this nonlinear, stage-like process of coarse-to-fine differentiation in the model proved key to explaining several critical phenomena in the study of human semantic abilities. To see why the model behaves in this fashion, first consider how the network learns about the following four objects: oak, pine, daisy, and salmon. Early in learning, when the weights are small and random, all of these inputs produce a similar meaningless pattern of activity throughout the network. Because oaks and pines share many output properties, this pattern results in a similar error signal for the two items, and the weights leaving the oak and pine units move in similar directions. Because the salmon shares few properties with the oak and pine, the same initial pattern of output activations produces a different error signal, and the weights leaving the salmon input unit move in a different direction. What about the daisy? It shares more properties with the oak and the pine than it does with the salmon or any of the other animals, and so it tends to move in a similar direction as the other plants. Similarly, the rose tends to be pushed in the same direction as all of the other plants, and the other animals tend to be pushed in the same direction as the salmon. As a consequence, on the next pass, the pattern of activity across the representation units will remain similar for all the plants, but will tend to differ between the plants and the animals.

This explanation captures part of what is going on in the early stages of learning in the model, but does not fully explain why there is such a strong tendency to learn the superordinate structure first. Why is it that so little intermediate-level information is acquired until after the superordinate-level information? Put another way, why don't the points in similarity space for different items move in straight lines toward their final locations?

To understand the stage-like pattern of differentiation, consider the fact that the animals all share some properties (e.g., they all can move, they all have skin, they are all called animals). Early in training, all the animals have the same representation. When this is so, if the weights going forward from the representation layer "work" to capture these shared properties for one of the animals, they must simultaneously work to capture them for all of the others. Similarly, any weight change that is made to capture the shared properties for one of the items will produce the same benefit in capturing these properties for all of the other items: If the representations of all of the items are the same, then changes applied to the forward-projecting weights for one of the items will affect all of the other items equally, and so the changes made when processing each individual item will tend to accumulate with those made in processing the others. On the other hand, weight changes made to capture a property of an item that is not shared by others with the same representation will tend to be detrimental for the other items, and when these other items are processed, the changes will actually be reversed. For example, two of the animals (canary and robin) can fly but not swim, and the other two (salmon and sunfish) can swim but not fly. If the four animals all have the same representation, what is right for half of the animals is wrong for the other half, and the weight changes across different patterns will tend to cancel each other out. The consequence is that properties shared by items with similar representations will be learned faster than the properties that differentiate such items.

The preceding paragraph considers how representational similarity structure at a given point in time influences the speed with which various kinds of attributes are learned in the model in the weights projecting forward from the Representation layer. But what about the weights from the input units to the Representation layer? These determine the representational similarity structure between items in the first place. As previously stated, items with similar outputs will have their representations pushed in the same direction, whereas items with dissimilar outputs will have their representations pushed in different directions. The question remaining is why the dissimilarity between, say, the fish and the birds does not push the representations apart very much from the very beginning.

The answer to this question lies in understanding that the magnitude of the changes made to the representation weights depends on the extent to which such changes will reduce error at the output. This in turn depends on the particular configuration of weight projecting forward from the Representation layer. For instance, if the network activated "has wings" and "has scales" to an equal degree for all animals (because half the animals have wings and the other half have scales), then there is no way of adjusting the representation of, say, the canary that will simultaneously reduce error on both the "has wings" and "has scales" units. Consequently, these properties will not exert much influence on the weights projecting into the Representation layer and will not affect how the representation of canary changes. In other words, error propagates much more strongly from properties that the network has begun to master.

Rogers and McClelland (2004) illustrated this phenomenon by observing the derivative of the error signal propagated back to the Representation units for the canary item. Specifically, this derivative was calculated across three different kinds of output units: those that reliably discriminate plants from animals (such as *can move* and *has roots*), those that reliably discriminate birds from fish (such as *can fly* and *has gills*), and those that differentiate the canary from the robin (such as *is red* and *can sing*). Because weights projecting into the Representation units are adjusted in proportion to these error derivatives, the calculation indicates to what extent these three different kinds of features are influencing representational change at different points in time. Figure 8.4 shows how the error derivatives from these three kinds of properties change throughout training when the model is given the canary (middle plot). This is graphed alongside measures of the distance between the two bird representations, between the birds and the fish, and between the animals and the plants (bottom plot); and also alongside of measures of activation of the output units for *sing*, *fly* and *move* (top plot). The figure shows that there comes a point at which the network is beginning to differentiate the plants and the animals, and is beginning to activate *move* correctly for all of the animals. At this time, properties like *can move* (reliably differentiating plants from animals) are producing a much stronger error derivative at the Representation units than are properties like *can fly* or *can sing*. As a consequence, these properties are contributing much more strongly to changing the representation weights than are the properties that reliably differentiate birds from fish or the canary from the robin. Put differently, the knowledge that the canary can move is more "important" for determining how it should be represented than the information that it can fly and sing at this stage of learning. (The error signal for *move* eventually dies out as the correct activation reaches asymptote, because there is no longer any error signal to propagate once the model has learned to produce the correct activation.)

The overall situation can be summarized as follows. Initially, the network assigns virtually the same representation to all items,

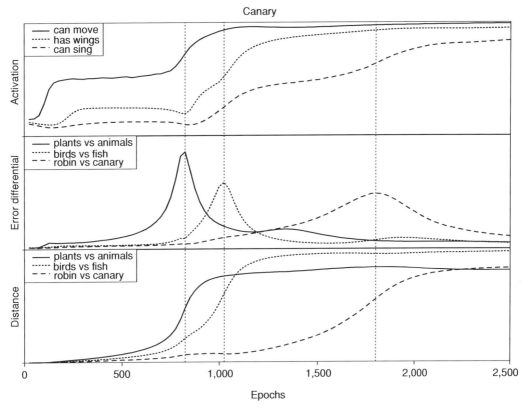

Figure 8.4. Bottom: Mean Euclidean distance between plant and animal, bird and fish, and robin and canary internal representations throughout training of the Rumelhart model. Middle: Average magnitude of the error signal propagating back to representation units from properties that reliably discriminate plants from animals, birds from fish, or the canary from the robin, when the network is presented with the canary as input at different points during learning. Top: Activation of different output properties when the network is queried about the canary. The properties include one shared by animals (can move), one shared by birds (can fly), and one unique to the canary (can sing). Reprinted with permission from Rogers and McClelland (2004), *Semantic cognition: A parallel distributed processing approach*, Figure 3.4, p. 94, Cambridge, MA: MIT Press.

and the only properties that vary systematically with these representations are those that are shared by all items (e.g., can grow, is living). All other properties have their influence on the weights almost completely cancelled out, because changes that favor one item will hinder another. Because there are many properties common to the animals and not shared by plants (and vice versa), however, weak error signals from these properties begin to move the various animal representations away from the plant representations. When this happens, the shared animal representation can begin to drive learning (in the forward weights) for properties that the animals have in common; and the shared plant representation can begin to drive learning for properties common to plants. These properties thus begin to exert a much stronger influence on the network's internal representations than do, for instance, the properties that differentiate birds from fish. The result is that the individual animal representations remain similar to one another, but are rapidly propelled away from the individual plant representations. Gradually, the weak error signals propagated from the properties that discriminate more fine-grained categories begin to accumulate, causing these subgroups to differentiate slightly and providing the basis for another "wave" of differentiation. This process eventually propagates down to the subordinate level, where individual items are differentiated from one another.

The network's tendency to differentiate its internal representations in this way does not arise from some general bias toward discovering superordinate category structure per se. Instead, it comes from patterns of higher-order covariation exhibited among the output properties themselves. The first wave of differentiation in the model will distinguish those subgroups whose shared properties show the strongest tendency to consistently covary together across the corpus (corresponding to those with the highest eigenvalues in the property covariance matrix; see Rogers and McClelland, 2004, Chapter 3, for further detail) that is, properties that show the strongest tendency to *covary coherently*. In the model corpus, and perhaps in real experience, such subgroups will correspond to very general semantic domains. For instance, animals share many properties – self-initiated and biological movement, biological contours and textures, facial features, and so on – that are not observed in plants or manmade objects. The system will not be pressured, however, to differentiate superordinate groups that do not have cohesive structure (e.g., toys vs. tools). Further waves of differentiation will then distinguish groupings whose shared properties show the next strongest patterns of coherent covariation.

It is worth noting that these interesting phenomena depend on three aspects of the network architecture. First, semantic representations for all different kinds of objects must be processed through the same weights and units at some point in the network, so that learning about one item influences representations for all items. This *convergence* in the architecture forces the network to find weights that work for all items in its experience, which in turn promotes sensitivity to high-order covariation among item properties. Second, the network must begin with very similar representations for all items, so that learning generalizes across all items until they are differentiated from one another. Third, learning must be slow and inter-

leaved, so that new learning does not destroy traces of previous learning. These architectural elements are critical to the theory and are taken as important design constraints on the actual cortical semantic system (see the last section of this chapter and Chapter 7 on episodic memory in this volume). It is also worth noting that the effects do not depend upon the use of the backpropagation learning algorithm per se. Any learning algorithm that serves the function of reducing error at the output (e.g. contrastive Hebbian learning, GeneRec, Leabra, etc.) could potentially yield similar results as long as they permit new learning to generalize relatively broadly. For instance, learning algorithms that promote representational sparsity (e.g., some parameterizations of Leabra) will diminish the degree to which learning generalizes across different items and so may not show the same sensitivity to higher-order covariation.

Rogers and McClelland's (2004) analysis of learning in the Rumelhart model provides a basis for understanding two of the pressing questions summarized earlier:

1. *Category coherence.* Why do some groupings of items seem to form "good" categories that support induction whereas others do not? The model suggests that "good" categories consist of items that share sets of properties that vary coherently together across many situations and contexts. Because these properties strongly influence representational change early in learning, they strongly constrain the degree to which different items are represented as similar/dissimilar to one another, which in turn constrains how newly learned information will generalize from one item to another. Rogers and McClelland (2004) showed how this property of the model can address phenomena as diverse as the progressive differentiation of semantic representations in infancy (Mandler, 2000), basic-level advantages in word-learning in later childhood (Mervis, 1987), "illusory correlations" in induction tasks (Gelman, 1990), and sensitivity to higher-order covariation in category-learning experiments (Billman & Knutson, 1996).

2. *Selective feature weighting.* Why are certain properties "important" for representing some categories and not others? The PDP account suggests that a given property becomes "important" for a given category when it covaries coherently with many other properties. This "importance" is reflected in two aspects of the system's behavior. First, coherently covarying properties are the main force organizing the system's internal representations so that items with a few such properties in common are represented as similar, even if they have many incoherent properties that differ. Second, coherent properties are learned much more rapidly: Because items that share such properties are represented as similar, learning for one item tends to generalize well to all other items that share the property. In simulation experiments, Rogers and McClelland showed that this emergent "feature weighting" provided a natural account of several phenomena sometimes thought to require innate knowledge structures. These include sensitivity to "conceptual" over perceptual similarity structure in infancy (Pauen, 2002), domain-specific patterns of feature-weighting (Keil, 1989; Macario, 1991), and the strong weighting of "causal" properties in determining conceptual similarity relations (Ahn, 1998; Gopnik & Sobel, 2000).

3.4. *Context-Sensitivity*

It is worth touching on one further aspect of the Rumelhart model because it relates to issues central to the next two sections. The analyses summarized previously pertain to the item representations that arise across the Representation units in the Rumelhart model. These units receive input from the localist input units corresponding to individual items, but they do not receive input from the Context input units. Instead, the distributed item representations feed forward to the Hidden units, which also receive inputs from the Context inputs and then pass activation forward to the output units. The pattern of activation arising across Hidden units may thus be viewed as a learned internal representation of an item occurring in a particular context. That is, in addition to learning context-independent representations (across the Representation units), the Rumelhart network also learns how these representations should be adapted to suit the particular context in which the item is encountered. These context-sensitive representations allow the network to produce different outputs in response to the same item – a key aspect of semantic cognition discussed in the introduction.

It turns out that this context-sensitivity also explains a puzzling aspect of human cognition – the tendency to generalize different kinds of newly learned information in different ways. For instance, Carey (1985) showed that older children inductively generalize biological facts (such as "eats" or "breathes") to a much broader range of living things than they do psychological facts ("thinks," "feels"). Because the Rumelhart model suggests that the same items get represented differently in different contexts, it provides a way of understanding why different "kinds" of properties might generalize in different ways.

Rogers and McClelland (2004) trained a variant of the Rumelhart model with a corpus of sixteen items from the same four categories as the original (birds, fish, trees, and flowers) and examined the patterns of activation that arose across the Representation and Hidden units for these sixteen items in different contexts. Figure 8.5 shows a multidimensional scaling of these patterns. The middle plot shows the learned similarities between item representations in the context-independent layer; the top plot shows the similarities across Hidden units for the same items in the *is* context; and the bottom plot shows these similarities in the *can* context. In the *can* context, all the plants receive very similar representations, because they all have exactly the same set of behaviors in the training environment – the only thing a plant can do, as far as the model knows, is grow. By contrast, in the *is* context, there are few properties shared among objects of the same kind, so that the network is pressured to strongly differentiate items in this context. The context-weighted

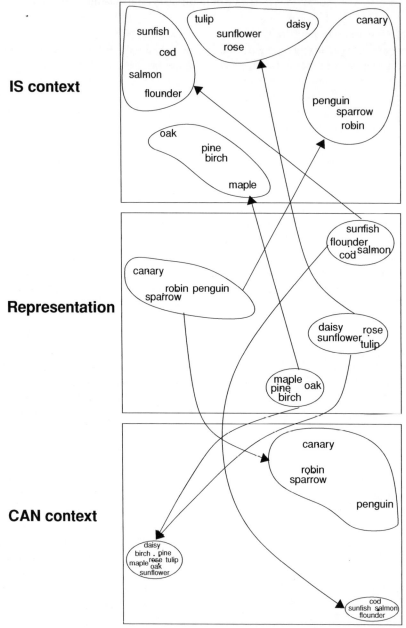

Figure 8.5. Multidimensional scaling showing the similarities represented by the Rumelhart model for objects in different relation contexts. The middle plot shows the similarities among object representations in the Representation layer. The top graph shows the similarities among the same objects in the Hidden layer, when the *is* relation unit is activated. The bottom graph shows the similarities across these same units when the *can* relation unit is activated. The *is* relation context exaggerates differences among related objects; for example, relative to the similarities in the Representation layer, the trees are fairly well spread out in the *is* context. Moreover, similarities in object appearances are preserved in these representations; for example, the canary is as close to the flowers as to the other birds in the *is* context, by virtue of being pretty. By contrast, the *can* context collapses differences among the plants, because in the network's world, all plants can do only one thing: grow. Reprinted with permission from Rogers and McClelland (2004), *Semantic Cognition: A Parallel Distributed Processing Approach*, MIT Press: Cambridge, MA.

similarities illustrated in the figure determine how newly learned properties will generalize in different contexts. If the network is taught, for instance, that the maple tree "can queem" (where "queem" is some novel property), this fact will tend to generalize strongly to all of the plants because these are represented as very similar in the "can" context. If it is taught that the maple tree "is queem," the new fact will not generalize strongly to all plants, but will weakly generalize to other items that, in the "is" context, are somewhat similar to the maple. In short, because the model's internal representations are sensitive to contextual constraints, the "base" representations learned in the context-independent Representation can be reconfigured to capture similarity relationships better suited to a given context. This reshaping can then influence how newly learned information will generalize.

3.5. *Summary*

This thread of research offers a promising theoretical framework for semantic cognition that addresses some of the core issues discussed in the introduction. The framework suggests that the semantic system allows us, when presented with a perceptual or linguistic stimulus in some particular situation, to make context-appropriate inferences about properties of the item denoted by the stimulus. It suggests that these inferences are supported by distributed internal representations that capture semantic similarity relations and that these relations can be adapted to suit particular contexts. It further suggests that the internal representations are learned through experience and shows how the learning dynamics that arise within the framework provide an explanation of category coherence, feature selection, and context-sensitivity in semantics. The framework does not explicitly address other key challenges for a theory of semantics specifically – the representation of abstract concepts, events, and multiple objects and relationships. These are the main focus of the next section.

4. Temporal Structure, Events, and Abstract Concepts

4.1. *Simple Recurrent Networks*

The second important thread of research derives in part from the seminal work of Elman (1990). Elman was interested not only in semantics, but in several different aspects of language, including the ability to segment the auditory stream into words, to organize words into different syntactic classes, and to use information about word order to constrain the interpretation of sentences. The key insight of this work was that all of these different abilities may derive from a similar underlying learning and processing mechanism – one that is sensitive to statistical structure existing in events that unfold over time. The catalyst for this insight was the invention of neural network architecture that permitted sensitivity to temporal structure – the simple recurrent network (SRN), or "Elman net," shown in Figure 8.6.

The three leftmost layers of the SRN shown in the figure constitute a feedforward connectionist network similar to that used by Rumelhart: units in the input layer are set directly by the environment; activation feeds forward through weighted connections to the Hidden layer and from there to the output layer. What makes the model "recurrent" is the Context layer shown on the right of the figure. Activation of these units feeds forward through weighted connections to influence the Hidden units, just as do the input units. The activations of the Context units are not set by inputs from the environment however. Instead, they contain a direct copy of the activation of the Hidden units from the previous time-step. It is this "memory" of the previous Hidden-unit state that allows the network to detect and respond to temporal structure.

As a simple example, suppose that the network's inputs code the perception of a spoken phoneme and that the network's task is to predict in its outputs what the next phoneme will be. Each individual input and

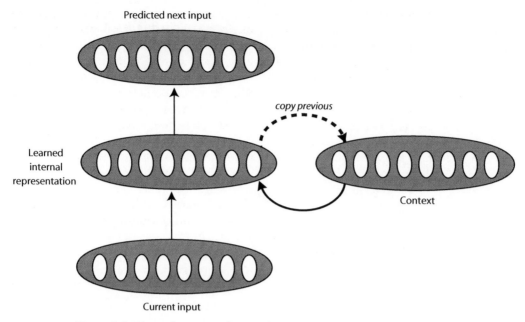

Predicted next input

copy previous

Learned
internal
representation

Context

Current input

Figure 8.6. The architecture of a simple recurrent network (Elman, 1990).

output unit might, for instance, be stipulated to represent a different syllable in English. To process a statement such as "pretty baby," the network would first be presented with the initial syllable (/pre/). Activation would spread forward to the Hidden units and then to the output units through the interconnecting weights. On the next step of the sequence, the Hidden unit pattern representing /pre/ would be copied to the Context layer, and the network would be given the next syllable in the phrase (/ti/). On this step, the Hidden unit activations will be influenced both by this new input and by the activations of the Context units, which contain the trace of the preceding Hidden representation. In other words, the new Hidden representation will code a representation of /ti/ in the context of having previously seen /pre/. Activation again feeds forward to the outputs, which code the network's "best guess" as to the likely next phoneme. On the third step, the Hidden unit representation is again copied to the Context layer, and the next syllable (/ba/) is presented as input. Again, the Hidden representations are influenced both by the input and by the Context unit activations; but this time, the Context representation has been influenced by two

previous steps (/pre/ followed by /ti/). In other words, the new Hidden representation now codes /ba/ in the context of previously encountering /pre/ followed by /ti/. In this manner, new inputs are successively "folded in" to the Context representation, so that this representation constitutes a distributed internal representation of the sequence up to the present point in time. As a consequence of this "holding on" to previously presented information, the model can produce different outputs for exactly the same input, depending on previously occurring inputs. That is, it is sensitive to the temporal context in which a given input is encountered.

SRNs can be trained with backpropagation just like a standard feed-forward network. In the syllable-prediction example, the presentation of each input syllable would provoke a pattern of activation across output units (via hidden units) that can be compared to a target pattern to generate a measure of error. Because the task is prediction in this example, the target is simply the next-occurring syllable in the speech stream. Weights throughout the network can then be adjusted to reduce the error. These weight adjustments are typically applied to all forward-going weights, including those projecting from the Context to Hidden layers. Learning on the weights projecting from Context to Hidden layers allows the network to adjust exactly how the sequence history coded in the Context influences the Hidden representation on the current time-step; and this in turn influences which steps of the sequence are robustly preserved in the Context representation itself. If there is no temporal structure, so that the sequence history has no implication for how a current input is processed, the weights from Context → Hidden will never grow large, and the Hidden representation will be driven almost exclusively by the Input and not by the Context. As a consequence, the Context representation itself will only reflect the representation of the preceding item and will not "build up" a representation of the sequence preceding that item. On the other hand, if there is temporal structure, so that predictions derived from a given input can be improved by "taking into account" the preceding items in the sequence, then the weights projecting from Context to Hidden units will be structured by the learning algorithm to captialize on these relationships, so that the Hidden states come to be more strongly influenced by the Context, and preceding states get "folded in" to the new context representation.

The SRN turned out to be a valuable tool for understanding a variety of linguistic phenomena precisely because language has temporal structure at many different time-scales. At a relatively small time-scale, for instance, it is the case that syllable-to-syllable transitions that occur within words tend to be much more predictable than the transitions that occur between words. From the earlier example, the transition from /pre/→/ti/ is much more frequent in English than the transition /ti/→/ba/ (Saffran, Aslin, & Newport, 1996). Because this is true, a syllable-prediction network like the one sketched out previously can provide a strategy for detecting word-boundaries in a continuous speech stream: Simply place the boundaries wherever prediction error is high. At broader time-scales, SRNs provide

a way of thinking about processing of syntactic information in languages like English where such information is often carried by word order. And, it turns out, SRNs and related approaches offer important insights into the acquisition and representation of semantic information.

Here again, the critical insight was offered by Elman (1990), who trained an SRN in which the input and output units, of corresponding to individual syllables, represented individual words. The network's task, just as before, was prediction, in this case, prediction of the next word in a sentence, given the current word as input. Elman trained the model with a sequence of simple two- and three-word sentences (e.g., "Woman smashes plate," "Cat moves," and so on) presented to the network in a long series. He then examined the internal representations arising across Hidden units in response to the activation of each individual word. The interesting observation was that words with similar meanings tended to be represented with similar patterns of activation across these units, even though inputs and outputs in the model were all localist, so that there was no pattern overlap between different words in either the input or output. Somehow, the network had acquired information about semantic relatedness solely by trying to predict what word would come next in a sentence!

Why should this be? The answer is that words with similar meanings, precisely *because* they have similar meanings, tend to occur in similar linguistic contexts. For instance, because dogs and cats are both kinds of pet, we tend to use similar words when referring to them in speech. We say things like, "I have to feed the dog/cat," "Don't worry, the dog/cat doesn't bite," "Please let the dog/cat outside," and so on. Elman's simulations suggested that the more similar two words are in meaning, the more similar are the range of linguistic contexts in which they are encountered. Because the representation of a given item is, in the SRN, influenced by the temporal contexts in which it is encountered, then items that occur in similar contexts tend to receive similar representations.

Just as the Rumelhart network learns to represent items as similar when they overlap in their output properties, so the SRN learns to represent items as similar when they overlap in the distribution of items that precede and follow them. Because items with similar meanings tend to be preceded and followed by similar distributions of words in speech, this suggests that the acquisition of semantic similarity relations may be at least partially supported by a learning mechanism that is sensitive to the context in which the words occur.

There are three aspects of this research that offer leverage on the theoretical issues listed previously. First, the internal representations acquired by an SRN are, like the representations that arise across the Hidden layer of the Rumelhart network, context-sensitive. In both cases, the distributed patterns that promote the correct output capture both the current input and the context in which it is encountered. As a consequence, both kinds of network can produce different responses to the same item, depending on the context. In an SRN, the context need not be represented as a separate input from the environment (as it is in the Rumelhart network), but can consist solely of a learned internal representation of the sequence of previously encountered inputs.

Second, Elman's approach suggests one way of thinking about representation of meanings for abstract concepts. Because semantic similarity relations are apparent (at least to some degree) from overlap in the linguistic contexts in which words tend to appear in meaningful speech, then such relations might be derived even for words with abstract meanings. Words like "fair" and "just" may not be associated with obvious perceptual-motor attributes in the environment, but they likely occur within similar linguistic contexts ("The decision was just," "The decision was fair"). The insight that word-meanings may partially inhere in the set of contexts in which the word is encountered may therefore provide some explanation as to how learning of such meanings is possible.

Third, the representations arising in the Context layer of an SRN capture information, not just about a single input, but also about a series of inputs encountered over time. That is, these representations are inherently representations of whole events rather than individual items. The SRN thus offers a tool for understanding how the semantic system might construct internal representations that capture the meaning of a whole event, instead of just the meaning of a single object or word.

The remainder of this section discusses some of the implications of these ideas for theories of semantic memory as they have been cashed out in two influential modeling approaches: LSA (Landauer & Dumais, 1997) and related approaches (Burgess & Lund, 1997; Steyvers et al., 2006), and the "Sentence Gestalt" models described by St. John and McClelland (McClelland et al., 1989; St. John & McClelland, 1990; St. John, 1992).

4.2. *Latent Semantic Analysis*

LSA is an approach to understanding the semantic representation of words (and larger samples of text) that capitalizes on the previously mentioned observation that words with similar meanings tend to occur in similar linguistic contexts (Landauer, Foltz, & Laham, 1998). Elman (1990) had illustrated the face validity of the idea by training an SRN with a small corpus of sentences constructed from a limited set of words. The pioneers of LSA and related approaches established the power of the idea by investigating precisely how much information about semantic relatedness among words can be extracted from linguistic context in large corpora of written text.

The basic computations behind LSA are fairly straightforward. The process begins with a large set of samples of text, such as an encyclopedia in which each article is considered a separate sample in the set. From this set, a matrix is constructed. Each row of the matrix corresponds to a single word appearing at least once in the set, and each column corresponds to one of the text samples in the set. The elements of the matrix indicate the frequency with which a word was encountered within the sample. For instance, the word "date" might occur ten times in an encyclopedia article on calendars, once in an article on Egypt; three times in an article on dried fruit, zero times in an article on lasers, and so on. So each word is associated with a row vector of frequencies across text samples, and each text sample is associated with a column vector of frequencies across words. If it is true that words with similar meanings occur in similar contexts, then the vectors for words with similar meanings should point in similar directions. The similarity structure of the word-to-text co-occurrence matrix thus captures information about the semantic relatedness of the individual words. To get at this structure, the elements of the matrix are usually transformed to minimize variation due to overall word frequencies (for instance, by taking the log of the frequencies in each cell); the co-occurrence matrix is converted to a similarity matrix by computing the pairwise correlation between all rows; and the similarity matrix is then subject to a singular value decomposition (a computationally efficient means of estimating eigenvectors in a very large similarity matrix). The singular-value decomposition returns a large set of orthogonal vectors that re-describe the similarity matrix (one for each word in the corpus); typically all but the first 300 or so of these vectors are then discarded. The resulting representation contains a description of each word in the corpus as a vector in approximately a 300-dimensional space.

What is remarkable about this process is that the similarity structure of the resulting vectors appears to parallel, sometimes with surprising accuracy, the semantic similarities discerned by human subjects among the words in the corpus. Semantic distances yielded by LSA and similar measures correlate with the magnitude of contextual semantic priming effects in lexical decision tasks (Landauer & Dumais, 1997), with normative estimates of the semantic relatedness between pairs of words and with word-sorting (Landauer et al., 1998),

with the likelihood of confusing two items in free-recall list-learning tasks (Howard & Kahana, 2002), and so on. Such correspondences would seem to suggest some nonarbitrary relationship between the representations computed by LSA-like methods and the word-meaning representations existing in our minds. But what, specifically, is the nature of this relationship?

At the very least, LSA demonstrates that overlap in linguistic context can convey considerable information about the degree to which different words have similar meanings. In short, Elman's (1990) speculation – that words with similar meanings appear in similar contexts – appears to be true in actual language. So a learning mechanism that is sensitive to the temporal context in which words occur may help to promote the learning of semantic similarity relationships. Nevertheless, the skeptic might justly question the conclusion that semantic representations can be derived solely from a "dumb" word- or phrase-prediction algorithm (Glenberg & Robertson, 2000). Surely, there is more to meaning than simply being able to anticipate which words are likely to follow one another in speech – you cannot learn a language just by listening to the radio. And indeed, as a theory of semantic processing, LSA raises many questions. How are the semantic representations it computes – abstract vectors in a high-dimensional space – accessed by perceptual and linguistic input? How do they support naming, action, and other behaviors? How are they influenced by these nonlinguistic aspects of experience? What *content* do they have?

One response to these criticisms is as follows. LSA shows that sensitivity to high-order temporal structure in language can yield important information about semantic similarity structure. Empirical studies show that the human semantic system is sensitive to the similarity structure computed by LSA-like measures; so it is possible that the human semantic system is also sensitive in some degree to high-order temporal structure in language. But this is not to say that the semantic system is not *also* sensitive to structure in other aspects of experience.

The same learning mechanisms that extract information from statistical structure in speech may also operate on nonlinguistic perceptual information to support predictions about future events or appropriate actions; and such a mechanism might even assimilate high-order patterns of covariation between linguistic and nonlinguistic sources of information, so that the resulting representations support predictions, not just about what words are likely to follow a given statement, but also about upcoming perceptual experiences as well. That is, LSA demonstrates that the human mind is sensitive to temporal structure in one aspect of experience (linguistic experience), and the same mechanism that gives rise this sensitivity may also mediate learning in other perceptual and motor domains.

4.3. *The Sentence Gestalt Model*

The notion that the semantic system might capitalize on statistical structure both within language and between language and other aspects of experience is apparent in many current theories of conceptual knowledge. This idea has not been very directly implemented in any computational model, for obvious reasons – it requires fairly explicit theories about perception, action, speech production, and comprehension, all of which constitute broad and controversial domains of study in their own right! Important progress in this vein was made, however, by St. John and McClelland (McClelland et al., 1989; St. John & McClelland, 1990; St. John, 1992).

St. John and McClelland were interested in investigating verbal comprehension, not just for individual words, but for full sentences describing mini-events. Each sentence described an agent performing some action on some recipient, often with a particular instrument, thus, understanding of each event required knowledge of who the actor was, which action was taken, what item was acted on, and what instrument was used. When one comprehends a sentence such as "The lawyer ate the spaghetti with the fork," for instance, one knows that the lawyer is the thing doing the eating; the spaghetti, and not the fork, is what is eaten; the fork is being used by the lawyer to eat the spaghetti; and so on. Comprehension of such utterances requires combining the meanings of the individual constituent words, as they come into the semantic system, into some whole or *Gestalt* representation of the event.

Exactly how such combination is accomplished is the subject of considerable research in psycholinguistics, extending well beyond the scope of this chapter. To illustrate just one of the complexities attending the question, consider the sentence, "The lawyer ate the spaghetti with the sauce." Structurally, it is identical to the example sentence in the preceding paragraph; but the interpretation of the final noun ("fork" vs. "sauce") is strikingly different. In the former sentence, the noun is interpreted as the instrument of the action "ate"; in the latter, the noun is interpreted as a modifier of the recipient "spaghetti." Understanding how the final noun "attaches" to the other concepts in the sentence seems to require knowledge of certain constraints deriving from the meaning of the full event, for instance, that it is impossible to use sauce to pick up and eat spaghetti noodles or that it is unlikely that the spaghetti was served with a topping made of forks. That is, the attachment of the noun derives neither from the structural/syntactic properties of words (which should be identical in the two sentences), nor from the meanings of individual words taken in isolation (e.g., "not used as a topping for spaghetti" is not likely to be a salient property of the concept "fork").

St. John and McClelland were interested both in providing a general framework for thinking about comprehension of the "whole meaning" of sentences and in addressing attachment phenomena like that just summarized. The model they used to exemplify the framework is illustrated in Figure 8.7. The first bank of input units consists of localist representations of the individual words that occur in sentences. These feed forward to a bank of hidden units which in turn feed forward to a simple recurrent

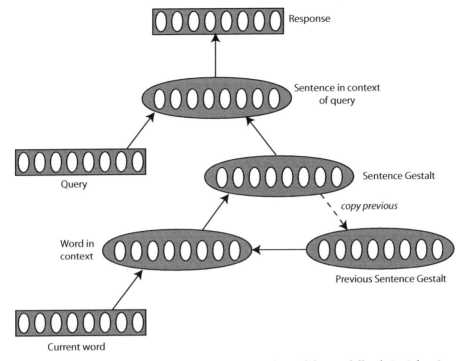

Figure 8.7. The architecture of the Sentence Gestalt Model (McClelland, St. John, & Taraban, 1989).

layer labeled "Sentence Gestalt." The "copying over" of patterns from the Sentence Gestalt to a Context layer (labeled "Previous Sentence Gestalt") allows the network to retain an internal representation of the full sequence of words preceding a current input. This context representation, rather than feeding back directly to the Sentence Gestalt, instead feeds forward into the first Hidden layer, thus influencing the pattern of activation that arises there in response to a particular word input. That is, the first Hidden layer forms a representation of a particular word encountered in a given sentence context; this context-sensitive word representation then feeds forward to influence the current Sentence Gestalt.

Finally, the Sentence Gestalt units feed forward to another bank of Hidden units, but these also receive inputs from the layer labeled "Query." The Query units themselves are set directly by the environment and contain localist representations of basic questions one can pose to the network about the meaning of the sentence – questions such as "Who is the actor?"; "Who is the recipient?"; "What was the action?"; "What was the instrument?"; and so on. The output layer, then, contains localist representations of the words that constitute answers to these questions: single units coding the various potential agents, recipients, actions, instruments, and so on. So the full model can be viewed as containing two parts: a "comprehension" or input system that retains representations of sequences of words in the sentence to be comprehended, and a "query" or output system that "interrogates" the model's internal representations to answer questions about the meaning of the sentence. The Sentence Gestalt layer codes the representations that intermediate between these two networks.

The model's task is to take in a series of words corresponding to a meaningful sentence and to correctly respond to queries about the sentence's meaning (i.e., answer questions about "who did what to whom with what"). To find a set of weights that accomplish this task, the model is trained with backpropagation. The unit corresponding to the first word of the sentence is activated in the input, and activation flows forward through the network to the output. The network is then "queried" by activating each of the possible question-inputs in turn. With each query, the network's actual response is compared with the correct response, and the error is computed and backpropagated through all the weights in the network. Next, the activation of the Sentence Gestalt layer is copied over to the Context layer; the next word in the sentence is activated in the input; input flows forward through the network to the outputs; and the model is queried again with all the various question-inputs. Effectively, the model is "asked" about the full meaning of the sentence as each word comes into the input and is trained with backpropagation to make its "best guess" as to the answers to those questions at each step in processing.

Setting aside for a moment questions about the naturalness of this training regime, let us consider the model's behavior after it has been learned. The trained network could be presented with a full sentence (each word coming in, one at a time, in order), leading it to build up a distributed pattern of activity in the Sentence Gestalt layer. The information coded in this representation could then be probed by activating different "Query" units, effectively asking the network to answer questions about the meaning of the sentence. The first remarkable thing was that the network could indeed successfully answer the questions. That is, although the model's internal representation of the sentence – the pattern of activity across the Sentence Gestalt layer – was not directly interpretable in and of itself, it produced the correct answers to all of the probe questions, indicating that it somehow "contained" the full meaning of the test sentences.

The second remarkable thing was that this ability generalized fairly well to test-sentences the network had never before seen. For instance, when given a sentence like "The policeman ate the spaghetti with the fork," the network could correctly state that the policeman was the actor and the fork was the instrument, despite never having seen a sentence in which the policeman used a fork. The third remarkable thing was that the network's generalization behavior was sensitive to just the kinds of conceptual constraints exemplified previously. When given a sentence like "The policeman ate the spaghetti with the sauce," for instance, it correctly concluded that "sauce" must be a modifier of "spaghetti," and not an instrument of "policeman" (again, despite never having been trained on sentences involving policemen and spaghetti). In general, instruments associated with human beings (e.g., "fork") would tend to attach to nouns describing human beings, even when the pairings had never before been encountered, and nouns that tended not to be used as instruments did not attach to agents, even in novel sentences. The basis for this generalization should be apparent from the previous discussion of Elman's (1990) work. Human agents tend to engage in many of the same kinds of activities, using some of the same kinds of instruments; this overlap leads the Sentence Gestalt model to represent the various human nouns as somewhat similar to one another in the first Hidden layer (and different from nonhuman agents), and this similarity promotes generalization to new sentence contexts.

There are other appealing aspects of the Sentence Gestalt model that will not be reviewed here. Instead, it is worth focusing briefly on a seemingly artificial nature of the training regime: the fact that the model is "queried" with all possible questions with each new word presentation and gets faithful answers to every question during training. To what could such training possibly correspond in the real world? One answer to this question is that the training regime in St. John and McClelland's (1990) work provides a coarse proxy to the covariation of language with other aspects of experience. The verbal statements that children are trying to understand as they learn a language do not occur in isolation, but together with other sensory-motor information. When daddy says, "Look, mommy's eating her dinner with a fork!" the infant may look up to see mommy holding a fork, jamming it into the spaghetti noodles, and raising it to her mouth. The agent, action, recipient, and instrument information is all contained in this event. Although children may not be explicitly querying themselves about these relationships as the Sentence Gestalt model does, they may be doing something related – trying to anticipate who will pick up the fork, or what mommy is holding on to, or what will go into the mouth, and so on, when they hear daddy's statement and look up toward mommy. That is, correspondences between verbal statements and actual observed events may provide the statistical basis for learning to represent the meanings of full sentences.

4.4. *Summary*

The thread of research described in Section 3 suggested that the semantic system may serve a particular functional role: the ability to make context-appropriate inferences about the properties of objects, given their name or some other perceptual input. To accomplish this role, it is necessary for the semantic system to represent conceptual similarity relationships among familiar items and to adapt these relationships as necessary according to the situation or context. Section 3 suggested that some of the information necessary to acquire such knowledge may be present in the overlap of sensory and motor properties across different modalities and across different situations. The work précised in the current section adds to this suggestion by showing how the semantic system can become sensitive to temporal structure, both within language and between language and other aspects of experience. Elman's (1990) work provided a simple mechanism for learning temporal structure; the work of Landauer and Dumais (1997), Burgess and Lund (1997), and others has shown how rich such structure can be, even just considering temporal structure in natural language; and the Gestalt models described by McClelland and St. John (St. John & McClelland, 1990; St. John, 1992) provide a simple framework for thinking about how coherent covariation between linguistic structure and other aspects of experience can promote the representation of meaning

for full sentences and events. These developments thus begin to offer leverage on the three issues that remained unaddressed or only partially addressed at the end of the last section: the context-sensitive nature of concepts, the representation of meaning for abstract words, and the representation and processing of full events encompassing multiple items.

5. Neurocognitive Models

All of the models reviewed thus far are best construed as cognitive models – they offer limited insight at best into the nature of the neural systems and processes that support semantic abilities. The final thread of research considered here encompasses neurocognitive models. The majority of this work has focused on understanding impairments to semantic abilities following brain damage. Two principal questions addressed by this work are: (1) How can patterns of observed semantic impairment be explained given what we know about the cortical organization of information-processing systems in the brain, and (2) what do patterns of semantic impairment tell us about the neuroanatomical organization of the semantic system?

Until very recently, these questions have been pursued more-or-less independently of the computational issues discussed in the previous two sections. In this final section, the two most widely studied forms of semantic impairment and the models that have been proposed to explain them are considered. Although these models share many properties in common, they differ in important respects that have implications for the view of semantic abilities considered in Sections 3 and 4.

5.1. *Category-Specific Semantic Impairment*

The first form of semantic impairment is *category-specific* impairment: semantic deficits that appear to be restricted to one semantic domain while largely sparing others. By far the most commonly observed category-specific impairment involves seriously degraded knowledge of living things, with comparatively good knowledge of manmade objects (Capitani et al., 2003; Martin & Caramazza, 2003; Warrington & McCarthy, 1983). The reverse dissociation has, however, also been reported (Warrington & McCarthy, 1987; Warrington & Shallice, 1984), along with other apparently selective semantic deficits (Crutch & Warrington, 2003; Samson & Pillon, 2003), seeming to indicate that different forms of brain damage can differentially affect knowledge of different semantic domains. One straightforward interpretation of this impairment is that different parts of the brain have been "specialized" over the course of evolution for storing and retrieving semantic information about living and nonliving things (Caramazza, 1998). In early discussions of apparent category-specific impairments, however, Warrington and Shallice (1984) suggested an alternative explanation: Perhaps semantic representations of living things depend to a greater extent on knowledge of perceptual qualities, whereas semantic representations of manmade objects depend more on knowledge of their functional characteristics. If so, then damage to regions of the brain that support knowledge of visual attributes may produce a seeming "living things" deficit, whereas damage to regions that support knowledge of action or function may produce an apparent "manmade object" impairment.

This hypothesis had appeal for at least two reasons. First, it was consistent with what was already known about the functional organization of cortex. That is, cortical regions supporting visual perception of objects are quite removed from those that support action/object use, so the hypothesis offered a means of understanding the pattern without requiring the ad-hoc proposal of separate cortical regions for representing different kinds of concepts. Second, the hypothesis explained a few apparent exceptions to the supposed "category-specific" patterns. For instance, some patients with living things impairments were also seriously impaired at naming and recognizing

musical instruments and minerals – artifacts that might well depend to a greater extent than usual on knowledge of perceptual characteristics. Similarly, some patients with "manmade object" impairments also showed deficits for recognizing body parts, arguably, living things that are closely tied to knowledge of action and function (Warrington & Shallice, 1984).

An influential computational implementation of the sensory-functional hypothesis was put forward by Farah and McClelland (1991). In addition to demonstrating that the theory was indeed tractable, simulations with the model showed that it also had some counterintuitive implications. The model, illustrated in the top panel of Figure 8.8, is a fully recurrent network, in which activation may flow in either direction between connected layers. For instance, visual input to the Visual layer can flow up to the Semantic layer, and then in turn to the Verbal layer; or alternatively, input from the Verbal layer can flow to the Semantic layer and back to the Visual layer. Thus, the units in the Semantic layer may be construed as computing mappings between visual and verbal information presented from the environment.

Representations of objects in the model take the form of distributed patterns of activity across groups of units. The units themselves can be thought of as each responding to some aspect of the entity represented by the whole pattern, although these aspects need not be nameable features or correspond in any simple way to intuitions about the featural decomposition of the concept. In the Semantic layer, some units may respond to objects with some particular visual property, whereas others may respond to aspects of the object's functional role. In the Visual layer, patterns of activity correspond to more peripheral visual representations, whereas patterns of activity in the Verbal layer form representations of words. To present a visual stimulus to the network, the corresponding pattern of activation is clamped across Visual units; these activations feed forward to Semantic units, then on to Verbal units. The activations of Verbal units can then feed back to the Semantic

A. Farah-McClelland model

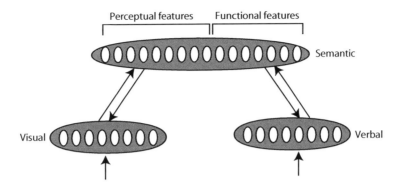

B. The Convergence theory

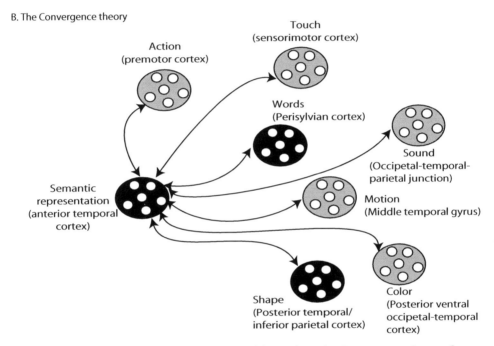

Figure 8.8. Panel A. The Farah-McClelland model. Panel B: The Convergence theory of semantic memory. Unit pools shown in black were implemented in the models described by Rogers et al. (2004) and Lambon Ralph, Lowe, and Rogers (2007).

units, and this dynamic flow of activation proceeds until the unit states stop changing, at which point the network is said to have settled into a steady state or attractor. The location of such stable configurations depends on the connection weight matrix. The role of learning in this model is to configure the weights in such a way that, when the network is presented with a particular word or picture as input, it will settle into a stable state in which the correct pattern of

activity is observed across units in the visual, verbal, and semantic layers.

Farah and McClelland (1991) created representations for ten "living" and ten "non-living" objects, by generating random patterns of −1 and +1 across all three layers of units in the model. Each unique pattern corresponded to a representation of an individual item. Representations of living and non-living things differed only in the proportion of active semantic units in the "functional" and "perceptual" pools. These were set to match the observed ratio of perceptual to functional features of objects in dictionary definitions. Living things in the model were represented with an average of 16.1 visual and 2.1 functional units active, whereas nonliving things were represented with an average of 9.4 visual and 6.7 functional units active. All patterns had some units active in both semantic pools. The verbal and visual representations were random patterns generated in the same way for living and nonliving items. To find a configuration of weights that would allow the network to perform correctly, the model was trained with the delta rule (McClelland & Rumelhart, 1985) to associate Visual and Verbal patterns with the appropriate Semantic pattern. When the model had finished learning, it could generate the correct Semantic pattern from any Verbal or Visual input, and activation of this pattern would then correctly "fill in" the corresponding Verbal or Visual pattern.

Of interest was the model's behavior when its semantic units were damaged. Under the sensory-functional hypothesis, units representing the functional-semantic aspects of an item can be damaged independently of the units representing the item's perceptual-semantic properties. How did the model's performance deteriorate with increasing damage to each of these pools of units? To simulate neural trauma in the network, Farah and McClelland (1991) simply deleted some proportion of the units in either the perceptual-semantic pool or the functional-semantic pool. They then tested the network's ability to perform model analogues of picture naming and match-to-sample tasks. In the former, the model was presented with the picture of an object (by applying a pattern of activity to the visual units) and allowed to settle to a steady state. The resulting pattern of activity across the word units could then be read off and compared with all the patterns in the training corpus. The model's response was considered correct if the pattern of activity across word units was more similar to the correct pattern than to any other pattern. The same procedure was employed in the match-to-

sample task, using a word as input and examining patterns of activity across visual units to determine the response.

Two aspects of their results are of interest. First, the model showed a clear double dissociation in its ability to name and match living and nonliving things. When visual semantic units were destroyed, the model exhibited a greater naming impairment for living relative to nonliving objects. The opposite was true when functional units were destroyed. Second, and more interesting, in neither case was the model completely unimpaired in the "spared" domain. Although the model was worse at naming living things when perceptual-semantic features were destroyed, it was also impaired at naming nonliving things. Living things rely more heavily on perceptual-semantic features in the model, but such features inform the representation of both living and nonliving objects to some degree. As this knowledge deteriorates in the model, it tends to affect naming performance for both domains, albeit to differing degrees. The same graded impairments are also witnessed in the patient data – profound impairments in one domain are almost without exception accompanied by mild impairments in the relatively spared domain.

Farah and McClelland (1991) also examined the network's ability to retrieve functional- and perceptual-semantic information when given a picture or a word as input. Considering only the perceptual or the functional unit pools, they compared the pattern of activity in the damaged network when it had settled to the correct pattern for each object. The network was considered to have spared knowledge of the perceptual properties of an item if the observed pattern of activity across perceptual-semantic units was closest to the correct pattern and spared knowledge of functional properties if the observed pattern across functional-semantic units was closest to the correct pattern.

The simulations showed that the loss of semantic features in one modality had important consequences for the model's ability to retrieve properties in the spared modality. When perceptual semantic features were lost, the model had a tendency to generate an incorrect pattern of activity across functional-semantic units, especially for living things. The reason is that the reciprocal connections among semantic features lead the network to rely on activity in perceptual-semantic units to help produce the appropriate patterns across functional units. When this activation is reduced or disrupted as a result of damage, these lateral connections can interfere with the model's ability to find the correct states, even in the spared units. Thus, the loss of "perceptual"-semantic knowledge can precipitate a disruption of knowledge about *functional* properties, especially for categories that rely to a large extent on perceptual information in their representation. Of course, the reverse is true when functional-semantic features are damaged. So, counterintuitively, it is not the case that patients with worse knowledge of animals than artifacts should always show preserved knowledge of functional properties under the theory, even though the theory attributes the apparent category effect to the loss of knowledge about sensory properties of objects.

5.2. *The Convergence Model*

The second well-studied form of semantic impairment is the progressive and profound degeneration of semantic knowledge observed in the syndrome known as *semantic dementia* (SD). There are three remarkable facts about SD that constrain theories about the neural basis of semantic abilities. First, the semantic impairment appears to encompass knowledge of all kinds of concepts, tested in all modalities of reception and expression. In contrast to the "category-specific" cases described earlier, for instance, patients with SD show equally poor knowledge about living and nonliving things (Garrard, Lambon Ralph, & Hodges, 2002). They are profoundly anomic (Hodges, Graham, & Patterson, 1995; Lambon Ralph et al., 1998; Rogers et al., 2006), but their impairments are not restricted to language: they show serious deficits recognizing line drawings of common objects (Rogers et al.,

2003), drawing pictures of objects after a brief delay (Bozeat et al., 2003), coloring black-and-white line drawings of common objects (Rogers et al., 2007), assessing the usual function of everyday objects (Bozeat et al., 2002), matching a sound (such as a telephone ring) to a picture of the item that makes the sound (Adlam et al., 2006, Bozeat et al., 2000) – effectively any task that requires them to make an inference about an object's properties (regardless of whether the item is depicted or denoted by a word).

Second, other aspects of cognitive functioning are remarkably spared in the disorder. Patients with SD are generally well oriented in space and time; show comparatively normal episodic and recognition memory; have speech that is grammatical and, apart from word-finding problems, fluent; have normal or near-normal perception; show no attentional dysfunction; and perform well on tests of reasoning and problem solving (Patterson & Hodges, 2000).

Third, the neuropathology that produces SD is not widespread in the brain, but is relatively circumscribed. The condition follows from the temporal-lobe variant of frontotemporal dementia, a disease that produces a slowly progressing deterioration of cortical gray matter in the anterior temporal lobes of the brain. Although the pathology is often more pronounced in the left hemisphere, it is virtually always bilateral and, in some cases, can be worse in the right hemisphere.

On the basis of these observations, Rogers et al. (2004) proposed a theory about the neural basis of semantic memory, illustrated in the bottom panel of Figure 8.8. Like the approaches discussed in Sections 3 and 4, the theory proposes that semantic memory serves a key function: to promote inferences about the properties of objects and events that are not directly perceived in the environment. For instance, when encountering a line drawing of a banana, representation of the depicted object's shape may depend predominantly on perceptual and not semantic processes; but the semantic system then promotes retrieval of the item's name, its characteristic color, its taste, the actions required to peel it, and so on. In this sense, the "meaning" of the image inheres in the coactivation of various associated sensory, motor, and linguistic representations.

Different kinds of sensory, motor, and linguistic information are known to be coded in widely distributed and functionally specialized cortical regions, with some regions specialized, for instance, for color perception, others for motion perception, others for representation of orthographic or phonological words forms, and so on (Chao, Haxby, & Martin, 1999; Martin & Chao, 2001). On the basis of the neuroanatomical observations from SD, Rogers et al. (2004) suggested that these widely distributed sensory, motor, and linguistic representations communicate with one another via the anterior temporal-lobe regions affected in SD. That is, the anterior temporal lobes act as a kind of "hub" or "convergence zone" (Damasio & Damasio, 1994) that promotes the interactive activation of linguistic, perceptual, and motor representations. When the hub deteriorates as a consequence of disease, this degrades the ability to map between such surface forms.

Rogers et al. (2004) used a simplified implementation of the theory to illustrate some desirable consequences of this proposal. The model's architecture (the black ovals in the second panel of Figure 8.8) was similar to that of the Farah-McClelland (Farah & McClelland, 1991) model: It included a layer to code visual shape representations, a layer to code verbal inputs-outputs, and an intermediating Hidden layer (labeled "Semantic" in the figure). Units in the Visual layer were understood to represent visual properties of objects that could be directly perceived, whereas units in the Verbal layer were understood to represent individual words. Visual and Verbal units could get direct input from the environment, and both layers sent connections to and received connections from the intermediating Semantic units. Thus, the model could be presented with a visual input (corresponding to a pattern of activity across Visual units), a single name or word (cor-responding to activation of a single Verbal unit), or a phrase describing an object's properties (corresponding to a pattern of activation across Verbal units).

This *Convergence* model contrasted with the Farah-McClelland (Farrah & McClelland, 1991) model in three important ways. First, the patterns of activity that constituted the Visual and Verbal representations were not random vectors, but instead captured aspects of similarity apparent in line drawings of common objects and in the verbal statements we tend to make about such objects. That is, items with many visual properties in common were represented with overlapping patterns in the Visual layer, whereas items to which similar spoken predicates apply were represented with similar patterns in the Verbal layer. Second, no "semantic" representations were assigned. Instead, the model was simply trained (using a backpropagation algorithm suited to recurrent networks) to complete mappings between individual names, visual representations, and verbal descriptions of various objects. The patterns of activation that arose across Semantic units in the trained models thus constituted learned internal representations, just as in the models described in Sections 3 and 4. Third, the Convergence model proposed no functional specialization of the intermediating semantic units.

Rogers et al. (2004) simulated the neuropathology of SD by removing an increasing proportion of the weights projecting into or out from the Semantic layer. The simulation experiments were able to replicate several interesting aspects of impairment in SD and made a variety of new predictions about the consequences of temporal-lobe damage for semantic memory (Lambon Ralph et al., 2007; Rogers et al., 2004). Rather than reviewing all of these results, one aspect of the simulations that provides a clue as to *why* the cortical semantic network might employ a convergent architecture will be discussed.

The key observation concerns the fact that the learned internal representations in the model end up capturing the semantic similarity relations existing among the items in the training corpus for essentially the same reasons discussed earlier with respect to the Rumelhart model. More interestingly, the authors showed that these acquired similarity relations differed from those apparent in the overlap of the model's Visual and Verbal patterns considered independently. Specifically, from overlap in visual features, the category of fruits was largely intermingled with manmade objects, whereas, from overlap in verbal features, the same items were represented as quite distinct from both manmade objects and from animals. The internal representations formed across Semantic units in the Convergence model captured a blend of these similarity relations: Fruits were represented as (1) similar to one another, (2) distinct from both manmade objects and animals, but (3) considerably more similar to the former than the latter. This counter intuitive finding (that fruits may be represented as more similar to manmade objects than to animals) predicted that patients with SD should be more likely to confuse fruits with artifacts than with animals, a prediction that was confirmed in a subsequent sorting experiment (Rogers et al., 2004).

In other words, the simulation showed that the intermediating representations that arise from learning in a convergent architecture can capture similarity structure that is not directly apparent in any individual surface representation. This observation is important precisely because surface representations – the sensory, motor, and linguistic representations from which "meanings" are thought to arise – often do not seem to faithfully capture semantic/conceptual similarities. Light bulbs and pears may have similar shapes, fire engines and strawberries have similar colors, potato-mashers and plungers engage similar motor programs; and so on. The Convergence model suggests that, although conceptual similarity structure may not be directly captured by any of these surface representations, it may be apparent in the pattern of overlap across the different kinds of representation. Thus, the explanation as to why, computationally, the cortex should employ a convergent architecture is as follows: To acquire representations that capture conceptual similarity relations (and thus promote appropriate generalization of stored information to newly encountered items), the semantic system must be sensitive to overlap across widely distributed surface representations, and such sensitivity depends in turn on there being, somewhere in the cortical semantic network, a region where all these different kinds of information converge.

5.3. *Summary*

The two previously described semantic syndromes seem to point to different conclusions about the neuroanatomical organization of the semantic system. Studies of patients with apparent category-specific impairment seem to suggest that there exists a certain degree of functional specialization within the semantic system, and theorists vary considerably in their opinions as to the degree and nature of such functional specialization. On the other hand, studies of patients with SD seem to suggest that there exists in the anterior temporal cortex a relatively circumscribed region that is critical to semantic processing for all variety of concepts and all modes of reception and expression. The Farah-McClelland model may be viewed as an effort to find a middle way between a complete balkanization of the semantic system and a fully homogeneous system. Related efforts have been put forward by Plaut (2002), Humphreys and Forde (2001), Tyler and colleagues (Tyler et al., 2000), Devlin and colleagues (Devlin et al., 1998), Lambon Ralph et al. (2007), and many others. Although there is as yet no clear consensus as to the resolution of these issues, it is apparent that computational models are providing important tools for an increasing number of researchers interested in the neural basis of semantic abilities.

An important direction for future efforts will be to relate these neurocognitive models back to the computational issues motivating the more abstract models reviewed in earlier sections of this chapter. That is, rather than asking, "What architecture best explains the pattern of sparing and impairment observed from different forms of brain damage," one may ask, "What architectures yield the computational properties that, from more abstract semantic theories, we believe the semantic system must possess?"

6. Conclusion and Open Issues

This overview indicates that, for many of the challenging puzzles currently facing research in human semantic memory, the beginnings of answers exist in the literature. Important questions about category coherence and feature weighting may be addressed by the fact that certain network architectures promote sensitivity to high-order covariance structure among stimulus properties across different modalities of reception and expression. Context-sensitivity may also reflect sensitivity to higher-order correlational structure in that any particular situation or context constrains which of an item's properties are "important" or relevant and which similarity relationships are best used to govern generalization and induction. One way of understanding such influences is to propose that the distributed semantic representations that govern performance in the moment are shaped not only by the particular item in question, but also by a representation of the current context, as is the case in the Rumelhart model (see also Chapter 15 on cognitive control in this volume). Finally, the semantic system's ability to comprehend full events, as well as its knowledge of "abstract" properties – properties that are not plausibly instantiated directly in sensory and motor systems – may derive, at least in part, from its sensitivity to temporal structure.

Important directions for future work involve drawing these various threads together in three different respects. First, the existing work is dispersed across a variety of models employing quite different architectures, differing degrees of abstraction, and different assumptions about the nature of learning and the information available to the semantic system. It is not clear how the differ-

ent pieces fit together into a single framework – a model in which coherent covariation among perceptual, motor, and linguistic properties, sensitivity to temporal structure, and representation of task context all contribute together to semantic representation and processing. Clearly, the development of such a model is beyond the current state of the art, but important next steps will involve addressing at least some components of this uber-system.

Second, this chapter focuses predominantly on PDP approaches to semantic memory, not because there are no other computational approaches, but because these other approaches typically focus on a slightly different set of issues. For instance, semantic memory is clearly important for human induction and inference; but induction and inference also constitute seperate domains of study in their own right, in which Bayesian approaches are probably most influential. Similarly, studies of categorization, although clearly overlapping with issues addressed here, also constitute a separate domain of study in which mathematical approaches (including prototype and instance-trace models) are the norm. As previously mentioned, these overlapping domains of study, and the methods they adopt, are reviewed in other chapters of this volume. An important direction for future research in semantic cognition and in these other domains will be to understand whether the theoretical approaches adopted there differ fundamentally from those described in the current chapter or whether they constitute different formal descriptions of the same underlying processes.

Finally, there is clearly much to be done in relating computational theories of semantic abilities to information processing in the brain. Although most theories about the neural basis of semantic cognition support the notion that semantic memory arises from the association of perceptual, motor, and linguistic representations that are widely distributed in the brain, there remain many open questions about the structure and properties of the cortical semantic network. For instance, how can sensory-motor learning lead to knowledge of conceptual similarity relations? How are abstract properties represented in the brain, if the semantic system is built on sensory and motor properties? How does the brain achieve the flexibility and context-sensitivity observed in the semantic system? What cortical mechanisms support conceptual development, and to what extent are these driven by experience versus maturation? The simulations reviewed in the current chapter provide intriguing clues about the answers to these questions; the next decade of research will need to integrate these computational ideas with the emerging picture from neuroscience.

References

Adlam, A.-L., Rogers, T. T., Salmond, C. H., Patterson, K., & Hodges, J. R. (2006). Semantic dementia and fluent primary progressive aphasia: Two sides of the same coin? *Brain*, *129*, 3066–3080.

Ahn, W. (1998). Why are different features central for natural kinds and artifacts? The role of causal status in determining feature centrality. *Cognition*, *69*, 135–178.

Anderson, J. R. (1991). The adaptive nature of human categorization. *Psychological Review*, *98*(3), 409–426.

Bertenthal, B. (1993). Infants' perception of biomechanical motions: Intrinsic image and knowledge-based constraints. In C. Grandrud (Ed.), *Visual perception and cognition in infancy* (pp. 175–214). Hillsdale, NJ: Lawrence Erlbaum.

Billman, D., & Knutson, J. (1996). Unsupervised concept learning and value systematicity: A complex whole aids learning the parts. *Journal of Experimental Psychology: Learning, Memory, and Cognition*, *22*, 458–475.

Bodner, G. E., & Masson, M. E. (2003). Beyond spreading activation: An influence of relatedness proportion on masked semantic priming. *Psychonomic Bulletin and Review*, *10*(3), 645–652.

Bozeat, S., Lambon Ralph, M. A., Graham, K. S., Patterson, K., Wilkin, H., Rowland, J., et al. (2003). A duck with four legs: Investigating the structure of conceptual knowledge using picture drawing in semantic dementia. *Cognitive Neuropsychology*, *20*(1), 27–47.

Bozeat, S., Lambon Ralph, M. A., Patterson, K., Garrard, P., & Hodges, J. R. (2000). Nonverbal semantic impairment in semantic dementia. *Neuropsychologia*, *38*, 1207–1215.

Bozeat, S., Lambon Ralph, M. A., Patterson, K., & Hodges, J. R. (2002). When objects lose their meaning: What happens to their use? *Cognitive, Affective, and Behavioral Neuroscience*, *2*(3), 236–251.

Bruner, J. S., Goodnow, J. J., & Austin, G. A. (1956). *A study of thinking*. New York: Wiley.

Burgess, C., & Lund, K. Modelling parsing constraints with high-dimensional context space. *Language and Cognitive Processes*, *12*(2), 177–210.

Capitani, E., Laiacona, M., Mahon, B. Z., & Caramazza, A. (2003). What are the facts of semantic category-specific deficits? A critical review of the clinical evidence. *Cognitive Neuropsychology*, *20*(3–6), 213–261.

Caramazza, A. (1998). The interpretation of semantic category-specific deficits: What do they reveal about the organization of conceptual knowledge in the brain? *Neurocase*, *4*, 265–272.

Carey, S. (1985). *Conceptual change in childhood*. Cambridge, MA: MIT Press.

Chao, L. L., Haxby, J. V., & Martin, A. (1999). Attribute-based neural substrates in temporal cortex for perceiving and knowing about objects. *Nature Neuroscience*, *2*(10), 913–919.

Collins, A. M., & Loftus, E. F. (1975). A spreading-activation theory of semantic processing. *Psychological Review*, *82*, 407–428.

Collins, A. M., & Quillian, M. R. (1969). Retrieval time from semantic memory. *Journal of Verbal Learning and Verbal Behavior*, *8*, 240–247.

Crestani, F. (1997). Application of spreading activation techniques in information retrieval. *Artificial Intelligence Review*, *11*(6), 453–482.

Crutch, S. J., & Warrington, E. K. (2003). The selective impairment of fruit and vegetable knowledge: A multiple processing channels account of fine-grain category-specificity. *Cognitive Neuropsychology*, *20*(3–6), 355–372.

Csibra, G., Gergely, G., Biro, S., Koos, O., & Brockbank, M. (1999). Goal attribution without agency cues: The perception of 'pure reason' in infancy. *Cognition*, *72*(3), 237–267.

Damasio, A. R., & Damasio, H. (1994). Cortical systems underlying knowledge retrieval. In C. Koch (Ed.), *Large-scale neuronal theories of the brain* (pp. 61–74). Cambridge, MA: MIT Press.

Dell, G. S. (1986). A spreading-activation theory of retrieval in sentence production. *Psychological Review, 93*(3), 283–321.

Devlin, J. T., Gonnerman, L. M., Andersen, E. S., & Seidenberg, M. S. (1998). Category-specific semantic deficits in focal and widespread brain damage: A computational account. *Journal of Cognitive Neuroscience, 10*(1), 77–94.

Elman, J. L. (1990). Finding structure in time. *Cognitive Science, 14,* 179–211.

Farah, M., & McClelland, J. L. (1991). A computational model of semantic memory impairment: Modality-specificity and emergent category-specificity. *Journal of Experimental Psychology: General, 120,* 339–357.

Garrard, P., Lambon Ralph, M. A., & Hodges, J. R. (2002). Semantic dementia: A category-specific paradox. In E. M. Forde & G. W. Humphreys (Eds.), *Category specificity in brain and mind* (pp. 149–179). Hove, UK: Psychology Press.

Gelman, R. (1990). First principles organize attention to and learning about relevant data: Number and the animate/inanimate distinction as examples. *Cognitive Science, 14,* 79–106.

Gelman, R., & Williams, E. M. (1998). Enabling constraints for cognitive development and learning: A domain-specific epigenetic theory. In D. Kuhn and R. Siegler (Eds.), *Handbook of child psychology, Volume II: Cognition, perception and development* (Vol. 2, pp. 575–630). New York: John Wiley.

Glenberg, A., & Robertson, D. A. (2000). Symbol grounding and meaning: A comparison of high-dimensional and embodied theories of meaning. *Journal of Memory and Language, 43,* 379–401.

Gopnik, A., & Sobel, D. M. (2000). Detecting blickets: How young children use information about novel causal powers in categorization and induction. *Child Development, 71*(5), 1205–1222.

Hinton, G. E. (1981). Implementing semantic networks in parallel hardware. In G. E. Hinton and J. A. Anderson (Eds.), *Parallel models of associative memory* (pp. 161–187). Hillsdale, NJ: Lawrence Erlbaum.

Hodges, J. R., Graham, N., & Patterson, K. (1995). Charting the progression in semantic dementia: Implications for the organisation of semantic memory. *Memory, 3,* 463–495.

Howard, M. W., & Kahana, M. J. (2002). When does semantic similarity help episodic retrieval? *Journal of Memory and Language, 46,* 85–98.

Humphreys, G. W., & Forde, E. M. (2001). Hierarchies, similarity, and interactivity in object-recognition: On the multiplicity of 'category-specific' deficits in neuropsychological populations. *Behavioral and Brain Sciences, 24*(3), 453–509.

Johnson, S. (2000). The recognition of mentalistic agents in infancy. *Trends in Cognitive Science, 4,* 22–28.

Jolicoeur, P., Gluck, M., & Kosslyn, S. M. (1984). Pictures and names: Making the connection. *Cognitive Psychology, 19,* 31–53.

Jones, S. S., Smith, L. B., & Landau, B. (1991). Object properties and knowledge in early lexical learning. *Child Development, 62*(3), 499–516.

Keil, F. (1989). *Concepts, kinds, and cognitive development.* Cambridge, MA: MIT Press.

Kruschke, J. K. (1992). ALCOVE: An exemplar-based connectionist model of category learning. *Psychological Review, 99*(1), 22–44.

Lambon Ralph, M. A., Graham, K., Ellis, E., & Hodges, J. R. (1998). Naming in semantic dementia–What matters? *Neuropsychologia, 36,* 125–142.

Lambon Ralph, M. A., Lowe, C., & Rogers, T. T. (2007). The neural basis of category-specific semantic deficits for living things: Evidence from semantic dementia, HSVE and a neural network model. *Brain, 130,* 1127–1137.

Landau, B., Smith, L., & Jones, S. (1988). The importance of shape in early lexical learning. *Cognitive Development, 3,* 299–321.

Landauer, T. K., & Dumais, S. T. (1997). A solution to Plato's problem: The Latent Semantic Analysis theory of acquisition, induction, and representation of knowledge. *Psychological Review, 104*(2), 211–240.

Landauer, T. K., Foltz, P. W., & Laham, D. (1998). An introduction to Latent Semantic Analysis. *Discourse Processes, 25,* 259–284.

Macario, J. F. (1991). Young children's use of color in classification: Foods and canonically colored objects. *Cognitive Development, 6,* 17–46.

Mandler, J. M. (2000). Perceptual and conceptual processes in infancy. *Journal of Cognition and Development, 1,* 3–36.

Martin, A., & Caramazza, A. (2003). Neuropsychological and neuroimaging perspectives on conceptual knowledge: An introduction. *Cognitive Neuropsychology, 20*(3–6), 195–212.

Martin, A., & Chao, L. L. (2001). Semantic memory in the brain: Structure and processes. *Current Opinion in Neurobiology, 11*, 194–201.

McClelland, J. L., & Rumelhart, D. E. (1985). Distributed memory and the representation of general and specific information. *Journal of Experimental Psychology: General, 114*, 159–188.

McClelland, J. L., St. John, M. F., & Taraban, R. (1989). Sentence comprehension: A Parallel Distibuted Processing Approach. *Language and Cognitive Processes, 4*, 287–335.

Medin, D. L., & Shaffer, M. M. (1978). Context theory of classification learning. *Psychological Review, 85*, 207–238.

Mervis, C. B. (1987). Child-basic object categories and early lexical development. In U. Neisser (Ed.), *Concepts and conceptual development: Ecological and intellectual factors in categorization* (pp. 201–233). Cambridge, UK: Cambridge University Press.

Mervis, C. B., & Rosch, E. (1981). Categorization of natural objects. *Annual Review of Psychology, 32*, 89–115.

Murphy, G. L., & Medin, D. L. (1985). The role of theories in conceptual coherence. *Psychological Review, 92*, 289–316.

Nosofsky, R. (1984). Choice, similarity, and the context theory of classification. *Journal of experimental psychology: Learning, memory, and cognition, 10*, 104–110.

Nosofsky, R. M. (1986). Attention, similarity and the identification-categorization relationship. *Journal of Experimental Psychology: Learning, Memory and Cognition, 115*(1), 39–57.

Patterson, K., & Hodges, J. (2000). Semantic dementia: One window on the structure and organisation of semantic memory. In J. Cermak (Ed.), *Handbook of neuropsychology Vol. 2: Memory and its disorders* (pp. 313–333). Amsterdam: Elsevier Science.

Pauen, S. (2002). Evidence for knowledge-based category discrimination in infancy. *Child Development, 73*(4), 1016–1033.

Plaut, D. C. (2002). Graded modality-specific specialisation in semantics: A computational account of optic aphasia. *Cognitive Neuropsychology, 19*(7), 603–639.

Rips, L. J., Shoben, E. J., & Smith, E. E. (1973). Semantic distance and the verification of semantic relations. *Journal of Verbal Learning and Verbal Behavior, 12*, 1–20.

Rogers, T. T., Ivanoiu, A., Patterson, K., & Hodges, J. (2006). Semantic memory in Alzheimer's disease and the fronto-temporal dementias: A longitudinal study of 236 patients. *Neuropsychology, 20*(3), 319–335.

Rogers, T. T., Lambon Ralph, M. A., Garrard, P., Bozeat, S., McClelland, J. L., Hodges, J. R., et al. (2004). The structure and deterioration of semantic memory: A computational and neuropsychological investigation. *Psychological Review, 111*(1), 205–235.

Rogers, T. T., Lambon Ralph, M. A., Hodges, J. R., & Patterson, K. (2003). Object recognition under semantic impairment: The effects of conceptual regularities on perceptual decisions. *Language and Cognitive Processes, 18*(5/6), 625–662.

Rogers, T. T., & McClelland, J. L. (2004). *Semantic Cognition: A Parallel Distributed Processing Approach*. Cambridge, MA: MIT Press.

Rogers, T. T., Patterson, K., & Graham, K. (2007). Colour knowledge in semantic dementia: It's not all black and white. *Neuropsychologia, 45*, 3285–3298.

Rosch, E. (1978). Principles of categorization. In E. Rosch & B. Lloyd (Eds.), *Cognition and categorization*. Hillsdale, NJ: Lawrence Erlbaum.

Rosch, E., & Mervis, C. B. (1975). Family resemblances: Studies in the internal structure of categories. *Cognitive Psychology, 7*, 573–605.

Rosch, E., Mervis, C. B., Gray, W., Johnson, D., & Boyes-Braem, P. (1976). Basic objects in natural categories. *Cognitive Psychology, 8*, 382–439.

Rosch, E., Simpson, C., & Miller, R. S. (1976). Structural bases of typicality effects. *Journal of Experimental Psychology: Human Perception and Performance, 2*, 491–502.

Rumelhart, D. E. (1990). Brain style computation: Learning and generalization. In S.F. Zornetzer, J. L. Davis & C. Lau (Eds.), *An introduction to neural and electronic networks* (pp. 405–420). San Diego, CA: Academic Press.

Rumelhart, D. E., Hinton, G. E., & Williams, R. J. (1986). Learning internal representations by error propagation. In D. E. Rumelhart, J. L. McClelland and the PDP Research Group (Eds.), *Parallel distributed processing: Explorations in the microstructure of cognition* (Vol. 1, pp. 318–362). Cambridge, MA: MIT Press.

Rumelhart, D. E., & Todd, P. M. (1993). Learning and connectionist representations. In D. E. Meyer & S. Kornblum (Eds.), *Attention and performance XIV: Synergies in experimental psychology, artificial intelligence, and cognitive neuroscience* (pp. 3–30). Cambridge, MA: MIT Press.

Saffran, J. R., Aslin, R. N., & Newport, E. L. (1996). Statistical learning by 8-month-olds. *Science, 274*(5294), 1926–1928.

Samson, D. S., & Pillon, A. (2003). A case of impaired knowledge for fruits and vegetables. *Cognitive Neuropsychology, 20*(3–6), 373–400.

Smith, J. D. (2002). Exemplar theory's predicted typicality gradient can be tested and disconfirmed. *Psychological Science, 13*, 437–442.

St. John, M. A., & McClelland, J. L. (1990). Learning and applying contextual constraints in sentence comprehension. *Artificial Intelligence, 46*, 217–257.

St. John, M. F. (1992). The story gestalt: A model of knowledge-intensive processes in text comprehension. *Cognitive Science, 16*, 271–306.

Steyvers, M., Griffiths, T. L., & Dennis, S. (2006). Probabilistic inference in human semantic memory. *Trends in Cognitive Science, 10*(7), 327–334.

Tulving, E. (1972). Episodic and semantic memory. In E. Tulving & W. Donaldson (Eds.), *Organization of memory* (pp. 381–403). New York: Academic Press.

Tyler, L., Moss, H. E., Durrant-Peatfield, M. R., & Levy, J. P. (2000). Conceptual structure and the structure of concepts: A distributed account of category-specific deficits. *Brain and Language, 75*(2), 195–231.

Warrington, E. K., & McCarthy, R. (1983). Category-specific access dysphasia. *Brain, 106*, 859–878.

Warrington, E. K., & McCarthy, R. (1987). Categories of knowledge: Further fractionation and an attempted integration. *Brain, 110*, 1273–1296.

Warrington, E. K., & Shallice, T. (1984). Category specific semantic impairments. *Brain, 107*, 829–854.

Wilson, R. A., & Keil, F. C. (2000). The shadows and shallows of explanation. In F. C. Keil & R. A. Wilson (Eds.), *Explanation and cognition* (pp. 87–114). Boston, MA: MIT Press.

Wittgenstein, L. (1953). *Philosophical investigations*. Oxford, UK: Blackwell.

Yeh, W., & Barsalou, L. (2006). The situated nature of concepts. *American Journal of Psychology, 119*(3), 349–384.

Zaki, S. F., & Nosofsky, R. (2004). False prototype enhancement effects in dot pattern categorization. *Memory and Cognition, 32*(3), 390–398.

CHAPTER 9

Models of Categorization

John K. Kruschke

1. Introduction

This chapter surveys a variety of formal models of categorization, with emphasis on exemplar models. The chapter reviews exemplar models' similarity functions, learning algorithms, mechanisms for exemplar recruitment, formalizations of response probability, and response dynamics. The intended audience of this chapter is students and researchers who are beginning the daunting task of digesting the literature regarding formal models of categorization. There are numerous variations for formalizing the component processes in exemplar models of categorization, and one of the contributions of the chapter is a direct comparison of component functions across models. For example, the similarity functions of several different models are expressed in a shared notational format, and formulas for the special case of present/absent features are derived, which permits direct comparison of their behaviors. No previous review cuts across models this way, also including comparisons of learning, exemplar recruitment, and so forth.

By decomposing the models and displaying corresponding components side by side, the chapter intends to reveal some of the issues that motivate model builders, and to identify some of the unresolved issues for future investigators. Along the way, a few promising but undeveloped ideas are pointed out, such as an identity-sensitive similarity function (Kruschke, 1993), a new gradient-descent learning rule for the Supervised and Unsupervised Stratified Adaptive Incremental Network (SUSTAIN) model (Love, Medin, & Gureckis, 2004), an attentionally modulated exemplar recruitment mechanism (Kruschke, 2003b), a proposal for cascaded activation in Attentional Learning Covering map (ALCOVE; Kruschke, 1992), among others.

Whereas this chapter is specifically intended to survey exemplar model formalisms, it avoids discussions of the various empirical effects explained or unexplained by each model variation. A survey of empirical phenomena can be found in the highly readable book by Murphy (2002). A chapter by Goldstone and Kersten (2003) describes the various roles of categorization in cognition. Another chapter by Kruschke (2005) surveys models of categorization with special emphasis on the role of selective attention and attentional learning. Previous reviews by Estes (1993, 1994) emphasize particular exemplar models and associated empirical results through the early 1990s.

1.1. *Everyday Categorization*

Everyone does categorization. For example, if you were in an office, and your companion pointed to the piece of furniture by the desk and asked, "What's that?" you would easily reply, "It's a *chair*." Such facility in categorization is not to be taken sitting down: There are hundreds of different styles of chairs, many of them novel, seen from thousands of different angles, yet all can be effortlessly categorized as *chair*. Whereas people include many items in the category *chair*, they also exclude similar items that are categorized instead as a park *bench* or a car *seat*. Putting those examples behind us, we conclude, a posteriori, that categorization is a complex process.

Categorization is not just an armchair amusement. It has consequences with costs or benefits. If you mistakenly categorize a dog as a chair and try sitting on it, the category of teeth might suddenly leap to mind. You might think it is ridiculous to confuse a dog with a chair, but there are children's chairs manufactured to resemble dogs. Moreover, categorizing a dog as a dog is not always easy; a Labrador is doggier than a Pekinese. A humorous consequence of category atypicality was revealed in a 1933 cartoon by Rea Gardner in the *New Yorker Magazine*: A rotund wealthy lady enters a posh restaurant clutching her tiny lap dog, to which the snooty maitre d' remarks, "I'm sorry, Madam, but *if* that's a dog, it's not allowed." For a more thorough review of the many uses and consequences of categorization, see the chapter by Goldstone and Kersten (2003).

1.2. *Categorization in the Laboratory*

Models of categorization are usually designed to address data from laboratory ex-

periments, so "categorization" might be best defined as the class of behavioral data generated by experiments that ostensibly study categorization. Perhaps the iconic categorization experiment is one that presents a stimulus to an observer and asks him or her to select a classification label for the stimulus. In some experiments, corrective feedback is then supplied.

There are many kinds of procedures and measurements in categorization experiments, which can assay many different aspects of behavior. One such measure is the proportion of times each category label is chosen when a stimulus is presented repeatedly on different occasions. Experimenters can also measure confidence ratings, response times, typicality ratings, eye gaze, recognition accuracy or rating, and so forth. Those dependent variables can be assessed as a function of many different independent variables. For example, behavior can be tracked as a function of the number of stimulus exposures, whereby the experimenter can assess learning, priming, habituation, and so forth. Experimenters can also manipulate category structure, that is, how the stimuli from different categories are situated relative to each other. (For example, the categories "stars in Orion" and "stars in the Big Dipper" are fairly easy to distinguish because their structures put them in distinct regions of the sky. But the categories "stars closer than 50 light years" and "stars farther than 50 light years" are more difficult to distinguish because stars from those categories are scattered in overlapping regions of the sky.) The variety of independent variables is bounded only by the experimenter's imagination. A very accessible review of the empirical literature has been presented by Murphy (2002).

1.3. *Informal and Formal Models*

It is the constellation of categorization phenomena that theorists want to explain. Informal theories provide some insights into the possible shapes behind that constellation. For instance, one may informally hypothesize that a bird is defined by necessary and sufficient features: A bird is something that flies, sings, and has feathers. By that definition, however, a bird can be an opera diva wearing a feather boa in an airplane. So, instead, one might informally hypothesize that a bird is defined by similarity to a prototype: A bird is something like a robin, which is an often-seen bird for North Americans.

Informal theories are a very useful first step in creating explanations of complex behaviors. Unfortunately, informal theories rarely make precise predictions and are often difficult to distinguish empirically. Sometimes, it is only intuition that generates predictions from an informal theory, so different theorists can make different predictions from the same informal theory.

All branches of science progress from informal theory to formal model. If all that Isaac Newton did was propose informally that there is a mysterious force that acts on apples and the moon in the same way, it is unlikely that his theory would be remembered today. It was the precision and veracity of his *formal* model of gravity that made his idea famous. Whereas Newton invented a formal model of how apples and moons interact among themselves, cognitive scientists have been inventing formal theories of how apples and moons are mentally categorized by observers. Just as there are many possible aspects of objects that could be formally specified in a model of gravitational behavior, there are many aspects of mental processing that could be formally specified in a model of categorical behavior.

1.4. *Types of Representation and Process*

Any model must assume that the stimulus is represented by some formal description.[1] This input representation could be de-

rived from multidimensional scaling (e.g., Kruskal, 1964; Shepard, 1962). For example, an animal might be represented by its precise coordinates in a psychological space that includes dimensions of size, length of hair/fur, and ferocity. Other methods for deriving a stimulus representation include feature extraction from additive clustering or factor analysis. Any model must also assume a formal representation of the cognizer's response. In the case when the cognizer is asked to produce a category label for a presented stimulus, the formal representation of the response could be a simple 1/0 coding for the presence/absence of each possible category label.

Some key differences among models are the representations and transformations that link the input and response representations. These intermediate representations and transformations are supposed to describe mental processes.[2] In general, a model of categorization specifies three things: (1) the content and format of the internal categorical knowledge representation, (2) the process of matching a to-be-classified stimulus to that knowledge, and (3) a process of selecting a category (or other response) based on the results of the matching process.

It can be useful to categorize models of categorization according to the content and format of their internal knowledge. Essentially, this content and format describe the type of representation that models use to mediate the mapping from input to output. The usual five types of representation are exemplars, prototypes, rules, boundaries, and theories. Many models of categorization are explicitly designed to be a clear case of one of those representational types, and some models are explicitly designed to be hybrids of those types, whereas yet other models are not easily classified as one of the five.

1 This representational assumption for a model does not necessarily imply that the mind makes a formal representation of the stimulus. Only the formal model requires a formal description. This is exactly analogous to formal models of motion: Newton's formal model uses representations of mass and distance to determine force and acceleration, but the objects themselves do not necessarily measure their masses and distances and then compute their force and acceleration. The representations in the model help us understand the behavior, but those repre-

sentations need not be reified in the behavior being modeled.

2 Just as input and output representations are in the model but not necessarily in the world, an intermediate transformation and representation in the model need not be reified in the mind being modeled.

1.4.1. EXEMPLAR MODELS

The canonical exemplar model simply stores every (distinct) occurrence of a stimulus and its category label. To classify a stimulus, the model determines the similarity of the stimulus to all the known exemplars, aggregates the similarities, and then decides the categorization of the stimulus. Exemplar models are the primary focus of this chapter and will be discussed extensively later. The other types of models are only briefly described to establish a context for exemplar models.

1.4.2. PROTOTYPE MODELS

A prototype model operates analogously to an exemplar model, but instead of storing information about every instance, the model only stores a summary representation of the many instances in a category. This representative stimulus could be a central tendency that expresses an average of the category. This average need not be the same as any actually experienced instance. The representative prototype could instead be a modal stimulus defined either as the most frequent instance or as a derived stimulus that is a combination of all the most frequent features. In the latter case, this modal stimulus need not be the same as any actually experienced instance. Finally, the prototype could instead be an "ideal" exemplar or caricature that indicates not only the content of the items in the category but also emphasizes those features that distinguish the category from others. This ideal need not be actually attained by any real instance of the category.

In "pure" prototype models, the models take a stimulus as input, compute its similarity to various explicitly specified prototypes, and then generate categorical response tendencies. A famous early application of a prototype model to human classification of schematic faces was conducted by Reed (1972). Any one-layer feed-forward connectionist model can be construed as a prototype model; an example is the component-cue model of Gluck and Bower (1988), in which a category is defined by a vector of weighted connections from features. (For a discussion of connectionist models, see Chapter 2 in this volume.)

Pure prototype models have a single explicit prototype per category. It is possible instead to represent a category with multiple prototypes, especially if the category is multimodal or has "jagged" boundaries with adjacent categories. Taken to the limit, this multiple-prototype approach can assign one prototype per instance, so it becomes an exemplar model. Some examples of models that recruit multiple prototypes during learning of labeled categories will be discussed later, but there are also models that recruit multiple prototypes while trying to learn clusterings among unlabeled items (e.g., Carpenter & Grossberg, 1987; Rumelhart & Zipser, 1985).

In another form of prototype model, the prototypes for the categories are implicit and dynamic (and in fact, it might be debatable to assert that these models "have" prototypes at all). An example of this sort of model is a recurrent connectionist network. When a few nodes in the network are clamped "on," activation spreads via weighted connections to other nodes. Some other nodes will be stably activated, whereas other nodes will be suppressed. If each node represents a feature, then the collection of co-activated nodes can be interpreted as having filled in the typical features of the category to which the initially clamped-on features belonged. Models that implement this approach include the "brain state in a box" model of Anderson et al. (1977) and the constraint-satisfaction network of Rumelhart et al. (1986).

1.4.3. RULE MODELS

Another type of model that specifies a category by a summary of its content is a rule model. A rule is a list of necessary and sufficient features for category membership. For example, a bachelor is anything that is human, male, unmarried, and eligible. (Notice that the features themselves are categories.) Examples of rule models include the hypothesis-testing approach of Levine (1975) and the RULEX model of Nosofsky et al. (Nosofsky & Palmeri, 1998; Nosofsky, Palmeri, & McKinley, 1994).

1.4.4. BOUNDARY MODELS

Unlike the previously described types of models, a boundary model does not explicitly specify the content of a category but instead specifies the boundaries between categories. For example, one might define a skyscraper as any building that is at least twenty stories tall. The value, twenty stories, is the boundary between skyscraper and non-skyscraper. Sometimes, boundary models are also referred to as rule models, because the boundary is a specific condition for category membership just like necessary and sufficient features are a specific condition. The usage here emphasizes that rules specify interior content, whereas boundaries specify edges between. The best developed boundary models have been expounded in a series of publications by Ashby and collaborators (e.g., Ashby & Gott, 1988; Ashby & Maddox, 1992)

1.4.5. CONTENT/BOUNDARY DUALITY AND ON-THE-FLY EQUIVALENCE

In some cases, it is only a matter of emphasis to think of a model as specifying content or boundary, because there may be ways to convert a content model to an equivalent boundary model and vice versa. For example, suppose two categories are represented by one prototype for each category, and the categorization is made by classifying a stimulus as whichever prototype is closer. From this it can be easily inferred that the model makes a linear boundary between the two categories, and an equivalent model states that the stimulus is classified by whichever side of the linear boundary it falls on.

It might be possible in principle to convert any content model to an equivalent boundary model and vice versa, but that does not mean that the two types of models are equally useful. Especially when category structure is complex, when there are many categories involved, and when new categories might be created, it is probably easier to describe a category by content than by boundary. For example, if new category members are observed that are somewhat different from previously learned instances, it is easy to simply add the new items to memory, but potentially difficult to add explicit "dents" in all the category boundaries between that category and many others. The actual difficulty depends on the particular formalization of boundaries, so this intuitive argument must be considered with caution.

There is another way in which a pure exemplar model encompasses the others. If a cognizer has perfect memory of all instances encountered, then the cognizer could, in principle, generate prototypes, rules, or theories at any moment, on the fly, and use those derived representations to categorize stimuli. Although this process is possible, presumably it would generate long response latencies compared with a process that has those representations immediately available because of previously deriving them during learning.

1.4.6. THEORY MODELS

The fifth approach to models of categorization is the "theory theory." This approach asserts that people have theories about the world, and people use those theories to categorize things. This approach can explain a variety of complex phenomena that are difficult for simpler models to address. The primary statement of this approach was written by Murphy and Medin (1985), and more recent reviews have been writtten by Murphy (1993, 2002). Theory theories have had limited formalizations, however, in part because it can be difficult to formally specify all the details of a complex knowledge structure. Some recent models that include formalizations of previous knowledge, if not full-blown theories, are those by Heit and Bott (2000); Heit, Briggs, and Bott (2004) and Rehder (2003a, 2003b).

1.4.7. HYBRID MODELS

The various representations and processes described in previous sections have different properties, and it may turn out to be the case that no single representation captures all of human behavior. It is plausible that the breadth of human behavior is best explained by a model that uses multiple representations. The challenge to the theorist then goes beyond specifying the details of any one representational type. The theorist must also specify exactly how the different representations interact and the circumstances under which each subsystem is selected for action or learning. Only a few combinations of representation have been explored.

Busemeyer, Dewey, and Medin (1984) combined prototype and exemplar models and found no consistent benefit of including prototypes. A model proposed by Smith and Minda (2000) combined prototypes with *punctate* exemplars, in which only exact matches to the exemplars have an influence; but Nosofsky (2000) showed that this particular hybrid model has serious shortcomings.

Other models have combined rules or boundaries with exemplars or multiple prototypes. For example, the COVIS model (Ashby et al., 1998; Ashby & Maddox, 2005) includes two subsystems, an explicit verbal subsystem that learns boundaries aligned with stimulus dimensions and an implicit system that learns to map exemplars or regions of stimulus space to responses. As another example, a "mixture of experts" approach (Erickson & Kruschke, 1998, 2002; Kalish, Lewandowsky, & Kruschke, 2004; Kruschke, 2001a; Kruschke & Erickson, 1994; Yang & Lewandowsky, 2004) combines modules that learn boundaries and modules that learn exemplar mappings. The mixture-of-expert approach also incorporates a gating system that learns to allocate attention to the various modules.

1.5. *Learning of Categories*

A model of categorization can specify a mapping from input to output without specifying how that mapping was learned. Theories of learning make additional assumptions about how internal representations change with exposure to stimuli. Different types of representation may require different types of learning. This section merely mentions some of the various possibilities for learning algorithms. Examples of each are described in Section 2.

Perhaps the simplest learning mechanism is a tally of how many times a particular feature co-occurs with a category label. Somewhat more general are simple Hebbian learning algorithms that increment a connection weight by a constant amount whenever the two nodes at the ends of that connection are co-activated. More sophisticated Hebbian algorithms adjust the size of the increment so that the magnitude of the weight is limited. Notice that in these schemes the weights are adjusted independently of how well the system is performing its categorization.

Alternatively, learning could be driven by categorization performance, not by mere co-occurrence of stimuli. The model can compare its predicted categorization with the actual category and, from the discrepancy, adjust its internal states to reduce the error. Thus, error minimization can be one goal for learning. In other approaches to learning, the goal is to adjust the internal representation such that it maximizes economy of description or the amount of information transmitted through the system.

Yet another scheme is learning by Bayesian updating of beliefs regarding alternative hypotheses. In the previous non-Bayesian schemes, learning was a matter of adjusting the values of a set of parameters, such as associative weights. By contrast, in a Bayesian framework, there are a large set of hypothetical fixed parameter values, each with a certain degree of belief. Bayesian learning consists of shifting belief away from hypotheses that fail to fit observations, toward hypotheses that better fit the observations.

2. Exemplar Models

The previous section provided a brief informal description of some of the concepts that will be formally expressed in the remainder of the chapter. From here on, the chapter unabashedly employs many mathematical formulas to express ideas.

In recent decades, theories of categorization emphasized rule-based theories (e.g., Bourne, 1966; Bruner, Goodnow, & Austin, 1956), then changed to prototype-based theories (e.g., Reed, 1972; Rosch & Mervis, 1975), and then moved to boundary (e.g., Ashby & Gott, 1988) and exemplar theories (e.g., Medin & Schaffer, 1978; Nosofsky, 1986). Although a variety of representations have been formalized, exemplar models have been especially richly explored in recent years, in no small part because they have been shown to fit a wide variety of empirical data. Exemplar models also form a nice display case for illustrating the issues mentioned in the preceding introductory paragraphs.

2.1. *Exemplary Exemplar Models*

Exemplar models have appeared in domains other than categorization, such as perception, memory, and language (e.g., Edelman & Weinshall, 1991; Hintzman, 1988; Logan, 2002; Regier, 2005). Within the categorization literature, however, a dominant family line of exemplar models centers on the Generalized Context Model (GCM; Nosofsky, 1986). The GCM is a formal generalization of the context model of Medin and Schaffer (1978). In these models, a stimulus is stored in memory as a complete exemplar that includes the full combination of stimulus features. It is not the case that each feature is stored independently of other features. Thus, the "context" for a feature is the other features with which it co-occurs. Exemplar representation allows the models to capture many aspects of human categorization, including the ability to learn nonlinear category distinctions and correlated features, while at the same time producing typicality gradients.

In the context model and GCM, perhaps just as important as exemplar representation is selective attention to features. With selective attention, the same underlying exemplar representation can be used to represent different category structures in which different features are relevant or irrelevant to the categorization. The context model and GCM had no learning mechanism for attention, however. Kruschke (1992) provided such a learning mechanism for attention in the ALCOVE model and at the same time

provided an error-driven learning mechanism for associations between exemplars and categories (unlike the simple frequency counting used in the GCM). Hurwitz (1994) independently developed a similar idea but based on the formalism of the context model, not the GCM. Attentional shifting in ALCOVE was assumed to be gradual over trials, but human attentional shifting is probably much more rapid within trials while retention is gradual across trials. Rapid attention shifts were implemented in the Rapid Attention Shifts 'N' Learning (RASHNL) model of Kruschke and Johansen (1999). The basic formulas for the GCM and ALCOVE are presented next, so that subsequent researchers' variations of these formulas can be provided.

The GCM assumes that stimuli are points in an interval-scaled multidimensional space. For example, a stimulus might have a value of 47 on the dimension of perceived size and a value of 225 on the dimension of perceived hue. Formally, exemplar x has value x_i on dimension i.

The similarity between memory exemplar x and stimulus y is computed in two steps. First, the psychological distance between x and y is computed:

$$d(x, y) = \sum_i \alpha_i |x_i - y_i| \qquad (9.1)$$

where α_i is the attention allocated to dimension i. Equation 9.1 simply says that for each dimension i, the absolute difference between x and y is computed, and then those dimensional differences are added up to determine the overall distance. Each dimension contributes to the total distance only to the extent that it is being attended to; the degree of attention to dimension i is captured by the coefficient α_i (which is non-negative). Notice that when α_i gets larger, the difference on dimension i is weighted more heavily in the overall distance function. Equation 9.1 applies when the dimensions are psychologically separable; that is, when they can be selectively attended. In some applications, the attention strengths are assumed to sum to 1.0, to

GCM/ALCOVE: c=0.5,α=(0.5,0.5)

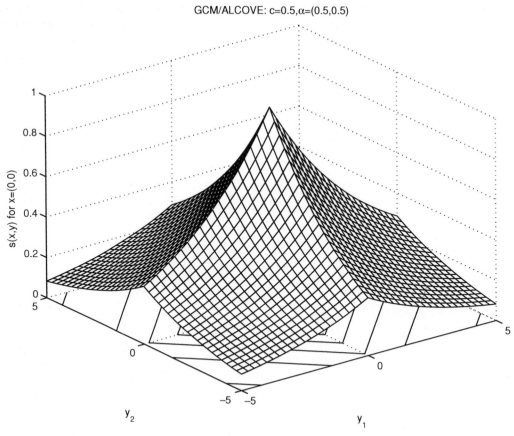

Figure 9.1. Similarity function in Generalized Concept Model (GCM) and Attentional Learning Covering (ALCOVE) map. A memory exemplar is located at position $x = (0, 0)$, and the height of the surface is the similarity of stimulus $y = (y_1, y_2)$ to x. The closer y is to $(0, 0)$, the more similar it is to x, so that the similarity peaks when $y = x$ at $(0, 0)$. Notice that the level contours, which can be glimpsed on the floor of the plot, are diamond shaped. These diamonds mark points of equal distance from the exemplar, using the "city-block" metric of Equation 9.1. The curved surface drops exponentially as a function of distance, as dictated by Equation 9.2.

reflect the notion that dimensions compete for attention.

After the distance is computed, the similarity is determined as an exponentially decaying function of distance:

$$s(x, y) = \exp(-c\, d(x, y)) \qquad (9.2)$$

where $c > 0$ is a scaling parameter. Thus, when the distance is zero, that is, $d(x, y) = 0$, then the similarity is 1, that is, $s(x, y) = 1$. As the distance increases, the similarity drops off toward zero. The rapidity of the decrease in similarity, as a function of distance, is governed by the scaling parame-

ter, c: When c is large, the similarity drops off more rapidly with distance. The exponential form of the similarity function has been motivated both empirically and theoretically (cf. Shepard, 1987; Tenenbaum & Griffiths, 2001a, but note that those analyses refer to generalization regarding a single category, not exemplars). Figure 9.1 shows a plot of this similarity function for an exemplar set arbitrarily at $x = (0, 0)$. The caption of the figure provides detailed discussion.

After similarity is computed, a categorical response is then generated on the basis of which category's exemplars are most similar to the stimulus and most frequently observed. In a sense, the exemplars "vote" for the category with which they are associated. The strength of the vote is determined by how strongly the exemplar is activated (by similarity) and how strongly it is associated with the category (by frequency of co-occurrence). The probability of choosing a category is then just the proportional number of votes it gets. Formally, in the original GCM (Nosofsky, 1986), the probability of category R given stimulus y is

$$p(R|y) = \frac{\beta_R \sum_{x \in R} N_{Rx} s(x, y)}{\sum_r \beta_r \sum_{k \in r} N_{rk} s(k, y)} \quad (9.3)$$

where β_r is the response bias for category r, and N_{rk} is the frequency that exemplar k has occurred as an instance of the category r. This rule is an extension of the similarity-choice model for stimulus identification (Luce, 1963; Shepard, 1957) and is often referred to as the ratio rule. The numerator of Equation 9.3 simply expresses the total weighted vote for category R, and the denominator simply expresses the grand total votes cast. Thus, Equation 9.3 expresses the proportion of votes cast for category R.

In summary, Equations 9.1, 9.2, and 9.3 describe how the GCM transforms a stimulus representation, y, to a categorical choice probability, $p(R \mid y)$. The transformation is mediated by similarity to exemplars in memory.

In the GCM, the attention weights (α_i in Equation 9.1) were either freely estimated to best fit data or set to values that optimized the model's performance for a given category structure. The ALCOVE model (Kruschke, 1992) instead provided a learning algorithm for the attention and associative strengths. For a training trial in which the correct classification is provided (as in human learning experiments), ALCOVE computes the discrepancy, or error, between its predicted classification and the actual classification. The model then adjusts the attention and associative weights to reduce the error. To describe this error reduction formally, let the correct (i.e., teacher) categorization be denoted t_k, such that $t_k = 1$ when category k is correct and $t_k = 0$ oth-

erwise. The model's predicted category activation, given stimulus y, is defined to be the sum of the weighted influences of the exemplars. Denote the associative weight to category k from exemplar x as w_{kx}. Then the predicted activation of category k is $a_k = \sum_x w_{kx} s(x, y)$. Notice that this sum is the same as the sum that appears in the GCM's Equation 9.3 if $w_{kx} = N_{kx}$. When a stimulus is presented, the model's error in categorization is then defined as

$$E = .5 \sum_k (t_k - a_k)^2. \quad (9.4)$$

The model strives to reduce this error by changing is attention and associative weights.

Of the many possible methods that could be used to adjust attention and associative weights, ALCOVE uses gradient descent on error. Generally in gradient descent, a parameter value is changed in the direction that most rapidly reduces error. Because the gradient (i.e., derivative) of a function specifies the direction of greatest increase, gradient descent follows the negative of the gradient. Gradient descent yields the following formulas for changing weights and attention:

$$\Delta w_{kx} = \lambda_w (t_k - a_k) s(x, y) \quad (9.5)$$

$$\Delta \alpha_i = -\lambda_\alpha \sum_x \sum_k (t_k - a_k)$$
$$\times w_{kx} s(x, y) c |x_i - y_i| \quad (9.6)$$

where λ_w and λ_α are constants of proportionality, called learning rates, that are freely estimated to best fit human learning data. Equation 9.5 says that the change in weight w_{kx}, which connects exemplar x to category k, is proportional to the error $(t_k - a_k)$ in the category node and the similarity $s(x, y)$ in the exemplar node. Equation 9.6 says that the error at the category nodes is propagated backwards to the exemplar nodes. Define the error at each exemplar as $\varepsilon_x = \sum_k (t_k - a_k) w_{kx} s(x, y) c$. Then the change in attention to dimension i is simply the sum, over exemplars, of each exemplar's error, times its closeness to the stimulus on that dimension: $\Delta\alpha_i = -\lambda_\alpha \sum_x \varepsilon_x |x_i - y_i|$.

The RASHNL model (Kruschke & Johansen, 1999) is an extension of ALCOVE that makes large attentional shifts on each trial and better mimics individual differences and human probabilistic category learning than ALCOVE. In particular, RASHNL includes a mechanism that gradually reduces the learning and shifting rates, so that a large shift of attention can be "frozen" into the learned structure.

The previous section summarized the GCM and ALCOVE models. They provide a reference point for exploring other exemplar models. The discussion of other exemplar models will emphasize the following processes: computing similarity, learning associations and attention, recruiting exemplars, choosing a response category, and their timing, that is, temporal dynamics. Each of these five aspects will be explored at length in the following sections. One of the goals is to show in detail how each of the five aspects can be formalized in a variety of ways. This side-by-side comparison of the internal components of each model is intended to clarify how the models do indeed have components, rather than being indivisible all-or-nothing entities. The juxtaposition of components also reveals the variety of formalisms that has evolved over the years and is suggestive of variation for future intelligent designers.

2.2. *Similarity*

The GCM and its relatives, such as ALCOVE, assume that stimuli can be represented as points on "interval" scales, such as size. Stimuli that are instead best represented on "nominal" scales, such as political party (e.g., Republican, Democrat, Libertarian, or Green Party), are not directly handled. Moreover, in the GCM and ALCOVE, all that affects similarity is *differences* between stimuli; the number of dimensions on which stimuli *match* has no impact. Empirical evidence demonstrates that the number of matching features can, in fact, affect subjective similarity (e.g., Gati & Tversky, 1984; Tversky, 1977).

Various researchers have contemplated alternative stimulus representations and similarity functions in attempts to expand the range of applicability of exemplar models. The variations can be analyzed on two factors (among others). First, the similarity models can address stimuli represented on either continuous, interval-scaled dimensions or discrete, nominally scaled dimensions. Second, similarity models can be sensitive to either stimulus differences only or stimulus commonalities as well. For example, imagine two schematic drawings of faces, composed merely of an oval outline and two dots that indicate eyes. The separation of the eyes differs between the two faces. The perceived similarity of these two faces is some baseline value denoted s_b. Now imagine including in both faces identical lines for mouths and noses. Still, the only difference between the faces is the eye separation; both faces merely have additional identical features. The perceived similarity of the augmented faces is denoted s_a. If $s_a \neq s_b$, then the similarity is affected by the number of matching features or dimensions.

Similarity models that are sensitive to the number of matching features can be further partitioned into two types. One type is sensitive to stimulus commonalities only when there is at least one difference between stimuli. In this type of model, when the stimuli are identical, then the similarity of the stimuli is 1.0 regardless of how many features or dimensions are present. In other words, the self-similarity of any stimulus is 1.0 regardless of how rich or sparse the stimulus is. In a different type of model, even self-similarity is affected by how many stimulus features or dimensions are present.

Table 9.1 lays out the two characteristics of similarity functions, with the columns corresponding to the type of scale used for representing the stimuli and the rows corresponding to how the similarity function is affected by the number of matching features or dimensions. The following paragraphs will first describe variations of models

Table 9.1: Characteristics of similarity functions for various models

Similarity is sensitive to:	Scale for stimulus representation		
	Binary features	N-ary features	Continuous (interval) scale
Mismatches only	Featural ALCOVE (Lee & Navarro, 2002)		GCM (Nosofsky, 1986), ALCOVE (Kruschke, 1992)
Number of matches, but only with a mismatch present	WRM (Lamberts, 1994), Configural Model (Pearce, 1994)	SUSTAIN (Love et al., 2004)	
Number of matches, including self-similarity	SDM (Kanerva, 1988), ADDCOVE (Verguts et al., 2004)	Rational Model (featural version; Anderson, 1990)	APPLE (Kruschke, 1993)

that handle continuous scaled stimuli and then describe several models that handle nominally scaled stimuli. Finally, a hybrid model will be presented.

A stimulus will be denoted y and the value of its ith feature is y_i. A copy of that stimulus in memory is called an exemplar and will be denoted $x = \{x_i\}$. This notation can be used regardless of whether the features are represented on continuous or nominal scales. In the special circumstance that every feature is simply present or absent, the presence of the ith feature is indicated by $y_i = 1$, and its absence is indicated by $y_i = 0$. As a reminder that this is a special situation, the stimulus will be denoted as uppercase Y (instead of lowercase y). When dealing with present/absent features, the number of features that match or differ across the stimulus Y and a memory exemplar X can be counted. The set of present features that are shared by X and Y is denoted $X \cap Y$, and the number of those features is denoted $n_{X \cap Y}$. Some models are also sensitive to the absence of features. The set of features absent from a stimulus is denoted $\overline{Y}$, and the number of features absent from both X and Y is denoted $n_{\overline{X} \cap \overline{Y}}$. The set of features present in X but absent from Y is denoted $X \neg Y \equiv X \cap \overline{Y}$, and the number of such features is denoted $n_{X \neg Y}$.

Similarity functions must specify, at least implicitly, the range of features over which the similarity is computed. In principle, there are an infinite number of features absent from any two stimuli (e.g., they both have no moustache, they both have no freckles, they both have no nose stud, etc.) and an infinite number of features present in both stimuli (e.g., they are both smaller than a battleship, they are both mounted on shoulders, they are both covered in skin, etc.). The following discussion assumes that the pool of candidate features over which similarity is computed has been prespecified.

2.2.1. CONTINUOUS SCALE, SENSITIVE TO DIFFERENCES ONLY

In the GCM and ALCOVE, stimuli are represented as values on continuously scaled dimensions. The similarity between a stimulus and an exemplar declines from 1.0 only if there are differences between the exemplar and the stimulus. If the exemplar and stimulus have no differences, then their similarity is 1.0, regardless of how many dimensions are involved. Therefore, the GCM and ALCOVE are listed in the upper right cell of Table 9.1.

Although the GCM/ALCOVE similarity function is meant to be applied to dimensions with continuous scales, it will be useful for comparison with other models to consider the special case when all dimensions have only present/absent values. To simplify even further, assume that $\alpha_i = 1$ for all i and that $c = 1$. In this special case, Equations 9.1 and 9.2 reduce to

$$s(X, Y) = \exp(-[n_{X \neg Y} + n_{Y \neg X}]). \quad (9.7)$$

Clearly, the similarity depends only on the number of differing features and not on the number of matching features. The term in Equation 9.7 will arise again when discussing the featural ALCOVE model of Lee and Navarro (2002).

2.2.2. CONTINUOUS SCALE, SENSITIVE TO MATCHES

The similarity function in GCM/ALCOVE proceeds in two steps. First, as expressed in Equation 9.1, the model computes an overall distance between exemplar and stimulus by summing across dimensions. Second, as expressed in Equation 9.2, the model generates the similarity by applying an exponentially decaying function to the overall distance.

In the Approximately ALCOVE (APPLE) model of Kruschke (1993), that ordering of computations is reversed. First, a similarity is computed on each dimension separately, using an exponentially decaying function of distance within each dimension:

$$s_i(x, y) = \exp(-\alpha_i |x_i - y_i|). \quad (9.8)$$

Second, an overall similarity is computed by combining the dimensional similarities via a sigmoid (also known as squashing or logistic) function:

$$
\begin{aligned}
s(x, y) \\
= \mathrm{sig}\left(\sum_i s_i(x, y); g, \theta\right) \\
= \left[1 + \exp\left(-g\left\{\sum_i s_i(x, y) - \theta\right\}\right)\right]^{-1}
\end{aligned}
$$

$$(9.9)$$

where the gain, $g > 0$, is the steepness of the sigmoid and θ is a threshold that is typically somewhat less than the number of dimensions being summed.

Figure 9.2 shows a plot of this similarity function, which should be contrasted with the GCM/ALCOVE similarity function shown in Figure 9.1. This similarity function has some attractive characteristics, one being that individual featural matches can have disproportionately strong influence on overall similarity. This is revealed in Figure 9.2 as the "ridges" where either $x_1 = y_1$ or $x_2 = y_2$. Another useful property of the similarity function is that self-similarity (i.e., when $y = x$) can vary from exemplar to exemplar if they have different thresholds or gains. In particular, the self-similarity can be less than 1.0 when the threshold, θ, is high. Finally, when there are more dimensions on which the stimuli match, then the similarity is larger. This can be inferred from Equation 9.9: When there are more dimensional $s_i(x, y)$ terms contributing to the sum, the overall $s(x, y)$ is larger. Thus, APPLE's similarity function operates on continuously scaled stimuli and is affected by the number of matching dimensions, even for identical stimuli. Therefore, it is listed in Table 9.1 in the lower right cell.

When the continuously scaled dimensions assumed by APPLE are reduced to present/absent features represented by 1/0 values, the similarity function can be expressed in terms of the number of matching and differing features. Simplify by assuming $\alpha_i = 1$ for all i, then Equations 9.8 and 9.9 imply

$$
s(X, Y) = \mathrm{sig}\left(n_{X \cap Y} + n_{\overline{X} \cap \overline{Y}}\right.
$$

$$
\left. + \frac{1}{e}(n_{X \neg Y} + n_{Y \neg X}); g, \theta\right) \quad (9.10)
$$

where $e = 2.718$ is the base of the exponential function. Clearly, this similarity is a function of both the number of matching features and the number of mismatching features.

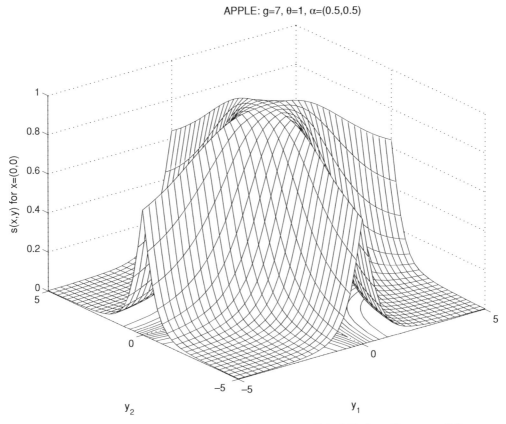

Figure 9.2. Similarity function in Approximately ALCOVE (APPLE), from Equations 9.8 and 9.9, using specific parameter values indicated in the title of the figure. Compare with Figure 9.1.

2.2.3. NOMINAL SCALE, SENSITIVE TO DIFFERENCES ONLY

Whereas the GCM, ALCOVE, and APPLE apply to stimuli represented on continuous scales, there are also many models of categorization that apply to stimulus representations composed of nominally scaled dimensions. This section reviews several such models that are sensitive only to stimulus differences, not to stimulus commonalities (analogous to GCM/ALCOVE). A later section addresses similarity functions in which commonalities do have an influence (analogous to APPLE).

Lee and Navarro (2002) discussed a *featural ALCOVE model* in which stimuli are represented as features derived from additive clustering techniques. Let x_i denote the presence or absence of feature i in stimu-

lus x, such that $x_i = 1$ if x has features i, and $x_i = 0$ otherwise. The distance between exemplar x and stimulus y is given by

$$d(x, y) = \sum_i \alpha_i \left[x_i(1 - y_i) + (1 - x_i)y_i \right].$$

$$(9.11)$$

Notice in Equation 9.11 that the term inside the square brackets is simply 1 if feature i mismatches and 0 otherwise. The distance is algebraically equivalent to $\sum_i \alpha_i |x_i - y_i|$, which is an expression seen before in Equation 9.1 and which will be seen again in Equation 9.14. Lee and Navarro (2002) preferred to express the distance as shown in Equation 9.11 because it suggests discrete values for x_i and y_i rather than continuous values. Lee and Navarro (2002) then defined similarity as the usual exponentially decaying function of distance. In the special case that $\alpha_i = 1$ for all i, the similarity function becomes exactly Equation 9.7. This similarity function is not sensitive to matching features, so this model is listed in the upper left cell of Table 9.1. Lee and Navarro (2002) collected human learning data for stimuli that were well described by present/absent features, and found that AL-COVE with the featural representation fit the data better than the original continuous-scaled ALCOVE.

2.2.4. NOMINAL SCALE, SENSITIVE TO MATCHES

Several models are considered in this section. This section first describes models that assume binary valued (present/absent) features and then moves on to models that assume features with m values. Within each of those, the discussion first addresses models that are sensitive to the number of matching features only when at least one mismatch is present and then addresses models that are sensitive to the number of matching features, even when there are no mismatching features.

Pearce (1987) developed a model in which similarity is a function of both matching and distinctive features. He defined the similarity of two stimuli, X and Y, to be

$$s(X, Y) = \frac{f(X \cap Y) f(X \cap Y)}{f(X) f(Y)} \qquad (9.12)$$

where $f(X)$ is a monotonic function of the number of features in X and of the individual saliences of the features.

Pearce (1994) proposed a specific version of that function in his *configural model* of associative learning. First, restrict consideration to a situation where all features are equally salient. Let the number of features in stimulus X be denoted n_X. When exemplar X is perceived, its features compete for limited attention, such that each feature is activated to a level $1/\sqrt{n_X}$. This level of activation implies that the sum of the squared

activations is unity. Every distinct stimulus recruits a copy of that stimulus activation in exemplar memory. Pearce (1994) referred to those exemplars as configurations of features, hence, the moniker of the configural model.

The similarity of a memory exemplar and a stimulus was then defined to be simply the sum over features of the products of the feature activations. Because absent features have zero activation, the sum over all features reduces to a sum over matching present features; hence, the similarity is given by:

$$
\begin{aligned}
s&(X, Y) \\
&= \sum_{i \in X \cap Y} \frac{1}{\sqrt{n_X}} \frac{1}{\sqrt{n_Y}} \\
&= n_{X \cap Y} \frac{1}{\sqrt{n_X}} \frac{1}{\sqrt{n_Y}} \\
&= \left[\frac{n_{X \cap Y}}{(n_{X \cap Y} + n_{X \neg Y})} \frac{n_{X \cap Y}}{(n_{X \cap Y} + n_{Y \neg X})} \right]^{1/2}.
\end{aligned}
$$
$$(9.13)$$

Notice that the similarity increases when the number of matching features increases, as long as there is at least one differing feature. Hence, the configural model is listed in the middle-left cell of Table 9.1.

Young and Wasserman (2002) compared Pearce's (1994) model and ALCOVE on a task involving learning about stimuli with present/absent features. ALCOVE was not designed for present/absent features, and Pearce's model does not have selective attention. Young and Wasserman (2002) found that neither model accurately captured the learning trends in their set of category structures, but suggested that it might be possible to modify the attentional capacity constraints in the models to address their findings.

Lamberts (1994) explored another similarity function that is sensitive to matching features and distinctive features. Again, consider features that are binary valued, either present or absent, and coded as 1 or 0, respectively. In Lamberts's Weighted Ratio

Model (WRM), the similarity of exemplar x to stimulus y is given by

$$s(x, y)$$
$$= \frac{\mu \sum_i \alpha_i (1 - |x_i - y_i|)}{\mu \sum_i \alpha_i (1 - |x_i - y_i|) + (1 - \mu) \sum_i \alpha_i |x_i - y_i|} \quad (9.14)$$

where $(1 - |x_i - y_i|)$ is 1 if and only if the exemplar and stimulus match on dimension i, and $|x_i - y_i|$ is 1 if and only if the exemplar and stimulus differ on dimension i. The value of μ (between 0 and 1) in Equation 9.14 determines the influence of matching features relative to differing features. As in previous sections, α_i is the attention allocated to dimension i. Lamberts (1994) explored some aspects of this similarity function in model fitting, but the similarity function has not been extensively pursued in subsequent work.

Notice that in Equation 9.14, the component of the denominator that measures featural differences, $\sum_i \alpha_i |x_i - y_i|$, is the same as Equation 9.1 and is algebraically equivalent to Equation 9.11 used by Lee and Navarro (2002). The WRM goes beyond the GCM by including the influence of matching features in addition to mismatching features. The number of matching features only affects the similarity, however, when there is at least one mismatch; therefore, the WRM is listed in the middle-left cell of Table 9.1. Again it is worth emphasizing that, despite the comparison of the WRM with the GCM, the GCM applies to continuous dimensions, whereas the WRM applies to present-absent features.

The similarity function of the WRM can be expressed in terms of the number of matching and differing features. Just as Pearce (1994) assumed equal salience for all features, set $\alpha_i = 1$ for all i, which implies that $\sum_i \alpha_i (1 - |x_i - y_i|) = n_{X \cap Y} + n_{\overline{X} \cap \overline{Y}}$ and $\sum_i \alpha_i |x_i - y_i| = n_{X \neg Y} + n_{Y \neg X}$. When $\mu = 0.5$, Equation 9.14 becomes

$$s(x, y) = \frac{n_{X \cap Y} + n_{\overline{X} \cap \overline{Y}}}{n_{X \cap Y} + n_{\overline{X} \cap \overline{Y}} + n_{X \neg Y} + n_{Y \neg X}}. \quad (9.15)$$

Equation 9.14 reduces to the similarity function of the configural model under slightly different special circumstances. First, suppose that $n_{\overline{X} \cap \overline{Y}} = 0$; second, set $\mu = 2/3$, that is, put twice as much weight on matching features than differing features; third, suppose $n_{X \neg Y} = n_{Y \neg X}$. Then the WRM similarity of Equation 9.15 becomes

$$s(x, y) = \frac{n_{X \cap Y}}{n_{X \cap Y} + n_{X \neg Y}} = \frac{n_{X \cap Y}}{n_{X \cap Y} + n_{Y \neg X}}. \quad (9.16)$$

When those final two (equal) expressions in Equation 9.16 are multiplied times each other and square-rooted, the result is an expression that matches the configural model's similarity in Equation 9.13. In their general forms, however, the WRM similarity allows differential salience (i.e., attention) to features and differential weighting of matching and differing features, whereas the configural model predicts that the effect of increasing $n_{X \neg Y}$ can be different than the effect of increasing $n_{Y \neg X}$.

The Sparse Distributed Memory (SDM) model of Kanerva (1988) can be interpreted as a form of exemplar model. In SDM, stimuli are assumed to be represented as points in a high-dimensional binary-valued space, such that $y_i \in \{1, 0\}$. Memory exemplars are represented by weights such that $x_i = 1$ for a present feature, but, unlike previous models, $x_i = -1$ for an absent feature (and $x_i = 0$ for a feature about which the exemplar is indifferent, but such a case will not be considered here). A memory exemplar is activated when $\sum_i x_i y_i > \theta_x$, where θ_x is the threshold of the exemplar. This activation can be interpreted as the similarity of the stimulus to the exemplar; here, the similarity has just two values. Thus,

$$s(X, Y) = \begin{cases} 1 & \text{if } \sum_i x_i y_i \geq \theta_x \\ 0 & \text{otherwise} \end{cases}$$
$$= \text{step}\,(n_{X \cap Y} - n_{Y \neg X} - \theta_x) \quad (9.17)$$

where $\text{step}(n) = 1$ when $n \geq 0$ and $\text{step}(n) = 0$ when $n < 0$. Clearly, the similarity function in SDM is sensitive to both matching and differing features, and it is listed in the lower-left cell of Table 9.1. SDM has not been extensively applied to many behavioral phenomena, but it is included here as an example of the variety of possible similarity functions.

Verguts et al. (2004) developed a variation of ALCOVE that they called Additive ALCOVE (ADDCOVE) because the first step in its similarity computation is an additive weighting of features. Specifically, suppose a stimulus consists of features x_i. The corresponding exemplar in memory is given feature weights $w_i = x_i/\sqrt{\sum_j x_j^2} = x_i/\|x\|$. When presented with stimulus y, a baseline exemplar activation is computed by adding weighted features as follows:

$$a(x, y) = \sum_i \frac{x_i}{\|x\|} y_i. \tag{9.18}$$

When x and y consist of 0/1 bits, Equation 9.18 becomes

$$a(x, y) = \sum_{i \in X \cap Y} \frac{1}{\sqrt{n_X}}$$
$$= n_{X \cap Y}/\sqrt{n_X}, \tag{9.19}$$

which is like the configural model (Equation 9.13), except that here, $y_i = 1$, not $1/\sqrt{n_Y}$.

These baseline activations are then normalized relative to other exemplar activations. Included in the set of other exemplar activations is a novelty detector, which has $a_N(y) = \theta\|y\| = \sqrt{n_Y}$ with θ close to 1.0, for example, 0.99. The similarity of exemplar x to stimulus y is then given as

$$s(x, y) = a(x, y)^\phi \bigg/ \left[\sum_k a(k, y)^\phi + a_N(y)^\phi\right] \tag{9.20}$$

where the index, k, varies over all exemplars in memory. When x and y consist of 0/1 bits,

Equation 9.20 becomes

$$s(x, y)$$
$$= \frac{(n_{X \cap Y}/\sqrt{n_X})^\phi}{\left[\sum_K (n_{K \cap Y}/\sqrt{n_K})^\phi + (\theta\sqrt{n_Y})^\phi\right]}$$
$$= \frac{(n_{X \cap Y}/\sqrt{n_{X \cap Y} + n_{X \neg Y}})^\phi}{\left[\sum_K (n_{K \cap Y}/\sqrt{n_{K \cap Y} + n_{K \neg Y}})^\phi + (\theta\sqrt{n_Y})^\phi\right]}. \tag{9.21}$$

As can be gleaned from Equation 9.21, this similarity function depends on both the shared and the distinctive features between the exemplar and the stimulus.

Notice that the similarity function of Equation 9.21 can be asymmetric: $s(x, y) \neq s(y, x)$ when $X \neg Y \neq Y \neg X$. In other words, if a memory exemplar has, say, one feature that a stimulus does not have, but that stimulus has two features that the memory exemplar does not have, then the similarity of the stimulus to the exemplar is different from the similarity of the exemplar to the stimulus. This asymmetry might be useful for addressing analogous asymmetries in human similarity judgments. (Another example of an asymmetric similarity function can be found in Sun, 1995, p. 258.) Interestingly, moreover, the similarity in Equation 9.21 also depends on what other exemplars are currently in memory. Thus, a stimulus might be fairly similar to an exemplar at one moment, but after another highly similar exemplar is added to memory, the similarity to the first exemplar will be reduced.

The *SUSTAIN model* of Love et al. (2004) employs a similarity function that operates on multivalued (not just binary valued) nominal dimensions. Different nominal dimensions can have different numbers of values. For example, the dimension of marital status might have three values (single, married, divorced), and the dimension of political affiliation might have four values (Democrat, Republican, Green, Libertarian). If dimension i has m_i values, then a stimulus is represented by a bit vector of length $\sum_i m_i$ that has 1's in positions of present features and 0's elsewhere.

In SUSTAIN, what is here being referred to as "exemplars" are not just copies of individual stimuli, but are instead central tendencies of clusters of stimuli. In certain conditions, SUSTAIN could recruit a cluster node for every presented instance and could therefore become a pure exemplar model. The representation for a cluster is also a vector of $\sum_i m_i$ values, but the values are the means (between 0 and 1) of the instances represented by the cluster. The components of the vectors are denoted x_{iv}, where the subscript indicates the vth element of the ith dimension. The similarity of a cluster node x to a stimulus y is then defined as

$$s(x, y) = \frac{1}{\sum_i \alpha_i^\gamma}$$
$$\times \sum_i \alpha_i^\gamma \exp\left(-.5\alpha_i \sum_{v \in i} |x_{iv} - y_{iv}|\right)$$
$$(9.22)$$

where $\gamma \geq 0$ governs the relative dominance of the most attended dimension over the less attended dimensions. Notice that if $x = y$ then $s(x, y) = 1$ regardless of how many dimensions are involved.

It should be noted that Love et al. (2004) never asserted that Equation 9.22 is a model of similarity; rather, they simply defined the activation of a cluster node when a stimulus is presented. It is merely by analogy to other models that it is here being called similarity. Moreover, the final activation of cluster nodes in SUSTAIN is another step away: There is competition and then only the winner retains any activation at all. Because the SUSTAIN model incorporates several other mechanisms that distinguish it from other exemplar models, it is not clear which aspects of the specific formalization in Equation 9.22 are central to the model's behavior. The function is described here primarily as an example of how similarity can be defined on multivalued nominal dimensions.

SUSTAIN's similarity function can be related to previous approaches that assumed binary valued features. Suppose that every feature is binary valued, suppose that $\alpha_i = 1$ for all features, and suppose that clusters represent single exemplars (so that $x_i \in \{0, 1\}$). Then Equation 9.22 becomes

$$s(x, y) = \frac{(n_{X \cap Y} + n_{\overline{X} \cap \overline{Y}}) + \frac{1}{e}(n_{X \neg Y} + n_{Y \neg X})}{(n_{X \cap Y} + n_{\overline{X} \cap \overline{Y}}) + (n_{X \neg Y} + n_{Y \neg X})}$$
$$(9.23)$$

where $e = 2.718$ is the base of the exponential function. This special case of the similarity function clearly decomposes the influence of matching and differing features. The numerator of this equation appeared before, specifically in Equation 9.10, which expressed the APPLE model when applied to the special case of binary features. The APPLE model compresses the range of that numerator by passing it through a sigmoidal squashing function. The SUSTAIN model compresses the range of that numerator by dividing by the total number of features. However, unlike APPLE, the ratio in SUSTAIN is only sensitive to the number of matching features when there is at least one mismatching feature; hence, SUSTAIN is listed in the center cell of Table 9.1.

Another approach to similarity, and the last that will be considered here, is provided by the rational model of Anderson (1990, 1991). Like SUSTAIN, the rational model recruits cluster nodes as training progresses. In the limit, it can recruit one cluster per (distinct) exemplar and behave much like the GCM (Nosofsky, 1991).

The rational model takes a Bayesian approach, which entails fundamental ontological differences from the previous approaches. (For a discussion of Bayesian models more generally, see Chapter 3 in this volume.) The goal of the rational model is to mimic the probability distribution of features observed in instances. Each cluster node represents the probability of sampling any particular feature value, and the model overall represents the probability of instances as a mixture of cluster-node distributions. But that statement does not capture an important subtlety of the Bayesian approach: Each cluster node represents an entire distribution of beliefs about possible probabilities of features values.

For example, suppose a cluster node is representing the distribution of heads and tails (i.e., the feature values) in a sequence of coin flips (i.e., the instances). Denote the underlying probability of heads as θ_1 and the probability of tails as θ_2 $(= 1 - \theta_1)$. One possible belief about the underlying probability of heads is that $\theta_1 = 0.5$, that is, the coin is fair. But there are other possible beliefs that the coin is biased, such as $\theta_1 = 0.1$ or $\theta_1 = 0.9$. The cluster node represents the degree of belief in every possible value of θ_1 and θ_2. By assumption, the model begins (before seeing any instances) with beliefs spread out uniformly over all possible values of θ. Gradually, the model loads up its beliefs onto those values of θ that best mimic the observed values, simultaneously reducing its belief in values of θ that do not easily predict the observed values. Figure 9.3 illustrates this process of updating belief distributions.

In general, when a feature has V values, any *particular* belief specifies the probability θ_v of each of the V feature values. A cluster node represents a degree of belief in every possible particular combination of probabilities. The degree of belief is a distribution over the space of all possible values of $\theta_1, \ldots, \theta_V$. Such a distribution could, in principle, be specified in a variety of ways; typically, the specification of the distribution will involve parameter values. Anderson (1990) uses the Dirichlet distribution, which has parameters, a_v, one per feature value, that determine the distribution's central tendency and shape. In the earlier example with two scale values (i.e., heads and tails), the Dirichlet distribution has two parameters, a_1 and a_2 (and in this case is commonly called the Beta distribution). Examples of the Dirichlet distribution are shown in Figure 9.3. Anderson assumes that clusters begin with unbiased beliefs, parameterized by $a_v = 1$ for all values v. With each observation of an instance, the distribution of beliefs is updated according to Bayes' theorem. Conveniently, the updated ("poste-

rior") distribution of beliefs turns out also to be a Dirichlet distribution in which the a parameter of the observed feature value is incremented by one. Again, see the caption of Figure 9.3 for an example of this process. Thus, after m_v instances with value v, the parameters of the belief distribution are $a_v = m_v + 1$.

The value θ_v is, by definition, the probability that the feature value would be generated by the cluster if the value θ_v were true. So the cluster's predicted probability of feature value v is the integral over all possible values of θ_v weighted by the probability of believing it is true. Thus, $p(v) = \int \cdots \int d\theta_1 \cdots d\theta_V \, \theta_v \, p(\theta_1, \ldots, \theta_V | a_1, \ldots, a_V)$. For the Dirichlet distribution, the integral simplifies to

$$p(v) = a_v \Big/ \sum_w a_w$$

$$= (m_v + 1) \Big/ \sum_w (m_w + 1). \quad (9.24)$$

To reiterate, Equation 9.24 provides the probability that a cluster would generate feature value v within a particular featural dimension.

Stimuli do not usually have just one featural dimension, however. For example, they might have the features of political party, marital status, ethnicity, and so forth. The rational model assumes that, within any cluster, the features are independent of each other. Because of this assumed independence, the probability of observing value v_1 on feature 1 in conjunction with value v_2 on feature 2, and so forth, is the product of their individual probabilities: $p(\{v_d\}) = \prod_d p(v_d)$. Anderson used that overall probability of the stimulus as a measure of how similar the stimulus is to the cluster. Formally, for a stimulus $y = \{v_d\}$ and a cluster $x = \{a_{v_d}\}$, the "similarity" of y to x is

$$s(x, y) = \prod_d p(v_d)$$

$$= \prod_d \frac{m_{v_d} + 1}{\sum_{w \in d} (m_w + 1)}. \quad (9.25)$$

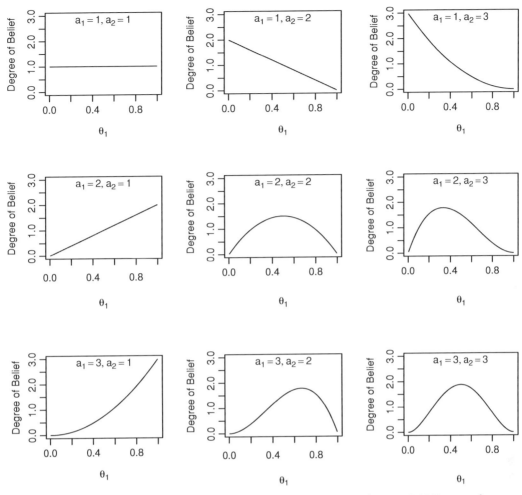

Figure 9.3. Each panel corresponds to the state of a cluster node in Anderson's (1990) rational model. Here, the cluster node is representing a single featural dimension that has two possible values. In each panel, the horizontal axis shows θ_1, which indicates the probability that the feature takes on its first value. (Of course, $\theta_2 = 1 - \theta_1$.) The vertical axis indicates the degree of belief in values of θ_1. Before observing any instances, the cluster begins in the top-left state, believing uniformly in any possible value of θ_1, which is parameterized as $a_1 = 1$ and $a_2 = 1$. If the first observed instance displays value 1, then the cluster node adjusts its distribution of beliefs to reflect that observation, moving to the left-middle state, parameterized as $a_1 = 2$ and $a_2 = 1$. If the next observed instance displays value 2, then the cluster node changes its beliefs to the center state, parameterized as $a_1 = 2$ and $a_2 = 2$. At this point, because 50% of the instances have shown value 1, the cluster believes most strongly that $\theta_1 = 0.50$, but because there have only been two observations, beliefs are still spread out over other possible values of θ_1.

Anderson intended this as similarity only metaphorically and not as an actual model of similarity ratings (Anderson, 1990, p. 105).

Consider the special circumstances wherein all dimensions are binary valued and a cluster represents a single exemplar.

When the cluster represents a single exemplar, it implies that $m_v = 0$ for all v but one. If the represented instance occurred r times, then $m_v = r$ for the feature value that actually appeared in the instance. In this particular situation, the similarity formula can be expressed in terms of the number of features that match or mismatch between the cluster and the stimulus. Equation 9.25 becomes

$$s(x, y) = \left(\frac{r+1}{r+2}\right)^{n_{X \cap Y} + n_{\bar{X} \cap \bar{Y}}}$$
$$\times \left(\frac{1}{r+2}\right)^{n_{X \neg Y} + n_{Y \neg X}} . \quad (9.26)$$

Because similarity of an instance to its corresponding exemplar is influenced by how often the instance has previously appeared, the rational model is listed in the lower-center cell of Table 9.1.

2.2.5. HYBRID SCALE

Nosofsky and Zaki (2003) proposed a similarity function that incorporates aspects of the standard spatial similarity metric of Equation 9.2 with coefficients that express discrete-feature matching and mismatching. Their hybrid similarity function defined similarity as

$$s_h(x, y) = C D \exp(-c \, d(x, y)) \quad (9.27)$$

where $C > 1$ expresses the boost in similarity from matching features, and $0 < D < 1$ expresses the decrease in similarity from distinctive features. Notice in particular that the similarity of an item to itself is $C > 1$. Nosofsky and Zaki (2003) found that the hybrid-similarity model fit their recognition data very well, whereas the standard similarity function did not.

2.2.6. ATTENTION IN SIMILARITY

Finally, a crucial aspect of similarity that has not been yet emphasized is selective attention to dimensions or features. Most of the models reviewed earlier do explicitly allow for differential weighting of dimensions. Even the SDM model permits differential feature weights (Kanerva, 1988, p. 46). Only the configural model (Pearce, 1994) and the rational model (Anderson, 1990) do not have explicit mechanisms for selective attention.[3] This lack of selective at-

---

3 Anderson (1990, pp. 116–117) describes a way to differentially weigh the *prior* importance of each

tention leaves those models unable to generate some well-established learning phenomena, such as the relative ease of categories for which fewer dimensions are relevant (e.g., Nosofsky et al., 1994). See Chapter 9 in this volume for a review that emphasizes the role of attention.

2.2.7. SUMMARY OF SIMILARITY FORMALIZATIONS

One of the contributions of this chapter is a review of these various models of similarity in a common notation to facilitate comparing and contrasting the approaches. In particular, expressions were derived for the similarity functions in terms of the number of matching and mismatching features when the models are applied to the special case of present/absent features, with equal attention on all the features. This restriction to a special case permits a direct comparison of the similarity functions in terms of the influence of the number of features in each stimulus, the number of distinctive features, and so forth.

If nothing else, what can be concluded from the variety of similarity functions reviewed in this section is that the best formal expression of similarity is still an open issue. The shared commitment in this variety is the claim that categorization is based on computing the similarity of the stimulus to exemplars in memory. Although the review of similarity functions has revealed that there are a variety of formalizations that different researchers have found useful in different circumstances, what is lacking is specific guidance regarding which formalization is appropriate for which situation. A general answer to this question is a foundational issue for future research. A thought-provoking review of how people make similarity judgments has been

---

featural dimension, but this is opposite from learned selective attention. In Anderson's approach, the model begins with strong prior selectivity that subsequently gets overwhelmed with continued learning. But in human learning, the prior state is, presumably, noncommittal regarding selectivity and subsequently gets stronger with continued learning.

provided by Medin, Goldstone, and Gentner (1993). A perspective on similarity judgment, as a case of Bayesian integration over candidate hypotheses for generalization, has been presented by Tenenbaum and Griffiths (2001a).

2.3. *Learning of Associations*

Exemplar models assume that at least three aspects of the model get learned. First, the stimulus exemplars themselves must be stored. This aspect is discussed in a subsequent section. Second, once the exemplars are in memory, the associations between exemplars and category labels must be established. Third, the allocation of attention to stimulus dimensions must be determined. In principle, other aspects of the model could also be adjusted through learning. For example, the steepness of the generalization gradient (e.g., parameter c in Equation 9.2) could be learned, or the decisiveness of choice (e.g., parameter ϕ in Equation 9.36) could be learned. These intriguing possibilities will not be further explored here.

This section focuses on how the associations between exemplars and category labels are learned. Learned attentional allocation can also be implemented as learned associations to attentional gates, and therefore attentional learning is also a topic of this section. (For a discussion of associative learning in humans and animals, see Chapter 22 in this volume.)

Associative strengths can be adjusted many different ways. Perhaps the simplest way is adding a constant increment to the weight whenever both its source and target node are simultaneously activated. More sophisticated schemes include adjusting the weight so that the predicted activation at the target node better matches the true target activation. These and other methods are discussed en route.

2.3.1. CO-OCCURRENCE COUNTING
The GCM establishes associations between exemplars and categories by simply counting the number of co-occurrences. This can be

understood in the context of Equation 9.3, wherein the effective associative influence between exemplar x and response r is N_{rx}, that is, the number of times that response r has occurred with instance x. Somewhat analogously, in SDM (Kanerva, 1988), associative weights from exemplar nodes to output nodes are incremented (by 1) if both the exemplar and the output are co-activated, and associative weights are decremented (by 1) if either is active whereas the other is not.

A related approach is taken by the rational model (Anderson, 1990, p. 136). When implemented in a network architecture, the weight from cluster node k to category-label node r can be thought of as $p(r|k) = (m_r + 1)/\sum_\ell (m_\ell + 1)$, where m_ℓ is the number of times that category label ℓ has co-occurred with an instance of cluster k. Thus, the change in the associative weight is affected only by the co-occurrence of the cluster and the label. (The assignment of the stimulus to the cluster is affected by past learning, however.)

In all these models, regardless of whether the model is classifying a stimulus well or badly, the associative links are incremented the same amount. Other models adjust their weights only to the extent that there is error in performance (as described in the next section).

In none of these models is there learned allocation of selective attention. In the GCM, attention is left as a free parameter that is estimated by fits to data. In some early work (e.g., Nosofsky, 1984), it was assumed that attention is allocated optimally for the categorization, but there was no mechanism suggested for how the subject learns that optimal allocation.

2.3.2. GRADIENT DESCENT ON ERROR
ALCOVE uses gradient descent on error to learn associative weights and attentional strengths. On every trial, the error between the correct and predicted categorization is determined (see Equation 9.4), and then the gradient of that error is computed, followed by adjustments in the direction of the gradient (see Equations 9.5 and 9.6).

RASHNL also uses gradient descent, iterated to achieve large shifts of attention on single trials.

In the SUSTAIN model of Love et al. (2004), only the winning cluster (exemplar) node learns, and only its output weights learn by gradient descent on categorization *error*. The dimensional attention strengths and cluster coordinates learn (almost) by gradient ascent on *similarity*. That is, the attention strengths are adjusted to increase the similarity of the winning cluster node to the stimulus, and the coordinates of the winning cluster node are moved to increase its similarity to the stimulus. The particular formulas used in SUSTAIN for learning attention and cluster coordinates are not exactly gradient ascent on similarity, however. The goal for the remainder of this section is to demonstrate how gradient ascent on similarity yields learning formulas that are much like the ones used in SUSTAIN.

The SUSTAIN model adjusts the winning cluster's coordinates, x_{iv}, by applying a learning formula from Kohonen (1982):

$$\Delta x_{iv} = \eta \left(y_{iv} - x_{iv} \right) \qquad (9.28)$$

where η is a constant of proportionality. (The Kohonen learning rule can be derived as gradient ascent on a Gaussian density function with respect to its mean.) Gradient ascent on the winning cluster's similarity, with respect to its coordinates, yields almost the same formula:

$$\Delta x_{iv} \propto \frac{\partial}{\partial x_{iv}} s(x, y)$$
$$= \eta_i \, \mathrm{sgn}(y_{iv} - x_{iv}) \qquad (9.29)$$

where $\mathrm{sgn}(z)$ is the sign of z, such that $\mathrm{sgn}(z) = +1$ if $z > 0$, $\mathrm{sgn}(z) = -1$ if $z < 0$, and $\mathrm{sgn}(z) = 0$ if $z = 0$. Equation 9.29 involves coefficients η_i that depend on the dimension i: $\eta_i = .5\alpha_i^{\gamma+1}$ $\exp(-.5\alpha_i \sum_{v \in i} |x_{iv} - y_{iv}|)/ \sum_j \alpha_j^{\gamma}$.

To adjust attention, Love et al. (2004, p. 314, discussion of their Equation 3) consider the gradient of each dimension's individual similarity with respect to attention, and heuristically use the formula (their Equation 13):

$$\Delta\alpha_j \propto \exp(-\alpha_j d_j) \left(1 - \alpha_j d_j\right). \qquad (9.30)$$

This can be recognized as a truncated form of gradient ascent on the winning cluster's overall similarity to the stimulus, as follows. Computation of the derivative yields

$$\Delta\alpha_j \propto \frac{\partial}{\partial \alpha_j} s(x, y)$$
$$= \frac{1}{\sum_i \alpha_i^{\gamma}} \left\{ \exp(-\alpha_j d_j) \right.$$
$$\times \left(\gamma \alpha_j^{\gamma-1} - \alpha_j^{\gamma} d_j \right) - \gamma \alpha_j^{\gamma-1} s(x, y) \right\}$$
$$(9.31)$$

where $d_j = (1/2) \sum_{v_j} |x_{jv_j} - y_{jv_j}|$. In the special circumstances when $\gamma = 1$ and $\sum_i \alpha_i = 1$, Equation 9.31 reduces to

$$\Delta\alpha_j \propto \exp(-\alpha_j d_j) \left(1 - \alpha_j d_j\right) - s(x, y),$$
$$(9.32)$$

which is very similar to the formula used by Love et al. (2004).

In summary, although it is not clear that the formulas used by SUSTAIN always increase the similarity of the winning cluster to the stimulus (because the formulas do not implement gradient ascent), the formulas are analogous to true gradient ascent on similarity. The goal of the formulas in SUSTAIN is to increase the winning cluster's representativeness of the instances it wins. True gradient ascent on similarity would be one way to achieve that goal. Notice, however, that increasing the similarity of the winning cluster to the stimulus might not necessarily reduce error in predicting the category label.

2.3.3. SYSTEMATIC OR RANDOM HILL-CLIMBING

Error reduction can be achieved without explicit computation of the gradient. In principle, any method for function optimization could be used. Indeed, if the parameter space is small enough, a dense search of parameter combinations could be undertaken. But when the parameter space is large, as in most learning situations, there are various "hill-climbing" algorithms that probe the error near the current parameter values and creep their way down the error surface (e.g., Press et al. 1992, pp. 394–455). Some algorithms, for example, numerically estimate the gradient of the error without an explicit formula for the gradient by trying two different values of a parameter, say w and $w + \Delta w$; computing the error generated by each value, E and $E + \Delta E$; and approximating the gradient as $\Delta E / \Delta w$. The algorithms then use the estimates of gradient (and sometimes also curvature) to make systematic jumps to new parameter values.

Other algorithms do not bother computing the gradient at all and simply probe nearby values of the parameters, changing to those values if the error is reduced. The algorithms differ in how they decide which nearby values to probe. The Stochastic COntext DEpendent Learning (SCODEL) model of Matsuka (2005) is a noisy hill-climbing algorithm for learning associative weights and attention strengths in ALCOVE. SCODEL *randomly* tries new values that are close to its current values. If a candidate value decreases error, then the value is kept. But even if the candidate value increases error, there is a nonzero probability that the change is kept. This procedure can allow the model to jump over local minima in the error surface and produces large individual differences between different runs of the model that may mimic the large variance seen in human learners.

2.3.4. BAYESIAN LEARNING

A rather different approach to learning is taken by Bayesian parameter estimation. In a Bayesian conceptualization, the mind of the learner is conceived to contain a large set of hypotheses, with each hypothesis specifying particular parameter values. Learning does not change the parameter values within each hypothesis. Instead, learning changes how strongly one believes each hypothesis.

This type of idea was encountered earlier in the context of the rational model (Anderson, 1990). There were various hypotheses about the underlying probabilities, θ_v, of encountering feature values v. For example, the model could believe strongly that a feature value v has probability $\theta_v = 0.2$ and believe only weakly that the feature value has probability $\theta_v = 0.9$. The degree of belief was governed by a parameterized (Dirichlet) distribution, and Bayesian learning adjusted the parameters of the distribution (see the discussion accompanying Figure 9.3).

Instead of entertaining hypotheses about feature probabilities, consider hypotheses about the magnitude of associative weights in an associative network. For example, one might have two hypotheses about an association between an exemplar and a category. Hypothesis $H+$ specifies an associative weight of $+1$, and hypothesis $H-$ specifies an associative weight of -1. At first, one might have no preference for one hypothesis over the other. This state of beliefs can be expressed as $p(H+) = .5$ and $p(H-) = .5$. Suppose that a learning trial is then experienced, in which the instance occurs and is taught to be a member of the category. This occurrence is consistent with $H+$, so beliefs should shift toward $H+$; perhaps then $p(H+) = .9$ and $p(H-) = .1$. Notice that none of the associative weights has changed, but the degree of belief in each one has changed.

A useful property of Bayesian learning is that changes in degree of belief about one hypothesis must affect degree of belief in other hypotheses. This is because it is assumed that the hypotheses in the hypothesis space are mutually exclusive and exhaust all possible hypotheses. So if evidence compels you to believe less strongly in one hypothesis, you must believe more strongly in other hypotheses. Conversely, if evidence makes you believe more strongly in one hypothesis, you must believe less strongly in other hypotheses. There has been much empirical research demonstrating that people are not very accurate Bayesian reasoners (e.g., Edwards, 1968; Van Wallendael & Hastie, 1990). But in simple situations, people do show Bayesian-like trade-offs in beliefs. For example, when you find an object d'art fallen from its shelf, you might hypothesize that the cause was either the cat or the toddler. When you then see the cat lying on the shelf where the object d'art was, you exonerate the toddler. Conversely, if you learn that the cat has the alibi of having been outside, the toddler is implicated more strongly.

Bayesian learning of associative weights in connectionist networks has been actively explored in recent years (e.g., MacKay, 2003; Neal, 1996). Psychologists have successfully applied other Bayesian models of learning to associative and causal learning paradigms (e.g., Anderson, 1990, 1991; Courville et al., 2004; Courville, Daw, & Touretzky, 2004; Dayan & Kakade, 2001; Dayan, Kakade, & Montague, 2000; Gopnik et al., 2004; Sobel, Tenenbaum, & Gopnik, 2004; Steyvers et al., 2003; Tenenbaum & Griffiths, 2001b, and Chapter 3 in this volume).

In most existing Bayesian models of category learning, the model has a (possibly infinite) set of hypotheses in which each hypothesis constitutes a complete mapping from stimulus to categorical response. Bayesian learning consists of updating the degree of belief in each of these complete mappings. An alternative new approach uses Bayesian updating within successive subcomponents of the mapping Kruschke (2006). For example, a model such as ALCOVE can be thought of as a succession of two components: The first component maps a stimulus to an allocation of attention across stimulus dimensions; the second component maps attentionally weighted similarities to categorical responses (Kruschke, 2003a). In a typical globally Bayesian approach to ALCOVE, a hypothesis would consist of particular weights on the attention in combination with particular weights on category associations, that is, a hypothesis would be a complete mapping from stimulus to response. In a locally Bayesian approach, there are hypotheses about attention weights separate from hypotheses about category association weights, and Bayesian updating occurs separately on the two hypothesis spaces. The hypothesis space regarding category associative weights is updated by using the corrective feedback about the categories. But the hypothesis space regarding attention strengths needs target attention values, analogous to the target category values used for the associative weights. The target attention strengths are determined by choosing those values that maximize (or at least improve) the predictive accuracy of the current associative beliefs. Thus, the internal attentional targets are chosen to be maximally consistent with current beliefs, and only then are beliefs updated with respect to external targets. The approach combines the ability of Bayesian updating to exhibit trade-offs among hypotheses, with the ability of selective attention to produce phenomena such as trial-order effects seen in human learning. See Kruschke (2006) for a description of various phenomena addressed by the locally Bayesian approach.

2.4. *Exemplar Recruitment*

The previous section described learning of associative strengths, assuming that the exemplars were already in memory. But getting those exemplars into memory is itself a learning process. This section describes a variety of exemplar recruitment models.

2.4.1. NO RECRUITMENT: PRE-LOADED EXEMPLARS

In SDM (Kanerva, 1988), memory consists of a set of randomly scattered exemplars, but these memory exemplars need not be copies of presented instances. Instead, the memory exemplars are pre-loaded and form a covering map of the stimulus space. This idea influenced the development of ALCOVE. SDM generates interesting behavior because it assumes high-dimensional spaces for input, exemplars, and output.

One interpretation of the GCM assumes that every distinct trial instance is pre-loaded as an exemplar in memory. This simplification, although expedient for illustrating the power of the model, is logically dissatisfying because it assumes knowledge is in the model before it could have been learned. The original ALCOVE model finessed the issue by assuming the stimulus space was initially covered by a random covering map of exemplars as in SDM; that covering map was the impetus for ALCOVE's name. It turned out that fits to selected data sets were affected little by whether a random covering map or a set of pre-loaded exemplars was used, so most reported fits of ALCOVE use the exemplar version.

2.4.2. INCESSANT RECRUITMENT

Instead of thinking of the GCM as preloading the exemplars and then incrementing their weights on subsequent presentations, the GCM can be thought of as recruiting a new exemplar with every training instance and creating a link that has weight +1 between the newly recruited exemplar and the correct category node (Nosofsky, Kruschke, & McKinley, 1992, p. 215). The associative weights of exemplars are unaffected by the specifics of subsequent training. In this way, exemplar learning and associative learning occur with the same magnitude on every trial. Denote the tth repetition of instance x by x^t, where the superscript is merely an index, not a power. Then Equation 9.3 becomes

$$p(R|y) = \frac{\beta_R \sum_{x \in R} \sum_t^{N_x} s(x^t, y)}{\sum_r \beta_r \sum_{k \in r} \sum_t^{N_k} s(k^t, y)}.$$
(9.33)

This is formally equivalent to constant increments on the associative weights (via cooccurrence counting), but a benefit is that each instance merely recruits a new exemplar, rather than having to check if there is already an exemplar that matches it.

2.4.3. NOVELTY DRIVEN RECRUITMENT

The ADDCOVE model (Verguts et al., 2004), described earlier beginning with Equation 9.18, has exemplar recruitment. When a stimulus occurs that does not match an existing exemplar in memory, then a new exemplar is recruited into memory that exactly copies the current stimulus. Notice that this recruitment process is driven by stimulus novelty alone, regardless of the performance of the model. Thus, if a novel stimulus appears, a new exemplar is recruited even if the novel item is correctly classified by the model (but the newly recruited exemplar might not learn a very large associative weight to the category nodes if there is little error).

2.4.4. PERFORMANCE DRIVEN RECRUITMENT

Incessant recruitment does not solve a basic problem of frequency counting models: They can become entrenched by large numbers of repeated items in early training. If the correct categorization changes, the model can only slowly learn the change by accumulating vast numbers of subsequent countervailing exemplars. People, however, are quick to relearn after shifts in categories. One solution to this problem is to allow the exemplars to be probabilistically forgotten (e.g., Estes, 1994, p. 63) or for the associative strengths to decay (Nosofsky et al., 1992). In either of those approaches, the initial learning of any exemplar is full strength. As an alternative new approach, suppose that the initial learning of exemplars should depend on the current performance of the model. An exemplar should be recruited for a stimulus depending on the degree of error generated on that stimulus.[4] When there is a large error, there should be a high probability of recruiting an exemplar. When there is a small error, there should be a small probability of recruiting an exemplar. A challenge to this proposed approach is that probabilistic mappings would continually generate error and endlessly recruit exemplars.

The SUSTAIN model of Love et al. (2004) recruits new cluster nodes under certain conditions, depending on the type of training. For supervised training, that is, when category labels are provided as feedback, a new cluster node is recruited when an instance is presented for which the

---

4 Previous exemplar theorists have described probabilistic remembering of features or exemplars (e.g., Hintzman, 1986, 1988), but not such that the probability depends on the momentary accuracy of the model.

maximally activated category label is not the correct label. For unsupervised training, a new cluster node is recruited when an instance is sufficiently novel, that is, when no existing cluster node is strongly activated (analogous to ADDCOVE). In the unified SUSTAIN (uSUSTAIN) model of Gureckis and Love (2003), the recruitment condition for supervised training is modified to be more consistent with the character of the unsupervised condition. A new cluster node is recruited when no existing cluster node *for that category label* is strongly activated. The recruitment rule presumes deterministic mappings of instances to category labels, so that there is no ambiguity regarding which label a cluster belongs to.

An attentionally based approach to exemplar recruitment was proposed by Kruschke (2003b, 2003c). In this framework, every node in the network has its output gated by a corresponding attentional multiplier. Even the exemplars are attentionally modulated. When an instance is presented at the input nodes, a novel candidate exemplar node is recruited. Attention is distributed to the novel candidate exemplar node, and to all previously recruited nodes, according to the similarity of the nodes to the input and according to any previously learned allocation of attention. When the corrective feedback is provided, the discrepancy between the correct and predicted output is computed, and attention is shifted to reduce that discrepancy. If the error-reducing attentional shift causes a shift away from the candidate exemplar node, toward previously existing nodes, then the candidate is immediately retired. But if the error-reducing attentional shift brings more attention to the candidate node, it is retained.

Another model with performance-based exemplar recruitment is the rational model of Anderson (1990, 1991). When an instance appears, the rational model computes the probability that the instance belongs to each cluster and the probability that the instance belongs to a novel cluster. If the highest probability is for a novel cluster, the model recruits a new cluster and assigns the instance to that cluster. Equation 9.25 stated the probability of an instance $y = \{v_d\}$ for a particular cluster node x, that is, $p(\{v_d\}|x) = \prod_d p_x(v_d)$. For cluster recruitment, however, what is needed is the probability of the cluster given the instance, that is, the reverse conditional probability. Bayes' theorem provides the relation between reversed conditional probabilities: $p(x|\{v_d\}) \propto p(\{v_d\}|x)p(x)$ where $p(x)$ is the probability of the cluster prior to seeing an information about the particular instance.

Anderson (1990, 1991) derived an expression for the prior cluster probabilities analogous to those used for feature values within clusters, but now with a free parameter called a coupling probability, which is a fixed background probability c ($0 \leq c \leq 1$) that two random instances come from the same cluster. The probability that a random instance belongs to an existing cluster x, prior to actually having any information about the instance, is $p(x) = cq_x/((1 - c) + cq)$, where q is the total number of instances seen so far, and q_x is the number of instances assigned to cluster x. The probability that a random instance belongs to a novel cluster x_0, prior to actually having any information about the instance, is $p(x_0) = (1 - c)/((1 - c) + cq)$. Notice that before seeing any instances, when $q = 0$, the probability of assigning the first instance to a novel cluster is $p(x_0) = 1.0$. After seeing one instance, that is, when $q = 1$, then the background probability of another instance being in the same cluster is $p(x) = c$, and the probability of being in a different cluster is $p(x_0) = 1 - c$. After seeing many instances, q_x dominates c, so $p(x) \approx q_x/q$ and $p(x_0) \approx 0$. To recapitulate: A new cluster node is recruited for instance $\{v_d\}$ when $p(\{v_d\}|x_0)p(x_0) > p(\{v_d\}|x)p(x)$ for all existing clusters x. Although $p(x)$ can increase across trials as more instances are included in the cluster, $p(\{v_d\}|x)$ can decrease because the cluster can become more sharply tuned to the specific instances it represents (cf. Equation 9.26). In particular, new clusters can be recruited when existing clusters are tuned to particular feature combinations, and the current instance is not similar enough to any existing cluster.

It might turn out to be the case that an entirely different approach mimics human performance best. For example, rather than explicitly constructing new nodes "from thin air," it might be possible to perform something functionally analogous in a distributed representation. In such a scheme, there would be a fixed array of representational nodes, but their various parameter values (weights, thresholds, gains, etc.) are adjusted such that the array as a whole behaves as if a new exemplar node were recruited. Alas, it remains for future research to evaluate the relative merits of these various recruitment algorithms.

2.5. *Response Probability*

Exemplar models are committed to the notions of exemplar representation and selective attention to features. They are not committed to a particular response function, however. Different response functions have been explored.

One simple modification to the ratio rule (Equation 9.3) is the inclusion of a guessing parameter, G:

$$p(R|y) = \frac{\beta_R \left(\sum_{x \in R} N_{Rx}\, s(x, y) + G \right)}{\sum_r \beta_r \left(\sum_{k \in r} N_{rk}\, s(k, y) + G \right)}$$
(9.34)

The guessing parameter keeps the choice probabilities early in learning (when the N_{rk} are small) close to chance levels, instead of being unduly influenced by just a few cases. The guessing parameter also reduces the extremity of choices when a stimulus is presented that is not very similar to any memory exemplars (Nosofsky et al., 1992).

Ashby and Maddox (1993) extended the original GCM response rule to modulate its decisiveness with a power parameter γ:

$$p(R|y) = \frac{\left(\sum_{x \in R} s(x, y) \right)^{\gamma}}{\sum_r \left(\sum_{k \in r} s(k, y) \right)^{\gamma}}.$$
(9.35)

When γ is large, it converts a small advantage in summed similarity to a strong preference; conversely, when γ is small, choice probabilities are less extreme. Nosofsky and Palmeri (1997) provided a process interpretation of the γ parameter in terms of how much exemplar-based evidence needs to be accumulated before a response is made. The γ parameter is especially useful for fitting data from individual subjects, as opposed to group average data (for a review, see Nosofsky & Zaki, 2002) and can be crucial for fitting other data, such as inferences of missing features (Kruschke, Johansen, & Blair, 1999).

Another variation of the ratio rule for response choice was used in the ALCOVE model (Kruschke, 1992). There, the response function is the normalized exponential, or softmax rule,

$$p(R|y) = \frac{\exp\left(\phi \sum_x w_{Rx}\, s(x, y) \right)}{\sum_r \exp\left(\phi \sum_x w_{rx}\, s(x, y) \right)},$$
(9.36)

which has been used previously in connectionist models (e.g., Bridle, 1990). The exponential transformation is especially important in models for which the summed similarities can be negative because of negative associative weights. This is not an issue in the GCM, but in ALCOVE, it is crucial because learned association weights can become negative. The ϕ parameter in Equation 9.36 governs the decisiveness of the model: When ϕ is large, a small advantage in summed similarity translates into a big choice preference; conversely, when ϕ is small, choice preferences are muted.

Wills et al. (2000) examined the ratio rule in a general way and presented empirical results that they argued were difficult for the ratio rule to explain. They proposed instead a winner-take-all response network, which implements competition between response nodes in a recurrent network.

Juslin, Wennerholm, and Winman (2001) appended an additional response strategy called eliminative inference, which supercedes the ratio rule when the stimulus is too different from known exemplars. The reasoning goes as follows: When a stimulus appears that is clearly unlike previously learned stimuli, then the response given to it should also be unlike previously learned responses. That is, for an unknown stimulus, eliminate the known categories, and guess at random from the remaining categories. There clearly are circumstances in which people will spontaneously use this strategy (Juslin et al., 2001; Kruschke & Bradley, 1995), but its impact on categorization phenomena more broadly has not been demonstrated (Kruschke, 2001b). More generally, however, this raises the point that there are many possible response strategies that people could use, in addition to or instead of the ratio rule.

2.6. *Response Time and Choice as a Function of Time*

The GCM has no temporal dynamics within or across trials. ALCOVE and RASHNL have dynamics across trials because they learn, but they have no dynamics within trials. Thus, these models make no predictions about response times after onset of a stimulus.

The Exemplar-Based Random Walk model (EBRW; Nosofsky & Palmeri, 1997; Nosofsky & Stanton, 2005) addresses the dynamics of the response process. In the EBRW, exemplars are conceived to be instantly and fully activated by the onset of the stimulus, but then the response is generated by an iterative race to cross response thresholds for each category. Think of each category as having its own horse, racing to cross its response threshold. The race is conceptualized as a series of brief moments of time. In each moment of time, a spinner is spun that points to one of the exemplars at random. The pointed-at exemplar belongs to one of the categories, and the horse for that category moves ahead one unit toward its response threshold (and the other horses move back one unit). The probability of the spinner pointing to an exemplar, that is, the amount of space an exemplar gets on the spinner, is proportional to the exemplar's similarity to the stimulus. More exactly, the EBRW is applied to two-category situations, and when one horse is moved ahead, the other horse is moved backward.

It is as if there is just one horse, moving either toward one threshold for category A or moving in the opposite direction toward the threshold for category B. The response time is assumed to be proportional to the number of iterations needed until a category threshold is crossed. If the response thresholds for A and B are γ units away from the starting position (in opposite directions), then the probability of choosing category A turns out to be exactly the choice rule described earlier in Equation 9.35 (for a derivation, see Nosofsky & Palmeri, 1997).

Other models of response dynamics include models with recurrent activation and lateral inhibition (Usher & McClelland, 2001; Wills et al., 2000). These models are based on different assumptions than the diffusion/race model assumptions of EBRW. Usher and McClelland (2001) compared the recurrent activation approach with the diffusion model approach (but not the EBRW itself). Wills et al. (2000) applied a winner-take-all recurrent activation network to responses in category learning, but their emphasis was response proportions, not response times.

The EBRW has been applied to domains with integral dimensions, where it is not unreasonable to suppose that exemplars are activated in one fell swoop. When stimulus dimensions are separable, however, then issues about the temporal processing of dimensions loom large. The EBRW was intended primarily as a model of response time dynamics and not so much as a model of perceptual dynamics.

The Extended Generalized Context Model (EGCM) of Lamberts (1995, 1997, 2000) addresses the dynamics of exemplar processing, not just response processing. In the EGCM (Lamberts, 1995, 1998), similarity is a function of time:

$$s(t, x, y) = \exp\left(-c \sum_i \alpha_i [\pi_i(t)|x_i - y_i|]\right)$$

(9.37)

where α_i is the utility of dimension i for the categorization, just as in the GCM or ALCOVE, but a new term, $\pi_i(t)$, is the (cumulative) *inclusion probability* of dimension i at time t. Lamberts (1995, 1998) suggests that the inclusion rate for a dimension should be constant through time and that therefore the cumulative inclusion probability can be expressed as

$$\pi_i(t) = 1 - \exp(-q_i t) \qquad (9.38)$$

where q_i is the *inclusion rate* for dimension i. The inclusion rate for a dimension is tied to its physical salience, irrespective of the dimension's relevance for the particular categorization. Notice that a dimension with a fast inclusion rate has a relatively high probability of being included in the similarity computation. When the time t is small, the inclusion probabilities of all dimensions are small, so the similarity is close to 1 for all exemplars. When the time t is very large, the inclusion probabilities of all dimensions are nearly 1, so the similarities shrink to the values they would be in the basic GCM.

One of the interesting predictions of the EGCM is that categorization tendencies can change nonmonotonically after stimulus onset. One such situation can occur because salient dimensions (i.e., those with high inclusion rates) dominate response tendencies early in processing, but those salient dimensions might not be the most relevant to the categorical distinction. That is, the relevant dimensions with high α_i might be nonsalient dimensions with low π_i when t is small. Nonmonotonic response tendencies can also be produced when an exemplar of one category is set in the midst of several exemplars from a different category. Early in processing, all the π_i are small, and therefore the surrounded exemplar is highly similar to its many neighbors that belong to the other category. Consequently, it is classified as a case of the neighbor's category. Later in processing, the π_i have grown large, and the surrounded exemplar is less similar to its neighbors. Consequently, it is classified in its own correct category. Lamberts and collaborators have documented several such nonmonotonicities; for example, Experiment 2 of Lamberts and Freeman (1999) examined a case of a surrounded exemplar. The EBRW cannot account for these nonmonotonici-

ties because its similarity values are fixed through time, and its random walks are (on average) monotonically related to the relative similarities.

The EGCM (Lamberts, 1995, 1998) models similarity and choice tendency as a function of time, but it does not predict specific latencies to respond. The EGCM Response Time (EGCM-RT) (Lamberts, 2000) is a model of response time per se. It generates RTs by sampling elements from separable dimensions, and after each sample determining a probability of stopping (i.e., making a response) that is related to the current summed similarity of the stimulus to all exemplars (Lamberts, 2000, Equation 14, p. 230). Lambert's mechanism for gradual dimension accumulation was combined with the EBRW's response race mechanism into a model called "EBRW with perceptual encoding" (EBRW-PE) by Cohen and Nosofsky (2003). They found comparable fits to data by EBRW-PE and EGCM-RT, and suggested that although future experiments might better distinguish the models, the random-walk response mechanism in the EBRW-PE is more thoroughly studied in the literature than the stopping-rule mechanism in EGCM-RT. Future research will have to explore potential differences between the models; but there are yet other possibilities for dynamic mechanisms to consider, described next.

In the connectionist literature, processing analogous to Lamberts's inclusion rate can be found in McClelland's cascaded activation approach (McClelland, 1979). That approach assumes that the ith node's net input accumulates through time, according to the temporal integration equation

$$\text{net}_i(t) = \kappa \sum_j w_{ij} a_j(t)$$
$$+ (1 - \kappa) \text{net}_i(t-1) \qquad (9.39)$$

where w_{ij} is the connection weight to node i from node j, $a_j(t)$ is the activation of node j at time t, and κ is the cascade rate for the node. It can easily be seen from Equation 9.39 that $\text{net}_i = \sum_j w_{ij} a_j$ is a stable value: Just plug that into the right side and notice that it comes out again on the left side. Moreover, this value is reached asymptotically. At each moment in time, the net input is (instantaneously) transformed into activation by the usual sigmoidal squashing function:

$$a_i(t) = 1/[1 + \exp(-\text{net}_i(t))]. \qquad (9.40)$$

McClelland and Rumelhart (1988, pp. 153–155, 304–305) showed that cascaded activation networks can produce nonmonotonic outputs through time. In particular, consider two hidden nodes that converge on a single output node. The first hidden node has large positive incoming weights and a weak positive outgoing weight to the output node. The second hidden node has small positive incoming weights, but a strong negative outgoing weight to the output node. When the input nodes are activated, the first hidden node will become activated more quickly than the second hidden node, because the first hidden node has larger incoming weights. Hence, the output node will initially feel the positive connection from the first hidden node and be activated. Later, however, the second hidden node will become as activated as the first hidden node, and then its stronger negative output weight will be felt at the output. Hence, the output activation will have changed from initially growing to asymptotically low. Such nonmonotonicities were exhibited by a model of memory for arithmetic described by Dallaway (1992, 1994). His network, when queried with "$3 \times 8 =$," initially activated a response of 27 before settling to the correct response of 24.

Although it has not been previously described in the literature, it would be straightforward to implement cascaded activation in the ALCOVE or APPLE networks. Simply let each dimensional distance accumulate through time:

$$d_i(t, x, y) = \kappa\, \alpha_i |x_i - y_i| + (1 - \kappa)$$
$$\times d_i(t - 1, x, y). \qquad (9.41)$$

This formula has dimensional salience already implicit in the stimulus coordinates, because a more salient dimension has feature values that are farther apart in psychological space. Alternatively, salience could be explicitly marked by another multiplicative factor, analogous to the inclusion rate in the ECGM. The cascaded dimensional distance is used in the natural ways in ALCOVE and APPLE: For ALCOVE, the overall distance is $d(t, x, y) = \sum_i d_i(t, x, y)$ (cf. Equation 9.1), and for APPLE, $s_i(t, x, y) = \exp(-d_i(t, x, y))$ (cf. Equation 9.8). At asymptote, $d_i(t, x, y)$ converges to $\alpha_i |x_i - y_i|$, so asymptotic choice proportions are as in the original models. Presumably, the cascaded activation versions of the models would generate dynamic behaviors much like the EGCM, but combined with the additional ability to learn associative weights and attentional allocations. (Learning takes place once the activations have reached asymptote, without any change in algorithm.) Analogous cascaded similarity functions could be implemented in a variety of models discussed earlier.

3. Conclusion

This chapter began with a quick overview of the representational options for models of categorization. These options included exemplars, prototypes, rules, boundaries, and theories. A mutual goal of different formal models is to account for detailed quantitative data from laboratory experiments in categorization. These data can include information about what stimuli or categories are learned more or less easily, the degree to which categorical responses are generalized from learned stimuli to novel stimuli, and the speed with which categorical responses are made.

Although a variety of representational formats have been formalized, exemplar models have been especially richly explored by many researchers. The main goal of the chapter has been to slice across numerous exemplar models, to excise their functional components, and to examine those components side by side. The main functional components included the computation of similarity, the learning of associations and attention, the recruitment of exemplars, the determination of response probability, and the generation of response times. This dissection revealed a variety of formalizations available for expressing any given psychological process. The analysis also suggested numerous directions for novel research.

References

Anderson, J. A., Silverstein, J. W., Ritz, S. A., & Jones, R. S. (1977). Distinctive features, categorical perception, and probability learning: Some applications of a neural model. *Psychological Review, 84*(5), 413–451.

Anderson, J. R. (1990). *The adaptive character of thought.* Hillsdale, NJ: Lawrence Erlbaum.

Anderson, J. R. (1991). The adaptive nature of human categorization. *Psychological Review, 98*(3), 409–429.

Ashby, F. G., Alfonso-Reese, L. A., Turken, A. U., & Waldron, E. M. (1998). A neuropsychological theory of multiple systems in category learning. *Psychological Review, 105*(3), 442–481.

Ashby, F. G., & Gott, R. E. (1988). Decision rules in the perception and categorization of multidimensional stimuli. *Journal of Experimental Psychology: Learning, Memory, and Cognition, 14*(1), 33–53.

Ashby, F. G., & Maddox, W. T. (1992). Complex decision rules in categorization: Contrasting novice and experienced performance. *Journal of Experimental Psychology: Human Perception & Performance, 18*, 50–71.

Ashby, F. G., & Maddox, W. T. (1993). Relations between prototype, exemplar and decision bound models of categorization. *Journal of Mathematical Psychology, 37*, 372–400.

Ashby, F. G., & Maddox, W. T. (2005). Human category learning. *Annual Review of Psychology, 56*, 149–178.

Bourne, L. E. (1966). *Human conceptual behavior.* Boston: Allyn and Bacon.

Bridle, J. S. (1990). Probabilistic interpretation of feedforward classification network outputs, with relationships to statistical pattern recognition. In F. Fogelman Soulié & J. Hérault (Eds.), *Neurocomputing: Algorithms, architectures and applications* (pp. 227–236). New York: Springer-Verlag.

Bruner, J. S., Goodnow, J. J., & Austin, G. A. (1956). *A study of thinking.* New York: Wiley.

Busemeyer, J. R., Dewey, G. I., & Medin, D. L. (1984). Evaluation of exemplar-based generalization and the abstraction of categorical information. *Journal of Experimental Psychology: Learning, Memory, & Cognition, 10*(4), 638–648.

Carpenter, G. A., & Grossberg, S. (1987). A massively parallel architecture for a self-organizing neural pattern recognition machine. *Computer Vision, Graphics, and Image Processing, 37*, 54–115.

Cohen, A. L., & Nosofsky, R. M. (2003). An extension of the exemplar-based random-walk model to separable-dimension stimuli. *Journal of Mathematical Psychology, 47*, 150–165.

Courville, A. C., Daw, N. D., Gordon, G. J., & Touretzky, D. S. (2004). Model uncertainty in classical conditioning. In S. Thrun, L. K. Saul, & B. Schölkopf (Eds.), *Advances in neural information processing systems* (Vol. 16, pp. 977–984). Cambridge, MA: MIT Press.

Courville, A. C., Daw, N. D., & Touretzky, D. S. (2004). Similarity and discrimination in classical conditioning: A latent variable account. In L. K. Saul, Y. Weiss, & L. Bottou (Eds.), *Advances in neural information processing systems* (Vol. 17). Cambridge, MA: MIT Press.

Dallaway, R. (1992). Memory for multiplication facts. In J. K. Kruschke (Ed.), *Proceedings of the Fourteenth Annual Conference of the Cognitive Science Society* (pp. 558–563). Hillsdale, NJ: Lawrence Erlbaum.

Dallaway, R. (1994). *Dynamics of arithmetic: A connectionist view of arithmetic skills.* Unpublished doctoral dissertation, University of Sussex at Brighton, UK.

Dayan, P., & Kakade, S. (2001). Explaining away in weight space. In T. Leen, T. Dietterich, & V. Tresp (Eds.), *Advances in neural information processing systems* (Vol. 13, pp. 451–457). Cambridge, MA: MIT Press.

Dayan, P., Kakade, S., & Montague, P. R. (2000). Learning and selective attention. *Nature Neuroscience, 3*, 1218–1223.

Edelman, S., & Weinshall, D. (1991). A self-organizing multiple-view representation of 3D objects. *Biological Cybernetics, 64*, 209–219.

Edwards, W. (1968). Conservatism in human information processing. In B. Kleinmuntz (Ed.), *Formal representation of human judgment.* New York: Wiley.

Erickson, M. A., & Kruschke, J. K. (1998). Rules and exemplars in category learning. *Journal of Experimental Psychology: General, 127*(2), 107–140.

Erickson, M. A., & Kruschke, J. K. (2002). Rule-based extrapolation in perceptual categorization. *Psychonomic Bulletin & Review*, 9(1), 160–168.

Estes, W. K. (1993). Models of categorization and category learning. In G. Nakamura, R. Taraban, & D. L. Medin (Eds.), *Psychology of learning and motivation* (Vol. 29, pp. 15–56). San Diego, CA: Academic Press.

Estes, W. K. (1994). *Classification and cognition*. New York: Oxford University Press.

Gati, I., & Tversky, A. (1984). Weighting common and distinctive features in perceptual and conceptual judgments. *Cognitive Psychology*, 16(3), 341–370.

Gluck, M. A., & Bower, G. H. (1988). From conditioning to category learning: An adaptive network model. *Journal of Experimental Psychology: General*, 117(3), 227–247.

Goldstone, R. L., & Kersten, A. (2003). Concepts and categorization. In A. F. Healy & R. W. Proctor (Eds.), *Comprehensive handbook of psychology, volume 4: Experimental psychology* (pp. 599–621). Hoboken, NJ: Wiley.

Gopnik, A., Glymour, C., Sobel, D. M., Schulz, L. E., Kushnir, T., & Danks, D. (2004). A theory of causal learning in children: Causal maps and Bayes nets. *Psychological Review*, 111, 3–32.

Gureckis, T. M., & Love, B. C. (2003). Human unsupervised and supervised learning as a quantitative distinction. *International Journal of Pattern Recognition and Artificial Intelligence*, 17(5), 885–901.

Heit, E., & Bott, L. (2000). Knowledge selection in category learning. In D. L. Medin (Ed.), *The psychology of learning and motivation* (Vol. 39, pp. 163–199). San Diego, CA: Academic Press.

Heit, E., Briggs, J., & Bott, L. (2004). Modeling the effects of prior knowledge on learning incongruent features of category members. *Journal of Experimental Psychology: Learning, Memory and Cognition*, 30(5), 1065–1081.

Hintzman, D. L. (1986). "Schema abstraction" in a multiple-trace memory model. *Psychological Review*, 93, 411–428.

Hintzman, D. L. (1988). Judgments of frequency and recognition memory in a multiple-trace memory model. *Psychological Review*, 95, 528–551.

Hurwitz, J. B. (1994). Retrieval of exemplar and feature information in category learning. *Journal of Experimental Psychology: Learning, Memory and Cognition*, 20, 887–903.

Juslin, P., Wennerholm, P., & Winman, A. (2001). High level reasoning and base-rate use: Do we need cue competition to explain the inverse base-rate effect? *Journal of Experimental Psychology: Learning, Memory and Cognition*, 27, 849–871.

Kalish, M. L., Lewandowsky, S., & Kruschke, J. K. (2004). Population of linear experts: Knowledge partitioning and function learning. *Psychological Review*, 111(4), 1072–1099.

Kanerva, P. (1988). *Sparse distributed memory*. Cambridge, MA: MIT Press.

Kohonen, T. (1982). *Self-organized formation of topologically correct feature maps. Biological Cybernetics*, 43, 59–69.

Kruschke, J. K. (1992). ALCOVE: An exemplar-based connectionist model of category learning. *Psychological Review*, 99, 22–44.

Kruschke, J. K. (1993). Human category learning: Implications for backpropagation models. *Connection Science*, 5, 3–36.

Kruschke, J. K. (2001a). Toward a unified model of attention in associative learning. *Journal of Mathematical Psychology*, 45, 812–863.

Kruschke, J. K. (2001b). The inverse base rate effect is not explained by eliminative inference. *Journal of Experimental Psychology: Learning, Memory and Cognition*, 27, 1385–1400.

Kruschke, J. K. (2003a). Attention in learning. *Current Directions in Psychological Science*, 12, 171–175.

Kruschke, J. K. (2003b, April). *Attentionally modulated exemplars and exemplar mediated attention*. Keynote Address to the Associative Learning Conference, University of Cardiff, Wales.

Kruschke, J. K. (2003c, May). *Attentionally modulated exemplars and exemplar mediated attention*. Invited talk at the Seventh International Conference on Cognitive and Neural Systems, Boston University. Boston, MA.

Kruschke, J. K. (2005). Category learning. In K. Lamberts & R. L. Goldstone (Eds.), *The handbook of cognition* (pp. 183–201). London: Sage.

Kruschke, J. K. (2006). Locally Bayesian learning with applications to retrospective revaluation and highlighting. *Psychological Review*, 113, 677–699.

Kruschke, J. K., & Bradley, A. L. (1995). *Extensions to the delta rule for associative learning* (Indiana University Cognitive Science Research Report #141). Retrieved June 26, 2007, from http://www.indiana.edu/~kruschke/articles/KruschkeB1995.pdf.

Kruschke, J. K., & Erickson, M. A. (1994). Learning of rules that have high-frequency exceptions: New empirical data and a hybrid connectionist model. In *Proceedings of the Sixteenth Annual Conference of the Cognitive Science Society* (pp. 514–519). Hillsdale, NJ: Lawrence Erlbaum.

Kruschke, J. K., & Johansen, M. K. (1999). A model of probabilistic category learning. *Journal of Experimental Psychology: Learning, Memory and Cognition, 25*(5), 1083–1119.

Kruschke, J. K., Johansen, M. K., & Blair, N. J. (1999, June). *Exemplar model account of inference learning.* Unpublished manuscript. Retrieved June 26, 2007, from http://www.indiana.edu/~kruschke/articles/KruschkeJB1999.pdf.

Kruskal, J. B. (1964). Nonmetric multidimensional scaling: A numerical method. *Psychometrika, 29*, 115–129.

Lamberts, K. (1994). Flexible tuning of similarity in exemplar-based categorization. *Journal of Experimental Psychology: Learning, Memory, and Cognition, 20*(5), 1003–1021.

Lamberts, K. (1995). Categorization under time pressure. *Journal of Experimental Psychology: General, 124*, 161–180.

Lamberts, K. (1997). Process models of categorization. In K. Lamberts & D. Shanks (Eds.), *Knowledge, concepts and categories* (pp. 371–403). Cambridge, MA: MIT Press.

Lamberts, K. (1998). The time course of categorization. *Journal of Experimental Psychology: Learning, Memory, and Cognition, 24*(3), 695–711.

Lamberts, K. (2000). Information-accumulation theory of speeded categorization. *Psychological Review, 107*(2), 227–260.

Lamberts, K., & Freeman, R. P. J. (1999). Building object representations from parts: Tests of a stochastic sampling model. *Journal of Experimental Psychology: Human Perception & Performance, 25*(4), 904–926.

Lee, M. D., & Navarro, D. J. (2002). Extending the ALCOVE model of category learning to featural stimulus domains. *Psychonomic Bulletin & Review, 9*(1), 43–58.

Levine, M. (1975). *A cognitive theory of learning: reseach on hypothesis testing.* Hillsdale, NJ: Lawrence Erlbaum.

Logan, G. D. (2002). An instance theory of attention and memory. *Psychological Review, 109*(2), 376–400.

Love, B. C., Medin, D. L., & Gureckis, T. M. (2004). SUSTAIN: A network model of category learning. *Psychological Review, 111*(2), 309–332.

Luce, R. D. (1963). Detection and recognition. In R. D. Luce, R. R. Bush, & E. Galanter (Eds.), *Handbook of mathematical psychology* (pp. 103–189). New York: Wiley.

MacKay, D. J. C. (2003). *Information theory, inference & learning algorithms.* Cambridge, UK: Cambridge University Press.

Matsuka, T. (2005). Simple, individually unique, and context-dependent learning methods for models of human category learning. *Behavior Research Methods, 37*(2), 240–255.

McClelland, J. L. (1979). On the time-relations of mental processes: An examination of systems of processes in cascade. *Psychological Review, 86*, 287–330.

McClelland, J. L., & Rumelhart, D. E. (1988). *Explorations in parallel distributed processing.* Cambridge, MA: MIT Press.

Medin, D. L., & Goldstone, R. L., & Gentner, D. (1993). Respects for similarity. *Psychological Review, 100*(2), 254–278.

Medin, D. L., & Schaffer, M. M. (1978). Context theory of classification learning. *Psychological Review, 85*, 207–238.

Murphy, G. L. (1993). Theories in concept formation. In I. Van Mechelen, J. Hampton, R. S. Michalski, & P. Theuns (Eds.), *Categories and concepts: Theoretical views and inductive data analysis* (pp. 173–200). London: Academic Press.

Murphy, G. L. (2002). *The big book of concepts.* Cambridge, MA: MIT Press.

Murphy, G. L., & Medin, D. L. (1985). The role of theories in conceptual coherence. *Psychological Review, 9*(3), 289–316.

Neal, R. M. (1996). *Bayesian learning for neural networks.* New York: Springer.

Nosofsky, R. M. (1984). Choice, similarity, and the context theory of classification. *Journal of Experimental Psychology: Learning, Memory, and Cognition, 10*, 104–114.

Nosofsky, R. M. (1986). Attention, similarity, and the identification-categorization relationship. *Journal of Experimental Psychology, 115*, 39–57.

Nosofsky, R. M. (1991). Relation between the rational model and the context model of categorization. *Psychological Science, 2*(6), 416–421.

Nosofsky, R. M. (2000). Exemplar representation without generalization? Comment on Smith and Minda (2000) "Thirty categorization results in search of a model." *Journal of*

Experimental Psychology: Learning, Memory, and Cognition, 26, 1735–1743.

Nosofsky, R. M., Gluck, M. A., Palmeri, T. J., McKinley, S. C., & Glauthier, P. (1994). Comparing models of rule-based classification learning: A replication of Shepard, Hovland, and Jenkins (1961). *Memory & Cognition, 22*, 352–369.

Nosofsky, R. M., Kruschke, J. K., & McKinley, S. C. (1992). Combining exemplar-based category representations and connectionist learning rules. *Journal of Experimental Psychology: Learning, Memory, and Cognition, 18*(2), 211–233.

Nosofsky, R. M., & Palmeri, T. J. (1997). An exemplar-based random walk model of speeded classification. *Psychological Review, 104*(2), 266–300.

Nosofsky, R. M., & Palmeri, T. J. (1998). A rule-plus-exception model for classifying objects in continuous-dimension spaces. *Psychonomic Bulletin & Review, 5*, 345–369.

Nosofsky, R. M., Palmeri, T. J., & McKinley, S. C. (1994). Rule-plus-exception model of classification learning. *Psychological Review, 101*, 53–79.

Nosofsky, R. M., & Stanton, R. D. (2005). Speeded classification in a probabilistic category structure: Contrasting exemplar-retrieval, decision-boundary, and prototype models. *Journal of Experimental Psychology: Human Perception and Performance, 31*(3), 608–629.

Nosofsky, R. M., & Zaki, S. (2002). Exemplar and prototype models revisited: Response strategies selective attention and stimulus generalization. *Journal of Experimental Psychology: Learning, Memory, and Cognition, 28*(5), 924–940.

Nosofsky, R. M., & Zaki, S. R. (2003). A hybrid-similarity exemplar model for predicting distinctiveness effects in perceptual old-new recognition. *Journal of Experimental Psychology: Learning, Memory, & Cognition, 29*(6), 1194–1209.

Pearce, J. M. (1987). A model for stimulus generalization in Pavlovian conditioning. *Psychological Review, 94*(1), 61–71.

Pearce, J. M. (1994). Similarity and discrimination: A selective review and a connectionist model. *Psychological Review, 101*, 587–607.

Press, W. H., Teukolsky, S. A., Vetterling, W. T., & Flannery, B. P. (1992). *Numerical recipes in C* (2nd ed.). Cambridge, UK: Cambridge University Press.

Reed, S. K. (1972). Pattern recognition and categorization. *Cognitive Psychology, 3*, 382–407.

Regier, T. (2005). The emergence of words: Attentional learning in form and meaning. *Cognitive Science, 29*, 819–865.

Rehder, B. (2003a). Categorization as causal reasoning. *Cognitive Science, 27*, 709–748.

Rehder, B. (2003b). A causal-model theory of conceptual representation and categorization. *Journal of Experimental Psychology: Learning, Memory, and Cognition, 29*(6), 1141–1159.

Rosch, E. H., & Mervis, C. B. (1975). Family resemblances: Studies in the internal structure of categories. *Cognitive Psychology, 7*, 573–605.

Rumelhart, D. E., Smolensky, P., McClelland, J. L., & Hinton, G. E. (1986). Schemata and sequential thought processes in PDP models. In J. L. McClelland & D. E. Rumelhart (Eds.), *Parallel distributed processing* (Vol. 2, pp. 7–57). Cambridge, MA: MIT Press.

Rumelhart, D. E., & Zipser, D. (1985). Feature discovery by competitive learning. *Cognitive Science, 9*, 75–112.

Shepard, R. N. (1957). Stimulus and response generalization: A stochastic model relating generalization to distance in psychological space. *Psychometrika, 22*, 325–345.

Shepard, R. N. (1962). The analysis of proximities: Multidimensional scaling with an unknown distance function, I and II. *Psychometrika, 27*, 125–140, 219–246.

Shepard, R. N. (1987). Toward a universal law of generalization for psychological science. *Science, 237*, 1317–1323.

Smith, J. D., & Minda, J. P. (2000). Thirty categorization results in search of a model. *Journal of Experimental Psychology: Learning, Memory, and Cognition, 26*, 3–27.

Sobel, D. M., Tenenbaum, J. B., & Gopnik, A. (2004). Children's causal inferences from indirect evidence: Backwards blocking and Bayesian reasoning in preschoolers. *Cognitive Science, 28*, 303–333.

Steyvers, M., Tenenbaum, J. B., Wagenmakers, E. J., & Blum, B. (2003). Inferring causal networks from observations and interventions. *Cognitive Science, 27*, 453–489.

Sun, R. (1995). Robust reasoning: Integrating rule-based and similarity-based reasoning. *Artificial Intelligence, 75*(2), 241–296.

Tenenbaum, J. B., & Griffiths, T. L. (2001a). Generalization, similarity and Bayesian inference. *Behavioral & Brain Sciences, 24*(4), 629–640.

Tenenbaum, J. B., & Griffiths, T. L. (2001b). Structure learning in human causal induction. In T. K. Leen, T. G. Dietterich, & V. Tresp (Eds.), *Advances in neural information processing systems* (Vol. 13, pp. 59–65). Cambridge, MA: MIT Press.

Tversky, A. (1977). Features of similarity. *Psychological Review, 84*(4), 327–352.

Usher, M., & McClelland, J. L. (2001). The time course of perceptual choice: The leaky, competing accumulator model. *Psychological Review, 108*(3), 550–592.

Van Wallendael, L. R., & Hastie, R. (1990). Tracing the footsteps of Sherlock Holmes: Cognitive representations of hypothesis testing. *Memory & Cognition, 18*, 240–250.

Verguts, T., Ameel, E., & Storms, G. (2004). Measures of similarity in models of categorization. *Memory & Cognition, 32*(3), 379–389.

Wills, A. J., Reimers, S., Stewart, N., Suret, M., & McLaren, I. P. (2000). Tests of the ratio rule in categorization. *Quarterly Journal of Experimental Psychology, 53A*, 983–1011.

Yang, L.-X., & Lewandowsky, S. (2004). Knowledge partitioning in categorization: Constraints on exemplar models. *Journal of Experimental Psychology: Learning, Memory, & Cognition, 30*(5), 1045–1064.

Young, M. E., & Wasserman, E. A. (2002). Limited attention and cue order consistency affect predictive learning: A test of similarity measures. *Journal of Experimental Psychology: Learning, Memory, and Cognition, 28*(3), 484–496.

CHAPTER 10

Micro-Process Models of Decision Making

Jerome R. Busemeyer and Joseph G. Johnson

1. Introduction

Computational models are like the new kids in town for the field of decision making. This field is largely dominated by axiomatic utility theories (Bell, Raiffa, & Tversky, 1998; Luce, 2000) or simple heuristic rule models (Gigerenzer, Todd, & the ABC Research Group, 1999; Payne, Bettman, & Johnson, 1993). It is difficult for the new kids to break into this field for a very important reason: They just seem too complex in comparison. Computational models are constructed from a large number of elementary units that are tightly interconnected to form a complex dynamic system. So the question, "what does this extra complexity buy us?," is raised. Computational theorists first have to prove that their models are worth the extra complexity. This chapter provides some answers to that challenge.

First, the current state of decision research applied to preferences under uncertainty is reviewed. The evolution of the algebraic utility approach that has dominated the field of decision making is described, showing a steady progression away from a simple and intuitive principle of maximizing expected value. The development of utility theories into their current form has included modifications for the subjective assessment of objective value and probability, with the most recent work focusing on finer specification of the latter. The impetus for these modifications is then discussed; in particular, specific and pervasive "paradoxes" of human choice behavior are briefly reviewed. This section arrives at the conclusion that no single utility theory provides an accurate descriptive model of human choice behavior.

Then, computational approaches to decision making are introduced, which seem more promising in their ability to capture robust trends in human choice behavior. This advantage is due to their common focus on the micro-mechanisms of the underlying deliberation process, rather than solely on the overt choice behavior driven by choice stimuli. A number of different approaches are introduced, providing a broad survey of the current corpus of computational models of decision making. The fourth section focuses on one particular model to offer a detailed example of the computational approach. Specifically, decision field theory is discussed, which has benefit from the most extensive (to date) application to a variety of choice domains and empirical phenomena.

The fifth section provides concrete illustration of how the computational approach can account for all of the behavioral paradoxes in the second section that have contested utility theories. Again, decision field theory is recruited for this analysis because of its success in accounting for all the relevant phenomena. However, the extent to which the other computational models have been successful in accounting for the results is also discussed. We conclude with comparisons among the computational models introduced, and summary comparisons between the computational approach and utility-based models of decision making.

2. Decision Models: State of the Art

2.1. *The Evolution of Utility-Based Models*

Decision theory has a long history, starting as early as the seventeenth century with probabilistic theories of gambling by Blaise Pascal and Pierre Fermat. Consider an option, or prospect, that offers some n number of quantifiable outcomes, $\{x_1, \ldots, x_n\}$, each with some specified probability, $\{p_1, \ldots, p_n\}$, respectively. The initial idea was that the decision maker should choose to maximize the long run average value or *expected value* (EV), $EV = \sum p_j \cdot x_j$. But the EV principle soon came under attack because it prescribes paying absurd prices to play a celedraft-brated gamble known as the St. Petersburg paradox. It was also criticized because it fails to explain why people buy insurance (the premium exceeds the expected value). To fix these problems, Daniel Bernoulli (1738) proposed that the objective outcome x_j be replaced with the subjective utility of this outcome $u(x_j)$, and recommended that the decision maker should choose to maximize the *expected utility* (EU), $EU = \sum p_j \cdot u(x_j)$.

For many years, Bernoulli's EU theory was disregarded by economists because it lacked a rational or axiomatic foundation. For example, why should one choose on the basis of expectation if the game is played only once? Von Neumann and Morgenstern (1947) rectified this problem by (a) proposing a set of rational axioms (e.g., transitivity, independence, solvability), and (b) proving that the EU principle uniquely satisfies these axioms. This led to EU theory being accepted by economists as the rational basis for making decisions. Thus far, EU theory was restricted to decisions with objectively known probabilities (e.g., well-defined lotteries). Shortly afterward, Savage (1954) provided an axiomatic foundation for assigning personal probabilities to uncertain events (e.g., presidential elections).

Unfortunately, people are not always rational, and subsequent empirical research soon demonstrated systematic violations of these rational axioms (see Allais, 1961; Ellsberg, 1953). To explain these violations, Kahneman and Tversky (1979) developed *prospect theory*, which changed EU theory in two important ways. Following an earlier suggestion by Edwards (1962), they replaced the objective probabilities p_i with subjective decision weights $\pi(p_i)$, where π is an inverse S shaped function. Unlike Savage's (1954) theory, these decision weights are not constrained to obey the laws of probability. Second, the utility function was defined with respect to a reference point: for losses (below the reference), the function is convex (risk seeking); for gains (above the reference), the function is concave (risk averse); and the function is steeper on the loss compared with the gain side (loss aversion). The initial prospect theory was severely criticized for two main reasons (see Starmer, 2000): (1) it predicted preferences for stochastically dominated options that are never empirically observed (anomalies that had to be removed by ad hoc editing operations); and (2) the theory was limited to binary outcomes, and it broke down and made poor predictions for a larger number of outcomes (Lopes & Oden, 1999).

Recognizing these limitations, Tversky and Kahneman (1992) modified and extended prospect theory to form cumulative prospect theory (CPT), which builds on earlier ideas of rank dependent utility (RDU) theories (Quiggin, 1982). The problem to be solved was the following: On the one hand, nonlinear decision weights were needed to explain violations of the rational axioms; but on the other hand, nonlinear transformations of outcome probabilities led to absurd predictions. To overcome this problem, RDU theories such as CPT employ a more sophisticated method for computing decision weights.[1] Suppose payoffs are rank-ordered in preference according to the index j so $u(x_{j+1}) > u(x_j)$. The rank dependent decision weight for outcome x_j is then defined by the formula: $w(x_j) = \pi(\sum_j^n p_j) - \pi(\sum_{j+1}^n p_j)$ for $j = n - 1, n - 2, \ldots, 2, 1$, and $w(x_n) = \pi(p_n)$.

Here, π is a monotonically increasing weight function designed to capture optimistic (more weight to higher outcomes) or pessimistic (more weight to lower outcomes) beliefs of a decision maker. The term $(\sum_j^n p_j)$ is called the decumulative probability (one minus the cumulative probability), which is the probability of getting a payoff at least as good as x_j. Whereas prospect theory transformed the outcome probabilities, $\pi(p_j)$, CPT transforms the decumulative probabilities, $\pi(\sum_j^n p_j)$. By doing this, one can account for systematic violations of the EU axioms, while at the same time avoid making absurd predictions about dominated options. This is the current state of utility theories.

2.2. *Problems with Utility Models: Paradoxes in Decision Making*

This section briefly and selectively reviews some important paradoxes of decision making (for a more complete review, see Rieskamp, Busemeyer, & Mellers, 2006; Starmer, 2000) and points out shortcomings of utility theories in explaining these phenomena.

---

1 Note that CPT is one exemplar from the class of RDU, which in turn are a subset of the more general EU approach. For the current chapter, reference to one class subsumes the more specific model(s); e.g., claims regarding RDU theory apply also to CPT.

2.2.1. ALLAIS PARADOX

This most famous paradox of decision making (Allais, 1979; see also Kahneman & Tversky, 1979) was designed to test expected utility theory. In one example, the following choice was given:

> A: "win \$1 M (million) dollars for sure,"
> B: "win \$5 M with probability .10, or \$1 M with probability .89, or nothing."

Most people preferred prospect A even though prospect B has a higher expected value. This preference alone is no violation of expected utility theory – it simply reflects a risk averse utility function. The violation occurs when this first preference is compared with a second preference obtained from a choice between two other prospects:

> A': "win \$1 million dollars with probability .11, or nothing,"
> B': "win \$5 million dollars with probability .10, or nothing."

Most people preferred prospect B', and the (A, B') preference pattern is the paradox.

To see the paradox, one needs to analyze this problem according to expected utility theory. These prospects involve a total of three possible final outcomes: $\{x_1 = \$0, x_2 = \$1 \text{ M}, x_3 = \$5 \text{ M}\}$. Each prospect is a probability distribution, (p_1, p_2, p_3), over these three outcomes, where p_j is the probability of getting payoff x_j. Thus, the prospects are:

$$A = (0, 1, 0) \qquad A' = (.89, .11, 0)$$
$$B = (.01, .89, .10) \quad B' = (.90, 0, .10).$$

Now define three new prospects:

$$O = (0, 1, 0) \qquad Z = (1, 0, 0)$$
$$F = (1/11, 0, 10/11).$$

It can be seen that $A = (.11) \cdot O + (.89) \cdot O$ and $B = (.11) \cdot F + (.89) \cdot O$, producing $EU(A) - EU(B) = [(.11) \cdot EU(O) + (.89) \cdot EU(O)] - [(.11) \cdot EU(F) + (.89) \cdot EU(O)]$. The common branch, $(.89) \cdot EU(O)$, cancels out, making the comparison of utilities between A and B reduce to a comparison of utilities for O and F. It can also be seen that:

$A' = (.11) \cdot O + (.89) \cdot Z$ and $B' = (.11) \cdot F + (.89) \cdot Z$, producing $EU(A') - EU(B')$ $= [(.11) \cdot EU(O) + (.89) \cdot EU(Z)] - [(.11) \cdot EU(F) + (.89) \cdot EU(Z)]$.

Again a common branch, $(.89) \cdot EU(Z)$, cancels out, making the comparison between A' and B' reduce to the same comparison between O and F. More generally, EU theory requires the following *independence axiom*: for any three prospects $\{A, B, C\}$, if A is preferred to B, then $A' = p \cdot A + (1 - p) \cdot C$ is preferred to $p \cdot B + (1 - p) \cdot C = B'$. The Allais preference pattern (A, B') violates this axiom.

To account for these empirical violations, the independence axiom has been replaced by weaker axioms (see Luce, 2000, for a review). The new axioms have led to the development of the RDU class of theories introduced earlier, including CPT, which can account for the Allais paradox. However, the RDU theories (including CPT) must satisfy another property called stochastic dominance.

2.2.2. STOCHASTIC DOMINANCE

Assume again that the payoffs are rank ordered in preference according to the index j, so $u(x_{j+1}) > u(x_j)$. Define X as the random outcome produced by choosing a prospect. Prospect A stochastically dominates prospect B if and only if $\Pr[u(X) \geq u(x_j) \mid A] \geq \Pr[u(X) \geq u(x_j) \mid B]$ for all x_j.

In other words, if A offers at least as good a chance as B of obtaining each possible outcome or better, then A stochastically dominates B.[2] The reason RDU theories (e.g., CPT) must satisfy stochastic dominance (predict choice of stochastically dominating prospects) is straightforward. If A stochastically dominates B with respect to the payoff probabilities, then it follows that A stochastically dominates B with respect to the decision weights, which implies that the RDU for A is greater than that for B, and this finally implies that A is preferred to

B. Unfortunately for decision theorists, human preferences do not obey this property either – systematic violations of stochastic dominance have been reported (Birnbaum & Navarrete, 1998; Birnbaum, 2004). In one example, the following choice was presented:

> F: "win $98 with .85, or $90 with .05, or $12 with .10,"
> G: "win $98 with .90, or $14 with .05, or $12 with .05."

Most people chose F in this case, but it is stochastically dominated by G. To see this, we can rewrite the prospects as follows:

> F': "win $98 with .85, or $90 with .05, or $12 with .05, or $12 with .05,"
> G': "win $98 with .85, or $98 with .05, or $14 with .05, or $12 with .05."

Most people chose G' in this case. The choice of F violates the principle of stochastic dominance, which is contrary to RDU theories such as CPT. More complex decision weight models, such as Birnbaum's Tax model, are required to not only explain violations of stochastic dominance, but to simultaneously account for the pattern (F, G'; see Birnbaum, 2004).

2.2.3. PREFERENCE REVERSALS

Violations of independence and stochastic dominance are two of the classic paradoxes of decision making. Perhaps the most serious challenge for all utility theories is one that calls into question the fundamental concept of preference. According to most utility theories (including prospect theory), there are two equally valid methods for measuring preference – one based on choice, and a second based on price. If prospect A is chosen over prospect B, then $u(A) > u(B)$, which implies that the price equivalent for prospect A should be greater than the price equivalent for prospect B (this follows from the relations, $\$_A = A > B = \$_B$, where $\$_K$ is the price equivalent of prospect K). Contrary to this fundamental prediction, systematic reversals of preferences have been found between choices

2 Note that, technically, A must also offer a better chance of obtaining at least one outcome. That is, the inequality must be strict for at least one outcome, otherwise the prospects A and B are identical.

and prices (Grether & Plott, 1979; Lichten-stein & Slovic, 1971; Lindman, 1971; Slovic & Lichtenstein, 1983). In one example, the following prospects were presented:

P: "win $4 with 35/36 probability,"
D: "win $16 with 11/36 probability."

Most people chose prospect P over prospect D, even though D has a higher expected value – they tend to be risk averse with choices. The same people, however, most frequently gave a higher price equivalent to prospect D than to prospect P. Further-more, another interesting finding in need of explanation is that the variance of the prices for prospect D is much larger than that for prospect P (Bostic, Herrnstein, & Luce, 1990).

Tversky, Sattath, and Slovic (1988) ini-tially explained preference reversals be-tween choice and price by arguing that deci-sion makers place more weight on the prob-ability dimension when making choices, whereas the price task shifts weight to the price dimension. Alternatively, Mellers, Schwartz, and Cooke (1998) argued that de-cision makers use different strategies when making choices versus prices. However, a se-rious problem for both of these explanations is that preferences also reverse when individ-uals are asked to give two different types of prices, such as minimum selling prices (will-ingness to accept [WTA]) versus maximum buying prices (willingness to pay [WTP]), for the same prospects (Birnbaum & Zim-merman, 1998). Consider the following two prospects:

F: "win $60 with probability .50, other-wise $48."
G: "win $96 with probability .50, other-wise $12."

People gave a higher WTA for prospect G compared with prospect F, but the opposite order was found for WTP. So, not only do preferences change depending on whether choices or prices are used, but also when dif-ferent types of prices are used. Furthermore, such violations extend beyond trivial tasks involving hypothetical or low-stakes gam-bles to situations involving more realistic consequences, such as managerial decisions, medical decisions, environmental protection policies, and highway safety programs.

Neither choice-pricing nor WTP-WTA reversals can be explained with a single utility model such as prospect theory, but only by assuming arbitrary task-dependent changes in the decision weights and/or util-ity function and/or combination of weight and utility. These unnerving findings have led researchers to question stability of pref-erences and to argue instead that prefer-ences are constructed on the fly in a task-dependent manner (e.g., Slovic, 1995).

2.2.4. CONTEXT-DEPENDENT PREFERENCES

A final challenge for utility theories is that preferences seem to depend not only on changes in the task, but also in changes in the context produced by the choice set for a single task. These preference reversals in-volve violations of a principle called *indepen-dence from irrelevant alternatives*. According to this principle, if option A is chosen most frequently over option B in a choice set that includes only {A, B}, then A should be cho-sen more frequently over B in a larger choice set {A, B, C} that includes a new option C. This principle is required by a large class of utility models called simple scalable utility models (see Tversky, 1972). However, em-pirical evidence points to at least three direct violations of this principle.

The first violation is produced by what is called the similarity effect (Tversky, 1972; Tversky & Sattath, 1979), in which case the new option, labeled S, is designed to be sim-ilar and competitive with the common op-tion B. In one example, participants chose among hypothetical candidates for graduate school that varied in terms of intelligence and motivation scores:

Candidate A: Intelligence = 60, Motiva-tion = 90,
Candidate B: Intelligence = 78, Motiva-tion = 25,

Candidate S: Intelligence = 75, Motivation = 35.

Participants chose B more frequently than A in a binary choice. However, when candidate S was added to the set, then preferences reversed and candidate A became the most popular choice. The similarity effect rules out all simple scalable utility models, but it can be explained by a heuristic choice model called the elimination by aspects (EBA) model (Tversky, 1972). According to this model, decision makers sample a feature based on its importance and eliminate any option that does not contain the selected feature; the process continues until there is only one option left, and the last surviving option is then chosen. Applying EBA to the previous example, if grade-point average is most important, then A is most likely to be eliminated at the first stage, leaving B as the most frequent choice; however, when S is added to the set, then both B and S survive the first elimination, and S reduces the share of B.

The second violation is produced by what is called the attraction effect (Huber, Payne, & Puto, 1982; Huber & Puto, 1983; Simonson, 1989), in which case the new option, labeled D, is similar to A but dominated by A. In one example, participants chose among cars varying in miles per gallon and ride quality:

Brand A: 73 rating on ride quality, 33 miles per gallon (mpg),
Brand B: 83 rating on ride quality, 24 mpg,
Brand D: 70 rating on ride quality, 33 mpg.

Brand B was more frequently chosen over brand A on a binary choice; however, adding option D to the choice set reversed preferences so that brand A became most popular. In this second case, the new option helps rather than hurts the similar option. The attraction effect is important because it violates another principle called *regularity*, which states that adding an option to the set can never increase the popularity of one

of the original options from the subset. The EBA model satisfies regularity, and therefore it cannot explain the attraction effect (Tversky, 1972).

The third violation is produced by what is called the compromise effect (Simonson, 1989; Simonson & Tversky, 1992), in which a new extreme option A is added to the choice set. In one example, participants chose among batteries varying in expected life and corrosion rate:

Brand A: 6% corrosion rate, 16 hours duration,
Brand B: 2% corrosion rate, 12 hours duration,
Brand C: 4% corrosion rate, 14 hours duration.

When given a binary choice between B and C, brand B was more frequently chosen over brand C. However, when option A was added to the choice set, then brand C was chosen more often than brand B. Thus, adding an extreme option A, which turns option C into a compromise, reverses the preference orders obtained between the binary and triadic choice methods. The compromise effect is interesting because it rules out another heuristic choice rule called the lexicographic (LEX), or "take the best," strategy. According to this strategy, the decision maker first considers the most important dimension and picks the best alternative on this dimension, but if there is a tie, then the decision maker turns to the second most important dimension and picks the best on this dimension, and so forth. According to the LEX strategy, individuals should never choose the compromise option!

The collection of results presented in this section indicate that preferences among a set of options are not subject to the calculus of probability and are dependent on the choice context and the elicitation method. These results are only a subset of the decades of research showing that human decisions do not correspond to those predicted by utility models. Any serious model of decision making must account for effects such as the robust and representative examples mentioned in this section. We now turn to examining a distinctly different type of modeling approach that shows promise in this respect.

3. Computational Models of Decision Making: A Survey

In an attempt to retain the basic utility framework, constraints on utility theories are being relaxed, and the formulas are becoming more deformed. Recently, many researchers have responded to the growing corpus of phenomena that challenge traditional utility models by applying wholly different approaches. That is, rather than continuing to modify utility equations to accommodate each new empirical trend, these researchers have adopted alternative representations of human decision making. The common thread among these approaches is their attention to the processes, or computations, that are assumed to produce observable decision behavior. Beyond this, the popular approaches outlined in this section diverge in precisely how they model decision making.

3.1. *Heuristic Rule-Based Systems*

Payne, Bettman, and Johnson (1992, 1993) propose an adaptive approach to decision making. Essentially, this approach assumes that decision makers possess a repertoire of distinct decision strategies that they may apply to any given task. The repertoire of strategies usually includes noncompensatory rules that do not require trade-offs among attributes, such as EBA and LEX, as well as compensatory rules that are based on attribute trade-offs such as a weighted additive (WADD) rule or EU rule. Furthermore, it is assumed that the strategy applied is selected as a trade-off between the mental effort required to apply the strategy and the accuracy or performance of the strategy. Thus, in trivial situations or those involving extreme time pressure, individuals may employ relatively simple strategies that do not involve complex calculations such as the LEX or EBA rules. In contrast, in important situations where a high level of performance is required, decision makers may apply more cognitively intensive strategies such as the WADD or EU rule.

This approach assumes that each possible strategy is assembled from elementary information processing units, such as "retrieve," "store," "move," "compare," "add," "multiply," and so forth (Payne et al., 1993). For example, the EBA rule might be instantiated by a "retrieve" of a prospect's attribute value, followed by a "compare" to some threshold value defining deficiency. EU could be formalized by a "multiply" of subjective probability and utility values, the "store" of each product, and an "add" across products; choice is defined by a "compare" operation among expected utilities. Mental effort is defined by the sum of processing times for these elementary mental operations, and accuracy is typically defined by performance relative to the WADD or EU rule.

Gigerenzer and colleagues (Gigerenzer et al., 1999) have developed a closely related approach. Their simple heuristics are formulated in terms of their rules for (a) searching through information, (b) stopping this search, and (c) selecting an option once the search concludes. For example, Brandstätter, Gigerenzer, and Hertwig (2006) recently proposed a LEX model called the "priority heuristic," which assumes the following process for positively valued gambles: (1) first compare the lowest outcomes for each prospect, and if this difference exceeds a cutoff, then choose the best on this comparison; otherwise (2) compare the probabilities associated with the lowest payoffs, and if this difference exceeds a cutoff then choose the best on this comparison; otherwise (3) compare the maximum possible payoff for each prospect and choose the best on this maximum.

The strength of heuristic models is their ability to explain effects of effort, conflict, time pressure, and emotional content on choices and other processing measures (e.g., amount of information searched, order of search) in terms of changes in decision strategies. However, one drawback to these models is their lack of specification across applications; it is often difficult to determine exactly which strategy is used in any given situation. Furthermore, when considering the findings summarized earlier, the heuristic models cannot account for all of the results reviewed previously despite this flexibility. They have been used to explain violations of independence for risky choices but not the violations of stochastic dominance. They also have been used to explain preference reversals between choice and prices, but not between buying and selling prices. Finally they can explain the similarity effect but not the compromise or attraction effect.

3.2. Dynamic Systems/Connectionist Networks

Many researchers prefer to adopt a single dynamic process model of decision making rather than proposing a tool box of strategies. This idea has led to the development of several computational models that are formulated as connectionist models or dynamic systems (see Chapter 2 on connectionist models and Chapter 4 on dynamic systems in this volume).

3.2.1. AFFECTIVE BALANCE THEORY

Grossberg and Gutowski (1987) presented a dynamic theory of affective evaluation based on an opponent processing network called a gated dipole neural circuit. Habituating transmitters within the circuit determine an affective adaptation level, or reference point, against which later events are evaluated. Neutral events can become affectively charged either through direct activation or antagonistic rebound within the habituated dipole circuit. This neural circuit was used to provide an explanation for the probability weighting and value functions of Kahneman and Tversky's (1979) prospect theory, and preference reversals between choices and prices. However, this theory cannot explain preference reversals between buying and selling prices, nor can it explain violations of stochastic dominance. Finally, the

affective balance theory has never been applied to more than two choice options, so it is not clear how it would explain the similarity, attraction, and compromise context effects.

3.2.2. ECHO

Holyoak and Simon (1999) and Guo and Holyoak (2002) proposed a connectionist network, called ECHO, adapted from Thagard and Millgram (1995). According to this theory, there is a special node, called the external driver, representing the goal to make a decision, which is turned on when a decision is presented. The driver node is directly connected to attribute nodes, with a constant connection weight. Each attribute node is connected to an alternative node with a bidirectional link, which allows activation to pass back and forth from the attribute node to the alternative node. The connection weight between an attribute node and an alternative node is determined by the value of the alternative on that attribute. There are also constant lateral inhibitory connections between the alternative nodes to produce a competitive recurrent network.

The decision process works as follows. On presentation of a decision problem, the driver is turned on and applies constant input activation into the attribute nodes, and each attribute node then activates each alternative node (differentially depending on value). Then each alternative node provides positive feedback to each attribute node and negative feedback to the other alternative nodes. Activation in the network evolves over time according to a nonlinear dynamic system, which keeps the activations bounded between zero and one. The decision process stops as soon as the changes in activations fall below some threshold. At that point, the probability of choosing an option is determined by a ratio of activation strengths.

The ECHO model has been shown to account for the similarity and attraction effect, but it cannot account for the compromise effect. It has not been applied to risky choices, so it remains unclear how it would explain violations of independence or stochastic dominance. Finally, this theory is restricted to choice behavior, and it has no mechanisms for making predictions about prices. One interesting prediction of the ECHO model is that the weight of an attribute changes during deliberation in the direction of the currently favored alternative. Evidence supporting this prediction was reported by Simon, Krawczyk, and Holyoak (2004).

3.2.3. LEAKY COMPETING ACCUMULATOR MODEL

Usher and McClelland (2004) proposed a connectionist network model of decision making called the leaky competing accumulator model. Preference is based on the sequential evaluation of attributes, where each evaluation compares the relative advantages and disadvantages of each prospect. These comparisons are integrated over time for each option by a recursive network. The accumulation continues until a threshold is crossed, and the first option to reach the threshold is chosen.

This theory is closely related to decision field theory (described later), with the following important exceptions. First, the activation for each option is restricted to remain positive at all times, which requires the temporal integration to be nonlinear. Second, the leaky competing accumulator model adopts Tversky and Kahneman's (1991) loss aversion hypothesis so that disadvantages have a larger impact than advantages.

Usher and McClelland (2004) have shown that the leaky competing accumulator can explain the similarity, attraction, and compromise effects using a common set of parameters. However, this model has not been applied to risky choices or to preference reversals.

3.3. Models Cast in Cognitive Architectures

Some researchers have taken advantage of the extensive work that has been done in developing comprehensive cognitive architectures that can then be specified for al-

most any conceivable individual task (see Chapter 6 on cognitive architectures in this volume). In particular, researchers have recently formulated models within two popular cognitive architectures for choice tasks that are the focus of the current chapter.

3.3.1. SUBSYMBOLIC AND SYMBOLIC COMPUTATION IN ACT-R

Although one of the most popular cognitive architectures, ACT-R, incorporates a simple expected utility mechanism by default, other researchers have realized the drawbacks with the expected utility approach and developed alternative models within ACT-R. Specifically, Belavkin (2006) has developed two models that can correctly predict the Allais paradox (it has not been applied to the other paradoxes). In fact, these decision models are not unique to the ACT-R implementation proposed by Belavkin (2006); each model is actually a probabilistic extension of earlier simple heuristic rules guiding choice.

The first model essentially reduces to a simple rule of maximizing the probability of the largest outcome possible. Due to the negative correlation that typically exists between outcome and probability (e.g., to maintain constant expected value across gambles), this first rule results in the likelihood of choosing the option with the larger outcome to be equal to the probability of this outcome. The second model is formulated at the symbolic rule level in ACT-R and defines preference relations on each component of the stimuli (i.e., first outcome, probability of first outcome, second outcome, and probability of second outcome). A simple tally rule is assumed, and the proportion of total relations (including indifference) that favor each option produces the probability of choosing the option. Although each of these simple rule models can predict choices that produce the Allais paradox, they cannot predict a number of more basic results. For example, in both models, changing the value of an outcome does not affect choice if the rank order is preserved, contrary to empirical evidence.

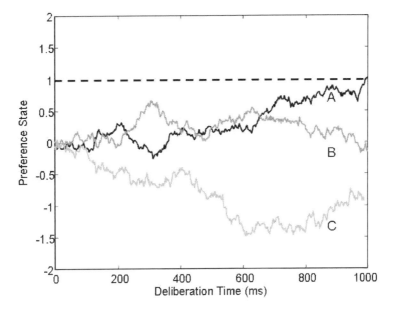

Figure 10.1. Illustration of preference evolution for three options (A, B, and C), according to decision field theory. The threshold is shown as a dashed line; the three options are shown as solid lines of different darkness.

4. Computational Models of Decision Making: A Detailed Example

It is impossible to describe all of the previously mentioned computational models in detail, so this section will focus on one, called decision field theory (DFT; Busemeyer & Townsend, 1993; Diederich, 1997; Roe, Busemeyer, Townsend, 2001; Johnson & Busemeyer, 2005a).[3] This model has been more broadly applied to decision-making phenomena compared with the other computational models at this point.

4.1. *Sequential Sampling Deliberation Process*

DFT is a member of a general class of sequential sampling models that are commonly used in a variety of fields in cognition (Ashby, 2000; Laming, 1968; Link & Heath, 1975; Nosofsky & Palmeri, 1997; Ratcliff,

3 The name "decision field theory" reflects the influence of Kurt Lewin's (1936) field theory of conflict.

1978; Smith, 1995; Usher & McClelland, 2001). The basic ideas underlying the decision process for sequential sampling models are illustrated in Figure 10.1. Suppose the decision maker is initially presented with a choice between three risky prospects, A, B, C, at time $t = 0$. The horizontal axis on the figure represents deliberation time (in milliseconds), and the vertical axis represents preference strength. Each trajectory in the figure represents the preference state for one of the risky prospects at each moment in time.

Intuitively, at each moment in time, the decision maker thinks about various payoffs of each prospect, which produces an affective reaction, or *valence*, to each prospect. These valences are integrated across time to produce the preference state at each moment. In this example, during the early stages of processing (between 200 and 300 ms), attention is focused on advantages favoring prospect B, but later (after 600 ms), attention is shifted toward advantages favoring prospect A. The stopping rule

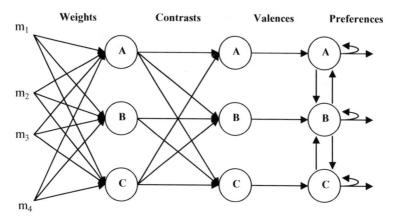

Figure 10.2. Connectionist network representation of decision field theory.

for this process is controlled by a threshold (which is set equal to 1.0 in this example): The first prospect to reach the top threshold is accepted, which in this case is prospect *A* after about 1 second. Choice probability is determined by the first option to win the race and cross the upper threshold, and decision time is equal to the deliberation time required by one of the prospects to reach this threshold.

The threshold is an important parameter for controlling speed-accuracy trade-offs. If the threshold is set to a lower value (about .50) in Figure 10.1, then prospect *B* would be chosen instead of prospect *A* (and done so earlier). Thus, decisions can reverse under time pressure (see Diederich, 2003). High thresholds require a strong preference state to be reached, which allows more information about the prospects to be sampled, prolonging the deliberation process and increasing accuracy. Low thresholds allow a weak preference state to determine the decision, which cuts off sampling information about the prospects, shortening the deliberation process and decreasing accuracy. There are many examples of task and individual variables that could determine the threshold for an individual application. As an example of the former, under high time pressure, decision makers must choose a low threshold; but under low time pressure, a higher threshold can be used to increase accuracy. Concerning personal variables, very careful

and deliberative decision makers tend to use a high threshold, and impulsive or careless decision makers can be described as using a low threshold.

4.2. *Connectionist Network Interpretation*

Figure 10.2 provides a connectionist interpretation of DFT for the example shown in Figure 10.1. Assume once again that the decision maker has a choice among three risky prospects, and also suppose for simplicity that there are only four possible final outcomes. Thus, each prospect is defined by a probability distribution across these same four payoffs. The subjective, affective values produced by each payoff are represented by the inputs, m_j, shown on the far left side of this network. At any moment in time, the decision maker anticipates the payoff of each prospect, which produces a momentary evaluation, $U_i(t)$, for prospect i, shown as the first layer of nodes in Figure 10.2. This momentary evaluation is an attention-weighted average of the affective evaluation of each payoff: $U_i(t) = \sum W_{ij}(t) \cdot m_j$. The attention weight at time t, $W_{ij}(t)$, for payoff j offered by prospect i, is assumed to fluctuate according to a stationary stochastic process. This reflects the idea that attention is shifting from moment to moment, causing changes in the anticipated payoff of each prospect across time.

The momentary evaluation of each prospect is compared with other prospects to form a valence for each prospect at each moment, $v_i(t) = U_i(t) - U_.(t)$, where $U_.(t)$ equals the average momentary evaluation across all the prospects. The valence $v_i(t)$ represents the relative advantage or disadvantage of prospect i at time t, and this is shown as the second layer of nodes in Figure 10.2. The total valence balances out to zero so that all the options cannot become attractive simultaneously.

Finally, the valences are the inputs to a dynamic system that integrates the valences over time to generate the output preference states. The output preference state for prospect i at time t is symbolized as $P_i(t)$, which is represented by the last layer of nodes in Figure 10.2 (and plotted as the trajectories in Figure 10.1). The dynamic system is described by the following linear stochastic difference equation for a small time step h in the deliberation process:

$$P_i(t + h) = \sum_j s_{ij} \cdot P_j(t) + v_i(t + h)$$

$$(10.1)$$

The positive self-feedback coefficient, $s_{ii} = s > 0$, controls the memory for past input valences for a preference state. Values of $s_{ii} < 1$ suggest decay in the memory or impact of previous valences over time, whereas values of $s_{ii} > 1$ suggest growth in impact over time (primacy effects). The negative lateral feedback coefficients, $s_{ij} = s_{ji} < 0$ for $i \neq j$, produce competition among actions so that the strong inhibit the weak. In other words, as preference for one prospect grows stronger, then this moderates the preference for other prospects. The magnitudes of the lateral inhibitory coefficients are assumed to be an increasing function of the similarity between choice options. These lateral inhibitory coefficients are important for explaining context effects on preference.

Formally, this decision process is a Markov process, and matrix formulas have been mathematically derived for computing the choice probabilities and distribution of choice response times (for details, see Buse-

meyer & Diederich, 2002; Busemeyer & Townsend, 1992; Diederich & Busemeyer, 2003). Alternatively, Monte Carlo computer simulation can be used to generate predictions from the model.

4.3. Attention Switching Mechanism

What is the psychological source of decision weights? According to DFT, an attention process is used to generate the predicted payoff for each prospect at each time step of the sequential sampling process. In this context, the decision weight for a payoff equals the average amount of time an individual spends paying attention to that payoff. Consequently, the decision weights are derived from a micro-process model of attention (Johnson & Busemeyer, 2006).

Consider a prospect with payoffs $x_1 \leq x_2, \ldots, \leq x_n$ and associated probabilities $(p_1, \ldots, p_n)$. The attention process starts at the lowest payoff and works its way up the ranks. Given that the attention process is focused on a particular payoff x_j for $1 < j < n$, it can make four transitions: predict x_j with probability p_j; do not predict this right away, but remain focused on it with probability $\beta \cdot (1 - p_j)$; or switch the focus up to the next highest payoff or down to the next lowest payoff with equal probability, $(1 - \beta) \cdot (1 - p_j)/2$. If attention is focused on the lowest (highest) payoff, then focus may only switch to the next lowest (highest) payoff; that is, the probability of switching focus is $(1 - \beta) \cdot (1 - p_j)$, for $j = \{1, n\}$. This attention mechanism is then used to mathematically derive (again using Markov chain theory) the mean attention weights, $w_{ij} = E[W_{ij}(t)]$, for DFT (see Johnson & Busemeyer, 2006). In this way, all of the decision weight parameters are derived on the basis of a single attention parameter, $0 \leq \beta \leq 1$, that represents the tendency to dwell on any given outcome once focused on the outcome.

4.4. Response Mechanism

How can a choice process be used to determine prices, yet still produce preference reversals? According to DFT, a sequential comparison process is used to search and find a price that makes the decision maker indifferent when faced with a choice between a prospect and a price (Johnson & Busemeyer, 2005a).

Consider, for example, the task of finding a price for the D bet given earlier, "win $16 with probability 11/36." For simplicity, assume the feasible set of candidate prices includes the dollar values $0, $1, $2, . . . , $16. For a simple price equivalent, the most efficient place to start searching is in the middle of this set ($8); when buying, it is advantageous to start bargaining with the lowest possible bid ($0); and it is advantageous for sellers to start by asking for the highest price ($16). The sequential comparison then inserts this starting value into a binary choice process (the D prospect is compared with the candidate dollar value). This comparison process can result in one of three outputs: (a) if the process results in (implicit) choice favoring the prospect D over the candidate value, then the price is too low, and it is incremented by a dollar; (b) if the process results in preference for the candidate value over the prospect D, then the price is too high, and the price is reduced by a dollar; however, (c) each time that the comparison process transits through the zero (indifference) preference state, then there is some probability, r, that the comparison process will stop and exit, and report finding a price equivalent. This sequential comparison process is then used to mathematically derive (again using Markov chain theory) the entire distribution of prices for gambles (see Johnson & Busemeyer, 2005a).

4.5. Model Parameters

It is now possible to identify and compare the parameters of DFT model with those of RDU theories, such as CPT. First, DFT has a set of affective values, m_j, that correspond to the utilities of outcomes, $u(x_j)$, used in RDU theories. Second, DFT has a set of mean attention weights, w_{ij}, that correspond to the decision weights, $w_i(x_j)$, of RDU theories. However, the weights for DFT are generated from an attention mech-

anism, which requires only one parameter, β. To account for prices, DFT requires only one additional parameter, the exit rate parameter r, whereas RDU theories require a new set of weights for choices and prices to account for preference reversals.

In addition, DFT includes three types of parameters to describe properties of human decision making that RDU models (including CPT) cannot. First, DFT uses a threshold-bound parameter to account for speed-accuracy trade-offs (RDU theories fail to do this because they are static). Second, DFT includes a variance term to account for the probabilistic nature of choice (RDU theories are deterministic, and probabilistic extensions require additional parameters). A parameter for the self-feedback coefficient, $s_{ii} = s$, is needed to account for primacy/recency effects on the growth of preferences over time, and parameters for the lateral inhibition coefficients, $s_{ij} = s_{ji}$ for $i \neq j$, are needed to explain context-dependent preferences.

5. Accounting for Paradoxes in Decision Making

As indicated by the selective survey of results in Section 2.2, human decision-making behavior is complex, even under extremely simple decision situations. Can the computational models account for this daunting collection of empirical results? In this section, we will show how DFT is able to account for all of the findings introduced in Section 2.2. Although this is the only theory that has been shown to account for this entire collection of results, we also mention where appropriate the success or failure of other computational approaches in accounting for some of these findings.

5.1. Accounting for Violations of Independence and Stochastic Dominance

Recall that RDU theories (including CPT) are unable to account for violations of stochastic dominance. The attention-switching mechanism of DFT is responsible for its ability to predict violations of

Table 10.1: Predictions derived from micro-process model of attention to payoffs

Prospect	Probabilities	Weights	Mean value
Allais problem			
A	0, 1, 0	0, 1, 0	1.00
B	.01, .89, .10	.03, .96, .01	.986
A'	.89, .11, 0	.99, .01, 0	.011
B'	.90, 0, .10	.99, 0, .01	.045
Stochastic dominance problem			
F	.10, .05, .85	.40, .16, .44	62.65
G	.05, .05, .90	.24, .20, .56	60.64
F'	.05, .05, .05, .85	.27, .28, .12, .33	49.85
G'	.05, .05, .05, .85	.27, .28, .12, .33	51.38

independence and stochastic dominance (see Johnson & Busemeyer, 2006). Table 10.1 presents the predictions for both the Allais and the stochastic dominance choice problems from Section 2.2, when the "dwell parameter" was set to $\beta = .70$. The columns show the prospect, the probabilities, the weights, and the mean values (assuming $E[U_i(t)] = u_i = \sum w_{ij} \cdot m_j$ with $m_j = x_j$). As can be seen in this table, both paradoxes are explained using the same attention mechanism and the same parameter value. Intuitively, the tendency to begin by considering low outcomes, coupled with a moderate dwelling probability, results in "overweighting" of the small probabilities associated with the lowest outcomes of the prospects. Note that the β parameter and/or m_j values could be fit to amplify or moderate the effects shown in Table 10.1 However, we avoid this in order to illustrate that a simple and consistent application can produce the paradox. Furthermore, Johnson and Busemeyer (2006) show how the attention process accounts for several other findings that are not reviewed here, using the same assumptions and parameter value.

5.2. Accounting for Preference Reversals

As noted earlier, strategy switching between tasks can explain reversals between choices and prices, but they fail to explain reversals

between buying and selling prices. To illustrate the predictions of the DFT model for reversals between choice and pricing, consider prospects P and D introduced in Section 2.2.3, for which robust preference reversals have been observed. The first result that must be predicted is the risk-averse tendency found with choices (a higher proportion of P choices). To obtain this, Johnson and Busemeyer (2005a) assumed the affective values of the payoffs to be a concave function of the payoffs (specifically, $m_j = x_j^{0.7}$). This produces a higher predicted choice probability (0.68) for prospect P compared with prospect D. To generate price equivalents, the exit rate parameter for indifference was set equal to $r = .02$. This generates both a higher predicted mean price for prospect D ($4.82) compared with prospect P ($3.42), as well as a larger predicted variance in the prices for prospect D ($4.13) compared with prospect P ($.31).

Next, consider the application to prospects F and G described in Section 2.2.3. Using exactly the same parameter values and assumptions as those applied to P and D produces the following results: the mean buying price for prospect F ($52) exceeds that for prospect G ($38), but the mean selling price for prospect G ($64) is higher than that for prospect F ($56). More generally, this sequential comparison process is able to reproduce the observed preference orders for five different measures of preference

Table 10.2: Choice probabilities predicted by decision field theory for similarity, attraction, and compromise effects

Similarity		Attraction		Compromise	
Options	Probability	Options	Probability	Options	Probability
A: (1.0, 3.0)	.39	A: (1.0, 3.0)	.59	A: (1.0, 3.0)	.31
B: (3.0, 1.0)	.31	B: (3.0, 1.0)	.40	B: (3.0, 1.0)	.25
S: (2.99, 1.01)	.30	D: (1.0, 2.5)	.01	C: (2.0, 2.0)	.44

Note: Simulation results based on 10,000 replications.

(see Johnson & Busemeyer, 2005a): choices, price equivalents, minimum selling prices, maximum buying prices, and probability equivalents.

5.3. *Accounting for Context Dependent Preferences*

Can a single theory account for similarity, attraction, and compromise effects, using a common set of assumptions and a single set of parameter values? Recall that simple scalable utility models fail to explain the similarity effect, the EBA model fails to account for the attraction effect, and the LEX model fails to account for the compromise effect. Roe et al. (2001) initially demonstrated that DFT provides a robust and comprehensive account for all three effects. For multi-attribute choice tasks, attention is assumed to drift back and forth between attributes across time (Diederich, 1997). For example, when choosing among consumer products, attention shifts between thinking about quality and price. Although mathematical formulas have been derived for calculating the model predictions for this process (see Diederich, 1997; Roe et al., 2001), it is simpler (albeit slower) to generate predictions from computer simulations, especially when the number of alternatives is large.[4]

Predictions from DFT for an example of all three context effects are presented in Table 10.2. The values of the alternatives on

each attribute are shown in the table (these determine the inputs, m_{ij}, for the network). For all three effects, the same set of parameters were used: the mean attention weight for the two attributes was set equal to .51 and .49 (reflecting slightly greater weight on the first dimension); the threshold bound was set equal to 12; the variance parameter for the valence was set equal to 1; the self-feedback coefficient was set equal to .93; the lateral inhibitory coefficient connection between the two most extremely different options, A and B, was set to zero; and the lateral inhibitory coefficient between similar option pairs was set to $-.07$.

Option B tends to be chosen more frequently in a binary choice (.55 for B for all three conditions), because of the larger weight given to the first attribute. However, as shown in Table 10.2, this preference is reversed by the introduction of a third option in the triadic choice sets. As shown in Table 10.2, the model successfully reproduces all three effects: for the similarity effect, the addition of a new similar competitive option hurt option B; for the attraction effect, the addition of a new similar dominated option helped option A; and for the compromise effect, the addition of the extreme option made the compromise option C most popular.

According to DFT, the attention switching mechanism is crucial for producing the similarity effect, but the lateral inhibitory connections are critical for explaining the compromise and attraction effects. If the attention switching process is eliminated, then the similarity effect disappears, and if the lateral connections are all set to zero,

---

4 The predictions in Table 10.2 were generated from a simulation program available at http://mypage.iu.edu/~jbusemey/lab/sim_mdf.m.

then the attraction and compromise effects disappear. This property of the theory entails an interesting prediction about the effects of time pressure on preferences. The contrast effects produced by lateral inhibition require time to build up, which implies that the attraction and compromise effects should become larger under prolonged deliberation (see Roe et al., 2001). Alternatively, if context effects are produced by switching from a weighted average rule under binary choice to a quick heuristic strategy for the triadic choice, then these effects should get larger under time pressure. Empirical tests show that prolonging the decision process indeed increases the effects (Simonson, 1989) and time pressure decreases the effects (Dhar, Nowlis, & Sherman, 2000).

6. Discussion

This chapter began with a challenge to computational models: What can they contribute that goes beyond the explanatory power of the more popular approaches to decision making based on algebraic utility or heuristic rules? Following, a synopsis is provided that is based on the detailed discussions presented in the earlier sections. The issue of complexity of computational models is also addressed, followed by a discussion of some connections to work on computational models in other domains of judgment.

6.1. *Comparison Among Models*

Modern rank dependent utility theories, such as cumulative prospect theory, are able to explain some old paradoxes of risky decision making, such as the Allais paradox. But they fail to explain new paradoxes of risky decision making, such as stochastic dominance violations. Furthermore, they cannot explain preference reversals between choice and prices without postulating entirely new utility functions for each measure. Finally, they are unable to account for context effects on choice including similarity, attraction, and compromise effects.

Simple heuristic rule-based models allow for changes in strategy from compensatory rules (e.g., WADD or EU) to noncompensatory rules (e.g., EBA and LEX). These switches occur under time pressure or with increases in choice set size and may depend on the response measure. Simple heuristic rules can explain the Allais paradox with risky decisions, but not violations of stochastic dominance. Strategy switching between response measures can account for preference reversals between choice and prices, but not between buying and selling prices. Finally, simple heuristic rules can account for similarity effects on choice, but they are unable to account for attraction and compromise effects. In short, despite the increased flexibility provided by allowing mixtures of strategies, these models have not yet proven capable of providing a coherent explanation for many of the well-established findings.

Several computational models were presented, but two in particular stand out as most promising for meeting the challenge of this chapter. Both DFT and the leaky accumulator model provide coherent explanations for similarity, attraction, and compromise effects on choice. Furthermore, both of these models can predict how time pressure moderates these effects. In fact, the two models are based on very similar principles for making a choice, that is, a race between accumulators of preference to a threshold. The models differ in terms of their details concerning lateral inhibition and nonlinear accumulation. However, DFT has been applied more broadly than the leaky accumulator; the former also accounts for preference reversal among different measures of preference (choice vs. prices and buying prices vs. selling prices) as well as the paradoxes of risky decision making (Allais and stochastic dominance paradoxes). In conclusion, these two "accumulation to threshold" models provide explanatory power that goes beyond the algebraic utility models and the simple heuristic models.

Critics of computational models may claim that the power of these models comes at a cost of increased complexity. However, it is important to note that computational models may have the same number of (or even fewer) free parameters than the algebraic utility models applied to the same domain (see Section 3.4; cf. Johnson & Busemeyer, 2005a). By focusing on underlying cognitive processes, computational models can provide parsimonious explanations for broad collections of puzzling behavioral phenomena. In addition, computational models make precise predictions not possible with other approaches. Unlike typical utility models, computational models are dynamic and thus offer deliberation time predictions. Many of these models – including DFT, the focus of the current chapter – also account for variability in human behavior, in contrast to deterministic approaches, such as RDU theory and simple heuristic models.

6.2. Connections to Computational Modeling in Judgment

There are now a variety of computational models relevant to judgment and decision making research. Connectionist models of social reasoning are reviewed in Chapter 18 in this volume, and Stasser (2000) has considered computational models for information sharing in group decision making. Instance-based memory models of Bayesian inference (Dougherty, Gettys, & Ogden, 1999) and decision making (Stewart, Chater, & Brown, 2006) have been developed. Stochastic models of confidence judgments have been proposed (Brenner, Griffin, & Koehler, 2005; Erev, Wallsten & Budescu, 1994; Wallsten & Barton, 1982; Wallsten & Gonzalez-Vallejo, 1994). Several computational models of strategy learning have appeared (Busemeyer & Myung, 1992; Johnson & Busemeyer, 2005b; Rieskamp & Otto, 2006). This chapter is directed at decision making rather than reasoning or inference (but see Chapter 11 in this volume); it is focused on performance rather than memory or learning models; and it concerns individual as opposed to group decision processes.

7. Conclusion

This chapter discussed how a particular computational model could account for a wide variety of empirical trends that have resisted a coherent explanation by models cast in the dominant framework. This accomplishment was made possible by considering an alternative level of analysis, rather than attempting to further modify the utility framework. In addition, computational models have distinct advantages – both theoretical and practical – over contemporary approaches toward the study of decision making. Hopefully, more and more researchers will appreciate these advantages and contribute to an expanding and interesting literature involving computational models.

References

Allais, M. (1953). Le comportement de l'homme rationnel devant le riske: Critique des postulats et axiomes de l'ecole Americaine. *Econometrica, 21,* 503–546.

Allais, M. (1979). The so-called Allais paradox and rational decisions under uncertainty. In O. Hagen & M. Allais (Eds.), *Expected utility hypotheses and the Allais paradox* (pp. 437–681). Dordrecht: Reidel.

Ashby, F. G. (2000). A stochastic version of general recognition theory. *Journal of Mathematical Psychology, 44,* 310–329.

Belavkin, R. V. (2006). Towards a theory of decision-making without paradoxes. In D. Fum, F. D. Missier, & A. Stocco (Eds.), *Proceedings of the seventh international conference on Cognitive Modeling* (pp. 38–43). Trieste, Italy: Edizioni: Goliardiche.

Bell, D. E., Raiffa, H., & Tversky, A. (1988). *Decision making: Descriptive, normative, and prescriptive interactions.* Cambridge, UK: Cambridge University Press.

Birnbaum, M. H. (2004). Causes of Allais common consequence paradoxes: An experimental dissection. *Journal of Mathematical Psychology, 48*(2), 87–106.

Birnbaum, M. H., & Navarrete, J. B. (1998). Testing descriptive utility theories: Violations of stochastic dominance and cumulative independence. *Journal of Risk and Uncertainty, 17,* 49–78.

Birnbaum, M. H., & Zimmermann, J. M. (1998). Buying and selling prices of investments: Configural weight model of interactions predicts violations of joint independence. *Organizational Behavior & Human Decision Processes, 74*(2), 145–187.

Bostic, R., Herrnstein, R. J., & Luce, R. D. (1990). The effect on the preference-reversal phenomenon of using choice indifference. *Journal of Economic Behavior and Organization, 13*, 193–212.

Brandstätter, E., Gigerenzer, G., & Hertwig, R. (2006). The priority heuristic: Making choices without trade-offs. *Psychological Review, 113*, 409–432.

Brenner, L., Griffin, D., & Koehler, D. J. (2005). Modeling patterns of probability calibration with random support theory: Diagnosing case-based judgment. *Organizational Behavior and Human Decision Processes, 97*(1), 64–81.

Busemeyer, J. R., & Diederich, A. (2002). Survey of decision field theory. *Mathematical Social Sciences, 43*, 345–370.

Busemeyer, J. R., & Myung, I. J. (1992). An adaptive approach to human decision making: Learning theory, decision theory, and human performance. *Journal of Experimental Psychology:General, 121*, 177–194.

Busemeyer, J. R., & Townsend, J. T. (1992). Fundamental derivations for decision field theory. *Mathematical Social Sciences, 23*, 255–282.

Busemeyer, J. R., & Townsend, J. T. (1993). Decision field theory: A dynamic-cognitive approach to decision making in an uncertain environment. *Psychological Review, 100*, 432–459.

Dhar, R., Nowlis, S. M., & Sherman, S. J. (2000). Trying hard or hardly trying: An analysis of context effects in choice. *Journal of Consumer Psychology, 9*, 189–200.

Diederich, A. (1997). Dynamic stochastic models for decision making under time constraints. *Journal of Mathematical Psychology, 41*, 260–274.

Diederich, A. (2003). MDFT account of decision making under time pressure. *Psychonomic Bulletin and Review, 10*(1), 157–166.

Diederich, A., & Busemeyer, J. R. (2003). Simple matrix methods for analyzing diffusion models of choice probability, choice response time, and simple response time. *Journal of Mathematical Psychology, 47*, 304–322.

Dougherty, M. R. P., Gettys, C. F., & Ogden, E. E. (1999). MINERVA-DM: A memory process model for judgments of likelihood. *Psychological Review, 106*, 108–209.

Edwards, W. (1962). Subjective probabilities inferred from decisions. *Psychological Review, 69*, 109–135.

Ellsberg, D. (1961). Risk, ambiguity, and the Savage axioms. *Quarterly Journal of Economics, 75*, 643–669.

Erev, I., Wallsten, T. S., & Budescu, D. V. (1994). Simultaneous over- and underconfidence: The role of error in judgment processes. *Psychological Review, 101*(3), 519–527.

Gigerenzer, G., Todd, P.M., & the ABC Research Group. (1999). *Simple heuristics that make us smart.* New York: Oxford University Press.

Grether, D. M., & Plott, C. R. (1979). Economic theory of choice and the preference reversal phenomenon. *American Economic Review, 69*, 623–638.

Grossberg, S., & Gutowski, W. E. (1987). Neural dynamics of decision making under risk: Affective balance and cognitive-emotional interactions. *Psychological Review, 94*, 300–318.

Guo, F. Y., & Holyoak, K. J. (2002). Understanding similarity in choice behavior: A connectionist model. In W. Gray & C. Schunn (Eds.), *Proceedings of the twenty-fourth annual conference of the Cognitive Science Society* (pp. 393–398). Hillsdale, NJ: Lawrence Erlbaum.

Holyoak, K. J., & Simon, D. (1999). Bidirectional reasoning in decision making by constraint satisfaction. *Journal of Experimental Psychology: General, 128*, 3–31.

Huber, J., Payne, J. W., & Puto, C. (1982). Adding asymmetrically dominated alternatives: Violations of regularity and the similarity hypothesis. *Journal of Consumer Research, 9*, 90–98.

Huber, J., & Puto, C. (1983). Market boundaries and product choice: Illustrating attraction and substitution effects. *Journal of Consumer Research, 10*(1), 31–44.

Johnson, J. G., & Busemeyer, J. R. (2005a). A dynamic, stochastic, computational model of preference reversal phenomena. *Psychological Review, 112*(4), 841–861.

Johnson, J. G., & Busemeyer, J. R. (2005b). Rule-based Decision Field Theory: A dynamic computational model of transitions among decision-making strategies. In T. Betsch, & S. Haberstroh, (Eds.), *The routines of decision making* (pp. 3–20). Mahwah, NJ: Lawrence Erlbaum.

Johnson, J. G., & Busemeyer, J. R. (2006). Trading "as if" for "as is" models of cognition: A computational model of the attention processes used to generate decision weights in risky choice. *Cognitive Psychology*. Manuscript submitted for publication.

Kahneman, D., & Tversky, A. (1979). Prospect theory. *Econometrica, 47*, 263–292.

Laming, D. R. (1968). *Information theory of choice reaction times*. New York: Academic Press.

Leland, H. E. (1998). Agency costs, risk management, and capital structure. *Journal of Finance, 53*, 1213–1243.

Lichtenstein, S., & Slovic, P. (1971). Reversals of preference between bids and choices in gambling decisions. *Journal of Experimental Psychology, 89*, 46–55.

Lindman, H. R. (1971). Inconsistent preferences among gambles. *Journal of Experimental Psychology, 89*, 390–397.

Link, S. W., & Heath, R. A. (1975). A sequential theory of psychological discrimination. *Psychometrika, 40*, 77–105.

Loomes, G., Starmer, C., & Sugden, R. (1992). Are preferences monotonic? Testing some predictions of regret theory. *Economica, 59*(233), 17–33.

Lopes, L. L., & Oden, G. C. (1999). The role of aspiration level in risky choice: A comparison of cumulative prospect theory and SP/A Theory. *Journal of Mathematical Psychology, 43*, 286–313.

Luce, R. D. (2000). *Utility of gains and losses*. NJ: Lawrence Erlbaum.

Mellers, B. A., Schwartz, A., & Cooke, A. D. J. (1998). Judgment and decision making. *Annual Review of Psychology, 49*, 447–477.

Nosofsky, R. M., & Palmeri, T. J. (1997). An exemplar-based random walk model of speeded classification. *Psychological Review, 104*, 226–300.

Payne, J. W., Bettman, J. R., & Johnson, E. J. (1992). Behavioral decision research: A constructive processing perspective. *Annual Review of Psychology, 43*, 87–131.

Payne, J. W., Bettman, J. R., & Johnson, E. J. (1993). *The adaptive decision maker*. New York: Cambridge University Press.

Quiggin, J. (1982). A theory of anticipated utility. *Journal of Economic Behavior and Organizations, 3*, 323–343.

Ratcliff, R. (1978). A theory of memory retrieval. *Psychological Review, 85*, 59–108.

Rieskamp, J., Busemeyer, J. R., & Mellers, B. A. (2006). Extending the bounds of rationality: A review of research on preferential choice. *Journal of Economic Literature. 44* 631–636.

Rieskamp, J., & Otto, P. E. (2006). SSL: A theory of how people learn to select strategies. *Journal of Experimental Psychology: General, 135*, 207–236.

Roe, R. M., Busemeyer, J. R., & Townsend, J. T. (2001). Multi-alternative decision field theory: A dynamic connectionist model of decision-making. *Psychological Review, 108*, 370–392.

Savage, L. J. (1954) *The foundations of statistics*. New York: Wiley.

Simon, D., Krawczyk, D. C., & Holyoak, K. J. (2004). Construction of preferences by constraint satisfaction. *Psychological Science, 15*, 331–336.

Simonson, I. (1989). Choice based on reasons: The case of attraction and compromise effects. *Journal of Consumer Research, 16*, 158–174.

Simonson, I., & Tversky, A. (1992). Choice in context: Tradeoff contrast and extremeness aversion. *Journal of Marketing Research, 29*(3), 281–295.

Slovic, P. (1995). The construction of preference. *American Psychologist, 50*(5), 364–371.

Slovic, P., & Lichtenstein, S. (1983). Preference reversals: A broader perspective. *American Economic Review, 73*, 596–605.

Smith, P. L. (1995). Psychophysically principled models of visual simple reaction time. *Psychological Review, 102*(3), 567–593.

Starmer, C. (2000). Developments in non-expected utility theory: The hunt for a descriptive theory of choice under risk. *Journal of Economic Literature, 38*, 332–382.

Stasser, G. (2000). Information distribution, participation, and group decision: Explorations with the DISCUSS and SPEAK models. In *Computational modeling of behavior in organizations: The third scientific discipline* (pp. 135–161). Washington, DC: American Psychological Association.

Stewart, N., Chater, N., & Brown, G. D. A. (2006). Decision by sampling. *Cognitive Psychology*.

Thagard, P., & Millgram, E. (1995). Inference to the best plan: A coherence theory of decision. In A. Ram & D. B. Leake (Eds.), *Goal-driven learning* (pp. 439–454). Cambridge, MA: MIT Press.

Tversky, A. (1972a). Elimination by aspects: A theory of choice. *Psychological Review, 79,* 281–299.

Tversky, A., & Kahneman, D. (1991). Loss aversion in riskless choice: A reference dependent model. *Quarterly Journal of Economics, 106,* 1039–1061.

Tversky, A.,& Kahneman, D. (1992). Advances in prospect theory: Commulative representation of uncertainty. *Journal of Risk and Uncertainty, 5,* 297–323.

Tversky, A., & Sattath, S. (1979). Preference trees. *Psychological Review, 86,* 542– 573.

Tversky, A., Sattath, S., & Slovic, P. (1988). Contingent weighting in judgment and choice. *Psychological Review, 95,* 371–384.

Usher, M., & McClelland, J. L. (2001). The time course of perceptual choice: The leaky, competing accumulator model. *Psychological Review, 102*(3), 550–592.

Usher, M., & McClelland, J. L. (2004). Loss aversion and inhibition in dynamic models of multi-alternative choice. *Psychological Review, 111,* 757–769.

von Neumann, J., & Morgenstern, O. (1947). *Theory of games and economic behavior.* Princeton, NJ: Princeton University Press.

Wallsten, T. S., & Barton, C. (1982). Processing probabilistic multidimensional information for decisions. *Journal of Experimental Psychology: Learning, Memory, and Cognition, 8,* 361–384.

Wallsten, T. S., & Gonzalez-Vallejo, C. (1994). Statement verification: A stochastic model of judgment and response. *Psychological Review, 101,* 490–504.

CHAPTER 11

Models of Inductive Reasoning

Evan Heit

1. Introduction

How do you make a prediction about the unpredictable? Inductive reasoning is about drawing conclusions that are not certain or logically valid, but still likely. Suppose you are buying a new CD for your friend. It is impossible to know with certainty what she will like, and it does not seem that the rules of logic will tell you which CD to buy. There is no correct answer. Nonetheless, you can make an informed guess, and indeed she will probably like the CD that you buy. The more you know about her taste in music and which categories of music she likes and does not like, the more likely it is that your prediction will be correct. Our everyday experiences are filled with predictions of this nature – we use inductive reasoning to make likely but not certain predictions about how people will act and about things we have not seen. For example, when we open a door to a room, we predict that the room will have a floor and ceiling. In spite of the uncertainty, we manage to be fairly successful in our predic-

tions – we can buy gifts that our friends will enjoy and avoid walking into rooms without floors.

When it comes to making predictions about the unpredictable, computational models are in a similar position to people. Because the judgments being modeled are themselves uncertain, it is unlikely that models of inductive reasoning will be perfectly correct. Any computational model of inductive reasoning could probably be improved by taking account of more knowledge or more principles of prediction. Nonetheless, current models of inductive reasoning already do a fairly good job of capturing patterns and regularities in how people make likely predictions.

This chapter first reviews some of the empirical work on inductive reasoning, summarizing regularities that people show. The second part of the chapter describes computational models of inductive reasoning, particularly from the psychology literature. The concluding section addresses more general issues in modeling inductive reasoning and other cognitive activities.

2. Human Inductive Reasoning: The Data

Inductive reasoning is potentially an extremely large topic, especially because it is often defined as reasoning about problems that do not involve perfectly certain conclusions (Heit, 2007). The class of problems that have perfectly certain conclusions is much more circumscribed, for example, it could be defined in terms of a set of logical rules about what conclusions must follow from a given set of premises. In comparison, the set of problems for which inductive reasoning applies is potentially "everything else," and that is indeed a large and varied set. It is instructive to examine several textbooks on cognitive psychology. They will each no doubt have a section on inductive reasoning, but one is likely to find that different textbooks cover different topics under this heading. These topics will include analogical reasoning (Gentner, Holyoak, & Kokinov, 2001; for some connections to inductive reasoning, see Lassaline, 1996; Thagard, 2007; Wu & Gentner, 1998), categorization (see Chapter 9 in this volume), judgment and decision making (see Chapter 10 in this volume), and causal reasoning (Sloman, 2005). Likewise, inductive reasoning has been an important issue in artificial intelligence and computer science (e.g., Collins & Michalski, 1989; Sun, 1995; Sun & Zhang, 2006). Some of these topics are referred to indirectly over the course of this chapter; however, this chapter necessarily has a focus. It addresses one important aspect of inductive reasoning, namely, psychological research on category-based induction, or how people use categories to make likely inferences.

Categories and inductive reasoning go hand in hand. For example, Anderson (1991) suggested that the most important function of categories is not that they allow us to categorize things, but rather that they allow us to draw inferences. Returning to the example of buying your friend a CD, let us say that you know that your friend likes some 1960s music and hates Celine Dion. In predicting which CDs she will like, it seems safer to choose something from within the 1960s category than from within the Celine Dion category. Category-based induction has been studied extensively by psychologists, although usually not with musical categories but with more structured categories that are part of people's basic knowledge, such as different kinds of animals.

In one of the earliest studies of category-based induction, Rips (1975) examined how people project properties of one category of animal to another. Subjects were told to imagine that on an island, all members of a species of mammals catch a particular disease; then they were asked what proportion of other species will catch the disease. For example, knowing that all horses have the disease, what proportion of cows will have the disease? What proportion of dogs? Mice?

This was a very useful task, but before reviewing results in inductive reasoning, another important step in studying inductive reasoning will be described. A limitation of the Rips (1975) task was that it was best suited for drawing inferences from one category to another, whereas inductive reasoning usually involves more pieces of information. Osherson et al. (1990) made an influential contribution to the study of inductive reasoning by having subjects evaluate written inductive arguments in the format usually used for logic problems.

```
All horses have property X.   (1)
All cows have property X.
All mice have property X.
All lions have property X.
-------------------------
All mammals have property X.
```

In argument (1), the premise statements above the line are taken to be true, and the task is to judge the degree to which the conclusion statement, below the line, follows from the premises. Essentially this is a judgment of argument strength. This task is very flexible in the sense that any number of premises can be used, and various properties could be swapped for property X (or the uninformative property X could be used).

Osherson et al. reported eleven main phenomena or regularities regarding how people perform inductive reasoning. A later review paper by Heit (2000) split things up differently, considering some newer data, and reported eight main phenomena in inductive reasoning. In the next sections of this chapter, some of these phenomena will be described, setting the stage for the presentation of computational models of inductive reasoning. Note that results from adults only will be discussed here. There is also a rich literature on inductive reasoning by children that could be used to constrain modeling; for reviews, see Heit (2000; Heit, Hahn, & Feeney, 2005; Heit & Hayes, 2005), as well as Hayes (2007).

2.1. *Similarity Effects*

The idea that similarity should guide inductive reasoning has a distinguished history. Mill (1874, Book III, Chapter III, Section I) argued that "what happens once, will, under a sufficient degree of similarity of circumstances, happen again." Going back to the example of buying a CD for your friend, if you know that she likes 1960s albums by the Rolling Stones and does not like Celine Dion, the most promising strategy is no doubt to buy her a CD by a similar 1960s band rather than by someone else who sings like Celine Dion. These similarity effects are backed up by a lot of laboratory evidence – similarity effects are the most robust result in inductive reasoning. For example, Rips (1975) found a strong correlation between strength of inferences and measures based on similarity judgments. If all horses had the disease, then most cows would have the disease, but fewer dogs and yet fewer mice. Likewise, Osherson et al. (2000) found that given a choice such as between argument (2) and argument (3), about 95% of people chose argument (2) because of the greater similarity of sparrows to robins and bluejays versus geese to robins and bluejays.

```
Robins use serotonin as a neurotransmitter.(2)
Bluejays use serotonin as a neurotransmitter.
---------------------------------------------
Sparrows use serotonin as a neurotransmitter.
```

```
Robins use serotonin as a neurotransmitter.(3)
Bluejays use serotonin as a neurotransmitter.
---------------------------------------------
Geese use serotonin as a neurotransmitter.
```

Despite this strong evidence, there are some exceptions to similarity effects and some complications, as will soon be described. Yet, clearly any computational model of induction will have to address similarity effects (and ideally the exceptions and complications, too).

2.2. *Typicality Effects*

Another very robust finding in inductive reasoning is the typicality effect. This phenomenon is closely tied to categorization research, in particular, the idea that not all category members are equal, but instead some are more prototypical than others (e.g., Rosch & Mervis, 1975). Returning to buying a CD for your friend, if you know that she likes albums by the Rolling Stones, a prototypical 1960s guitar-based rock band, there would seem to be a lot of similar 1960s bands to choose from. On the other hand, if you know that she likes albums by the Moody Blues, a much less typical 1960s band that recorded with a symphony orchestra, it would seem harder to choose another 1960s band that she would like – she might only like rock bands that use classical music.

Like similarity effects, typicality effects have been well documented in laboratory research. For example, Rips (1975) found that when a more typical mammal, such as horses, had the disease, people generally drew stronger inferences to other mammals, compared with a situation in which a less typical mammal, such as mice, had the disease. There was an additional effect of typicality beyond what might be predicted based only on similarity. Intuitively, if a typical mammal, such as horses, have the disease, then perhaps all mammals have it, that is, the property applies to the superordinate category. On the other hand, if mice have the disease, it might be restricted to a subcategory of mammals, such as rodents.

Indeed, Osherson et al. (1990) addressed this intuition directly. They compared arguments like (4) and (5). Here, knowing a fact about robins seems to license a stronger inference about all birds compared with knowing a fact about penguins. More than 90% of people chose argument (4).

```
Robins have a higher potassium concentration
in their blood than humans.   (4)
-----------------------------------------------
All birds have a higher potassium concentration
in their blood than humans.
```

```
Penguins have a higher potassium concentration
in their blood than humans.   (5)
-----------------------------------------------
All birds have a higher potassium concentration
in their blood than humans.
```

In sum, the typicality effect is another robust phenomenon that must be addressed by models of inductive reasoning.

2.3. *Diversity Effects*

The diversity effect is somewhat more elusive than similarity or typicality, but it, too, has a distinguished history (Heit et al., 2005). Bacon (1620) argued that before drawing inferences about a category, such as things possessing heat, diverse instances of this category should be examined. In making this point, he listed twenty-eight different kinds of heat and hot things, including the rays of the sun, steam, burning hay, and the insides of animals. The diversity effect is also well illustrated in the example of buying CDs. If your friend actually likes both the Rolling Stones and Celine Dion, then you might infer that she has broad tastes in music, and it would be safe to buy her one of many styles of music. On the other hand, if you know she likes the Rolling Stones and The Who, another guitar-based 1960s band, you might infer that her musical tastes are fairly narrow after all, and you should not stray too far from similar bands.

Studying the diversity effect in laboratory experiments requires giving people at least two pieces of information and varying the diversity of these two items. In the study by Rips (1975), subjects were only given one fact at a time, so diversity effects were not addressed. It was the Osherson et al. (1990) study that first focused on diversity effects in inductive reasoning by adults, using arguments such as the following:

```
Hippos have a higher sodium concentration in
their blood than humans.   (6)
Hamsters have a higher sodium concentration in
their blood than humans.
-----------------------------------------------
All mammals have a higher sodium concentration
in their blood than humans.
```

```
Hippos have a higher sodium concentration in
their blood than humans.   (7)
Rhinos have a higher sodium concentration in
their blood than humans.
-----------------------------------------------
All mammals have a higher sodium concentration
in their blood than humans.
```

About 75% of people chose argument (6), with the more diverse set of category members, over argument (7), with the less diverse set. In essence, diverse evidence is stronger than nondiverse evidence. Osherson et al.'s own explanation for this phenomenon was in terms of coverage: Hippos and hamsters cover, or span, the category of mammals better than do hippos and rhinos. Hence, a property of hippos and hamsters is more likely to generalize to other mammals.

Although diversity effects have been found in other laboratory experiments, there are more exceptions compared with similarity and typicality effects (see Heit, 2000, and Heit et al., 2005, for reviews). Still, because of the very nature of inductive reasoning, namely, that it is probabilistic, there are likely to be exceptions to any regularity that is found. Hence, diversity is another effect that computational models will need to address.

2.4. *Other Phenomena, Including Background Knowledge Effects*

Although similarity, typicality, and diversity are three of the most important phenomena, there are several others summarized by Osherson et al. (1990) and Heit (2000), and reported by other researchers. Some of these are fairly straightforward, encompassing other points about the structure of inductive arguments. For example, Osherson et al. reported that more evidence leads to stronger generalizations than less evidence (see also Nisbett et al., 1983). Looking back at argument (1), this argument with four premises seems fairly strong, and it would be stronger than another argument with just a single premise, for example, that only horses have property X.

There is another class of phenomena that is much messier but much more interesting, both in its own right and as challenges for computational models. These phenomena involve the use of more background knowledge, and as such, are closely linked to the nature of inductive reasoning. That is, because inductive reasoning is uncertain by nature, there is always room for improvement by drawing on some other source of knowledge. (This makes a sharp contrast with deductive reasoning, or logical reasoning, where the conclusion is certain and using background knowledge is usually considered an error.) Returning to the example of buying a CD that your friend will like, the more information that you can accumulate about her musical tastes and listening habits, the more successful you will be in choosing a CD for her. In fact, with enough knowledge about her habits, you might be able to make detailed and sophisticated predictions, such as music to play in the car versus while at home studying.

Heit and Rubinstein (1994) reported one such phenomenon based on background knowledge, showing a kind of exception to the similarity effect. Suppose there are two inductive arguments as follows:

```
Bears have property X.          (8)
-----------------------------------
Whales have property X.

Tuna have property X.           (9)
-----------------------------------
Whales have property X.
```

Which argument is stronger, (8) or (9)? Heit and Rubinstein showed that the answer depends on X. If property X is filled in with an anatomical property, such as having a liver with two chambers, then (8) is considered stronger than (9) by virtue of other shared anatomical properties of the two mammals, bears and whales. On the other hand, if property X is filled in with a behavioral property, such as traveling shorter distances in extreme heat, then (9) is considered stronger than (8). Here, shared behavioral properties are considered, and the two swimmers, tuna and whales, have more in common on this basis. Heit and Rubinstein concluded that the basic similarity effect in inductive reasoning is not a singular phenomenon but instead is mediated by background knowledge.

There have been many other demonstrations of background knowledge effects in inductive reasoning (Lopez et al., 1997; Medin et al., 2003; Proffitt, Coley, & Medin, 2000; Rehder, 2006; Ross & Murphy, 1999; Shafto & Coley, 2003; Sloman, 1994). For example, Medin et al. (2003) reported an exception to the diversity effect, known as the nondiversity by property reinforcement effect. The idea behind nondiversity by property reinforcement is that two diverse categories may nonetheless have some characteristic in common and tend to generalize only to other categories with this same characteristic. This phenomenon is illustrated by the following arguments.

```
Polar bears have property X.     (10)
Antelopes have property X.
-----------------------------------
All animals have property X.

Polar bears have property X.     (11)
Penguins have property X.
-----------------------------------
All animals have property X.
```

When given a choice between polar bears and antelopes versus polar bears and penguins, people judged the two animals from the same biological class, polar bears and antelopes, to be more similar than the two animals from different biological classes, polar bears and penguins. However, when asked to assess the inductive strength of each argument, argument (11) was judged to be less convincing than argument (10). That is, argument (10) had less diverse evidence, yet it was the stronger argument. Intuitively, although polar bears and penguins are from different biological classes, people use their knowledge that both live in a cold climate and infer that property X does not apply to all animals but only to animals living in cold climates (see Heit & Feeney, 2005, for further discussion).

The more general point is that when people evaluate inductive arguments, they potentially draw on a variety of resources. When people use background knowledge, it is illuminating to think of what people are doing as causal reasoning, that is, they are reasoning about relations between causes and effects (Rehder, 2006). People are reasoning about what causes whales to move more slowly in extreme heat, what causes two cold-weather animals to have other properties in common, and so on. One consideration to keep in mind as computational models are presented is whether they have any facility for addressing not only similarity, typicality, and diversity effects, but also background knowledge effects and indeed whether they show any capacity for causal reasoning.

3. Human Inductive Reasoning: The Computational Models

Having reviewed some of the important empirical phenomena, it is time to turn to models of inductive reasoning. A representative sample will be given rather than complete details on all models. First, two earlier models by Osherson et al. (1990) and Sloman (1993) will be described. These models do an excellent job of addressing many structural phenomena in inductive reasoning, but do not address background knowledge effects sufficiently. Next, an alternative kind of model based on Bayesian hypothesis testing is presented in some detail (Heit, 1998). Bayesian models have the potential to address some background knowledge ef-

fects, and further applications by Tenenbaum and colleagues (Kemp & Tenenbaum, 2003; Tenenbaum & Griffiths, 2001; Tenenbaum, Kemp, & Shafto, 2007) are described. Other modeling work in the psychology literature, not described here, can be found in papers by Rips (1975), Smith, Shafir, and Osherson (1993), McDonald, Samuels, and Rispoli (1996), Sloutsky and Fisher (2004), Heit and Hayes (2005), and Blok, Osherson, and Medin (2007). Likewise, some of the empirical regularities documented and modeled by psychologists were anticipated in a seminal paper in artificial intelligence by Collins and Michalski (1989).

3.1. *Osherson et al. (1990)*

The most influential computational model of inductive reasoning was proposed by Osherson et al. (1990). This model has two main components. The first component assesses the similarity between the premise categories and the conclusion category. In the most straightforward application of the model, this information is simply taken from people's similarity judgments for various pairs of categories. The model predicts that the basic similarity effect that is pervasive in inductive reasoning. The second component measures how well the premise categories cover the superordinate category that includes all the categories mentioned in an argument. For single-premise arguments, coverage more or less reduces to typicality, but for multiple-premise arguments, coverage gives something closer to a measure of diversity. Coverage is most easily explained with examples.

```
Mice have property X.            (12)
---------------------------------
All mammals have property X.


Horses have property X.          (13)
---------------------------------
All mammals have property X.


Hippos have property X.          (14)
Rhinos have property X.
---------------------------------
All mammals have property X.
```

```
Hippos have property X.          (15)
Hamsters have property X.
----------------------------------
All mammals have property X.
```

For arguments (12) and (13), the lowest-level superordinate that includes all the categories is *mammal.* Coverage is assessed in terms of the average similarity of the premise category to members of the superordinate. To the extent that horses are more typical mammals than are mice and therefore more similar to other kinds of mammals, argument (13) will have greater coverage than argument (12). This is how the model addresses typicality effects.

The remaining arguments have multiple premises. When assessing similarity between members of the superordinate category and the multiple premises, only the maximum similarity for any one premise category is considered. So for argument (14), very large mammals tend to be similar to both hippos and rhinos, and smalls mammals tend not to be similar to hippos and rhinos. So including rhino as a premise category does not add much information beyond just having hippo as a premise category alone. In contrast, for argument (15), some mammals are similar to hippos and other mammals are similar to hamsters. Therefore, the hamster premise adds information, and the coverage for argument (15) is greater than for argument (14). Hence, the Osherson et al. (1990) model addresses diversity effects to the extent that greater coverage is correlated with greater diversity.

The Osherson et al. (1990) model can be written out more formally, as shown in Equation (11.1)

$$Strength = \alpha SIM(P_1, \ldots P_n; C) + (1 - \alpha)$$
$$\times SIM(P_1, \ldots P_n; [P_1, \ldots P_n, C]).$$
$$(11.1)$$

Here, α refers to the relative influence of the similarity component (ranging from 0 to 1) and $(1 - \alpha)$ is the influence of the coverage component. This equation applies when there are n premise categories P

and one conclusion category C. When the premise and conclusion categories are all at the same taxonomic level (e.g., robins, bluejays; sparrows), then SIM returns the maximum of the pairwise similarities between each P_i and C. When the conclusion category is at a higher taxonomic level than the premise categories (e.g., robins, bluejays; birds), then SIM is applied recursively to known c that are members of C and averaged over these c. For example, SIM(robins, bluejays; birds) = AVERAGE(SIM(robins, bluejays; sparrows), SIM(robins, bluejays; penguins), SIM(robins, bluejays; chickens), SIM(robins, bluejays; pigeons), ...). Finally, the bracket function [] returns the lowest-level superordinate covering all of the included categories, for example, [robins, bluejays, sparrows]=birds; [robins, bluejays, birds]=birds; [robins, bluejays, dogs]=animals.

Generally speaking, the Osherson et al. (1990) model addressed a wide variety of structural phenomena in inductive reasoning and is particularly impressive in how it puts together information from multiple premises, because of the powerful combination of similarity and coverage components. Although the model does incorporate some information about categories and similarity, it does not address background knowledge effects, such as the differential use of similarity and properties in Heit and Rubinstein (1994), exceptions to diversity in Medin et al. (2003), or, more generally, any use of causal knowledge or causal reasoning.

3.2. *Sloman (1993)*

The model by Sloman (1993) is particularly interesting because it asks the question of whether the coverage component in the Osherson et al. (1990) model is really necessary. Sloman's model was implemented as a connectionist network, and it can account for many of the same phenomena as the Osherson et al. model. (For comparison, see an alternate connectionist model in the artificial intelligence literature in Sun, 1995.) The way Sloman's model works is that premises of an argument are encoded by training the connectionist network to learn associations between input nodes representing the features of the premise categories and an output node for the property to be considered, using the classic delta rule (e.g., Sutton & Barto, 1981). For example, for the model to learn that apples have property X, it would learn to associate a vector of features such as {is round, is red, is edible, . . .} with an output node representing property X. Then the model is tested by presenting the features of the conclusion category and measuring the activation of the same output node. For example, to evaluate the strength of the conclusion that oranges have property X, the model would use a somewhat different input vector of features {is round, is orange, is edible, . . . } and measure the degree of activation for the output unit corresponding to property X.

The model accounts for similarity effects because training and testing on similar input vectors will lead to strong outputs during testing. Going back to arguments (2) and (3), the model would first be trained to associate input representations for robins and bluejays with an output node representing the property in the conclusion. Because the representation for sparrows would have a lot of overlap with representations of robins and bluejays, presenting sparrow to the network would also activate the output node strongly. In comparison, the representation of geese would have much less overlap with representations for robins and bluejays. Hence, presenting geese to the network would only weakly activate the output node.

The activation function is as follows:

$$a(C \mid P_i, \ldots, P_n) = \frac{W(P_i, \ldots, P_n) \bullet C}{|C|^2}.$$

(11.2)

This function refers to the output activation given a set of n premise categories P and a conclusion category C. W is a vector corresponding to the already-trained weights in the network after the premise categories have been learned. C is a vector corresponding to the featural representation of the conclusion category. The dot product between W and C is computed, yielding a value corresponding to the similarity between the premise categories and the conclusion category. For example, donkey and mule would have many features in common, and there would be a fairly high, positive dot product between the two vectors. On the other hand, donkey and ostrich would have fewer features in common and a lower dot product, perhaps close to zero. Finally, the activation is scaled in the denominator, by the squared length of the vector C, essentially a measure of the number of known features of C. If C corresponds to a well-known category, such as dogs, it will be relatively difficult to draw a new conclusion. If C corresponds to a poorly known category, such as ocelots, it will be easier to draw new conclusions about the category.

The model accounts for diversity effects because training on a diverse set of categories will tend to strengthen a greater number of connections in W than training on a narrow range of categories. In terms of arguments (6) and (7), training the network that both hippos and hamsters have a certain property would activate a broad range of features that apply to various mammals, leading to a strong conclusion that all mammals have that property. That is, hippos and hamsters would activate different features and different connections. In comparison, training the network that hippos and rhinos have a property would only activate a narrow range of features and connections. Although this model does have a notion of breadth of features, there is no distinct component for assessing coverage of a superordinate category, as in the Osherson et al. (1990) model, and indeed Sloman's (1993) model does not even rely on knowledge about superordinate categories (see also Sloman, 1998, and see Sun & Zhang, 2006, for an alternative account). Nonetheless, the Sloman model can account for not only diversity effects but a variety of other phenomena involving multiple premises.

The treatment of typicality effects is slightly less straightforward. The model would correctly predict that argument (4) is stronger than argument (5), namely, that robins lead to stronger inferences about all birds than do penguins. The Sloman (1993) model makes this prediction in terms of overlap in representations. On the assumption that the featural representations for robins and birds are closer than the representations for penguins and birds, the model predicts greater activation for birds after training on robins compared with training on penguins. Yet the model essentially predicts the typicality effect in the same way as the similarity effect. This seems to be at odds with a finding by Rips (1975) of an independent contribution of typicality beyond similarity. Still, at a broad level, the Sloman model predicts a kind of typicality effect (see Heit, 2000, for further discussion).

More importantly, the Sloman (1993) model, like the Osherson et al. (1990) model, can account for many structural phenomena in inductive reasoning, but it does not address background knowledge effects and does not use knowledge about the properties being reasoned about to guide the use of similarity or information about causality.

3.3. Bayesian Model

The next model to be discussed is the Bayesian model, applied to inductive reasoning problems by Heit (1998; see also Tenenbaum & Griffiths, 2001, as well as Chapter 3 in this volume). According to the Bayesian model, evaluating an inductive argument is conceived of as learning about a property, in particular, learning for which categories the property is true or false. For example, in argument (16),

Cows have property X.   (16)

Sheep have property X.

the goal is to learn which animals have property X and which do not. The model assumes that for a novel property X, people would rely on prior knowledge about familiar properties to derive a set of hypotheses about what property X may be like. For example, people know some facts that are true of all mammals, including cows and sheep,

but they also know some facts that are true just of cows and some facts that are true just of sheep. The question is which kind of property is property X. Is it a cow-and-sheep property, a cow-only property, or a sheep-only property? To answer this question, the Bayesian model treats the premise or premises in an inductive argument as evidence, which is used to revise beliefs about the prior hypotheses according to Bayes' theorem. Once these beliefs have been revised, then the plausibility of the conclusion is estimated.

People know quite a few properties of animals, but these known properties must fall into four types: properties that are true of cows and sheep, properties that are true of cows but not sheep, properties that are true of sheep but not cows, and properties that are not true of either cows or sheep. These types of known properties can serve as four hypotheses when reasoning about novel properties, because any new property must also be one of these four types, as listed in Table 11.1. As shown in the table, a person would have prior beliefs about these hypotheses. For example, the value of .70 for hypothesis 1 represents the belief that there is a 70% chance that a new property would be true of both cows and sheep. This high value could reflect the high degree of similarity between cows and sheep, and that people know many other properties that are true of both cows and sheep. (The particular numbers are used only for illustration.) However, the person might see a 5% chance that a new property would be true of cows and not sheep, a 5% chance that a new property would be true of sheep and not cows, and a 20% chance that the property is true of neither category.

The next step is to combine these prior beliefs with new evidence, using Bayes' theorem as shown in Equation (11.3). The given premise, "Cows have property X," is used to update beliefs about the four hypotheses, so that the conclusion, "Sheep have property X," can be evaluated. In applying Bayes' theorem in Equation (11.3), the premise is treated as the data, D. The prior degree of belief in each hypothesis is indicated by $P(H_i)$. (Note that there are

Table 11.1: Sample application of the Heit (1998) model

Hypothesis number	Cows?	Sheep?	Degree of prior belief $P(H_i)$	$P(D \mid H_i)$	Posterior belief $P(H_i \mid D)$
1	True	True	.70	1	.93
2	True	False	.05	1	.07
3	False	True	.05	0	.00
4	False	False	.20	0	.00

four hypotheses, so $n = 4$ here.) The task is to estimate $P(Hi \mid D)$, that is, the posterior degree of belief in each hypothesis given the data.

$$P(H_i \mid D) = \frac{P(H_i)P(D \mid H_i)}{\sum_{j=1}^{n} P(H_j)P(D \mid H_j)}$$

(11.3)

The calculations are shown for all four hypotheses, given the data that cows have property X. The calculation of $P(D \mid H_i)$ is easy. Under hypotheses 1 and 2, cows have the property in question, so obtaining the data (that cows have the property) has a probability of 1. But under hypotheses 3 and 4, cows do not have the property, so the probability of obtaining the data must be 0 under these hypotheses. The final column, indicating the posterior beliefs in the four types of properties, is calculated using Bayes' theorem. Notably, hypothesis 1, that cows and sheep have the property, and hypothesis 2, that just cows have the property, have been strengthened, and the two remaining hypotheses have been eliminated from consideration.

Finally, the values in Table 11.1 may be used to evaluate the conclusion, that sheep have property X. The degree of belief in this conclusion is simply the sum of the posterior beliefs for hypotheses 1 and 3, or .93. Recall that before the introduction of evidence that cows have the property, the prior belief that sheep have the property was only .75. Hence, the premise that cows have the property led to an increase in the belief that sheep have the property.

The Bayesian model addresses many of the key phenomena in inductive reasoning. For example, the model predicts the similarity effect because novel properties would be assumed to follow the same distributions as familiar properties. Generalizing from cows to sheep seems plausible because many known properties are true of both categories. In contrast, generalizing from cows to mice seems weaker because prior knowledge indicates that there are fewer properties in common for these two categories. The Bayesian model also addresses typicality effects under the assumption that according to prior beliefs, atypical categories, such as mice, would have a number of idiosyncratic features. A premise asserting a novel property about mice would suggest that this property is likewise idiosyncratic and not to be widely generalized. In comparison, prior beliefs about typical categories would indicate that they have many features in common with other categories; hence, a novel property of a typical category should generalize well to other categories.

The Bayesian model also addresses diversity effects, with a rationale similar to that for typicality effects. An argument with two similar premise categories, such as hippos and rhinos, could bring to mind a lot of idiosyncratic properties that are true just of large mammals. Therefore, a novel property of hippos and rhinos might seem idiosyncratic as well. In contrast, an argument with two diverse premise categories, such as hippos and hamsters, could not bring to mind familiar idiosyncratic properties that are true of just these two animals. Instead, the prior hypotheses would be derived from known properties that are true of all mammals or all animals. Hence, a novel property of hippos and hamsters should generalize fairly broadly. More generally, Heit (1998) showed that the Bayesian model addresses about the same range of structural phenomena in inductive reasoning as does the Osherson et al. (1990) and Sloman (1993) models.

Although it is by no means a complete model of the use of background knowledge in inductive reasoning, the Bayesian model does make a start at addressing background knowledge effects. For example, when reasoning about the anatomical and behavioral properties in Heit and Rubinstein (1994), subjects could have drawn on different priors for the two kinds of properties. Reasoning about anatomical properties led people to rely on prior knowledge about familiar anatomical properties, so there was stronger generalization from bears to whales than from tunas to whales. In contrast, when reasoning about a behavioral property, the prior hypotheses could be drawn from knowledge about familiar behavioral properties. These priors would tend to promote inferences between animals such as tunas and whales that are similar behaviorally rather than anatomically. Although by no means does the Bayesian model itself perform causal reasoning, the priors used in the model could be the end-product of causal reasoning.

Indeed, a fair criticism of the Bayesian model would be that its predictions are captive to assumptions about distributions of prior beliefs. Heit (1998) responded to this criticism, in part, by stating that the exact values of priors do not usually matter, for example, the values for prior beliefs in Table 11.1 could be somewhat different and the same general pattern would emerge. Also, Heit argued that priors would be derived from psychologically plausible mechanisms. It could be assumed that priors are determined by the number of known properties of each type that are brought to mind in the context of evaluating an inductive argument. In this way, prior beliefs for new properties would be estimated using something like an availability heuristic (Tversky & Kahneman, 1973) based on known properties.

Still, it would be a major improvement to the Bayesian model if assumptions about prior beliefs could be generated by a model rather than just simply assumed. Tenenbaum and colleagues (Chapter 3 in this volume; Kemp & Tenenbaum, 2003; Tenenbaum et al., 2007) have made improvements in this regard. Their central idea is that properties of living things have come about due to a process, rather than being arbitrarily distributed. That is, because of an evolutionary process, living things can be thought of as being on the branches of a tree. Two very similar animals probably have a relatively recent common ancestor, whereas two animals that are very different probably only have a common ancestor from very long ago. The starting point for Tenenbaum and colleagues was a large set of ratings on whether different animals possess various known properties. From principles of branching evolution as well as mutation, they derived a tree structure, in effect, inferring common ancestors for each pair of animals. Tenenbaum and colleagues then used the tree structure to set the priors for the Bayesian model. It was found that priors derived from the tree structure were much more successful at predicting people's judgments than priors derived from their property ratings. Interestingly, Tenenbaum and colleagues have argued that this method of setting priors is particularly successful because it represents people's causal knowledge of how properties of living things come about and the mechanisms by which they could be shared.

To sum up the description of Bayesian modeling of inductive reasoning, this kind of modeling does address many phenomena and regularities. The greatest weakness of Bayesian models, that they are subject to assumptions about priors, may also be their greatest strength, in the sense that many predictions are robust over different assumptions about priors, and furthermore, the priors themselves could be derived from other reasoning processes that likewise could be modeled.

4. Causal Learning and Causal Reasoning

An interim summary of the chapter so far could be that current models of inductive reasoning can account for much of what people do, but they especially fall short when it comes to causal knowledge. Part of the problem, from the modeling perspective, is that research on modeling of inductive reasoning has largely proceeded separately from research on modeling the use of causal knowledge. Research on modeling the use of causal knowledge has itself largely taken two separate approaches. One approach focuses on causal learning, or causal induction, namely, how people infer a causal structure from a set of observations. For example, a novice DJ at a party could observe that playing some songs makes people get up and dance, whereas playing other songs makes people sit quietly, and could draw inferences about what kinds of songs are associated with different behaviors. The other approach focuses on causal reasoning, which mainly addresses how often complex knowledge structures can be used to make fresh inferences. For example, an expert with years of experience in the music industry could make detailed predictions about which new performers will succeed and which will not, and give an elaborate causal explanation in terms of market forces, demographics, current trends, and so forth. Of course, there is much overlap between causal learning and causal reasoning, but the emphasis in causal learning research is more on the acquisition of causal knowledge and in causal reasoning research, it is on the use of causal knowledge.

The question of how to infer causation from a set of observations has been considered a central problem of induction at least since the time of Hume (1777). If event B tends to follow event A, does A cause B? At the simplest level, this is the most important question faced by animals seeking food or other necessities – which cues are predictive of obtaining nourishment or some other needed reward? Indeed, one of the most important models of causal learning has its origins in animal conditioning research (Rescorla & Wagner, 1972). The Rescorla-Wagner model can be written as shown in Equation (11.4).

$$V_A(n + 1) = V_A(n) + \beta(\lambda(n) - V_A(n))$$

(11.4)

This formula gives the associative strength, V, of stimulus A, on trial $n + 1$, as a function of the associative strength of A, on trial n, a learning rate β, and a level of reinforcement, $\lambda(n)$, on trial n. In the asymptote, the associative strength of A will tend toward the expected value of the level of reinforcement. The consequence is that stimuli that are followed by reinforcement tend to gain higher levels of associative strength than stimuli that are not reinforced. Of course, the Rescorla-Wagner model can also be extended to situations where there is more than one stimulus on each learning trial. In these situations, the stimuli compete with each other to be the best predictor of reinforcement. For example, once the animal learns that A is associated with reinforcement, if the compound stimulus $A + X$ is reinforced, the animal will be blocked from learning an association between X and reinforcement, because A alone sufficiently predicts the outcome.

There is a lively debate about whether such associative mechanisms are good accounts of people's causal learning (e.g., see Buehner & Cheng, 2005; Luhmann & Ahn, 2004; Novick & Cheng, 2004; Shanks, 2007; Waldmann, 2000; White, 2005), to which the reader is referred. However, there is no doubt that people do acquire causal beliefs. Hence, the next question is how do people represent and reason using this causal information.

The current state of the art in cognitive science is that people represent causal knowledge in the form of a causal network, akin to a formalization known as Bayes nets (Gopnik et al., 2004; Pearl, 2000; Sloman, 2005; Spirtes, Glymour, & Scheines, 2001). These networks allow for the representation of complex causal configurations, such as a causal chain (e.g., the boy threw the ball that broke the window that woke the cat), a common effect from multiple causes (e.g., a fire is caused by a spark in the presence of oxygen and some kind of fuel), and common effects from a single cause (e.g., a cold caused a runny nose, fever, and redness of the eyes). Bayes nets provide a formalism for using this structured knowledge to draw inferences, for example, to estimate the probability that the cat will wake. Although this kind of modeling no doubt provides a valuable framework for describing causal reasoning, further work needs to be done to integrate this framework with human data. Although there have been some efforts to relate this kind of formalism to results from inductive reasoning (Rehder, 2006, 2007; Rehder & Burnett, 2005), for the most part, modeling of causal reasoning stands apart from modeling of inductive reasoning as captured by the results in this chapter. It remains a challenge for Bayes nets or some related model of causal reasoning to show that they cannot only explain what the current models of inductive reasoning can explain but also do a better job by incorporating the use of causal knowledge.

5. Conclusion

5.1. *Summary*

Although inductive reasoning is by its very nature uncertain reasoning, there are nonetheless regularities and patterns that people show when performing inductive reasoning. These regularities include similarity effects, typicality effects, diversity effects, and several others. Current models of inductive reasoning, such as the influential Osherson et al. (1990) model, are successful at explaining these regularities, but have problems addressing the exceptions to these regularities, particularly when people use other kinds of background knowledge outside the scope of these models, such as causal knowledge. There are also extant models of causal induction and causal reasoning, but these models have generally been used to address other sets of results. It remains an im-

portant task for future research to integrate computational modeling work on inductive reasoning, causal induction, and causal reasoning, as applied to a diverse set of human results.

This chapter concludes by discussing two general issues that arise in modeling inductive reasoning, but also arise in computational modeling of other cognitive activities. The first issue is that cognitive activities do not fall neatly into pigeonholes. The second is that putting background knowledge into models is the necessary next step.

5.2. *Everything Is Intertwingled*

As Nelson (1987) noted, everything is deeply intertwingled. Although it is convenient for books to have separate chapters about different cognitive activities, and likewise, it is convenient for researchers to have separate model for different cognitive activities, the truth is that cognitive activities are not as separate as they are portrayed. For example, there is a traditional split between inductive reasoning and deductive reasoning, yet it is still not known where the dividing line is or even if inductive reasoning and deductive reasoning involve distinct cognitive processes (Heit, 2007; Heit & Rotello, 2005). The well-known mental model theory of reasoning (Johnson-Laird & Yhang, this volume), usually applied to deductive reasoning problems, has also been applied to inductive reasoning problems (Johnson-Laird, 1994; Johnson-Laird et al., 1999). An alternative to mental model theory is the probabilistic account, which aims to account for a variety of reasoning phenomena, particularly traditional deduction problems, in terms of probabilistic formulas (Chater & Oaksford, 2000). The probabilistic account says that people solve deduction problems by means of induction processes. Likewise, Osherson et al. (1990) applied their model of inductive reasoning to some problems involving deductively valid conclusions, and some modeling work in the artificial intelligence literature has addressed both deductive reasoning and inductive reasoning to some extent (Collins & Michalski, 1989;

Sun, 1995). Although there are likely some important differences in the reasoning processes involved in induction versus deduction (Rips, 2001), it would be ideal if models of reasoning addressed both rather than focusing on one or the other. Likewise, causal reasoning is another kind of probabilistic reasoning, and as noted, models of inductive reasoning would no doubt be improved by capturing causal reasoning, particularly when addressing effects of background knowledge. The same point can be made about models of judgment and decision making (e.g., Chapter 10 in this volume) – these models essentially address inductive phenomena.

Inductive reasoning is related to not only other kinds of reasoning, but also to other cognitive activities, such as categorization and recognition memory. For example, in a set of experiments, Sloutsky and Fisher (2004) examined relations between inductive reasoning, categorization, and recognition memory. For sets of various animals, subjects either made inductive reasoning judgments, inferring hidden properties, or made categorization judgments, assigning the animals to categories. There was a strong correlation between inductive reasoning and categorization (see also Rehder & Hastie, 2001). Moreover, Sloutsky and Fisher found systematic relations between inductive reasoning and recognition memory. For example, after seeing some pictures of cats with a particular property and inferring that all cats have this property, people tended to falsely recognize other pictures of cats, that is, remember them as having been seen when they had not been seen. In assessing this work, Heit and Hayes (2005) argued that the boundaries between induction, categorization, and recognition are fuzzy. Inductive reasoning can be thought of as a kind of categorization, categorization itself can be said to involve reasoning, and likewise a recognition judgment can be thought of as a kind of categorization. Heit and Hayes concluded that induction, categorization, and recognition should not be modeled separately, but instead, it would be desirable for models to capture the theoretical relations among these activities and likewise the empirical relations, such as how one kind of judgment is correlated with another or even how one kind of judgment directly affects another.

5.3. *Knowledge Is Power*

The second, and final general issue to be raised about modeling is that incorporating background knowledge into models is usually the most important next step and the most difficult. Taking a point from Sir Francis Bacon, knowledge is power. Again, comparing inductive reasoning to categorization is useful in terms of historical progression. Following years of research in which computational models of categorization had been compared to each other, for example, exemplar models versus prototype models, Murphy and Medin (1985) concluded that all the current models were wrong! Exemplar models, prototype models, and alternatives would not be able to, say, categorize someone who jumps into a swimming pool with all his clothes on as a drunk, because categorization models did not take account of people's background knowledge, intuitive theories, and use of causal reasoning and explanations. Since that time, most research on computational modeling of categorization has still focused on structural issues that do not depend heavily on background knowledge and for which models might make different predictions only in the fine details. Still, there have been some efforts to incorporate background knowledge into categorization models (Heit, 1997; Heit & Bott, 2000, Heit, Briggs, & Bott, 2004; Rehder & Murphy, 2003).

Computational modeling of inductive reasoning is now at a similar point in its own history. The models reviewed in this chapter by Osherson et al. (1990), Sloman (1993), and Heit (1998) are successful at addressing largely the same set of structural phenomena in inductive reasoning without addressing important background knowledge effects. (See also Heit and Hayes, 2005, for further examples of current models of induction making very similar predictions.)

Although it is no doubt possible to conduct experiments splitting apart the detailed predictions of these models, what is needed most is new efforts on modeling, incorporating background knowledge and causal reasoning.

Returning to the themes at the start of this chapter, models of inductive reasoning have a particularly hard job, because they are addressing a form of reasoning that is itself uncertain and does not have a correct answer. In such a situation, the success of the models can only be improved by taking account of additional knowledge. Doing so is especially important because the structural phenomena, such as similarity, typicality, and diversity effects, have exceptions and can indeed be overridden by other knowledge. In addressing these knowledge effects, models of inductive reasoning will need to become closer to models of causal reasoning. Going back to the example of buying a CD for your friend, it may be useful to buy CDs that are similar to what she already has. But the most successful strategy for predicting the unpredictable would no doubt to be to discover *why* she likes some CDs and does not like others.

References

Anderson, J. R. (1991). The adaptive nature of human categorization. *Psychological Review, 98*, 409–429.

Bacon, F. (1620). *Novum organum*. London: George Bell and Sons.

Blok, S. V., Osherson, D. N., & Medin, D. L. (2007). From similarity to chance. In A. Feeney & E. Heit (Eds.), *Inductive reasoning* (pp. 137–166). New York: Cambridge University Press.

Buehner, M., & Cheng, P. W. (2005). Causal learning. In K. J. Holyoak & R. G. Morrison (Eds.), *Cambridge handbook of thinking and reasoning* (pp. 143–168). New York: Cambridge University Press.

Chater, N., & Oaksford, M. (2000). The rational analysis of mind and behavior. *Synthese, 122*, 93–131.

Collins, A., & Michalski, R. S. (1989). The logic of plausible reasoning: A core theory. *Cognitive Science, 13*, 1–49.

Gentner, D., Holyoak, K., & Kokinov, B. (Eds.). (2001). *The analogical mind: Perspectives from cognitive science*. Cambridge, MA: MIT Press.

Gopnik, A., Glymour, C., Sobel, D., Schulz, L., Kushnir, T., & Danks, D. (2004). A theory of causal learning in children: Causal maps and Bayes nets. *Psychological Review, 111*, 1–31.

Hayes, B. K. (2007). The development of inductive reasoning. In A. Feeney & E. Heit (Eds.), *Inductive reasoning* (pp. 25–54). Cambridge, UK: Cambridge University Press.

Heit, E. (1997). Knowledge and concept learning. In K. Lamberts & D. Shanks (Eds.), *Knowledge, concepts, and categories* (pp. 7–14). London: Psychology Press.

Heit, E. (1998). A Bayesian analysis of some forms of inductive reasoning. In M. Oaksford & N. Chater (Eds.), *Rational models of cognition* (pp. 248–274). Oxford, UK: Oxford University Press.

Heit, E. (2000). Properties of inductive reasoning. *Psychonomic Bulletin & Review, 7*, 569–592.

Heit, E. (2007). What is induction and why study it? In A. Feeney & E. Heit (Eds.), *Inductive reasoning* (pp. 1–24). Cambridge, UK: Cambridge University Press.

Heit, E., & Bott, L. (2000). Knowledge selection in category learning. In D. L. Medin (Ed.), *Psychology of learning and motivation* (Vol. 39, pp. 163–199). San Diego, CA: Academic Press.

Heit, E., Briggs, J., & Bott, L. (2004). Modeling the effects of prior knowledge on learning incongruent features of category members. *Journal of Experimental Psychology: Learning, Memory, and Cognition, 30*, 1065–1081.

Heit, E., & Feeney, A. (2005). Relations between premise similarity and inductive strength. *Psychonomic Bulletin & Review, 12*, 340–344.

Heit, E., Hahn, U., & Feeney, A. (2005). Defending diversity. In W. Ahn, R. Goldstone, B. Love, A. Markman, & P. Wolff (Eds.), *Categorization inside and outside of the laboratory: Essays in honor of Douglas L. Medin* (pp. 87–99). Washington DC: APA.

Heit, E., & Hayes, B. K. (2005). Relations among categorization, induction, recognition, and similarity. *Journal of Experimental Psychology: General, 134*, 596–605.

Heit, E., & Rotello, C. M. (2005). Are there two kinds of reasoning? In *Proceedings of the Twenty-Seventh Annual Conference of the Cognitive Science Society* (pp. 923–928). Hillsdale, NJ: Lawrence Erlbaum.

Heit, E., & Rubinstein, J. (1994). Similarity and property effects in inductive reasoning. *Journal of Experimental Psychology: Learning, Memory, and Cognition, 20,* 411–422.

Hume, D. (1777). *An enquiry concerning human understanding.* Oxford, UK: Clarendon Press.

Johnson-Laird, P. N. (1994). Mental models and probabilistic thinking. *Cognition, 50,* 189–209.

Johnson-Laird, P. N., Legrenzi, P., Girotto, V., Legrenzi, M. A., & Caverni, J. P. (1999). Naive probability: A mental model theory of extensional reasoning. *Psychological Review, 106,* 62–88.

Kemp, C. S., & Tenenbaum, J. B. (2003). Theory-based induction. In *Proceedings of the Twenty-Fifth Annual Conference of the Cognitive Science Society* (pp. 658–663). Hillsdale, NJ: Lawrence Erlbaum.

Lassaline, M. E. (1996). Structural alignment in induction and similarity. *Journal of Experimental Psychology: Learning, Memory, & Cognition, 22,* 754–770.

Lopez, A., Atran, S., Coley, J. D., Medin, D. L., & Smith, E. E. (1997). The tree of life: Universal and cultural features of folkbiological taxonomies and inductions. *Cognitive Psychology, 32,* 251–295.

Luhmann, C. C., & Ahn, W. (2005). The meaning and computation of causal power: A critique of Cheng (1997) and Novick and Cheng (2004). *Psychological Review, 112,* 685–693.

McDonald, J., Samuels, M., & Rispoli, J. (1996). A hypothesis-assessment model of categorical argument strength. *Cognition, 59,* 199–217.

Medin, D. L., Coley, J. D., Storms, G., & Hayes, B. K. (2003). A relevance theory of induction. *Psychonomic Bulletin & Review, 10,* 517–532.

Mill, J. S. (1874). *A System of logic, ratiocinative and inductive.* New York: Harper & Row.

Murphy, G. L., & Medin, D. L. (1985). The role of theories in conceptual coherence. *Psychological Review, 92,* 289–316.

Nelson, T. H. (1987). *Computer lib / Dream machines.* Redmond, WA: Microsoft.

Nisbett, R. E., Krantz, D. H., Jepson, C., & Kunda, Z. (1983). The use of statistical heuristics in everyday inductive reasoning. *Psychological Review, 90,* 339–363.

Novick, L. R., & Cheng, P. W. (2004). Assessing interactive causal influence. *Psychological Review, 111,* 455–485.

Osherson, D. N., Smith, E. E., Wilkie, O., Lopez, A., & Shafir, E. (1990). Category-based induction. *Psychological Review, 97,* 185–200.

Pearl, J. (2000). *Causality.* New York: Oxford University Press.

Proffitt, J. B., Coley, J. D., & Medin, D. L. (2000). Expertise and category-based induction. *Journal of Experimental Psychology: Learning, Memory, & Cognition, 26,* 811–828.

Rehder, B. (2006). When causality and similarity compete in category-based property induction. *Memory & Cognition, 34,* 3–16.

Rehder, B. (2007). Property generalization as causal reasoning In A. Feeney & E. Heit (Eds.), *Inductive reasoning* (pp. 81–113). Cambridge, UK: Cambridge University Press.

Rehder, B., & Burnett, R. (2005). Feature inference and the causal structure of categories. *Cognitive Psychology, 50,* 264–314.

Rehder, B., & Hastie, R. (2001). Causal knowledge and categories: The effects of causal beliefs on categorization, induction, and similarity. *Journal of Experimental Psychology: General, 130,* 323–360.

Rehder, B., & Murphy, G. L. (2003). A knowledge-resonance (KRES) model of knowledge-based category learning. *Psychonomic Bulletin & Review, 10,* 759–784.

Rescorla, R. A., & Wagner, A. R. (1972). A theory of Pavlovian conditioning: Variations in the effectiveness of reinforcement and nonreinforcement. In A. H. Black & W. F. Prokasy (Eds.), *Classical conditioning II: Current research and theory* (pp. 64–99). New York: Appleton-Century-Crofts.

Rips, L. J. (1975). Inductive judgments about natural categories. *Journal of Verbal Learning and Verbal Behavior, 14,* 665–681.

Rips, L. J. (2001). Two kinds of reasoning. *Psychological Science, 12,* 129–134.

Rosch, E., & Mervis, C. B. (1975). Family resemblances: Studies in the internal structure of categories. *Cognitive Psychology, 7,* 573–605.

Ross, B. H., & Murphy, G. L. (1999). Food for thought: Cross-classification and category organization in a complex real-world domain. *Cognitive Psychology, 38,* 495–553.

Shafto, P., & Coley, J. D. (2003). Development of categorization and reasoning in the natural world: Novices to experts, native similarity to ecological knowledge. *Journal of Experimental Psychology: Learning, Memory, and Cognition, 29,* 641–649.

Shanks, D. R. (2007). Associationism and cognition: Human contingency learning at 25. *Quarterly Journal of Experimental Psychology, 60,* 291–309.

Sloman, S. A. (1993). Feature-based induction. *Cognitive Psychology, 25,* 231–280.

Sloman, S. A. (1994). When explanations compete: The role of explanatory coherence on judgments of likelihood. *Cognition, 52,* 1–21.

Sloman, S. A. (1998). Categorical inference is not a tree: The myth of inheritance hierarchies. *Cognitive Psychology, 35,* 1–33.

Sloman, S. A. (2005). *Causal models: How we think about the world and its alternatives.* New York: Oxford University Press.

Sloutsky, V. M., & Fisher, A. V. (2004). Induction and categorization in young children: A similarity-based model. *Journal of Experimental Psychology: General, 133,* 166–188.

Smith, E. E., Shafir, E., & Osherson, D. (1993). Similarity, plausibility, and judgments of probability. *Cognition, 49,* 67–96.

Spirtes, P., Glymour, C., & Scheines, R. (2001). *Causation, prediction, and search* (2nd ed.). Cambridge, MA: MIT Press.

Sun, R. (1995). Robust reasoning: integrating rule-based and similarity-based reasoning. *Artificial Intelligence, 75,* 241–296.

Sun, R., & Zhang, X. (2006). Accounting for a variety of reasoning data within a cognitive architecture. *Journal of Experimental & Theoretical Artificial Intelligence, 18,* 169–191.

Sutton, R., & Barto, A. (1981). Towards a modern theory of adaptive networks: expectation and prediction. *Psychological Review, 88,* 135–170.

Tenenbaum, J. B., & Griffiths, T. L. (2001). Generalization, similarity, and Bayesian inference. *Behavioral and Brain Sciences, 24,* 629–641.

Tenenbaum, J. B., Kemp, C., & Shafto, P. (2007). Theory-based Bayesian models of inductive reasoning. In A. Feeney, & E. Heit, (Eds.), *Inductive reasoning* (pp. 167–207). Cambridge, UK: Cambridge University Press.

Thagard, P. (2007). Abductive inference: From philosophical analysis to neural mechanisms. In A. Feeney & E. Heit (Eds.), *Inductive reasoning.* Cambridge, UK: Cambridge University Press.

Tversky, A., & Kahneman, D. (1973). Availability: A heuristic for judging frequency and probability. *Cognitive Psychology, 5,* 207–232.

Waldmann, M. R. (2000). Competition among causes but not effects in predictive and diagnostic learning. *Journal of Experimental Psychology: Learning, Memory, and Cognition, 26,* 53–76.

White, P. A. (2005). The power PC theory and causal powers: Reply to Cheng (1997) and Novick and Cheng (2004). *Psychological Review, 112,* 675–682.

Wu, M., & Gentner, D. (1998). Structure in category-based induction. In *Proceedings of the Twentieth Annual Conference of the Cognitive Science Society* (pp. 1154–1158). Hillsdale, NJ: Lawrence Erlbaum.

CHAPTER 12

Mental Logic, Mental Models, and Simulations of Human Deductive Reasoning

Philip N. Johnson-Laird and Yingrui Yang

1. Introduction

Individuals who know no logic are able to make deductive inferences. Given a problem such as:

> If the printer test was run then the printer produced a document.
> The printer test was run.
> What follows?

they draw the conclusion:

> The printer produced a document.

The conclusion is the result of a *valid* deduction, that is, if the premises are true, then the conclusion must be true also. How naive individuals – those untrained in logic – are able to draw valid conclusions is a matter of controversy, because no one has access to the mental processes underlying inferences. Some cognitive scientists believe that these processes are analogous to those of "proof" theory in logic (see Chapter 5 in this volume on logic-based modeling); some believe that they are analogous to those of "model"

theory in logic; and some believe that logic is irrelevant and that the probability calculus is a better guide to human deductive reasoning. The present chapter focuses on simulations based on proof theory and model theory, but it has something to say about the probabilistic theory.

The chapter starts with an outline of how psychological theories based on formal rules of inference – proof theory, that is – can be implemented to simulate reasoning. It uses as a test-bed so-called sentential reasoning based on negation and connectives, such as "if," "and," and "or." This sort of reasoning lies at the heart of our everyday deductions, although we are soon defeated by complex inferences in this domain. The chapter then turns to programs simulating the theory inspired by "model" theory in logic, that is, the theory of *mental* models, which posits that the engine of human reasoning relies on content. It illustrates two simulations of the theory. One program simulates spatial reasoning, and it shows how valid inferences can be drawn without explicit representations of the logical properties of relations. Instead, they emerge from the representations of the meanings of relational terms. The other program concerns sentential reasoning, and it shows how an apparently unexceptional assumption leads to a striking prediction of systematic fallacies in reasoning – a case that yields crucial predictions about the nature of human deductive reasoning. The chapter concludes with an attempt to weigh up the nature of human rationality in the light of these and other simulation programs.

2. The Simulation of Formal Theories of Reasoning

For many years, psychologists argued that deduction depends on an unconscious system of formal rules of inference akin to those in proof-theoretic logic. The inference in the opening example, for example, could be drawn using the formal rule of inference known as *modus ponens*:

> If A then B
> A
> Therefore, B.

The human inference engine matches the form of the premises to this rule, where *A* has as its value: *the printer test was run*, and *B* has as its value: *the printer produced a document*. The use of the rule proves the conclusion, *B*. This sort of theory has its proponents both in artificial intelligence and in cognitive psychology. Its intellectual godfather in psychology was the Swiss theorist, Jean Piaget (see, e.g., Beth & Piaget, 1966), but many theorists have proposed versions of the doctrine (e.g., Braine, 1978; Braine & O'Brien, 1998; Johnson-Laird, 1975; Osherson, 1974–1976; Rips, 1983, 1994).

Rips (1994) describes an implementation of his version of the theory, and the proponents of the other leading formal rule theory (Braine & O'Brien, 1998) have described an algorithm for it, although they did not implement a program. Hence, this section focuses on Rips's (1994) program. He argues that formal rules, such as modus ponens, are central to human cognition, underlying not just deduction but all thinking. Hence, formal rules on his account are part of cognitive architecture and akin to a general-purpose programming system in which any sort of theory can be implemented, even, say, Newell's (1990) Soar theory (see Chapter 6 in this volume on cognitive architecture). Soar is a so-called production system, which is made up of a large number of productions, that is, conditional rules with specific contents. They have the form: *if condition X holds then carry out action Y*, and a production can be triggered whenever its antecedent condition is satisfied. Rips argues that this method of applying the rules is akin to the use of modus ponens, but that Newell's theory is "too unconstrained to explain what is essential about deduction" (Rips, 1994, p. 30).

At the heart of Rips's (1994) theory is the notion of a mental proof, so theorists need to devise psychologically plausible formal rules of inference and a psychologically plausible mechanism to use them in constructing mental proofs. Like several proposals in the mid-1970s (e.g., Braine, 1978; Johnson-Laird, 1975; Osherson, 1974–1976), Rips adopts the "natural deduction" approach to rules of inference. Each logical connective has its own rules. Each quantifier, such as "every" and "some," also has its rules, too, although Rips presupposes an input to the program that captures the logical form of premises (see Chapter 5 in this volume on logic-based modeling). This section accordingly focuses on Rips's system for reasoning with sentential connectives. It has rules to introduce each connective into a proof, for example:

> A
> B _____
> A and B

where the proposition beneath the line signifies the conclusion. And the system has rules to eliminate connectives, for example:

> If A then B
> A _____
> B.

Natural deduction can yield intuitive proofs, and it was popular in logic texts, although the so-called "tree" method supplanted it (e.g., Jeffrey, 1981). Rips refers to the tree method, which simulates the search for counterexamples, but he considers it to be psychologically implausible, because "the tree method is based on a reductio ad absurdum strategy" (p. 75), that is, the assumption for the sake of argument of the *negation* of the conclusion to be proved. In fact, the tree method can be used to derive conclusions without using the reductio strategy (see Jeffrey 1981, Chapter 2).

Natural deduction relies on suppositions, which are sentences that are assumed for the sake of argument and which must be "discharged" if a derivation is to yield a conclusion. One way to discharge a supposition is to make it explicit in a conditional conclusion (conditional proof), and another way is to show that it leads to a contradiction and must therefore be false (reductio ad absurdum). An example is the following proof of an inference in the form known as *modus tollens*:

1. If the printer test was run then the printer produced a document.
2. The printer did not produce a document.
3. The printer test was run. (Supposition)
4. The printer produced a document. (Modus ponens applied to 1 and 3)

At this point, a contradiction occurs between one of the premises and the most recent conclusion. The rule of reductio ad absurdum discharges the supposition by negating it:

5. The printer test was not run.

Rips (1994) could have adopted a single rule for modus tollens, but it is a more difficult inference than modus ponens, so he assumes that it depends on the chain of inferential steps illustrated here. The main problems in developing a formal system are to ensure that it is computationally viable and that it explains robust psychological findings. An example of a computational difficulty is that the rule for introducing "and" can run amok, leading to such futile derivations as:

$$A$$
$$B$$
$$\therefore \quad A \text{ and } B$$
$$\therefore \quad A \text{ and } (A \text{ and } B)$$
$$\therefore \quad A \text{ and } (A \text{ and } (A \text{ and } B))$$

and so on ad infinitum. The rules that are dangerous are those that introduce a connective or a supposition. Programs in artificial intelligence, however, can use a rule in two ways: either to derive a step in a *forward* chain leading from the premises to the conclusion or to derive a step in a *backward* chain leading from the conclusion to the premises. In a backward chain, the effect of a rule is to create subgoals, for example, given the goal of proving a conclusion of the form, *A and B*, the rule for "and" creates a subgoal to prove *A* and a subgoal to prove *B*. If the program satisfies these two subgoals, then it has in effect proved the conjunction: *A and B*, and it terminates there with no further application of the rule. Rips (1994) prevents rules from running amok by using those that introduce connectives or suppositions only in backward chains. His system therefore has three sorts of rules: those that it uses forward, those that it uses backward, and those that it uses in either direction. Table 12.1 summarizes these rules in Rips's system.

The formal rules postulated in a psychological theory should be ones that naive individuals recognize as "intuitively sound" (Rips, 1994, p. 104). One worry about the rules in Table 12.1 is whether they are all intuitive. The rule for introducing "or," for example, was used appropriately by only 20% of participants in Rips's own study. Indeed, this rule is not part of other formal theories (e.g., Braine, 1978). What complicates matters is that Rips allows that individuals may differ in the rules they possess, they may learn new rules, and they may even use nonstandard rules that lead them to conclusions not sanctioned by classical logic (Rips, 1994, p. 103).

Table 12.1: The forward, backward, and bidirectional rules in Rips's (1994) system

Forward rules

IF P THEN Q*	IF P OR Q THEN R*	IF P AND Q THEN R
P	P	P
___	___	Q
Q	R	R

P AND Q*	NOT (P AND Q)*	NOT (P AND Q)*
P	(NOT P) OR (NOT Q)	P
		NOT Q

P OR Q*	NOT (P OR Q)
NOT P	NOT P
Q	

P OR Q	NOT NOT P*
IF P THEN R	P
IF Q THEN R	
R	

Backward rules

+P	+NOT P	+P
:	:	:
Q	Q AND (NOT Q)	Q AND (NOT Q)
IF P THEN Q	P	NOT P

P	P
Q	___
P AND Q	P OR Q

P OR Q	NOT (P OR Q)
+P	(NOT P) AND (NOT Q)
:	
R	
+Q	
:	
R	
R	

---

* Signifies that a rule can also be used backward. Rules, such as the one eliminating AND, are shown leading to the conclusion P; other versions of such rules yield the conclusion Q. Plus sign (+) designates a supposition and colon (:) designates a subsequent derivation.

A major problem for systems implementing proofs is to embody an efficient method of searching for the correct sequence of inferential steps. The process is computationally intractable, and the space of possible sequences of inferential steps grows very rapidly (Cook, 1971). Rips's system uses a fixed deterministic search procedure in evaluating an inference with a given conclusion. It tries each of its applicable forward rules in a breadth-first search until they yield no new conclusions. It checks whether the conclusion is among the results. If not, it tries to work backward from the conclusion, pursuing a chain of inference depth first until it finds the sentences that satisfy the subgoals or until it has run out of rules to apply (Rips, 1994, p. 105). Either it succeeds in deriving the conclusion or else it returns to an earlier choice point in the chain and tries to satisfy an alternative subgoal. If all the subgoals fail, it gives up. However, Rips's system is incomplete, that is, there are valid inferences that it cannot prove. As Barwise (1993, p. 338) comments: "The 'search till you're exhausted' strategy gives one at best an educated, correct guess that something does not follow." In other words, when Rips's system fails to find a proof, it may do so because an inference is invalid or else because it is valid but the incomplete rules fail to yield its proof.

Rips's system constrains the use of suppositions. They can be made only in a backward chain of inference from a given conclusion, so reasoners can use suppositions only when there is a given conclusion or they can somehow guess a conclusion. In everyday life, reasoners are not constrained to making suppositions only when they have a conclusion in mind. "Suppose everyone suddenly became dyslexic," they say to themselves, and then they follow up the consequences to an unexpected conclusion, for example, the sale of dictionaries would decline. In an earlier account, Rips (1989) allowed suppositions to occur in forward chains of reasoning. But, in that case, how can they be prevented from running amok? One possibility is to distinguish between the strategies that reasoners adopt and the lower level mechanisms that sanction inferential steps. One strategy is to make a supposition, but the strategic machinery must keep the lower level mechanisms in check to prevent them from losing track of the purpose of the exercise. Indeed, human reasoners develop a variety of strategies for sentential reasoning, and they use suppositions in ways not always sanctioned by Rips's theory (van der Henst, Yang, & Johnson-Laird, 2002).

Braine and colleagues have described a series of theories based on natural deduction (see, e.g., Braine, 1978; Braine & O'Brien, 1998). Their rules differ from Rips's rules in

two main ways. First, "and" and "or" can apply to any number of propositions, so they formulate the following rule to introduce "and":

$$\frac{P_1, P_2, \ldots P_n}{P_1 \text{ and } P_2 \ldots \text{ and } P_n.}$$

Second, they do not distinguish between forward and backward rules. Instead, they try to build the effects of dangerous rules, such as: P; therefore, P or Q, into other rules. Hence, they have a rule of the form: *If P_1 or $P_2, \ldots$ or P_n then Q; P_1; therefore, Q.* Their idea is to obviate the need for the rule introducing disjunction. Like Rips, however, they appear to postulate a single deterministic search strategy in which individuals apply simple rules before they apply rules that make suppositions. A problem that both Rips and Braine share is that it is often not obvious what conclusion, if any, their theories predict that individuals should draw spontaneously from a set of premises. At this point, the first author should declare an interest. At one time, he was a proponent of formal rules of inference (see Johnson-Laird, 1975), but, as the next section illustrates, he has now come to believe that the human inference engine relies, not on form, but on content.

3. The Simulation of Spatial Reasoning Using Mental Models

The theory of mental models postulates that when individuals understand discourse, they construct models of the possibilities consistent with the discourse (e.g., Johnson-Laird & Byrne, 1991; Johnson-Laird, 2006). Each mental model represents a possibility. A frequent misunderstanding is that mental models are images. In fact, they are more akin to three-dimensional models of the world of the sort that underlie the phenomena of mental rotation (Metzler & Shepard 1982). Because each model represents a possibility, a conclusion is necessary if it holds in all the models of the premises, it is possible if it holds in at least one model of the premises, and it is probable if it holds in most of the models of the premises given that the models are equiprobable. The theory accordingly embraces deductions, reasoning about possibilities, and probabilistic reasoning, at least of the sort that depends on the various ways in which events can occur (Johnson-Laird et al., 1999).

The first mental model theory was for simple inferences based on quantifiers, and programs have simulated various versions of this theory (see Bucciarelli & Johnson-Laird, 1999, for a review). Polk and Newell (1995) simulated a model theory in which counterexamples played no role, but more recent evidence implies that human reasoners do make use of them (Bucciarelli & Johnson-Laird, 1999; Johnson-Laird & Hasson, 2003). Bara, Bucciarelli, and Lombardo (2001) developed a program that simulated both sentential and quantified reasoning in a single model-based program. In contrast, Johnson-Laird has written a series of small-scale programs that simulate various sorts of reasoning. The general design of these programs is the same. Each program has a lexicon that specifies the meanings of the key words in the input, which, depending on the domain, may be sentential connectives, quantifiers, causal verbs, deontic verbs, relational terms, or nouns referring to objects. The program also has a grammar of the relevant fragment of English. In many cases, this fragment is infinite in size because the grammar contains recursive rules. Such a grammar is illustrated in the next section. Associated with each grammatical rule is a function that carries out the corresponding semantic interpretation. The parser is a "shift-and-reduce" one familiar in the design of compilers (see, e.g., Aho & Ullman, 1972). It constructs a representation of the meaning of each sentence as it uses the grammar to parse the sentence. The program accordingly implements a "compositional" semantics (Montague, 1974), that is, the meanings of the words in a sentence are composed to yield the meaning of the sentence from its grammatical structure. The resulting meaning can then be used to update the model, or models, of the discourse so far, which represent the context of each sentence. The present section illustrates how such a system works in a program for spatial reasoning.

The program simulates three-dimensional spatial reasoning based on mental models (Byrne & Johnson-Laird, 1989). The input to the program is a description with, or without, a given conclusion. There can be any number of premises, and they can describe complex three-dimensional relations. But a simple inference best shows how the program works:

> The triangle is to the right of the circle.
> The circle is to the right of the diamond.
> Therefore, the triangle is to the right of the diamond.

The program composes a representation of the meaning of the first premise, which it uses to build a model. It uses the meaning of *the circle* to insert a token representing the circle into a minimal three-dimensional spatial model:

○

The meaning of *to the right of* specifies that the model-building system scans in a rightward direction from the circle, so the program increments the left-to-right axis from the circle while holding constant the values on the other two axes (up-and-down and front-and-back). It uses the meaning of *the triangle* to insert a representation of the triangle into an empty location in the model:

○   △

The left-to-right axis in this diagram corresponds to the left-to-right spatial axis of the model.

The program can search for referents in its spatial models. Hence, given the second premise:

> The circle is to the right of the diamond

it discovers that the circle is already represented in its current model of the premises.

Table 12.2: Seven procedures for reasoning using models

1. Start a new model. The procedure inserts a new referent into the model according to a premise.
2. Update a model with a new referent in relation to an existing referent.
3. Update a model with a new property or relation.
4. Join two separate models into one according to a relation between referents in them.
5. Verify whether a proposition is true or false in models.
6. Search for a counterexample to refute a proposition. If the search fails, then the proposition follows validly from the previous propositions in the description.
7. Search for an example to make a proposition true. If the search fails, then the proposition is inconsistent with the previous propositions.

It uses the meaning of the sentence to update this model. It therefore inserts a representation of the diamond into an appropriate position in the model:

◇　　○　　△

With the first premise, human reasoners can scan from the circle in the direction that the relation specifies to find a location for the triangle. But, with the second premise, this natural procedure is not feasible, because the subject of the sentence is already in the model. The program therefore scans in the opposite direction to the one that the relation specifies – from the circle to a location for the diamond. This task ought to be a little bit harder, and psychological evidence shows that it is (e.g., Oberauer & Wilhelm, 2000). If a premise refers to nothing in the current model, then the program constructs a new model. Later, given an appropriate premise, it can integrate the two separate models into a single model. This case also adds to the difficulty of human reasoning.

Given the putative conclusion in the example:

The triangle is to the right of the diamond

the program discovers that both referents are already represented in its current model. It checks whether the appropriate relation holds between them. It scans in a rightward direction from the diamond until it finds the triangle. The relation holds. Next, it checks whether any other model of the premises is a counterexample to the conclusion. It

finds none, so it declares that the inference is valid. In case a conclusion does not hold in the current model, the program checks whether any other model of the previous premises allows the relation to hold. If not, the program declares that the proposition is inconsistent with what has gone before. Table 12.2 summarizes the main procedures used in the program. If the human inferential system uses models, it needs such procedures, too.

In formal systems, the previous inference can be proved only if an additional premise specifies the transitivity of "to the right of":

For any x, y, and z, if x is to the right of y, and y is to the right of z, then x is to the right of z.

This premise functions as an axiom for any inference concerning the relation, and for obvious reasons, logicians refer to such axioms as *meaning postulates*. Proof theory in logic and formal rule theories in psychology need meaning postulates to allow deductions whose validity depends on the meanings of relations. In contrast, as the program shows, the model theory does not need meaning postulates, because the validity of inferences emerges from the meanings of relations, which specify the direction in which to scan models, and from the procedures that construct models and search for counterexamples.

One point is easy to overlook. The program's search for counterexamples works because it has access to the representations of the *meanings* of the premises. Without these representations, if the program were to change a model, it would have no way to check whether the result was still a model of the premises. Any inferential system that constructs alternative models therefore needs an independent record of the premises. It must either have a memory for their meanings, or be able to return to each premise to re-interpret it.

The strategy embodied in the spatial reasoning program is to construct a single model at a time. When a description is consistent with more than one layout, the program builds whichever model requires the least work. An alternative strategy, which is implemented in a program for reasoning about temporal relations, is to try to build all the different possible models. Still another strategy is to represent the alternative possibilities within a single model using a way to indicate the uncertain positions of entities in the model. Human reasoners can probably develop any of these strategies, depending on the particulars of the problems that they tackle (see, e.g., Carreiras & Santamaría, 1997; Jahn, Knauff, & Johnson-Laird, 2007; Schaeken, Johnson-Laird, & d'Ydewalle, 1996a, 1996b; Vandierendonck, Dierckx, & De Vooght, 2004).

The evidence corroborates the use of models in spatial reasoning. Participants in experiments report that they imagine layouts. They often make gestures with their hands that suggest they have a spatial model in mind. Likewise, if they have paper and pencil, they draw diagrams. Yet, such evidence does not rule out the possibility that deep down, the unconscious inferential processes are guided by form rather than content. Several experiments, however, provide crucial evidence supporting the model theory. One experiment used descriptions of two-dimensional spatial layouts of household objects and showed that inferences that depend on a single model are easier than those that depend on multiple models. Yet, the one-model problems called for longer formal proofs than the multiple-model problems (Byrne & Johnson-Laird, 1989).

A recent study demonstrated a still greater difficulty for meaning postulates

(Goodwin & Johnson-Laird, 2005). It examined such inferences as:

> Alice is a blood relative of Brian.
> Brian is a blood relative of Charlie.
> What follows?

The participants tended to infer that Alice is a blood relative of Charlie. They presumably thought of a set of siblings or a line of descendants. Yet, there are counterexamples to the conclusion. Suppose, for instance, that Alice is Brian's mother, and Charlie is his father. Alice is related to Brian, and he is related to Charlie, but his mother and father are probably not blood relatives. These "pseudo-transitive" inferences depend on relations that are neither transitive nor intransitive, but that yield models of typical situations in which a transitive conclusion holds. The model theory therefore predicts that the way to block these inferences is to get the participants to search harder for counterexamples. Hence, when the problem about "blood relatives" was prefaced with the clue that people can be related either by blood or by marriage, the proportion of transitive inferences was reduced reliably.

If human reasoners use formal rules to reason, then they need meaning postulates that capture the transitivity of relations. So what sorts of relations should be tagged as transitive? The reader might suppose that good candidates would be comparative relations, such as "taller than." But, consider this problem:

> Cate is taller than Belle.
> Belle *was* taller than Alice.
> Who is tallest?

The change in tense no longer guarantees transitivity, and again individuals are much less inclined to draw the transitive conclusion (Goodwin & Johnson-Laird, 2005). It follows that no comparative terms, not even "taller than," can be classified as transitive in all cases. In other words, the logical form of an assertion depends on its significance, which in turn depends on its tense, its context, and general knowledge. The obvious route to discover its correct logical form is to use this information to construct models of the situations to which it refers. But once one has constructed such models, they can be used directly in reasoning: There is no need to recover the assertion's logical form. Hence, if the system builds models, then it no longer needs meaning postulates. The models either support a transitive conclusion or not.

4. The Simulation of Sentential Reasoning Using Mental Models

Sentential reasoning hinges on negation and such connectives as "if," "or," and "and," which interconnect *atomic* propositions, that is, those that do not contain negation or connectives. Section 2 illustrated how sentential reasoning could be simulated using formal rules. Connectives have idealized meanings in logic, so that the truth-values of sentences formed with them depend solely on the truth-values of those atomic propositions or their negations that they interconnect. For example, an exclusive disjunction of the form: *A or else B but not both*, is true if one proposition is true and the other false, and in any other case the disjunction is false. Model theory in logic captures this analysis in a truth-table, as shown in Table 12.3. Each row in the table represents a different possibility, for example, the first row represents the case in which both *A* and *B* are true, and it shows that the disjunction is false in this case. Truth-tables can be used to determine the validity of sentential inferences: An inference is valid if any row in its truth-table in which the premises are true is also one in which its conclusion is true. However, truth-tables double in size with each additional atomic proposition in an inference, whereas the psychological difficulty of inferences does not increase at anything like the same rate (Osherson, 1974–1976).

The theory of mental models is based on a fundamental assumption that obviates this problem and that is known as the principle of *truth*:

Table 12.3: A truth-table for an exclusive disjunction

A	B	A or else B but not both
True	True	False
True	False	True
False	True	True
False	False	False

Mental models represent only what is true, that is, they represent only true possibilities and within them they represent only those atomic propositions or their negations in the premises that are true.

As an example, consider an exclusive disjunction, such as:

The machine does not work or else the setting is high, but not both.

The principle of truth implies that individuals envisage only the two true possibilities. They therefore construct the following two mental models shown in the rows of the following diagram, where "¬" designates negation:

¬ Machine works

　　　　　　　Setting high

The principle of truth has a further, less obvious, consequence. When individuals think about the first possibility, they tend to neglect the fact that it is false that the setting is high in this case. Likewise, when they think about the second possibility, they tend to neglect the fact that it is false that the machine does not work in this case, that is, the machine *does* work. The relation between these mental models and the truth-table for an exclusive disjunction is transparent (see Table 12.3). The mental models correspond to those rows in the table in which the disjunction is true, and they represent only those *literals* in the premises that are true in the row, where a literal is an atomic proposition or its negation.

The principle of truth postulates that individuals normally represent what is true, but not what is false. It does not imply, however, that they never represent falsity. Indeed, the theory proposes that they represent what is false in "mental footnotes," but that these footnotes are ephemeral. People tend to forget them. But as long as they are remembered, they can be used to construct *fully explicit* models, which represent the true possibilities in a fully explicit way. Hence, the footnotes about what is false allow reasoners to flesh out the models of the proposition:

> The machine does not work or else the setting is high, but not both.

to make them fully explicit:

> ¬ Machine works   ¬ Setting high
> Machine works   Setting high

where a true negation is used to represent a false affirmative proposition. This representation of negation makes models more abstract than images, because you cannot form an image of negation. Even if you imagine, say, a large red cross superimposed on whatever is to be negated, nothing in the image alone captures the meaning of negation.

The meanings of conditional propositions, such as:

> If the machine works then the setting is high

are a matter of controversy. Their meanings depend both on context and on the semantic relations, if any, between their two clauses – the *antecedent* clause following "if" and the *consequent* clause following "then" (see Johnson-Laird & Byrne, 2002). The core logical meaning of a conditional is independent of its context and of the meanings and referents of its antecedent and consequent clauses. It yields two mental models. One mental model represents the salient possibility in which both the antecedent and the consequent are true. The other model is wholly implicit, that is, it has no explicit content, but allows for possibilities in which the antecedent of the conditional is false. The mental models for the preceding conditional are accordingly:

> Machine works   Setting high
>   . . .

where the ellipsis denotes the implicit model, and a mental footnote indicates the falsity of the antecedent in the implicit possibilities. A biconditional, such as:

> The machine works if and only if the setting is high

has exactly the same mental models, but a footnote indicates that both the antecedent and the consequent are false in the possibilities that the implicit model represents. It is the implicit model that distinguishes the models of a conditional from the model of a conjunction, such as:

> The machine works and the setting is high

which has only a single model:

> Machine works   Setting high

The fully explicit models of the conditional can be constructed from the mental models and the footnote on the implicit model. They are as follows:

> Machine works   Setting high
> ¬ Machine works   Setting high
> ¬ Machine works   ¬ Setting high

Likewise, the fully explicit models of the biconditional are:

> Machine works   Setting high
> ¬ Machine works   ¬ Setting high

One point bears emphasis: These diagrams refer to mental models, but mental models themselves represent entities in the world – they are not merely strings of words. Table 12.4 summarizes the mental models and the fully explicit models of sentences formed from the main sentential connectives in their "logical" senses.

Table 12.4: The mental models and fully explicit models for sentences based on the main sentential connectives

Connective	Mental models		Fully explicit models	
A and B:	A	B	A	B
A or else B:	A		A	¬ B
		B	¬ A	B
A or B, or both:	A		A	¬ B
		B	¬ A	B
	A	B	A	B
If A then B:	A	B	A	B
	. . .		¬ A	B
			¬ A	¬ B
If and only if A then B:	A	B	A	B
	. . .		¬ A	¬ B

"¬" denotes negation and ". . ." denotes a wholly implicit model. Each line represents a model of a possibility.

How are sentential inferences made with mental models? A computer program simulates the process (see Johnson-Laird & Byrne, 1991). The program takes as input a set of sentences. It is sensitive to the occurrence of the following sentential connectives: *and* (conjunction), *or* (inclusive disjunction), *ore* (exclusive disjunction), *if* (conditional), *iff* (biconditional), and *then*, which serves only a syntactic role.

The program has a grammar that can be summarized as follows, where the items in parentheses may, or may not, occur in a sentence, and *comma* is a syntactic element:

sentence = (negation) variable
= negation sentence
= (comma) sentence connective sentence
= (comma) *if* sentence *then* sentence.

These four rules allow for different sorts of sentences, but because "sentence" occurs on both the left- and right-hand sides of some rules, the rules can be used recursively to

analyze complex sentences, such as:

if not A and B then, C or D

where A, B, C, and D are all variables. *Not A*, for example, is analyzed as a sentence according to the first rule in the set shown previously, and *C or D* is analyzed as a sentence according to the third rule. Each of the rules in the grammar has an associated function for carrying out the appropriate semantics, so that the parser controls the process of interpretation, too.

The program's process of inference can be illustrated by the following example:

A ore B.
Not A.
What follows?

The exclusive disjunction symbolized by "ore" yields the mental models:

A
   B

The categorical premise yields the model:

¬ A

This model eliminates the first model of the disjunction because they cannot both be true. But it is consistent with the second model of the disjunction. Their conjunction:

¬ A   B

yields the conclusion:

B.

This conclusion is valid, because it holds in all the models – in this case, the single model – consistent with the premises.

The principles for conjoining mental models seem straightforward, but contain some subtleties. If one model represents a proposition, A, among others, and another model represents its negation, $\neg A$, their conjunction yields the empty (or null) model that represents contradictions. The previous example illustrated this principle. But what happens if the two models to be conjoined contain nothing in common? An example illustrating this case occurs with these premises:

>   If C then D.
>   E ore C.

The reader is invited to consider what possibilities are compatible with the two premises. Most individuals think that there are two:

>   C   D
>   E

The mental models of the first premise are:

>   C   D
>   . . .

and the mental models of the second premise are:

>   E
>   C

One possibility according to the second premise is E, so the program conjoins:

>   C   D   and   E

C occurs in the set of models of the disjunction from which E is drawn, so the interpretative system takes the absence of C in the model of E to mean *not* C:

>   C   D   and   E   ¬ C

Because there is now a contradiction – one model contains C and the other its negation – the result is the null model. The program next conjoins the pair:

>   C   D   and   C

D does not occur elsewhere in the set of models of the disjunction containing C, so the two models are compatible with one another. Their conjunction yields:

>   C   D

The program now constructs conjunctions with the implicit model of the conditional. The conjunction:

>   . . . and E

yields E, because E does not occur in the models of the conditional containing the implicit model. The final conjunction:

>   . . . and C

yields the null model, because C occurs in the models of the conditional, so its absence in the implicit model is treated as akin to its negation. The mental models of the conjunction of the premises are accordingly:

>   C   D
>   E

The null models are not shown because they do not represent possibilities. The two models of possibilities yield the valid conclusion:

>   C and D, ore E.

Table 12.5 summarizes the mechanisms for forming conjunctions of pairs of models. These principles apply both to the combination of sets of models, as in the preceding disjunctive inference, but they also apply to the combination of possible individuals in models of quantified propositions (Johnson-Laird, 2006).

The same mechanisms apply to the conjunction of fully explicit models except that the first mechanism in the table does not come into play. Here are the previous premises again:

>   If C then D.
>   E ore C.

A mechanism that uses mental footnotes can flesh our mental models into fully explicit

Table 12.5: The mechanisms for forming conjunctions of pairs of mental models and pairs of fully explicit models

---

1. If one model represents a proposition, A, which is not represented in the second model, then if A occurs in at least one of the models from which the second model is drawn, then its absence in the second model is treated as its negation (and mechanism 2 applies); otherwise, its absence is treated as its affirmation (and mechanism 3 applies). This mechanism applies only to mental models.
2. The conjunction of a pair of models containing respectively a proposition and its negation yield the null model, e.g.:

   A   B and ¬ A   B yield nil.
3. The conjunction of a pair of models that are not contradictory yields a model representing all the propositions in the models, e.g.:

   A   B and B   C yield A   B   C
4. The conjunction of a null model with any model yields the null model, e.g.:
   A   B and nil   yield nil.

---

models. The fully explicit models of the conditional and the disjunction (see Table 12.4) are, respectively:

$$
\begin{array}{ll}
\begin{array}{ll}
C & D \\
\neg C & D \\
\neg C & \neg D
\end{array}
&
\begin{array}{ll}
E & \neg C \\
\neg E & C
\end{array}
\end{array}
$$

There are six pair-wise conjunctions, but three of them are contradictions yielding the null model. The remaining pairs yield the following models:

$$
\begin{array}{lll}
C & D & \neg E \\
\neg C & D & E \\
\neg C & \neg D & E
\end{array}
$$

The same conclusion follows as before:

C and D, ore E.

But reasoners who rely on mental models will fail to think of the second of the these three possibilities.

A problem for formal rule theories is to find the right sequence of inferential steps to prove that a conclusion follows from the premises. The model-based program does not have a search problem, because it merely updates its set of models for each new premise. As the number of distinct atomic propositions in the premises increases, the number of models tends to increase, but it does so much less rapidly than the number of rows in a truth-table. Nevertheless, the intractability of sentential reasoning does catch up with the program and with human reasoners as the number of distinct atoms in a problem increases.

The principles for constructing conjunctions of mental models seem innocuous – just a slight variation on those for fully explicit models, which yield a complete account of sentential reasoning. After the program was written, however, it was given a test of the following sort of premises based on a hand of cards:

If there is a king then there is an ace ore if there is not a king then there is an ace.
There is a king.

When the program reasoned using mental models, it returned a single mental model:

King   Ace

But when it reasoned using fully explicit models, it returned the fully explicit model:

King   ¬ Ace

Did it really follow that there is *not* an ace? This result was so bizarre that Johnson-Laird spent half a day searching for a bug in his program, but at last discovered it in his own mind. The force of the exclusive disjunction in the first premise is that one of the two conditionals is false, and the falsity of either conditional implies that there is not an ace, so the fully explicit models did yield a valid conclusion. Given an inclusive interpretation of the disjunction, or a biconditional interpretation of the conditionals, or both, mental models still yield the (invalid) conclusion that there is an ace, whereas fully explicit models do not. Nothing definite follows from the premises with these interpretations: There may, or may not, be an ace. Yet, as experiments showed (Johnson-Laird & Savary, 1999), nearly everyone succumbs to the illusion that there *is* an ace. Johnson-Laird modified the program so that it would search for illusions by generating a vast number of premises and comparing their mental models with their fully explicit models. Subsequent experiments corroborated the occurrence of various sorts of illusory inference in sentential reasoning (Walsh & Johnson-Laird, 2004), modal reasoning about what is possible (Goldvarg & Johnson-Laird, 2000), deontic reasoning about what is permissible (Bucciarelli & Johnson-Laird, 2005), reasoning about probabilities (Johnson-Laird et al., 1999), and reasoning with quantifiers (Yang & Johnson-Laird, 2000a, 2000b). The theories based on formal rules did not predict the illusory inferences, and they have no way of postdicting them unless they posit invalid rules of inference. But in that case, they then run the risk of inconsistency. Illusory inferences are therefore a crucial corroboration of the use of mental models in reasoning, and their discovery was a result of a simulation of the theory.

5. Concepts, Models, and Minimization

Because infinitely many valid conclusions follow from any set of premises, computer programs for proving theorems do not normally draw conclusions, but instead evaluate given conclusions (see, e.g., Pelletier, 1986). Human reasoners, however, exercise real intelligence because they can draw conclusions for themselves. They abide by two principal constraints (Johnson-Laird & Byrne, 1991). First, they do not normally throw semantic information away by adding disjunctive alternatives. Second, they aim for conclusions that re-express the semantic information in the premises parsimoniously. They never, for example, draw a conclusion that merely forms a conjunction of all the premises. Of course, human performance degrades with complex problems, but the goal of parsimony provides a rational solution to the problem of which conclusions intelligent programs should draw. They should express all the semantic information in the premises in a minimal description. The logic of negation, conjunction, and disjunction is often referred to as "Boolean," after the logician George Boole. Minimization accordingly has a two-fold importance. On the one hand, it is equivalent to the minimization of electronic circuits made up from Boolean units, which are powerful enough for the central processing units of computers (Brayton et al., 1984). On the other hand, cognitive scientists have argued that simplicity is a cognitive universal (Chater & Vitányi, 2003) and that the difficulty of the human learning of Boolean concepts depends on the length of their minimal descriptions (Feldman, 2000).

A simple algorithm to find a minimal description of a set of possibilities checks all possible descriptions, gradually increasing the number of literals and connectives in them, until it discovers one that describes the set. The problem is computationally intractable, and this method is grossly inefficient. Hence, various other methods exist (e.g., Quine, 1955), but, because of the intractability of the problem, circuit designers use approximations to minimal circuits (Brayton et al., 1984). Another version of the program described in the previous section uses the notation of the sentential calculus: & (conjunction), v (inclusive disjunction), ∇ (exclusive disjunction), → (conditional), and ↔ (biconditional). It finds minimal descriptions using fully explicit

Table 12.6: The possibilities compatible with four Boolean concepts, putatively minimal descriptions of them, and true minimal descriptions discovered by the program using fully explicit models

III.   a   ¬ b   c
       ¬ a   b   ¬ c
       ¬ a   ¬ b   c
       ¬ a   ¬ b   ¬ c
Putative minimal description: (¬ a & ¬ (b & c)) v (a & (¬ b & c))

The program's description: (¬ a v c) & (¬ b v ¬ c)

IV.   a   ¬ b   ¬ c
       ¬ a   b   ¬ c
       ¬ a   ¬ b   c
       ¬ a   ¬ b   ¬ c
Putative minimal description: (¬ a & ¬ (b & c)) v (a & (¬ b & ¬ c))

The program's description: (c → (¬ a & ¬ b)) & (a → ¬ b)

V.   a   b   c
       ¬ a   b   ¬ c
       ¬ a   ¬ b   c
       ¬ a   ¬ b   ¬ c
Putative minimal description: ((¬ a & ¬ (b & c)) v (a & (b & c)))

The program's description: a ↔ (b & c)

VI.   a   b   ¬ c
        a   ¬ b   c
       ¬ a   b   c
       ¬ a   ¬ b   ¬ c
Putative minimal description: (a & ((¬ b & c) v (b & ¬ c)) v ¬ a & ((¬ b & ¬ c) v (b & c))

The program's description: (a ∇ b) ↔ c

The Roman numbers are the labels of the problems in Shepard et al. (1961).

models. Table 12.6 presents four Boolean concepts, first studied by Shepard et al. (1961), with Feldman's (2000) putative minimal descriptions and, as the program revealed, actual minimal descriptions. Shepard et al. (1961) found that concepts III, IV, and V were roughly equally difficult for their participants to learn but VI was reliably harder, so Feldman concluded that subjective difficulty is well predicted by his putative descriptions. But, as the table shows, true minimal length does not correlate with psychological complexity. In fairness to Feldman, he used only approximations to minimal descriptions, and he restricted his vocabulary to negation, conjunction, and in-

clusive disjunction on the grounds that these are the traditional Boolean primitives. However, Goodwin (2006) has shown that when concepts concern patterns of switch positions that cause a light to come on, naive individuals neither restrict their vocabulary to these primitives nor are they able to discover minimal descriptions (less than 4% of their descriptions were minimal). Parsimonious descriptions are hard to find, and they may not relate to the psychological difficulty of learning concepts.

When the program builds models from premises, it multiplies them together to interpret conjunctions. Hence, to *describe* a given set of models, it works backward, dividing the set up into subsets of models that can be multiplied together to get back to the original set. The process of division proceeds recursively until it reaches models that each contain only two items. Pairs of items are easy to describe, because the standard connectives do the job. Consider, for example, the following description (of concept V in Table 12.6):

$$((\neg a \,\&\, \neg (b \,\&\, c)) \vee (a \,\&\, (b \,\&\, c))).$$

It yields these fully explicit models of possibilities:

$$
\begin{array}{ccc}
a & b & c \\
\neg a & b & \neg c \\
\neg a & \neg b & c \\
\neg a & \neg b & \neg c
\end{array}
$$

The reader may notice, as the program does, that all four possible combinations of b and c, and their negations, occur in these possibilities. The program therefore recodes the models as:

$$
\begin{array}{cc}
a & X \\
\neg a & \neg X
\end{array}
$$

where the value of the variable X is: b & c. The program compares these two models with each of its connectives and finds the description: a ↔ X. It plugs in the description of X to yield the overall minimal description: a ↔ (b & c).

There are six sorts of decomposition of a set of models depending on whether or not any pairs of propositions or variables occur in all four possible contingencies and how the other elements relate to them. Any procedure for minimization is necessarily intractable, but the program is more efficient than some algorithms. Table 12.7 presents some typical examples of its performance with examples from logic textbooks. Each example shows the input, and the program's output, which in each of these cases are both an evaluation of the given conclusion (the last assertion in the input) and a minimal valid conclusion expressing all the information in the premises.

6. General Discussion: The Nature of Human Deductive Reasoning

Does the engine of inference rely on form or content? Indeed, might it rely on entirely different principles? For example, Shastri and Ajjanagadde (1993) describe a "connectionist" system of simulating a network of idealized nerve cells capable of simple inferences (see also Chapter 2 in this volume on connectionist models). Likewise, in a series of striking studies, Oaksford and Chater (e.g., 1998) have argued that logic is irrelevant to our everyday reasoning and to our deductions in the psychological laboratory. The right criterion to assess them is the probability calculus, and they even claim that this calculus *describes* our deductions. Our reasoning, they say, is a rational adaptation to the world, and it depends on a tractable process. Because the probability calculus is not tractable, they argue that we use heuristics rather than the calculus itself. Yet, they reject Tversky and Kahneman's (e.g., 1973) findings that heuristics can lead to into errors in probabilistic thinking. They advocate instead different heuristics, which they claim are rational. Their theory is ingenious, and, granted certain assumptions about the interpretations of premises, it gives a good account of three sorts of reasoning: performance in a hypothesis-testing task, reasoning from simple quantified assertions, and simple inferences from conditional assertions (Oaksford & Chater, 1998). Yet, serious difficulties exist for the theses of rationality, tractability, and probability: Any heuristic process that seeks to circumvent the intractability of sentential reasoning is bound to lead to systematic error, for example, the illusory inferences described earlier. And recent empirical studies have shown that the probabilistic theory often makes unsatisfactory predictions (e.g., Espino et al., 2005; Schroyens, Schaeken, & d'Ydewalle, 2001). But the decisive issue is that the preservation of truth in a valid deduction transcends validity in the probability calculus (Rips, 2002).

Many observations suggest that human deductive reasoning does not rely on form.

Table 12.7: Some examples of the program using fully explicit models

1. Input: a v b
            a → c
            b → d
            c v d
Output: This premise follows from those that preceded it: c v d

Premises are equivalent to: (a → c) & ((b → d) & (a v b))

2. Input: w v (p → i)
            i → (c v s)
            s → u
            ¬ c & ¬ u
            ¬ w
Output: This premise follows from those that preceded it: ¬ w

Premises are equivalent to: ¬ w & (¬ p & (¬ i & (¬ c & (¬ s & ¬ u))))

3. Input: (a → b) & (c → d)
            (b → e) & (d → f)
            ¬(e & f)
            a → c
            ¬ a
Output: This premise follows from those that preceded it: ¬ a.

Premises are equivalent to: ¬ a & ((b → e) & ((e → ¬ f) & ((d → f) & (c → d))))

4. Input: (v → (s & (p & m)))
            (r → (g → (¬ l → ¬ m)))
            s → r
            (p → (c → g))
            l → ¬ c
            c
            ¬ v
Output: This premise follows from those that preceded it: ¬ v.

Premises are equivalent to: ¬ v & (¬ l & (c & ((p → g) & ((s → r) & ((m & g) → ¬ r)))))

One observation is that theorists have yet to devise an algorithm for recovering the logical form of propositions. Another observation is that the inferential properties of relations and connectives are impossible to capture in a simple way. Reasoners use their knowledge of meaning, reference, and the world to modulate their interpretation of these terms. Hence, no sentential connectives in everyday language, such as "if" and "or," can be treated as they are in logic. For example, the truth of a conjunction, such as, "He fell off his bicycle and he broke his leg," depends on more than the truth of its two clauses: The events must also be in the cor-rect temporal order for the proposition to be true. Likewise, a conditional, such as "If she's in Brazil then she is not in Rio," has an interpretation that blocks a modus tollens inference (Johnson-Laird & Byrne, 2002), whereas a counterfactual conditional, such as "If she had been in Rio then she would have been in Brazil," facilitates the inference (Byrne, 2005). The use of axioms to spec-ify the logical properties of relations, such as "taller than," faces similar problems. Logical properties depend on the proposition as a whole and its context. Instead, as the sim-ulation program in Section 3 showed, rea-soners can use the meanings of propositions to construct appropriate models from which logical consequences emerge. A more recent simulation has shown how context, depending both on the current models of the discourse and on general knowledge, overrules the "logical" interpretations of connectives (Johnson-Laird, Girotto, & Legrenzi, 2004).

Because human working memory is limited in capacity, human reasoners cannot rely on truth-tables. Their mental models represent atomic propositions and their negations only when they are true in a possibility. The failure to represent what is false seems innocuous. Indeed, for several years, no one was aware of its serious consequences. However, the simulation program implementing the theory revealed for some inferences radical discrepancies between mental models and fully explicit models. These discrepancies predicted the occurrence of illusory inferences, which subsequent experiments corroborated. Some commentators argue that human reasoning depends on both formal rules and on mental models, and that the evidence shows only that sometimes human reasoners do not rely on logic, not that they never use formal rules. No conceivable evidence could ever rule out the use of formal rules on at least some occasions, but theoretical parsimony suggests that in general, human reasoners rely on mental models.

7. Conclusions

If humans err so much, how can they be rational enough to invent logic and mathematics, and science and technology? At the heart of human rationality are some simple principles that almost everyone recognizes: A conclusion must be the case if it holds in all the possibilities compatible with the premises. It does not follow from the premises if it runs into a counterexample, that is, a possibility that is consistent with the premises, but not with the conclusion. The foundation of rationality is our knowledge of these principles, and they are embodied in the programs simulating the theory of mental models.

References

Aho, A. V., & Ullman, J. D. (1972). *The theory of parsing, translation, and compiling, Vol. 1: Parsing.* Englewood Cliffs, NJ: Prentice Hall.

Bara, B., Bucciarelli M., & Lombardo V. (2001). Model theory of deduction: A unified computational approach. *Cognitive Science, 25,* 839–901.

Barwise, J. (1993). Everyday reasoning and logical inference. *Behavioral and Brain Sciences, 16,* 337–338.

Beth, E. W., & Piaget, J. (1966). *Mathematical epistemology and psychology.* Dordrecht, Netherlands: Reidel.

Braine, M. D. S. (1978). On the relation between the natural logic of reasoning and standard logic. *Psychological Review, 85,* 1–21.

Braine, M. D. S., & O'Brien, D. P. (Eds). (1998). *Mental logic.* Mahwah, NJ: Lawrence Erlbaum.

Brayton, R. K., Hachtel, G. D., McMullen, C. T., & Sangiovanni-Vincentelli, A. L. (1984). *Logic minimization algorithms for VLSI synthesis.* New York: Kluwer.

Bucciarelli, M., & Johnson-Laird, P. N. (1999). Strategies in syllogistic reasoning. *Cognitive Science, 23,* 247–303.

Bucciarelli, M., & Johnson-Laird, P. N. (2005). Naïve deontics: A theory of meaning, representation, and reasoning. *Cognitive Psychology, 50,* 159–193.

Byrne, R. M. J. (2005). *The rational imagination: How people create alternatives to reality.* Cambridge, MA: MIT Press.

Byrne, R. M. J., & Johnson-Laird, P. N. (1989). Spatial reasoning. *Journal of Memory and Language, 28,* 564–575.

Carreiras, M., & Santamaría, C. (1997). Reasoning about relations: Spatial and nonspatial problems. *Thinking & Reasoning, 3,* 191–208.

Chater, N., & Vitányi, P. (2003). Simplicity: A unifying principle in cognitive science? *Trends in Cognitive Science, 7,* 19–22.

Cook, S. A. (1971). The complexity of theorem proving procedures. In *Proceedings of the Third Annual Association of Computing Machinery Symposium on the Theory of Computing* (pp. 151–158).

Espino, O., Santamaría, C., Meseguer, E., & Carreiras, M. (2005). Early and late processes in syllogistic reasoning: Evidence from eye-movements. *Cognition, 98,* B1–B9.

Feldman, J. (2000). Minimization of Boolean complexity in human concept learning. *Nature, 407,* 630–633.

Goldvarg, Y., & Johnson-Laird, P. N. (2000). Illusions in modal reasoning. *Memory & Cognition, 28,* 282–294.

Goodwin, G. P. (2006). *How individuals learn simple Boolean systems and diagnose their faults.* Unpublished doctoral thesis, Princeton University, Princeton, NJ.

Goodwin, G., & Johnson-Laird, P. N. (2005). Reasoning about relations. *Psychological Review, 112,* 468–493.

Jahn, G., Knauff, M., & Johnson-Laird, P. N. (2007). Preferred mental models in reasoning about spatial relations. *Memory & Cognition,* in press.

Jeffrey, R. (1981). *Formal logic: Its scope and limits* (2nd ed.). New York: McGraw-Hill.

Johnson-Laird, P. N. (1975). Models of deduction. In Falmagne, R. J. (Ed.), *Reasoning: Representation and process in children and adults* (pp. 7–54). Hillsdale, NJ: Lawrence Erlbaum.

Johnson-Laird, P. N. (2006). *How we reason.* Oxford, UK: Oxford University Press.

Johnson-Laird, P. N., & Byrne, R. M. J. (1991). *Deduction.* Hillsdale, NJ: Lawrence Erlbaum.

Johnson-Laird, P. N., & Byrne, R. M. J. (2002). Conditionals: A theory of meaning, pragmatics, and inference. *Psychological Review, 109,* 646–678.

Johnson-Laird, P. N., Girotto, V., & Legrenzi, P. (2004). Reasoning from inconsistency to consistency. *Psychological Review, 111,* 640–661.

Johnson-Laird, P. N., & Hasson, U. (2003). Counterexamples in sentential reasoning. *Memory & Cognition, 31,* 1105–1113.

Johnson-Laird, P. N., Legrenzi, P., Girotto, V., Legrenzi, M., & Caverni, J-P. (1999) Naive probability: A mental model theory of extensional reasoning. *Psychological Review, 106,* 62–88.

Johnson-Laird, P. N., & Savary, F. (1999). Illusory inferences: A novel class of erroneous deductions. *Cognition, 71,* 191–229.

Metzler, J., & Shepard, R. N. (1982). Transformational studies of the internal representations of three-dimensional objects. In Shepard, R. N., & Cooper, L. A., *Mental images and their transformations* (pp. 25–71). Cambridge, MA: MIT Press.

Montague, R. (1974). *Formal philosophy: Selected papers.* New Haven, CT: Yale University Press.

Newell, A. (1990). *Unified theories of cognition.* Cambridge, MA: Harvard University Press.

Oaksford, M., & Chater, N. (1998). *Rationality in an uncertain world.* Hove, UK: Psychology Press.

Oberauer, K., & Wilhelm, O. (2000). Effects of directionality in deductive reasoning: I. The comprehension of single relational premises. *Journal of Experimental Psychology: Learning, Memory, and Cognition, 26,* 1702–1712.

Osherson, D. N. (1974–1976). *Logical abilities in children* (Vols. 1–4). Hillsdale, NJ: Lawrence Erlbaum.

Pelletier, F. J. (1986). Seventy-five problems for testing automatic theorem provers. *Journal of Automated Reasoning, 2,* 191–216.

Polk, T. A., & Newell, A. (1995). Deduction as verbal reasoning. *Psychological Review, 102,* 533–566.

Quine, W. V. O. (1955). A way to simplify truth functions, *American Mathematical Monthly, 59,* 521–531.

Rips, L. J. (1983). Cognitive processes in propositional reasoning. *Psychological Review, 90,* 38–71.

Rips, L. J. (1989). The psychology of knights and knaves. *Cognition, 31,* 85–116.

Rips, L. J. (1994). *The psychology of proof.* Cambridge, MA: MIT Press.

Rips, L. J. (2002). Reasoning. In Medin, D. (Ed.), *Stevens' handbook of experimental psychology, vol. 2: Memory and cognitive processes* (3rd ed., pp. 317–362). New York: John Wiley.

Schaeken, W. S., Johnson-Laird, P. N., & d'Ydewalle, G. (1996a). Mental models and temporal reasoning. *Cognition, 60,* 205–234.

Schaeken, W. S., Johnson-Laird, P. N., & d'Ydewalle, G. (1996b). Tense, aspect, and temporal reasoning. *Thinking and Reasoning, 2,* 309–327.

Schroyens, W., Schaeken, W., & d'Ydewalle, G. (2001). The processing of negations in conditional reasoning: A meta-analytical case study in mental models and/or mental logic theory. *Thinking & Reasoning, 7,* 121–172.

Shastri, L., & Ajjanagadde, V. (1993). From simple associations to systematic reasoning: A connectionist representation of rules, variables and dynamic bindings using temporal synchrony. *Behavioral and Brain Sciences, 16,* 417–494.

Shepard, R., Hovland, C. L., & Jenkins, H. M. (1961). Learning and memorization of classifications. *Psychological Monographs: General and Applied, 75,* 1–42.

Tversky, A., & Kahneman, D. (1973). Availability: A heuristic for judging frequency and
probability. *Cognitive Psychology, 5*, 207–232.

Van der Henst, J.-B., Yang, Y., & Johnson-Laird,
P. N. (2002). Strategies in sentential reasoning. *Cognitive Science, 26*, 425–468.

Vandierendonck, A., Dierckx, V., & De Vooght,
G. (2004). Mental model construction in linear reasoning: Evidence for the construction
of initial annotated models. *Quarterly Journal
of Experimental Psychology, 57A*, 1369–1391.

Walsh, C., & Johnson-Laird, P. N. (2004). Co-
reference and reasoning. *Memory & Cognition,
32*, 96–106.

Yang, Y., & Johnson-Laird, P. N. (2000a). Illusory inferences with quantified assertions:
How to make the impossible seem possible,
and *vice versa*. *Memory & Cognition, 28*, 452–
465.

Yang, Y., & Johnson-Laird, P. N. (2000b) How
to eliminate illusions in quantified reasoning.
Memory & Cognition, 28, 1050–1059.

CHAPTER 13

Computational Models of Skill Acquisition

Stellan Ohlsson

1. Introduction: Topic, Scope and Viewpoint

Daily life is a sequence of tasks: cook breakfast; drive to work; make phone calls; use a word processor or a spread sheet; take an order from a customer, operate a steel lathe or diagnose a patient; plan a charity event; play tennis; shop for groceries; cook dinner; load the dishwasher; tutor children in arithmetic; make a cup of tea; brush teeth; and set the alarm for next morning. The number of distinct tasks a person learns to perform in a lifetime is certainly in the hundreds, probably in the thousands.

There is no entirely satisfactory way to refer to the type of knowledge that supports task performance. The phrase *know-how* has entered the popular lexicon but is stylistically unbearable. The philosopher Gilbert Ryle (1949/1968) famously distinguished *knowing how* from *knowing that*. Psychometricians talk about *abilities* (Carroll, 1993), whereas artificial intelligence researchers talk about *procedural knowledge* (Winograd, 1975); both terms are somewhat misleading or awkward. The alterna-

tive term *practical knowledge* resonates with other relevant usages, such as the verb *to practice*, the cognitive anthropologist's concept of *a practice*, the philosopher's concept of *practical inference*, and the common sense distinction *theory versus practice*. In this review, the term "practical knowledge" refers to whatever a person knows about how to perform tasks, achieve desired effects, or reach goals, whereas "declarative knowledge" refers to knowledge about how things are.

How is practical knowledge acquired? How can a person – or some other intelligent agent, if any – bootstrap himself or herself from inability to mastery? The purpose of this chapter is to organize the stock of current answers to this question in a way that facilitates overview, comparison, and future use.

This chapter focuses on cognitive as opposed to sensori-motor skills. The distinguishing feature of a cognitive skill is that the physical characteristics of the relevant actions (amplitude, force, speed, torque, etc.) are not essential for task performance. Compare tennis with chess in this respect. The success of a tennis serve is a function of the exact trajectory of the racket, but a chess move is the same move, from the point of view of chess, whether it is executed by moving the piece by hand, foot, or mouth, physically very different movements. The equivalence class of movements that count as making *chess move so-and-so* abstracts over the physical characteristics of those movements, and its success, as a chess move, is not a function of those characteristics. Many skills have both cognitive and sensori-motor components, but the hypotheses discussed in this chapter were not designed to explain the acquisition of the latter.

A second boundary of this review derives from its focus on computer models. It is possible and useful to reason with informal hypotheses, but for inclusion here, a hypothesis has to be implemented as a running computer program, and there must be at least one publication that reports results of a simulation run. Also, this chapter emphasizes models that have been proposed as explanations for human learning over contributions to machine learning research or robotics. This chapter focuses on models that create or alter symbolic knowledge representations and deals only briefly with models that learn by adjusting quantitative properties of knowledge structures. Although occasionally refering to empirical studies, this chapter is primarily a review of theoretical concepts. This chapter does not attempt to pass judgment on the empirical adequacy of the different models, for reasons that are spelled out in the last section. Although no current hypothesis explains all skill acquisition phenomena, this chapter proceeds on the assumption that each hypothesis contains some grain of truth to be extracted and incorporated into future models.

The unit of analysis throughout is the individual *learning mechanism*. A learning mechanism is specified by its *triggering conditions*, that is, the conditions under which it will execute, and by the particular *change* that occurs under those conditions. As an illustration, consider the classical concept of association: If two concepts are active simultaneously, a memory link is created between them. The triggering condition is in this case the simultaneous occurrence of the two concepts in working memory; the change is the creation of a link. The learning mechanisms considered in this chapter are considerably more complicated, but their descriptions can nevertheless be parsed into a set of triggering conditions and a change process.

The learning mechanism is a more fine-grained unit than the model or the cognitive architecture because a model might include multiple learning mechanisms and, in fact, some models do. Slicing models into their component learning mechanisms facilitates comparisons among the latter. This chapter does not review every application of every model, but focuses on publications that introduce, explain, or demonstrate learning mechanisms.

Improvements in a skill cannot come out of thin air, so a learning mechanism must draw on some source of information. Different mechanisms operate on different sources: Learning from instruction is not the same process as learning from error. In general, each learning mechanism takes a specific type of information as input. I refer to this as the *Information Specificity Principle*. (see Figure 13.1).

It is highly unlikely that all phenomena associated with the acquisition of cognitive skills can be explained by a single learning mechanism. We do not know how many distinct modes of cognitive change there are, but it is assumed that the observable changes in overt behavior are a product of multiple, interacting mechanisms.

In short, to explain skill acquisition is to specify a repertoire of learning mechanisms, each mechanism consisting of a triggering condition and a change process, to implement these within some performance system and to demonstrate, by running the resulting simulation model, that the cumulative outcome of the interactions among the specified mechanisms mimics the acquisition of ecologically relevant cognitive skills across tasks, initial knowledge states, and learning scenarios. This formulation of the skill acquisition problem is the product of a century of scientific progress.

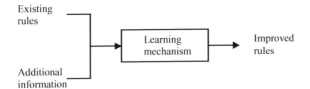

Figure 13.1. Schema for learning mechanisms.

2. History

In William James' (1980) comprehensive summary of the principles of psychology, there is a chapter on habit formation but no chapter on learning. Systematic empirical research on the acquisition of cognitive (as opposed to sensori-motor) skills began with Edward Thorndike's PhD thesis, begun in 1896 under James at Harvard University but issued a few years later from Teachers College at Columbia University. Thorndike (1898) investigated how various species of animals learned to escape from cages with nonobvious door-opening mechanisms. He displayed the time it took individual animals to escape from a box as a function of trial number. Although Hermann Ebbinghaus (1885/1964) had already published curves for the memorization and forgetting of lists of syllables, Thorndike was the first person to plot what we now call practice curves for complex skills. He formulated the Law of Effect, which says that the probability that a learner will perform a particular action is increased when the action is followed by a positive outcome (a "satisfier" in Thorndike's terminology) and decreased when followed by a negative outcome ("annoyer"; Thorndike, 1927). This proved to be an enduring insight.

Learning became the major theme of the behaviorist movement, conventionally dated as beginning with Watson's (1913) article, "Psychology as the Behaviorist Views It." During the 1913–1955 period, *experimental psychology* and *learning theory* became almost synonymous in the United States, but the dominant experimental paradigm for the study of learning was the memorization of lists of letters, syllables, or words. Woodworth's (1938) attempt to replicate

James's comprehensive summary from fifty years earlier included a chapter on practice and skill that mentioned twenty-seven studies that tracked learning in complex tasks, like archery, telegraphy, and typing (pp. 156–175). The negatively accelerated shape of the practice curve was well established, and the search for a mathematical equation had begun (pp. 170–173). The idea that the process of acquiring a new skill goes through phases that involve different types of changes was stated but not developed. Both ideas have turned out to be enduring (Ackerman, 1990; Newell & Rosenbloom, 1981).

During World War II, psychologists in Britain and the United States were prompted to move away from list learning and focus on complex skills by the need to contribute to the war effort (Gardner, 1985). The war posed novel problems, such as how to train anti-aircraft gunners. (Anti-aircraft guns were still aimed manually.) A second transforming influence was that psychologists worked alongside engineers, scientists, and mathematicians who were in the process of creating new information technologies. Code breaking and other information processing problems led researchers to realize that information can be measured and processed in objective and systematic ways, making it possible both to build information processing systems and to view humans and animals as examples of such systems.

Immediately after the war, Norbert Weiner at the Massachusetts Institute of Technology envisioned an interdisciplinary science – called *cybernetics* – which was to study complex information-based systems, encompassing humans, machines, and animals, in terms of *feedback circles*. The idea of replacing the stimulus–response reflex with the feedback circle as the central concept of psychology played the star role in Miller, Galanter, and Pribram's (1960) sketch of what we now call the cognitive architecture. Although the concept of feedback remains important, a variety of factors, including Wiener's focus on continuous feedback, which can only be manipulated with complex mathematics, reduced the influence of the cybernetic approach (Conway & Siegelman, 2005). It was soon overtaken by the digital approach, variously called *complex information processing* and, eventually, *artificial intelligence*, launched by Newell, Shaw, and Simon (1958) with an article describing the Logic Theorist, the first symbol-processing computer program that performed a task, logical deduction, that is recognized as requiring intelligence when done by people. The program formalized the notion of *heuristic search*, another enduring concept. Significantly, the article was published in *Psychological Review* rather than an engineering journal, and the authors offered speculations on the relation between their program and human reasoning. The article thus simultaneously established the two fields of artificial intelligence and cognitive modeling (Crevier, 1993).

Paradoxically, the success of the digital symbol manipulating approach had a detrimental effect on the study of learning. In the period 1958–1979, few leading cognitive psychologists studied the effects of practice or other problems related to skill acquisition (but see Welford, 1968, for an exception). The new modeling techniques were at first applied to steady-state performance. This was difficult enough with the crude programming tools available at the time. Success in simulating human behavior – any behavior – was recognized as an achievement in and of itself, even if a model did not simulate changes in that behavior over time.

The era of computational skill acquisition models was inaugurated with a *Psychological Review* article by Anzai and Simon (1979). They presented a computer program that modeled the successive strategy changes of a single person who solved the Tower of Hanoi problem multiple times. The article

demonstrated the feasibility of simulating the acquisition and not only the execution of cognitive skills. The article was closely followed by the first set of learning assumptions associated with J. R. Anderson's ACT model. Anderson, Kline, and Beasley (1978) laid out a design for a cognitive architecture with multiple learning mechanisms, later published in Anderson (1982, 1983, 1987, 1993).

Several of the early simulation efforts were formulated within the production system framework (Davis & King, 1977; Neches, Langley, & Klahr, 1987; Newell, 1972, 1973; Newell & Simon, 1972; Waterman & Hayes-Roth, 1978). In this framework, practical knowledge is encoded in *rules*, knowledge structures of the form *if the current goal is G, and the current situation is S, then consider performing action A.* A production system architecture executes a collection of such rules through a cyclic process: Match the G and S components against the current goal and the current situation (as represented in working memory); enter all matching rules into a *conflict set*; select a rule by resolving the conflict; and execute (the action of) the selected rule. The action alters the state of the world, and the cycle repeats. The production rule notation

Goal, Situation → Action

is as close as the field has come to a *lingua franca* for the analysis of cognitive skills.

The Anzai and Simon (1979) article, the emergence of production systems as a shared formalism, the launching of Anderson's ACT project, and other events collectively triggered an unprecedented explosion of the theoretical imagination. More new hypotheses about the mechanisms behind the acquisition of cognitive skills were proposed in the years 1979–1995 than in the previous century. The success of the initial models established computer simulation as a workable and even indispensable theoretical tool. Informal arguments to the effect that this or that learning mechanism has such-and-such behavioral consequences remain acceptable, but they are clearly inferior to predictions produced by running a simulation model. The last twenty years have seen a proliferation of formal approaches, including neural networks (Chapter 2 in this volume), genetic algorithms (De Jong, 1990; Holland, 1975), and dynamic systems (Chapter 4 in this volume). However, the invention of novel learning mechanisms appears to have slowed.

The following four sections review the skill acquisition mechanisms that have been proposed since Thorndike's experimental subjects clawed, pecked, and pushed their way out of his problem boxes. The explanatory power of these mechanisms disproves the pessimists who would argue that cognitive modeling of learning has made little progress. The task of disproving the optimists is postponed until the last section.

3. How Does Skill Practice Begin?

The three phases of skill acquisition sketched by Woodworth (1938) and articulated further by Fitts (1964) and others provide a useful framework for thinking about skill acquisition. At the outset of practice, the learner's main problem is how to get started, how to construct an initial strategy for the target task. Once the learner is acting vis-à-vis the task, the challenge is to improve that initial strategy until the task has been mastered. Finally, in the long run, the challenge is to optimize the mastered strategy. Each phase provides different sources of information and hence affords different learning mechanisms. This section reviews learning mechanisms that primarily operate within the first phase, while the following two sections focus on the second and third phases. Within each phase, learning mechanisms are distinguished on the basis of the source of information that they draw on, their triggering conditions, and the type of change they compute.

The grouping of learning mechanisms by phase should not be interpreted as a claim that the phases are created by a big switch in the mind that turns mechanisms on and off. I assume that all learning mechanisms operate continuously and in parallel, but the types of information they require as input might vary in abundance and accessibility over time. The phases emerge out of the fact that some types of information becomes less accessible, frequent, or useful as learning progresses, whereas other types of information increase, producing a gradual shift in the relative importance of different types of changes across the successive phases. The final behavior – the fast, accurate, smooth, and nearly effortless expert performance – is the composite and aggregate outcome of the mechanisms operating in all three phases.

For present purposes, the first phase is defined as starting when the learner encounters the task and as ending when the learner completes the task for the first time. The learning mechanisms that dominate this phase are answers to the question, *how can skill practice begin?* How does a learner know what to do before he or she has learned what to do? There are at least four principled approaches to this paradox, corresponding to four distinct sources of information that can be available at the outset of practice: instructions, abstract declarative knowledge, prior skills, and someone else's solution.

3.1. *Interpret Exhortations*

Unfamiliar tasks often come with written or spoken recipes for what to do, variously referred to as *advice* or *instructions*; in linguistic terminology, *exhortations*. Dispensing spoken advice is a large part of what coaches and tutors do. Written sources include cook books, manuals for electronic devices, instruction sheets for assembly-required furniture, and software manuals. Exhortations are presumably understood via the standard discourse comprehension processes studied in psycholinguistics (word recognition, mental lexicon look-up, disambiguation, syntactic parsing, implicit inferences and so on; see Gernsbacher, 1994), but people cannot follow complex instructions without hesitation, backtracking, errors, and repeated rehearsals, even when those instructions are fully understood, so additional processes are required to translate the output of discourse comprehension into executable practical knowledge.

In McCarthy's (1959, 1963)[1] early design for an advice taker system, reasoning
about exhortations and actions was assimilated to logical deduction via axioms that
define nonlogical operators like *can* and *do*.
Instructions are propositional grist for the
deductive mill; no special process needed
(see also Simon, 1972). This deductive reasoning approach continues within logic programming (Amir & Maynard-Zhang, 2004;
Giunchiglia et al., 2004) but remains largely
unexplored by psychologists modeling human skill acquisition (but see Chapter 5 in
this volume).

The Advice Taker model described by
Mostow (1983) and Hayes-Roth, Klahr, and
Mostow (1981) was designed to opera-
tionalize exhortations by transforming them
into executable plans. In the context of the
game of hearts, a novice might be told *if you
can't take all the points in a round, take as few
as possible*. If the learner does not yet know
how to take few points, he or she has to refer
to the definitions of *take*, *few*, and *points* to
expand the advice into an action he or she
knows how to do, for example, *play a low
card*. This amounts to a top-down search
through all alternative transformations allowed by concept definitions, background
knowledge, and so on. Mostow (1983) reports using a repertoire of approximately
200 transformation rules to find a 100-step
expansion of the advice *avoid taking points*
into the executable action *play a low card*
(given a particular state of knowledge about
the game).

Nonlogical operators and transformation
rules have to be general across domains to
serve their purpose, so they share the difficult question of their origin. A contrasting approach is employed in Instructo-Soar
(Huffman & Laird, 1995). An exhortation
is operationalized by constructing an explanation for why it is good advice. The

system conducts an internal search (look-
ahead) from the current situation (or a hypothetical situation specified in the conditional part of an exhortation like, *if the red
light is flashing, sound the alarm*) until it finds
a path to the relevant goal that includes the
recommended step. Soar's chunking mechanism – a form of explanation-based learning[2] – is then applied to create a new rule (or
rules) that can generate that path in the future without search. This technique allows
Instructo-Soar to acquire complex actions
as well as other types of knowledge from
task instructions. Instructo-Soar is equipped
with a natural language front end and receives instructions in English. An alternative approach to translating instructions
for a radar operting task into production
rules in the ACT-R system is described by
Taatgen (2005). A simpler translation of instructions into production rules was implemented in the Instructable Production System (Rychener, 1983; Rychener & Newell,
1978).

Doane et al. (2000) described a system,
UNICOM, that learns to use the Unix
operating system from instructions. An
updated version, called ADAPT-PILOT,
accurately models the effect of on-line instructions on the behavior of jet pilots during training (Doane & Sohn, 2000; Sohn
& Doane, 2002). These models are based on
the construction-integration theory of discourse comprehension proposed by Kintsch
(1998). General background knowledge and
knowledge of the current state of the
world are represented as propositions, and
plan elements – internal representations of
executable actions – are represented in

---

1 The two papers referenced here were reprinted as
sections 7.1 and 7.2, respectively, of a chapter titled
"Programs with Common Sense" in Minsky (1968).
Note that the chapter with that same title in Lif-
schitz (1990) corresponds to section 7.1, i.e., to
McCarthy (1959), but leaves out the content in
McCarthy (1963).

2 Explanation-based learning, henceforth EBL, is a
machine learning technique that compresses a deductive proof or a sequence of rule executions
into a single knowledge structure that connects the
premises and the conclusion. The key aspect of
the technique is that it aligns variable bindings in
the successive steps in such a way as to identify
which constants can be replaced by variables. That
is, it produces a motivated, conservative generalization of the compressed structure. What kind of
learning EBL implements depends on context, origin of its input, and the use made of its output. See
Russell and Norvig (1995) for an introduction.

terms of their preconditions and outcomes. All of these are linked in a single associative network on the basis of overlap of predicates. Links can be excitatory or inhibitory. In each cycle of operation, a standard network algorithm is used to compute the current activation level of each node (proposition or plan element). The plan element with the highest activation level is chosen for execution. Its outcome is recorded in the network, and the cycle starts over. Learning occurs by incorporating verbal prompts, for example, *you will need to use the arrow symbol "≥" that redirects the output from a command to a file*, into the associative network. This alters the set of connections, hence, the outcome of the construction-integration process, and, ultimately, which plan element is executed.

There are other applications of the network concept to the problem of learning from instruction. The CAP2 network model described by Schneider and Oliver (1991) and Schneider and Chein (2003) is instructable in the related sense that a symbolic representation of the target skill can inform and speed up learning in a neural network.

The proposed mechanisms capture the complexity of learning from exhortations, but the psychological validity of their details is open to question. Also, these mechanisms apply primarily to initial instructions. They do not model learning from tutorial feedback, because they do not relate what is said to what was just done. Models of learning from instruction are potentially useful in educational research (Ohlsson, 1992; Ohlsson, Ernst & Rees, 1992; VanLehn, Ohlsson, & Nason 1994).

3.2. *Reason from Abstract Declarative Knowledge*

An intelligent agent who desires to travel southward but who is facing north, and who knows something about the compass, should be able to infer that his or her next action ought to be *turn around*. The abstract declarative principles that hold in this situation – the agent's mental model of the Earth, the

compass, and their relation – can guide action, and it is tempting to believe that the flexibility of human beings is, in part, a function of cognitive processes that make such guidance explicit. How else did Christoffer Columbus decide that *the Earth is round* implies *sail West*? The strength of the intuition belies the difficulty of specifying the relevant processes.

The *proceduralization* mechanism proposed by Anderson (1982, 1983) processes abstract declarative knowledge with interpretative production rules, which match parts of declarative representations and create new production rules. To illustrate the flavor of the approach, consider the following didactive example (not identical to any of the author's own examples): *If you want to achieve G, and you know the proposition "if S, then G," then form the new production rule: if you want to achieve G, then set the subgoal to achieve S.* Execution of this interpretative rule has two important consequences: It incorporates the declarative principle *if S, then G* into the learner's practical knowledge, and it eliminates the need to retrieve that piece of knowledge from memory. Neves and Anderson (1981) demonstrated how a collection of interpretative rules can produce executable rules for proof finding in plane geometry from declarative representations of geometry theorems.

The principles-to-actions transformation has been studied in depth in the domain of counting. Empirical studies indicate that children know very early some relevant principles, for example, that the counting words form a linear sequence, that the mapping from words to objects is supposed to be one-one, and that the last counting word represents the cardinality of the set that is counted (Gelman & Gallistel, 1978). In the COUNTPLAN model (Greeno, Riley, & Gelman, 1984; Smith, Greeno, & Vitolo, 1989), these principles are represented as action schemata, which are processed by a planning-like process to yield a plan for how to count a set of objects. A strong feature of the model is that it can generate plans for nonstandard counting tasks, for example, *count the yellow objects before the blue ones*. A very different process for turning the counting principles into practical knowledge is described in Ohlsson and Rees (1991a).

That these mechanisms operate in the domains of geometry and counting is no accident. The idea that action is – or ought to be – derived from principles is entrenched in mathematics education research (Hiebert, 1986). To the extent that the principled knowledge is communicated via written or spoken discourse, the problem of deriving action from abstract knowledge and of learning from instruction become intertwined. But proceduralization and planning apply equally well to knowledge retrieved from long-term memory.

3.3. *Transfer Prior Knowledge*

Initial rules for an unfamiliar task can be generated by adapting previously learned rules. That is, the problem of how practice gets under way can be subsumed under the problem of transfer of training. There are three principled ideas about how learners can utilize this source of information: identical elements, analogy, and subsumption.

3.3.1. IDENTITY

If the unfamiliar task is identical in some respects to an already familiar task, then components of the previously learned skill might apply to the unfamiliar task without change (*the identical elements hypothesis*; Thorndike, 1911, pp. 243–245). This hypothesis comes for free with a production system architecture because rules are automatically considered whenever they match the current situation. Kieras and Bovair (1986), Singley and Anderson (1989), and Pirolli and Recker (1994) report success in predicting the magnitude of transfer effects by counting the number of rules shared between two methods. However, the identical rules hypothesis predicts that positive transfer effects are necessarily symmetrical in magnitude, a dubious prediction (Ohlsson, 2007). Also, identity is a very restrictive criterion for the re-use of practical knowledge.

3.3.2. ANALOGY

The hypothesis of *analogical transfer* assumes a mapping process that identifies structural similarities between the task at hand and some already mastered task. The mapping is used to construct a method or a solution for the unfamiliar task, using the familiar one as a template. For example, consider a situation described by *Block A is on the table, Block B is on the table*, and *Block C is on top of Block B*. If the goal is to *put Block C on Block A*, then the successful action sequence is to *grasp C, lift C up, move C sideways*, and *put C down*. When the learner encounters a second situation in which *Box R is inside Box X, Box S is inside Box X, Box T is inside Box S*, and the goal is to *put T inside R*, the mapping

$$\{table \rightarrow Box \ X,$$
$$on \ top \ of \rightarrow inside,$$
$$Block \ A \rightarrow Box \ R,$$
$$etc.\}$$

leads to the analogous solution *grasp T, take T out of X, move T sideways*, and *put T inside R*. The two analogues are not similar in any perceptual sense, but they share the same relational structure, so one can serve as a template for the other.

There are multiple ways to implement the two processes of analogical mapping and inference. The structure mapping principle proposed by Gentner (1983) and implemented in the Structure Mapping Engine (Falkenhainer, Forbus, & Gentner, 1989; Forbus, Gentner, & Law, 1994) says that higher-order relations should weigh more in choosing a mapping than lower-order relations and perceptual features. Holyoak and colleagues (Holyoak, 1985; Holyoak & Thagard, 1989a; Spellman & Holyoak, 1996) emphasized pragmatic factors, that is, which mapping seems best from the point of view of the learner's current purpose. The mapping processes by Keane, Ledgeway, and Duff (1994) and Wilson et al. (2001) are designed to minimize cognitive load, the former by satisfying a variety of constraints, for example, *map only objects of the same type*, and the latter by only mapping a single pair of propositions at a time. The path-mapping process proposed by Salvucci and Anderson (2001), however, pursues flexibility by separating a low-level, object-to-object mapping process from the higher-order, acquired, and hence potentially domain-specific processes that use it. Mapping processes can be implemented as connectionist networks (Holyoak & Thagard, 1989b; Hummel & Holyoak, 1997, 2003). Anderson and Thompson (1989) and Kokinov and Petrov (2001) emphasize the need to integrate analogical reasoning with other cognitive functions.

Of particular interest from the point of view of skill acquisition is the distinction between different types of analogical inferences. In some models, an analogical mapping is used to construct a solution *path* for the target problem, as in the previous didactic block/box example. Carbonell (1983, 1986; Veloso & Carbonell, 1993) proposed a *derivational analogy* mechanism of this sort. The learner infers a solution to the target problem, a sequence of actions, but no general strategy or method, so this conservative process will primarily affect behavior on the current task. In other models, an analogical mapping is used to infer a solution *method*; see VanLehn and Brown (1980) for an early attempt in terms of planning nets. At a more fine-grained level, the analogy might generate a part of a method, such as a single production rule (Anderson & Thompson, 1989; Blessing & Anderson, 1996; Pirolli, 1986, 1991). In these cases, the learner gains new practical knowledge that might apply not only to the target task but also to future tasks, a riskier type of analogical inference.

In yet another variation on the analogy theme, the EUREKA system by Jones and Langley (2005) uses analogical mapping to infer how a fully specified, past problem-solving step can be applied to the current situation. The Cascade model (VanLehn & Jones, 1993) uses a closely related mechanism. Although this application of analogy – *analogical operator retrieval* – is a part of the performance mechanism rather than a learning mechanism, it allows past steps, derivations, or problem-solving episodes, even if completely specific, to affect future behavior.

3.3.3. SUBSUMPTION
Some prior cognitive skills transfer to the target task because they are general enough to subsume the unfamiliar task at hand. The idea of wide applicability through abstraction or generality goes back to antiquity, but takes a rather different form in the context of practical as opposed to declarative knowledge. General or *weak methods* make few assumptions about the task to which they are applied, so the learner does not need to know much about the task to use them (Newell, 1990; Newell & Simon, 1972). By the same token, such methods do not provide strong guidance. Different weak methods structure search in different ways. Hill-climbing (take only steps that improve the current situation), backward search (identify what the last step before achieving the current goal would have to be and pose its requirements as subgoals, then iterate) and means–ends analysis (identify differences between the current state and the goal and think of ways to reduce each one) are the most well-known weak methods. For example, Elio and Scharf's (1990) EUREKA model initially solves physics problems via means–ends analysis, but accumulates problem-solving experiences into problem schemas that gradually come to direct future problem-solving efforts.

People also possess a repertoire of slightly more specific but still weak heuristics such as *if you want to figure out how to use an unfamiliar device, push buttons at random and see what happens*, and *if you want to know how to get to location X, ask someone*. Weak methods and heuristics are not learning mechanisms – they do not create new practical knowledge – but they serve to generate task-relevant actions. The actions produce new information about the task, which in turn can be used by a variety learning mechanisms; see the following section. When weak methods dominate initial task behavior, skill acquisition is a process of *specialization*, because it transforms those methods into domain-specific heuristics and strategies. This is a widely adopted principle (Anderson, 1987; Jones, Ritter & Wood, 2000; Langley, 1985; Ohlsson, 1996; Rosenbloom, Laird, & Newell, 1993; Sun, Slusarz, & Terry, 2005; VanLehn, 1999; VanLehn & Jones, 1993). It represents an important insight, because common sense suggests that learning proceeds in the opposite direction, from concrete actions to more abstract competencies.

There is no reason to doubt the psychological reality of either of these three transfer relations – identity, analogy, and subsumption – but there are different ways to exploit each one. Both analogy and subsumption are relaxations of the strict criterion of identity. They make prior skills more widely applicable by allowing for some differences between past and current tasks.

3.4. *Study Someone Else's Solution*

A fourth source of information on which to base initial behavior vis-à-vis an unfamiliar task is a solution provided by someone else. In an educational setting, a teacher or helpful textbook author might provide a written representation of a correct solution, a so-called *solved example*. To learn from a solved example, the learner has to study the successive steps and infer how each step was generated. There are at least three key challenges to learning from solved examples: The example might be incomplete, suppressing some (presumed obvious) steps for the sake of conciseness, which forces the learner to interpolate the missing steps. Also, a solved example might not explain why each step is the correct step where it occurs, which forces the learner to guess the correct conditions on the actions. Finally, because a solved example is specific (by definition of "example"), there is the issue how, and how far, to generalize each step.

The Sierra model (VanLehn, 1983, 1987) learned procedures from sequences of solved examples, organized into lessons, in the domain of place-value arithmetic. The examples were parsed both top-down and bottom-up. Various constraints were applied to choose a possible way to close the gap, especially the *one-subprocedure per lesson* constraint (VanLehn, 1987). Sierra produced a set of initial ("core") procedures that were not guaranteed to be complete and hence might generate impasses when executed, necessitating further learning. The main purpose of Sierra was to explain, in conjunction with Repair Theory, the origin of errors in children's arithmetic (see Section 4.2 on learning at impasses).

The Cascade model (VanLehn, 1999; VanLehn & Jones, 1993; VanLehn, Jones, & Chi, 1992) learns from solved examples in the domain of physics. The model studies examples consisting of sequences of lines. It attempts to derive each line, using its domain-specific knowledge. If the derivation succeeds, it stores the derivation itself; because Cascade uses analogies with past derivations to guide search, stored derivations can affect future processing. If the derivation fails, the system engages background knowledge that can be of various types but is likely to be overly general. If the derivation succeeds using overly general knowledge, the system applies an EBL technique called *explanation-based learning of correctness* to create a specialized version. Once it has proven its worth, the new rule is added to the learner's domain-specific knowledge. Finally, if Cascade cannot derive the line even with its general knowledge, it stores the line itself in a form that facilitates future use by analogy. Reimann, Schult, and Wichman (1993) described a closely related model of learning to solve physics problems via solved examples, using both rules and cases. The X system described by Pirolli (1986, 1991) uses analogies to solved examples to guide initial problem solving rather than overly general background knowledge, and it uses the knowledge compilation mechanism of the ACT* model rather than EBL to cache the solution for future use, but its principled approach to initial learning is similar.

In some instructional settings, it is common for a coach to *demonstrate* the correct solution, that is, to perform the task while the pupil is observing. Learning from demonstrations poses all the same problems as learning from solved examples (except possibly incompleteness), plus the problems of visual perception and learning under real-time constraints. Having to explain vision as well as learning is not a simplification, and I know of no cognitive model of human learning that learns by observing demonstrations. Learning by mimicry has played a central role in social learning theory (Bandura, 1977). Donald (1991) has made the interesting suggestion that mimicry was the first representational system to appear in hominid evolution and that remnants of it can still be seen in the play of children.

3.5. *Discussion*

The four principled answers to the question of how a learner can start practicing – follow exhortations; reason from abstract declarative knowledge; transfer identical, analogous, or general prior skills; and study someone else's solution – can be implemented in multiple ways. The diversity of approaches to the generation of initial rules is highlighted in Table 13.1. All four modes of learning have a high degree of psychological plausibility, but the validity of the exact processing details of the competing mechanisms is difficult to ascertain. Each mode is likely to produce initial rules that are incorrect or incomplete: Details might be lost in the translation of verbal recipes, reasoning can be faulty, identical elements might be incomplete, analogies might not be exact, search by weak methods might not find an optimal path, and solved examples and real-time demonstrations can be misunderstood. Exhortations, principles, prior skills, and solved examples are sources of initial rules that are likely to require fine tuning by other learning mechanisms.

4. How Are Partially Mastered Skills Improved?

The second phase of skill acquisition begins after the first correct performance and ends with mastery, that is, reliably correct performance. The learning mechanisms that are responsible for improvement during this phase answer the question, *how can an initial, incomplete, and perhaps erroneous method improve in the course of practice?* Although the mechanisms that dominate in the first phase necessarily draw on information sources available before action begins, the mechanisms that dominate this phase capitalize on the information that is generated by acting. The latter includes information to the effect that the learner is on the right track (*positive feedback*). An important subtype of positive feedback is *subgoal satisfaction*. The discovery that a subgoal has been achieved is very similar to the reception of environmental feedback in its implications for learning – the main difference is whether the information originates internally or externally – and the two will be discussed together. The environment can also produce information to the effect that an action was incorrect, inappropriate, or unproductive in some way (*negative feedback*). Feedback is both a triggering condition and a source of information, but learning from positive and negative feedback requires different processes. Another important type of triggering event is the occurrence of an *impasse*, a situation in which the learner cannot resolve what to do next.

4.1. *Positive Feedback and Subgoal Satisfaction*

As the learner acts vis-à-vis the task on the basis of initial rules, he or she will sooner or later perform a correct action or obtain some useful or desirable intermediate result. Information that designates an action or its outcome as correct or useful can originate internally (*well, that worked*), in causal consequences (*if the apple falls in your hand, you know you shook the tree hard enough*), or in utterances by an instructor (*well done*). The receipt of positive feedback is a trigger for learning. The theoretical question is what is learned. If the learner takes a correct step knowing that it is correct, there is nothing to learn. Yet, positive feedback facilitates

Table 13.1: Sample of learning mechanisms that operate in the initial phase of skill acquisition

Information source	Name of mechanism	A key concept	Example model	Example domain	Select reference
Instructions	Chunking	Search for a path that contains the recommended action; then contract that path into new rules.	Instructo-Soar	Blocks world	Huffman & Laird (1995)
	Construction-integration	Add instructions to a semantic network, then re-compute the distribution of activation.	ADAPT	Piloting jet airplanes	Doane & Sohn (2000)
Abstract declarative knowledge	Proceduralization	Use general interpretive rules to translate declarative principles into production rules.	ACT*	Plane geometry	Neves & Anderson (1981)
Prior practical knowledge	Identical rules	Tasks share rules, so some rules apply to a new task without change.	ACT*	Word processing	Singley & Anderson (1989)
	Structure mapping	Higher-order relations are given more weight in mapping than lower-order relations and features.	SME	Physics	Falkenhainer, Forbus, & Gentner (1989)
	Multiconstraint mapping	Select a mapping on the basis of pragmatic constraints, i.e., its relevance for the current goal.	ACME	Radiation problems	Holyoak & Thagard (1989b)
	Derivational analogy	Use analogical mapping to revise the derivation of the solution to a base problem so as to fit the target, as to fit the current task.	Prodigy	Simulated logistics	Veloso & Carbonell (1993)
Solved example provided by somebody else.	EBL of correctness	Derive the next step in a solved example, then cache the derivation into a new problem-solving rule.	Cascade	Mechanics	VanLehn (1999)

ACT* = Adaptive Cognitive Theory. SME = Structure Mapping Engine. ACME = Analogical Constraint Mapping Engine.

human learning, presumably because many steps generated by initial rules are tentative, and positive feedback reduces uncertainty about their correctness.

4.1.1. INCREASE RULE STRENGTH

The simplest mechanism for uncertainty reduction is described in the first half of Thorndike's Law of Effect (Thorndike, 1927): Increase the strength of the rule that generated the feedback-producing action. Variants of this *strengthening* idea are incorporated into a wide range of cognitive models.

The EUREKA model described by Jones and Langley (2005) stores past problem-solving steps, fully instantiated, in a semantic network memory. When faced with a decision as to what to do in a current situation S, the model spreads activation across the network to retrieve a set of past steps that are relevant for S. A step is selected for execution based on degree of similarity to the current situation. (When a problem is encountered a second time, the exact same step that led to success last time is presumably maximally similar and hence guaranteed to be selected for execution.) Finally, analogical mapping between the past step and S is used to apply the step to S. As experience accumulates, the knowledge base of past steps grows. Positive and negative feedback are used to adjust the strengths of the relevant network links, which in turn alters the outcome of future retrieval processes. In the GIPS model, Jones and Van-Lehn (1994) interpreted positive feedback as evidence in favor of the hypothesis that the action was the right one under the circumstances and increased the probability of that hypothesis with a probabilistic concept learning algorithm, a very different concept of strengthening.

There are multiple implementation issues: By what function is the strength increment to be computed? How is the strength increment propagated backward through the solution path if the feedback-producing outcome required N steps? How is the strength increment to be propagated upward in the goal hierarchy? Should a higher-order goal be strengthened more, less, or by the same amount as a lower-order goal (Corrigan-Halpern & Ohlsson, 2002)? Strengthening increases the probability that the feedback-producing rule will be executed in every situation in which it can, in principle, apply. But a rule that is useful in some class of situations {S} is not necessarily useful in some other class of situations {S'}. The purpose of learning must be to separate these two classes of situations, something strengthening does not accomplish.

4.1.2. CREATE A NEW RULE

Positive feedback following a tentative action A can trigger the bottom-up creation of a new rule that recommends the successful action in future encounters with the same situation. The theoretical problem is that the situation S itself is history by the time the feedback arrives and will never recur. The purpose thus cannot be to create a rule that executes A in S, but in *situations like* S. A mechanism for creating a new rule following success must provide for some level of generality.

One solution is to create a very specific rule by using the entire situation S as its condition and then rely on other learning mechanisms to generalize it. This is the solution used in the CLARION system (Sun, Merril, & Peterson, 2001; Sun et al., 2005), which is a hybrid model with both subsymbolic and symbolic learning. Actions can be chosen on the basis of a quantitative measure called a Q-value, computed by a connectionist network. When an action chosen in this way is rewarded with a positive outcome, and there is no symbolic rule that would have proposed that action in that situation, the system creates a new rule with the current state as the condition on that action. (If such a rule already exists, the rule is generalized.) The opposite solution is to create a maximally general rule and rely on other learning mechanisms to restrict its application. This solution has received less attention (but see Bhatnagar & Mostow, 1994; Ohlsson, 1987a).

The more common solution is to generalize the specific step conservatively, usually by replacing (some) constants with variables. An early model of this sort was described by Larkin (1981). It responded to successful derivations of physics quantities by creating new rules that could duplicate the derivations. Particular values of physical magnitudes were replaced with variables, on what basis was not stated. Lewis (1988) combined analogy from existing productions and explanation-based generalization to create new rules in response to positive outcomes.

Later systems have used some version of EBL to contract derivations or search paths into single rules and to provide a judicious level of generality. This principle is at the center of the Soar system (Newell, 1990; Rosenbloom et al., 1993). Soar carries out all activities through problem space search. When the goal that gave rise to a problem space is reached, Soar retrieves the search path that led to it and applies an EBL-like mechanism called *chunking* (Newell & Rosenbloom, 1981; Rosenbloom & Newell, 1986, 1987). The result is a rule of grounded generality that can regenerate the positive outcome without search. The theme of searching until you find and then using EBL or some related technique to cache the successful path with an eye toward future use recurs in several otherwise different models (e.g., VanLehn, 1999).

4.1.3. GENERALIZE RULES

When a rule already exists and generates a positive outcome, a possible response is to generalize that rule. If it is allowed to apply in more situations, it might generate more positive outcomes. In the CLARION model (Sun et al., 2001, 2005), when an action proposed by a rule generates positive feedback, the rule is generalized. Curiously, this is done by *adding* a condition element, a value on some dimension describing the current situation, to the rule. In a pattern-matching architecture, adding a condition element *restricts* the range of situations in which a rule matches, but CLARION *counts* the number of matches, so one more condition element provides one more chance

of scoring a match, giving the rule more chances to apply.

If multiple rule applications and their consequences – an execution history – are stored in memory, rule generalization can be carried out inductively. In ACT*, a collection of specific rules (or rule instances) that all recommended the same action and produced positive feedback can serve as input to an inductive mechanism that extracts what the rules have in common and creates a new rule based on the common features (Anderson, 1983; Anderson, Kline, & Beasley, 1979). However, inductive, commonalities-extracting mechanisms that operate on syntactic similarities have never been shown to be powerful. Life is full of inconsequential similarities and differences, so getting to what matters usually requires analysis.

Indeed, Lenat (1983) made the intriguing observation that heuristics of intermediate generality appear to be less useful than either very specific or very general heuristics. For example, the specific heuristic, *to turn on the printer in Dr. Ohlsson's office, lean as far toward the far wall as you can, reach into the gap between the wall and the printer with your left arm, and push the button that is located toward the back of the printer*, is useful because it provides very specific guidance, whereas the general heuristic, *to turn on any electric device, push its power button*, is useful because it is so widely applicable. The intermediate heuristic, *if you want to turn on a printer, push its power button*, provides neither advantage. An inductive rule generalization mechanism is likely to produce rules of such intermediate generality.

4.2. Interlude: Learning at Impasses

Impasses are execution states in which the cognitive architecture cannot resolve what to do next. An impasse is a sign that the current method for the target task is incomplete in some way, so impasses should trigger learning. The mere occurrence of an impasse is not in and of itself very informative, so the question is how the inability to proceed can be turned into an opportunity to improve. The general answer is that some trick must be found that resolves the impasse and enables problem solving to continue; learning occurs when the latter produces a positive outcome. Different models differ in how they break out of the impasse as well as in how they learn from the subsequent success.

In Repair Theory (Brown & VanLehn, 1980; VanLehn, 1983, 1990), the cognitive architecture has access to a short list of *repairs*, processes it can execute when it does not know what action to take next. VanLehn (1983, p. 57) described five repairs: pass over the current step (*No-op*); return to a previous execution state and do something different (*Back-up*); give up and go to the next problem (*Quit*); revise the execution state (technically, the arguments in the top goal) so as to avoid the impasse (*Refocus*); and relax the criteria on the application of the current step (*Force*). Although applications of a repair can be saved for future use (VanLehn, 1990, pp. 43, 188), repairs are not learning mechanisms. They enable task-relevant behavior to continue and are in that respect analogous to weak methods. The purpose of Repair Theory was to explain, in combination with the Sierra model of induction from solved example, the emergence of children's incorrect subtraction procedures.

The previously mentioned Cascade model (VanLehn, 1988, 1999; VanLehn & Jones, 1993; VanLehn et al., 1992) of learning from solved examples also learns at impasses while solving physics problems. If a subgoal cannot be achieved with the system's current strategy, it brings to bear background knowledge that might be overly general. If the knowledge allows the impasse to be resolved and if a positive outcome eventually results, then a new, domain-specific rule is created using explanation-based learning of correctness. The new rule is added tentatively to the model's domain knowledge until further evidence is available as to its appropriateness or usefulness. The new domain rule is a special case of the overly general rule, so this is yet another case of specialization. If an impasse cannot be re-

solved even by engaging general background knowledge, the system uses a version of analogy to continue problem solving (not unlike applying a repair), but does not learn a new rule. Similarly, Pirolli's (1986, 1991) X model responded to impasses through analogies with available examples. If an analogy was successful in resolving an impasse, the resolution was stored as production rules for future use.

In the Soar system (Newell, 1990; Rosenbloom, Laird & Newell, 1993; Rosenbloom & Newell, 1986, 1987), an impasse causes the creation of a subgoal that poses the resolution of the impasse as a problem in its own right. That subgoal is pursued by searching the relevant problem space, bringing to bear whatever knowledge might be relevant and otherwise falling back on weak methods. When the search satisfies the subgoal, the problem-solving process is captured in one or more production rules through *chunking*, an EBL-like mechanism that compresses the successful search path into a single rule of appropriate generality. Another model, Icarus, which also engages in problem solving in response to an impasse, has been described by Langley and Choi (2006). This model uses a variant of backward chaining to resolve a situation in which no existing skill is sufficient to reach the current subgoal. When the solution has been found, it is stored for future use.

These models differ in how they resolve an impasse: call on repairs, apply weak methods like search and backward chaining, reason from general background knowledge, and use analogy to past problem-solving experiences. These mechanisms are not learning mechanisms; they do not change the current strategy. Their function is to allow task-oriented behavior to continue. Once the impasse is broken and problem solving continues, learning occurs at the next positive outcome via the same learning mechanisms that are used to learn from positive outcomes in general. Impasses trigger learning but do not provide unique information, so learning at impasses is a special case of learning from positive outcomes.

4.3. *Negative Feedback*

Much of the information generated by tentative actions resides in errors, failures, and undesirable outcomes. There are multiple mechanisms for making use of such information. The basic response is to avoid repeating the action that generated the negative feedback. More precisely, the problem of learning from negative feedback can be stated as follows: If rule R recommends action A in situation S, and A turns out to be incorrect, inappropriate or unproductive vis-à-vis the current goal, then what is the indicated revision of R? The objective of the revision is not so much to prevent the offending rule from executing in S, or situations like S, but to prevent it from generating similar errors in the future.

4.3.1. REDUCE STRENGTH

The simplest response to failure is described in the second half of Thorndike's Law of Effect: Decrease the strength of the feedback-producing rule. As a consequence, that rule will have a lower probability of being executed. Like strengthening, this *weakening* mechanism is a common component of cognitive models (e.g., Jones & Langley, 2005). As with strengthening, there are multiple issues: By what function should the strength values be decremented, and how should the strength decrement be propagated backward through prior steps or upward through the goal hierarchy (Corrigan-Halpern & Ohlsson, 2002)? Weakening lowers the probability that the rule will execute in any future situation. The purpose of learning from negative feedback is to discriminate between those situations in which the rule is useful from those in which it is incorrect, and a strength decrement is not an effective way to accomplish this. Jones and VanLehn (1994) instead interpreted negative feedback as evidence against the hypothesis that the action was the right one under the circumstances and reduced the probability of that hypothesis with a probabilistic concept learning algorithm.

4.3.2. SPECIALIZATION

Ohlsson (1993, 1996, 2007; see also Ohlsson et al., 1992; Ohlsson & Rees, 1991a, 1991b) has described *constraint-based rule specialization*, a mechanism for learning from a single error. It presupposes that the learner has sufficient (declarative) background knowledge, expressed in terms of constraints, to judge the outcomes of his or her actions as correct or incorrect. A constraint is a binary pair <R, C> of conditions, the first determining when the constraint is relevant and the second determining whether it is satisfied. When an action violates a constraint, that is, creates a situation in which the relevance condition is satisfied but the satisfaction condition is not, the violation is processed to create a more restricted version of the offending rule. The constraint-based rule specialization mechanism identifies the weakest set of conditions that will prevent the rule from violating the same constraint in the future. For example, if the rule is *if the goal is G and the situation is S, then do A*, and it turns out that doing A in S violated some constraint <R, C>, then the constraint-based mechanism specializes the rule by creating two new rules, one that includes the new condition *not-R* (do not recommend A when the constraint applies) and one that includes the condition C (recommend A only when the constraint is guaranteed to be satisfied); see Ohlsson and Rees (1991a) for a formal description of the algorithm. The purpose of constraint-based specialization is not primarily to prevent the rule from executing in the current situation or in situations like it, but to prevent it from violating the same constraint in the future. The algorithm is related to EBL as applied to learning from errors, but does not require the combinatorial process of constructing an explanation of the negative outcome.

The CLARION model (Sun et al., 2001, 2005) contains a different specialization mechanism: If an action is executed and followed by negative feedback, and there is a rule that proposed that action in that situation, then the application of that rule is restricted. This is done by removing a *value*, that is, a measure on some dimension used to describe the current situation. In the context of CLARION, this decreases the number of possible matches and hence restricts the range of situations in which the rule will be the strongest candidate.

A rather different conception of specialization underpins systems that respond to negative feedback by learning *critics*, rules that vote against performing in action during conflict resolution. The ability to encode missteps into critics removes the need to specialize overly general rules, because their rash proposals are weeded out during conflict resolution (Ohlsson, 1987a). This idea has been explored in machine learning research (Bhatnage & Mostow, 1994), where critics are sometimes called *censors* or *censor rules* (Bharadwaj & Jain, 1992; Jain & Bharadwaj, 1998; Winston, 1986).

The previous mechanisms improve practical knowledge by making it more specific and thereby restricting its application, in direct contrast to the idea that practical knowledge becomes generalized and more abstract over time. The latter view is common among lay people and researchers in the fields of educational and developmental psychology, in part, perhaps, as a legacy of Jean Piaget's (1950) and his followers' claim that cognitive development progresses from sensori-motor schemas to formal logical operations. "Representations are literally built from sensory-motor interactions" (Fischer, 1980, p. 481).

4.3.3. DISCRIMINATION

Restle (1955) and others tried to accommodate discrimination within the behaviorist framework, but an explanation of discrimination requires symbolic representations. Langley (1983, 1987) described SAGE, a system that included a discrimination mechanism. The model assumes that each application of a production rule, including any positive and negative feedback, and the state of the world in which the rule applied are recorded in memory. Once memory contains some instances that were followed by positive feedback and some that were fol-lowed by negative feedback, the two sets of situations can be compared with the purpose of identifying features that differentiate them, that is, that hold in the situations in which the rule generated positive outcomes but not in the situations in which it generated negative outcomes, or vice versa. One or more new rules are created by adding the discriminating features to the condition side of the original rule. A very similar mechanism was included in the 1983 version of the ACT* theory (Anderson, 1983). A rather different mechanism for making use of an execution history that records both successful and unsuccessful actions, based on quantitative concept learning methods, was incorporated into the GIPS system described by Jones and VanLehn (1994).

Implementation of a discrimination mechanism raises at least the following issues: What information should be stored for each rule application? The instantiated rule? The entire state of working memory? How many examples of negative and positive outcomes are needed before it is worth searching for discriminating features? By what criterion are the discriminating features to be identified? Which new rules are created? All possible ones? If not, then how are the new rules selected?

4.4. *Discussion*

Positive and negative outcomes are simultaneously triggers for learning and inputs to learning mechanisms. Learning from feedback is not as straightforward as Thorndike (1927) presupposed when he formulated the Law of Effect. The simplicity of early formulations hid the complexity of deciding to which class of situations the feedback refers. If doing A in S led to the attainment of goal G, what is the class {S} of situations in which A will have this happy outcome? If I see a movie by director X and lead actor Y on topic Z, and I enjoy the movie, what is the conclusion? It takes more than syntactic induction to realize that *see more movies by director X* is a more sensible conclusion than *see more movies on topic Z*. If A leads to an error, the even harder question is which revision of the responsible rule will prevent it from causing similar errors in the future. The variety of approaches to learning from feedback is highlighted in Table 13.2.

5. How Do Skills Improve Beyond Mastery?

The third phase of skill acquisition begins when the learner exhibits reliably correct performance and lasts as long as the learner keeps performing the task. During this period, the performance becomes more streamlined. Long after the error rate has moved close to zero, time to solution keeps decreasing (Crossman, 1959), possibly throughout the learner's entire lifetime, or at least until the onset of cognitive aging (Salthouse, 1996). The learning mechanisms operating during this phase are answers to the question, *how can an already mastered skill undergo further improvement?* What is changing, once the strategy for the task is correct? Even a strategy that consistently delivers correct answers or solutions might contain inefficient, redundant, or unnecessary steps. Changes of this sort are devided into three types: changes in the sequence of overt actions (optimization at the knowledge level), changes in the mental code for generating a fixed sequence of actions (optimization at the computational level), and the replacement of computation with memory retrieval. The main source of information to support these types of changes is the current *execution state* and, to the extent that past execution states are stored in memory, the *execution history* of the learner's current strategy.

5.1. *Optimization at the Knowledge Level*

The strategy a learner acquires in the course of practice might be correct but inefficient. Over time, he or she might discover or invent a shorter sequence of actions to accomplish the same task. The challenge is to explain what drives the learner to find a shorter solution when he or she cannot know ahead of time whether one exists and when there is no negative feedback (because his or her current strategy leads to correct answers).

A well-documented example of short-cut detection is the so-called SUM-to-MIN transition in the context of simple mental additions. Problems like $5 + 3 = ?$ is at a certain age solved by counting out loud, *one, two, three, four, five, six, seven, eight – so eight is the answer*. Only after considerable practice do children discover that the first five steps are unnecessary and transition to the more economical MIN-strategy, in which they choose the larger addend and count up: *five, six, seven, eight – eight*.

Neches (1987) described seven different types of optimization mechanisms in the context of the HPM model, including deleting redundant steps, replacing a subprocedure, and reordering steps, and he showed that they collectively suffice to produce the SUM-to-MIN transformation. Jones and VanLehn (1994) modeled the same shortcut discovery in their GIPS model. Each condition on a GIPS action is associated with two numerical values, *sufficiency* and *necessity*. Conflict resolution uses these values to compute the odds that the action is worth selecting, and the action with the highest odds wins. The two values are updated on the basis of successes and failures with a probabilistic concept learning algorithm. A more recent model, the Strategy Choice and Discovery Simulation (SCADS), was proposed by Shrager and Siegler (1998; see also Siegler & Araya, 2005). SCADS has limited attentional resources, so at the outset of practice, it merely executes its given strategy. Once the answers to some problems can be retrieved from memory and hence require little attention, attention is allocated to strategy change processes that (a) inspect the execution trace and delete redundant steps, and (b) evaluate the efficiency of different orders of execution of the steps in the current strategy and fixate the more efficient one (p. 408). These two change mechanisms turn out to be sufficient to discover the MIN strategy.

Another strategy shift that results in different overt behavior transforms the

Table 13.2: Sample of learning mechanisms that operate in the mastery phase of skill acquisition

Information source	Name of mechanism	A key concept	Example model	Example domain	Select reference
Positive feedback	Strengthening; Law of Effect, 1st part	When a positive outcome is encountered, increase the strength of the responsible action or rule.	Eureka	Tower of Hanoi	Jones & Langley (2005)
	Chunking	Search until the current goal is satisfied, then cache the path to it into a new rule.	Soar	Simulated job shop scheduling	Nerb, Ritter, & Krems (1999)
	Bottom-up creation of a new rule	If implicit choice of action leads to success, create a symbolic rule with the entire situation as its condition.	CLARION	Simulated submarine navigation	Sun, Merrill, & Peterson (2001)
	Inductive rule generalization	Extract features common to several successful rule applications and encode them as a new rule.	ACT	Categorization	Anderson, Kline, & Beasley (1979)
Negative feedback	Weakening; Law of Effect, 2nd part	When a negative outcome is encountered, decrease the strength of the responsible action or rule.	Eureka	Tower of Hanoi	Jones & Langley (2005)
	Adaptive search	Encode each unsuccessful rule application as a censor rule.	FAIL-SAFE-2	Blocks world	Bhatnagar & Mostow (1994)
	Constraint-based rule specialization	Extract new rule conditions from the mismatch between constraints and the outcomes of actions.	HS	Structural formulas in chemistry	Ohlsson (1996)
	Discrimination	Compare successful and unsuccessful rule applications; add discriminating features to rule.	SAGE	Balance scale task	Langley (1987)

CLARION = Connectionist Learning with Adaptive Rule Induction ONline. ACT = Adaptive Cognitive Theory. HS = Heuristic Self-Improvement. SAGE = Strategic Acquisition Governed by Experimentation.

novice's laborious problem solving through means–ends analysis or backward chaining into the expert's forward-inference process that develops the knowledge about a problem until the desired answer can be found, perhaps without ever setting any subgoals. The ABLE model of physics problem solving by Larkin (1981) simulated this transformation in the domain of physics. Elio and Scharf (1990) achieved the same effect, also in the domain of physics, with sophisticated indexing of successful problem-solving episodes in memory. Their EUREKA model created problem solving schemas and used positive and negative outcomes to adjust the level of generality of the schemas. Over time, it relied increasingly on the forward-inference schemas and less on means–ends analysis.

Anderson (1982, 1983) explained both the transition from backward to forward chaining and the transition from serial to parallel search in the Sternberg short-term memory task by showing that rule composition can squeeze subgoals out of rules. In contrast, Koedinger and Anderson (1990) attributed the forward-inference behavior of geometry experts to a repertoire of diagram chunks that allow experts to quickly identify possible inferences in a geometric diagram, thus seemingly arriving at conclusions before they derive them, but Koedinger and Anderson did not model the acquisition of those diagram chunks. Taking a different tack, Blessing and Anderson (1996) argued that rule-level analogies suffice to discover strategic shortcuts.

Another empirically documented strategy discovery is the invention of the pyramid recursion strategy of Tower of Hanoi. Unlike the MIN-to-SUM and backward-to-forward transitions, the transition from moving single discs to moving pyramids of discs requires an *increase* in the complexity of internal processing to simplify overt behavior. Ruiz and Newell (1993) modeled this strategy discovery in the Soar system by adding special productions that (a) notice subpyramids and (b) reason about spatial arrangements like stacks of objects, but without postulating any other learning mechanisms

than Soar's standard impasse-driven chunking mechanism.

A different hypothesis about shortcut detection is that the mind reasons from declarative background knowledge to new production rules that may represent shortcuts (Ohlsson, 1987b). For example, if the current strategy contains a production rule that matches goal G and produces some partial result B, and there is in memory a general implication A_1 *and* A_2 *implies* B, then it makes sense to create the new rule, *if you want G and you have A_1, set the subgoal to get A_2*, as well as, *if you want G and you have both A_1 and A_2, infer B*. The first rule encodes a backward-chaining subgoaling step – get the prerequisites for the target conclusion – and the second new rule is akin to the result of the proceduralization process discussed previously. This and two other mechanisms for reasoning about a set of rules on the basis of general *if–then* propositions were implemented in a model called PSS3, which reduced the simulated time for performing a simple spatial reasoning task by two orders of magnitude.

Several of these learning mechanisms require that production rules can test for properties of other production rules – the mental code, not merely traces of executions – a psychologically problematic assumption. Although these mechanisms are intended to explain success in strategy revision, Fu and Gray (2004) provide a useful counterpoint by specifying some of the conditions and factors that might prevent optimization mechanisms from operating and hence keep the performer on a stable but suboptimal solution path.

5.2. Optimization at the Computational Level

Even when the learner cannot find a shorter action sequence, he or she might be able to save on the mental computations required to generate the relevant sequence. In this case, overt behavior does not change, but the learner produces that behavior with fewer or less capacity-demanding cognitive steps.

An optimization mechanism, *rule composition*, was invented by Lewis (1987) and included in the ACT* model (Anderson, 1983; Neves & Anderson, 1981). This mechanism requires a less extensive access to the execution trace than shortcut detection: It need only keep track of the temporal sequence of rule executions. If two rules are repeatedly executed in sequence, then a new rule is created that performs the same work as the two rules. To illustrate the flavor of this type of change, imagine that G, $S_1 \rightarrow A_1$ and G, $S_2 \rightarrow A_2$ are two rules that repeatedly execute in sequence. A plausible new rule would be G, $S_1 \rightarrow A_1$; A_2, which is executed in a single production system cycle. Given that A_2 is always performed after A_1, there is no need to evaluate the state of the world after A_1. A full specification of this contraction mechanism needs to take interactions between the action of the first rule and the conditions of the second rule into account. In ACT*, composition worked in concert with proceduralization. The combination of the two mechanisms was referred to as *knowledge compilation*.

Recently, the composition mechanism has been replaced by the related *production compilation* mechanism (Taatgen, 2002, 2005; Taatgen & Anderson, 2002; Taatgen & Lee, 2003). The triggering condition for this learning mechanism is also that two rules repeatedly execute in temporal sequence, and, again like composition, it creates a single new rule. The resulting rule is specialized by incorporating the results of retrievals of declarative information into the resulting rule. The combination process eliminates memory retrieval requests in the first rule and tests on retrieved elements in the second rule. For example, if the two rules *if calling X, then retrieve his area code* and *if calling X and his area code is remembered to be Y, then dial Y* are executed in the course of calling a guy called John with area code 412, production compilation will create the new rule *if calling John, then dial 412*. Because there can only be a single request on memory in any one ACT-R production rule, eliminating such requests saves production system cycles.

However, there is more to combining rules than mere speed-up. Anderson (1986) argued that knowledge compilation can mimic the effects of other learning mechanisms, such as discrimination and generalization, and produce qualitatively new practical knowledge. In the same vain, Taatgen and Anderson (2002) modeled the transition from incorrect use of regular past tense for irregular verbs like "break" to the correct irregular form, using nothing but production compilation. The effects of optimization by contraction are more complicated than they first appear and deserve further study.

The issues in designing a rule combination mechanism include: What is the triggering criterion? How many times do the two rules have to execute in sequence for there to be sufficient reason to compose them? Does the new rule replace the previous rules or is it added to them? Are there counterindications? If the learner's execution history for the relevant rules *also* contains situations in which the two rules did not execute in sequence, should the rules nevertheless be combined?

5.3. *Retrieve Solutions from Memory*

If people perform the same tasks over and over again, they eventually remember the answers and hence need not perform any other processing than retrieving those answers from long-term memory. In a restricted domain such as arithmetic, the balance between computing and retrieving might over time shift in favor of retrieval. A shift from, for example, 60% of answers being calculated and 40% retrieved to the opposite percentages might have a strong effect on the mean solution time.

This shift toward memory-based responding is central to the instance-based model by Logan (1998) and the series of models of children's strategy choices in arithmetic described by R. S. Siegler and associates: the distribution of associations model (Siegler & Shrager, 1984); the Adaptive Strategy Choice Model (ASCM; Siegler & Shipley, 1995); and the SCADS model (Shrager & Siegler, 1998). All three models use the idea that associations between particular problems and their answers are gradually strengthened until they can provide a solid basis for answering. Hence, the proportion of memory-based responses increases with practice.

The psychological reality of instance memorization and a gradual shift toward memory-based responding as experience of a task domain accumulates is hardly in doubt (everyone knows the multiplication table), but this type of learning cannot be important in all domains. For example, it does not apply to buying a house because few people buy the same house multiple times.

5.4. *Discussion*

Cognitive psychologists discuss the long-term consequences of practice in terms of two concepts that in certain respects are each others' opposites: *automaticity* and *expertise*. The essential characteristics of automaticity include rigidity in execution and a high probability of being triggered when the relevant stimuli are present (Schneider & Chein, 2003). The consequences include capture errors (Reason, 1990), *Einstellung* effects (Luchins & Luchins, 1959), and negative transfer (Woltz, Gardner & Bell, 2000). But we think of experts as exhibiting a high degree of awareness, flexibility, and ability to adapt to novel situations (Ericsson et al., 2006). Which view is correct? If one practices four hours a day, six days a week, for ten years, does one end up a rigid robot or an elastic expert? Both end states are well documented, so the question is which factors determine which end state will be realized in any one case. Ericsson, Krampe, and Tesch-Rober (1993) have proposed that experts engage in deliberate practice, but they have not offered a computational model of how deliberate practice might differ from mere repetitive activity in terms of the cognitive processes involved. Deliberate practice is undertaken with the intent to improve, but how does that affect the operation of the relevant learning mechanisms? Salomon and Perkins (1989) has summarized studies that indicate that

the variability of practice is the key, with more variability creating more flexible skills. Another hypothesis, popular among educational researchers, is that flexibility is a side effect of conceptual understanding. To explain the difference between automaticity and expertise, a model cannot postulate two sets of learning mechanisms, one that produces rigidity and one that leads to flexibility. The theoretical challenge is to show how one and the same learning mechanism (or set of mechanisms) can produce either automaticity or expertise, depending on the properties of the training problems (complexity, variability, etc.), the learner, the learning scenario, or other factors. It is not clear whether the current repertoire of optimization mechanisms (see Table 13.3 for an overview) is sufficient in this respect.

6. Capture the Statistical Structure of the Environment

As the learner becomes familiar with a particular task environment, he or she accumulates information about its quantitative and statistical properties. For example, the members of a tribe of foraging hunter-gatherers might have implicit but nevertheless accurate estimates of the average distance between food sources and the probability of discovering a new food source in a given amount of time, for example, before the sun sets or before winter sets in (Simon, 1956). Quantitative information of this sort was abundant in the environments in which human beings evolved (*How often has such and such an animal been sighted recently? How many days of rain in a row should we expect? How high up the banks will the river flood?*), so it is plausible that they evolved cognitive mechanisms to capture it. A modern descendant might use such mechanisms to estimate the expected travel time to the airport or the probability that a sports team will win its next match.

The behaviorist learning theories of the 1895–1945 era were the first psychological theories to focus on the effect of environmental quantities, especially the frequency,

Table 13.3: Sample of learning mechnisms that operate in the optimization phase of skill acquisition

Information source	Name of mechanism	A key concept	Example model	Strategy transition	Select reference
Execution trace	Redundancy elimination	The execution trace is inspected for redundant steps.	HPM	Arithmetic: SUM-to-MIN	Neches (1987)
	Reordering	Steps are ordered in the most efficient sequence.	SCADS	Arithmetic: SUM-to-MIN	Shrager & Siegler (1998)
	Chunking	If production rules notice complex situation features, chunking will incorporate them into rules.	Soar	Tower of Hanoi: disk-to-pyramid	Ruiz & Newell (1993)
	Rational learning	Use general implications to deduce a short cut; create rules that compute the shorter path.	PSS3	Reasoning: center-to-periphery	Ohlsson (1987b)
	Indexing	Solutions are accumulated in memory and indexed with abstract problem features.	EUREKA	Physics: backward-to-forward	Elio & Scharf (1990)
Temporal sequence of rule executions	Composition	Two production rules that fire in sequence are contracted into a single rule.	ACT*	Sternberg: serial-to-parallel	Anderson (1982)
	Production compilation	Two production rules that fire in sequence are contracted into a single rule.	ACT-R	Vocabulary: regular-to-irregular	Taatgen & Anderson (2002)
Memory of past answers	Association strengthening	Problem-answer associations grow stronger with use, so more answers are retrieved rather than computed.	ACSM	Arithmetic: computation-to-retrieval	Siegler & Shipley (1995)

Each example simulates some empirically documented strategy transition. HPM = Heuristic Procedure Modification. SCADS = Strategy Choice and Discovery Simulation. PSS3 = Production System Stockholm 3. ACT = Adaptive Cognitive Theory. ACSM = Adaptive Strategy Choice Model.

type, and amount of feedback (also known as reinforcement), on skill acquisition. The first theories of this sort were proposed by E. Thorndike, E. R. Guthrie, C. L. Hull, E. C. Tolman, B. F. Skinner, and others; Hilgard and Bower (1966) wrote the classical review. These theorists conceptualized the effect of feedback in cause–effect and motivational terms: Each event impacts the learner, and the effect of multiple events is merely the sum of their impacts. The strength of the disposition to perform an action could not yet be seen as an estimate of the relative frequency of environmental events like positive and negative feedback, because the learner was not yet seen as an information processor.

Mathematical psychologists in the 1945–1975 period discovered and investigated several types of adaptation to quantitative properties of the environment (see, e.g., Neimark & Estes, 1967). In a standard laboratory paradigm called *probability matching*, subjects are presented with a long sequence of binary choices (e.g., left, right) and given right–wrong feedback on each. The relative frequencies of trials on which "left" or "right" is the correct response is varied between groups. Over time, the relative frequencies of the subjects' responses begin to match the relative frequencies of the feedback, so if "left" is the correct response 80% of the time, then the subject tends to say "left" 80% of the time. In the absence of other sources of information, probability matching provides a lower hit rate than choosing the response that is more often followed by positive feedback on every trial. Other well-documented sensitivities to event frequencies include word frequency effects, prototype effects in classification, the impact of co-occurrences on causal reasoning, the role of estimated outcome probabilities in decision making, and many more.

Two distinct lines of research laid the foundation for the contemporary concept of *implicit* or *subsymbolic* learning (see Chapter 14 in this volume). Models of *semantic networks* (Anderson & Pirolli, 1984; Collins & Loftus, 1975; see Chapter 8 in this volume) contributed the important idea of

splitting the quantity associated with a knowledge unit into two. The *strength* of a unit is an estimate of its past usefulness. It moves up or down according to the feedback generated when the unit is active. *Activation* is a transient quantity that estimates the moment-to-moment relevance for the situation at hand. When activation spreads across the network, the amount of activation each unit receives from other nodes is proportional to its strength. Models of *neural networks*, also known as connectionist models, have extended this basic idea with mathematically sophisticated studies of different schemes and regimens for the propagation of strength adjustments throughout a network (see Chapter 2 in this volume).

Although connectionist and symbolic network models were initially conceived as competing accounts of human learning, modelers have come to realize that it is more fruitful to see them as complementary. Schneider and Oliver (1991) and Schneider and Chein (2003) described CAP2, a hybrid model that could transfer information from the symbolic to the subsymbolic level, thus speeding up learning at the notoriously slow connectionist level. In the CLARION model (Sun et al., 2001, 2005), a connectionist network is used to represent actions and to select an action to perform in a particular situation. A combination of two connectionist learning algorithms are used to adjust the network to experience. The distributed representation models implicit skill. CLARION extracts explicit rules from such implicit knowledge and generalizes and specializes them in response to positive and negative feedback, thus relating the symbolic and subsymbolic levels in the opposite way compared with CAP2. In yet another twist on this two-roads-to-mastery theme, the Soar architecture has been revised to augment its symbolic chunking mechanism with mechanisms for so-called reinforcement learning, that is, the learning of a quantitative function for predicting the value of executing a particular action in a given situation (Nason & Laird, 2005). In this case, symbolic and statistical learning mechanisms are conceptualized to run in parallel and to be mutually supporting, without either level dictating what should be learned at the other.

In a series of path-breaking analyses, Anderson (1989, 1990) has developed the idea that mental quantities, like strengths, are estimates of environmental magnitudes, not repositories of causal impacts, into a radical new approach to the modeling of learning. The starting point for his *rational analysis* is that the mind is maximally efficient, that is, it solves each information processing task as well as the nature of the task allows. Consequently, the structure of the mind mirrors the structure of the task environment, a fundamental point often illustrated with a mythical beast called Simon's ant; its winding path across a beach reflects the topology of the beach more than its decision-making mechanism (Simon, 1970). In humans, the task of the long-term memory system is to correctly estimate, for each memory entry, the probability that it is the entry that needs to be retrieved in the next unit of time, given the person's current situation and goal. This probability can be estimated from prior experience: How often has the entry been needed in the past, how much time has gone by since it was needed last, and how does the probability that an entry is needed depend on the time since it was needed last? The memory entry to be retrieved is the one with the highest estimated probability of being the one that is needed. When the outcome of the retrieval becomes available – did the retrieved entry support goal attainment? – the relevant probabilities can be updated with Bayes' rule, a sound statistical inference rule (see Chapter 3 in this volume).

When a rational analysis is integrated into a cognitive architecture, the combination extends cognitive modeling in multiple ways. First, seeing mental quantities as estimates of environmental quantities focuses modelers' attention on the need for a serious analysis of the latter; which environmental quantities are people sensitive to, and how do those quantities, in fact, behave? Astonishing regularities have been found. The probability that an email address is the next one to be needed declines over time according to the same function as the probabil-ity that a particular word is the next one to appear in a newspaper headline (Anderson & Schooler, 1991, p. 401). To make accurate estimates, our brains must be sensitive to the shape of such functions. To make accurate models, modelers have to identify those functions by studying the environment, an unfamiliar type of activity. Second, the rationality assumption and the use of Bayes' rule and other sound inference rules emphasizes the question of how closely the operation of the mind approximates the maximally possible performance. If the approximation is close, then behavior can be predicted by asking how a maximally efficient system would behave. It turns out that at least some behavioral regularities, including forgetting curves, can indeed be predicted this way (Anderson & Schooler, 1991) without any processing assumptions.

The theory and practice of rational analysis is a growing enterprise (Anderson & Lebiere, 1998; Oaksford & Chater, 1998; Petrov & Anderson, 2005; Schooler & Hertwig, 2005), Indeed, the practice of modeling adaptation as a process of adjusting cognitive magnitudes so as to estimate environmental magnitudes is, in general, a growing enterprise, and it has been applied to many types of mental quantities (e.g., Altmann & Burns, 2005; Gray, Shoelles, & Sims, 2005).

How do mental estimates of environmental magnitudes help optimize a cognitive skill in the long run? Consider the following everyday example: Many of the operations I perform during word processing cause a dialogue window to appear with a request for confirmation of the operation; for example, do I really intend to shut down my computer, print this file, and so forth. After using the same computer and the same software for several years, I know exactly where on my computer screen the dialogue box and hence the confirmation button will appear. Before my computer presents the dialogue box, I have already moved my cursor to that position, so there is zero time lag between the appearance of the button and the click (see Gray & Boehm-Davis, 2000, for other examples of such micro-strategies). This rather extreme adaptation to the task environment is a case of computational optimization (clicking fast and clicking slow are equally correct), and it depends crucially on having sufficient experience for the estimate of the button location to become stable and accurate. Other quantities affect processing in other ways, optimizing memory retrieval, conflict resolution, goal setting, attention allocation, and so on. As practice progresses, the internal estimates of the relevant environmental quantities become more accurate and less noisy, and enable fine tuning of the relevant processes. Capturing the statistical structure of task environment is likely to be responsible for a significant proportion of the speed-up that accompanies practice in the long run.

7. Obstacles and Paths to Further Progress

Research on skill acquisition draws on a century of scientific progress. The computational models proposed since 1979 address a wide range of theoretical questions, and they are more detailed, more precise, and more explanatory than the verbal formulations and mathematical equations that preceded them. Nevertheless, there are reasons to despair.

What is the next step? According to the textbook definition of research, the next wave of skill acquisition research should consist of empirical studies to test which of the many hypotheses previously reviewed is correct. Researchers are supposed to derive the behavioral predictions from each hypothesized learning mechanism and test them against empirical data. The hypotheses that remain standing at the end of the day are the true ones.

There are several problems with this cartoon of research. The most serious for present purposes is the implicit assumption that we can test hypothesized learning mechanisms one at a time. But it is unlikely that the human capacity for change relies on a single learning mechanism, so we should not expect a single learning mechanism to explain all behavioral phenomena

associated with skill acquisition. Instead, we should expect the theory we seek to include a repertoire of N interacting learning mechanisms (Anderson, 1983; Gagné, 1970). The total amount of behavioral change that occurs in each successive phase of training is divided among the members of that repertoire, and the relative contributions of the different mechanisms shift gradually as practice continues. Figure 13.2 shows a didactic example. The relative contributions of four sources of information are plotted in terms of the proportion of the total behavioral change within each phase that each source accounts for, in a hypothetical learner who has a single learning mechanism for each source. The character of each phase is determined by the relative contributions of different types of information and associated learning mechanisms, and these contributions shift across time. In the figure, instructions and solved examples account for almost all change in the initial phase, whereas responding to feedback is the most important type of learning in the middle phase and memory-based responding becomes dominant in the optimization phase. This is a hypothetical, didactic case. Each repertoire of learning mechanisms will exhibit its own succession of shifts.

The methodological difficulty is that we have no way of disabling N-1 of the mechanisms to test different models of the Nth one. Instead, all N mechanisms must be assumed to be operating continuously and in parallel. If so, then the overt, observable change in behavior is a product of the interactions among the N learning mechanisms. Behavioral data cannot speak to the existence or nature of any one mechanism but only to some ensemble of mechanisms. Hence, we cannot test hypotheses about, for example, analogical transfer per se, only about analogical transfer in the context of whichever other learning mechanisms we believe that people possess. Attempts to derive a specific phenomenon like the power law of practice from a single learning mechanism (a widespread misdemeanor; see, e.g., Anderson, 1982; Logan, 1998; Newell & Rosenbloom, 1981; Ohlsson,

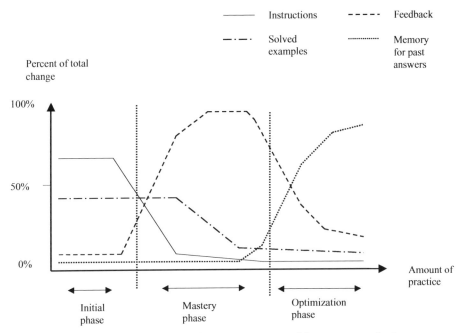

Figure 13.2. Successive shift in the relative importance of four sources of information across the three phases of skill practice in a hypothetical learner. Instruction = task instructions, exhortations, and so forth. Examples = solved examples and demonstrations. Feedback = positive and negative on-line feedback from the environment during practice. Memory = accumulated store of information about the task, including past solutions and answers, execution history of the skill, and cumulative statistics about the task environment.

1996; Shrager, Hogg, & Huberman, 1988) are unwarranted, and the outcomes of such single-mechanism derivations are uninterpretable (Ohlsson & Jewett, 1997).

Pursuing the interaction argument to its natural end point, we reach a radically counterintuitive conclusion: If a single learning mechanism successfully predicts a particular behavioral phenomenon, the hypothesis it represents must be false. Furthermore, the better the fit between the hypothesis and the data, the stronger the reason to reject the hypothesis. These conclusions follow because the behavior that results from the interactions among N learning mechanisms is highly likely to differ from the behavior that would result if the mind only possessed a single mechanism. Hence, if a single-mechanism hypothesis accounts for certain data *in the absence of interactions with other learning mechanisms*, then it is highly *unlikely* that it will fit those same data in the presence of such interactions. In other words, fit to data in a single-mechanism simulation is good reason to doubt that good fit would result if the interactions with other mechanisms were factored into the generation of the predictions. Because we have stronger reasons for believing in the existence of multiple learning mechanisms than for believing in any one mechanism, the rational response to a good fit by a model built around a single learning mechanism is to reject that model.

This methodological conundrum prevents modelers from carrying out the divide-and-test program of cartoon science. Modelers have to investigate and test entire repertoires of learning mechanisms. The resulting theory space is immense. For example, with ten different potential learning mechanisms, each of which can be either included or excluded, there are 2^{10}, or 1,024 different models to test. If it takes 10 years to evaluate each one, we will know the true theory in the spring of the year 12,246 A.D.

The standard response to a large search space is to apply information to prune the possibilities. However, the interaction argument applies to falsification as well as confirmation: If a single-mechanism model fails to fit a data set, nothing follows. That mechanism might account for those data very well in interaction with other mechanisms (Ohlsson & Jewett, 1997). It is not obvious how cognitive modelers are to claw, peck, or push their way out of this problem box.

One approach is to adopt the spirit of rational analysis. Human beings are such good learners – we are not merely superior, but orders of magnitude superior to other animals in this respect – that we might in fact be maximally efficient learners. Once prehumans adopted the evolutionary strategy of relying on learned rather than innate competencies, selective pressures propelled the evolution of multiple distinct learning mechanisms, one for every type of information that might be available to the learner during skill practice. Each mechanism is designed to make maximal use of the type of information it takes as input, and, in conjunction, the mechanisms cover all potentially available sources of information. As the retinas in our eyes are maximally sensitive in the sense that they can react to a single photon, so the learning mechanisms in our head are collectively sufficient to make use of every bit of information. I call this rationality principle the *Principle of Maximally Efficient Learning.*

To evaluate the plausibility of this proposal, the reader might try the thought experiment of imagining a model of skill acquisition that lacks one or more modes of learning reviewed in the previous sections. Which one might turn out false if we could make the appropriate empirical test? Is it plausible that we would ever conclude that people cannot benefit from instructions and exhortations? That they cannot re-use prior skills? Are unable to capitalize on positive outcomes produced by tentative steps? Cannot learn from their errors? Have no way of responding to impasses? Cannot find shortcuts or optimize their mental code? Do not absorb the statistical structure of the envi-

ronment? The idea that we would ever reject any one of these hypotheses on the basis of data is quixotic, because the intuition that people can learn in each and every one of these ways is stronger than our belief in any one experimental study.

The previous sections identified nine distinct sources of information for learning: exhortations, abstract declarative knowledge, prior skills, solved examples and demonstrations, positive feedback (including subgoal satisfaction), negative feedback and errors, execution states and histories, memory for problem-answer links, and the statistical properties of the environment. Recognition of the fact that these different sources of information are available to a learner is by itself a conceptual advance in the study of skill acquisition. If we assume that people can use each type of information and that different processes are needed to use each type, as per the Information Specificity Principle, then a first-approximation model of skill acquisition should be equipped with at least nine different learning mechanisms, one for each source of information.

The first mission for such a model might be to simulate the broad functionality of human learning. The model should be able to acquire the entire range of cognitive skills that people can learn (universality); draw on information from diverse sources during learning (integration); be able to make progress even when insufficient information is available (graceful degradation); override prior experience when what is learned turns out to be a mistake or the task environment changes (defeasibility); and accumulate learning effects over long periods of practice (accumulation). Once a set of learning mechanisms has been shown to capture these and other broad features of human learning, quantitative data can be brought to bear to identify the exact details of each mechanism. If the model has N learning mechanisms, the implementation of each mechanism can be seen as a parameter. By varying the implementations, we might be able to improve the model's fit to empirical phenomena. This *functionality first, fit later* research strategy requires complex models, but it takes the logic of the interaction argument seriously.

A breakthrough in our understanding of skill acquisition can be sought along two other lines of inquiry. The set of possible or plausible learning mechanisms is constrained by the structure of the knowledge representations they operate on. Different representations afford or suggest different types of changes. One reason the production rule format has attracted skill acquisition researchers is that the rule notation is fertile in such suggestions: The ideas of adding or deleting conditions elements or of composing rules are irresistibly suggested by the notation itself. Likewise, nodes and links in a semantic network afford the ideas of creating and deleting links, whereas propositional representations afford the replacement of constants with variables (or vice versa). Although a deeper understanding of the space of possible knowledge representations was heralded in the early years of cognitive science as one of the field's major goals and potentially unique contributions, the problem of identifying exactly how the mind encodes information turned out to be intractable. For example, debates about the different roles of phonetic and semantic codes in short-term memory (Baddeley & Levy, 1971; Kintsch & Buschke, 1969; Wickelgren, 1969) and about holistic versus propositional encodings of images (Anderson, 1978, 1979; Pylyshyn, 1979) were intensively engaged but put aside without resolution. By the 1990s, the field had settled for an irregular collection of partial solutions, including semantic networks, sets of propositions, production rules, and schemas (Markman, 1999). Each of these representations captures some but not all features of human knowledge, and collectively they have no principled rationale over and above the fact that we know how to implement them in computer code.

A second wave of inquiry into knowledge representation might provide us with a new and psychologically accurate representation which, in turn, will suggest the right set of learning mechanisms. Because the individual concept is the building block for any knowledge representation, such an enterprise might benefit from linking skill acquisition research to theories of semantics. If we could understand the mental representation of a single concept (e.g., *make tea*), perhaps we could understand how the mind links concepts into the larger structures that make up practical knowledge. Whether such a project would benefit most from reaching back to the semantic theories proposed in decades past (Jackendoff, 1983; Lakoff, 1971; Miller & Johnson-Laird, 1976), attending to more recent semantic endeavors (e.g., Engelberg, 2004; Pustejovsky, 2005), or striking out in an entirely new direction (e.g., Fauconnier & Turner, 2002; Gärdenfors. 2000) is an open question, but a grounded theory of representation might constrain the set of plausible learning mechanisms.

A similar situation holds with respect to motor action. The field of computational modeling has settled on the so-called STRIPS operator as the standard representation for actions (Fikes & Nilsson, 1993), but this representation bears little relation to motor schemas and other types of representations that are discussed in the neighboring and yet so distant field of motor skill learning (Adams, 1987; Fischer, 1980; Gallistel, 1980; Wolpert, Ghahramani & Flanagan, 2001; see Chapter 24 in this volume). Again, an empirically grounded theory of the representation of elementary actions might suggest novel learning mechanisms or help modelers to choose among those already under consideration.

Another promising but as yet untapped source of constraints on the repertoire of learning mechanisms is the brain. There is no evidence that the mind is a blob of ectoplasm hovering somewhere just out of sight from scientific observation, so it must be assumed that every learning mechanism will one day be understood as implemented in neural matter. Cognitive descriptions of processes in the mind are functional descriptions of what this or that piece of wetware is doing, what function it carries out. This perspective points to the need to understand the relation between learning mechanisms like those reviewed in this chapter and modes of neural plasticity. How does the neural matter change when a learner changes his or her mind in some particular way, for example, by collapsing two production rules into one, creating a new subgoal, or lowering the strength of a link?

How many distinct modes of neural plasticity are there? One or one hundred? The cognitive neuroscience literature indicates that the answer is somewhere in between. There is *long-term potentiation* (the lowering of the threshold for signal transmission between one neuron and a downstream neuron consequent on repeated transmissions), *consolidation*, and *synaptic pruning*, but also the creation of new synapses and even wholesale replacement of brain cells. The challenge is to understand how these changes in neural matter relate to changes of mind as described at the cognitive level. For example, is long-term potentiation the same as strengthening? That is, can we reasonably assume that long-term potentiation is operating each time one of our simulation models upgrades the strength of a link as a function of frequency of use (Martin, Grimwood, & Morris, 2000; Martin & Morris, 2002)? Or is it not possible to map cognitive change mechanisms onto modes of neural plasticity in this way? Once we are past the potentiation-strengthening linkage, it becomes suspiciously difficult to make further mappings of this sort. For example, which type of neural plasticity should we conceive as implementing discrimination learning? Perhaps synaptic pruning can serve that purpose? But is pruning sensitivity to feedback? So little is understood about how to make such mind-brain mappings that it is unclear whether this approach is a tool or a problem, but it seems likely that an exhaustive list of the modes of neural plasticity would have implications for the plausibility of rival learning mechanisms defined at the cognitive level.

In the end, what is needed for further progress is a brilliant guess. Somebody has to propose a repertoire of learning mechanisms that happens to be close enough to the truth so that incremental improvement of fit to data can be pursued through the hypothesis-testing and parameter-fitting procedures of normal science. Cognitive skill acquisition awaits its Newton.

Acknowledgments

The preparation of this chapter was supported by Grant No. N00014-00-1-0640 from the Cognitive Science Program of the Office of Naval Research (ONR) to Barbara Di Eugenio and Stellan Ohlsson. The opinions expressed are those of the author. No endorsement should be inferred.

References

Ackerman, P. L. (1990). A correlational analysis of skill specificity: Learning, abilities, and individual differences. *Journal of Experimental Psychology: Learning, Memory, and Cognition, 16*, 883–901.

Adams, J. A. (1987). Historical review and appraisal of research on the learning, retention, and transfer of human motor skills. *Psychological Bulletin, 101*, 41–74.

Altmann, E. M., & Burns, B. D. (2005). Streak biases in decision making: Data and a memory model. *Cognitive Systems Research, 6*, 5–16.

Amir, E., & Maynard-Zhang, P. (2004). Logic-based subsumption architecture. *Artificial Intelligence, 153*, 167–237.

Anderson, J. R. (1978). Arguments concerning representations for mental imagery. *Psychological Review, 85*, 249–277.

Anderson, J. R. (1979). Further arguments concerning representations for mental imagery: A response to Hayes-Roth and Pylyshyn. *Psychological Review, 86*, 395–406.

Anderson, J. R. (1982). Acquisition of cognitive skill. *Psychological Review, 89*, 369–406.

Anderson, J. R. (1983). *The architecture of cognition*. Cambridge, MA: Harvard University Press.

Anderson, J. R. (1986). Knowledge compilation: The general learning mechanism. In R. S. Michalski, J. G. Carbonell, & T. M. Mitchell (Eds.), *Machine learning: An artificial intelligence approach* (Vol. 2, pp. 289–310). Los Altos, CA: Kaufmann.

Anderson, J. R. (1987). Skill acquisition: Compilation of weak-method problem solutions. *Psychological Review, 94*, 192–210.

Anderson, J. R. (1989). A rational analysis of human memory. In H. L. Roediger III & F. I. M. Craik (Eds.), *Varieties of memory and consciousness* (pp. 195–210). Hillsdale, NJ: Lawrence Erlbaum.

Anderson, J. R. (1990). *The adaptive character of thought*. Hillsdale, NJ: Lawrence Erlbaum.

Anderson, J. R. (1993). *Rules of the mind*. Hillsdale, NJ: Lawrence Erlbaum.

Anderson, J. R., Kline, P., & Beasley, C. M. (1978, February). *A theory of the acquisition of cognitive skills* (Technical Report 77-1). New Haven, CT: Yale University.

Anderson, J. R., Kline, P. J., & Beasley, C. M. (1979). A general learning theory and its application to schema abstraction. In G. H. Bower (Ed.), *The psychology of learning and motivation: Advances in research and theory* (Vol. 13, pp. 277–318). New York: Academic Press.

Anderson, J. R., & Lebiere, C. (1998). *The atomic components of thought*. Mahwah, NJ: Lawrence Erlbaum.

Anderson, J. R., & Pirolli, P. L. (1984). Spread of activation. *Journal of Experimental Psychology: Learning, Memory, and Cognition, 10*, 791–798.

Anderson, J. R., & Schooler, L. J. (1991). Reflections of the environment in memory. *Psychological Science, 2*, 396–408.

Anderson, J. R., & Thompson, R. (1989). Use of analogy in a production system architecture. In S. Vosniadou & A. Ortony (Eds.), *Similarity and analogical reasoning* (pp. 267–297). Cambridge, UK: Cambridge University Press.

Anzai, Y., & Simon, H. A. (1979). The theory of learning by doing. *Psychological Review, 86*, 124–140.

Baddeley, A. D., & Levy, B. A. (1971). Semantic coding and short-term memory. *Journal of Experimental Psychology, 89*, 132–136.

Bandura, A. (1977). *Social learning theory*. Upper Saddle River, NJ: Prentice Hall.

Bharadwaj, K. K., & Jain, N. K. (1992). Hierarchical censored production rule (HCPRs) system. *Data & Knowledge Engineering, 8*, 19–34.

Bhatnagar, N., & Mostow, J. (1994). On-line learning from search failure. *Machine Learning, 15*, 69–117.

Blessing, S. B., & Anderson, J. R. (1996). How people learn to skip steps. *Journal of Experimental Psychology: Learning, Memory, & Cognition, 22*, 576–598. [Reprinted in T. A. Polk & C. M. Seifert (Eds.). (2002). *Cognitive modeling* (pp. 577–620). Cambridge, MA: MIT Press.]

Brown, J. S., & VanLehn, K. (1980). Repair theory: A generative theory of bugs in procedural skills. *Cognitive Science, 4*, 379–426.

Carbonell, J. G. (1983). Learning by analogy: Formulating and generalizing plans from past experience. In R. S. Michalski, J. G. Carbonell, & T. M. Mitchell (Eds.), *Machine learning: An artificial intelligence approach* (pp. 137–161). Palo Alto, CA: Tioga.

Carbonell, J. G. (1986). Derivational analogy: A theory of reconstructive problem solving and expertise acquisition. In R. S. Michalski, J. G. Carbonell, & T. M. Mitchell (Eds.), *Machine learning: An artificial intelligence approach* (Vol. 2, pp. 371–392). Los Altos, CA: Morgan Kauffmann.

Carroll, J. B. (1993). *Human cognitive abilities*. Cambridge, UK: Cambridge University Press.

Collins, A. M., & Loftus, E. F. (1975). A spreading-activation theory of semantic processing. *Psychological Review, 82*, 407–428.

Conway, F., & Siegelman, J. (2005). *Dark hero of the information age: In search of Norbert Wiener the father of cybernetics*. New York: Basic Books.

Corrigan-Halpern, A., & Ohlsson, S. (2002). Feedback effects in the acquisition of a hierarchical skill. In W. D. Gray & C.D. Schunn (Eds.), *Proceedings of the Twenty-Fourth Annual Conference of the Cognitive Science Society* (pp. 226–231). Mahwah, NJ: Lawrence Erlbaum.

Crevier, D. (1993). *AI: The tumultuous history of the search for artificial intelligence*. New York: Basic Books.

Crossman, E. (1959). A theory of the acquisition of speed-skill. *Ergonomics, 2*, 152–166.

Davis, R., & King, J. (1977). An overview of production systems. In E. Elcock & D. Michie (Eds.), *Machine intelligence* (Vol. 8, pp. 300–332). Chichester, UK: Horwood.

Doane, S. M., & Sohn, Y. W. (2000). ADAPT: A predictive cognitive model of user visual attention and action planning. *User Modeling and User-Adapted Interaction, 10*, 1–45.

Doane, S. M., Sohn, Y. W., McNamara, D. S., & Adams, D. (2000). Comprehension-based skill acquisition. *Cognitive Science, 24*, 1–52.

De Jong, K. (1990). Genetic-algorithm-based learning. In Y. Kodratoff & R. S. Michalski (Eds.), *Machine learning: An artificial intelligence approach* (Vol. 3, pp. 611–638). San Mateo, CA: Morgan Kauffmann.

Donald, M. (1991). *Origins of the modern mind: Three stages in the evolution of culture and cognition.* Cambridge, MA: Harvard University Press.

Ebbinghaus, H. (1885/1964). *Memory: A contribution to experimental psychology.* New York: Dover.

Elio, R., & Scharf, P. B. (1990). Modeling novice-to-expert shifts in problem-solving strategy and knowledge organization. *Cognitive Science, 14,* 579–639.

Engelberg, S. (2004). Lexical event structures for verb semantics. *Journal of Language and Linguistics, 3,* 62–108.

Ericsson, K. A., Charness, N., Feltovich, P. J., & Hoffman, R. R. (Eds.). (2006). *The Cambridge handbook of expertise and expert performance.* Cambridge, UK: Cambridge University Press.

Ericsson, K. A., Krampe, R. Th., & Tesch-Romer, C. (1993). The role of deliberate practice in the acquisition of expert performance. *Psychological Review, 100,* 363–406.

Falkenhainer, B., Forbus, K. D., & Gentner, D. (1989). The structure-mapping engine: Algorithm and examples. *Artificial Intelligence, 41,* 1–63.

Fauconnier, G., & Turner, M. (2002). *The way we think: Conceptual blending and the mind's hidden complexities.* New York: Basic Books.

Fikes, R. E., & Nilsson, N. J. (1993). STRIPS, a retrospective. *Artificial Intelligence, 59,* 227–232.

Fischer, K. W. (1980). A theory of cognitive development: The control and construction of hierarchies of skills. *Psychological Review, 87,* 477–531.

Fitts, P. (1964). Perceptual-motor skill learning. In A. Melton (Ed.), *Categories of human learning* (pp. 243–285). New York: Academic Press.

Forbus, K. D., Gentner, D., & Law, K. (1994). MAC/FAC: A model of similarity-based retrieval. *Cognitive Science, 19,* 141–205.

Fu, W.-T., & Gray, W. D. (2004). Resolving the paradox of the active user: Stable suboptimal performance in interactive tasks. *Cognitive Science, 28,* 901–935.

Gagne, R. M. (1970). *The conditions of learning* (2nd ed.). London, UK: Holt, Rinehart & Winston.

Gallistel, C. R. (1980). *The organization of action: A new synthesis.* Hillsdale, NJ: Lawrence Erlbaum.

Gärdenfors, P. (2000). *Conceptual spaces: The geometry of thought.* Cambridge, MA: MIT Press.

Gardner, H. (1985). *The mind's new science: A history of the cognitive revolution.* New York: Basic Books.

Gelman, R., & Gallistel, C. R. (1978). *The child's understanding of number.* Cambridge, MA: Harvard University Press.

Gentner, D. (1983). Structure-mapping: A theoretical framework for analogy. *Cognitive Science, 7,* 155–170.

Gernsbacher, M. A. (Ed.). (1994). *Handbook of psycholinguistics.* San Diego, CA: Academic Press.

Giunchiglia, E., Lee, J., Lifschitz, V., McCain, N. & Tuner, H. (2004). Nonmonotonic causal theories. *Artificial Intelligence, 153,* 49–104.

Greeno, J. G., Riley, M. S., & Gelman, R. (1984). Conceptual competence for children's counting. *Cognitive Psychology, 16,* 94–143.

Gray, W. D., & Boehm-Davis, D. A. (2000). Milliseconds matter: An introduction to microstrategies and to their use in describing and predicting interactive behavior. *Journal of Experimental Psychology: Applied, 6,* 322–335.

Gray, W. D., Schoelles, M. J., & Sims, C. R. (2005). Adapting to the task environment: Explorations in expected value. *Cognitive Systems Research, 6,* 27–40.

Hayes-Roth, F., Klahr, P., & Mostow, D. (1981). Advice taking and knowledge refinement: An iterative view of skill acquisition. In J. Anderson (Ed.), *Cognitive skills and their acquisition* (pp. 231–253). Hillsdale, NJ: Lawrence Erlbaum.

Hiebert, J., (Ed.). (1986). *Conceptual and procedural knowledge: The case of mathematics.* Hillsdale, NJ: Lawrence Erlbaum.

Hilgard, E. R., & Bower, G. H. (1966). *Theories of learning* (3rd ed.). New York: Appleton-Century-Crofts.

Holland, J. H. (1975). *Adaptation in natural and artificial systems: An introductory analysis with applications to biology, control, and artificial intelligence.* Ann Arbor: University of Michigan Press.

Holyoak, K. J. (1985). The pragmatics of analogical transfer. In G. H. Bower (Ed.), *The psychology of learning and motivation* (Vol. 19, pp. 59–87). New York: Academic Press.

Holyoak, K. J., & Thagard, P. R. (1989a). A computational model of analogical problem solving. In S. Vosniadou & A. Ortony (Eds.), *Similarity and analogical reasoning* (pp. 242–266). Cambridge, UK: Cambridge University Press.

Holyoak, K. J., & Thagard, P. (1989b). Analogical mapping by constraint satisfaction. *Cognitive Science, 13*, 295–355.

Huffman, S. B., & Laird, J. E. (1995). Flexibly instructable agents. *Journal of Artificial Intelligence Research, 3*, 271–324.

Hummel, J. E., & Holyoak, K. J. (1997). Distributed representations of structure: A theory of analogical access and mapping. *Psychological Review, 104*, 427–466.

Hummel, J. E., & Holyoak, K. J. (2003). A symbolic-connectionist theory of relational inference and generalization. *Psychological Review, 110*, 220–264.

Jackendoff, R. (1983). *Semantics and cognition.* Cambridge, MA: MIT Press.

Jain, N. K., & Bharadwaj, K. K. (1998). Some learning techniques in hierarchical censored production rules (HCPRs) system. *International Journal of Intelligent Systems, 13*, 319–344.

James, W. (1890). *Principles of psychology* (Vols. 1 & 2). London, UK: Macmillan.

Jones, G., Ritter, F. E., & Wood, D. J. (2000). Using a cognitive architecture to examine what develops. *Psychological Science, 11*, 93–100.

Jones, R. M., & Langley, P. A. (2005). A constrained architecture for learning and problem solving. *Computational Intelligence, 21*, 480–502.

Jones, R. M., & VanLehn, K. (1994). Acquisition of children's addition strategies: A model of impasse-free, knowledge-level learning. *Machine Learning, 16*, 11–36. [Reprinted in T. A. Polk & C. M. Seifert (Eds.). (2002). *Cognitive modeling* (pp. 623–646). Cambridge, MA: MIT Press.]

Keane, M. T., & Ledgeway, T., & Duff, S. (1994). Constraints on analogical mapping: A comparison of three models. *Cognitive Science, 18*, 387–338.

Kieras, D., & Bovair, S. (1986). The acquisition of procedures from text: A production-system analysis of transfer of training. *Journal of Memory and Language, 25*, 507–524.

Kintsch, W. (1998). *Comprehension: A paradigm for cognition.* Cambridge, UK: Cambridge University Press.

Kintsch, W., & Buschke, H. (1969). Homophones and synonyms in short-term memory. *Journal of Experimental Psychology, 80*, 403–407.

Koedinger, K. R., & Anderson, J. R. (1990). Abstract planning and perceptual chunks: Elements of expertise in geometry. *Cognitive Science, 14*, 511–550.

Kokinov, B. N., & Petrov, A. A. (2001). Integrating memory and reasoning in analogy-making: The AMBR model. In D. Gentner, K. J. Holyoak & B. N. Kokinov (Eds.), *The analogical mind: Perspectives from cognitive science* (pp. 59–124). Cambridge, MA: MIT Press.

Lakoff, G. (1971). On generative semantics. In D. D. Steinberg & L. A. Jakobovits (Eds.), *Semantics: An interdisciplinary reader in philosophy, linguistics and psychology* (pp. 232–296). Cambridge, UK: Cambridge University Press.

Langley, P. (1983). Learning search strategies through discrimination. *International Journal of Man-Machine Studies, 18*, 513–541.

Langley, P. (1985). Learning to search: From weak methods to domain-specific heuristics. *Cognitive Science, 9*, 217–260.

Langley, P. (1987). A general theory of discrimination learning. In D. Klahr, P. Langley, & R. Neches (Eds.), *Production system models of learning and development* (pp. 99–161). Cambridge, MA: MIT Press.

Langley, P., & Choi, D. (2006). Learning recursive control programs from problem solving. *Journal of Machine Learning Research, 7*, 493–518.

Larkin, J. H. (1981). Enriching formal knowledge: A model for learning to solve textbook physics problems. In J. R. Anderson (Ed.), *Cognitive skills and their acquisition* (pp. 311–334). Hillsdale, NJ: Lawrence Erlbaum.

Lenat, D. B. (1983). Toward a theory of heuristics. In R. Groner, M. Groner & W. F. Bischof (Eds.), *Methods of heuristics* (pp. 351–404). Hillsdale, NJ: Lawrence Erlbaum.

Lewis, C. (1987). Composition of productions. In D. Klahr, P. Langley & R. Neches (Eds.), *Production system models of learning and development* (pp. 329–358). Cambridge, MA: MIT Press.

Lewis, C. (1988). Why and how to learn why: Analysis-based generalization of procedures. *Cognitive Science, 12*, 211–356.

Lifschitz, V., (Ed.). (1990). *Formalizing common sense: Papers by John McCarthy.* Norwoord, NJ: Ablex.

Logan, G. D. (1998). Toward an instance theory of automatization. *Psychological Review, 95*, 492–527.

Luchins, A. S., & Luchins, E. H. (1959). *Rigidity of behavior.* Eugene: University of Oregon Press.

Markman, A. B. (1999). *Knowledge representation*. Mahwah, NJ: Lawrence Erlbaum.

Martin, S. J., Grimwood, P. D., & Morris, R. G. M. (2000). Synaptic plasticity and memory: An evaluation of the hypothesis. *Annual Review of Neuroscience, 23*, 649–711.

Martin, S. J., & Morris, R. G. M. (2002). New life in an old idea: The synaptic plasticity and memory hypothesis revisited. *Hippocampus, 12*, 609–636.

McCarthy, J. (1959). Programs with common sense. In *Proceedings of the Teddington Conference on the Mechanization of Thought Processes* (pp. 75–91). London: Her Majesty's Stationary Office. [Reprinted as Section 7.1 of J. McCarthy, Programs with common sense, in Minsky (1968).]

McCarthy, J. (1963, July). *Situations, actions and causal laws*. Stanford Artificial Intelligence Project Memo No. 2. Stanford, CA: Stanford University. [Reprinted as Section 7.2 of J. McCarthy, Programs with common sense, in Minsky (1968).]

Miller, G. A., Galanter, E., & Pribram, K. H. (1960). *Plans and the structure of behavior*. New York: Holt, Rinehart & Winston.

Miller, G. A., & Johnson-Laird, P. N. (1976). *Language and perception*. Cambridge, MA: Harvard University Press.

Minsky, M., (Ed.). (1968). *Semantic information processing*. Cambridge, MA: MIT Press.

Mostow, D. J. (1983). Machine transformation of advice into a heuristic search procedure. In R. S. Michalski, J. G. Carbonell & T. M. Mitchell (Eds.), *Machine learning: An artificial intelligence approach* (pp. 367–404). Palo Alto, CA: Tioga.

Nason, S., & Laird, J. E. (2005). Soar-RL: integrating reinforcement learning with Soar. *Cognitive Systems Research, 6*, 51–59.

Neches, R. (1987). Learning through incremental refinement of procedures. In D. Klahr, P. Langley, & R. Neches (Eds.), *Production system models of learning and development* (pp. 163–219). Cambridge, MA: MIT Press.

Neches, R., Langley, P., & Klahr, D. (1987). Learning, development, and production systems. In D. Klahr, P. Langley, & R. Neches (Eds.), *Production system models of learning and development* (pp. 1–53). Cambridge, MA: The MIT Press.

Neimark, E. D., & Estes, W. K., (Eds.). (1967). *Stimulus sampling theory*. San Francisco: Holden-Day.

Nerb, J., Ritter, F. E., & Krems. J. F. (1999). Knowledge level learning and the power law: A Soar model of skill acquisition in scheduling. *Kognitionswissenschaft, 8*, 20–29.

Neves, D. M., & Anderson, J. R. (1981). Knowledge compilation: Mechanisms for the automatization of cognitive skills. In J. R, Anderson (Ed.), *Cognitive skills and their acquisition* (pp. 57–84). Hillsdale, NJ: Lawrence Erlbaum.

Newell, A. (1972). A theoretical exploration of mechanisms for coding the stimulus. In A. W. Melton & E. Martin (Eds.), *Coding processes in human memory* (pp. 373–434). New York: Wiley.

Newell, A. (1973). Production systems: Models of control structures. In W. G. Chase (Ed.), *Visual information processing* (pp. 463–526). New York: Academic Press.

Newell, A. (1990). *Unified theories of cognition*. Cambridge, MA: Harvard University Press.

Newell, A., & Rosenbloom, P. (1981). Mechanisms of skill acquisition and the law of practice. In J. Anderson (Ed.), *Cognitive skills and their acquisition* (pp. 1–55). Hillsdale, NJ: Lawrence Erlbaum.

Newell, A., Shaw, J. C., & Simon, H. A. (1958). Elements of a theory of human problem solving. *Psychological Review, 65*, 151–166.

Newell, A., & Simon, H. (1972). *Human problem solving*. Englewood Cliffs, NJ: Prentice Hall.

Oaksford, M., & Chater, N., (Eds.). (1998). *Rational models of cognition*. Oxford, UK: Oxford University Press.

Ohlsson, S. (1987a). Transfer of training in procedural learning: A matter of conjectures and refutations? In L. Bolc (Ed.), *Computational models of learning* (pp. 55–88). Berlin, West Germany: Springer-Verlag.

Ohlsson, S. (1987b). Truth versus appropriateness: Relating declarative to procedural knowledge. In D. Klahr, P. Langley, & R. Neches (Eds.), *Production system models of learning and development* (pp. 287–327). Cambridge, MA: MIT Press.

Ohlsson, S. (1992). Artificial instruction: A method for relating learning theory to instructional design. In P. Winne & M. Jones (Eds.), *Foundations and frontiers in instructional computing systems* (pp. 55–83). New York: Springer-Verlag.

Ohlsson, S. (1993). The interaction between knowledge and practice in the acquisition of cognitive skills. In S. Chipman & A. L. Meyrowitz (Eds.), *Foundations of knowledge* acquisition: Cognitive models of complex learning (pp. 147–208). Boston: Kluwer.

Ohlsson, S. (1996). Learning from performance errors. Psychological Review, 103, 241–262.

Ohlsson, S. (2007). The effects of order: A constraint-based explanation. In F. E. Ritter, J. Nerb, E. Lehtinen, & T. O'Shea (Eds.), In order to learn: How the sequence of topics in fluences learing (pp. 151–165). New York: Oxford University Press.

Ohlsson, S., Ernst, A. M., & Rees, E. (1992). The cognitive complexity of doing and learning arithmetic. Journal of Research in Mathematics Education, 23, 441–467.

Ohlsson, S., & Jewett, J. J. (1997). Ideal adaptive agents and the learning curve. In J. Brzezinski, B. Krause & T. Maruszewski (Eds.), Idealization VIII: Modelling in psychology (pp. 139–176) Amsterdam: Rodopi.

Ohlsson, S., & Rees, E. (1991a). The function of conceptual understanding in the learning of arithmetic procedures. Cognition and Instruction, 8, 103–179.

Ohlsson, S., & Rees, E. (1991b). Adaptive search through constraint violation. Journal of Experimental and Theoretical Artificial Intelligence, 3, 33–42.

Petrov, A. A., & Anderson, J. R. (2005). The dynamics of scaling: A memory-based anchor model of category rating and absolute identification. Psychological Review, 112, 383–416.

Piaget, J. (1950). The psychology of intelligence. London: Routledge & Kegan Paul.

Pirolli, P. (1986). A cognitive model and computer tutor for programming recursion. Human-Computer Interaction, 2, 319–355.

Pirolli, P. (1991). Effects of examples and their explanations in a lesson on recursion: A production system analysis. Cognition and Instruction, 8, 207–259.

Pirolli, P., & Recker, M. (1994). Learning strategies and transfer in the domain of programming. Cognition & Instruction, 12, 235–275.

Pustejovsky, J. (2005). Meaning in context. Cambridge, MA: MIT Press.

Pylyshyn, Z. W. (1979). Validating computational models: A critique of Anderson's indeterminacy of representation claim. Psychological Review, 86, 383–394.

Reason, J. (1990). Human error. Cambridge, UK: Cambridge University Press.

Restle, R. (1955). A theory of discrimination learning. Psychological Review, 62, 11–19.

Reimann, P., Schult, T. J., & Wichmann, S. (1993). Understanding and using worked-out examples: A computational model. In G. Strube & K. Wender (Eds.), The cognitive psychology of knowledge (pp. 177–201). Amsterdam: North-Holland.

Rosenbloom, P. S., Laird, J. E., & Newell, A., (Eds.). (1993). The Soar papers: Research on integrated intelligence (Vols. 1 & 2). Cambridge, MA: MIT Press.

Rosenbloom, P., & Newell, A. (1986). The chunking of goal hierarchies: A generalized model of practice. In R. S. Michalski, J. G. Carbonell & T. M. Mitchell (Eds.), Machine learning: An artificial intelligence approach (Vol. 2, pp. 247–288). Los Altos, CA: Kaufmann.

Rosenbloom, P., & Newell, A. (1987). Learning by chunking: A production system model of practice. In D. Klahr, P. Langley & R. Neches (Eds.), Production system models of learning and development (pp. 221–286). Cambridge, MA: MIT Press.

Ruiz, D., & Newell, A. (1993). Tower-noticing triggers strategy-change in the Tower of Hanoi: A Soar model. In P. S. Rosenbloom, J. E. Laird, & A. Newell (Eds.), The Soar papers: Research on integrated intelligence (Vol. 2, pp. 934–941). Cambridge, MA: MIT Press.

Russell, S., & Norvig, P. (1995). Artificial intelligence: A modern approach. Los Altos, CA: Morgan Kaufman.

Rychener, M. D. (1983). The instructible production system: A retrospective approach. In R. S. Michalski, J. G. Carbonell, & T. M. Mitchell (Eds.), Machine learning: An artificial intelligence approach (pp. 429–459). Palo Alto, CA: Tioga.

Rychener, M. D., & Newell, A. (1978). An instructible production system: Basic design issues. In D. A. Waterman & F. Hayes-Roth (Eds.), Pattern-directed inference systems (pp. 135–153). New York: Academic Press.

Ryle, G. (1949/1968). The concept of mind. London: Penguin.

Salomon, G., & Perkins, D. N. (1989). Rocky roads to transfer: Rethinking mechanisms of a neglected phenomenon. Educational Psychologist, 24, 113–142.

Salthouse, T. A. (1996). The processing-speed theory of adult age differences in cognition. Psychology Review, 103, 403–428.

Salvucci, D. D., & Anderson, J. R. (2001). Integrating analogical mapping and general problem solving: the path-mapping theory. Cognitive Science, 25, 67–110.

Schooler, L. J., & Hertwig, R. (2005). How forgetting aids heuristic inference. *Psychological Review, 112,* 610–628.

Schneider, W., & Chein, J. M. (2003). Controlled & automatic processing: Behavior, theory, and biological mechanisms. *Cognitive Science, 27,* 525–559.

Schneider, W., & Oliver, W. L. (1991). An instructable connectionist/control architecture: Using rule-based instructions to accomplish connectionist learning in a human time scale. In K. VanLehn (Ed.), *Architectures for intelligence* (pp. 113–145). Hillsdale, NJ: Lawrence Erlbaum.

Shrager, J., Hogg, T., & Huberman, B. A. (1988). A graph-dynamic model of the power low of practice and the problem-solving fan effect. *Science, 242,* 414–416.

Shrager, J., & Siegler, R. S. (1998). A model of children's strategy choices and strategy discoveries. *Psychological Science, 9,* 405–410.

Siegler, R., & Araya, R. (2005). A computational model of conscious and unconscious strategy discovery. In R. V. Kail (Ed.), *Advances in child development and behavior* (Vol. 33, pp. 1–42). Oxford, UK: Elsevier.

Siegler, R. S., & Shipley, C. (1995). Variation, selection, and cognitive change. In T. J. Simon & G. S. Halford (Eds.), *Developing cognitive competencies: New approaches to process modeling* (pp. 31–76). Hillsdale, NJ: Lawrence Erlbaum.

Siegler, R. S., & Shrager, J. (1984). Strategy choices in addition and subtraction: How do children know what to do? In C. Sophian (Ed.), *Origins of cognitive skills* (pp. 229–293). Hillsdale, NJ: Lawrence Erlbaum.

Simon, H. A. (1956). Rational choice and the structure of the environment. *Psychological Review, 63,* 129–138.

Simon, H. A. (1970). *The sciences of the artificial.* Cambridge, MA: MIT Press.

Simon, H. A. (1972). On reasoning about actions. In H. A. Simon & L. Siklossy, (Eds.), *Representation and meaning* (pp. 414–430). Englewood Cliffs, NJ: Prentice Hall.

Singley, M. K., & Anderson, J. R. (1989). *The transfer of cognitive skill.* Cambridge, MA: Harvard University Press.

Smith, D. A., Greeno, J. G., & Vitolo, T. M. (1989). A model of competence for counting. *Cognitive Science, 13,* 183–211.

Sohn, Y. W., & Doane, S. M. (2002). Evaluating comprehension-based user models: Predicting individual user planning and action. *User Modeling and User-Adapted Interaction, 12,* 171–205.

Spellman, B. A., & Holyoak, K. J. (1996). Pragmatics in analogical mapping. *Cognitive Psychology, 31,* 307–346.

Sun R., Merrill, E., & Peterson, T. (2001). From implicit skills to explicit knowledge: A bottom-up model of skill learning. *Cognitive Science, 25,* 203–244.

Sun, R., Slusarz, P., & Terry, C. (2005). The interaction of the explicit and the implicit in skill learning: A dual-process approach. *Psychological Review, 112,* 159–192.

Taatgen, N. A. (2002). A model of the individual differences in skill acquisition in the Kanfer-Ackerman air traffic control task. *Cognitive Systems Research, 3,* 103–112.

Taatgen, N. A. (2005). Modeling parallelization and flexibility improvements in skill acquisition: From dual tasks to complex dynamic skills. *Cognitive Science, 29,* 421–455.

Taatgen, N. A., & Anderson, J. R. (2002). Why do children learn to say "Broke"? A model of learning the past tense without feedback. *Cognition, 86,* 123–155.

Taatgen, N. A., & Lee, F. J. (2003). Production compilation: A simple mechanism to model complex skill acquisition. *Human Factors, 45,* 61–76.

Thorndike, E. L. (1898). *Animal intelligence: An experimental study of the associative processes in animals.* Unpublished doctoral dissertation, Columbia University, New York.

Thorndike, E. L. (1911). *The principles of teaching based on psychology.* New York: A. G. Seiler.

Thorndike, E. L. (1927). The law of effect. *American Journal of Psychology, 39,* 212–222.

VanLehn, K. (1983, November). *Felicity conditions for human skill acquisition: Validating an AI based theory* (Technical Report CIS 21). Palo Alto, CA: Xerox Palo Alto Research Centers.

VanLehn, K. (1987). Learning one subprocedure per lesson. *Artificial Intelligence, 31,* 1–40.

VanLehn, K. (1988). Toward a theory of impasse-driven learning. In H. Mandl & A. Lesgold (Eds.), *Learning issues for intelligent tutoring systems* (pp. 19–41). New York: Springer-Verlag.

VanLehn, K. (1990). *Mind bugs: The origins of procedural misconceptions.* Cambridge, MA: MIT Press.

VanLehn, K. (1999). Rule-learning events in the acquisition of a complex skill: An evaluation of Cascade. *The Journal of the Learning Sciences, 8,* 71–125.

VanLehn, K., & Brown, J. S. (1980). Planning nets: A representation for formalizing analogies and semantic models of procedural skills. In R. E. Snow, P.-A. Federico & W. E. Montague (Eds.), *Aptitude, learning, and instruction: Cognitive process analyses of learning and problem solving* (Vol. 2, pp. 95–137). Hillsdale, NJ: Lawrence Erlbaum.

VanLehn, K., & Jones, R. (1993). Learning by explaining examples to oneself: A computational model. In S. Chipman & A. L. Meyrowitz (Eds.), *Foundations of knowledge acquisition: Cognitive models of complex learning* (pp. 25–82). Boston: Kluwer.

VanLehn, K., Jones, R. M., & Chi, M. T. H. (1992). A model of the self-explanation effect. *The Journal of the Learning Sciences, 2,* 1–59.

VanLehn, K., Ohlsson, S., & Nason, R. (1994). Applications of simulated students: An exploration. *Journal of Artificial Intelligence and Education, 5,* 135–175.

Veloso, M. M., & Carbonell, J. G. (1993). Derivational analogy in Prodigy: Automating case acquisition, storage and utilization. *Machine Learning, 10,* 249–278.

Waterman, D., & Hayes-Roth, F. (1978). An overview of pattern-directed inference systems. In D. Waterman & F. Hayes-Roth (Eds.), *Pattern-directed inference systems* (pp. 3–22). New York: Academic Press.

Watson, J. B. (1913). Psychology as the behaviorist views it. *Psychological Review, 20,* 158–177.

Welford, A. T. (1968). *Fundamentals of skill.* London: Methuen.

Wickelgren, W. A. (1969). Auditory or articulatory coding in verbal short-term memory. *Psychological Review, 76,* 232–235.

Wilson, W. H., Halford, G. S., Gray, B., & Phillips, S. (2001). The STAR-2 model for mapping hierarchically structured analogs. In D. Gentner, K. J. Holyoak & B. N. Kokinov (Eds.), *The analogical mind: Perspectives from cognitive science* (pp. 125–159). Cambridge, MA: MIT Press.

Winograd, T. (1975). Frame representations and the declarative/procedural controversy. In D. Bobrow & A. Collins (Eds.), *Representation and understanding: Studies in cognitive science* (pp. 185–210). New York: Academic Press.

Winston, P. H. (1986). Learning by augmenting rules and accumulating censors. In R. S. Michalski, J. G. Carbonell, & T. M. Mitchell (Eds.), *Machine learning: An artificial intelligence approach* (Vol. 3, pp. 45–61). Los Altos, CA: Kaufmann.

Wolpert, D. M., Ghahramani, Z., & Flanagan, J. R. (2001). Perspectives and problems in motor learning. *Trends in Cognitive Sciences, 5,* 487–494.

Woltz, D. J., Gardner, M. K., & Bell, B. G. (2000). Negative transfer errors in sequential skills: Strong-but-wrong sequence application. *Journal of Experimental Psychology: Learning, Memory, and Cognition, 26,* 601–625.

Woodworth, R. S. (1938). *Experimental psychology.* New York: Henry Holt.

CHAPTER 14

Computational Models of Implicit Learning

Axel Cleeremans and Zoltán Dienes

1. Introduction

Implicit learning – broadly construed as learning without awareness – is a complex, multifaceted phenomenon that defies easy definition. Frensch (1998) listed as many as eleven definitions in an overview, a diversity that is undoubtedly symptomatic of the conceptual and methodological challenges that continue to pervade the field forty years after the term first appeared in the literature (Reber, 1967). According to Berry and Dienes (1993), learning is *implicit* when an individual acquires new information without intending to do so and in such a way that the resulting knowledge is difficult to express. In this, implicit learning thus contrasts strongly with explicit learning (e.g., as when learning how to solve a problem or learning a concept), which is typically hypothesis-driven and fully conscious. Implicit learning is the process through which one becomes sensitive to certain regularities in the environment: (1) without trying to learn regularities, (2) without knowing that one is learning regularities, and (3) in such a way that the resulting knowledge is unconscious.

Over the last twenty years, the field of implicit learning has come to embody ongoing questioning about three fundamental issues in the cognitive sciences: (1) consciousness (how one should conceptualize and measure the relationships between conscious and unconscious cognition); (2) mental representation (in particular, the complex issue of abstraction); and (3) modularity and the architecture of the cognitive system (whether one should think of implicit and explicit learning as being subtended by separable systems of the brain or not). Computational modeling plays a central role in addressing these issues.

2. Implicit Cognition: The Phenomena

Everyday experience suggests that implicit learning is a ubiquitous phenomenon. For instance, we often seem to know more than we can tell. Riding a bicycle, using chopsticks or driving a car all involve mastering complex sets of motor skills that we find very difficult to describe verbally. These dissociations between our ability to report on cognitive processes and the behaviors that involve these processes are not limited to action but also extend to high-level cognition. Most native speakers of a language are unable to articulate the grammatical rules they nevertheless follow when uttering expressions of the language. Likewise, expertise in domains such as medical diagnosis or chess, as well as social or aesthetic judgments, all involve intuitive knowledge that one seems to have little introspective access to.

We also often seem to tell more than we can know. In a classic article, social psychologists Nisbett and Wilson (1977) reported on many experimental demonstrations that verbal reports on our own behavior often reflect reconstructive and interpretative processes rather than genuine introspection. Although it is often agreed that cognitive *processes* are not in and of themselves open to any sort of introspection, Nisbett and Wilson further claimed that we can sometimes be "(a) unaware of the existence of a stimulus that importantly influenced a response, (b) unaware of the existence of the response, and (c) unaware that the stimulus has affected the response" (p. 231).

Demonstrations of dissociations between subjective experience and various cognitive processes have now been reported in many domains of cognitive science. For instance, dissociations have been reported between conscious awareness and memory. Memory for previous events can be expressed explicitly, as a conscious recollection, or implicitly, as automatic, unconscious influences on behavior. Numerous studies have demonstrated dissociations between implicit and explicit memory, both in normal participants (see Schacter, 1987) as well in special populations. Amnesic patients, for instance, who exhibit severe or total loss in their ability to explicitly recall previous experiences (conscious recollection) nevertheless retain the ability to learn novel procedural skills or to exhibit sensitivity to past experiences of which they are not conscious.

Findings of "learning without awareness" have also been reported with normal subjects (Cleeremans, Destrebecqz, & Boyer, 1998). Arthur Reber, in a classic series of studies conducted in 1965 (see Reber, 1967), first coined the term "implicit learning" (although the phenomenon as such was discussed before Reber, e.g., in Clark Hull's PhD dissertation, published in 1920). Implicit learning contrasts with implicit memory in that implicit learning focuses on generalization to new stimuli rather than sensitivity to processing the same stimulus again. Implicit learning also contrasts with subliminal perception in that it can involve consciously perceived stimuli.

Implicit learning research has essentially been focused on three experimental paradigms: artificial grammar learning (AGL), dynamic system control, and sequence learning (SL). Paradigms that will not be discussed include probability learning (Millward & Reber, 1968), hidden covariation detection (Lewicki, 1986), acquisition of invariant characteristics (Lewicki, Hill, & Czyzewska, 1992), and visual search in complex stimulus environments (Chun & Jiang, 1999).

In Reber's (1967) seminal study of AGL, subjects were asked to memorize meaningless letter strings generated by a simple set of rules embodied in a finite-state grammar (Figure 14.1). After this memorization phase, subjects were told that the strings followed the rules of a grammar and were asked to classify novel strings as grammatical or not. In this experiment and in many subsequent replications, subjects were able to perform this classification task better than chance despite remaining unable to describe the rules of the grammar in verbal reports. This dissociation between classification performance and verbal report is the finding that prompted Reber to describe learning as implicit because subjects appeared sensitive to and could apply knowledge that they remained unable to describe and had had no intention to learn.

In a series of studies that attracted renewed interest in implicit learning, Berry and Broadbent (1984, 1988) showed that success in learning how to control a simulated system (e.g., a "sugar factory") so as to make it reach certain goal states was

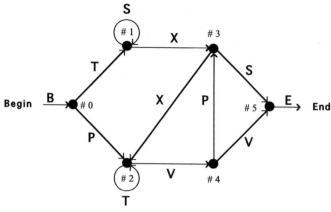

Figure 14.1. A finite-state grammar (Reber, 1976) is a simple directed graph consisting of nodes connected by labeled arcs. Sequences of symbols can be generated by entering the grammar through a "begin" node and moving from node to node until an "end" node is reached. Each transition between one node and the next produces the label associated with the arc linking the two nodes. Concatenating the symbols together produces strings of symbols, in this case, letters of the alphabet. Finite-state grammars have been used both in the context of Sequence Learning studies and in the context of artificial grammar learning studies.

independent from ability to answer questions about the principles governing the subject's inputs and the system's output: Practice selectively influenced ability to control the system, whereas verbal explanations about how the system worked selectively influenced ability to answer questions.

Today, another paradigm, SL, has become dominant in the study of implicit learning. In SL situations (Clegg, DiGirolamo, & Keele, 1998), participants are asked to react to each element of a sequentially structured visual sequence of events in the context of a serial reaction time (SRT) task. On each trial, subjects see a stimulus that appears at one of several locations on a computer screen and are asked to press as fast and as accurately as possible on the key corresponding to its current location. Nissen and Bullemer (1987) first demonstrated that subjects progressively learned about the sequential structure of a repeating series of stimuli in spite of showing little evidence of being aware that the material was so structured. To establish that reaction time (RT) savings reflect sequence knowledge rather

than mere familiarization with the task, a different sequence is typically presented during an unannounced transfer block, expected to elicit slower reaction times to the extent that people use their knowledge of the sequence so as to anticipate the location of the next event. Cleeremans and McClelland (1991) used a different design in which the stimulus' location was probabilistically determined based on a finite-state grammar similar to that shown in Figure 14.1 and in which nongrammatical stimuli were randomly interspersed with those produced by the grammar. Numerous subsequent studies have indicated that subjects can learn about complex sequential relationships despite remaining unable to fully deploy this knowledge in corresponding direct tasks.

Most of the modeling work has focused on the AGL and SL tasks, and this chapter therefore focuses on these paradigms (see Dienes & Fahey, 1995; Gibson, Fichman, & Plaut, 1997; Lebiere, Wallach, & Taatgen, 1998; and Sun, 2002, for simulations of process control tasks). Both the AGL and SL tasks involve learning sequential dependencies and thus involve similar computational problems. To put the computational modeling work in perspective and to highlight the challenging methodological and conceptual issues that characterize the domain, however, the next section is dedicated to discussing how to explore implicit learning empirically.

3. Demonstrating That Implicit Learning Is Implicit

The findings briefly reviewed earlier all suggest that unconscious influences on behavior are pervasive. This raises the question of how to best characterize the relationships between conscious and unconscious processes, and in particular, whether one should consider that mental representations can be unconscious. Settling the conceptual question of what conscious awareness is would help settle the methodological question of how to measure it. But there is no general agreement concerning what it means for an agent to be conscious of some state of affairs. There is a sense in which any perception of an object involves one being conscious of it. Thus, if by looking, a person can discriminate the presence or absence of an object then they are, in that sense, conscious of it being there. This sense of being "conscious of" methodologically leads one to using direct forced choice tests as measures of awareness. If a person can discriminate whether an object is moving up or down when forced to say "up" or "down" on each trial, then in the sense we are talking about, the person is conscious of the object's direction of movement. In a similar way, if a person can discriminate whether a set of stimuli shared common features, one should conclude that they are conscious of that regularity. In this sense, subjects in implicit learning experiments are conscious of many regularities (e.g., Dulany, Carlson, & Dewey, 1984; Perruchet & Pacteau, 1990). For example, in AGL, subjects can indicate relevant parts of strings of letters that make them grammatical or non-grammatical (Dulany et al., 1984) and they can say

whether particular bigrams (sequences of two letters) are allowed by a grammar or not (Perruchet & Pacteau, 1990). In SL, subjects can recognize parts or all of the sequence as old or new (e.g., Shanks & Johnstone, 1999). Further, in this sense of being conscious of regularities, the process of becoming conscious of the regularities can be simulated by computational models that learn to make the same discriminations as people do, as described in Section 4.

However, the useful distinction between implicit and explicit knowledge may not hinge on whether or not one is conscious of a regularity. It may hinge on whether a person is conscious of the regularity with a conscious rather than unconscious mental state. For example, in the sense we have been using, a "blindsight" patient is conscious of whether an object is moving up or down because the patient can discriminate direction of motion. But the seeing by which the patient is conscious of the object is not conscious seeing: The blindsight patient is conscious of the object with an unconscious mental state; one could say that the patient is *sensitive* to the object.

As a matter of general terminology, some people reserve the phrase "conscious of" for cases in which one is conscious of something by a conscious mental state; others use the phrase more generally, as is done here. In any case, there is now the problem of determining what a mental state's being conscious consists of. The conceptual answer to this question suggests both the methodology for determining whether people have conscious or unconscious knowledge in an implicit learning experiment and the sort of computational model needed for simulating conscious rather than unconscious knowledge. Three approaches to defining the conscious status of mental states will be considered.

One approach claims that a mental state's being conscious is its being inferentially promiscuous, globally accessible (Baars, 1988; Block, 1995), or part of a suitable global pattern of activity (Tononi & Edelman, 1998). According to this approach, a person has conscious knowledge of a regularity if that knowledge can be expressed in different ways, for example, in verbal report or in different structured tests (Lewicki, 1986; Reber, 1967). The knowledge in implicit learning experiments is typically difficult to express in verbal report; indeed, this is the original finding that prompted Reber to conclude his AGL paradigm elicited unconscious knowledge. Further, the knowledge generated in implicit learning experiments can often be expressed only in some structured tasks but not in others. For example, Jiménez, Mendez, and Cleeremans (1996) measured the expression of knowledge learned through an SRT task using both reaction time and the ability to subsequently generate the sequence. Through detailed correlational analyses, they were able to show there was knowledge that was only expressed through the reaction time responses, but not through the sequence generation measure. The knowledge was thus not globally available. This type of study is more concincing than those using free report, as free report is often taken after a delay, without all retrieval cues present, and gives the subject the option of not reporting some conscious knowledge (Dulany, 1968). Thus, knowledge may be globally available yet not elicited on a test that is insensitive or not asking for the same knowledge (Shanks & St. John, 1994). These issues can be addressed, for example, by asking subjects to predict the next element under the same conditions that they initially reacted to it, as Jimenez et al. did. Computational models based on defining a conscious mental state in terms of global access include those of Tononi (2005) and Dehaene and collaborators (e.g., Dehaene, Sergent, & Changeux, 2003), but will not be discussed here.

Another approach is to identify conscious knowledge with knowledge that can be used according to one's *intentions* (Jacoby, 1991). This is a restricted form of inferential promiscuity that Jacoby operationally defines by his *process dissociation procedure*. In the process dissociation procedure, a subject is asked in two different conditions ("inclusion" and "exclusion") to do opposite things with a piece of knowledge. If the knowledge can be used according to opposing intentions, the knowledge is taken to be conscious (and unconscious otherwise). For example, Destrebecqz and Cleeremans (2001) applied the process dissociation procedure to SL, asking trained participants to either generate a sequence that resembled the training sequence (inclusion) or a sequence that was as different as possible from the training sequence (exclusion). Results indicated that although subjects could include the sequence when instructed, under certain conditions, participants were unable to exclude familiar sequence fragments, thus suggesting that they had no control over the knowledge acquired during training. Subjects could use the knowledge according to the intention to include but not the intention to exclude. Use was thus not determined by intentions. Destrebecqz and Cleeremans concluded that this knowledge was best described as implicit, for its expression was not under conscious control. They also produced a computational model of performance in the process dissociation task, discussed later (see also Tunney & Shanks, 2003; Vokey & Higham, 2004).

A third approach is to identify conscious mental states with states one is conscious of (Rosenthal, 2006), that is, with higher-order states (i.e., mental states about mental states). On this approach, one must *know that one knows* for knowledge to be conscious. This approach suggests the use of subjective measures of awareness, such as confidence ratings. For example, individuals may say, for each discrimination they perform in an AGL task, whether they were just *guessing* or whether they *knew* the correct answer. Two common criteria based on the confidence responses are the guessing and zero correlation criteria. According to the guessing criterion, if people can discriminate above chance when they believe they are guessing, the knowledge is unconscious. According to the zero correlation criterion, if people cannot discriminate with their "guess" and "know" responses between when they did and did not know, the knowledge is unconscious. According to both criteria, the knowledge acquired in AGL and SL paradigms is partly unconscious. The problem for computer simulation is to determine how a network could come to represent its own states as internal states and specifically as knowledge states. The problem is not trivial and as yet not fully resolved (Cleeremans, 2005).

Despite the considerable methodological advances achieved over the past decade or so, assessing awareness in implicit learning and related fields remains particularly challenging. There is no conceptual consensus on what a mental state's being conscious consists of and hence no methodological consensus for determining the conscious status of knowledge. Although the central issue of the extent to which information processing can occur in the absence of conscious awareness remains as controversial today as it was forty years ago, the conceptual and methodological tools are certainly more refined today.

A further challenge is to determine how to best interpret dissociations between conscious and unconscious knowledge in terms of systems or processes. Dunn and Kirsner (1988) pointed out that even crossed double dissociations between two tasks do not necessarily indicate the involvement of separable, independent processes. Many authors have described nonmodular architectures that can nevertheless produce double dissociations. Plaut (1995) explored these issues in the context of cognitive neuropsychology. In a compelling series of simulation studies, Plaut not only showed that lesioning a single connectionist network in various ways could account for the double dissociations between concrete and abstract word reading exhibited by deep dyslexic patients, but also that lesions in a single site produced *both* patterns of dissociations observed with patients. In other words, the observed dissociations can clearly not be attributed to architectural specialization, but can instead be a consequence of *functional specialization* (functional modularity) in the representational system of the network. These issues are also debated in the context of implicit learning research.

Computational modeling plays a key part in resolving such issues, just as it has in other domains. The process of implementing core conceptual ideas concerning the nature of conscious versus unconscious states together with ideas concerning the nature of human learning, testing implementations against human data, revising core concepts, and so on, cyclically, will help the field get beyond simple dichotomies. The brain is both in a sense one system, yet it is also inhomogeneous. The verbal question of how many learning systems there are is in danger of being vacuous. If God were to tell us how many learning systems there were with a single number (one? two? three?), we would have learned nothing. What we really need to know are the principles by which a working computational model of human learning could be built. It is still early, and models of implicit learning have focused more on the mechanisms of learning rather than on the conscious versus unconscious distinction (but see Sun, 2002). Future developments are eagerly awaited.

4. Computational Models of Implicit Learning

Computational modeling has played a central role in deconstructing early verbal theories of the nature of what is learned in implicit learning paradigms (1) by offering "proof of existence" demonstrations that elementary, associative learning processes (as opposed to rule-based learning) are in fact often sufficient to account for the data, (2) by making it possible to cast specific predictions that can then be contrasted with those of competing models, and (3) by making it possible to explore how specific computational principles can offer novel, unitary accounts of the data. Detailed computational models have now been proposed for all three main paradigms of implicit learning. Two families of models are currently most influential: neural network models and fragment-based, or "chunking," models. Both approaches find their roots in exemplar-based models (Estes, 1957; Hintzmann, 1986; Medin & Schaffer, 1978), which had already captured the central

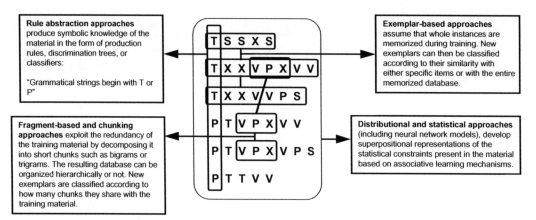

Rule abstraction approaches produce symbolic knowledge of the material in the form of production rules, discrimination trees, or classifiers:

"Grammatical strings begin with T or P"

Fragment-based and chunking approaches exploit the redundancy of the training material by decomposing it into short chunks such as bigrams or trigrams. The resulting database can be organized hierarchically or not. New exemplars are classified according to how many chunks they share with the training material.

Exemplar-based approaches assume that whole instances are memorized during training. New exemplars can then be classified according to their similarity with either specific items or with the entire memorized database.

Distributional and statistical approaches (including neural network models), develop superpositional representations of the statistical constraints present in the material based on associative learning mechanisms.

Figure 14.2. A representation of different computational approaches to artificial grammar learning (see text for details).

intuition that rule-following behavior can emerge out of the processing of exemplars in a germane domain – categorization.

Neural network models typically consist of simple auto-associator models (Dienes, 1992) or of networks capable of processing sequences of events, such as the simple recurrent network (SRN) introduced by Elman (1990) and first applied to SL by Cleeremans and McClelland (1991). Chunking models (e.g., Perruchet and Vinter, 1998), in contrast, are variants of exemplar-based models that assume that learning results in the acquisition of memory traces such as whole exemplars or fragments thereof. Although no type of model can currently claim generality, both approaches share a number of central assumptions: (1) learning involves elementary association or recoding processes that are highly sensitive to the statistical features of the training set, (2) learning is viewed essentially as a mandatory by-product of ongoing processing, (3) learning is based on the processing of *exemplars* and produces *distributed* knowledge, and (4) learning is *unsupervised* and *self-organizing*. More recently, hybrid models that specifically attempt to capture the relationships between symbolic and subsymbolic processes in learning have also been proposed. Sun (2002), for instance, has introduced models that specifically attempt to link the subsymbolic, associative, statistics-based processes characteristic of implicit learning with the symbolic, declarative, rule-based processes characteristic of explicit learning.

These different models have been essentially directed at addressing the questions of (1) what can be learned implicitly and (2) what are the computational principles characteristic of the mechanisms involved in implicit learning. In discussing the models, a third, important question will also be considered: How does one determine whether a model provides a good explanation of human learning? This issue is particularly acute in the domain of implicit learning because there are often competing and overlapping accounts of the data. For example, consider what could be learned based on having memorized a few letter strings from a finite-state grammar (Figure 14.2). People could learn about the rules that govern string generation; they could memorize a few frequent fragments of the training strings; they could learn about the statistical features of the material (e.g., the probability that each letter follows others); or they could simply memorize entire strings. Each of these possibilities would result in better-than-chance performance in a subsequent task asking participants to make decisions concerning the grammaticality of novel strings, and it remains a significant methodological challenge to design experimental situations that make it possible to successfully discriminate between the different competing accounts.

Computational modeling is of great help in this respect because it forces modelers to be explicit about their theories, but modeling raises its own challenge when it comes to comparing different models with a joint set of empirical data.

Section 5 is dedicated to considering the extent to which demonstrated dissociations between conscious and unconscious knowledge in people should be interpreted as reflecting the involvement of separable learning systems. The basic features of the connectionist, chunking, and hybrid approaches are examined in the following sections.

4.1. *Connectionist Models of Implicit Learning*

The first fully implemented connectionist models of implicit learning are found in the early efforts of Dienes (1992) and Cleeremans and McClelland (1991). Although authors such as Brooks (1978) and Berry and Broadbent (1984) had already suggested that performance in implicit learning tasks such as AGL or process control may be based on retrieving exemplar information stored in memory arrays (see Chapter 9 in this volume), such models have in general been more concerned with accounting for performance at retrieval rather than accounting for learning itself. The connectionist approach (see Chapter 2 in this volume), by contrast, has been centrally concerned with the mechanisms involved during learning since its inception and therefore constitutes an excellent candidate framework with which to examine the processes involved in implicit learning. Because long-term knowledge in connectionist networks accrues in connection weights as a mandatory consequence of information processing, connectionist models capture, without any further assumptions, two of the most important characteristics of implicit learning: (1) the fact that learning is incidental and mandatory, and (2) the fact that the resulting knowledge is difficult to express. A typical connectionist network, indeed, does not have direct access to the knowledge stored in connection weights. Instead, this knowledge

can only be expressed through the influence that it exerts on the model's representations, and such representations may or may not contain readily accessible information (i.e., information that can be retrieved with low or no computational cost; see Kirsh, 1991).

An important distinction in this regard is the distinction between supervised and unsupervised learning. O'Reilly and Munakata (2000) have characterized this distinction as a contrast between *model learning* (Hebbian, unsupervised learning) and *task learning* (error-driven, supervised learning). Their analysis is framed in terms of the different computational objectives the two types of learning fulfill: capturing the statistical structure of the environment so as to develop appropriate models of it on the one hand, and learning specific input-output mappings so as to solve specific problems (tasks) in accordance with one's goals on the other hand. Although many connectionist models of implicit learning have used supervised learning procedures, often, such models can also be interpreted as involving unsupervised learning (e.g., auto-associator networks).

Turning now to specific connectionist models of implicit learning, we will consider first a simple auto-associator as applied to AGL; then the more powerful SRN, which has been applied to both SL and AGL tasks; and finally the memory buffer model, which has also been applied to both SL and AGL tasks.

4.1.1. THE AUTO-ASSOCIATOR NETWORK
Dienes (1992) proposed that performance in an AGL task could be accounted for based on the idea that, over training, people incidentally accumulate knowledge concerning the structure of the exemplars of the domain and subsequently use that knowledge to make decisions concerning the grammaticality of novel exemplars in the transfer task. Dienes compared several instantiations of this basic idea in auto-associator networks trained with either the Hebb Rule or the Delta Rule.

In auto-associator networks, the task of the model is simply to reproduce the input pattern on its output units. The first problem in constructing a neural network is to decide how to encode the input. Dienes's models had no "hidden" units and used simple localist representation on both their input and output units, that is, each unit in the network represented the occurrence of a particular letter at a particular position in a string or the occurrence of a particular bigram. The second problem is to decide what pattern of connection to implement. Dienes had each unit connected to all other units, that is, the network attempted to predict each unit based on all other units in the network. Finally, one has to decide what learning rule to use. Dienes used either the Hebb rule or the delta rule. The learning rules were factorially crossed with different coding schemes.

The two learning rules produce different types of knowledge. The Hebb rule, that is, the notion that "units that fire together wire together," learns the association between two units independently of any association those units may have with other units. After Hebbian learning, the weights are like first-order correlations. The delta rule, by contrast, involves competition between units in making predictions, so the weights are like multiple regression coefficients. The consequence was that for bigram models, the delta rule network could perfectly reproduce the training strings used and also any new string that could be formed by adding or subtracting any training strings. That is, simple associative learning produced rule-like behavior – perfect reproduction of any linear combination of the training strings without that rule being explicitly represented anywhere in the network – definitely one of the most important insights gained through connectionist modeling in this context.

All networks could classify test strings as well as people could, that is, all networks tended to reproduce grammatical test strings more faithfully than nongrammatical test strings. This raises a methodological problem: Why should one model be preferred over another as an account of human implicit learning? This question will be considered in the context of examining the different models of implicit learning that have been developed.

A key aspect of this problem is that networks in general have free parameters – numbers, like the learning rate, that have to be assigned some value for the network to give simulated behavior. The delta rule network, for example, requires a learning rate; different learning rates lead to different behaviors. Dienes dealt with this problem by producing parameter-free predictions. With a sufficiently small learning rate and sufficiently many training epochs the delta rule converges in the limit to producing multiple regression coefficients. The Hebb rule was parameter free in any case because it is a one-shot learning rule. The parameter-free models were tested by determining how well they predicted the order of difficulty human subjects had with classifying the strings. The delta rule model could predict the order of difficulty better than the Hebb rule.[1]

The delta rule auto-associator models passed the tests they were subjected to, but they have a couple of serious weaknesses. First, those models entail that people can learn to predict a letter in one position by the letters in any other position, no matter how far away; distance is irrelevant. But this entailment is false: People find long-distance dependencies in AGL hard to learn (Mathews et al., 1989). Second, those models entail that the association between two letters in two positions should not generalize to knowing the association between those letters in different positions. This entailment is very unlikely. Cleeremans and McClelland (1991) simulated implicit learning with a connectionist model that dealt with both these problems.

---

1 Dienes (1992) also considered variants of exemplar-based models (Estes, 1957; Hintzmann, 1986; Medin & Schaffer, 1978). These will not be elaborated on further here, but such models all share the assumption that grammaticality decisions are taken based on an item's similarity with the stored exemplars, accumulated over training with the material. These models turned out not to be good at predicting the order of difficulty of the test items, given the coding assumptions used.

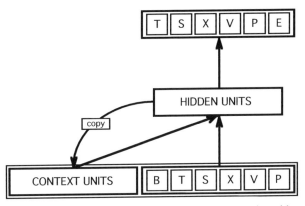

Figure 14.3. The simple recurrent network introduced by Elman (1990). The network takes the current element of a sequence as input and is trained to predict the next element using backpropagation. Context units, which on time step contain a copy of the activation pattern that existed over the network's hidden units on the previous time step, enable previous information to influence current predictions.

4.1.2. THE SIMPLE RECURRENT NETWORK
Cleeremans and McClelland (1991) simulated performance in the SRT task. The network, Elman's (1990) SRN (Figure 14.3), is a three-layer backpropagation network that is trained to predict each element of a sequence presented on its input units (see also Chapter 2 in this volume). Thus, on each trial, element t of a sequence is presented to the network (by activating a single input unit), and the network has to predict element $t + 1$ of the sequence by activating the corresponding output unit. To make this prediction task possible, the network is equipped with so-called *context units*, which, on each time step through the sequence, contain a copy of the network's pattern of activity over its hidden units. Over time, the network learns to use these representations of its own activity in such a way as to refine its ability to predict the successor of each sequence element. Detailed analyses of the network's performance in learning sequential material have shown that the SRN's responses come to approximate the conditional probability of occurrence of each element in the temporal context set by its predecessors (Cleeremans, Servan-Schreiber, & McClelland, 1989).

Servan-Schreiber, Cleeremans, and McClelland (1991) have shown that learning progresses through three qualitatively different phases when the network is trained on material generated from a finite-state grammar such as the one illustrated in Figure 14.1.

During a first phase, the network tends to ignore the context information. This is a direct consequence of the fact that the patterns of activation on the hidden layer – and hence the context layer – are continuously changing from one epoch to the next as the weights from the input units (the letters) to the hidden layer are modified. Consequently, adjustments made to the weights from the context layer to the hidden layer are inconsistent from epoch to epoch and cancel each other. In contrast, the network is able to pick up the stable association between each *letter* and all its possible successors. In a second phase, patterns copied on the context layer are now represented by a unique code designating which letter preceded the current letter, and the network can exploit this stability of the context information to start distinguishing between different occurrences of the same letter – different arcs in the grammar. Finally, in a third phase, small differences in the context information that reflect the occurrence of previous elements can be used to differentiate position-dependent predictions resulting from length constraints.

The internal representations that result from such training can be surprisingly rich and structured. Cluster analysis of the patterns of activation obtained over the network's hidden units after training on material generated from the probabilistic finite-state grammar revealed that the internal representations learned by the network are organized in clusters, each of which corresponds to a node of the finite-state grammar. This turns out to be the most efficient representation of the input material from the point of view of a system that continuously attempts to predict what the next element will be, because knowing at which node a given sequence fragment terminates provides the best possible information concerning its possible successors. Just as the simple auto-associator considered by Dienes (1992) in some sense acquired abstract knowledge, so did the SRN. Cleeremans (1993) suggested that it is useful to think of abstractness as lying on a continuum and that verbal disputes over whether implicit knowledge is or is not abstract may be ill formed. The knowledge acquired by the SRN, in any case, has a level of abstractness somewhere between that of rote learning exemplars and learning the finite-state grammar propositionally.

As a model of human performance in SRT tasks, the SRN model has been shown to account for about 80% of the variance in the reaction time data (Cleeremans & McClelland, 1991). To capture reaction time data, one simply assumes that the normalized activation of each output unit is inversely proportional to reaction time. This is obviously a crude simplification, made necessary by the fact that backpropagation is unable to capture the time course of processing. Other connectionist models have been more successful in this respect, such as Dominey's (1998) "Temporal Recurrent Network."

In modeling people's behavior with the SRN, there are a number of free parameters, including the learning rate, number of hidden units, and momentum. There is no easy way of obtaining parameter-free predictions. This is a methodological issue that will be addressed shortly in terms of what it means for assessing the SRN as an account for human learning.

The SRN model has also been applied to AGL tasks. For instance, Boucher and Dienes (2003) contrasted the SRN with a fragment-based model. Similarly, Kinder and Shanks (2001) used the SRN to model AGL in considering the question of how many learning systems there are (see Section 5).

Both AGL and the SL task require the subject to learn sequential dependencies, so it is not surprising that the same model has been brought to bear on the two tasks. To what extent learning principles are the same in different domains of implicit learning is an interesting question. There is one key difference between AGL and SL stimuli, however. In AGL, the whole string is typically presented at once; in SRT, there is only one element of the sequence presented at a time. In fact, in AGL, performance decreases when the string is presented sequentially rather than simultaneously (Boucher & Dienes, 2003), implying that some modification of either coding or learning is needed when modelling standard AGL with the SRN. This point has not yet been addressed.

Dienes, Altmann, and Gao (1999) considered a simple adaptation of the SRN to model the phenomenon of transfer between domains. Significantly, Reber (1969) showed that people trained on a finite-state grammar with one set of letters can classify new strings using a different set of letters (but the same grammar). The problem for the standard SRN is that the knowledge embedded in the connection weights is linked to particular letters. If new input units were activated, no previous learning would be relevant. Indeed, Marcus (2001) has regarded the inability to generalize outside the training space to be a general problem for connectionist models. Dienes et al. (1999) solved this problem by introducing an extra encoding layer between the

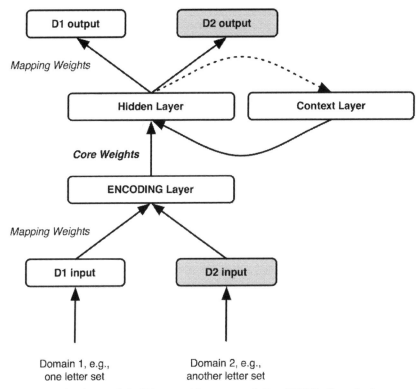

Figure 14.4. The model of Dienes, Altmann, and Gao (1999). Transfer between domains is achieved by augmenting a simple recurrent network with "mapping" weights that make it possible for the knowledge embedded in the "core" weights to be preserved and used for generalization when switching to a different set of stimuli.

input units and the hidden units, as shown in Figure 14.4.

In the training phase, the network adjusts weights between the "domain one" input units all the way up to the "domain one" output units. The weights from the encoding layer to the hidden units and from the context units to the hidden units – called the "core weights" – encode structural properties of the stimuli not tied to any particular letter set. In testing, the "domain two" input units are activated, and activation flows through the core weights to the output units. The core weights are frozen, and the network learns the weights from the core part of the network to the input and output units in the new domain. Thus, the network learns how to best map the new domain onto the structures already present in its core weights. In this way, the network can indeed generalize outside of its

training space and reveal various detailed properties shown by people (including infants) in transfer between domains in AGL. Although the freezing of the core weights is simplistic, it shows that connectionist networks can generalize beyond their training space. The freezing idea is similar to that of a switching device that determines how and when neural networks interface with each other (Jacobs, Jordan, & Barto, 1991).

Dienes et al. (1999) showed that the augmented SRN could predict a number of characteristics of human performance to within the 95% confidence limits of the effects. Fitting any more accurately would be fitting noise. Still, we must confront the methodological problem that the model has many free parameters. The required qualitative behavior of the model was not restricted to a small region of parameter space. Nonetheless, simply showing that a model

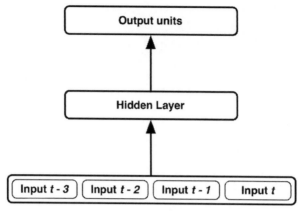

Figure 14.5. The buffer network. A fixed-width time window is implemented by input units dedicated for each time slot.

can fit some behavior is a weak scientific test. In general, if a model could produce a wide range of behavior when the parameters are chosen appropriately, in what sense can the model *explain* any specific behavior? Compare the exhortations of Popper (1959) that a *theory that can explain everything explains nothing* and likewise, *the more a theory rules out, the more it explains*. The discussion of the memory buffer model will methodologically squarely face up to these exhortations.

4.1.3. THE MEMORY BUFFER MODEL

The SRN is just one way, albeit an elegant way, of instantiating a memory buffer. The context units allow the SRN to learn (fallibly) how far into the past it needs a memory to reduce error. The SRN can be contrasted with a fixed memory buffer model, similar to the SRN in operating characteristics, learning rule, and so forth, except for how time is coded. The architecture of the memory buffer model is similar to the SRN except that it has no context units (see Figure 14.5).

Rather than storing information about the previous events in the recurrent context units, the input units of the memory buffer model not only encode the input presented at time t, but also at time t-1, t-2, and t-3. The size of the memory buffer is specified by the number of time steps that are encoded. Moreover, the number of time steps that have been encoded will determine defini-

tively the length of the non-local dependency that can be learned. The simplicity of this means of encoding time (i.e., unfolded in space) has often recommended itself to researchers (see Sejnowski & Rosenberg, 1987, who developed NETtalk). Cleeremans (1993) fit a buffer network, coding four time steps into the past, to the reactions times of people learning the SRT task. He found that people became gradually sensitive in their reaction times to information contained up to four time-steps into the past, and the buffer network could behave in a similar way. The SRN and the buffer model were about equally good in this respect. He found that where the buffer model (with a buffer of four time steps) and the SRN made different predictions, and where the data differed significantly in that respect, the buffer model performed better than the SRN. Specifically, both the buffer model and people could learn a certain probabilistic difference over random intervening material, whereas the SRN could not.

Human learning in general requires a buffer. Aspects of language and music that can be learned in the lab rely on non-local dependencies, that is, dependencies that take the form of two dependent items that are separated by a varying number of embedded items. Several studies have shown that under certain circumstances, people can learn non-local dependencies that go

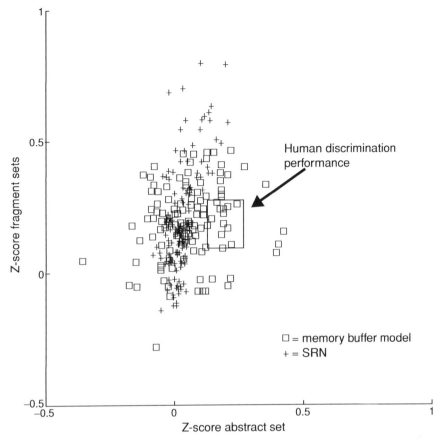

Figure 14.6. Performance of the memory buffer network and of the simple recurrent network (SRN) on music stimuli over a full range of parameters. The box shows a standard error above and below human means. The buffer network is characteristically more like human behavior than is the SRN. See text for a full explanation.

beyond the learning of adjacent regularities. Kuhn and Dienes (2005) investigated the implicit learning of music with the AGL paradigm. People heard eight-note tunes in which the first note predicted the fifth, the second the sixth, and so on. (In fact, to be precise, the last four notes were the musical inversion of the first four.) After sufficient exposure, people came to like melodies respecting these mapping rules rather than other melodies. Some of the test melodies respecting the mapping rules had repeated sequences of notes from the training strings (the fragment set) and others were made from new note bigrams (the abstract set). People liked both sets equally; they had learned the long-distance dependencies, and

this requires that people had a buffer. But what sort of buffer do the mechanisms that subtend implicit learning use?

Kuhn and Dienes (in press) investigated how the SRN and the buffer network would learn the material. They found that with suitable encoding and parameter values, both networks could fit the subjects' level of performance. Figure 14.6 shows the behavior of the SRN and memory buffer model over a full range of parameter values on both fragment and abstract test sets, with one input unit coding each musical note. The square in the figure represents a standard error above and below the human performance means. The SRN was relatively more sensitive to adjacent associations than long distance ones; the fixed buffer model was equally sensitive to each. As people with these musical stimuli found the abstract and fragment sets equally difficult, the characteristic behavior of the memory buffer model was more like that of people than the characteristic behavior of the SRN. In fact, significantly more memory buffer models fell in the box defining human behavior than SRN models.

With neural network models, one always has to consider whether different methods of coding the input would change the behavior of the model. With different, more musically relevant coding schemes, more SRN models fell in the box defining human behavior. That is, the SRN could fit the data. But there were always significantly more memory buffer models in the box than SRN models. The methodological moral is that to explain human data, find out if the model's characteristic behavior matches that of people. The point is thus not so much whether the model can "*fit*" the data; rather, it is whether the model can *explain* the data because its processing principles and hypotheses about encoding entail a characteristic behavior that matches that of people.

In sum, at this point, there is no clear "victor neural network model" of implicit learning. Perhaps the memory buffer model, although used in only two studies in the implicit learning literature, has an edge in SL and AGL applied to music. Future work needs to explore its use for AGL generally and whether it can be extended in the manner of Dienes et al. (1999) to allow transfer to different domains. However, it may be that different domains are learned in different ways. People do not implicitly learn long distance contingencies with strings of letters very easily at all. What we learn about letters in everyday life is which letters chunk together, not what long distance dependencies there may be.

4.2. Fragment-Based Models of Implicit Learning

Although connectionist models of implicit learning have been highly successful, one

might argue that they fail to capture the fact that people, particularly in the AGL paradigm, typically perform a memorization task and hence end up consciously memorizing fragments, or chunks, of the material. There is ample evidence that this knowledge is available for verbal report (Reber & Lewis, 1977), and it is therefore but a short step to assume that this knowledge is what drives people's ability to classify novel strings above chance (Perruchet & Gallego, 1997). These ideas are nicely captured by models that assume that learning involves accumulating fragmentary knowledge of the training material and that performance at test involves using this knowledge to decide on the grammaticality of each novel string, for instance, by comparing its overlap in terms of fragments. The first such model was proposed by Servan-Schreiber and Anderson (1990) in the context of AGL. The model was called "Competitive Chunking" (CC). The central idea, well-known in the memory literature (Miller, 1956) but also in other domains (Newell, 1990) is that learning involves chunking of information: Production rules are combined so as to form larger units that execute faster; complex percepts are formed by combining elementary features in different ways; items are committed to memory by organizing information so as to make it possible to exploit the redundancy of the material. In an AGL task, people asked to memorize meaningless letter strings chunk the material in short fragments (e.g., bigrams and trigrams). The CC model assumes that processing a letter string (or any other combination of elements) proceeds by recursively combining fragments of it until a single chunk can be used to represent the entire string. Thus, for instance, a string such as TTXVPS might first be analyzed as (TT)X(VPS), then as (TT(X))(VPS), and then finally as ((TT(X))(VPS)). At this point, the entire string is represented as a single unit in the model and is said to be maximally familiar. Chunk formation in the model is a competitive process in which different potential chunks compete with each other: Each chunk receives bottom-up "support" from its constituent chunks, and its activation decays over time (see the Appendix for technical details). Servan-Schreiber and Anderson (1990) showed that competitive chunking offered a good account of performance in AGL tasks. More recently, Perruchet and Vinter (1998) have elaborated on these ideas by introducing a chunking model dubbed PARSER, based on similar principles (see the Appendix for further details concerning PARSER and a comparison with CC). Although the model has not yet been applied in detail to implicit learning data, it shows great promise in capturing the fact that people naturally come to perceive AGL strings as composed of chunks that they can report (Perruchet & Pacton, 2006; Servan-Schreiber & Anderson, 1990).

Boucher and Dienes (2003) contrasted the CC with the SRN as models of AGL. At one level, both models learn the sequential dependencies produced by frequent bigrams and other chunks in the training strings. But the principles through which they learn are very different. The SRN is based on error-correction. If the bigram "BV" occurs frequently in training, the SRN learns to predict that whenever B occurs, then V is likely to happen next. If BV no longer occurs but BX does, the SRN unlearns the BV connection and now comes to predict X given a B has occurred. This is a form of "catastrophic interference" (McCloskey & Cohen, 1989) that some neural networks are subject to. On the other hand, once the competitive chunker has learned BV, it can then learn that BX is a chunk without unlearning that BV is also a chunk.

Boucher and Dienes (2003) presented people with training stimuli in which one bigram, BV, occurred in the first half of training and another in the last half. In the conflict condition, the other bigram was BX. In a control group, PX occurred in the last half instead of BX. The question is, to what extent did people unlearn in the conflict condition. People were asked to endorse different bigrams at the end of the test phase. The SRN and competitive chunker models were trained and tested in the same way over a full range of parameter values. Figure 14.7 shows the relative tendency of the models over a full range of parameter values to endorse bigram BV and also shows the mean value for people with confidence intervals. Note that the SRN is spread out all over the space; the competitive chunker's behavior is more compact. Importantly, although the SRN models could "fit" the data, it was the characteristic behavior of the competitive chunker that best matched people's behavior.

To summarize the main points so far, connectionist modeling is an excellent way of exploring theories of implicit learning. The SRN offers an elegant account of the data, but people show less interference and more sensitivity to long-distance dependencies. Chunking models can capture the former, but not the latter (the long-distance dependencies learned by Kuhn and Dienes's (in press) subjects cannot be learned by current chunking models). A memory buffer model can capture the latter point but not the former, as it depends on error correction. Thus, there remains a problem of getting one model to exhibit all characteristics of human implicit learning! Perhaps this state of affairs will act as a spur to people interested in computational modeling. Finally, a simple but important point is worth stressing: In comparing models, do not merely attempt to fit the data. Instead, look at the characteristic performance of models.

4.3. Hybrid Models of Implicit Learning

Although the connectionist and fragment-based models reviewed previously have proven extremely successful in accounting for implicit learning data, none have successfully addressed the central issue of how implicit knowledge may turn into explicit knowledge. This, however, is a central issue in the cognitive sciences (Smolensky, 1988). Clark and Karmiloff-Smith (1993) pointed out that connectionist networks (and, by extension, any association-based model) have no "self-generated means of analyzing their own activity so as to form symbolic representations of their own

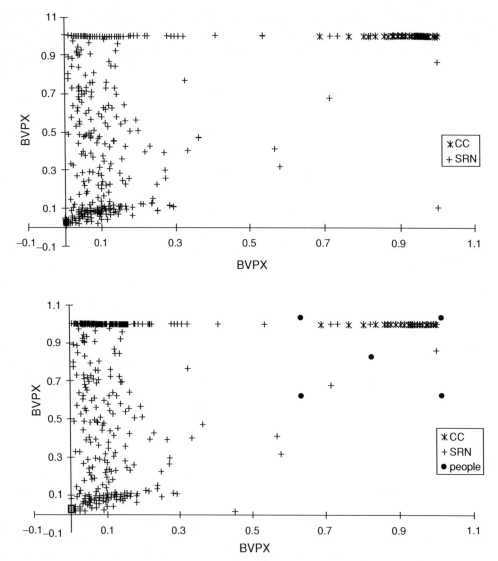

Figure 14.7. Performance of the competitive chunker (CC) and simple recurrent network (SRN) models in dealing with prediction conflicts. The competitive chunker is resistant to conflict, whereas the SRN shows a range of sensitivity to it. Humans are resistant, like the competitive chunker. See text for full explanation.

processing. Their knowledge of rules always *remains* implicit unless an external theorist intervenes" (p. 504). It is therefore a genuine, singular challenge, as Pinker (1999) suggests, to figure out how to best combine symbolic and subsymbolic approaches to cognition. In this respect, there are essentially four possible points of view about this, humorously summarized (from the perspective of die-hard connectionists) by Clark and Karmiloff-Smith (1993, pp. 504–505):

(1) *Give up connectionism entirely and revert to a thoroughly classical approach (despair)*

(2) *Augment connectionist-style networks with the symbol structures of natural language (a representational leap)*

(3) *Combine elements of connectionism and classicism in a single system (hybridization)*

(4) *Use thoroughly connectionist resources in increasingly sophisticated ways (more of the same).*

Recently, several models of implicit learning have been specifically directed at addressing the synergy between implicit and explicit learning. This approach makes a lot of sense because participants, even when placed in experimental situations designed to minimize the possibility of their becoming aware of the relevant regularities, will always attempt to infer explicit, conscious rules based on their experience of the situation. Further, many often also turn out to know something that they can verbalize about the material. In other words, one cannot simply turn awareness off, and there are good reasons to believe that performance in typical implicit learning situations always involve a mixture of implicit and explicit learning. Sun and colleagues (Sun, 1997, 2002; Sun, Slusarz, & Terry, 2005) have attempted to address this issue by proposing a hybrid model of implicit learning called CLARION. The model uses both bottom-up, neural-network-based learning mechanisms and top-down, rule-based learning mechanisms. The model is thus genuinely hybrid in that it assumes continuous interaction between two separable components: one that is essentially symbolic in its representations and learning mechanisms and another that is clearly subsymbolic. Sun has applied CLARION to SL and process control tasks, simulating, for instance, the data of Curran and Keele (1993), in great details, which interestingly contrasted the influence of different instructions manipulating orientation to learn (i.e., incidental vs. intentional) in the task and the resulting differing degree of awareness of the material. Sun was able to capture these differences by manipulating the extent to which CLARION's symbolic component is allowed to extract rules from its subsymbolic component.

In the same spirit, Lebiere and collaborators (Lebiere et al., 1998; Wallach & Lebiere, 2000) have proposed ACT-R (Anderson, 1993) models of performance in SL and in process control tasks. Learning in ACT-R (see Chapter 6 in this volume) assumes that information processing is driven by the interaction between declarative knowledge structures (e.g., chunks of the stimulus material) and procedural knowledge, which in ACT-R take the form of production rules that implement the system's goals. The basic goal, for instance, in an SL situation, is to encode each stimulus and to respond to it using through a specific key. This and other productions operate on the declarative chunks acquired over training by the model, retrieving previously encoded chunks whenever appropriate to anticipate the location of the next stimulus. In such a model, explicit knowledge thus consists of the learned chunks, and implicit knowledge consists in the association strength between different co-occuring chunks that the model learns automatically. Despite the appeal of hybrid models in accounting for the complex interactions between implicit and explicit learning (Domangue et al., 2004), detailed assessment of how well they compare with fragment-based and connectionist models in accounting for the human data must await further research.

5. Theoretical and Conceptual Implications

In this section, three central issues are addressed: whether performance in implicit learning situations result in abstract knowledge, whether the data and the modeling suggest the involvment of single or multiple systems; and whether modeling is relevant to addressing the conscious versus unconscious nature of the acquired knowledge.

5.1. *Rules versus Statistics*

As discussed previously, early characterizations of implicit knowledge have tended to describe it as *abstract*, based essentially on findings that subjects exhibit better-than-chance *transfer* performance, as when asked to make grammaticality judgments on novel strings in the context of AGL situations (Reber, 1989). Likewise, it has often been assumed that the reaction time savings observed in SRT tasks reflect the acquisition of "deep" knowledge about the rules used to generate the stimulus material (Lewicki, Czyzewska, & Hoffman, 1987). These *abstractionist* accounts have generally left the exact form of the acquired knowledge unspecified, short of noting that it must somehow represent the structure of the stimuli and their relationships and be independent of the surface features of the material. The latter claim was further substantiated by findings that AGL knowledge transfers to strings based on the same grammar but instantiated with a different letter set, or even across modalities, as when training involves letter strings but transfer involves tone sequences.

However, as overviewed earlier, there now is considerable evidence that *nonabstractionist* mechanisms are largely sufficient to account for the data. Brooks (1978) first suggested that subjects in AGL experiments were classifying novel strings based not on abstract knowledge of the rules, but simply based on the extent to which novel grammatical or ungrammatical strings are similar to *whole exemplars* memorized during training. Perruchet and Pacteau (1990) showed that the knowledge acquired in both AGL and SL tasks might consist of little more than explicitly memorized short fragments or *chunks* of the training material, such as bigrams or trigrams, or simple frequency counts, which are perhaps the simplest form of abstraction. Both learning and transfer performance can then be accounted for by the extent to which novel material contains memorized chunks, as pointed out by Redington and Chater (1996, 2002), who emphasized that rule-like behavior does not necessarily entail rule-based representations – a point also made clear by many of the computational models reviewed here, such as Dienes et al. (1999)'s augmented SRN.

Overall, although it is clear that the knowledge acquired in typical implicit learning situations need not be based on the unconscious acquisition of symbolic rules, significant areas of debate remain about the extent to which unitary, fragment-based, or associative mechanisms are sufficient to account for sensitivity to both the general and specific features of the training material. Simulation models have generally suggested that such mechanisms can in fact be sufficient to account simultaneously for both grammaticality and similarity effects, partly because some instantiations of these mechanisms produce knowledge that lies on a continuum of abstractness. They can produce sets of weights that specify very precise rule-like behavior (Dienes, 1992) that form graded finite-state patterns (Cleeremans, 1993) and that learn the specific lags over which dependencies occur (Kuhn & Dienes, in press); (Boyer, Destrebecqz, & Cleeremans, 2005).

The fact that both rule-based and exemplar-based approaches produce identical predictions over a large range of data is a significant issue that Pacton et al. (2001) attempted to address by examining the untaught (and hence, incidental) acquisition of orthographic regularities over five years in a school setting. One prediction that rule-based approaches make is that after sufficient training, any acquired rules should generalize perfectly. Any learning mechanism based on the operation of associative learning mechanisms, however, would predict that performance on novel material will always lag behind performance on familiar material (*the transfer decrement*) These conditions are impossible to obtain in the laboratory, which motivated Pacton et al.'s longitudinal study. They found that performance on novel material indeed tended to lag, by a constant amount, behind performance on familiar material, a result that reinforces the idea that what people learn when they learn incidentally is essentially associative, rule-like knowledge, rather than rule-based knowledge.

5.2. *Separable Systems?*

Dissociations between implicit and explicit learning or processing have often been interpreted as suggesting the existence of separable memory systems. For instance, Knowlton et al. (1992) have shown that AGL is largely preserved in amnesia to the extent that amnesic patients perform at the same level as normal controls when asked to classify strings as grammatical or not, but are impaired when asked to discriminate between familiar and novel instances (or fragments) of the strings. These results suggest that the processes that subtend declarative and nondeclarative memory depend on separable brain systems respectively dedicated to representing either information about the specific features of each encountered exemplar, on the one hand (the hippocampus and related structures), and information about the features shared by many exemplars, on the other hand (the neocortex).

In this case also, however, computational modeling often casts the empirical findings in a different light. For instance, Kinder and Shanks (2001) were able to simulate the observed dissociations by tuning a single parameter (the learning rate) in an SRN trained on the same material as used in the behavioral studies and therefore concluded that a single-system account is in fact sufficient to account for the data. The finding arises from the fact that the classification task and the recognition task were based on different test stimuli. The classification test consisted of new grammatical and new ungrammatical strings. The recognition task consisted of old grammatical and new grammatical material. The discriminations turned out to be differentially sensitive to changes in learning rate.

Not all learning by people consists of gradual change in sensitivity to distributional statistics, however. People consider possibilities and test hypotheses. The models overviewed in this chapter only function to model reality as it actually is. In the terms of Perner (1991), the models constitute "single updating models." As new information comes in, the model updates itself in an attempt to match reality more closely. The weights try to match the statistical structure of the world and the input units the occurrent stimulus. People can, however, in Perner's terms, consider *multiple* models of the world – the real and the possible or the counterfactual. Our ability to engage with multiple models underlies much of our explicit learning. Integrating implicit and explicit learning processes in a single model certainly deserves more work, following the example of Sun (2002).

5.3. *Conscious versus Unconscious Knowledge*

As discussed in the Introduction, there is no sense in which current computational models can say much about the distinction between conscious and unconscious knowledge as observed in implicit learning tasks or, for that matter, in any other task (but see Dehaene et al., 2003 and Mathis & Mozer, 1996, for interesting attempts). Nevertheless, there have been a few attempts at capturing the functional consequences of the distinction in terms of performance on different tasks (e.g., Sun, 2002, as discussed earlier). For instance, the SRN model as it stands fails to distinguish between anticipation and prediction responses, yet this difference is at the heart of the difference between the (largely implicit) facilitation observed when processing a sequence in the context of the SRT task and the (largely explicit) performance of participants asked to produce the same or a different sequence in the subsequent generation task. Destrebecqz and Cleeremans (2003) sought to address this limitation of the SRN by combining it with an auto-associator, so as to reflect the fact that people's task during the SRT task merely consists of mapping the current stimulus onto the correct response, whereas in the generation task, they are expected to predict the location of the next element. The model was successful in capturing human data obtained over a range of conditions that either facilitated or promoted the acquisition of conscious knowledge. Likewise, Destrebecqz (2004) was able to capture the effects of manipulating orientation to learn and information both in an SRT task and on the subsequent generation task by pretraining an SRN to different degrees, thus reflecting the idea that differences in availability to consciousness in this task reflect differences in the strength of the stored representations.

6. Conclusions

Implicit learning has proven to be a rich domain not only for the exploration of the differences between information processing with and without consciousness, but also for the development of computational models of the mechanisms involved in elementary learning. Because implicit learning situations typically involve incidental instructions, the mechanisms of change in such situations necessarily involve unsupervised processes that characterize learning as a byproduct of information processing rather than as hypothesis-driven. Because the resulting knowledge is typically difficult to express, the most successful models all share the characteristic that they only involve elementary, associative learning mechanisms that result in distributed knowledge.

Based on the principles of successful models of implicit learning, it is appealing to consider it as a complex form of priming whereby experience continuously shapes memory and through which stored traces in turn continuously influence further processing. Implicit learning studies suggest that such priming is far more interesting than the mere reinstatement of specific past experiences: The processes that produce it lead to quasi-abstract knowledge structures that allow the interesting generalizations that are at the heart of implicit learning.

Finally, although both fragment-based and neural network models make it clear how sensitivity to the distributional properties of an ensemble of stimuli can emerge out of the processing of exemplars, they differ in whether they assume that the shared features of the training materials are represented as such or merely computed when needed. This *locus of abstraction* issue is a difficult one that is unlikely to be resolved by modeling alone. Thus, it appears that the knowledge acquired through implicit learning is best described as lying somewhere on a continuum between purely exemplar-based representations and more general, abstract representations – a characteristic that neural network models have been particularly apt at capturing. Further research is needed to develop unified models of implicit learning and to gain insight into the computational principles that differentiate conscious from unconscious processing.

Appendix

The equations for the two main chunking models in the implicit learning literature, the Competitive Chunker (CC) of Servan-Scheiber and Anderson (1990) and the PARSER model of Perruchet and Vinter (1998), are presented here.

Competitive Chunker

CC perceives a stimulus by successively chunking together the basic components of that stimulus until a single chunk represents it. So, using brackets to denote a chunk, the exemplar "MTVR" might be perceived at first as "MTVR," that is, as "(M)(T)(V)(R)," then "(MT)VR," then "(MT)(VR)," and finally "((MT)(VR))." Once a stimulus is fully chunked, it is said to be maximally familiar, or memorized.

Initially, CC is given elementary chunks, for example, letters. Each chunk has a strength. Strength is increased by one unit every time the chunk is used or recreated. However, strength decays with time. At any point in time, the strength of a chunk is the sum of its successive individually decaying strengthenings:

$$strength = \Sigma_i T_i^{-d} \qquad (14.1)$$

where T_i is the time elapsed since the ith strengthening, and d is the *decay parameter* $(0 < d < 1)$.

Given "MTVR," it will consider all possible combinations of two adjacent existing chunks as possible new chunks, that is, "MT," "TV," and "VR." Each possibility has a support, given by the sum of the strengths of each of its subchunks. The probability that a new chunk will be formed is given by:

$$(1 - e^{-c*support})/(1 + e^{-c*support}) \qquad (14.2)$$

where c is the *competition parameter*, c > 0. Only one new chunk is formed at a time. Thus, the three chunks "MT," "TV," and "VR" will compete with each other to be created. If "MT" is formed as a chunk, next time the stimulus is seen, possible new chunks are "MTV," and "VR," which will compete to be formed by the same process.

When a stimulus is presented, the mere existence of a chunk that matches part of the stimulus does not mean it will be retrieved. The probability of retrieving a chunk is given by equation (2), the same equation as for chunk creation. Thus, it may be that two competing chunks are retrieved, for example, both "MTV" and "VR". In that case, the stronger chunk wins. The greater the value of c, the more likely it is that chunks will be retrieved, and hence the greater the probability of competition. After a first pass, another pass is made to see if the existing chunks can be perceived as higher-order chunks. At a certain point, no further chunks are retrieved. At this stage, if the resulting percept is not one single chunk, a further chunk may be created, as described.

The familiarity of a stimulus is given by the number of active chunks resulting from the perceptual process, for example:

$$\text{familiarity} = e^{1 - n_{\text{active}}} \qquad (14.3)$$

This familiarity value can then be used to classify strings as grammatical, old, and so forth.

Parser

Like CC, PARSER begins with a set of primitives, for example, letters. When presented with a string like "MTVRXX," it randomly considers perceiving groups of 1, 2, or 3 primitives reading from left to right. (PARSER differs from CC in parsing from left to right: PARSER was originally used to model the perception of auditory strings, and CC was developed to model visual strings.) For example, if it randomly produced "1, 3, 2," it would see the string as (M)(TVR) (XX). Because TVR and XX do not exist as units, they become new per-

ceptual units and are assigned weights (like CC's strengths; e.g., all new units could be assigned weights of 1). "M" already exists, and its weight is incremented (by an amount *a*). At each time step, all units are affected by forgetting and interference. Forgetting is simulated by decreasing all the units by a fixed value *f*. Interference is simulated by decreasing the weights of the units in which any of the letters involved in the currently processed unit are embedded (by an amount *i*). Once new units have been formed, they act in the cycle described just like primitive units. All units can contribute to perception as long as their weight exceeds a threshold (*t*). As for CC, the number of chunks a string is perceived as could be used to determine its familiarity.

Comparison

CC and PARSER both postulate that learning occurs by chunking in which (a) the use of a chunk increments its weight, and (b) each chunk decays in weight on each time step; they theoretically differ in that (c) PARSER, but not CC, has an interference process by which chunks that are not used but that contain an element that was used are decremented in weight. Because of (a) and (b), both models correctly predict that with the strengthening of common chunks and fading of infrequent ones, people will come to perceive stimuli as made of the commonly occurring chunks.

PARSER's interference parameter has two effects. One is that it tends to eliminate long items (long items are obviously very prone to interference, because many small items interfere with them). But perhaps more importantly, it makes PARSER sensitive to both forward transitional probabilities (the conditional probability of a second event given a first) and backward transitional probabilities (the conditional probability of a first event given a second). CC is mainly sensitive to the frequency of co-occurrence of two items next to each other rather than transitional probabilities. The SRN is sensitive to forward but not backward transitional probabilities.

Perruchet and Peereman (2004) showed that in rating the goodness of nonwords as being words, people were sensitive to both forward and backward transitional probabilities, consistent with PARSER but not with the SRN or with CC. Further, in many statistical learning situations, people are sensitive to transition probabilities (e.g., Aslin, Saffran, & Newport, 1998). Conversely, Boucher and Dienes (2003) found support for CC over the SRN in artificial grammar learning because people were mainly sensitive to co-occurrence frequency. Thus, it is likely that PARSER could fit the Boucher and Dienes data by letting the interference parameter go to 0, but that would be an ad-hoc solution because PARSER's characteristic behavior is sensitivity to transition probabilities. Nonetheless, PARSER provides a framework for future research to establish a meaningful way of indicating when its interference parameter should go to 0 and when it should not.

Acknowledgments

Axel Cleeremans is a research director with the Fund for Scientific Research (F.R.S.-F.N.R.S., Belgium). This work was supported by an institutional grant from the Université Libre de Bruxelles to Axel Cleeremans, by Concerted Research Action 06/11-342 titled "Culturally Modified Organisms: What It Means to Be Human in the Age of Culture," financed by the Ministère de la Communauté Française – Direction Générale l'Enseignement non obligatoire et de la Recherche scientifique (Belgium), and by F.R.F.C. grant 2.4577.06.

References

Anderson, J. R. (1993). *Rules of the mind.* Hillsdale, NJ: Lawrence Erlbaum.

Aslin, R. N., Saffran, J. R., & Newport, E. L. (1998). Computation of conditional probability statistics by 8-month-old infants. *Psychological Science, 9,* 321–324.

Baars, B. J. (1988). *A cognitive theory of consciousness.* Cambridge, UK: Cambridge University Press.

Berry, D. C., & Broadbent, D. E. (1984). On the relationship between task performance and associated verbalizable knowledge. *Quarterly Journal of Experimental Psychology, 36A,* 209–231.

Berry, D. C., & Broadbent, D. E. (1988). Interactive tasks and the implicit-explicit distinction. *British Journal of Psychology, 79,* 251–272.

Berry, D. C., & Dienes, Z. (1993). *Implicit learning: Theoretical and empirical issues.* Hove, UK: Lawrence Erlbaum.

Block, N. (1995). On a confusion about a function of consciousness. *Behavioral and Brain Sciences, 18,* 227–287.

Boucher, L., & Dienes, Z. (2003). Two ways of learning associations. *Cognitive Science, 27,* 807–842.

Boyer, M., Destrebecqz, A., & Cleeremans, A. (2005). Processing abstract sequence structure: Learning without knowing, or knowing without learning? *Psychological Research, 69,* 383–398.

Brooks, L. R. (1978). Non-analytic concept formation and memory for instances. In E. Rosch & B. Lloyd (Eds.), *Cognition and concepts* (pp. 16–211). Mahwah, NJ: Lawrence Erlbaum.

Chun, M. M., & Jiang, Y. (1999). Top-down attentional guidance based on implicit learning of visual covariation. *Psychological Science, 10,* 360–365.

Clark, A., & Karmiloff-Smith, A. (1993). The cognizer's innards: A psychological and philosophical perspective on the development of thought. *Mind and Language, 8,* 487–519.

Cleeremans, A. (1993). *Mechanisms of implicit learning: Connectionist models of sequence processing.* Cambridge, MA: MIT Press.

Cleeremans, A. (2005). Computational correlates of consciousness. In S. Laureys (Ed.), *Progress in brain research* (Vol. 150, pp. 81–98). Amsterdam: Elsevier.

Cleeremans, A., Destrebecqz, A., & Boyer, M. (1998). Implicit learning: News from the front. *Trends in Cognitive Sciences, 2,* 406–416.

Cleeremans, A., & McClelland, J. L. (1991). Learning the structure of event sequences. *Journal of Experimental Psychology: General, 120,* 235–253.

Cleeremans, A., Servan-Schreiber, D., & McClelland, J. L. (1989). Finite state automata and simple recurrent networks. *Neural Computation, 1,* 372–381.

Clegg, B. A., DiGirolamo, G. J., & Keele, S. W. (1998). Sequence learning. *Trends in Cognitive Sciences, 2,* 275–281.

Curran, T., & Keele, S. W. (1993). Attentional and nonattentional forms of sequence learning. *Journal of Experimental Psychology: Learning, Memory and Cognition, 19,* 189–202.

Dehaene, S., Sergent, C., & Changeux, J.-P. (2003). A neuronal network model linking subjective reports and objective physiological data during conscious perception. *Proceedings of the National Academy of Sciences of the U.S.A., 100*(14), 8520–8525.

Destrebecqz, A. (2004). The effect of explicit knowledge on sequence learning: A graded account. *Psychological Belgica, 44*(4), 217–248.

Destrebecqz, A., & Cleeremans, A. (2001). Can sequence learning be implicit? New evidence with the Process Dissociation Procedure. *Psychonomic Bulletin & Review, 8*(2), 343–350.

Destrebecqz, A., & Cleeremans, A. (2003). Temporal effects in sequence learning. In L. Jiménez (Ed.), *Attention and implicit learning* (pp. 181–213). Amsterdam: John Benjamins.

Dienes, Z. (1992). Connectionist and memory-array models of artificial grammar learning. *Cognitive Science, 16,* 41–79.

Dienes, Z., Altmann, G., & Gao, S.-J. (1999). Mapping across domains without feedback: A neural network model of transfer of implicit knowledge. *Cognitive Science, 23,* 53–82.

Dienes, Z., & Fahey, R. (1995). Role of specific instances in controlling a dynamic system. *Journal of Experimental Psychology: Learning, Memory, and Cognition, 21,* 848–862.

Domangue, T., Mathews, R. C., Sun, R., Roussel, L. G., & Guidry, C. (2004). The effects of model-based and memory-based processing on speed and accuracy of grammar string generation. *Journal of Experimental Psychology: Learning, Memory and Cognition, 30*(5), 1002–1011.

Dominey, P. F. (1998). Influences of temporal organization on sequence learning and transfer: Comments on Stadler (1995) and Curran and Keele (1993). *Journal of Experimental Psychology: Learning, Memory and Cognition, 24,* 234–248.

Dulany, D. E. (1968). Awareness, rules, and propositional control: A confrontation with S-R behavior theory. In T. Dixon & D. Horton (Eds.), *Verbal behavior and behavior theory* (pp. 340–387). New York: Prentice Hall.

Dulany, D. E., Carlson, R. A., & Dewey, G. I. (1984). A case of syntactical learning and judgement: How conscious and how abstract? *Journal of Experimental Psychology: General, 113,* 541–555.

Dunn, J. C., & Kirsner, K. (1988). Discovering functionally independent mental process: The principle of reversed association. *Psychological Review, 95,* 91–101.

Elman, J. L. (1990). Finding structure in time. *Cognitive Science, 14,* 179–211.

Estes, W. K. (1957). Toward a statistical theory of learning. *Psychological Review, 57,* 94–107.

Frensch, P. A. (1998). One concept, multiple meanings: On how to define the concept of implicit learning. In M. A. Stadler & P. A. Frensch (Eds.), *Handbook of implicit learning* (pp. 47–104). Thousand Oaks, CA: Sage Publications.

Gibson, F., Fichman, M., & Plaut, D. C. (1997). Learning in dynamic decision task: Computational models and empirical evidence. *Organizational Behavior and Human Decision Processes, 71,* 1–35.

Hintzmann, D. (1986). "Schema abstraction" in a multiple-trace memory model. *Psychological Review, 93,* 411–428.

Hull, C. L. (1920). Quantitative aspects of the evolution of concepts: An experimental study. *Psychological Monographs, 28,* 123.

Jacobs, R. A., Jordan, M. I., & Barto, A. G. (1991). Task decomposition through competition in a modular connectionist architecture: The what and where of vision tasks. *Cognitive Science, 15,* 219–250.

Jacoby, L. L. (1991). A process dissociation framework: Separating automatic from intentional uses of memory. *Journal of Memory and Language, 30,* 513–541.

Jiménez, L., Mendez, C., & Cleeremans, A. (1996). Comparing direct and indirect measures of sequence learning. *Journal of Experimental Psychology-Learning Memory and Cognition, 22*(4), 948–969.

Kinder, A., & Shanks, D. R. (2001). Amnesia and the Declarative/Nondeclarative distinction: A recurrent network model of classification, recognition, and repetition priming. *Journal of Cognitive Neuroscience, 13*(5), 648–669.

Kirsh, D. (1991). When is information explicitly represented? In P. P. Hanson (Ed.), *Information, language, and cognition.* New York: Oxford University Press.

Knowlton, B. J., Ramus, S. J., & Squire L. R. (1992). Intact artificial grammar learning in amnesia: Dissociation of classification learning and explicit memory for specific instances. *Psychological Science, 3,* 172–179.

Kuhn, G., & Dienes, Z. (2005). Implicit learning of non-local musical rules: Implicitly learning more than chunks. *Journal of Experimental Psychology: Learning, Memory and Cognition, 31*(6), 1417–1432.

Kuhn, G., & Dienes, Z. (in press). Learning nonlocal dependencies. *Cognition*.

Lebiere, C., Wallach, D. P., & Taatgen, N. A. (1998). Implicit and explicit learning in ACT-R. In F. Ritter & R. Young (Eds.), *Cognitive modeling* (Vol. II, pp. 183–193). Nottingham, UK: Notthingam University Press.

Lewicki, P. (1986). Processing information about covariations that cannot be articulated. *Journal of Experimental Psychology: Learning, Memory and Cognition, 12*, 135–146.

Lewicki, P., Czyzewska, M., & Hoffman, H. (1987). Unconscious acquisition of complex procedural knowledge. *Journal of Experimental Psychology: Learning, Memory and Cognition, 13*, 523–530.

Lewicki, P., Hill, T., & Czyzewska, M. (1992). Nonconscious acquisition of information. *American Psychologist, 47*, 796–801.

Marcus, G. F. (2001). *The algebraic mind. Integrating connectionism and cognitive science.* Cambridge, MA: MIT Press.

Mathews, R. C., Buss, R. R., Stanley, W. B., Blanchard-Fields, F., Cho, J. R., & Druhan, B. (1989). Role of implicit and explicit process in learning from examples: A synergistic effet. *Journal of Experimental Psychology: Learning, Memory and Cognition, 15*, 1083–1100.

Mathis, W. D., & Mozer, M. C. (1996). Conscious and unconscious perception: A computational theory. In Garrison W. Cottrell (Ed.), *Proceedings of the Eighteenth Annual Conference of the Cognitive Science Society* (pp. 324–328). Hillsdale, NJ: Lawrence Erlbaum.

McCloskey, M., & Cohen, N. (1989). Catastrophic interference in connectionist networks: The sequential learning problem. In G. H. Bower (Ed.), *The psychology of learning and motivation* (Vol. 24, pp. 109–164). New York: Academic Press.

Medin, D. L., & Schaffer, M. M. (1978). Context theory of classification learning. *Psychological Review, 85*, 207–238.

Miller, G. A. (1956). The magical number Seven, plus or minus two. *Psychological Review, 63*, 81–97.

Millward, R. B., & Reber, A. S. (1968). Event-recall in probability learning. *Journal of Verbal Learning and Verbal Behavior, 7*, 980–989.

Newell, A. (1990). *Unified theories of cognition.* Cambridge, MA: Harvard University Press.

Nisbett, R. E., & Wilson, T. D. (1977). Telling more than we can do: Verbal reports on mental processes. *Psychological Review, 84*, 231–259.

Nissen, M. J., & Bullemer, P. (1987). Attentional requirement of learning: Evidence from performance measures. *Cognitive Psychology, 19*, 1–32.

O'Reilly, R. C., & Munakata, Y. (2000). *Computational explorations in cognitive neuroscience: Understanding the mind by simulating the brain.* Cambridge, MA: MIT Press.

Pacton, S., Perruchet, P., Fayol, M., & Cleeremans, A. (2001). Implicit learning out of the lab: The case of orthographic regularities. *Journal of Experimental Psychology: General, 130*(3), 401–426.

Perner, J. (1991). *Understanding the representational mind.* Cambridge, MA: MIT Press.

Perruchet, P., & Gallego, G. (1997). A subjective unit formation account of implicit learning. In D. Berry (Ed.), *How implicit is implicit knowledge?* (pp. 124–161). Oxford, UK: Oxford University Press.

Perruchet, P., & Pacteau, C. (1990). Synthetic grammar learning: Implicit rule abstraction or explicit fragmentary knowledge? *Journal of Experimental Psychology: General, 119*, 264–275.

Perruchet, P., & Pacton, S. (2006). Implicit learning and statistical learning: Two approaches, one phenomenon? *Trends in Cognitive Sciences, 10*, 233–238.

Perruchet, P., & Peereman, R. (2004). The exploitation of distributional information in syllable processing. *Journal of Neurolinguistics, 17*, 97–119.

Perruchet, P., & Vinter, A. (1998). PARSER: A model for word segmentation. *Journal of Memory and Language, 39*, 246–263.

Pinker, S. (1999). Out of the mind of babes. *Science, 283*, 40–41.

Plaut, D. C. (1995). Double dissociation without modularity: Evidence from connectionist neuropsychology. *Journal of Clinical and Experimental Neuropschology, 17*, 291–326.

Popper, K. (1959). The *logic of scientific discovery.* London: Hutchinson.

Reber, A. S. (1967). Implicit learning of artificial grammars. *Journal of Verbal Learning and Verbal Behavior, 5*, 855–863.

Reber, A. S. (1969). Transfer of syntactic structure in synthetic languages. *Journal of Experimental Psychology, 81*, 115–119.

Reber, A. S. (1976). Implicit learning of synthetic languages. *Journal of Experimental Psychology: Human Learning and Memory, 2,* 88–94.

Reber, A. S., & Lewis, S. (1977). Implicit learning: An analysis of the form and structure of a body of tacit knowledge. *Cognition, 114,* 14–24.

Reber, A. S. (1989). Implicit learning and tacit knowledge. *Journal of Experimental Psychology: General, 118,* 219–235.

Redington, M., & Chater, N. (1996). Transfer in artificial grammar learning: A reevaluation. *Journal of Experimental Psychology: General, 125,* 123–138.

Redington, M., & Chater, N. (2002). Knowledge representation and transfer in artificial grammar learning. In R. M. French & A. Cleeremans (Eds.), *Implicit learning and consciousness* (pp. 121–123). Hove, UK: Psychology Press.

Rosenthal, D. (2006). *Consciousness and mind.* Oxford, UK: Oxford University Press.

Schacter, D. L. (1987). Implicit memory: History and current status. *Journal of Experimental Psychology: Learning, Memory, and Cognition, 13,* 501–518.

Sejnowski, T. J., & Rosenberg, C. R. (1987). Parallel networks that learn to pronounce English text. *Complex Systems, 1,* 145–168.

Servan-Schreiber, D., Cleeremans, A., & McClelland, J. L. (1991). Graded State Machines: The representation of temporal contingencies in simple recurrent networks. *Machine Learning, 7,* 161–193.

Servan-Schreiber, E., & Anderson, J. R. (1990). Learning artificial grammar with competitive chunking. *Journal of Experimental Psychology: Learning, Memory and Cognition, 16,* 592–608.

Shanks, D. R., & Johnstone, T. (1999). Evaluating the relationship between explicit and implicit knowledge in a serial reaction time task.

Journal of Experimental Psychology: Learning, Memory, & Cognition, 25, 1435–1451.

Shanks, D. R., & St. John, M. F. (1994). Characteristics of dissociable human learning systems. *Behavioral and Brain Sciences, 17,* 367–447.

Smolensky, P. (1988). On the proper treatment of connectionism. *Behavioral and Brain Sciences, 11,* 1–74.

Sun, R. (1997). Learning, action, and consciousness: A hybrid approach towards modeling consciousness. *Neural Networks, 10*(7), 1317–1331.

Sun, R. (2002). *Duality of the mind.* Mahwah, NJ: Lawrence Erlbaum.

Sun, R., Slusarz, P., & Terry, C. (2005). The interaction of the implicit and the explicit in skill learning: A dual-process approach. *Psycological Review, 112*(1), 159–192.

Tononi, G. (2005). Consciousness, information integration, and the brain. In S. Laureys (Ed.), *Progress in brain research* (Vol. 150, pp. 109–126). Amsterdam: Elsevier.

Tononi, G., & Edelman, G. M. (1998). Consciousness and complexity. *Science, 282*(5395), 1846–1851.

Tunney, R. J., & Shanks, D. R. (2003). Does opposition logic provide evidence for conscious and unconscious processes in artificial grammar learning? *Consciousness and Cognition, 12,* 201–218.

Vokey, J. R., & Higham, P. A. (2004). Opposition logic and neural network models in artificial grammar learning. *Consciousness and Cognition, 3,* 565–578.

Wallach, D. P., & Lebiere, C. (2000). Learning of event sequences: An architectural approach. In N. A. Taatgen (Ed.), *Proceedings of the Third International Conference on Cognitive Modeling* (pp. 271–279). Gröningen, The Netherlands: Universal Press.

CHAPTER 15

Computational Models of Attention
and Cognitive Control

Nicola De Pisapia, Grega Repovš, and Todd S. Braver

1. Introduction

The study of attention is central to understanding how information is processed in cognitive systems. Modern cognitive research interprets attention as the capacity to select and enhance limited aspects of currently processed information, while suppressing the remaining aspects. Cognitive scientists interpret attention as a solution to a fundamental computational trade-off that limited agents face in complex environments: on one side, the necessity to focus on as much information as possible in order to be vigilant and opportunistic, on the other side, the necessity to optimize performance by allocating, in a coherent and continuous manner, cognitive resources to the most salient and behaviorally relevant events and actions (Allport, 1989). As such, attention turns out not to be a unitary phenomenon, but instead is present at many stages of cognitive information processing, involves many different brain regions, and relates to almost all psychological processes.

This chapter reviews the existing literature on computational models of atten-

tion, with the aim of fleshing out the progress that has been made in elucidating the core mechanisms of attentional modulation and attentional control. The chapter starts with a description of work that focuses on visual selective attention and the computational mechanisms that exist at the site of attentional influence within visual perceptual pathways. Subsequent sections focus on work at the intersection of attention and executive control, which emphasizes the mechanisms by which goal-driven attentional control signals are represented, shaped, and propagated according to the various constraints and dynamics of task processing. In the concluding section, the focus is on the contrast or continuum between attentional control and automaticity, an issue that becomes crystallized when examining the distinctions between, or transitions from, novice to expert cognitive task performance.

It is important to begin with a caveat – this chapter is not intended to be comprehensive or exhaustive in the coverage of computational cognitive modeling work on attention. Instead, the goal is to provide a road map to the relevant literature, highlighting example models that best reflect the core mechanistic principles that are emerging from recent research or that illustrate new directions in which the field is headed. Moreover, the coverage is admittedly biased toward connectionist or neural network models. The reason for this bias is not only due to the expertise of the authors, but also to an overarching interest in computational models that have the most potential for integrating the large emerging corpus of literature, arising not only out of cognitive behavioral research, but also cognitive neuroscience and animal neurophysiology studies. Traditionally, this approach has been most closely aligned with connectionist/neural network models, although recent trends suggest that this traditional dichotomy between connectionist and symbolic models is beginning to blur (e.g., Anderson et al., 2004).

Nevertheless, it is still our belief that models that make strong attempts to incorporate as many core principles of neural information processing and computation as possible are the ones most likely to explain empirical data regarding attentional phenomena across the widest range of explanatory levels, from single-cell neurophysiology to observable behavior. Although this philosophical bias is reflected throughout the chapter, influential examples are also reviewed from work in symbolic, hybrid, or production system modeling, as well as more abstract mathematical models. Readers interested in learning more about both neurally oriented models of attention and symbolic ones are directed toward the many additional reviews of this literature arising from a variety of different theoretical perspectives and focus (i.e., Anderson et al., 2004; Itti & Koch, 2001; O'Reilly & Munakata, 2000).

2. Visual Attention

When we observe and interact with our environment, the focus of what we are attending to constantly changes. There are a variety of theoretical views regarding why attention selectively focuses on some aspects of the environment and away from others. Perhaps the oldest argument is that our processing capabilities are limited whereas the computational demands of processing visual input are huge. Under this account, the role of attention is to filter this spatiotemporal stream of information to a manageable size (Broadbent, 1958; Mozer, Sitton, & Pashler, 1998). A second theoretical argument regarding selection in visual attention is that not all of the information present in the visual environment is equally relevant at a given point in time. Under this account, the role of attention is to quickly detect, orient, and select the aspects of the visual environment that are most informative or of greatest relevance at the time, so as to produce efficient and optimized perceptual processing and subsequent behavior (Chang et al., 2001; van der Heijden & Bem, 1997). Yet, a third theoretical perspective is that the primary role of visual attention is to solve the binding problem: to produce a coherent interpretation of the visual environment based on integration of visual features into a unified whole. Under this account, selective attention enables visual perceptual processing to be concentrated on a restricted set of visual features to enable these to be correctly bound together into higher-level object representations (Treisman, 1999; Treisman & Gelade, 1980). And, lastly, a more recent theoretical view is the biased competition framework, which postulates that attention should be interpreted primarily as an emergent phenomenon of activation dynamics arising in a system in which inhibitory competition and constraint satisfaction is a ubiquitous component of the network (Desimone & Duncan, 1995; O'Reilly & Munakata, 2000).

Regardless of the particular theoretical perspective one adopts, there is clearly a consensus among theorists that: (1) attention is a core component of visual perceptual processing; (2) focus of attention is determined by an interaction of bottom-up processes that compute the "importance" of visual stimuli and top-down processes that modulate visual processing according to goals and intentions; and (3) top-down processes can operate by directing attention either to locations in space or to specific objects or object features in the visual field.

A number of theories of visual attention have been implemented in computational models. The design and scope of the existing computational models of visual attention vary widely and are determined by the problems they are meant to resolve. Some models were built to explicitly test specific aspects of existing theories of visual attention or to account for empirical data that apply to specific experimental domains, such as stimulus filtering, visual search, and perceptual cueing (Cave, 1999; Deco & Zihl, 2001a; Heinke & Humphreys, 2003; Humphreys & Mueller, 1993; Mozer et al., 1998; Phaf, Van der Heijden, & Hudson 1990; Wolfe, 1994). Other models were particularly geared toward explaining the mechanisms underlying particular neuropsychological deficits, such as attentional neglect (Cohen et al., 1994; Deco & Rolls, 2002; Heinke & Humphreys, 2003). Still other models were designed primarily from a neurophysiological perspective to account for basic aspects of early visual processing and identification of salient locations in visual field (Itti & Koch, 2000; Koch & Ullman, 1985; Lee et al., 1999; Parkhurst, Law, & Niebur, 2002) or to understand the core neurobiological mechanisms involved in attention (Braun, Koch, & Davis, 2001; Hamker, 2003). Finally, some models were built primarily from a machine learning rather than cognitive, neuropsychological, or neurobiological perspective, such as advancing the development of computer vision systems (Tsotsos et al., 1995). Rather than detailing each one of these models, the following subsections focus on what might be considered a "consensual" model that contains core features common to many of the specific implementations.

2.1. The Base Model

Computational models of visual attention share a very similar overall organization, which follows at least coarsely the structure and organization of the visual percep-

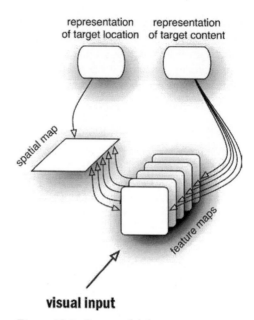

representation of target location   representation of target content

spatial map

feature maps

visual input

Figure 15.1. Base model depicting core elements of the visual system and their connections, within which attention is implemented.

tual system. This commonality enables the description of a core consensual model architecture, consisting of a set of primary cognitive elements that are present in different forms throughout a variety of computational models. The base model provides a joint reference for reviewing and comparing specific computational solutions proposed by the individual models. It consists of topographically and hierarchically organized feature maps, a spatial map coding locations, and two modules providing top-down bias by coding target location and content, respectively (Figure 15.1).

Feature maps are postulated to code for specific properties of visual input. Such feature maps were first proposed in the influential feature integration theory of attention (Treisman, 1999; Treisman & Gelade, 1980), which assumed that basic visual features are represented in separate topographical maps, each of them linked to a master map of locations that allows later binding of individual features for further processing. Feature maps, at least in their initial computational implementation, were assumed to code low-level basic features of visual input, such as color, orientation, and intensity (Koch & Ullman, 1985) that could be represented in primary visual cortex (VI). Yet, it has also been appreciated that such maps might as well be used to code progressively more complex features, such as motion, shape, and object identity, depending on the focus and complexity of the model. In cognitive neuroscience terms, these maps represent different stages of visual analysis of the ventral, or "what," stream, starting from the primary visual cortex to the inferotemporal cortex (IT). Although the initial feature maps coding low-level features are supposed to be independent, their combination to ever higher levels of representation can be seen as comprising a hierarchical system dedicated to object recognition (Mozer et al., 1998). The maps are topographically organized with the nodes in the initial maps having relatively small reception fields, and the nodes in the higher feature maps having large receptive fields, ultimately covering the whole visual field.

Whereas feature maps deal with what is present in visual input, spatial maps code information about where visual input is present. Such coding occurs through topographical representation of locations in the visual field. In feed-forward models of attention, the spatial map also frequently serves as the map that explicitly codes spatial attention, earning the name saliency map (Koch & Ullman, 1985), activation map (Wolfe, 1994), or simply attentional map (Mozer et al., 1998). The spatial map is supposed to be instantiated in the dorsal, or "where," stream of visual processing, most frequently in the posterior parietal (PP) cortex. Feature maps and the spatial map are densely interconnected. Most models assume each of the feature maps to be connected to the location map. In many models, these connections are unidirectional, leading primarily from low-level feature maps to the spatial map (e.g. Koch & Ullman, 1985); however, other models include recurrent feedback connections, from the spatial map back to low-level feature maps (e.g., Deco, 2001).

The feature maps and spatial map represent the most frequent core of the model, where attentional influences emerge and are expressed. To also model the top-down influence on attention, most models assume modulatory connections from structures coding goals and intentions. In the base model, the top-down modulatory effect is exerted by an element that is holding a representation of target location and an element that is holding a representation of target content. The former projects to the spatial map and the latter to the feature maps. Both are assumed to be located in the anterior part of the brain (i.e., in the prefrontal cortex [PFC]), closely connected to cognitive control processes and the production of goal-directed behavior.

2.2. Explicit Computation and Representation of Attention

Within the architecture of the base model, various computational models of attention can be implemented, differing significantly in the pattern of connectivity, the functional roles played by individual components, and the ensuing dynamics and behavior of the model. One conceptualization of attention assumes it is a distinct, explicitly computed and represented feature of the system enabling selection and filtering of visual input for further analysis. Attentional dynamics are assumed to evolve through two clearly defined steps. In the first step, stimulus features are used to compute and identify most salient locations in the visual field, representing the focus of attention. In the second step, the representation of spatial attention is used to focus the flow of visual information in an object processing stream.

Computation of visual attention using the saliency map was first explicitly proposed in the model of Koch and Ullman (1985) and led to a number of similar implementations in other models (Mozer et al., 1998; Wolfe, 1994) as well as more detailed refinements and additions to the original proposed mechanisms of feature extraction and saliency computation (Itti & Baldi, 2005; Itti, Koch, & Niebur, 1998; Lee et al., 1999). As proposed by Koch and Ullman (1985; see Figure 15.2), the visual input is first

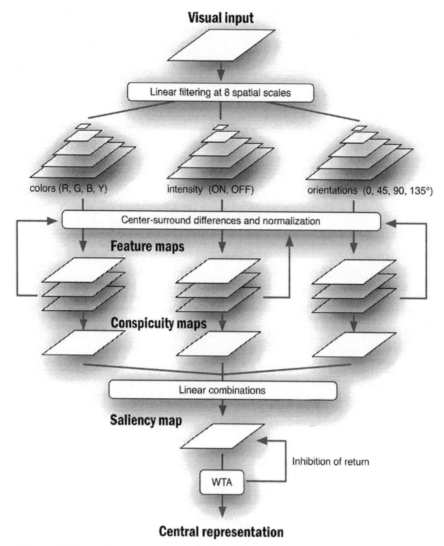

Figure 15.2. A schematic representation of the saliency map based on the computational model of visual attention initially proposed by Koch and Ullman (1985) and fully implemented by Itti et al. (1998).

decomposed by several feature detection mechanisms working in parallel at different spatial scales. Resulting individual feature maps represent the salience of locations in regard to the basic visual features being represented. The key element in determining the saliency of a location is not the intensity of the feature, but rather its local contrast judged in the context of the rest of the visual field. A red dot is more likely to attract attention than a uniform field of red. Furthermore, a particular red dot is more likely to attract attention when it is the only red dot in the visual field than when it is just one of many in a field of red dots. To take both properties of attention into account, the computation of saliency is proposed to be based on both short-range center-surround differences, which identify the presence of local contrast, as well as long-range spatial normalization, which estimates its importance in regard to the entire visual field. Resulting activity in feature maps is combined in "conspicuity maps" for each feature type and summed into a single, "master" saliency map coding overall saliency of stimuli within a given location in a topographical representation of the visual field. In this manner, the model collapses the representation of saliency over specific visual features, making the map blind and indifferent to which feature caused specific locations to be salient.

Once saliency is computed, the model has to be able to select a single location on which to focus attention. This step in ensured through a separate winner-take-all (WTA) network. Receiving topographical input from the saliency map and implementing strong global inhibition, the WTA network quickly settles on the winning neuron (or a population of them) receiving highest activation from the saliency map and representing the focus of attention.

Given a static display, the described network would compute and lock on to the most salient location in the visual field. To be able to disengage from the winning location and explore other salient locations, the model has to incorporate an "inhibition of return" (IOR) mechanism that temporarily inhibits the activity in the winning location. This inhibition then enables the second most active location in the saliency map to drive the shift in activity in the WTA network, representing a new focus of attention. Such IOR in covert shifts of attention has been experimentally well demonstrated (Kwak & Egeth, 1992; Posner, Cohen, & Rafal, 1982). In the Itti and Koch (2000) implementation of the model, it is realized through inhibitory feedback from the WTA network back to the saliency map. Other models have been developed that use similar types of active or passive (e.g., fatigue-like) inhibition mechanisms (Houghton & Tipper, 1996; O'Reilly & Munakata, 2000). Depending on the parameters of the model, IOR enables a network to sequentially select or search through a number of the most salient locations in the visual field before returning to the initial one.

A number of implementations of the saliency-based computational models have shown it to be successful in predicting human performance in psychophysical experiments and visual search tasks (Itti & Koch, 2000; van de Laar, Heskes, & Gielen, 1997), as well as accounting for the pattern of human eye movements made during the viewing of images containing complex natural and artificial scenes (Parkhurst et al., 2002). For an excellent review of saliency-based computation of attention, see Itti and Koch (2001).

Once attention is focused on a specific location, the mechanism of guiding further visual processing needs to be specified. The most straightforward solution uses saliency representation as a gating signal modulating the flow of information from lower-level feature maps to higher levels of visual analysis. In a model proposed by Mozer et al. (1998), the information coming from low-level feature maps is multiplied by the activity in the topographically equivalent area of the saliency map, limiting further processing to salient locations while attenuating the rest. Significantly more complex solutions are based on a dynamical routing approach proposed by Olshausen, Anderson, and Van Essen (1993) and recently instantiated by Heinke and Humphreys (2003) in their Selective Attention for Identification Model (SAIM). The routing and SAIM models build on the idea that translation-invariant pattern recognition can be achieved by an attentional window that can be moved over the visual field, focusing on its relevant sections and feeding that partial image to a recognition network. The task is realized by a complex network of connections (termed the "contents network") that map retinal input through a number of stages to a smaller "focus of attention" (FOA) layer. The appropriate mapping is ensured by a selection network (spatial map analogue), whose mutually inhibitory units activate only those connections of the contents network that project from the currently relevant part of the input layer to the FOA layer. In this manner, the network not only gates the visual input, but also translates it to a single layer for further analysis. Both models are successful in accounting for a number of empirical findings relating to both normal as well as pathological attentional phenomena.

For a review, see Heinke and Humphreys (2005).

Although bottom-up influences are important in drawing our attention to objects in the environment, models of visual attention must also appropriately account for voluntary top-down control. The models considered so far allow for both spatially based as well as feature-based top-down control of attention. Intentional guidance of spatial attention is presumed to occur via top-down inputs to the spatial map, which either bias or directly determine its pattern of activation. On the other hand, feature- or object-based attention is assumed to be brought about by biasing the computation of saliency. Searching for red horizontal bars in the visual scene would, for instance, entail selectively enhancing the contribution of feature maps coding red color and horizontal orientation to the master map of saliency, leading to the highest buildup of activity in location(s) where a conjunction of both features is present (Wolfe, 1994). As recently shown by Navalpakkam and Itti (2005), top-down control of attention using biased computation of the saliency map is not limited to simple features. Using learned sets of low-level features related to different views of an object, their model was successful in locating complex visual objects in natural scenes.

2.3. Interactive Emergence of Attention

An alternative approach to conceptualizing attention has been to consider it an emergent property of the system evolving seamlessly through competitive interactions between modules. Dense bidirectional (i.e., recurrent) connections between processing modules enable the active representation in any module to be the source or the target of a biasing signal affecting the local competition between representations, hence, the name "biased competition models." This bidirectional connectivity enables a dynamic settling process to occur that stabilizes on a coherent representation expressed throughout the system. Attention is not computed explicitly through distinct steps but rather emerges continuously as a property of activation dynamics in the system (Desimone

& Duncan, 1995). The initial proposal for these types of models can be traced to Phaf et al. (1990) and Desimone and Duncan (1995), with more recent models being proposed by Ward (1999) and Deco (2001; Deco & Rolls, 2005a).

Representative biased competition models of visual attention have been developed, described and explored by Deco and colleagues (Deco, 2001; Deco & Lee, 2004; Deco, Polatos, & Zihl, 2002; Deco & Rolls, 2002, 2003, 2004, 2005a; Deco & Zihl, 2004). The simplest instantiation of the model assumes existence of three processing modules, V1, PP, and IT, respectively corresponding to low-level feature maps, the spatial map, and the high-level feature map in the base model (Figure 15.3). Each module consists of a number of units, each representing a pool of neurons with similar properties. The activity of each unit is described using mean field approximation, where each unit i is characterized by its activation x_i, reflecting an average firing rate of the pool and an activity level of the input current A_i. The input-output relationship is defined as:

$$x_i = F(A_i(t)) = \frac{1}{T_r - \tau \log(1 - 1/\tau A_i(t))}$$

in which T_r denotes the cell's absolute refractory period (e.g., 1 ms) and τ stands for the membrane time constant. The dynamics of each excitatory unit within a module is described by:

$$\tau \frac{\delta}{\delta t} A_i(t) = -A_i + a F(A_i(t)) - b F(A^I(t)) + I_i^B(t) + I_i^T(t) + I_0 + v.$$

The first term is a habituation decay term. The second term represents the recurrent self-excitation that maintains the activity of the cells and mediates their cooperative interaction within the unit ($a = 0.95$). The third term represents a local inhibitory input from the inhibitory unit providing the basis for local competition between excitatory units within the module ($b = 0.8$). I_i^B denotes a specific bottom-up input from a lower cortical module, whereas I_i^T represents a specific top-down bias from higher

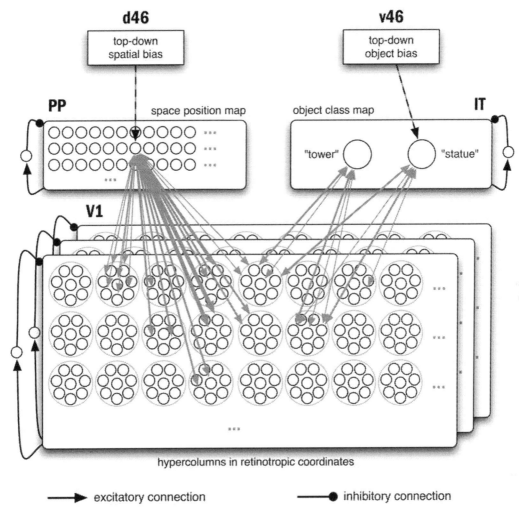

Figure 15.3. Schematic representation of biased competition model (Deco, 2001). Units within V1 hypercolumns coding eight orientations at three spatial scales are connected to (PP) units bidirectionally with Gaussian spatial distribution of weights. Units in IT are bidirectionally connected to every unit in V1 with variable weights defined through supervised Hebbian learning rule. (Only sample connections with various weights are shown.)

cortical modules. I_0 denotes a spontaneous background input, and v is an additive Gaussian noise in the system.

The inhibitory unit integrates information from all the excitatory units within the module and feeds back nonspecific inhibition to all excitatory units in the module. Its dynamics is defined by:

$$\tau_I \frac{\delta}{\delta t} A^I(t) = -A^I - c F(A^I(t))$$

$$+ d \sum_{i=1}^{m} F(A_i(t)).$$

With $\tau_I = 7$ ms, $c = 0.1$, and $d = 0.1$, the first two terms describe decay and self-excitation, respectively, whereas the third term is a function of activities of all excitatory units within the module connected to the inhibitory unit.

Input I_i^S of any connected module that provides either bottom-up input or top-down bias is described by:

$$I_i^S(t) = \alpha \sum_{j=1}^{n} w_{ij} F\left(A_j^S(t)\right),$$

where A_j^S denotes the activity level of the source module unit, w_{ij} denotes the connection weight between source unit j and target unit i, and $1/\alpha$ reflects an attenuation factor. Setting $\alpha = 1$ for bottom-up input and $\alpha = 0.6$ for top-down bias prevents the latter from dominating V1 units, and allows lower level representations to change the state of higher-order modules. The V1 module represents the input layer of the visual system and consists of a lattice of 33×33 hypercolumns topographically covering a 66- $\times$ -66-pixel scene. Each hypercolumn consists of twenty-four excitatory feature detector units (pools) representing eight spatial orientations in three spatial scales. The sensory input to the excitatory units is computed using 2D-Gabor functions, which act as local spatial bandpass filters detecting the presence of sensory input in a given orientation at a given spatial scale in the relevant location of the presented input image (for additional details, see Deco, 2001 and Lee, 1996). An additional inhibitory unit per scale is used to mediate global normalization within units at each scale.

The PP module encodes spatial location in the visual field, representing the function of the PPC. It consists of a lattice of 66×66 units, each of them receiving input from a limited spatial neighborhood of V1 hypercolumns. To capture the Gaussian-like nature of the spread of activation, the mutual connection weights between the units at hypercolumn pq in V1 and unit ij in PP are given by equation:

$$w_{pqij} = Ce^{-\frac{(i-p)^2+(j-q)^2}{2\sigma_w^2}} - B.$$

With $C = 1.5$, $B = 0.5$, and $\sigma_w = 2$, the resulting center-excitatory, surround-inhibitory weight profile connects bilaterally each PP unit to a spatial neighborhood of about 5×5 V1 hypercolumns, giving an effective receptive field of about 17 pixels in diameter. Local competition between PP units is ensured by one inhibitory unit that receives input from all excitatory units and inhibits all units uniformly, enabling WTA competition within PP.

The IT module encodes object class or categorical information corresponding to the function of inferotemporal cortex. IT consists of a finite set of units, each receiving connections from all units in V1 and returning attenuated symmetrical reciprocal feedback connections to V1. Similarly to PP, local competition is ensured by an additional inhibitory unit receiving excitatory input from and returning inhibitory feedback to all excitatory units in IT. Connection weights between V1 an IT are trained by supervised Hebbian learning. During learning, a target image is presented as input to V1 whereas top-down bias is imposed on PP unit coding for location of the target and IT unit coding for its identity. The network is allowed to settle into a steady state, after which all the relevant V1–IT connection weights are updated using Hebbian learning rule:

$$w_{ij} = w_{ij} + \eta F\left(A_i^{V1}(t)\right) F\left(A_j^{IT}(t)\right)$$

where η denotes the learning coefficient and t is large enough to allow for convergence. Having successfully learned to perform translation invariant object recognition, the model can operate in three modes: preattentive mode, spatial attention mode, and object attention mode (Deco, 2001; Deco & Lee, 2004). In the preattentive mode, no top-down biasing signal is provided. The perceptually most salient object in the visual field will cause a stronger input from feature maps to the representation of its location in the spatial map. This enhanced activation of the relevant location in the spatial map is then fed back to the feature maps, biasing their activation and thus the flow of information to the object recognition pathway. The recurrent, bidirectional flow of activity occurring in biased competition models results in a positive feedback loop that leads to iterative convergence on a single winning representation both in the spatial map as well as in the feature maps and the object identity module. This winning representation effectively marks both the position and the identity of the most salient object in the visual field.

In the spatial attention mode, object recognition at the attended location is implemented through preselecting a particular location in the representation of target location, presumably hosted in the dorsal PFC, which provides a top-down bias causing the activation of appropriate units in the spatial map. Feedback connections from the spatial map to the low-level feature maps enhance the activation of corresponding units, acting as a spatial attention beam. Excited by both the sensory input and the top-down signal from the spatial map, those units representing the features at the attended location will provide a stronger input to the related identity units in the higher-level maps, enabling them to win the local competition leading to identification of the object present at the attended location. In a model simulation, implementing a top-down spatial bias to PP results in an early differentiation of activity between the cell assemblies coding the target and distractor locations, respectively. The differentiation spreads both to V1 and IT, causing the cell assemblies coding the target object to be significantly more active than the ones coding the distractor object, signaling object identification.

The dynamics of the "object attention" mode mirrors that of the "spatial attention" mode. A biasing signal arising presumably from the ventral PFC leads to activation of the higher-level map units coding the identity of the attended object. Feedback connections to the low-level feature maps enhance the activity of units coding visual features of the attended object, effectively "back-projecting" the response pattern associated with the object across all retinotopic locations in parallel. The units receiving input from an appropriate visual stimulus will resonate best with the feedback signals leading to their enhanced activation. Providing stronger input to the units in the spatial map that code the position of the attended object will enable them to win the local competition, effectively completing visual search. Monitoring the dynamics of the model simulation reveals that the local competition is first resolved in the IT module, which then drives the competition in V1 and PP modules in favor of the units corresponding to the target object. The object is considered found when competition is eventually resolved in PP.

Simulations using the biased competition model were found to be successful in accounting for a number of empirical results in visual search (Deco & Lee, 2004; Deco & Zihl, 2001b). For example, the model showed that added difficulty of constraints in conjunction search tasks causes the network to take longer to settle. Congruent with behavioral findings, the times for the network to settle were independent of the number of distractors in a feature set task, whereas the times in conjunction search tasks were progressively longer with increasing number of distractors. Furthermore, reaction time slopes related to different types of conjunction search obtained by model simulations were successful in predicting subsequent psychophysical investigations (Deco et al., 2002). The model thus demonstrated that some, seemingly serial cognitive tasks may actually be a result of neuronal dynamics in a fully parallel system, bypassing the need for a dedicated implementation of a serial process guiding attentional spotlight from one item to the other.

Introducing artificial lesions in the model, enables testing of possible accounts of attentional deficits caused by brain lesions. Selective damage to the right side of the PP module reproduced some of the symptoms of the left spatial hemineglect typically caused by lesions to the right parietal cortex (Heinke et al., 2002). Replacing global inhibition with the local lateral inhibition enabled the model to also account for object-based neglect in which only the left side of the objects in the visual field is not seen (Deco & Rolls, 2002). Additionally, it also provided novel predictions about how patients with object-based neglect might perceive objects when they are joined with cross-links or brought toward each other (Deco & Rolls, 2002).

2.4. Key Issues in Models of Visual Attention

The present overview of visual attention models offers only selected highlights of some of the important progress being made in recent years. Advances in understanding

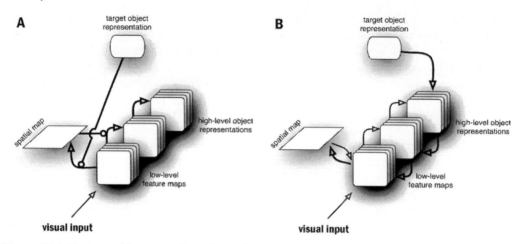

Figure 15.4. Two possible routes of top-down object attention. (A) In feedforward models, attention is guided by biasing input from the low-level feature maps to the spatial map that gates the flow of information to the higher levels of visual processing. (B) In biased competition account, the attention is guided by propagation of bias over rich recurrent connections from a high-level object representation to the low-level feature maps and through them, to the spatial map, ultimately leading the network to settle in a state representing the target object and its location.

of the architectural structure of the visual system have enabled the design of computational models that closely mimic the known neurophysiology of vision and are able to qualitatively match a wide variety of neurophysiological findings. They also agree with behavioral results coming from the basic experimental paradigms and with the data from brain-damaged patients suffering from attentional impairments. Nevertheless, despite convergence in a number of areas, important dilemmas still remain, most of them illustrated by the differences between the two basic categories of attentional architecture described earlier: feedforward versus biased competition (see Figure 15.4).

The core dilemma relates to the question of representation of attention: Should attention be represented explicitly in a single or perhaps in multiple spatial maps that code saliency of visual areas, or should it be represented implicitly in the interactive dynamics of the network? The first alternative is embodied in the models of attention centered around a feed-forward saliency map mechanism, which can be traced back to the proposal by Koch and Ullman (1985). In focusing on the problem of effective computation of saliency, these models have been effective in capturing the known neurobiology of

low-level visual processing, while simulating findings from the empirical visual search and natural scene viewing, and providing a successful architecture for various computer vision applications.

The second alternative builds on the conceptualization of attention as an emergent property of activation dynamics. It relies on rich recurrent connections between processing modules that bias local competition between representations. Although successful in replicating visual search findings, the true strength of these models lies in their ability to model the qualitative pattern of impairments associated with neuropsychologically based attentional disorders, such as the spatial neglect syndrome (Deco & Rolls, 2002), and in providing a coherent and seamless neural architecture that relates perception to action (Ward, 1999).

Both types of models exhibit a range of specific strengths and weaknesses. Their future development will depend on their ability to relate to the known brain anatomy and physiology (Shipp, 2004). In this regard, those models that incorporate a detailed mathematical description of neuronal dynamics are already successful in replicating and predicting spiking activity of single neurons (Deco & Rolls, 2003, 2005b), as well as local population dynamics, as reflected in the hemodynamical response observed with functional magnetic resonance imaging (fMRI; Deco et al., 2004). Besides the models presented here, there are also other contenders providing alternative approaches that should be considered, among them, Bundesen's Theory of Visual Attention (TVA). It started as a formal mathematical theory describing behavioral results (Bundesen, 1990, 1998), but was recently developed into a neural theory (Bundesen, Habekost, & Kyllingsbaek, 2005), which successfully applies the same basic equations to provide both a quantitative account of human performance on a set of attentional experimental paradigms and an account of a range of attentional phenomena studied at the single cell level using electrophysiology.

Furthermore, the models of visual attention will also need to successfully scale up toward the more complex visual tasks, including higher-level cognitive processing (Deco & Rolls, 2005a; Navalpakkam & Itti, 2005). Moreover, to provide a comprehensive description of visual attention and to eliminate any remnant of the "ghost in the machine," the models of attention in visual processing will have to be related to those explaining the ways in which top-down, goal-driven intentions are represented, manipulated, and controlled. These models have been developed and explored within the research of cognitive control, which will be addressed in the following section.

3. Models of Goal-Driven Attentional Control

For many theorists, the terms executive control, cognitive control, controlled attention, and executive attention are interchangeable (and they will be used somewhat interchangeably here as well), referring to the notion that sometimes attention appears to be directed in a top-down, volitional fashion according to abstract, internally represented goals, rather than by detection or extraction of specific perceptual features or objects. Similarly, in some cases, attention appears to have its effect in biasing the selection of

actions rather than inputs, or more globally, in modulating whole task-processing pathways rather than specific components of perception.

Cognitive control is often described in opposition to automaticity. Automaticity refers to the capacity of a cognitive system to streamline well-practiced behavior, so that task-relevant actions can be executed with minimal effort. As a complement to automatic behavior, cognitive control refers instead to the effortful biasing or inhibiting of sensory-motor information in the service of novel and unpracticed goal-directed behaviors. Top-down attention is what arises out of the neuronal activity shift guided by cognitive control, and it is typically assumed to be the product of biasing representations (such as intentions, rules, goals, and task demands) in the PFC that compete with perceptually based representations in the posterior cortex. Cognitive control is the mechanism that guides the entire cognitive system and orchestrates thinking and acting, and top-down attention is interpreted as its main emergent consequence.

Computational models seem best positioned to describe how top-down attentional control is engaged during the course of task processing and to indicate the consequences of such engagement. Critically, the explanations that arrive out of computational models are explicitly mechanistic in character, and they minimize the reliance on a hidden homunculus. Although formal theoretical investigations in the study of cognitive control have not advanced to the same degree as those in visual selective attention, there have been a number of computational models developed in this domain. Many of these models adopt the biased competition framework discussed in the preceding section as a core architectural assumption. Additionally, a primary focus of most models has been to address human experimental data, arising from basic cognitive performance, neuropsychological impairment, and neuroimaging findings, particularly regarding PFC function. This may be because many of the core phenomena of cognitive control relate to tasks most easily examined in humans, although this

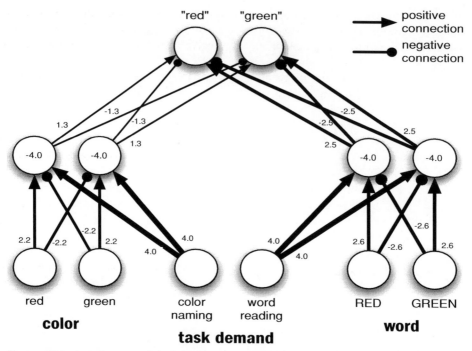

Figure 15.5. J. Cohen's model of the Stroop test (Cohen et al., 1990) This model provides a minimal account of top-down attentional biasing effects emerging from prefrontal cortex-based task-set representations.

has begun to change more recently (e.g., Miller & Cohen, 2001). In the next section, a fundamental but minimal model that illustrates the core principles of cognitive control is described first, then other key cognitive control models and the attentional issues they address are discussed.

3.1. *The Base Model*

A basic model that illustrates the key hypothesized mechanisms of attentional control is one developed by Cohen, Dunbar, and McClelland (1990) to account for processing and behavioral performance during the classic Stroop test (Stroop, 1935) of selective attention. The Stroop test may represent the paradigmatic example of the relationship and contrast between automaticity and cognitive control. The basic paradigm (although there have been many different variants) involves processing of colored word stimuli and selectively attending to either the word name or ink color. Attention is thought to be more critical for color nam-

ing than word reading, because the latter skill is so highly overlearned and practiced for most literate adults. The role of attention is especially critical for color naming in incongruent trials in which there is a direct conflict between the ink color and the color indicated by the word name (e.g., the word "GREEN" in red ink). In such a case, cognitive control over attention must enable preferential processing in a weaker task pathway (color naming) over a competing and stronger but task-irrelevant one (word reading).

The Cohen et al. (1990) model put forth a highly influential framework for understanding the mechanisms of cognitive control and attention in the Stroop task. Critically, the model illustrates very simple principles of biased competition in that attention is just another source of input that serves to strengthen the activation of hidden layer units, which then leads to a shift in the outcome of competition within a response layer (see Figure 15.5). The original model is feed-forward, although later models have used a fully bidirectional architecture (Cohen & Huston, 1994; O'Reilly & Munakata, 2000) that includes more natural lateral inhibitory mechanisms. The model uses a standard connectionist activation framework in which the activation a_j of each unit j at time t is a logistic function of the net input:

$$a_j(t) = \frac{1}{1 + e^{-net_j(t)}}.$$

The net input from every unit i into unit j is first computed as:

$$rawnet_j(t) = \sum_i a_i(t)w_{ij}$$

where w_{ij} is the weight from each unit i to unit j. This raw net input is then transformed into a "cascade" form (McClelland, 1979) to simulate continuous time dynamics:

$$net_j(t) = ((1 - \tau)^* net_j(t - 1))$$
$$+ (\tau^* rawnet_j(t))$$

where τ is a constant.

Attention demands arise in the model because of the asymmetry of weight strengths in the word-reading versus color-naming task pathways. This asymmetry arises during a learning phase in which the network receives greater practice in word reading than color naming. Because the training phase is accomplished with the backpropagation learning algorithm (Rumelhart & McClelland, 1986), weight strengths change in direct proportion to training experience. The key attentional mechanism arises from the task demand units, which represent top-down attentional effects arising out of the PFC. These units have a sensitizing effect on hidden-layer activation, particularly for the color pathway, such that with task demand (attentional) input, the color hidden units are maximally sensitive to stimulus input and can compete strongly with activation arising out of the word pathway. The magnitude of the attentional effects depend on

the size of the weights from the task demand units to the hidden layer, and they are computed as a cascading net input defined as in the previous equation.

Another core principle behind this model, which was also present in the original Norman and Shallice (1986) theory of cognitive control, is that the attentional system does not directly enable task processing, but only modulates its efficacy. This can be illustrated in the model in that the two task pathways, representing word reading and color naming, can each work in isolation (i.e., for unidimensional stimuli) to produce task-appropriate processing and responses, even in the absence of attentional signals. However, when both the word-reading and color-naming pathways are simultaneously engaged, competition between the two dimensions that occurs at the level of overlapping response representations produces a demand for attentional intervention. This demand for attention is most acute when performing color naming under competition conditions, because of the weaker strength of the color pathway. Thus, in the absence of attentional modulation, the word-reading pathway will dominate processing competition at the response layer.

In contrast, when there is an attentional influence from the task demand input on the color pathway, this pathway can successfully compete with the otherwise stronger word pathway by providing a stronger input to the response layer from the color-naming hidden layer. In the model, the mechanism of attentional modulation occurs via a nonlinearity of the activation function in task-processing units, such that, under the influence of top-down control, the activation function will be in its most sensitive region to be activated by bottom-up input, whereas without such an influence, the sensitivity to input is greatly reduced. Such top-down biasing mechanisms cause the color pathway to be more sensitive to the presence of color stimuli. This effect leads to a shift in the outcome of competition such that the color dimension successfully drives the response.

It is important to note that in the Stroop model, attention serves as an emergent influence in that the activity in the task demand unit has a top-down biasing effect on the information processing taking place in the rest of the network. But this top-down biasing role does not have any special property, that is, these higher-level units are conceptually identical to the other units in the network. Therefore, attention is framed as a very general property that can arise out of the influence that representations of any kind can have on processing of information taking place in any other area.

A further postulate of the Cohen et al. model of attentional control, which was further elaborated in later papers (Cohen, Braver, & O'Reilly, 1996; Cohen & Huston, 1994; Cohen & Servan-Schreiber, 1992), goal-driven attentional biasing effects are critically related to the functions of PFC. In this region, goal-related contextual information is thought to be actively represented and feeds back into other regions of the posterior neocortex, where it can exert a top-down bias on competitive interactions occurring among local populations (Miller & Cohen, 2001). As a consequence of this coordinative activity, the PFC can both implement a top-down sustained attentional function (to keep active and operate on representations elsewhere in the brain) and also an inhibitory one (to suppress task-irrelevant pathways), but with this latter function emerging as an indirect consequence of excitatory attentional bias on local competitions, rather than via a direct top-down inhibitory signal.

3.2. Extensions and Alternatives to the Base Model

This basic mechanism of PFC-mediated top-down attentional biasing that forms the core of the Stroop model has provided a relatively comprehensive and influential account of a range of empirical phenomena. Moreover, the same architectural framework has been utilized to simulate a range of other attentional phenomena in the Stroop task and in other attention and cognitive control paradigms (e.g., Barch et al., 1999; Braver

& Cohen, 2001; Carter et al., 1998; Cohen et al., 1994; Dehaene & Changeux, 1991; Servan-Schreiber et al., 1998). A recent extension of the basic model was utilized to address fMRI data regarding the activation of PFC and posterior cortical regions during Stroop performance (Herd, Banich, & O'Reilly, 2006). A key feature of this recent model was the addition of a separate task demand unit coding for general color-related representations, both perceptual and linguistic. In other studies using the Stroop model as a theoretical framework, the primary motivation was to investigate the cognitive impairments in schizophrenia, a psychiatric condition believed to involve impairments of cognitive control due to alterations in the transmission of dopamine in the PFC. Individuals with schizophrenia, for example, are well known to show particularly large interference effects in the Stroop task, although recent data have suggested that the empirical phenomena are more complex than originally thought (Barch, Carter, & Cohen, 2004). The Cohen et al. (1990) model suggests that weakened attentional representations in schizophrenia patients impair the ability to successfully bias competition in favor of color naming over word reading, even when required by task conditions (Cohen & Servan-Schreiber, 1992).

Given the role of the Stroop task as the paradigmatic example of selective attention, it is perhaps not surprising that a variety of alternative computational models have been developed to explain attention in the Stroop. Yet, in many ways, these alternative models, which have been developed in both connectionist and symbolic architectures, can be seen as being formally very analogous in terms of attentional mechanisms to the Cohen et al. (1990) account. However, some of the models have had different emphasis, such as to try to explain Stroop phenomena within more generic and comprehensive architectural frameworks, such as modeling of visual attention more broadly (Phaf et al., 1990) and word reading (Roelofs, 2000), or to account for potential high-level strategic variability (Lovett, 2002).

However, another recent model, put forth by Melara and Algom (2003), may provide an important conceptual alternative to the Cohen et al. (1990) Stroop model. In this so-called tectonic model, Stroop attentional effects are conceived of as being due to a continuous process of experience-dependent learning within two memory-based structures (the name *tectonic* for this theory, from the ancient Greek word *tektonikon*, meaning *to structure*, is due to this central feature of the model). One structure is a short-term memory of the dimensional uncertainty of the most recent trials, where values along the word dimension are more varied perceptually than values along the color dimension. The other structure is a long-term memory of the dimensional unbalance, storing asymmetry in the record of the observer's past efficiency in accessing the target dimension relative to the distractor dimension. This structure reflects the relative difficulty with which the currently accessed representations can be activated in long-term memory. Each structure contributes to building up excitation of the task-relevant dimension and inhibition of the task-irrelevant dimension. This complex model (see Melara & Algom, 2003, for equations and all technical details) has been shown to account for an impressive set of empirical behavioral phenomena that extend from the standard Stroop findings to other related effects, such as Garner interference. Nevertheless, the differences in the models may relate not to top-down attentional mechanisms per se, but to their interaction with a dynamically changing perceptual representation. Further work should be conducted to test the relationship between the Cohen et al. (1990) and tectonic model framework more systematically.

Subsequent models have attempted to expand the scope of the basic Stroop account by addressing the issue of the relationship of attention to the related construct of working memory. In particular, Cohen, Braver, and colleagues developed a model that integrated top-down biasing with the well-established active maintenance functions of PFC and also attempted to more thoroughly capture both the facilitation and inhibition effects of attention (Braver, Cohen, & Barch, 2002; Braver, Cohen, & Servan-Schreiber, 1995; Cohen et al., 1996). In this model, the central role of PFC is still to adapt the behavior of the entire cognitive system to the task demands via active representation of goal-related context, but additionally, the later models incorporated explicit mechanisms by which PFC representations could be actively maintained over time. Thus, in these models, top-down attentional effects could emerge following a delay interposed after presentation of a contextual cue. A further feature of this work was explicit incorporation of dopamine-mediated neuromodulation of PFC representations (Barch & Cohen, 1999; Braver & Cohen, 2000; Braver et al., 1995; Cohen, Braver & Brown, 2002). This dopamine modulatory input served both to stabilize active maintenance processes (via tonic dopamine activation in PFC) and to enable appropriate updating of PFC representations (via phasic dopamine activation, synchronous with cues indicating a new task goal or context). Other recent work has explored how norepinephrine neuromodulation, in addition to dopamine, might also play a particular role in modulating attentional focus (Aston-Jones & Cohen, 2005; Usher & Cohen, 1999; Yu & Dayan, 2005). More recently, a number of other models have been developed by distinct groups of investigators to address similar issues, but with more biologically detailed and realistic computational architectures (e.g., spiking units, distinct synaptic currents; Brunel & Wang, 2001; Durstewitz, Kelc, & Gunturkun, 1999). Nevertheless, these models have converged on similar prinicples regarding the role of biased competition mechanisms, active maintenance in PFC, and also dopaminergic neuromodulation in accounting for attentional effects in Stroop-like and other selective attention and working memory paradigms (for reviews of this work, see Cohen et al., 2002; Durstewitz et al., 2000; O'Reilly, 2006).

Another key issue first addressed by the Stroop model but expanded in subsequent work is the role of inhibitory mechanisms in attention. In the Stroop model and many other biased competition based models of top-down attentional control, inhibition effects emerge as an indirect consequence of local competition, rather than as a direct explicit inhibitory mechanism. Yet, it is still controversial as to whether or not top-down attentional mechanisms might include a special inhibitory function, at least in some cases, such as in response inhibition tasks (Aron & Poldrack, 2006). There have been computational models developed that postulate a specialized role for direct attentional inhibition mechanisms as an alternative to the standard biased competition account as a means of explaining distractor suppression and negative priming type effects (Houghton & Tipper, 1996). However, even in this model, there is no "central" top-down inhibition mechanism; rather, the inhibitory effects are achieved by local positive and negative feedback circuits thought to be widely distributed throughout the brain.

A final area of recent activity in elaborating on the computational mechanisms of goal-driven attention concerns mechanisms by which attentional biases arise or are modulated during the course of task performance. In particular, one influential account has suggested that top-down attentional biases are modulated in response to mechanisms that monitor dimensions of ongoing performance. Specifically, it has been postulated that the anterior cingulate cortex (ACC) detects response conflict present during task performance and translates this conflict index into an output signal that modulates attentional biases within lateral PFC (Botvinick et al., 2001). The basic hypothesis is that when high conflict occurs between different motor or behavioral responses, cognitive control mechanisms intervene to bias the relevant response versus the others, thus overcoming the conflict. These interactions have been characterized

in terms of a single conflict-control loop mechanism, where the performance of certain task conditions leads to detection of response conflict, which in turn leads to the engagement or increase of cognitive control, and in improved conflict resolution in subsequent performance. However, a new model proposes that ACC–PFC interactions are described by two, rather than one, distinct conflict-control loops (De Pisapia & Braver, 2006). The first loop implements a reactive control mechanism in which conflict detected in ACC over a short-time scale transiently modulates PFC activity to adjust within-trial attentional biases. The second loop implements a proactive control mechanism, in which long-time scale conflict is also detected in ACC and more slowly adjusts attentional biases in PFC across trials. The model was used to successfully account for detailed aspects of behavioral and brain activation patterns in the Stroop task.

3.3. *Multi-Tasking*

The previous sections described computational models of attention that operate at different levels of information processing, from fine-grained influence on visual perception to representations of goal information actively maintained in working memory. An intriguing question that has recently been garnering a great deal of theoretical interest is whether there are even higher forms of attention, such as those that can aid in the selection of one out of many possible tasks to perform. In particular, the question is whether the attentional biasing effects discussed previously can operate not just at the level of perceptual features (e.g., red vs. green colors) or dimensions (color vs. word), but that can also influence the activation of whole task pathways over competing pathways. This issue becomes more clear when considering multitasking situations, which seem to approximate well the real-world demands of everyday cognition. In the so-called multi-tasking situations, more than one task needs to be performed at a time, either through simultaneous (i.e., nested or interleaved) engagement or through rapid

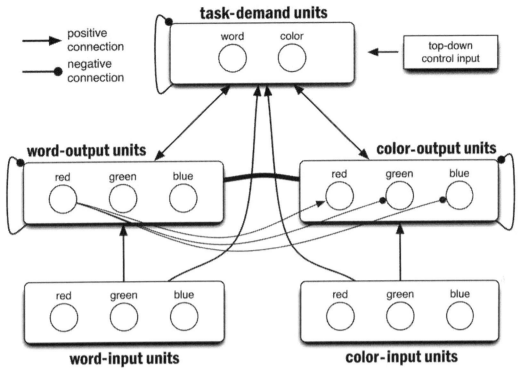

Figure 15.6. The Gilbert and Shallice (2002) model of task switching. This model is built on and extends earlier connectionist models of the Stroop task (Cohen et al., 1990; Cohen & Huston, 1994).

sequential alternation. Such situations seem to pose heavy attentional demands, and therefore they provide an excellent test bed for cognitive theories on attention at the task or dimensional level, rather than at the featural level of the stimuli.

One particular focus has been on *task switching*, an experimental paradigm requiring rapid switching among two or more tasks, in either an uncued-but-predictable or cued-but-random sequence. One consistent finding of such task-switching experiments is that there are reliable and robust *switch costs*; for example, performance is poorer on a trial in which the task is switched, in terms of both longer reaction times and a higher percentage of errors, compared with when the task is repeated. The original explanation for this finding is that a special time-consuming internal reconfiguration process is required to switch between tasks, which enables the engagement or "loading in" of the appropriate task representations that can bias attention appropriately during task per-

formance. However, an important question is whether this task-set reconfiguration process actually requires a dedicated mechanism that enables the appropriate form of attentional shift. A few theoretical models have been developed that provide an account of the types of attentional control and reconfiguration mechanisms involved in task switching.

One influential theoretical account of task switching that has been instantiated as a computational model is that of Gilbert & Shallice (2002; see Figure 15.6), which adopted the basic interactive architecture used in later models of the Stroop task (Cohen & Huston, 1994; O'Reilly & Munakata, 2000). The network consists of two separate input and output layers for words and colors, and a task-demand layer. In addition to top-down attentional effects, the task-demand units receive bottom-up connections from the input layers and the response layer. These bottom-up inputs allow for associative learning effects and item-specific priming based on past experiences. The task-demand layer has one unit for the color-naming task and one unit for the word-reading task. Thus, the model has the potential to implement task-switching paradigms by shifting which task-set unit is active. Lateral inhibition between task pathways provides a means for top-down excitatory input to bias the outcome of representational competition. Task-demand units receive an input from a top-down control input, which specifies which of the two tasks the network has to execute for a particular trial.

All units in the model compute activations in response to the weighted sum of all incoming inputs, both top-down and bottom-up. Thus, as in the Cohen et al. (1990) Stroop model, there is no distinction between task-demand (attentional) input and bottom-up perceptual signals. The activations themselves are computed as in the standard interactive activation equations (McClelland & Rumelhart, 1981), where the increase in activation for each cycle is given by:

if the net input is positive:
$$\Delta act = step^* net^* (max - act)$$

if the net input is negative:
$$\Delta act = step^* net^* (act - min)$$

where *step* is the step size (establishing the speed of the activation update in each cycle), *net* is the net input, *max* is the maximum activation value allowed, and *min* is the minimum activation value. A random Gaussian noise is also added to the activation values of each unit.

The core feature of this model is that the task-demand units retain a residual level of activation even after that task is completed. This type of mechanism implements a version of the task-carryover account (Allport, Styles, & Hsieh, 1994), which postulates that switch costs are due to interference between this residual task-set activation and the engagement of a new task-set representation corresponding to the cur-

rently relevant task. Importantly, however, the model suggests that there is no specialized reconfiguration mechanism that is only engaged on switch trials. Activation of the relevant task-set representation occurs in the same way on every trial; it is just that on switch trials, there is increased competition between this new representation and the residual activation from the previously engaged task representation. Such competition does not occur on task-repeat trials when the same task-set representation as the previous trial is activated again.

A second important attentional mechanism implemented in the Gilbert and Shallice (2002) model is the bottom-up activation of task-set representations from features of task stimuli. The model implements a Hebbian (i.e., activity-dependent) learning mechanism. The weights between the stimulus input j and task demand units i are set with the learning rate *lrate* according following equation:

$$w_{ij} = lrate^* a_j^* a_i$$

This equation does not establish an update of the weights based on previous values, but instead the weights are calculated as new at the end of each trial, and the weights derived only affect the model's performance in the next trial. This mechanism allows the learning of associations between an active task-set representation and the particular stimulus features present on a task trial. This learning effect means that if such features are presented again on the subsequent trial, they will have the ability to "prime" the previously associated task-set representation due to strengthened associative weights.

Gilbert and Shallice (2002) applied their model to a task-switching version of the Stroop task (in which word reading and color naming randomly alternate across trials). The model was able to account for a wide range of experimental phenomena, including not only switch-cost effects and their temporal dynamics, but also phenomena related to item-specific priming effects as well. Importantly, the model's ability to account for task-related attention does not rely on any type of specialized representations or mechanisms, but instead generalized mechanisms of biased competition, which play out not only in task-specific processing layers but also within the task-demand layer. Moreover, because the model is fully bidirectional and interactive, attention effects are fully emergent and can arise not only because of task-demand inputs, but also via effects emanating from the input level. However, one limitation of the Gilbert and Shallice (2002) model is that it does not address the question of whether task-demand representations themselves involve specialized content or coding schemes or how such "global" representations develop. This issue is taken up again in the concluding section of the chapter.

The Gilbert and Shallice (2002) model provides a useful starting point for understanding some of the core issues regarding computational mechanisms of task switching. In the last few years, other researchers have begun developing models that address some additional key issues in this literature. One issue concerns the mechanisms of task-set updating and advance task preparation and biasing. Some models have suggested that updating and advance preparation may occur in an all-or-none manner, but probabilistically across trials (Reynolds et al., 2006), or across the preparation interval (Sohn & Anderson, 2001). Interestingly, the Reynolds et al. (2006) model also makes contact with earlier models by postulating that dopamine neuromodulation is the source of the task-set updating and maintenance signal. In a second set of mathematical models, Logan and colleagues have argued that it is not necessary to postulate mechanisms of advance preparation and that task switching can occur purely retroactively as a retrieval process driven by the target presentation (Schneider & Logan, 2005). A different issue that has been addressed is the role of higher-order sequential processes in task switching (Brown, Reynolds, & Braver, 2006). In this work, conflict-control loops similar to those postulated in the previously described models of ACC–PFC interactions (i.e., Botvinick et al., 2001) adjust both attentional biases and response speed across trials in response to the experience of interference due to either task switches or the processing of task-irrelevant features.

3.4. Dual-Task Coordination

A second important component of multi-tasking arises in dual-task conditions, where two tasks must be performed in an overlapping period of time, such that some coordination or time sharing of processing resources is needed. Within this latter domain, there has been a great deal of interest in the so-called psychological refractory period (PRP) paradigm. In this dual-task paradigm, the relative timing of the two tasks is strictly controlled by manipulating the onset time of the target stimulus for the second task (termed T2) relative to the timing of the first task stimulus (termed T1). The basic finding is that that when the T2 onset time is short (relative to T1 reaction times), this causes an additional slowing of T2 reaction time (but not T1), which is termed the PRP effect. The primary theoretical interpretation of this effect is that there are certain stages of task processing that are particularly sensitive to dual-task overlap or interference and that some form of coordination mechanism is invoked to "serialize" processing as a means of minimizing this interference (Pashler, 1994).

Logan and Gordon (2001) developed a formal mathematical model that accounts for dual-task situations and used the model to extensively investigate the PRP effect. They found that only a model with a dedicated attention-switching mechanism was capable of fitting the behavioral data, thus suggesting that some form of reconfiguration of attention control takes place in overlapping task situations. Specifically, according to the model, a task-set refers to a particular set of control parameters that govern strategic aspects of how task stimuli are processed. When processing must rapidly shift from one task to another, new control parameters have to be loaded, which may take a fixed amount of time. Ironically, as discussed earlier, this attention-switching mechanism was not found to be necessary to account for switch-cost effects in explicit task-switching paradigms (Logan, 2005). This is because the model does not assume any form of persistent storage of old control parameters after a task trial has been completed. In other words, according to the model, task-set switching processes will only affect performance latency when two tasks are overlapping in time.

Kieras and colleagues (Meyer & Kieras, 1997) have also modeled PRP effects in multitasking situations using the Executive-Process Interactive Control (EPIC) symbolic computational architecture. Their account of PRP phenomena assumes that dual-task coordination is purely under strategic control and that any form of serializing, time-sharing, or switching processes are not mandatory for performance. Instead, scheduling and task deferment is introduced in PRP situations to avoid potential interference or ordering confusions between tasks (e.g., responding to T2 before T1). Task deferment is accomplished by activation of a time-consuming control mechanism that implements lock and unlock commands on T2 processing. Thus, the engagement of this control mechanism is the source of PRP effects. Nevertheless, a key aspect of the model is that the point at which further T2 processing is "locked-out" (and then "unlocked" again) can depend on complex relationships between the two tasks and other experimental demands. Such flexible deferment implies an attentional control system that is strategic and subject to adjustments based on task experience. Typically, in simulations with the model, the primary determinant of changes in task-scheduling and deferment strategies is the presence of response level conflict or cross-talk. Thus, although as yet unexplored, the EPIC model may provide an account of the PRP effect that relies on dynamic conflict-control loop mechanisms similar to that postulated in the conflict monitoring account.

Other symbolic architectures, such as ACT-R, have also addressed the issue of dual-task coordination and PRP effects (Byrne & Anderson, 2001). In the ACT-R framework, the different modules – containing production rules – are intrinsically serial. Thus, in overlapping dual-task situations, ACT-R naturally implements a task-processing bottleneck that can induce PRP-type slowing. The inherent seriality of ACT-R sets it apart from both EPIC and other cognitive architectures in the treatment of dual-task attentional control.

A final issue that is just beginning to be explored is the more generic role of task-scheduling processes during multitask environments. The critical problem is that many multitask situations require a continuous and repeated inter-leaving of processing across different tasks due to the tasks' complexity and duration. Thus, in addition to the problem of time sharing, multitask coordination in these situations also requires mechanisms that can handle more complex scheduling processes, such as interruption and time-dependent resumption. Such complexity might seem to require a more general-purpose high-level controller that can carry out the appropriate scheduling and coordination functions when needed, across a wide variety of multitask situations. A recent model using the ACT-R architecture has been used to examine the functionality of a general purpose executive controller (Salvucci, 2005). The model proposes that generic multitasking abilities are accomplished through a goal-queuing mechanism that sets time-based priorities on the execution of different goals, and thus allows effective scheduling within the constraints of a serialized goal-execution process. The model was effectively applied to the task of driving in a virtual environment, with required control and monitoring of all its subtask components. It seems clear that this form of generic goal-queuing mechanism may represent the highest form of attentional control by specifying not only how attention gets allocated to a particular task, but also when and with what priority the attentional allocation process occurs.

3.5. *Automaticity: Actions Without Attention?*

The general concept that behaviors executed repeatedly become less demanding and less effortful – a view that is clearly in line with subjective experience – has been studied at least since the dawn of modern psychology (James, 1890). More recently, this idea of automaticity has been considered to describe a specific mode of functioning in the mind/brain after extensive training in the execution of tasks. This automatic mode of processing enables performance to be qualitatively more efficient, robust, and rapid (Posner & Snyder, 1975; Schneider & Shiffrin, 1977). The key aspects that define automatic task processing are: (1) a decrease in effort, (2) an increase in speed along with practice, (3) no dependency on voluntary control, and (4) no interference with concurrent processes. A hybrid symbolic-connectionist computational architecture (CAP2) that accounts for these aspects can be found in Schneider and Chein (2003). It consists of a network of task-processing modules, each of which is a connectionist network linked with a central control system sending priority signals. The key process in this framework that enables a transition from controlled to automatic processing is a reduction in the requirement for such control signal intervention to ensure appropriate processing and selection in the distributed network of task-processing modules. Specifically, in the controlled processing state, control signal input is required for selection and amplification of the output of task-relevant processing modules, such that these outputs can be broadcast to other modules (e.g., those involved in response generation). In the automatic state, learning has occurred that enables certain outputs of a module to be coded as high priority, which then enables transmission to other modules, even in the absence of control system inputs. Thus, the transition from controlled to au-

tomatic processing in this model can be seen as a shift in whether attentional selection is governed by top-down or bottom-up biasing mechanisms.

One question that has been debated is whether automaticity reduces or even stops the demands of attention. The view taken in connectionist modeling is that automaticity does not completely shut off the requirement of attention, but simply reduces it. In other words, the role of controlled attention in task execution is not of the all-or-none variety. Graded and continuous attributes of automaticity, as well as of attention, should instead be considered. In the Stroop models of Cohen et al. (1990) described earlier, color naming is considered in need of attention. However, word reading, even though considered to be automatic, also still requires a top-down modulatory input from the task-demand units to generate a response within an appropriate timeframe. Therefore, word reading requires attentional control, although to a much lesser extent than color naming due to the stronger weights on the word-reading pathway.

A rather detailed analysis and model of the processes associated with automaticity can be found in the ACT-R framework (e.g., in Anderson, 1992). The basic view is that automaticity is due to the progressive compilation and associative linking of task-related production rules due to extensive training. The ACT-R framework has provided the most successful and comprehensive account to date regarding phenomena associated with automatization of processing, such as the power law rule of learning.

Another formal theory of automaticity can be found in Logan (2005). The key principle of this theory is that novel actions must be executed sequentially, according to a step-by-step algorithm. However, after the completion of each such action, a memory trace of its execution is formed. In the future, when that action is required again, it can be executed step by step as before or by accessing its memory, depending on which is faster. Each performance of an action and accumulation of experience leads to the storage of further (discrete) instances of the action in memory, which in turn leads to a higher likelihood that one of these instances will be retrieved from memory and faster than the algorithm, thus producing automaticity.

3.6. *Unresolved Issues and Future Directions*

Several key issues remain unresolved in research on attentional control, and many research challenges still await a solution. A fundamental issue concerns the well-known capacity-limited nature of attention and cognitive control. Cognitive control is effortful, and the capacity to maintain task-relevant representations active even for intervals of seconds is a very limited ability, as several studies on these constraints have shown (Ansorge, 2004; Cowan, 2001; Engle, Kane, & Tuholski, 1999; Schneider & Shiffrin, 1977). But a clear theoretical justification for capacity constraints is still lacking, except for speculations that they are due to limitations of metabolic resources (Just et al., 2001) or that they are an emergent computational property arising from the necessity to constrain a massively parallel computer (the brain) into actions that have to be performed serially and unequivocally (Allport, 1989). A further speculation may have to do with competitive interactions between actively maintained goal representations in PFC, such that only a limited number can be sustained simultaneously without mutual interference or decay (O'Reilly, Braver, & Cohen, 1999; Usher & Cohen, 1999).

Another issue relates to exactly how attentional control is engaged and implemented and its relationship with conflict. The conflict-monitoring hypothesis of ACC–PFC interactions starts to tackle this issue, but convincing explanations and experimental verification of how conflict modulates control is still an open question. Is the information conveyed by the conflict signal precise enough to even address specific attentional control strategies that may be implemented in PFC? Other more general issues relate to the nature and function-

ing of the attention-related representations thought to be housed in PFC. These are usually referred to as rules, task demands, intentions, or goals, but explanations of how the anterior part of the neocortex implements and develops these representations is only just beginning. Such theoretical developments are critical for understanding the potentially specialized role of PFC representations in attention and for understanding their power in enabling flexible behavior.

One attempt to examine and understand the nature and development of PFC goal representations involved simulations training a single model to perform several different cognitive control tasks through an interleaved learning protocol (Rougier et al., 2005). As a result of this training, the model self-organized to develop abstract rule-like representations that preferentially coded dimensional properties of task stimuli. These representations were found to be sufficient to enable the model to successfully perform new attentional tasks, such as the Stroop without additional specialized training. Most importantly, the developed representations also enabled a high degree of within-task generalization, such that appropriate performance could be exhibited by the model for stimuli that it had never previously encountered during training. However, this model constitutes only a first attempt to understand the nature of PFC representations and their functionality. More complex forms of complex symbolic reasoning still remain to be addressed, for example, the dynamical recombination of different representations and how these interact with other cognitive systems. Nonetheless, it is an important manifestation of how computational modeling can provide an understanding of even hard dilemmas, such as flexible attentional control, without recourse to the homunculus.

Even setting aside questions of how goal-related representations develop, there are other important questions of the activation dynamics of such representations. For one, how is it possible to maintain a goal or intention for days and years, and not just seconds, as is usually modeled? These representations cannot be explained just by active representations in PFC, but necessarily by some other flexible mechanism acting in a much larger time scale. One such mechanism may involve the storage and retrieval of goal information in episodic memory. However, the specifics of whether, how, and when such storage occurs are as yet unknown. A related issue concerns the scheduling of attentional control for goals and subgoals in the execution of complex tasks. The precise neural mechanisms involved in the coordination, transformation, and integration of stored and hierarchically organized information in complex task situations are still poorly understood. Recent empirical studies have begun to focus investigation on the most anterior part of the PFC as critical for a variety of goal-scheduling functions, such as branching (Koechlin et al., 1999), deferral (Burgess et al., 2003) and integration/coordination (Braver & Bongiolatti, 2002; De Pisapia & Braver, in press) during multitask conditions. But, as yet, there have been no computational models developed that can integrate and synthesize the accumulating data into an account of how anterior PFC mechanisms might specifically contribute to high-level multitasking functions.

A final important issue relates to how attention relates to other critical constructs and motivation, such as emotion, motivation, and consciousness. With regard to emotion, it is clear that any comprehensive theory of attention will need to address how attentional mechanisms are modulated by internal estimates of value. Yet, at this point, models of attention have been developed independently of affective/motivational considerations and vice versa. Nevertheless, the inclusion of neural mechanisms in attentional models that are also thought to have affective and motivational functions, such as the ACC and dopamine neurotransmitter system, may point to the route for these constructs to be eventually integrated within a unified framework.

With regard to consciousness, it seems critical to understand why voluntary attentional control and the effort it requires seem very prominent in subjective experience, whereas other forms of attentional modulation seem to go on in the absence of awareness. A recent review (Maia & Cleeremans, 2005) suggests the intriguing possibility that computational modeling of cognitive control and the biased competition framework could provide the theoretical path for an integration of attentional control with consciousness and working memory based on the idea of global competition between representations with the top-down biasing from PFC. These and other questions on attentional control and related cognitive constructs, as interesting as they are, remain without convincing answers.

4. Conclusion

This chapter has reviewed key computational models and theoretical directions pursued by researchers trying to understand the multifaceted phenomenon of attention. A broad division is drawn between theories and models addressing the mechanisms by which attention modulates specific aspects of perception (primarily visual) and those that have focused on goal-driven and task-oriented components of attention. Although the scope of the field is broad, the various accounts that have been put forth all seem to converge on the idea that attention can be understood as the mechanisms of focused selection and enhancement of currently processed information, and the suppression of perceived background aspects. Inquiring more specifically into how these mechanisms actually work has produced many more questions than answers, and this proliferation of unresolved issues likely will not end soon. On the other hand, over the last twenty years, there has been tremendous progress in the number and success of attempts to embody theoretical hypothesis into explicit computational and mathematical models. A particularly noteworthy point of convergence has been the widespread adoption of the biased competition framework as the core computational backbone of many attention models. More islands of growing convergence will probably emerge in the coming years. Implemented models are the main instrument that researchers have available to substantiate or falsify their theories. The use of formal models that serve as explicit information-processing devices and that do not assume an internal observer or hidden homunculus will be critical in the effort to eventually fit, predict, and decompose human data from complex cognitive activities down to the most elemental components.

References

Allport, A. (1989). Visual attention. In M. I. Posner (Ed.), *Foundations of cognitive science* (pp. 631–682). Cambridge, MA: The MIT Press.

Allport, A., Styles, E. A., & Hsieh, S. (1994). Shifting intentional set: Exploring the dynamic control of tasks. In C. Umilta & M. Moscovitch (Eds.), *Attention and performance XV* (pp. 421–452). Cambridge, MA: MIT Press.

Anderson, J. R. (1992). Automaticity and the ACT* theory. *American Journal of Psychology, 105*(2), 165–180.

Anderson, J. R., Bothell, D., Byrne, M. D., Douglass, S., Lebiere, C., & Qin, Y. (2004). An integrated theory of the mind. *Psychological Review, 4*(111), 1036–1060.

Ansorge, U. (2004). Top-down contingencies of nonconscious priming revealed by dual-task interference. *The Quarterly Journal of Experimental Psychology: A, Human Experimental Psychology, 57*(6), 1123–1148.

Aron, A. R., & Poldrack, R. A. (2006). Cortical and subcortical contributions to Stop signal response inhibition: Role of the subthalamic nucleus. *The Journal of Neuroscience, 26*(9), 2424–2433.

Aston-Jones, G., & Cohen, J. D. (2005). An integrative theory of locus coeruleus-norepinephrine function: Adaptive gain and optimal performance. *Annual Review of Neuroscience, 28*, 403–450.

Barch, D. M., Carter, C. S., Braver, T. S., Sabb, F. W., Noll, D. C., & Cohen, J. C. (1999). Overt verbal responding during fMRI scanning: Empirical investigations of problems and potential solutions. *Neuroimage, 10*(6), 642–657.

Barch, D. M., Carter, C. S., & Cohen, J. D. (2004). Factors influencing Stroop performance in schizophrenia. *Neuropsychology, 18*(3), 477–484.

Botvinick, M. M., Braver, T. S., Barch, D. M., Carter, C. S., & Cohen, J. D. (2001). Conflict monitoring and cognitive control. *Psychological Review, 108*(3), 624–652.

Braun, J., Koch, C., & Davis, L. J. (2001). *Visual attention and cortical circuits.* Cambridge, MA: MIT Press.

Braver, T. S., Barch, D. M., & Cohen, J. D. (1999). Cognition and control in schizophrenia: A computational model of dopamine and prefrontal function. *Biological Psychiatry, 46*, 312–328.

Braver, T. S., & Bongiolatti, S. R. (2002). The role of frontopolar cortex in subgoal processing during working memory. *Neuroimage, 15*(3), 523–536.

Braver T. S., & Cohen J. D. (2000). On the control of control: The role of dopamine in regulating prefrontal function and working memory. In S. Monsell & J. Driver (Eds.), *Attention and performance XVIII; control of cognitive processes* (pp.713–737). Cambridge, MA: MIT Press.

Braver, T. S., & Cohen, J. D. (2001). Working memory, cognitive control, and the prefrontal cortex: Computational and empirical studies. *Cognitive Processing, 2*, 25–55.

Braver, T. S., Cohen, J. D., & Barch, D. M. (2002). The role of the prefrontal cortex in normal and disordered cognitive control: A cognitive neuroscience perspective. In D. T. Stuss & R. T. Knight (Eds.), *Principles of frontal lobe function* (pp. 428–448). Oxford, UK: Oxford University Press.

Braver, T. S., Cohen, J. D., & Servan-Schreiber, D. (1995). Neural network simulations of schizophrenic performance in a variant of the CPT-AX: A predicted double dissociation. *Schizophrenia Research, 15*(1–2), 110.

Broadbent, E. D. (1958). *Perception and communication.* London: Pergamon.

Brown, J. W., & Braver, T. S. (2005). Learned predictions of error likelihood in the anterior cingulate cortex. *Science, 307*(5712), 1118–1121.

Brown, J. W., Reynolds, J. R., & Braver, T. S. (2007). A computational model of fractionated conflict-control mechanisms in task-switching. *Cognitive Psychology, 55*, 37–85.

Brunel, N., & Wang, X.-J. (2001). Effects of neuromodulation in a cortical network model of object working memory dominated by recurrent inhibition. *Journal of Computational Neuroscience, 11*, 63–85.

Bundesen, C. (1990). A theory of visual attention. *Psychological Review, 97*(4), 523–547.

Bundesen, C. (1998). A computational theory of visual attention. *Philosophical Transactions of the Royal Society of London. Series B, Biological Sciences, 353*(1373), 1271–1281.

Bundesen, C., Habekost, T., & Kyllingsbaek, S. (2005). A neural theory of visual attention: Bridging cognition and neurophysiology. *Psychological Review, 112*(2), 291–328.

Burgess, P. W., Scott, S. K., & Frith, C. D. (2003). The role of the rostral frontal cortex (area 10) in prospective memory: A lateral versus medial dissociation. *Neuropsychologia 41*(8), 906–918.

Byrne, M. D., & Anderson, J. R. (2001). Serial modules in parallel: The psychological refractory period and perfect time-sharing. *Psychological Review, 108*(4), 847–869.

Carter, C. S., Braver, T. S., Barch, D. M., Botvinick, M. M., Noll, D., & Cohen, J. D. (1998). Anterior cingulate cortex, error detection, and the online monitoring of performance. *Science, 280*(5364), 747–749.

Cave, K. R. (1999). The FeatureGate model of visual selection. *Psychological Research, 62*(2–3), 182–194.

Chang, L., Speck, O., Miller, E. N., Braun, J., Jovicich, J., Koch, C. et al. (2001). Neural correlates of attention and working memory deficits in HIV patients. *Neurology, 57*(6), 1001–1007.

Cohen, J. D., Braver, T. S., & Brown, J. W. (2002). Computational perspectives on dopamine function in prefrontal cortex. *Current Opinion in Neurobiology 12*, 223–229.

Cohen, J. D., Braver, T. S., & O'Reilly, R. C. (1996). A computational approach to prefrontal cortex, cognitive control and schizophrenia: Recent developments and current challenges. *Philosophical Transactions of the Royal Society of London. Series B, Biological Sciences, 351*(1346), 1515–1527.

Cohen, J. D., Dunbar, K., & McClelland, J. L. (1990). On the control of automatic processes: A parallel distributed processing account of the Stroop effect. *Psychological Review, 97*(3), 332–361.

Cohen, J. D., & Huston, T. A. (1994). Progress in the use of interactive models for understanding attention and performance. In C. Umiltà & M. Moscovitch (Eds.), *Attention and performance XV* (pp. 1–19). Cambridge, MA: MIT Press.

Cohen, J. D., Romero, R. D., Farah, M. J., & Servan-Schreiber, D. (1994). Mechanisms of spatial attention: The relation of macrostructure to microstructure in parietal neglect. *Journal of Cognitive Neuroscience, 6*(4), 377–387.

Cohen, J. D., & Servan-Schreiber, D. (1992). Context, cortex, and dopamine: A connectionist approach to behaviour and biology in schizophrenia. *Psychological Review, 99*, 45–77.

Cowan, N. (2001). The magical number 4 in short-term memory: A reconsideration of mental storage capacity. *Behavioral and Brain Sciences, 24*, 87–185.

De Pisapia, N., & Braver, T. S. (2006). A model of dual control mechanisms through anterior cingulate and prefrontal cortex interactions. *Neurocomputing, 69*(10–12), 1322–1326.

De Pisapia, N., & Braver, T. S. (2007). Functional specializations in lateral prefrontal cortex associated with the integration and segregation of information in working memory. *Cerebral Cortex, 17*, 993–1006.

Deco, G. (2001). Biased competition mechanisms for visual attention in a multimodular neurodynamical system. In S. Wermter, J. Austin, D. Willshaw, and M. Elshaw (eds.), *Emergent neural computational architectures based on neuroscience: Towards neuroscience-inspired computing* (pp. 114–126). Berlin: Springer.

Deco, G., & Lee, T. S. (2004). The role of early visual cortex in visual integration: A neural model of recurrent interaction. *The European Journal of Neuroscience, 20*(4), 1089–1100.

Deco, G., Pollatos, O., & Zihl, J. (2002). The time course of selective visual attention: Theory and experiments. *Vision Research, 42*(27), 2925–2945.

Deco, G., & Rolls, E. T. (2002). Object-based visual neglect: A computational hypothesis. *The European Journal of Neuroscience, 16*(10), 1994–2000.

Deco, G., & Rolls, E. T. (2003). Attention and working memory: A dynamical model of neuronal activity in the prefrontal cortex. *The European Journal of Neuroscience, 18*(8), 2374–2390.

Deco, G., & Rolls, E. T. (2004). A neurodynamical cortical model of visual attention and invariant object recognition. *Vision Research, 44*(6), 621–642.

Deco, G., & Rolls, E. T. (2005a). Attention, short-term memory, and action selection: A unifying theory. *Progress in Neurobiology*, 76(4), 236–256.

Deco, G., & Rolls, E. T. (2005b). Neurodynamics of biased competition and cooperation for attention: A model with spiking neurons. *Journal of Neurophysiology*, 94(1), 295–313.

Deco, G., Rolls, E. T., & Horwitz, B. (2004). "What" and "where" in visual working memory: A computational neurodynamical perspective for integrating FMRI and single-neuron data. *Journal of Cognitive Neuroscience*, 16(4), 683–701.

Deco, G., & Zihl, J. (2001a). A neurodynamical model of visual attention: Feedback enhancement of spatial resolution in a hierarchical system. *Journal of Computational Neuroscience*, 10(3), 231–253.

Deco, G., & Zihl, J. (2001b). Top-down selective visual attention: A neurodynamical approach. *Visual Cognition*, 8(1), 119–140.

Deco, G., & Zihl, J. (2004). A biased competition based neurodynamical model of visual neglect. *Medical Engineering & Physics*, 26(9), 733–743.

Dehaene, S., & Changeux, J. P. (1991). The Wisconsin card sorting test: Theoretical analysis and modeling in a neuronal network. *Cerebral Cortex*, 1(1), 62–79.

Desimone, R., & Duncan, J. (1995). Neural mechanisms of selective visual attention. *Annual Review of Neuroscience*, 18, 193–222.

Durstewitz, D., Kelc, M., & Gunturkun, O. (1999). A neurocomputational theory of the dopaminergic modulation of working memory functions. *Journal of Neuroscience*, 19(7), 2807–2822.

Durstewitz, D., Seamans, J. K., & Sejnowski, T. J. (2000). Neurocomputational models of working memory. *Nature Neuroscience*, 3(Suppl) 1184–1191.

Engle, R. W., Kane, M. J., & Tuholski, S. W. (1999). Individual differences in working memory capacity and what they tell us about controlled attention, general fluid intelligence, and functions of the prefrontal cortex. In A. Miyake & P. Shah (Eds.), *Models of working memory* (pp. 102–134). New York: Cambridge University Press.

Gilbert, S. J., & Shallice, T. (2002). Task switching: A PDP model. *Cognitive Psychology*, 44(3), 297–337.

Hamker, F. H. (2003). The reentry hypothesis: Linking eye movements to visual perception. *Journal of Vision*, 3(11), 808–816.

Heinke, D., Deco, G., Zihl, J., & Humphreys, G. (2002). A computational neuroscience account of visual neglect. *Neurocomputing*, 44–46, 811–816.

Heinke, D., & Humphreys, G. W. (2003). Attention, spatial representation, and visual neglect: Simulating emergent attention and spatial memory in the selective attention for identification model (SAIM). *Psychological Review*, 110(1), 29–87.

Heinke, D., & Humphreys, G. W. (2005). Computational models of visual selective attention: A review. In G. Houghton (Ed.), *Connectionist models in psychology* (pp. 273–312). London: Psychology Press.

Herd, S. A., Banich, M. T., & O'Reilly, R. C. (2006). Neural mechanisms of cognitive control: An integrative model of stroop task performance and FMRI data. *Journal of Cognitive Neuroscience*, 18(1), 22–32.

Houghton, G., & Tipper, S. P. (1996). Inhibitory mechanisms of neural and cognitive control: Applications to selective attention and sequential action. *Brain and Cognition*, 30(1), 20–43.

Humphreys, G. W., & Muller, H. J. (1993). SEarch via Recursive Rejection (SERR): A connectionist model of visual search. *Cognitive Psychology*, 25(1), 43–110.

Itti, L., & Baldi, P. (2005). A principled approach to detecting surprising events in video. *IEEE Computer Society Conference on Computer Vision and Pattern Recognition (CVPR'05)*, 1, 631–637.

Itti, L., & Koch, C. (2000). A saliency-based search mechanism for overt and covert shifts of visual attention. *Vision Research*, 40(10–12), 1489–1506.

Itti, L., & Koch, C. (2001). Computational modelling of visual attention. *Nature reviews. Neuroscience*, 2(3), 194–203.

Itti, L., Koch, C., & Niebur, E. (1998). A model of saliency-based visual attention for rapid scene analysis. *IEEE Transactions on Pattern Analysis and Machine Intelligence*, 20(11), 1254–1259.

James, W. (1890). *Principle of Psychology*. Dover Publications 1950, vol. 1.

Just, M. A., Carpenter, P. A., Keller, T. A., Emery, L., Zajac, H., & Thulborn, K. R. (2001). Interdependence of nonoverlapping cortical systems in dual cognitive tasks. *Neuroimage, 14*(2), 417–426.

Koch, C., & Ullman, S. (1985). Shifts in selective visual attention: Towards the underlying neural circuitry. *Human Neurobiology, 4*(4), 219–227.

Koechlin, E., Basso, G., Pietrini, P., Panzer, S., & Grafman, J. (1999). The role of the anterior prefrontal cortex in human cognition. *Nature, 399*, 148–151.

Kwak, H. W., & Egeth, H. (1992). Consequences of allocating attention to locations and to other attributes. *Perception & Psychophysics, 51*(5), 455–464.

Lee, D. K., Itti, L., Koch, C., & Braun, J. (1999). Attention activates winner-take-all competition among visual filters. *Nature Neuroscience, 2*(4), 375–381.

Lee, T. S. (1996). Image representation using 2D gabor wavelets. *IEEE Transactions on Pattern Analysis and Machine Intelligence, 18*(10), 959–971.

Logan, G. D. (2005). The time it takes to switch attention. *Psychonomic Bulletin & Review, 12*(4), 647–653.

Logan, G. D., & Gordon, R. D. (2001). Executive control of visual attention in dual-task situations. *Psychological Review, 108*(2), 393–434.

Lovett, M. C. (2002). Modeling selective attention: Not just another model of Stroop. *Cognitive Systems Research, 3*(1), 67–76.

Maia, T. V., & Cleeremans, A. (2005). Consciousness: Converging insights from connectionist modeling and neuroscience. *Trends in Cognitive Sciences, 9*(8), 397–404.

McClelland, J. L. (1979). On the time relations of mental processes: An examination of systems of processes in cascade. *Psychological Review, 86*, 287–330.

McClelland, J. L., & Rumelhart, D. E. (1981). An interative activation model of context effects in letter perception: Part 1. An account of basic findings. *Psychological Review, 88*, 375–407.

Melara, R. D., & Algom, D. (2003). Driven by information: A tectonic theory of Stroop effects. *Psychological Review, 110*, 422–471.

Meyer, D. E., & Kieras, D. E. (1997). A computational theory of executive cognitive processes and multiple-task performance: Part 1. Basic mechanisms. *Psychological Review, 104*, 3–65.

Miller, E. K., & Cohen, J. D. (2001). An integrative theory of prefrontal cortex function. *Annual Review of Neuroscience, 21*, 167–202.

Mozer, M. C., Shettel, M., & Vecera, S. (2006). Top-down control of visual attention: A rational account. In Y. Weiss, B. Schoelkopf, & J. Platt (Eds.), *Neural information processing systems* (pp. 923–930). Cambridge, MA: MIT Press.

Mozer, M. C., & Sitton, M. (1998). Computational modeling of spatial attention. In H. Pashler (Ed.), *Attention* (pp. 341–393). London: Psychology Press.

Navalpakkam, V., & Itti, L. (2005). Modeling the influence of task on attention. *Vision Research, 45*(2), 205–231.

Norman, D. A., & Shallice, T. (1986). Attention to action: Willed and automatic control of behavior. In R. J. Davidson, G. E. Schwartz, & D. Shapiro (Eds.), *Consciousness and Self-regulation* (Vol. 4, pp. 1–18). New York: Plenum Press.

Olshausen, B. A., Anderson, C. H., & Van Essen, D. C. (1993). A neurobiological model of visual attention and invariant pattern recognition based on dynamic routing of information. *The Journal of Neuroscience, 13*(11), 4700–4719.

O'Reilly, R. C. (2006). Biologically based computational models of high-level cognition. *Science, 314*, 91–94.

O'Reilly, R. C., Braver, T. S., & Cohen, J. D. (1999). A biologically-based computational model of working memory. In A. Miyake & P. Shah (Eds.), *Models of working memory: Mechanisms of active maintenance and executive control*. New York: Cambridge University Press.

O'Reilly, R. C., & Munakata, Y. (2000). *Computational explorations in cognitive neuroscience: Understanding the ming by simulating the brain*. Cambridge, MA: MIT Press.

Parkhurst, D., Law, K., & Niebur, E. (2002). Modeling the role of salience in the allocation of overt visual attention. *Vision Research, 42*(1), 107–123.

Pashler, H. (1994). Dual-task interference in simple tasks: Data and theory. *Psychological Bulletin, 116*(2), 220–244.

Phaf, R. H., Van der Heijden, A. H., & Hudson, P. T. (1990). SLAM: A connectionist model for attention in visual selection tasks. *Cognitive Psychology, 22*(3), 273–341.

Posner, M. I., Cohen, Y., & Rafal, R. D. (1982). Neural systems control of spatial orienting.

Philosophical Transactions of the Royal Society of London. Series B, Biological sciences, 298(1089), 187–198.

Posner, M. I., & Snyder, C. R. R. (1975). Attention and cognitive control. In R. L. Solso (Ed.), *Information processing and cognition* (pp. 55–85). Hillsdale, NJ: Erlbaum.

Reynolds, J. R., Braver, T. S., Brown, J. W., & Stigchel, S. (2006). Computational and neural mechanisms of task-switching. *Neurocomputing,* 69, 1332–1336.

Roelofs, A. (2000). Control of language: A computational account of the Stroop asymmetry. In *Proceedings of the Third International Conference on Cognitive Modeling.* Veenendaal, The Netherlands: Universal Press.

Rougier, N. P., Noelle, D., Braver, T. S., Cohen, J. D., & O'Reilly, R. C. (2005). Prefrontal cortex and the flexibility of cognitive control: Rules without symbols. *Proceedings of the National Academy of Sciences,* 102(20), 7338–7343.

Rumelhart, D. E., & McClelland, J. L. (1986). *Parallel distributed processing: Explorations in the microstructure of cognition* (Vol. 1 and 2). Cambridge, MA: MIT Press.

Salvucci, D. D. (2005). A multitasking general executive for compound continuous tasks. *Cognitive Science,* 29, 457–492.

Schneider, D. W., & Logan, G. D. (2005). Modeling task switching without switching tasks: A short-term priming account of explicitly cued performance. *Journal of Experimental Psychology: General,* 34(3), 343–367.

Schneider, W., & Chein, J. M. (2003). Controlled and automatic processing: Behavior, theory, and biological mechanisms. *Cognitive Science,* 27(3), 525–559.

Schneider, W., & Shiffrin, R. M. (1977). Controlled and automatic human information processing: I. Detection, search, and attention. *Psychological Review,* 84, 1–66.

Servan-Schreiber, D., Bruno, R., Carter, C., & Cohen, J. (1998). Dopamine and the mechanisms of cognition: Part I. A neural network model predicting dopamine effects on selective attention. *Biological Psychiatry,* 43(10), 713–722.

Shipp, S. (2004). The brain circuitry of attention. *Trends in Cognitive Sciences,* 8(5), 223–230.

Sohn, M.-H., & Anderson, J. R. (2003). Stimulus-related priming during task switching. *Memory & Cognition,* 31(5), 775–780.

Stroop, J. R. (1935). Studies of interference in serial verbal reactions. *Journal of Experimental Psychology,* 18, 643–662.

Treisman, A. (1999). Feature binding, attention and object perception. In J. W. Humphreys & J. Duncan (Eds.), *Attention space and action* (pp. 91–111). Oxford, UK: Oxford University Press.

Treisman, A. M., & Gelade, G. (1980). A feature-integration theory of attention. *Cognitive Psychology,* 12(1), 97–136.

Tsotsos, K. J., Culhane, M. S., Wai, K. W. Y., Lai, Y., Davis, N., & Nuflo, F. (1995). Modeling visual attention via selective tuning. *Artificial Intelligence,* 78, 507–545.

Usher, M., & Cohen, J. D. (1999). Short term memory and selection processes in a frontal-lobe model. In D. Heinke, G. W. Humphries, & A. Olsen (Eds.), *Connectionist models in cognitive neuroscience* (pp. 78–91). The 5th Neural Computation and Psychology Workshop. Springer Verlag, University of Birmingham, UK.

van de Laar, P., Heskes, T., & Gielen, S. (1997). Task-dependent learning of attention. *Neural Networks,* 10(6), 981–992.

van der Heijden, A. H., & Bem, S. (1997). Successive approximations to an adequate model of attention. *Consciousness and Cognition,* 6(2–3), 413–428.

Yu, A. J., & Dayan, P. (2005). Uncertainty, neuromodulation, and attention. *Neuron,* 46, 681–692.

Ward, R. (1999). Interaction between perception and action systems: A model for selective action. In W. G. Humphreys, J. Duncan, & A. Treisman (Eds.), *Attention, space and action – Studies in cognitive neuroscience* (pp. 311–332). Oxford, UK: Oxford University Press.

Wolfe, C. D., & Bell, M. A. (2004). Working memory and inhibitory control in early childhood: Contributions from physiology, temperament, and language. *Developmental Psychobiology,* 44(1), 68–83.

Wolfe, J. (1994). Guided search 2.0: A revised model of visual search. *Psychonomic Bulletin & Review,* 1, 202–238.

CHAPTER 16

Computational Models of Developmental Psychology

Thomas R. Shultz and Sylvain Sirois

1. Introduction

This chapter provides a comparative survey of computational models of psychological development. Because it is impossible to cover everything in this active field in such limited space, the chapter focuses on compelling simulations in domains that have attracted a range of competing models. This has the advantage of allowing comparisons between different types of models. After outlining some important developmental issues and identifying the main computational techniques applied to developmental phenomena, modeling in the areas of the balance scale, past tense, object permanence, artificial syntax, similarity-to-correlation shifts in category learning, discrimination-shift learning, concept and word learning, and abnormal development is discussed. This is followed by preliminary conclusions about the relative success of various types of models.

2. Developmental Issues

To understand how computational modeling can contribute to the study of psychological development, it is important to appreciate the enduring issues in developmental psychology. These include issues of how knowledge is represented and processed at various ages and stages, how children make transitions from one stage to another, and explanations of the ordering of psychological stages. Although many ideas about these issues have emerged from standard psychological research, these ideas often lack sufficient clarity and precision. Computational modeling forces precision because models that are not clearly specified will either not run or will produce inappropriate results.

3. Computational Techniques

The most common computational techniques applied to psychological development are production systems, connectionist networks, dynamic systems, robotics, and Bayesian inference. Production systems represent long-term knowledge in the form of condition-action rules that specify actions to be taken or conclusions to be drawn under particular conditions (see Chapter 6 in this volume). Conditions and actions are composed of symbolic expressions containing constants as well as variables that can be bound to particular values. The rules are processed by matching problem conditions (contained in a working-memory buffer) against the condition side of rules. Ordinarily, one rule with satisfied conditions is selected and then fired, meaning that its actions are taken or its conclusions drawn. Throughout matching and firing, variable bindings must be consistently maintained so that the identities of particular objects referred to in conditions and actions are not confused.

Although first-generation production system models involved programmers writing rules by hand (Klahr & Wallace, 1976; Siegler, 1976), it is more interesting for understanding developmental transitions if rules can be acquired by the model in realistic circumstances. Several such rule-learning systems have been developed, including Soar (Newell, 1990), which learns rules by saving the results of look-ahead search through a problem space; ACT-R (Anderson, 1993), which learns rules by analogy to existing rules or by compiling less efficient rules into more efficient ones; and C4.5 (Quinlan, 1993), which learns rules by extracting information from examples of objects or events. Rule learning is a challenging computational problem because an indefinitely large number of rules can be consistent with a given data set, and because it is often unclear which rules should be modified and how they should be modified (e.g., by changing existing conditions, adding new conditions, or altering the certainty of conclusions).

Connectionism represents knowledge in a subsymbolic fashion via activation patterns on neuron-like units (see Chapter 2 in this volume). Connectionist networks process information by passing activation among units. Although some networks, including connection weight values, are designed by hand, it is more common in developmental applications for programer-designed networks to learn their connection weights (roughly equivalent to neuronal synapses) from examples. Some other neural networks also construct their own topology, typically by recruiting new hidden units. The neural learning algorithms most commonly applied to development include back-propagation (BP) and its variants, cascade-correlation (CC) and its variants, simple recurrent networks (SRNs), encoder networks, auto-association (AA), feature-mapping, and contrastive Hebbian learning.

A dynamic system is a set of quantitative variables that change continually, concurrently, and interdependently over time in accordance with differential equations (see Chapter 4 in this volume). Such systems can be understood geometrically as changes of position over time in a space of possible system states. Dynamic systems overlap connectionism in that neural networks are often dynamic systems. In recurrent networks, activation updates depend in part on current activation values; and in learning networks, weight updates depend in part on current weight values. However, it is also common for dynamic-system models to be implemented without networks, in differential equations where a change in a dependent variable depends in part on its current value.

Another relatively new approach is developmental robotics, a seemingly unlikely marriage of robotics and developmental psychology (Berthouze & Ziemke, 2003). A principal attraction for roboticists is to create generic robots that begin with infant skills and learn their tasks through interacting with adults and possibly other robots. The primary hook for developmentalists is the challenge of placing their computational models inside of robots operating in real environments in real time.

Bayesian inference, which is rapidly gaining ground in modeling a variety of cognitive phenomena, is starting to be applied to developmental problems (see Chapter 3 in this volume). At its heart is the use of Bayes' rule to infer posterior probabilities (of a hypothesis given some data) from products of prior and likelihood probabilities divided by the sum of such products across all known hypotheses. The CC and C4.5 algorithms are discussed here in some detail because they are not treated elsewhere in this volume, but have been used in a variety of developmental simulations.

4. Cascade-Correlation

CC networks begin with just input and output units, ordinarily fully connected. They are feed-forward networks trained in a supervised fashion with patterns representing particular input and target output values. Any internal, hidden units required to deal with nonlinearities in the training patterns are recruited one at time, as needed. The CC algorithm alternates between output and input phases to reduce error and recruit helpful hidden units, respectively (Fahlman & Lebiere, 1990). The function to minimize during output phase is error at the output units:

$$E = \sum_o \sum_p (A_{op} - T_{op})^2 \qquad (16.1)$$

where A is actual output activation and T is target output activation for unit o and pattern p. Error minimization is typically accomplished with the Quickprop algorithm (Fahlman, 1988), a fast variant of the generalized delta rule that uses curvature as well as slope of the error surface to compute weight changes. When error can no longer be reduced by adjusting weights entering the output units, CC switches to input phase to recruit a hidden unit to supply more computational power.

In input phase, a pool of usually eight candidate hidden units with typically sigmoid activation functions have random trainable weights from the input units and any existing hidden units. These weights are trained by attempting to maximize a covariance

C between candidate-hidden-unit activation and network error:

$$C = \frac{\sum_o \left| \sum_p (h_p - \langle h \rangle)(e_{op} - \langle e_o \rangle) \right|}{\sum_o \sum_p (e_{op} - \langle e_o \rangle)^2} \qquad (16.2)$$

where h_p is activation of the candidate hidden unit for pattern p, $<h>$ is mean activation of the candidate hidden unit for all patterns, e_{op} is residual error at output o for pattern p, and $<e_o>$ is mean residual error at output o for all patterns. C represents the absolute covariance between hidden-unit activation and network error summed across patterns and output units and standardized by the sum of squared error deviations. The same Quickprop algorithm used for output training is used here, but with the goal of maximizing these correlations rather than reducing network error. When the correlations stop increasing, the candidate with the highest absolute covariance is installed into the network, with its just-trained input weights frozen, and a random set of output weights with the negative of the sign of the covariance C. The other candidates are discarded.

The basic idea of input phase is to select a candidate whose activation variations track current network error. Once a new recruit is installed, CC returns to output phase to resume training of weights entering output units to decide how to best use the new recruit to reduce network error. Standard CC networks have a deep topology with each hidden unit occupying its own layer.

A variant called sibling-descendant CC (SDCC) dynamically decides whether to install each new recruit on the current highest layer of hidden units (as a sibling) or on its own new layer (as a descendant; Baluja & Fahlman, 1994). SDCC creates a wider variety of network topologies, normally with less depth, but otherwise performs much the same as standard CC on simulations (Shultz, 2006).

CC and SDCC are constructivist algorithms that are theoretically compatible with verbally formulated constructivist theories of development (Piaget, 1954). Qualitative changes in cognition and behavior potentially can be attributed to qualitative changes in underlying computational resources, namely recruited hidden units and their connectivity.

5. C4.5

In some ways, C4.5 is the symbolic analog of CC and accordingly has been applied to several developmental domains. To learn to classify examples, C4.5 builds a decision tree that can be transformed into production rules (Quinlan, 1993). C4.5 processes a set of examples in attribute-value format and learns how to classify them into discrete categories using information on the correct category of each example. A decision tree contains leaves, each indicating a class, and branching nodes, each specifying a test of a single attribute with a subtree for each attribute value. C4.5 learning proceeds as follows:

1. If every example has the same predicted attribute value, return it as a leaf node.
2. If there are no attributes, return the most common attribute value.
3. Otherwise, pick the best attribute, partition the examples by values, and recursively learn to grow subtrees below this node after removing the best attribute from further consideration.

C4.5 creates smaller and more general trees by picking the attribute that maximizes information gain. Symbolic rules can be derived from a decision tree by following the branches (rule conditions) out to the leaves (rule actions). C4.5 is a reasonable choice for modeling development because it learns rules from examples, just as connectionist models do, and without the background knowledge that Soar and ACT-R often require. Like CC, C4.5 grows as it learns, building its later knowledge on top of existing knowledge as a decision tree is being constructed. The two algorithms thus make an interesting and parallel contrast between constructive neural and symbolic systems.

A hybrid learning system that does Connectionist Learning with Adaptive Rule Induction Online (CLARION; Sun, Slusarz, & Terry, 2005) may also be worth trying in a developmental context. CLARION works on two levels: BP networks learn from examples, and explicit rules can be extracted from these networks.

6. Balance Scale

One of the first developmental tasks to attract a wide range of computational models was the balance scale. This task presents a child with a rigid beam balanced on a fulcrum (Siegler, 1976). This beam has pegs spaced at regular intervals to the left and right of the fulcrum. An experimenter places a number of identical weights on a peg on the left side and a number of weights on a peg on the right side. While supporting blocks prevent the beam from tipping, the child predicts which side of the beam will descend, or whether the scale will balance, if the supporting blocks are removed.

Children are typically tested with six types of problems on this task. Two of these problems are simple because one cue (weight or distance from the fulcrum) perfectly predicts the outcome, whereas the other cue is constant on both sides. A third is even simpler, with identical cues on each side of the fulcrum. The other three problem types are more complex because the two cues conflict, weight predicting one outcome and distance predicting a different outcome. The pattern of predictions across these problem types helps to diagnose how a child solves these problems.

Despite ongoing debate about details, it is generally agreed that there are two major psychological regularities in the balance-scale literature: stage progressions and the torque-difference effect. In stage 1, children use weight information to predict that the side with more weights will descend or

Table 16.1: Characteristics of balance-scale models

Author	Model	All 4 stages	Torque-difference effect
Langley (1987)	Sage	no[a]	no
Newell (1990)	Soar	no[b]	no
Schmidt & Ling (1996)	C4.5	yes[c]	yes[d]
van Rijn et al. (2003)	ACT-R	yes[e]	yes[f]
McClelland (1989)	BP	no[g]	yes
Shultz et al. (1994)	CC	yes	yes

[a]Sage only learned stage 3, not stages 1, 2, and 4.

[b]Soar learned stages 1–3, but not stage 4.

[c]C4.5 learned all four stages, but to get the correct ordering of the first two stages, it was necessary to list the weight attributes before the distance attributes because C4.5 breaks ties in information gain by picking the first-listed attribute with the highest information gain.

[d]To capture the torque-difference effect, C4.5 required a redundant coding of weight and distance differences between one side of the scale and the other. In addition to doing a lot of the work that a learning algorithm should be able to do on its own, this produced strange rules that children never show.

[e]The ordering of stages 1 and 2 and the late appearance of addition and torque rules in ACT-R were engineered by programmer settings; they were not a natural result of learning or development. The relatively modern ACT-R model is the only balance-scale simulation to clearly distinguish between an addition rule (comparing the weight + distance sums on each side) and the torque rule.

[f]ACT-R showed a torque-difference effect only with respect to differences in distance but not weight and only in the vicinity of stage transitions, not throughout development as children apparently do.

[g]BP oscillated between stages 3 and 4, never settling in stage 4.

that the scale will balance when the two sides have equal weights (Siegler, 1976). In stage 2, children start to use distance information when the weights are equal on each side, predicting that in such cases the side with greater distance will descend. In stage 3, weight and distance information are emphasized equally, and the child guesses when weight and distance information conflict on complex problems. In stage 4, children respond correctly on all problem types. The torque-difference effect is that problems with large torque-differences are easier for children to solve than problems with small torque differences (Ferretti & Butterfield, 1986). Torque is the product of weight × distance on a given side; torque difference is the absolute difference between the torque on one side and the torque on the other side.

The ability of several different computational models to capture these phenomena is summarized in Table 16.1. The first four rows in Table 16.1 describe symbolic, rule-based models, and the last two rows describe connectionist models.

In one of the first developmental connectionist simulations, McClelland (1989) found that a static BP network with two groups of hidden units segregated for either weight or distance information developed through the first three of these stages and into the fourth stage. However, these networks did not settle in stage 4, instead continuing to cycle between stages 3 and 4. The first CC model of cognitive development naturally captured all four balance-scale stages, without requiring segregation of hidden units (Shultz, Mareschal et al., 1994).

The ability of these network models to capture stages 1 and 2 is due to a bias toward equal-distance problems in the training set, that is, problems with weights placed equally distant from the fulcrum on each side. This bias, justified by noting that children rarely place objects at differing distances from a fulcrum but have considerable experience lifting differing numbers of objects, forces a network to emphasize weight information first because weight information is more relevant to reducing network error. When weight-induced error has been reduced, then the network can turn its attention to distance information. A learning algorithm needs to find a region of connection-weight space that allows it to emphasize the numbers of weights on the scale before moving to another region of weight space that allows correct performance on most balance-scale problems. A static network such as BP, once committed to using weight information in stage 1, cannot easily find its way to a stage-4 region by continuing to reduce error. In contrast, a constructive algorithm such as CC has an easier time with this move because each newly recruited hidden unit changes the shape of connection-weight space by adding a new dimension.

Both of the connectionist models readily captured the torque-difference effect. Such perceptual effects are natural for neural models that compute a weighted sum of inputs when updating downstream units. This ensures that larger differences on the inputs create clearer activation patterns downstream at the hidden and output units. In contrast, crisp symbolic rules care more about direction of input differences than about input amounts, so the torque-difference effect is more awkward to capture in rule-based systems.

7. Past Tense

The morphology of the English past tense has generated considerable psychological and modeling attention. Most English verbs form the past tense by adding the suffix -ed to the stem, but about 180 have irregular past-tense forms. Seven psychological regularities have been identified:

1. Children begin to overregularize irregular verbs after having correctly produced them.
2. Frequent irregulars are more likely to be correct than infrequent ones.
3. Irregular and regular verbs that are similar to frequent verbs are more likely to be correct. (Two regularities are combined here into one sentence.)
4. Past-tense formation is quicker with consistent regulars (e.g., *like*) than with inconsistent regulars (e.g., *bake*), which are in turn quicker than irregulars (e.g., *make*).
5. Migrations occurred over the centuries from Old English such that some irregulars became regular and some regulars became irregular.
6. Double-dissociations exist between regulars and irregulars in neurological disorders, such as specific language impairment and Williams syndrome.

The classical rule-rote hypothesis holds that the irregulars are memorized, and the add −ed rule applied when no irregular memory is retrieved (Pinker, 1999), but this has not resulted in a successful published computational model. The ability of several different computational models to capture past-tense phenomena is summarized in Table 16.2. All of the models were trained to take a present-tense verb stem as input and provide the correct past-tense form.

One symbolic model used ID3, a predecessor of the C4.5 algorithm that was discussed in Section 5, to learn past-tense forms from labeled examples (Ling & Marinov, 1993). Like C4.5, ID3 constructs a decision tree in which the branch nodes are attributes, such as a particular phoneme in a particular position, and the leaves are suffixes, such as the phoneme −t. Each example describes a verb stem, for example, *talk*, in terms of its phonemes and their positions, and is labeled with a particular past-tense ending, for example, *talk-t*. Actually, because there are several such endings, the

Table 16.2: Coverage of English past-tense acquisition

Authors	Ling & Marinov (1993)	Taatgen & Anderson (2002)	Plunkett & Marchman (1996)	Daugherty & Seidenberg (1992)	Hare & Elman (1995)	Westermann (1998)
Model	ID3	ACT-R	BP	BP	BP	CNN[a]
Over-regularization	yes	yes	yes	–	–	yes
Frequency	yes	yes	–	yes	–	yes
Similarity-irregulars	no	no	–	yes	–	yes
Similarity-regulars	no	no	–	yes	–	–
Reaction time	no	no	–	yes	–	–
Migration	no	no	–	–	yes	–
Double-dissociation	no	no	–	–	–	yes

[a]CNN is a Constructivist Neural Network model with Gaussian hidden units.

model used a small grove of trees. Instead of a single rule for the past tense as in the rule-rote hypothesis, this grove implemented several rules for regular verbs and many rules for irregular verbs. Coverage of over-regularization in the ID3 model was due to inconsistent and arbitrary use of the *m* parameter that was originally designed to control the depth of decision trees (Quinlan, 1993). Although *m* was claimed by the authors to implement some unspecified mental capacity, it was decreased here to capture development, but increased to capture development in other simulations, such as the balance scale (Schmidt & Ling, 1996).

The ACT-R models started with three handwritten rules: a *zero rule*, which does not change the verb stem; an *analogy rule*, which looks for analogies to labeled examples and thus discovers the *–ed* rule; and a *retrieval rule*, which retrieves the past tense form from memory (Taatgen & Anderson, 2002). Curiously, this model rarely applied the *–ed* rule because it mostly used retrieval; the *–ed* rule was reserved for rare words, novel words, and nonsense words.

As shown in Table 16.2, none of the computational models cover many past-tense phenomena, but collectively, a series of neural-network models do fairly well. Several of these phenomena naturally emerge from neural models, where different past-tense patterns are represented in common hidden units. In these neural models, less frequent and highly idiosyncratic verbs cannot easily resist the pull of regularization and other sources of error. Being similar to other verbs can substitute for high frequency. These effects occur because weight change is proportional to network error, and frequency and similarity effects create more initial error. In symbolic models, memory for irregular forms is searched before the regular rule is applied, thus slowing responses to regular verbs and creating reaction times opposite to those found in people.

8. Object Permanence

A cornerstone acquisition in the first two years is belief in the continued existence of hidden objects. Piaget (1954) found that object permanence was acquired through six stages, that the ability to find hidden objects emerged in the fourth stage between the ages of eight and twelve months, and that a full-blown concept of permanent objects independent of perception did not occur until about two years. Although data collected using Piaget's object-search methods were robust, recent work using different methodologies suggested that he might have underestimated the cognitive abilities of very young infants.

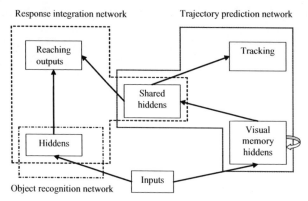

Figure 16.1. Modular network topology for looking and reaching. The network in the lower left learns to recognize objects based on their static features. The network on the right learns to follow the trajectory of moving objects. The network in the upper left learns to reach for objects by integrating visual tracking and object recognition. (Adapted, with permission, from Mareschal et al., 1999).

An influential series of experiments suggested that infants as young as 3.5 months understand the continued existence of hidden objects if tested by where they look rather than where they reach (Baillargeon, 1987). Infants were familiarized to a simple perceptual sequence and then shown two different test events: one that was perceptually more novel but consistent with the continued existence of objects and one that was perceptually more familiar but that violated the notion that hidden objects continue to exist. Infants looked longer at the impossible event, which was interpreted as evidence that they understand the continued existence of occluded objects.

Computational modeling has clarified how infants could reveal an object concept with looking but not by reaching. In one model, perceptual input about occluded objects fed a hidden layer with recurrent connections, which in turn fed two distinct output systems: a looking system and a reaching system (Munakata et al., 1997). Both systems learned to predict the location of an input object, but the reaching system lagged developmentally behind the looking system because of differential learning rates. The same underlying competence (understanding where an object should be) thus led to different patterns of performance, depending on which system was used to assess that competence.

A different model of the lag between looking and reaching (Mareschal, Plunkett, & Harris, 1999) used a modular neural network system implementing the dual-route hypothesis of visual processing (i.e., that visual information is segregated into a *what* ventral stream and a *where* dorsal stream). Like the previous model, this one had a shared bank of hidden units receiving input from a recurrent bank of visual-memory inputs. As shown in Figure 16.1, these hidden units fed two output modules: a trajectory-prediction module and a response-integration module. The former was trained to predict the position of an object on a subsequent time step. The latter was trained to combine hidden-unit activations in the trajectory module with object-recognition inputs. Here, the time lag between looking and reaching was explained by the *what* and *where* streams needing to be integrated in reaching tasks, but not in looking tasks, which can rely solely on the *where* stream. The model uniquely predicted developmental lags for any task requiring integration of the two visual routes.

Although both models simulated a lag between looking and reaching, some embodied simulations integrated the *what* and *where* functions into a *how* function (Schlesinger, 2004; Schlesinger, Parisi, & Langer, 2000). Here, the problem of reaching was constrained by mechanical and kinematic properties of the task that facilitate learning.

A novel experiment used a primitive robot to produce looking-time data in an object-permanence experiment measuring looking (Baillargeon, 1986). This robot knew nothing about objects and their permanence, but was designed to habituate to visual stimuli that it captured through video cameras (Lovett & Scassellati, 2004). Its behavior as a surrogate participant in the infant experiment suggested that looking-time differences between possible and impossible events could be due to mere habituation to stimuli, having nothing to do with knowledge of objects or their permanence.

A major subtopic in development of the object concept concerns the so-called *A-not-B* error. Between seven and twelve months of age, infants search for a hidden object in one location (conventionally called location A), but when it is moved to another hiding place (location B), they persevere in searching at A (Piaget, 1954). Ten major regularities have been noted in the extensive psychological literature on the A-not-B error.

1. *Age.* Before seven to eight months, infants do not search for a hidden object. Between seven and twelve months, they perseverate in searching A. After twelve months, they search in B.
2. *Delay.* No error with no delay between hiding and search; error increases with amount of delay.
3. *Décalage.* Well before twelve months, infants look longer at an event in which the hidden object is retrieved from a different place than where they last saw it.
4. *Distinctiveness.* Making the hiding places more distinctive reduces error, for example, by using distinctive covers, landmarks, or familiar environments. Conversely, using identical covers increases error.
5. *Multiple locations.* Decrease error.

6. *Reaching to A.* The more reaches to A, the more likely the error.
7. *Interestingness.* Less error the more interesting the toy; hiding a cookie reduces error.
8. *Objectless.* Cuing a cover is sufficient to elicit the error without any hidden object.
9. *Object helpful.* Less error in covers-only condition when a toy is hidden at B.
10. *Adult error.* Even adults can make this error under certain conditions.

Two quite different computational models addressed these regularities, one using a feed-forward neural network with self-recurrent excitatory connections within hidden and output layers to maintain representations over time and inhibitory connections within these layers to implement competition (Munakata, 1998). The network received sequential input about three hiding locations, two types of cover, and two toys. These inputs fed a bank of self-recursive hidden units representing the three locations. These hidden units fed two separate banks of outputs: gaze/expectation units, representing where infants look, and reach units representing where infants reach. Because reaching was permitted only near the end of a trial, these units were updated less frequently than the gaze/expectation units, which produced earlier looking than reaching. The network was trained with a few standard A-not-B observations. Learning of feed-forward weights was done with a zero-sum Hebbian rule that increased a weight when its sending unit's activation was higher than the mean of its layer and decreased a weight when its sending unit activation was lower than the mean of its layer. Recurrent and inhibitory weights were fixed. Age effects were covered by increasing the recurrent weights from .3 to .5, that is, stronger recurrence with increasing age.

The other model of the A-not-B error was a dynamic-system model (Thelen et al., 2001). A decision to reach in a particular direction (A or B) was modeled as activation in a dynamic field, expressed in a differential equation, the details of which can be found elsewhere (Thelen et al., 2001). Somewhat informally,

$$\begin{aligned} activation = {} & -decay + cooperativity + h \\ & + noise + task + cue \\ & + reach.memory \end{aligned} \quad (16.3)$$

where *decay* was a linear decrease in activation, *cooperativity* included both local excitation and distant inhibition integrated over field positions, *h* was the resting activation level of the field, Gaussian *noise* ensured that activations were probabilistic rather than deterministic, *task* reflected persisting features of the task environment, *cue* reflected the location of the object or attention to a specific cover, and *reach memory* reflected the frequency and recency of reaching in a particular direction. Development relied on the resting activation level of the field. When *h* was low, strong inputs predominated and activation was driven largely by inputs and less by local interactions, a condition known as noncooperation. When *h* was large, many field sites interacted, and local excitation was amplified by neighboring excitation and distant inhibition, allowing cooperation and self-sustained excitation, even without continual input. Parameter *h* was set to -6 for cooperation and -12 for noncooperation. All parameters but *h* were differential functions of field position and time. Variation of the cue parameter implemented different experimental conditions. Other parameters were held constant, but estimated to fit psychological data.

The differential equation simulated up to 10 sec of delay in steps of 50 msec. An above-threshold activation peak indicated a perseverative reach when centered on the A location or a correct reach when centered on the B location. This idea was supported by findings that activity in populations of neurons in monkey motor and premotor cortex became active in the 150 msec between cue and reach, and predicted the direction of ordinary reaching (Amirikian & Georgopoulos, 2003). See Figure 4.3 in this volume, which shows that

Table 16.3: Model coverage of the A-not-B error in object permanence

	Model	
Regularity	Munakata (1998)	Thelen et al. (2001)
Age	yes	yes
Delay	yes	yes
Décalage	yes	no
Distinctiveness	yes	yes
Multiple locations	yes	no
Reaching to A	yes	no
Interestingness	no	no
Objectless	yes	yes
Object helpful	yes	no
Adult error	no	no

neighboring excitation sustains local activation peaks whereas global inhibition prevents diffusion of peaks and stabilizes against competing inputs.

In simulation of younger infants, implemented by noncooperation ($h = -12$), a cue to location B initially elicited activation, which then decayed rapidly, allowing memory of previous reaching to A to predominate. But in simulations of young infants allowed to reach without delay, the initial B activation tended to override memory of previous A reaches. In simulation of older infants, implemented by cooperation ($h = -6$), the ability to sustain initial B activation across delays produced correct B reaches despite memory of reaching to A. This model suggested that the A-not-B error has more to do with the dynamics of reaching for objects than with the emergence of a concept of permanence.

Comparative coverage of the psychological regularities by these two models is indicated in Table 16.3. The neural-network model covered almost all of these regularities, and it is possible that the dynamic-system model could also achieve this by manipulation of its existing parameters. It would be interesting to see if the dynamic-system model could be implemented in a neurally plausible way. Both models were highly designed by fixing weights in the neural model and by writing equations and fitting parameters in the dynamic-system model. Modeler-designed parameter changes were used to implement age-related development in both models.

9. Artificial Syntax

An issue that attracted considerable simulation activity concerns whether cognition should be interpreted in terms of symbolic rules or subsymbolic neural networks. For example, it was argued that infants' ability to distinguish one syntactic pattern from another could only be explained by a symbolic rule-based account (Marcus et al., 1999). After being familiarized to sentences in an artificial language with a particular syntactic pattern (such as ABA), infants preferred to listen to sentences with an inconsistent syntactic form (such as ABB). The claim about the necessity of rule-based processing was contradicted by a number of neural-network models showing more interest in novel than familiar syntactic patterns (Altmann & Dienes, 1999; Elman, 1999; Negishi, 1999; Shultz, 1999; Shultz & Bale, 2001; Sirois, Buckingham, & Shultz, 2000). This principal effect from one simple experiment is rather easy for a variety of connectionist learning algorithms to cover, probably due to their basic ability to learn and generalize. In addition to this novelty preference, there were a few infants who exhibited a slight familiarity preference, as evidenced by slightly more recovery to consistent novel sentences than to familiar sentences.

One of the connectionist simulations (Shultz & Bale, 2001) was replicated (Vilcu & Hadley, 2005) using batches of CC encoder networks, but it was claimed that this model did not generalize well and merely learned sound contours rather than syntax. Like other encoder networks, these networks learned to reproduce their inputs on their output units. Discrepancy between inputs and outputs is considered as error, which networks learn to reduce. Infants are thought to construct an internal model of stimuli to which they are being exposed and then differentially attend to novel stimuli that deviate from their representations (Cohen & Arthur, 1983). Because neural learning is directed at reducing the largest sources of error, network error can be considered as an index of future attention and learning.

The CC simulations captured the essentials of the infant data: more interest in sentences inconsistent with the familiar pattern than in sentences consistent with that pattern and occasional familiarity preferences (Shultz & Bale, 2001). In addition, CC networks showed the usual exponential decreases in attention to a repeated stimulus pattern that are customary in habituation experiments and generalized both inside and outside of the range of training patterns. Follow-up simulations clarified that CC networks were sensitive to both phonemic content and syntactic structure, as infants probably are (Shultz & Bale, 2006).

A simple AA network model contained a single layer of interconnected units, allowing internal circulation of unit activations over multiple time cycles (Sirois et al., 2000). After learning the habituation sentences with a delta rule, these networks needed more processing cycles to learn inconsistent than consistent test sentences. The mapping of processing cycles to recovery from habituation seems particularly natural in this model.

A series of C4.5 models failed to capture any essential features of the infant data (Shultz, 2003). C4.5 could not simulate familiarization because it trivially learned to expect the only category to which it was exposed. When trained instead to discriminate the syntactic patterns, it did not learn the desired rules except when these rules were virtually encoded in the inputs.

Three different SRN models covered the principal finding of a novelty preference, but two of these models showed such a strong novelty preference that they would not likely show any familiarity preference. Two of these SRN models also were not replicated by other researchers (Vilcu & Hadley, 2001, 2005). Failure to replicate seems surprising with computational models and probably deserves further study.

Table 16.4: Coverage of artificial syntax phenomena

Author	Model	Novelty preference	Regularity Familiarity preference	Simulation replicated
Altmann & Diennes (1999)	SRN	yes	–	no
Elman (1999)	SRN	yes	no	no
Negishi (1999)	SRN	yes	no	–
Shultz & Bale (2001)	CC	yes	yes	yes
Sirois et al. (2000)	AA	yes	yes	–
Shultz (2003)	C4.5	no	no	–

Comparative performance of each of these models is summarized in Table 16.4. Dashes in the table indicate uncertainty. It is possible that the SRN models and the AA model might be able to show some slight familiarity preference if not so deeply trained.

10. Similarity-to-Correlation Shift in Category Learning

Research on category learning with a familiarization paradigm showed that four-month-olds process information about independent features of visual stimuli, whereas ten-month-olds additionally abstract relations among those features (Younger & Cohen, 1986). These results addressed a classic controversy about whether perceptual development involves integration or differentiation of stimulus information, integration being favored by developing the ability to understand relations among already discovered features. Following repetitions of visual stimuli with correlated features, four-month-olds recovered attention to stimuli with novel features more than to stimuli with either correlated or uncorrelated familiar features. However, ten-month-olds recovered attention both to stimuli with novel features and to stimuli with familiar uncorrelated features more than to stimuli with familiar correlated features. Uncorrelated test items violated the correlations in the training items. The four-month-old finding is termed a *similarity* effect because the uncorrelated test item was most similar to those in the familiarization set. The ten-month-old finding is termed a *correlation* effect. Both groups learned about individual stimulus features, but older infants also learned how these features correlate.

These effects, including the shift from similarity to correlation, were simulated with three different neural-network algorithms: BP networks with shrinking receptive fields (Shrink-BP; Westermann & Mareschal, 2004), *Sustain* networks (Gureckis & Love, 2004), and CC encoder networks (Shultz & Cohen, 2004). Westermann and Mareschal (2004) used more Gaussian hidden units than inputs and shrank the width of Gaussian receptive fields for older infants to mimic developing visual acuity. Increased acuity arising from decreased field size presumably enhances selective response to unique conjunctions of feature values. The Sustain algorithm tries to assimilate new stimuli to existing prototypes and recruits a new prototype when stimuli are sufficiently novel. A parameter controlled the number of prototypes that could be recruited and was set higher for older infants. Alternatively, Sustain could capture the infant data if the inputs were randomized to mimic poor visual acuity in younger infants. In CC networks, age was implemented by setting the score-threshold parameter higher for four-month-olds than for ten-month-olds, an approach that has been used successfully to model other age-related changes in learning tasks (Shultz, 2003). Training continues until all output activations are within a score threshold of their

Table 16.5: Coverage of the shift from features to correlations in category learning

Authors	Model	Effect			
		Similarity	Correlation	Shift	Habituation
Westermann & Mareschal (2004)	Shrink-BP	yes	yes	yes	no
Gureckis & Love (2004)	Sustain	yes	yes	yes	no
Shultz & Cohen (2004)	CC	yes	yes	yes	yes
Shultz & Cohen (2004)	BP	no	no	no	no

target values for all training patterns. Thus, a lower score-threshold parameter produces deeper learning.

In contrast to these successful models, a wide range of topologies of ordinary BP networks failed to capture any of these effects (Shultz & Cohen, 2004). Comparative patterns of data coverage are summarized in Table 16.5.

The three successful models shared several commonalities. They all employed unsupervised (or self-supervised in the case of encoder networks) connectionist learning, and they explained apparent qualitative shifts in learning by quantitative variation in learning parameters. Also, the Shrink-BP and Sustain (in the randomized-input version) models both emphasized increased visual acuity as an underlying cause of learning change. Finally, both the Sustain and CC models grew in computational power.

When CC networks with a low score threshold were repeatedly tested over the familiarization phase, they predicted an early similarity effect followed by a correlation effect. Tests of this *habituation* prediction found that ten-month-olds who habituated to training stimuli looked longer at uncorrelated than correlated test stimuli, but those who did not habituate did the opposite, looking longer at correlated than uncorrelated test stimuli (Cohen & Arthur, 2003).

CC might be preferred over Sustain because: (a) the effects in Sustain are smaller than in infants, necessitating 10,000 networks to reach statistical significance, whereas the number of CC networks matched the nine infants run in each condition, (b) parameter values had to be op-

timally fit in Sustain, but not in CC, and (c) like the well-known ALCOVE, concept-learning algorithm, Sustain employs an attention mechanism that CC does not require. One could say that Sustain attends to learn, whereas CC learns to attend. Likewise, CC seems preferable over Shrink-BP because CC learns much faster (tens vs. thousands of epochs), thus making a better match to the few minutes of familiarization in the infant experiments. CC is so far the only model to capture the *habituation* effect across an experimental session at a single age level. Shrink-BP and Sustain would not capture this effect because their mechanisms operate over ages, not over trials; CC mechanisms operate over both trials and ages.

11. Discrimination-Shift Learning

Discrimination-shift learning tasks stretch back to early behaviorism (Spence, 1952) and have a substantial human literature with robust, age-related effects well suited to learning models. In a typical discrimination-shift task, a learner is shown pairs of stimuli with mutually exclusive attributes along two perceptual dimensions (e.g., a black square and a white circle or a white square and a black circle, creating four stimulus pairs when left-right position is counterbalanced). The task involves learning to pick the consistently-rewarded stimulus in each pair, where reward is linked to an attribute (e.g., black). When the learner consistently picks the target stimulus (usually eight times or more in ten consecutive trials), various shifts in reward contingencies are introduced. A within-dimension shift involves an attribute from the initially relevant dimension as the new learning target (e.g., shifting from black to white). Conversely, a between-dimensions shift involves a new learning target from the previously irrelevant dimension (e.g., from black to circle).

Children above ten years and adults typically exhibit dimensional transfer on these tasks, whereby within-dimension shifts are easier (i.e., require fewer learning trials) than between-dimension shifts, and generalization of shift learning is observed on untrained stimuli. In contrast, preschoolers do not show dimensional transfer, and their learning is often explained as stimulus-response association. A popular interpretation of this age-related change in performance was that development involves a change from associative to mediated information processing during childhood (Kendler, 1979).

A simulation of these tasks with BP networks (Raijmakers, van Koten, & Molenaar, 1996) found that performance was comparable to that of preschoolers because networks failed to show dimensional transfer and generalization. Even though these networks included hidden units, which might mediate between inputs and outputs, they failed to exhibit mediated processing typical of older children and adults. The authors concluded that feed-forward neural networks were unable to capture the rule-like behavior of adults who abstract the relevant dimensions of variation in a problem.

However, research with CC networks showed that these shift-learning tasks are linearly separable problems and that multilayered BP nets make the problem more complicated than necessary (Sirois & Shultz, 1998). These authors argued, based on psychological evidence, that preschoolers and adults differ in depth of processing rather than on qualitatively different representational structures. They further suggested that adults acquire more focused representations through extensive iterative processing, which can be simulated in neural networks by lowering the score-threshold parameter.

These CC networks provided successful coverage of a wide range of discrimination-shift phenomena, capturing the performance of both preschoolers and adults. Two empirical predictions were made. One was that adults would perform like preschoolers if iterative processing were blocked. Overtraining research had already shown that preschoolers would perform like adults through additional learning trials. New research using a cognitive load during discriminative learning confirmed that adults do perform like preschoolers (Sirois & Shultz, 2006), revealing a continuity of representations between preschoolers and adults.

The second prediction concerned associative learning in preschoolers and was counterintuitive. Researchers had suggested that preschoolers do not respond on the basis of perceptual attributes but rather treat stimuli as perceptual compounds. The idea was that preschoolers are under object control, whereas adults are under dimensional control. But networks were sometimes correct on stimulus pairs and incorrect for each stimulus in a pair (Sirois & Shultz, 1998). The prediction here was that preschoolers would be under *pair* control rather than *object* control, such that they would have difficulty categorizing individual stimuli following successful pairwise learning. This has since been confirmed in experiments with children (Sirois, 2002).

12. Concept and Word Learning

The classic developmental problem of how children learn concepts and words is attracting a flurry of interest from both Bayesian and connectionist modelers. Four-year-olds and adults were reported to be consistently Bayesian in the way they generalized a novel word beyond a few provided examples (Xu & Tenenbaum, 2007). When three examples of a novel word were generated by a teacher, learners were justified in assuming that these examples represented a random sample from the word's extension. As a result, they restricted generalization to a specific, subordinate meaning. In contrast, when three examples were provided but only one of them was a randomly selected instance of the word meaning (the other two examples having been chosen by the learner), subjects generalized more broadly, to the basic level, just as in previous studies that had provided only one example of the word's extension. The authors argued that other theories and models that do not explicitly address example sampling could not naturally account for these results.

Other, related phenomena that are attracting modeling concern shape and material biases in generalizing new word meanings. Six regularities from the psychological literature deserve model coverage:

1. Shape and material bias. When shown a single novel solid object and told its novel name, 2.5-year-olds generalized the name to objects with the same shape. In contrast, when shown a single novel nonsolid substance and told its novel name, children of the same age typically generalized the name to instances of the same material (Colunga & Smith, 2003; Imai & Gentner, 1997; Soja, Carey, & Spelke, 1992). These biases are termed overhypotheses because they help to structure a hypothesis space at a more specific level (Goodman, 1955/1983).

2. Development of shape bias and material bias. The foregoing biases emerge only after children have learned some names for solid and nonsolid things (Samuelson & Smith, 1999). One-year-old infants applied a novel name to objects identical to the trained object but not to merely similar objects. Furthermore, the training of infants on object naming typically requires familiar categories and multiple examples. This is in contrast to 2.5-year-olds' attentional shifts being evoked by naming a single novel example.

3. Shape bias before material bias. At two years, children exhibit shape bias on these tasks, but not material bias (Imai & Gentner, 1997; Kobayashi, 1997; Landau, Smith, & Jones, 1988; Samuelson & Smith, 1999; Soja, Carey, & Spelke, 1991; Subrahmanyam, Landau, & Gelman, 1999).

4. Syntax. Name generalization in these tasks is influenced by syntactic cues marking the noun as a count noun or mass noun (Dickinson, 1988; Imai & Gentner, 1997; Soja, 1992). If an English noun is preceded by the article *a* or *the*, it yields a shape bias, but if preceded by *some* or *much* it shows a material bias.

5. Ontology bias. Names for things tend to not refer to categories that span the boundary between solids and nonsolids, for example, water versus ice (Colunga & Smith, 2005). This underscores greater complexity than a mere shape bias for solids and material bias for nonsolids. Solid things do not typically receive the same name as nonsolid stuff does.

6. Material-nonsolid bias. In young children, there is an initial material bias for nonsolids (Colunga & Smith, 2005).

All six of these phenomena were covered by a constraint-satisfaction neural network trained with contrastive Hebbian learning (see Figure 2.2 in this volume) that adjusts weights on the basis of correlations between unit activations (Colunga & Smith, 2005). Regularities 5 and 6 were actually predicted by the network simulations before being documented in children. Each word and the solidity and syntax of each example were represented locally by turning on a particular unit. Distributed activation patterns represented the shape and material of each individual object or substance. Hidden units learned to represent the correlations between shape, material, solidity, syntax, and words. After networks learned a vocabulary via examples that paired names with perceptual instances, they were tested on how they would categorize novel things. Statistical distributions of the training patterns matched adult judgments (Samuelson & Smith, 1999). The recurrent connection scheme is illustrated by the arrows in Figure 16.2.

A hierarchical Bayesian model covered the mature shape bias and material bias described in regularity 1 and probably could

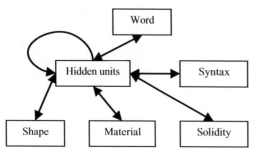

Figure 16.2. Topology of the network used by Colunga and Smith (2005). (Adapted with permission.)

be extended to cover regularities 4 and 5 (Kemp, Perfors, & Tenenbaum, 2007). Such models include representations at several levels of abstraction and show how knowledge can be acquired at levels remote from experiential data, thus providing for both top-down and bottom-up learning. Hypotheses at some intermediate level are conditional on both data at a lower level and overhypotheses at a higher level (see Chapter 3 in this volume).

This model also generated several predictions that may prove to be somewhat unique. For example, the optimal number of examples per category is two, assuming a fixed number of total examples. Also, learning is sometimes faster at higher than lower levels of abstraction, thus explaining why abstract knowledge might appear to be innate even when it is learnable. This is likely to happen in situations when a child encounters sparse or noisy observations such that any individual observation is difficult to interpret, although the observations taken together might support some hypothesis.

As is typical, this Bayesian model is pitched at a computational level of analysis, whereas connectionist models operate at more of an implementation level. As such, a computational-level Bayesian model may apply to a variety of implementations. The other side of this coin is that Bayes' rule does not generate representations – it instead computes statistics over structures designed by the modelers. In contrast, connectionist approaches sometimes are able to show how structures emerge.

Kemp et al. (2007) note that a common objection is that the success of Bayesian models depends on the modeler's skill in choosing prior probabilities. Interestingly, hierarchical Bayesian models can solve this problem because abstract knowledge can be learned rather than specified in advance.

A final point is that the correlations between syntax, solidity, shape, and material that underlie learning and generalization in this domain are far from perfect (Samuelson & Smith, 1999). For example, according to adult raters, *bubble* names a nonsolid but shape-based category; *soap* names a solid but material-based category; *crayon*, *key*, and *nail* name categories that are based on both shape and material. The many exceptions to these statistical regularities suggest that symbolic rule-based models would be nonstarters in this domain.

Particularly challenging to learn are so-called *deictic* words, such as personal pronouns, whose meaning shifts with point of view. Although most children acquire personal pronouns such as *me* and *you* without notable errors (Charney, 1980; Chiat, 1981; Clark, 1978), a small minority of children show persistent pronoun errors before getting them right (Clark, 1978; Oshima-Takane, 1992; Schiff-Meyers, 1983). The correct semantics are such that *me* refers to the person using the pronoun and *you* refers to the person who is addressed by the pronoun (Barwise & Perry, 1983). Unlike most words, the referent of these pronouns is not fixed, but instead shifts with conversational role. Although a mother calls herself *me* and calls her child *you*, these pronouns must be reversed when the child utters them. Because the referent of a personal pronoun shifts with conversational role, an imitative model for correct usage can be difficult to find. If children simply imitated what they heard in speech that was directly addressed to them, they would incorrectly refer to themselves as *you* and to the mother as *me*. These are indeed the typical errors made by a few children before sorting out the shifting references. A challenge for computational modelers is to explain both this rare sequence and the virtually errorless acquisition observed in most children.

The most coherent explanation and evidence focused on the extent to which children were exposed to speech directly addressed to them versus speech that they overheard (Oshima-Takane, 1988). In overheard speech, children can observe that *you* refers to a person other than themselves and that *me* and *you* reciprocate each other with shifts of speaker, addressee, and referent. But in directly addressed speech, children would observe that *you* always refers to themselves and that *me* refers to the speaker. Thus, the correct semantics are better understood as children listen to others addressing each other.

This idea was supported by a training experiment using the so-called *me-you* game for several weeks with nineteen-month-olds who were just starting to acquire personal pronouns (Oshima-Takane, 1988). Correct pronoun production benefited more from listening to overheard speech (for example, the mother looks at the father, points to herself, and says *me*) than from listening to directly addressed speech (e.g., the father looks at the child, points to the child, and says *you*). Only those children assigned to the overheard speech condition could produce pronouns without errors. Also supportive was a naturalistic study in which second-borns acquired these pronouns earlier than did first-borns, even though these two groups of children did not differ on other measures of language development (Oshima-Takane, Goodz, & Derevensky, 1996). The explanation is that second-born children have relatively more opportunities to hear pronouns used in speech not addressed to them in conversations between a parent and an older sibling.

There are some theoretically interesting, albeit extreme, conditions of pronoun experience that cannot be found with children, such as exclusive exposure to either directly addressed speech or overheard speech. One advantage of simulation work is that such variations can be systematically explored. Several simulations with CC networks manipulated the relative amounts of directly addressed speech and overheard speech (Oshima-Takane, Takane, & Shultz, 1999; Shultz, Buckingham, & Oshima-Takane, 1994). As in the psychology experiment (Oshima-Takane, 1988), the networks had input information on speaker, addressee, and referent, and learned to predict the correct pronoun. As with children, error-free pronoun acquisition by networks was achieved with a high proportion of overheard speech patterns, whereas persistent reversal errors resulted from a high proportion of directly addressed speech patterns. Thus, both errorless acquisition and a progression from reversal errors to correct usage can be achieved, depending on the relative proportions of directly addressed and overheard speech. In an attempt to find effective therapeutic techniques for persistent reversal errors, simulations pointed to the benefits of massive amounts of overheard speech. Attempts to correct pronoun reversal errors using directly addressed speech are notoriously difficult because the child misunderstands the correction (Oshima-Takane, 1992), and this difficulty was verified with simulations.

Simulation of first- and second-person pronoun acquisition was also implemented within a developmental robotics approach (Gold & Scassellati, 2006). Instead of learning a pronoun-production function of speaker, addressee, and referent, $p = f(s, a, r)$, as in Oshima-Takane's psychology experiment and the CC network simulations, a humanoid robot learned a pronoun-comprehension function, referent as a function of speaker, addressee, and pronoun, $r = f(s, a, p)$. This comprehension function was learned in a game of catch with a ball between two humans and the robot. The robot's video camera captured both visual and auditory information, the latter being processed by a speech-recognition system. The humans tossed the ball back and forth and occasionally to the robot, while commenting on the action with utterances such as, "I got the ball" or "You got the ball." Once reference was established, word counts for each pronoun were updated by the robot's computer in 2×2 tables for each pronoun-property pair. The highest significant *chi-square* value indicated the meaning of the utterance. Results revealed that *you* as addressee was acquired first and more strongly than *I* as speaker. Although the robot's distinction between *I* and *you* captures the correct semantics, it is not generally true that children acquire second- before first-person pronouns. If anything, there is a tendency for children to show the reverse order: first-person pronouns before second-person pronouns (Oshima-Takane, 1992; Oshima-Takane et al., 1996).

In a simulation of blind children, the robot in another condition could not see which of the humans had the ball, but could sense whether it (the robot) had the ball. This blind robot fell into the reversal error of interpreting *you* as the robot, as do young blind children (Andersen, Dunlea, & Kekelis, 1984).

The game of catch seems like an interesting and natural method to facilitate personal pronoun acquisition. Although tabulating word-property counts in 2×2 tables and then analyzing these tables with *chi-square* tests is a common technique in the study of computational semantics, it is unclear whether this could be implemented with neural realism.

A major difference between the psychology experiment and neural-network model on the one hand and the robotic model on the other hand concerns the use of gestures. Both the psychology experiment and the neural-network model liberally used pointing gestures to convey information about the referent, as well as eye-gaze information, to convey information about the addressee. In contrast, the robotic model eschewed gestures on the grounds that pointing is rude, unnecessary, and difficult for robots to understand. Paradoxically then, even though developmental robotics holds the promise of understanding embodied cognition, this robotic model ignored both gestural and eye-gaze information. The game of catch, accompanied by appropriate verbal commentary, nicely compensated for the absence of such information in the robot. However, humans are well known to both use and interpret gestures to complement verbal communication (Goldin-Meadow, 1999), and deictic (or pointing) gestures (McNeill, 1992) are among the first to appear in young children, as early as ten months of age (Bates, 1979). Hence, future humanoid robotic modelers might want to incorporate gesture production and interpretation in an effort to more closely follow human strategies.

It would seem interesting to explore computational systems that could learn all the functions relating speaker, addressee, referent, and pronoun to each other as well as extended functions that included third-person pronouns. Could learning some of these functions afford inferences about other functional relations? Or would every function have to be separately and explicitly learned? Bayesian methods and neural networks with recurrent connections might be good candidates for systems that could make inferences in various directions.

13. Abnormal Development

One of the promising ideas supported by connectionist modeling of development is that developmental disorders might emerge from early differences that lead to abnormal developmental trajectories (Thomas & Karmiloff-Smith, 2002). One such simulation was inspired by evidence that larger brains favor local connectivity and smaller brains favor long-distance connections (Zhang & Sejnowski, 2000) and that children destined to become autistic show abnormally rapid brain growth in the months preceding the appearance of autistic symptoms (Courchesne, Carper, & Akshoomoff, 2003). Neural networks modeled the computational effects of such changes in brain size (Lewis & Elman, 2008). The networks were feed-forward pattern associators, trained with backpropagation of error. As pictured in Figure 16.3, each of two *hemispheres* of ten units was fed by a bank of five input units. Units within a hemisphere were

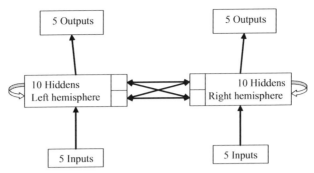

Figure 16.3. Topology of the autism network. Each of two hemispheres of ten units was fed by a bank of five input units. Units within a hemisphere were recurrently connected, and two units in each hemisphere were fully connected across hemispheres. Each hemisphere, in turn, fed a bank of five output units.

recurrently connected, and two units in each hemisphere were fully connected across hemispheres. Each hemisphere, in turn, fed a bank of five output units. Both inter- and intra-hemispheric connections exhibited conduction delays, implemented by periodically adding or subtracting copy units forming a transmission chain – the more links in the chain, the longer the conduction delay. The networks simulated inter-hemispheric interaction by growing in spatial extent, with consequent transmission delays, at the rate of either typically developing children or those in the process of becoming autistic.

Those networks that simulated autistic growth (marked by rapid increases in the space taken up by the network) were less affected by removal of inter-hemispheric connections than those networks that grew at a normal rate, indicating a reduced reliance on long-distance connections in the autistic networks. As these differences accelerated, they were reflected in declining connectivity and deteriorating performance. The simulation offers a computational demonstration of how brain overgrowth could produce neural reorganization and behavioral deficits.

In a similar vein, researchers have examined the role of initial conditions in developmental dyslexia (Harm & Seidenberg, 1999), specific language impairments (Hoeffner &

McClelland, 1994), and Williams syndrome (Thomas & Karmiloff-Smith, 2002).

14. Conclusions

14.1. *Computational Diversity*

Computational modeling of development is now blessed with several different techniques. It started in the 1970s with production systems, which were joined in the late 1980s by neural networks. But by the early twenty-first century, there were also dynamic system, robotic, and Bayesian approaches to development. This diversity is welcome because each approach has already made valuable contributions to the study of development, just as they have in other areas of psychology. All of these approaches have contributed to the notion that an understanding of development can be facilitated by making theoretical ideas precise and systematic, covering various phenomena of interest, linking several different findings together, explaining them, and predicting new phenomena. Such activities significantly accelerate the scientific process.

Production systems are to be admired for their precision and clarity in specifying both knowledge representations and processes that operate on these representations to produce new knowledge. Connectionist systems have the advantage of graded knowledge representations and relative closeness to biological neural systems in terms of activation functions, connectivity, and learning processes. Dynamic systems illustrate how the many different features of a complex computational system may interact to yield emergent behavior and ability. Developmental robotics forces modelers to deal with the complexities of real environments and the constraints of operating in real time. Bayesian methods contribute tools for making inferences despite incomplete and uncertain knowledge.

14.2. *Complementary Computation*

These different modeling approaches tend to complement each other, partly by being pitched at various levels. Marr's (1982) levels of computational analysis, imperfect as they are, can be used to explore this. Marr argued that explanations of a complex system can be found in at least three levels: analysis of the system's competence, design of an algorithm and representational format, and implementation. Analyzing a system's competence has been addressed by task analysis in symbolic approaches, differential equations in a dynamic system approach, and Bayesian optimization.

Every computational model must cope with the algorithmic level. Symbolic rule-based models do this with the mechanics of production systems: the matching and firing of rules, and the consequent updating of working memory. In neural networks, patterns of unit activations represent active memory, whereas weight updates represent the learning of long-term memory. Activation fields geometrically represent the changing positions of a dynamic system. Bayesian approaches borrow structures from symbolic approaches and compute statistics over these structures to identify the most probable hypothesis or structure given current evidence.

The implementation level can be taken to refer to the details of how a particular model is instantiated. In this context, higher-level approaches, such as production systems (Lebiere & Anderson, 1993) and

dynamic systems (van Gelder, 1998), have sometimes been implemented as neural networks. One can also be concerned with how a system is implemented in neural tissue. Of the approaches considered in this chapter, neural networks come closest to simulating how this might be done because these networks were largely inspired by principles of how the brain and its neurons work. Growth of brain structure within a network and integration of brain structures across networks have both been stressed in this and other reviews (Westermann et al., 2006). As noted, dynamic systems can also be inspired by neuroscience discoveries. There is, of course, a continuum of neural realism in such implementations.

If the different modeling approaches do exist at different levels, wouldn't it make sense to use the lowest level to obtain the finest grain of detail, perhaps to a biologically realistic model of actual neural circuits? Remembering the reductionist cruncher argument (Block, 1995), the answer would be negative because different levels may be better for different purposes. It is preferable to work at the most appropriate level for one's goals and questions, rather than always trying to reduce to some lower level. Nonetheless, one of the convincing rationales for cognitive science was that different levels of analysis can constrain each other, as when psychologists try to build computational models that are biologically realistic.

14.3. *Computational Bakeoffs*

Even if computational algorithms exist at somewhat different levels, so-called *bakeoff* competitions are still possible and interesting, both between and within various approaches. This is because different approaches and models sometimes make different, and even conflicting, predictions about psychological phenomena. Focusing on phenomena that have attracted a lot of modeling attention, as in this chapter, provides some ready-made bakeoff scenarios.

Symbolic and connectionist models were sharply contrasted here in the cases of the balance scale, past tense, artificial syntax, and pronouns. In balance-scale simulations, rule-based models, but not connectionist models, had difficulty with the torque-difference effect. This is a graded, perceptual effect that is awkward for crisp symbolic rules but natural for neural systems with graded representations and update processes that propagate these gradations. Past-tense formation was likewise natural for neural approaches, which can implement regularities and exceptions in a homogeneous system and thus capture various phenomena by letting them play off against each other, but awkward for symbolic systems that isolate rule processing from other processes. Several connectionist models captured the novelty preference in learning an artificial syntax, but the one rule-based approach that was tried could not do so. Although no rule-based models have yet been applied to pronoun acquisition, the graded effects of variation in amount of experience with overheard versus directly addressed speech would pose a challenge to rule-based models.

Attractive modeling targets, such as the balance scale, artificial syntax, similarity-to-correlation shift, and discrimination shift also afforded some bakeoff competitions within the neural approach in terms of static (BP) versus constructive (CC) network models. On the balance scale, CC networks uniquely captured final, stage-4 performance and did so without having to segregate inputs by weight and distance. CC also captured more phenomena than did static BP models in simulations of the similarity-to-correlation shift. This was probably because CC naturally focused first on identifying stimulus features while underpowered and only later with additional computational power abstracted correlations among these features. In discrimination-shift learning, the advantage of CC over static BP was a bit different. Here, BP modelers were led to incorrect conclusions about the inability of neural networks to learn a mediated approach to this problem by virtue of trying BP networks with designed hidden units. Because CC networks only recruit hidden units as needed, they were able to verify

that these simple learning problems were actually linearly separable, suggesting that hidden units were making learning more difficult than it needed to be. Other constructive versus static network competitions have also favored constructive networks on developmental problems (Shultz, 2006). To simulate stages and transitions between stages, there is an advantage in starting small and increasing in computational power as needed.

The notion of underlying *qualitative* changes causing qualitative changes in psychological functioning differs from the idea of underlying small *quantitative* changes causing qualitative shifts in behavior, as in mere weight adjustment in static neural networks or quantitative changes in dynamic-system parameters. There are analogous qualitative structural changes at the neurological level in terms of synaptogenesis and neurogenesis, both of which have been demonstrated to be under the control of pressures to learn in mature as well as developing animals (Shultz, Mysore, & Quartz, 2007). The CC algorithm is neutral with respect to whether hidden-unit recruitment implements synaptogenesis or neurogenesis, depending on whether the recruit already exists in the system or is freshly created. But it is clear that brains do grow in structure and there seem to be computational advantages in such growth, particularly for simulating qualitative changes in behavioral development (Shultz, 2006).

This is not to imply that static connectionist models do not occupy a prominent place in developmental modeling. On the contrary, this review highlights several cases in which static networks offered compelling and informative models of developmental phenomena. Static networks may be particularly appropriate in cases for which evolution has prepared organisms with either network topologies or a combination of connection weights and topologies (Shultz & Mareschal, 1997). When relevant biological constraints are known, as in a model of object permanence (Mareschal et al., 1999), they can guide design of static network topologies. In some studies, the process of network evolution itself has been modeled (Schlesinger et al., 2000). Ultimately, models showing how networks evolve, develop, and learn would be a worthy target.

The more recently applied modeling techniques (dynamic systems, developmental robotics, Bayesian) do not yet have enough bakeoff experience to draw firm conclusions about their relative effectiveness in modeling development. For example, in the A-not-B error, the dynamic system approach seemed promising but did not cover as many phenomena as BP networks did. However, as noted, this dynamic system has several parameters whose variation could be explored to cover additional phenomena.

Likewise, although Bayesian approaches are only just starting to be applied to development, they have already made some apparently unique predictions in the domain of word learning: inferences allowed by random sampling of examples and estimates of the optimal number of examples for Bayesian inference. Also in the word-learning domain, the Bayesian approach covered only a portion of the shape-and-material-bias phenomena covered by the neural-network model. Nonetheless, the hierarchical Bayesian model employed there seems to have the potential to integrate phenomena across different explanatory levels. Before leaving these biases, it is perhaps worth remembering, in a bakeoff sense, that rule-based methods would likely be bothered by the many exceptions that exist in this domain.

In the domain of pronoun acquisition, the robotics model did not address the same psychology experiment as did the CC model, so the robot could not realistically cover the findings of that experiment. However, a blind catch-playing robot did simulate the reversal errors made by blind children. However, a sighted robot developed *you* before *I*, something that is not true of children.

The domain of syntax learning proved to be too easy for a variety of connectionist models, so it was difficult to discriminate among them – they all captured the main infant finding of a novelty preference. This problem was not so easy for C4.5, though, which could not capture any phenomena from the infant experiment. Moving to realistically complex syntactic patterns will likely prove challenging for all sorts of models.

Simulation of abnormal development has a number of promising connectionist models, but it is too early to tell which particular approaches will best capture which particular developmental disorders.

14.4. *Development via Parameter Settings?*

Some of the models reviewed in this chapter simulated development with programmer-designed parameter changes. Variations in such parameter settings were used to implement age-related changes in both connectionist and dynamic-systems models of the A-not-B error, the CC model of discrimination-shift learning, all three models of the similarity-to-correlation shift, and the autism model. Granted that this technique captured developmental effects and arguably could be justified on various grounds, but does it really constitute a good explanation of developmental change? Or is this a case of divine intervention, manually implementing changes that should occur naturally and spontaneously? ACT-R simulations of development also have this character as programmers change activation settings to allow different rules to come to the fore. Perhaps such parameter settings could be viewed as a preliminary step in identifying those changes a system needs to advance. One hopes that this could be followed by model improvements that would allow for more natural and spontaneous development.

Acknowledgments

This work was supported by a grant from the Natural Sciences and Engineering Research Council of Canada to the first author. Frédéric Dandurand, J-P Thivierge, and Yuriko Oshima-Takane provided helpful comments.

References

Altmann, G. T. M., & Dienes, Z. (1999). Rule learning by seven-month-old infants and neural networks. *Science, 284,* 875.

Amirikian, B., & Georgopoulos, A. P. (2003). Modular organization of directionally tuned cells in the motor cortex: Is there short-range order? *Proceedings of the National Academy of Sciences U.S.A., 100,* 12474–12479.

Andersen, E. S., Dunlea, A., & Kekelis, L. S. (1984). Blind children's language: Resolving some differences. *Journal of Child Language, 11,* 645–664.

Anderson, J. R. (1993). *Rules of the mind.* Hillsdale, NJ: Lawrence Erlbaum.

Baillargeon, R. (1986). Representing the existence and the location of hidden objects: Object permanence in 6- and 8-month-old infants. *Cognition, 23,* 21–41.

Baillargeon, R. (1987). Object permanence in 3 1/2- and 4 1/2-month-old infants. *Developmental Psychology, 23,* 655–664.

Baluja, S., & Fahlman, S. E. (1994). *Reducing network depth in the cascade-correlation learning architecture* (Technical Report No. CMU-CS-94-209). Pittsburgh PA: School of Computer Science, Carnegie Mellon University.

Barwise, J., & Perry, J. (1983). *Situations and attitudes.* Cambridge, MA: MIT Press.

Bates, E. (1979). *The emergence of symbols: Cognition and communication in infancy.* New York: Academic Press.

Berthouze, L., & Ziemke, T. (2003). Epigenetic robotics – modelling cognitive development in robotic systems. *Connection Science, 15,* 147–150.

Block, N. (1995). The mind as the software of the brain. In E. E. Smith & D. N. Osherson (Eds.), *Thinking: An invitation to cognitive science* (Vol. 3, 2nd ed.). Cambridge, MA: MIT Press.

Charney, R. (1980). Speech roles and the development of personal pronouns. *Journal of Child Language, 7,* 509–528.

Chiat, S. (1981). Context-specificity and generalization in the acquisition of pronominal distinctions. *Journal of Child Language, 8,* 75–91.

Clark, E. V. (1978). From gesture to word: On the natural history of deixis in language acquisition. In J. S. Bruner & A. Garton (Eds.), *Human growth and development* (pp. 85–120). Oxford, UK: Oxford University Press.

Cohen, L. B., & Arthur, A. E. (1983). Perceptual categorization in the infant. In E. Scholnick (Ed.), *New trends in conceptual representation* (pp. 197–220). Hillsdale, NJ: Lawrence Erlbaum.

Cohen, L. B., & Arthur, A. E. (2003). *The role of habituation in 10-month-olds' categorization.* Unpublished manuscript.

Colunga, E., & Smith, L. B. (2003). The emergence of abstract ideas: Evidence from networks and babies. *Philosophical Transactions by the Royal Society, 358,* 1205–1214.

Colunga, E., & Smith, L. B. (2005). From the lexicon to expectations about kinds: A role for associative learning. *Psychological Review 112,* 347–382.

Courchesne, E., Carper, R., & Akshoomoff, N. (2003). Evidence of brain overgrowth in the first year of life in autism. *Journal of the American Medical Association, 290,* 337–344.

Daugherty, K., & Seidenberg, M. S. (1992). Rules or connections? The past tense revisited. In *Proceedings of the Fourteenth Annual Conference of the Cognitive Science Society* (pp. 259–264). Hillsdale, NJ: Lawrence Erlbaum.

Dickinson, D. K. (1988). Learning names for materials: Factors constraining and limiting hypotheses about word meaning. *Cognitive Development, 3,* 15–35.

Elman, J. L. (1999). *Generalization, rules, and neural networks: A simulation of Marcus et al.* Retrieved April 27, 1999, from http//www.crl.ucsd.edu/~elman/Papers/MVRVsim.html

Fahlman, S. E. (1988). Faster-learning variations on back-propagation: An empirical study. In D. S. Touretzky, G. E. Hinton, & T. J. Sejnowski (Eds.), *Proceedings of the 1988 Connectionist Models Summer School* (pp. 38–51). Los Altos, CA: Morgan Kaufmann.

Fahlman, S. E., & Lebiere, C. (1990). The cascade-correlation learning architecture. In D. S. Touretzky (Ed.), *Advances in neural information processing systems 2* (pp. 524–532). Los Altos, CA: Morgan Kaufmann.

Ferretti, R. P., & Butterfield, E. C. (1986). Are children's rule-assessment classifications invariant across instances of problem types? *Child Development, 57,* 1419–1428.

Gold, K., & Scassellati, B. (2006). Grounded pronoun learning and pronoun reversal. In *Proceedings of the Fifth International Conference on Development and Learning ICDL 2006.* Bloomington: Department of Psychological and Brain Sciences, Indiana University.

Goldin-Meadow, S. (1999). The role of gesture in communication and thinking. *Trends in Cognitive Sciences, 3,* 419–429.

Goodman, N. (1955/1983). *Fact, fiction, and forecast*. New York: Bobbs-Merrill.

Gureckis, T. M., & Love, B. C. (2004). Common mechanisms in infant and adult category learning. *Infancy, 5*, 173–198.

Hare, M., & Elman, J. L. (1995). Learning and morphological change. *Cognition, 56*, 61–98.

Harm, M. W., & Seidenberg, M. S. (1999). Phonology, reading acquisition, and dyslexia: Insights from connectionist models. *Psychological Review, 106*, 491–528.

Hoeffner, J. H., & McClelland, J. L. (1994). Can a perceptual processing deficit explain the impairment of inflectional morphology in development dysphasia – a computational investigation? In *Proceedings of the Twenty-Fifth Annual Child Language Research Forum* (pp. 38–49). Center for the Study of Language and Information, Stanford University, Stanford, CA.

Imai, M., & Gentner, D. (1997). A cross-linguistic study of early word meaning: Universal ontology and linguistic influence. *Cognition, 62*, 169–200.

Kemp, C., Perfors, A., & Tenenbaum, J. B. (2007). Learning overhypotheses with hierarchical Bayesian models. *Developmental Science, 10*, 307–321.

Kendler, T. S. (1979). The development of discrimination learning: A levels-of-functioning explanation. In H. Reese (Ed.), *Advances in child development and behavior* (Vol. 13, pp. 83–117). New York: Academic Press.

Klahr, D., & Wallace, J. G. (1976). *Cognitive development: An information processing view*. Hillsdale, NJ: Lawrence Erlbaum.

Kobayashi, H. (1997). The role of actions in making inferences about the shape and material of solid objects among 2-year-old children. *Cognition, 63*, 251–269.

Landau, B., Smith, L. B., & Jones, S. S. (1988). The importance of shape in early lexical learning. *Cognitive Development, 3*, 299–321.

Langley, P. (1987). A general theory of discrimination learning. In D. Klahr, P. Langley, & R. Neches (Eds.), *Production systems models of learning and development* (pp. 99–161). Cambridge, MA: MIT Press.

Lebiere, C., & Anderson, J. R. (1993). A connectionist implementation of the ACT-R production system. In *Proceedings of the Fifteenth Annual Conference of the Cognitive Science Society* (pp. 635–640). Hillsdale, NJ: Lawrence Erlbaum.

Lewis, J. D., & Elman, J. L. (2008). Growth-related neural neural reorganization and the autism phenotype: a test of the hypothesis that altered brain growth leads to altered connectivity. *Developmental Science, 11*, 135–155.

Ling, C. X., & Marinov, M. (1993). Answering the connectionist challenge: A symbolic model of learning the past tenses of English verbs. *Cognition, 49*, 235–290.

Lovett, A., & Scassellati, B. (August 2004). Using a robot to reexamine looking time experiments. Paper presented at the *Fourth International Conference on Development and Learning*, San Diego, CA.

Marcus, G. F., Vijayan, S., Bandi Rao, S., & Vishton, P. M. (1999). Rule learning by seven-month-old infants. *Science, 283*, 77–80.

Mareschal, D., Plunkett, K., & Harris, P. (1999). A computational and neuropsychological account of object-oriented behaviours in infancy. *Developmental Science, 2*, 306–317.

Marr, D. (1982). *Vision: A computational investigation into the human representation and processing of visual information*. San Francisco: W. H. Freeman.

McClelland, J. L. (1989). Parallel distributed processing: Implications for cognition and development. In R. G. M. Morris (Ed.), *Parallel distributed processing: Implications for psychology and neurobiology* (pp. 8–45). Oxford, UK: Oxford University Press.

McNeill, D. (1992). *Hand and mind*. Chicago: University of Chicago Press.

Munakata, Y. (1998). Infant perseveration and implications for object permanence theories: A PDP model of the AB task. *Developmental Science, 1*, 161–184.

Munakata, Y., McClelland, J. L., Johnson, M. H., & Siegler, R. S. (1997). Rethinking infant knowledge: Toward an adaptive process account of successes and failures in object permanence tasks. *Psychological Review, 104*, 686–713.

Negishi, M. (1999). Do infants learn grammar with algebra or statistics? *Science, 284*, 433.

Newell, A. (1990). *Unified theories of cognition*. Cambridge, MA: Harvard University Press.

Oshima-Takane, Y. (1988). Children learn from speech not addressed to them: The case of personal pronouns. *Journal of Child Language, 15*, 95–108.

Oshima-Takane, Y. (1992). Analysis of pronominal errors: A case study. *Journal of Child Language, 19*, 111–131.

Oshima-Takane, Y., Goodz, E., & Derevensky, J. L. (1996). Birth order effects on early language development: Do secondborn children learn from overheard speech? *Child Development, 67,* 621–634.

Oshima-Takane, Y., Takane, Y., & Shultz, T. R. (1999). The learning of first and second pronouns in English: Network models and analysis. *Journal of Child Language, 26,* 545–575.

Piaget, J. (1954). *The construction of reality in the child.* New York: Basic Books.

Pinker, S. (1999). *Words and rules: The ingredients of language.* New York: Basic Books.

Plunkett, K., & Marchman, V. (1996). Learning from a connectionist model of the acquisition of the English past tense. *Cognition, 61,* 299–308.

Quinlan, J. R. (1993). *C4.5: Programs for machine learning.* San Mateo, CA: Morgan Kaufmann.

Raijmakers, M. E. J., van Koten, S., & Molenaar, P. C. M. (1996). On the validity of simulating stagewise development by means of PDP networks: Application of catastrophe analysis and an experimental test of rule-like network performance. *Cognitive Science, 20,* 101–136.

Samuelson, L., & Smith, L. B. (1999). Early noun vocabularies: Do ontology, category structure and syntax correspond? *Cognition, 73,* 1–33.

Schiff-Meyers, N. (1983). From pronoun reversals to correct pronoun usage: A case study of a normally developing child. *Journal of Speech and Hearing Disorders, 48,* 385–394.

Schlesinger, M. (2004). Evolving agents as a metaphor for the developing child. *Developmental Science, 7,* 158–164.

Schlesinger, M., Parisi, D., & Langer, J. (2000). Learning to reach by constraining the movement search space. *Developmental Science, 3,* 67–80.

Schmidt, W. C., & Ling, C. X. (1996). A decision-tree model of balance scale development. *Machine Learning, 24,* 203–229.

Shultz, T. R. (1999). Rule learning by habituation can be simulated in neural networks. In M. Hahn & S.C. Stoness (Eds.), *Proceedings of the Twenty-first Annual Conference of the Cognitive Science Society* (pp. 665–670). Mahwah, NJ: Lawrence Erlbaum.

Shultz, T. R. (2003). *Computational developmental psychology.* Cambridge, MA: MIT Press.

Shultz, T. R. (2006). Constructive learning in the modeling of psychological development. In Y. Munakata & M. H. Johnson (Eds.), *Processes of change in brain and cognitive development: Attention and performance XXI.* (pp. 61–86). Oxford, UK: Oxford University Press.

Shultz, T. R., & Bale, A. C. (2001). Neural network simulation of infant familiarization to artificial sentences: Rule-like behavior without explicit rules and variables. *Infancy, 2,* 501–536.

Shultz, T. R., & Bale, A. C. (2006). Neural networks discover a near-identity relation to distinguish simple syntactic forms. *Minds and Machines, 16,* 107–139.

Shultz, T. R., Buckingham, D., & Oshima-Takane, Y. (1994). A connectionist model of the learning of personal pronouns in English. In S. J. Hanson, T. Petsche, M. Kearns, & R. L. Rivest (Eds.), *Computational learning theory and natural learning systems, Vol. 2: Intersection between theory and experiment* (pp. 347–362). Cambridge, MA: MIT Press.

Shultz, T. R., & Cohen, L. B. (2004). Modeling age differences in infant category learning. *Infancy, 5,* 153–171.

Shultz, T. R., & Mareschal, D. (1997). Rethinking innateness, learning, and constructivism: Connectionist perspectives on development. *Cognitive Development, 12,* 563–586.

Shultz, T. R., Mareschal, D., & Schmidt, W. C. (1994). Modeling cognitive development on balance scale phenomena. *Machine Learning, 16,* 57–86.

Shultz, T. R., Mysore, S. P., & Quartz, S. R. (2007). Why let networks grow? In D. Mareschal, S. Sirois, G. Westermann, & M. H. Johnson (Eds.), *Neuroconstructivism: Perspectives and prospects* (Vol. 2). Oxford, UK: Oxford University Press.

Siegler, R. S. (1976). Three aspects of cognitive development. *Cognitive Psychology, 8,* 481–520.

Sirois, S. (September 2002). Rethinking object compounds in preschoolers: The case of pairwise learning. Paper presented at the British Psychological Society Developmental Section Conference, University of Sussex, UK.

Sirois, S., Buckingham, D., & Shultz, T. R. (2000). Artificial grammar learning by infants: An auto-associator perspective. *Developmental Science, 4,* 442–456.

Sirois, S., & Shultz, T. R. (1998). Neural network modeling of developmental effects in discrimination shifts. *Journal of Experimental Child Psychology, 71,* 235–274.

Sirois, S., & Shultz, T. R. (2006). Preschoolers out of adults: Discriminative learning with a cognitive load. *Quarterly Journal of Experimental Psychology, 59,* 1357–1377.

Soja, N. N. (1992). Inferences about the meaning of nouns: The relationship between perception and syntax. *Cognitive Development, 7,* 29–45.

Soja, N. N., Carey, S., & Spelke, E. S. (1991). Ontological categories guide young children's inductions of word meaning: Object terms and substance terms. *Cognition, 38,* 179–211.

Soja, N. N., Carey, S., & Spelke, E. S. (1992). Perception, ontology, and word meaning. *Cognition, 45,* 101–107.

Spence, K. W. (1952). The nature of the response in discrimination learning. *Psychological Review, 59,* 89–93.

Subrahmanyam, K., Landau, B., & Gelman, R. (1999). Shape, material, and syntax: Interacting forces in children's learning in novel words for objects and substances. *Language & Cognitive Processes, 14,* 249–281.

Sun, R., Slusarz, P., & Terry, C. (2005). The interaction of the explicit and the implicit in skill learning: A dual-process approach. *Psychological Review, 112,* 159–192.

Taatgen, N. A., & Anderson, J. R. (2002). Why do children learn to say "broke"? A model of learning the past tense without feedback. *Cognition, 86,* 123–155.

Thelen, E., Schoener, G., Scheier, C., & Smith, L. (2001). The dynamics of embodiment: A field theory of infant perseverative reaching. *Brain and Behavioral Sciences, 24,* 1–33.

Thomas, M. S. C., & Karmiloff-Smith, A. (2002). Are developmental disorders like cases of adult brain damage? Implications from connectionist modelling. *Behavioral and Brain Sciences, 25,* 727–787.

van Gelder, T. J. (1998). The dynamical hypothesis in cognitive science. *Behavioral and Brain Sciences, 21,* 1–14.

van Rijn, H., van Someren, M., & van der Maas, H. (2003). Modeling developmental transitions on the balance scale task. *Cognitive Science, 27,* 227–257.

Vilcu, M., & Hadley, R. F. (2001). Generalization in simple recurrent networks. In J. B. Moore & K. Stenning (Eds.), *Proceedings of the Twenty-third Annual Conference of the Cognitive Science Society* (pp. 1072–1077). Mahwah, NJ: Lawrence Erlbaum.

Vilcu, M., & Hadley, R. F. (2005). Two apparent "Counterexamples" to Marcus: A closer look. *Minds and Machines, 15,* 359–382.

Westermann, G. (1998). Emergent modularity and U-shaped learning in a constructivist neural network learning the English past tense. In M. A. Gernsbacher & S. J. Derry (Eds.), *Proceedings of the Twentieth Annual Conference of the Cognitive Science Society* (pp. 1130–1135). Mahwah, NJ: Lawrence Erlbaum.

Westermann, G., & Mareschal, D. (2004). From parts to wholes: Mechanisms of development in infant visual object processing. *Infancy, 5,* 131–151.

Westermann, G., Sirois, S., Shultz, T. R., & Mareschal, D. (2006). Modeling developmental cognitive neuroscience. *Trends in Cognitive Sciences, 10,* 227–232.

Xu, F., & Tenenbaum, J. B. (2007). Sensitivity to sampling in Bayesian word learning. *Developmental Science, 10,* 288–297.

Younger, B. A., & Cohen, L. B. (1986). Developmental change in infants' perception of correlations among attributes. *Child Development, 57,* 803–815.

Zhang, K., & Sejnowski, T. J. (2000). A universal scaling law between gray matter and white matter of cerebral cortex. *Proceedings of the National Academy of Sciences USA, 97,* 5621–5626.

CHAPTER 17

Computational Models of Psycholinguistics

Nick Chater and Morten H. Christiansen

1. Introduction

The computational mechanisms that underlie how people process and acquire language has been a central topic for cognitive science research since the beginning of the field. Indeed, Chomsky's revolutionary impact on linguistics (e.g., 1957, 1959, 1965) involved the attempt to align linguistics with the project of cognitive science. The project of linguistics was viewed as providing a formally specified account of the knowledge that underpins linguistic behavior. This specification took the form of a generative grammar – a set of rules that determined which linguistic forms (strings of phonemes, strings of words, etc.) are linguistically acceptable and which are not. Generative grammars themselves had direct relationships to models of formal languages in automata theory and are used to specify formal languages, both in logic and the development of programming languages.

For Chomsky, computational ideas were also fundamental to understanding human language in another way. He defined a formal hierarchy of grammars and associated languages (regular, context-free, context-sensitive, unrestricted grammars), each of which relates elegantly to the kind of language-processing operations that can parse and produce them (Chomsky & Schützenberger, 1963). Thus, for example, a finite state automaton can parse and produce only finite-state languages, a push-down automaton can deal with finite-state and context-free languages, and so on. Moreover, Chomsky used these observations to devastating effect, in considering existing behaviorist theories of linguistic behavior (Chomsky, 1959; Skinner, 1957). He argued that human languages correspond to the highest level in the Chomsky hierarchy and, hence, cannot be accounted for by existing associative theories, which appear to be limited to processing mechanisms that correspond to a finite state machine. Indeed, Chomsky's arguments concerning the formal and computational properties of human language were one of the strongest and most influential lines of argument behind the development of the field of cognitive science, in opposition to behaviorism. Moreover, Chomsky's (1968, 1980) arguments concerning the poverty of the linguistic input available to the child in relation to the spectacular intricacy of the linguistic system that children acquire became a major impetus for strongly nativist theories of language (e.g., Berwick, 1986; Crain, 1991; Lightfoot, 1991; Pinker, 1984), but also, by extension, nativist theories across a wide range of cognitive domains (e.g., Hirschfeld & Gelman, 1994; Pinker, 1997).

Given this historical background, it is perhaps not surprising that computational models of language processing and acquisition have been theoretically central to the development of cognitive science over the past fifty years. But the direction that these models have taken has been much less predictable. Chomsky's initial suggestion that a formal theory of linguistic knowledge should integrate smoothly with computational theories of processing and acquisition has run into a number of difficulties. Reactions to these difficulties vary widely, with the result that computational models in psycholinguistics have fragmented into different traditions, which are not readily integrated into a single perspective. The resulting work has been rich and varied, and has led to considerable qualitative insights into many aspects of human language processing and acquisition; but it is by no means clear how to synthesize the variety of computational methods and insights into anything resembling an integrated theoretical framework. This chapter outlines the historical origins and the state of the art of computational models of psycholinguistic processes. Also considered are the interrelationships between the different theoretical traditions that have emerged from, and in reaction to, the Chomskyan revolution. This survey is necessarily highly selective, both in terms of the topics covered and the research within each topic. The survey aims, though, to focus attention on topics that have the widest general theoretical implications, both for other fields of computational cognitive modeling and for the project of cognitive science more broadly.

The next section, *Three Computational Frameworks for Psycholinguistics*, begins by outlining and contrasting symbolic, connectionist, and probabilistic approaches to the computational modeling of psycholinguistic phenomena (see Chapter 1 in this volume). There are important overlaps and relationships between these traditions, and each tradition itself contains a range of incompatible viewpoints. Nonetheless, this three-way division is at least a convenient starting point for discussion. Next, attention turns to specific computational proposals and associated theoretical positions across specific psycholinguistic topics. *From Signal to Word* considers word segmentation and recognition, and single word reading. *Sentence Processing* primarily focusses on parsing, relating connectionist and probabilistic models to the symbolic models of grammar and processing associated with Chomsky's program. *Language Acquisition* reviews formal and computational models of language learning and re-evaluates, in the light of current computational work, Chomsky's early theoretical arguments for a strong nativist view of the computational mechanisms involved. Finally, in *Where Next?* the future of computational models of psycholinguistics is considered.

2. Three Computational Frameworks for Psycholinguistics

2.1. *Chomsky and the Symbolic Tradition*

Chomsky's initiation of the cognitive science of language proposed that human language should be assimilated into the domain of formal languages, and this immediately suggests that the computational mechanisms involved in parsing and producing formal languages, which is a rich area of research in computer science, (e.g., Aho & Ullman, 1972; Hopcroft, Motwani, & Ullman, 2000), might be co-opted and extended to provide models of human language processing. This is a rigorously *symbolic* perspective on the structure of language and the nature of the computational processes operating over language – a perspective that meshed well with the prevalent computational models of mind, inspired by spectacular theoretical and technical advances in symbolic computation (e.g., Winograd, 1972).

This perspective provides an attractively crisp picture of the relationship between knowledge of the language, and the processing operations used in parsing or producing it. The knowledge of the language is embodied in a set of declarative rules (i.e., the rules are explicitly represented in symbolic form), and a set of processing operations applies these rules in parsing and production. In parsing, the problem is to find a syntactic derivation (typically corresponding to a tree structure), using the rules, that yields the observed sequence of words; in production, there is the converse problem of using the rules to construct a derivation and then to output the resulting sequence of words. From this point of view, too, the problem of language learning can be stated as a problem of induction, that is, inducing a grammar (i.e., a set of symbolic linguistic rules) from a set of observed sentences, and this problem yields readily to formal analysis, using techniques from theoretical computer science.

Yet, despite these evident strengths, and moreover, extensive developments in linguistic theory based on the symbolic approach, the expected program of computational models of psycholinguistic phenomena rapidly ran into difficulties. Initial grammar formalisms proposed that the derivation of a sentence required the operation of a succession of transformations, leading to the natural assumption that a computational model of language parsing and production would need to recapitulate these transformations and that the number and complexity of transformations should therefore correlate with processing time and difficulty in psycholinguistic experiments. This derivational theory of complexity (Miller, 1962) proved to be a poor computational model when compared with empirical data and was rapidly abandoned. In the generative grammar tradition, the relationship between linguistic theory and processing was assumed to be indirect (e.g., Fodor, Bever, & Garrett, 1974), and this led subsequent developments in the

Chomskyan tradition in generative grammar to disengage from work on computational modeling.

Yet, in parallel with this, a wide range of research in computational linguistics took the generative approach to linguistic theory and attempted to build computational mechanisms for language processing that could serve as potential cognitive models. For example, early debates concerned alternative mechanisms for parsing versions of transformational grammar or related but simpler formalisms, for example, Wanner and Maratsos's (1978) Augmented Transition Networks and Frazier and Fodor's (1978) "sausage machine." Work on cognitive models of symbolic parsing has also continued (e.g., Crocker, 1996; Gibson, 1998). Early and recurring issues arising from these models concerned how to deal with the huge local ambiguity of natural language, which appears to lead to a combinatorically explosive number of possible parses. Are many parallel parses computed at once? If not, what constraints determine which parse is pursued? (Marcus, 1980).

Psycholinguistic theories focusing on the generative tradition tended to assume that language processing is an autonomous domain (Ferreira & Clifton, 1986), that is, language processing can be separated from processes of general world knowledge (Fodor, 1983). Moreover, it is typically assumed that structural, rather than probabilistic, features of language are central. The idea is that the cognitively represented linguistic rules determine what it is possible to say (the linguistic rules aim to capture linguistic *competence*; Chomsky, 1965); all manner of pragmatic, and knowledge-based constraints, as well as processing limitations, will determine what people actually say (such matters are assumed to be theoretically secondary issues of *performance*, Chomsky, 1965). For these reasons, early proposals concerning parsing and production assumed these processes to be determined by aspects of syntactic structure, that is, that the processing system may aim to build a tree with as few nodes as possible (the core of Frazier's [1979] proposal of minimal attachment).

Attempts to model psycholinguistic data have, however, been relatively rare, in the symbolic tradition. Purely structural features of language appear to be just one of the factors that determine performance in psycholinguistic experiments, for example. Predictably enough, experimental results are strongly influenced by the very probabilistic and world-knowledge factors that the Chomskyan viewpoint aims to relegate to the realm of "performance" (e.g., MacDonald, Pearlmutter, & Seidenberg, 1994; Trueswell & Tanenhaus, 1992). One approach is to view psycholinguistic paradigms as highly imperfect measures of the "pure" language module – and, indeed, classical linguistics has typically taken this perspective and ignored experimental psycholinguistic evidence concerning the structure of language to the exclusion of direct linguistic acceptability judgments from native speakers. Another approach is to propose that structural factors determine which options the processor considers and that probability and world knowledge may arise purely in pruning such proposals (Crain & Steedman, 1985; Fodor, 1983). From the point of view of building computational models of psycholinguistic processes, it seems inevitable that probabilistic aspects of language processing must take center stage. This observation has been one line of impetus behind two rather different, but related, alternative computational frameworks: connectionist and probabilistic models of language, which are discussed in the following subsections.

2.2. Connectionist Psycholinguistics

A symbolic perspective on language processing fits well with, and was a strong motivation for, the broader view of the mind as a symbol-processing system, based on principles analogous to the digital computer (Newell & Simon, 1972). Connectionism has a different origin in attempts to design computers inspired by the brain (see Chapter 2 in this volume). At a coarse level, the brain consists of a very large number of densely interconnected neurons, each of which is computationally relatively simple. These neurons do not appear to operate individually in tackling information processing problems; rather, large numbers of neurons operate simultaneously and co-operatively to process information. Furthermore, neurons appear to communicate real numbers (approximately encoded by firing rate) rather than symbolic messages, and therefore neurons can be viewed as mapping real-valued inputs (from other neurons) onto a real-valued output (which is transmitted to other neurons). Connectionist nets mimic these properties, although typically without attempting high levels of biological realism (although see Dayan & Abbott, 2001). Connectionist methods also provide interesting "bottom-up" models of learning – learning occurs by a multitude of small adjustments to the "weights" of the connections between processing units, which can be determined purely locally; this is a very different picture of learning from the traditional serial hypothesis-generation and test envisaged by typical symbolic models of learning. This raises the possibility that connectionism may shed new light on processes underlying language acquisition (Bates & Elman, 1993; Elman 1993, 2003; Redington & Charter, 1998).

The relative merits of connectionist and symbolic models of language are, as noted earlier, hotly debated. But should they be in competition at all? Advocates of symbolic models of language processing assume that symbolic processes are somehow implemented in the brain: They, too, are connectionists, at the level of *implementation*. They assume that language processing can be described both at the psychological level, in terms of symbol processing, and at an implementational level, in neuroscientific terms (to which connectionism approximates). If this is right, then connectionist modeling should start with symbol processing models of language processing and implement these in connectionist nets. Advocates of this view (Fodor & Pylyshyn, 1988; Marcus, 1998; Pinker & Prince, 1988) typically assume that it implies that symbolic modeling is entirely autonomous from connectionism;

symbolic theories set the goalposts for connectionism, but not the reverse. Chater and Oaksford (1990) argued that, even according to this view, there will be a two-way influence between symbolic and connectionist theories, since many symbolic accounts can be ruled out precisely because they could not be neurally implemented to run in real time. Indeed, some computational proposals concerning, for example, morphology or reading single words, have a hybrid character, in which aspects of what is fundamentally a symbolic process are implemented in connectionist terms, to explain, for example, complex statistical patterns in dealing with irregular items, alongside apparently rigid rule-based patterns, for regular items (e.g., Coltheart et al., 2001; Marcus, 2000).

Many connectionists in the field of language processing have a more radical agenda: to challenge, rather than reimplement, the symbolic approach. They see many aspects of language as consisting of a multitude of "soft" regularities, more naturally captured by connectionist, rather than rule-based, methods (e.g., Seidenberg, 1997). There are also theoretical positions that take inspiration from both symbolic and connectionist paradigms: In linguistics, optimality theory attempts to define a middle ground of ranked, violable linguistic constraints, used particularly to explain phonological regularities (Smolensky & Legendre, 2006). And in morphology, there is debate over whether "rule + exception" regularities (e.g., English past tense, German plural) are better explained by a single stochastic process (Hahn & Nakisa, 2000; Marcus et al., 1995). Overall, then, a central theoretical question is how far connectionist models complement, or compete with, symbolic models of language processing and acquisition (Marcus, 1998; Seidenberg & Elman, 1999; Smolensky, 1999; Steedman, 1999).

2.3. *Probabilistic Models of Language*

As noted earlier, according to Chomsky (1965), the study of language should primarily focus on *competence*, rather than performance, that is, what is linguistically ac-

ceptable, rather than the statistical properties of what people actually say. This has led to the downplaying of probabilistic features of language, more generally, in favor of the putatively rigid linguistic rules (although there has been a long tradition of interest in statistical properties of language in sociolinguistics, e.g., Labov, 1972).

Yet, recent work, particularly in computational linguistics and, as is described later, connectionist psycholinguistics, has suggested that a probabilistic viewpoint may be central to understanding language processing, language acquisition, and perhaps the structure of language itself (Chater & Manning, 2006). Thus, for example, whereas from a symbolic perspective, parsing is naturally viewed as the problem of constructing a logical derivation from grammatical rules to a string of words generated by the application of those rules (Pereira & Warren, 1983), from a probabilistic point of view, the problem is not merely to find *any* derivation, but to find the *most probable* derivation (or the most probable derivations, ranked by their probability). Moreover, given the notorious local ambiguity of language (where large numbers of lexical items are syntactically ambiguous and can combine locally in many ways), focusing on the most probable local derivation can potentially lead to a dramatic reduction in the problem of searching for globally viable parses.

In particular, probabilistic Bayesian methods (see Chapter 3 in this volume) specify a framework showing how information about the probability of generating different grammatical structures and their associated word strings can be used to infer grammatical structure from a string of words. An elegant feature of the probabilistic viewpoint is that the same Bayesian machinery can also be turned to the problem of learning: of showing how information about the degree to which different probabilistic grammars have different probabilities of generating observed linguistic data and using this to infer grammars, at least to a limited extent, from linguistic data. Moreover, this Bayesian framework is analogous to probabilistic models of vision, inference, and learning (Chater, Tenenbaum, & Yuille, 2006); what is distinctive is the specific structures (e.g., syntactic trees, dependency diagrams) relevant for language.

As with the relationship between symbolic and connectionist viewpoints, the relationship between probabilistic and symbolic views can be viewed as complementary or competitive. The complementary viewpoint needs assume only that probabilities are *added* to existing linguistic rules to indicate how often rules of each type are used; a clean separation between nonprobabilistic linguistic competence and probabilistic information and processing used in linguistic *performance* can thus be maintained. But the more radical viewpoint is that some, and perhaps many, aspects of language structure should be viewed probabilistically (Bod, Hay, & Jannedy, 2003).

In linguistics, there has been renewed interest in phenomena that seem inherently graded and/or stochastic, from phonology to syntax (Fanselow et al., in press; Hay & Baayen, 2005). There have also been revisionist perspectives on the strict symbolic rules thought to underlie language and an increasing emphasis on nonrule-based processes, for example, processes based on individual linguistic constructions (Goldberg, 2006; Tomasello, 2003). Indeed, some theorists suggest that many aspects of language processing and acquisition may be best understood in terms of retrieving similar previous cases from a large store of prior instances of linguistic structure (Bod, 1998; Daelemans & van den Bosch, 2005). Memory, or instance-based, views are currently widely used across many fields of cognitive science.

3. From Signal to Word

Early theories of speech processing adopted a symbolic viewpoint in which a set of symbolically represented word forms were matched against the acoustic or visual input, in some cases, assuming a sequential search in memory, by analogy with the operation of memory retrieval in digital computers (Forster, 1976). Other early models assumed that multiple word forms could be activated in parallel, and choice was resolved by a process of competition (Morton, 1969); and, in the context of speech, this competition was assumed to proceed incrementally, and very rapidly, as the speech signal was encountered (Marslen-Wilson & Welsh, 1978).

These models were typically not implemented, however, and hence not quantitatively matched against empirical data. Two sources of candidate computational models began to emerge, however. The first arose from the application of sophisticated probabilistic and mathematical techniques, such as from hidden Markov models, vector quantization, and dynamic programming, in the development of speech technology (Juang & Rabiner, 1991). These technical developments had relatively little impact on psychological theories of speech processing, although the probabilistic tradition that they embody has more recently had a substantial impact, as will become clear. The second source of candidate models arose from connectionism, which led to a range of important detailed cognitive models. Connectionist modeling of speech processing begins with TRACE, which has an "interactive activation" architecture, with a sequence of "layers" of units (Figure 17.1A), for phonetic features, phonemes, and words (McClelland & Elman, 1986). Speech input corresponds to activation of phonetic features, which allow the recognition of phonemes and the words; at each level, representations compete via mutually inhibitory links. Hence, alternative phonemes compete to explain particular bundles of phonetic features, and different hypothetical words inhibit each other. Between layers, mutually consistent hypotheses support each other, for example, phonetic features consistent with a particular phoneme reinforce each other; a word and its constituent phonemes are mutually reinforcing. The bidirectional, interactive character of these links underpins TRACE's ability to capture apparently top-down effects – if there is evidence that a particular word has been heard, that word will support a constituent phoneme for which the input at the phonetic level might be ambiguous.

A. Interactive Activation Network

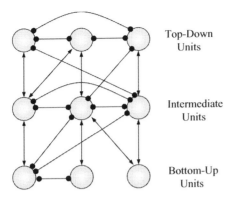

Top-Down Units

Intermediate Units

Bottom-Up Units

B. Feed-Forward Network

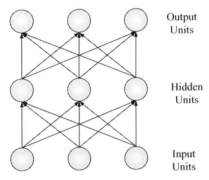

Output Units

Hidden Units

Input Units

Figure 17.1. Interactive and feed-forward connectionist architectures. A fundamental divide between neural network architectures concerns whether the input is processed unidirectionally or whether top-down feedback is allowed. (A) Top-down feedback is a distinctive feature of the *interactive activation network* (as used in TRACE; McClelland & Elman, 1986). The network has bidirectional excitatory (arrows) or inhibitory (filled circles) links. Activation flows bottom-up and top-down, reinforcing mutually consistent states and inhibiting inconsistent states. Inhibitory connections within layers implement competition between alternative words, phonemes, or phonetic features. The weights in TRACE are hand-coded rather than learned. (B) A *feedforward network* passes information in one direction, with no feedback connections. Feedforward networks are typically not hand-coded, but are trained using backpropagation, which minimizes the discrepancy between the network's actual and desired output. Information flows bottom-up from input to output units (see Chapter 2 in this volume).

TRACE captured a wide range of empirical data and made important novel predictions. TRACE is most controversial because it is interactive – the bidirectional links between units mean that information flows top-down as well as bottom-up. Other connectionist models, by contrast, assume purely bottom-up information flow (Norris, 1994). TRACE provided an impetus for the interactive versus bottom-up debate, with a prediction apparently incompatible with bottom-up models.

To understand this novel prediction, it is necessary to sketch two background results on speech perception. First, note that if an ambiguous phoneme is sometimes resolved by the word context in which that phoneme is embedded. Thus, if an ambiguous /s/-/š/ phoneme (the /s/ and /š/ are pronounced as in the onsets of the words *sip* and *ship*) is presented at the end of fooli-, it is heard as a /š/, because *foolish* is a word and *fooliss* is not; conversely, in the context *Christma-*, the same ambiguous phoneme is heard as a /s/, because *Christmas* is a word, whereas *Christmash* is not. This is the Ganong effect (Ganong, 1980), and it follows naturally from an interactive viewpoint, where word recognition can feed back to phoneme recognition. But it can be equally well explained by bottom-up models by assuming that the participant's responses concerning phoneme identity are simultaneously influenced by both the phoneme and lexical levels (Fodor, 1983). The second background result to motivate Elman and McClelland's (1988) prediction comes from the observation that, in natural speech, the pronunciation of a phoneme is affected by surrounding phonemes: this is "coarticulation." Thus, for example, /t/ and /k/ differ only by the phonetic feature of place of articulation, that is, tongue position. But the location of the tongue for the current phoneme is also influenced by its previous position and hence by the previous phoneme. In particular, for example, /s/ and /t/ have the same place of articulation; but after a /š/, the place of articulation of the /t/ is dragged somewhat toward that which is normal for a /k/. The opposite pattern occurs for /k/, which is dragged somewhat toward the pronunciation of a /t/

when preceded by a /s/. Mann and Repp (1981) put an ambiguous /k/-/t/ phoneme in the context of –*apes*, so that when heard alone, the input was judged equally often to the *capes* or *tapes*. After the word *Christmas*, the ambiguous input is most often heard as *capes* – the ambiguous phoneme is "explained" by the speech processor by the influence of the previous /š/ context. Conversely, after the word *foolish*, the same ambiguous phoneme is heard as *tapes*. Thus, Mann and Repp (1981) concluded that the speech processor engages in "compensation for coarticulation" (CFC); it compensates for the coarticulation that arises in speech production.

Elman and McClelland (1988) observed that TRACE makes an interesting prediction where the preceding phoneme is also ambiguous – between /š/ and /s/. If the word level directly influences the phoneme level (and this type of direct interactive influence is what leads to the Ganong effect), then the compensation of the /k/ should occur even when the /s/ relies on lexical input for its identity (i.e., with an ambiguous /s/-/š/ in *Christmas*, the /s/ should be restored and thus CFC should occur as normal, so that the following ambiguous /k/-/t/ should be perceived as /k/). TRACE's novel prediction was experimentally confirmed (Elman & McClelland 1988).

3.1. Bottom-Up Connectionist Models Capture "Top-Down" Effects

Yet, bottom-up connectionist models *can* capture these results. One study used a simple recurrent network (SRN; Elman, 1990) to map phonetic input onto phoneme output (Norris, 1993). The SRN is a standard feedforward network (Figure 17.1B), where hidden units are copied back at a given time-step and presented to the network at the next time-step, so that the network's behavior is determined by a sequence of inputs, rather than just the current input (Figure 17.2A). In Norris's model, when the SRN received phonetic input with an ambiguous first word-final phoneme and ambiguous initial segments of the second word, an analog of CFC was observed. The percentages of

/t/ and /k/ responses to the first phoneme of the second word depended on the identity of the first word (as in Elman & McClelland, 1988). Importantly, the explanation for this pattern of results cannot be top-down influence from word units, because there *are* no word units. Nonetheless, the presence of "feedback" connections in the hidden layer of the SRN might suggest that some form of interactive processing occurs in this model. But this is misleading – the feedback occurs within the hidden layer (i.e., from its previous to its present state), rather than flowing from top to bottom. This model, although an important demonstration, is small-scale – it deals with just twelve words. However, a subsequent study scaled up these results using a similar network trained on phonologically transcribed conversational English (Cairns et al., 1997).

How is it possible that bottom-up processes can mimic what appear to be top-down effects from the lexicon? It was argued that restoration depends on local statistical regularities between the phonemes within a word, rather than depending on access to lexical representations, thus, individual phonemes are supported by phonemes in the same word, not via links to an abstract word-level representation but instead by lateral connections between the phonemes, exploiting the statistical dependencies between neighboring phonemes. More recent experiments have since shown that CFC is indeed determined by statistical regularities for nonword stimuli, and that, for word stimuli, there appear to be no residual effects of lexical status once statistical regularities are taken into account (Pitt & McQueen, 1998). It is not clear, though, whether bottom-up models can model other evidence that phoneme identification is affected by the lexicon, for example, from signal detection analyses of phoneme restoration (Kraljic & Samuel, 2005; Norris, McQueen, & Cutler, 2000; Samuel, 1996).

3.2. Exploiting Distributed Representations

A different line of results provides additional evidence that bottom-up models

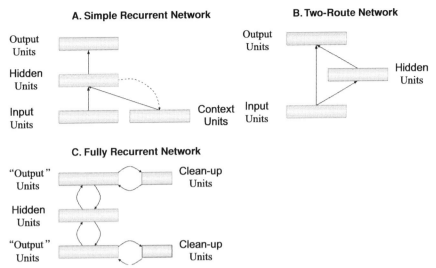

A. Simple Recurrent Network

Output Units

Hidden Units

Input Units

Context Units

B. Two-Route Network

Output Units

Hidden Units

Input Units

C. Fully Recurrent Network

"Output" Units

Clean-up Units

Hidden Units

"Output" Units

Clean-up Units

Figure 17.2. Connectionist architectures for cognitive models. The structure of the network is represented more schematically than in Figure 17.1. Each block represents a bank of units, and arrows between blocks indicate full connectivity between each unit in the relevant blocks. (A) A *simple recurrent network* is essentially a standard feedforward network equipped with an extra layer of so-called context units. At each-time step, an input propagates through the hidden units to the outputs (solid arrows). The hidden-unit activation at the previous time-step is copied back to the context layer (dashed arrows) and paired with the current input (solid arrows). Thus, the hidden units influence the processing of subsequent inputs, providing a limited ability to deal sequential inputs. (B) Here, there are two routes from input to output – one that is direct and can only encode simple relationships and one that is indirect and can encode more complex relationships between input and output. Zorzi, Houghton, & Butterworth (1998) use this structure to illustrate how a single network can simultaneously learn both simple patterns (the basic grapheme-phoneme correspondences of English) using one route while simultaneously learning a complex pattern of exceptions with the other route. Note that the resulting model of reading differs from standard dual-route models (Coltheart et al., 2001) because the route encoding lexical exceptions can operate by "correcting" the simpler route rather than proceeding independently of it. (C) A fully recurrent network in which activation flows both up and down the network and also recirculates between banks of units (Allen & Seidenberg, 1999). The network can be trained using the backpropagation-through-time learning algorithm (e.g., Williams & Zipser, 1990). The recirculation within banks of units serves to "clean up" any errors that may have been introduced. The labels "input" and "output" are shown in quotes because all connections are bidirectional. Thus, although the network can be used to map form to meaning (as in Allen & Seidenberg, 1999), it could equally be used to map meaning to form.

can accommodate apparently top-down effects (Gaskell & Marslen-Wilson, 1995). An SRN was trained to map a systematically altered featural representation of speech onto a phonemic and semantic representation of the same speech (following previous work, Kawamoto, 1993). After training, the network showed evidence of lexical effects in modeling lexical and phonetic decision data (Marslen-Wilson & Warren, 1994). This work was extended by an SRN trained to map sequential phonetic input onto corresponding distributed representations of phonological surface forms and semantics (Gaskell & Marslen-Wilson, 1997a, 1997b). This style of representation contrasts with the localist representations used in TRACE. The ability of the SRN to model the integration of partial cues to phonetic identity and the time course of lexical access provides support for a distributed approach. An important challenge for such distributed models is to model the simultaneous activation of multiple lexical candidates necessitated by the temporal ambiguity of the speech input (e.g., /kæp/ could continue*captain* and *captive*; see Allopenna, Magnuson, & Tanenhaus, 1998, for a generalization of this phenomenon). The "coactivation" of several lexical candidates in a distributed model results in a semantic "blend" vector. Computational explorations (Gaskell & Marslen-Wilson, 1999) of such semantic blends provide explanations of recent empirical results aimed at measuring lexical coactivation (Gaskell & Marslen-Wilson, 1997a, 1997b) and more generally provide a concrete implementation of theoretical proposals that were previously expressed informally (Marslen-Wilson & Warren, 1994).

3.3. Speech Segmentation

Further evidence for the bottom-up approach to speech processing comes from the modeling of speech segmentation (Christiansen, Allen, & Seidenberg, 1998). An SRN was trained to integrate sets of phonetic features with information about lexical stress (strong or weak) and utterance boundary information (encoded as a binary unit) derived from a corpus of child-directed speech. The network was trained to predict the appropriate values of these three cues for the next segment. After training, the network was able to generalize patterns of cue information that occurred at the end of utterances to when the same patterns occurred elsewhere in the utterance. Relying entirely on bottom-up information, the model performed well on the word segmentation task and captured important aspects of infant speech segmentation. Speech segmentation has also been the subject a wide variety of alternative computational proposals (e.g., Hockema, in press).

3.4. Reading Aloud

Connectionist research on reading aloud has focused on single words. A classic early model used a feedforward network (Figure 17.1B) to map from a distributed orthographic representation to a distributed phonological representation for monosyllabic English words (Seidenberg & McClelland, 1989). The net's performance captured a wide range of experimental data on the assumption that network error maps onto response time. This model contrasts with standard views of reading, which assume both a "phonological route," applying rules of pronunciation, and a "lexical route," which is a list of words and their pronunciations. Regular words (e.g., *sing*) can be read using either route, exception words (e.g., *colonel*) by the lexical route, and nonwords by the phonological route. It was claimed that, instead, a single connectionist route can pronounce both exception words and nonwords. Critics have responded that the network's nonword reading is well below human performance (Besner et al., 1990, although see Seidenberg & McClelland, 1990). Another difficulty is the model's reliance on (log) frequency compression during training (otherwise exception words are not learned successfully). Subsequent research has addressed both limitations, showing that a network trained on actual word frequencies can achieve human levels of performance on both word and nonword pronunciation, which has led to a range of new connectionist models (e.g., Plaut, 1999).

3.5. Explaining the Acquired Dyslexias

The number of routes by which words can be recognized is a central point of theoretical debate. It is widely agreed that both semantic (where orthography is mapped to meaning and then to phonology) and nonsemantic routes (which map orothography to phonology without going through semantics) are available. The key controversy is whether there are one or two *non-semantic* routes. Dual-route theorists typically argue that there are two such routes – a phonological route that uses the rules of regular orthography/phonology to pronounce words piecemeal and a "lexical" route, which maps whole orthographic inputs to whole phonological outputs by a process akin to table look-up. Some connectionists take a single nonsemantic route viewpoint, arguing, for example, that the division of labor between phonological and semantic routes can explain diverse neuropsychological syndromes that have been taken to require a dual-route account (Plaut et al., 1996). One viewpoint is that a division of labor emerges between the phonological and the semantic pathway during reading acquisition: the phonological pathway specializes in regular orthography-to-phonology mappings at the expense of exceptions, which are read by the semantic pathway. Damage to the semantic pathway causes "surface dyslexia" (where exceptions are selectively impaired), and damage to the phonological pathway causes "phonological dyslexia" (where nonwords are selectively impaired). According to this viewpoint, the syndrome of "deep dyslexia" (severe reading impairment, with meaning-based errors, such as reading the word *peach* as *apricot*) occurs when the phonological route is damaged and the semantic route is also partially impaired (which leads to semantic errors that are characteristic of the syndrome). Other highly successful connectionist models take the opposite line and directly implement both phonological routes, in line with standard views in cognitive neuropsychology (Coltheart et al., 1993). As well as exploring data on the breakdown of reading, there has also been a lively literature of (primarily) connectionist computational models of acquisition, although this issue is not explored here (Brown & Chater, 2003; Harm, McCandliss, & Seidenberg, 2003).

3.6. *Capturing the Psycholinguistic Data*

Moving from neuropsychological to experimental data, connectionist models of reading have been criticized for not modeling effects of specific lexical items (Spieler & Balota, 1997). One defense is that current models are too partial (e.g., containing no letter recognition and phonological output components) to model word-level effects (Seidenberg & Plaut, 1998). However, this challenge is taken up in a study in which an SRN is trained to pronounce words phoneme-by-phoneme (Plaut, 1999). The network can also refixate the input when unable to pronounce part of a word. The model performs well on words and nonwords, and fits empirical data on word length effects (Rastle & Coltheart, 1998; Weekes, 1997). Complementary work using a recurrent network focuses on providing a richer model of phonological knowledge and processing (Harm & Seidenberg, 1999, 2004), which may be importantly related to reading development (Bradley & Bryant, 1983).

Finally, it has been shown how a two-route model of reading might emerge naturally from a connectionist learning architecture (Zorzi et al., 1998). Direct links between orthographic input and phonological output learn to encode letter-to-phoneme correspondences (a phonological route) whereas links via hidden units spontaneously learn to handle exception words (a lexical route; Figure 17.2B). Here, as elsewhere, connectionist and indeed probabilistic models can provide persuasive instantiations of a range of theoretical positions.

3.7. *Probabilistic Approaches*

In recent work, there has been a trend toward developing probabilistic models of reading. One attraction of this approach is that it allows a clearer and more direct explanation of how the statistical structure of the orthography-phonology mapping and other factors such as word frequency lead to variations in reading performance. This approach can, to some degree, be viewed as providing a theoretical analysis of why some of the connectionist models work as they do. For example, many aspects of network behavior can be understood as depending on the regularity of the orthography-phonology mapping at different levels of analysis (individual phonemes, trigrams, onsets/rimes, etc.); probabilistic models can provide a principled way of synthesizing regularities at different levels to produce predictions about how non-words should be read; dissonances between levels will suggest that processing is likely to be slowed (Brown, 1998). A comprehensive model by Norris (2006) provides examples of this approach. Moreover, probabilistic methods have also been extended recently to provide an "ideal" model of how eye movements should be controlled to maximize the expected information throughput to the reading system (Legge, Klitz, & Tjan, 1997).

4. Sentence Processing

Although symbolic models of sentence processing have been extensively developed in computational linguistics and many proposals concerning sentence processing have been framed in symbolic terms (e.g., Berwick & Weinberg, 1984; Crocker, 1996; Kurtzman, 1985; Yngve, 1960), much recent work oriented toward explaining specific psycholinguistic data has been carried out within the connectionist and probabilistic traditions.

Sentence processing provides a considerable challenge for connectionism. Some connectionists (Miyata, Smolensky, & Legendre, 1993) have built symbolic structures directly into the network, whereas others have chosen to construct a modular system of networks, each tailored to acquire different aspects of syntactic processing (Miikkulainen, 1996). However, the approach that has had the most impact involves directly training networks to discover syntactic structure from word sequences (Elman, 1991). This approach is the most radical approach, that is, it aims to dispense with traditional rule-based models of language and, indeed, any rigid distinction between grammar and processing, or competence and performance (Christiansen, 1992).

4.1. Capturing Complexity Judgment and Reading Time Data

One study has explored the learning of different types of recursion by training an SRN on small artificial languages (Christiansen & Chater, 1999). Christiansen and Chater reasoned that processing will be difficult to the extent that each piece of subsequent linguistic input is not predicted. They measured the average prediction error for the network, when trained on different sentence types, and predicted that errors should correlate with psycholinguistic data on processing difficulty. The results provided a good match with human data concerning the greater perceived difficulty associated with center-embedding in German compared with cross-serial dependencies in Dutch (Bach, Brown, & Marslen-Wilson, 1986). Moreover, error scores considered word by word from a related model were mapped directly onto reading times, providing an experience-based account for human data concerning the differential processing of singly center-embedded subject and object relative clauses by good and poor comprehenders (MacDonald & Christiansen, 2002).

Another approach to sentence processing involves a two-component model of ambiguity resolution, combining an SRN with a "gravitational" mechanism (Tabor, Juliano, & Tanenhaus, 1997). The SRN was trained in the usual way on sentences derived from a grammar. After training, SRN hidden unit representations for individual words were placed in the gravitational mechanism, and the latter was allowed to settle into a stable state. Settling times were then mapped onto word-reading times. The two-component model was able to fit data from several experiments concerning the interaction of lexical and structural constraints on the resolution of temporary syntactic ambiguities (i.e., garden path effects) in sentence comprehension. The two-component model has also been extended (Tabor & Tanenhaus, 1999) to account for empirical findings reflecting the influence of semantic role expectations on syntactic ambiguity resolution in sentence processing (McRae, Spivey-Knowlton, & Tanenhaus, 1998).

4.2. *Capturing Grammaticality Rratings in Aphasia*

Some headway has also been made in accounting for data concerning the effects of acquired aphasia (i.e., language processing difficulties, typically resulting from damage to, or degeneration of, brain areas involved with language) on grammaticality judgments (Allen & Seidenberg, 1999). A bidirectional recurrent network (Figure 17.2C) was trained mutually to associate two input sequences: a sequence of word forms and a corresponding sequence of word meanings. The network was able to learn a small artificial language successfully, enabling it to regenerate word forms from meanings and vice versa. Grammaticality judgments were simulated by testing how well the network could recreate a given input sequence, allowing activation to flow from the provided input forms to meaning and then back again. Ungrammatical sentences were recreated less accurately than grammatical sentences; hence, the network was able to distinguish grammatical from ungrammatical sentences. The network was then "lesioned" by removing 10% of the weights in the network. Grammaticality judgments were then elicited from the impaired network for ten different sentence types from a classic study of aphasic grammaticality judgments (Linebarger, Schwartz, & Saffran 1983). The aphasic patients had problems with three of these sentence types, and the network fitted this pattern of performance impairment. Computational models of aphasia have also been formulated within the symbolic tradition (Haarmann, Just, & Carpenter 1997).

4.3. *Probabilistic Approaches to Sentence Processing*

In contrast to the connectionist models described earlier, probabilistic models have typically been viewed as complementary to symbolic linguistic representations, al-

though many theorists take probabilistic methods to have substantial revisionist implications for traditional linguistic representations (e.g., Bod et al., 2003). Here, the focus is on how probabilistic ideas have led to a rethinking of structural accounts of parsing, such as minimal attachment (Frazier, 1979), as mentioned previously.

Structural principles have come under threat from psycholinguistic data that indicates that parsing preferences over structural ambiguities, such as prepositional phrase attachment, differ across languages, often in line with variations in observed corpus frequencies in these languages (e.g., Mitchell et al., 1995). Psycholinguists are increasingly exploring corpus statistics across languages, and parsing preferences seem to fit the probabilities evident in each language (Desmet et al., in press; Desmet & Gibson, 2003).

Structural parsing principles also have difficulty capturing the probabilistic influence of lexical information. Thus, a structural principle finds it difficult to account for the difference in parsing preference between *the astronomer saw the planet with a telescope* and *the astronomer saw the star with a moon*. The probabilistic approach seems useful here because it seems important to integrate the constraint that seeing-with-telescopes is much more likely than seeing-with-moons.

One way to capture these constraints aims to capture statistical (or even rigid) regularities between words. For example, "lexicalized" grammars, which carry information about what material co-occurs with specific words, substantially improve computational parsing performance (Charniak, 1997; Collins, 2003). More generally, the view that parsing preferences are determined by the integration of many "soft" constraints, rather than by any single principle, structural or otherwise, is compatible with both connectionist and probabilistic frameworks (Seidenberg & MacDonald, 1999).

4.4. *Plausibility and Statistics*

Statistical constraints between words are, however, a crude approximation of what sentences are *plausible*. In off-line judgement tasks, for example, where people assign explicit ratings of plausibility, people can use world knowledge, the understanding of the social and environmental context, pragmatic principles, and much more, to determine what people might plausibly say or mean. Determining whether a statement is plausible may involve determining how likely it is to be true, but also whether, given the present context, it might plausibly be *said*. The first issue requires a probabilistic model of general knowledge (Pearl, 1988). The second issue requires engaging "theory of mind" (inferring the other's mental states) and invoking principles of pragmatics. Models of these processes, probabilistic or otherwise, are very preliminary (Jurafsky, 2003).

A fundamental theoretical debate concerns whether plausibility is used on-line in parsing decisions. Are statistical dependencies between words used as a computationally cheap surrogate for plausibility? Or are both statistics and plausibility deployed on-line, perhaps in separate mechanisms? Eye-tracking paradigms (Tanenhaus et al., 1995; McDonald & Shillcock, 2003) have been used to suggest that both factors are used on-line, although this interpretations is controversial. However, recent work indicates that probabilistic grammar models often predict the time course of processing (Hale, 2003; Jurafsky, 1996; Narayanan & Jurafsky, 2002).

4.5. *Is the Most Likely Parse Favored?*

In the probabilistic framework, it is typically assumed that on-line ambiguity resolution favors the most probable parse. Yet, Chater, Crocker, and Pickering (1998) suggest that, for a serial parser, whose chance of "recovery" is highest if the "mistake" is discovered soon, this is an oversimplification. In particular, they suggest that because parsing decisions are made *on-line* (Pickering, Traxler, & Crocker, 2000), there should be a bias to choose interpretations that make *specific* predictions, which might rapidly be falsified. For example, in the phrase *John realized his . . .*, the more probable interpretation is that *realized* introduces a sentential complement (i.e., *John realized [that] his . . .*). On this interpretation, the rest of the noun phrase after *his* is unconstrained. By contrast, the less probable transitive reading (*John realized his goals/potential/objectives*) places very strong constraints on the subsequent noun phrase. Perhaps, then, the parser should favor the more specific reading because if wrong, it may rapidly and successfully be corrected. Chater, Pickering, and Crocker (1998) provide a Bayesian analysis of "optimal ambiguity resolution" capturing such cases. The empirical issue of whether the human parser follows this analysis (Pickering et al., 2000) is not fully resolved. Note, too, that parsing preferences appear to be influenced by additional factors, including the linear distance between the incoming word and the prior words to which it has a dependency relation (Grodner & Gibson, 2005).

Overall, connectionist and probabilistic computational proposals have allowed a more fine-grained match with psycholinguistic data than obtained by early symbolic models. The question of how far models of sentence processing, considering the full complexity of natural language syntax and the subtlety of compositional semantics, can avoid adopting traditional symbolic representations, as postulated by linguistic theory, remains controversial.

5. Language Acquisition

Chomsky (1965) frames the problem of language acquisition as follows: The child has a hypothesis-space of candidate grammars and must choose, on the basis of (primarily linguistic) experience, one of these grammars. From a probabilistic standpoint, each candidate grammar is associated with a prior probability, and these probabilities will be modified by experience using Bayes' theorem (see Chapter 3 in this volume). The learner will presumably choose a language with high, and perhaps the highest, posterior probability.

A. Overlap

B. Undergeneral grammar

C. Overgeneral grammar

D. Probabilistic evidence against an overgeneral grammar

 Target language

 Guess

 Example sentence

Figure 17.3. The problem of recovery from overgeneral grammars. Suppose that sentences (gray triangles) are generated according to a true grammar, indicated by the unbroken circles. The learner considers an alternative, incorrect, grammar, shown by the broken circles. How can the learner realize that its current guess is incorrect and that it needs to search for an alternative grammar? (A) When the grammars partially overlap, a sentence will eventually be encountered that is outside the hypothesized grammar. (B) The same is true when the learner's proposed grammar is undergeneral, that is, the sentences of the hypothesized grammar are all allowed in the true language, but the proposed grammar does not allow some sentences that are grammatical. (C) A problem arises when the learner's grammar is overgeneral because all the sentences that are encountered by the learner fit the overgeneral language; hence, there is no decisive way of falsifying the overgeneral language from observed sentences. Of course, if the learner *produces* an illegitimate sentence, it may obtain feedback that this sentence is not acceptable, but it is widely, although controversially, argued that such feedback is not required for language acquisition. The puzzle of how to recover from postulating an overgeneral grammar, which arises in a range of guises, has been seen as so serious as to pose a "logical" problem for language acquisition (e.g., Baker & McCarthy, 1981; see MacWhinney, 2004, for discussion). (D) If, however, the learner finds that only a portion of the space of possible sentences is actually used, for example,

5.1. The Poverty of the Stimulus?

Chomsky (1968, 1980) influentially argued, as noted earlier, that the learning problem is unsolvable without strong prior constraints on the language, given the "poverty" (i.e., partiality and errorfulness) of the linguistic stimulus. Indeed, Chomsky (1981) argued that almost all syntactic structure, aside from a finite number of binary parameters, must be innate. Independent mathematical results by Gold (1967) indicated that, under certain assumptions, learners provably cannot converge on a language even "in the limit" as the corpus becomes indefinitely large (for discussion, see MacWhinney, 2004; Rohde & Plaut, 1999). In essence, the problem is that the learner seems to have no way of guaranteeing recovery from formulating an overgeneral grammar, at least if it is restricted to observing sentences in the language. This is because all the sentences that it hears are allowed by the overgeneral grammar, and hence the learner appears to have no impetus to switch to a new grammar (Figure 17.3).

A probabilistic standpoint yields more positive learnability results. For example, Horning (1969) proved that phrase structure grammars are learnable (with high probability) to within a statistical tolerance if sentences are sampled as independent, identically distributed data. Chater and Vitányi (2007; Chater, 2004, gives a brief summary) generalize to a language that is generated by any computable process (i.e., sentences may be interdependent,

Figure 17.3 (cont.)
those that fit with some other grammar, then the learner should become increasingly persuaded that the grammar is overgeneral. This argument, although intuitively appealing, is not straightforward, however, because, of course, the learner's experience of the language is always a finite subset of an infinite set of possible sentences. A key observation is that an alternative *simple* and less general grammar is available that captures all observed sentences. This type of argument can be made rigorous (e.g., Horning, 1969; Chater, 2004).

as they are in real language corpora, and sentences may be generated by any computable process, i.e., the highest level in the Chomsky hierarchy). They show that prediction, grammaticality, and semantics are all learnable to a statistical tolerance. These results are "ideal"; however, they consider what would be learned if the learner could find the shortest representation of linguistic data and use this representation as the basis for prediction, grammaticality judgements, and so on. In practice, the learner may find a short code, but not the shortest, and theoretical results are not available for this case. Nonetheless, from a probabilistic standpoint, learning looks less intractable, partly because learning need only succeed with high probability and to an approximation (speakers may learn slightly different idiolects).

5.2. *Computational Models of Language Learning*

Yet, the question of learnability and the potential need for innate constraints remain. Machine learning methods have successfully learned small artificial context-free languages (e.g., Anderson, 1977; Lari & Young, 1990), but profound difficulties in extending these results to real language corpora have led computational linguists to focus on learning from parsed trees (Charniak, 1997; Collins, 2003), presumably not available to the child. Connectionist models are restricted to small artificial languages (Elman, 1990; Christiansen & Chater, 1999) and, despite having considerable psychological interest, they often do not scale well (though see Reali, Christiansen, & Monaghan, 2003).

Klein and Manning (2002, 2004) have recently made substantial steps toward solving the problem of deriving syntactic constituency from a corpus of unlabelled, unparsed text. Klein and Manning (2002) extended the success of distributional clustering methods for learning word classes (Redington et al., 1998; Schütze 1998), discussed later. Roughly, they classify the categories of phrases by grouping together

phrases that have similar contexts (context here concerns the word immediately preceding and immediately following the phrase). As discussed later, this corresponds to a statistical version of the distributional test in linguistics. Klein and Manning (2004) combine this work with a system for learning linguistic dependency relations. The dependency model uses data on which words occur together, with two additional and crucial constraints: that dependencies between nearby words are preferred and a preference for words to have few dependencies. Klein and Manning's work shows that central features of language, phrase structure and dependency relations can be learned to a good approximation from unlabelled language – clearly a task crucial to child language acquisition.

This work is a promising demonstration of empirical language learning from a probabilistic standpoint, but most linguistic theories use richer structures than surface phrase structure trees. Moreover, learning the syntactic regularities of language should, presumably, be in the service of learning how to map linguistic forms to meanings. In the probabilistic tradition, there is some work on mapping to meaning representations of simple data sets (Zettlemoyer & Collins, 2005) and work on unsupervised learning of a mapping from surface text to semantic role representations (Swier & Stevenson, 2005). There is also a related tradition of work, especially on thematic role assignment, in the connectionist tradition (Lupyan & Christiansen, 2002; McClelland & Kawamoto, 1986; St. John, 1992).

5.3. *Poverty of the Stimulus, Again*

The status of Chomsky's (1965) poverty of the stimulus argument remains unclear, beginning with the question of whether children really do face a poverty of linguistic data (see the debate between Pullum & Scholz, 2002, and Legate & Yang, 2002). Perhaps no large and complex grammar can be learned from the child's input, or perhaps certain specific linguistic patterns (e.g., perhaps encoded in an innate universal grammar) are in principle unlearnable. Interestingly, however, Reali and Christiansen (2005) have shown that both probabilistic and connectionist methods can successfully be applied to learning an apparently problematic linguistic construction, auxiliary fronting, suggesting that more linguistic phenomena may be learnable than is typically assumed in linguistics (e.g., Chomsky, 1957).

Presently, theorists using probabilistic methods diverge widely on the severity of the prior "innate" constraints they assume. Some theorists focus on applying probability to learning parameters of Chomskyan Universal Grammar (Gibson & Wexler, 1994; Niyogi, 2006); others focus on learning relatively simple aspects of language, such as learning morphological structure, or learning approximate syntactic or semantic categories, with relatively weak prior assumptions.

5.4. *Acquiring Morphological Structure*

A key issue in computational models of morphological processing and acquisition is how computational analysis has addressed a key theoretical question: whether inflectional morphology requires two "routes," one to handle regular morphology (e.g., "go" → "went") or whether a single computational mechanism can account for both rules and exceptions paralleling the single route vs. dual route debate in reading, discussed previously. Studies with idealized languages patterned on English past tense morphology suggest that a single route may handle both cases (Hahn & Nakisa, 2000). However, Prasada and Pinker (1993) argued that the success of these models results from the distributional statistics of English. Many regular English /-ed/ verbs have low token frequencies, which a connectionist model can handle by learning to add /-ed/ as a default. For irregular verbs, token frequency is typically high, allowing the network to override the default. Prasada and Pinker argued that a default regular mapping with both low type and token frequency could not be learned by a connectionist network. The pu-

tative default /-s/ inflection of plural nouns in German appears to provide an example of such a "minority default mapping." Marcus et al. (1995) proposed that the German plural system must be modeled by two routes: a pattern associator, which memorizes specific cases (both irregular and regular), and a default rule (add /s/), which applies when the connectionist pattern associator fails.

Hahn and Nakisa (2000) asked whether single route associative models (they tested two exemplar-based learning models and a simple feed-forward connectionist net with one hidden layer) could learn the German plural system and generalize appropriately to novel regular and irregular nouns. Their models' task was to predict to which of 15 different plural types the input stem belonged. The inputs to the learning mechanisms were phonetic representations of 4,000 German nouns taken from the CELEX database (token frequency was ignored). All models showed good performance in predicting the plural form of 4,000 unseen nouns, and the connectionist model obtained the best performance, at over 80% correct.

Crucially, Hahn and Nakisa (2000) also simulated the Marcus et al. (1995) model by assuming that any test word which is not close to a training word, according to the associative model (for which the lexical memory fails), will be dealt with by a default "add /-s/" rule. The associative models were trained on the irregular nouns, and the models were tested as before. They found that for all three models, the presence of the rule led to a decrement in performance. In general, the higher the threshold for memory failure (the more similar a test item had to be to a training item to be irregularized via the associative memory), the greater the decrement in performance. The use of a default rule could only have improved performance for regular nouns occupying regions of phonemic space surrounding clusters of irregulars. Hahn and Nakisa's findings demonstrate that very few regular nouns occur in these regions in the German lexicon. The extension of Hahn and Nakisa's findings to the production of the plural form (instead of merely indicating the plural type) and to more realistic input (for instance, taking account of token frequency) remains to be performed. Further work might also focus on the extent to which different single- and dual-route models are able to capture changes in detailed error patterns of under-regularization- and overregularization during development. Another interesting topic for future work is the processing of derivational, rather than inflectional, morphology (e.g., Plaut & Gonnerman, 2000).

5.5. *Acquiring Syntactic Categories*

The problem of categorizing phrases using distributional methods from unlabelled text (Klein & Manning, 2002) has been discussed. A more basic question is how does the child acquire lexical syntactic categories, such as noun and verb. This problem encompasses both discovering that there are different classes and ascertaining which words belong to each class. Even for theorists who assume that the child innately possesses a universal grammar and syntactic categories (as is assumed in the traditional Chomskyan framework), identifying the category of particular words must primarily be a matter of learning. Universal grammatical features can only be mapped on to the specific surface appearance of a particular natural language once the identification of words with syntactic categories has been made, although once some identifications have been made, it may be possible to use prior grammatical knowledge to facilitate further identifications. The contribution of innate knowledge to initial linguistic categories must be relatively slight. Both language-external and language-internal cues may be relevant to learning syntactic categories. One language-external approach, semantic bootstrapping, exploits the putative correlation between linguistic categories (in particular, noun and verb) and the child's perception of the environment (in terms of objects and actions). This may provide a means of "breaking in" to the system of syntactic categories. Also, there may be many

relevant language-internal factors: regularities between phonology, prosody and distributional analysis, both over morphological variations between lexical items (e.g., affixes such as "-ed" are correlated with syntactic category; Maratsos & Chalkley, 1980; see also Onnis & Christiansen, 2005), and at the word level.

Here, the focus is on this last approach, which has a long history, although this method of finding word classes has often been dismissed on a priori grounds within the language learning literature. The "distributional test" in linguistics is based on the observation that if all occurrences of word A can be replaced by word B without loss of syntactic acceptability, then they share the same syntactic category. For example, dog can be substituted freely for cat in phrases such as: *the cat sat on the mat, nine out of ten cats prefer . . .* , indicating that these items have the same category. The distributional test is not a foolproof method of grouping words by their syntactic category, because distribution is a function of many factors other than syntactic category (such as word meaning). Thus, for example, *cat* and *barnacle* might appear in very different contexts in some corpora, although they have the same word class. Nevertheless, it may be possible to exploit the general principle underlying the distributional test to obtain useful information about word classes. One approach is to record the contexts in which the words to be classified appear in a corpus of language and group together words with similar distributions of contexts. Here, context is defined in terms of co-occurrence statistics.

Redington et al. (1998) used a window of two words before and after each target word as context. Vectors representing the co-occurrence statistics for these positions were constructed from a 2.5 million-word corpus of transcribed adult speech taken from the CHILDES corpus (MacWhinney & Snow, 1985), much of which was child-directed. The vectors for each position were concatenated to form a single vector for each of 1,000 target words. The similarity of distribution between the vectors was calculated using Spearman's rank correlation, and hierarchical cluster analysis was used to group similar words together.

This approach does not partition words into distinct groups corresponding to the syntactic categories, but produces a hierarchical tree, or dendrogram, whose structure reflects to some extent the syntactic relationships between words. Figure 17.4A shows the high-level structure of the dendrogram resulting from the previous analysis. Figure 17.4B shows part of the Adjective cluster in Figure 17.4A, illustrating how statistical distributional analysis reflects syntactic and semantic information at a very fine level.

A quantitative analysis of the mutual information between the structure of the dendrogram and a canonical syntactic classification of the target words (defined as their most common syntactic usage in English) as a percentage of the joint information in both the derived and canonical classifications revealed that at all levels of similarity, the dendrogram conveyed useful information about the syntactic structure of English. Words that were clustered together tended to belong to the same syntactic category, and words that were clustered apart tended to belong to different syntactic categories. Thus, computational analysis of real language corpora shows that distributional information at the word level is highly informative about syntactic category, despite a priori objections to its utility (see Monaghan, Chater, & Christiansen, 2005). Similar results, typically on a smaller scale, have been obtained from hidden-unit analysis of connectionist networks (e.g., Elman, 1990; although such results also arise when the network is untrained; Kolen, 1994).

5.6. *Acquiring Lexical Semantics*

Acquiring lexical semantics involves identifying the meanings of particular words. Even for concrete nouns, this problem is complicated by the difficulty of detecting which part of the physical environment a speaker is referring to. Even if this can be ascertained, it may still remain unclear whether the term used by the speaker refers to a particular object, a part of that object, or a class of objects. For abstract nouns and other words that have no concrete referents, these difficulties are compounded further.

Presumably, the primary sources of information for the development of lexical semantics are language-external. Relationships between the child and the physical environment, and especially the social environment, are likely to play a major role in the development of lexical semantic knowledge. However, it also seems plausible that language-internal information might be used to constrain the identification of the possible meaning of words. For instance, just as semantics might constrain the identity of a word's syntactic category (words referring to concrete objects are likely to be nouns), knowing a word's syntactic category provides some constraint on its meaning; in general, knowing that a word is a noun, perhaps because it occurs in a particular set of local contexts, implies that it will refer to a concrete object or an abstract concept, rather than an action or process.

Because there are potentially informative relationships between aspects of language at all levels, this means that even relatively low-level properties of language, such as morphology and phonology, might provide some constraints on lexical semantics. Gleitman has proposed that syntax is a potentially powerful cue for the acquisition of meaning. Gleitman assumes that the child possesses a relatively high degree of syntactic knowledge. However, an examination of Figure 17.4B shows that the distributional method used earlier to provide information about syntactic categories also captures some degree of semantic relatedness without any knowledge of syntax proper. More direct methods for deriving semantic relationships have been proposed (e.g., Landauer & Dumais, 1997; Lund & Burgess, 1996; Schütze, 1993).

These statistical approaches do, however, have a somewhat arbitrary quality. Griffiths and Steyvers (2004) have more recently developed a more rigorous Bayesian approach, in which the words in a text are viewed as generated from a mixture of "topics,"

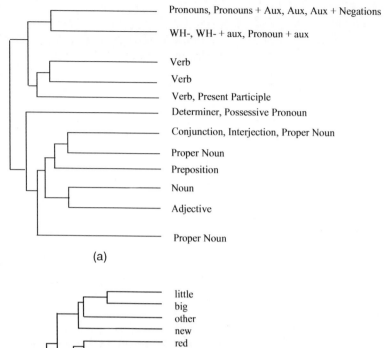

(a)

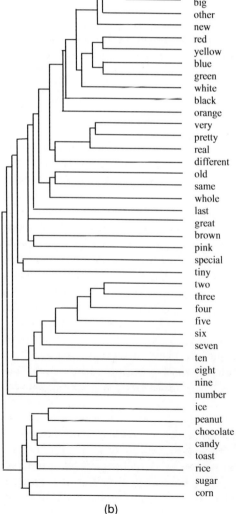

(b)

Figure 17.4 Word clusters from distributional information, based on Redington, Chater, and Finch (1998). Analysis was conducted over a large corpus of transcribed adult speech from the CHILDES database (MacWhinney & Snow, 1985). (A) The overall structure of a cluster of the lexicon in which the syntactic labels, added by hand, classify the category of the vast majority of the words correctly compared with standard classifications. The numbers in parentheses indicate the number of lexical items in each category. (B) A close-up of part of the adjective cluster. Note the fine-grained semantic groupings obtained, such as groupings of color and number words. (Reprinted with permission of the Cognitive Science Society, from Redington, M., Chater, N., & Finch, S. [1998]. Distributional information: A powerful cue for acquiring syntactic categories. *Cognitive Science*, *22*, 425–469.)

TRANSPORTATION	BEANS	ROOM	BARN	CREEK	SAVINGS
CARS	POTATOES	HOUSE	CHICKENS	BANK	MONEY
TRUCKS	POTATO	BED	HOUSE	STREAM	ACCOUNT
ROADS	TOMATOES	TABLE	HEN	SIDE	INTEREST
TRAVEL	SWEET	KITCHEN	BIG	WOODS	ACCOUNTS
TRAINS	VEGETABLES	ROOMS	FARM	FEET	FUNDS
AIRPLANES	CORN	BEDROOM	COWS	MEADOW	LOAN
AUTOMOBILES	LETTUCE	DOOR	HAY	DEEP	BANK
HIGHWAYS	CARROTS	WALLS	STRAW	RIVER	DEPOSITS
CARRY	BEAN	FLOOR	LANTERN	BUSHES	MUTUAL
TRANSPORT	EAT	CHAIR	HENS	RAN	DEPOSIT
GOODS	SQUASH	WALL	HORSE	BROOK	CHECKING
BUSES	CABBAGE	LIVING	STALL	STOOD	HIGHER
BUILT	TOMATO	WINDOWS	SHED	POOL	INSTITUTION
CITIES	PEAS	HALL	PIGS	WATER	OFFER
MOVE	BANANAS	DINING	ROOSTER	EDGE	FUND
FREIGHT	PEPPERS	FURNITURE	COW	BRANCHES	ASSOCIATIONS
RAILROADS	CABBAGES	CHAIRS	HORSES	TREES	PROVIDE
PASSENGERS	SPROUTS	CURTAINS	CHICKEN	LAY	INVEST
SHIPS	PEANUTS	SHELVES	STALLS	WALKED	EARN

Figure 17.5. Semantic relations between lexical items, learned from distributional information. Six semantic "topics" derived from a large text corpus (the TASA corpus), using the method of Griffiths & Steyvers (2004) and chosen from 1,700 topics used in this analysis. The top twenty most frequent words for each topic are shown in rank order. They correspond to transport, food, furniture, barnyard animals, pastoral, and finance topics. Note that *bank* occurs in both the latter contexts, indicating that multiple readings of a word can be recognized.

and the topics themselves are inferred from the data. This Bayesian approach provides an elegant way of finding semantic categories from text. Thus, good approximations to syntactic categories and semantic classes have been learned by clustering items based on their linear distributional contexts (e.g., the distribution over the word that precedes and follows each token of a type) or broad topical contexts (see Figure 17.5). One can even simultaneously cluster words exploiting local syntactic and topical similarity (Griffiths et al., 2005).

Grouping words that are semantically related is only a small part of the problem of learning lexical semantics, of course. One particularly pressing problem is that such analyses merely relate words to each other, rather than connecting them to objects in the world. The problem of relating words to the referents (e.g., as presented in perceptual input for words with concrete referents) raises very large computational challenges. Nonetheless, some interesting work has been carried out that begins to address this problem (e.g., Regier, 2005; Roy, 2005).

6. Conclusion and Future Directions

Linguistics has traditionally viewed language as a symbolic system, governed by a rich system of rules; yet, computational models of human language processing have focused on graded and probabilistic aspects of language structure and processing. Connectionist and probabilistic computational accounts of psycholinguistic phenomena have been proposed, ranging from speech processing to phonology, morphology, reading, syntax, semantics, and language production. Moreover, as has been seen, connectionist and probabilistic approaches have provided both new theoretical perspectives and specific computational models of a range of aspects of language acquisition, typically emphasizing the importance of information in the linguistic input far more than the strongly nativist tradition in Chomskyan linguistics.

There is reason to expect, nonetheless, that future developments in computational modeling of psycholinguistic phenomena will involve an interplay between all three perspectives on language. Language has a substantial symbolic component, even if it also has much graded and probabilistic structure; a wide variety of recent work in linguistics, much of it inspired by or directly rooted in computational modeling, proposes that symbolic and probabilistic aspects of language must be explained simultaneously (e.g., Goldberg, 2006). There is a variety of overlapping ways in which rule-based and probabilistic factors may interact: The set of potentially conflicting linguistic rules to apply may be determined using probabilistic methods (e.g., Smolensky & Legendre, 2006); rules may be embodied directly in stochastic grammars (e.g., Charniak, 1997); rules, and perhaps also their exceptions, may be probabilistically approximated using connectionist networks (Christiansen & Chater, 2001). The project of building deeper models of human language processing and acquisition involves paying attention to both rules and to graded/probabilistic structure in language. At the same time, the project of computational modeling must be in close dialogue with both theoretical work in linguistics and, perhaps most crucially, with the increasingly sophisticated and detailed body of empirical data on how people use and acquire language.

Acknowledgments

We would like to thank Tom Griffiths, Chris Manning, and Martin Redington for input into this work and two anonymous reviewers for their comments on an earlier draft of this chapter. Nick Chater was partially supported by ESRC grant RES-000-22-1120 and a Leverhulme Trust Major Research Grant. Morten Christiansen was supported by a Charles A. Ryskamp Research Fellowship from the American Council of Learned Societies.

References

Aho, A. V., & Ullman, J. D. (1972). *The theory of parsing, translation and compiling* (Vol. 1). Englewood Cliffs, NJ: Prentice Hall.

Allen, J., & Seidenberg, M. S. (1999). The emergence of grammaticality in connectionist networks. In B. MacWhinney (Ed.), *The emergence of language* (pp. 115–151). Mahwah, NJ: Lawrence Erlbaum.

Allopenna, P. D., Magnuson, J. S., & Tanenhaus, M. K. (1998). Tracking the time course of spoken word recognition using eye movements: Evidence for continuous mapping models. *Journal of Memory and Language, 38*, 419–439.

Anderson, J. A. (1977). Induction of augmented transition networks. *Cognitive Science, 1*, 125–157.

Bach, E., Brown, C., & Marslen-Wilson, W. (1986). Crossed and nested dependencies in German and Dutch: A psycholinguistic study. *Language and Cognitive Processes, 1*, 249–262.

Baker, C. L., & McCarthy, J. J. (Eds.). (1981). *The logical problem of language acquisition.* Cambridge, MA: MIT Press.

Bates, E. A., & Elman, J. L. (1993). Connectionism and the study of change. In M. H. Johnson (Ed.), *Brain and cognitive development: A reader* (pp. 623–642). Oxford, UK: Blackwell.

Berwick, R., (1986). *The acquisition of linguistic knowledge.* Cambridge, MA: MIT Press.

Berwick, R., & Weinberg, A. (1984). *The grammatical basis of linguistic performance.* Cambridge, MA: MIT Press.

Besner, D., Twilley, L., McCann, R. S., & Seergobin, K. (1990). On the connection between connectionism and data: are a few words necessary? *Psychological Review, 97*, 432–446.

Bod, R. (1998). *Beyond grammar: An experience-based theory theory of language.* Stanford, CA: CSLI Publications.

Bod, R., Hay, J., & Jannedy, S. (Eds.). (2003). *Probabilistic linguistics.* Cambridge, MA: MIT Press.

Bradley, L., & Bryant, P. (1983). Categorizing sounds and learning to read: a causal connection. *Nature, 301*, 419–421.

Brown, G. D. A. (1998). The endpoint of reading instruction: The ROAR model. In J. L. Metsala & L. C. Ehri (Eds.), *Word recognition in beginning Literacy* (pp. 121–138). Mahwah, NJ: Erlbaun.

Brown, G. D. A., & Chater, N. (2003). Connectionist models of children's reading. In T. Nunes & P. E. Bryant (Eds.), *Handbook of children's literacy* (pp. 67–89). Dordrecht: Kluwer.

Cairns, P., Shillcock, R. C., Chater, N., & Levy, J. (1997). Bootstrapping word boundaries: A bottom-up corpus-based approach to speech segmentation. *Cognitive Psychology, 33,* 111–153.

Charniak, E. (1997). Statistical parsing with a context-free grammar and word statistics. In B. F. Kuipers & B. Webber (Eds.), *Proceedings of the 14th National Conference on Artificial Intelligence* (pp. 598–603). Cambridge, MA: AAAI Press.

Chater, N. (2004). What can be learned from positive evidence? *Journal of Child Language, 31,* 915–918.

Chater, N., Crocker, M. W., & Pickering, M. J. (1998). The rational analysis of inquiry: The case of parsing. In M. Oaksford, & N. Chater (Eds.), *Rational models of cognition* (pp. 441–469). Oxford, UK: Oxford University Press.

Chater, N., & Manning, C. (2006). Probabilistic models of language processing and acquisition. *Trends in Cognitive Sciences, 10,* 335–344.

Chater, N., & Oaksford, M. (1990). Autonomy, implementation and cognitive architecture: A reply to Fodor and Pylyshyn. *Cognition, 34,* 93–107.

Chater, N., Tenenbaum, J. B., & Yuille, A. (Eds.) (2006). Probabilistic models of cognition [Special issue]. *Trends in Cognitive Sciences, 10.*

Chater, N., & Vitányi, P. M. B. (2007). 'Ideal learning' of natural language: Positive results about learning from positive evidence. *Journal of Mathematical Psychology, 51,* 135–163.

Chomsky, N. (1957). *Syntactic structures.* The Hague, Mouton.

Chomsky, N. (1959). A review of B.F. Skinner's verbal behavior. *Language, 35,* 26–58.

Chomsky, N. (1965). *Aspects of the theory of syntax.* Cambridge, MA: MIT Press.

Chomsky, N. (1968). *Language and mind.* New York: Harcourt Brace Jovanovich.

Chomsky, N. (1980). Rules and representations. *Behavioral and Brain Sciences, 3,* 1–61.

Chomsky, N. (1981). *Lectures on government and binding.* Dordrecht: Foris.

Chomsky, N., & Schützenberger, M. P. (1963). The algebraic theory of context free languages. In P. Braffort & D. Hirschberg (Eds.), *Computer programming and formal languages* (pp. 118–161). Amsterdam: North-Holland.

Christiansen, M. H. (1992). The (non) necessity of recursion in natural language processing. In J. Kolodner & C. Riesbeck (Eds.), *Proceedings of the 14th Annual Cognitive Science So-*

ciety Conference (pp. 665–670). Hillsdale, NJ: Lawrence Erlbaum.

Christiansen, M. H., Allen, J., & Seidenberg, M. S. (1998). Learning to segment speech using multiple cues: a connectionist model. *Language and Cognitive Processes, 13,* 221–268.

Christiansen, M. H., & Chater, N. (1999). Toward a connectionist model of recursion in human linguistic performance. *Cognitive Science, 23,* 157–205.

Christiansen, M. H., & Chater, N. (Eds.). (2001). *Connectionist psycholinguistics.* Westport, CT: Ablex.

Collins, M. (2003). Head-driven statistical models for natural language parsing. *Computational Linguistics, 29*(4), 589–637.

Coltheart, M., Curtis, B., Atkins, P., & Haller, M. (1993). Models of reading aloud: Dual-route and parallel-distributed-processing approaches. *Psychological Review, 100,* 589–608.

Coltheart, M., Rastle, K., Perry, C., Langdon, R., & Ziegler, J. (2001). DRC: A dual route cascaded model of visual word recognition and reading aloud. *Psychological Review, 108,* 204–256.

Crain, S. (1991). Language acquisition in the absence of experience. *Behavioral and Brain Sciences, 14,* 597–650.

Crain, S., & Steedman, M. (1985). On not being led up the garden path: The use of context by the psychological parser. In D. R. Dowty, L. Kartunnen, & A. Zwicky (Eds.), *Natural language parsing: Psychological, computational, and theoretical perspectives* (pp. 320–358). New York: Cambridge University Press.

Crocker, M. W. (1996). *Computational psycholinguistics: An interdisciplinary approach to the study of language.* Boston: Kluwer.

Daelemans, W., & Van den Bosch, A. (2005). *Memory-based language processing.* Cambridge, UK: Cambridge University Press.

Dayan, P., & Abbott, L. F. (2001). *Theoretical neuroscience: Computational and mathematical modelling of neural systems.* Cambridge, MA: MIT Press.

Desmet, T., De Baecke, C., Drieghe, D., Brysbaert, M., & Vonk, W. (in press). Relative clause attachment in Dutch: On-line comprehension corresponds to corpus frequencies when lexical variables are taken into account. *Language and Cognitive Processes.*

Desmet, T., & Gibson, E. (2003). Disambiguation preferences and corpus frequencies in noun phrase conjunction. *Journal of Memory and Language, 49,* 353–374.

Elman, J. L. (1990). Finding structure in time. *Cognitive Science, 14,* 179–211.

Elman, J. L. (1991). Distributed representation, simple recurrent networks, and grammatical structure. *Machine Learning, 7,* 195–225.

Elman, J. L. (1993). Learning and development in neural networks: The importance of starting small. *Cognition, 48,* 71–99.

Elman, J. L. (2003). Generalization from sparse input. In *Proceedings of the 38th Annual Meeting of the Chicago Linguistic Society.* Chicago: Chicago Linguistic Society.

Elman, J. L., & McClelland, J. L. (1988). Cognitive penetration of the mechanisms of perception: Compensation for coarticulation of lexically restored phonemes. *Journal of Memory and Language, 27,* 143–165.

Fanselow, G., Féry, C., Vogel, R., & Schlesewsky, M. (Eds.). (in press). *Gradience in grammar: Generative perspectives.* Oxford, UK: Oxford University Press.

Ferreira, F., & Clifton, C. J. R. (1986). The independence of syntactic processing. *Journal of Memory and Language, 25,* 348–368.

Fodor, J. A. (1983). *Modularity of mind.* Cambridge, MA: MIT Press.

Fodor, J. A., Bever, T. G., & Garrett, M. F. (1974). *The psychology of language: An introduction to psycholinguistics and generative grammar.* New York: McGraw-Hill.

Fodor, J. A., & Pylyshyn, Z. W. (1988). Connectionism and cognitive architecture: A critical analysis. *Cognition, 28,* 3–71.

Forster, K. I. (1976). Accessing the mental lexicon. In R. J. Wales & E. Walker (Eds.), *New approaches to language mechanisms* (pp. 257–287). Amsterdam: North-Holland.

Frazier, L. (1979). *On comprehending sentences: Syntactic parsing strategies.* Bloomington: Indiana University Linguistics Club.

Frazier, L., & Fodor, J. D. (1978). The sausage machine: A new two-stage parsing model. *Cognition, 13,* 187–222.

Ganong, W. F. I. (1980). Phonetic categorisation in auditory word perception. *Journal of Experimental Psychology: Human Perception and Performance, 6,* 110–125.

Gaskell, M. G., & Marslen-Wilson, W. D. (1995). Modeling the perception of spoken words. In *Proceedings of the 17th Annual Cognitive Science Conference* (pp. 19–24). Hillsdale, NJ: Lawrence Erlbaum.

Gaskell, M. G., & Marslen-Wilson, W. D. (1997a). Discriminating local and distributed models of competition in spoken word recognition. In M. G. Shafto & P. Langley (Eds.), *Proceedings of the 19th Annual Cognitive Science Conference* (pp. 247–252). Hillsdale, NJ: Lawrence Erlbaum.

Gaskell, M. G., & Marslen-Wilson, W. D. (1997b). Integrating form and meaning: A distributed model of speech perception. *Language and Cognitive Processes, 12,* 613–656.

Gaskell, M. G., & Marslen-Wilson, W. D. (1999). Ambiguity, competition, and blending in spoken word recognition. *Cognitive Science, 23,* 439–462

Gibson, E. (1998). Linguistic complexity: Locality of syntactic dependencies. *Cognition, 68,* 1–76.

Gibson, E., & Wexler, K. (1994). Triggers. *Linguistic Inquiry, 25,* 407–454.

Gold, E. M. (1967). Language identification in the limit. *Information and Control, 10,* 447–474.

Goldberg, A. E. (2006). *Constructions at work: The nature of generalization in language.* Oxford, UK: Oxford University Press.

Griffiths, T., & Steyvers, M. (2004). Finding scientific topics. *Proceedings of the National Academy of Sciences, 101*(Suppl. 1), 5228–5235.

Griffiths, T. L., Steyvers, M., Blei, D. M., & Tenenbaum, J. B. (2005). Integrating topics and syntax. In B. Schölkopf, J. Platt & T. Hofmann (Eds.), *Advances in Neural Information Processing Systems, 17.*

Grodner, D., & Gibson, E. (2005). Consequences of the serial nature of linguistic input. *Cognitive Science, 29,* 261–291.

Haarmann, H. J., Just, M. A., & Carpenter, P. A. (1997). Aphasic sentence comprehension as a resource deficit: A computational approach. *Brain and Language, 59,* 76–120.

Hahn, U., & Nakisa, R. C. (2000). German inflection: Single or dual route? *Cognitive Psychology, 41,* 313–360.

Hale, J. (2003). The information conveyed by words in sentences. *Journal of Psycholinguistic Research, 32,* 101–123.

Harm, M., McCandliss, B. D., & Seidenberg, M. S. (2003). Modeling the successes and failures of interventions for disabled readers. *Scientific Studies of Reading, 7,* 155–182.

Harm, M. W., & Seidenberg, M. S. (1999). Phonology, reading acquisition, and dyslexia: Insights from connectionist models. *Psychological Review, 106,* 491–528.

Harm, M. W., & Seidenberg, M. S. (2004). Computing the meanings of words in reading:

Division of labor between visual and phonological processes. *Psychological Review, 111,* 662–720.

Hay, J., & Baayen, H. (2005). Shifting paradigms: Gradient structure in morphology. *Trends in Cognitive Sciences, 9,* 342–348.

Hirschfeld, L. A., & Gelman, S. A. (Eds). (1994). *Mapping the mind: Domain specificity in cognition and Culture.* New York: Cambridge University Press.

Hockema, S. A. (in press). Finding words in speech: An investigation of American English. *Language Learning and Development.*

Hopcroft, J. E., Motwani, R., & Ullman, J. D. (2000). *Introduction to automata theory, languages and computability.* Boston: Addison-Wesley.

Horning, J. J. (1969). *A study of grammatical inference* (Tech. Rep. CS 139). Stanford, CA: Computer Science Department, Stanford University.

Juang, B. H., & Rabiner, L. R. (1991). Hidden Markov models for speech recognition, *Technometrics, 33,* 251–272.

Jurafsky, D. (1996). A probabilistic model of lexical and syntactic access and disambiguation. *Cognitive Science, 20,* 137–194.

Jurafsky, D. (2003). Pragmatics and computational linguistics. In L. R. Horn & G. Ward (Eds.), *Handbook of pragmatics.* Oxford, UK: Blackwell.

Kawamoto, A. H. (1993). Nonlinear dynamics in the resolution of lexical ambiguity: A parallel distributed processing account. *Journal of Memory and Language, 32,* 474–516.

Klein, D., & Manning, C. (2002). A generative constituent-context model for improved grammar induction. In *Proceedings of the 40th Annual Meeting of the ACL, 2004* (pp. 128–135).

Klein, D., &. Manning, C. (2004). Corpus-based induction of syntactic structure: Models of dependency and constituency. In *Proceedings of the 42nd Annual Meeting of the ACL.*

Kolen, J. F. (1994). The origin of clusters in recurrent network state space. In A. Ram & K. Eiselt (Eds.), *The Proceedings Sixteenth Annual Conference of the Cognitive Science Society.* Hillsdale, NJ: Lawrence Erlbaum.

Kraljic, T., & Samuel, A. G. (2005). Perceptual learning for speech: Is there a return to normal? *Cognitive Psychology, 51,* 141–178.

Kurtzman, H. (1985). *Studies in syntactic ambiguity resolution.* Unpublished doctoral dissertation, MIT, Cambridge, MA.

Labov, W. (1972). *Sociolinguistic patterns.* Philadelphia: University of Pennsylvania Press.

Landauer, T. K., & Dumais, S. T. (1997). A solution to Plato's problem: The latent semantic analysis theory of acquisition, induction, and representation of knowledge. *Psychological Review, 104,* 211–240.

Lari, K., & Young., S. Y. (1990). The estimation of stochastic context-free grammars using the inside-outside algorithm. *Computer Speech and Language, 4,* 35–56.

Legate, J. A., & Yang, C. D. (2002). Empirical re-assessment of stimulus poverty arguments. *The Linguistic Review, 19,* 151–162.

Legge G. E., Klitz T. S., & Tjan B. S. (1997). Mr. Chips: An ideal observer model of reading. *Psychological Review, 104,* 524–553.

Lightfoot, D. (1991). *How to set parameters: Arguments from language change.* Cambridge, MA: MIT Press.

Linebarger, M. C., Schwartz, M. F., & Saffran, E. M. (1983). Sensitivity to grammatical structure in so-called agrammatic aphasics. *Cognition, 13,* 361–392.

Lund, K., & Burgess, C. (1996). Producing high-dimensional semantic spaces from lexical co-occurrence. *Behavior Research Methods, Instrumentation, and Computers, 28,* 203–208.

Lupyan, G., & Christiansen, M. H. (2002). Case, word order, connectionist modeling. In L. R. Gleitman & A. K. Joshi (Eds.), *Proceedings of the 24th Annual Conference of the Cognitive Science Society* (pp. 596–601). Mahwah, NJ: Erlbaum.

MacDonald, M. C., & Christiansen, M. H. (2002). Reassessing working memory: A comment on Just and Carpenter (1992) and Waters and Caplan (1996). *Psychological Review, 109,* 35–54.

MacDonald, M. C., Pearlmutter, N. J., & Seideberg, M. S. (1994). The lexical nature of syntactic ambiguity resolution. *Psychological Review, 101,* 676–703.

MacWhinney, B. (2004). Multiple solutions to the logical problem of language acquisition. *Journal of Child Language, 31,* 883–914.

MacWhinney, B., & Snow, C. (1985). The child language data exchange system. *Journal of Child Language, 12,* 271–296.

Mann, V. A., & Repp, B. H. (1981). Influence of preceding fricative on stop consonant perception. *Journal of the Acoustical Society of America, 69,* 548–558.

Maratsos, M., & Chalkley, M. (1980). The internal language of children's syntax: The ontogenesis and representation of syntactic categories. In K. Nelson (Ed.), *Children's language* (Vol. 2). (pp. 127–214). New York: Gardner Press.

Marcus, G. F. (1998). Rethinking eliminative connectionism. *Cognitive Psychology, 37,* 243–282.

Marcus, G. F. (2000). Children's overregularization and its implications for cognition. In P. Broeder & J. Murre (Eds.), *Models of language acquisition: Inductive and deductive approaches* (pp. 154–176). New York: Oxford University Press.

Marcus. G. F., Brinkman, U., Clahsen, H., Weise, R., & Pinker, S. (1995). German inflection: The exception that proves the rule. *Cognitive Psychology, 29,* 189–256.

Marcus, M. P. (1980). *A theory of syntactic recognition for natural language.* Cambridge, MA: MIT Press.

Marslen-Wilson, W., & Warren, P. (1994). Levels of perceptual representation and process in lexical access: Words, phonemes, and features. *Psychological Review, 101,* 653–675.

Marslen-Wilson, W., & Welsh, A. (1978). Processing instructions and lexical access during word recognition in continuous speech. *Cognitive Psychology, 10,* 29–63.

McClelland, J. L., & Elman, J. L. (1986). The TRACE model of speech perception. *Cognitive Psychology, 18,* 1–86.

McClelland, J. L., & Kawamoto, A. H. (1986). Mechanisms of sentence processing: Assigning roles to constituents. In J. L. McClelland, & D. E. Rumelhart (Eds.), *Parallel distributed processing* (pp. 272–325). Cambridge, MA: MIT Press.

McDonald, S. A., & Shillcock, R. C. (2003). Eye movements reveal the on-line computation of lexical probabilities. *Psychological Science, 14,* 648–652.

McRae, K., Spivey-Knowlton, M. J., & Tanenhaus, M. T. (1998). Modeling the influence of thematic fit (and other constraints) in on-line sentence comprehension. *Journal of Memory and Language, 38,* 282–312.

Miikkulainen, R. (1996). Subsymbolic case-role analysis of sentences with embedded clauses. *Cognitive Science, 20,* 47–73.

Miller, G. A. (1962). Some psychological studies of grammar. *American Psychologist, 17,* 748–762.

Mitchell, D. C., Cuetos, F., Corley, M. M. B., & Brysbaert, M. (1995). Exposure-based models of human parsing: Evidence for the use of coarse-grained (nonlexical) statistical records. *Journal of Psycholinguistic Research, 24,* 469–488.

Miyata, Y., Smolensky, P., & Legendre, G. (1993). Distributed representation and parallel distributed processing of recursive structures. In W. Kintsch (Ed.), *Proceedings of the Fifteenth Annual Meeting of the Cognitive Science Society* (pp. 759–764). Hillsdale, NJ: Lawrence Erlbaum.

Monaghan, P., Chater, N., & Christiansen, M. H. (2005). The differential contribution of phonological and distributional cues in grammatical categorisation. *Cognition, 96,* 143–182.

Morton, J. (1969). The interaction of information in word recognition. *Psychological Review, 76,* 165–178.

Narayanan, S., & Jurafsky, D. (2002). A Bayesian model predicts human parse preference and reading time in sentence processing. In T. G. Dietterich, S. Becker, & Z. Ghahramani (Eds.), *Advances in neural information processing systems 14* (pp. 59–65), Cambridge, MA: MIT Press.

Niyogi, P. (2006). *The computational nature of language learning and evolution.* Cambridge, MA: MIT Press.

Norris, D. (1993). Bottom-up connectionist models of "interaction." In G. T. M. Altmann & R. Shillock (Eds.), *Cognitive models of speech processing* (pp. 211–234), Hillsdale, NJ: Lawrence Erlbaum.

Norris, D. (1994). Shortlist: A connectionist model of continuous speech recognition. *Cognition, 52,* 189–234.

Norris, D. (2006). The Bayesian reader: Explaining word recognition as an optimal Bayesian decision process. *Psychological Review, 113,* 327–357.

Norris, D., McQueen, J. M., & Cutler, A. (2000). Merging information in speech recognition: Feedback is never necessary. *Behavioral and Brain Sciences, 23,* 299–370.

Onnis, L., & Christiansen, M. (2005). New beginnings and happy endings: Psychological plausibility in computational models of language acquisition. In B. G. Bara, L. Barsalov & M. Bucciarelli (Eds.), *Proceedings of the 27th Annual Meeting of the Cognitive Science Society.* Hillsdale, NJ: Lawrence Erlbaum.

Pearl, J. (1988). *Probabilistic reasoning in intelligent systems: Networks of plausible inference.* San Mateo, CA: Morgan Kaufman.

Pereira, F. C. N., & Warren, D. H. D. (1983). Parsing as deduction. In M. Marcus (Ed.),

Proceedings of the 21st Annual Conference of the Association for Computational Linguistics (pp. 137–144). Cambridge, MA: Association for Computational Linguistics.

Pickering, M. J., Traxler, M. J., & Crocker, M. W. (2000). Ambiguity resolution in sentence processing: Evidence against frequency-based accounts. *Journal of Memory and Language, 43*, 447–475.

Pinker, S. (1984). *Language learnability and language development.* Cambridge, MA: MIT Press.

Pinker, S. (1997). *How the mind works.* New York: Norton.

Pinker, S., & Prince, A. (1988). On language and connectionism: Analysis of a parallel distributed processing model of language acquisition. *Cognition, 28*, 73–193.

Pitt, M. A., & McQueen, J. M. (1998). Is compensation for coarticulation mediated by the lexicon? *Journal of Memory and Language, 39*, 347–370

Plaut, D. C. (1999). A connectionist approach to word reading and acquired dyslexia: Extension to sequential processing. *Cognitive Science, 23*, 543–568.

Plaut, D. C., & Gonnerman, L. M. (2000). Are non-semantic morphological effects incompatible with a distributed connectionist approach to lexical processing? *Language and Cognitive Processes, 15*, 445–485.

Plaut, D. C., McClelland, J. L., Seidenberg, M. S., & Patterson, K. E. (1996). Understanding normal and impaired word reading: computational principles in quasi-regular domains. *Psychological Review, 103*, 56–115.

Prasada, S., & Pinker, S. (1993). Similarity-based and rule-based generalizations in inflectional morphology. *Language and Cognitive Processes, 8*, 1–56.

Pullum, G., & Scholz, B. (2002). Empirical assessment of stimulus poverty arguments. *The Linguistic Review, 19*, 9–50.

Rastle, K., & Coltheart, M. (1998). Whammies and double whammies: the effect of length on nonword reading. *Psychonomic Bulletin and Review, 5*, 277–282.

Reali, F., & Christiansen, M. H. (2005). Uncovering the richness of the stimulus: Structure dependence and indirect statistical evidence. *Cognitive Science, 29*, 1007–1028.

Reali, F., Christiansen, M. H., & Monaghan, P. (2003). Phonological and distributional cues in syntax acquisition: Scaling up the connectionist approach to multiple-cue integration.

In A. Markman & L. Barsalov (Eds.), *Proceedings of the 25th Annual Conference of the Cognitive Science Society* (pp. 970–975). Mahwah, NJ: Lawrence Erlbaum.

Redington, M., & Chater, N. (1998). Connectionist and statistical approaches to language acquisition. *Language and Cognitive Processes, 13*, 129–191.

Redington, M., Chater, N., & Finch, S. (1998). Distributional information: A powerful cue for acquiring syntactic categories. *Cognitive Science, 22*, 425–469.

Regier, T. (2005). The emergence of words: Attentional learning in form and meaning. *Cognitive Science, 29*, 819–865.

Rohde, D. L. T., & Plaut, D. C. (1999). Language acquisition in the absence of explicit negative evidence: How important is starting small? *Cognition, 72*, 68–109.

Roy, D. (2005). Grounding words in perception and action: Insights from computational models. *Trends in Cognitive Science, 9*, 389–396.

Samuel, A. C. (1996). Does lexical information influence the perceptual restoration of phonemes? *Journal of Expermental Psychology: General, 125*, 28–51.

Schütze, H. (1993). Word space. In S. J. Hanson, J. D. Cowan, & C. L. (Eds.), *Neural information processing systems 5*(pp. 895–902). San Mateo, CA: Morgan Kaufmann.

Schütze, H. (1998). Automatic word sense discrimination. *Computational Linguistics, 24*, 97–123.

Seidenberg, M. S. (1997). Language acquisition and use: Learning and applying probabilistic constraints. *Science, 275*, 1599–1603.

Seidenberg, M. S., & Elman, J. L. (1999). Do infants learn grammar with algebra or statistics? *Science, 284*, 434–435.

Seidenberg, M. S., & MacDonald, M. C. (1999). A probabilistic constraints approach to language acquisition and processing. *Cognitive Science, 23*, 569–588.

Seidenberg, M. S., & McClelland, J. L. (1989). A distributed, developmental model of word recognition and naming. *Psychological Review, 96*, 523–568.

Seidenberg, M. S., & McClelland, J. L. (1990). More words but still no lexicon. Reply to Besner *et al.* (1990). *Psychological Review, 97*, 447–452.

Seidenberg, M. S., & Plaut, D. C. (1998). Evaluating word-reading models at the item level: Matching the grain of theory and data. *Psychological Science, 9*, 234–237.

Skinner, B. F. (1957). *Verbal behavior*. New York: Appleton-Century-Crofts.

Smolensky, P. (1999). Grammar-based connectionist approaches to language. *Cognitive Science, 23*, 589–613.

Smolensky, P., & Legendre, G. (2006). *The harmonic mind* (2 vols). Cambridge, MA: MIT Press.

Spieler, D. H., & Balota, D. A. (1997). Bringing computational models of word recognition down to the item level. *Psychological Science, 8*, 411–416.

St. John, M. F. (1992). The story Gestalt: A model of knowledge-intensive processes in text comprehension. *Cognitive Science, 16*, 271–206.

Steedman, M. (1999). Connectionist sentence processing in perspective. *Cognitive Science, 23*, 615–634.

Swier, R., & Stevenson, S. (2005). Exploiting a verb lexicon in automatic semantic role labelling. In R. J. Mooney (Ed.), *Proceedings of the Joint Human Language Technology Conference and Conference on Empirical Methods in Natural Language Processing* (HLT/EMNLP-05) (pp. 883–890).

Tabor, W., Juliano, C., & Tanenhaus, M. K. (1997). Parsing in a dynamical system: An attractor-based account of the interaction of lexical and structural constraints in sentence processing. *Language and Cognitive Processes, 12*, 211–271.

Tabor, W., & Tanenhaus, M. K. (1999). Dynamical models of sentence processing. *Cognitive Science, 23*, 491–515.

Tanenhaus, M. K., Spivey-Knowlton, M. J., Eberhard, K. M., & Sedivy, J. E. (1995). Integration of visual and linguistic information in spoken language comprehension. *Science, 268*, 632–634.

Tomasello, M. (2003). *Constructing language*. Cambridge, MA: Harvard University Press.

Trueswell, J. C., & Tanenhaus, M. K. (1992). Toward a lexicalist framework for constraint-based ambiguity resolution. In J. C. Clifton, L. Frazier, & K. Rayner (Eds.), *Perspectives on sentence processing* (pp. 155–179). Hillsdale, NJ: Lawrence Erlbaum.

Wanner, E., & Maratsos, M. (1978). An ATN approach to comprehension. In M. Halle, J. W. Bresnam, & G. A. Miller (Eds.), *Linguistic theory and psychological reality* (pp. 119–161). Cambridge, MA: MIT Press.

Weekes, B. S. (1997). Differential effects of number of letters on word and nonword latency. *Quarterly Journal of Experimental Psychology, 50A*, 439–456.

Williams, R. J., & Zipser, D. (1990). *Gradient-based learning algorithms for recurrent connectionist networks* (Tech. Rep. NU-CCS-90-9). College of Computer Science, Northeastern University.

Winograd, T. (1972). *Understanding natural language*. New York: Academic Press.

Yngve, V. H. (1960). A model and an hypothesis for language structure. *Proceedings of the American Philosophical Society, 104*, 444–466.

Zettlemoyer, L. S., & Collins, M. (2005). Learning to map sentences to logical form: Structured classification with probabilistic categorical grammars. In *Proceedings of the Twenty-First Conference on Uncertainty in Artificial Intelligence* (UAI-05).

Zorzi, M., Houghton, G., & Butterworth, B. (1998). Two routes or one in reading aloud? A connectionist dual-process model. *Journal of Experimental Psychology: Human Perception and Performance, 24*, 1131–1161.

CHAPTER 18

Computational Models in Personality and Social Psychology

Stephen J. Read and Brian M. Monroe

1. Introduction

This chapter focuses on computational models in social psychology and personality. Although there has been a considerable amount of simulation work of social behavior in other fields such as anthropology, sociology, and political science, that work will not be reviewed here. Some of the work in those fields is covered in Chapter 19 in this volume. Computational modeling in social psychology and personality started in the early days of computational modeling of human psychology; however, this chapter focuses on work over roughly the last fifteen years, occasionally referring to earlier work.

Coverage of various simulations is largely organized in terms of the substantive questions being addressed, rather than by the particular simulation technique being used. It was felt that most readers of this chapter would be more interested in how they could address a particular issue and less interested in learning about the different ways that a particular simulation technique has been used.

Currently, the most frequently used computational models in social psychology are probably various kinds of connectionist models, such as constraint satisfaction networks, feedforward pattern associators with delta-rule learning, and multilayer recurrent networks with learning (see Chapter 2 in this volume). Another frequently used modeling technique is cellular automata. Although multiagent systems (see Chapter 19 in this volume) have been widely used in other fields studying social behavior, such as anthropology, sociology, and organizational behavior, this technique has only occasionally been used in social psychology.

Several authors have used sets of difference equations as the basis of simulations of personality or of personality stability. Others have used *coupled* logistic equations to simulate aspects of dyadic interaction. Despite the popularity of production system models, such as ACT-R (Anderson, 1993; Anderson & Lebiere, 1998) and CLARION (Sun, Slusarz, & Terry, 2005), and other symbolic models in cognitive psychology and cognitive science, symbolic models are largely absent in current modeling in social psychology or personality. However, symbolic models were important in early work in computational modeling in personality and social psychology, as exemplified by such work as Abelson and Carroll's (1965) simulation of conservative ideology, the Goldwater machine, Gullahorn and Gullahorn's (1963) simulation of social interaction, Loehlin's (1968) personality model, and Colby's (1975, 1981) model of paranoid personality (for overviews of this early work, see Abelson, 1968; Loehlin, 1968; Tomkins & Messick, 1963).

Although the discussion is largely organized around particular substantive topics, there tends to be a strong correlation between the types of topics being addressed and the simulation techniques that are used. Work on intra-personal or individual cognitive and emotional phenomena, such as causal reasoning, impression formation, stereotyping, attitude formation and attitude change, and personality, have largely relied on various kinds of connectionist models. In contrast, work that has focused on interpersonal phenomena, such as dyadic relationships, mating choice, social influence and group discussion, and decision making, has tended to focus on techniques such as cellular automata, multiagent systems, and symbolic models.

The chapter begins with work on causal learning, causal reasoning, and impression formation for several reasons. First, it has been one of the most active areas of work in social modeling over the last ten to fifteen years, involving a relatively wide range of researchers. Second, it has historically been a central area in social psychology, although one that is currently less active. Third, because it deals with many of the models that are used in other substantive areas, it provides a useful introduction to this other work.

2. Computational Models

2.1. *Causal Learning, Causal Reasoning, and Impression Formation*

Research in this area has examined both the learning of causal relationships and the use of such previously learned relationships in causal reasoning and impression formation.

2.1.1. CAUSAL LEARNING

Several different sets of researchers (e.g., Shanks, 1991; Van Overwalle, 1998; Van Overwalle & Van Rooy, 1998, 2001; see Chapter 12 in this volume) have used a feedforward network, with delta-rule learning, to capture a number of different phenomena in human and animal causal learning, such as *overshadowing* (cues compete for associative strength), *blocking* (a previously learned cue blocks the learning of a new cue), and *conditioned inhibition* (learning that one cue inhibits an outcome increases the strength of a countervailing cue). These researchers have noted that the standard delta rule (Widrow & Hoff, 1960), used in neural network models, is almost identical to the well-known Rescorla-Wagner (Rescorla & Wagner, 1972) model of animal learning. Both are error-correcting rules that modify the weight strength or strength of association between an input or cue and an output or response in such a way as to reduce the error of prediction from the input to output. One aspect of this kind of error-correcting rule is that it models the impact of competition between cues for predicting outcomes. For example, if two cues simultaneously predict the same outcome, then associative strength is divided between them (overshadowing). Or if an organism first strongly learns that cue A predicts C, if they are then presented situations in which cue A and B predict C, they will fail to learn that B also predicts C (blocking). This occurs because A already predicts C, and in the absence of an error signal for C, there can be no change in associative strength between B and C.

This work has shown that a feedforward network, with delta-rule learning, can model essentially all of the classic human and animal causal learning phenomena that can be captured by the Rescorla-Wagner rule. However, one important limitation of these models is that because they are feedforward networks, they can only capture the forward associations from input to output or cue to response. They cannot model any backward associations from the output to the input. This is a limitation that is shared by the standard version of the Rescorla-Wagner model.

2.1.2. CAUSAL REASONING

Other researchers have used Thagard's (1989, 2000) ECHO model of explanatory coherence as the basis of a model of causal reasoning and impression formation. ECHO is a bidirectionally connected, recurrent network that functions as a constraint satisfaction network and implements a number of principles of explanatory coherence, such as *breadth of explanation* and *simplicity of explanation* or *parsimony*. In this model, nodes represent the evidence to be explained, as well as the proposed explanatory hypotheses. Evidence nodes are connected to a special node that provides activation to them.

Explanatory hypotheses have positive links to the data they explain and negative links to data that contradicts them. Further, hypotheses that are contradictory have negative or inhibitory links to each other, whereas hypotheses that support one another have positive links. Principles of explanatory coherence are instantiated in terms of patterns of connectivity. For example, breadth of explanation follows because an explanation that explains more facts will receive more activation from those connected facts. And simplicity is implemented by dividing the weights between explanations and facts as a function of the number of explanatory hypotheses needed to explain a given fact. Thus, more hypotheses mean smaller weights from each one.

Goodness of explanations is evaluated by passing activation through the recurrent connections among the evidence and hypotheses until the activation levels asymptote. Thagard has shown that such a constraint satisfaction network can capture a number of different aspects of causal reasoning, specifically scientific reasoning (Thagard, 2000) and jury decision making (Thagard, 2003).

Read and Marcus-Newhall (1993) showed that human subjects' patterns of social causal reasoning followed the principles of goodness of explanation that are em-

bedded in ECHO's constraint satisfaction network. They tested this by developing a number of scenarios in which they could manipulate the influence of different principles of *explanatory coherence* and then had subjects rate the goodness of various explanations. They showed that ECHO could simulate their experimental results.

Read and Miller (1993) also showed how the same kind of network could capture several fundamental phenomena in social psychological work on causal reasoning, including the well-known *correspondence bias* (or *fundamental attribution error*), which is the tendency to overattribute behavior to a trait and underweight the importance of situational forces. They suggested that the correspondence bias could be captured by assuming that decreased attention to a potential cause (here, the situation) leads to a decrease in the spreading of activation from that node, thus making it less able to inhibit the alternative explanation, the individual's trait.

Subsequently, in response to a critique by Van Overwalle (1998) that noted (accurately) that ECHO did not include learning and which expressed doubt that a constraint satisfaction network, such as ECHO, could include learning, Read and Montoya (1999a, 1999b) presented a combined model of causal learning and causal reasoning that combined the constraint satisfaction capabilities of a recurrent, auto-associative network with the error-correcting learning of the delta rule. Their model was based on McClelland and Rumelhart's (1986, 1988) auto-associator, which is a recurrent or feedback network that implements delta-rule learning. Read and Montoya showed that this integrated model was just as capable as feedforward, pattern associators of capturing classic phenomena in human and animal causal learning, such as blocking, overshadowing, and conditioned inhibition. At the same time, it could capture many aspects of causal reasoning from previously learned causal relationships. First, it could capture the impact of principles of explanatory coherence that were previously captured by ECHO (Read & Marcus-Newhall, 1993). Second, it could model classic phenomena in causal reasoning, such as *augmenting* and *discounting*. Discounting, for example, is the tendency to reduce the strength of an hypothesized explanation to the extent that there is a plausible alternative. It can be implemented by a negative or inhibitory link among alternative causes. Augmenting is the tendency to judge a cause to be stronger if it results in an outcome in the face of countervailing or inhibitory forces. Third, Montoya and Read (1998) showed how this auto-associator could also model the correspondence bias (or fundamental attribution error) in terms of accessibility of competing explanations. The basic idea is that, at least among Americans, trait explanations are more chronically accessible than are situational explanations. And a more accessible trait explanation can send more activation and inhibit competing situational explanations. In summary, this auto-associator integrated a wide range of phenomena in causal learning and reasoning.

2.2. *Impression Formation*

Constraint satisfaction models have also been used to model impression formation. Read and Miller (1993) showed how an ECHO-type model could be used to simulate how social perceivers formed trait impressions of others from sequences of behaviors, or narratives. They also described how conceptual combinations could be formed from different combinations of traits by modeling how the underlying conceptual components of several traits were interconnected by excitatory and inhibitory links. After the network settled, the underlying concepts that remained activated would represent the meaning of the conceptual combination.

Kunda and Thagard (1996) used a related constraint satisfaction model, IMP (IMPression formation model), in their discussion and simulation of a wide range of research in impression formation, including the integration of stereotypes and individuating information in forming impressions. They contrast their approach with Brewer's (1988) and Fiske and Neuberg's (1990) models of impression formation. Both models distinguish between top-down, stereotype-driven processing and bottom-up, attribute-based processing. Both are serial process models and hypothesize that stereotype-driven processing occurs first and then, under the right circumstances, may be followed by attribute-based processes.

In contrast, Kunda and Thagard (1996) argue that both stereotype- and attribute-based information are processed in parallel in a constraint satisfaction network. Their model assumes that stereotypes, traits, and behaviors are represented as interconnected nodes in a constraint satisfaction network. They use this model to investigate a number of phenomena in impression formation. For example, they show that stereotypes can constrain the meaning of both behaviors and traits as a result of the stereotypes' patterns of connectivity with alternative interpretations of the traits and behaviors. Conversely, they also show that individuating information can influence the interpretation of a stereotype. Further, they demonstrate that a stereotype will affect judgments of an individual's traits when individuating information is ambiguous, but not when the individuating information is unambiguous. Overall, they demonstrate that a parallel process, constraint satisfaction model can successfully capture a wide range of data in impression formation that had been previously argued to be the result of a serial process.

Van Overwalle and Labiouse (2004) used a recurrent network with delta-rule learning to simulate a number of findings in person perception. However, although this network has bidirectional weights, it is not a constraint satisfaction system, as it only allows one cycle of updating of internal activations. This is not enough cycles for the passage of activation to solve the constraints imposed by the connections among the nodes. The model attempts to capture various phenomena in terms of differences in learning history and the role of error-correcting learning. Among the phenomena they seek to model are primacy and recency effects in impression formation, assimilation and contrast effects in priming, increased recall for trait-inconsistent information, and asymmetric diagnosticity of ability- and morality-related traits.

Hastie (1988) presented a model of impression formation and person memory that focused on simulating the impact on impressions and memory of personality-relevant information that was congruent or incongruent with an initial impression. Impressions were represented as vectors of values on impression dimensions (e.g., intelligent, sociable), and impression formation was modeled as a weighted average or anchoring and adjustment process applied to sequentially presented personality-relevant behaviors. Memory was modeled by representing behaviors as propositions that started in working memory and that subsequently moved to long-term memory. The probability of forming links among behaviors and the impact of a behavior on an impression increased with greater residence in working memory, with residence time being a positive function of the discrepancy between the current impression and the implications of the item. Retrieval of items from long-term memory proceeded by a search of the associative memory so that items with more links were more likely to be retrieved. Hastie showed that his model could capture many of the findings on the impact of incongruent information on impressions and memory. For example, his model predicted that incongruent behaviors that were relatively infrequent were more likely to be recalled than congruent behaviors and had a greater impact on impressions.

Another topic in impression formation that has received considerable research attention is the impact of category accessibility effects, whereby priming a category leads to greater use of that category in forming an impression from an individual's behavior (e.g., Higgins, Bargh, & Lombardi, 1985; Higgins, Rholes, & Jones, 1977; Srull & Wyer, 1979; Wyer & Srull, 1986). Smith (1988) used Hintzman's (1988) exemplar-only memory model to simulate several different aspects of category accessibility effects. In Hintzman's model, phenomena like categorization and recognition are modeled by re-

trieval of exemplars (represented as a vector of binary features) from memory, rather than in terms of abstractions or schemas. A key assumption of the model is that when exemplars are learned, each exemplar is separately stored in memory. Then, when the individual is asked to make a categorization judgment or to recall something, a probe is entered into memory that activates related exemplars. The strength of activation of exemplars is a function of their similarity to the probe.

Smith argued that priming effects can be viewed as entering additional exemplars into memory. He showed that Hintzman's model could simulate three different category accessibility effects: (1) greater priming with more instances, (2) greater priming by trait-related behaviors than by trait labels alone, and (3) slower decay of priming when there are more primes.

2.3. Group Perception and Stereotyping

Models that have addressed group perception and related phenomena have, on the whole, focused on showing that the phenomena are a natural result of the structure of information in the environment and/or learning processes, and do not require sophisticated schema or motivated processing to produce (although motivation can be involved). Initially, the attempts in this domain were based on analysis of the information environment, with models by Smith (1991) and Fiedler (1996) looking at phenomena such as illusory correlation (perception of a nonexistent relation between minority group members and negative characteristics) and the outgroup homogeneity effect (the perception that outgroup members are less variable on important attributes than the ingroup). The basic argument was that these phenomena could be understood in terms of the distribution of information in the environment and did not depend on the assumptions of a process model for explanation. Later, these models will be compared with the more recent ones.

A family of fully recurrent auto-associator models, based on McClelland and

Rumelhart's (1988) auto-associator, have been used to explain various aspects of group perception in terms of learning processes. The earliest model (Smith & DeCoster, 1998) argued that several seemingly disparate phenomena all have a common underlying mechanism. They show that their forty-unit autoassociator, which represents information in a distributed fashion and uses delta-rule learning, makes inferences based on the natural correlations that arise from the learning experience. Once the network has learned, it will fill in missing information with stereotypical information for new (unlearned) individuals and can also make complex inferences based on these learned schemas. Additionally, they replicated recency and frequency-related accessibility effects, and made novel predictions about the rapid recovery of schema information after decay.

In a follow-up model, Queller & Smith (2002) show that their auto-associator's behavior, based on the constraint satisfaction module of PDP++ (O'Reilly & Munakata, 2000), is consistent with empirical data on several different models of stereotype change. It predicts that counterstereotypic information that is distributed across a number of individuals (rather than being clustered in a few counterstereotypic individuals within a larger sample) results in gradual change in the stereotype, which is consistent with the "bookkeeping" model (this model suggests that stereotype change should be dispersed across all members of the group). However, the model also predicts that when the same amount of counterstereotypic information is clustered within a small number of individuals within a larger sample, the result is subtyping, where the perceiver differentiates a new subtype or category for this small group of individuals and maintains the original stereotype of the other individuals. They show that these different kinds of change are due to differences in the patterns of correlations among the counterstereotypic features and the resulting pattern of weights. When the counterstereotypic features are clustered in a small number of individuals, the features are highly correlated and develop strong interconnections and a

coherent subgroup. When the same features are distributed among a larger number of individuals, the features are not correlated and no strong interconnections develop. Thus, the subtyping process does not require anything beyond the learning process (i.e., there is no need for a reasoning process to explain away the counterstereotypic information).

Van Rooy et al. (2003) used a semilocalist representation in an auto-associator to examine the same general phenomena. Their model used delta-rule learning with one cycle of updating (although it was also tested with multiple cycles and generally gave the same results). In their model, subtyping is produced by the competition property of delta-rule learning. Consistent with the Queller and Smith (2002) model, they also found that counterstereotypic information that was dispersed among exemplars (as opposed to being concentrated in one exemplar) helped to prevent subtyping.

Other important group impression phenomena that have been the focus of concentrated modeling attention are illusory correlations and the outgroup homogeneity effect (OHE). Illusory correlation is a perceived (illusory) positive association between membership in a smaller group and an infrequent behavior, despite the fact that the larger group is proportionally just as likely to exhibit the behavior. Smith (1991), using an exemplar-based memory model by Hintzman (1988), and Fielder (1996) proposed information aggregation models, showing that illusory correlation could be a natural product of information sampling and aggregation with different sized groups. Sampling and aggregating larger samples of information lead to more precise and less variable estimates of parameters. In comparison, the Van Rooy et al. (2003) model claims that this phenomenon is caused by differences in weight strength due to differences in the number of group members encountered.

The OHE is the perception of the outgroup as having less person-to-person (within-group) variability than one's own group. Linville, Fischer, and Salovey (1989) developed an exemplar-based simulation of the OHE (PDIST). In their model, group variability estimates are not calculated at encoding, but rather at the time of judgment, using exemplars retrieved from memory. When there are more exemplars in a group, it probabilistically follows that the range of values of group attributes will tend to be larger, thus, variability estimates should be larger for the ingroup (with which one typically has much more experience) than for the outgroup.

The information-based models (Fiedler, 1996; Smith, 1991) attempt to show that the OHE depends on noisy inputs masking variability. The noise is more likely to be averaged out for larger samples, as would be the case with the more familiar ingroup.

Van Rooy et al. (2003), using an autoassociator, suggest that the OHE is a natural product of learning, as do Read and Urada (2003) using a recurrent version of McClelland and Rumelhart's (1988) autoassociator. Both models essentially argue that learning of the extremes of the distribution is better for larger samples (typically the ingroup). Read and Urada further conclude that "the OHE follows from fundamental assumptions about how information is represented in memory," and depends upon the number of members of the ingroup and outgroup encountered, without the additional assumption that one has more information *per individual* for the ingroup members. They emphasize, however, that their model cannot account for all proposed (noncognitive) mechanisms that bias the type of information we get, such as secondhand exposure to exemplars through the media.

Kashima and colleagues have taken a unique approach within social psychology with their tensor product model (TPM) of group perception (Kashima, Woolcock, & Kashima, 2000; Kashima, Woolcock, & King, 1998). In this model, inputs are all vectors of distributed representations for the event, the group, the person, and the context of an episode. These vectors are encoded and combined to form a tensor product, which encodes the relations among the vectors. Various judgments are based on operations on this tensor product. They are able to reproduce empirical results on group impression formation and sequential exposure to exemplars. One conclusion is that stereotype-inconsistent information changes the representation of the individual in memory. Their model shares with the previously discussed auto-associators the finding that no attributional processes are needed to explain the phenomena, but instead, that the phenomena can be explained by information distribution and basic learning processes. This is perhaps the most significant conclusion of this line of research.

2.4. *Emotional Coherence*

Thagard and colleagues (e.g., Sahdra & Thagard, 2003; Thagard, 2003; Thagard & Nerb, 2002) have also used an ECHO-like constraint satisfaction model, HOTCO, to capture the influence of emotions on reasoning and decision making. The general idea is that an emotion or evaluation is represented as an additional node in an ECHO-like coherence network that sends activation to connected nodes. Thus, a highly activated emotion or valence node will influence or "bias" the activation of related hypotheses and beliefs. In one example, Thagard (2003) analyzed juror decision making in the O. J. Simpson murder trial and showed how pre-existing liking for O. J. among the jurors' may have biased the jurors willingness to accept the defense's account of the evidence in the trial and their subsequent verdict.

Nerb and Spada (2001) presented a coherence model of cognition and emotion that integrates assumptions from appraisal models of emotion (e.g., Lazarus, 2001; Ortony, Clore, & Collins, 1988; Roseman, 2001; Scherer, 2001) into a constraint satisfaction network similar to ECHO (Thagard, 2000) and IMP (Kunda & Thagard, 1996). They examine cognitions and emotions, and their interaction in the context of making decisions about environmental problems.

2.5. *Face Perception*

A recent area of interest in social psychology is how perception of facial features and emotional expressions affects the inferences we draw about lasting personality traits. This phenomenon has been proposed to account for popularity and voting outcomes in presidential elections as well as more mundane interactions we have with people every day.

Zebrowitz and colleagues (Zebrowitz et al., 2003; Zebrowitz, Kikuchi, & Fellous, 2005) argue that many of these social perception effects are driven by overgeneralizations from evolutionarily adaptive responses to types of individuals such as babies and those with anomalous faces. Zebrowitz et al. (2003) used a neural network with an input, hidden, and output layer, and a backpropagation learning algorithm, and trained it to classify a complement of normal, anomalous, and infant faces. They then showed that trait inferences for test or generalization faces could be predicted by how they were classified by the network. For example, ratings of adult faces on sociable were predicted by the extent to which they activated the baby output unit. And higher activation of the anomaly output unit by a test adult face predicted lower ratings on attractiveness, healthy, and intelligent.

In a subsequent study, Zebrowitz et al. (2005) focused on reactions to emotional expressions, arguing that these may be evolutionarily adaptive generalizations from responses to baby and mature faces. Using the same network architecture, they found that impressions of emotion faces were partially mediated by their degree of resemblance to baby and mature faces. Anger faces, like mature faces, created impressions of high dominance and low affiliation, whereas surprise faces, like baby faces, led to impressions of high affiliation and low dominance. The authors emphasize that the success of these models (which are based solely on the information structure in the faces) in predicting impressions, suggests that resorting to cultural explanations for the associations between facial features and trait inferences is not always necessary. These results, along with several other models of unrelated phenomena in social psychology, such as the OHE and illusory correlations, show how empirical effects can be reproduced relying only on very basic properties of learning systems and information structure, and do not require complex motivational or other processes to arise.

2.6. *Attitudes and Attitude Change*

One of the earliest computational models in social psychology was Abelson and Carroll's (1965) "Goldwater Machine," which was an attempt to model the ideological belief systems and attitudes of a conservative (also see Abelson, 1963, 1973). This line of work led to Abelson's collaboration with Roger Schank (Schank & Abelson, 1977) on scripts, plans, goals, beliefs, and understanding, and the Yale artificial intelligence approach. Unfortunately, this early modeling work by Abelson was not followed up by other social psychologists and seems to have had little direct influence on computational modeling in social psychology.

However, there has been a recent resurgence of modeling of attitudes, primarily motivated by interest in cognitive consistency. Theories of cognitive consistency were in their heyday in the 1960s (see Abelson et al., 1968), but interest then declined dramatically. However, the advent of computational modeling has added a somewhat fresh perspective on this and related phenomena, such as attitude formation and change, and cognitive dissonance. The classical formulations of cognitive consistency theory (Abelson et al., 1968; Festinger, 1957) argue that attitudes and evaluations are the result of a balancing act among competing cognitions; for people to make sense of the world, these cognitions must end up being organized in such a way as to mutually support each other, maintaining consistency in one's world view. For example, as it does not make much sense to think both that one needs to drive the latest oversized sports utility vehicle and that we should conserve natural resources and protect the environment; one of these beliefs must be adjusted, or some other way of reducing the disparity between them needs to be found, for example, by introducing intervening cognitions like "my one car doesn't make much difference when the problem is a global one."

This sounds quite similar to processing in coherence-type networks, such as ECHO. Not surprisingly, cognitive consistency has recently been reconceptualized in terms of constraint satisfaction or coherence networks. Two variants of ECHO have been used to simulate cognitive consistency as parallel constraint satisfaction networks. First, Spellman, Ullman, and Holyoak (1993) asked students their opinions on the Persian Gulf conflict of 1991 at two times, two weeks apart. They constructed ECHO models of students' opinions, where all concepts were only indirectly related to each other through the overall opinion node. The way the network settled predicted students' attitude changes over the two-week period.

Read and Miller (1994) also used ECHO to model a variety of balance and dissonance situations. One addition they made is that differences in the initial degree of belief in a cognition were represented. This model was able to describe how different modes of inconsistency resolution could be implemented, mainly by adding nodes that denied or bolstered the ambivalent cognitions. The mode of resolution that ultimately gets chosen in this model is determined by the pattern of coherence settling.

Shultz and Lepper (1996, 1998) developed their own constraint satisfaction model to account specifically for cognitive dissonance. The model was designed to maximize the coherence quantity, defined as:

$$C = \sum_i \sum_j w_{ij} a_i a_j.$$

In this equation, a_i and a_j are the activations of the two nodes that are being evaluated and w_{ij} is the weight between the two nodes. As in the preceding models, the weights are bidirectional and fixed – the activations change during the settling process. They introduced an additional change resistance parameter to represent how "changeable" a particular node is, due to things like attitude importance and embeddedness in a web of beliefs. The simulations reproduced the results in several well-established disso-

nance paradigms, and the model was also able to reproduce annoyance effects, mood effects, and locus of change effects found empirically in the original studies that are not predicted by classical dissonance theory per se. Further lab studies (Shultz, Léveille, & Lepper, 1999) tested novel predictions of this model, where it succeeded in predicting the pattern of evaluation changes among chosen and rejected wall posters by thirteen-year olds.

Van Overwalle and colleagues (Van Overwalle & Jordens, 2002; Van Overwalle & Siebler, 2005) have noted that a shortcoming of the previous models is that they lack the ability to represent long-term changes in attitudes, because weights are not allowed to change. To attempt to remedy this, Van Overwalle and Jordens (2002) represented attitudes in a feedforward neural network with delta-rule learning, with input nodes representing the features of the environment and two output nodes: behavior and affect. The average of the activation of the behavior and affect nodes are treated as the measure of attitude. They defined dissonance as "the discrepancy between expected and actual outcomes," and thus dissonance reduction, in their model, is the adjustment of the connection weights to the behavior and affect nodes; in other words, they characterized cognitive dissonance as an error of prediction and dissonance reduction as error-correcting learning. The model uses a training phase and then a one-trial experimental phase, after which weights are allowed to adjust. They modeled the same experiments as Shultz and Lepper (1996).

Although coherence-based models of dissonance have not captured long-term attitude change, it is not clear how Van Overwalle and Jordens' (2002) model actually accounts for the experience of dissonance or the attitude change that follows an experience of dissonance. Their model simply changes the strength of association between an attitude object and an affective response, once the experimenter tells the network what the target affect is. The network does not provide any insight into how the affective response arises. For example, let's take their simulation of the forbidden toy paradigm. In one condition in this paradigm, children receive a mild threat to not play with an attractive toy and are then left alone with the toy. These children are much more likely to derogate the toy than children who are watched after the mild threat or than children who receive a severe threat, regardless of whether they are watched. The typical explanation of this result is that the child in the mild threat, no surveillance condition, finds it dissonant that she is not playing with this attractive toy, even though there do not seem to be any good reasons not to. To rationalize this, she decides that the toy is not particularly attractive.

To simulate this, Van Overwalle and Jordens' (2002) network first learns that the presence of an attractive toy predicts both playing and positive affect, whereas the presence of a severe threat predicts not playing with the toy and negative affect. Then the network receives an experimental trial in which there is an attractive toy and a mild threat. Initial learning of weights is set up so that a mild threat is not sufficient to inhibit activation of the behavior and affect nodes. Thus, the network predicts that the child will play with the toy and will feel mildly positive. Yet, empirically, we know that the child in this condition does not play with the toy.

What Van Overwalle and Jordens (2002) do is to then tell the network that the child did *not* play with the toy *and* that the child felt negative affect, resulting in a discrepancy between the prediction and the outcome for the behavior and the affect. Delta-rule learning leads to the weights from the attractive toy to the play and affect nodes becoming more negative. But note one very important thing. This network does *not infer* how the child felt. It is *told* how the child supposedly felt. This is essential to the ability of this network to simulate dissonance effects.

One virtue of the various constraint satisfaction models is that they have something to say about making the affective inference

in the first place. Van Overwalle and Jordens' (2002) model does not. Instead, it simply shows that the network will learn to associate the toy with negative affect, *once* the experimenter has told the network that the child feels bad. But because the experimenter has to tell the network how the individual feels, it does not seem that this tells us much about dissonance. There is already extensive evidence in other domains that people will learn to associate cues to negative emotions that are paired with them.

A constraint satisfaction network, in which weights are updated after the network settles (such as McClelland and Rumelhart's (1988) auto-associator, which has been used in several simulations discussed previously), would seem to make more theoretical sense. In the typical dissonance study, the individual is faced with two or more inconsistent beliefs (e.g., "the toy is attractive" and "I didn't play with it, even though there aren't good reasons not to"). One way to resolve this inconsistency is for the belief "I didn't play with this toy, even though there aren't good reasons not to" to inhibit the belief "the toy is attractive" and excite the alternate belief "the toy is dumb." After the network settles, weights could be adjusted, with the result that subsequently thinking about the toy would activate the cognition "the toy is dumb."

Subsequently, Van Overwalle and Siebler (2005) presented a model aimed at explaining other attitude-change phenomena. The model is a recurrent network with delta-rule learning and is based on an auto-associative model originally presented by McClelland and Rumelhart (1988). It attempts to account for various phenomena including several heuristics and central versus peripheral (e.g., systematic vs. heuristic) processing. Although this network has bidirectional weights, it does not function as a constraint satisfaction network because the authors restrict the model to one cycle of updating of internal activation and use a linear updating function. Further, they make several ad hoc adjustments to the original McClelland and Rumelhart (1988) auto-associator, especially to its learning mechanisms. For example, to have McClelland and Rumelhart's variation of delta-rule learning work, Van Overwalle and Siebler treat the internal activation of a node as both the internal (predicted) outcome and the external (actual) outcome.

The network represents the various heuristics (including the consensus, expertise, and ease of retrieval heuristics) as weights between those cues and attitude valence. The simulation to recreate the effect of central versus peripheral processing uses a researcher-controlled attention mechanism and a learning phase to set up the initial associations. The model is able to account for this processing distinction, closely related to the Elaboration Likelihood Model (ELM; Petty & Cacioppo, 1986) and Heuristic Systematic Model (Eagley & Chaiken, 1993) of attitude change.

Other, non-constraint-satisfaction networks have been used to model attitude phenomena. Eiser et al. (2003) used a feedforward network with an input, output, and hidden layer to show how attitude perseverance naturally results from an uneven payoff matrix and reinforcement learning. Using a "good beans, bad beans" paradigm, their simulations showed how individuals naturally avoided novel items to avoid possible negative outcomes, and in the process, preserved their existing attitudes by not being exposed to disconfirming information.

And Mosler et al.'s (2001) model of the ELM used a complicated symbolic architecture, one requiring many control structures. Calculations are performed in many subprocesses and involve diverse inputs, such as personal relevance, distraction, and source argument quality. This computational model was able to replicate many empirical results and make many qualitative predictions regarding the ELM, but at the cost of being unable to account for other attitude-relevant processes.

2.7. Personality

Computational modeling of personality has been an active area and has a long history (Colby, 1975; Loehlin, 1968; Tomkins & Messick, 1963). Of the more recent models, Mischel and Shoda's (1995) Cognitive-Affective Processing System (CAPS) model is a recurrent, localist network, which functions as a constraint satisfaction system. It has an input layer consisting of nodes representing different situations (or situational features), which are recurrently connected to a set of nodes representing the cognitive-affective units (CAUs). These CAUs are then recurrently connected to behavior nodes. The CAUs represent various beliefs, goals, and emotions that an individual may have. In the CAPS model, individual differences are represented by different patterns of weights among the CAUs. In a series of simulations, Mischel and Shoda have generated an array of different CAPS networks with different randomly generated weights and then exposed the different networks to the same sequence of situations. They have shown that these differently connected networks have distinctive behavioral signatures, giving different behavioral responses to the same situation.

Mischel and Shoda (1995) are trying to deal with an apparent paradox in the personality literature: There is clear evidence for individual differences in personality, yet there is little evidence for strong general cross-situational consistency in behavior. They propose their CAPS model as a possible solution to that paradox. They argue that people have consistent behavioral signatures in that individuals respond consistently to the same situations, although different individuals will respond differently to different situations. In their various simulations, they show that different patterns of connection of the CAUs do lead to consistent behavioral signatures for different individuals. However, they make no attempt to try to capture major differences in personality structure (e.g., the big five: *extraversion, agreeableness, neuroticism, conscientiousness,* and *openness to experience*).

More recently, Read and Miller (Read & Miller, 2002; Read et al., 2008) have used a multilayer, recurrent neural network model, using the Leabra++ architecture in PDP++ (O'Reilly & Munakata, 2000), to model personality structure and dynamics. This model is designed to capture major distinctions in personality structure, specifically what has sometimes been referred to as the big three: *extraversion, neuroticism,* and *conscientiousness.*

One of the major ideas driving Read and Miller's model is that personality traits are goal-based structures; goals and motives are central to the meaning of individual traits. Essentially, personality can be understood largely in terms of individual differences in the behavior of underlying motivational systems. Thus, a central focus of this model is to capture personality dynamics in terms of the structure and behavior of motivational systems.

Read and Miller's (2002) initial model had an input layer with eight situational features, with one-to-one recurrent links to nodes in a goal layer (with nodes corresponding to eight goals), and one-to-one recurrent links from the goal layer to the behavior layer (with eight behaviors). The goal layer was divided into an *Approach* layer and an *Avoidance* layer, to correspond to a key motivational distinction between an approach system, which governs sensitivity to reward and loss of reward, and an avoidance system, which governs sensitivity to the possibility of punishment or threat (Gray, 1987). The sensitivity of the approach and avoid layers to input was manipulated by a gain parameter. In addition, an attempt was made to capture basic aspects of conscientiousness by using the degree of overall inhibition in the network. Overall inhibition in this model functions to enhance the difference between the most highly activated nodes and less activated nodes. This model did not have learning: the authors set the weights.

Read and Miller (2002) were able to use the gain parameters for the approach and avoid layers to successfully simulate broad individual differences in extraversion and neuroticism. They also showed that degree of inhibition could capture what could be termed as goal focus and thus could model certain aspects of conscientiousness.

Read et al., (2006) have recently developed a more ambitious version of the Virtual Personality model. It uses a semidistributed representation of situational features in the input layer (twenty-nine in all) that allows them to specify a wide variety of specific situations that can arise in two general contexts: work and parties. The input layer connects, through a hidden layer, to the goal layer, which is again divided into approach (twelve goals) and avoid layers (eight goals). The situational features, the goal layer, and a resource layer (with eleven units) are then connected through a hidden layer to the behavior layer, which has a wide variety (forty-three) of different behaviors that can be enacted in work and party settings (e.g., give orders, work extra hard, dance, drink alcohol, tell jokes, etc.).

In addition to being much more detailed than the original virtual personality network, this network learns. Weights develop as a result of exposure to learning environments. Also, hidden layers are included so it can learn conjunctive or nonlinear relationships of cues to particular outcomes (e.g., situational features to goal nodes).

Various aspects of the network can be manipulated to capture personality differences. First, the relative sensitivities of the approach and avoid systems in the goal layer can be manipulated to capture individual differences in sensitivity to reward and threat, and thereby capture general differences in extraversion and neuroticism. This is done by manipulating the relative reward values of of approach and avoidance goals during learning. For instance, greater reward value of an approach goal during training will subsequently make that goal more likely to be highly activated when appropriate inputs are encountered.

Second, the bias inputs of individual goals can be manipulated to capture individual differences in the extent to which different goals are chronically activated and are likely to direct behavior. Third, the overall degree of inhibition within various layers (especially goal and behavior) can be manipulated to enhance or reduce the differences in activation between the most highly activated concepts and less activated concepts. This can be interpreted as influencing differences in "goal focus" and thus can capture certain aspects of the broad trait of conscientiousness.

Although it has not been done, it should be possible to capture other major aspects of personality by organizing the goals into further subclusters. In the current model, all the goals in a layer should have moderately correlated impacts on behavior because they are all influenced by a common gain or sensitivity parameter. As an example of further structure, the general approach layer could be organized into major subclasses of human goals. For example, Depue and Morrone-Strupinsky (2005) have argued that the general trait of extroversion can actually be divided into two subcomponents that correspond to partially independent neurobiological systems and separate classes of goals. One subcomponent corresponds to what is typically viewed as the general trait of agreeableness and the other is typically viewed as the general trait of extraversion. Agreeableness includes more *collectivistic* or relationally oriented sets of goals and motives, whereas extraversion includes more *individualistic* or *agentic* goals and motives. This analysis could be pushed further by assuming that the trait of openness to experience corresponds to a third subcluster of goals and motives in the approach system. These goals may have to do with *play* and *fun* (Panksepp, 1998, 2000) or with curiosity, a desire for knowledge. The basic idea is that the results of analyses of personality structure can be captured by the organization of the motivational systems in the Virtual Personality model.

This attempt to simulate major personality distinctions is one major difference between this model and Mischel and Shoda's (1995) CAPS model of personality. In Mischel and Shoda's model there is little structure to the cognitive affective units (goals, beliefs, etc.) or their interrelationships. And there is no attempt to relate the structure of their model to the structure of human personality, as exemplified in structural models of personality.

Recently Zachary et al. (2005a, 2005b) presented a symbolic model that is based on the conceptual distinctions of the Virtual Personality model. This implementation is intended for the construction of software agents, with realistic personalities.

Other simulation work has examined temporal stability in personality. Fraley has developed a set of difference equations and related simulations to represent alternative models of both personality stability (Fraley & Roberts, 2005) and stability of attachment styles (Fraley, 2002; Fraley & Brumbaugh, 2004). He compared what is essentially an autoregressive function, in which behavior is a function of the previous state of the individual plus random variation, with an equation in which there is an additional parameter that models the consistent impact of a stable trait (related to Kenny & Zautra's (1995, 2001) trait-state-error model). Fraley notes that over time, the autoregressive model essentially becomes a random walk model in which the initial impact of an individual's behavior on his or her environment is eventually swamped by the random variation. This model predicts that over time, the stability coefficient for a trait or for attachment styles approaches zero. In contrast, for the model with the stable trait (such as early attachment style or early temperament differences), the simulated stability coefficient approaches an asymptote that is roughly equal to the value of the parameter that describes the influence of the "trait" on the individual's behavior. Fraley argues that this consistent influence acts as an anchor or constraint against the impact of random variation. According to Fraley's metaanalytic results, the stability coefficient for both neuroticism and attachment styles are nonzero, even after twenty years, contradicting the auto-regressive model, but consistent with the trait model.

Probably the earliest work on simulating personality was summarized in Tomkins and Messick (1963). Subsequent work was presented by Loehlin (1968), who simulated personality dynamics, Atkinson and Birch (1978), who presented a numerical simulation of the dynamics of the activation of motivational systems over the course of a day, and Colby (1975, 1981), who simulated a paranoid personality. More recently, Sorrentino et al. (2003) have presented a simulation of Sorrentino's trait of *uncertainty orientation*, which has some conceptual similarities to the earlier Atkinson and Birch (1978) work.

2.8. *Personality and Dyadic Interactions*

The previous simulations focus on individual behaviors. In other work, Shoda, LeeTiernan, and Mischel (2002) have used the CAPS constraint satisfaction architecture to simulate dyadic interactions among individuals with different personalities (for other simulations of social interaction, see Chapter 19 in this volume). In Shoda et al.'s simulations, the behavioral output of one member's network is the input to the other member's network. When two individuals' networks are linked in this way, the joined networks exhibit new attractors that are not characteristic of either of the individual networks. Thus, these simulations suggest that the behavior of two individuals, when joined in a dyad, are different from their behavior in isolation, and it provides a mechanism for that difference.

Nowak and Vallacher have done dynamical systems simulations of a wide range of different social and personality phenomena (e.g., Nowak & Vallacher, 1998; Nowak, Vallacher, & Zochowski, 2002). Only a subset of that work is discussed here. In one series of simulations, they used coupled logistic equations to investigate both the conditions under which synchronization of behavior occurs in dyadic interactions and the role of individual differences in the extent to which behavior is affected by the characteristics of the other with whom they are interacting. In these coupled logistic equations, an individual's behavior is a function of both his or her state on the previous time-step $(x_1(t))$, as well as the preceding behavior of his or her partner $(x_2(t))$. The parameter r is a control parameter that determines the extent to which the current behavior is due to the previous state of the individual,

and the parameter α is the extent to which the current behavior of the individual is influenced by the preceding behavior of his or her partner. This is the degree of coupling between the two individuals.

$$x_1(t+1) = [r_1 x_1(t)(1 - x_1(t))$$
$$+ \alpha r_2 x_2(t)(1 - x_2(t))]/[1 + \alpha]$$
$$x_2(t+1) = [r_2 x_2(t)(1 - x_2(t))$$
$$+ \alpha r_1 x_1(t)(1 - x_1(t))]/[1 + \alpha].$$

In a series of simulations, they found that the degree of synchronization between the members of the dyad was higher when the degree of coupling, α, was higher and when the control parameters r for the two individuals were more similar. They also found that synchronization between two individuals could occur, even with weak coupling, when the control parameters (r) were similar. Interestingly, they found that with moderate degrees of coupling, the two individuals tended to stabilize each other's behavior. These simulations provide an interesting way to think about how individuals in interactions influence each other.

In further simulations, they argued that individual differences could be partially captured by the location, depth, and breadth of attractors for equilibrium values of a particular state of an individual. They show that these factors affect the extent to which the behavior of one member of a dyad is affected by and becomes synchronized to the behavior of the other member. For example, the behavior of A is more likely to become synchronized to the behavior of B when their attractors are close together or when the attractor for A is shallow. Further, the behavior of A is less likely to become synchronized to B when A has a deep attractor.

2.9. *The Self*

The self is a central concept in social psychology, but its properties have remained somewhat nebulous. It seems unlikely that any one model would be able to satisfactorily capture it, but researchers have begun to investigate aspects of it with different types of models.

Greenwald and Banaji (1989) examined whether an ordinary associative semantic memory model could capture memory and recall effects related to the self. Using an existing general associative framework, they found that no special adjustments were required to replicate their lab results (recall of self-generated names and subsequent learned associations to objects vs. other-generated names). They concluded that this implies there is nothing extraordinary about the structure of the self in memory.

Smith, Coats, and Walling (1999) investigated the self's overlap with relationship partners and ingroup members. Using the Interactive Activation and Competition model (McClelland & Rumelhart, 1981), a localist connectionist model with nodes for the self, others, and particular traits connected by bidirectional links, they tested response times as proxies for the activation flow between concepts in the cognitive structure. They found the self is implicitly accessed when the subject was asked about its relationship partner. Additionally, they concluded that the exact representation of the self (i.e., the pattern of activation relevant to the self-concept) varies with context. In lay terms, the findings are consistent with the notion that a romantic partner's traits (and presumably actions as well) really do reflect on oneself.

Nowak et al.'s (2000) innovative approach to examining this topic was to use cellular automata to represent different aspects of the self and to investigate how the mind can self-organize the self-concept with respect to a positive versus negative evaluation. Cellular automata consist of sets of simple processing elements that can take on a limited number of values of a single variable that can change dynamically as the result of influence from other elements (e.g., an attitude of an individual in a community can change as a result of influence from other individuals). Elements are typically arranged in simple spatial arrangements, such as a grid (e.g., checkerboard), and on each time-step they change their internal state

on the basis of an updating rule that takes into account the state of communicating elements. Communication among the elements is typically determined by their spatial arrangement. For example, a cell on a grid may communicate only with the four cells on its sides, it may communicate with those on its sides as well as on the directly adjacent diagonals, or it may use other kinds of communication rules. Various updating rules can be used: One example is a majority rule, where a unit may change its current "attitude" depending on the "attitude" of the majority of the other units with which it communicates. Such cellular automata have interesting dynamic properties and have been used in various domains.

In Nowak et al.'s (2000) simulation, each unit in the lattice was influenced by its adjacent neighbors, and this influence was modified by a centrality (in the self-concept) parameter representing a particular aspect's resistance to change. The model did indeed self-organize, with the initially more prevalent positively evaluated aspects gaining even more units. The negative units that did survive tended to be highly central ones. Even more thought-provoking were their simulations of what happened when information was introduced to a preintegrated network. They found that high pressure for integration (a tunable parameter of the model) prevented external information from influencing the network, yet under lower pressure, external information actually facilitated integration of the network. Further, when the influence of the information was particularly strong, the random nature of it overwhelmed the existing structure of the network and reduced organization. Finally, the system was relatively "immune" to contradictory information.

2.10. *Social Influence*

Researchers have used also cellular automata to model various aspects of social influence, the process by which we influence and are influenced by others. The subject of influence has ranged from attitudes and group opinions to belief and enforcement of group norms. Latané and colleagues (e.g., Latane, 1996; Latané, 2000; Latane, Nowak, & Liu, 1994; Nowak, Szamrej, & Latane, 1990) have focused on trying to predict system order parameters under different circumstances. These parameters include: (1) polarization/consolidation – the degree to which the proportion that adopts the majority/minority opinion changes over the course of interaction; (2) dynamism – the likelihood of an individual changing his or her position; and (3) clustering – the degree of spatial organization in the distribution of positions held by individuals.

A critical step in these simulations is determining the influence function: how an individual is influenced by his or her neighbors. The parameters that investigators have chosen to focus on are the strength of attitude/conviction in the influencee (who also serves a dual role as an influencer), the persuasiveness of an influencer in changing the influencee's attitude, the supportiveness of the influencer in defending the influencee's current attitude, the social distance between influencer and influencee, and the number of people within the influence horizon (which can also be affected by the geometries of contact, e.g., full connectivity, where everyone is connected to everyone else no matter how extensive the network vs. a family geometry, where individuals are limited to contacting only their family members plus a few selected friends). The investigators suggest that different influence rules might be applicable under different circumstances; for example, when groups and issues are well-defined, the influence horizon can include the whole population, but when issues and groups are not well formed, a purely incremental influence function is more appropriate (Latane et al., 1994). Once the parameters for the simulation are determined, a random seed or other specified initial conditions representing the number, location, and spatial mixing parameter for the initial attitudes is used to run a trial. The simulation then iterates until an equilibrium solution is found.

The results from these simulations show that the equilibrium (final) distributions are highly dependent on small changes in initial conditions. Reproducible patterns are found throughout the simulations: Initial majorities tend to get bigger, leaving clusters of minorities with strong convictions (Latane, 1996; Latane et al., 1994; Nowak et al., 1990). Subsequent lab experiments were carried out with these simulations in mind: Generally, the simulations reproduced the lab results well, with the caveat that the more strongly held the opinions/attitudes, the less well the lab results were predicted by the simulations (Latane & Burgeois, 2001).

Latane's (2000) simulations of group opinion change have shown results similar to those previously discussed with an influence function, where an individual's attitude is the average of his or her neighbors. Clusters of similar attitudes develop, and majorities tend to gain more control. This model also implemented social comparison processes as an additional source of influence. In this case, if a neighbor's outcome was better, an individual adopted that neighbor's effort level. Simulating several parallel work groups, the results showed remarkable within-group homogeneity, but large between-group differences.

Centola, Willer, and Macy (2005) modeled social influence in one particular context: the enforcement of privately unpopular social norms (also known as the Emperor's dilemma.) Their model suggests that this can happen when the strength of social influence exceeds the strength of conviction of the individuals. The process requires a few true believers (individuals with imperturbable convictions) to induce a cascade of norm enforcement that happens because the people with the weakest convictions adopt enforcement rather quickly, which increases the influence further on the remaining individuals until most everyone enforces the unpopular norm. Note that this effect only occurs in networks where only local influence is allowed.

2.11. Dynamics of Human Mating Strategies

Extensive research has shown that couples are similar on almost any personal attribute that one can think of, including physical attractiveness. An obvious hypothesis about how similarity on physical attractiveness comes about is that people choose partners who are similar to them on physical attractiveness. However, there is little evidence for this. When given a choice, people almost always choose the most attractive partner available. For example, when college students are given a choice of partners for a date, they will almost always choose the most attractive partner available. So this raises the question of how we can get attractiveness matching when people do not seem to be choosing partners who are similar to them on attractiveness.

Kalick and Hamilton (1986) ran a simulation with a set of very simple agents to test the possibility that in a population of individuals who choose the most attractive partner, the result could still be attractiveness matching. In one simulation, they generated a large number of "men" and "women" who randomly varied on "attractiveness." Male and female participants were randomly paired on a date and decided whether to accept their partner as a mate. The likelihood of accepting the partner was a function of the partner's attractiveness. To form a "couple," each member had to accept the other. Because of these factors, two partners of the highest level of attractiveness would be almost certain to accept each other, and two partners of the lowest level would be extremely unlikely to do so. Once a couple was formed, they were removed from the dating pool, and a new set of pairings were made. Kalick and Hamilton showed that over time, matching on attractiveness moved to levels comparable to those found with real couples. Thus, attractiveness matching did not require choosing a similar mate, but instead could result from people choosing the most attractive mate available who would reciprocate.

Kenrick et al. (2003) used cellular automata to examine hypotheses about the distribution of human mating strategies. Work in evolutionary approaches has noted that human males and females differ in the amount of investment in their offspring. Such differential investment is typically re-

lated to different mating strategies for males and females in a species, with the sex that makes the greater investment being more selective and having a more restricted mating strategy. However, it is not clear whether men and women actually have such biologically based differences in mating strategies. As Kenrick et al. note, mating strategies are not just a function of the individual; they are also a function of the strategies of their potential mates and the surrounding population. For example, a man who might prefer an unrestricted mating strategy might follow a restricted strategy if that is what most available women desire.

In one set of simulations, individuals in a standard checkerboard pattern made decisions about their mating strategy on the basis of the mating strategies of their contiguous possible partners. All individuals had either a restricted or an unrestricted mating strategy and followed a decision rule about whether to change their strategy as a function of the proportion of surrounding individuals who followed a specific strategy. Kenrick et al. (2003) then varied both the initial distribution of mating strategies among men and women, as well as the decision rule (proportion of surrounding others) for changing a strategy.

In their initial simulations, although both men and women needed more than a majority of the surrounding population to have a different rule in order to change, men had a lower threshold for switching from restricted to unrestricted than for switching from unrestricted to restricted. Women had the reverse pattern: it was harder for them to switch from restricted to unrestricted than the reverse. With these sets of rules and over a wide range of initial distributions of mating strategies, most of the populations ended up with more restricted members (both men and women). In another simulation, they found that if both sexes used male decision rules, the populations moved toward more unrestricted distributions, whereas if both sexes used female decision rules, the populations moved toward more restricted populations.

Conrey and Smith (2005) used a multiagent system to study the evolution of different mating choice rules. Research on mating choice has shown that women tend to end up with mates who have more resources than they do, and men tend to end up with mates who are younger than they are. Conrey and Smith note that the typical approach in evolutionary psychology is to identify a pattern of behavior such as this and then assume that there is an evolved mechanism or "module" that directly corresponds to the behavior. Thus, evolutionary psychologists assume that men and women have evolved sexually dimorphic decision rules: Men have an evolved preference for younger mates, and women have an evolved preference for men with resources. However, Conrey and Smith note that behavior is the result of genes, environment, and their interaction, which makes it possible that there is no direct correspondence between decision rules and behavior and that men and women have the same decision rule.

They ran a series of simulations in which numerous agents are born, enter reproductive age, have children (if they succeed in getting a mate), and then die. Women invest more resources in their offspring than men do. Agents who do not maintain enough resources die. Once agents reach reproductive age, they make offers to potential mates. Individuals make offers to the most desirable available partners, given their decision rule. And pairing off requires mutual agreement. This is similar to a key assumption in Kalick and Hamilton (1986).

In the first study, Conrey and Smith (2005) simulate several different combinations of decision rules for men and women. All agents can have no decision rule, they prefer the partner with the most resources, they can prefer the partner who is youngest, or they can prefer a partner with both. Perhaps not surprisingly, populations in which women want a mate with resources and men want a youthful partner exhibit patterns of mate choice that match what is empirically observed.

However, they also find that a simulation in which both men and women prefer a partner with resources gives the same pattern of mate choice. Thus, there does not have to be a direct correspondence between the decision rule and the pattern of mate choice.

In a second study, they start with a population with no decision rules, but in which it is possible for a resource rule and a youth rule to evolve by a process of mutation and selection. They find that a pattern of resource attention evolves quite quickly in both sexes, whereas a pattern of sensitivity to youth never evolves. Yet, the result is a population in which women end up with men with resources and men end up with women who are younger. Conrey and Smith (2005) note that such a shared decision rule can result in sex differences in mate choice because of very different correlations between age and resources for men and women. In their simulations, the correlation between age and resources is quite high for men, but fairly modest for women. Thus, sex differences in behavior do not require sex differences in underlying decision rules. Environmental constraints can also play a major role in the pattern of choices.

2.12. *Group Discussion*

Modeling of group discussion processes and related decisions (including jury deliberations) appears to have more immediate applications than most of the models in social psychology, because many of the parameters can be deliberately and fairly easily controlled in a real context. The first attempts at modeling group decisions were essentially focused on predicting the probabilities of jurors changing their opinions in the face of an opposing faction. The DICE model (Penrod & Hastie, 1980) and the SIS model (Stasser & Davis, 1981) depended most critically on total group size and faction size of the two opposing viewpoints, with some variability parameters to account for individual differences. They were able to fit a wide range of experimental data with these parameters, but glossed over the actual mechanics of the discussion/deliberation process.

This next step was bridged with Stasser's (1988) DISCUSS model, which focused on how the information exchange affected discussion outcomes. This model was a simulation of a discussion as a series of events: who talks, what is said, the effect on members' recall of all information, and ultimately their preference. Discussion terminates when the decision rule (unanimity, majority, etc.) is satisfied. Importantly, each member values individual arguments slightly differently, and an individual participation parameter determines the distribution over members of participation. Members' preferences are based on the combined weight of currently salient information. This model was able to reproduce empirical results from Stasser & Titus (1985) on information exchange, but the insights the simulation results provided are perhaps more interesting. The results showed that a search of the available information biased by motivational factors was not necessary to reproduce the results: Information sampling based on the participation distribution alone could account for the results. Notwithstanding, biased information presentation (either advocacy or nonadvocacy conditions) also produced differences in the outcome. Also, the resolution was critically dependent on the discussion being able to resolve differences in the evaluation of individual pieces of evidence. In addition to Stasser's information-based model, a model by Larson (1997) based on information sampling predicts that shared information gets introduced earlier and unshared information tends to get discussed later. Together, these models are able to explain a fair amount of the empirical results and processes within this area without resorting to more complex interpersonal accounts.

The SPEAK model (Stasser & Taylor, 1991) provided a more detailed account of how speaker patterns affected discussion processes, based on variations around dyadic exchanges. The model includes "three basic processes: formation of speaking hierarchies within a group, intermittent fluctuations in members' tendencies to speak, and competition among members for speaking time (p. 683)." It used a sequential speaking likelihood decay function to implement the process structure. The model successfully reproduced four-person data with a model fit with parameters derived from six-person data. The model did not cover a wider range of group sizes, and it does not attempt to implement "individual characteristics [that] mediate patterns of speaking" (p. 683). The SPEAK model was subsequently combined with the DISCUSS model (Stasser & Vaughan, 1996). The results of these simulations showed the interesting result that minorities who wanted to overcome ill-informed majorities might be most successful when they were forceful about their viewpoint.

3. Conclusion

In looking back over this chapter, several themes come through. One is that a large number of central phenomena in social psychology can be captured by a fairly simple feedback or recurrent network with learning. Important findings on causal learning, causal reasoning, individual and group impression formation, and attitude change can all be captured within the same basic architecture. This suggests that we might be close to being able to provide an integrated theory or account of a wide range of social psychological phenomena. It also suggests that underlying the apparent high degree of complexity of social and personality phenomena may be a more fundamental simplicity. Some of the complexity of social psychological theory may be due to the current lack of understanding of the underlying principles. The success of a relatively simple model in providing an account for such a wide range of phenomena suggests that once we understand the basic underlying principles we will be able to integrate a wide range of social psychology.

Another theme that comes through in many of the models is the emphasis on self-organization and coherence mechanisms, the role of constraint satisfaction principles that seek to satisfy multiple, simultaneous constraints. As Read, Vanman, and Miller (1997) indicated, this is not a new trend, but goes back to the gestalt psychological roots of much of social psychology. Theories of cognitive consistency (e.g., cognitive dissonance, Festinger, 1957; balance, Heider, 1958), impression formation

(Asch, 1946), personality and goal-directed behavior (Lewin, 1935), and group dynamics (Lewin, 1947a, 1947b), all central topics in social psychology, were based on gestalt principles. Gestalt psychology, with its emphasis on cognition as the result of interacting fields of forces and holistic processing, was essentially focused on constraint satisfaction principles, although this term was not used. Other authors (e.g., Rumelhart & McClelland, 1986) have also noted the parallels between constraint satisfaction principles and the basic principles of gestalt psychology.

Another interesting, although not surprising, theme is that the type of computational model tends to be strongly related to whether the investigator is interested in intra-personal or inter-personal phenomena. Connectionist models strongly tend to be used to model intra-personal phenomena, whereas cellular automata and multiagent models are typically used for inter-personal phenomena, such as social influence and development of mating strategies.

Social and personality psychologists have been interested in computational models since the early days of computational modeling, with work by Abelson on hot cognition (Abelson, 1963) and on ideology (Abelson, 1973; Abelson & Carroll, 1965) and by Loehlin (1968) and Colby (1975, 1981) on personality (see also Tomkins & Messick, 1963). However, it is only recently that computational modeling has started to become more widely used in the field. And even now, computational modeling is much rarer in social and personality psychology than it is in cognitive psychology and cognitive science. However, given the complexity of social and personality dynamics and the requirements for theories that can adequately handle that complexity, there should be an increasing focus on computational modeling.

References

Abelson, R. P. (1963). Computer simulation of "hot cognition." In S. S. Tomkins & S. Messick (Eds.), *Computer simulation of personality* (pp. 277–298). New York: Wiley.

Abelson, R. P. (1968). Simulation of social behavior. In G. Lindzey & E. Aronson (Eds.), *Handbook of social psychology* (Revised edition). Cambridge, MA: Addison-Wesley.

Abelson, R. P. (1973). The structure of belief systems. In R. C. Schank & K. Colby (Eds.), *Computer models of thought and language* (pp. 287–339). San Francisco: Freeman.

Abelson, R. P., & Carroll, J. (1965). Computer simulation of individual belief systems. *American Behavioral Scientist, 8*, 24–30.

Abelson, R. P., Aronson, E., McGuire, W. J., Newcomb, T. M., Rosenberg, M. J., & Tannenbaum, P. H. (Eds.). (1968). *Theories of cognitive consistency: A sourcebook*. Chicago: Rand-McNally.

Anderson, J. R. (1993). *Rules of the mind*. Hillsdale, NJ: Lawrence Erlbaum.

Anderson, J. R., & Lebiere, C. (1998). *The atomic components of thought*. Mahwah, NJ: Lawrence Erlbaum.

Asch, S. E. (1946). Forming impressions of personality. *Journal of Abnormal and Social Psychology, 41*, 258–290.

Atkinson, J. W., & Birch, D. (1978). *An introduction to motivation*. New York: Van Nostrand.

Brewer, M. B. (1988). A dual process model of impression formation. In T. K. Srull & R. S. Wyer, Jr. (Eds.), *Advances in social cognition* (pp. 1–36). Hillsdale, NJ: Lawrence Erlbaum.

Centola, D., Willer, R., & Macy, M. (2005). The emperor's dilemma: A computational model of self-enforcing norms. *American Journal of Sociology, 110*(4), 1009–1040.

Colby, K. M. (1975) *Artificial paranoia: A computer simulation of paranoid processes*. New York: Pergamon Press.

Colby, K. M. (1981). Modeling a paranoid mind. *The Behavioral and Brain Sciences, 4*, 515–560.

Conrey, F. R., & Smith, E. (2005). *Multi-agent simulation of men's and women's mate choice: Sex differences in mate characteristics need not reflect sex differences in mate preferences*. Unpublished manuscript, Indiana University.

Depue, R. A., & Morrone-Strupinsky, J. V. (2005). A neurobehavioral model of affiliative bonding: Implications for conceptualizing a human trait of affiliation. *Behavioral and Brain Sciences, 28*, 313–350

Eagley, A. H., & Chaiken, S. (1993). *The psychology of attitudes*. Fort Worth, TX: Harcourt Brace Jovanovich.

Eiser, J. R., Fazio, R. H., Stafford, T., & Prescott, T. J. (2003). Connectionist simulation of attitude learning: Asymmetries in the acquisition of positive and negative evaluations. *Personality and Social Psychology Bulletin, 29*(10), 1221–1235.

Festinger, L. (1957). *A theory of cognitive dissonance.* Evanston, IL: Row, Peterson.

Fiedler, K. (1996). Explaining and simulating judgment biases as an aggregation phenomenon in probabilistic, multiple-cue environments. *Psychological Review, 103*(1), 193–214.

Fiske, S. T., & Neuberg, S. L. (1990). A continuum of impression formation, from category-based to individuating processes: Influences of information and motivation on attention and interpretation. In M. Zanna (Ed.), *Advances in experimental social psychology* (pp. 1–74). San Diego, CA: Academic Press.

Fraley, R. C. (2002). Attachment stability from infancy to adulthood: Meta-analysis and dynamic modeling of developmental mechanisms. *Personality and Social Psychology Review, 6*(2), 123–151.

Fraley, R. C., & Brumbaugh, C. C. (2004). A dynamical systems approach to understanding stability and change in attachment security. In W. S. Rholes & J. A. Simpson (Eds.), *Adult attachment: Theory, research, and clinical implications* (pp. 86–132). New York: Guilford Press.

Fraley, R. C., & Roberts, B. W. (2005). Patterns of continuity: A dynamic model for conceptualizing the stability of individual differences in psychological constructs across the life course. *Psychological Review, 112*(1), 60–74.

Gray, J. A. (1987). *The psychology of fear and stress* (2nd ed.). New York: Cambridge University Press.

Greenwald, A. G., & Banaji, M. R. (1989). The self as a memory system: Powerful, but ordinary. *Journal of Personality and Social Psychology, 57*(1), 41–54.

Gullahorn, J., & Gullahorn, J. E. (1963). A computer model of elementary social behavior. *Behavioral Science, 8,* 354–362.

Hastie, R. (1988). A computer simulation model of person memory *Journal of Experimental Social Psychology, 24*(5), 423–447.

Heider, F. (1958). *The psychology of interpersonal relations.* New York: Wiley.

Higgins, E. T., Bargh, J. A., & Lombardi, W. (1985). The nature of priming effects on categorization. *Journal of Experimental Psychology: Learning, Memory, and Cognition, 11,* 59–69.

Higgins, E. T., Rholes, W. S., & Jones, C. R. (1977). Category accessibility and impression formation. *Journal of Experimental Social Psychology, 13,* 141–154.

Hintzman, D. L. (1988). Judgments of frequency and recognition memory in a multiple trace memory model. *Psychological Review, 95,* 528–551.

Kalick, S. M., & Hamilton, T. E. (1986). The matching hypothesis reexamined. *Journal of Personality and Social Psychology, 51*(4), 673–682.

Kashima, Y., Woolcock, J., & Kashima, E. S. (2000). Group impressions as dynamic configurations: The tensor product model of group impression formation and change. *Psychological Review, 107*(4), 914–942.

Kashima, Y., Woolcock, J., & King, D. (1998). The dynamics of group impression formation: The tensor product model of exemplar-based social category learning. In S. J. Read & L. C. Miler (Eds.), *Connectionist models of social reasoning and social behavior* (pp. 71–109). Mahwah, NJ: Lawrence Erlbaum.

Kenny, D. A., & Zautra, A. (1995). The trait-state-error model for multiwave data. *Journal of Consulting and Clinical Psychology, 63,* 52–59.

Kenny, D. A., & Zautra, A. (2001). Trait-state models for longitudinal data. In L. M., Collins & A. G. Sayer (Eds.), *New methods for the analysis of change: Decade of behavior* (pp. 243–263). Washington, DC: American Psychological Association.

Kenrick, D. T., Li, N. P., & Butner, J. (2003). Dynamical evolutionary psychology: Individual decision rules and emergent social norms. *Psychological Review, 110*(1), 3–28.

Kunda, Z., & Thagard, P. (1996). Forming impressions from stereotypes, traits, and behaviors: A parallel constraint-satisfaction theory. *Psychological Review, 103,* 284–308.

Larson, J. R. J. (1997). Modeling the entry of shared and unshared information into group discussion: A review and BASIC language computer program. *Small Group Research, 28*(3), 454–479.

Latané, B. (1996). Strength from weakness: The fate of opinion minorities in spatially distributed groups. In E. H. Witte & J. H. Davis (Eds.), *Understanding group behavior, Vol. 1: Consensual action by small groups* (pp.193–219). Hillsdale, NJ: Lawrence Erlbaum.

Latané, B. (2000). Pressures to uniformity and the evolution of cultural norms: Modeling dynamic social impact. In D. R. Ilgen & C. H. Hulin (Eds.), *Computational modeling of behavior in organizations: The third scientific discipline* (pp. 189–220). Washington, DC: American Psychological Association.

Latané, B., & Bourgeois, M. J. (2001). Successfully simulating dynamic social impact: Three levels of prediction. In J. P. Forgaz & K. D. Williams (Eds.), *Social influence: Direct and indirect processes* (pp. 61–76). New York: Psychology Press.

Latané, B., Nowak, A., & Liu, J. H. (1994). Measuring emergent social phenomena: Dynamism, polarization, and clustering as order parameters of social systems. *Behavioral Science, 39*(1), 1–24.

Lazarus, R. S. (2001). Relational meaning and discrete emotions. In K. R. Scherer, A. Schorr, & T. Johnstone (Eds.), *Appraisal processes in emotion: Theory, methods, research* (pp. 37–67). Oxford, UK: Oxford University Press.

Lewin, K. (1935). *A dynamic theory of personality*. New York: McGraw-Hill.

Lewin, K. (1947a). Frontiers in group dynamics: I. *Human Relations, 1*, 2–38.

Lewin, K. (1947b). Frontiers in group dynamics: II. *Human Relations, 1*, 143–153.

Linville, P. W., Fischer, G. W., & Salovey, P. (1989). Perceived distributions of the characteristics of in-group and out-group members: Empirical evidence and a computer simulation. *Journal of Personality and Social Psychology, 57*, 165–188.

Loehlin, J. C. (1968). *Computer models of personality*. New York: Random House.

McClelland, J. L., & Rumelhart, D. E. (1981). An interactive activation model of context effects in leter perception: Part I. An account of basic findings. *Psychological Review, 88*, 375–407.

McClelland, J. L., & Rumelhart, D. E. (1986). (Eds.). *Parallel distributed processing: Explorations in the microstructure of cognition. Vol. 2: Psychological and biological models*. Cambridge, MA: MIT Press/Bradford Books.

McClelland, J. L., & Rumelhart, D. E. (1988). *Explorations in parallel distributed processing: A handbook of models, programs, and exercises*. Cambridge, MA: MIT Press/Bradford Books.

Mischel, W., & Shoda, Y. (1995). A cognitive-affective system theory of personality: Reconceptualizing situations, dispositions, dynamics, and invariance in personality structure. *Psychological Review, 102*(2), 246–268.

Montoya, J. A., & Read, S. J. (1998). A constraint satisfaction model of the correspondence bias: The role of accessibility and applicability of explanations. In M. A. Gernsbacher, S. J. Derry (Eds.), *The Proceedings of the Twentieth Annual Cognitive Science Society Conference* (pp. 722–727). Mahwah, NJ: Lawrence Erlbaum.

Mosler, H., Schwarz, K., Ammann, F., & Gutscher, H. (2001). Computer simulation as a method of further developing a theory: Simulating the elaboration likelihood model. *Personality and Social Psychology Review, 5*(3), 201–215.

Nerb, J., & Spada, H. (2001). Evaluation of environmental problems: A coherence model of cognition and emotion. *Cognition & Emotion, 15*(4), 521–551.

Nowak, A., Szamrej, J., & Latané, B. (1990). From private attitude to public opinion: A dynamic theory of social impact. *Psychological Review, 97*(3), 362–376.

Nowak, A., & Vallacher, R. R. (1998). *Toward computational social psychology: Cellular automata and neural network models of interpersonal dynamics*. In S. J. Read & L. C. Miller (Eds.), *Connectionist models of social reasoning and social behavior*. (pp. 277–311). Mahwah, NJ: Lawrence Erlbaum.

Nowalk, A., Vallacher, R. R., Tesser, A., & Borkowski, W. (2000). Society of self: The emergence of collective properties in self-structure. *Psychological Review, 107*(1), 39–61.

Nowak, A., Vallacher, R. R., & Zochowski, M. (2002). The emergence of personality: Personal stability through interpersonal synchronization. In D. Cervone & W. Mischel (Eds.), *Advances in personality science* (Vol. 1, pp. 292–331). New York: Guilford Press.

O'Reilly, R. C., & Munakata, Y. (2000). *Computational explorations in cognitive neuroscience*. Cambridge, MA: MIT Press.

Ortony, A., Clore, G. L., & Collins, A. (1988). *The cognitive structure of emotions*. New York: Cambridge University Press.

Panksepp, J. (1998). *Affective neuroscience: The foundations of human and animal emotions*. New York: Oxford University Press.

Panksepp, J. (2000). Emotions as natural kinds in the mammalian brain. In M. Lewis & J. M. Haviland-Jones (Ed.), *Handbook of emotions* (2nd ed., pp. 137–156). New York: Guilford.

Penrod, S., & Hastie, R. (1980). A computer simulation of jury decision making. *Psychological Review, 87*(2), 133–159.

Petty, R. E., & Cacioppo, J. T. (1986). *Communication and persuasion*. New York: Springer-Verlag.

Queller, S., & Smith, E. R. (2002). Subtyping versus bookkeeping in stereotype learning and change: Connectionist simulations and empirical findings. *Journal of Personality and Social Psychology, 82*(3), 300–313.

Read, S. J., & Marcus-Newhall, A. (1993). Explanatory coherence in social explanations: A parallel distributed processing account. *Journal of Personality and Social Psychology, 65*, 429–447.

Read, S. J., & Miller, L.C. (1993). Rapist or "regular guy": Explanatory coherence in the construction of mental models of others. *Personality and Social Psychology Bulletin, 19*, 526–540.

Read, S. J., & Miller, L. C. (1994). Dissonance and balance in belief systems: The promise of parallel constraint satisfaction processes and connectionist modeling approaches. In R. C. Schank & E. Langer (Eds.), *Beliefs, reasoning, and decision-making: Psycho-logic in honor of Bob Abelson*. Hillsdale, NJ: Lawrence Erlbaum.

Read, S. J., & Miller, L. C. (2002). Virtual personalities: A neural network model of personality. *Personality and Social Psychology Review, 6*(4), 357–369.

Read, S. J., Monroe, B. M., Brownstein, A. L., Yang, Y., Chopra, G., & Miller, L. C. (2008). *Virtual personality II: A motivationally based neural network model of personality structure and dynamics*. Unpublished manuscript, University of Southern California.

Read, S. J., & Montoya, J. A. (1999a). An autoassociative model of causal learning and causal reasoning. *Journal of Personality and Social Psychology, 76*, 728–742.

Read, S. J., & Montoya, J. A. (1999b). A feedback neural network model of causal learning and causal reasoning. In M. Hahn, & S. C. Stoness (Eds.), *The Proceedings of the Twenty-first Annual Cognitive Science Society Conference* (pp. 578–583). Mahwah, NJ: Lawrence Erlbaum.

Read, S. J., & Urada, D. I. (2003). A neural network simulation of the outgroup homogeneity effect. *Personality and Social Psychology Review, 7*(2), 146–159.

Read, S. J., Vanman, E. J., & Miller, L. C. (1997). Connectionism, parallel constraint satisfaction processes, and gestalt principles: (Re) introducing cognitive dynamics to social psychology. *Personality and Social Psychology Review, 1*, 26–53.

Rescorla, R. A., & Wagner, A. R. (1972). A theory of Pavlovian conditioning: Variations in the effectiveness of reinforcement and non-reinforcement. In A. H. Black & W. F. Prokasy (Eds.), *Classical conditioning II: Current research and theory*. New York: Appleton-Century-Crofts.

Roseman, J. J. (2001). A model of appraisal in the emotion system: Integrating theory, research, and applications. In K. R. Scherer, A. Schorr, & T. Johnstone (Eds.), *Appraisal processes in emotion: Theory, methods, research* (pp. 68–91). Oxford, UK: Oxford University Press.

Rumelhart, D. E., & McClelland, J. L. (Eds.), (1986). *Parallel distributed processing: Explorations in the microstructure of cognition: Vol. 1: Foundations*. Cambridge, MA: MIT Press/Bradford.

Sahdra, B., & Thagard, P. (2003). Self-deception and emotional coherence. *Minds and Machines, 13*(2), 213–231.

Schank, R. C., & Abelson, R. P. (1977). *Scripts, plans, goals and understanding: An inquiry into human knowledge structures*. Hillsdale, NJ: Lawrence Erlbaum.

Scherer, K. R. (2001). Appraisal considered as a process of multilevel sequential checking. In K. R. Scherer, A. Schorr, & T. Johnstone (Eds.), *Appraisal processes in emotion: Theory, methods*, research (pp. 92–120). Oxford, UK: Oxford University Press.

Shanks, D. R. (1991). Categorization by a connectionist network. *Journal of Experimental Psychology: Learning, Memory, and Cognition, 17*, 433–443.

Shoda, Y., LeeTiernan, S., & Mischel, W. (2002). Personality as a dynamical system: Emergency of stability and distinctiveness from intra- and interpersonal interactions. *Personality and Social Psychology Review, 6*(4), 316–325.

Shultz, T. R., & Lepper, M. R. (1996). Cognitive dissonance reduction as constraint satisfaction. *Psychological Review, 103*(2), 219–240.

Shultz, T. R., & Lepper, M. R. (1998). The consonance model of dissonance reduction. In S. J. Read, & L. C. Miller (Eds.), *Connectionist models of social reasoning and social behavior* (pp. 211–244). Hillsdale, NJ: Erlbaum.

Shultz, T. R., Léveillé, E., & Lepper, M. R. (1999). Free choice and cognitive dissonance revisited: Choosing "lesser evils" versus "greater goods." *Personality and Social Psychology Bulletin, 25*(1), 40–48.

Smith, E. R. (1998). Category accessibility effects in a simulated exemplar-based memory. *Journal of experimental social psychology*, 24(5), 448–463.

Smith, E. R. (1991). Illusory correlation in a simulated exemplar-based memory. *Journal of Experimental Social Psychology*, 27(2), 107–123.

Smith, E. R., Coats, S., & Walling, D. (1999). Overlapping mental representations of self, in-group, and partner: Further response time evidence and a connectionist model. *Personality and Social Psychology Bulletin*, 25(7), 873–882.

Smith, E. R., & DeCoster, J. (1998). Knowledge acquisition, accessibility, and use in person perception and stereotyping: Simulation with a recurrent connectionist network. *Journal of Personality and Social Psychology*, 74(1), 21–35.

Sorrentino, R. M., Smithson, M., Hodson, G., Roney, C. J. R., & Walker, A. M. (2003). The theory of uncertainty orientation: A mathematical reformulation. *Journal of Mathematical Psychology*, 47(2), 132–149.

Spellman, B. A., Ullman, J. B., & Holyoak, K. J. (1993). A coherence model of cognitive consistency: Dynamics of attitude change during the Persian Gulf war. *Journal of Social Issues*, 49(4), 147–165.

Srull, T. K., & Wyer, R. S. (1979). The role of category accessibility in the interpretation of information about other people: Some determinants and implications. *Journal of Personality and Social Psychology*, 37, 1660–1672.

Stasser, G. (1988). Computer simulation as a research tool: The DISCUSS model of group decision making. *Journal of Experimental Social Psychology*, 24(5), 393–422.

Stasser, G., & Davis, J. H. (1981). Group decision making and social influence: A social interaction sequence model. *Psychological Review*, 88(6), 523–551.

Stasser, G., & Taylor, L. A. (1991). Speaking turns in face-to-face discussions. *Journal of Personality and Social Psychology*, 60(5), 675–684.

Stasser, G., & Titus, W. (1985). Pooling of unshared information in group decision making: Biased information sampling during discussion. *Journal of personality and social psychology*, 48(6), 1467–1478.

Stasser, G., & Vaughan, S. I. (1996). *Models of participation during face-to-face unstructured discussion*. In E. H. Witte & J. H. Davis (Eds.), Understanding group behavior, Vol.1: Con-

sensual action by small groups (pp. 165–192). Hillsdale, NJ: Lawrence Erlbaum.

Sun, R., Slusarz, P., & Terry, C. (2005). The interaction of the explicit and the implicit in skill learning: A dual-process approach. *Psychological Review*, 112, 159–192.

Thagard, P. (1989). Explanatory coherence. *Behavioral and Brain Sciences*, 12(3), 435–502.

Thagard, P. (2000). Probabilistic networks and explanatory coherence. *Cognitive Science Quarterly*, 1(1), 91–114.

Thagard, P. (2003). Why wasn't O. J. convicted: Emotional coherence in legal inference. *Cognition and Emotion*, 17, 361–383.

Thagard, P., & Nerb, J. (2002). Emotional gestalts: Appraisal, change and the dynamics of affect. *Personality and Social Psychology Review*, 6(4), 274–282.

Tomkins, S. S., & Messick, S. (Eds.). (1963). *Computer simulations of personality*. New York: Wiley.

Van Overwalle, F. (1998). Causal explanation as constraint satisfaction: A critique and a feedforward connectionist alternative. *Journal of Personality and Social Psychology*, 74, 312–328.

Van Overwalle, F., & Jordens, K. (2002). An adaptive connectionist model of cognitive dissonance. *Personality and Social Psychology Review*, 6(3), 204–231.

Van Overwalle, F., & Labiouse, C. (2004). A recurrent connectionist model of person impression formation. *Personality and Social Psychology Review*, 8(1), 28–61.

Van Overwalle, F., & Siebler, F. (2005). A connectionist model of attitude formation and change. *Personality and Social Psychology Review*, 9(3), 231–274.

Van Overwalle, F., & Van Rooy, D. (1998). A connectionist approach to causal attribution. In S. J. Read & L. C. Miller (Eds.), *Connectionist models of social reasoning and social behavior*. (pp. 143–171). Mahwah, NJ: Lawrence Erlbaum.

Van Overwalle, F., & Van Rooy, D. (2001). How one cause discounts or augments another: A connectionist account of causal competition. *Personality and Social Psychology Bulletin*, 27(12), 1613–1626.

Van Rooy, D., Van Overwalle, F., Vanhoomissen, T., Labiouse, C., & French, R. (2003). A recurrent connectionist model of group biases. *Psychological Review*, 110(3), 536–563.

Widrow, G., & Hoff, M. E. (1960). Adaptive switching circuits. *Institute of Radio Engineers*,

Western Electronic Show and Convention, Convention Record, Part 4, 96–104.

Wyer, R. S., & Srull, T. K. (1986). Human cognition in its social context. *Psychological Review*, 93, 322–359.

Zachary, W., LeMentec, J-C., Miller, L. C., Read, S. J., & Thomas-Meyers, G. (2005). Steps toward a Personality-based Architecture for Cognition. In *Proceedings of the Annual Conference on Behavioral Representation in Modeling and Simulation*, Los Angeles, CA.

Zachary, W., Le Mentec, J-C., Miller, L. C., Read, S. J., & Thomas-Meyers, G. (2005). Human behavioral representations with realistic personality and cultural characteristics. In *Pro-*

ceedings of the Tenth International Command and Control Research and Technology Symposium, McLean, VA.

Zebrowitz, L. A., Fellous, J., Mignault, A., & Andreoletti, C. (2003). Trait impressions as overgeneralized responses to adaptively significant facial qualities: Evidence from connectionist modeling. *Personality and Social Psychology Review*, 7(3), 194–215.

Zebrowitz, L. A., Kikuchi, M., & Fellous, J. (2005). *Trait impressions from emotion expression, facial resemblance to emotions, and facial maturity: Evidence from connectionist modeling.* Unpublished manuscript, Brandeis University.

CHAPTER 19

Cognitive Social Simulation

Ron Sun

1. Introduction

One feature of the current state of the social and behavioral sciences is the lack of integration and communication between cognitive and social disciplines. Each discipline considers a particular aspect and ignores (more or less) the rest. Consequently, they often talk past each other instead of to each other.

For instance, over the years, the notions of agent and agency have occupied a major role in defining research in the social and behavioral sciences. Computational models of agents have been developed. In cognitive science, they are often known as "cognitive architectures," that is, the overall, essential structure and process of cognition in the form of a broadly scoped, domain-generic computational cognitive model. They are often used for broad, cross-domain analysis of cognition and behavior (Newell, 1990; Sun, 2002). In particular, cognitive architectures provide a new avenue for specifying a range of cognitive processes together in tangible ways, although traditionally, the focus of research in cognitive science has been on specific components of cognition.[1] Computational cognitive modeling, especially with cognitive architectures, has become an essential area of research on cognition (Anderson & Lebiere, 1998; Sun, 2004). Such developments, however, need to be extended to issues of multiagent interaction. By and large, models of agents used in the social sciences have been extremely simple, not even remotely comparable to the work on cognitive architectures.[2]

---

1 A cognitive architecture provides a concrete framework for more detailed modeling of cognitive phenomena through specifying essential structures, divisions of modules, relations among modules, and a variety of other essential aspects (Sun, 2004). As discussed in Chapter 1, they help to narrow down possibilities, provide scaffolding structures, and embody fundamental theoretical assumptions. The value of cognitive architectures has been argued many times before; see, for example, Newell (1990), Anderson and Lebiere (1998), Sun (2002, 2004), and so on. See also Chapter 6 in this volume.
2 However, there have been some promising developments in this regard. See, for example, a number of recent articles in this area in the journal *Cognitive Systems Research* or the book *Cognition and Multi-Agent Interaction* (Sun, 2006a).

Two approaches dominate the traditional social sciences. The first approach may be termed the "deductive" approach (Axelrod, 1997; Moss, 1999), exemplified by much research in classical economics. It proceeds with the construction of mathematical models of social phenomena, usually expressed as a set of closed-form mathematical equations. Such models may be mathematically elegant. Deduction may be used to find consequences of assumptions in order to achieve better understanding of relevant phenomena. Their predictive power may also result from the analysis of various states (equilibria) through applying the equations.

The second approach may be termed the "inductive" approach, exemplified by many traditional approaches to sociology. With such an approach, insights are obtained by generating generalizations from (hopefully a large number of) observations. Insights are usually qualitative and describe social phenomena in terms of general categories and characterizations of these general categories.

However, a new approach has emerged relatively recently. It involves computational modeling and simulation of social phenomena. It starts with a set of assumptions (in the forms of rules, mechanisms, or processes). But unlike deduction, it does not prove theorems. Instead, simulations lead to data that can be analyzed inductively to come up with interesting generalizations. However, unlike typical induction in empirical social sciences, simulation data come from prespecified rules, mechanisms, and processes, not from direct measurements of social processes. With simulation data, both inductive and deductive methods may be applied: Induction can be used to find patterns in data, and deduction can be used to find consequences of assumptions (i.e., rules, mechanisms, and processes specified for simulations). Thus, simulations are useful as an aid to developing theories, in both directions and in their combinations thereof (Axelrod, 1997; Moss, 1999).

Within this third approach, a particularly interesting development is the focus on agent-based social simulations, that is, simulations based on autonomous individual entities. Naturally, such simulations focus on the interaction among agents. From their interactions, complex patterns may emerge. Thus, the interactions among agents provide explanations for corresponding social phenomena (Gilbert, 1995). Agent-based social simulations have seen tremendous growth in the past decade. Researchers hoping to go beyond the limitations of traditional approaches to the social sciences have increasingly turned to agents for studying a wide range of theoretical and practical issues (Conte, Hegselmann, & Terna, 1997; Epstein & Axtell, 1996; Gilbert & Conte, 1995; Gilbert & Doran, 1994; Moss & Davidsson, 2001; Prietula, Carley, & Gasser, 1998).

Axelrod (1984) was one of the first to use agent-based modeling and simulation in his study of evolution of cooperation. In this early work, computational simulations were used to study strategic behavior in the iterated prisoner's dilemma game. Even today, this work is still influencing research in various fields.

In the mid-1980s, a new area of research, artificial life, emerged. The idea was to simulate life to understand basic principles of life. This led to the application in social simulation of many interesting ideas, such as complexity, evolution, self-organization, and emergence. These ideas have significantly influenced social scientists in developing and conducting social simulations.

Recently, another topic area appeared, dealing with the study of the formation and the dynamics of social networks, that is, social structures (made of individuals or organizations) connected through social familiarities ranging from casual acquaintance to close familial bonds. To understand the spread of information as well as social beliefs, one has to consider the underlying social networks that influence those processes.

Issues addressed thus far by social simulation have been diverse. They include, for example, social beliefs, social norms, language evolution, resource allocation, traffic patterns, social cooperation, tribal customs, culture formation, stock market dynamics, group interaction and dynamics, organizational decision making, organization design, and countless others.

In all, agent-based social simulation is becoming an increasingly more important research methodology in the social sciences. It has become widely used to test theoretical models or to investigate their properties when analytical solutions are not possible. A simulation may even serve as a theory or an explanation of a social phenomenon by itself (Sun, 2005).

A particularly important advantage of social simulation is that it can provide support for "functionalist" explanations of social phenomena. For example, functionalists in the social sciences often argued that some specific forms of social structures were functional for society. However, functionalist explanations were viewed with suspicion in the social sciences because of the difficulty in verifying such explanations (Gilbert, 1995). The problem with functionalism in the social sciences is that it involves explaining a cause by its effect. Whereas it is customary to explain an effect by its cause, it seems post hoc to explain a cause by its effect. A related problem is that it tends to ignore historical processes in leading up to a specific social phenomenon, while focusing on a specific moment in history. Social simulation, however, can help to substantiate functionalist explanations by remedying both of these problems. First, social simulation focuses on processes, and thus it helps to provide some forms of historical perspectives in explaining social phenomena. For example, Cecconi and Parisi (1998) focused on the evolution of survival strategies in tribal societies. Similarly, Doran et al. (1994) provided explanations for the increasing complexity of tribal societies in the Upper Paleolithic period. Reynolds (1994) simulated the Sunay ritual of the llama herders in the Peruvian Andes and provided explanations for the emergence of the ritual. Second, the effect of a cause can be verified through experimentation with social simulation. Consequently, functionalist explanations can be better validated, and thus they become more convincing with the use of social simulation.

However, most of the work in social simulation assumes rudimentary cognition on the part of agents. There have been relatively few attempts to accurately capture human cognition (as argued in Sun, 2006a; Thagard, 1992). Agent models have frequently been custom tailored to the task at hand, often amounting to little more than a restricted set of highly domain-specific rules. Although this approach may be adequate for achieving the limited objectives of some social simulations, it is overall unsatisfactory. It not only limits the realism, and hence applicability of social simulation, but also precludes any possibility of resolving the theoretical question of the micro-macro link (Alexander et al., 1987; Castelfranchi, 2001; Sawyer, 2003). At the same time, researchers in cognitive science, although studying individual cognition in depth, have paid relatively little attention to social phenomena (with some notable exceptions, of course). The separation of the two fields can be seen (1) in the different journals dedicated to the two fields (e.g., *Journal of Artificial Society and Social Simulation* and *Computational and Mathematical Organization Theory* for social simulation, vs. *Cognitive Science* and *Cognitive Systems Research* for cognitive modeling); (2) in the different conferences for these two different fields (e.g., *the International Conference on Social Simulation* vs. *the International Conference on Cognitive Modeling*); (3) in the different professional organizations (e.g., *the North American Association for Computational Social and Organizational Science* and *the European Social Simulation Association* vs. *the Cognitive Science Society*); and (4) in the scant overlap of authors in these two fields. Moreover, most of the commonly used social simulation tools (e.g., *Swarm* and *RePast*) embody simplistic agent models, not even remotely comparable to what has been developed within the field of cognitive architectures (e.g., Anderson & Lebiere, 1998, and Sun, 2002; although there have been simulation tools with more complex agent models).

Nevertheless, there are reasons to believe that investigation, modeling, and simulation of social phenomena need cognitive science (Sun, 2001) because such endeavors need a better understanding, and better models, of individual cognition, only on the basis of which it can develop better models of aggregate processes through multiagent interaction. Cognitive models may provide better grounding for understanding multiagent interaction by incorporating realistic constraints, capabilities, and tendencies of individual agents in terms of their cognitive processes (and maybe even in terms of their physical embodiment) in their interaction with their environments (which include both physical and social environments). This point was argued at length in Sun (2001). This point has also been made, for example, in the context of cognitive realism of game theory (Camerer, 1997; Kahan & Rapaport, 1984), in the context of deeper models for addressing human-computer interaction (Gray & Altmann, 2001), or in the context of understanding social networks from a cognitive perspective (Krackhardt, 1987; Mason, Conrey, & Smith, in press). Related to this, Mithen (1996), Zerubavel (1997), Turner (2000), Rizzello and Turvani (2000), Boyer and Ramble (2001), Atran and Norenzayan (2004), Andersen, Barker, and Chen (2006), Kim, Lodge, and Tabor (2007), and others also explored the cognitive basis of social, political, and cultural processes and representations. Although some cognitive details may ultimately prove to be irrelevant, they cannot be determined a priori, and thus modeling may be useful in determining which aspects of cognition can be safely abstracted away.

Conversely, cognitive science also needs social simulation and the social sciences in general. Cognitive science is very much in need of new theoretical frameworks and new conceptual tools, especially for analyzing sociocultural aspects of cognition (e.g., Nisbett et al., 2001; Vygotsky, 1962) and cognitive processes involved in multiagent interaction (e.g., Andersen & Chen, 2002). It needs computational models and theories from multiagent work (in artificial intelligence and in social simulation), and also broader conceptual frameworks that can be found in sociological and anthropological work (as well as in social psychology to some extent). In particular, cognitive modeling, as a field, can be enriched through the incorporation of these disparate strands of ideas.

Although, generally speaking, computational modeling is often limited to within a particular "level" at a time (inter-agent, agent, intra-agent, etc.), this need not be the case: As discussed earlier in Chapter 1, cross-level analysis and modeling, such as combining cognitive modeling and social simulation, could be intellectually enlightening and might even be essential to the progress of this field (Sun & Naveh, 2004). These "levels" do interact with each other (e.g., by constraining each other) and may not be easily isolated and tackled alone. Moreover, their respective territories are often intermingled, without clear-cut boundaries. One may start with purely social descriptions but then substitute cognitive principles and cognitive processing details for simpler descriptions of agents (examples of such substitution will be described later). Thus, the differences and the separations among "levels" should be viewed as rather fluid.

It should be noted that, within a multi-"level" framework, Sun, Coward and Zenzen (2005) provided detailed arguments for crossing and mixing levels: the social, the psychological, and so on. Hence, the case for the integration of social simulation with cognitive modeling was presented there (which opened the way for a more detailed discussion of integrating social simulation and cognitive modeling in Sun, 2006a; see also Helmhout, 2006). Sun et al. (2005) also argued for the role of computational modeling and simulation in understanding the social-cognitive interaction, especially the role of complex computational social simulation with realistic cognitive models (i.e., cognitive social simulation), utilizing cognitive architectures in particular. The argument based on *complexity* and *expressive power* of computational models did the bulk of the work in this regard (Sun et al., 2005).

In the remainder of this chapter, three representative examples of cognitive social simulation are presented. Then, a more general discussion of types, issues, and directions of cognitive social simulation follows. Finally, a summary completes this chapter.

2. Examples of Cognitive Social Simulation

Below, let us look into a few representative examples of the kind of social simulation that takes cognition of individual agents into consideration seriously. These examples are drawn from West and Lebiere (2001), West, Lebiere, and Bothell (2006), Sun and Naveh (2004), Naveh and Sun (2006), Sun and Naveh (2007), and Clancey et al. (2006). The reader is referred to Sun (2006a) for further examples.

2.1. *A Cognitive Simulation of Games*

Game-theoretical interaction is an excellent domain for researching multiagent interactions. Although it is customary to use game theory (von Neumann & Morgenstern, 1944) to calculate optimal strategies for various games, as described in West and Lebiere (2001) and West et al. (2006), human players often do not play according to optimal game theoretical strategies. According to West and Lebiere (2001) and West et al. (2006), human players can be understood in terms of how they deviate from optimal strategies. They explored this approach for understanding human game-playing behavior and presented a different perspective based on cognitive modeling.

They found that human players did not use a fixed way of responding. Instead, they attempted to adjust their responses to exploit perceived weaknesses in their opponents' way of playing. West et al. (2006) argued that humans had evolved to be such players rather than the optimal players. Furthermore, they argued that evolution had evolved the human cognitive system to support a superior ability to operate as such a player.

The use of cognitive architectures addresses the need to unify various subfields of psychology by providing computational accounts of the findings of specialized areas in an integrated architecture of cognition (Sun, 2004; see also Chapter 6 in this volume). Cognitive architectures specify, often in considerable computational detail, the mechanisms underlying cognition (Sun, 2004). One of them, ACT-R (Anderson & Lebiere, 1998), is a cognitive architecture that has accounted for hundreds of phenomena from the cognitive psychology and the human factors literature. In West and Lebiere (2001) and West et al. (2006), it was used to explain human game-playing behavior.

Applying ACT-R to game playing, West et al. (2006) created a cognitive model of how people play games and then compared it with the behavior of human players. Although providing qualitative rather than definitive answers, this approach has led to interesting insights.

One issue is that the standard game theory requires that players be able to select moves randomly in accordance with preset probabilities. However, research has repeatedly shown that people are very poor at doing this (see, e.g., Wagenaar, 1972, for a review), suggesting that the evolutionary success of humans is not based on this ability. Instead of trying to learn advantageous move probabilities, people try to detect sequential dependencies in the opponent's play and use this information to predict the opponent's moves (West & Lebiere, 2001; West et al., 2006). This is consistent with a large amount of psychological research showing that when sequential dependencies exist, people can detect and exploit them (e.g., Anderson, 1960; Estes, 1972). It also explains why people tend to do poorly on tasks that are truly random – because they persist in trying to predict the outcomes, even though it leads to suboptimal results (e.g., Gazzaniga, 1998; Ward, 1973).

West and Lebiere (2001) and West et al. (2006) examined this process using ACT-R designed to detect sequential dependencies in the game of Paper, Rock, Scissors. The inputs were the opponent's moves at previous lags, and the outputs were the moves the player would make on the current play.

As ACT-R gained experience in a task, the parameter values were adjusted to reflect a rational adaptation to the task.[3]

Using the ACT-R model, West et al. (2006) found four interesting results (regarding the model): (1) the interaction between two agents of this type produced chaos-like behavior, and this was the primary source of randomness; (2) the sequential dependencies that were produced by this process were temporary and short lived; (3) processing more lags created an advantage; (4) treating ties as losses (i.e., punishing the system for ties) created an advantage.

West et al. (2006) also tested human subjects and found that they played similarly to a lag two network that was punished for ties. That is, people were able to predict their opponents' moves by using information from the previous two moves, and people treated ties as losses. Although both the ACT-R model and game theory predicted that people would play Paper, Rock, Scissors with equal frequency, the ACT-R model predicted that people would be able to beat a lag one network that was punished for ties and a lag two network that was not punished for ties, whereas game theory predicted they would tie with these opponents. The results showed that people were reliably able to beat these opponents, demonstrating that game theory could not account for all the results.

The model described above was based directly on the ACT-R architecture and therefore represented a strong prediction about the way people detected sequential dependencies. The simulation results did not depend on parameter tweaking. All parameters relevant for this model were set at the default values found to work in other ACT-R models. Simulations and testing with human subjects confirmed that the model could account for the human performance in Paper,

Rock, Scissors (West & Lebiere, 2001; West et al., 2006). This was significant because the aspects of the architecture that were used were developed to model the human declarative memory system, not the specific ability to play games. It suggests that the evolutionary processes that shaped declarative memory may have been influenced by competition (in the game theory sense), for example, for resources and mating privileges. It also indicates design efficiency, as it suggests that humans use the same system for competition as they do for learning facts about the world.

West et al. (2006) argued, based on the evolutionary success of humans, that the way with which people played games likely constituted a good general-purpose design. To test this, the ACT-R model was entered in the 1999 International RoShamBo Programming Competition. Overall, the model placed thirteenth out of fifty-five entries in the round-robin competition (with scores calculated based on margin of victory across games, e.g., plus five for winning by five and minus five for losing by five). In the open event, where the ACT-R model faced all the models, ACT-R placed fifteenth in terms of margin of victory and ninth in terms of wins and losses. That is, the ACT-R model, with no modifications, was able to beat most of the other models. This result demonstrated the power of cognitively based social simulation (Sun, 2006a).

2.2. A Cognitive Simulation of Organizations

As described in Sun and Naveh (2004), a simulation of simple organizations was conducted based on the CLARION cognitive architecture (see Chapter 6 in this volume), which helped to shed light on the role of cognition in organizations and the interaction between cognitive factors and organizational structures.

A typical task faced by organizations is classification decision making. In a classification task, agents gather information about problems, classify them, and then make further decisions based on the classification. In

---

3 Using this approach, characteristics of human cognition previously thought of as shortcomings could actually be viewed as optimal adaptations to the environment. For example, forgetting provides a graceful way of addressing the fact that the relevance of information decreases with time (Andersion & Lebiere, 1998).

Table 19.1: Human and simulation data for the organizational task from Carley et al. (1998)

Agent	Team (B)	Team (D)	Hierarchy (B)	Hierarchy (D)
Human	50.0	56.7	46.7	55.0
Radar-Soar	73.3	63.3	63.3	53.3
CORP-P-ELM	78.3	71.7	40.0	36.7
CORP-ELM	88.3	85.0	45.0	50.0
CORP-SOP	81.7	85.0	81.7	85.0

D indicates distributed information access; B indicates blocked information access. All numbers are percent correct.

this case, the task is to determine whether a blip on a screen is a hostile aircraft, a flock of geese, or a civilian aircraft. It has been used extensively before in studying organizational design (e.g., Carley, Prietula, & Lin, 1998).

In each case, there is a single object in the air space. The object has nine different attributes, each of which can take on one of three possible values (e.g., its speed can be low, medium, or high). An organization must determine the status of an observed object: whether it is friendly, neutral, or hostile. There are a total of 19,683 possible objects, and 100 problems are chosen randomly (without replacement) from this set.

No one single agent has access to all the information necessary to make a choice. Decisions are made by integrating separate decisions made by different agents, each of which is based on a different subset of information.

In terms of organizational structures, there are two major types of interest: (1) teams, in which decision makers act autonomously, individual decisions are treated as votes, and the organization decision is the majority decision; and (2) hierarchies, which are characterized by agents organized in a chain of command, such that information is passed from subordinates to superiors, and the decision of a superior is based solely on the recommendations of his or her subordinates. In this task, only a two-level hierarchy with nine subordinates and one supervisor is considered.

In addition, organizations are distinguished by the structure of information accessible to each agent. There are two types of information access: (1) distributed access, in which each agent sees a different subset of three attributes (no two agents see the same subset of three attributes); and (2) blocked access, in which three agents see exactly the same subset of attributes. In both cases, each attribute is accessible to three agents.

The human experiments by Carley et al. (1998) were done in a 2×2 fashion (organization $\times$ information access). In addition, the human data from the experiments were compared with the results of the four agent-based models: CORP-SOP, CORP-ELM, CORP-P-ELM, and Radar-Soar.[4] The human data and the simulation results from this study (Carley et al. 1998) are shown in Table 19.1.

The data showed that humans generally performed better in team situations, especially when distributed information access was in place. Moreover, distributed information access was generally better than blocked

---

4 Among them, CORP-ELM produced the most probable classification (based on an agent's own experience), CORP-P-ELM stochastically produced a classification in accordance with the estimate of the probability of each classification (based on the agent's own experience), CORP-SOP followed the organizationally prescribed standard operating procedure (which involved summing up the values of the attributes available to an agent) and thus was not adaptive, and Radar-Soar was a somewhat cognitive model built in Soar, which was based on explicit, elaborate search in problem spaces. See Carley et al. (1998) for details of the models.

Table 19.2: Simulation data for CLARION running for 3,000 cycles

Agent	Team (B)	Team (D)	Hierarchy (B)	Hierarchy (D)
Human	50.0	56.7	46.7	55.0
CLARION	53.2	59.3	45.0	49.4

The human data from Carley et al. (1998) are reproduced here for ease of comparison. Performance for CLARION is computed as percent correct over the last 1,000 cycles.

information access. The worst performance occurred when hierarchical organizational structure and blocked information access were used in conjunction.

From the point of view of matching human performance, the agent models used were simplistic. The "intelligence" level in these models was rather low (including, to a large extent, the Soar model, which essentially encoded a set of simple rules). Moreover, learning in these simulations was rudimentary: There was no complex learning process as one might observe in humans. With these shortcomings in mind, it seemed worthwhile to undertake a simulation that involved more comprehensive agent models that more accurately captured human performance. Moreover, with the use of more cognitively realistic agent models, one might investigate individually the importance of different cognitive capacities and process details in affecting the overall organizational performance. With cognitive architectures, one could easily vary parameters that corresponded to different cognitive capacities and test the resulting performance.

The CLARION cognitive architecture is intended for capturing all the essential cognitive processes (as broadly defined) within an individual cognitive agent (Sun, 2002, 2003; Sun et al., 2005). CLARION consists of a number of distinct subsystems, with a dual representational structure in each subsystem (implicit vs. explicit representations). Its subsystems include the action-centered subsystem, the non-action-centered subsystem, the motivational subsystem, and the meta-cognitive subsystem. The role of the action-centered subsystem is to control actions, regardless of whether the actions are for external physical movements or internal mental operations. The role of the non-action-centered subsystem is to maintain general knowledge, either implicit or explicit. The role of the motivational subsystem is to provide underlying motivations for perception, action, and cognition, in terms of providing impetus and feedback (e.g., indicating whether outcomes are satisfactory or not). The role of the meta-cognitive subsystem is to monitor, direct, and modify the operations of the action-centered subsystem dynamically as well as the operations of all the other subsystems. Each of these interacting subsystems consists of two levels of representation (i.e., a dual representational structure): The top level encodes explicit knowledge, and the bottom level encodes implicit knowledge (this implicit-explicit distinction has been amply argued for before; see Reber, 1989; Seger, 1994; Sun, 2002). The explicit knowledge at the top level is implemented with symbolic representations, whereas the implicit knowledge at the bottom level is implemented with distributed connectionist representations. Hence, it is a hybrid symbolic-connectionist architecture (Sun, 2002, 2003). A variety of parameters exist that control, for example, learning rate, generalization threshold, probability of using implicit versus explicit processing (i.e., using the bottom level vs. the top level), and so on (see Sun 2002, 2003, for details).

The results of the CLARION simulations, with 3,000 training cycles for each group, are shown in Table 19.2. As can be seen, the results closely accord with the patterns of the human data, with teams outperforming hierarchal structures and distributed access being superior to blocked access. Also, as in humans, performance is not grossly skewed toward one condition or the other, unlike some of the simulation results from Carley et al. (1998) shown earlier. The match with the human data is far better than the previous simulations, which shows, at least in part, the advantage of cognitively based social simulation (Sun, 2006a).

Next, there is the question of what happens when cognitive parameters are varied. Addressing this question would allow us to see the variability of results and thus avoid overgeneralization. Because CLARION captures a wide range of cognitive processes, its parameters are generic (rather than task specific). Thus, one has the opportunity of studying social and organizational issues in the context of a general theory of cognition.

An ANOVA (analysis of variance) on the results of the experiments confirmed the significance of the effects of organization and information access. Moreover, the interaction of these two factors with length of training was also significant. These interactions reflected the following trends: the superiority of team and distributed information access at the start of the learning process, and either the disappearance or reversal of these trends toward the end. The finding from ANOVA showed that these trends persisted robustly across a wide variety of settings of cognitive parameters and did not critically depend on any one setting of these parameters.

The effect of probability of using implicit versus explicit processing was likewise significant. More interestingly, however, its interaction with length of training was significant as well. Explicit rule learning was far more useful at the early stages of learning, when increased reliance on them tended to boost performance, than toward the end of the learning process. This is because explicit rules are crisp guidelines that are based on past success, and as such, they provide a useful anchor at the uncertain early stages of learning. However, by the end of the

learning process, they become no more reliable than highly trained networks. This corresponds to findings in human cognition, where there are indications that rule-based learning is more widely used in the early stages of learning, but is later increasingly supplanted by similarity-based processes and skilled performance. Such trends may partially explain why hierarchies did not perform well initially: Because a hierarchy's supervisor was burdened with a higher input dimensionality, it took a longer time to encode rules (which were nevertheless essential at the early stages of learning).

Predictably, the effect of learning rate was significant according to ANOVA. Those groups with a higher learning rate outperformed the groups with a lower learning rate. However, there was no significant interaction between learning rate and organization or information access. This suggests that quicker learners did not differentially benefit, say, a hierarchy versus a team. By the same token, the poorer performance of slower learners could not be mitigated by recourse to a particular combination of organization and information access.

ANOVA confirmed the significance of the effect of generalization threshold. Generalization threshold determines how readily an agent generalizes a successful rule. It was better to have a higher rule generalization threshold than a lower one (up to a point). That is, if one restricts the generalization of rules to those rules that have proven relatively successful (by selecting a fairly high generalization threshold), the result is a higher-quality rule set, which leads to better performance in the long run.

This simulation showed that some cognitive parameters (e.g., learning rate) had a monolithic, across-the-board effect under all conditions, whereas in other cases, complex interactions of factors were at work. See Sun and Naveh (2004) for the full details of the analysis. This illustrates the importance of limiting one's social simulation conclusions to the specific cognitive context in which human data were obtained (in contrast to the practice of some existing social simulations).

In sum, by using CLARION, Sun and Naveh (2004) have been able to more accurately capture organizational performance data and, moreover, to formulate deeper explanations for the results observed (see Sun and Naveh, 2004, for details of this aspect). In CLARION, one can vary parameters and options that correspond to cognitive processes and test their effects on collective performance. In this way, CLARION may be used to predict human performance in social/organizational settings and, furthermore, to help to improve collective performance by prescribing optimal or near-optimal cognitive abilities for individuals for specific collective tasks and/or organizational structures (Sun & Naveh, 2004).

2.3. A Cognitive Simulation of Group Interaction

As described by Clancey et al. (2006), group activities may be understood and captured through cognitive modeling of individuals involved. To integrate cognitive modeling with social studies (which stress how relationships and informal practices drive behavior), Clancey et al. believe that it requires a shift from modeling goals and tasks to modeling behavioral patterns as agents are engaged in purposeful activities. According to Clancey et al. instead of exclusively deducing actions from goals, behaviors are primarily driven by broader patterns of chronological and spatially located activities (see also Sun, 2002). In a way, conceptualization of activities drives behavior, which includes how knowledge is called into play and applied. How problems are discovered and framed, what methods are called into play, and who cares or has the authority to act are constrained by norms, which are conceived and enacted by individuals. Norms are reinforced through their reproduction, but also adapted and even purposefully violated.

The goal of Clancey et al. (2006) was to understand this social notion of activity (Lave, 1988; Suchman, 1987) and to ground it in a cognitive architecture. To illustrate these ideas, they conducted a simulation of the Flashline Mars Arctic Research Station, in which a crew of six people lived and worked. Here the focus is on one part – the simulation of a planning meeting. How people behave during the meeting (e.g., standing at the table) exemplifies the nature of norms and is modeled at the individual agent level. The simulation showed how physiological constraints (e.g., hunger and fatigue), facilities (e.g., the habitat's layout), and group decision making interacted. This approach to the simulation focuses on modeling the context in which behavior occurs and how it unfolds over time through the interaction of people, places, and tools. Such a simulation model of practice is a useful complement to task analysis and (knowledge-based) modeling of reasoning.[5]

Often, a cognitive model is of an individual's knowledge and reasoning, organized around problem-solving goals. In contrast, an activity model is a kind of cognitive model organized around activities (i.e., what people do, when, and where), with conditional actions called workframes (Clancey et al., 2006), which specify subactivities or primitive actions (e.g., moving and communicating). An activity model uses familiar cognitive constructs, but relates and uses them in a different way:

- Activities are conceptualizations of what an agent is doing (e.g., participating in a planning meeting).
- Activities are activated hierarchically in parallel (e.g., while participating in a planning meeting, an individual is also living in the mars habitat, as well as being a computer scientist).
- Workframes for each activity remain potentially active, such that interruptions may occur at higher levels to redirect attention (as in a subsumption architecture; Brooks, 1991).
- Perception is modeled by "detectables" associated with workframe actions. Thus, what an agent notices in the environment

---

5 It may also have potential practical applications for work system design, operations management, and training (Clancey et al., 2006).

and how it is interpreted may depend on the agent's current activity.

- The conditional part of a workframe matches the agent's beliefs. A belief is not necessarily a conscious proposition. Agents may infer new beliefs through forward reasoning (called "thoughtframes"). Agents may also receive new beliefs through communication with another agent or by reading them from objects (e.g., documents, displays, etc.).

Thus, the simulation of the planning meeting is a type of cognitive model, although the model contains no examples of goal-directed reasoning. Developing the model in this way was an experiment to determine to what extent purposeful, interactive behavior of a group could be simulated based on conditional activity patterns.

Clancey et al. (2006) found that focusing on the agents' activities and interactions with objects provided significant challenges. They focused on postures (to understand what constrained them and what they conveyed), coordination of multiagent activity (e.g., how individual agents transitioned into a group activity), and biological motives (e.g., hunger and fatigue). With this perspective, they uncovered interesting issues that shed a different light on what cognition accomplished and how perception and action were related through conceptualization of activity, without modeling discourse, planning, and goal-directed inference.

The topics of a planning meeting, such as discussing the weather and reviewing the habitat's power or water systems, were modeled as a sequence of events, with fixed temporal durations. Even within such a restricted framework, individual agents could opportunistically change the topic (a subactivity) of the meeting or carry out a given subactivity in a way that changed what other agents were doing. For example, if there was a fire alarm, the meeting would be interrupted, and the activity of dealing with the fire would begin. This flexibility resulted from the combination of detectables, thoughtframes, communications, inheritance of activities through group membership, and the mechanism for interrupting and resuming activities (i.e., the subsumption architecture).

Social analyses have suggested (e.g., Wenger, 1998) that activity conceptualizations involve dynamic blending of identities. For example, crew members are always improvising their roles, as seen through their prior conceptualizations (e.g., being a scientist on an expedition, being a NASA representative, and so on). In some ways, in the model, the interleaving of actions in different parallel activity conceptualizations captured this blending.

In the model, Clancey et al. (2006) included biological drivers of behavior, such as fatigue, hunger, and the need to use the bathroom. The activity model revealed that how people accomplished tasks within an activity was affected by biological concerns (e.g., interrupting work to put on a sweater). Biological needs were modeled in a simple way. Each factor was represented by a single parameter (physical energy, hunger, urine in the bladder) that accumulated over time and was reset by a compensating action (rest, eating, elimination). Relatedly, activities such as eating were interleaved with group activities (such as the planning meeting), and how they were carried out reflected the group's norms.

It was found that behavior might be determined by many physiological, personal, social, and environmental functions at the same time, and these did not need to be articulated by the person (Sun, 2006b). Although a goal-based analysis tended to ascribe a single purpose to an action, a broad analysis of a day-in-the-life of the crew showed that all human activity was purposeful, but not every activity accomplished a task (i.e., the work of the crew), nor could it be easily assigned to a single goal (i.e., a conscious proposition). This followed especially from the fact that multiple activities on different levels were affecting behavior by inhibiting, enabling, or blending actions.

Obviously, when the crew discussed what to do on a particular day, they were clearly engaged in goal articulation and planning. However, what was revealing was how much else was occurring that was modulated by perception of the environment and each other, physiological needs, and relationships, and could be modeled in the simulation without reasoning about goals and plans of action. Conventional goal/task analysis is a descriptive abstraction of human behavior imposed by an observer. Goal/task analysis has implied that every action has a direct goal as its cause. In contrast, the simulation represented a nesting of activities, each of which had many implicit goal structures, so any behavior might make sense from multiple perspectives. Clancey et al. (2006) concluded that it was highly problematic (if not theoretically impossible) to explain by goals the actions that had not been deliberately planned. Instead, in the activity model, the context in which the action occurred was explored, and an attempt was made to descriptively capture all movements, sequences, and communications (cf. Sun, 2002).

In short, by modeling how individual agents carried out a group activity as conditional actions organized into activity conceptualizations, Clancey et al. (2006) explored how collective (social) behavior related to individual cognition (in a broad sense, involving perception, motives, and actions). The simulation of a planning meeting, with realistic timing, involved integrating diverse information (topography, agent beliefs, posture, meeting structure, etc.). Recognizing in this way how norms were manifested, violated, adapted, and so on, in a cognitively based way, may lead to better and broader understanding of group interactions.

3. Types, Issues, and Directions of Cognitive Social Simulation

3.1. *Dimensions of Cognitive Social Simulation*

Given the preceding examples of different types of cognitive social simulation, let us look into some possible dimensions for categorizing cognitive social simulation. We have discussed embedding cognitive agents in social simulation, and at the heart of this approach lies the conceptions of how *agents* should be modeled in simulations. Therefore, we need to compare different ways of representing agents in social simulation.

The first approach, the equation-based approach, involves abstracting the agents away altogether. Agents in such simulations are not explicitly represented as part of the model, and their role is only indirectly captured by equations. A second approach involves representing agents as autonomous computational entities. Such an approach may lack the elegance of an equation-based approach, but its greater accessibility allows it to be evaluated by a wider range of researchers. Moreover, using such agents enables, in many cases, a more detailed representation of target phenomena.

However, simulations vary widely in the level of detail of their agents, ranging from very simple models, such as those used in some early simulations of the prisoner's dilemma (Axelrod, 1984) to more detailed cognitive models, such as ACT-R (Anderson & Lebiere, 1998) or CLARION (Sun, 2002).

Agents in simulations can be further distinguished based on their computational complexity (as expressed by computer scientists by using "Big-O" and other similar measures). Such measures have important implications with respect to a model's scalability, because they determine whether its running time and memory requirements vary linearly, polynomially, or exponentially with the size of its input.

Simulations also differ in the degree of rationality imputed to their agents. Some simulations (for instance, in traditional economics) assume perfectly rational agents, whereas others consist of boundedly rational agents that aim merely for satisficing solutions, rather than optimal ones.

More importantly, simulations differ in terms of their cognitive realism (and amount of cognitive details). Social simulation models can be completely noncognitive by using, for example, a finite-state automaton for modeling an individual agent (Axelrod, 1984). Social simulation models can also be completely "cognitive" by using well-developed cognitive architectures, such as CLARION (Schreiber, 2004; Sun, 2006b; Sun & Naveh, 2004, 2007). In between, there can be models that include more cognitive details than a finite-state machine but fewer details than a typical cognitive architecture (e.g., Burns & Roszkowska, 2006; Carley & Newell, 1994; Clancey et al., 2006; Goldspink, 2000).

The distinctions above lead us to a set of dimensions for classifying simulations according to their representation of agents. These dimensions include, first, whether or not a model is agent based; second, the granularity, or detailedness, of the model; third, the model's computational complexity; fourth, whether rationality is bounded or unbounded in the model; and fifth, the degree of cognitive realism in the model (including its emotional, motivational, and meta-cognitive aspects). In actuality, these dimensions may be correlated to some extent, but they should be separately evaluated nevertheless, for us to gain a better understanding of the relative position of a model with regard to other existing or potential models. In particular, the final dimension above is seldom used in the evaluation of simulations, but it is important, for reasons mentioned earlier (see also Naveh & Sun, 2006; Sun & Naveh, 2004).

By referring to this classificatory system, one can arrive at sets of limitations common to certain classes of simulations. For instance, using the dimensions discussed, one can categorize the afore-described CLARION simulation of organizations (Sun & Naveh, 2004) as an agent-based simulation, reasonably detailed, computationally complex, boundedly rational, and cognitively realistic. This simulation therefore inherits the limitations associated with each of these five characteristics. Thus, as a high-granularity model, CLARION can make it hard to disentangle the respective contributions of different factors to the results of simulations. Likewise, its relatively high computational complexity can raise issues of scalability. Bounded rationality may hinder the ability to generalize from the results of simulations (Ahlert, 2003). Finally, the choice of a cognitively realistic agent model may itself rest on particular ontological conceptions of the target phenomenon, and thus the CLARION cognitive architecture may not be appropriate for all simulations. For another instance, the ACT-R simulation described earlier (West & Lebiere, 2001; West et al., 2006) is also agent based. However, it is slightly less detailed, boundedly rational, and somewhat cognitively realistic (although it does not cover some cognitive factors; see Sun, 2006b). Its computational complexity is also somewhat high.

Some of the other, additional dimensions that are also relevant here include: level of noncognitive details (as opposed to level of cognitive details), type of interactivity, number of agents involved in a simulation, and so on. Let us look into these additional dimensions.

Evidently, the dimension of level of details (mentioned earlier) may be subdivided into two subdimensions: level of cognitive details and level of noncognitive details. The dimension of cognitive realism mentioned before essentially determines level of cognitive details: High levels of cognitive realism necessarily entail high levels of cognitive details (including emotional, motivational, and metacognitive details; Sun, 2006b). However, level of noncognitive details can be varied more independently. In terms of level of noncognitive details, one may include in a model only highly abstract social scenarios, for example, as described by game theory (e.g., West et al., 2006), or one may include a lot more details of the scenarios, as captured in ethnographical studies (e.g., Clancey et al., 2006).

In terms of interactivity, there can be the following different types (among others): no interactions; indirect interactions, such as in simple game theoretical situations (e.g., West & Lebiere, 2001, West et al., 2006); restricted interactions, such as in some organizational simulations (e.g., Carley et al., 1998, Sun & Naveh, 2004); and direct interactions, such as in some very detailed ethnographical simulations (e.g., Clancey et al., 2006).

Number of agents involved in a simulation is also a relevant dimension. The more agents there are in a simulation, the more difficult it is to conduct the simulation. This factor affects choices in other dimensions: For example, when a large number of agents are required in a simulation, the level of cognitive and noncognitive details may have to be low somehow.

3.2. Issues in Cognitive Social Simulation

Next, let us examine a few important issues in cognitive social simulation. First, whether or not to use detailed cognitive models in social simulation is a decision that should be made on a case-by-case basis. There are many reasons for using or not using cognitive models in social simulation. The reasons for using detailed cognitive models include: (1) the fact that cognitive realism in social simulation may lead to models that more accurately capture human data; (2) the fact that with cognitive realism, one will be able to formulate deeper explanations for results observed by basing explanations on cognitive factors rather than somewhat arbitrary assumptions; and (3) the fact that with detailed cognitive models, one can vary parameters that correspond to cognitive processes and test their effects on performance, and in this way, simulations may be used to predict performance based on cognitive factors or to improve performance by prescribing optimal (or near-optimal) cognitive abilities for specific tasks.

On the other hand, the reasons for not using detailed cognitive models in social simulation include: (1) the fact that it is sometimes possible to describe causal relationships at higher levels without referring to relationships at lower levels (Goldstone & Janssen, 2005); (2) the issue of complexity, which can make it difficult to interpret results of complex cognitively based social simulations in terms of their precise contributing factors; and (3) the fact that complexity also leads to longer running times

and hence raises issues of scalability (as discussed earlier).

Another issue facing cognitive social simulation is the validation of simulation results, including the validation of cognitive models as part of social simulation models. It is well known that validation of complex simulation models is extremely difficult (Axtell, Axelrod, & Cohen, 1996; Moss, 2006; Pew & Mavor, 1998; Sun, 2005). Full validation of models, especially when detailed cognitive models (e.g., cognitive architectures) are used, is clearly not possible currently (due to, among other things, complexity). However, in this regard, adopting existing cognitive models as part of a cognitive social simulation may be beneficial. If one adopts a well-established cognitive model (a cognitive architecture in particular), the prior validation of that cognitive model, to whatever extent it may exist, may be leveraged in validating the overall simulation results. Therefore, there is a significant advantage in adopting an existing cognitive model, especially an existing cognitive architecture (Anderson & Lebiere, 1998; Sun, 2002). However, even when existing cognitive architectures are adopted, validation of cognitive social simulation models is still a difficult task, due to complexity and other issues.

Yet another issue facing cognitive social simulation is the relationship between simulation and theory: Can a simulation constitute a theory of cognitive-social processes? Or does it merely represent some experimentation in data generation (see Sun, 2005; van Fraasen, 2002)? One viewpoint is that computational modeling and simulation, including those based on cognitive architectures, should not be taken as theories. According to this view, a simulation is a generator of data and phenomena: Although simulation is important for building cognitive-social theories (e.g., through testing theories), it is not a theory by itself (cf. Axtell et al., 1996; Gilbert, 1995). However, there is a rather different position based roughly on the idea that a model may be a theory (Newell, 1990), which may serve well as a meta-theoretical foundation for computational cognitive social simulation (cf. van Fraasen, 2002). According to this view, a computational simulation (and the model thereof) is a formal description of a relevant phenomenon and may thus be a theory of the phenomenon. The language of a model is, by itself, a distinct symbol system for formulating a theory (Newell, 1990). See Chapter 1 in this volume for a further discussion of this issue (see also Sun, 2005).

3.3. *Directions of Cognitive Social Simulation*

There are a number of interesting research directions involving combining cognitive modeling and social simulation that are currently being actively pursued. It is possible that these research directions may lead to some significant advances in understanding social and cognitive processes and their interactions.

Some work has been done in extending existing formal frameworks of agent interaction in order to take into consideration cognitive processes more realistically. For instance, there have been various modifications of, and extensions to, game theory in the direction of enhanced cognitive realism so as to better address psychological and/or sociological issues. West and Lebiere (2001) and West et al. (2006) modeled game-theoretical situations using a cognitive architecture to supplement existing formal descriptions. Burns and Roszkowska (2006) extended standard game-theoretical constructs significantly to include various social and cognitive factors in the description of social interactions.

A variety of modeling work has been done on group and/or organizational dynamics on the basis of cognitive models, which may be useful for understanding or even designing organizational structures for improving organizational performance in various situations. Carley and associates have worked extensively on this topic (see, e.g., Carley et al., 1998). They occasionally applied rudimentary cognitive models (such as simple models based on the Soar architecture) to organizational modeling. Sun and Naveh (2004)

applied a more sophisticated cognitive architecture to the simulation of organizational decision making, which led to the better understanding of the significance of cognitive factors in organizational decision making (as described before). Clancey et al. (2006), in contrast, conducted ethnographical studies of a crew on a simulated space mission and produced interesting simulations of crew interaction (as described earlier in detail).

There is work ongoing in robotics that involves, in a sense, both social simulation and cognitive modeling. For example, the work by Mataric and associates (see Mataric, 2001; Shell & Mataric, 2006) is representative of this line of work. In their work, various cognitive constructs have been deployed and explored in an effort to generate useful social behavior among a group of robots. Such work, beside constituting interesting cognitive social simulation, is also relevant to building useful application systems.

There have also been evolutionary social simulation models on top of cognitive modeling. Sun and Naveh (2007) described an evolutionary simulation of social survival strategies on the basis of the earlier work by Cecconi and Parisi (1998). Sun and Naveh's (2007) work used the CLARION cognitive architecture for modeling individual agents and an genetic algorithm for modeling evolution. Social survival strategies evolved through evolutionary changes of individual cognition. Thus, in the work, social phenomena were explained by cognitive factors through an evolutionary process. Kluver et al. (2003) also addressed issues relevant to the evolution of cognitive processes in social simulation (see also Kenrick, Li, & Butner, 2003).

Finally, there is also ongoing work on modeling emotion, motivation, and other socially relevant aspects of cognition (broadly defined), which may serve as foundations for combining social simulation and cognitive modeling. For example, Gratch, Mao, and Marsella (2006) addressed specifically the modeling of emotions in computational terms and used the resulting model in realistic simulations of social interactions (see also Thagard and Kroon, in press). In contrast, the CLARION cognitive architecture (see, e.g., Sun, 2003) included motivational processes as an integral part of the cognitive architecture. It described, in computational terms, various motivational forces and their dynamic interactions in determining behavior.

In all, many directions of research are being pursued in cognitive social simulation. They may eventually lead to better, more cognitively and socially realistic simulations that address fundamental theoretical issues and practical problems facing social scientists. They may have significant theoretical and practical implications in the future.

4. Conclusion

This chapter surveys the field of cognitive social simulation, which is at the intersection of cognitive modeling and social simulation. By combining cognitive models and social simulation models, cognitive social simulation is poised to address issues of the interaction of cognition and sociality, in addition to advancing the state of the art in understanding cognitive and social processes. Cognitive social simulation may even find some practical applications (as in, e.g., Best & Lebiere, 2006).

Overall, the field is at an early stage of development, given the relatively recent emergence of the two fields on which this field is based: social simulation and cognitive modeling (including cognitive architectures). There are many research issues to explore and intellectual challenges to address. Given the importance of its topic and the novelty of its methodology, it is reasonable to expect that this field will eventually come to fruition in helping to better understand both cognition and sociality, as well as their interaction (Sun, 2006a).

Acknowledgments

The work represented by this chapter was carried out while the author was supported (in part) by ARI contracts DASW01-00-K-0012 and W74V8H-05-K-0002 (to Ron Sun and Robert Mathews). The author benefited from discussions with Isaac (Yizchak) Naveh. Thanks are due to Paul Thagard and Stephen Read for their comments on the draft version of this chapter.

References

Ahlert, M. (2003, September). *An axiomatic approach to bounded rationality in negotiations*. Paper presented at the 2003 European Meeting of the Economic Science Association, Erfurt, Germany.

Alexander, J., Giesen, B., Munch, R., & Smelser, N. (Eds.). (1987). *The micro-macro link*. Berkeley: University of California Press.

Andersen, H., Barker, P., & Chen, X. (2006). *The cognitive structure of scientific revolution*. New York: Cambridge University Press.

Andersen, S., & Chen, S. (2002). The relational self: An interpersonal social-cognitive theory. *Psychological Review, 109*(4), 619–645.

Anderson, J., & Lebiere, C. (1998). *The atomic components of thought*. Mahwah, NJ: Lawrence Erlbaum.

Anderson, N. (1960). Effect of first-order probability in a two choice learning situation. *Journal of Experimental Psychology, 59*, 73–93.

Atran, S., & Norenzayan, A. (2004). Religion's evolutionary landscape: Counterintuition, commitment, compassion, and communion. *Brain and Behavioral Sciences, 27*, 713–770.

Axelrod, R. (1984). *The evolution of cooperation*. New York: Basic Books.

Axelrod, R. (1997). Advancing the art of simulation in the social sciences. In R. Conte, R. Hegselmann, & P. Terna (Eds.), *Simulating social phenomena* (pp. 21–40), Berlin: Springer.

Axtell, R., Axelrod, J., & Cohen, M. (1996). Aligning simulation models: A case study and results. *Computational and Mathematical Organization Theory, 1*(2), 123–141.

Best, B., & Lebiere, C. (2006). Cognitive Agents Interacting in Real and Virtual Worlds. In: R. Sun (Ed.), *Cognition And Multi-Agent Interaction: From Cognitive Modeling To Social Simulation*. New York: Cambridge University Press.

Boyer, P., & Ramble, C. (2001). Cognitive templates for religious concepts: Cross-cultural evidence for recall of counter-intuitive representations. *Cognitive Science, 25*, 535–564.

Brooks, R. (1991). Intelligence without representation. *Artificial Intelligence, 47*, 139–159.

Burns, T., & Roszkowska, E. (2006). Social judgment in multi-agent systems. In R. Sun (Ed.), *Cognition and multi-agent interaction: From cognitive modeling to social simulation*. New York: Cambridge University Press.

Camerer, C. (1997). Progress in behavioral game theory. *Journal of Economic Perspectives, 11*(4), 167–188.

Carley, K., & Newell, A. (1994). The nature of social agent. *Journal of Mathematical Sociology, 19*(4), 221–262.

Carley, K., M. J., Prietula, & Lin, Z. (1998). Design versus cognition: The interaction of agent cognition and organizational design on organizational performance. *Journal of Artificial Societies and Social Simulation, 1*(3), http://www.soc.surrey.ac.uk/JASSS/1/3/4.html

Castelfranchi, C. (2001). The theory of social functions: Challenges for computational social science and multi-agent learning. *Cognitive Systems Research* [Special issue]. *2*(1), 5–38.

Cecconi, F., & Parisi, D. (1998). Individual versus social survival strategies. *Journal of Artificial Societies and Social Simulation, 1*(2). http://www.soc.surrey.ac.uk/JASSS/1/2/1.html

Clancey, W., Sierhuis, M., Damer, B., & Brodsky, B. (2006). Cognitive modeling of social behaviors. In R. Sun (Ed.), *Cognition and multi-agent interaction: From cognitive modeling to social simulation*. New York: Cambridge University Press.

Conte, R., Hegselmann, R., & Terna, P. (Eds.). (1997). *Simulating social phenomena*. Berlin, Germany: Springer.

Doran, J., Palmer, M., Gilbert, N., & Mellars, P. (1994). The EOS project: Modeling upper Palaeolithic social change. In N. Gilbert & J. Doran (Eds.), *Simulating societies*. London: UCL Press.

Epstein, J., & Axtell, R. (1996). *Growing artificial societies*. Cambridge, MA: MIT Press.

Estes, W. (1972). Research and theory on the learning of probabilities. *Journal of the American Statistical Association, 67*, 81–102.

Gazzaniga, M. (1998, July). The split brain revisited. *Scientific American*, 50–55.

Gilbert, N. (1995). Simulation: An emergent perspective. Paper presented at the Conference on New Technologies in the Social Sciences, Bournemouth, UK.

Gilbert, N., & Conte, R. (Eds.). (1995). *Artificial societies*. London: UCL Press.

Gilbert, N., & Doran, J. (1994). *Simulating societies: The computer simulation of social phenomena*. London: UCL Press.

Goldspink, C. (2000). Modelling social systems as complex: Towards a social simulation meta-model. *Journal of Artificial Societies and Social Simulation, 3*(2). http://www.soc.surrey.ac.uk/JASSS/3/2/1.html

Goldstone, R., & Janssen, M. (2005). Computational models of collective behavior. *Trends in Cognitive Sciences, 9*(9), 424–430.

Gratch, J., Mao, W., & Marsella, S. (2006). Modeling social emotions and social attributions. In R. Sun (Ed.), *Cognition and multi-agent interaction: From cognitive modeling to social simulation*. New York: Cambridge University Press.

Gray, W., & Altmann, E. (2001). Cognitive modeling and human-computer interaction. In W. Karwowski (Ed.), *International encyclopedia of ergonomics and human factors* (Vol 1, pp. 387–391). New York: Taylor and Francis.

Helmhout, M. (2006). *The social cognitive actor: A multi actor simulation of organisations*. Unpublished doctoral dissertation, University of Groningen, Groningen, Netherlands.

Kahan, J., & Rapoport, A. (1984). *Theories of coalition formation*. Mahwah, NJ: Lawrence Erlbaum Associates.

Kenrick, D., Li, N., & Butner, J. (2003). Dynamical evolutionary psychology: Individual decision rules and emergent social norms. *Psychological Review, 110*(1), 3–28.

Kim, S., Lodge, M., & Tabor, C. (2007). A model of political preference: The dynamics of candidate evaluation in the 2000 presidential election. Manuscript submitted for publication.

Kluver, J., Malecki, R., Schmidt, J., & Stoica, C. (2003). Sociocultural evolution and cognitive ontogenesis: A sociocultural-cognitive algorithm. *Computational and Mathematical Organization Theory, 9*, 255–273.

Krackhardt, D. (1987). Cognitive social structures. *Social Networks, 9*, 109–134.

Lave, J. (1988). *Cognition in practice*. Cambridge, UK: Cambridge University Press.

Mason, W., Conrey, F., & Smith, E. (in press). Situating social influence processes: Dynamic, multidirectional flows of influence within social networks. *Personality and Social Psychology Review*.

Mataric, M. (2001). Learning in behavior-based multi-robot systems: Policies, models, and other agents. *Cognitive Systems Research* [Special issue], 2(1), 81–93.

Mithen, S. (1996). *The prehistory of the mind: The cognitive origins of art, religion, and science.* London: Thames and Hudson.

Moss, S. (1999). *Relevance, realism and rigour: A third way for social and economic research* (CPM Report No. 99–56). Manchester, UK: Center for Policy Analysis, Manchester Metropolitan University.

Moss, S. (2006). Cognitive science and good social science. In R. Sun (Ed.), *Cognition and multi-agent interaction: From cognitive modeling to social Simulation.* New York: Cambridge University Press.

Moss, S., & Davidsson, P. (Eds.). (2001). *Multi-agent-based simulation.* Berlin, Germany: Springer.

Naveh, I., & Sun, R. (2006). A cognitively based simulation of academic science. *Computational and Mathematical Organization Theory, 12,* 313–337.

Newell, A. (1990). *Unified theories of cognition.* Cambridge, MA: Harvard University Press.

Nisbett, R., Peng, K., Choi, I., & Norenzayan, A. (2001). Culture and systems of thought: Holistic versus analytic cognition. *Psychological Review, 108*(2), 291–310.

Pew, R., & Mavor, A. (Eds.). (1998). *Modeling human and organizational Behavior: Application to Military Simulations.* Washington, DC: National Academy Press.

Prietula, M., Carley, K., & Gasser, L. (Eds.). (1998). *Simulating organizations: Computational models of institutions and groups.* Cambridge, MA: MIT Press.

Reber, A. (1989). Implicit learning and tacit knowledge. *Journal of Experimental Psychology: General, 118*(3), 219–235.

Reynolds, R. (1994). Learning to co-operate using cultural algorithms. In N. Gilbert & J. Doran (Eds.), *Simulating societies: The computer simulation of social phenomena.* London, UK: UCL Press.

Rizzello, S., & Turvani, M. (2000). Institutions meet mind: The way out of an impasse. *Constitutional Political Economy, 11,* 165–180.

Sawyer, R. (2003). Multiagent systems and the micro-macro link in sociological theory. *Sociological Methods and Research, 31*(3), 325–363.

Schreiber, D. (2004, March). *A hybrid model of political cognition.* Paper presented at the Mid-

western Political Science Association Annual Meeting, Chicago.

Seger, C. (1994). Implicit learning. *Psychological Bulletin, 115*(2), 163–196.

Shell, D., & Mataric, M. (2006). Behavior-based methods for modeling and structuring control of social robots. In R. Sun (Ed.), *Cognition and multiagent interaction: From cognitive modeling to social simulation.* New York: Cambridge University Press.

Suchman, L. (1987). *Plans and situated actions: The problem of human machine communication.* Oxford, UK: Oxford University Press.

Sun, R. (2001). Cognitive science meets multi-agent systems: A prolegomenon. *Philosophical Psychology, 14*(1), 5–28.

Sun, R. (2002). *Duality of the mind.* Mahwah, NJ: Lawrence Erlbaum.

Sun, R. (2003). *A tutorial on CLARION* [Technical report]. Troy, NY: Cognitive Science Department, Rensselaer Polytechnic Institute. http://www.cogsci.rpi.edu/~rsun/sun. tutorial. pdf

Sun, R. (2004). Desiderata for cognitive architectures. *Philosophical Psychology, 17*(3), 341–373.

Sun, R. (2005). Theoretical status of computational cognitive modeling [Technical report]. Troy, NY: Cognitive Science Department, Rensselaer Polytechnic Institute.

Sun, R. (Ed.). (2006a). *Cognition and multi-agent interaction: From cognitive modeling to social simulation.* New York: Cambridge University Press.

Sun, R. (2006b). The CLARION cognitive architecture: Extending cognitive modeling to social simulation. In R. Sun (Ed.), *Cognition and multi-agent interaction: From cognitive modeling to social simulation.* New York: Cambridge University Press.

Sun, R., Coward, A., & Zenzen, M. (2005). On levels of cognitive modeling. *Philosophical Psychology, 18*(5), 613–637.

Sun, R., & Naveh, I. (2004). Simulating organizational decision making with a cognitive architecture CLARION. *Journal of Artificial Society and Social Simulation, 7*(3). http://jasss.soc.surrey.ac.uk/7/3/5.html

Sun, R., & Naveh, I. (2007). Social institution, cognition, and survival: A cognitive-social simulation. *Mind and Society, 6*(2), 115–142.

Thagard, P. (1992). Adversarial problem solving: modeling an opponent using explanatory coherence. *Cognitive Science, 16,* 123–149.

Thagard, P., & F. W. Kroon (in press). Emotional consensus in group decision making. *Mind and Society*.

Turner, M. (2000). *Cognitive dimensions of social science*. New York: Oxford University Press.

van Fraasen, B. (2002). *The empirical stance*. New Haven, CT: Yale University Press.

von Neumann, J., & Morgenstern, O. (1944). *Theory of games and economic behaviour*. Princeton, NJ: Princeton University Press.

Vygotsky, L. (1962). *Thought and language*. Cambridge, MA: MIT Press.

Wagenaar, W. (1972). Generation of random sequences by human subjects: A critical survey of the literature. *Psychological Bulletin, 77*, 65–72.

Ward, L. (1973). Use of Markov-encoded sequential information in numerical signal detection. *Perception and Psychophysics, 14*, 337–342.

Wenger, E. (1998). *Communities of practice: Learning, meaning, and identity*. New York: Cambridge University Press.

West, R., & Lebiere, C. (2001). Simple games as dynamic coupled systems: Randomness and other emergent properties. *Cognitive Systems Research, 1*(4), 221–239.

West, R., Lebiere, C., & Bothell, D. (2006). Cognitive architectures, game playing, and human evolution. In R. Sun (Ed.), *Cognition and multi-agent interaction: From cognitive modeling to social simulation*. New York: Cambridge University Press.

Zerubavel, E. (1997). *Social mindscapes: An invitation to cognitive sociology*. Cambridge, MA: Harvard University Press.

CHAPTER 20

Models of Scientific Explanation

Paul Thagard and Abninder Litt

1. Introduction

Explanation of why things happen is one of humans' most important cognitive operations. In everyday life, people are continually generating explanations of why other people behave the way they do, why they get sick, why computers or cars are not working properly, and of many other puzzling occurrences. More systematically, scientists develop theories to provide general explanations of physical phenomena, such as why objects fall to earth; chemical phenomena, such as why elements combine; biological phenomena, such as why species evolve; medical phenomena, such as why organisms develop diseases; and psychological phenomena, such as why people sometimes make mental errors.

This chapter reviews computational models of the cognitive processes that underlie these kinds of explanations of *why* events happen. It is not concerned with another sense of explanation that just means clarification, as when someone explains the U.S. constitution. The focus will be on scientific explanations, but more mundane examples will occasionally be used on the grounds that the cognitive processes for explaining why events happen are much the same in everyday life and in science, although scientific explanations tend to be more systematic and rigorous than everyday ones. In addition to providing a concise review of previous computational models of explanation, this chapter describes a new neural network model that shows how explanations can be performed by multimodal distributed representations.

Before proceeding with accounts of particular computational models of explanation, let us characterize more generally the three major processes involved in explanation and the four major theoretical approaches that have been taken in computational models of it. The three major processes are: providing an explanation from available information, generating new hypotheses that provide explanations, and evaluating competing explanations. The four major theoretical approaches are: deductive, using logic or rule-based systems; schematic, using explanation patterns or analogies; probabilistic, using Bayesian networks; and neural, using networks of artificial neurons. For each of these theoretical approaches, it is possible to characterize the different ways in which the provision, generation, and evaluation of explanations are understood computationally.

The processes of providing, generating, and evaluating explanations can be illustrated with a simple medical example. Suppose you arrive at your doctor's office with a high fever, headache, extreme fatigue, a bad cough, and major muscle aches. Your doctor will probably tell you that you have been infected by the influenza virus, with an explanation like:

> People infected by the flu virus often have the symptoms you describe.
> You have been exposed to and infected by the flu virus.
> So, you have these symptoms.

If influenza is widespread in your community and your doctor has been seeing many patients with similar symptoms, it will not require much reasoning to provide this explanation by stating that the flu virus is the likely cause of your symptoms.

Sometimes, however, a larger inferential leap is required to provide an explanation. If your symptoms also include a stiff neck and confusion, your doctor may make the less common and more serious diagnosis of meningitis. This diagnosis requires generating the hypothesis that you have been exposed to bacteria or viruses that have infected the lining surrounding the brain. In this case, the doctor is not simply applying knowledge already available to provide an explanation, but generating a hypothesis about you that makes it possible to provide an explanation. This hypothesis presupposes a history of medical research that led to the identification of meningitis as a disease caused by particular kinds of bacteria and viruses, research that required the generation of new general hypotheses that made explanation of particular cases of the disease possible.

In addition to providing and generating explanations, scientists and ordinary people sometimes need to evaluate competing explanations. If your symptoms are ambiguous, your doctor may be unsure whether you have influenza or meningitis and therefore may consider them as competing explanations of your symptoms. The doctor's task is then to figure out which hypothesis, that you have influenza or meningitis, is the *best* explanation of your disease. Similarly, at a more general level, scientific researchers had to consider alternative explanations of the causes of meningitis and select the best one. This selection presupposed the generation and provision of candidate explanations and involved the additional cognitive processes of comparing the candidates in order to decide which was most plausible.

Provision, generation, and evaluation of explanations can all be modeled computationally, but the forms these models take depend on background theories about what constitutes an explanation. One view, prominent in both philosophy of science and artificial intelligence, is that explanations are deductive arguments. An explanation consists of a deduction in which the explanatory target, to be explained, follows logically from the explaining set of propositions. Here is a simple example:

> Anyone with influenza has fever, aches, and cough.
> You have influenza.
> So, you have fever, aches, and cough.

In this oversimplified case, it is plausible that the explanatory target follows deductively from the explaining propositions.

Often, however, the relation between explainers and explanatory targets is looser than logical deduction, and an explanation can be characterized as a causal schema rather than a deductive argument. A schema is a conceptual pattern that specifies a typical situation, as in the following example:

> Explanatory pattern: Typically, influenza causes fever, aches, and cough.
> Explanatory target: You have fever, aches, and cough.

Schema instantiation: Maybe you have influenza.

In medical research, the explanatory pattern is much more complex, as scientists can provide a much richer description of the genetic, biological, and immunological causes of infection. Like deductive explanations, schematic ones can be viewed as providing causes, but with a more flexible relation between explainers and what is explained.

Probability theory can also be used to provide a less rigid conception of explanation than logical deducibility. A target can be explained by specifying that it is probable given the state of affairs described by the explainers. In the flu case, the explanation has this kind of structure:

The probability of having fever, aches, and coughs given influenza is high.
So influenza explains why you have fever, aches, and cough.

On this view, explanation is a matter of conditional probability rather than logical deducibility or schematic fit. Like deduction and schema views, the probabilistic view of explanation has inspired interesting computational models, particularly ones involving Bayesian networks that will be described later.

A fourth computational way of modeling explanation derives from artificial neural networks, which attempt to approximate how brains use large groups of neurons, operating in parallel to accomplish complex cognitive tasks. The neural approach to explanation is not in itself a theory of explanation in the way that the deductive, schema, and probabilistic views are, but it offers new ways of thinking about the nature of the provision, generation, and evaluation of explanations. This quick overview sets the stage for the more detailed analysis of computational models of scientific explanation that follows. For a concise review of philosophical theories of explanation, see Woodward (2003); for more detail, see Kitcher and Salmon (1989).

2. Deductive Models

The view that explanations are deductive arguments has been prominent in the philosophy of science. According to Hempel (1965, p. 336), an explanation is an argument of the form:

$$C_1, C_2, \ldots, C_k$$
$$L_1, L_2, \ldots, L_r$$
$$\overline{}$$
$$E.$$

Here, Cs are sentences describing particular facts, Ls are general laws, and E is the sentence explained by virtue of being a logical consequence of the other sentences. This sort of explanation does occur in some areas of science, such as physics, where laws stated as mathematical formulas enable deductive predictions.

Many computational models in artificial intelligence have presupposed that explanation is deductive, including ones found in logic programming, truth maintenance systems, explanation-based learning, qualitative reasoning, and in some approaches to abduction (a form of inference that involves the generation and evaluation of explanatory hypotheses); see, for example, Russell and Norvig (2003), Bylander et al. (1991), and Konolige (1992). These artificial intelligence approaches are not intended as models of human cognition, but see Chapter 5 in this volume for a discussion of the use of formal logic in cognitive modeling.

Deductive explanation also operates in rule-based models, which have been proposed for many kinds of human thinking (Anderson, 1983, 1993; Holland et al., 1986; Newell, 1990; Newell & Simon, 1972; see also Chapter 6 in this volume). A rule-based system is a set of rules with an IF part consisting of conditions (antecedents) and a THEN part consisting of actions (consequents). Rule-based systems have often been used to model human problem solving in which people need to figure out how to get from a starting state to a goal state by applying a series of rules. This is a kind of deduction in that the application of rules in a series of if–then inferences amounts to a series of applications of the rule of deductive inference, modus ponens, which licenses inferences from p and *if p then q* to q. Most rule-based systems, however, do not always proceed just from starting states to goal states, but can also work backward from a goal state to find a series of rules that can be used to get from the starting state to the goal state.

Explanation can be understood as a special kind of problem solving, in which the goal state is a target to be explained. Rule-based systems do not have the full logical complexity to express the laws required for Hempel's model of explanation, but they can perform a useful approximation. For instance, the medical example used in the introduction can be expressed by a rule like:

IF X has influenza, THEN X has fever,
   cough, and aches.
Paul has influenza.

_____

Paul has fever, cough, and aches.

Modus ponens provides the connection between the rule and what is to be explained. In more complex cases, the connection would come from a sequence of applications of modus ponens as multiple rules get applied. In contrast to Hempel's account in which an explanation is a static argument, rule-based explanation is usually a dynamic process involving application of multiple rules. For a concrete example of a running program that accomplishes explanations in this way, see the PI cognitive model of Thagard (1988; code is available at http://cogsci.uwaterloo.ca/). The main scientific example to which PI has been applied is the discovery of the wave theory of sound, which occurs in the context of an attempt to explain why sounds propagate and reflect.

Thus, rule-based systems can model the provisions of explanations construed deductively, but what about the generation and evaluation of explanations? A simple form of abductive inference that generates hypotheses can be modeled as a kind of backward chaining. Forward chaining means running rules forward in the deductive process that proceeds from the starting state toward a goal to be solved. Backward chaining occurs when a system works backward from a goal state to find rules that could produce it from the starting state. Human problem solving on tasks such as solving mathematics problems often involves a combination of forward and backward reasoning, in which a problem solver looks both at how the problem is described and the answer that is required, attempting to make them meet. At the level of a single rule, backward chaining has the form: goal G is to be accomplished; there is the rule IF A THEN G, that is, action A would accomplish G; so set A as a new subgoal to be accomplished. Analogously, people can backchain to find a possible explanation: fact F is to be explained; there is a rule IF H THEN F, that is, hypothesis H would explain F; so hypothesize that H is true. Thus, if you know that Paul has fever, aches, and a cough, and the rule that IF X has influenza, THEN X has fever, cough, and aches, then you can run the rule backward to produce the hypothesis that Paul has influenza.

The computational model PI performs this simple kind of hypothesis generation, but it also can generate other kinds of hypotheses (Thagard, 1988). For example, from the observation that the orbit of Uranus is perturbed, and the rule that IF a planet has another planet near it THEN its orbit is perturbed, PI infers that there is some planet near Uranus; this is called existential abduction. PI also performs abduction to rules that constitute the wave theory of sound: the attempt to explain why an arbitrary sound propagates generates not only the hypothesis that it consists of a wave but the general theory that all sounds are waves. PI also performs a kind of analogical abduction, a topic discussed in the next section on schemas.

Abductive inference that generates explanatory hypotheses is an inherently risky form of reasoning because of the possibility of alternative explanations. Inferring that Paul has influenza because it explains his fever, aches, and cough is risky because other diseases, such as meningitis, can cause the same symptoms. People should only accept an explanatory hypothesis if it is better than its competitors, a form of inference that philosophers call *inference to the best explanation* (Harman, 1973; Lipton, 2004). The PI cognitive model performs this kind of inference by taking into account three criteria for the best explanation: consilience, which is a measure of how much a hypothesis explains; simplicity, which is a measure of how few additional assumptions a hypothesis needs to carry out an explanation; and analogy, which favors hypotheses whose explanations are analogous to accepted ones. A more psychologically elegant way of performing inference to the best explanation, the model ECHO, is described later in the section on neural networks. Neither the PI nor the ECHO way of evaluating competing explanations requires that explanations be deductive.

In artificial intelligence, the term "abduction" is often used to describe inference to the best explanation as well as the generation of hypotheses. In actual systems, these two processes can be continuous, for example in the PEIRCE tool for abductive inference described by Josephson and Josephson (1994). This is primarily an engineering tool rather than a cognitive model, but is mentioned here as another approach to generating and evaluating scientific explanations, in particular, medical ones involving interpretation of blood tests. The PEIRCE system accomplishes the goal of generating the best explanatory hypothesis by achieving three subgoals:

1. generation of a set of plausible hypotheses,
2. construction of a compound explanation for all the findings, and
3. criticism and improvement of the compound explanation.

PEIRCE employs computationally effective algorithms for each of these subgoals, but does not attempt to do so in a way that corresponds to how people accomplish them.

3. Schema and Analogy Models

In ordinary life and in many areas of science less mathematical than physics, the relation between what is explained and what does the explaining is usually looser than deduction. An alternative conception of this relation is provided by understanding an explanation as the application of a causal schema, which is a pattern that describes the relation between causes and effects. For example, cognitive science uses a general explanation schema that has the following structure (Thagard, 2005):

> *Explanation target:* Why do people have a particular kind of **intelligent behavior**?
> *Explanatory pattern:*
> People have mental **representations.**
> People have algorithmic **processes** that operate on those **representations.**
> The **processes**, applied to the **representations**, produce the **behavior**.

This schema provides explanations when the terms shown in boldface are filled in with specifics and subsumes schemas that describe particular kinds of mental representations, such as concepts, rules, and neural networks. Philosophers of science have discussed the importance of explanation schemas or patterns (Kitcher, 1993; Thagard, 1999).

A computational cognitive model of explanation schemas was developed in the SWALE project (Leake, 1992; Schank, 1986). This project modeled people's attempts to explain the unexpected 1984 death of a racehorse, Swale. Given an occurrence, the program SWALE attempts to fit it into memory. If a problem arises indicating an anomaly, then the program attempts to find an explanation pattern stored in memory. The explanation patterns are derived from previous cases, such as other unexpected deaths. If SWALE finds more than one relevant explanation pattern, it evaluates them to determine which is most relevant to the intellectual goals of the person seeking understanding. If the best explanation pattern does not quite fit the case to be explained, it can be tweaked (adapted) to provide a better fit, and the tweaked version is stored in memory for future use. The explanation patterns in SWALE's database included both general schemas, such as *exertion + heart defect causes fatal heart attack*, and particular examples, which are used for case-based reasoning, a kind of analogical thinking. Leake (1992) describes how competing explanation patterns can be evaluated according to various criteria, including a reasoner's pragmatic goals.

Explaining something by applying a general schema involves the same processes as explaining using analogies. In both cases, reasoning proceeds as follows:

Identify the case to be explained.
Search memory for a matching schema or case.
Adapt the found schema or case to provide an explanation of the case to be explained.

In deductive explanation, there is a tight logical relation between what is explained and the sentences that imply it, but in schematic or analogical explanation, there need only be a roughly specified causal relation.

Falkenhainer (1990) describes a program, PHINEAS, that provides analogical explanations of scientific phenomena. The program uses Forbus's (1984) qualitative process theory to represent and reason about physical change and is provided with knowledge about liquid flow. When presented with other phenomena to be explained, such as osmosis and heat flow, it can generate new explanations analogically by computing similarities in relational structure, using the Structure Mapping Engine (Falkenhainer, Forbus, & Gentner, 1989). PHINEAS operates in four stages: access, mapping/transfer, qualitative simulation, and revision. For example, it can generate an explanation of the behavior of a hot brick in cold water by analogy to what happens when liquid flows between two containers. Another computational model that generates analogical explanations is the PI system (Thagard, 1988), which simulates the discovery of the

wave theory of sound by analogy to water waves.

Thus, computational models of explanation that rely on matching schematic or analogical structures based on causal fit provide an alternative to models of deductive explanation. These two approaches are not competing theories of explanation, because explanation can take different forms in different areas of science. In areas such as physics that are rich in mathematically expressed knowledge, deductive explanations may be available. But in more qualitative areas of science and everyday life, explanations are usually less exact and may be better modeled by application of causal schemas or as a kind of analogical inference.

4. Probabilistic Models

Another, more quantitative way of establishing a looser relation than deduction between explainers and their targets is to use probability theory. Salmon (1970) proposed that the key to explanation is *statistical relevance*, where a property B in a population A is relevant to a property C if the probability of B given A and C is different from the probability of B given A alone: $P(B|A \& C) \neq P(B|A)$. Salmon later moved away from a statistical understanding of explanation toward a causal mechanism account (Salmon, 1984), but other philosophers and artificial intelligence researchers have focused on probabilistic accounts of causality and explanation. The core idea here is that people explain why something happened by citing the factors that made it more probable than it would have been otherwise.

The main computational method for modeling explanation probabilistically is Bayesian networks, developed by Pearl (1988, 2000) and other researchers in philosophy and computer science (e.g., Glymour, 2001; Neapolitain, 1990; Spirtes, Glymour, & Scheines, 1993; see also Chapter 3 in this volume). A Bayesian network is a directed graph in which the nodes are statistical variables, the edges between them represent conditional probabilities, and no

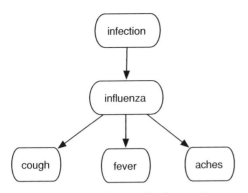

Figure 20.1. Causal map of a disease. In a Bayesian network, each node is a variable, and the arrow indicates causality represented by conditional probability.

cycles are allowed: you cannot have A influencing B which influences A. Causal structure and probability are connected by the Markov assumption, which says that a variable A in a causal graph is independent of all other variables that are not its effects, conditional on its direct causes in the graph (Glymour, 2003).

Bayesian networks are convenient ways for representing causal relationships, as in Figure 20.1. Powerful algorithms have been developed for making probabilistic inferences in Bayesian networks and for learning causal relationships in these networks. Applications have included scientific examples, such as developing models in the social sciences (Spirtes et al., 1993). Bayesian networks provide an excellent tool for computational and normative philosophical applications, but the relevant question for this chapter is how they might contribute to cognitive modeling of scientific explanation.

The psychological plausibility of Bayesian networks has been advocated by Glymour (2001) and Gopnik et al. (2004). They show the potential for using Bayesian networks to explain a variety of kinds of reasoning and learning studied by cognitive and developmental psychologists. Gopnik et al. (2004) argue that children's causal learning and inference may involve computations similar to those for learning Bayesian networks and for predicting with them. If they are right about children, it would be plausible that

the causal inferences of scientists are also well modeled by Bayesian networks. From this perspective, explaining something consists of instantiating it in a causal network and using probabilistic inference to indicate how it depends causally on other factors. Generating an explanation consists of producing a Bayesian network, and evaluating competing explanations consists of calculating the comparative probability of different causes.

Despite their computational and philosophical power, there are reasons to doubt the psychological relevance of Bayesian networks. Although it is plausible that people's mental representations contain something like rough causal maps depicted in Figure 20.1, it is much less plausible that these maps have all the properties of Bayesian networks. First, there is abundant experimental evidence that reasoning with probabilities is not a natural part of people's inferential practice (Gilovich, Griffin, & Kahneman, 2002; Kahneman, Slovic, & Tversky, 1982). Computing with Bayesian networks requires a very large number of conditional probabilities that people not working in statistics have had no chance to acquire. Second, there is no reason to believe that people have the sort of information about independence that is required to satisfy the Markov condition and to make inference in Bayesian networks computationally tractable. Third, although it is natural to represent causal knowledge as directed graphs, there are many scientific and everyday contexts in which such graphs should have cycles because of feedback loops. For example, marriage breakdown often occurs because of escalating negative affect, in which the negative emotions of one partner produces behaviors that increase negative emotions of the other, which then produces behavior that increases the negative emotions of the first partner (Gottman et al., 2003). Such feedback loops are also common in biochemical pathways needed to explain disease (Thagard, 2003). Fourth, probability by itself is not adequate to capture people's understanding of causality, as argued in the last section of this chapter. Hence, it is not at all

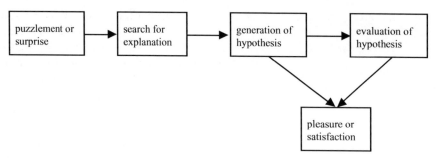

Figure 20.2. The process of abductive inference (Thagard, 2007).

obvious that Bayesian networks are the best way to model explanation by human scientists. Even in statistically rich fields, such as the social sciences, scientists rely on an intuitive, nonprobabilistic sense of causality of the sort discussed later.

5. Neural Network Models

The most important approach to cognitive modeling not yet discussed employs artificial neural networks. Applying this approach to high-level reasoning faces many challenges, particularly in representing the complex kinds of information contained in scientific hypotheses and causal relations. Thagard (1989) provided a neural network model of how competing scientific explanations can be evaluated, but did so using a localist network in which entire propositions are represented by single artificial neurons and in which relations between propositions are represented by excitatory and inhibitory links between the neurons. Although this model provides an extensive account of explanation evaluation that is reviewed later, it reveals nothing about what an explanation is or how explanations are generated. Neural network modelers have been concerned mostly with applications to low-level psychological phenomena, such as perception, categorization, and memory, rather than high-level ones, such as problem solving and inference (O'Reilly & Munakata, 2000). However, this section shows how a neurologically complex model of explanation and abductive inference can be constructed. For a review of neural network ap-

proaches to cognitive modeling, see Chapter 2 in this volume.

One benefit of attempting neural analyses of explanation is that it becomes possible to incorporate multimodal aspects of cognitive processing that tend to be ignored from deductive, schematic, and probabilistic perspectives. Thagard (2007) describes how both explainers and explanation targets are sometimes represented nonverbally. In medicine, for example, doctors and researchers may employ visual hypotheses (say about the shape and location of a tumor) to explain observations that can be represented using sight, touch, and smell as well as words. Moreover, the process of abductive inference has emotional inputs and outputs, because it is usually initiated when an observation is found to be surprising or puzzling, and it often results in a sense of pleasure or satisfaction when a satisfactory hypothesis is used to generate an explanation. Figure 20.2 provides an outline of this process. Let us now look at an implementation of a neural network model of this sketch.

The model of abduction described here follows the Neural Engineering Framework (NEF) outlined in Eliasmith and Anderson (2003) and is implemented using the MATLAB-based NEF simulation software *NESim*. The NEF proposes three basic principles of neural computation (Eliasmith & Anderson, p. 15):

1. Neural representations are defined by a combination of nonlinear encoding and linear decoding.
2. Transformations of neural representations are linearly decoded functions of

variables that are represented by a neural population.

3. Neural dynamics are characterized by considering neural representations as control theoretic state variables.

These principles are applied to a particular neural system by identifying the interconnectivity of its subsystems, neuron response functions, neuron tuning curves, subsystem functional relations, and overall system behavior. For cognitive modeling, the NEF is useful because it provides a mathematically rigorous way of building more realistic neural models of cognitive functions.

The NEF characterizes neural populations and activities in terms of mathematical representations and transformations. The complexity of a representation is constrained by the *dimensionality* of the neural population that represents it. In rough terms, a single dimension in such a representation can correspond to one discrete "aspect" of that representation (e.g., speed and direction are the dimensional components of the vector quantity velocity). A hierarchy of representational complexity thus follows from neural activity defined in terms of one-dimensional scalars; vectors, with a finite but arbitrarily large number of dimensions; or functions, which are essentially *continuous* indexings of vector elements, thus ranging over infinite dimensional spaces.

The NEF provides for arbitrary computations to be performed in biologically realistic neural populations and has been successfully applied to phenomena as diverse as lamprey locomotion (Eliasmith & Anderson, 2003), path integration by rats (Conklin & Eliasmith, 2005), and the Wason card selection task (Eliasmith, 2005). The Wason task model, in particular, is structured very similarly to the model of abductive inference discussed here. Both employ *holographic reduced representations*, a high-dimensional form of distributed representation.

First developed by Plate (2003), holographic reduced representations (HRRs) combine the neurological plausibility of distributed representations with the ability to maintain complex, embedded structural relations in a computationally efficient manner. This ability is common in symbolic models and is often singled out as deficient in distributed connectionist frameworks; for a comprehensive review of HRRs in the context of the distributed versus symbolic representation debate, see Eliasmith and Thagard (2001). HRRs consist of high-dimensional vectors combined via multiplicative operations and are similar to the tensor products used by Smolensky (1990) as the basis for a connectionist model of cognition. But HRRs have the important advantage of *fixed dimensionality*: the combination of two n-dimensional HRRs produces another n-dimensional HRR, rather than the 2n or even n^2 dimensionality one would obtain using tensor products. This avoids the explosive computational resource requirements of tensor products to represent arbitrary, complex structural relationships.

HRR representations are constructed through the multiplicative *circular convolution* (denoted by $\otimes$) and are decoded by the approximate inverse operation, *circular correlation* (denoted by #). The details of these operations are given in the appendices of Eliasmith & Thagard (2001), but in general if $C = A \otimes B$ is encoded, then $C \# A \approx B$ and $C \# B \approx A$. The approximate nature of the unbinding process introduces a degree of noise, proportional to the complexity of the HRR encoding in question and in inverse proportion to the dimensionality of the HRR (Plate, 1994). As noise tolerance is a requirement of any neurologically plausible model, this loss of representation information is acceptable, and the "cleanup" method of recognizing encoded HRR vectors using the dot product can be used to find the vector that best fits what was decoded (Eliasmith & Thagard, 2001). Note that HRRs may also be combined by simple superposition (i.e., addition): $P = Q \otimes R + X \otimes Y$, where $P \# R \approx Q$, $P \# X \approx Y$, and so on. The operations required for convolution and correlation can be implemented in a recurrent connectionist network (Plate, 1993) and, in particular, under the NEF (Eliasmith, 2005).

In brief, the new model of abductive inference involves several large, high-dimensional populations to represent the data stored via HRRs and learned HRR transformations (the main output of the model), and a smaller population representing emotional valence information (abduction only requires considering emotion scaling from surprise to satisfactions and hence only needs a single dimension represented by as few as 100 neurons to represent emotional changes). The model is initialized with a base set of causal encodings consisting of 100-dimensional HRRs combined in the form

$$\text{antecedent} \otimes a + \text{relation} \otimes \text{causes}$$
$$+ \text{consequent} \otimes b,$$

as well as HRRs that represent the successful explanation of a target x ($expl \otimes x$). For the purposes of this model, only six different "filler" values were used, representing three such causal rules (a causes b, c causes d, and e causes f). The populations used have between 2,000 and 3,200 neurons each and are 100- or 200-dimensional, which is at the lower-end of what is required for accurate HRR cleanup (Plate, 1994). More rules and filler values would require larger and higher-dimensional neural populations, an expansion that is unnecessary for a simple demonstration of abduction using biologically plausible neurons.

Following detection of a surprising b, which could be an event, proposition, or any sensory or cognitive data that can be represented via neurons, the change in emotional valence spurs activity in the output population toward generating a hypothesized explanation. This process involves employing several neural populations (representing the memorized rules and HRR convolution/correlation operations) to find an antecedent involved in a causal relationship that has b as the consequent. In terms of HRRs, this means producing (*rule # antecedent*) for [(*rule # relation* $\approx$ *causes*) and (*rule # consequent* $\approx b$)]. This production is accomplished in the 2,000-neuron, 100-dimensional output population by means of

associative learning through recurrent connectivity and connection weight updating (Eliasmith, 2005). As activity in this population settles, an HRR cleanup operation is performed to obtain the result of the learned transformation. Specifically, some answer is "chosen" if the cleanup result matches one encoded value significantly more than any of the others (i.e., is above some reasonable threshold value).

After the successful generation of an explanatory hypothesis, the emotional valence signal is reversed from surprise (which drove the search for an explanation) to what can be considered pleasure or satisfaction derived from having arrived at a plausible explanation. This, in turn, induces the output population to produce a representation corresponding to the successful dispatch of the explanandum b: namely, the HRR $expl_b = expl \otimes b$. On settling, it can thus be said that the model has accepted the hypothesized cause obtained in the previous stage as a valid explanation for the target b. Settling completes the abductive inference: Emotional valence returns to a neutral level, which suspends learning in the output population and causes population firing to return to basal levels of activity.

Figure 20.3 shows the result of performing the process of abductive inference in the neural model, with activity in the output population changing with respect to changing emotional valence and vice versa. The output population activity is displayed by dimension, rather than individual neuron, because the 100-dimensional HRR output of the neural ensemble as a whole is the real characterization of what is being represented. The boxed sets of numbers represent the results of HRR cleanups on the output population at different points in time; if one value reasonably dominates over the next few largest, it can be taken to be the "true" HRR represented by the population at that moment. In the first stage, the high emotional valence leads to the search for an antecedent of a causal rule for b, the surprising explanandum. The result is an HRR cleanup best fitting to a, which is indeed the correct response. Reaching an answer with a

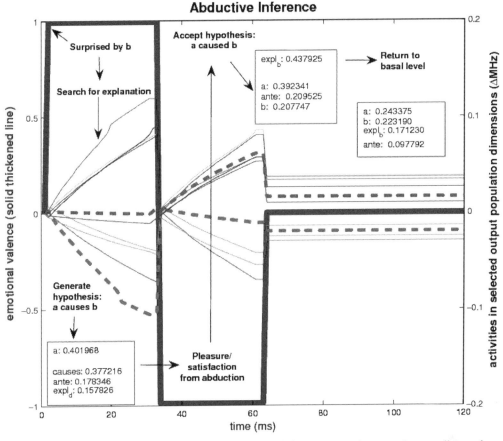

Figure 20.3. Neural activity in output population for abduction. For clarity, only a small (evenly spaced) selection of dimensional firing activities is displayed here (the full 2,000-neuron population has 100 dimensions). Activities for two specific population dimensions are highlighted by thickened dashed lines to demonstrate the neural activity changes in response to changing emotional valence (shown as a thickened solid line).

reasonably high degree of certainty triggers an emotional valence shift (from surprise to satisfaction), which in turn causes the output population to represent the fact that b has been successfully explained, as represented by the HRR cleanup in the second stage of the graph. Finally, the emotional arousal shifts to a neutral state as abduction is completed, and the population returns to representing nothing particularly strongly in the final stage.

The basic process of abduction outlined previously (see Figure 20.2) maps very well to the results obtained from the model. The output population generates a valid hypothesis when surprised (because "a causes b" is the best memorized rule available to handle surprising b), and reversal of emotional valence corresponds to an acceptance of the hypothesis and hence the successful explanation of b.

In sum, the model of abduction outlined here demonstrates how emotion can influence neural activity underlying a cognitive process. Emotional valence acts as a *context gate* that determines whether the output neural ensemble must conduct a search for some explanation for surprising input or whether some generated hypothesis needs to be evaluated as a suitable explanation for the surprising input.

The neural network model just described provides a mechanism for explanation, its emotional input and output, and a simple kind of abduction. It also does a very simple sort of explanation evaluation in that the causal rule that it selects from memory is chosen because it is a good match for the problem at hand, namely explaining *b*. Obviously, however, this model is too simple to account for the comparative evaluation of explanatory theories as performed by the cognitive model ECHO (Thagard, 1989, 1992, 2000). In ECHO, hypotheses and pieces of evidence are represented by simple artificial neurons called units, which are connected by excitatory or inhibitory links that correspond to constraints between the propositions they represent. For example, if a hypothesis explains a piece of evidence, then there is a symmetric excitatory link between the unit that represents the hypothesis and the unit that represents the evidence. If two hypotheses contradict each other, then there is a symmetric inhibitory link between the two units that represent them. Units have activations that spread between them until the network reaches stable activation levels, which typically takes 60 to 100 iterations. If a unit ends up with positive activation, the proposition that it represents is accepted, whereas if a unit ends up with negative activation, the proposition that it represents is rejected.

ECHO has been used to model numerous cases in the history of science and has also inspired experimental research in social and educational psychology (Read & Marcus-Newhall, 1993; Schank & Ranney, 1991) It shows how a very high-level kind of cognition, evaluating complex theories, can be performed by simple neural network performing parallel constraint satisfaction. ECHO has a degree of psychological plausibility, but for neurological plausibility it pales in comparison to the NEF model of abduction described earlier in this section. The largest ECHO model uses only around 200 units to encode the same number of propositions, whereas the NEF model uses thousands of spiking neurons to encode a few causal relations. Computationally, this seems inefficient, but of course, the brain has many billions of neurons that provide its distributed representations.

How might one implement comparative theory evaluation as performed by ECHO within the NEF framework? Thagard and Aubie (in press) use the NEF to encode ECHO networks by generating a population of thousands of neurons. Parallel constraint satisfaction is performed by transformations of neurons that carry out approximately the same calculations that occur more directly in ECHO's localist neural networks. Hence, it is now possible to model evaluation of competing explanations using more biologically realistic neural networks.

6. Causality

Like most other models of explanation, these neural network models presuppose some understanding of causality. In one sense that is common in both science and everyday life, to explain something involves stating its cause. For example, when people have influenza, the virus that infects them is the cause of their symptoms, such as fever. But what is a cause? Philosophical theories of explanation correlate with competing theories of causality; for example, the deductive view of explanation fits well with the Humean understanding of causality as constant conjunction. If all *A* are *B*, then someone can understand how being *A* can cause and explain being *B*. Unfortunately, universality is not a requisite of either explanation or causality. Smoking causes lung cancer, even though many smokers never get lung cancer, and some people with lung cancer never smoked. Schematic models of explanation presuppose a primitive concept of causation without being able to say much about it. Probability theory may look like a promising approach to causality in that causes make their effects more probable than they would be otherwise, but such increased probability may be accidental or the result of some common cause. For example, the probability of someone drowning is greater on a day when much ice cream is consumed, but that is because of the common cause that more people go swimming on hot days. Sorting out causal probabilistic information from misleading correlations requires much information about probability and independence that people usually lack.

Thagard (2007) conjectured that it might be possible to give a neural network account of how organisms understand causality. Suppose, in keeping with research on infants' grasp of causality, that cause is a preverbal concept based on perception and motor control (Baillargeon, Kotovsky, & Needham, 1995; Mandler, 2004). Consider an infant of a few months old, lying on its back, swiping at a mobile suspended over its head. The infant has already acquired an image schema of the following form:

perception of situation + motor behavior

→ perception of new situation.

Perhaps this schema is innate, but alternatively, it may have been acquired from very early perceptual/motor experiences in which the infant acted on the world and perceived its changes. A simple instance of the schema would be:

stationary object + hand hitting object

→ moving object.

The idea of a preverbal image schema for causality is consistent with the views of some philosophers that manipulability and intervention are central features of causality (Woodward, 2004). The difference between A causing B and A merely being correlated with B is that manipulating A also manipulates B in the former case but not the latter. Conceptually, the concepts of manipulation and intervention seem to presuppose the concept of causation, because making something happen is on the surface no different from causing it to happen. However, although there is circularity at the verbal level, psychologically, it is possible to break out of the circle by supposing that people have from infancy a neural encoding of the causality image schema described earlier. This nonverbal schema is the basis for understanding the difference between one event making another event happen and one event just occurring after the other.

The causality image schema is naturally implemented within the NEF used to construct the model of abductive inference. Neural populations are capable of encoding both perceptions and motor behaviors, and are also capable of encoding relations between them. In the model of abductive inference described in the last section, *cause* (c, e) was represented by a neural population that encodes an HRR vector that captures the relation between a vector representing c and a vector representing e, where both of these can easily be nonverbal perceptions and actions as well as verbal representations. In the NEF model of abduction, there is no real understanding of causality, because the vector was generated automatically. In contrast, it is reasonable to conjecture that people have neural populations that encode the notion of causal connection as the result of their very early preverbal experience with manipulating objects. Because the connection is based on visual and kinesthetic experiences, it cannot be adequately formulated linguistically, but it provides the intellectual basis for the more verbal and mathematical characterizations of causality that develop later.

If this account of causality is correct, then a full cognitive model of explanation cannot be purely verbal or probabilistic. Many philosophers and cognitive scientists currently maintain that scientific explanation of phenomena consists of providing mechanisms that produce them (e.g., Bechtel & Abrahamsen, 2005; Sun, Coward, & Zenzen, 2005). A mechanism is a system of objects whose interactions regularly produce changes. All of the computational models described in this chapter are mechanistic, although they differ in what they take to be the parts and interactions that are central to explaining human thinking; for the neural network approaches, the computational mechanisms are also biological ones. But understanding of mechanism presupposes understanding of causality in that there must be a relation between the interactions of the parts that constitute production of the

Table 20.1: Summary of approaches to computational modeling of explanation

	Target of explanation	Explainers	Relation between target and explainers	Mode of generation
Deductive	Sentence	Sentences	Deduction	Backward chaining
Schema	Sentence	Pattern of Sentences	Fit	Search for fit, schema generation
Probabilistic	Variable node	Bayesian network	Conditional probability	Bayesian learning
Neural network	Neural group: multimodal representation	Neural groups	Gated activation, connectivity	Search, associative learning

relevant phenomena. Because scientific explanation depends on the notion of causality, and because understanding of causality is in part visual and kinesthetic, future comprehensive cognitive models of explanation will need to incorporate neural network simulations of people's nonverbal understanding of causality.

7. Conclusion

This chapter has reviewed four major computational approaches to understanding scientific explanations: deductive, schematic, probabilistic, and neural network. Table 20.1 summarizes the different approaches to providing and generating explanations. To some extent, the approaches are complementary rather than competitive, because explanation can take different forms in different areas of science and everyday life. However, at the root of scientific and everyday explanation is an understanding of causality represented nonverbally in human brains by populations of neurons encoding how physical manipulations produce sensory changes. Another advantage of taking a neural network approach to explanation is that it becomes possible to model how abductive inference, the generation of explanatory hypotheses, is a process that is multimodal, involving not only verbal representations but

also visual and emotional ones that constitute inputs and outputs to reasoning.

Acknowledgments

This research was supported by the Natural Sciences and Engineering Research Council of Canada. The authors are very grateful to Chris Eliasmith for much help in applying the Neural Engineering Framework.

References

Anderson, J. R. (1983). *The architecture of cognition.* Cambridge, MA: Harvard University Press.

Anderson, J. R. (1993). *Rules of the mind.* Hillsdale, NJ: Lawrence Erlbaum.

Baillargeon, R., Kotovsky, L., & Needham, A. (1995). The acquisition of physical knowledge in infancy. In D. Sperber, D. Premack, & A. J. Premack (Eds.), *Causal cognition: A multidisciplinary debate* (pp. 79–116). Oxford, UK: Clarendon Press.

Bechtel, W., & Abrahamsen, A. A. (2005). Explanation: A mechanistic alternative. *Studies in History and Philosophy of Biology and Biomedical Sciences, 36,* 421–441.

Bylander, T., Allemang, D., Tanner, M., & Josephson, J. (1991). The computational complexity of abduction. *Artificial Intelligence, 49,* 25–60.

Conklin, J., & Eliasmith, C. (2005). An attractor network model of path integration in the rat. *Journal of Computational Neuroscience, 18*, 183–203.

Eliasmith, C. (2005). Cognition with neurons: A large-scale, biologically realistic model of the Wason task. In B. Bara, L. Barasalou, & M. Bucciarelli (Eds.), *Proceedings of the XXVII Annual Conference of the Cognitive Science Society* (pp. 624–629). Mahwah, NJ: Lawrence Erlbaum.

Eliasmith, C., & Anderson, C. H. (2003). *Neural engineering: Computation, representation and dynamics in neurobiological systems.* Cambridge, MA: MIT Press.

Eliasmith, C., & Thagard, P. (2001). Integrating structure and meaning: A distributed model of analogical mapping. *Cognitive Science, 25,* 245–286.

Falkenhainer, B. (1990). A unified approach to explanation and theory formation. In J. Shrager & P. Langley (Eds.), *Computational models of discovery and theory formation.* (pp. 157–196). San Mateo, CA: Morgan Kaufman.

Falkenhainer, B., Forbus, K. D., & Gentner, D. (1989). The structure-mapping engine: Algorithms and examples. *Artificial Intelligence, 41,* 1–63.

Forbus, K. D. (1984). Qualitative process theory. *Artificial Intelligence, 24,* 85–168.

Gilovich, T., Griffin, D., & Kahneman, D. (Eds.). (2002). *Heuristics and biases: The psychology of intuitive judgment.* Cambridge, UK: Cambridge University Press.

Glymour, C. (2001). *The mind's arrows: Bayes nets and graphical causal models in psychology.* Cambridge, MA: MIT Press.

Glymour, C. (2003). Learning, prediction, and causal Bayes nets. *Trends in Cognitive Sciences, 7,* 43–48.

Gopnik, A., Glymour, C., Sobel, D. M., Schultz, L. E., Kushur, T., & Danks, D. (2004). A theory of causal learning in children: Causal maps and Bayes nets. *Psychological Review, 2004,* 3–32.

Gottman, J. M., Tyson, R., Swanson, K. R., Swanson, C. C., & Murray, J. D. (2003). *The mathematics of marriage: Dynamic nonlinear models.* Cambridge, MA: MIT Press.

Harman, G. (1973). *Thought.* Princeton, NJ: Princeton University Press.

Hempel, C. G. (1965). *Aspects of scientific explanation.* New York: The Free Press.

Holland, J. H., Holyoak, K. J., Nisbett, R. E., & Thagard, P. R. (1986). *Induction: Processes of inference, learning, and discovery.* Cambridge, MA: MIT Press/Bradford Books.

Josephson, J. R., & Josephson, S. G. (Eds.). (1994). *Abductive inference: Computation, philosophy, technology.* Cambridge, UK: Cambridge University Press.

Kahneman, D., Slovic, P., & Tversky, A. (1982). *Judgment under uncertainty: Heuristics and biases.* New York: Cambridge University Press.

Kitcher, P. (1993). *The advancement of science.* Oxford, UK: Oxford University Press.

Kitcher, P., & Salmon, W. (1989). *Scientific explanation.* Minneapolis: University of Minnesota Press.

Konolige, K. (1992). Abduction versus closure in causal theories. *Artificial Intelligence, 53,* 255–272.

Leake, D. B. (1992). *Evaluating explanations: A content theory.* Hillsdale, NJ: Lawrence Erlbaum.

Lipton, P. (2004). *Inference to the best explanation* (2nd ed.). London: Routledge.

Mandler, J. M. (2004). *The foundations of mind: Origins of conceptual thought.* Oxford, UK: Oxford University Press.

Neapolitan, R. (1990). *Probabilistic reasoning in expert systems.* New York: John Wiley.

Newell, A. (1990). *Unified theories of cognition.* Cambridge, MA: Harvard University Press.

Newell, A., & Simon, H. A. (1972). *Human problem solving.* Englewood Cliffs, NJ: Prentice Hall.

O'Reilly, R. C., & Munakata, Y. (2000). *Computational explorations in cognitive neuroscience.* Cambridge, MA: MIT Press.

Pearl, J. (1988). *Probabilistic reasoning in intelligent systems.* San Mateo, CA: Morgan Kaufman.

Pearl, J. (2000). *Causality: Models, reasoning, and inference.* Cambridge, UK: Cambridge University Press.

Plate, T. (2003). *Holographic reduced representations.* Stanford, CA: CSLI.

Read, S., & Marcus-Newhall, A. (1993). The role of explanatory coherence in the construction of social explanations. *Journal of Personality and Social Psychology, 65,* 429–447.

Russell, S., & Norvig, P. (2003). *Artificial intelligence: A modern approach* (2nd ed.). Upper Saddle River, NJ: Prentice Hall.

Salmon, W. (1970). Statistical explanation. In R. Colodny (Ed.), *The nature and function of scientific theories* (pp. 173–231). Pittsburgh, PA: University of Pittsburgh Press.

Salmon, W. (1984). *Scientific explanation and the causal structure of the world.* Princeton, NJ: Princeton University Press.

Schank, P., & Ranney, M. (1991). Modeling an experimental study of explanatory coherence. In *Proceedings of the Thirteenth Annual Conference of the Cognitive Science Society* (pp. 892–897). Hillsdale, NJ: Lawrence Erlbaum.

Schank, R. C. (1986). *Explanation patterns: Understanding mechanically and creatively.* Hillsdale, NJ: Lawrence Erlbaum.

Smolensky, P. (1990). Tensor product variable binding and the representation of symbolic structures in connectionist systems. *Artificial Intelligence, 46,* 159–217.

Spirtes, P., Glymour, C., & Scheines, R. (1993). *Causation, prediction, and search.* New York: Springer-Verlag.

Sun, R., Coward, L. A., & Zenzen, M. J. (2005). On levels of cognitive modeling. *Philosophical Psychology, 18,* 613–637.

Thagard, P. (1988). *Computational philosophy of science.* Cambridge, MA: MIT Press/Bradford Books.

Thagard, P. (1989). Explanatory coherence. *Behavioral and Brain Sciences, 12,* 435–467.

Thagard, P. (1992). *Conceptual revolutions.* Princeton, NJ: Princeton University Press.

Thagard, P. (1999). *How scientists explain disease.* Princeton, NJ: Princeton University Press.

Thagard, P. (2000). *Coherence in thought and action.* Cambridge, MA: MIT Press.

Thagard, P. (2003). Pathways to biomedical discovery. *Philosophy of Science, 70,* 235–254.

Thagard, P. (2005). *Mind: Introduction to cognitive science* (2nd ed.). Cambridge, MA: MIT Press.

Thagard, P. (2007). Abductive inference: From philosophical analysis to neural mechanisms. In A. Feeney & E. Heit (Eds.), *Inductive reasoning: Experimental, developmental, and computational approaches* (pp. 226–247). Cambridge: Cambridge University Press.

Thagard, P., & Aubie, B. (forthcoming). Emotional consciousness: A neural model of how cognitive appraisal and somatic perception interact to produce qualitative experience. *Consciousness and Cognition.*

Woodward, J. (2003). *Scientific explanation.* Retrieved August 11, 2005, from http://plato.stanford.edu/entries/scientific-explanation/

Woodward, J. (2004). *Making things happen: A theory of causal explanation.* Oxford, UK: Oxford University Press.

CHAPTER 21

Cognitive Modeling for Cognitive Engineering

Wayne D. Gray

1. Introduction

Cognitive engineering is the application of cognitive science theories to human factors practice. As this description suggests, there are strong symbioses between cognitive engineering and cognitive science, but there are also strong differences.

Symbiosis implies a mutual influence, and the history of cognitive engineering supports this characterization in two key areas: the development of cognitive theory and the development of computational modeling software. For theory development, a stringent test of our understanding of cognitive processes is whether we can apply our knowledge to real-world problems. The degree to which we succeed at this task is the degree to which we have developed robust and powerful theories. The degree to which we fail at this task is the degree to which more research and stronger theories are required (Gray, Schoelles, & Myers, 2004).

The development of the production-system-based architectures most strongly associated with cognitive engineering (ACT-R

[Anderson, 1993], EPIC [Kieras & Meyer, 1997], and Soar [Newell, 1990]) was motivated by the desire to explore basic cognitive processes. However, each has been strongly influenced by a formalism for cognitive task analysis that was developed explicitly for the application of cognitive science to human-computer interaction (Card, Moran, & Newell, 1980a, 1980b, 1983). Indeed, it can be argued that the modern form of ACT-R (Anderson et al., 2004) and the development of EPIC (Kieras & Meyer, 1997), with their modules that run in parallel, owes a great intellectual debt to the development of CPM-GOMS (Gray & Boehm-Davis, 2000; John, 1988, 1993). It is definitely the case that the potential of these architectures for application has long been recognized (Elkind et al., 1989; Pew, 2007; Pew & Mavor, 1998) and that much recent development of these basic research architectures has been funded at least partly because of their potential in tutoring systems (S. F. Chipman, personal communication, April 2, 2007), human-computer interaction (Chipman & Kieras, 2004; Freed et al., 2003; Williams, 2000), or human-system integration (Gluck & Pew, 2005; Gray & Pew, 2004).

On the other hand, the engineering enterprise of building systems that are in some way directly relevant to real-world problems is fundamentally different from the basic research enterprise of developing or elaborating cognitive theory. Cognitive science and cognitive engineering can be viewed as differing along five dimensions. Although these differences do not imply a dichotomy, they can be viewed as capturing some of the characteristic differences of these two endeavors.

First is the nature of the problems picked. As an applied discipline, the problems addressed by cognitive engineering are often not picked by the researcher, but are defined for the researcher in terms of safety, workload, design, operational need, or financial impact.

Second is the amount of prior study of the task and task domain. Many of our best models of cognitive theory rest on years of exploring a small number of experimental paradigms within a well-specific domain. Great examples of this would be models of reasoning (Johnson-Laird, 1993; Rips, 1994), models of category learning (Love, Medin, & Gureckis, 2004; Nosofsky & Palmeri, 1997; Shepard, Hovland, & Jenkins, 1961), as well as models of memory retrieval (Anderson & Schooler, 1991; Hintzman, 2005). In contrast, many computational models for cognitive engineering tend to be first-generation attempts in that little, if any, prior empirical or modeling work exists. Two examples that are discussed in this chapter are Byrne and Kirlik's (2005) work on modeling the taxiing behavior of commercial airline pilots and Gluck's work on modeling uninhabited air vehicle operators (Gluck, Ball, & Krusmark, 2007).

Third, many but not all computational models for cognitive engineering entail domain-specific expertise. This characterization applies to both the development of tutoring systems for the training of novices as well as to the modeling of expert performance. It is definitely the case that much has been learned about basic cognitive processes by studying the acquisition or execution of expertise (Chi, Feltovich, & Glaser, 1981).

It is also the case that there is a vast middle ground of educational research in which the distinction between basic versus domain-specific work is often blurred (Anderson, Conrad, & Corbett, 1989; Corbett & Anderson, 1988; Singley & Anderson, 1989). However, at the further extreme are the attempts to model rare forms of expertise, such as that possessed by Submarine Commanders (Ehret, Gray, & Kirschenbaum, 2000; Gray & Kirschenbaum, 2000; Gray, Kirschenbaum, & Ehret, 1997; Kirschenbaum & Gray, 2000), uninhabited air vehicle (UAV) operators (Gluck et al., 2007), or airline pilots (Byrne & Kirlik, 2005). Although, arguably, insights and progress into basic research issues have emerged from these studies, it is undoubtedly true that the motivation and funding to study and the particular expertise of such small populations[1] stems from the need to solve very important applied problems.

Fourth, computational modeling for cognitive engineering operates in an arena where the demand for answers is more important than the demand for understanding. Newell warned us about such arenas (Newell & Card, 1985); if another discipline can reduce human errors, increase productivity, and in general augment cognition, then who cares if those advances rely on an in-depth understanding of the human cognitive architecture? The issue for cognitive science is one of relevance.[2]

---

1 For example, the active duty population of submarine commanders is estimated to be less than 100.

2 A reviewer for this chapter proposed astronomy as an example in which public funding continues to flow in the absence of any immediate relevance to the human condition. It is not clear, however, that this example actually makes that case. Indeed, the evidence suggests just the opposite. Astronomy is the smallest field that the National Science Foundation tracks in its surveys of doctoral scientists and engineers in the United States (Tsapogas, 2003). Staying just within the NSF-defined category of physical sciences, in 2003, there were 4,280 living astronomers in the United States (including retired, unemployed, and employed) compared with 69,460 chemists (excluding biochemistry), 20,220 earth scientists, and 40,440 physicists. Astronomers are fond of pointing out that expensive space programs, such as the Shuttle, are not astronomy and that the bulk of the money in expensive "big science" programs, such as the Hubble telescope

Fifth, whereas many of our best cognitive science models focus on the distilled essence of a cognitive functionality, such as memory or categorization, cognitive engineering models are called on to predict performance in task environments that entail many cognitive functionalities. Hence, the particular challenge of computational modeling for cognitive engineering is to model not just the pieces but also the control of an integrated cognitive system (Gray, 2007b).

These characteristic differences between basic and applied computational cognitive modeling are not meant as dichotomies, but rather to illustrate the different sets of challenges faced by cognitive engineering. To some degree, these challenges can be seen as challenges for the basic science, especially the need for cognitive engineering to model the control of integrated cognitive systems (the last item on my list). Unfortunately, neither the list nor the efforts that instantiate it are tidy.

The next section reviews the seminal work of Card, Moran, and Newell (Card et al., 1983) from the modern perspective. We then jump to the 2000s to discuss the issues and applications of cognitive engineering, first for the broad category of complex systems and then for the classic area of human-computer interaction, with a focus on human interaction with quantitative information, that is, visual analytics.[3] The chapter ends with a summary and discussion of cognitive engineering.

2. Initial Approaches to Cognitive Modeling for Cognitive Engineering

Attempts to apply computational and mathematical modeling techniques to human factors issues have a long and detailed history.

Unfortunately, we cannot review that history here; however, we can do the next best thing and point the reader to Pew's (2007) very personal history of human performance modeling from the 1950s on. In this section, we pick up the cognitive science side of the story with Card et al.'s (1983) seminal GOMS[4] framework for applying the information-processing approach to developing cognitive task analysis.[5]

Before the cognitive revolution and, arguably, continuing today, most researchers studying cognitive human behavior were trained in experimental psychology. This tradition focuses on teasing and torturing secrets from nature by tightly controlled studies in which small manipulations are made, and humans perform many nearly identical trials. People with this background and training often cannot conceive how someone could possibly study, let alone model, something as complex as VCR programming (Gray, 2000), driving (Salvucci, 2006), the influence of the layout of a graph on performance (Peebles & Cheng, 2003), information search on the World Wide Web (Blackmon, Kitajima, & Polson, 2005; Kaur & Hornof, 2005; Pirolli, 2005), or air traffic control issues (ATC) (Byrne & Kirlik, 2005).

Although the study of such issues is complex and demanding, it is made possible by an open secret long exploited by the human factors community (Kirwan & Ainsworth, 1992) and long recognized by cognitive science (see Simon, 1996, Chapter 8, "The Architecture of Complexity," and his discussion therein of "near decomposability"); namely, that most any human behavior that extends in time longer than a few minutes can be conceived of as a hierarchical series of tasks, subtasks, and subsubtasks. The

---

and deep space probes, goes to engineering, not astronomy.

3 Where visual analytics is defined as the visual representation of quantitative data (Thomas & Cook, 2005; Wong & Thomas, 2004). The human-computer interaction interest in visual analytics lies in the building of interfaces that support the search and representation of massive quantities of quantitative data.

4 A GOMS task analysis analyzes human behavior in terms of its goals, the operators needed to accomplish the goals, sequences of operators and subgoals that constitute methods for accomplishing a goal, and selection rules for choosing a method when alternative methods for accomplishing the same goal exist.

5 Different approaches to the topic of cognitive engineering and cognitive engineering models are possible and two excellent chapters that are very different from the current chapter have been authored by Kieras (2007) and Byrne (2007a).

structure of this hierarchy is, for the most part, determined by the nature of the task and task environment and less so by the human operator. Rather than having to deal with hours of behavior as one unit, the human factors analyst can break the behavior down to the level required by the goals of the analysis.

For the human factors professional, this *task analysis* approach works well for designing complex industrial operations in which the lowest unit of analysis is the human operator as well as designing procedures for individual humans in which each low-level task requires minutes or hours to perform (Kirwan & Ainsworth, 1992; Shepherd, 1998, 2001). For the cognitive scientist interested in interactive behavior, arguably, the job is even easier. Although behaviors may extend indefinitely in time, most interactive behavior results from and results in changes to the task environment. For the pilot of an F-16, the driver of a car, or the user of a VCR, the paradigm comes down to (a) do something, (b) evaluate change in the world, and (c) return to (a). Although interactive behavior is complex, the complexity lies not in planning and executing a long sequence of behavior, but (a) evaluating the current state of the task environment, (b) deciding what can be done "now" that will advance the user's goals, given the current state of the task environment, (c) evaluating the strategies available to the human operator for accomplishing the current, momentary goal, and (d) executing (c) to accomplish (b). The key to this interactive cycle is the *unit task*.

2.1. The Unit Task as a Control Construct for Human Interactive Behavior

Card, Moran, and Newell's conceptual breakthrough was that even tasks which lasted only minutes were composed from a series of smaller "*unit tasks* within which behavior is highly integrated and between which dependencies are minimal. This quasi-independence of unit tasks means that their effects are approximately additive" (Card et al., 1983, p. 313). The "unit task is fundamentally a control construct, not a task construct" (Card et al., 1983, p. 386). The unit task is not given by the task environment, but results from the interaction of the task structure with the control problems faced by the user.

The prototypical example of a unit task (from Chapter 11 in Card et al., 1983) is the structure imposed by a typist on transcription typing. The physical task environment for transcription typing consists of the dictated speech, a word processor, and a foot pedal that controls how much of a recording is played back. As speech is typically much faster than skilled typing, the basic problem faced by the typist is how much of the recording to listen to before shutting it off. The efficient typist listens while typing, and the longer he or she listens, the greater the lag between what they are hearing and what they are typing. At some point, the typist shuts off the recording and continues to type until he or she can remember no more of the recording with certainty. With some experience with the particular speaker and maybe with the particular topic, a skilled transcription typist will minimize the amount of rewind and replay, and maximize the amount typed per unit task. This chopping up of the physical task environment into unit tasks reflects a control process that adjusts performance to the characteristics of the task (the speed of dictation and clarity of speech), the typist's general typing skill (number of words per minute), and the typist's cognitive, perceptual, and motor limits.

2.2. The Path from Unit Tasks through Interactive Routines to Embodiment

A typical GOMS unit task is shown in Table 21.1. This sample unit task is one of approximately twenty needed to model Lovett's (Lovett & Anderson, 1996) building sticks task, a simple game whose objective is to match the length of a target stick by building a new stick from pieces of various sizes (a dry analogue to the better-known water jug problem). This unit task would be invoked to subtract length from the built stick when it is larger than the target stick. This example shows that each

Table 21.1: Example unit task for the "building sticks task" using NGOMSL format (Kieras, 1997)

Step	Description	Stmt time	Op	# Ops	Op time	Total time
Method for goal: Subtract stick<position>		0.1				0.1
Step 1	Point to stick<position>	0.1	P	1	1.1	1.2
Step 2	Mouse click stick<position>	0.1	BB	1	0.2	0.3
Step 3	Confirm: Stick is now black	0.1	M	1	1.2	1.3
Step 4	Point to inside of "your stick"	0.1	P	1	1.1	1.2
Step 6	Click mouse	0.1	BB	1	0.2	0.3
Step 7	Confirm: Change in stick size	0.1	M	1	1.2	1.3
Step 8	Return with goal accomplished	0.1				0.1
						5.8

Stmt time = statement time; Op = operator; P = point operator, BB = button click; M = mental operator, All times ore in second.

line or statement has an execution overhead (Stmt Time) of 0.1 second. There are three types of operators (Ops) used. P is a point operator that is assumed to have a time of 1.1 seconds. BB is a button click (up and down) with the duration of 0.2 sec. M is a mental operator with the duration of 1.2 sec. The entire method for accomplishing this unit task lasts 5.8 sec.

As suggested by the table, the NGOMSL format reduces all operators to one of a small set. The duration of each operator is based on empirical data, mathematical descriptions of behavior such as Fitts' Law or Hicks Law, and so on. Much of what goes into an NGOMSL analysis comes out of Card et al.'s (1983, Chapter 2) Model Human Processor. That chapter summarizes many important regularities gleaned from experimental psychology but cast into a form that could be used by human factors analysts.

GOMS was intended as a tool for cognitive engineering. Hence, whereas each line of the NGOMSL analysis could be made more precise and more tailored to, say, the exact distance moved, a large motivation for GOMS was to derive engineering-style approximations for predicting human behavior. However, for some applied purposes, the grain size of GOMS analyses in Table 21.1 is too gross. Indeed, to model transcription typing, John (1996) had to develop a version of GOMS that went below the grain size of normal GOMS. John (1988) rep-

resented the dependencies between cognitive, perceptual, and motor operations during task performance (see Figure 21.1) in an activity network formalism (Schweickert, Fisher, & Proctor, 2003) that allowed the computation of critical paths. This version of GOMS is called CPM-GOMS, where the CPM has a double meaning as both critical path method and cognitive, perceptual, and motor operations.

The power of this representation received a boost from its ability to predict performance times in a very prominent field test of two workstations for telephone toll and assistance operators (TAOs; Gray, John, & Atwood, 1993). Not only did CPM-GOMS models predict the counterintuitive finding that TAOs using a proposed new workstation would perform more slowly than those who used the older workstations, but after a field trial confirmed this prediction, the models provided a diagnosis in terms of the procedures imposed by workstations on the TAO as to how and why newer, faster technology could perform more slowly than older technology.

2.3. The Legacy of Card, Moran, and Newell

Representations have a power to make certain things obvious, and the GOMS and CPM-GOMS representations did so in several ways. First was the basic insight offered

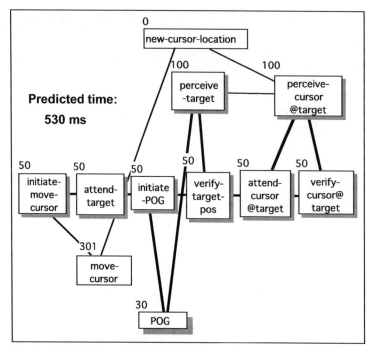

Figure 21.1. A CPM-GOMS model of an interactive routine. This interactive routine could be instantiated as Step 1 and Step 4 in Table 21.1. It shows the cognitive, perceptual, and motor operations required to move a mouse to a predetermined location on a computer screen. Total predicted time is 530 ms. The middle row shows cognitive operators with a default execution time of 50 ms each. Above that line are the perceptual operators, and below it are the motor operators. The flow of operators is from left to right, with connecting lines indicating dependencies. Within an operator type, the dependencies are sequential. However, between operator types, the dependencies may be parallel. The numbers above each operator indicate the time, in milliseconds, for that operator to execute. Time is accumulated from left to right along the critical path. The critical path is indicated by bold lines connecting the shadowed boxes. Loc = location; POG = point of gaze. See Gray and Boehm-Davis (2000) for more detailed information.

by the unit task, namely, that functional units of behavior resulted from an interaction between the task being performed, detailed elements of the design of the task environment, and limits of human cognitive, perceptual, and motor operations. Second, the notation of CPM-GOMS made it very clear that all human behavior was embodied behavior. Indeed, the mechanistic representations of CPM-GOMS were very compatible with the views of embodiment expressed by modelers such as Ballard (Ballard, Hayhoe, & Pelz, 1995; Ballard

et al., 1997; Ballard & Sprague, 2007) and Kieras (Kieras & Meyer, 1997) and, at the same time, completely side-stepped the extreme, philosophical claims that are sometimes attached to this concept (Wilson, 2002). Third, whereas standard GOMS and NGOMSL (Kieras, 1997) emphasized control of cognition, CPM-GOMS provided a representation that showed that this control was far from linear, but entailed a complex interleaving of various parallel activities.

Whether as part of the Zeitgeist or as a driving force, the 1990s saw many of the insights of CPM-GOMS become standard among modelers. Kieras and Myers (1997) built a new cognitive architecture, EPIC, by expanding Kieras's parsimonious production system (Bovair, Kieras, & Polson, 1990; Kieras & Bovair, 1986) to include separate modules for motor movement, eye movements, and so on. ACT-R (Anderson, 1993) flirted with the addition of a module for visual attention (Anderson, Matessa, & Lebiere, 1997), experimented with a graft of EPIC's modules (Byrne & Anderson, 1998), and completely restructured itself so that all cognitive activity (not simply that which required interactive behavior) entailed puts and calls to a modular mind (Anderson et al., 2004). During the same period, Ballard's notions of embodiment (Ballard et al., 1997) took literal form in Walter – a virtual human who could follow a path while avoiding obstacles, picking up trash, and stopping to check traffic before he crossed the street (Ballard & Sprague, 2007).

GOMS and the concept of the unit task were conceived as tools to develop "an engineering-style theory of how the user interacts with the computer" (Newell & Card, 1985, p. 215) in an effort to "harden" the science base for cognitive engineering. During the 1990s, the attention of the basic research cognitive science community turned to issues of control of cognition, exactly those issues that were highlighted first by the unit task and then by CPM-GOMS. Although by no means complete, by the turn of the twenty-first century, the theoretical tools and modeling techniques were in place to accelerate progress on the cognitive engineering agenda.

3. Issues and Applications of Computational Modeling for Cognitive Engineering

To illustrate the differences between contemporary cognitive engineering and contemporary cognitive science, a very selective review of two areas of recent research is provided. The first is the broad area of complex systems. Work in this area has the typical human factors character of one team of researchers working on one applied problem. The second area is the human-computer interaction topic of visual analytics – how best to design computer interfaces (where "interface" includes "interactive procedures") to facilitate the search and understanding of abstract data presented in visual form. Work in this area resembles the type of distributed research activity familiar to researchers in areas such as visual attention, memory, or categorization.

The position adopted in this section is that the contribution of cognitive engineering is in solving applied problems and in identifying gaps in the underlying cognitive theory. To address this first point, more time than the reader might expect is spent on explaining the domain as well as explaining the nature of the problem that is being solved. To address the second point, details of the model are not discussed. As most cognitive engineering relies on modeling techniques developed elsewhere, those interested in these details may turn to the original sources. Rather, the focus here will be on identifying the special problems that the modelers faced, theoretical mechanisms that contributed to the success of the applied model, and identifying the gaps in cognitive theory that the applied model revealed.

3.1. Complex Systems

A major goal of cognitive engineering is to design high-fidelity models of the demands on human cognitive, perceptual, and action resources during the operation of complex, technological systems. The level of analysis of cognitive engineering is much like that of cognitive science. However, a characteristic difference is that in the typical laboratory study for, say, memory or visual search, the task being studied is the main task being performed. In contrast, cognitive engineering tends not to focus on the main task per se, but on a piece of the main task. So in the arena of commercial aviation, the focus is not on the successful operation of an air traffic control system or even on the take-off, flight, and successful landing of individual flights. Much more typically, the focus would be on a small portion of the flight, such as why pilots get lost while taxiing to their gate after landing. Likewise, for the case of driving a car on a crowded highway, cognitive engineering is not concerned with variables such as the number of drivers on the road, miles driven, number of accidents, and so on. Rather, cognitive engineering would focus on basic questions concerning how best to design instrument panels and what sorts of guidelines should be given to manufacturers regarding the design of in-vehicle systems, such as car radios, navigation systems, and cell phones (Green, 1999, 2002).

3.1.1. THE PREDATOR UNINHABITED AIR VEHICLE

An important challenge for cognitive engineering is the design of new systems, especially those that create new roles for human operators. One such system is UAVs. UAVs are increasingly used by the military and intelligence agencies in place of humanly piloted aircraft for a variety of missions. There is also some thought that in the foreseeable future, UAVs may replace some portion of human-piloted commercial aviation (Gluck et al., 2005).

Remotely piloting a slow-moving aircraft while searching for ground targets is a mission that is difficult for even experienced Air Force pilots. A complete model that could take off, perform missions, and return safely would entail the detailed integration of most, if not all, functional subsystems studied by cognitive scientists today as well as raising challenging issues in the control of integrated cognitive systems. Such a complete system is beyond our current state-of-the-art. However, partial systems can be useful in determining limits of human performance and identifying strategies that work. Such partial models have been built by Gluck and colleagues (Gluck et al., 2007) to study the challenges to the human pilot in three routine UAV maneuvers. These researchers modeled two alternative sets of strategies and were able to show that one set would not meet the per-

formance demands of the UAV, whereas the other set would. Close analysis of human performance data suggested that the best human pilots used the strategies incorporated into the best performing model.

Unlike tasks such as simple decision making or categorization, a key challenge to the modelers was obtaining access to an adequate simulation of the pilot's task environment, namely the aerodynamics of a UAV in flight. The flight dynamics of a UAV are very different from those of manned vehicles, and understanding these dynamics presents a challenge for even experienced Air Force pilots. Given that the UAV is traveling at such and such an altitude and speed, what needs to be done to turn it right by 25 degrees while descending by 1,000 feet and slowing by 50 mph within a given period of time without stalling? Computing the effect of such changes on UAV flight in such a dynamic task environment is not trivial and, indeed, is a significant aerodynamic engineering effort. An additional problem not faced by basic theory cognitive science modelers is that UAVs are artifacts that are being constantly upgraded. Indeed, the most recent UAVs have very different flight dynamics than the UAV used by Gluck and associates (2007). This interesting program of research has slowed to a halt, as the flight characteristics of the new UAVs are sufficiently different from the old UAVs to make cognitive modeling impossible without a new aerodynamic model.

3.1.2. RUNWAY INCURSIONS

Making a wrong turn while driving is frustrating. Making a wrong turn after landing your passenger jet and trying to taxi to your gate is a *runway incursion*, which is considered by air traffic control as "creating a collision hazard with another aircraft taking off or landing or intending to take off or land" (Byrne & Kirlik, 2005; Wald, 2006, p. 137). Such errors are serious enough that they are tabulated in a nationwide database and were the focus of a National Aeronautics & Space Administration (NASA) funded effort to find a systematic explanation for their occurrence.

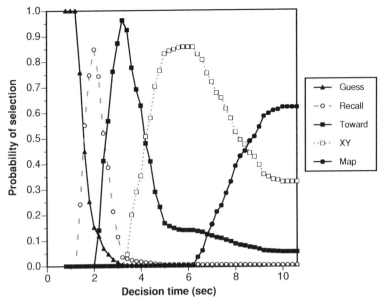

Figure 21.2. Predicted selection probability for each turn heuristic by decision-time horizon. (From Byrne & Kirlik, 2005).

The modeling effort by Byrne and Kirlik (2005) had three key components; (1) interviews with pilots to elicit the knowledge and strategies used to navigate from the runway to gate; (2) an analysis of 284 routes from landing to gate at nine major U.S. airports; (3) an analysis of the time-horizon for making a decision to turn an aircraft as a function of intersection distance and aircraft dynamics (when on the ground, large aircraft are neither graceful nor easy to turn).

From their knowledge engineering effort, the researchers obtained five heuristics that pilots used to determine which direction to turn at an intersection. The cognitive modeling focused on strategy selection as a function of the time remaining before a decision had to be made and a turn initiated. As in the UAV example, an important component of the model was aircraft dynamics; however, in the passenger jet case, it was the dynamics of a lumbering 870,000-pound passenger jet as it taxied on the ground toward its gate, specifically, an algorithm "to calculate the maximum speed with which a turn of a given type could be negotiated" (Byrne & Kirlik, 2005, p. 148). The model was based on the ACT-R cognitive architecture but run as a Monte Carlo simulation for 300 repetitions at each of 50 time-horizons. The results predicted the selection probability for each of five heuristics. The details of the model and the heuristics are beyond the scope of the current chapter, but a glance at Figure 21.2 shows large differences between predicted strategy as a function of the decision-time horizon.

The Byrne and Kirlik (2005) work focused on errors in decision making and showed a good match to the data set of real errors as well as to a better documented set of errors collected from experienced airline pilots in a high-fidelity flight simulator. Making an error while taxiing is a low-probability event. The chance of a serious, loss-of-life incident resulting from such an error is an even lower probability event. However, in an ATC system that supervises thousands of takeoffs and landings each day, even extremely low-probability events may come to pass. The low actual probability makes the empirical data difficult to collect as the event is occurring.

When a terrible, low-probability event does occur, all too often, the public and official response is to find someone to blame – in aviation, this usually means blaming the pilot or the air traffic controller. Model-based analysis such as Byrne and Kirlik's (2005) does not eliminate the human responsibility from the accident equation, but it does show that properties of the designed task environment contribute to such accidents in all-too-predictable ways. The simplest and oldest way to augment human cognition is by the design of the task environment. Byrne and Kirlik's analyses point to how this might be done to reduce errors while taxiing.

3.1.3. DRIVING AND DRIVING WHILE DIALING

An especially notable attempt to model a complex task is Salvucci's program of research to model driving (Salvucci, 2001, 2006; Salvucci & Gray, 2004; Salvucci & Macuga, 2001). Driving is such an everyday, mundane, expertise that it may be necessary to step back and remind the reader of its cognitive complexity:

> The task of driving is in fact an everchanging set of basic tasks that must be integrated and interleaved. Michon (1985) identifies three classes of task processes for driving: operational processes that involve manipulating control inputs for stable driving, tactical processes that govern safe interactions with the environment and other vehicles, and strategic processes for higher-level reasoning and planning. Driving typically involves all three types of processes working together to achieve safe, stable navigation – for instance, monitoring a traffic light and controlling the vehicle to stop and start, or deciding to make a turn and controlling the vehicle through the turn. Some tasks are not continual but intermittent, arising in specific situations – for instance, parking a vehicle at a final destination. In addition, driving may include secondary tasks, perhaps related to the primary driving task (e.g., using a navigation device), or perhaps mostly or entirely unrelated (e.g., tuning a radio or dialing a cellular phone). (Salvucci, 2006, p. 363)

Salvucci's modeling work has evolved over the last several years. The most complete report of his work is contained in the *Human Factors* article (Salvucci, 2006). In that work, Salvucci presents the results of comparing the models with human behavior on several dependent variables related to lane keeping, curve negotiation, and lane changing. The dependent variables include performance-based measures, such as steering angle and lateral position, as well as eye data measures thought to be closely related to visual attention. Salvucci's modeling is done within the ACT-R architecture of cognition. In all cases, his work benefits from ACT-R's ability to use the same simulation software as used by his human subjects. This means that the same type of log files are generated by models and humans, and the same types of analyses can be easily applied.

Salvucci's basic model of driving has been integrated with models of dialing different cell phones (Salvucci, 2001). The results have practical implications in yielding clear predictions for the differential effect of cell phone design on driving performance. The efforts to integrate models of two individual tasks (driving and dialing) also have implications for the control of integrated cognitive systems (Salvucci, 2005). This later work nicely illustrates the importance of cognitive engineering for identifying important gaps in basic cognitive theory.

3.1.4. PREDICTING SKILLED PERFORMANCE FROM ANALYSES OF NOVICES

Verifying a task analysis of a complex system is itself a complex task, with little guidance and few shortcuts suggested by the literature (Kirwan & Ainsworth, 1992; Shepherd, 2001). In some sense, the knowledge contained in the computational cognitive model can be considered a verification of a task analysis if the model is able to perform the task at human levels of competence. Perhaps a more stringent validation of a task analysis is that, with experience at the task, the knowledge taught to human novices suffices to produce expert-level performance. Taatgen and Lee (2003) take up this challenge with modest but noteworthy results.

The acquisition of skilled performance is an enduring topic in both the basic and applied literature. Indeed, the dominant characterization of skilled performance as passing through three phases (Fitts & Posner,

1967) comes from a researcher, Paul Fitts, who made contributions to both experimental psychology and human factors research. Taatgen and Lee (2003) embrace Anderson's (1982) characterizations of the improvement in performance between stages as a shift from declarative to procedural knowledge with practice. The model they built was written in ACT-R and was seeded with basic knowledge (how to click on buttons, where the various information items were on the display and what they represented), as well as a declarative representation of the instructions to human subjects.

The vehicle they chose for their test is the Kanfer-Ackerman air traffic controller (KA-ATC) task (Ackerman & Kanfer, 1994); a game-like simplification of the air traffic controller's task. The model used Taatgen's production compilation enhancement (Taatgen & Anderson, 2002) to ACT-R. With experience, production compilation converts declarative knowledge and very general productions into task-specific productions. Through production compilation, many fewer production cycles are required to perform the task, and many retrievals from memory are replaced by incorporating specific declarative knowledge into the specialized productions.

The Taatgen and Lee (2003) model incorporated the knowledge and declarative representation of procedures that humans would acquire through a thorough reading of task instructions. All parameters used by the model were the default ACT-R parameters. The model played the game for ten, 10-minute periods (trials). Model and human performance were compared at three increasingly detailed levels of analysis; overall performance, unit task performance, and key-stroke levels. Across all three levels of comparison, the model mimicked the qualitative changes in human performance (as shown by generally high r^2 values). The absolute match of the model to human data (such as would be tested by RMSE comparisons, although these were not provided by the authors) showed mixed results. In several cases, the models were right on top of the human data. For overall performance, the models started out better than the humans, but began to match human performance after the fifth 10-minute trial. For two of the three unit tasks, the model provided a good match to human performance. In the third unit task, the model was slower. For the key-stroke data presented, the model also was generally slower than the humans.

The authors attribute the differences in model and human performance to several factors. First, other analyses (John & Lallement, 1997; Schunn & Reder, 2001) have established that different humans bring different strategies to bear on this task, whereas the model only used one strategy. Furthermore, human performance as it speeds up seems to exhibit more parallelism than does model performance. These differences reflect limits of the current ACT-R architecture that does not learn new strategies with experience or by exploration and can only deploy the strategies provided by the modeler. On the other hand, the general quantitative fit of model to data is good, and the qualitative fit captures the speed up in human performance with experience. In general, the Taatgen and Lee (2003) work is a successful demonstration of the ability of cognitive engineering to predict expert patterns of performance given a novice task analysis and instructions.

3.1.5. SUMMARY: COMPLEX SYSTEMS
The previous four cases are good examples of cognitive engineering applied to complex systems. Although the applications may seem modest, each of the computational cognitive models is built on an architecture, ACT-R, that was intended as a vehicle for basic research, not applied. In this usage, the ACT-R architecture becomes a vehicle for applying basic research to applied problems.

The question of "why ACT-R" arises. The answer is straightforward and rests more on the nature of cognitive engineering than on ACT-R's claims as an architecture of cognition (although this aspect certainly does not hurt!). First, compared with connectionist models, it is much easier to write ACT-R models that interact with tasks that consist of multiple components that extend serially in time (e.g., such as piloting a UAV). Second, compared with Soar, over the past 15 years, ACT-R (like EPIC) has changed dramatically to incorporate many of the theoretical advances of cognitive science. Of prime importance for modeling interactive behavior has been ACT-R's (like EPIC's) emphasis on modeling the interaction of cognitive, perceptual, and motor operations. Third, and probably foremost, the current ACT-R software (ACT-R 6.0; see Anderson et al., 2004) reflects over a decade of software engineering. One result of this software engineering is that it is now relatively easy to incorporate new modules into ACT-R to either supplement or replace existing modules. Fourth, in the last eight years (Byrne & Anderson, 1998), a significant part of the software engineering effort has been focused on enabling ACT-R models to directly interact with the same software task environments as human users. Fifth, a concomitant of this software engineering has been a decade-long effort to produce tutorial materials and conduct a series of summer schools to train a wide variety of users in ACT-R.

Whatever the particular merits of ACT-R, it is clear that the last two decades have seen a significant expansion in the scope of cognitive engineering. We have gone from a focus on small, self-paced tasks, such as text editing (Card et al., 1983), to larger and much more dynamic tasks, such as piloting UAVs and driving cars.

3.2. Visual Analytics: Human-Computer Interaction during the Search and Exploration of Massive Sets of Qualitative Data

Visual analytics is a new label (Thomas & Cook, 2005; Wong & Thomas, 2004) for efforts to present abstract information in visual form in both structured and unstructured displays. Structured displays include the traditional bar charts and line graphs (Wainer & Velleman, 2001), as well as newer technologies that allow us to dynamically create multiple, multidimensional, complex representations of selected subsets of vast data sets (for an excellent sampling of recent innovative visualizations for visual analytic displays, see the special issue organized by Keim et al., 2006). The most common example of unstructured displays is the World Wide Web. Although individual Web pages or Web sites may be well structured, the Web as a whole is not.

Motivation for work in this area is high. Knowledge may be power, but data is not knowledge until it can be processed and presented so that a human can understand and use it. Techniques for displaying data are key to transforming data into knowledge. These techniques need to support the human user in rapid, exploratory search and in comprehending what is found. Unfortunately, modern techniques for visualization are not only prey to well-known usability problems (Andre & Wickens, 1995) but can introduce new and debilitating distortions. For example, three-dimensional representations of terrain, favored by many new military systems, make it extremely difficult to accurately judge relative and absolute distances (Smallman & St. John, 2005). Identifying and guarding against such alluring and subtle distortions should be one of the goals of cognitive engineering.

The following section begins with a brief history of visual analytics as treated by cognitive science. Next is a sampling of recent work on structured displays. This sampling is followed by a discussion of work on seeking and extracting information from the unstructured environment of the World Wide Web.

3.2.1. A BRIEF HISTORY
In large part, the history of visual analytics has been driven by two very different communities; judgment and decision making, and human-computer interaction.

3.2.1.1. *Judgment and Decision-Making Beginnings.* In the 1980s, Payne, Bettman, and Johnson (as summarized in their 1993 book) acknowledged borrowing the construct of elementary information processes (EIPs) from Newell and Simon (1972) to quantify the cognitive effort involved in various judgment and decision-making strategies.

By demonstrating that people would adopt strategies that traded off decision-making effectiveness (accuracy) for cognitive efficiency (effort), this research had a large and important influence on both the judgment and decision-making as well as the cognitive science communities (e.g., Anderson, 1990; Anderson, 1991).

The EIPs construct provides a framework for thinking about the cognition involved in various decision strategies under a variety of conditions by comparing the effectiveness and efficiency of alternative strategies that use partial information against that of a decision strategy that uses complete information. However, the EIP construct is limited in that it is not embedded in a theory of the control of cognition. For example, efficiency is assessed by simply comparing the number of EIPs used by alternative strategies with the number used by the total information strategy.

The original work ignored how the information was displayed and factors associated with the cost of information extraction, manipulation, and retention. This emphasis began to change in the 1990s. Researchers in the judgment and decision-making tradition began to focus on the influence of the organization, form, and sequence of information on strategy selection (e.g., Fennema & Kleinmuntz, 1995; Kleinmuntz & Schkade, 1993; Schkade & Kleinmuntz, 1994). Other research looked at how individual differences in working memory capacity interacted with interface design to affect performance on decision-making tasks (Lohse, 1997). At least one study investigated how the cost of information access affects strategy selection (Lohse & Johnson, 1996). Other studies looked at how the design of decision aids may have unintended consequences for the decision strategies that people adopt (Adelman et al., 1996; Benbasat & Todd, 1996; Rose & Wolfe, 2000; Todd & Benbasat, 1994, 1999, 2000).

3.2.1.2. *Human-Computer Interaction Beginnings.* The growth of research in cognitive modeling of information search provides a case study on the role of technology in scientific research. Although other work

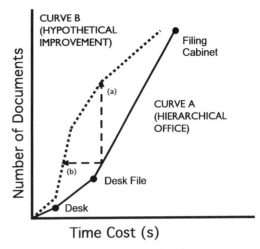

Figure 21.3. Cost of knowledge characteristic function (adapted from Card et al., 1994, Figure 21.1). Notice that improvement (Curve B, the dotted line) can come in one of two ways. By keeping the time costs the same we can access more documents (arrow A). By keeping the number of documents the same we can access them at a lower cost.

focused on the cognitive factor implications of interface design (Gray et al., 1993; Lohse, 1993), few groups had access to the advanced technologies that were creating new designs and new visualizations (see Card, Mackinlay, & Shneiderman, 1999, for a compendium of many of the key papers from the 1980s and 1990s on this topic.). In the early 1990s many advanced visualizations were emerging from PARC and the cognitive modeling group led by Card took full advantage of these opportunities (Card, Pirolli, & Mackinlay, 1994; Mackinlay, Robertson, & Card, 1991; Pirolli & Card, 1995; Russell et al., 1993).

An early project focused on the "cost of knowledge" for extracting information from dynamic, visual analytic displays (Card et al., 1994). This effort framed the information search problem in terms of the number of documents that could be found within a given time period. Different technologies allowed different efficiencies, with "technologies" widely defined to include everything from computer programs to stacks on the desktop, to papers tucked away in filing cabinets (see Figure 21.3). The work identified several ways in which such searches could be sped up, including alternative ways of organizing the documents, making more efficient methods available to the user, and advances in computer technologies (hardware and networks) that would allow the same procedures to be performed more quickly. These analyses illustrated the effect that trade-offs in system design issues, very broadly defined, would have on human productivity.

3.2.2. REASONING FROM GRAPHS

Understanding information presented in line graphs may be the prototypical example of reasoning from structured displays. At the very least, it is a topic that has been well studied for a number of years (many of the key papers are listed in the bibliography provided by Gillan et al., 1998; Tufte, 1983). However, people still have trouble extracting information from graphs and, as anyone who has had to perform this task might suspect, researchers still have problems creating graphs that make their data transparent to their readers.

There are two basic decisions made in creating a data graph: (a) what to display and (b) how to display it. Most discussions of line graphs assume that the display incorporates the intended data and no more. If the "what to display" assumption is correct, then alternative displays of the same data would be informationally equivalent (Larkin & Simon, 1987; Peebles & Cheng, 2003) in that no information could be inferred from one that could not be inferred from another. Of course, the assumption that the graph designer has displayed no more and no less information than needed can be problematic. Displaying too little information means that the "point" of the display can never be taken. Displaying too much means that the reader may be confused as to the point or may extract information irrelevant to the point.

If we assume that no more and no less information than is needed is being displayed, then how to display it becomes an important topic. Alternative representations may be informationally equivalent without being computationally equivalent. Computational

equivalence (Larkin & Simon, 1987) refers to the number of operations, the resources required by these operations (e.g., memory, attention, perceptual-motor), or the time required to extract information from the graph. Informational equivalence is a function of the displays, whereas computational equivalence is a function of the cognitive, perceptual, and motor operations required to extract equivalent information from the displays.

Peebles and Cheng (2003) studied the basic graph-reading task (see also, Lohse, 1997) of determining the value of one variable that corresponds to the given value of another variable (e.g., for the year in which oil consumption was six, what was gas consumption?). They created two informationally equivalent versions of each graph and for each one asked three types of questions of each participant. Their intention was two-fold. First, they wished to compare human behavior in this task with the predictions of their Graph-Based Reasoning model (Peebles, Cheng, & Shadbolt, 1999). The Graph-Based Reasoning predictions were based on a task analysis, which assumes that the eye movements made will follow the optimal sequence required to achieve the current informational goal. Second, they wished to evaluate the value-added of building a computational cognitive model of embodied cognition that incorporated detailed assumptions regarding the use of memory, visual attention, motor movement, and perceptual operations. The model was built using ACT-R. An example of the data they collected from their human subjects and their model subjects is presented in Figure 21.4.

Peebles and Cheng (2003) found an interaction between question type and graph type. The efficiency with which questions were answered varied across the two graph types. The eye movement data revealed patterns that could be interpreted as due to perceptual and cognitive limitations of the participants. The Graph-Based Reasoning model did not predict these patterns; however, the ACT-R model did. Compared with predictions from the Graph-Based Reasoning model, the ACT-R model required more

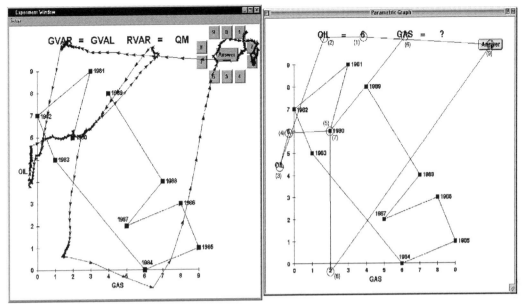

Figure 21.4. Screen shots from Peebles and Cheng (2003) showing a human subject's eye movement path (left) and the ACT-R models visual attention path (right). Both scan paths are in pursuit of the answer to a specific query. (For a discussion of the query and the layout of this particular graph, see Peebles & Cheng, 2003.)

glances back to the question toward the end of each trial. These glances varied with question type and graph type, and reflect different demands made on memory for the location of graph elements, the association between symbol and variable, and the effect of practice.

Traditional approaches to graph understanding have focused on two elements: the visual properties of the graph and the requirements of the task. The model built by Peebles and Cheng (2003) incorporates a third element, namely, the demands on embodied cognition (cognitive, perceptual, and motor operations). The interaction among these three elements is complex. Compared with the other tasks discussed in this chapter, the familiarity of graph reading to the readers of this chapter may make it seem a cut-and-dried proposition. However mundane the task may be, it is clearly a task that even the most experienced of scientists struggle with when reading the work in their field. It may not be too far-fetched to think that the day may be near when each author could have a graph-reading program that would provide real-time feedback as to how much difficulty a novice (one unfamiliar with the terminology) and expert would have in extracting different amounts of information from a display. If this comes to pass, it would be through the application of cognitive science theory for cognitive engineering purposes.

3.2.3. COGNITIVE ENGINEERING MODELS OF SURFING THE WEB (AND OTHER INFORMATIONAL DISPLAYS): INFORMATION SEARCH OF MASSIVE DATA SETS IN HETEROGENEOUSLY DESIGNED SPACES

A prime example of unstructured displays for representing and accessing massive amounts of quantitative data visually is the World Wide Web. Although surfing the Web represents a mundane expertise (i.e., something that many people in the population of readers do daily and are very good at), understanding and predicting human Web search behavior presents a considerable challenge to the theoretical mechanisms of contemporary cognitive science. In particular, a full accounting of Web search requires an understanding of information scent, semantic relatedness, visual saliency, general knowledge of page layouts and idioms, and the control of integrated cognitive systems.

3.2.3.1. *Theory Development.* Analogies are important in making progress in science. In the mid-1990s, researchers at PARC (Russell, et al., 1993) hit on the analogy between people searching for information and animals searching for food. This tie between information search and animal foraging was productive, due in large part to the existence of *optimal foraging theory* (Stephens & Krebs, 1986), which cast animal foraging behavior into an abstract, quantitative, modeling framework that proved possible to adapt and extend to human information seeking (Pirolli & Card, 1999; Pirolli, 2007).

By this analogy, *information scent* is the construct that relates the semantic relatedness of the current information context to the goals of the user's search. The higher the information scent, the more related the current context is to the search goals and the more likely the searcher would be to remain in the current *information patch*. The searcher will likely remain in the current patch for as long as the information scent remains above some threshold. When the information scent falls below this threshold, the searcher will likely leave (Card et al., 2001; Fu & Pirolli, 2007; Pirolli & Fu, 2003). In Web terms, a query to a search engine may return a link with a high information scent to the user's query. The user will click on the link and begin to search the Web site. As long as the information at that site has a high semantic relatedness to the searched-for information, the user will remain. However, if the information turns out to be less useful than expected, the user will leave the current site and attempt to find one with a higher information scent.

The theory of information scent has played a key role in developing the cognitive engineering approach to information search and retrieval. However, it is the first step, not the last in building cognitive engineering models of human information search. If our goal is to design cognitively congruent interactive procedures for searching information displays, then nothing less than a *cognitive theory of embodied information search* is required. Some of the issues and cognitive technologies for achieving this goal are discussed in the following sections.

3.2.3.2. *Semantic Relatedness Measures.* For the development of models of information search, an all-but-prerequisite codevelopment was that of statistical measures of semantic relatedness (Harman, 1993; Landauer & Dumais, 1997; Lemaire & Denhiére, 2004; Turney, 2001). To appreciate the development of these measures, consider how the modeling of interactions with semantic content would have been handled without these measures.

For decades, the only means available of estimating associative strength within experimental psychology was to have participants in psychology studies estimate the link between two items on, say, a seven-point scale. By this method, obtaining reliable and valid estimates of associative strength between, say, each of 100 words would require human judgments on 4,950 word pairs. As such, human judgments are notoriously noisy; a reliable and valid estimate of relatedness required large numbers of human subjects to judge the associative relatedness of each pair of words. At the end of all of this work, there would be good estimates of relatedness between each of the 100 words in the list. Obviously, such methods of obtaining word associations means that human search among the unlimited diversity of the World Wide Web would be all but impossible to model and study.

Statistical measures of semantic similarity parse large corpora (measured in the millions of documents) to develop families of measures that purport to provide humanlike judgments of the relatedness of one word to another or of an entire text to the topic of a query. A review of these measures is beyond the scope of the current chapter (see Lemaire & Denhiére, 2004, for a cogent and succinct overview of several of these measures.) However, it is clear

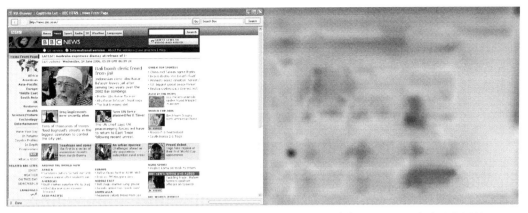

Figure 21.5. Visual saliency map on right of Web page shown on left using Rosenholtz' (1999) measure of visual saliency. To produce the "map," for each screen pixel, the score for each dimension is translated to a 256-bit vector, averaged with the other two dimensions and mapped onto a 256-bit gray-scale.

that the research in this area has gone from demonstrating that various measures can be generated that mimic human judgment to examining the cognitive fidelity of these statistically derived judgments across a variety of search tasks (Blackmon et al., 2005; Kaur & Hornof, 2005; Veksler & Gray, 2006). The current goals include understanding the limits and best application of current methods (Juvina et al., 2005; Lemaire & Denhiére, 2004; Matveeva et al., 2005) and developing new measures as needed.

3.2.3.3. *Stimulus-Driven Factors in Visual Search.* The human visual system seems hard-wired by evolution to allocate attention and resources to certain visual stimuli (Wolfe, 1998), such as abrupt onsets or patterns of motion against otherwise still backgrounds (Ware & Bobrow, 2004). It also seems the case that certain combinations of stimulus characteristics are easier to allocate visual attention to in some visual environments than in others. For example, searching for a red L amid a field of green Ls is quite easy. Searching for a red L amid a field of green Ls and red Ts is much harder (Wolfe, 1998).

Recent work has made progress in developing statistical visual saliency measures (Itti & Koch, 2001; Rao & Ballard, 1995; Rosenholtz, 2001; Verghese & McKee, 2004) that are somewhat analogous to the statistical semantic relatedness measures discussed ear-

lier. These measures allow the computation of differences between elements of a visual display along one or more visual dimensions. For example, Figure 21.5 shows a visual saliency map of a Web page using Rosenholtz's (1999) measure of visual saliency. This measure computes a similarity score for each of three dimensions (color, orientation, and contrast) between every element on the screen and every other element.

It is certainly not the case that visual saliency determines where the eye looks. If this issue were in doubt, it has been laid to rest by a variety of small, experimental psychology demonstrations (Henderson et al., 2007; Underwood & Foulsham, 2006). However, contemporary theory asserts that eye movement location is determined by activation at a saccade map (Trappenberg et al., 2001) and that where the activation builds up is influenced by stimulus-driven as well as goal-directed factors (Godijn & Theeuwes, 2002; Pomplun, 2007). It seems clear that visual saliency has an important role to play in the direction, or misdirection, of visual attention during information search. Given the visually dramatic nature of modern structured and unstructured (e.g., the left side of Figure 21.5) visual analytic displays, it is clear that visual saliency is a factor that must be taken into account in predicting the success and time costs of information search.

3.2.3.4. *Knowledge-Driven Factors in Visual Search.* Knowledge-driven factors are those that influence visual search because of explicitly *adopted* strategies (Everling & Fischer, 1998; Godijn & Theeuwes, 2002), *adapting* search to the statistical structure of a specific search environment (Reder et al., 2003), or general knowledge and experience with the layout of visually presented information (e.g., books have tables of content, indexes, and chapters; chapters have introductions, subsections, and summaries; and so on). It is clear that even unstructured information spaces such as Web pages often enable knowledge-driven search. For example, most Web pages have headers and footers that contain navigation information or information specific to the page or Web site itself, that is, not content information. Likewise, menus come in many forms, but most of these forms are visually distinctive and, when present, are often on the right, the left, or toward the top of a Web page (Rigutti & Gerbino, 2004). At present, we know of no computational cognitive model that factors such knowledge into its predictions, although there are several in which such factors are explicitly eliminated by the modelers (Blackmon et al., 2005; Kaur & Hornof, 2005).

3.2.4. SUMMARY: COGNITIVE ENGINEERING MODELS FOR HUMAN-INFORMATION INTERACTION

The purpose of building cognitive engineering models that can surf the Web, extract information from line graphs, or make sense of a complex visual display of qualitative information is to optimize human performance by identifying design elements or decisions that may lead to stable but suboptimal human performance (Fu, 2007; Fu & Gray, 2004, 2006). Achieving this goal will require advances in cognitive science theories of semantic comprehension and visual attention as well as in advances in our understanding of the composition and control of integrated cognitive systems (Gray, 2007a). The symbiosis between cognitive science and cognitive engineering shows no sign of abating.

4. Conclusions

This chapter began with a discussion of five dimensions on which cognitive science and cognitive engineering sometimes differ. First discussed was the manner in which the problems were picked. As in the case of runway incursions (Byrne & Kirlik, 2005; Kirlik, 2007) or UAVs (Gluck et al., 2007), the problem is often picked for the researcher, and the research is unlikely to continue without a larger organization that provides substantive support in terms of equipment and specialized expertise.

Second was the amount of prior empirical data. Certainly, the models discussed previously rest on a broad base of empirical data. However, the breadth of that base meant that much of it, usually the part closest to the task being modeled, was very shallow. Hence, the Peebles and Cheng (2003) model rested on years of research on memory and visual attention as well as studies of reading line graphs. However, theirs is the first model that put these elements together to predict graph reading. The shallowness of this base was fully exposed in the discussion of Visual Analytics, in which a common everyday task (i.e., surfing the Web) presents a challenge to both applied and basic cognitive science.

Third was the expertise factor. Key to modeling the UAV, runway incursions, and driving tasks was access to human experts. This factor was not as important to the graph-reading task and not at all applicable to the ATC game, where the focus was on understanding the transition from novice to skilled performance. It is unclear how this dimension of expertise will play itself out in the domain of visual analytics. Certainly, the strong reliance on statistical measures of semantic relatedness suggest that much mundane human expertise will have to be assumed before progress on building cognitive engineering models of visual analytic performance can progress.

Fourth was a different sort of factor. The areas in which cognitive engineering has been applied are areas with strong demands for answers. What are the implications for cognitive science if cognitive engineering cannot meet those demands? If cognitive engineering is "cognitive science theories applied to human factors practice," then if we cannot meet the demands for cognitive engineering, a strong implication might be that the cognitive science enterprise has little relevance to our modern world. Pursuit of knowledge for knowledge's sake may be a fine ideal, but the successful advancement of physics and biology in the last century was due less to knowledge for knowledge's sake and more to knowledge that was able to address key concerns of our society. Compared with disciplines such as philosophy and linguistics, research in cognitive science is well funded. The basic questions that cognitive science addresses are no more compelling than those in these other fields. What accounts for our better funding is our promise to society that advances in cognitive science theory will result in tangible improvements.

Fifth was the view that cognitive engineering dealt with integrated cognitive systems and that such systems had been largely ignored by a basic research community that was content to dive deeply into artificially isolated areas such as reasoning, decision making, memory, and visual attention (Byrne, 2007b). Not only is the control of integrated cognitive systems a challenging basic research question, the importance of understanding the control of integrated cognitive systems for cognitive engineering purposes suggests that research on control issues should become a high priority among basic researchers as well as those agencies that fund basic research.

References

Ackerman, P. L., & Kanfer, R. (1994). Kanfer-Ackerman air traffic controller task © CD-ROM database, data collection program, and playback program. Arlington, VA: Office of Naval Research, Cognitive Science Program.

Adelman, L., Bresnick, T., Black, P. K., Marvin, F. F., & Sak, S. G. (1996). Research with Patriot Air Defense officers: Examining information order effects. *Human Factors, 38*(2), 250–261.

Anderson, J. R. (1982). Acquisition of cognitive skill. *Psychological Review, 89*(4), 369–406.

Anderson, J. R. (1990). *The adaptive character of thought.* Hillsdale, NJ: Lawrence Erlbaum.

Anderson, J. R. (1991). Is human cognition adaptive? *Behavioral and Brain Sciences, 14*(3), 471–517.

Anderson, J. R. (1993). *Rules of the mind.* Hillsdale, NJ: Lawrence Erlbaum.

Anderson, J. R., Bothell, D., Byrne, M. D., Douglas, S., Lebiere, C., & Quin, Y. (2004). An integrated theory of the mind. *Psychological Review, 111*(4), 1036–1060.

Anderson, J. R., Conrad, F. G., & Corbett, A. T. (1989). Skill acquisition and the LISP Tutor. *Cognitive Science, 13*(4), 467–505.

Anderson, J. R., Matessa, M., & Lebiere, C. (1997). ACT-R: A theory of higher-level cognition and its relation to visual attention. *Human-Computer Interaction, 12*(4), 439–462.

Anderson, J. R., & Schooler, L. J. (1991). Reflections of the environment in memory. *Psychological Science, 2*, 396–408.

Andre, A. D., & Wickens, C. D. (1995, October). When users want what's not best for them. *Ergonomics in Design*, 10–14.

Ballard, D. H., Hayhoe, M. M., & Pelz, J. B. (1995). Memory representations in natural tasks. *Journal of Cognitive Neuroscience, 7*(1), 66–80.

Ballard, D. H., Hayhoe, M. M., Pook, P. K., & Rao, R. P. N. (1997). Deictic codes for the embodiment of cognition. *Behavioral and Brain Sciences, 20*(4), 723–742.

Ballard, D. H., & Sprague, N. (2007). On the role of embodiment in modeling natural behaviors. In W. D. Gray (Ed.), *Integrated models of cognitive systems.* New York: Oxford University Press.

Benbasat, I., & Todd, P. (1996). The effects of decision support and task contingencies on model formulation: A cognitive perspective. *Decision Support Systems, 17*(4), 241–252.

Blackmon, M. H., Kitajima, M., & Polson, P. G. (2005). Tool for accurately predicting website navigation problems, non-problems, problem severity, and effectiveness of repairs. In W. Kellogg, S. Zhai, G. v. d. Veer & C. Gale (Eds.), *Proceedings of the SIGCHI Conference on Human Factors in Computing Systems* (pp. 31–40). New York: ACM Press.

Bovair, S., Kieras, D. E., & Polson, P. G. (1990). The acquisition and performance of text-editing skill: A cognitive complexity analysis. *Human-Computer Interaction, 5*(1), 1–48.

Byrne, M. D. (2007a). Cognitive architecture. In A. Sears & J. A. Jacko (Eds.), *The human-computer interaction handbook* (2nd ed.). Mahwah, NJ: Lawrence Erlbaum.

Byrne, M. D. (2007b). Local theories vs. comprehensive architectures: The cognitive science jigsaw puzzle. In W. D. Gray (Ed.), *Integrated models of cognitive systems* (pp. 431–443). New York: Oxford University Press.

Byrne, M. D., & Anderson, J. R. (1998). Perception and action. In J. R. Anderson & C. Lebiére (Eds.), *The atomic components of thought* (pp. 167–200). Hillsdale, NJ: Lawrence Erlbaum.

Byrne, M. D., & Kirlik, A. (2005). Using computational cognitive modeling to diagnose possible sources of aviation error. *International Journal of Aviation Psychology, 15*, 135–155.

Card, S. K., Mackinlay, J. D., & Shneiderman, B. (Eds.). (1999). *Information visualization: Using vision to think.* New York: Morgan Kaufmann.

Card, S. K., Moran, T. P., & Newell, A. (1980a). Computer text editing: An information processing analysis of a routine cognitive skill. *Cognitive Psychology, 12*, 32–74.

Card, S. K., Moran, T. P., & Newell, A. (1980b). The keystroke-level model for user performance time with interactive systems. *Communications of the ACM, 23*(7), 396–410.

Card, S. K., Moran, T. P., & Newell, A. (1983). *The psychology of human-computer interaction.* Hillsdale, NJ: Lawrence Erlbaum.

Card, S. K., Pirolli, P., & Mackinlay, J. D. (1994). The cost-of-knowledge characteristic function: Display evaluation for direct-walk dynamic information visualizations. In B. Adelson, S. Dumais, & J. Olson (Eds.), *ACM CHI'94 Conference on Human Factors in Computing Systems* (Vol. 1, pp. 238–244). New York: ACM Press.

Card, S. K., Pirolli, P., Van Der Wege, M., Morrison, J. B., Reeder, R. W., Schraedley, P. K., et al. (2001). Information scent as a driver of Web behavior graphs: Results of a protocol analysis method for Web usability. *CHI Letters, 3*(1), 498–505.

Chi, M. T. H., Feltovich, P. J., & Glaser, R. (1981). Categorization and representation of physics problems by experts and novices. *Cognitive Science, 5*(2), 121–152.

Chipman, S. F., & Kieras, D. E. (2004, March 17–18). *Operator centered design of ship systems.*

Paper presented at the Engineering the Total Ship Symposium, NIST, Gaithersburg, MD.

Corbett, A. T., & Anderson, J. R. (1988). The LISP intelligent tutoring system: Research in skill acquisition. In J. Larkin, R. Chabay, & C. Scheftic (Eds.), *Computer assisted instruction and intelligent tutoring systems: Establishing communciations and collaboration.* Hillsdale, NJ: Lawrence Erlbaum.

Ehret, B. D., Gray, W. D., & Kirschenbaum, S. S. (2000). Contending with complexity: Developing and using a scaled world in applied cognitive research. *Human Factors, 42*(1), 8–23.

Elkind, J. I., Card, S. K., Hochberg, J., & Huey, B. M. (1989). *Human performance models for computer-aided engineering.* Washington, DC: National Academy Press.

Everling, S., & Fischer, B. (1998). The antisaccade: A review of basic research and clinical studies. *Neuropsychologia, 36*(9), 885–899.

Fennema, M. G., & Kleinmuntz, D. N. (1995). Anticipations of effort and accuracy in multiattribute choice. *Organizational Behavior & Human Decision Processes, 63*(1), 21–32.

Fitts, P. M., & Posner, M. I. (1967). *Human performance.* Belmont, CA: Brooks Cole.

Freed, M., Matessa, M., Remington, R. W., & Vera, A. (2003, March). *How Apex automates CPM-GOMS.* Paper presented at the Fifth International Conference on Cognitive Modeling, Bamberg, GE.

Fu, W.-T. (2007). A rational–ecological approach to the exploration/exploitation trade-offs: Bounded rationality and suboptimal performance. In W. D. Gray (Ed.), *Integrated models of cognitive systems* (pp. 165–179). New York: Oxford University Press.

Fu, W.-T., & Gray, W. D. (2004). Resolving the paradox of the active user: Stable suboptimal performance in interactive tasks. *Cognitive Science, 28*(6), 901–935.

Fu, W.-T., & Gray, W. D. (2006). Suboptimal tradeoffs in information seeking. *Cognitive Psychology, 52*(3), 195–242.

Fu, W.-T., & Pirolli, P. (in press). SNIF-ACT: A cognitive model of user navigation on the World Wide Web. *Human-Computer Interaction.*

Gillan, D. J., Wickens, C. D., Hollands, J. G., & Carswell, C. M. (1998). Guidelines for presenting quantitative data in HFES publications. *Human Factors, 40*(1), 28–41.

Gluck, K. A., Ball, J. T., Gunzelmann, G., Krusmark, M. A., Lyon, D. R., & Cooke, N. J.

(2005). *A Prospective Look at Synthetic Team-mate for UAV Applications*. Paper presented at the American Institute of Aeronautics and Astronautics "Infotech@Aerospace" Conference, Reston VA.

Gluck, K. A., Ball, J. T., & Krusmark, M. A. (2007). Cognitive control in a computational model of the predator pilot. In W. D. Gray (Ed.), *Integrated models of cognitive systems* (pp. 13–28). New York: Oxford University Press.

Gluck, K. A., & Pew, R. W. (2005). *Modeling human behavior with integrated cognitive architectures: Comparison, evaluation, and validation*. Mahwah, NJ: Lawrence Erlbaum.

Godijn, R., & Theeuwes, J. (2002). Programming of endogenous and exogenous saccades: Evidence for a competitive integration model. *Journal of Experimental Psychology: Human Perception and Performance, 28*(5), 1039–1054.

Gray, W. D. (2000). The nature and processing of errors in interactive behavior. *Cognitive Science, 24*(2), 205–248.

Gray, W. D. (2007a). Composition and control of integrated cognitive systems. In W. D. Gray (Ed.), *Integrated models of cognitive systems* (pp. 3–12). New York: Oxford University Press.

Gray, W. D. (Ed.). (2007b). *Integrated models of cognitive systems*. New York: Oxford University Press.

Gray, W. D., & Boehm-Davis, D. A. (2000). Milliseconds matter: An introduction to microstrategies and to their use in describing and predicting interactive behavior. *Journal of Experimental Psychology: Applied, 6*(4), 322–335.

Gray, W. D., John, B. E., & Atwood, M. E. (1993). Project Ernestine: Validating a GOMS analysis for predicting and explaining real-world performance. *Human-Computer Interaction, 8*(3), 237–309.

Gray, W. D., & Kirschenbaum, S. S. (2000). Analyzing a novel expertise: An unmarked road. In J. M. C. Schraagen, S. F. Chipman, & V. L. Shalin (Eds.), *Cognitive task analysis* (pp. 275–290). Mahwah, NJ: Lawrence Erlbaum.

Gray, W. D., Kirschenbaum, S. S., & Ehret, B. D. (1997). The précis of Project Nemo, phase 1: Subgoaling and subschemas for submariners. In M. G. Shafto & P. Langley (Eds.), *Nineteenth Annual Conference of the Cognitive Science Society* (pp. 283–288). Hillsdale, NJ: Lawrence Erlbaum Associates.

Gray, W. D., & Pew, R. W. (2004). Introduction to human performance modeling (HPM) and to this symposium on cognitive HPM. In *48th Annual Conference of the Human Factors and Ergonomics Society* (pp. 2109–2110). Santa Monica, CA: Human Factors and Ergonomics Society.

Gray, W. D., Schoelles, M. J., & Myers, C. W. (2004). Meeting Newell's other challenge: Cognitive architectures as the basis for cognitive engineering. *Behavioral & Brain Sciences, 26*(5), 609–610.

Green, P. A. (1999). Estimating compliance with the 15-second rule for driver-interface usabilty and safety. In *Proceedings of the Human Factors and Ergonomics Society 43rd Annual Meeting*. Santa Monica, CA: Human Factors and Ergonomics Society.

Green, P. A. (2002). *Calculation of the time to complete in-vehicle navigation and route guidance tasks* (No. SAE J2365). Warrendale, PA: SAE International.

Harman, D. (1993). Overview of the first TREC conference. In *Proceedings of the 16th annual international ACM SIGIR conference on Research and development in information retrieval*. Pittsburgh, PA: ACM Press.

Henderson, J. M., Brockmole, J. R., Castelhano, M. S., & Mack, M. (2007). Visual saliency does not account for eye movements during visual search in real-world scenes. In R. van Gompel, M. Fischer, W. Murray & R. Hill (Eds.), *Eye movement: A window on mind and brain*. Oxford: Elsevier.

Hintzman, D. L. (2005). Memory strength and recency judgments. *Psychonomic Bulletin & Review, 12*(5), 858–864.

Itti, L., & Koch, C. (2001). Computational modelling of visual attention. *Nature Reviews Neuroscience, 2*(3), 194–203.

John, B. E. (1988). *Contributions to engineering models of human-computer interaction*. Unpublished doctoral dissertation, Carnegie Mellon University, Pittsburgh, PA.

John, B. E. (1993). *A quantitative model of expert transcription typing* (No. CMU-CS-93-120). Pittsburgh, PA: Carnegie Mellon University School of Computer Science.

John, B. E. (1996). TYPIST: A theory of performance in skilled typing. *Human-Computer Interaction, 11*(4), 321–355.

John, B. E., & Lallement, Y. (1997). Strategy use while learning to perform the Kanfer-Ackerman Air Traffic Controller task. In M. G. Shafto & P. Langley (Eds.) *Nineteenth*

Annual Conference of the Cognitive Science Society (pp. 337–342). Hillsdale, NJ: Lawrence Erlbaum Associates.

Johnson-Laird, P. N. (1993). *Human and machine thinking.* Hillsdale, NJ: Lawrence Erlbaum Associates.

Juvina, I., van Oostendorp, H., Karbor, P., & Pauw, B. (2005). Towards modeling contextual information in web navigation. In B. G. Bara, L. Barsalou, & M. Bucciarelli (Eds.), *27th Annual Meeting of the Cognitive Science Society, CogSci2005* (pp. 1078–1083). Austin, Tx: The Cognitive Science Society.

Kaur, I., & Hornof, A. J. (2005). A comparison of LSA, WordNet, and PMI-IR for predicting user click behavior. In W. Kellogg, S. Zhai, G. v. d. Veer & C. Gale (Eds.), *ACM CHI 2005 Conference on Human Factors in Computing Systems* (pp. 51–60). New York: ACM Press.

Keim, D. A., Robertson, G. G., Thomas, J. J., & van Wijk, J. J. (2006). Guest editorial: Special section on visual analytics. *IEEE Transactions on Visualization and Computer Graphics, 12*(6), 1361–1362.

Kieras, D. E. (1997). A guide to GOMS model usability evaluation using NGOMSL. In M. Helander, T. K. Landauer, & P. Prabhu (Eds.), *Handbook of human-computer interaction* (2nd ed., pp. 733–766). New York: Elsevier.

Kieras, D. E. (2007). Model-based evaluation. In A. Sears & J. A. Jacko (Eds.), *The human-computer interaction handbook* (2nd ed.). Mahwah, NJ: Lawrence Erlbaum.

Kieras, D. E., & Bovair, S. (1986). The acquisition of procedures from text: A production-system analysis of transfer of training. *Journal of Memory and Language, 25,* 507–524.

Kieras, D. E., & Meyer, D. E. (1997). An overview of the EPIC architecture for cognition and performance with application to human-computer interaction. *Human-Computer Interaction, 12*(4), 391–438.

Kirlik, A. (2007). Ecological resources for modeling interactive cognition and behavior. In W. D. Gray (Ed.), *Integrated models of cognitive systems* (pp. 194–210). New York: Oxford University Press.

Kirschenbaum, S. S., & Gray, W. D. (2000). The précis of Project Nemo, phase 2: Levels of expertise. In L. R. Gleitman & A. K. Joshi (Eds.), *Twenty-second Annual Conference of the Cognitive Science Society* (pp. 753–758). Mahwah, NJ: Lawrence Erlbaum.

Kirwan, B., & Ainsworth, L. K. (Eds.). (1992). *A guide to task analysis.* Washington, DC: Taylor & Francis.

Kleinmuntz, D. N., & Schkade, D. A. (1993). Information displays and decision processes. *Psychological Science, 4*(4), 221–227.

Landauer, T. K., & Dumais, S. T. (1997). A solution to Plato's problem: The latent semantic analysis theory of acquisition, induction, and representation of knowledge. *Psychological Review, 104*(2), 211–240.

Larkin, J. H., & Simon, H. A. (1987). Why a diagram is (sometimes) worth ten thousand words. *Cognitive Science, 11,* 65–99.

Lemaire, B., & Denhiére, G. (2004). Incremental construction of an associative network from a corpus. In K. D. Forbus, D. Gentner & T. Regier (Eds.), *26th Annual Meeting of the Cognitive Science Society, CogSci2004* (pp. 825–830). Hillsdale, NJ: Lawrence Erlbaum.

Lohse, G. L. (1993). A cognitive model for understanding graphical perception. *Human-Computer Interaction, 8*(4), 353–388.

Lohse, G. L. (1997). The role of working memory on graphical information processing. *Behaviour & Information Technology, 16*(6), 297–308.

Lohse, G. L., & Johnson, E. J. (1996). A comparison of two process tracing methods for choice tasks. *Organizational Behavior and Human Decision Processes, 68*(1), 28–43.

Love, B. C., Medin, D. L., & Gureckis, T. M. (2004). SUSTAIN: A network model of category learning. *Psychological Review, 111*(2), 309–332.

Lovett, M. C., & Anderson, J. R. (1996). History of success and current context in problem solving: Combined influences on operator selection. *Cognitive Psychology, 31,* 168–217.

Mackinlay, J. D., Robertson, G. G., & Card, S. K. (1991). The perspective wall: detail and context smoothly integrated. In S. P. Robertson, G. M. Olson & J. S. Olson (Eds.), *Proceedings of the SIGCHI conference on Human factors in computing systems: Reaching through technology* (pp. 173–176). New York: ACM Press.

Matveeva, I., Levow, G., Farahat, A., & Royer, C. (2005, September). *Term representation with generalized latent semantic analysis.* Paper presented at the 2005 Conference on Recent Advances in Natural Language Processing, Borovets, Bulgaria.

Newell, A. (1990). *Unified theories of cognition.* Cambridge, MA: Harvard University Press.

Newell, A., & Card, S. K. (1985). The prospects for psychological science in human-computer interaction. *Human-Computer Interaction, 1*(3), 209–242.

Newell, A., & Simon, H. A. (1972). *Human problem solving*. Englewood Cliffs, NJ: Prentice Hall.

Nosofsky, R. M., & Palmeri, T. J. (1997). An exemplar-based random walk model of speeded classification. *Psychological Review, 104*(2), 266–300.

Payne, J. W., Bettman, J. R., & Johnson, E. J. (1993). *The adaptive decision maker*. New York: Cambridge University Press.

Peebles, D., & Cheng, P. C. H. (2003). Modeling the effect of task and graphical representation on response latency in a graph reading task. *Human Factors, 45*(1), 28–46.

Peebles, D., Cheng, P. C.-H., & Shadbolt, N. (1999). Multiple processes in graph-based reasoning. In M. Hahn & S. C. Stoness (Eds.), *Twenty-First Annual Conference of the Cognitive Science Society* (pp. 531–536). Hillsdale, NJ: Lawrence Erlbaum.

Pew, R. W. (2007). Some history of human performance modeling. In W. D. Gray (Ed.), *Integrated models of cognitive systems*. New York: Oxford University Press.

Pew, R. W., & Mavor, A. S. (Eds.). (1998). *Modeling human and organizational behavior: Application to military simulations*. Washington, DC: National Academy Press.

Pirolli, P. (2005). Rational analyses of information foraging on the Web. *Cognitive Science, 29*(3), 343–373.

Pirolli, P., & Card, S. K. (1995). Information foraging in information access environments. In I. R. Katz, R. Mack, L. Marks, M. B. Rosson & J. Nielsen (Eds.), *Proceedings of the SIGCHI conference on Human factors in computing systems* (pp. 51–58). New York: ACM Press.

Pirolli, P., & Card, S. K. (1999). Information foraging. *Psychological Review, 106*(4), 643–675.

Pirolli, P., & Fu, W.-T. (2003). SNIF-ACT: A model of information foraging on the World Wide Web. *Lecture Notes in Computer Science, 2702*, 45–54.

Pomplun, M. (2007). Advancing area activation towards a general model of eye movements in visual search. In W. D. Gray (Ed.), *Integrated models of cognitive systems* (pp. 120–131). New York: Oxford University Press.

Rao, R. P. N., & Ballard, D. H. (1995). An active vision architecture based on iconic representations. *Artificial Intelligence, 78*(1–2), 461–505.

Reder, L. M., Weber, K., Shang, J., & Vanyukov, P. M. (2003). The adaptive character of the attentional system: Statistical sensitivity in a target localization task. *Journal of Experimental Psychology-Human Perception and Performance, 29*(3), 631–649.

Rigutti, S., & Gerbino, W. (2004). Navigating within a web site: the WebStep model. In M. C. Lovett, C. D. Schunn, C. Lebiere & P. Munro (Eds.), *Abstract presented at the Sixth International Conference on Cognitive Modeling, ICCM2004* (pp. 378–379). Mahwah, NJ: Erlbaum.

Rips, L. J. (1994). *The psychology of proof: Deductive reasoning in human thinking*. Cambridge, MA: The MIT Press.

Rose, J. M., & Wolfe, C. J. (2000). The effects of system design alternatives on the acquisition of tax knowledge from a computerized tax decision aid. *Accounting Organizations and Society, 25*(3), 285–306.

Rosenholtz, R. (1999). A simple saliency model predicts a number of motion popout phenomena. *Vision Research, 39*, 3157–3163.

Rosenholtz, R. (2001). Search asymmetries? What search asymmetries? *Perception & Psychophysics, 63*(3), 476–489.

Russell, D. M., Stefik, M. J., Pirolli, P., & Card, S. K. (1993). *The cost structure of sensemaking*. Amsterdam, The Netherlands: ACM Press.

Salvucci, D. D. (2001). Predicting the effects of in-car interface use on driver performance: An integrated model approach. *International Journal of Human-Computer Studies, 55*(1), 85–107.

Salvucci, D. D. (2005). A multitasking general executive for compound continuous tasks. *Cognitive Science, 29*(3), 457–492.

Salvucci, D. D. (2006). Modeling driver behavior in a cognitive architecture. *Human Factors, 48*(2), 362–380.

Salvucci, D. D., & Gray, R. (2004). A two-point visual control model of steering. *Perception, 33*(10), 1233–1248.

Salvucci, D. D., & Macuga, K. L. (2001). Predicting the effects of cell-phone dialing on driver performance. In E. M. Altmann, A. Cleeremans, C. D. Schunn & W. D. Gray (Eds.), *Fourth International Conference on Cognitive Modeling* (pp. 25–30). Mahwah, NJ: Lawrence Erlbaum Associates.

Schkade, D. A., & Kleinmuntz, D. N. (1994). Information displays and choice processes: Differential effects of organization, form, and sequence. *Organizational Behavior & Human Decision Processes, 57*(3), 319–337.

Schunn, C. D., & Reder, L. M. (2001). Another source of individual differences: Strategy adaptivity to changing rates of success.

Journal of Experimental Psychology-General, *130*(1), 59–76.

Schweickert, R., Fisher, D. L., & Proctor, R. W. (2003). Steps toward building mathematical and computer models from cognitive task analyses. *Human Factors, 45*(1), 77–103.

Shepard, R. N., Hovland, C. I., & Jenkins, H. M. (1961). Learning and memorization of classifications. *Psychological Monographs, 75*(13), 42–42.

Shepherd, A. (1998). HTA as a framework for task analysis. *Ergonomics, 41*(11), 1537–1552.

Shepherd, A. (2001). *Hierarchical task analysis.* New York: Taylor & Francis.

Simon, H. A. (1996). *The sciences of the artificial* (3rd ed.). Cambridge, MA: The MIT Press.

Singley, M. K., & Anderson, J. R. (1989). *The transfer of cognitive skill.* Cambridge, MA: Harvard University Press.

Smallman, H. S., & St. John, M. (2005). Naïve realism: Misplaced faith in the utility of realistic displays. *Ergonomics in Design, 13*(3), 6–13.

Stephens, D. W., & Krebs, J. R. (1986). *Foraging theory.* Princeton, NJ: Princeton University Press.

Taatgen, N. A., & Anderson, J. R. (2002). Why do children learn to say "broke"? A model of learning the past without feedback. *Cognition, 86*(2), 123–155.

Taatgen, N. A., & Lee, F. J. (2003). Production composition: A simple mechanism to model complex skill acquisition. *Human Factors, 45*(1), 61–76.

Thomas, J. J., & Cook, K. A. (Eds.). (2005). *Illuminating the path: The research and development agenda for visual analytics*: Washington, DC: IEEE Press.

Todd, P., & Benbasat, I. (1994). The influence of decision aids on choice strategies – an experimental-analysis of the role of cognitive effort. *Organizational Behavior and Human Decision Processes, 60*(1), 36–74.

Todd, P., & Benbasat, I. (1999). Evaluating the impact of DSS, cognitive effort, and incentives on strategy selection. *Information Systems Research, 10*(4), 356–374.

Todd, P., & Benbasat, I. (2000). Inducing compensatory information processing through decision aids that facilitate effort reduction: An experimental assessment. *Journal of Behavioral Decision Making, 13*(1), 91–106.

Trappenberg, T. P., Dorris, M. C., Munoz, D. P., & Klein, R. M. (2001). A model of saccade initiation based on the competitive integration of exogenous and endogenous signals in the superior colliculus. *Journal of Cognitive Neuroscience, 13*(2), 256–271.

Tsapogas, J. (2003). *Characteristics of doctoral scientists and engineers in the United States* (No. NSF 06-320). Arlington, VA: National Science Foundation.

Tufte, E. R. (1983). *The visual display of quantitative information.* Chesire, CT: Graphics Press.

Turney, P. (2001). Mining the Web for Synonyms: PMI-IR versus LSA on TOEFL. In L. De Raedt & P. Flach (Eds.), *Proceedings of the Twelfth European Conference on Machine Learning (ECML-2001)* (pp. 491–502). New York: Springer.

Underwood, G., & Foulsham, T. (2006). Visual saliency and semantic incongruency influence eye movements when inspecting pictures. *Quarterly Journal of Experimental Psychology, 59*(11), 1931–1949.

Veksler, V. D., & Gray, W. D. (2006). Test case selection for evaluating measures of semantic distance. In R. Sun (Ed.), *Proceedings of the 28th Annual Meeting of the Cognitive Science Society* (pp. 2624). Austin, TX: Cognitive Science Society.

Verghese, P., & McKee, S. P. (2004). Visual search in clutter. *Vision Research, 44*(12), 1217–1225.

Wainer, H., & Velleman, P. F. (2001). Statistical graphics: Mapping the pathways of science. *Annual Review of Psychology, 52*, 305–335.

Wald, M. L. (2006, November 3). F.A.A. finds more errors on runways. *New York Times.*

Ware, C., & Bobrow, R. (2004). Motion to support rapid iterative queries on node-link diagrams. *ACM Transactions on Applied Perception, 1*(1), 3–18.

Williams, K. E. (2000). An automated aid for modeling human-computer interaction. In J. M. Schraagen, S. F. Chipman, & V. L. Shalin (Eds.), *Cognitive task analysis* (pp. 165–180). Mahwah, NJ: Lawrence Erlbaum.

Wilson, M. (2002). Six views of embodied cognition. *Psychonomic Bulletin & Review, 9*(4), 625–636.

Wolfe, J. M. (1998). Visual search. In H. Pashler (Ed.), *Attention* (pp. 13–73). East Sussex, UK: Psychology Press.

Wong, P. C., & Thomas, J. (2004). Visual analytics. *IEEE Computer Graphics and Applications, 24*(5), 20–21.

CHAPTER 22

Models of Animal Learning and Their Relations to Human Learning

Francisco J. López and David R. Shanks

1. Introduction

Since the earliest modern laboratory studies of animal learning by Pavlov, Thorndike, and others, there has been a widespread consensus about the theoretical importance of associationism, the idea that bonds may be formed among mental representations of stimuli and responses such that presentation of one stimulus may elicit activation of another or of a response. Pavlov, for instance, proposed that the elementary form of learning he discovered, conditioning, resulted from the acquisition of a connection between the representations of the conditioned stimulus (CS) and unconditioned stimulus (US) such that the CS came to "substitute" for the US. In the study of human as opposed to animal learning, however, associationism has had a much more difficult history. Indeed, only thirty or so years ago, a standard textbook on human learning and memory (Crowder, 1976) made no reference to this concept, nor did it mention conditioning. At that time, cognitive psychologists were more concerned with the role of meaning in learning and believed the associative framework to be wholly inadequate to deal with it.

Since the 1970s, however, there has been acceptance of the view that associative learning does contribute significantly to human cognition, although its relationship to more cognitive, meaning-based or inferential processes is still poorly understood. One reason for this rapprochement has been the opening up of a relatively new area of human research, contingency learning, which possesses many characteristics that seem to invite an associative view. In the present chapter, this research field is reviewed against the background of recent formal models of animal learning. In addition to showing the great usefulness of these models in explaining human judgment and behavior, consideration will also be given to some of the powerful arguments that have gone in the opposite direction, namely, the view that contingency learning (and, for some researchers, animal conditioning, too) can only be adequately understood from a cognitive, not an associationist, perspective. The ongoing confrontation between these approaches has generated vigorous debate and a wealth of new knowledge about human learning.

Although the basic features of animal conditioning preparations (classical or instrumental) are familiar, a broader range of procedures has been used to study contingency learning. However, in many studies, the basic task has involved asking participants to study a series of trials or cases, each made up of a set of cues or features. On the basis of these cues, the participant predicts the trial outcome prior to receiving feedback about the true outcome. Finally, some judgment is made about the cue-outcome relationships (contingencies) or else responding is observed in test trials with new combinations of cues. This general description encompasses (with numerous variations) a very substantial amount of research including not only human causal and predictive learning but also category learning and multiple-cue probability learning. Here, of course, only a tiny portion of the findings from all this research will be reviewed.

A typical instantiation of this task methodology would be a situation in which the participant is asked to imagine that she is an allergist trying to work out the causes of allergic reactions in a hypothetical patient, Mr. X. On each trial, information is provided about the foods (cues) that Mr. X eats in a particular meal, and the participant predicts which of several possible types of allergic reaction (or no reaction) will occur on that occasion. After receiving outcome feedback, the next trial is presented. Across several dozen trials in such a task, the participant will quickly begin to learn the food-allergy contingencies, and such knowledge can be expressed either as judgments on a simple rating scale or inferred from responding to test trials. The main question research has sought to address is what is the function that maps particular cue-outcome contingencies onto participants' responses. This deceptively simple question goes to the heart of the understanding of basic learning processes which, in turn, arguably lie at the heart of human adaptation and plasticity.

2. Associative Models of Predictive Learning

2.1. *The Rescorla-Wagner (1972) Model*

The development of theoretical models of predictive learning has been stimulated to an enormous extent by demonstrations that cues compete with each other to gain control over behavior (so-called cue interaction effects). These phenomena emerge in experiments in which the learner has to infer the predictive value of a target cue from incomplete information. For example, in one of these effects, blocking (originally shown in the animal conditioning literature by Kamin, 1968), the participant has to evaluate the predictive value of a target cue T when the only information received concerning the direct predictive value of this cue is through trials in which it is paired with another cue, X, and the outcome (i.e., TX+ trials where + is the outcome). The situation is uncertain because there is no clear way to establish which cue, T, X, or both, has true predictive value in relation to the outcome. In a blocking situation, the uncertainty is partially resolved because participants are additionally shown, via X+ trials, that cue X on its own is consistently followed by the same outcome (see Table 22.1). The typical resolution of this uncertainty, the blocking effect, consists in attributing low predictive value to target cue T compared with a situation in which X+ trials are not included (or are replaced by trials with a completely different cue, Y+). Thus, the solution involves attributing little predictive value to cue T on the basis that its presence or absence does not make any difference concerning the outcome: Provided that cue X occurs, the outcome will always occur regardless of whether cue T is present (TX+ trials) or absent (X+ trials).

The theoretical interpretation of this type of cue interaction effect prompted the development of the Rescorla-Wagner model (RW) in 1972. According to this theory, the predictive value of a cue (i.e., in the original animal learning terminology, the level of conditioning evoked by the cue) is directly related to the magnitude of the mental

Table 22.1: Design of blocking and higher-order retrospective revaluation experiments

	Stage 1	Stage 2	Test
Blocking	X+	TX+	T
Blocking control		TX+	T
Backward blocking	TX+	X+	T
Recovery from overshadowing	TX+	X−	T

	Stage 1	Stage 2	Stage 3	Test
Higher-order retrospective revaluation	TX+	XY+	Y+	T
Control	TX+	XY+	Y−	T

bond that develops between the representations of the cue and the outcome in the learner's memory. The formation of these associations depends on two principal factors that are applied on a trial-by-trial basis:

(a) the amount of processing that the cognitive system allocates to the cue, a constant factor (i.e., nonmodifiable through experience) that depends on its salience, that is, the relative intensity of the cue compared with other cues; and

(b) the amount of processing that is allocated to the outcome, a factor that is, at least in part, modifiable through experience. Specifically, the processing of the outcome depends on how surprising it is. This level of surprise depends, in turn, on how predictable the outcome is, given the cues present on that trial. In addition, its processing also depends on its fixed salience, as is the case for the processing of the cue.

More formally, these two general principles are incorporated into two basic equations that regulate the formation of associative links between cues and outcomes:

$$\Delta V_{ij} = \alpha_i \beta_j (\lambda_j - \Sigma V) \qquad (22.1)$$

$$V_{ij}(t) = V_{ij}(t-1) + \Delta V_{ij}(t), \qquad (22.2)$$

where $V_{ij}(t)$ (i.e., the associative strength of cue i for outcome j on trial t) repre-

sents the degree to which cue i predicts outcome j and ΔV_{ij} designates its variation on the current trial; α_i and β_j are the saliences of the cue and the outcome, respectively, and both parameters are within the $[0,1]$ interval; λ_j represents the maximum associative strength that the outcome can support and represents the actual status of the outcome in the current trial (i.e., $\lambda_j = 1$ or $\lambda_j = 0$ when it is present or absent, respectively); and ΣV represents the degree to which the combination of cues present on the trial predict the outcome. The core of the model is the difference or error term, $\lambda_j - \Sigma V$, which is a formalization of the second principle stated previously regarding the variable amount of processing that the cognitive system allocates to the outcome. This error term represents the discrepancy between the expectation of the outcome (ΣV) and its actual status on the current trial (λ_j) or, in other words, the level of surprise produced by that outcome. Equation 2, therefore, describes the incremental nature of the associative strength accrued by a cue across trials: The associative strength on trial t, $V_{ij}(t)$, is simply the sum of its associative strength in trial $t - 1$, $V_{ij}(t-1)$, and the variation produced on the current trial t, $\Delta V_{ij}(t)$.

In terms of the theory, then, the low predictive value attributed to cue T in a blocking situation is caused by the low processing devoted to the outcome on those trials where the cue is present, which in turn prevents the acquisition of any associative link between cue T and the outcome. This weak processing in turn is due to the low degree of surprise engendered by the outcome on trials where cue T is present, as the outcome is fully predicted by the accompanying cue X as a consequence of the prior X+ trials. In terms of Equation 1, the error term should approach 0 as a result of 2 conditions: (a) $\lambda_j = 1$ on TX+ trials, and (b) following the X+ trials, ΣV must also approach 1 because cue X should have acquired all of the associative strength that the outcome can support.

In a computational sense, the learning algorithm postulated in the RW model (equivalent to the delta rule frequently used in connectionist modeling, given certain assumptions; see Sutton & Barto, 1981) has the capacity to extract, from the different pairings between cues and outcomes that constitute the learning input, normative statistical information that is crucial to compute the true predictive value of a cue. The asymptotic associative strength of a cue converges into the normative ΔP contingency measure (at least if certain conditions, such as those involved in the blocking design, are met; see Chapman & Robbins, 1990; Cheng, 1997, for formal demonstrations):

$$\Delta P = P(O/C \cdot K) - P(O/-C \cdot K),$$

(22.3)

where the predictive value of a cue equals the difference between the probability of the outcome given the cue and the probability of the outcome in the cue's absence, provided that the status of potential alternative predictive cues, K, is controlled. Thus, the asymptotic associative strength of the cue represents a normative statistic (López, Cobos et al., 1998; Shanks, 1995). In fact, in the RW theory, this is the only knowledge that is stored in the learner's memory regarding the predictive value of the cue: Nothing about the history that led to the current value is retained. As will be shown, this probably constitutes an oversimplification of what is acquired in predictive learning situations.

Despite its simplicity (e.g., the small number of free parameters postulated and the simplicity of the equations described earlier), the RW model has demonstrated a remarkable capacity to explain empirical phenomena in animal and human predictive learning. Focusing on human learning, phenomena such as (1) the gradual acquisition of predictive knowledge (i.e., acquisition curves, Shanks, 1987); (2) cue interaction effects like blocking, overshadowing, and relative validity effects (Chapman & Robbins, 1990; Shanks, 1985; Wasserman, 1990); (3) trial order effects (e.g., recency effects; see López, Shanks et al., 1998); (4) sensitivity of participants' performance to the programmed cue-outcome contingency (Wasserman et al., 1993); and (5) some examples of biased judgments in the detection of noncontingency (e.g., density bias; Shanks, 1987; Shanks, López et al., 1996) are all empirical findings for which the RW model offers a detailed explanation (see Allan, 1993; Shanks, 1995; Shanks, Holyoak, & Medin, 1996, for extensive reviews of these phenomena).

However, although simplicity is a virtue of any theory in science, it must not be achieved at the cost of failing to provide a comprehensive account. Thus, much of the work dedicated to the development of new associative models of predictive learning has tried to solve some oversimplifications intrinsic to the original RW formulation. It is fair to say that the RW model has become a yardstick against which more recent theoretical proposals are measured. In what follows, some of these phenomena that go beyond the scope of the RW model in the human predictive learning literature will be reviewed and will form a platform for considering more recent theoretical accounts (see Miller, Barnet, & Grahame, 1995, for a review of the model and its major weaknesses in the animal conditioning field).

2.2. Models That Learn about the Predictive Values of Absent Cues

Recall that in a blocking situation, the participant evaluates the predictive value of a target cue T from information that is to some extent incomplete, TX+ trials (see previous discussion). The uncertainty is resolved because the participant also learns that cue X, on its own, is paired with the outcome on X+ trials and, hence, can infer that cue T has no true predictive value with respect to the outcome: Its presence or absence makes no difference. Notice that the RW theory's explanation of blocking crucially depends on when exactly the X+ trials are provided. In terms of the model, predictive learning about cue T depends on the surprisingness of the outcome on trials where that cue is present. As mentioned earlier, cue T will not acquire associative strength (i.e., blocking will occur) if X+ trials precede TX+ trial, as under these circumstances, the outcome will be unsurprising on the TX+ trials due to the presence of a good predictor, cue X. However, if the TX+ trials precede the X+ trials (see Table 22.1), the outcome will be to some degree surprising (at least, initially) on trials where cue T is present, and consequently, it will accrue associative strength or predictive value. Subsequent X+ trials will not affect the already acquired associative strength of cue T, as those trials do not involve T's occurrence (i.e., its salience will be 0), and thus, no blocking will take place. Blocking, therefore, depends on trial order. However, contrary to the model's predictions, blocking occurs regardless of the order in which the X+ trials are presented, both in animal and human learning. It is true (Miller & Matute, 1996; Shanks, 1985) that it seems to be of greater magnitude when X+ trials precede TX+ trials (forward blocking) than when they follow the TX+ trials (backward blocking), but the reality of backward blocking is beyond dispute.

Other similar phenomena concerning cue interaction effects have been reported demonstrating revaluation of the predictive value of absent cues, such as recovery from overshadowing (Dickinson & Burke, 1996; Kaufman & Bolles, 1981). In a recovery from overshadowing situation (Table 22.1), the uncertainty regarding the predictive value of target cue T on TX+ trials is resolved because participants are later provided with X− trials (i.e., in which no outcome accompanies cue X). In this case, and unlike the blocking situation, cue T demonstrates positive predictive value, as its presence does matter for the occurrence of the outcome. But, again, according to the RW model, no new learning or revaluation should occur regarding cue T on X− trials, as it is not present (its salience is 0). Participants' performance, though, shows that the predictive value attributed to cue T is revalued (i.e., increased) compared with a situation in which no X− trials are provided.

Thus, these two phenomena, backward blocking and recovery from overshadowing, suggest that individuals may retrospectively revalue a predictive cue, even when that cue is not present. Retrospective revaluation effects reveal a fundamental limitation of the original RW account of predictive learning. Although these phenomena may be initially viewed as implying logical inferential reasoning on the part of the individual, they have prompted the development of new associative models that are compatible with them and, importantly, new predictions have been derived and tested from these modified models. Later, additional empirical data will be considered that represent a challenge for an associative account of retrospective revaluation effects.

Although the surprising occurrence of backward blocking and other examples of retrospective revaluation (De Houwer & Beckers, 2002; Larkin, Aitken, & Dickinson, 1998; Melchers, Lachnit, & Shanks, 2004; Williams, 1996) certainly adds weight to alternative cognitive approaches, another way to react to such findings is to ask whether they can be observed in animal learning and, if so, whether a better response might not be to revise the associative theories. Research has now documented fairly convincingly the occurrence of retrospective revaluation in animal conditioning (Balleine, Espinet, & González, 2005; Denniston et al., 2003; Shevill & Hall, 2004), and this has been followed by modifications of associative theories, some of them fairly straightforward (Dickinson & Burke, 1996; Ghirlanda, 2005), which allow them to generate retrospective changes in response strength.

The first proposal of a modified RW model comes from van Hamme and Wasserman (1994). This modification involves changes in how the salience of a cue is determined. According to the modified model, even an absent cue may undergo changes in its associative strength, as it is still processed by the learning system. These changes, however, run in the opposite direction of those experienced by present cues. More formally, the salience of a cue is defined within the $[-1,1]$ rather than the $[0,1]$ interval. Consequently, if a presented cue were to gain associative strength in a given trial (e.g., were paired with the outcome), then a nonpresented cue would correspondingly lose strength; and vice versa, if a presented cue were to lose associative strength, then the nonpresented cue would gain associative strength. However, an absent cue is only processed on a trial (i.e., gains a negative salience) if its presence is expected on that trial. Thus, only cues that are both absent and expected will be processed with a negative salience. This apparently minor change in the rules that determine the salience of a cue allows the retrospective revaluation effects just described to be explained (see Perales & Shanks, 2003, for its implications regarding asymptotic predictions in the associative strength of a cue compared with RW predictions). For example, in the backward blocking effect, on X+ trials, the absence of target cue T will be processed because the presence of cue X will retrieve a memory of this cue due to prior pairings of T and X formed on TX+ trials. The negative salience of cue T will ensure that its associative strength will be diminished as the absence of cue T is paired with the outcome in X+ trials (i.e., a backward blocking effect on cue T). Wasserman and Castro (2005) provide more details concerning the predictions of van Hamme and Wasserman's (1994) modification of the RW model.

A related proposal for an associative model that learns about absent, though expected, cues is Dickinson and Burke's

(1996) modification of Wagner's (1981) Standard Operating Procedures (SOP) model of animal Pavlovian conditioning. In SOP, cues are represented by nodes in associative memory, each composed of a number of elements. These elements can be in any of three different activation states: an inactive state, I, or two active states, A1 and A2. The unpredicted presentation of a cue or outcome activates a proportion of its elements in the corresponding node from I into the A1 state. These active states are transient so that, over time, the A1 state of these elements decays into A2 and then back again into I. Activating a node by an associative connection, though, bypasses the A1 state and leads to a direct transition of the elements of the node from I to the A2 state. According to Wagner's original formulation, the associative strength of a cue will only develop provided that its presentation is not expected, that is, its elements are in the A1 active state. In Dickinson and Burke's modified version, a cue may develop changes in its associative strength even when it is not present provided that it is expected, that is, its elements are in the A2 active state. According to this new version, if both the elements of the cue and the outcome are in the A2 state, excitatory learning will occur between them, whereas if the elements of the cue are in the A2 state but those of the outcome are in the A1 state (i.e., the outcome is present), inhibitory learning will develop. As in the original formulation of Wagner (1981), it is assumed that the overall associative strength of a cue corresponds to an aggregation across its excitatory and inhibitory associations with the outcome. The explanation of retrospective revaluation follows straightforwardly. For example, in the recovery from overshadowing effect (Table 22.1), on X− trials, the elements of target cue T will be in the A2 state due to the T–X association formed on prior TX+ trials and so will be the elements of the outcome node due to the prior X-outcome association formed in TX+ trials. Thus, as T and the outcome elements will be in the A2 state, an excitatory association will develop between them, increasing the net associative strength of cue T compared with a control situation in which X− trials are not included. Hence, the recovery from overshadowing effect will occur through learning that takes place about an absent cue.

Fortunately, in addition to offering an ad hoc explanation of retrospective revaluation effects, both models also make new predictions that have obtained empirical support. For example, absent cues should update their associative strength in the opposite direction compared with their updating when they are present. Wasserman and Castro (2005) provide a review of evidence supporting this prediction, whereas Dwyer (2001) describes the conditions that induce the opposite pattern, namely, mediated conditioning. A second example is the critical role that both models grant to the formation of associations between cues ("within-compound" associations) in the explanation of retrospective revaluation effects, as these are the associations that cause a cue to be expected and hence guarantee its processing. Evidence shows that retrospective revaluation effects are indeed mediated by such within compound associations (see Aitken, Larkin, & Dickinson, 2001; Melchers et al., 2004; Wasserman & Berglan, 1998).

Although van Hamme and Wasserman's (1994) model and Dickinson and Burke's (1996) modified version of SOP make different predictions concerning the specific details of these retrospective revaluation effects, there is as yet no conclusive evidence that distinguishes between them (see Aitken & Dickinson, 2005; Wasserman & Castro, 2005). Moreover, these two associative accounts are far from the only possible explanations for retrospective revaluation effects (see Le Pelley & McLaren, 2001; Melchers et al., 2004, for further possibilities). However, they demonstrate fairly plainly that learning about an absent cue is not necessarily beyond the scope of an associative account and that there are specific models that prove their empirical viability through relatively basic associative learning principles. Future evidence will clarify the relative merits of these different accounts of retrospective revaluation.

2.3. Models That Learn about the Predictive Values of Configurations of Cues

All the models discussed so far assume that the predictive value of a compound cue (i.e., a cue consisting of two or more cues as in the TX trials described earlier) corresponds to the aggregate or combination of the predictive values of its constituent elements. However, there is evidence that individuals do not always treat the predictive value of a compound cue just as the sum of its elements and that instead a compound cue may acquire a predictive value that is to some extent independent of the predictive value of its constituents. Some of this evidence comes from "negative patterning" discrimination learning in animal and human studies. In this problem, individuals are able to solve a discrimination in which A+, B+, and AB− trials are intermixed and, as is evident, what is learned about the predictive value of the single cues A and B cannot be transferred to its aggregate, AB. In another illustration, Shanks et al. (1998) trained participants on an A+, AB− discrimination prior to presenting several B+ trials. The initial trials should have endowed B with an inhibitory or negative weight, which should then have been replaced by a positive weight during the B+ trials. If the predictive value of a compound is the sum of the values of its constituents, presentation at test of the compound AB should have evoked high levels of responding, as it is composed of two elements each of which should have positive value. However, this was not what Shanks et al. observed. Instead, participants were able to retain intact across the B+ trials the information that the AB compound predicted no outcome. These and other results that violate this aggregation principle have led some theorists to propose configurational models of learning which assume that whole configurations of cues are able to acquire their own independent associative strengths for an outcome (e.g., Pearce, 1994).

According to Pearce's (1994, 2002) model, the predictive value of a compound cue (or any cue, in general) involves (1) the associative strength acquired by the configural node that has been recruited to represent it in memory, and (2) the associative strength generalizing to it from other similar cues. The degree of similarity between any two cues is a linear function of the number of elements they share. As was the case for the RW model, Pearce's model assumes that changes in the associative strength of a cue in a given trial are determined by the surprisingness of the outcome when that cue is present. Thus, the greater the amount of generalized associative strength a cue receives from other cues, the less its intrinsic associative link to the outcome is changed as the outcome is less surprising. Also, as in the RW model, only cues that are present on a trial may undergo changes in their associative strengths (hence, retrospective revaluation effects are not dealt with by this model, although the learning rules could be suitably modified).

In addition to results involving configural processing of cues (e.g., Shanks et al., 1998), Pearce's model has been successfully applied to a number of learning phenomena, such as blocking (see Pearce, 1994, for details). Other successful applications that are problematic for the original RW model (and for some standard connectionist models; Lewandowsky & Li, 1995) include the lack of catastrophic forgetting exhibited by human learners, whereby new learning does not seem to completely override previous learning. The particular solution to this problem offered by Pearce's model is based on the assignment of exclusive configural representations to each new pattern of cues the system is exposed to (which preserves old knowledge and prevents it from being catastrophically interfered with) and the generalization mechanism based on pattern similarity (which ensures a certain level of transfer between old and more recent knowledge; see López, Shanks, et al., 1998, for details on the predictions of Pearce's model regarding this effect).

Pearce and Bouton (2001) recently reviewed the relative merits of configural and more traditional elemental approaches in the field of animal learning. Regarding

human predictive learning, new evidence shows an enormous flexibility in an individual's representational scheme for cues (Melchers, Lachnit, & Shanks, in press; Shanks, 2005). For example, Williams, Sagness, and McPhee (1994) and, more recently, Melchers et al. (2005; in a human conditioning preparation) have shown that depending on different pretraining treatments, either an elemental or a configural representation of cues may occur during a later target training stage. A compound such as TX may, under some circumstances, be coded as the sum of its elements and, under others, may be coded as being a configuration whose associative value is unrelated to those of its elements. Thus, the coding of cues does not seem to be fixed (as assumed by all current associative accounts, including Pearce's model), but may instead vary according to a range of factors. For example, Melchers et al.'s (2005) participants either received a pretraining discrimination problem that encouraged an elemental solution (i.e., elemental coding of the cues was sufficient to solve the problem) or a configural solution (i.e., configural coding was necessary) and evaluated the influence of such pretraining treatments on a later target discrimination problem that required configural coding (e.g., the negative patterning problem described earlier). In two experiments, it was found that participants who had received elemental pretraining discriminations were hindered in solving the later configural problem compared with participants who had received configural pretraining.

Much research has been devoted to the possible selective role of the hippocampus in configural coding. A claim with a long history (Wickelgren, 1979) is that the hippocampus is particularly involved in tasks that require the formation of configural representations. This idea was made most explicitly by Sutherland and Rudy (1989) and is supported by a range of evidence, mostly from animal conditioning studies, to the effect that hippocampal lesions impair the acquisition of certain configural or nonlinear discriminations but do not impair acquisition of elemental or linear ones. For instance, McDonald et al. (1997) found that lesions in the hippocampus but not in the fornix-fimbria (a major input-output pathway for the hippocampus) in rats impaired acquisition of a negative patterning discrimination that cannot be solved elementally. The current status of this hypothesis is extensively discussed by O'Reilly and Rudy (2001).

Overall, the results in this section imply that individuals can learn about the predictive value of a compound cue and that this value may be relatively independent of the predictive values of the compound's constituent elements. This is inconsistent with the original summation assumption of the RW model, but alternative associative models (such as Pearce's, 1994) are able to capture these effects. However, recently revealed experimental findings concerning representational flexibility are at variance with all current associative accounts, as it has been shown that the coding of cues is variable (either elemental or configural) depending on factors such as the specific pretraining treatments provided.

2.4. Models That Learn about the Relevance of Cues

In previous models, if there is a single core assumption that explains the process of acquisition of associative strength, it concerns the level of surprise that the outcome produces in a given trial: the so-called error term. Remember that this error term is modifiable through experience, whereas the processing of the cue is a fixed parameter (the cue's salience). This principle of a fixed amount of cue processing was soon called into question in the animal conditioning field. Data accumulated in Pavlovian conditioning showing the limitations of such a principle, and new models were developed to specifically address this problem (see Le Pelley, 2004; Mackintosh, 1975; Pearce & Hall, 1980; Wasserman & Miller, 1997, for reviews). In terms of these models, the amount of processing that a cue receives is not fixed but varies according to its predic-

tive value. These changes may be conceived as changes in the level of associability of the cue (captured by the parameter α_i in Equation 1) and may be interpreted as showing varying degrees of its susceptibility to form new associative links with the same or different outcomes.

It is only more recently that related evidence on associability changes has started to accumulate in the field of human predictive learning. Kruschke and Blair (2000), using the now familiar blocking design (both in forward and backward versions), showed that individuals actively learn to ignore the target blocked cue T of the blocking design (see Table 22.1) when this cue is made relevant in a completely new predictive learning task (i.e., when it is subsequently paired reliably with a different outcome). After training with X+ and TX+ trials and comparing the predictive value of cue T with that of a control cue in a condition in which X+ trials did not occur, training with target cue T continued, but now this cue was consistently paired with a different outcome (equivalent training was programmed for the control cue). The key result was that the predictive value of the control cue for the new outcome was perceived as greater than that of the target cue T. According to a traditional associative account of blocking, the ability of the target cue T to form new associations with a different outcome should not have been altered by the blocking procedure. However, the results showed that its ability to enter into new associations was attenuated after having been part of either a forward or a backward blocking training regime (see Le Pelley & McLaren, 2003; Le Pelley, Oakeshott, & McLaren, 2005, for results that may be interpreted in a similar fashion).

These types of results have encouraged the formulation of new mechanisms within associative theory that incorporate principled variations in the processing of a cue according to its predictive history. For example, Kruschke's (1996) ADIT model conceives these variations in the processing of a cue as variations in the amount of attention allocated to it. On this approach, during initial X+ trials in a blocking design, cue X attracts attention as a result of being a good predictor of the outcome. On the later TX+ trials, attention to cue T is reduced, as there is a limit on the availability of attentional resources. This reduced attentional allocation will diminish the expectation of the outcome in the presence of T as attention is directed to the cue that already has an associative link to the outcome, cue X. Consequently, attention is shifted away from cue T to cue X and will remain diminished for cue T into the later training stage in which it is again involved. Hence, the results obtained by Kruschke and Blair (2000) will emerge.

Another recently discovered and rather striking effect may also require an attentional explanation. Consider a compound stimulus AB, which is paired with an outcome on AB+ trials. According to the error-correction process embodied in Equation (1) and assuming that A and B have equal saliences, then any changes to A and B's separate associative strengths should be identical, as the error term is common to all present cues. Now, imagine that A has a prior history as an excitor (resulting from A+ trials), whereas B's history is that of an inhibitor (resulting from BC+, B− trials). Will it still be the case that, as the RW and many other models predict, equal associative changes occur for A and B? Modeled on an animal experiment by Rescorla (2000), Le Pelley and McLaren (2004, 2005) recently addressed this issue in human contingency learning and found that the excitor A gained more additional weight than the inhibitor B from an AB+ trial. When the AB compound was extinguished rather than reinforced (i.e., AB−), B underwent a greater loss of excitatory strength (or, equivalently, greater gain of inhibitory strength) than A. Curiously, Rescorla found the exact opposite in his animal experiments, with the inhibitor gaining more weight on AB+ trials and the excitor more on AB− trials. Lastly, Le Pelley and McLaren showed that retrospective changes induced in a backward blocking procedure were also different, depending on prior history.

A plausible explanation for these results – putting aside the divergence from the animal data – is that the associability of the A and B elements changed differentially during their initial history. Consider the case where the AB compound is reinforced (AB+). Having previously been trained as an excitor, A's associability for the outcome would have been maintained at a high level, thus ensuring a substantial weight change on the compound trials. During its training as an inhibitor, in contrast, B would have lost associability for the outcome and not undergone a substantial weight change on the AB+ trials. Le Pelley and McLaren (2004, 2005) speculated that different outcomes (including the presence vs. absence of a given reinforcer) might maintain independent saliences. Thus, the patterns of differential associative changes they observed would be accommodated.

There are other associative explanations of these associability effects (see, e.g., Le Pelley, 2004), and it is still not clear how these different accounts may be integrated into a single formulation, if that is possible. However, all of them emphasize the general idea that the relevance of a cue (or the amount of processing that the system allocates to it) is subject to variations that depend on its past predictive history.

2.5. *Late Computation Models*

The empirical phenomena reviewed thus far are interpreted – according to associative models – as the product of mental operations accomplished during the course of learning. Although different in the specific learning processes they postulate, all these models have in common the assumption that the behavioral response prompted by a test cue directly reflects its predictive value as computed during training in the form of a unique associative strength attached to that particular cue. Thus, these models may be referred to as early computation models (see Estes, 1986, for this distinction in the context of categorization models). However, there are other associative accounts that envision a different way in which the test cue prompts a behavioural response. According to these models, at the time of testing, the learner is conceived to consult all the relevant associations previously acquired and performs whatever computations are required to combine these associations to produce a behavioral response to that particular test cue. These are late computation models (see Miller & Escobar, 2001, for the distinction between acquisition and performance-based models). Consistent with Marr's Principle of Least Commitment (Marr, 1976), under this view, the bulk of the information-processing operations an intelligent system performs is put off until the last possible moment (i.e, the time of testing in this context), avoiding doing anything that may later have to be undone. That is, the organism is not committed to a particular processing strategy early on, but acts under a more conservative principle of trying not to impose too many restrictions on the incoming information so that later demands, which are unknown at present, may be satisfied (Cole, Barnet, & Miller, 1995).

A prominent example of these late computation models is the comparator theory of Miller and colleagues (Miller & Matzel, 1988). This theory posits a specific rule determining how the different associative links formed during training are later retrieved from memory and combined to produce a response. Although the theory was initially developed as an account of animal Pavlovian conditioning, it should come as no surprise that it has been extensively applied to human predictive learning, too (e.g., Matute, Arcediano, & Miller, 1996). The theory represents an alternative way to interpret cue interaction effects like blocking.

The comparator theory assumes that the acquisition of associative links is determined by pairings between the cue and the outcome in temporal and spatial contiguity (see Stout & Miller, 2007, for a computational version of the theory). Thus, X+ trials will induce the formation of an associative link between these two events. In addition, on TX+ trials, the contiguity-based process will ensure the formation of T–X associations, as well as an association between the target cue T and the outcome (note that on pre-vious early computation-based accounts of blocking, no significant association was assumed to be formed between the blocked cue and the outcome), plus the strengthening of the previously formed X-outcome association. Thus, when the predictive value of target cue T is assessed, there are two distinct ways in which the memory of the outcome can be retrieved: through what may be called a direct route (the cue T-outcome association), and through an indirect route (the T–X association and, in turn, the X-outcome association). The predictive value of cue T (and the corresponding behavioral response) is, in this theory, the result of a process that compares the outcome activation due to the direct T-outcome route and its activation due to the indirect X-outcome route. In a blocking group, the memory of the outcome is strongly activated by the indirect X-outcome route, so the target cue T has a limited ability to signal the outcome beyond that degree of activation. In a control condition in which X+ trials are not included, the comparator process yields a stronger activation of the outcome due to the direct T-outcome route, because the indirect X-outcome association is weaker. Hence, the blocking effect is explained.

In a recent extension of the theory (Denniston, Savastano, & Miller, 2001), the comparator process idea is applied recursively so that higher order comparator processes also modulate the effectiveness of the primary comparator process. Returning to the blocking situation, in its extended version, a comparator process also determines the effectiveness with which both the T–X and the X-outcome associations will modulate the expression of the target T-outcome association (i.e., a direct and an indirect route are envisaged for activating both the memory of cue X and that of the outcome).

An empirical phenomenon that illustrates the operation of this higher order comparator process is so-called higher-order retrospective revaluation, recently shown in human predictive learning (see De Houwer & Beckers, 2002; Melchers et al., 2004) and animal conditioning (Denniston et al., 2001, 2003). In these studies, for example, a target cue T is paired with cue X and the outcome on TX+ trials (see Table 22.1). In addition, the same cue X is paired with cue Y and the outcome on XY+ trials. Cue Y is then presented on its own either accompanied by the outcome in one condition (i.e., Y+ trials) or its absence in another condition (i.e., Y– trials). Similar to other retrospective revaluation effects considered earlier, the predictive value of cue X is lower in the condition where Y was associated with the outcome than in the condition where it was associated with its absence. Note that in accordance with associative models that learn about absent but expected cues, such revaluation effects are expected due to the X–Y within compound association. But in addition to this, and crucially, the predictive value of target cue T is also revalued so that this cue is perceived as having a greater predictive value in the condition where cue Y was paired with the outcome than in the condition where it was unpaired with it. As cue T was never paired with cue Y, T– Y within-compound associations should not have been formed, and thus, nothing further should have been learned about target cue T on trials where Y occurred on its own. Consequently, early computation-based models, even ones that account for backward blocking (e.g., Dickinson & Burke, 1996; van Hamme & Wasserman, 1994), should not expect any revaluation of the predictive value of cue T because it was absent and not expected during cue Y trial types.

The extended comparator hypothesis, though, provides an interpretation of this further revaluation process on cue T. As in the standard version of the theory, the predictive value of target cue T corresponds to the output of the primary comparator process (i.e., the cue's associative strength relative to the ability of its comparator cue X to retrieve the memory of the outcome). But in the extended version, there is a further comparator process that determines this primary comparator process (i.e., the higher-order comparator process). Accord-

ing to this, cue X's associative strength for the outcome is rendered more or less effective, as its comparator stimulus cue Y, in turn, has a stronger or weaker association with the outcome (depending on the condition). Thus, after prior experience with TX+ and XY+ trials, Y+ trials should make the cue X-outcome association less effective and thereby increase the predictive value of cue T. Similarly, Y– trials should make the X-outcome association more effective and thereby decrease the predictive value of target cue T. Hence, varying the effectiveness of the primary comparator stimulus X for target cue T (through cue Y training trials) will indirectly affect its predictive value in the direction of the empirical results obtained (see Denniston et al., 2001, for a more detailed discussion).

Despite the ability of the extended version of the comparator hypothesis to offer an account of both first and higher-order retrospective revaluation effects, the theory is not without its problems. For example, according to the explanation provided earlier, blocking, both in its forward and backward versions, critically depends on the formation of within-compound associations between the cues on compound cue trial types. However, there is evidence that whereas the formation of within-compound associations plays a critical role in retrospective revaluation effects (e.g., the backward version of the blocking effect), it does not seem to play such a role in the corresponding forward versions (see, e.g., Aitken et al., 2001; Dickinson & Burke, 1996; Melchers et al., 2004).

Because it can provide an explanation of higher-order retrospective revaluation effects, which are not easy to reconcile with other early computation-based associative models (though see Melchers et al., 2004, for an explanation in terms of an alternative hypothesis based on a memory rehearsal mechanism), a complete explanation of predictive learning should probably contemplate the sort of elaborated memory retrieval process envisaged by the comparator hypothesis. However, the exact explanatory scope of the specific proposal made by Miller and collaborators (Denniston et al., 2001) remains to be precisely determined.

In this section, a variety of empirical phenomena have been reviewed that characterize human predictive learning. The diversity of the models that have been developed since the original formulation of Rescorla and Wagner (1972) in response to these phenomena has been reviewed. However, no single model accommodates the entire range of empirical diversity. Different models emphasize different aspects of the learning mechanisms involved. For example, there are models that include specific mechanisms for allowing revaluation of the predictive weight of cues when those cues are absent, whereas others assume that learning takes place on entire configurations of cues. Others conceive that the relevance of a cue determines the amount of processing that is allocated to it and, consequently, will determine the degree of learning that will accrue to that cue. The present section has considered the explanatory value that is gained when a retrieval process across stored associations in memory is assumed.

Despite all these differences between models, there are also significant similarities that lend support to the fundamental principles of an associative account of human predictive learning. These principles reflect a coherent picture of the process of predictive learning, which views it as automatic and bottom-up, not demanding cognitively complex operations, and mediated by knowledge concerning cue-outcome associations that is evoked in an automatic fashion by a test target cue. In the next section, new evidence will show that this associative approach is not without its limits as a complete account of contingency learning.

3. Challenges for Associative Accounts of Predictive Learning

Many of the empirical phenomena that have resisted explanation by extant associative models depend on the learner's sensitivity to prior knowledge, that is, knowledge that antecedes his or her brief encounter with the experimental task but which nevertheless influences performance. This evidence suggests that when individuals are faced with predictive learning tasks, they retrieve from memory prior knowledge that actively guides learning (see Alloy & Tabachnik, 1984, for a review of the influence of prior knowledge on contingency learning). It is important to note that such influences are typically obtained despite the best efforts of the experimenter to minimize their impact by using, for example, experimental scenarios for which participants are unlikely to possess specific cue-outcome knowledge (e.g., the effect of a particular type of radiation on mutation in a butterfly). However, this engagement of prior knowledge is perhaps hardly surprising, given the adaptive pressure for accurate detection of predictive relationships. There is no obvious advantage to ignoring knowledge that the individual understands is relevant to solving the task, taking advantage of his or her own experience with related tasks.

The exact nature of this knowledge, what its origin might be, or when exactly during task processing it intervenes are all important questions for which there are no clear answers yet. However, one of the situations in which these effects of prior knowledge has been extensively studied involves (unsurprisingly) cue interaction, specifically, the blocking effect. In the present section, this evidence will be reviewed.

This research is easier to reconcile with a much more complex, active, and cognitively demanding role for the learner than is assumed in associative models. For example, individuals seem to give sense to the learning input (cue-outcome pairings) by the active search for a coherent "model" that to some extent "explains" this learning input, unravelling some of its abstract or structural properties. In this search, individuals seem to go beyond the information provided by the input and take into consideration their prior knowledge. Under this view, the learner is regarded much more as an "inferential reasoner" than as someone whose knowledge is automatically evoked by a target cue during the test phase of the experimental task.

The evidence also shows that this conception of the processes of predictive learning should not be viewed as being in strict opposition to associative models, but rather as complementary (see also, for example, Sloman, 1996, or Sun, Slusarz & Terry, 2005, for a related perspective on other domains of cognition). This is because the evidence has also shown that there are specific factors that modulate participants' performance, so that it conforms to one process or the other. That is, although the use of prior knowledge in predictive learning has been revealed and challenges current associative explanations, there is also evidence showing that in some circumstances, this knowledge may be inert, and processing becomes closer to that envisaged by associative models.

3.1. *Use of Prior Knowledge about the Structure of Causal Relationships*

Although the interest in this chapter has been focused on human predictive learning in general, most of the evidence that reveals an influence of prior knowledge is based on a particular example of predictive learning, namely, causal learning. In causal learning scenarios, the cue and outcome are provided, via the instructions, with particular causal roles. In most cases, then, the cues are not only potentially predictive of the outcome but also *cause* it (e.g., predictive relationships are arranged between different types of food that may be eaten – cues – potentially causing allergic reactions in patients – outcomes). These results are relevant for the present analysis, given that since the work of Dickinson, Shanks, and Evenden (1984), associative models have been proposed as plausible accounts of causal learning.

In what follows, evidence showing the use of prior knowledge concerning structural properties of causal relationships is reviewed. Part of the interest in using this kind of knowledge in the induction of causal relationships is that it serves to impose restrictions on specific characteristics of the learning input; thus, it may guide effective learning of predictive relationships. In other words, this knowledge may suggest that certain cue-outcome pairings or certain properties of the outcome are more probable than others. These restrictions, though, should not necessarily be understood as being independent of the specific content they refer to; that is, they may not be universal or true across all possible causal scenarios where the cues and the outcomes of the task are defined.

As an illustration, individuals may have general knowledge (i.e., valid across multiple cases of causal relationships experienced previously) that causes follow a principle of additivity when producing an effect. According to this principle, when two valid causes of a certain effect co-occur, the resulting effect should be of a greater magnitude than when the causes are found in isolation. Notice that this prior knowledge or assumption may suffice to explain the familiar blocking effect. If participants know that cue X is able to produce the effect on X+ trials, and then are presented with TX+ trials (but the effect that occurs is no greater in magnitude than that produced by X on its own), they should discount target cue T as a true cause of the effect, as its presence has added nothing to the situation. In the control condition, no X+ trials are included, so T cannot be discounted on the basis on TX+ trials only – it may have causal value. Thus, the causal value of T should be greater in the control condition, leading to the blocking effect. In agreement with the view that participants use this sort of general causal knowledge, Lovibond et al. (2003) recently found that pretraining manipulations affecting prior assumptions about the additivity of causes (e.g., making the additivity principle more or less credible to participants) correspondingly affected the magnitude of the blocking effect obtained.

Relatedly, other forms of prior knowledge may modulate the magnitude of the blocking effect found. For example, participants have previous causal knowledge that if a given effect is produced at a ceiling level by a given cause, X, then the addition of another effective noninteracting cause, T, should produce no difference. Hence, from the point of view of causal induction, T is indistinguishable from a spurious cause. Contrarily, if the effect is produced at a submaximal level, the addition of cause T should increase the level of the effect. Thus, from the point of view of induction, there should be a difference between adding T and adding a spurious cause. According to this, the blocking effect should increase if participants are informed that the effect is at a submaximal level compared with a situation in which they are informed that the effect is produced at its maximal level. This is because, only in the former case, participants receiving X+ trials can be sure that target cue T does not play any role in producing the outcome. This prediction has been empirically confirmed by recent studies (De Houwer, Beckers, & Glautier, 2002; see also Beckers et al., 2005, and Mitchell, Lovibond, & Condoleon, 2005, for recent evidence showing an independent modulatory effect of prior ideas about additivity and ceiling effects on the magnitude of blocking).

Because blocking has been a touchstone of associative theory for several decades, these findings are particularly striking, as they suggest the intervention of rather different processes. Whereas blocking is normally thought of as arising from a process of reinforcement driven by prediction error, the studies of additivity and maximality are seemingly more congenial with the intervention of cognitive processes in which participants try to figure out an underlying rational explanation of predictive roles. There have been some attempts (e.g., Livesey & Boakes, 2004) to reconcile additivity pretraining effects with associative theory by considering the balance induced by the pretraining between elemental and configural processing. As discussed in Section 2.3, it is well known that stimuli can sometimes be treated as composed of independent elements and sometimes as configural "wholes."

Indeed, people can be induced to code the same stimulus either elementally or configurally (Shanks, 2005; Williams et al., 1994). Thus, the possibility arises that additivity pretraining has its effect via switching the balance between elemental and configural training. Specifically, if it tended to induce a more elemental approach, then an enhancement of blocking would be expected, as blocking requires treating the two cues as separate elements. Indeed, Livesey and Boakes (2004) showed that additivity instructions are rendered inadequate to generate blocking if the cues are presented in a way that strongly encourages configural processing. The fact, however, that additivity training can enhance blocking, even when it is given *after* the blocking trials (Beckers et al., 2005), is a particularly powerful piece of evidence for the inferential account, as it would seem to rule out an explanation solely in terms of elemental/configural processing, although there may be some contribution from this shift.

Another source of evidence of the influence of general causal knowledge on people's performance in causal learning situations comes from studies by Waldmann and colleagues (Waldmann, 2000, 2001; Waldmann & Hagmayer, 2001; Waldmann & Holyoak, 1992; Waldmann & Walker, 2005). These show that participants may be sensitive to the causal role that the instructions provide to cues and outcomes (i.e., whether they are causes or effects). This sensitivity is relevant from a causal perspective. Let us once again consider the interpretation of TX+ trials. If cues and outcome are interpreted as causes and effect, respectively, then these trials indicate that two potential causes produce a single effect (in the jargon of causal models, this is a common-effect situation); but if the cues and the outcome are interpreted as effects and cause, respectively, then a single cause (the outcome) is producing two different effects (the cues; i.e., a common-cause situation). In the common-effect situation, the predictive value of cue T is unclear, as the true causal value of the cue to produce the effect cannot be unambiguously determined: Cue X or even both cues may well be necessary to produce the effect. In this situation, both causes compete to gain predictive or causal value. In the common-cause situation, on the other hand, the predictive value of cue T should not be affected by the presence of the other effect, X, as both effects are systematically produced by the cause. In fact, both effects (T and X) seem to corroborate to diagnose the presence of their single cause. Thus, cue T is perfectly indicative of the presence of the cause. Hence, whereas in the common-effect situation, the true predictive value of cue T remains undetermined or ambiguous, in the common-cause situation, it reliably indicates the presence of its cause. To the extent that participants' performance is sensitive to variations in the causal interpretation of cues and outcomes, it should be sensitive to this sort of general causal knowledge. According to this knowledge, causes, but not effects, compete to gain causal or predictive credit. Waldmann's research suggests, at the very least, that there are some circumstances in which the cue-outcome interpretation offered by the instructions dramatically affects cue competition, even when the actual trial sequence presented to participants is identical (see also López, Cobos, & Caño, 2005). Such results therefore implicate background knowledge in basic contingency learning.

3.2. *Rule Learning*

Another line of evidence that seems to go beyond an associative approach to predictive learning comes from studies in which participants apparently do not learn a pattern of predictive relationships between specific cues and outcomes, but instead gain knowledge of the rules that govern those predictive relationships and are able to transfer such knowledge to a different set of cues and outcomes. This suggests that individuals are able to grasp structural knowledge that is independent of the physical or perceptual properties of the events.

Shanks and Darby (1998) offer an illustration of this rule learning (see Winman

et al., 2005, for related evidence). In their experiments, participants were able to master the negative patterning discrimination learning described earlier, in which a compound cue and its constituent elements lead to completely opposite outcomes (e.g., a compound cue is paired with the absence of the outcome, whereas its constituent elements predict the outcome: A+, B+, AB−). The key demonstration of rule learning, though, was shown in participants who were able to transfer a newly learned abstract rule of the sort "compound cues and their constituent elements are associated with opposite outcomes" to new sets of cues for which they had had no specific experience. For example, they could predict on the basis of having observed a compound cue paired with the absence of the outcome that its constituent elements would be associated with the outcome. Notice that this rule-learning effect goes beyond even Pearce's (1994) configural model. To illustrate, consider the situation in which a negative patterning rule transfers to a new set of cues. If cues X and Y are both paired with the outcome, and participants behave according to the rule (as in Shanks & Darby, 1998), the never-before-experienced compound XY would induce expectation of the absence of the outcome. However, in terms of Pearce's model, despite the configural XY unit being able to maintain its own associative strength, it is expected that learning about its constituent elements will generalize to the compound cue due to their similarity and, hence, some expectation of the outcome would occur. Paradoxically, it may be argued that Pearce's configural model is not configural enough to support this kind of rule-learning effect.

4. The Search for Boundary Conditions for Different Processes

Despite the challenging nature of the evidence against an associative perspective as a unique account of human predictive learning, there is also evidence that the influence of causal knowledge or rule learning is not necessarily pervasive (Cobos et al., 2002; Matute et al., 1996; Price & Yates, 1995; Shanks & Darby, 1998; Shanks & López, 1996; Winman et al., 2005). Thus, it may be difficult to formulate an alternative account to associative models in terms of controlled inferential reasoning processes (De Houwer, Beckers, & Vandorpe, 2005; Lovibond, 2003; Waldmann, 1996), which offers a complete explanation for human predictive learning. In addition, there is also evidence that goes beyond the predictions of such inferential reasoning accounts and is more in line with associative models' predictions (see, e.g., Le Pelley et al., 2005), including recent functional magnetic resonance imaging (fMRI) data that appear to favor the involvement of associative error-correction process in various predictive learning phenomena (Corlett et al., 2004).

Therefore, a much more promising line of research to further the understanding of the processes involved would entail a specification of the circumstances under which different operations (either associative, inferential, or of any other form) are involved in participants' performance in predictive learning tasks. In fact, this strategy has started to provide suggestive results establishing some of the boundary conditions for the different processes.

For example, De Houwer and Beckers (2003) and Waldmann and Walker (2005) have shown that – as the inferential reasoning account predicts – asking participants to perform a secondary task while carrying out a predictive learning task may interfere with their competence to use causal knowledge and consequently induce them to rely on default, more simple, less cognitively demanding associative processes. Another factor that has been suggested as a boundary condition is the complexity of the task, measured, for example, in terms of the number of cues and outcomes that need to be memorized (see, e.g., Aitken & Dickinson, 2005; Le Pelley et al., 2005). In general, experiments that reveal an influence of prior knowledge on performance tend to use fewer cues and outcomes (e.g., Waldmann,

2001) than those which do not (e.g., Cobos et al., 2002). Relatedly, Tangen and Allan (2004) have found that the number of trials in the task may be another factor that qualitatively influences participants' performance. In their results, as the number of trials increased, responses were less sensitive to prior causal knowledge, suggesting that as responding becomes more habitual, it is less influenced by top-down knowledge.

Another factor that may affect the balance between associative and inferential processes is the credibility, plausibility, and tangibility of the causal scenario in which the cues and outcomes are embedded in the task instructions (López et al., 2005; Waldmann & Walker, 2005). Given the cognitive effort required to deploy prior causal knowledge in predictive learning, participants may refrain from accessing it unless the causal scenario meets these requirements, and their performance, hence, will be guided by more simple, default processes like those described by associative models.

Other factors relating to individual differences or even motivational factors have been suggested as relevant issues for understanding these boundary conditions. For example, Shanks and Darby (1998) and Winman et al. (2005) demonstrated that rule learning was correlated with performance during the learning task. Specifically, participants who demonstrated the greatest accuracy during training also learned the rules governing the cue-outcome relationships in the training input better (Winman et al., 2005, also documented age-related individual differences). López et al. (2005) showed that there needs to be some additional motivation for participants to perform in a way consistent with the use of general and abstract causal knowledge (i.e., the causal role of cues and outcomes). For example, the results from one of their experiments showed that unless participants were cued, through the instructions, to perceive the relevance of the causal scenario, they did not use prior causal knowledge and relied on more simple associative processes (see also Goedert & Spellman, 2005, for related effects of motivational factors and the complexity of participants' performance). Thus, these results seem to show that participants do not always necessarily have the ability or motivational resources to actively engage in a more complex resolution of the task at hand and, instead, rely on more simple associative processes.

At present, there are very interesting questions that remain unanswered regarding these delimiting factors, such as how they interact, what other factors are relevant, what their exact nature might be, and how they relate to representative examples of predictive learning in more natural settings. Another relevant question that future research will have to address is whether distinct dissociable processes are necessarily demanded by the data or whether a unified account can be envisaged. At present, more modestly, these results question the viability of current explanations of human predictive learning.

5. New Directions in Associative Models of Predictive Learning

The bulk of the evidence that challenges associative accounts of predictive learning comes from studies revealing an influence of prior knowledge on participants' behavior. It should be emphasized, though, that the problem for an associative account is not the use of prior knowledge per se. For example, prior knowledge concerning specific cue-outcome relationships may be conceived as being previously acquired and stored in terms of the cues' associative links. Rather, it is the nature of the knowledge that has been shown to exert an influence that is crucial. This knowledge is of a general and abstract nature, relatively independent of the specific physical properties of cues and outcomes, and captures what may be regarded as structural properties of the learning input.

Thus, the challenging nature of these results reduces to the question of whether the acquisition of such knowledge is beyond associative principles. A positive answer to this question would severely restrict the scope of associative accounts. A negative answer would open up the prospect of an associative explanation of how this kind of knowledge influences a learner's performance. It now seems clear that such a positive answer is unlikely to be found in the simple sort of associative analysis that has been considered in this chapter. However, it may not necessarily be beyond the scope of more complex connectionist models (see other chapters in this volume). Ever since the classic work of Hinton (1991), these complex models, using sophisticated architectures and learning algorithms, have demonstrated that the abstraction of general structural properties of objects within a given domain and its transfer to new situations may not be beyond their scope. The extent to which the acquisition of this more complex knowledge suffices to offer an explanation for the challenging evidence reviewed here remains an open question. In line with this perspective, Rogers and McClelland (2004) have offered a tentative proposal of the potential of a sequential recurrent network-based model to explain the role of abstract, general causal knowledge in individuals' performance on semantic memory tasks after experiencing causal event sequences.

Acknowledgments

The writing of this chapter was supported by a research grant from Junta de Andalucía (EXCEL-SEJ0406), Spain. We would like to thank Julián Almaraz, Pedro L. Cobos, David Luque, Helena Matute, and Miguel A. Vadillo for their helpful comments on previous versions of the chapter.

References

Aitken, M. R. F., & Dickinson, A. (2005). Simulations of a modified SOP model applied to retrospective revaluation of human causal learning. *Learning & Behavior, 33*, 147–159.

Aitken, M. R. F., Larkin, M. J. W., & Dickinson, A. (2001). Re-examination of the role of within-compound associations in the retrospective revaluation of causal judgements.

Quarterly Journal of Experimental Psychology, 54B, 27–51.

Allan, L. G. (1993). Human contingency judgments: Rule-based or associative? *Psychological Bulletin, 114,* 435–448.

Alloy, L. B., & Tabachnik, N. (1984). Assessment of covariation by humans and animals: The joint influence of prior expectations and current situational information. *Psychological Review, 91,* 112–149.

Balleine, B. W., Espinet, A., & González, F. (2005). Perceptual learning enhances retrospective revaluation of conditioned flavor preferences in rats. *Journal of Experimental Psychology: Animal Behavior Processes, 31,* 341–350.

Beckers, T., De Houwer, J., Pineño, O., & Miller, R. R. (2005). Outcome additivity and outcome maximality influence cue competition in human causal learning. *Journal of Experimental Psychology: Learning, Memory, and Cognition, 31,* 238–249.

Chapman, G. B., & Robbins, S. J. (1990). Cue interaction in human contingency judgment. *Memory & Cognition, 18,* 537–545.

Cheng, P. W. (1997). From covariation to causation: A causal power theory. *Psychological Review, 104,* 367–405.

Cobos, P. L., López, F. J., Caño, A., Almaraz, J., & Shanks, D. R. (2002). Mechanisms of predictive and diagnostic causal induction. *Journal of Experimental Psychology: Animal Behavior Processes, 28,* 331–346.

Cole, R. P., Barnet, R. C., & Miller, R. R. (1995). Effect of relative stimulus validity: Learning or performance deficit? *Journal of Experimental Psychology: Animal Behavior Processes, 21,* 293–303.

Corlett, P. R., Aitken, M. R. F., Dickinson, A., Shanks, D. R., Honey, G. D., Honey, R. A. E., et al. (2004). Prediction error during retrospective revaluation of causal associations in humans: fMRI evidence in favor of an associative model of learning. *Neuron, 44,* 877–888.

Crowder, R. G. (1976). *Principles of learning and memory.* Hillsdale, NJ: Lawrence Erlbaum.

De Houwer, J., & Beckers, T. (2002). Higher-order retrospective revaluation in human causal learning. *Quarterly Journal of Experimental Psychology, 55B,* 137–151.

De Houwer, J., & Beckers, T. (2003). Secondary task difficulty modulates forward blocking in human contingency learning. *Quarterly Journal of Experimental Psychology, 56B,* 345–357.

De Houwer, J., Beckers, T., & Glautier, S. (2002). Outcome and cue properties modulate blocking. *Quarterly Journal of Experimental Psychology, 55A,* 965–985.

De Houwer, J., Beckers, T., & Vandorpe, S. (2005). Evidence for the role of higher order reasoning processes in cue competition and other learning phenomena. *Learning & Behavior, 33,* 239–249.

Denniston, J. C., Savastano, H. I., Blaisdell, A. P., & Miller, R. R. (2003). Cue competition as a retrieval deficit. *Learning and Motivation, 34,* 1–31.

Denniston, J. C., Savastano, H. I., & Miller, R. R. (2001). The extended comparator hypothesis: Learning by contiguity, responding by relative strength. In R. R. Mowrer & S. B. Klein (Eds.), *Handbook of contemporary learning theories* (pp. 65–117). Hillsdale, NJ: Lawrence Erlbaum.

Dickinson, A., & Burke, J. (1996). Within-compound associations mediate the retrospective revaluation of causality judgements. *Quarterly Journal of Experimental Psychology, 49B,* 60–80.

Dickinson, A., Shanks, D. R., & Evenden, J. L. (1984). Judgement of act-outcome contingency: The role of selective attribution. *Quarterly Journal of Experimental Psychology, 36A,* 29–50.

Dwyer, D. M. (2001). Mediated conditioning and retrospective revaluation with LiCl then flavour pairings. *Quarterly Journal of Experimental Psychology, 54B,* 145–165.

Estes, W. K. (1986). Array models for category learning. *Cognitive Psychology, 18,* 500–549.

Ghirlanda, S. (2005). Retrospective revaluation as simple associative learning. *Journal of Experimental Psychology: Animal Behavior Processes, 31,* 107–111.

Goedert, K. M., & Spellman, B. A. (2005). Non-normative discounting: There is more to cue interaction effects than controlling for alternative causes. *Learning & Behavior, 33,* 197–210.

Hinton, G. E. (1991). Mapping part-whole hierarchies into connectionist networks. In G. E. Hinton (Ed.), *Connectionist symbol processing* (pp. 47–76). Cambridge, MA: MIT Press.

Kamin, L. J. (1968). "Attention-like" processes in classical conditioning. In M. R. Jones (Ed.), *Miami symposium on the prediction of behavior, 1967: Aversive stimulation* (pp. 9–31). Coral Gables, FL: University of Miami Press.

Kaufman, M. A., & Bolles, R. C. (1981). A nonassociative aspect of overshadowing. *Bulletin of the Psychonomic Society, 18*, 318–320.

Kruschke, J. K. (1996). Base rates in category learning. *Journal of Experimental Psychology: Learning, Memory, and Cognition, 22*, 3–26.

Kruschke, J. K., & Blair, N. J. (2000). Blocking and backward blocking involve learned inattention. *Psychonomic Bulletin & Review, 7*, 636–645.

Larkin, M. J. W., Aitken, M. R. F., & Dickinson, A. (1998). Retrospective revaluation of causal judgments under positive and negative contingencies. *Journal of Experimental Psychology: Learning, Memory, and Cognition, 24*, 1331–1352.

Le Pelley, M. E. (2004). The role of associative history in models of associative learning: A selective review and a hybrid model. *Quarterly Journal of Experimental Psychology, 57*, 193–243.

Le Pelley, M. E., & McLaren, I. P. L. (2001). Retrospective revaluation in humans: Learning or memory? *Quarterly Journal of Experimental Psychology, 54B*, 311–352.

Le Pelley, M. E., & McLaren, I. P. L. (2003). Learned associability and associative change in human causal learning. *Quarterly Journal of Experimental Psychology, 56B*, 68–79.

Le Pelley, M. E., & McLaren, I. P. L. (2004). Associative history affects the associative change undergone by both presented and absent cues in human causal learning. *Journal of Experimental Psychology: Animal Behavior Processes, 30*, 67–73.

Le Pelley, M. E., & McLaren, I. P. L. (2005). The role of associative history in human causal learning. In A. J. Wills (Ed.), *New directions in human associative learning* (pp. 125–153). Mahwah, NJ: Lawrence Erlbaum.

Le Pelley, M. E., Oakeshott, S. M., & McLaren, I. P. L. (2005). Blocking and unblocking in human causal learning. *Journal of Experimental Psychology: Animal Behavior Processes, 31*, 56–70.

Lewandowsky, S., & Li, S.-C. (1995). Catastrophic interference in neural networks: Causes, solutions, and data. In F. N. Dempster & C. J. Brainerd (Eds.), *Interference and inhibition in cognition* (pp. 329–361). San Diego, CA: Academic Press.

Livesey, E. J., & Boakes, R. A. (2004). Outcome additivity, elemental processing and blocking in human causality judgements. *Quarterly Journal of Experimental Psychology, 57B*, 361–379.

López, F. J., Cobos, P. L., & Caño, A. (2005). Associative and causal reasoning accounts of causal induction: Symmetries and asymmetries in predictive and diagnostic inferences. *Memory & Cognition, 33*, 1388–1398.

López, F. J., Cobos, P. L., Caño, A., & Shanks, D. R. (1998). The rational analysis of human causal and probability judgment. In M. Oaksford & N. Chater (Eds.), *Rational models of cognition* (pp. 314–352). Oxford, UK: Oxford University Press.

López, F. J., Shanks, D. R., Almaraz, J., & Fernández, P. (1998). Effects of trial order on contingency judgments: A comparison of associative and probabilistic contrast accounts. *Journal of Experimental Psychology: Learning, Memory, and Cognition, 24*, 672–694.

Lovibond, P. F. (2003). Causal beliefs and conditioned responses: Retrospective revaluation induced by experience and by instruction. *Journal of Experimental Psychology: Learning, Memory, and Cognition, 29*, 97–106.

Lovibond, P. F., Been, S.-L., Mitchell, C. J., Bouton, M. E., & Frohardt, R. (2003). Forward and backward blocking of causal judgment is enhanced by additivity of effect magnitude. *Memory & Cognition, 31*, 133–142.

Mackintosh, N. J. (1975). A theory of attention: Variations in the associability of stimuli with reinforcement. *Psychological Review, 82*, 276–298.

Marr, D. (1976). Early processing of visual information. *Transactions of the Royal Society of London, 275B*, 483–519.

Matute, H., Arcediano, F., & Miller, R. R. (1996). Test question modulates cue competition between causes and between effects. *Journal of Experimental Psychology: Learning, Memory, and Cognition, 22*, 182–196.

McDonald, R. J., Murphy, R. A., Guarraci, F. A., Gortler, J. R., White, N. M., & Baker, A. G. (1997). Systematic comparison of the effects of hippocampal and fornix-fimbria lesions on acquisition of three configural discriminations. *Hippocampus, 7*, 371–388.

Melchers, K. G., Lachnit, H., & Shanks, D. R. (2004). Within-compound associations in retrospective revaluation and in direct learning: A challenge for comparator theory. *Quarterly Journal of Experimental Psychology, 57B*, 25–53.

Melchers, K. G., Lachnit, H., & Shanks, D. R. (in press). Stimulus coding in human associative learning: Flexible represntations of parts and wholes. *Behavioural Processes*.

Melchers, K. G., Lachnit, H., Üngör, M., & Shanks, D. R. (2005). Past experience can influence whether the whole is different from the sum of its parts. *Learning and Motivation, 36*, 20–41.

Miller, R. R., Barnet, R. C., & Grahame, N. J. (1995). Assessment of the Rescorla-Wagner model. *Psychological Bulletin, 117*, 363–386.

Miller, R. R., & Escobar, M. (2001). Contrasting acquisition-focused and performance-focused models of acquired behavior. *Current Directions in Psychological Science, 10*, 141–145.

Miller, R. R., & Matute, H. (1996). Biological significance in forward and backward blocking: Resolution of a discrepancy between animal conditioning and human causal judgment. *Journal of Experimental Psychology: General, 125*, 370–386.

Miller, R. R., & Matzel, L. D. (1988). The comparator hypothesis: A response rule for the expression of associations. In G. H. Bower (Ed.), *The psychology of learning and motivation* (Vol. 22, pp. 51–92). San Diego, CA: Academic Press.

Mitchell, C. J., Lovibond, P. F., & Condoleon, M. (2005). Evidence for deductive reasoning in blocking of causal judgments. *Learning and Motivation, 36*, 77–87.

O'Reilly, R. C., & Rudy, J. W. (2001). Conjunctive representations in learning and memory: Principles of cortical and hippocampal function. *Psychological Review, 108*, 311–345.

Pearce, J. M. (1994). Similarity and discrimination: A selective review and a connectionist model. *Psychological Review, 101*, 587–607.

Pearce, J. M. (2002). Evaluation and development of a connectionist theory of configural learning. *Animal Learning & Behavior, 30*, 73–95.

Pearce, J. M., & Bouton, M. E. (2001). Theories of associative learning in animals. *Annual Review of Psychology, 52*, 111–139.

Pearce, J. M., & Hall, G. (1980). A model for Pavlovian conditioning: Variations in the effectiveness of conditioned but not of unconditioned stimuli. *Psychological Review, 87*, 532–552.

Perales, J. C., & Shanks, D. R. (2003). Normative and descriptive accounts of the influence of power and contingency on causal judgment. *Quarterly Journal of Experimental Psychology, 56A*, 977–1007.

Price, P. C., & Yates, J. F. (1995). Associative and rule-based accounts of cue interaction in contingency judgment. *Journal of Experimental Psychology: Learning, Memory, and Cognition, 21*, 1639–1655.

Rescorla, R. A. (2000). Associative changes in excitors and inhibitors differ when they are conditioned in compound. *Journal of Experimental Psychology: Animal Behavior Processes, 26*, 428–438.

Rescorla, R. A., & Wagner, A. R. (1972). A theory of Pavlovian conditioning: Variations in the effectiveness of reinforcement and nonreinforcement. In A. H. Black & W. F. Prokasy (Eds.), *Classical conditioning II: Current theory and research* (pp. 64–99). New York: Appleton-Century-Crofts.

Rogers, T. T., & McClelland, J. L. (2004). *Semantic cognition: A parallel distributed processing approach*. Cambridge, MA: MIT Press.

Savastano, H. I., Arcediano, F., Stout, S. C., & Miller, R. R. (2003). Interaction between preexposure and overshadowing: Further analysis of the extended comparator hypothesis. *Quarterly Journal of Experimental Psychology, 56B*, 371–395.

Shanks, D. R. (1985). Forward and backward blocking in human contingency judgement. *Quarterly Journal of Experimental Psychology, 37B*, 1–21.

Shanks, D. R. (1987). Acquisition functions in causality judgment. *Learning and Motivation, 18*, 147–166.

Shanks, D. R. (1995). *The psychology of associative learning*. Cambridge, UK: Cambridge University Press.

Shanks, D. R. (2005). Connectionist models of basic human learning processes. In G. Houghton (Ed.), *Connectionist models in cognitive psychology* (pp. 45–82). Hove, UK: Psychology Press.

Shanks, D. R., Charles, D., Darby, R. J., & Azmi, A. (1998). Configural processes in human associative learning. *Journal of Experimental Psychology: Learning, Memory, and Cognition, 24*, 1353–1378.

Shanks, D. R., & Darby, R. J. (1998). Feature- and rule-based generalization in human associative learning. *Journal of Experimental Psychology: Animal Behavior Processes, 24*, 405–415.

Shanks, D. R., Holyoak, K. J., & Medin, D. L. (Eds.). (1996). *The psychology of learning and motivation: Causal learning* (Vol. 34). San Diego, CA: Academic Press.

Shanks, D. R., & López, F. J. (1996). Causal order does not affect cue selection in human associative learning. *Memory & Cognition, 24,* 511–522.

Shanks, D. R., López, F. J., Darby, R. J., & Dickinson, A. (1996). Distinguishing associative and probabilistic contrast theories of human contingency judgment. In D. R. Shanks, K. J. Holyoak, & D. L. Medin (Eds.), *The psychology of learning and motivation: Causal learning* (Vol. 34, pp. 265–311). San Diego, CA: Academic Press.

Shevill, I., & Hall, G. (2004). Retrospective revaluation effects in the conditioned suppression procedure. *Quarterly Journal of Experimental Psychology, 57B,* 331–347.

Sloman, S. A. (1996). The empirical case for two systems of reasoning. *Psychological Bulletin, 119,* 3–22.

Stout, S. C., & Miller, R. R. (2007). Sometimes-competing retrieval (SOCR): A formalization of the comparator hypothesis. *Psychological Review, 114,* 759–783.

Sun, R., Slusarz, P., & Terry, C. (2005). The interaction of the explicit and the implicit in skill learning: A dual-process approach. *Psychological Review, 112,* 159–192.

Sutherland, R. J., & Rudy, J. W. (1989). Configural association theory: The role of the hippocampal formation in learning, memory, and amnesia. *Psychobiology, 17,* 129–144.

Sutton, R. S., & Barto, A. G. (1981). Toward a modern theory of adaptive networks: Expectation and prediction. *Psychological Review, 88,* 135–170.

Tangen, J. M., & Allan, L. G. (2004). Cue interaction and judgments of causality: Contributions of causal and associative processes. *Memory & Cognition, 32,* 107–124.

van Hamme, L. J., & Wasserman, E. A. (1994). Cue competition in causality judgments: The role of nonpresentation of compound stimulus elements. *Learning and Motivation, 25,* 127–151.

Wagner, A. R. (1981). SOP: A model of automatic memory processing in animal behaviour. In N. E. Spear & R. R. Miller (Eds.), *Information processing in animals: Memory mechanisms* (pp. 5–47). Hillsdale, NJ: Lawrence Erlbaum.

Waldmann, M. R. (1996). Knowledge-based causal induction. In D. R. Shanks, K. J. Holyoak, & D. L. Medin (Eds.), *The psychology of learning and motivation: Causal learning*

(Vol. 34, pp. 47–88). San Diego, CA: Academic Press.

Waldmann, M. R. (2000). Competition among causes but not effects in predictive and diagnostic learning. *Journal of Experimental Psychology: Learning, Memory, and Cognition, 26,* 53–76.

Waldmann, M. R. (2001). Predictive versus diagnostic causal learning: Evidence from an overshadowing paradigm. *Psychonomic Bulletin & Review, 8,* 600–608.

Waldmann, M. R., & Hagmayer, Y. (2001). Estimating causal strength: The role of structural knowledge and processing effort. *Cognition, 82,* 27–58.

Waldmann, M. R., & Holyoak, K. J. (1992). Predictive and diagnostic learning within causal models: Asymmetries in cue competition. *Journal of Experimental Psychology: General, 121,* 222–236.

Waldmann, M. R., & Walker, J. M. (2005). Competence and performance in causal learning. *Learning & Behavior, 33,* 211–229.

Wasserman, E. A. (1990). Detecting response-outcome relations: Toward an understanding of the causal texture of the environment. In G. H. Bower (Ed.), *The psychology of learning and motivation* (Vol. 26, pp. 27–82). New York: Academic Press.

Wasserman, E. A., & Berglan, L. R. (1998). Backward blocking and recovery from overshadowing in human causal judgement: The role of within-compound associations. *Quarterly Journal of Experimental Psychology, 51B,* 121–138.

Wasserman, E. A., & Castro, L. (2005). Surprise and change: Variations in the strength of present and absent cues in causal learning. *Learning & Behavior, 33,* 131–146.

Wasserman, E. A., Elek, S. M., Chatlosh, D. L., & Baker, A. G. (1993). Rating causal relations: The role of probability in judgments of response-outcome contingency. *Journal of Experimental Psychology: Learning, Memory, and Cognition, 19,* 174–188.

Wasserman, E. A., & Miller, R. R. (1997). What's elementary about associative learning? *Annual Review of Psychology, 48,* 573–607.

Wickelgren, W. A. (1979). Chunking and consolidation: A theoretical synthesis of semantic networks, configuring in conditioning, S-R versus cognitive learning, normal forgetting, the amnesic syndrome, and the hippocampal arousal system. *Psychological Review, 86,* 44–60.

Williams, D. A. (1996). A comparative analysis of negative contingency learning in humans and nonhumans. In D. R. Shanks, K. J. Holyoak, & D. L. Medin (Eds.), *The psychology of learning and motivation: Causal learning* (Vol. 34, pp. 89–131). San Diego, CA: Academic Press.

Williams, D. A., Sagness, K. E., & McPhee, J. E. (1994). Configural and elemental strategies in predictive learning. *Journal of Experimental Psychology: Learning, Memory, and Cognition, 20,* 694–709.

Winman, A., Wennerholm, P., Juslin, P., & Shanks, D. R. (2005). Evidence for rule-based processes in the inverse base-rate effect. *Quarterly Journal of Experimental Psychology, 58A,* 789–815.

CHAPTER 23

Computational Modeling of Visual Information Processing

Pawan Sinha and Benjamin J. Balas

1. Introduction

Vision is one of the most actively researched subdomains of neuroscience. This is not surprising, given that the visual sense provides perhaps the most significant conduit for the acquisition of information around the world. Over 30% of the primate brain is devoted to visual analysis. The interpretation of visual images presents a host of interesting questions and excellent opportunities for the development of novel computational models.

Visual processing can be conceptualized as a series of inter-related stages. The early stages serve as sophisticated pre-processors of the visual image, highlighting some aspects of the input signal and suppressing others. The later stages operate on this filtered signal to perform tasks like recognizing the objects in the visual array. Our understanding of exactly how the primate brain accomplishes this processing is still relatively limited. However, the experimental data thus far have guided the development of computational models, which in turn have helped refine the experimental hypotheses.

Over the past several decades, numerous computational models have been proposed for various aspects of visual analysis. It is difficult to summarize the rich literature in computational modeling of vision in just one chapter. What is discussed in this chapter instead is a description of some fundamental issues related to computational modeling that transcend specific problems and presentation of a few specific proposals that span early and late visual processes and their interactions.

The enterprise of computational modeling of visual function received a significant boost with the far-reaching ideas of David Marr in the early 1980s (Marr, 1982). Although some of Marr's specific proposals are now not considered entirely accurate, his legacy is the formulation of the notion of levels of analysis. He suggested that any model of a particular aspect of visual processing can be considered to have three distinct levels:

1. Computational theory level: What is the information-processing problem the model is trying to solve?

2. Algorithmic level: What algorithm can, in principle, solve the problem?
3. Implementation level: How can the algorithm be implemented in neural hardware?

Some researchers have criticized this proposal as enforcing an unnatural separation of the levels of analysis (see Chapter 1 in this volume). The assessment of viability of an algorithm for a certain vision task cannot be entirely divorced from its eventual implementation constraints. For instance, an algorithm that uses the Radon transform (which computes the one-dimensional projections of a two-dimensional image across several orientations) to detect extended linear structures in images is less viable as a biological model than one that uses local interactions among a network of small edge detectors. However, notwithstanding such caveats, it is perhaps fair to say that this proposal has helped catalyze and systematize the effort of computational modeling over the past two decades. Conceptualizing vision as an information-processing task has allowed researchers to think more abstractly about the input-output mappings they are attempting to accomplish. It has helped them understand what information is needed to solve a problem theoretically and then guided experimentation to examine the neural mechanisms responsible for analyzing such information.

Regardless of what specific visual task a model is designed for, it typically has to contend with a few of the following ubiquitous challenges:

1. *The inputs are often highly impoverished.* Our eyes are notoriously prone to refractive and chromatic errors. Also, observing objects at a distance reduces the effective resolution of their images falling over the retina. This, combined with atmospheric haze, scotomas, blur induced by object or self-motion, and a host of other factors, ensures that the image the visual system has to work with is of rather poor quality. For instance, a small half-toned newspaper image of a car has very limited information about luminance gradients across the car's body. Yet, we have no trouble using our shape from shading processes to estimate the curvature of the hood and even the glossiness of the paint. For a model to mimic the human visual system, it needs to be able to handle such degraded images.

2. *The problems are severely underconstrained.* The process of projecting a three-dimensional world onto a two-dimensional imaging surface, along with the degradations mentioned previously, results in a many-to-one mapping between objects and images. Corresponding to any given two-dimensional (2-D) image, there are infinitely many three-dimensional (3-D) objects that are projectionally consistent with it. Inverting this mapping is, therefore, an underconstrained problem. In some circumstances, one can acquire multiple images to reduce this underconstrainedness, but often, there is no way to entirely avoid it. How the human visual system overcomes this problem has been one of the persistent open questions in the domain of computational vision. Much of the work has attempted to identify and formalize the biases needed to uniquely (or nearly so) invert the object-to-image mapping. For instance, given a single two-dimensional line drawing, one can try to limit the search for likely three-dimensional objects that gave rise to it by using biases toward symmetry.

3. *The "answer" needs to be computed rapidly.* The human visual system is designed to allow us to interact with a highly dynamic world. We can catch fast-moving balls and get out of the way of speeding cars. To aid survival, the visual system simply does not have the luxury of long compute times. Any plausible computational model of a visual process must necessarily respect this constraint. Algorithms requiring hundreds or thousands of iterations are effectively ruled out. Of course, given the speed of computational hardware today, executing a few thousand iterations in a fraction of a second is not a tall order. However, it is worth remembering that neurons, the computational

units of the nervous system, are rather slug-gish and are capped at about 200 Hz in terms of their maximal spike firing rates. For a downstream neuron to estimate their fir-ing rate, an integration time of a few mil-liseconds appears necessary. Each neuronal transmission, therefore, is a slow process and places strong constraints on the number of such serial steps the overall computation can have.

4. *Many aspects of vision are subject to cog-nitive influences.* The sensory signal only partly determines our eventual percept. Our prior knowledge, expectations, attention, and emotional states all contribute to this process. A computational model that did not take these "higher-level" influences into ac-count will likely not be a comprehensive or accurate account of the biological process. Even a task as simple as detecting contours in an image, which one might think of as an early vision problem, solvable by convolv-ing the image with Gabor filters, can be af-fected by prior knowledge of the kinds of objects expected to be seen in the input. For instance, in looking at a facial image, most observers can readily detect the contour sep-arating the jaw and chin from the neck. In reality, however, most facial images have lit-tle or no luminance gradient at that location. Somehow, our prior familiarity with faces allows us to enhance, or even "hallucinate," contours where we expect them to be. A big challenge for computational models is to in-corporate such cognitive influences in their operation.

This chapter illustrates some of these problems, and tentative computational re-sponses, in the specific domain of object recognition. This allows presentation of con-crete examples of models, rather than talk-ing in generalities. Object recognition, as a problem domain, is well suited to serve an illustrative function. It provides striking in-stances of the problems described earlier. A person's face, for instance, subtends less than a third of a degree of visual angle from a distance of a hundred feet. The effective resolution of the resulting image (given the discrete sampling of the photoreceptor mo-saic) is quite modest. However, we typically have no problem recognizing people at these distances. The many-to-one mapping men-tioned previously shows up in a particularly difficult form in the context of recognition. Not only is any single image consistent with an infinite number of real-world objects, a recognition system also needs to treat many different images, which correspond to dif-ferent appearances of an object, as denot-ing the same entity. The time constraints on recognition are also stringent. We need to, and often are able to, recognize objects and people at a glance. Recognition responses are evident in the brain less than 150 ms after stimulus presentation. Given the neuronal latencies described earlier, this leaves very little time for iterative loops in the compu-tation. Finally, our recognition performance is highly prone to high-level influences. Priming enhances recognition accuracy and speed. We are better able to tolerate image degradations in images of objects that we are more familiar with. Additionally, recog-nition serves as an important prerequisite for bringing to bear high-level influences on other visual tasks. For instance, influencing the shape-from-shading computation for the small half-toned image of the car mentioned earlier requires that we know that the object depicted is a car.

To contextualize the discussion, let us start by considering the overall framework of visual processing, as illustrated in Fig-ure 23.1. Very roughly, it can be partitioned into two stages – an "early" stage concerned with image representation in terms of a ba-sic vocabulary of filters and a "late" stage concerned with recognition. To span this processing framework, three computational models are described:

1. Models of early visual processing that suggest why neurons in the initial stages of the visual pathway have the particu-lar filter properties that they do.
2. Models that link early vision with recog-nition.
3. A model of how recognition might in-fluence early vision.

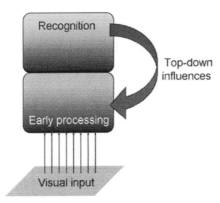

Figure 23.1. Visual processing can be approximated as a cascade of processing stages, ranging from generalized image filtering to object recognition. In this chapter, we consider computational models of these stages and also of feedback influences from later to early stages.

Although far from comprehensive, these proposals provide illustrations of how experimentation and modeling can aid each other.

2. Modeling Early Visual Processing

To characterize the relationship between early visual areas and downstream recognition processes, the discussion must begin with the current understanding of what is being computed in early vision and why. Put another way, what is the basic vocabulary of features used to encode images in cortex? Further, what visual tasks is this vocabulary is suited to?

The pioneering electrophysiological work of Hubel and Wiesel provided a first look at what features neurons in early visual areas are sensitive to (Hubel & Wiesel, 1959). The nature of these cells' preferred stimuli was very surprising at the time, as the tuning of these neurons is quite different from the properties of earlier visual areas. Unlike cells in the lateral geniculate nucleus (LGN), stationary spots of light are usually not enough to produce a strong response in a V1 cell. Instead, oriented bars (often with a preferred direction of movement) elicit strong responses. Cells can also be categorized as "simple" or "complex" depending on their willingness to generalize over contrast polarity and edge position. Figure 23.2a shows response curves from four V1 neurons. As is evident, the response is maximal for a specific orientation of the visual stimulus (a bar) and decays rapidly as the orientation is changed. Hubel and Wiesel (1962) proposed a simple linear model for constructing oriented receptive fields in V1 from the unoriented fields of the lateral geniculate nucleus (Figure 23.2b). More recent simultaneous recordings from the LGN and V1 have suggested that this model might indeed be correct to a large extent (Alonso, Usrey, & Reid, 2001; Kara et al., 2002; Usrey, Alonso, & Reid, 2000; Jones & Palmer, 1987).

For computational purposes, many researchers have summarized the physiological studies of early vision in felines and primates primarily in terms of edge extraction. Descriptive models of early visual receptive fields usually take the form of Gabor patches or wavelets, both of which provide a means of representing image structure in terms of local oriented edges at multiple scales.

But why should early vision choose this encoding scheme as opposed to any other? A compelling explanation that has been explored extensively is that the features computed by early visual areas permit optimal redundancy reduction. It has been argued that an important goal of any sensory system is to formulate a representation that takes advantage of latent structures in the input to obtain an efficient code for incoming stimuli (Atick, 1992; Attneave, 1954; Barlow, 1961). Natural scenes are highly structured, having a characteristic power spectrum of approximately $1/f$ (Field, 1987). It is thus reasonable to ask about the form of the features that compose an efficient code for vision.

Various methods of redundancy reduction have been applied to libraries of natural image patches in order to answer this question, including principal components analysis, independent components analysis, and "sparsification" of outputs (Bell & Sejnowski, 1997; Hancock, Baddeley, & Smith, 1992; Olshausen & Field, 1996;

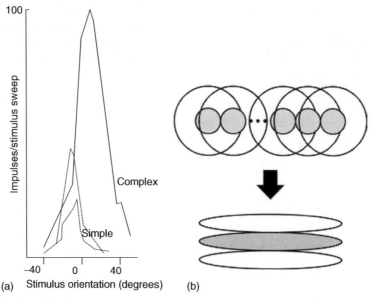

Figure 23.2. (a) Orientation tuning curves of V1 neurons (Adapted from Watkins & Berkley, 1974). (b) A simple model proposed by Hubel and Wiesel to account for orientation tuning in V1. Linearly aligned sets of unoriented receptive fields of the LGN neurons are posited as the substrate for the orientation-tuned receptive fields of V1 neurons. (Adapted from Hubel & Wiesel, 1962.)

Olshausen, & Field, 1997). These methods make different assumptions about the statistical realization of an efficient code, but generally agree that Gabor or wavelet-like features emerge as a robust solution to visual redundancy reduction. The approximate convergence between these computational results and the physiological findings described earlier have led to a wealth of studies attempting to forge a stronger link between visual cortex and the reduction of statistical redundancy. Color, stereo, and motion selectivity in early visual areas have all recently been modeled with some success using redundancy reduction techniques (Hoyer & Hyvaarinen, 2000; Olshausen, 2003), indicating that the link between computational theory and physiology is relatively robust.

There are, however, a great many aspects of V1 function that are likely not captured by the current methods of carrying out redundancy reduction. Although computational modelers are generally content to consider multiscale representations

of oriented luminance-defined edges as "biologically plausible," there remains much to be understood regarding early visual function. For example, the distribution of preferred frequencies usually present in computational solutions does not seem to capture the full spectrum of observed receptive fields in primate V1 (Ringach, 2002).

It is unclear why this should be so, but a prime reason for this discrepancy may be that current redundancy reduction techniques typically model neurons as purely linear systems, whereas it is known that real neurons exhibit strong nonlinear behavior. Assumptions such as this that grossly simplify the physiological properties of early visual areas make it possible that redundancy reduction as currently formulated only explains a small portion of visual function in primary visual cortex. (For an excellent review of this topic, see Olshausen & Field, 2005.) Real visual neurons with classical and "nonclassical" receptive fields and horizontal connections between neighboring cells may carry out computations far richer than the linear weighting of image pixels assumed by many.

Despite an ongoing debate over how well simple Gabor or wavelet models of V1 receptive fields accurately characterize visual processing, the modeling community has embraced such features as a useful first step in a wide range of computational tasks. For object and face recognition, representing images with a multiscale "pyramid" of oriented edge information (Freeman & Adelson, 1991) or information closely related to this has become a standard pre-processing step for many successful algorithms (Riesenhuber & Poggio, 1999, Wiskott et al., 1997). Although there may be more complex processing going on in visual cortex, oriented edges provide a versatile feature vocabulary that is supported to some extent by computational and biological principles. In the next section, a model of recognition based on the use of this feature vocabulary is discussed.

3. Modeling Recognition Based on the Outputs of Early Visual Stages

3.1. Overview

In Marr's (1982) original conceptualization of visual processing, recognition was situated at the very top of the hierarchy and operated on the outputs of "midlevel" modules. These included modules for estimating 3-D shape based on texture gradients, stereo, and shape from shading, among others. The matching was to be executed between the 3-D shape information extracted from the current input and that extracted from previous exposures. The use of 3-D information, in principle, imbued the model with an ability to recognize objects despite significant variations in the viewpoint; because 3-D shape estimation was unaffected by the direction of observation, the resulting recognition performance was expected to be viewpoint independent. However, several years of work revealed significant problems with this proposal.

Real-world images were found to be too noisy and degraded to permit accurate 3-D shape recovery. More fundamentally, even if the practical difficulties of 3-D shape estimation could be set aside, the model's recognition performance did not accurately mirror human performance. A growing body of results has shown that humans are not viewpoint independent in their recognition abilities. Performance is best from the previously experienced vantage points and falls off significantly as the viewpoint changes. The proposal by Marr did not reflect this aspect of human recognition. This shortcoming led to modifications of the original scheme.

A particularly influential proposal from Biederman (1987) alleviated the requirement of 3-D reconstruction. This idea, referred to as "recognition by components," (RBC) suggested that objects are represented as collections of simple volumetric primitives ("geons") and their qualitative spatial relationships. Most significantly, the geon decomposition could, in principle, be accomplished using only 2-D image cues. Biederman's ideas have had great impact on the field. Artifactual objects, such as cups and tablelamps, do indeed lend themselves to decomposition into geon-like parts, and human recognition performance is modulated by the observability of these parts, just as the RBC scheme would suggest. However, some researchers worry that geon decompositions are difficult to accomplish for many natural objects. Even for simpler objects, image imperfections make it difficult to reliably identify the constituent geons.

Another proposal that arose in response to the shortcomings of the viewpoint independent recognition scheme is that of image-based recognition. The basic idea is straightforward: Instead of constructing sophisticated intermediate representations, try to match the currently seen images against a database of previously seen ones. This idea underlies some of the most successful recognition models today. Two are discussed in the following paragraphs.

Wiskott et al. (1997) proposed a scheme based on "Gabor jets." In effect, multiple points in any given image were filtered using banks of Gabors of different scales (a stack of differently sized and oriented Gabor filters is referred to as a Gabor jet). The collected vector of responses served as the representation of an image. Image matching was thus reduced to a problem of comparing Gabor jet vectors. The elements of a vector could be differentially weighted depending on whether high or low spatial frequencies were to be given more significance. The Gabor-jet model of recognition yielded good performance on real-world recognition tasks, such as face recognition, and was also roughly consistent with known physiology.

More recently, Reisenhuber and Poggio (1999) proposed a hierarchical model of recognition that builds on the earlier suggestions by Hubel and Wiesel (1959) of increasing feature complexity along the visual pathway. The model is structured as a series of stages wherein each stage pools the outputs of the previous one using a max operator (thus picking out the strongest input, rather than averaging across them). The early stages of the model perform simple feature detection via oriented filtering, and later stages achieve sensitivity to complex patterns through a cascade of neural pooling steps. Recent simulations have shown that this biologically plausible model is able to perform well on complex image-sets (Serre et al., 2007).

It is perhaps not entirely obvious how a model, like the two mentioned previously, that relies largely on simple filtering and pooling can achieve reasonable recognition performance across images that are highly variable in appearance. For instance, a face illuminated from the left is very different at the pixel level from a face illuminated from the right. How can a visual system generalize across such illumination variations? Filtering by fine edge-detectors in V1 has proved not to be too helpful for solving this problem. Although such filtering does de-emphasize in the low-spatial frequencies caused by illumination, the fine edge-maps are still found to be highly variable, belying the hopes of invariance. A recognition system they are embedded in consequently would be highly brittle and unsuited to the variabilities of

the real world. Does this mean that early filtering is inadequate to support robust recognition?

To explore this question, an illustrative model of face detection can be used. Even though the performance of this model is superseded by others in the literature, it serves a useful expository purpose due to its simplicity. Interestingly, the model gains its generalization abilities by discarding detailed spatial and photometric information in favor of a more "qualitative" code. Further details about this model may be found in Sinha (2002) and Sadr et al. (2002).

3.2. A "Qualitative" Model of Recognition

The starting point of this model lies in re-examining the response properties of neurons in the early stages of the visual pathway. These response properties constrain the kinds of measurements that can plausibly be included in a representation scheme for recognition. The conventional view of the V1 neurons, as described in the preceding section, is that they encode detailed spatial and photometric information. It turns out, however, that in contrast to this dogma, many neurons have receptive fields that cover a significant extent of visual space. In this sense, they encode the coarse, low-resolution structure of the image (comparing large regions) rather than extracting fine edges from image details. Additionally, as shown in Figure 23.3, many neurons have rapidly saturating contrast response functions (Albrecht & Hamilton, 1989; Anzai et al., 1995; DeAngelis, Ohzawa, & Freeman, 1993a, 1993b). Their tendency to reach ceiling level responses at low contrast values render these neurons sensitive primarily to ordinal, rather than metric, relations (hence, they can justifiably be called qualitative in their responses).

The model described here uses an idealization of such units as the basic vocabulary of its representation scheme. In this scheme, objects are encoded as sets of qualitative (ordinal) relations across large image regions. This very simple idea seems well suited to handling the photometric appearance

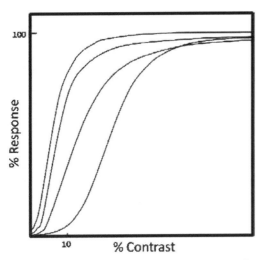

Figure 23.3. Response curves of four striate cells illustrating their rapid saturation as a function of edge contrast. Given their limited dynamic range, these neurons can be approximated as ordinal comparators of region luminance. (Adapted from Albrecht & Hamilton, 1989.)

variations that real-world objects exhibit. Let us examine the specific case of face detection as an illustration of how qualitative encoding can permit recognition despite significant appearance variations.

The three images in Figure 23.4 appear very different from each other. Variations in illumination, even without any viewpoint variations (as would be expected in the imaging setup of Figure 23.4) significantly alter the individual brightness of different parts of the face, such as the eyes, cheeks, and forehead. Therefore, absolute image brightness distributions are unlikely to be adequate for classifying all of these images as depicting the same underlying object. Even the contrast magnitudes across different parts of the face change greatly under different lighting conditions.

Although the absolute luminance and contrast magnitude information is highly variable across these images, some stable ordinal measurements can be identified. Consider Figure 23.5. It shows several pairs of average luminance values over localized patches for each of the three images included in Figure 23.4. Certain regularities are apparent. For instance, the average luminance of the left eye is always less than that of the forehead, regardless of the lighting conditions. The relative magnitudes of the two luminance values may change, but the sign of the inequality does not. In other words, the *ordinal* relationship between the average luminance of the left-eye-forehead pair is invariant under lighting changes. Figure 23.6 shows several other such pair-wise invariances. It seems, therefore that local ordinal relations may encode stable facial attributes across different illumination conditions. By putting all of these pair-wise

Figure 23.4. Three-dimensional objects imaged under varying illumination conditions can yield images that are very different at the pixel level, as shown here for the case of a human face.

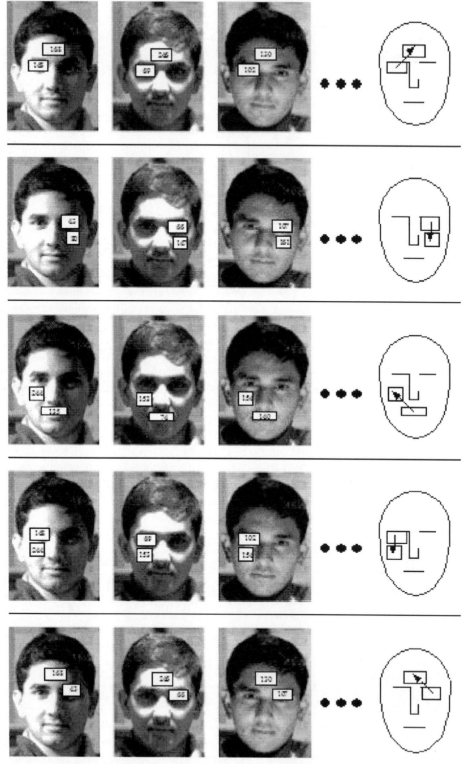

Figure 23.5. The absolute brightnesses and even their relative magnitudes change under different lighting conditions, but several pair-wise ordinal relationships are invariant.

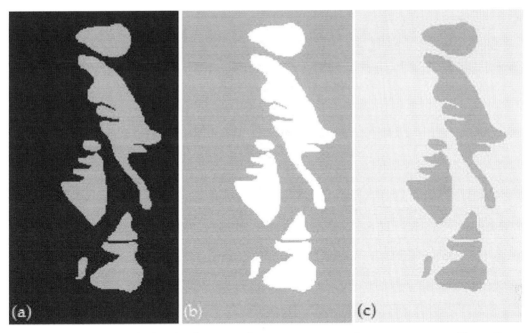

Figure 23.6. Preserving absolute brightnesses of image regions is neither necessary nor sufficient for recognition. The patches in (a) and (b) have very different brightnesses, yet they are perceived as depicting the same object. The patches in (a) and (c), however, are perceived very differently, even though they have identical absolute brightnesses. The direction of brightness contrast appears to have greater perceptual significance. (Mooney image courtesy of Patrick Cavanagh, Harvard University.)

invariances together, we obtain a larger composite invariant (Figure 23.7). This invariant is called a *ratio-template*, given that it is comprised of a set of binarized ratios of image luminance. It is worth noting that dispensing with precise measurements of image luminance not only leads to immunity to illumination variations, but also renders the ratio-template robust in the face of sensor noise. It also reconciles the design of the invariant with known perceptual limitations – the human visual system is far better at making relative brightness judgments than absolute ones (Figure 23.6).

The ratio-template is not a strict invariant in that special cases in which it breaks exist. One such situation arises when the face is strongly illuminated from below. However, for almost all "normal" lighting conditions (light sources at or above the level of the head), the ratio-template serves as a robust invariant. An additional advantage to using ordinal relations is their natural robustness to sensor noise due to the fact that they use coarse image structure, whereas sensor

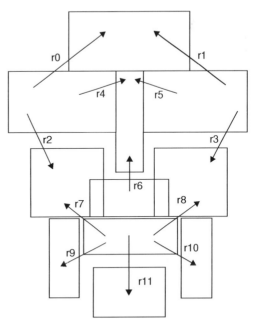

Figure 23.7. A ratio-template is a conjugation of several pair-wise invariants. This is a representation of the invariant ordinal structure of luminance on a human face under widely varying illumination conditions.

noise typically affects high spatial frequencies. Thus, it seems that local ordinal representations may be well suited for devising compact representations, robust against large photometric variations, for at least some classes of objects.

How a ratio-template may be used for face detection is discussed in the following section.

3.2.1. THE MATCH METRIC

Having decided on the structure of the ratio-template (which, in essence, is one model for a face under different illumination setups), let us now consider the problem of matching it against a given image fragment to determine whether or not that part of the image contains a face. The first step involves averaging the image intensities over the regions laid down in the ratio-template's design and then determining the prescribed pair-wise ratios. The next step is to determine whether the ratios measured in the image match the corresponding ones in the ratio-template. An intuitive way to think of this problem is to view it as an instance of the general graph matching problem. The patches over which the image intensities are averaged constitute the nodes of the graph and the inter-patch ratios constitute the edges. A directed edge exists between two nodes if the ratio-template has been designed to include the brightness ratio between the corresponding image patches. The direction of the edge is such that it points from the node corresponding to the brighter region to the node corresponding to the darker one. Each corresponding pair of edges in the two graphs is examined to determine whether the two edges have the same direction. If they do, a predetermined positive contribution is made to the overall match metric and a negative one otherwise. The magnitude of the contribution is proportional to the "significance" of the ratio. A ratio's significance, in turn, is dependent on its robustness. For instance, the eye-forehead ratio may be considered more significant than the nose-tip-cheek ratio because the latter is more susceptible to being affected by such factors as facial hair and is therefore less robust. The contributions to be associated with different ratios can be learned automatically from training examples. After all corresponding pairs of edges have been examined, the magnitude of the overall match metric can be used under a simple threshold-based scheme to declare whether or not the given image fragment contains a face. Alternatively, the vector indicating which graph edges match can be the input to a statistical classifier.

3.2.2. FIRST-ORDER ANALYSIS

It may seem that by discarding the brightness ratio magnitude information, we run the risk of rendering the ratio-template too permissive in terms of the patterns that it will accept as faces; several false positives would be expected to result. In this section, we present a simple analysis showing that the probability of false positives is actually quite small. We proceed by computing how likely it is for an *arbitrary* distribution of image brightnesses to match a ratio-template. In the following treatment, the graph representation of the spatial distribution of brightnesses in the image and the template is used.

Suppose that the ratio-template is represented as a graph with n nodes and e directed edges. Further suppose that if all the edges in this graph were to be replaced by undirected edges, it would have c simple cycles. We need to compute the cardinality of the set of all valid graphs defined on n nodes with e edges connecting the same pairs of nodes as in the template graph. A graph is "valid" if it represents a physically possible spatial distribution of intensities. A directed graph with a cycle, for instance, is invalid because it violates the principle of transitivity of intensities. Each of the e edges connecting two nodes (say, A and B) can take on one of three directions:

1. if A has higher intensity value than B, the edge is directed from A to B; or
2. if B has higher intensity value than A, the edge is directed from B to A; or
3. if A and B have the same intensity values, the edge is undirected.

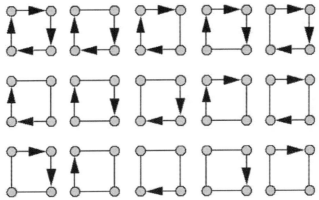

Figure 23.8. A cycle set of m edges yields $2(2^m - 1)$ invalid graphs. A cycle set of four edges, for instance, yields thirty invalid graphs, fifteen of which are shown in the figure (the other fifteen can be obtained by reversing the arrow directions). Each of these graphs leads to impossible relationships between intensity values (say, a and b) of the form $a > b$ & $b > a$ or $a > b$ & $a = b$.

The total number of graphs on n nodes and e edges, therefore, is 3^e. This number, however, includes several invalid graphs. A set of m edges that constitute a simple cycle when undirected, introduce $2(2^m - 1)$ invalid graphs, as illustrated in Figure 23.8. For c such sets, the total number of invalid graphs are

$$\sum_i = 1 \quad \text{to } c \; 2(2^{m_i} - 1)$$

where m_i is the number of edges in the "cycle set" i. Therefore, the total number of valid graphs on n nodes, e edges, and c cycles is

$$3^e - \sum_i = 1 \quad \text{to } c \; 2(2^{m_i} - 1).$$

Of all these graphs, only one is acceptable as representing a human face. For most practical ratio-template parameters, the total number of valid graphs is quite large, and the likelihood of an arbitrary distribution of image brightnesses accidentally being the same as that for a face is very small. For instance, for $e = 10$ and two cycle sets of sizes six and three, the number of valid graphs is nearly 59,000. If all the corresponding intensity distributions are equally likely,

the probability of a false positive is only $1.69 * 10^{-5}$.

3.2.3. IMPLEMENTATION ISSUES
As stated in the introductory section, for a model of visual processing to be consistent with human performance, the computation it embodies has to be sufficiently straightforward to be executed rapidly. The ratio-template approach meets this criterion well. It requires the computation of average intensities over image regions of different sizes. An efficient implementation can be obtained by adopting a multiresolution framework. In such a framework, the input image is repeatedly filtered and subsampled to create different levels of the image pyramid. The process of determining the average value for any image patch is reduced to picking out the appropriate pixel value from the bank of pre-computed pyramid levels, leading to a tremendous saving in computation. The appropriate scale of operation for a given ratio-template depends on the chosen spatial parameters, such as the patch sizes and the distances between them. By varying these parameters systematically, the face detection operation can be performed at multiple scales. Such a parameter variation is easily accomplished in a

Figure 23.9. Testing the face-detection scheme on real images. The program places a small white square at the center of, or a rectangle around, each face it detects. The results demonstrate the scheme's robustness in detecting varying identity, facial hair, skin tone, eyeglasses, and scale.

multiresolution implementation. By tapping different sets of the levels constituting the image pyramid, the presence of faces of different sizes can be determined. Therefore, the total amount of computational overhead involved in handling multiple scales is not excessive. The use of different pyramid levels is akin to using different sized Gabor filters in the multiresolution model of V1 described earlier.

3.2.4. TESTS

Figure 23.9 shows some of the results obtained on real images by using a ratio-template for face detection. Whenever it detects a face, the program pinpoints the location of the center of the head with a little white patch or a rectangle. The results are encouraging, with a correct detection rate of about 80% and very few false positives. The "errors" can likely be reduced even further by appropriately setting the threshold of acceptance. The results demonstrate the efficacy of the ratio-template as a face detector capable of handling changes in illumination, face identity, scale, facial expressions, skin tone, and degradations in image resolution.

The use of a qualitative face signature, a ratio-template, as a candidate scheme for detecting faces under significant illumination variations has been described. One can think of this specific scheme as an instance of a more general object recognition strategy that uses qualitative object signatures. Such a strategy would be attractive for the significant invariance to imaging conditions that it can potentially confer. However, it also has a potential drawback. Intuitively, it seems that the "coarseness" of the measurements it uses would limit the usefulness of qualitative signatures at tasks requiring fine discriminations. How might one obtain *precise* model indexing using qualitative invariants that are, by definition, comprised of *imprecise* measurements? Depicting this problem schematically, Figure 23.10a shows a collection of object models positioned in a space defined by three attribute axes. To precisely index into this model set, one of two approaches can be adopted: either be absolutely right in measuring at least one attribute value (Figure 23.10b), or be "approximately right" in measuring *all three* attributes (Figure 23.10e). Being

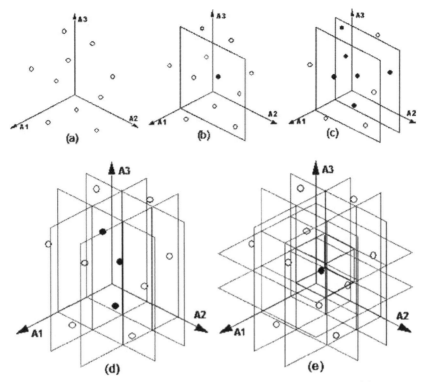

Figure 23.10. (a) A schematic depiction of a collection of object models positioned in a space defined by three attribute axes. To precisely index into this model set, one of two approaches can be adapted: either be absolutely right in measuring at least one attribute value (b), or be "approximately right" in measuring all three attributes (e). Being approximately right in just one or two attributes is not expected to yield unique indexing (c) and (d).

approximately right in just one or two attributes is not expected to yield unique indexing (Figures 23.10c and 23.10d).

The qualitative invariant approach constructs unique signatures for objects using several approximate measurements. The ratio-template is a case in point. It achieves its fine discriminability between face and nonface images by compositing several very imprecise binary comparisons of image brightnesses. In several real-world situations, there might in fact be no alternative to using approximate measurements. This could be either because precise invariants just might not exist or because of noise in the measurement process itself. The only recourse in these situations would be to exploit several attribute dimensions and be "approximately good" in measuring all of them. This is what qualitative invariants are designed to do. The "recognition by qualitative invariants" approach is eminently suited to a complex visual world such as ours. Most objects vary along several attribute dimensions, such as shape, color, texture, and motion, to name a few. The qualitative invariant approach can exploit this complexity by constructing unique object signatures from approximate measurements along all of these dimensions. Evidence for the generality of this approach is provided by the success of similar schemes at recognizing a diversity of objects and scenes, including natural landscapes, people, and cars (Lipson, Grimson, & Sinha, 1997; Oren et al., 1997).

A related observation is that the ratio-template representation is an image-based "holistic" encoding of object structure. Because each ordinal relation by itself is too coarse to provide a good discriminant function to distinguish between members and nonmembers of an object-class, many of the relations need to be considered together (implicitly processing object structure holistically) to obtain the desired performance. At least in the context of face detection, this holistic strategy appears to be supported by our recent studies of concept acquisition by children learning to see after treatment for congenital blindness (Bouvrie & Sinha, in press).

To summarize, the qualitative scheme for recognition does not require extensive pre-processing of the input image. It directly makes use of the outputs of "early" visual features and dispenses with the need for computations, such as 3-D shape recovery. This is significant because of the highly error-prone nature of these computations, as mentioned earlier. However, the difficulty in extracting these attributes is in contrast to our subjective experience. Given an image, we can typically generate a clean line-drawing (in essence, an edge-map) for it or estimate what the 3-D structure of the constituent objects is likely to be. How can we reconcile the poor performance of purely low-level visual mechanisms with the high-quality of our eventual percepts?

The idea explored next provides one solution. Simply stated, it proposes using the recognition of an object to facilitate the processing of its visual attributes, such as edge structure and 3-D shape. In the next section, whether recognition-dependent top-down influences on early vision can be modeled is addressed. This effectively brings the exposition of the modeling of visual processing full circle.

4. Modeling the Influence of Recognition on Early Vision

4.1. *Overview*

Before discussing a particular computational model for incorporating recognition-based influences in early perception, let us consider in conceptual terms what such a model has to do. The model's overall task is to esti-mate perceptual attributes of an object in an image based on previously acquired knowledge about that object or, more generally, its class. This task can be subdivided into four parts:

1. The model has to recognize objects in images.
2. The model has to access previously learned knowledge (such as 3-D shape or location of depth discontinuities) associated with the recognized object. This requirement involves a method for representing object/class-specific knowledge.
3. If the model's "knowledge base" does not have information corresponding to the specific object in the image, it (the model) has to be able to synthesize such information on the basis of class-specific knowledge.
4. Having generated perceptual attributes corresponding to the object in a top-down fashion, the model has to combine it with information about the same attributes estimated by the bottom-up processes.

It is evident that this list includes some very challenging tasks. For instance, we currently do not possess a general-purpose strategy for object recognition, nor do we know how top-down estimates are combined with bottom-up data under different circumstances. Clearly, a comprehensive model for all of these tasks is at present beyond our reach. However, proposals for restricted problem domains may be feasible. Indeed, several models for incorporating top-down influences in perception have been developed recently (Borenstein & Ullman, 2002; Cavanagh, 1991; Itti, 2006; Jones et al., 1997; Mumford, 1992; Ullman, 1995; Warren & Rayner, 2004). As in the previous section, one simple model to illustrate the general ideas is provided. The Jones et al. (1997) model has a simple architecture and is the one that will be presented here. It builds on proposals for recognition described in the previous section and focuses on items 2 and 3 from the previous list.

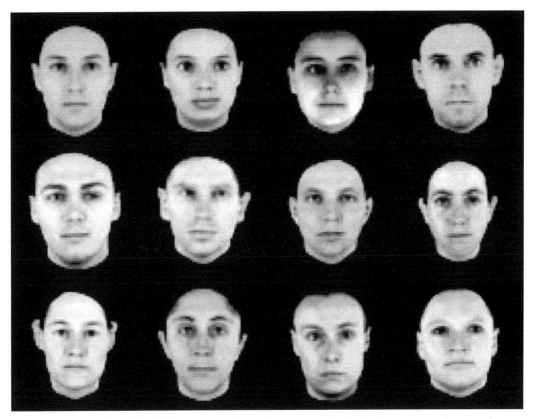

Figure 23.11. Twelve of the 100 prototype faces that were set in pixelwise correspondence and then used for a flexible model of human faces. (Adapted from Jones et al., 1997.)

4.2. Jones et al.'s Model for Incorporating Learned High-Level Influences in Early Perception

Jones et al.'s (1997) computational strategy for incorporating high-level influences in perception uses the concept of "flexible models" introduced by Vetter, Jones, and Poggio (Jones & Poggio, 1995; Poggio & Vetter, 1992). A flexible model is the affine closure of the linear space spanned by the shape and the texture vectors associated with a set of prototypical images (Figure 23.11). Pixelwise correspondences between a reference image and the other prototype images are obtained using an optical flow algorithm. Once the correspondences are computed, an image is represented as a "shape vector" and a "texture vector." The shape vector specifies how the 2-D shape of the example differs from a reference image and corresponds to the flow field between the two images. Analogously, the texture vector specifies how the texture differs from the reference texture. The term "texture" is used to mean simply the pixel intensities (gray level or color values) of the image. The flexible model for an object class is then a linear combination of the example shape and texture vectors. The matching of the model to a novel image consists of optimizing the linear coefficients of the shape and texture components.

Once estimated, the parameters of the flexible model can be used for effectively learning a simple visual task, like 3-D shape recovery, in the following way. Assume that a good 3-D shape estimate is available for each of the prototypical gray-level images (obtained initially in a bottom-up fashion perhaps via haptic inputs or binocular stereo). Then, given the image of a novel face, the approach is to estimate the parameters of the best-fitting gray-level flexible

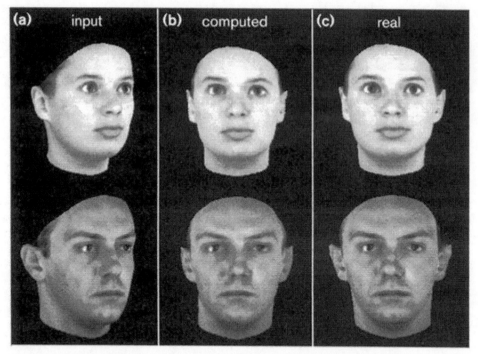

Figure 23.12. An illustration of how the top-down strategy can be used to generate virtual views of 3-D objects – here, two human heads: (a) input images, (b) computed virtual frontal views, and (c) the real frontal views.

model and to plug the same parameter values in a second flexible model built from the protoypical 3-D shape estimates. This approach can be regarded as learning from a set of examples of the mapping between a gray-level face image and its 3-D shape.

To demonstrate their ideas, Jones et al. (1997) implemented a slightly different version of the shape recovery task. Instead of explicit shape estimation (depth recovery for each point on the object), the authors focused on the task of implicit shape recovery in the form of novel view-estimation. The view-estimation problem is an implicit shape recovery task because even though it is tied to the 3-D shape of an object, it does not require an explicit computation of the 3-D structure. This problem arises in recognition tasks in which an object, for which only one example image is available, has to be recognized from a novel view. Jones et al., and Vetter and Poggio (1996) before them considered this problem for linear object classes. An object belongs to a linear class if its 3-D structure can be exactly described as a linear combination of the 3-D structure of a small number of prototypes. A new "virtual" view of an object that belongs to a linear class can be generated exactly from a single example view, represented as a 2-D shape vector, provided appropriate prototypical views of other objects in the same class are available (under orthographic projection). In this way, new views of a specific face with a different pose can be estimated and synthesized from a single view (the procedure is exact for linear classes; empirically, faces seem to be close to a linear class so that the procedure previously described provides a good approximation for pose and expression). Again, this procedure can be formulated in terms of the learning metaphor in which a learning box is trained with input-output pairs of prototypical views representing each prototype in the initial and in the desired pose. Then, for a new input image, the system synthesizes a virtual view in the desired pose (Figure 23.12).

The model is not limited to the task of implicit 3-D shape recovery. Explicit estimation of 3-D structure from a single image would proceed in a very similar way if the image and the 3-D structure of a sufficient number of prototypical objects of the same class are available. In Jones et al.'s (1997) learning box metaphor, the system, trained with pairs of prototype images as inputs (represented as 2-D shape vectors) and their 3-D shape as output, would effectively compute shape for novel images of the same class.

In discussing the generality of their model, Jones et al. (1997) suggested that a similar approach may be extended to other supposedly early perceptual tasks, such as edge-detection, color constancy, and motion analysis. In these cases, the desired information about edge-locations, color, or motion will need to be provided in a learning-from-examples scheme based on the use of a class-specific flexible model. To substantiate their claim of generality, Jones et al. considered the problem of edge-detection at length. Following is a brief summary of their approach and results on this task.

Jones et al. (1997) started with the premise that an edge-map corresponding to a gray-level image should ideally capture all the "relevant" edges of the object in a way similar to an artist's line-drawing. As many years of work on edge-detection have shown (for a review, see Haralick, 1980; Marr & Hildreth, 1980), the problem is difficult, in part because physical edges – meant as discontinuity in 3-D structure and albedo that convey information about the object's shape and identity – do not always generate intensity edges in the image. Conversely, intensity edges are often due to shading, therefore depending on illumination, and do not reflect invariant properties of the object. Several years ago, the Turing Institute circulated a photograph of a face and asked fellow scientists to mark "edges" in the image. Some of the edges that were found by the subjects of these informal experiments did not correspond to any change in intensity in the picture; they corresponded to locations where the subjects knew that the 3-D shape

had a discontinuity, for instance, the chin boundary. The traditional approach to edge-detection – to use a general purpose edge-detector, such as a directional derivative followed by a nonlinear operation – is bound to fail in the task of producing a good line drawing, even if coupled with algorithms that attempt to fill edge gaps, using general principles such as good continuation, and collinearity. A quite different approach, and the one adopted by Jones et al., is to exploit specific knowledge about faces in order to compute the line-drawing. This approach runs contrary to the traditional wisdom in computer vision, because it almost assumes that object recognition is used for edge-detection – almost a complete subversion of the usual paradigm. A possible implementation of this approach is based on a learning metaphor. Consider a set of prototypical (gray-level) face images and the corresponding line drawings, drawn by an artist. The task is to learn from these examples the mapping that associates to a gray-level image of a face its "ideal" line drawing. Computationally, this task is analogous to the problem of view-prediction that was described earlier.

Jones et al. (1997) implemented an even simpler version of the scheme. They assumed that the ideal line-drawing corresponding to the average prototype is available from an artist, as shown in Figure 23.13. The matching of the flexible model obtained from the prototypes (some of which are shown in Figure 23.13) to a novel gray-level image provided a shape vector that was a linear combination of the prototypes and that effectively prescribed how to warp the average shape of the gray-level prototype in order to match the shape of the novel gray-level image. Because the line-drawings were supported on a subset of the pixels of the corresponding gray-level images, the line drawings associated with novel images could be straightforwardly obtained by warping the line drawing associated with the reference prototype by using the estimated shape vector. Figure 23.14 shows a few examples of novel images (not contained in the set of Jones et al.'s prototypical examples set)

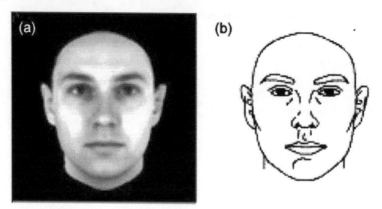

Figure 23.13. The reference face (a) and its corresponding line-drawing created by an artist (b).

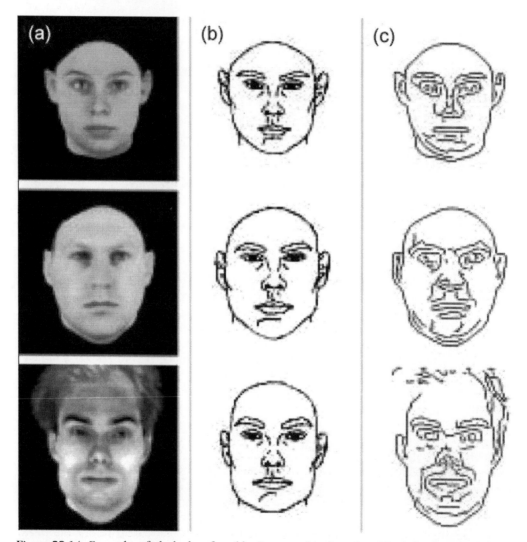

Figure 23.14. Examples of ideal edges found by Jones et al.'s algorithm. The left column (a) shows the input novel images. The middle column (b) shows the line-drawings estimated automatically by the algorithm, which matches the flexible models to the novel images and then appropriately modifies the ideal edges of the reference image. For comparison, the right column (c) shows the edges found by a bottom-up edge-detector (Canny, 1986). Note that the ideal edges emphasize the perceptually significant features of the face much better than the Canny edges.

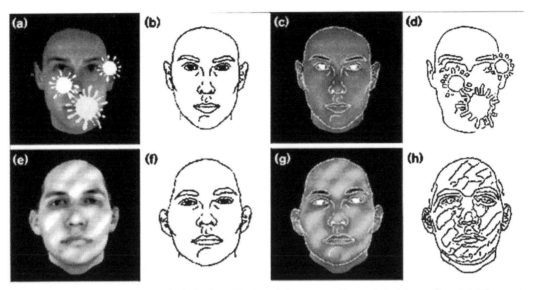

Figure 23.15. (a–d) Example of ideal edges (b) found for a partially occluded input face (a). The image (c) shows these edges overlaid on the unoccluded input face; (d) shows the Canny edge map for comparison. (e–h) An example of an image with nonintrinsic edges, such as those due to shadows (e). Jones et al.'s method for finding ideal edges effectively ignores the spurious edges (f). The accuracy of these edges can be assessed from the image in (g) showing the edges overlaid on the image; (h) highlights the susceptibility of bottom-up edge-extraction approaches to spurious image artifacts.

and the line-drawing estimated from each of them by Jones et al.'s "ideal edge detector." To contrast this approach to a low-level gradient-based approach, Figure 23.14 also shows the edges found for each face image by a Canny (1986) edge-detector. Figure 23.15 shows the ideal edge estimated for a partially occluded input image as well as for one with extraneous edges. As is evident from the examples, Jones et al.'s algorithm can detect and complete edges that do not correspond to any intensity gradients in the image. The power of the algorithm derives from the high-level knowledge about faces, learned from the set of prototypical images.

In summary, the scheme proposed by Jones et al. (1997) is an example of a class of algorithms that can be used to learn visual tasks in a top-down manner, specific to object classes. From the point of view of a neuroscientist, these demonstrations are plausibility proofs that a simple learning process can successfully incorporate object-specific knowledge and thereby learn to perform seemingly "low-level" visual tasks in a top-

down manner. Visual perception in humans may rely on similar processes to a greater extent than commonly assumed.

The encouraging performance of this model supports the conjecture that, at least in some cases, our visual system may solve low-level vision problems by exploiting prior information specific to the task and to the type of visual input. Furthermore, the visual system may learn algorithms specific to a class of objects by associating in each "prototypical" example an ideal output to the input view. The ideal outputs may be available through other sensory modalities, sequences of images in time or even explicit instruction. The notion of what constitutes an ideal output corresponding to a certain class of inputs may change and evolve over time as the learning process encounters new examples. This second part of the conjecture predicts that human subjects should be able to learn to associate arbitrary outputs to input images and to generalize from these learned associations. Recent psychophysical evidence strongly supports this prediction (Sinha & Poggio, 1996). It does not necessarily follow from Jones et al.'s (1997) work that learning follows the linear combination algorithm that they used in their plausibility demonstration. Further experimental work is required to determine which learning schemes are actually used by the visual system.

5. Conclusion

In this chapter, some of the challenges inherent in the computational modeling of vision were reviewed. The primary ones include poor input quality, severe underconstrainedness of the problems, the necessity of rapid computation of results, and the need for incorporating high-level or cognitive influences in the computations. These challenges via specific models that together span the range of visual processing have been illustrated, from early image filtering to recognition and then back again, in the form of recognition-based top-down influences. The model for face detection via ordinal relationships exemplifies how impairments in image quality can be handled via the use of multiple measurements that together constitute a robust representation of the object. This is likely to turn out to be a general operating principle in the domain of computational vision. It is unlikely, in most circumstances, that a model will be able to rely on just a unitary measurement; noise and poor image quality tend to rule out that strategy. What seems more workable is the use of multiple coarse measurements that in concert provide precise performance. A similar idea underlies the increasingly popular approach of boosting (for reviews, see Meir & Rätsch, 2003; Shapire, 2003), wherein good classification performance is obtained via a combination of multiple weak classifiers.

The Jones et al. (1997) model is a simple demonstration of the gains in performance that can be obtained by incorporating prior knowledge into seemingly low-level vision tasks. For a long time, the domain of computational vision struggled with developing purely data-driven models of various tasks, such as segmentation, stereocorrespondence, and shape from shading.

Increasingly, experimental results are suggesting that to achieve the kind of robustness that the human visual system exhibits on these tasks, guidance from prior experience might hold an important key. A trend that we can expect to become more popular in the coming years is the development of models that do not partition vision into early and late stages, but rather strive for a seamless integration between them.

Through the illustrative examples of this chapter, some of the big questions that computational neuroscientists are probing and some representative approaches they are taking in their modeling efforts have been presented. It is hoped that these examples highlight the strong synergy that exists between empirical and theoretical approaches to studying brain function.

References

Albrecht, D. G., & Hamilton, D. B. (1989). Striate cortex of monkey and cat: Contrast response function. *Journal of Neurophysiology*, 48, 217–237.

Alonso, J. M., Usrey, W. M., & Reid, R. C. (2001). Rules of connectivity between geniculate cells and simple cells in cat primary visual cortex. *Journal of Neuroscience 21*, 4002–4015.

Anzai, A., Bearse, M. A., Freeman, R. D., & Cai, D. (1995). Contrast coding by cells in the cat's striate cortex: Monocular versus binocular detection. *Visual Neuroscience*, 12, 77–93.

Atick, J. J. (1992). Could information theory provide an ecological theory of sensory processing? *Network*, 3, 213–251.

Attneave, F. (1954). Some informational aspects of visual perception. *Psychological Review*, 61, 183–193.

Barlow, H. B. (1961). Possible principles underlying the transformation of sensory messages. In W. Rosenblith (Ed.), *Sensory communication* (pp. 217–234). Cambridge, MA: MIT Press.

Bell, A. J., & Sejnowski, T. J. (1997). The "independent components" of natural scenes are edge filters. *Vision Research*, 37(23), 3327–3338.

Biederman, I. (1987). Recognition-by-components: A theory of human image understanding. *Psychological Review*, 94, 115–147.

Borenstein, E., & Ullman, S. (2002, May). *Class-specific, top-down segmentation*. Paper presented at the European Conference on Computer Vision. Copenhagen, Denmark.

Bouvrie, J. V., & Sinha, P. (in press). Object concept learning: Observations in congenitally blind children and a computational model. *Neurocomputing*.

Canny, J. F. (1986). A computational approach to edge-detection. *IEEE Trans Patt Anal Mach Vis, 8*, 679–698.

Cavanagh P. (1991). What's up in top-down processing? In A. Gorez (Ed.), *Representations of vision* (pp. 295–305). Cambridge, UK: Cambridge University Press.

DeAngelis, G. C., Ohzawa, I., & Freeman, R. D. (1993a). Spatiotemporal organization of simple-cell receptive fields in the cat's striate cortex. I. General characteristics and postnatal development. *Journal of Neurophysiology, 69*, 1091–1117.

DeAngelis, G. C., Ohzawa, I., & Freeman, R. D. (1993b). Spatiotemporal organization of simple-cell receptive fields in the cat's striate cortex. II. Linearity of temporal and spatial summation, *Journal of Neurophysiology, 69*, 1118–1135.

Field, D. J. (1987). Relations between the statistics of natural images and the response properties of cortical cells. *Journal of the Optical Society of America A, 4*, 2379–2394.

Freeman, W. T., & Adelson, E. H. (1991). The design and use of steerable filters. *IEEE Trans. On Pattern Analysis and Machine Intelligence, 13*, 891–906.

Hancock, P. J. B., Baddeley, R. J., & Smith, L. S. (1992). The principal components of natural images. *Network: Computation in Neural Systems, 3*, 61–70.

Haralick, R. M. (1980). Edge and region analysis for digital image data. *Comp Graph Image Proc, 12*, 60–73.

Hoyer, P. O., & Hyvaarinen, A. (2000). Independent component analysis applied to feature extraction from colour and stereo images. *Network: Computation in Neural Systems, 11*, 191–210.

Hubel, D. H., & Wiesel, T. N. (1959). Receptive fields of single neurones in the cat's striate cortex. *Journal of Physiology, 148*, 574–591.

Hubel, D., & Wiesel, T. (1962). Receptive fields, binocular interaction and functional architecture in the cat's visual cortex. *Journal of Physiology of London, 160*, 106–154.

Itti, L. (2006 month August). Bottom-up and top-down influences on visual attention during understanding of dynamic visual scenes. Paper presented at the Gordon Research Conference on Sensory Coding and the Natural Environment, Big Sky, Montana.

Jones, J. P., & Palmer, L. A. (1987). The two-dimensional spatial structure of simple receptive fields in cat striate cortex *J. Neurophysiol, 58*, 1187–1211.

Jones, M., & Poggio, T. (1995). Model-based matching by linear combinations of prototypes. In E. Grimson (Ed.), *Proceedings of the Fifth International Conference on Computer Vision* (pp. 531–536). Cambridge, MA: IEEE Computer Society Press.

Jones, M., Sinha, P., Vetter, T., & Poggio, T. (1997). Top-down learning of low-level vision tasks. *Current Biology, 7*, 991–994.

Kara, P., Pezaris, J. S., Yurgenson, S., & Reid, R. C. (2002). The spatial receptive field of thalamic inputs to single cortical simple cells revealed by the interaction of visual and electrical stimulation. *Proc. Natl. Acad. Sci., 99*, 16261–16266.

Lipson, P., Grimson, E., & Sinha, P. (1997). Configuration based scene classification and image-indexing. *Proceedings of the IEEE Computer Society Conference on Computer Vision and Pattern Recognition*, San Juan, Puerto Rico (pp. 1007–1012). Washington, DC: IEEE Computer Society.

Marr, D., & Hildreth, E. (1980). Theory of edge-detection. *Proceedings of the Royal Society of London [Biological], 207*, 187–217.

Marr, D. (1982). *Vision: A computational investigation into the human representation and processing of visual information*. New York: W. H. Freeman and Company.

Meir, R., & Rätsch, G. (2003). An introduction to boosting and leveraging. In S. Mendelson, A. J. Smolz (Eds.), *Advanced lectures on machine learning* (LNAI2600) (pp. 118–183). New York: Springer-Verlag.

Mumford, D. (1992). On the computational architecture of the neocortex. II. The role of cortico-cortical loops. *Biological Cybernetics, 66*, 241–251.

Olshausen, B. A. (2003). Learning sparse, overcomplete representations of time-varying natural images. In *IEEE International Conference on Image Processing*, Barcelona, Spain (pp. 41–44). Washington, DC: IEEE Computer Society.

Olshausen, B. A., & Field, D. J. (1996). Emergence of simple-cell receptive field properties by learning a sparse code for natural images. *Nature, 381*(6583), 607–609.

Olshausen, B. A., & Field, D. J. (1997). Sparse coding with an overcomplete basis set: A strategy employed by V1? *Vision Research, 37*(23), 3311–3325.

Olshausen, B. A., & Field, D. J. (2005). How close are we to understanding V1? *Neural Computation, 17,* 1665–1699.

Oren, M., Papageorgiou, C., Sinha, P., Osuna, E., & Poggio, T. (1997). Pedestrian detection using wavelet templates. *Proceedings of the IEEE Computer Society Conference on Computer Vision and Pattern Recognition,* San Juan, Puerto Rico (pp. 193–199). Washington, DC: IEEE Computer Society.

Poggio, T., & Vetter, T. (1992). *Recognition and structure from one 2D model view: Observations on prototypes, object classes and symmetries* (MIT A.I. Memo No. 1347). Cambridge, MA: MIT.

Riesenhuber, M., & Poggio, T. (1999). Hierarchical models of object recognition in cortex. *Nature Neuroscience, 2*(11), 1019–1025.

Ringach, D. L. (2002). Spatial structure and symmetry of simple-cell receptive fields in macaque primary visual cortex. *Journal of Neurophysiology, 88,* 455–463.

Sadr, J., Mukherjee, S., Thoresz, K., & Sinha, P. (2002). The fidelity of local ordinal encoding. In T. Dietterich, S. Becker, & Z. Ghahramani (Eds.), *Advances in neural information processing systems* (pp. 1279–1286). MIT Press: Cambridge, MA.

Schapire, R. E. (2003). The boosting approach to machine learning: An overview. In D. D. Denison, M. H. Hansen, C. Holmes, B. Mallick, & B. Yu (Eds.), *Nonlinear estimation and classification* (pp. 149–172). New York: Springer.

Serre, T., Wolf, L., Bileschi, S., Riesenhuber, M., & Poggio, T. (2007). Object recognition with cortex-like mechanisms. *IEEE Transactions on Pattern Analysis and Machine Intelligence, 29*(3), 411–426.

Sinha, P. (2002). Qualitative representations for recognition. In H. Bulthoff (Ed.), *Lecture notes in computer science* (pp. 249–262). Berlin: Springer-Verlag.

Sinha, P., & Poggio, T. (1996). Role of learning in three-dimensional form perception. *Nature, 384,* 460–463.

Ullman, S. (1995). Sequence seeking and counter streams: A model for bidirectional information flow in the visual cortex. *Cerebral Cortex, 5,* 1–11.

Usrey, W. M., Alonso, J-M., & Reid, R. C. (2000). Synaptic interactions between thalamic inputs to simple cells in cat visual cortex. *J. Neurosci. 20,* 5461–5467.

Warren, T., & Rayner, K. (2004). Top-down influences in the interactive alignment model: The power of the situation model. *Behavioral and Brain Sciences, 27*(2), page 211.

Watkins, D. W., & Berkley, M. A. (1974). The orientation selectivity of single neurons in cat striate cortex. *Experimental Brain Research, 19,* 433–446.

Wiskott, L., Fellous, J. M., Kruger, N., & von der Malsburg, C. (1997). Face recognition by elastic graph matching. *IEEE Transactions on Pattern Analysis and Machine Intelligence, 19,* 775–779.

CHAPTER 24

Models of Motor Control

Ferdinando A. Mussa-Ivaldi and Sara A. Solla

1. Introduction

The motor system is a complex machine. Even as we carry out the most mundane of operations, such as bringing food to our mouths, our brains must solve difficult problems, problems that robotic engineers have a hard time solving. Indeed, for quite some time, the neuroscience of motor behavior has avoided dealing with complexity by focusing on highly constrained behaviors, such as the one-dimensional flexion-extension motions of a limb about a single joint. Starting from the 1980s and perhaps under the influence of robotics research, scientists have become more aware of the importance of understanding natural behaviors: how they are planned, learned, and controlled. One of the earliest challenges came from the observation that the control of a multijoint limb, such as the human arm, cannot be implemented by combining single-joint controllers due to dynamical interactions between degrees of freedom; for example, the movements of the elbow generate torques that must be compensated at the shoulder and vice versa. This rela-

tively simple observation suffices to cast serious doubts over the applicability to natural behavior of earlier models of motor control based on the investigation of single-joint movements.

At least three general classes of theories in motor control have emerged in the last three decades. One such class is often referred to as the dynamical systems view (Kugler & Turvey, 1987; Lansner, Kotaleski, & Grillner, 1998; Saltzman & Kelso, 1987; Scott Kelso, 1995); it emphasizes the role of skeletal mechanics combined with neural processes in shaping time-dependent behaviors, such as cyclic kinematic patterns of locomotion. Another class is equilibrium point control models (Bizzi et al., 1984; Bizzi et al., 1992; Feldman, 1966; Feldman, 1986; Hogan, 1985; Latash, 1998), which highlight the existence of static attractors resulting from the interaction of neural feedback and muscle viscoelastic properties. The third class is optimization-based models (Hogan, 1984; Todorov & Jordan, 2002; Uno, Kawato, & Suzuki, 1989), suggesting that behavior emerges from the selection of control policies that maximize a gain or minimize a cost function. This chapter describes a theoretical framework that contains elements from each of these three approaches.

A fecund concept in motor control arose in the context of investigating reflexes (Sherrington, 1910); a reflex is a stereotyped action that deterministically follows a sensory input. The study of reflexes in combination with the engineering concept of feedback control led to early models of voluntary movements (Merton, 1972). In feedback control, the nervous system generates forces that tend to eliminate the sensed error between desired and actual states. This very simple concept is quite powerful, as its implementation does not involve complex operations. The plausibility of feedback control is supported by the presence of sensing organs, such as muscle spindles and the fusimotor system, that appear to supply the neural controller with state-error information. However, feedback control systems tend to exhibit severe instability problems in the presence of large delays (Hogan et al., 1987; Ogata, 1997). The delays associated with neural information processing of proprioceptive feedback are indeed quite large by common engineering standards: conventional estimates suggest 30 ms for the transmission delay in spinal reflex loops and about 100 ms for transcortical loops. These would be unacceptable values for the stable control of a robotic arm.

An alternative approach to the control of multijoint limbs was based on the computational idea of look-up tables. In a look-up table, the control signals that are needed to generate a movement are not computed explicitly from knowledge of the limb dynamics. Instead, patterns of neural activations are stored as they are produced, in conjunction with the movement that they cause, in an associative memory bank. Subsequently, when a movement is required, the desired movement is used as an address for retrieving the corresponding neural activations. Marr (1969) and Albus (1971) proposed this as a computational model of cerebellar motor control. Subsequently, Marr (1982) himself criticized this approach

based on its inability to capture and express the wide variety of movements that characterize natural behaviors. The failure of look-up models is due a combinatorial explosion arising from the structure of multijoint kinematics: The number of movement patterns that need to be stored grows exponentially with the number of degrees of freedom.

This chapter focuses on the computational models of motor control that have emerged from addressing the failures of earlier feedback and look-up models. These current views of motor control are characterized by an awareness of the geometrical complexity of natural behavior and of the coordinate transformations involved in the production of movements.

The discussion begins with a review of the geometrical framework of coordinate transformations involved in the mapping of motor plans into control signals. The key concept developed throughout this chapter is that the mechanical properties of the musculoskeletal system provide a basis for simplifying the computational demands of this transformation. The complexity arising from the large number of available muscles and joints underlies the great mobility of biological organisms. This abundance allows us to carry out any action in a variety of possible ways; this multiplicity of options is thus associated with computational problems of "redundancy" and, most notably, the ill-posed problem of associating a unique motor command with a desired plan of action. This ill-posed inverse mapping problem is related to the more general issue of developing a consistent internal representation of the Euclidean geometry of the environment in which the organism moves.

The following sections describe how the mechanics of the musculoskeletal system offer a natural framework for solving the computational problems of redundancy while preserving all the flexibility that redundancy affords. In this theoretical framework, musculoskeletal mechanics provides a basis for representing motor control signals through a combination of modules called, in analogy with linguistics, *motor primitives*. The transformation of a movement plan into control signals can then be described mathematically as a form of function approximation, thus bringing an extensive repertoire of powerful analytical tools into the study of motor control.

The discussion includes a review of some of the neurobiological evidence for the existence of such motor primitives and of combination rules based on the simple vectorial summation of the forces generated by specific groups of muscles. The computational value of motor primitives is not limited to the ability to generate a wide repertoire of movements, but also includes the ability of adapting the motor control signals to changes in mechanical properties of both the body and the external environment. The formalism of function approximation, when combined with probabilistic analysis, provides the means toward a conceptual framework for understanding motor control as based on internal representations of the controlled dynamics. The need for probabilistic analysis is due to the presence of noise and uncertainty in the environment as well as in the control system. Bayesian statistics provide tools for describing the adaptive development of internal representations that map a desired movement into a motor command and, conversely, for estimating the state of motion of the body given a known motor command. The presentation ends with a discussion of neural network architectures capable of implementing various aspects of the computational tasks associated with the use of motor primitives arising from the mechanics of the motor system.

It is worth stressing that the general domain of motor behavior is very broad and includes activities as diverse as reaching, walking, swallowing, speaking, manipulating objects, and playing musical instruments. This review focuses on a subset of these activities, mostly concerning the actions of moving multiarticular limbs and reaching for external targets. Although the computational problems associated with this particular class of actions are broad and complex, they constitute by no means a exhaustive description of the amazingly rich repertoire of biological motor behaviors.

2. Cordinate Systems for Motor Control

The geometrical nature of the operations that the brain must carry out in the recognition of objects and in the execution of movements is a central issue in neural information processing. In particular, some critical operations in the generation and control of movements can be formulated as coordinate transformations. Sensory information about the state of motion of the body comes from a variety of signal sources, each being concerned with particular mechanical variables. For example, skeletal muscles are endowed with sensors that measure the muscle strain and its rate of change (Nichols, 2002). Muscles are also endowed, at their junction with tendons, with Golgi tendon organs (Jami, 1992) that sense variations in muscle force. Other receptors are sensitive to the displacement of the joints, to pain, to temperature, and so forth. Signals from other sensory modalities, such as the eyes and the vestibular organs, provide information about the position of the body and its parts with respect to the environment. In contrast to this variety of sensory signals, the structures that generate movements are quite specific. The neural signals that control muscle contractions are generated by the motoneurons, which are located inside the grey matter of the spinal cord. Muscles are partitioned into groups of fibers – called motor units – that receive common innervation from a single motoneuron. The force generated by a muscle is graded by a distribution of neural activities over the motoneurons that innervate its motor units. Each motor unit contracts and generates tension; as motor units are connected both in parallel and in series within a muscle, either tensions (parallel) or strains (series) are combined additively.

The quantitative description of motor and sensory signals requires the use of a coordinate system. Although there are several possible coordinate systems for describing different signals, these coordinate systems fall quite naturally into three classes: actuator coordinates, generalized coordinates, and endpoint coordinates.

2.1. *Endpoint Coordinates*

Endpoint coordinates are appropriate for describing motor behavior of an organism as placed within the environment. An appropriate choice of such coordinates will reflect and incorporate the symmetries that characterize the external environment. Perhaps the most striking of these is the Euclidean symmetry: the invariance of distance between points under rotations and translations is an intrinsic symmetry of the environment within which organisms move. The dimensionality of endpoint space is generally rather low. Because the state of a moving rigid body is fully described by six coordinates (three translational and three angular), the force applied to the body is a six-dimensional force/torque vector. In a target reaching task, the position of a point target relative to the body is given by three coordinates (e.g., the Cartesian coordinates with respect to a frame fixed in the body). Human hand movements tend to be spontaneously organized in endpoint coordinates: The kinematics of reaching is generally a smooth trajectory, that is, a straight line with bell-shaped velocity profile, when described in the coordinates of the hand (Flash & Hogan, 1985; Morasso, 1981; Soechting & Lacquaniti, 1981; Figure 24.1). This is remarkable because the kinematics of a multijointed limb defines a curved manifold that does not match the symmetries of Euclidean space. For instance, a given angular excursion of the shoulder and elbow causes a net displacement of the hand that varies in amplitude and direction depending on its starting position; however, the length of a segment in Euclidean geometry does not depend on the location or the orientation of the segment. Similar observations have been made in different species. For example, Gutfreund et al. (1998) investigated reaching movements of the octopus and found that a stereotyped tentacle motion, characterized by a bending wave traveling along the tentacle, leads to a simple movement of the bending point, which travels in a radial, nearly rectilinear direction toward the target. This bending motion does not appear to be produced as a passive whip, but rather as a continuously propagating wave of muscle activity that insures a repeatable velocity profile and a quasi-planar motion of the tentacle.

2.2. *Actuator Coordinates*

Information about the position of the arm in space can be conveyed by specifying a collection of muscle lengths, $l = (l_1, l_2, \ldots, l_m)$. In this representation, each muscle is regarded as a coordinate, leading to a number of muscle coordinates that clearly exceeds the number of independent coordinates needed for specifying the position of the arm. In this coordinate system, a force is a collection of muscle tensions, $f = (f_1, f_2, \ldots, f_m)$. Such *actuator coordinates* (Holdefer & Miller, 2002) afford the most direct representation for the motor output of the central nervous system. The final output stage (or "final common path"; [Sherrington, 1906]) of the motor system is provided by the motoneurons in the spinal cord, whose activities determine the state of contraction of the muscles. The latter is measured by the receptors in the muscle spindles, which deliver this information to the nervous system via the dorsal root ganglia.

Although each muscle is operated by a distinct set of neural signals, actuator coordinates do not constitute a system of mechanically independent variables: One cannot set arbitrary values to all l_i without eventually violating a kinematic constraint. To determine the position of the arm from its representation in actuator coordinates, the nervous system must perform some form of analysis such as least squares estimation, as is typically the case for overdetermined systems.

Different approaches to the study of motor control may employ different levels of detail in the description of physiological processes, leading to actuator models with different dimensionality. For example, some approaches focus on simplified models in which a single joint is operated by a pair of muscles acting as reciprocal (agonist/antagonist) actuators. If the observed

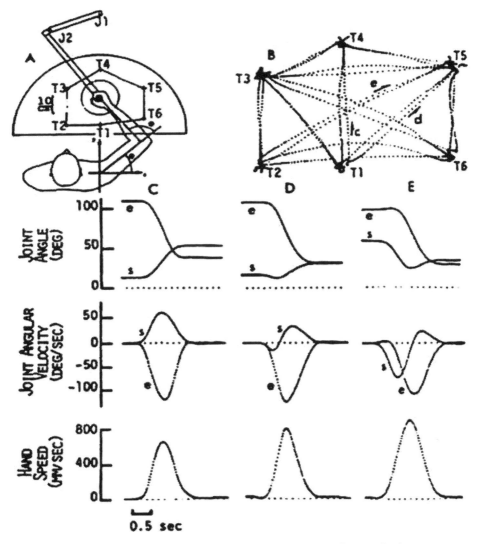

Figure 24.1. Spatial control of hand movements. (A) Plan view of a seated subject grasping the handle of a position transducer manipulandum. A horizontal semicircular plate located above the handle carries six visual targets (T1 through T6); the panel obstructs vision of the hand. (B) A series of digitized handle paths (sampling rate 100 Hz) performed by one subject in different parts of the movement space. Arrows show the direction of some of the hand movements. (C, D, E) Kinematic data for three selected movements whose paths are shown in (B). The correspondence is indicated by lowercase letters in (B); for example, data under (C) are for path c in (B); *e:* elbow joint angle, *s:* shoulder joint angle, both measured as indicated in (A). (Modified from Morasso, 1982).

motions involve several degrees of freedom and multiple muscle groups, the dimensionality of the actuator space will increase, typically by one order of magnitude. At the most detailed level of analysis, individual motor units may be considered as actuator elements. In this case, the dimensionality of

the actuator space can reach hundreds of thousands.

2.3. Generalized Coordinates

A different way of describing body motions is to specify the value of the joint angles that define the orientation of each skeletal segment either with respect to fixed axes in space or with respect to the neighboring segments. Joint angles are a particular instance of *generalized coordinates*. Generalized coordinates are a set of independent variables suitable for describing the dynamics of a mechanical system (Goldstein, 1980; Jose & Saletan, 1998). *Dynamics* refers to a description of how the state of motion of a limb evolves under the influence of the muscle forces, of the passive mechanical properties of the moving limb, and of the forces generated by the environment with which the limb comes in contact. Mathematically, dynamics are expressed by differential equations that relate these forces and the current state of motion of a limb – its position and velocity – to the rate of change of velocity, that is, the limb's acceleration. In discrete time, a dynamics equation allows one to derive the next state of motion given the current state and the applied forces. A typical problem in engineering is to find the forces that must be applied to the mechanical joints of a robotic arm so as to generate a desired trajectory. The solution to this problem requires representing the dynamics equation of the arm and calculating the applied force from the desired position, velocity, and acceleration of each joint.

The concept of *state* is critically important in a dynamical formulation. The state of a mechanical system is the smallest set of variables that suffices to describe the future evolution of a system, given its current value and the applied forces. This definition is quite general and many different specifications of state variables are usually possible. The laws of Newtonian mechanics establish that the acceleration of a point mass is given by the applied force divided by the mass. If one knows the current position and velocity of the point mass, and the forces that will be applied to it from this moment on, the application of Newton's law determines the value of all future positions and velocities. Thus, the state of a point mass is fully specified by its position and velocity. These two variables can be specified in different coordinates: Cartesian, cylindrical, spherical, and

so forth. Coordinates are typically chosen so as to further simplify the dynamical description, based on the symmetries of the forces that are applied to the system.

The idea that the state of a system is specified by its position and velocity is generally applicable to all mechanical systems, but specific applications require a careful definition of what is meant by "position" and "force." This extension to *generalized coordinates* and *generalized forces* was introduced shortly after Newton's early definition of force for simple point mass systems, and it involves the incorporation of constraints between the constituents of a composite system. For example, the position of a rigid rod pivoting at one of its ends can be fully specified by the angle formed between the rod and any fixed direction in space, such as the vertical direction of gravity. In this example, knowing the length of the rod, the position of its fixed end, and only one angular variable suffices to specify the instantaneous position of all points in the rod. This angle is therefore a generalized coordinate for the rod system, because the specification of its value defines the rod's *configuration*.

An example that involves the internal structure of a composite mechanical system is provided by the planar two-joint manipulandum shown in Figure 24.1A; in this case, the configuration is defined by the two angles, s for shoulder and e for elbow, formed by rigid segments at the two mobile joints. In the extension of Newtonian mechanics provided by Lagrange (Goldstein, 1980), the state of a system is specified by the value of its configurational variables and their first temporal derivative. This redefinition of the concepts of state as involving generalized definitions of position and velocity also carries with it a redefinition of the concept of force. The *generalized force* applied to a system causes a change of the system's state as described by its generalized coordinates. For the planar scenario illustrated in Figure 24.1A, the generalized force is given by the moments (or torques) applied to the joint angles by both the subject pushing on the handle of the manipulandum and by the motors acting directly on the manipulandum joints. It is important to note that the generalized coordinates and the generalized force share a common geometrical description. If the generalized coordinates are linear, then the generalized forces are ordinary forces causing linear accelerations. If the generalized coordinates are angular, then the generalized forces are angular "torques" causing rotational accelerations.

The kinematics of the body are often approximated by a tree of rigid links, interconnected by joints with one to three rotational degrees of freedom; the corresponding generalized forces are thus the torques generated at each joint by both the muscles and the external environment. The dynamics of the body, or of its parts, are then described by systems of coupled differential equations relating the generalized coordinates to their first and second time derivatives and to the generalized forces.

In vector notation, the dynamics equations for a multijoint limb can be written as:

$$I(q)\ddot{q} + G(q, \dot{q}) + E(q, \dot{q}, \ddot{q}, t)$$
$$= C(q, \dot{q}, u(t)), \quad (24.1)$$

where $q = (q_1, q_2, \ldots, q_n)$ describes the configuration of the limb though its n joint-angle coordinates $\dot{q}$ and $\ddot{q}$ are respectively the first (velocity) and second (acceleration) time derivatives of q, I is an $n \times n$ matrix of inertia (that depends on the configuration), $G(q, \dot{q})$ is a vector of centripetal and Coriolis torques (Sciavicco & Siciliano, 2000), and $E(q, \dot{q}, \ddot{q}, t)$ is a vector of external torques, which depends, in general, on the state of motion of the limb, its acceleration, and also, possibly, time. In a more compact notation, Coriolis and inertial forces are lumped in a single function $D(q, \dot{q}, \ddot{q})$ representing the passive dynamics of the limb, and Equation 24.1 becomes:

$$D(q, \dot{q}, \ddot{q}) + E(q, \dot{q}, \ddot{q}, t) = C(q, \dot{q}, u(t)).$$
$$(24.2)$$

The left side of Equations 24.1 and 24.2 represents the torque due to inertial properties and to the action of the environment (part of which may be considered "noise"). The term $C(\cdot)$ on the right side represents the net torque generated by the muscles. The time-dependent function $u(t)$ is a vector of control variables representing, for example, a set of neural signals directed to the motoneurons or the desired limb position at time t. An additional term, to be added to the right side of Equations 24.1 and 24.2, could represent the noise associated with $u(t)$.

3. The Problem of Kinematic Redundancy

A distinctive feature of biological control systems is what appears to be an overabundance of controlled components and of degrees of freedom (Bernstein, 1967). The term "kinematic redundancy" describes this prevalence. The presence of kinematic redundancy in biological limbs is in striking contrast to the traditional design of robotic systems, where the number of control actuators and degrees of freedom matches the dimension of the space associated with the task. As six coordinates are needed to position a rigid tool in space, a robotic arm with six degrees of freedom is in principle capable of placing such a tool in an arbitrary pose at an arbitrary position. However, advanced robotics technologies have recognized the value of design that allows for "extra" degrees of freedom in favor of greater versatility and dexterity (Brady et al., 1982; Leeser & Townsend, 1997; Mussa-Ivaldi & Hogan, 1991). Ultimately, the term redundancy could be considered as a misnomer because it does not acknowledge that the dimension associated with a task may well exceed the dimension of the kinematics space. For example, Hogan (1985) has pointed out the important role played by what appear to be extra degrees of freedom that modulate the impedance of the endpoint of a limb in the face of an expected impact.

The importance of redundancy as a means for providing alternative (or "equivalent") ways to achieve a goal in the face of variable operating conditions was

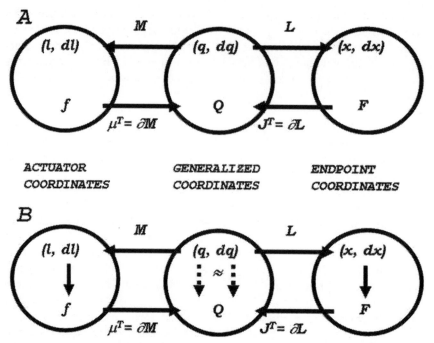

Figure 24.2. Coordinate systems and their transformations. (A) The functions *L* and *M* describe well-posed coordinate transformations. Forces are transformed back onto generalized coordinates through well-posed dual transformations based on Jacobians of partial first derivatives. (B) Motor primitives described as force fields in endpoint coordinates provide a basis for the approximation of generalized forces through superposition. The activation of forces in actuator coordinates specifies the selection coefficients that implement the linear combination (see text).

recognized a century ago by Bernstein (1967), who described the computational problems arising from the presence of an imbalance between the number of degrees of freedom and the demands of a task. The computational problem is illustrated in Figure 24.2A, representing the maps of force and position in a serial limb, such as the arm. On the right side of the diagram are representations of state and force variables in endpoint coordinates. These variables are observed at the interface with the environment, for example, the position of the fingertip and the contact force at this point. On the left side of the diagram are representations of state and force variables in actuator coordinates. Note that the force generated by the muscular system results from a function that maps the state of motion of the muscles – collectively indicated by the two vectors $l, \dot{l}$ of muscle lengths and their rates of change – and the muscle control signals $u(t)$ into a vector f of muscle tensions. This map into muscle tensions is in general nonlinear and noninvertible. The generalized coordinates, typically joint angle variables, are an intermediate representation between actuator and endpoint coordinates. The directions of the arrows in Figure 24.2A correspond to the directions in which kinematic and force transformations are well-posed. For example, joint angles map into endpoint position via a direct kinematics function L and into muscle length via a function M. Both functions are generally noninvertible, although for different reasons. The map L is noninvertible because a given endpoint position can be obtained through a large number of joint configurations that define a so called null space. The term "null space" refers to directions of variability in the space of generalized coordinates that result in no change of the endpoint location. In more formal terms, if A is a matrix acting on a vector space x, the null space of A is the set of all vectors x that satisfy $Ax = 0$. The map M is noninvertible because an arbitrary set of muscle lengths may not be realizable, as it may have no corresponding image in configuration space. Although the kinematic maps L and M refer to coordinate transformations, forces transform in a dual, reciprocal way, through the Jacobian derivatives ∂L and ∂M of the corresponding kinematic functions. Note the reversed direction of the corresponding arrows. The Jacobian of a map, such as a coordinate transformation, is a linear operator containing the partial derivatives of the output variables taken with respect to the input variables.

4. Motor Planning and the Representation of Euclidean Space

The remarkable ability of the visual system to capture the Euclidean invariance of object size and shape with respect to rigid translations and rotations has been extensively studied (Hatfield, 2003; Shepard, 2001). For example, (Shepard, 2001) proposed that the Euclidean metric of object space is implicitly learned and represented internally. In contrast to the long-standing interest in the visual perception and representation of space, little is known about how the fundamental geometrical properties of space are represented in the motor system, where neither sensory nor muscle command signals are characterized by Euclidean invariance. However, we are evidently able to formulate and execute motor plans, such as "move the hand 10 cm to the right", despite the fact that this simple act requires widely varying muscle activations and segmental coordination, depending on the starting position of the hand. Our ability to generate straight motions of our hands in different directions and from different starting points, without apparent effort, is a simple demonstration of our motor system's de facto ability to capture the Euclidean properties of the space in which we move.

In a recent study, Mosier et al. (2005) investigated how movement representations are reorganized by the central nervous system to capture the Euclidean properties of the space within which actions take place. In these experiments, subjects wore a data glove that allowed for the measurement of twenty-two signals related to hand and finger postures. A highly redundant linear mapping was used to transform these twenty-two signals into two coordinates defining the location of a cursor on a computer monitor (Figure 24.3). The study resulted in four main findings: (1) after about one hour of training with visual feedback of the final error but not of the ongoing cursor motion, subjects learned to map cursor locations into hand and finger configurations; (2) extended practice led to more rectilinear cursor movement, a trend that was facilitated by training under continuous visual feedback of cursor motions; (3) with practice, subjects reduced variability of both cursor and hand movements; and (4) the reduction of errors and the increase in linearity generalized beyond the set of movements used for training. Taken together, these findings suggested that subjects not only learned to produce novel coordinated movements to control the placement of the cursor, but that they also developed a representation of the two-dimensional space (the plane of the monitor) onto which hand movements were mapped. The emergence of this representation is evidenced by the practice-induced tendency to generate controlled trajectories that were both shorter and less variable. The construction of this representation appears to involve the subjects' ability to partition the degrees of freedom of the hand into combinations that contributed to cursor movements and null space combinations that did not generate any cursor movement.

5. Transforming Plans into Actions

The diagram in Figure 24.2A illustrates the computational challenge associated with the redundancy of the musculoskeletal apparatus, which manifests itself in the noninvertibility of the transformations between actuator, generalized, and endpoint coordinates.

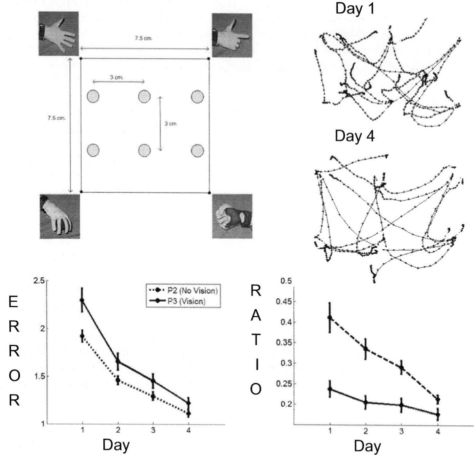

Figure 24.3. Reorganization of hand movements. Subjects were asked to control the movement of a cursor by changing the configuration of hand and fingers. The hand was instrumented with a data glove. Hand configuration controlled the position of a cursor on the screen via a smooth and linear map from a twenty-two dimensional vector of glove signals to the two coordinates of the monitor. Circular targets were presented, and subjects were asked to make a rapid movement to the target, stop, and then correct. Movements were executed under one of two training protocols: in the No-Vision (NV) protocol, the cursor was suppressed during the reaching movements. The cursor was only presented at the end of reaching to allow for a correction (not analyzed). In the Vision (V) protocol, the cursor was always visible. Subjects in the P2 group were trained and tested under the NV protocol. Subjects in the P3 group were trained under the V protocol and tested under the NV protocol. Data analysis was carried out only for test trials allowing comparison of how subjects executed reaching movements without visual guidance after having trained without (P2) and with (P3) visual guidance. *Top left:* The linear map from glove signals to screen coordinates was set up by asking the subjects to hold their hand in four "standard gestures" corresponding to the corners of a rectangular region on the monitor. *Top right:* Two sets of cursor trajectories obtained on Day 1 and on Day 4 of training from the same subject. *Bottom left:* Subjects in both P2 and P3 groups learned the reaching task with similar results. The two curves show the average reaching error measured in each of four sessions on consecutive days. The vertical bars are 99% confidence intervals. *Bottom right:* Under both training conditions, subjects tend to produce increasingly straighter cursor motions, as evidenced by the decreasing trend in "aspect ratio," the ratio of lateral deviation to movement extent. Subjects trained with vision generated significantly straighter trajectories than subjects trained without vision of cursor motion. (Modified from Mosier et al., 2005).

Based on this diagram, it is not evident how a movement plan such as a desired motion of the endpoint can be mapped by the nervous system into a corresponding set of commands for the muscles. An answer to this problem may be offered by the impedance properties of the muscular apparatus (Hill, 1938; Hogan, 1985; Huxley, 1957; Mussa-Ivaldi, Hogan, & Bizzi, 1985; Rack & Westbury, 1969). The spring-like and viscous properties of the muscles provide a computational "bridge" between motion and force variables, as illustrated in Figure 24.2B. Although the transformation from a desired motion to a set of control signals $u(t)$ may be ill defined, a plan of action may be implemented as an approximation of a desired *force field* by an appropriate tuning of viscoelastic actuators (Mussa-Ivaldi, 1997; Mussa-Ivaldi & Bizzi, 2000). The force field f generated by the combined viscoelastic behavior of the muscles under a pattern of control signals $u(t)$ is given by a function $f(l, \dot{l}, u(t))$. This force field can be expressed in terms of generalized coordinates through the Jacobian derivative of the map M, resulting in a computational structure that does not involve any ill-posed inverse mapping:

$$Q = \varphi_f(q, \dot{q}, u(t))$$
$$= \partial M(q)^T f(l(q), \dot{l}(q), u(t)). \quad (24.3)$$

The planning of a desired behavior can in turn be expressed as a force field F that maps a state of the endpoint (for example, a heading direction) into a corrective force $F(x, \dot{x}, t)$. This is a way to represent what some researchers would call a "policy" (Sutton & Barto, 1998), a prescribed action in response to an observed state. This policy can be represented as a force field in terms of generalized coordinates through the Jacobian derivative of the map L, resulting also in this case in a computational structure that does not involve any ill-posed inverse mapping:

$$Q = \psi_F(q, \dot{q}, t)$$
$$= \partial L(q)^T F(x(q), \dot{x}(q), t). \quad (24.4)$$

Therefore, the biological implementation of a planned policy can be seen as the approximation

$$\varphi_f(q, \dot{q}, u(t)) \approx \psi_F(q, \dot{q}, t), \quad (24.5)$$

to be achieved through the appropriate choice of $u(t)$. As an example of the application of this rather abstract computational structure, how this approximation may be implemented by the neural structures of the spinal cord is discussed in the following section.

6. The Organization of Muscle Synergies in the Spinal Cord

The spinal cord is the final output stage of the central nervous system. Every muscle is innervated by motoneurons located in the ventral portion of the spinal grey matter. This system of motoneurons is comparable to a switchboard in which each motoneuron drives a specific group of muscle fibers, a motor unit. But there is more than a switchboard in the spinal cord. In addition to the motoneurons, the spinal grey matter contains a large population of nerve cells, the interneurons, whose functions are not yet fully understood.

Spinal interneurons may form connections with motoneurons that innervate several different muscles. In a series of experiments (Bizzi, Mussa-Ivaldi, & Giszter, 1991; Giszter, Mussa-Ivaldi, & Bizzi, 1993; Lemay & Grill, 1999; Mussa-Ivaldi, Giszter, & Bizzi, 1990; Tresch & Bizzi, 1999), the activity induced by chemical and electrical stimulation of the spinal interneurons of the frog was found to spread to several groups of motoneurons. This distribution of activity was not random, but imposed a specific balance of muscle contractions. The mechanical outcome of the evoked synergistic contraction of multiple muscles was captured by a force field (Figure 24.4). The activation of a group of muscles generated a force that was recorded by a sensor at the endpoint of the limb. This force vector changed in amplitude and direction depending on the

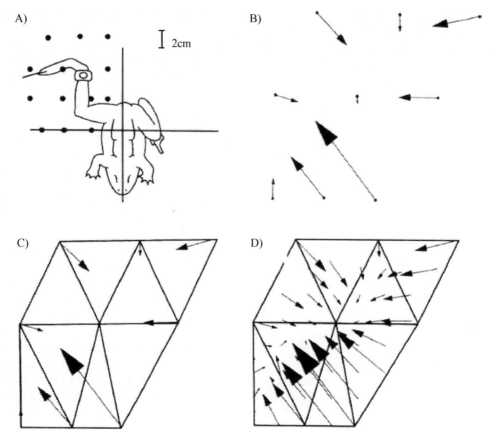

Figure 24.4. Force fields induced by microstimulation of the spinal cord in spinalized frogs. (A) The hind limb was placed at several locations on the horizontal plane, as indicated by the dots. At each location, a stimulus was applied at a fixed site in the lumbar spinal cord. The ensuing force was measured by a six-axes force transducer. (B) Peak force vectors recorded at nine of the locations shown in (A). The workspace of the hind limb was partitioned into a set of eight non-overlapping triangles for which each vertex is a tested point. The force vectors recorded on the three vertices of each triangle are used to estimate, by linear interpolation, the forces in the interior of the triangle. (D) Interpolated force field. (Modified from Bizzi et al., 1991).

position of the limb. The resulting force field converged toward a location in the reachable space of the limb – a stable equilibrium point. At this location, the force vanished, and a small displacement of the endpoint in any direction induced a restoring force. The analysis of the force field induced by stimulation of the spinal interneurons revealed that such activation leads to the generation of a stable posture.

In these experiments, the stimulating electrodes were placed in different loci of the lumbar spinal cord. The conclusion of these studies is that there were at least four areas from which distinct types of conver-gent force fields were elicited. This is a strikingly small number of distinct force fields, given the very large number of combinations that could in principle be generated by the set of leg muscles.

Perhaps the most interesting aspect of these investigations was the discovery that the fields induced by the focal activation of the cord follow a principle of vectorial summation (Mussa-Ivaldi, Giszter, & Bizzi, 1994): When two separate sites in the spinal cord were simultaneously active, the resulting force field was the vector sum of the force fields induced by the separate activation of each site. This discovery led to a novel hypothesis for explaining movement and posture, based on the combination of a few basic elements. The few distinct force fields encoded by the connectivity of the spinal cord may be viewed as representing motor primitives from which a vast number of movements can be formed through superposition, through impulses conveyed via supraspinal pathways. According to this view, the supraspinal signals would establish the level of activation with which each motor primitive contributes to the superposition.

In this discussion, the concept of *primitive* is defined quite generally as an elementary control function emerging from the combination of neural activity and muscle mechanics. The term "elementary" is not intended to mean "simple", but rather "basic" or "fundamental", in the same sense that is typically attributed to the components of a set of basis functions. The microstimulation experiments suggest that the circuitry in the spinal cord – and perhaps also in other areas of the nervous system – is organized in independent units, or modules, implementing individual motor primitives. Whereas each module generates a specific field, more complex behaviors are produced by superposition of the fields associated with concurrently active modules. Thus, one may regard these primitive force fields as independent elements, forming a basis for an internal model of limb dynamics. In particular, the experimentally observed vector summation suggests that under descending supraspinal commands, the fields expressed by the spinal cord may form a broad repertoire:

$$\Gamma = \left\{ C_S(q, \dot{q}, t \,|\, \{c_f\}) = \sum_f c_f \varphi_f(q, \dot{q}, t) \right\}. \tag{24.6}$$

Each element of the set Γ is generated by descending commands that select a group of primitives through the weighting coefficients c_f. In this view, the neural control system may approximate a target field $\psi_F(q, \dot{q}, t)$ (Equation 24.5) by finding the element of Γ that is closest to this target field.

Field approximation has been directly applied to the generation of a desired trajectory $q_D(t)$ in generalized coordinates (Mussa-Ivaldi, 1997, 2002). In this case, the attempt to generate the appropriate controller amounts to finding values for the parameters c_f so as to minimize the difference between forces generated by the passive dynamics and those generated by the control field along the desired trajectory. If the residual error could be reduced to zero, the corresponding controller would exactly produce the desired trajectory. If there is a nonzero residual, then the problem of obtaining acceptable approximations becomes a question of local stability. Residual forces may be regarded as a perturbation of the dynamics, and one needs to insure that this perturbation does not lead to a motion that diverges from the desired trajectory. A study by Lohmiller and Slotine (1998) showed that the combination of control modules is stable if their associated dynamics are "contracting," a condition germane to exponential stability.

7. Motor Primitives and Field Approximation

Consistent with the finding of vector summation, the net force field C induced by a pattern of K motor commands may be represented as a linear combination over the corresponding K primitive force fields, labeled by an index i running from 1 to K:

$$\sum_{i=1}^{K} c_i \varphi_i(q, \dot{q}, t). \tag{24.7}$$

In this expression, each spinal force is a field that depends on the state of motion of the limb, $(q, \dot{q})$ and on time t. The descending commands $(c_1, c_2, \ldots, c_K)$ modulate the degree with which each spinal field $(\varphi_1, \varphi_2, \ldots, \varphi_K)$ participates in the combination. These commands select the modules by determining how much each one contributes to the net control policy. The linear

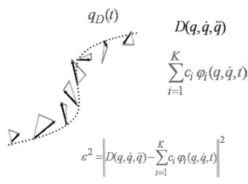

$q_D(t)$

$D(q, \dot{q}, \ddot{q})$

$$\sum_{i=1}^{K} c_i \, \varphi_i(q, \dot{q}, t)$$

$$\varepsilon^2 = \left| D(q, \dot{q}, \ddot{q}) - \sum_{i=1}^{K} c_i \, \varphi_i(q, \dot{q}, t) \right|^2$$

Figure 24.5. Control by field approximation. The desired trajectory is represented schematically in blue. The black arrows indicate the dynamic forces D needed to generate the desired trajectory. The green vectors are the forces generated by a linear combination of force fields. The red bars are the errors to be minimized.

combination of Equation 24.7 generates the torque, the generalized force that drives the limb inertia. Substituting it for the right-hand side of Equation 24.2 results in:

$$D(q, \dot{q}, \ddot{q}) + E(q, \dot{q}, \ddot{q}, t) = \sum_{i=1}^{K} c_i \varphi_i(q, \dot{q}, t).$$

(24.8)

For simplicity, let us start by analyzing the implications of Equation 24.8 in the case where the controlled limb is not affected by external forces, that is, $E = 0$. In this case, a least squares approximation (Figure 24.5) can efficiently determine the optimal set of coefficients $(c_1, c_2, \ldots, c_K)$ for a desired trajectory $q_D(t)$:

$$c_i = \sum_{j=1}^{K} [\Phi]_{i,j}^{-1} \Lambda_j$$

(24.9)

with

$$\begin{cases} \Phi_{l,m} = \int \varphi_l(q_D(t), \dot{q}_D(t), t) \bullet \\ \qquad \varphi_m(q_D(t), \dot{q}_D(t), t) \, dt \\ \Lambda_j = \int \varphi_j(q_D(t), \dot{q}_D(t), t) \bullet \\ \qquad D(q_D(t), \dot{q}_D(t), \ddot{q}_D(t)) \, dt \end{cases}$$

(24.10)

where the symbol $\bullet$ indicates the ordinary inner product.

While spinal force fields offer a practical way to generate movement, they also provide the central nervous system with a mechanism for movement representation. The possible movements of a limb can be considered as "points" in an abstract geometrical space in which the fields $\{\varphi_i\}$ provide a basis such as that provided by Cartesian axes, and the selection parameters $\{c_i\}$ that generate a particular movement may be regarded as generalized projections of this movement along the $\{\varphi_i\}$ axes.

8. A Computational Approach to Adaptive Learning

If the arm dynamics change while the modules remain unchanged, then the representation of the movement must change accordingly. Suppose that a desired trajectory, $q_D(t)$, is represented by a selection vector, $c = (c_1, c_2, \ldots, c_K)$, for a limb not affected by external forces, that is, $E = 0$. If the limb dynamics are suddenly modified by an external force, $E(q, \dot{q}, \ddot{q}, t)$, then the full form of Equation 24.8 must be considered:

$$D(q, \dot{q}, \ddot{q}) + E(q, \dot{q}, \ddot{q}, t) = \sum_{i=1}^{K} c_i \varphi_i(q, \dot{q}, t).$$

The solution to this equation will be a trajectory $\tilde{q}(t)$, generally different from the original $q_D(t)$ for $E = 0$. To recover the desired trajectory, the selection vector needs to be changed from c to a new vector $c' = c + e$, where the correction vector e satisfies

$$E(q_D(t), \dot{q}_D(t), \ddot{q}_D(t), t)$$

$$= \sum_{i=1}^{K} e_i \varphi_i(q_D(t), \dot{q}_D(t), t).$$

(24.11)

The modified coefficients $c' = c + e$ offer a new representation of the desired trajectory $q_D(t)$; the change reflects an alteration of the dynamic conditions within which the trajectory is to be executed. This computational procedure for forming a new representation and for recovering the original trajectory is consistent with the empirical observation of *after-effects* in force-field adaptation (Shad-mehr & Mussa-Ivaldi, 1994). If the force field is removed after the new representation is formed, the dynamics become

$$D(q, \dot{q}, \ddot{q}) = \sum_{i=1}^{K} (c_i + e_i)\, \varphi_i(q, \dot{q}, t),$$

$$(24.12)$$

which can be rewritten as:

$$D(q, \dot{q}, \ddot{q}) - \sum_{i=1}^{K} e_i\, \varphi_i(q, \dot{q}, t)$$

$$= \sum_{i=1}^{K} c_i \varphi_i(q, \dot{q}, t). \qquad (24.13)$$

Therefore, removing the load while maintaining the new representation will result in a trajectory that corresponds approximately to applying the opposite load with the old representation, in agreement with observed after effects.

The modification of motion representation through the selection coefficients thus provides a useful mechanism for rapidly adjusting to changes in limb dynamics. It is of interest to ask whether these representations need to be recalculated in response to every dynamical change or whether previously existing representations can be restored. From a computational point of view, whenever a dynamical change becomes permanent – as when due to growth or damage – it would be convenient for the central nervous system to have the ability to restore the previously learned motor skills (i.e., the previously learned movement representations) without the need to relearn them. It is possible for the adaptive system described here to do this by modifying the force fields expressed by the individual modules. A specific mechanism follows from expressing the coefficients $e = (e_1, e_2, \ldots, e_K)$ as a linear transformation of the original coefficients $c = (c_1, c_2, \ldots, c_K)$:

$$e = Wc. \qquad (24.14)$$

This is a simple coordinate transformation applied to the change e in selection vector;

a linear associative network can implement it. A few steps of algebra lead to

$$D(q, \dot{q}, \ddot{q}) + E(q, \dot{q}, \ddot{q})$$

$$= \sum_{i=1}^{K} c_i' \varphi_i(q, \dot{q}, t) = \sum_{i=1}^{K} (c_i + e_i)\varphi_i(q, \dot{q}, t)$$

$$= \sum_{i=1}^{K} c_i \bar{\varphi}_i(q, \dot{q}, t) \qquad (24.15)$$

where the old fields ϕ_i have been replaced by the new fields

$$\bar{\varphi}_i = \sum_{l=1}^{K} (\delta_{li} + W_{li})\varphi_l \quad \delta_{li} = \begin{cases} 1 & \text{if } l = i \\ 0 & \text{otherwise} \end{cases}.$$

$$(24.16)$$

This coordinate transformation is then made permanent through a change in the modules that represent individual force fields. By means of such coordinate transformation, one obtains the important result that the movement representation – that is, the selection vector c – can be maintained invariant after a change in limb dynamics.

9. Forward and Inverse Models as a Basis for Adaptive Behavior

The ability to generate a variety of complex behaviors cannot be attained by just storing the vector c of control signals for each action and recalling these selection coefficients when subsequently needed (Albus, 1971; Marr, 1969). Simple considerations about the geometrical space of meaningful behaviors are sufficient to establish that this approach would be inadequate (Bizzi & Mussa-Ivaldi, 1998). To achieve its typical competence, the motor system must take advantage of experience for going beyond experience itself by constructing internal representations of the controlled dynamics, such as, for example, the projections of D onto the fields $\{\varphi_i\}$, as in Equation 24.8 for $E = 0$. These representations need to allow the nervous system to generate new behaviors and to handle situations that have not yet been encountered. The term "internal model", used to indicate the collection of available internal representations, implies the ability to perform two distinct mathematical transformations: (1) the transformation from a motor command to the consequent behavior, and (2) the transformation from a desired behavior to the corresponding motor command (Bizzi & Mussa-Ivaldi, 1998; Flanagan & Wing, 1997; Jordan & Rumelhart, 1992; Kawato & Wolpert, 1998; McIntyre, Bertholz, & Lacquaniti, 1998; Shadmehr & Mussa-Ivaldi 1994). A model of the first kind is called a "forward model". Forward models provide the controller with the means not only to predict the expected outcome of a command, but also to estimate the current state of the limb in the presence of feedback delays (Hogan et al., 1987; Miall & Wolpert, 1996). Conversely, a representation of the transformation from desired actions to motor commands (as in Equations 24.9 and 24.10) is called an "inverse model". Studies by Kawato, Wolpert, and Miall (Wolpert & Kawato, 1998; Wolpert, Miall, & Kawato, 1998) have led to the proposal that neural structures within the cerebellum perform sensory-motor operations equivalent to a combination of multiple forward and inverse models. Strong evidence for the biological and behavioral relevance of internal models has been provided by numerous experiments (Hore, Ritchi, & Watts, 1999; Sabes, Jordan, & Wolpert, 1998). Some of these experiments involved the adaptation of arm movements to a perturbing force field generated by a manipulandum. The major findings of these studies are as follows (see Figure 24.6): (1) when exposed to a complex but deterministic field of velocity-dependent forces, arm movements are at first distorted, but the initial kinematics are recovered after repeated practice; (2) if, after adaptation, the field is suddenly removed, after-effects are clearly visible as mirror images of the initial perturbations, as described by Equation 24.13 (Shadmehr & Mussa-Ivaldi, 1994); (3) adaptation is achieved by the central nervous system through the formation of a local map that associates the states (positions and velocities) visited during the training period with the corresponding forces (Conditt, Gandolfo, & Mussa-Ivaldi, 1997; Conditt & Mussa-Ivaldi, 1999); (4) this map, which is the internal model of the field, undergoes a process of consolidation after adaptation (Brashers-Krug, Shadmehr, & Bizzi, 1996).

To generate the appropriate command for a desired movement of the arm, an inverse model must take into account that multijoint inertia depends on limb position and velocity. Therefore, an inverse model must be informed about the current state of motion of the limb. This information may come in one of two ways: (1) from the input to the inverse model that specifies where the limb should be, or (2) from a prediction of the current state based on delayed sensory feedback and on the past history of motor commands. Bhushan and Shadmehr (1999) have found compelling evidence for the second way. Their experimental results are consistent with the hypothesis that we learn to compensate changes in limb dynamics by a process that involves the combined adaptation of a forward and an inverse model of the limb.

10. Adaptation to State- and Time-Dependent Forces

The earliest studies on adaptation to force fields (Shadmehr & Mussa-Ivaldi, 1994) demonstrated the presence of after-effects when the perturbing forces were suddenly removed (Figure 24.6). This finding was consistent with the hypothesis that subjects formed a prediction of the external forces that they would encounter during the movement and that they used this prediction to compensate the disturbing force with an opposite force. However, the presence of after-effects is not sufficient to demonstrate that subjects formed a proper representation of the force field. The force field applied in these experiments was established by the manipulandum through the application of forces that depended on the velocity of the hand. These forces are expressed in endpoint coordinates, because they are applied at the

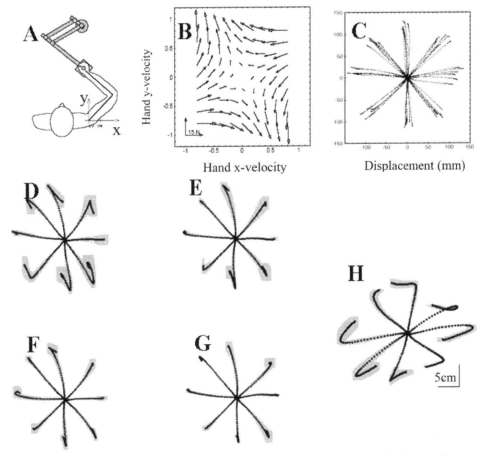

Figure 24.6. Force-field adaptation experiment. (A) Subjects hold the end-effector of a two-joint planar robot and execute reaching movements to a set of targets. (B) The robot can generate a force that depends on the measured velocity of the end-effector. (C) Typical hand trajectories generated by a subject in the absence of a force field. (D, E, F, G) Average +/− standard deviation of hand trajectories during the training period in the presence of a force field (B). The panels represent performance during four consecutive sets of 250 reaches. (H) After-effects of adaptation. These trajectories were obtained at the end of the training period by exposing the subject to random trials in which the field was unexpectedly removed. Note that the shape of these trajectories is approximately the mirror image of the trajectories in (D). (Modified from Shadmehr & Mussa-Ivaldi, 1994.)

interface between the limb and the planar manipulandum. Therefore, the applied field has the structure of a state-dependent force vector

$$F = E(\dot{x}), \tag{24.17}$$

where $\dot{x}$ is the two-dimensional vector that describes the instantaneous velocity of the hand. Learning the force field means forming an internal representation of this dependence.

An alternative mechanism would be to generate a "motor tape", that is, a representation of the time-varying forces as the hand moves through the environment:

$$F = \hat{E}(t) = E(\dot{x}(t)). \tag{24.18}$$

If this were the case, the perturbing force would be compensated as a function of time, not as a function of hand velocity. However, this "erroneous" or incomplete representation would still cause an after-effect to appear when the field is suddenly removed. To discriminate between a correct model of the force as a function of hand state and an inadequate representation of the force as a function of time, subjects need to be trained over a set of trajectories and then tested over trajectories that employ the same velocities but in a different temporal order. This test could not be successfully performed by subjects who have developed a time-based representation of the task. This experiment was carried out by Conditt et al. (1997), who trained subjects to execute reaching movements against a velocity-dependent field. After training, the same subjects were asked to execute circular movements in the same region of space. The circular movements lasted about two seconds, whereas the reaching movements lasted typically less than one second. The observed generalization was complete, and it was impossible to statistically distinguish the performance of these subjects from the performance of control subjects who were both trained and tested on the same circular movements. This finding is sufficient to rule out motor tape learning and provides strong evidence in favor of the formation of a correct state-dependent representation of the perturbing forces.

It is legitimate to suppose that we do indeed adapt to forces that are systematically encountered in the environment and that this adaptation involves developing a correct representation of these forces, whether they are a function of state or function of time. The experiments of Conditt et al. (1997) established that subjects do correctly represent the velocity-dependent forces generated by the manipulandum. The next obvious question was whether subjects would also develop correct representations of time-dependent forces that do not depend on the position or velocity of the hand. When such an experiment was carried out, it was found, surprisingly, that subjects were not able to form the correct representation of time-dependent forces (Conditt & Mussa-Ivaldi, 1999; Karniel & Mussa-Ivaldi, 2003). The paradigm of these experiments was similar to the paradigm for the velocity-

dependent force fields. Subjects were now trained to make reaching movements against a force that depended on time. At the end of training, they had learned to compensate the time-dependent forces, and they produced a clear after-effect if the forces were abruptly removed. However, when the subjects were subsequently asked to execute circular movements in the same region of space, they failed to compensate the time-varying forces. The same subjects were able to execute correct circular movements only if the time-dependent force was replaced by a field that depended on the velocity and the position of the hand and that produced the same forces as the time-dependent perturbation over the training movements. Taken together, these findings suggest that the adaptive controller of arm movements is able to form representations of state-dependent dynamics but not of time-dependent forces.

10.1. *State Space Models of Motor Learning*

The process of learning requires practice. In this respect, the formation of an internal model can be described as the temporal evolution of a dynamical system. This is the point of view taken by Thoroughman and Shadmehr (2000) and by Scheidt, Dingwell, and Mussa-Ivaldi (2001). Thoroughman and Shadmehr proposed to describe the adaptation to a force field as the temporal evolution of a system whose internal state is characterized by a hidden, unobservable variable z. The system produces an observable output to which a "performance error" y can be associated. An input signal p describes the applied perturbation through binary values that indicate the presence ($p = -1$) or absence ($p = +1$) of the applied field. The proposed state-space model is quite simple, as it involves only linear first-order dynamics over discrete time-steps counted by the index n:

$$z_{n+1} = az_n + bp_n$$
$$y_n = z_n + dp_n$$

(24.19)

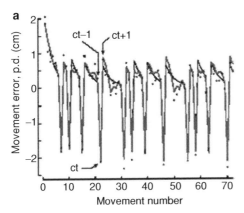

a

Figure 24.7. Unlearning effects captured by a state-space model. Plot of the time course of error in reaches along a specific direction. Circles indicate errors, measured as maximum lateral deviations from a straight line reach, for each subsequent reach during training. The field was suppressed at random trials ("catch trials") during this experiment. The field suppression during a catch trial caused an after-effect, indicated by a large negative spike in the error. Following this negative spike, the error returned to a level higher than its value immediately preceding the catch trial. Thus, catch trials cause unlearning. This effect is captured by state-space models of learning both in a scalar (black line) and in a vector (red line) form. (Modified from Thoroughman & Shadmehr, 2000).

In spite of its simplicity, the model proved adequate to capture a number of observed features of the learning process. One such feature is the time course of adaptation, as captured by the deviation of each movement from a straight line; this deviation was taken to be the observable error y. Thoroughman and Shadmehr (2000) noticed that following each "catch trial" – a trial in which the force field is unexpectedly removed – the experimental data indicated a brief but distinguishable unlearning period. The time course of this effect was adequately captured by the state-space model (Figure 24.7). Another important feature of this model is expressed by the value of the parameter b, which represents the effect on the current state (and therefore on the current error) of having experienced a force in the previous state. By estimating from the empirical error data the dependence of b on the

direction of the previous movement, Thoroughman and Shadmehr were able to derive "tuning curves", which demonstrate a destructive interference from previously experienced forces when there is a large difference between the current and the previous direction of movement.

An intriguing feature of this state-space model is its low order as a dynamical system. All that seems to matter is the experience that the learner has acquired in the previous repetition of the task. This conclusion is supported by observations of Scheidt et al. (2001), who exposed a group of subjects to randomly varying force fields. On each trial, subjects were exposed to velocity-dependent forces perpendicular to the direction of motion. The amplitude of the force was related to movement speed by a gain factor B. The actual value of this factor was randomly drawn on each trial from a Gaussian distribution. With practice, the best performance of the subjects (minimal error) was achieved for the mean value of the perturbing gain factor (Figure 24.8A and 24.8B). Most remarkably, the same result was observed when the random gain factor was drawn from a bimodal distribution (Figure 24.8C and 24.8D). This is apparently paradoxical, because in the bimodal case the mean value of the gain factor B is never experienced. The situation is reminiscent of the Buridan ass, who died of starvation because he could not choose between two identical stacks of hay placed in opposite directions. However, paradoxical as it may seem, a strategy based on the estimated mean value of the gain factor B is optimal in the sense of minimizing the mean square error.

These experimental observations indicate the existence of an underlying linear mechanism that guides the learning process. This suggests the possibility of using a simple linear time series – an autoregressive model with external input (Ljung, 1999) – to describe the learning behavior:

$$y_i = \sum_{j=1}^{L} a_j\, y_{i-j} + \sum_{k=0}^{M} b_k\, B_{i-k}. \qquad (24.20)$$

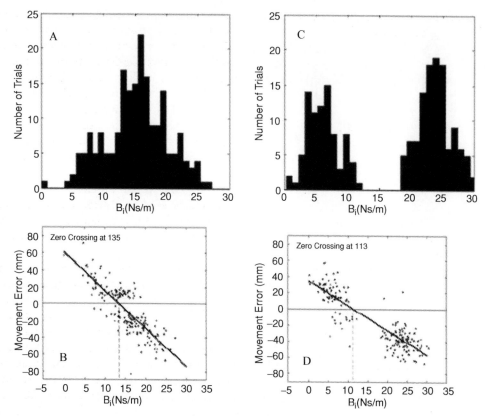

Figure 24.8. Adaptation to random force fields. Subjects were asked to move the hand against a velocity-dependent force field, whose gain varied randomly from trial to trial. For one group of subjects, the gain was drawn from a Gaussian probability distribution (A). The scatter plot of movement error versus field gain (B) exhibits a nearly linear relation (r = 0.82). Note that the zero crossing is near the mean value of the gain: The subjects have learned the mean value of the random field. For a second group of subjects, the gain was drawn from a bimodal distribution (C). The scatter plot of movement error versus field gain (D) shows a linear trend (r = 0.85), and the zero crossing is again in the vicinity of the mean value of the gain. This is remarkable because subjects have learned to compensate the mean perturbation, which in this case was never encountered during learning. (Modified from Scheidt et al., 2001).

In this model, y_n and B_n are, respectively, the error (deviation from linearity) and the input (field gain) at the nth trial. An estimation of the time windows L and M of the autoregressive process showed that the error at the current trial is only affected by the current input and by the immediately preceding input and error. The previous expression can then be rewritten as

$$y_i = a_1\, y_{i-1} + b_0\, B_i + b_1\, B_{i-1}. \qquad (24.21)$$

A simple transformation establishes the equivalence between this $L = M = 1$ model and

the formulation of Thoroughman and Shadmehr (2000), shown in Equation 24.19.

11. Noise and Uncertainty

The representation of motor plans and of actuator commands as force fields is directly related to the control of movements in uncertain and noisy environments. This is perhaps one of the most distinctive features of biological controllers. Unlike most robots, biological systems have evolved to interact with environments that change in unpredictable ways. In addition, muscles and sense organs are abundant but noisy and subject to variations in their transduction properties (van Beers, Baraduc, & Wolpert, 2002). Under these conditions, adaptability appears to be more valuable and achievable than precision. Indeed, the force-field approximation (Equation 24.8) does not insure the precise execution of a planned motion $q_D(t)$. The approximating field provides, at most, a prescription for driving the system in the face of external perturbations. Perhaps the most critical feature of this approach is that it ensures the stability of the resulting behavior. Biological organisms are not as precise as many machines, but they typically tolerate errors and recover from them much better.

The external environment is not the only source of noise. The analysis of motor unit activities (Matthews, 1996) indicates that the variance of these signals is tightly coupled to their amplitude. Harris and Wolpert (1998) have proposed that the smoothness of natural motions observed in different behaviors (e.g., arm and eye movements) may be accounted for by assuming that the biological controller minimizes the final error while being subject to signal-dependent noise. This proposal is based on the idea that violations of smoothness, such as a large swing in a trajectory, are associated with large-amplitude control signals. Given that the signal variance accumulates additively along a movement, the net expected outcome of a jerky motion is a larger variance at the final point. Similar considerations are consistent with a more general framework recently proposed by Todorov and Jordan (2002), who observed that in the presence of redundancy, one may identify within the space of control signals a lower-dimensional "task-relevant" manifold. This manifold contains the combinations of motor commands that have a direct impact on the achievement of the established goal. Because of redundancy, at each point of this manifold there is a null space of control signals that do not affect the execution of the task. For example, when we place the index finger on a letter key, we may do so through infinitely

many different arm configurations; it is these irrelevant combinations that are associated with control signals in the null space. A common observation across a variety of behaviors is that variability tends to be higher in the task-irrelevant dimensions. Todorov and Jordan (2002) consider this to be a direct consequence of optimal feedback control. In this formulation, the control system aims at minimizing the expected final error in the presence of signal-dependent noise. While the outcomes of the optimization may depend on the specific distribution of variability among the many actuators, the simulations presented by these authors indicate a general tendency of the control system to displace the variance into the task-irrelevant dimensions, so as to achieve a higher degree of precision in the task-relevant dimensions. This view of the biological control system brings about two important (although yet to be proven valid) concepts: (1) that the control system is not concerned with the explicit planning of trajectories but rather with the attainment of final goals with the least amount of variance, and (2) that the space spanned by the task-irrelevant dimensions plays the role of a "variance buffer", where the noise generated by the control signals may be concentrated so as to attain a more consistent performance in the relevant space as defined by the task.

Although this is a promising approach with interesting implications for the design of biomimetic controllers, the evidence for the explicit planning of trajectories remains rather strong. In some cases, the regularity of trajectories in endpoint coordinates is hard to be accounted for by mechanisms – such as the minimization of the effects of signal-dependent noise – that depend on the geometrical, mechanical, and control properties of the musculoskeletal system and of the neural controller.

The probabilistic framework of Bayes' theory provides a conceptual tool for connecting the formation of internal models with their stability in the face of variable environments. It is generally reasonable to assume that the perturbations caused by the environment and the fluctuations associated with a biological controller are not strictly deterministic. The uncertainty due to both the variability of the external world and the imperfect detection of its features would lead to internal models that are essentially probabilistic and thus represented as probability distributions over the possible values of a dynamical variable, such as the amplitude or direction of a perturbing force. Issues related to the ability of neural populations to both represent and manipulate probability distributions are the subject of active current research (Jazayeri & Movshon, 2006; Ma et al., 2006).

12. Bayesian Framework for Motor Learning

In the development of forward and inverse models for motor control, the central nervous system has to deal with the intrinsic variability of the external environment as well as noise in the detection of sensory inputs and the execution of motor commands. This scenario naturally leads to internal representations that are probabilistic in nature. A Bayesian approach then provides a powerful tool for the optimal estimation of policies (in the case of the inverse map) or states (in the case of the forward map). The Bayesian formulation discussed in this section results in an inference problem that is not necessarily easier to solve than the original control problem. However, it is posed in a computational language that is intrinsically probabilistic and thus quite natural to the workings of a central nervous system that relies on noisy inputs and noisy processors.

To examine the implications of variability, let us first consider motion in the absence of external forces (i.e., $E = 0$ in Equation 24.8). A given sequence of motor commands $u(t)$, if repeated many times, will not lead to a unique trajectory but to outcomes that are best described as a probability distribution over the state variables $(q(t), \dot{q}(t))$. The conditional probability distribution $P(q, \dot{q} \mid u)$ provides a statistical description of the expected trajectories given the control signal $u(t)$, as re-

quired of the forward model. A probabilistic forward model provides a tool for statistical state estimation; the ability to do so is crucial to compensate for the delays involved in the processing of sensory feedback.

Bayes theorem provides a simple relation for inverting conditional probability distributions (Bolstad, 2004):

$$P(u \mid q, \dot{q}) = \frac{P(q, \dot{q} \mid u) P(u)}{P(q, \dot{q})}. \quad (24.22)$$

This simple inversion formula expresses the conditional probability distribution that underlies the inverse model as a product of the conditional probability $P(q, \dot{q} \mid u)$ associated with the forward model and a prior distribution $P(u)$ that describes the available repertoire of motor commands, as established by previous experience. This prior can be used to bias the posterior distribution toward a particular class of control signals and to restrict the posterior distribution to the set of signals that are implementable by the biological controller. The denominator is a normalization factor obtained by summing the numerator over all possible motor commands; it guarantees that the right side of Equation 24.22 is a well-defined probability distribution over possible motor control signals u. A specific inverse map is obtained by choosing, for a desired trajectory $(q_D(t), \dot{q}_D(t))$, the motor command $\hat{u}$ that maximizes $P(u \mid q_D(t), \dot{q}_D(t))$. In the Bayesian framework, this optimization corresponds to the maximum-a-posteriori (MAP) estimate of u (DeGroot, 1970). This selection of an optimal policy through the maximization of a posterior distribution over possible control signals given the goal state $(q_D(t), \dot{q}_D(t))$ is similar to the approach of planning by probabilistic inference proposed by Attias (2003) for the case of discrete states and actions. Both formulations rely on the Bayesian inversion of Equation 24.22, and neither includes the effect of environmental influences that can affect the state.

The Bayesian formulation also provides a tool for incorporating the effect of external forces that modify the dynamics (i.e., $E \neq 0$ in Equation 24.8). In this case, a probabilistic characterization of the forward model requires knowledge of the full conditional distribution $P(q, \dot{q} \mid u, E)$. A simplified formulation suffices if the external forces correspond to a discrete number of possibilities $\{E_i\}$ with prior probabilities $\{p_i = P(E_i)\}$; this prior encodes information about the relative frequency of the various external environments, and it could also be formulated so as to incorporate information about the structured manner, if any, in which the environment changes over time.

In this discrete case, the Bayesian framework can be implemented through a modular architecture in which multiple forward models $P(q, \dot{q} \mid u, E_i)$ operate in parallel (Wolpert & Kawato, 1998). Each forward model provides a statistical description of the effect of a motor command $u(t)$ within a specific environment E_i. The current distribution of probabilities $\{p_i\}$ over the various models of the environment leads to the selection of the most likely forward model $P(q, \dot{q} \mid u, E_i^*)$, where E_i^* is the environment for which p_i is maximal. The corresponding inverse conditional probability $P(u \mid q, \dot{q}, E_i^*)$, defined as in Equation 24.23, guides the selection of an optimal motor command $\hat{u}(t)$ for the desired trajectory $(q_D(t), \dot{q}_D(t))$ in the environment E_i^*, currently estimated to be the most likely one. The resulting trajectory $(\bar{q}(t), \dot{\bar{q}}(t))$ can be used to evaluate the likelihood of every model; the likelihood is the probability $P(\bar{q}(t), \dot{\bar{q}}(t) \mid u, E_i)$ of the observed trajectory $(\bar{q}(t), \dot{\bar{q}}(t))$ in the environment E_i given the control signal $u(t)$. Within the computational variables accessible to the central nervous system, these likelihoods can be evaluated by comparing the optimal trajectory predicted by each forward model $P(q, \dot{q} \mid u, E_i)$ to the actual trajectory $(\bar{q}(t), \dot{\bar{q}}(t))$. The resulting difference is inversely related to the likelihood: The better the agreement between predicted and observed trajectories, the more likely the model E_i (Wolpert & Ghahramani, 2000). The probability of each model can then be re-evaluated by combining the prior and the likelihood according to Bayes rule:

$$P(E_i \mid \bar{q}(t), \dot{\bar{q}}(t), u)$$
$$= \frac{P(\bar{q}(t), \dot{\bar{q}}(t) \mid u, E_i) P(E_i \mid u)}{P(\bar{q}(t), \dot{\bar{q}}(t) \mid u)}. \quad (24.23)$$

The denominator is again a normalization constant, obtained in this case by summing over all environments $\{E_i\}$. The updated probabilities $P(E_i \mid q(t), \dot{q}(t), u)$ give a new ranking of the likely environments; a new winner E_i^* is chosen so as to maximize the posterior $P(E_i \mid q(t), \dot{q}(t), u)$. It is the inverse conditional probability $P(u \mid q, \dot{q}, E_i^*)$ associated with this newly selected model that now determines the optimal motor command $\hat{u}(t)$ to obtain a desired trajectory $(q_D(t), \dot{q}_D(t))$ (Wolpert & Ghahramani, 2000). The online implementation of this iterative Bayesian approach would lead to a continuous update of motor commands so as to reflect the current characterization of the environment; this is an adaptive inverse model based on the recursive use of probabilistic forward and inverse models.

An open question that might be amenable to Bayesian analysis is that of the formation of the forward conditional probabilities $P(q, \dot{q} \mid u, E_i)$. The existing ones need to be maintained, but also updated to reflect changes in the intrinsic dynamical properties of limbs, and novel forward conditional probabilities need to be developed as subjects confront novel environments. A tantalizing possibility is that a Bayesian description of the acquisition of such probabilistic maps could be formulated in the context of characterization of the environment through the superposition of primitive fields, as in Equation 24.11.

13. Architectures for Neural Computation

The problem of motor control, as reviewed in preceding sections, requires a variety of computational tasks to be implemented by neural ensembles. A large body of research in artificial neural networks has established some principles that relate network connectivity to computational functionality. Here, we review neural network models whose architecture is particularly well suited for the implementation of computational tasks relevant to motor control. For a related discussion, see Chapter 2 in this volume.

Force field vectors, whose amplitude and direction depend on the position of a limb as described by its endpoint coordinates x, have been mapped out in experiments based on microstimulation of spinal interneurons in the frog (Bizzi et al., 1991; Giszter et al., 1993). The resulting force fields exhibit an interesting property: They converge toward a stable equilibrium point within the two-dimensional space of attainable limb positions. To the extent that these force fields have zero curl, a condition met in related experiments on human subjects (Mussa-Ivaldi et al., 1985), it is possible to construct a scalar potential function $U(x)$ such that the observed force field is given by the gradient $\nabla U(x)$. The existence of a single stable equilibrium point for the force field corresponds to the existence of a unique minimum for the potential function $U(x)$. This observation, together with the dissipative nature of limb dynamics, suggest that the scalar potential $U(x)$ plays the role of an *energy function* that describes the dynamics of an *attractor neural network* (Amit, 1989). The existence of a relatively small number of distinct force fields associated with a large set of muscle elements could thus be modeled through an equivalently small number of attractor neural networks, each one of them constructed so as to reproduce the flow of the corresponding force field. The energy function associated with each one of these networks is the scalar function $U(x)$, whose local gradient maps a force field such as the one shown in Figure 24.4D. Movements generated as a combination of these few force-field primitives can be represented through a *mixture of experts* network (Jacobs et al., 1988), constructed as a linear superposition of individual modules. To implement the desired superposition, the modules would be attractor

neural networks associated with the force-field primitives (Wolpert & Ghahramani, 2000).

The implementation of a desired trajectory $x(t)$ in the endpoint coordinate representation requires a map from the state of the endpoint, as described by $(x, \dot{x})$, into a force $F(x, \dot{x}, t)$ that may also depend explicitly on time. This map from a *state* into an *action* can be easily captured in the framework of a *layered neural network* (Bishop, 1996). Training a layered neural network to implement the desired map from states into actions requires a training set, which can be acquired in the context of imitative learning (Atkeson & Schaal, 1997). The detailed observation of policies implemented so as to achieve a desired trajectory, in conjunction with the determination of endpoint state variables, could provide the data needed to train a layered neural network using standard algorithms for supervised learning (Bishop, 1996). Further training, based on generating actual trajectories and comparing them to desired trajectories so as to obtain an error signal, will be necessary to provide the layered network with some degree of robustness against noise and/or uncertainty in the input (sensory information on current state) or the output (actuated policy).

Of particular importance for the accurate execution of movements is the use of a control function $u(t)$ (see Equation 24.1), which can take the form of activation signals to motoneurons (in the language of actuator coordinates) or of a desired limb position (in the language of endpoint coordinates). The motion described by Equation 24.1 can be interpreted as an iterative map in a $2n$-dimensional tangent bundle (Jose & Saletan, 1998): This is the manifold spanned by the generalized coordinates $q = (q_1, q_2, \ldots, q_n)$ and the generalized velocities $\dot{q} = (\dot{q}_1, \dot{q}_2, \ldots, \dot{q}_n)$. When complemented with n equations of the form $\dot{q}_i = dq_i/dt$, $1 \leq i \leq n$, the n equations for $\ddot{q}_i$ (compactly expressed in vector form in Equation 24.1) define unique trajectories in the $(q, \dot{q})$ manifold of state variables. The state $(q, \dot{q})$ of the system at time $(t + dt)$

is uniquely and completely determined by the state at time t and by the control signal $u(t)$.

The appropriate neural network architecture to represent the action of the control signal on the $(q, \dot{q})$ manifold – that is to implement a forward model – is intermediate to the fully recurrent architecture of attractor neural networks and the purely feedforward architecture of layered neural networks. We specifically refer here to networks such as those described by Jordan and Elman (Elman, 1990; Jordan & Rosenbaum, 1989), which consist of a two-layered feedforward network whose intermediate layer receives as input not only the external input, but also a copy of its own state at the preceding time-step. This additional input provides mechanisms for implementing lateral connections that result in dynamical recurrence within the intermediate layer. For the control problem of interest here, the intermediate layer would encode the state $(q, \dot{q})$ of the system at time $(t + dt)$, as a function of its two inputs: the control signal and the state at time t. The connections from the intermediate layer to the output layer can be adjusted so as to implement the map L from generalized to endpoint coordinates (Figure 24.2). A comparison between actual and desired endpoint trajectories would generate an error signal to be fed back into the network for adjusting the connections that describe the effect of the control signal on the state and on the output of the system.

This brief discussion suggests that the computational demands of the execution and control of movements incorporates many facets, whose description in terms of neural computation involves different network models, ranging from fully recurrent to purely feedforward architectures and including hybrid models between these extremes. The choice of a suitable architecture in an artificial emulation of a neural system depends on the emphasis and the specific formulation of the problem, be it in the format of generating appropriate policies for endpoint coordinates or of characterizing the effects of control signals on the dynamics as described in generalized coordinates.

14. Conclusions

Current models of motor control emphasize the need to address the transformations that relate coordinates appropriate for the description of the external environment, the system of actuator signals and corresponding muscle activations, and the system of joint angles that describe the state of the skeletal system. A systematic investigation of the relations between these three different coordinate systems provides a framework for analyzing the redundancy of a musculoskeletal system controlled by a number of signals that far exceeds the number of independent degrees of freedom involved in the execution of specific motor tasks.

Carefully designed experiments reviewed in this chapter have revealed the emergence and consolidation of internal representations of extrinsic coordinates that describe the environment in which movements take place. When subjected to specific patterns of perturbations to the intrinsic dynamics of the limbs, additional representations of state-dependent forces are also easily acquired. The inability to generalize after adaptation to time-dependent forces that do not exhibit a reproducible dependence on state variables suggests that the adaptive controller fails to create an internal representation of time-dependent forces.

Two types of internal models are necessary for the successful implementation of desired movements: forward models able to predict the motor outcome of control signals, and inverse models able to identify the motor signals needed to produce a desired motor outcome. Forward models are comparatively easy to acquire, as the observation of discrepancies between the predicted and the actual movement triggered by repeated applications of specific control signals provides an error signal that can be used to iteratively train and improve forward models. The acquisition of inverse models is generally a more difficult task, due to the lack of a training signal in the form of an error that can be cast as a specific suggested change in motor control signals. A conceptual application of Bayesian statistics suggests that a probabilistic description, imposed by the intrinsic variability of the external environment as well as noise in the detection of sensory inputs and the execution of motor commands, might provide a mechanism for obtaining inverse models through a Bayesian inversion of the corresponding forward models.

Another powerful tool for the identification of control policies which are appropriate for the execution of desired movements follows from a particular formulation of the control problem. Specifically, we refer to the problem of choosing control signals that best approximate the required generalized forces to be generated by the muscular apparatus, and expressed as a field over the state space of the moving limb. This formulation is particularly well suited for the description of movements in terms of muscle synergies or motor primitives that provide a basis for the generation of a wide repertoire of movements. An open question for future research is the connection between this formulation and probabilistic descriptions.

References

Albus, J. (1971). The theory of cerebellar function. *Mathematical Biosciences*, *10*, 25–61.

Amit, D. (1989). *Modelling brain function: The world of attractor neural networks*. Cambridge, UK: Cambridge University Press.

Atkeson, C., & Schaal, S. (1997). *Robot learning from demonstration*. Paper presented at the Machine Learning: Proceedings of the Fourteenth International Conference (ICML '97), July 8–12, Nashville, TN.

Attias, H. (2003). Planning by probabilistic inference. In C. M. Bishop & B. J. Frey (Eds.), *Proceedings of the Ninth International Workshop on Artificial Intelligence and Statistics*. Key West, FL.

Bernstein, N. (1967). *The coordination and regulation of movement*. Oxford, UK: Pergamon Press.

Bhushan, N., & Shadmehr, R. (1999). Computational nature of human adaptive control during learning of reaching movements in force fields. *Biological Cybernetics*, *81*, 39–60.

Bishop, C. (1996). *Neural networks for pattern recognition*. Oxford, UK: Oxford University Press.

Bizzi, E., Accornero, N., Chapple, W., & Hogan, N. (1984). Posture control and trajectory formation during arm movement. *Journal of Neuroscience*, *4*(11), 2738–2744.

Bizzi, E., Hogan, N., Mussa-Ivaldi, F., & Giszter, S. (1992). Does the nervous system use equilibrium-point control to guide single and multiple joint movements? *Behavioral and Brain Sciences*, *15*, 603–613.

Bizzi, E., & Mussa-Ivaldi, F. (1998). The acquisition of motor behavior. *Daedalus*, *127*, 217–232.

Bizzi, E., Mussa-Ivaldi, F., & Giszter, S. (1991). Computations underlying the execution of movement: A biological perspective. *Science*, *253*, 287–291.

Bolstad, W. L. (2004). *Introduction to Bayesian statistics*. Hoboken, NJ: John Wiley and Sons.

Brady, M., Hollerbach, J., Johnson, T., Lozano-Perez, T., & Mason, M. (1982). *Robot motion: Planning and control*. Cambridge, MA: MIT Press.

Brashers-Krug, T., Shadmehr, R., & Bizzi, E. (1996). Consolidation in human motor memory. *Nature*, *382*, 252–255.

Conditt, M. A., Gandolfo, F., & Mussa-Ivaldi, F. A. (1997). The motor system does not learn the dynamics of the arm by rote memorization of past experience. *Journal of Neurophysiology*, *78*(1), 554–560.

Conditt, M. A., & Mussa-Ivaldi, F. A. (1999). Central representation of time during motor learning. *Proceedings of the National Academy of Sciences, USA*, *96*, 11625–11630.

DeGroot, M. (1970). *Optimal statistical decisions*. New York: McGraw-Hill.

Elman, J. L. (1990). Finding structure in time. *Cognitive Science*, *14*, 179–211.

Feldman, A. (1966). Functional tuning of the nervous system during control of movement or maintenance of a steady posture. II. Controllable parameters of the muscles. III. Mechanographic analysis of the execution by man of the simplest motor task. *Biophysics*, *11*, 565–578, 766–755.

Feldman, A. G. (1986). Once more on the equilibrium-point hypothesis (lambda model) for motor control. *Journal of Motor Behavior*, *18*, 17–54.

Flanagan, J., & Wing, A. (1997). The role of internal models in motion planning and control: Evidence from grip force adjustments during movements of hand-held loads. *Journal of Neuroscience*, *17*, 1519–1528.

Flash, T., & Hogan, N. (1985). The coordination of arm movements: An experimentally confirmed mathematical model. *Journal of Neuroscience, 5,* 1688–1703.

Giszter, S. F., Mussa-Ivaldi, F. A., & Bizzi, E. (1993). Convergent force fields organized in the frog's spinal cord. *Journal of Neuroscience, 13*(2), 467–491.

Goldstein, H. (1980). *Classical mechanics* (2nd ed.). Reading, MA: Addison-Wesley.

Gutfreund, Y., Flash, T., Fiorito, G., & Hochner, B. (1998). Patterns of arm muscle activation involved in octopus reaching movements. *18,* 5976–5987.

Harris, C. M., & Wolpert, D. M. (1998). Signal-dependent noise determines motor planning. *Nature, 394,* 780–784.

Hatfield, G. (2003). Representation and constraints: The inverse problem and the structure of visual space. *Acta Psychologica, 114,* 355–378.

Hill, A. V. (1938). The heat of shortening and the dynamic constants of muscle. *Proceeding of the Royal Society of London, Series B, Biological Sciences, 126,* 136–195.

Hogan, N. (1984). An organizing principle for a class of voluntary movements. *Journal of Neuroscience, 4,* 2745–2754.

Hogan, N. (1985). The mechanics of multi-joint posture and movement control. *Biological Cybernetics, 52,* 315–331.

Hogan, N., Bizzi, E., Mussa-Ivaldi, F., & Flash, T. (1987). Controlling multi-joint motor behavior. *Exercise and Sport Sciences Reviews, 15,* 153–190.

Holdefer, R. N., & Miller, L. E. (2002). Primary motor cortical neurons encode functional muscle synergies. *Experimental Brain Research, 146,* 233–243.

Hore, J., Ritchi, R., & Watts, S. (1999). Finger opening in an overarm throw is not triggered by proprioceptive feedback from elbow extension or wrist flexion. *Experimental Brain Research, 125,* 301–312.

Huxley, A. F. (1957). Muscle structure and theories of contraction. *Progress in Biophysics and BioPhysical Chemistry, 7,* 257–318.

Jacobs, R., Jordan, M. I., Nowlan, S. J., & Hinton, G. E. (1988). Adaptive mixtures of local experts. *Neural Computation, 3,* 79–87.

Jami, L. (1992). Golgi tendon organs in mammalian skeletal muscle: Functional properties and central actions. *Physiological Reviews, 72,* 623–666.

Jazayeri, M., & Movshon, J. A. (2006). Optimal representation of sensory information by neural populations. *Nature Neuroscience, 9,* 690–696.

Jordan, M., & Rumelhart, D. (1992). Forward models: Supervised learning with a distal teacher. *Cognitive Science, 16,* 307–354.

Jordan, M. I., & Rosenbaum, D. A. (1989). Action. In M. I. Posner (Ed.), *Foundations of cognitive science* (pp. 727–767). Cambridge, MA: MIT Press.

Jose, J. V., & Saletan, E. J. (1998). *Classical dynamics: A contemporary approach.* Cambridge, UK: Cambridge University Press.

Karniel, A., & Mussa-Ivaldi, F. A. (2003). Sequence, time or state representation: How does the motor control system adapt to variable environments? *Biological Cybernetics, 89,* 10–21.

Kawato, M., & Wolpert, D. (1998). Internal models for motor control. *Novartis Foundation Symposium, 218,* 291–304.

Kelso, J. A. S. (1995). *Dynamic patterns.* Cambridge, MA: MIT Press.

Kugler, P. N., & Turvey, M. T. (1987). *Information, natural law, and the self-assembly of rhythmic movement.* Mahwah, NJ: Lawrence Erlbaum.

Lansner, A., Kotaleski, J. H., & Grillner, S. (1998). Modeling of the spinal neuronal circuitry underlying locomotion in a lower vertebrate. *Annals of the New York Academy of Sciences, 860,* 239–249.

Latash, M. L. (1998). *Neurophysiological basis of movement.* Champaign, IL: Human Kinetics.

Leeser, K., & Townsend, W. T. (1997, December). Control and exploitation of kinematic redundancy in torque controllable manipulators via multiple-jacobian superposition. In *Proceedings of the First International Conference on Field and Service Robotics,* Canberra, Australia.

Lemay, M., & Grill, W. (1999, October). Endpoint forces evoked by microstimulation of the cat spinal cord. Paper presented at the 20th Annual International Conference of the IEEE Engineering in Medicine and Biology. Hong Kong, China.

Ljung, L. (1999). *System identification. Theory for the user.* Upper Saddle River, NJ: Prentice Hall.

Lohmiller, W., & Slotine, J.-J. E. (1998). On contraction analysis for nonlinear systems. *Automatica, 34,* 683–696.

Ma, W. J., Beck, J. M., Latham, P. E., & Pouget, A. (2006). Bayesian inference with probabilistic population codes. *Nature Neuroscience, 9,* 1432–1438.

Marr, D. (1969). A theory of cerebellar cortex. *Journal of Physiology, 202,* 437–470.

Marr, D. (1982). *Vision*. San Francisco: W. H. Freeman.

Matthews, P. B. (1996). Relationship of firing intervals of human motor units to the trajectory of post-spike after-hyperpolarization and synaptic noise. *Journal of Physiology, 492,* 597–682.

McIntyre, J., Berthoz, A., & Lacquaniti, F. (1998). Reference frames and internal models. *Brain Research Brain Research Reviews, 28*(1–2), 143–154.

Merton, P. (1972). How we control the contraction of our muscles. *Scientific American, 226,* 30–37.

Miall, R., & Wolpert, D. (1996). Forward models for physiological motor control. *Neural Networks, 9,* 1265–1279.

Morasso, P. (1981). Spatial control of arm movements. *Experimental Brain Research, 42,* 223–227.

Mosier, K. M., Sceidt, R. A., Acosta, S., & Mussa-Ivaldi, F. A. (2005). Remapping hand movements in a novel geometrical environment. *Journal of Neurophysiology, 94,* 4362–4372.

Mussa-Ivaldi, F., Giszter, S., & Bizzi, E. (1990). Motor-space coding in the central nervous system. *Cold Spring Harbor Symposium on Quantitative Biology: The Brain, 55,* 827–835.

Mussa-Ivaldi, F., Hogan, N., & Bizzi, E. (1985). Neural, mechanical and geometrical factors subserving arm posture in humans. *Journal of Neuroscience, 5,* 2732–2743.

Mussa-Ivaldi, F. A. (1997, July). Nonlinear force fields: A distributed system of control primitives for representing and learning movements. Paper presented at the 1997 IEEE International Symposium on Computational Intelligence in Robotics and Automation. (CIRA97), Monterey, CA.

Mussa-Ivaldi, F. A. (2002). Geometrical principles in motor control. In M. A. Arbib (Ed.), *Handbook of brain theory* (2nd ed.). Cambridge, MA: MIT Press.

Mussa-Ivaldi, F. A., & Bizzi, E. (2000). Motor learning through the combination of primitives. *Philosophical Transactions of the Royal Society. London B, 355,* 1755–1769.

Mussa-Ivaldi, F. A., Giszter, S. F., & Bizzi, E. (1994). Linear combinations of primitives in vertebrate motor control. *Proceedings of the National Academy of Sciences of the United States of America, 91,* 7534–7538.

Mussa-Ivaldi, F. A., & Hogan, N. (1991). Integrable solutions of kinematic redundancy via impedance control. *The International Journal of Robotics Research, 10,* 481–491.

Nichols, T. R. (2002). The contributions of muscles and reflexes to the regulation of joint and limb mechanics. *Clinical Orthopaedics and Related Research, 403* (Suppl.), S43-S50.

Ogata, K. (1997). *Modern control engineering.* Upper Saddle River, NJ: Prentice Hall.

Rack, P. M. H., & Westbury, D. R. (1969). The effects of length and stimulus rate on tension in the isometric cat soleus muscle. *Journal of Physiology, 204,* 443–460.

Sabes, P., Jordan, M., & Wolpert, D. (1998). The role of inertial sensitivity in motor planning. *Journal of Neuroscience, 18*(15), 5948–5957.

Saltzman, E., & Kelso, J. A. S. (1987). Skilled actions: A task-dynamic approach. *Psychological Reviews, 94,* 84–106.

Scheidt, R. A., Dingwell, J. B., & Mussa-Ivaldi, F. A. (2001). Learning to move amid uncertainty. *Journal of Neurophysiology, 86,* 971–985.

Sciavicco, L., & Siciliano, B. (2000). *Modeling and control of robot manipulators.* New York: Springer-Verlag.

Shadmehr, R., & Mussa-Ivaldi, F. A. (1994). Adaptive representation of dynamics during learning of a motor task. *Journal of Neuroscience, 14*(5), 3208–3224.

Shepard, R. N. (2001). Perceptual-cognitive universals as reflections of the world. *Behavioral and Brain Sciences, 24,* 581–601.

Sherrington, C. (1910). Flexion-reflex of the limb, crossed extension reflex and reflex stepping and standing. *Journal of Physiology, 40,* 28–121.

Sherrington, C. S. (1906). *The integrative action of the nervous system.* New York: Charles Scribner's Sons.

Soechting, J. F., & Lacquaniti, F. (1981). Invariant characteristics of a pointing movement in man. *Journal of Neuroscience, 1,* 710–720.

Sutton, R., & Barto, A. (1998). *Reinforcement learning: An introduction.* Cambridge, MA: MIT Press.

Thoroughman, K. A., & Shadmehr, R. (2000). Learning of action through adaptive combination of motor primitives. *Nature, 407,* 742–747.

Todorov, E., & Jordan, M. I. (2002). Optimal feedback control as a theory of motor coordination. *Nature Neuroscience, 5,* 1226–1235.

Tresch, M. C., & Bizzi, E. (1999). Responses to spinal microstimulation in the chronically spinalized rat and their relationship to spinal systems activated by low threshold cutaneous stimulation. *Experimental Brain Research, 129,* 401–416.

Uno, Y., Kawato, M., & Suzuki, R. (1989). Formation and control of optimal trajectory in human multijoint arm movement. *Biological Cybernetics, 61,* 89–101.

van Beers, R. J., Baraduc, P., & Wolpert, D. M. (2002). Role of uncertainty in sensorimotor control. *Philosophical Transactions of the Royal Society of London – Series B: Biological Sciences, 357,* 1137–1145.

Wolpert, D., & Kawato, M. (1998). Multiple paired forward and inverse models for motor control. *Neural Networks, 11,* 1317–1329.

Wolpert, D., Miall, R., & Kawato, M. (1998). Internal models in the cerebellum. *Trends in Cognitive Sciences, 2,* 338–347.

Wolpert, D. M., & Ghahramani, Z. (2000). Computational principles of movement neuroscience. *Nature Neuroscience, 3,* 1212–1217.

Part IV

Concluding Remarks

This part contains chapters that provide some historical and theoretical perspectives, as well as speculations, on computational psychology. They explore a range of issues relevant to computational cognitive modeling, and provide some evaluations and assessments.

CHAPTER 25

An Evaluation of Computational Modeling in Cognitive Science

Margaret A. Boden

1. Introduction

Computer modeling of specific psychological processes began over fifty years ago, with work on draughts playing, logical problem solving, and learning/conditioning (Boden, 2006: 6.iii, 10.i.c–e, 12.ii). Some of this work involved what is now called GOFAI, or good old-fashioned artificial intelligence (AI) (Haugeland, 1985: 112), and some involved what is now called connectionist AI (see Chapter 1 in this volume). In addition, cyberneticians were modeling very general principles believed to underlie intelligent behavior. Their physical simulations included robots representing reflex and adaptive behavior, self-organizing "homeostatic" machines, and chemical solutions undergoing dynamical change (Boden, 2006: 4.v.e, 4.viii). There was no ill-tempered rivalry between symbolists and connectionists then, as there would be later. The high points – or the low points, perhaps – of such passionate rivalry appeared on both sides of this intellectual divide.

The first prominent attack was Marvin Minsky and Seymour Papert's (1969) cri-

tique of perceptrons, an early form of connectionism (Rosenblatt, 1958). This caused something of a scandal at the time and is often blamed – to some extent, unjustly (Boden, 2006: 12.iii.e) – for the twenty-year connectionist "winter," in which virtually all the Defense Advanced Research Projects Agency (DARPA) funds for AI were devoted to symbolic approaches.

Some ten years after Minsky and Papert, Douglas Hofstadter (1979, 1983/1985) published a fundamental critique of symbolism, which aroused significant excitement, even in the media. In particular, he criticized the static nature of concepts as viewed by traditional AI, arguing instead that they are constantly changing, or "fluid." Hofstadter's attack on classical AI was soon echoed by the newly popular research on PDP, or parallel distributed processing, networks (McClelland, Rumelhart, & PDP Group, 1986; Rumelhart, McClelland, & PDP Group 1986). But the old "enemy" counterattacked: In response to the PDP challenge, an uncompromising defense of symbolism was mounted by Jerry Fodor and Zenon Pylyshyn (1988). As for Minsky and

Papert, they defiantly reissued their book – with a new Prologue and Epilogue – refusing to back down from their original position (Minsky & Papert, 1988).

The connectionist/symbolist divide was not the only one to cause people's tempers to rise. A more recent source of controversy was the (continuing) debate over situated cognition and robotics. The situationists stressed instant reactivity and embodiment, and played down the role of representations (Agre & Chapman, 1987, 1991; Brooks, 1991a, 1991b). Their opponents argued that representations and planning are essential for the higher mental processes, at least (Kirsh, 1991; Vera & Simon, 1993). (Ironically, one of the first to stress the reactive nature of much animal, and human, behavior had been the high-priest of symbolism himself, Simon [1969]).

This explicitly anti-Cartesian approach often drew from the phenomenological philosophers Martin Heidegger and Maurice Merleau-Ponty, as well as the later Wittgenstein (Clark, 1997; Wheeler, 2005). Indeed, these writers had inspired one of the earliest, and most venomous, attacks on AI and cognitive science (Dreyfus, 1965, 1972). Given the fact that phenomenological ("Continental") approaches have gained ground even among analytically trained philosophers over the last twenty years (McDowell, 1994), there are many people today who feel that Hubert Dreyfus had been right all along (e.g., Haugeland 1996). Predictably, however, many others disagree.

Much of the interest – and certainly much of the excitement – in the past forty years of research on cognitive modeling has been in the see-sawing dialectics of these two debates. But in the very earliest days, the debates had hardly begun. When they did surface, they were carried out with less passion and far less rhetorical invective. For at that time, the few afficionados shared a faith that all their pioneering activities were part of the same intellectual endeavor (Blake & Uttley, 1959; Feigenbaum & Feldman, 1963). This endeavor, later termed cognitive science, was a form of psychology (and neuroscience, linguistics, anthropology, and philosophy of mind) whose substantive theoretical concepts would be drawn from cybernetics and AI (Boden, 2006: 1.i–ii).

However, sharing a faith and expressing it persuasively are two different things. The nascent cognitive science needed a manifesto, to spread the ideas of the people already starting to think along these lines and to awaken others to the exciting possibilities that lay in the future. That manifesto, *Plans and the Structure of Behavior*, appeared in 1960. Written by George Miller, Eugene Galanter, and Karl Pribram (henceforth, MGP), it offered an intriguing, not to say intoxicating, picture of a future computational psychology.

It promised formal rigor. Psychological theories would be expressed as AI-inspired plans made up of TOTE-units (test, operate, test, exit). It also promised comprehensiveness. All psychological phenomena were included: animal and human; normal and pathological; cognitive and motivational/ emotional; instinctive and learned; perception, language, problem solving, and memory were covered or anyway briefly mentioned. In those behaviorist-dominated days, MGP's book made the blood race in its readers' veins.

The manifesto had glaring faults, visible even without the benefit of hindsight. It was unavoidably simplistic, for its authors had only half a dozen interesting computer models to draw on, plus Noam Chomsky's (1957) formal-generative theory of language. It was strongly biased toward symbolic AI, although connectionism was mentioned in the footnotes; the reason was that serial order, hierarchical behavior, and propositional inference were then better modeled by GOFAI, as they still are today (see following discussion). Although the concept of informational feedback was prominent, the cyberneticists' concern with dynamical self-organization was ignored. The book was careless in various ways. For instance, MGP's concept of "Image" was said by them to be very important, but was hardly discussed. And, last but not least, it was hugely overoptimistic.

Nevertheless, it was a work of vision. It enthused countless people to start thinking about the mind in a new manner. A good way of assessing today's computational psychology, then, is to compare it with MGP's hopes: How much have they been achieved, and how far are we on the road to their achievement?

Before addressing those questions directly, an important point must be made. A computational psychology is one whose theoretical concepts are drawn from cybernetics and AI. Similarly, computational anthropology and neuroscience focus on the information processing that is carried out in cultures or brains (Boden, 2006: chapters 8 and 14). So cognitive scientists do not use computers merely as tools to do their sums (as other scientists, including many noncomputational psychologists, often do), but also as inspiration about the nature of mental processes. However, whereas they all rely on computational ideas – interpreted very broadly here to include symbolic, connectionist, situationist, and/or dynamical approaches – they do not all get involved in computer modeling.

Sometimes, this is merely a matter of personal choice. Some computational psychologists lack the skills and/or resources that are required to build computer models. In such cases, other researchers may attempt to implement the new theory. Often, however, the lack of implementation is due to the forbidding complexity of the phenomena being considered. Computational theories of hypnosis, for example, or of the structure of the mind as a whole, are not expressed as functioning computer models (although, as shown in Section 3, some limited aspects of them may be fruitfully modeled).

Accordingly, nonmodeled computational theories as well as programmed simulations and robots will be discussed. After all, the theoretical concepts concerned are not based on mere speculative hand-waving: they are grounded in the theorists' experience with working AI systems. What is more, MGP themselves, despite all their brash optimism, were not suggesting that personality or paranoia would one day be modeled in detail. Rather, they were arguing that computational concepts could enable us to see how such phenomena are even possible. As discussed in Section 4, the demystification of puzzling possibilities is what science in general is about.

2. The Cognitive Aspects of Cognitive Science

The widely accepted name for this field is a misnomer: Cognitive science is not the science of cognition. Or rather, it is not the science of cognition alone.

In the beginning, indeed, a number of computer simulations were focussed on social and/or emotional matters (Colby, 1964, 1967; Tomkins & Messick, 1963). But the difficulties in modeling multigoal and/or interacting systems were too great. In addition, experimental psychology, largely inspired by information theory, was making important advances in the study of cognition: specifically, perception, attention, and concept formation (Broadbent, 1952a, 1952b, 1958; Bruner, Goodnow, & Austin, 1956). In neuropsychology, Donald Hebb's (1949) exciting ideas about cell assemblies were more readily applied to concepts and memory than to motivation and psychopathology, which he discussed only briefly. And the early AI scientists were more interested in modeling cognitive matters: logic, problem solving, game playing, learning, vision, or language (including translation). As a result, the early advances – and most of the later advances, too – concerned cognition.

Among the most significant work, which inspired MGP and whose influence still persists, was that of Allen Newell and Herbert Simon (Newell, Shaw, & Simon, 1957, 1958, 1959). These men provided examples of heuristic programming, wherein essentially fallible rules of thumb can be used to guide the system through the search space (itself a novel and hugely important, concept). They showed how means-end analysis can be used to generate hierarchically structured plans for problem solving. And Simon's stress on "bounded" rationality was especially important for psychologists. (For a recent, and very different, account of bounded rationality, see Gigerenzer, 2004; Gigerenzer & Goldstein, 1996).

Planning became the focus of a huge amount of research in AI and computational psychology. Increasing flexibility resulted: for instance, self-monitoring and correction, expressing plans at various levels of abstraction, and enabling the last-minute details to be decided during execution (Boden, 1977/1987: chapter 12). In addition, the flexibility exemplified by rapid reaction to interrupts was modeled by Newell and Simon using their new methodology of production systems (1972). Here, goals and plans were represented not by explicit top-down hierarchies but by a host of implicitly related if-then rules. This work was even more closely grounded in psychological experiments (and theories about the brain) than their earlier models had been and led to a wide range of production-system models of thought and motor behavior – from arithmetic, to typing, to seriation. Today, technologically motivated AI plans may comprise tens of thousands of steps (Russell & Norvig, 2003: viii, chapters 11–12).

Another advance seeks to defuse the first of the two often-vitriolic debates identified in Section 1. For although GOFAI and connectionist approaches are often presented as mutually exclusive, there are some interesting hybrid systems. In psychology, for instance, GOFAI plans have been combined with connectionist pattern-recognition and associative memory in computer models of human action and clinical apraxias (Norman & Shallice, 1980). Similarly, deliberative planning is being combined with reactive ("situated") behavior in modern robots (Sahota & Mackworth, 1994). Indeed, there is now a very wide range of hybrid systems, in both psychological and technological AI (Sun, 2001; Sun & Bookman, 1994). In other words, MGP's notion of plans as hierarchies of TOTE-units has been greatly advanced, with the hierarchy often being implicit and the "test" often being carried out by reactive and/or connectionist mechanisms.

The appeal of hybrid systems is that they can combine the advantages of both symbolic and connectionist approaches, for these two methodologies have broadly complementary strengths and weaknesses. As remarked earlier, serial order, hierarchical behavior, and propositional inference are better modeled by GOFAI. Indeed, much of the more recent connectionist research has attempted to provide (the first two of) these strengths to PDP systems (e.g., Elman, 1990, 1993; for other examples, see Boden, 2006: 12.viii–ix). In addition, symbolic models can offer precision (but many, though not all, "crash" in the presence of noise), whereas PDP offers multiple constraint satisfaction and graceful degradation (but is ill-suited to precise calculation wherein $2 + 2$ really does equal 4 and not 3.999 or probably 4).

Vision, too, was a key research area for computational modeling, not least because experimental psychologists had already learned a lot about it. The work on "scene analysis" in the 1960s and 1970s used top-down processing to interpret line-drawings of simple geometrical objects (Boden, 1977/1987: chapters 8–9). This fitted well with then-current ideas about the psychology of perception (Bruner, 1957), and some aspects of human vision were successfully explained in this way (Gregory, 1966, 1967).

In general, however, that approach was unrealistic. For example, if the computer input was a gray-scale image from a camera (as opposed to a line-drawing), it would be converted into a line-drawing by some line-finding program. Gibsonian psychologists complained that a huge amount of potential information was being lost in this way, and David Marr (among others) suggested that this could be captured by bottom-up connectionist processes designed/evolved to exploit the physics of the situation (Marr, 1976, 1982; Marr & Hildreth, 1980). (Marr went on to criticize top-down AI in general and what he saw as the theoretically unmotivated "explanations" offered by psychologists such as Newell and Simon; Marr, 1977. To simulate, he insisted, was not necessarily to explain.)

Work on low-level vision, including enactive vision (wherein much of the information comes as a result of the viewer's own movements, whether of eyes and/or body), has given rich returns over the past quarter-century (Hogg, 1996). But top-down models have been overly neglected. The recognition of indefinitely various objects, which must involve top-down processing exploiting learned categories, is still an unsolved problem. However, the complexity of visual processing, including the use of temporary representations at a number of levels, is now better appreciated. Indeed, computational work of this type has been cited as part inspiration for neuroscientific accounts of "dual-process" vision (Sloman, 1978: chapter 9, 1989; Goodale & Milner 1992; Milner & Goodale, 1993).

Language, which MGP (thanks to Chomsky) had seen as a prime target for their approach, has figured prominently in computational psychology. Both Chomsky's (1957) formalist discussion of grammar and Terry Winograd's (1972) GOFAI model of parsing influenced people to ask computational questions about psychology in general and about language use and development in particular (e.g., Miller & Johnson-Laird, 1976). But neither work was sufficiently tractable to be used as a base for computer models in later psycholinguistic research. (One exception was a model of parsing grounded in Chomskyan grammar, which attempted to explain "garden-path" sentences in terms of a limited working-memory buffer; Marcus, 1979.) Other types of modeling (such as augmented transition networks [ATNs]; Woods, 1973) and other theories of grammar were preferred.

All aspects of language use are now being studied in computational terms. With respect to syntax, many models have utilized a theory that is more computationally efficient than Chomskyan grammar (Gazdar et al., 1985). With respect to semantics, psychological models (and experiments) have been based in work ranging from conceptual dependencies (Schank, 1973), to the theory of scripts (Bransford & Johnson, 1972; Schank & Abelson 1977), to highly formal model-theoretic logic (Johnson-Laird, 1983). The use of language (and imagery) in problem solving has been explored in the theory of "mental models" (Johnson-Laird, 1983). More recently, both situation semantics and blending theory have offered cognitive versions of linguistics and analogical thinking that are deeply informed by the computational approach (Barsalou, 1999; Fauconnier & Turner, 2002). And with respect to pragmatics, computationalists have studied (for instance) speech-acts, focus, and plan-recognition in conversation (Cohen, Morgan, & Pollack, 1990; Cohen & Perrault, 1979; Grosz, 1977).

Machine translation has made significant advances, but has become increasingly statistical and corpus-based: it is an exercise in technological AI rather than computational psychology. Reference to machine translation reminds us that language, with its many ambiguities and rich associative subtleties, has long been regarded as the Achilles' heel of AI. But if perfect use/translation of elegant natural language is in practice (or even in principle) impossible for an AI system, it does not follow that useful language processing is impossible, too.

Still less does it follow that psychologists cannot learn anything about natural language by using a computational approach. What is more, important lessons about psychology in general may be learned in this way.

For instance, a connectionist program simulating the development of the past tense was seen by its authors as a challenge to psychological theories based on nativism and/or formalist rule realism (Rumelhart & McClelland, 1986). This network learned to produce the past tense of verbs in something apparently like how children do, including the temporary overregularization of irregulars (e.g., "goed" instead of "went") that Chomskyans had explained in terms of innate rules. This received (and still receives) attack and defense from Chomskyans and non-Chomskyans, respectively, including attention from developmentalists concerned with the growth of representational trajectories in general (Clark & Karmiloff-Smith,

1993; Pinker & Prince, 1988; Plunkett & Marchman, 1993). The verdict is not clearcut, for further similarities and also differences have been found when comparing network and child. Nevertheless, this is a good example of the use of computational models not only to throw light on specific psychological phenomena but also to explore foundational issues in theoretical psychology.

The computationally inspired, but nonprogrammed, theories of linguistic communication include blending theory, mentioned earlier. But perhaps the best example is Daniel Sperber and Deirdre Wilson's wideranging work on relevance (1986). This uses ideas about the efficiency of information processing to explain how we manage to interpret verbal communications, including those that seem to "break the rules" in various ways. There is no question of capturing the full extent of Sperber and Wilson's theory in a computer model: Language understanding is far too complex for that. But "toy" examples can be modeled. Moreover, their theoretical insights were grounded in their generally computational approach. In other words, even if individual examples of relevance-recognition cannot usually be modeled, their psychological possibility can be computationally understood (see Section 6).

Problem solving, vision, and language are obvious candidates for a cognitive psychology, whether computational or not. But MGP had set their sights even higher, to include, for example, hypnosis and hallucination (MGP 1960: 103f., 108–112). Recently, these phenomena, too, have been theorized by cognitive scientists.

For example, Zoltan Dienes and Josef Perner (in press) have explained hypnosis in terms of "cold control," wherein inference and behavior are directed by executive control but without conscious awareness. Conscious awareness, in their theory, involves higher-order thoughts (HOTs) that are reflexively accessible to (and reportable by) the person concerned. These authors outline computational mechanisms whereby hypnosis of varying types can occur, due to the suppression of HOTs of intention. In do-

ing so, they explain many puzzling facts observed by experimentalists over the years (such as the greater difficulty of inducing positive, as opposed to negative, hallucinations).

The most important topic about which MGP had little or nothing to say was development (see Chapter 16 in this volume). And indeed, for many years, most cognitive scientists ignored development as such. Most assimilated it to learning, as in the past-tense learner. A few used ideas from developmental psychology without considering their specifically developmental aspects, as Alan Kay, when designing human-computer interfaces, borrowed Jerome Bruner's classification of "cognitive technologies" and Jean Piaget's stress on construction and learning-by-doing (Boden, 2006: 13.v). A few Piagetians tried to model stage development (e.g., Young, 1976). But even they failed to take Piaget's core concept of epigenesis fully on board.

By the end of the century, that had changed. Epigenesis was now a word to conjure with even in robotics, never mind developmental psychology (see http://www.epigenetic-robotics.org and Chapter 16 in this volume). Forty years of "Piagetian" research in psychology (Elman et al., 1996; Karmiloff-Smith, 1979, 1986) and neuroscience (Changeux, 1985; Johnson, 1993) had led to theories, and computer models, in which epigenesis was a key feature. Instead of pre-programmed and sudden stage changes, development was conceptualized as a progression of detailed changes due in part to successive environmental influences. The simplistic nature-nurture controversy was rejected, as it had been by Piaget himself. Instead, the concept of innateness was enriched and redefined. This theoretical advance involved both (connectionist) computer modeling and the interdisciplinary integration of empirical research: an example of cognitive science at its best.

Researchers who took epigenesis seriously were naturally sceptical about modularity theories. The picture of the mind as a set of functionally isolated, inherited, and domain-specific modules had been suggested by Chomsky, championed by Jerry Fodor, and supported by evolutionary psychologists in general (Boden, 2006: 7.vi.d–e and i). Fodor (1983), in particular, expressed this twentieth-century version of "faculty psychology" in computational terms. The epigeneticists just mentioned, and especially Annette Karmiloff-Smith (1992), argued that the modularity apparent in the adult develops gradually, both before and after birth, from a source (i.e., a brain) that is much more plastic than orthodox modularity theorists had claimed.

To say (as just mentioned) that Fodor (1983) pictured the mind as a set of modules is not quite accurate. For he also posited "higher mental processes" – of inference, association, interpretation, and creative thinking – which lead us to accept an idiosyncratic collection of beliefs (and desires, intentions, hopes). These thought processes, he said, are domain-general and highly interactive: Were that not so, most poems (for instance) simply could not be written, and most everyday conversations could not happen, either.

However, his view was that such matters (unlike the functioning of modules) are wholly beyond the reach of a computational psychology. Because any two concepts can be combined in an intelligible image or belief, it follows that predicting (or even explaining post hoc) just why someone arrived at this belief rather than that one is impossible, in the general case. And since, according to him, computational psychology is the only psychology we've got, indeed the only psychology it is even worth wanting, there is no hope of our ever having a scientific explanation of beliefs or of the propositional attitudes in general. In short, modules are as good as it gets: The psychology of cognition is a much less wide-ranging enterprise than we had thought.

Whether Fodor was right depends on one's philosophical views about scientific explanation, whether computational or not. Must it involve detailed predictions of specific events (such as accepting a new belief or interpeting an analogy)? Or is it enough that it shows how certain general classes of events, some of which may be prima facie

very puzzling, are possible (and why certain other imaginable events are impossible)? This question will be discussed again in Section 6.

3. Emotions and Motivation

It is part of the human condition that we have many different, sometimes incompatible, motives and desires and that we are subject to a range of emotions that seem to interfere with rational problem solving. These banalities were touched on by MGP and discussed by several others at the outset of computational psychology (e.g., Simon, 1967). But such matters could then be modeled only to a very limited degree. It was difficult enough to write programs dealing with one goal (and its attendant subgoals), never mind more. And it was challenging enough to deal with problems of a well-understood ("logical") kind, in a relatively tractable ("rational") way.

In that context, conflicting motives and disturbing emotions seemed to be computational luxuries that no sensible programmer could afford. Simon himself, in his (and Newell's) huge book of 1972, mentioned emotions only in passing. This is largely why cognitive science is widely (though mistakenly) thought be the science only of cognition.

However, these matters could not be ignored forever. There were two reasons for this. First, emotions and motivation exist, so they should be featured in any comprehensive psychological approach. Second, they are intimately connected with cognitive phenomena, such as language and problem solving, so much so that a fully adequate model of cognition would not be a model of cognition alone. Indeed, both computationalists and neuroscientists have pointed out that in multimotive creatures such as ourselves, "pure" problem solving could not occur without emotional prioritizing.

The neuroscientists based this conclusion on clinical evidence. For example, the brain-damaged patient "Elliot" was, in effect, utterly incompetent, despite his intellect being unimpaired (Damasio, 1994). Asked to perform an individual subtask, he could do so easily. He could even work out all the relevant plans for the task as a whole and foresee the tests that (according to MGP) would be required in executing them. He could compare the possible consequences of different actions, construct contingency plans, and take moral principles and social conventions into account while doing so. What he could not do was choose sensibly between alternative goals or stick with a plan once he had chosen it, or assess other people's motives and personality effectively. His clinician felt that his deficit was not cognitive, but emotional. For he was unable to decide that one goal was more desirable than another (and showed no emotional reaction even to the most dreadful events happening in stories or real life): hence his inability to embark on a plan of action and/or to persevere with it if he did so.

Some cognitive scientists had long used principled computational arguments to arrive at a similar conclusion, namely, that rationality depends on emotion, which is not to deny that emotional response can sometimes make us act irrationally. By the end of the century, emotion had become a hot topic in AI and other areas of cognitive science, including the philosophy of mind (e.g., Evans, 2001; Evans & Druse, 2004). Even technological AI researchers were modeling emotional interrupts and prioritizing (Picard, 1997).

Among the most deeply thought out research on emotion was a longstanding theory, and a more recent computer model, developed by Aaron Sloman's group (Wright & Sloman, 1997; Wright, Sloman, & Beaudoin, 1996). Their program simulates the behavioral effects of several theoretically distinct varieties of anxiety. It represents a nursemaid dealing with several hungry, active babies, with an open door leading onto a water-filled ditch. She has seven different motives (which include feeding a baby if she believes it to be hungry, building a protective fence, and putting a baby behind the fence if it is nearing the ditch) and is subject to continual perceptual and emotional interrupts, which prompt appropriate changes of plan. Different types of anxiety arise because she has to distinguish between important and trivial goals and decide on urgency and postponement. (Feeding a baby is important but not highly urgent, whereas preventing it from falling into a ditch is both.) Because she cannot deal with everything at once, nor pursue all her motives at once, she must schedule her limited resources effectively, which is what emotion, according to Sloman, is basically about (see Section 4).

Such research is a huge advance on the models of emotion that were written over thirty years ago. These simulated the distortions of belief that are characteristic of neurosis and paranoia (Colby, 1964, 1975), and the effects of various (Freudian) types of anxiety on speech (Clippinger, 1977). Even though the virtual nursemaid does not form verbal beliefs, the role of anxiety in her mental economy is captured with some subtlety – and is grounded in an ambitious theory of mental architecture in general (see Section 4).

It is widely believed not only that cognitive science does not deal with emotions, but also that, in principle, it could not. In part, this belief springs from the notion that emotions are feelings and that computation cannot explain (and computers cannot experience) feelings. Whether conscious qualia (such as feelings) can be computationally explained is touched on in Section 5. Here, it must be said that emotions are not just feelings, but also scheduling mechanisms that have evolved to enable rational action in conflict-ridden minds – mechanisms, as we've seen, that can be computationally understood.

In part, however, the widespread belief that emotions – and their close cousins, moods – are beyond the reach of a computational psychology rests on the fact that they appear to depend less on connections than on chemistry. In other words, the neuroscientists tell us that chemical endorphins, and perhaps also rapidly diffusing small molecules such as nitric oxide, underlie very general psychological changes, such as alterations in mood. Because computation (so this objection goes) can model only specific decisions or neural connections, it is fundamentally ill suited to represent moods.

This objection has recently been countered by the development of computational systems called GasNets (Philippides, Husbands, & O'Shea, 1998; Philippides et al., 2005). In a nutshell, these are neural networks wherein the behavior of an individual unit can vary according to the location and concentration of (simulated) rapidly diffusing chemicals. The behavior of the system as a whole differs in distinct chemical circumstances, even though the neural connectivities do not change. GasNets are very different from GOFAI systems and even from orthodox neural networks, not to mention abstract models defined in terms of Turing-computation (see Section 6). As a result, they are able to simulate mental phenomena that seem intuitively to lie outside the range of a computational psychology.

GasNets and the virtual nursemaid reflect, respectively, the differing phenomenology of moods and emotions. Anxiety, for example, is normally directed onto a specific intentional object: that this baby will go hungry or that one will fall into the ditch. Admittedly, free-floating anxiety does seem to occur, but it is atypical. Moods (such as elation or depression), on the other hand, have no particular object but affect everything we do while in their grip. That, perhaps, is just what one would expect if their neurological base is some widely diffusing chemical, as opposed to the activation of a specific neural circuit or cell-assembly. Whether these speculative remarks are correct or not, however, the point is that these computer models show the potential scope of computational explanation to be much wider than most people assume.

4. Full-Fledged Humanity

Sloman's work on anxiety is just a small part of a much wider project, namely, his attempt to sketch the computational architecture of the mind – and possible minds

(Sloman, 1978, 1993, 2000). A similar project is underway at Massachusetts Institute of Technology, thanks to Minsky (2006).

Other examples of architectural research include ACT-R (Anderson, 1983, 1996), SOAR (Laird et al., 1987; Rosenbloom, Laird, & Newell, 1993), and CLARION (Sun, 2006; Sun, Peterson, & Merrill, 1999). These systems are both more and less ambitious than the other two just discussed. "More" because they are largely/fully implemented. "Less" because the range of psychological phenomena they model is narrower than those discussed by Minsky and Sloman (although CLARION, unlike the others, models social interactions: see Chapter 19 in this volume). In a nutshell, they are much more concerned with cognition than emotion and with effective problem solving rather than irrationality or psychopathology. In that sense, they are less relevant to "full-fledged humanity," however impressive they may be as implemented problem-solving systems.

Minsky and Sloman each see the mind as a "society" or "ecology" of agents or subsystems, both evolved and learned (Minsky, 1985; Sloman, 2003). Their overall designs, if successful, should not only illuminate the relation between cognition, motivation, and emotion, but also show how various types of essentially human psychology (and psychopathology) are possible.

For instance, consider the many debilitating effects of grief after bereavement (tearfulness, distractibility, lack of concentration, pangs of guilt, feelings of "meaninglessness") and the need for many months to engage in mourning. These phenomena are familiar to psychiatrists and psychotherapists, and, indeed, to most ordinary people. But being familiar is not the same as being theoretically intelligible. Why (and how) does grief affect us in such a variety of different ways? Why is so much time required for effective mourning? And what is "effective" mourning, anyway? These questions have been addressed in a highly illuminating way by Sloman, in the context of his architectural theory (Wright, Sloman, & Beaudoin, 1966). (If this seems counterintuitive, it is worth noting that the journal editor who published his article on grief is a psychiatrist, well acquainted with the ravages of this phenomenon from clinical practice.)

There is no question, in the foreseeable future, of implementing Sloman's (2003) or Minsky's (1985) systems as a whole. Improved versions of the nursemaid program, and equally limited models of other dimensions of their discussions, are about as much as we can hope for. A skeptic might infer, therefore, that these ambitious mind-mapping projects are mere hand-waving.

Compared with a fully functioning computer model, they are. However, one must recognize that the concepts used, and the hypotheses suggested, by both Sloman and Minsky are based on many years of experience with working AI systems, not to mention many years of thinking about architectural problems. They have been tried and tested separately countless times, in a host of AI models. The question is whether their integration, as sketched by these two writers, is plausible.

Success would involve more than computational plausibility, of course. It also requires consistency with the empirical evidence provided by psychology. So if one could show that the data about hypnosis (for example) or grief simply cannot be fitted within a particular architectural story, then that story would have to be modified. No matter how many improvements were made, of course, no implementation could in practice match the richness of a human mind (see Section 6). That drawback may be excused, however: If physicists are allowed to use inclined planes, psychologists also should be allowed to simplify their theoretical problems. Only if some psychological phenomena remain utterly untouched by the inclined-planes approach can it be criticized as a matter of principle.

It is often argued that consciousness is one such phenomenon that could not ever be illuminated or explained by a computational approach. In rebutting this view, one does not have to endorse the possibility of "machine consciousness," although some computationalists do (e.g., Aleksander, 2000),

and several conferences on "machine consciousness" have been held in recent years. One does not even have to endorse the denial of qualia, although, again, some cognitive scientists do (Dennett, 1991: chapter 12). One need only point out that "conscious" and "consciousness" are terms covering a mixed bag of psychological phenomena (Zelazo, Moscovitch, & Thompson, in press). These range from attention, to deliberate thinking, to self-reflection, even including the nonreciprocal co-consciousness typical of "multiple personality." Each of these has been hugely illuminated by computational approaches (Boden, 2006: 6.i.c–d, 6.iii, 7.i.h, and 7.iv). Indeed, these topics are what, in fact, the conferences on machine consciousness are mostly about.

In short, even if – and it is a philosophically controversial "if" – computational psychology cannot explain the existence of qualia, it can explain many other aspects of consciousness. (What is more, if it cannot do this, then neurophysiology cannot do it, either. Brain scans are not the solution, for correlation is not the same as explanation (Boden, 2006: x–xi.).)

One important aspect of human beings that is acknowledged – and explained – by theories of computational architecture such as these is freedom. To make a long story short (see Boden, 2006: 7.i.g), freedom is a flexibility of action that is not due to any fundamental indeterminacy, but is possible only because of the cognitive and motivational complexity of adult human minds. Various cognitive scientists argued this in the early days (e.g., Boden, 1972: 327–333; Minsky, 1965; Sloman, 1974). Now, with our increased understanding of the computational complexities concerned, the argument can be made more fully (e.g., Arbib & Hesse, 1986: 93–99; Dennett, 1984; Minsky, 1985).

5. Social Interaction

Implicit in MGP's manifesto was the notion that cognitive science could cover social, as well as individual, psychology. And, indeed, some of the early computational theories dealt with this theme. A prime example, systematizing the possible interactions between two people in different roles, was offered by the social psychologist Robert Abelson (1973). However, the topic was soon dropped (except in some models of conversation, e.g., Grosz, 1977; Cohen & Perrault, 1979), as it became clear that modeling even one purposive system was difficult enough. In the 1990s, however, interest in social interaction and distributed cognition burgeoned.

Distributed *representation* had already surfaced as PDP connectionism, wherein networks composed of many different units achieve a satisfactory result by means of mutual communications between those units. This is a form of distributed cognition in that no single unit has access to all of the relevant data and no single unit can represent ("know") the overall result. But PDP methodology was mostly used to model pattern recognition and learning (one highly controversial result was the network that learned to produce the past tense; see Section 2). It was hardly ever used to model social phenomena, because individual PDP units are too simple to be comparable to social beings.

One apparent exception is the work of the anthropologist Edwin Hutchins (1995). He uses communicating *networks* of PDP networks to study the collective problem solving that is involved in navigating a ship. The huge amount, and diversity, of knowledge required is distributed among the various crew members (and also in the nature, and spatial placement, of the instruments on board). Not even the captain knows it all. Moreover, the computer modeling showed that different patterns of communication between the crew members would lead to different types of success and failure. In some cases, then, failure was due not to human error on the part of a particular individual, but to an unfortunate choice – or an accepted tradition – of communicative strategy. However, this is a study of (distributed) cognition, not of social phenomena, as such.

The main root of the growing interest in distributed social cognition is technological AI's late-century concern with "agents" (Sun, 2006). This term was introduced into AI in the very early days by Oliver Selfridge (1959). He himself used it to cover both very simple reactive "demons" and (potentially) more complex, mindlike, subsystems. Since then, the term has increasingly been used to denote the latter (Boden, 2006: 13.iii.d).

Today's AI agents, then, include the members of groups of interacting robots, and, in particular, software agents cooperating within complex computer programs. Mindlike "softbots" are designed to enter into communications and negotiations of various types. Their activities include recognizing, representing, and aiding the goals and plans of other agents (including the human user); making deals, voting, and bargaining; asking and answering questions; and offering unsolicited but appropriate information to other agents (or, again, the human user).

It could fairly be said, however, that such agents – like the participants in most computer models, and many psychological theories (such as Abelson's, 1973), of social interaction – are conceptualized as solitary individuals who can affect and communicate with other individuals who happen to be around but whose nature is potentially solipsistic. There is no suggestion that they, or human beings, either, are *essentially* social.

The tension between individualistic and social views of the person, or self, is an old one. The key question is whether individual selves constitute society or whether they are largely constituted (not just influenced) by it. Opposing views are fiercely debated not only in political philosophy (e.g., Popper, 1957) but also in social science, including, of course, social psychology (Hollis, 1977; Mead, 1934).

Some recent modeling work by Ezequiel Di Paolo (1998, 1999) has specifically countered the individualistic viewpoint. In a nutshell, Di Paolo showed that cooperation need not depend (as Abelson, 1973, for instance, had assumed) on shared goals, nor on the attribution of intentions to the "partner." He showed, too, that communication need not be thought of (as is usual in cognitive science and in the multiagent systems mentioned earlier) as the transfer of information from the mind of one agent who has it to the mind of another agent, who does not. In one version of his model, for instance, the agents evolved cooperative activity without having internal representations of the task or of each other; the reward could not be gained by a sole agent, but was achieved only by a sequence of alternating actions of both agents.

Di Paolo (1998, 1999) is not the first to model cooperation and coordination between agents lacking representations of each others' intentions and plans (e.g., Goldberg & Mataric, 1999; Sun & Qi, 2000). But he explicitly draws an unorthodox philosophical moral, arguing that his work casts serious doubts on mainstream AI and cognitive science (Di Paolo, 1999: chapter 10). On the one hand, it does not rely on the internal state within the agents, so it goes against the representationalist assumptions of most cognitive scientists (including most connectionists). On the other hand, it goes against the individualistic bias of the field. Often, critics who complain that cognitive science is overly individualistic mean merely that the field, especially AI and computational psychology, has only very rarely considered social systems – these being understood as groups of two or more interacting (but potentially solitary) individuals. Di Paolo, by contrast, argues that an "individual" human being is in fact essentially social, so that orthodox cognitive science is not simply overly narrow in practice but radically inadequate in principle.

This fundamental debate cannot be resolved here; as discussed earlier, it has exercised social and political philosophers for over a century. For present purposes, the point is that although computer modeling has not yet paid much attention to social processes, it is not in principle impossible to do so. Indeed, Di Paolo's (1998, 1999) work shows that cooperation and communication between agents can be modeled even

when they are conceptualized in an essentially "nonindividualistic" way.

6. Conclusion

Computational psychology has a long way to go. There are many unanswered questions, plus some we do not even know just how to pose. One of those is the nature of computation. Alan Turing's definition is still the clearest, but it is not best suited to describe the practice of working AI scientists (Sloman, 2002). A number of people have suggested alternatives (e.g., Copeland, 2002; Smith, 1996; Scheutz, 2002).

This relates to a common criticism of computer-based approaches to the mind/brain. Critics often point out that crude analogies have repeatedly been drawn from contemporary technology, each of which has bitten the dust as knowledge has advanced (within living memory, steam engines, telegraphs, and jukeboxes). Why should not computers eventually bite the dust, too?

The short answer (distilled from Chrisley, 1999) is that computer science, here, is comparable to physics. Physicalists do not insist that everything can be explained (even in principle) by today's physics, but that everything is in principle explicable by whatever the best theory of physics turns out to be. Similarly, cognitive scientists believe that the mind/brain, which certainly cannot be fully understood in terms of today's computational concepts, is in principle intelligible in terms of whatever turns out to be the best theory of what computers can do. "What computers can do" has already been enriched way beyond MGP's imaginings. Very likely, it will be enriched beyond our current imaginings in the future.

A second common objection is that it is absurd to suggest that the subtle idiosyncracies of human lives could be represented, still less predicted, in a computer program. The very idea is felt to be insidiously dehumanizing. But whoever said that they could? Certainly not MGP. Even those (noncomputational) psychologists who specialize in individual differences or in clinical psychotherapy do not claim to be able to predict or explain every detail of individual minds. When such prediction/explanation does take place, it is usually based on human intuition/empathy rather than scientific theory (another long-standing opposition in psychology; Meehl, 1954).

Indeed, science in general is not primarily about prediction. Rather, it is about the identification and explanation of abstract structural possibilities – and impossibilities (Sloman, 1978: chapters 2–3; see also Boden, 2006: 7.iii.d). Correlational "laws" and event-predictions are sometimes available (as in most areas of physics), but they are a special case.

This, then, is the answer to Fodor's (1983) pessimism about the scope of computational psychology (see Section 2). He was right to say that we will never be able to predict every passing thought of a given individual. The human mind – as computational studies have helped us to realize – is far too rich for that. Nevertheless, to understand how mental phenomena are even possible is a genuine scientific advance.

The key problem faced by MGP was to show how such phenomena are possible. (As they put it, how to interpret the hyphen between the S and the R.) They waved their hands shamelessly in sketching their answer. But the overview of cognitive science given in this chapter should suffice to show that significant progress has been made since then.

References

Abelson, R. P. (1973). The structure of belief systems. In R. C. Schank & K. M. Colby (Eds.), *Computer models of thought and language* (pp. 287–339). San Francisco: Freeman.

Agre, P. E., & Chapman, D. (1987). Pengi: An implementation of a theory of activity. *Proceedings of AAAI-87* (Seattle), 268–272.

Agre, P. E., & Chapman, D. (1991). What are plans for? In P. Maes (Ed.), *Designing autonomous agents: Theory and practice from bi-*

ology to engineering and back (pp. 17–34). Cambridge, MA.: MIT Press.

Aleksander, I. (2000). *How to build a man: Dreams and diaries*. London: Weidenfeld & Nicolson.

Anderson, J. R. (1983). *The architecture of cognition*. Cambridge, MA: Harvard University Press.

Anderson, J. R. (1996). ACT: A simple theory of complex cognition. *American Psychologist, 5*, 355–365.

Arbib, M. A., & Hesse, M. B. (1986). *The construction of reality*. Cambridge, UK: Cambridge University Press. The Gifford Lectures, 1983.

Barsalou, L. W. (1999). Perceptual symbol systems. *Behavioral and Brain Sciences, 22*, 577–609.

Blake, D. V., & Uttley, A. M. (Eds.). (1959). *The Mechanization of Thought Processes* (Vols. 1–2). National Physical Laboratory Symposium No. 10. Proceedings of a Symposium held at NPL on 24–27 November 1958. London: Her Majesty's Stationery Office.

Boden, M. A. (1972). *Purposive explanation in psychology*. Cambridge, MA: Harvard University Press.

Boden, M. A. (1977/1987). *Artificial intelligence and natural man*. New York: Basic Books.

Boden, M. A. (2006). *Mind as machine: A history of cognitive science*. Oxford, UK: The Clarendon Press.

Bransford, J. D., & Johnson, M. K. (1972). Contextual prerequisites for understanding: Some investigations of comprehension and recall. *Journal of Verbal Learning and Verbal Behaviour, 11*, 717–726.

Broadbent, D. E. (1952a). Listening to one of two synchronous messages. *Journal of Experimental Psychology, 44*, 51–55.

Broadbent, D. E. (1952b). Failures of attention in selective listening. *Journal of Experimental Psychology, 44*, 428–433.

Broadbent, D. E. (1958). *Perception and communication*. Oxford, UK: Pergamon Press.

Brooks, R. A. (1991a). Intelligence without representation. *Artificial Intelligence, 47*, 139–159.

Brooks, R. A. (1991b). Intelligence without Reason. In *Proceedings of the Twelfth International Joint Conference on Artificial Intelligence*, Sydney, 1–27.

Bruner, J. S. (1957). Going beyond the information given. In H. Gruber, K. R. Hammond, & R. Jessor (Eds.), *Contemporary approaches to cognition* (pp. 41–69). Cambridge, MA: Harvard University Press. (Reprinted in Bruner 1974: 218–238.)

Bruner, J. S., Goodnow, J., & Austin, G. (1956). *A study of thinking.* New York: Wiley.

Changeux, J.-P. (1985). *Neuronal man: The biology of mind* (L. Garey, Trans.). New York: Pantheon.

Chomsky, A. N. (1957). *Syntactic structures.* 'S-Gravenhage, The Netherlands: Mouton.

Chrisley, R. L. (2000). Transparent computationalism. In M. Scheutz (Ed.), *Proceedings of the Workshop New Trends in Cognitive Science 1999: Computationalism – The Next Generation* (pp. 105–120). Vienna, Austria: Conceptus-Studien.

Clark, A. J. (1997). *Being there: Putting brain, body, and world together again.* Cambridge, MA: MIT Press.

Clark, A. J., & Karmiloff-Smith, A. (1993). The cognizer's innards: A psychological and philosophical perspective on the development of thought. *Mind and Language, 8,* 487–519.

Clippinger, J. H. (1977). *Meaning and discourse: A computer model of psychoanalytic discourse and cognition.* London: Johns Hopkins University Press.

Cohen, P. R., Morgan, J., & Pollack, M. E. (Eds.). (1990), *Intentions in communication.* Cambridge, MA: MIT Press.

Cohen, P. R., & Perrault, C. R. (1979). Elements of a plan-based theory of speech acts. *Cognitive Science, 3*(3), 177–212.

Colby, K. M. (1964). Experimental treatment of neurotic computer programs. *Archives of General Psychiatry, 10,* 220–227.

Colby, K. M. (1967). Computer simulation of change in personal belief systems. *Behavioral Science, 12,* 248–253.

Colby, K. M. (1975). *Artificial paranoia: A computer simulation of paranoid processes.* New York: Pergamon.

Copeland, B. J. (2002). Effective computation by humans and machines. *Minds and Machines, 13,* 281–300.

Damasio, A. R. (1994). *Descartes' error: Emotion, reason and the human brain.* New York: Putnam.

Dennett, D. C. (1984). *Elbow room: The varieties of free will worth wanting.* Cambridge, MA: MIT Press.

Dennett, D. C. (1991). *Consciousness explained.* London: Allen Lane.

Dienes, Z., & Perner, J. (in press). The cold control theory of hypnosis. In G. Jamieson (Ed.), *Hypnosis and conscious states: The cognitive neuroscience perspective.* Oxford, U.K.: Oxford University Press.

Di Paolo, E. A. (1998). An investigation into the evolution of communication. *Adaptive Behavior, 6,* 285–324.

Di Paolo, E. A. (1999). *On the evolutionary and behavioral dynamics of social coordination: Models and theoretical aspects.* Unpublished doctoral dissertation, University of Sussex, UK.

Dreyfus, H. L. (1965). *Alchemy and artificial intelligence* (Research Report P-3244). Santa Monica, CA: Rand Corporation.

Dreyfus, H. L. (1972). *What computers can't do: A critique of artificial reason.* (New York: Harper & Row).

Elman, J. L. (1990). Finding structure in time. *Cognitive Science, 14,* 179–212.

Elman, J. L. (1993). Learning and development in neural networks: The importance of starting small. *Cognition, 48,* 71–99.

Elman, J. L., Bates, E. A., Johnson, M. H., Karmiloff-Smith, A., Parisi, D., & Plunkett, K. (1996). *Rethinking innateness: A connectionist perspective on development.* Cambridge, MA: MIT Press.

Evans, D. (2001). *Emotion: The science of sentiment.* Oxford, UK: Oxford University Press.

Evans, D., & Cruse, P. (Eds.) (2004). *Emotion, evolution, and rationality.* Oxford, UK: Oxford University Press.

Fauconnier, G. R., & Turner, M. (2002). *The way we think: Conceptual blending and the mind's hidden complexities.* New York: Basic Books.

Feigenbaum, E. A., & Feldman, J. A. (Eds.). (1963). *Computers and thought.* New York: McGraw-Hill.

Fodor, J. A. (1983). *The modularity of mind: An essay in faculty psychology.* Cambridge, MA: MIT Press.

Fodor, J. A., & Pylyshyn, Z. W. (1988). Connectionism and cognitive architecture: A critical analysis. *Cognition, 28,* 3–71.

Gazdar, G. J. M., Klein, E., Pullum, G., & Sag, I. A. (1985). *Generalized phrase structure grammar.* Oxford, UK: Blackwell.

Gigerenzer, G. (2004). Fast and frugal heuristics: The tools of bounded rationality. In D. J. Koehler & N. Harvey (Eds.), *Blackwell handbook of judgment and decision making* (pp. 62–88). Oxford, UK: Blackwell.

Gigerenzer, G., & Goldstein, D. G. (1996). Reasoning the fast and frugal way: Models of bounded rationality. *Psychological Review,* *103,* 650–669.

Goldberg, D., & Mataric, M. J. (1999). Coordinating mobile robot group behavior using a model of interaction dynamics. In *Proceedings of Third International Conference on Autonomous Agents* (pp. 100–107). Seattle, WA: ACM Press.

Goodale, M. A., & Milner, A. D. (1992). Separate visual pathways for perception and action. *Trends in Neuroscience, 13,* 20–23.

Gregory, R. L. (1966). *Eye and brain: The psychology of seeing.* London: Weidenfeld and Nicolson.

Gregory, R. L. (1967). will seeing machines have illusions? In N. L. Collins & D. M. Michie (Eds.), *Machine intelligence* 1 (pp. 169–180). Edinburgh: Edinburgh University Press.

Grosz, B. (1977). The representation and use of focus in a system for understanding dialogs. *Proceedings of the Fifth International Joint Conference on Artificial Intelligence* (pp. 67–76). Cambridge, MA: Morgan Kaufman.

Haugeland, J. (1985). *Artificial intelligence: The very idea.* Cambridge, MA: MIT Press.

Haugeland, J. (1996). Body and world: A review of *What Computers Still Can't Do* (Hubert L. Dreyfus). *Artificial Intelligence, 80,* 119–128.

Hebb, D. O. (1949). *The organization of behavior: A neuropsychological theory.* New York: Wiley.

Hofstadter, D. R. (1979). *Godel, Escher, Bach: An eternal golden braid.* New York: Basic Books.

Hofstadter, D. R. (1985). *Metamagical themas: Questing for the essence of mind and pattern.* New York: Viking.

Hogg, D. C. (1996). Machine vision. In M. A. Boden (Ed.), *Artificial intelligence* (pp. 183–228). London: Academic Press.

Hollis, M. (1977). *Models of man: Philosophical thoughts on social action.* Cambridge, UK: Cambridge University Press.

Hutchins, E. L. (1995). *Cognition in the wild.* Cambridge, MA: MIT Press.

Johnson, M. H. (Ed.). (1993). *Brain development and cognition: A reader.* Oxford, UK: Blackwell.

Johnson-Laird, P. N. (1983). *Mental models: Towards a cognitive science of language, inference, and consciousness.* Cambridge, UK: Cambridge University Press.

Karmiloff-Smith, A. (1979). Micro- and macro-developmental changes in language acquisition and other representational systems. *Cognitive Science, 3,* 81–118.

Karmiloff-Smith, A. (1986). From meta-processes to conscious access: Evidence from children's metalinguistic and repair data. *Cognition, 23,* 95–147.

Karmiloff-Smith, A. (1992). *Beyond modularity: A developmental perspective on cognitive science.* London: MIT Press.

Kirsh, D. (1991). Today the earwig, tomorrow man? *Artificial Intelligence, 47,* 161–84.

Laird, J. E., Newell, A., & Rosenbloom, P. (1987). Soar: An architecture for general intelligence. *Artificial Intelligence, 33,* 1–64.

Marcus, M. (1979). A theory of syntactic recognition for natural language. In P. H. Winston & R. H. Brown (Eds.), *Artificial intelligence: An MIT perspective* (Vol. 1, pp. 193–230). Cambridge, MA: MIT Press.

Marr, D. C. (1976). Early processing of visual information. *Philosophical Transactions of the Royal Society: B, 275,* 483–524.

Marr, D. C. (1977). Artificial intelligence: A personal view. *Artificial Intelligence, 9,* 37–48.

Marr, D. C. (1982). *Vision: A computational investigation into the human representation and processing of visual information.* San Francisco: Freeman.

Marr, D. C., & Hildreth, E. (1980). Theory of edge-detection. *Proceedings of the Royal Society: B, 207,* 187–217.

McClelland, J. L., Rumelhart, D. E., & the PDP Research Group. (1986). *Parallel distributed processing: Explorations in the microstructure of cognition: Vol. 2. Psychological and biological models.* Cambridge, MA: MIT Press.

McDowell, J. (1994). *Mind and world.* Cambridge, MA: Harvard University Press.

Mead, G. H. (1934). *Mind, self, and society: From the standpoint of a social behaviorist.* Chicago: Chicago University Press.

Meehl, P. E. (1954). *Clinical versus statistical prediction: A theoretical analysis and a review of the evidence.* Minneapolis: University of Minnesota Press.

Miller, G. A., Galanter, E., & Pribram, K. H. (1960). *Plans and the structure of behavior.* New York: Holt.

Miller, G. A., & Johnson-Laird, P. N. (1976). *Language and perception.* Cambridge, UK: Cambridge University Press.

Milner, A. D., & Goodale, M. A. (1993). Visual pathways to perception and action. In T. P. Hicks, S. Molotchnikoff, & T. Ono (Eds.), *Progress in brain research* (Vol. 95, pp. 317–337). Amsterdam: Elsevier.

Minsky, M. L. (1965). Matter, mind, and models. In W. Kalenich (Ed.), *Proceedings of the International Federation of Information Processing Congress, 1* (pp. 45–49). Washington, DC: Spartan.

Minsky, M. L. (1985). *The soiety of mind.* New York: Simon & Schuster.

Minsky, M. L. (2006). *The emotion machine.* New York: Simon & Schuster.

Minsky, M. L., & Papert, S. A. (1969). *Perceptrons: An introduction to computational geometry.* Cambridge, MA: MIT Press.

Minsky, M. L., & Papert, S. A. (1988). Prologue: A view from 1988 and Epilogue: The new connectionism. In *Perceptrons: An introduction to computational geometry* (2nd ed., pp. viii–xv, 247–280). Cambridge, MA: MIT Press.

Newell, A., Shaw, J. C., & Simon, H. A. (1957). Empirical explorations with the logic theory machine. *Proceedings of the Western Joint Computer Conference, 15,* 218–239. (Reprinted [with added subtitle "A Case Study in Heuristics"] in Feigenbaum & Feldman 1963: pp. 109–133.)

Newell, A., Shaw, J. C., & Simon, H. A. (1958). Elements of a theory of human problem-solving. *Psychological Review, 65,* 151–166.

Newell, A., Shaw, J. C., & Simon, H. A. (1959). A general problem-solving program for a computer. In S. de Picciotto (Ed.), *Proceedings of the International Conference on Information Processing* (pp. 256–264). Paris: UNESCO.

Newell, A., & Simons, H. A. (1972). *Human Problem Solving.* Englewood Cliffs, NJ: Prentice Hall.

Norman, D. A., & Shallice, T. (1980). Attention to action: Willed and automatic control of behavior (CHIP Report 99). San Diego: University of California San Diego. Officially published in R. Davidson, G. Schwartz & D. Shapiro (Eds.), (1986). *Consciousness and self regulation: Advances in research and theory.* (Vol. 4, pp. 1–18). New York: Plenum.

Philippides, A., Husbands, P., & O'Shea, M. (1998). Neural signalling – It's a gas! In L. Niklasson, M. Boden, & T. Ziemke. (Eds.), *ICANN98: Proceedings of the 8th International Conference on Artificial Neural Networks* (pp. 51–63). London: Springer-Verlag.

Philippides, A., Ott, S. R., Husbands, P. N., Lovick, T. A., & O'Shea, M. (2005). Modeling cooperative volume signaling in a plexus of nitric oxide synthase-expressing neurons. *Journal of Neuroscience, 25*(28), 6520–6532.

Picard, R. W. (1997). *Affective computing.* Cambridge, MA: MIT Press.

Pinker, S., & Prince, A. (1988). On language and connectionism: Analysis of a parallel distributed model of language acquisition. *Cognition, 28,* 73–193.

Plunkett, K., & Marchman, V. (1993). From rote learning to system building: Acquiring verb-morphology in children and connectionist nets. *Cognition, 48,* 21–69.

Popper, K. R. (1957). *The poverty of historicism.* London: Routledge & Kegan Paul.

Rosenblatt, F. (1958). The perceptron: A probabilistic model for information storage and organization in the brain. *Psychological Review, 65,* 386–408.

Rosenbloom, P. S., Laird, J. E., & Newell, A. (Eds.) (1993). *The SOAR papers: research on integrated intelligence* (Vols. 1–2). Cambridge, MA: MIT Press.

Rumelhart, D. E., & McClelland, J. L. (1986). On learning the past tenses of English verbs. In McClelland, Rumelhart, & PDP Group, (pp. 216–271).

Rumelhart, D. E., McClelland, J. L., & the PDP Research Group (1986). *Parallel distributed processing: Explorations in the microstructure of cognition: Vol. 1. Foundations.* Cambridge, MA: MIT Press.

Russell, S., & Norvig, P. (2003). *Artificial Intelligence: A Modern Approach* (2nd ed.). London: Pearson Education.

Sahota, M., & Mackworth, A. K. (1994). Can situated robots play soccer? In *Proceedings of the Canadian Conference on Artificial Intelligence* (pp. 249–254). Banff, AB: Morgan Kaufmann.

Schank, R. C. (1973). Identification of conceptualizations underlying natural language. In Schank, R. C., & Colby K. M. (Eds.), *Computer Models of Thought and Language* (pp. 187–247). San Franscisco: Freeman.

Schank, R. C., & Abelson, R. P. (1977). *Scripts, plans, goals, and understanding.* Hillsdale, NJ: Lawrence Erlbaum.

Scheutz, M. (Ed.) (2002). *Computationalism: New directions.* Cambridge, MA: MIT Press.

Selfridge, O. G. (1959). Pandemonium: A paradigm for learning. In D. V. Blake & A. M. Uttley (Eds.), *The mechanization of thought processes* (Vol. 1, pp. 511–529). London: Her Majesty's Stationery Office.

Simon, H. A. (1967). *Motivational and emotional controls of cognition. Psychological Review, 74,* 29–39.

Simon, H. A. (1969). *The sciences of the artificial.* Cambridge, MA: MIT Press.

Sloman, A. (1974). Physicalism and the bogey of determinism. In S. C. Brown (Ed.), *Philosophy of psychology* (pp. 283–304). London: Macmillan.

Sloman, A. (1978). *The computer revolution in philosophy: Philosophy, science, and models of mind.* Brighton, UK: Harvester Press. Out of print, but available – and continually updated – online at http://www.cs.bham.ac.uk/research/cogaff/crp/

Sloman, A. (1989). On designing a visual system: Towards a Gibsonian computational model of vision. *Journal of Experimental and Theoretical AI, 1*, 289–337.

Sloman, A. (1993). The mind as a control system. In C. Hookway & D. Peterson (Eds.), *Philosophy and the Cognitive Sciences* (pp. 69–110). Cambridge: Cambridge University Press.

Sloman, A. (2000). Architectural requirements for human-like agents both natural and artificial. (What sorts of machines can love?). In K. Dautenhahn (Ed.), *Human cognition and social agent technology: Advances in consciousness research* (pp. 163–195). Amsterdam: John Benjamins.

Sloman, A. (2002). The irrelevance of turing machines to artificial intelligence. In Scheutz (pp. 87–127).

Sloman, A. (2003). How many separately evolved emotional beasties live within us? In R. Trappl, P. Petta & S. Payr (Eds.). *Emotions in humans and artifacts* (pp. 29–96). Cambridge, MA: MIT Press.

Smith, B. C. (1996). *On the origin of objects.* Cambridge, MA: MIT Press.

Sperber, D., & Wilson, D. (1986). *Relevance: Communication and cognition.* Oxford, UK: Blackwell.

Sun, R. (2001). Hybrid systems and connectionist implementationalism. In L. Nadel (Ed.), *Encyclopedia of cognitive science* (Vol. 2, pp. 697–703). New York: Macmillan.

Sun, R. (2006). The CLARION cognitive architecture: Extending cognitive modeling to social simulation. In R. Sun (Ed.), *Cognition and multi-agent interaction: From cognitive modeling to social simulation* (pp. 79–102). New York: Cambridge University Press.

Sun, R., & Bookman, L. (Eds.). (2001). *Computational architectures integrating neural and symbolic processes.* Needham, MA: Kluwer Academic.

Sun, R., Peterson, T., & Merrill, E. (1999). A hybrid architecture for situated learning of reactive sequential decision making. *Applied Intelligence, 11*, 109–127.

Sun, R., & Qi, D. (2000). Rationality assumptions and optimality of co-learning. In C. Zhang & V. Soo (Eds.), *Design and application of intelligent agents* (pp. 61–75). Heidelberg, Germany: Springer-Verlag.

Tomkins, S. S., & Messick, S. (Eds.), (1963). *Computer simulation of personality: Frontier of psychological research.* New York: Wiley.

Vera, A. H., & Simon, H. A. (1993). Situated action: A symbolic interpretation. *Cognitive Science, 17*, 7–48.

Wheeler, M. W. (2005). *Reconstructing the cognitive world: The next step.* Cambridge, MA: MIT Press.

Winograd, T. (1972). *Understanding natural language.* Edinburgh: Edinburgh University Press.

Woods, W. A. (1973). An experimental parsing system for transition network grammars. In R. Rustin (Ed.), *Natural language processing* (pp. 111–154). New York: Algorithmics Press.

Wright, I. P., & Sloman, A. (1997). MINDER1: An implementation of a protoemotional agent architecture. (Technical Report CSRP-97-1). Birmingham, UK: University of Birmingham, School of Computer Science. ftp://ftp.cs.bham.ac.uk/pub/tech-reports/1997/ CSRP-97-01.ps.gz

Wright, I. P., Sloman, A., & Beaudoin, L. P. (1996). Towards a design-based analysis of emotional episodes. *Philosophy, Psychiatry, and Psychology, 3*, 101–137.

Young, R. M. (1976). *Seriation by children: An artificial intelligence analysis of a piagetian task.* Basel, Switzerland: Birkhauser.

Zelazo, P. D., Moscovitch, M., & Thompson, E. (in press). *The Cambridge handbook of consciousness.* Cambridge, UK: Cambridge University Press.

CHAPTER 26

Putting the Pieces Together Again

Aaron Sloman

1. Introduction

Instead of attempting to sum up the *achievements* of the field, this chapter complements the review of requirements for work on integrated systems in Chapter 1, by presenting a personal view of some of the major unsolved problems and obstacles to solving them. In principle, this book should soon be out of date as a result of worldwide growth in research on cognitive systems. However, it is relatively easy to identify long-term ambitions in vague terms, for example the aim of modeling human flexibility, human learning, human cognitive development, human language understanding, or human creativity; but taking steps to achieve those goals is fraught with difficulties. So progress in modeling human and animal cognition is very slow despite many impressive narrow-focus successes, including those reported in earlier chapters.

An attempt is made to explain why progress in producing realistic models of human and animal competences is slow, namely, (1) the great difficulty of the problems; (2) failure to understand the breadth,

depth and diversity of the problems; (3) the fragmentation of the research community; and (4) social and institutional pressures against risky multidisciplinary, long-term research. Advances in computing power, theory, and techniques will not suffice to overcome these difficulties. Partial remedies will be offered, namely identifying some of the unrecognized problems and suggesting how to plan research on the basis of "backward-chaining" from long-term goals, in ways that may, perhaps, help warring factions to collaborate and provide new ways to select targets and assess progress.

1.1. *The Scope of Cognitive Modeling*

Although artificial intelligence (AI) and cognitive science have different aims, AI has always had two overlapping, mutually supporting strands, namely *science* (concerned with understanding what is and is not possible in natural and artificial intelligent systems) and *engineering* (concerned mainly with producing new useful kinds of machines). "Cognitive science" and "cognitive modeling" overlap significantly with the science strand of AI (as documented in great detail by Boden, 2006). However, the majority of AI researchers have a strong engineering orientation. In contrast, those who were responsible for many of the key ideas in AI were all interested in AI primarily as a contribution to the general "science of mind", including, for example, Turing (1950), McCarthy (2004), Minsky (2006), Simon (1997), and Newell (1990). Some people wish to restrict cognitive science to a *subset* of AI as science, namely the study of "natural" systems. Many are even more narrow and study only *human cognition*. Such restrictions reduce opportunities to understand how systems produced by evolution relate to the space of *possible* behaving systems – as if physicists restricted their studies to naturally occurring physical entities (e.g., plants and planets) while ignoring physical phenomena in artefacts like prisms, plasma lamps, and power stations. So, a full understanding of how minds work, deep enough to support realistic modeling, requires a broad multidisciplinary approach combining neuroscience, psychiatry, developmental psychology, linguistics, animal behavior studies (including insects and microbes), biology, computer science, mathematics, robotics, linguistics, and philosophy. It may also require physics and chemistry for reasons explained later. We need all those disciplines in order to understand the variety of possible ways of combining different kinds of competence within an integrated, embodied, organism-like agent, able to learn and develop as ants, antelopes, and humans do.

We cannot expect everyone working on highly focused research problems to switch immediately to long-term research on *integrated* biologically inspired systems combining multiple competences. But more researchers should think about these issues. In particular, we should inspire some of the brightest young researchers to do so, despite all the institutional and financial pressures to focus on narrow, more practical, goals and despite the deep intellectual difficulties discussed in the following sections.

1.2. *Levels of Analysis and Explanation*

Different kinds of commonality link natural and artificial systems, some concerned with physical mechanisms, some with high-level (virtual machine) design features, and some with task requirements. Organisms use many different physical mechanisms in their sensors, effectors, and internal information-processing systems. Not all of them have brains or nervous systems, although all acquire and use information from the environment in controlling behavior, for example determining direction of movement in microbes, of growth of shoots or roots, or orientation of leaves in plants. Likewise, artificial behaving systems differ in processor design and materials used, and at present use totally different physical mechanisms from those used in organisms, although those differences may be reduced in future.

Progress will depend not only on analysis of the variety of physical substrates and their trade-offs, but also investigation of types of form of representation, types of algorithm, types of dynamical system, and types of architectural decomposition – independently of how they are implemented in physical substrates. Many researchers ignore details in the hope of capturing important features of biological systems. For instance, people developing neural net models tend to ignore the roles of the many chemicals involved in biological information-processing, such as neurotransmitters and hormones. It could turn out that such omissions seriously undermine the long-term significance of their models, so more needs to be understood about the roles of physical and chemical information-processing in organisms (cf. Chapter 13 in this volume).

In addition to research on underlying mechanisms, and research on high-level virtual machine specifications, there is also a type of research that involves identifying the diverse *requirements* that the mechanisms and designs need to satisfy. This is sometimes called "task analysis", although organisms do not merely perform one type of task. Tasks that cognitive scientists need to analyze are more like the collection of requirements for travel to remote planets, compounded with use of diverse bodily forms in diverse environments. Requirements for a whole organism include a specification of the niche, or sequence of niches, in which it evolved or developed.

2. Difficulties and How to Address Them

Previous chapters have said much about explanatory mechanisms and architectures. Most of this chapter is about requirements (i.e., niches) and how to learn about them: a much harder task than many suppose. Contributing to a field like this requires several years of multidisciplinary postgraduate study in order to understand the problems. Unfortunately, both institutional features of current academic research environments and intrinsic features of the research problems make this difficult.

2.1. *Institutional Obstacles*

Severe institutional and financial deterrents obstruct multidisciplinary research, even when lip service is paid to the idea. It is especially risky for untenured researchers worried about getting research grants and building up publication lists – achieved more easily in work that focuses only on minor extensions or new applications of old techniques. That pressure prevents researchers from taking time to acquire the multidisciplinary knowledge required to investigate integrated systems (whole animals, whole robots) and makes them choose less risky research strategies. It also produces factions working on different subproblems who compete for funds, students, and attention, instead of collaborating, and whose teaching produces only partly educated students who believe myths such as that symbolic AI "failed", or, at the other extreme, that neural mechanisms are merely aspects of implementation. Although many funding agencies promote research that integrates subfields and disciplines (Hendler, 2005),

because of the career risks, research on integrated multifunctional ("whole-animal") systems remains impossible for younger researchers. (That is in addition to the intrinsic difficulties described in Section 2.2.) Reducing institutional pressures causing individuals to focus narrowly will require the academic community to teach politicians and managers that assessment by *measurable* results is no way to foster deep, high-calibre research or teaching. Sections 7 and 8 present a new research framework that may help to integrate future research communities, although that will require exceptionally able researchers.

2.2. *Intrinsic Difficulties in Making Progress*

Many researchers have identified detailed obstacles to progress. Some very high-level obstacles, however, appear not to have received much attention. The first difficulty arises because rival researchers argue about whose algorithm, architecture, or form of representation is best, instead of studying the structure of the space of alternatives and the trade-offs involving those options. There usually is no "best" alternative.

A related difficulty comes from studying only normal adult human capabilities in a specific community, ignoring not only the deep genetic heritage humans share with many other animals, but also the variations in human capabilities across ages, cultures, and personality types, and the varied consequences of brain damage or deterioration. Many of the facts that need to be explained are not even noticed.

Research planning is hard because identifying good ways to make progress toward very distant goals is hard when we do not yet have a clear vision of the intermediate research stages that can lead to those goals. A partial solution is suggested in Section 9.2.

Many further difficulties arise from limitations of our conceptual tools: After less than a century of intense investigation of mechanizable varieties of information-processing, what we still understand about forms of representation, about mechanisms for processing information, and about designs for architectures, is only a tiny fragment of what evolution produced over billions of years. Limitations of current materials science and mechatronic engineering capabilities may also have deep implications regarding still unknown requirements for varieties of information processing underlying animal intelligence, for example sharing of functions between hardware and software as described by Berthoz (2000).

3. Failing to See Problems: Ontological Blindness

Funding and institutional problems, and inadequacies of our concepts and tools have been listed as brakes on progress. A deeper hindrance is the difficulty of identifying what needs to be explained or modeled, often arising from "ontological blindness" discussed by Sloman and Chrisley (2005). Any information-user must use an ontology, which to a first approximation is the set of *types* of entities the user can refer to. Gaps or spurious types in the ontology can cause researchers to mis-identify what organisms are doing. So they fail to identify the various subfunctions that need to be modeled. Section 4 illustrates this in connection with modeling human vision, although the points are also applicable to other animals and other aspects of cognition.

Another common mis-identification concerns varieties of learning. It is often assumed that humans, and therefore human-like robots, necessarily start with very limited innate knowledge about the environment and have to use very general, knowledge-free forms of learning. This assumption ignores the fact that most organisms start with almost all the knowledge and competence they will require, because of their need to be independent from birth or hatching (like deer that walk to their mother's nipple and run with the herd very soon after birth). If evolution can produce so much information in the genome, for some species, why does it apparently produce helpless and ignorant

infants in altricial species, for example humans and hunting mammals. Chappell and Sloman (2007) propose that such animals start with deep meta-competences using generic information about the environment, including information about how to use the body to explore and learn about the details of a 3-D environment. This is an old idea as regards language learning (Chomsky, 1965), but language learning could be just a special case of the use of partly innately specified meta-competences that generate both new competences and new meta-competences through active investigation of the environment.

Other misrepresentations of the requirements for human-like systems include the assumption that intelligent agents must use a sense-think-act cycle. For example, the web page of a leading AI department states: "An intelligent agent should also learn to improve its performance over time, as it repeatedly performs this sense-think-act cycle", which ignores the fact that in humans and most other animals many kinds of information processing proceed in parallel, for example simultaneously walking, planning where to walk, enjoying the view and listening to what a companion is saying, concurrently with many bodily control functions. Different misrepresentations of requirements come from paying close attention to implementation details and concluding that all intelligence is to be explained in terms of the dynamics of sensori-motor control loops, ignoring the fact that many humans can listen to and understand a story, or look at and appreciate a complex scene without producing any relevant motor responses, and some can even prove theorems in their heads about transfinite ordinals, or plan a musical composition without producing any sounds.

4. What Are the Functions of Vision?

Marr (1982) suggested that the function of vision was to provide information about geometrical and physical properties of the environment, for example shape, size, location, motion, and color of objects. Many readers thought this obviously correct. However, in 1979, Gibson had pointed out that there are far more subtle functions of perception, namely providing information about "affordances" that are abstract properties of the environment related to possible actions and goals of the perceiver. This was generalized in Sloman (1982, 1989) by drawing attention to human abilities to learn to see states of mind and to read writing, music, and various other formal notations.

On the first view, vision is the same for a lion and a lamb surveying the same terrain, whereas the biological requirements and action capabilities are so different in hunting and grazing mammals that they need to perceive very different affordances, for which they have different genetically determined or learned visual mechanisms and capabilities. Requirements for catching and eating meat are very different from requirements for grazing: Vegetable matter does not attempt to escape, and grass does not require peeling or breaking open. Similar differences exist between birds that build nests from twigs and those that build nests using only mud, or between birds that fly and birds that do not, birds that dive for fish and birds that catch insects, and so on, suggesting that what is seen by two different animals looking at a scene can differ as much as what is seen by people who know different languages looking a page showing texts written in different languages.

4.1. *The Importance of Mobile Hands*

More subtle differences in requirements for vision depend on having hands that can move and manipulate objects. Animals that can manipulate things only using a mouth or beak will have very strong correlations between grasping actions and patterns of optical flow, because of the rigid link between eyes and mouth or beak, whereas animals with mobile hands or claws must be able to represent actions that move things without changing the viewpoint. Independently movable hands can perform essentially similar grasping actions producing vastly differ-

ent visual feedback, so using only sensorimotor relationships will make it difficult to represent what is common to many ways of grasping, namely:

> Two (or more) surfaces facing each other move together in 3-D space until they are in contact with opposite sides of some other object that can then be lifted, rotated, or moved horizontally.

An "exosomatic" ontology, referring to changing relationships in the external environment, is required for this, rather than a "somatic" ontology, referring only to changing sensory and motor signals. An exosomatic ontology makes it much simpler to transfer facts learned about grasping in one situation to grasping in another.

If grasping is represented amodally in terms of changing relations between 3-D surfaces, with changing causal consequences, then how the process is represented is independent of how it is sensed or what motor signals are required to produce it. Not representing the process in terms of "sensori-motor contingencies" has useful consequences. One is that information about the occurrence of such processes can be stored compactly if what needs to be remembered is that grasping defined as a process in 3-D space occurred, not how it was done or what sensor or motor signals were produced during the process. That allows generalisations to be learned at a high-level of abstraction, applicable to wide ranges of cases, such as grasping with the left hand, with the right hand, with both hands, or with teeth. Such amodal generalisations include such facts as: (a) a tightly grasped object undergoes the same translation and rotation as the two grasping surfaces, (b) the grasped object may fall if the pressure applied by the two surfaces is reduced, (c) when a grasped object is released it accelerates downwards, and (d) grasping changes the shape of non-rigid objects.

An amodal ontology allows what an individual learns by grasping to be transferred to grasping done by another individual, and vice versa. So actions done by others can be predicted, failures understood, and preventive measures taken (e.g., when a predator threatens, or a child is about to fail to reach a goal). Moreover, processes that are observed but produced by nobody (e.g., an apple falling) can suggest goals to be achieved. So-called mirror neurons might best be construed in terms of use of an ontology that abstracts from sensori-motor details. Perhaps "abstraction neurons" would have been a better label. Actor-independent representations of certain actions can allow parents to perceive "vicarious affordances" for offspring or predators, enabling them to use causal reasoning to help or protect offspring and to obstruct or avoid predators. This makes possible the "scaffolding" of learners by parents and teachers discussed by developmental psychologists. As noted in Chappell and Sloman (2007), there are hunting birds and mammals that give their young practice in dealing with prey, in a manner that suggests that they understand what their offspring need to do. Grasping is merely an example: Use of landmarks, observed in ants and wasps, may be another. Use of amodal, exosomatic representations of processes involved in actions is not a feature of all animal vision: but it is certainly a human competence. The extent to which other animals have it requires research.

All this imposes strong constraints on models of visual cognition that aim for completeness. Other constraints include the need to explain how visual servoing works, where precise, continuous motion is constantly monitored and modulated in sensori-motor feedback and feedforward loops.

This distinction between the use of vision in "online" control of fine details of actions and its use in acquiring more abstract reusable information applicable to many different situations, using dorsal and ventral pathways respectively, has, in recent years, been wrongly described as a difference in perception of "what" versus "where" or "what" versus "how". The mistake was corrected in Goodale and Milner (1992), albeit using a misleading contrast between perception and action, as opposed to two perceptual (visual) functions.

An "objective" (exosomatic, amodal) ontology can also be used to represent a hand moving to grasp an object that is not in view because the eyes have moved to get a view of something else, or the grasped object is obscured by something. Absence of sensori-motor details also allows representations to be useful in planning or predicting future actions where what motor and sensory signals will be involved can be left unspecified, because that can vary according to detailed circumstances at the time of action. Without use of amodal abstractions, the combinatorial complexity of the process of searching for a plan or prediction or explanation would be far greater.

Grasping is, of course, just one example. All this still leaves unexplained how a visual system manages to derive amodal descriptions of 3-D structures and processes from sensory input, but research on that is in progress in AI, psychology, and neuroscience (e.g., Hayworth & Biederman, 2006).

Ontological blindness to these possibilities leads some researchers to suppose that vision is merely (or mostly) object recognition, or that vision uses only image-based or more generally sensori-motor representations. There is now a vast amount of research on models of sensori-motor learning, using architectures that cannot do anything else (e.g., Lungarella & Sporns, 2006). Such models cannot explain most of the uses of vision.

4.2. Seeing Processes, Affordances, and Empty Spaces

Most vision researchers (including this author for many years) have concentrated on perception of *static* scenes, blind to the fact that perception occurs in an environment that is in motion much of the time, with constantly changing viewpoints as animals move. So a major function of a vision is to provide information about which *processes* are occurring, not just about structures and relationships. In that case, viewing static scenes is a special case of perceiving processes in which nothing much happens.

So perhaps the *primary* form of representation for visual information should be representations of processes extended in time and space, whereas many researchers (an exception being Grush, 2004), assume that vision produces information about objects, properties, and relationships. Of course, that is *part* of what needs to be explained, but only part. If vision uses representations of processes including affordances concerned with what can and cannot happen or be done the representations must be rich in *conditional* information about processes.

One test for whether a vision system perceives affordances is how it sees empty 3-D or 2-D spaces. If all the functions of a visual system are concerned with perception of objects, then empty space cannot be seen, whereas humans can see an empty space as full of potential for various kinds of occurrences, depending on where the space is, how big it is, how close we are to it, what other things are in the vicinity, and what our current capabilities and concerns are. A bird holding a twig to be added to its partially built nest needs to see places where that twig would be useful, and a route by which it can be inserted. Someone like Picasso can see potential in a blank surface that most people cannot. Harold Cohen's AARON program, described in Boden (1990) and accessible at http://www.kurzweilcyberart.com, also has some grasp of 2-D affordances and how they change as a painting grows. A mathematician wondering how to calculate the area of a circle may see the potential for inscribing and circumscribing an unending succession of regular polygons with ever-increasing numbers of sides just inside and just outside the circle – one of many cases of mathematical use of the visual ability to represent processes. Other cases can be found in Sloman (1978) and Anderson, Meyer, and Olivier (2001).

So, vision researchers who focus only the task of extracting from the optic array information about things *that exist in the scene*, exhibit ontological blindness insofar as they ignore the role of vision in seeing *what does not yet exist but could exist*, that is, the positive and negative affordances. Many also ignore the importance of seeing *ongoing processes* in which both structures and affordances are changed.

4.3. *Seeing Without Recognizing Objects*

A vast amount of vision research is concerned with recognition. But that fails to address seeing without recognizing objects, which involves acquiring information about spatial structure, relationships, affordances, and processes. Perception of structure involves recognition, not of whole objects, but of image and scene *fragments*, such as occluding edges, bumps, dents in surfaces, partially visible edges, changing curvature, and specularities. Perception of spatial structures and relations can be the basis of recognition, and may sometimes be facilitated by recognition. But systems designed only for recognition of "whole" objects must fail when confronted with new things! Nearly thirty years ago, Barrow and Tenenbaum (1978) drew attention to aspects of perception of shape properties and spatial relations of 3-D surface fragments that seem to be independent of object recognition, for example seeing the shape of the portion of the surface where a cup's handle meets the bowl, or seeing how the 3-D orientation of parts of the rim of a cup or jug vary around the rim, including the pouring lip if there is one. Range-finders have been used to obtain 3-D structure, but usually the aim of such work is to produce only the kind of mathematically precise 3-D information that suffices for generating images of the scene from multiple viewpoints, rather than the kind of "qualitative" information about surface shape and structure that supports perception of affordances. Várady, Martin, and Cox (1997) provide a useful survey.

Many animals appear to be able to see and make use of surface structure and shapes of fragments of objects they do not necessarily recognize (e.g., consider a carnivore's task in tearing open and eating its prey). Likewise, when Jackie Chappell presented parakeets with cardboard "polyflaps" (Sloman, 2006a), they played with, manipulated, and chewed them, despite never having seen them previously.

Infants spend much time developing competences related to various aspects of shape perception, including competences such as pushing, pulling, picking up, putting down, throwing, inserting, stacking, bending, twisting, breaking, assembling, disassembling, opening, and shutting, much of which precedes learning to talk, and often does not require the whole objects to be classified or recognized.

A good theory might explain ways in which brain damage can differentially affect abilities to see various kinds of surface features and affordances without removing the ability to see, as illustrated by *prosopagnosia*, an affliction in which the ability to recognize faces is lost.

In summary, there are deep and general forms of perception and learning that we need to understand in order to understand important aspects of vision on which many other competences build, in humans and other animals, including spatial and causal reasoning capabilities.

4.4. *Many Developmental Routes to Related Cognitive Competences*

We should not assume that human visual competence (or any cognitive competence) depends on having a specific bodily form, such as having hands that can manipulate things. Babies born without arms, as occurred in the thalidomide tragedy in the 1960s, can grow up into intelligent adults. This may depend on a powerful mixture of genetic endowments shared with normal humans, including a kind of *vicarious* learning capability used when watching others do things we cannot do ourselves, using an exosomatic ontology, as discussed in Section 4.1. Perhaps a shared evolutionary heritage provides the ability to develop a core set of amodal forms of representation that enables severely disabled children to learn about structures, processes, and affordances through watching others do things they cannot do. This ability to learn about, perceive,

and make use of vicarious affordances undermines some claims about cognition as intimately tied up with embodiment. It is arguable that having a human mind depends more on having had embodied ancestors than on being embodied.

4.5. *The Role of Perception in Ontology Extension*

At any particular time, an animal or child will have developed an ontology that is used in percepts, predictions, and plans, all of which represent entities, relationships, processes, and affordances in the environment. But things can go wrong: plans can fail and predictions can turn out false. The infant who takes a cut-out picture of an animal out of its recess and then later tries to replace it can fail, being surprised when it doesn't fit the recess. Such failures could trigger "debugging" processes that sometimes lead the child to extend the high-level ontology, possibly using low-level sensory features that were previously disregarded. For example the child may somehow extend his or her ontology to include the concept of the *boundary* of a flat object and the concept of two boundaries being *aligned*. After that change, the failure to get the puzzle piece into its recess may be overcome by performing additional actions to align the two boundaries. For this, the ontology will need to include processes like *sliding, rotating*, and *coming into alignment*.

Some toys are cleverly designed to require a less complex ontology. For stacking cups that are symmetrical, boundaries need not be aligned during insertion. Making cups conical allows small bases to be inserted into larger openings, reducing the need for precision in placing. Careful observation of actions of infants and toddlers at various stages of development reveals subtle ways in which they encounter difficulties that seem to be based on not yet having a rich enough ontology that they later extend – perhaps driven by detecting differences between actions previously seen as similar, or by modifying preconditions or consequences of actions to include relationships previously not representable. An eleven-month-old child is described in Sloman, Chappell, and CoSyTeam (2006) who was able to feed himself yogurt from a tub using a spoon to transfer the yogurt to his mouth, but failed to transfer yogurt to his leg because he merely placed the bowl of the spoon on his leg, apparently not realizing that it needed to be rotated. There are probably hundreds, or even thousands, of such processes of self-debugging leading to ontology extension in the first few years of a human child. Those extensions depend on types of objects (including types of food and clothing) in the environment, whose properties and behaviors can vary enormously from one part of the world to another and sometimes change as a result of cultural development. For example, many children born recently have acquired an ontology appropriate for interacting with a computer using a mouse, which none of their ancestors encountered. Some of the transitions in which new competences are acquired were studied by Piaget many years ago (1954), but the time may be ripe for renewed systematic study facilitated by the ability to use video recordings so that many different people can examine the same episode. Researchers with expertise in designing robots should have richer ontologies with which to perceive and think about what infants do, or fail to do.

5. Representational Capabilities

In order to explain how a child extends an ontology we need to know what representations are used. What sort of representation does a child or chimp have of a three dimensional curved surface such as various parts of a spoon? How are the causal capabilities represented? There are many mathematical ways of representing shapes, for instance using differential equations, or using very large vectors of point features. But those representations may not be adequate for cognitive purposes if they are too difficult to derive from the available sensory information (e.g., because of noise, low resolution of the parts of the visual field, or lack of suitable algorithms). The mathematical representations may also be unsuited to the derivation of affordances, and hard to use in planning or in controlling actions. Explaining cognitive competences in dealing with a 3-D environment may require new forms of representation that capture spatial structure in a manner that abstracts from the precise details that would be represented in differential equations and collections of point features, and are better tailored to facilitating action selection and control. It is likely that evolution "discovered" many more forms of representation and corresponding mechanisms than human mathematicians, scientists, and engineers have so far thought of.

Besides the difficulty of specifying the forms of representation used, there is the problem of explaining how they are implemented in brain mechanisms. My impression is that despite vast advances in detailed tracing of neuronal connections, the study of chemical brain process, and the recent development of more and more fine-grained brain imaging devices, there is still very little understanding of how the mechanisms so far discovered are capable of supporting most of the cognitive functions we believe humans and other animals are capable of. For example, standard neural models assume that all structures and processes can be represented in the contents of large vectors of values of sensory and motor signals, possibly at different levels of abstraction. We seem to need different sorts of computations, involving different information structures, in order to make progress in modeling cognitive processes. Some of the requirements are identified in Trehub (1991) and some hypothetical neural mechanisms proposed. But it is not clear whether they can meet all the requirements.

Research on these topics is extremely difficult. Perhaps that explains why the tasks identified by Barrow and Tenenbaum (mentioned in Section 4.3) have largely been forgotten, while most vision researchers work on other tasks that do not involve detailed understanding of spatial structure and affordances. Great progress has been made in developing mechanisms with narrow competences, like object recognition or classification, object tracking, trajectory prediction, pushing or grasping simple objects (e.g., Saxena, Driemeyer, Kearns, Osondu, & Ng, 2006) and path traversal – all of which are worthy research topics, of course, but form only a relatively small subset of functions of vision. Other functions, not discussed here, include the role of vision in fine-grained control of actions (visual servoing), posture-control, perceiving varieties of motion, developing many kinds of athletic capabilities using vision, parking a car or other vehicle, perceiving causal relationships, understanding the operation of a machine, perceiving social interactions, aesthetic appreciation of natural and artificial scenes and objects, communication, learning to read text first laboriously then later fluently, sight-reading music, and many more.

Some distinct visual capabilities can be exercised in parallel, for example when walking on difficult terrain while enjoying the view, or judging how to hit a moving tennis ball while seeing what the opponent is doing. This probably depends on the concurrent operation of mechanisms that perform fast and fluent well-learned tasks reactively and mechanisms that have more abstract and flexible deliberative capabilities (Sloman, 2006b).

It might be fruitful to set up a multi-disciplinary project to expand our ontology for thinking about vision, including a comprehensive taxonomy of functions of vision, along with requirements for mechanisms, forms of representation, types of learning, and architectures to support such functions, especially under the constraint of having only one or two eyes that have to be used to serve multiple concurrently active processes that perform different tasks while sharing lower-level resources. Similar things could be done for other major cognitive functions. Such projects will benefit from the scenario-driven research described in Section 7.

5.1. Is Language for Communication?

Similar kinds of ontological blindness can afflict students of language. A common assumption is that the sole function of language is communication: meanings are assumed to exist and language is used to convey them. But many are blind to the deeper problem of how it is possible for a person, animal or machine to have meanings to communicate. Thoughts, percepts, memories, suppositions, desires, puzzles, and intentions all have semantic content, and can therefore exist only where there is something that encodes or expresses their content.

Many animals clearly perceive things, want things, try to do things, and learn things, despite not having human language capabilities. Similarly, very young children have intentions, desires, information gained from the environment, and things they want to communicate before they have learned how to communicate in language (cf. Halliday, 1975). They can be very creative: before having learned to say "Look here", a child may move an adult's head to face something requiring attention.

Moreover, other animals can be attentive, afraid, puzzled, surprised, or repeatedly trying to do something, all of which involve states with semantic content. A dog that brings a stick to be thrown for it to catch need not have in its head a translation of the English sentence "Please throw this so that I can catch it", for it may not use the same ontology as we do nor the same mode of composition of meanings, nor the same varieties of speech-act. All we can be sure of is that they must have *some* internal states, processes, or structures that express or encode semantic content, and that allow the specific content to have consequences for internal and external behavior, even if the semantic content is not in a propositional form, or expressible in a language like English.

Many scientists now use "language" in a general sense referring to anything that expresses semantic content, whether for oneself or another agent, especially if it allows both structural variability and compositional semantics, providing the ability to cope with novel information items of varying complexity (Sloman, 2006b). Sloman and Chappell (2007) use "g[generalised]-language" to refer to such forms of representation, including propositional and analogical representations (Sloman, 1971). So the previous paragraph implies that many animals and prelinguistic children use g-languages. G-languages capable of expressing meanings with complex structures must therefore have evolved before communicative languages (Sloman, 1979), for use *within* individual animals, rather than for communication *between* animals. From this viewpoint, the functions of language include perceiving, thinking, wanting, intending, reasoning, planning, learning, deciding, and not just communication. (Unlike Fodor, 1975, we are not claiming that individuals use a fixed innate language into which they translate everything else.)

This leaves open what those inner languages are like. Despite the claims of Brooks (1991), intelligent systems must use representations, at least in the widely-used sense of "representation" that refers to something that provides, stores, or conveys usable information for some user. The requirements for g-languages are met by the forms of representation used in computational work on high-level vision, reasoning, planning, learning, problem solving, and are also met by external human languages; including both structural variability and compositional semantics, allowing fragments of information to be combined in different ways to form more complex information items that can then be combined with further information. Such representations can be used to express facts, hypotheses, conjectures, predictions, explanations, questions, problems, goals, and plans.

Not all mechanisms and architectures are capable of meeting the requirements: structural variability, for example, rules out forms of meaning that are expressed only in fixed size vectors with atomic components, such as are often used as inputs and outputs of neural nets. Although no human can actually cope with unbounded complexity, we can argue, echoing Chomsky's (1965) distinction between competence and performance, that humans have virtual machines with unbounded complexity but their implementations in physical machines impose limits. This is also true of most programming formalisms (Scheutz, 2002; Sloman, 2002).

We need more investigation of both the variety of requirements for forms of representation and the variety of possible representations, instead of assuming that known forms will suffice. We also need to stop assuming that human languages and linguistic meanings are *sui generis* and ask whether they are outgrowths of rich forms of syntactic and semantic competence provided by internal g-languages in other animals and in prelinguistic children. This is not to deny that external languages (including pictorial and other forms of communication) allowed rapid acceleration of both learning in individuals and cultural evolution that are unique to humans. In particular, individuals who have learned to use a human language for external communication are able to enrich the semantic contents expressed internally for their own purposes, for example in categorizing their thoughts as confused, their desires as selfish, or their knowledge as incomplete. (Cultural learning is discussed further in Section 6.2.)

5.2. *Varieties of Complexity: Scaling Up and Scaling Out*

Another common kind of ontological blindness involves varieties of complexity. Early AI researchers discovered that combinatorial explosions threatened progress. If the solution to a problem involves n actions and for every action there are k options, then there are k^n possible action sequences, a number that grows exponentially with n. Because this quickly makes problems intractable, a common demand is that models should "scale up", namely, continue to perform with reasonable space and time requirements as the complexity of the task increases. But another kind of complexity requirement often goes unnoticed, which requires what we call "scaling out". Vision and language illustrate this: Particular capabilities often depend on and contribute to other capabilities with which they can be combined. We have seen how impoverished theories of vision result from missing the role of vision in satisfying requirements for action and thought. Similarly, work on language that focuses entirely on linguistic phenomena, such as phonemics, morphology, syntax, and semantics, may fail to address such problems as:

- how language is used for non-communicative purposes (e.g., thinking, reasoning, having goals, desires, intentions, and puzzles);
- how it relates to and builds on capabilities that exist in young children or other animals that cannot use language;
- how it relates to forms of representations and mechanisms that evolved prior to human language; and
- how the process of learning a language relates to the evolutionary and developmental precursors of language.

A requirement for a model of how language or vision works, how plans are made and executed, how mathematical or other reasoning works, and how learning works, is that *the proposed mechanisms should be able to form a usefully functioning part of an integrated complete agent combining many other capabilities in different ways at different times.*

That "scaling out" requirement looks obvious once stated, but its implications for the various components of the system are not obvious, and are often ignored. The kinds of combination required can vary. In simple models, submodules are given tasks or other input, and run for a while (as "black boxes"), then produce results that can be used by other modules, like Fodor's (1983) modules. Many proposed architectures assume that sort of structure: they are represented by diagrams with arrows showing unidirectional flow of information between modules. As mentioned in Section 3, some designers assume that there is a *sense-think-act* cycle, in which a chunk of input comes in

via the senses, is processed by sending packets of derived information through various modules (some of which may be changed as a result) until some external behavior is produced, and then the cycle repeats, as in the TOTE (Test-Operate-Test-Exit) units of Miller, Galanter, and Pribram (1960), and many more recent designs.

This is clearly wrong. A deeper integration is required: different competences can interact while they are running in parallel and before specific tasks are complete. For humans, many other animals, and robots with complex bodies and multiple sensors acting in a fast changing environment, the *sense-think-act* model fails to account for the variety of extended, concurrent, interacting processes that are capable of mutual support and mutual modulation. (Cf. chapter 6 in Sloman, 1978.)

For instance, while looking for an object, if you hear someone say "Further to the left", what you hear can interact with how you see and help you recognize what you were looking for. Someone looking at the well-known puzzle picture of a dappled dalmation may become able to see the animal on hearing "It's a dog". Likewise, while you are trying to work out what someone means by saying "Put the bigger box on the shelf with more room, after making space for it" you may notice three shelves one of which is less cluttered than the others, and work out which shelf is being referred to and what might be meant by "making space for it" in the light of the perceived size of the bigger box. Some of these interactions were demonstrated several decades ago (Winograd, 1972). Others are explored in the work of Grice (e.g., Grice, 1975). The interactions need not be produced by first fully analyzing the sentence, deciding it is ambiguous, then setting up and acting on a goal to find more information to disambiguate it. What you see can help the interpretation of a heard sentence even before it is complete.

There are well-documented examples of close interaction between vision and spoken language comprehension, including the "McGurk effect" (McGurk & MacDonald, 1976) in which the same recorded utterance is heard to include different words when played with videos of speakers making different mouth movements. Interactions can also occur between active and currently suspended processes: Something you see or think of while doing one task may give you an idea about how to finish another task on which you are stuck, a common phenomenon in scientific and mathematical discovery.

That sort of interaction can even cause the current task to be dropped, with attention switching to a much more important, previously suspended task. "Anytime" planners, which can take account of time pressures and deliver partial results on request, are another well-studied example. There is growing interest in "incremental" processing in natural language, which may help to support such deep interactions between linguistic and non-linguistic capabilities. A workshop held in 2004 on incremental parsing has this Web site: http://homepages.inf.ed. ac.uk/keller/acl04_workshop/.

Yet another example is combining expert chess competence with knowledge of capabilities of a young opponent to produce chess moves and verbal comments suited to helping the youngster learn. Much teaching requires that sort of mixing of competences: another example of the ability to scale out.

The ability to "scale up" has received far more attention from cognitive modelers, who often try to design mechanisms that are able to cope with increasingly complex inputs without being defeated by a combinatorial explosion. But that is not a requirement for modeling human competence: humans do not scale up!

5.3. *Humans Scale Out, Not Up*

There are many human capabilities that are nowhere near being matched by current machines, yet all of them seem to be complexity-limited, a point related to what Donald Michie (1991) called "the human window". Moreover, there are already many specialized forms of competence where machines far outperform most, or all, humans. Such models scale up, but not out:

They have only very narrowly focused competence. Suitably programmed computers can do complex numerical calculations that would defeat all or most humans, but that does not enable those machines to explain what a number is or why it is useful to be able to do arithmetic. Chess programs, like Deep Blue, that use brute force mechanisms, can beat the vast majority of humans, but cannot teach a child to play chess, help a beginner think about his mistakes, modify its play so as to encourage a weaker player by losing sometimes, explain why it did not capture a piece, explain what its strategy is, or discuss the similarities and differences between playing chess and building something out of meccano.

Is any artificial chess system capable of being puzzled as to why its opponent did not make an obviously strong move? What are the requirements for being puzzled? Compare being surprised. Some of the representational and architectural requirements for such states are discussed in Sloman, Chrisley, and Scheutz (2005).

Occurrences of different competences interacting are part of our everyday life, but we may be blind to them when planning our research. Solving the problems of deep integration of cognitive systems with multiple functions may turn out to be much more difficult than anyone anticipates. For example, it is at least conceivable that some powerful forms of information-processing were discovered and used long ago by biological evolution that have not yet been understood by human scientists and engineers. Investigation of this issue is included in one of the U.K. Computing Research grand challenges on new forms of computation, summarized at this Web site: http://www.cs.york.ac.uk/nature/gc7/.

6. Are Humans Unique?

One of the curious facts about this question is that even among scientists who are supposed to be dispassionate seekers after knowledge there are both passionate claims that humans are unique, for example, because of their use of language, their self-consciousness, their ability to produce and appreciate art, their ability to share goals, or some other characteristics, and also equally passionate claims (some of them from champions of animal rights) that the continuity of evolution implies that we are not unique, merely slightly different from other animals, such as chimpanzees or foxes. It seems that both kinds of passion come from an unscientific commitment, for example to religious (or "romantic"?) reasons for *wanting* to think of humans as unique, or from a concern for animal welfare that uses Darwinian theory as a basis for claims that the similarity of other animals to humans gives them similar rights. The debate is misguided because the correct answer is obviously "Yes and No":

- Yes: Humans are unique because there are things humans do that no other (known) animals can do, such as prove theorems about infinite structures, compose poems, utter communications using subjunctive conditionals, send people and machines to the moon and outer space, or make tools to make tools to make tools to make tools . . . to make things we use for their own sake.
- No: Humans are not unique because there are huge numbers of facts about their bodies, their behavior, their needs, their modes of reproduction and development, and how they process information, that are also facts about other animals.

This is a shallow response, however, because there is so much we do not yet know about how humans and other animals work, and what the similarities and differences actually are, and what the implications of those differences are. We still understand relatively little about how most animals work, partly because we do not have clear and accurate knowledge about what their capabilities, especially their information-processing capabilities, actually are, and partly because many of the mechanisms and architectures supporting such capabilities are still unknown. Instead of wasting effort on spurious debates, we should try to deepen our understanding of the facts.

If we had a deep theory of the variety of types of information-processing architectures in nature and what capabilities they do and do not support, and if we knew which animals have which sorts, then such emotion-charged debates might give way to reasoned analysis and collection of relevant evidence to settle questions, or acknowledgment that many questions use concepts that are partly indeterminate (e.g., "cluster concepts") so that there are no answers. Similar comments can be made about the question whether a fetus is conscious or feels pain, whether various kinds of animals suffer, etc. Consequently the correct descriptions of future machines will be equally problematic.

6.1. *Altricial and Precocial Skills in Animals and Robots*

Many people are unaware of the great differences between

(a) the vast majority of species that seem to have their main competences determined genetically, for example grazing mammals that can run with the herd shortly after birth, and birds such as chickens that can peck for food soon after hatching, and

(b) the small subset of species that are born helpless, physiologically underdeveloped, and apparently cognitively incompetent, yet end up as adults with capabilities (e.g., nest-building in trees, hunting other mammals, use of hands to pick berries, and various kinds of tool use) that appear to be far more cognitively complex than those achieved by the former group.

The former species are labelled "precocial" species by biologists, and the latter "altricial". However, there is a spectrum of cases with different mixtures of precocial skills (genetically determined, preconfigured), and altricial skills ("meta-configured" competences generated by the individual and the environment through play, exploration, and learning, using powerful meta-level bootstrapping mechanisms). The nature/nurture trade-offs between different design options are not well understood although a preliminary analysis was offered in Sloman and Chappell (2005) and refined in Chappell and Sloman (2007) and Sloman and Chappell (2007). That analysis suggests that just as there is a spectrum of combinations of preconfigured (precocial) and meta-configured (altricial) skills in biological organisms, so will there also be such a spectrum in future robots, including robots developed as models of human cognition. Robots placed in environments where complex and unpredictable changes can occur over time will, like altricial animals, need to be able to bootstrap meta-configured competences their designers know nothing about, even though they start with a large collection of preconfigured skills, like precocial species. Where most of the environment is predictable in advance, a fully precocial design may function well, but it will not be a model of human, primate, or corvid cognition.

Some altricial species, especially humans, learn both very rapidly and in a wide range of environments, to cope with those environments. As a result, some young children have competences none of their ancestors had. In contrast, skills of precocial species (e.g., deer, chickens) are shaped only in minor ways by the environment in which they live, and altered mainly by slow, laborious training (e.g., circus training), unlike the spontaneous and rapid learning through play, in primates and some other species. At present the mechanisms supporting the latter learning are not well understood, and there are no learning mechanisms or self-constructing architectures under investigation that can account for this, although an idea suggested over twenty years ago by Oliver Selfridge is presented in Sloman and Chappell (2005).

Philipona, O'Regan, and Nadal (2003) present a type of learning-by-doing through finding invariants in sensori-motor patterns. This may explain some ontological extensions, but does not account for the human-like exosomatic, amodal ontology discussed in Section 4. Another important process may be selection of actions and percepts as "interesting" (Colton, Bundy, & Walsh, 2000). This requires architectural support for varieties of purely cognitive motivation as opposed to motivation based on physical and reproductive needs. We need to look closely at a variety of phenomena found in the animal world, including recent work on animal tool-making and use (e.g., Chappell & Kacelnik, 2002 and Chappell & Kacelnik, 2004). Related discussions and empirical data can be found in Cummins and Cummins (2005), Csibra and Gergely (2006) and Tomasello, Carpenter, Call, Behne, and Moll (2005). Perhaps future work on altricial robots will enable us to rewrite Piaget's (1954) theories.

6.2. Meta-semantic Competence

Another feature important in humans and possibly some other animals is meta-semantic competence: the ability not merely to perceive, think about, or have intentions involving physical things, such as rocks, trees, routes, food, and the bodies of animals (including one's own), but also to have semantic states that represent entities, states, and processes that themselves have semantic content, such as one's own thoughts, intentions, or planning strategies, or those of others. The label "meta-management" for an architectural layer with meta-semantic competence applied to the system itself was coined by Luc Beaudoin in his PhD thesis (1994). (The word "reflective" is sometimes used, but also often has other meanings – one of many examples of confused terminology in the study of architectures.) Closely related ideas have been developed by Minsky (2006) and Singh (2005), focusing mainly on attempts to model human competence. Sloman and Chrisley (2003) relate this to the concept of having qualia.

It seems that humans are not alone in having meta-semantic competence, but the richness of their meta-semantic competence, whether directed inwardly or outwardly is unmatched. We still do not know what sorts of forms of representation, mechanisms, and architectures support this, or how far they are genetically determined and how far a product of the environment, based, for example, on cultural learning. Late development does not rule out genetic determination, as should be clear from developments in puberty.

There is much discussion in many disciplines (e.g., philosophy, sociology, anthropology, psychology, ethology) of the ability of one individual to think about other intelligent individuals, to communicate with them, and to engage with them in various kinds of shared activities. There are deep problems concerned with referential opacity that need to be solved by such theories. For instance, normal modes of reasoning break down because things referred to in beliefs, desires, intentions, etc. need not exist. You cannot kick or eat something that does not exist, but you can think about it, talk about it or run away from it. Moreover, a stone or tree cannot be correct or mistaken – it just exists – but a thought or belief can be true or false. Developmental psychologists study growth of understanding of these matters in children, but do not explain the mechanisms. Perhaps roboticists will one day. Multidisciplinary research is needed to investigate when meta-semantic capabilities evolved, why they evolved, how much they depend on learning as opposed to being preconfigured or meta-configured, how they are influenced by a culture, and what their behavioral consequences are. There are very few discussions of architectural and representational requirements for an organism or machine to represent, refer to, or reason about, semantic contents. Exceptions include McCarthy (1995) and Minsky (2006). Further work is needed for progress on integrated cognitive systems that scale out.

7. Using Detailed Scenarios to Sharpen Vision

One way to reduce ontological blindness to some of the functions of natural cognition, is to formulate design goals in terms of *very de-*

tailed scenarios, an idea being taken up in the euCognition network's Research Roadmap project. If scenarios are described in minute detail, for example, using imaginary "film-scripts" for future demonstrations of human-like robots, then close attention to individual steps in the scenario can generate questions of the form: "How could it do that?" that might not be noticed if a competence is described at too general a level. Moreover, we must not focus only on scenarios involving useful "adult" robots. A three-year-old child who is well able to hold a pencil and make spirals and other things on a sheet of paper may be unable to copy a square drawn on the paper despite being able to trace a square and to join up dots forming the corners of a square. This could inspire a scenario in which a robot learns to perceive and produce pictures of various sorts on a blank sheet. By trying to design a robot that starts with the abilities and limitations of the three-year-old, and later extends its abilities, we may hope to gain new insights into hidden complexities in the original copying task. (Incidentally, this is one of many examples where the core issues could be studied using a simulated robot: the cognitive development is not dependent on physical embodiment.)

7.1. *Sample Competences to be Modeled*

As mentioned in Section 4.5, a young child may be able to lift cut-out pictures of various animals (e.g., a cat, a cow, an elephant) from a sheet of plywood, but be unable to replace them in their recesses until concepts like "boundary" and "alignment" have been added to his or her ontology. We can extend the example by analyzing a sequence of intermediate competences, each of which can be achieved without going on to the next step:

- being able to lift a picture from its recess (using its attached knob),
- being able to put down a picture,
- being able lift a picture from its recess and put it somewhere else,
- being able to lift a picture from the table and put it on the plywood sheet,

- being able to put the picture down in the general location of its recess,
- being able to see that the picture is not yet in its recess,
- being able to randomly move and rotate the picture until the picture drops into its recess,
- seeing that the explanation of the picture's not going into its recess is that its boundary is not aligned with the boundary of the recess,
- being able to use the perceived mismatch between the boundaries, to slide and rotate the picture till it drops into the recess,
- being able to say which picture should go into which recess,
- being able to explain why the non-aligned picture will not fit into its recess, and
- being able to help a younger child understand how to get the pictures back into their recesses.

This partially ordered collection of competences leaves out much of the fine detail in the progression, but indicates possible stages about which we can ask: What mechanisms, forms of representation, algorithms, or architectures. can account for this competence? What needs to be added to the child's ontology at each stage to enable competence to improve (e.g., boundary of a shape, alignment and misalignment of two boundaries)? What mechanisms can account for the development of the competence from precursor competences? What mechanisms can enable successor competences to develop from this competence? What sort of architecture can combine all these competences and the required forms of representation?

We should not assume that there is some *uniform* learning mechanism that is involved at all stages. Nor should we assume that all required forms of learning are present from the start: Some kinds of learning may themselves be learned. We need to distinguish kinds of meta-competence and ask which are learned, and how they are learned. The last example, the ability to help a younger child, has many precursor competences not in the list, that would need to be unpacked as part of a detailed analysis, including meta-semantic competences, such as being able to see and think about another individual as having goals, as perceiving objects, as performing intentional actions, as making mistakes, or as not knowing something.

7.2. *Fine-Grained Scenarios are Important*

The need for "fine grain" in scenario specifications is not always appreciated. Merely specifying that a robot will help infirm humans in their own homes does not generate as many questions as specifying that the robot will be able to see wine glasses on a table after a meal and put the used ones into a dishwasher without breaking them. How will it tell which have been used? Compare the differences between red and white wine. Will it also be able to do that for coffee cups? How will it control its movements in picking up the glasses? What difference does the design of its hand make? For example, does the task require force feedback? Will it pick up only one thing at a time or more than one in the same hand? How will it avoid bumping a glass against other objects in a partly loaded dishwasher? Under what conditions will it make a mistake and break a glass, and why? Can it improve its competence by practice, and if so, how will that happen, and what sorts of improvement will occur? Will it be able to modify its behavior appropriately if the lights are dimmed, or if its vision becomes blurred through camera damage, or if part of its hand is not functioning? Will it be able to explain why it picked up only two glasses at a time and not more? Can it explain how it would have changed its behavior if the glasses had been twice as big, or if they had had wine left in them?

Each question leads to bifurcations in the possible scenarios to be addressed, depending on whether the answer is "yes" or "no". If this attention to detail seems tedious, we need to remember that we are attempting to understand results of many millions of years of evolution.

7.3. *Behavior Specifications Are Not Enough*

Merely specifying a form of behavior to be demonstrated does not specify research goals, for, at one extreme, it may be that the behavior is largely pre-programmed by genetic mechanisms in an animal or by explicit programming in a robot (as in precocial species), or, at another extreme, it may be a result of a process of learning and development that is capable of producing a wide variety of end results depending on the environment in which it occurs (as in so-called altricial species). The scenario-based methodology avoids arguments over "best" target scenarios or "best" designs, allowing both extremes and also a variety of intermediate cases to be studied, so that we learn the detailed requirements for various combinations of competences, and their trade-offs.

Another way of generating task requirements is to bring people from different disciplines together to discuss one another's problems and results. A theory of ontological and representational development crying out for new research in computational models is presented in Karmiloff-Smith (1994). Compare the analysis of learning to count, in chapter 8 of Sloman (1978). Cognitive robotics researchers should attend to discoveries of psychologists, students of animal behavior, neuroscientists, and clinicians who identify failures of competence arising out of various kinds of brain damage or deterioration. Examples of "ritual behaviors" providing hints about the architecture are presented in Boyer and Lienard (2006).

8. Resolving Fruitless Disputes by Methodological "Lifting"

Many choices have to be made when designing explanatory models, including selecting forms of representation, algorithms, architectures, kinds of information to be used, types of hardware, design and testing procedures, programming languages, development environments, and other software tools, and, in recent years, debating whether robots can or cannot, should or should not have emotions: See (Arbib & Fellous, 2005; Simon, 1967; Sloman & Croucher, 1981). Too often the disagreements become pointless squabbles about which design option is right or best. They are pointless if the terms used are ill-defined, or if there is no *best* option, only a collection of *trade-offs*, as argued in the online presentation on whether intelligence requires emotions at this Web site: http://www.cs.bham.ac.uk/research/cogaff/talks/#cafe04.

8.1. *Analyze Before You Choose*

Instead of continuing these debates, we can shift the questions to a higher level, encouraging former opponents to become collaborators in a deeper project. Instead of debating whether neural or symbolic forms of representations should be used, we can instead explore the space of possible forms of representation, trying to understand the dimensions in which the formalisms differ, while trying to understand what the individual types are and are not good for, what mechanisms they require, and how they differ in relation to a range of meta-requirements such as speed, accuracy, reliability, extendability, and generality. Usually, the answers are not obvious, so if the options and trade-offs can be made clear by research addressing such "meta-level" questions, then future researchers can choose options wisely on the basis of detailed task requirements, instead of following fashions or prejudice. When we understand the trade-offs fully we shall be in a much better position to do empirical and theoretic research to support various design choices.

An example is Minsky's "causal diversity" depiction of trade-offs between symbolic and neural mechanisms (Minsky, 1992). His much older paper (Minsky, 1963) also includes many relevant observations about trade-offs between design alternatives. Another influential meta-level paper (McCarthy & Hayes, 1969) produced a first draft list of criteria for adequacy of forms of representation, namely, metaphysical adequacy, epistemological adequacy, and heuristic adequacy (to which, e.g., learnability and evolvability in various environments could be added). That paper's emphasis on logic provoked a charge of narrowness in Sloman (1971), and a response in Hayes (1984). A recent development of this thread is a PhD thesis on proofs using continuous diagrams Winterstein (2005). Some steps toward a more general overview of the space of possible forms of representation are in Sloman (1993, 1996). However, the analysis of varieties of information processing in biological systems still has a long way to go.

Many discussions of representations and mechanisms fail to take account of requirements for an integrated agent with a complex body embedded in a partially unknown and continuously changing richly structured environment. Such an agent will typically have concurrently active processes concerned with managing the state of the body, including controlling ongoing actions and continuously sensing the environment, in parallel with other internal processes, such as reminiscing, deliberating, thinking about what someone is saying, and planning a response, as well as aesthetic and emotional responses. Work on requirements for complete architectures in systems interacting with a rich dynamic environment has begun to address this complexity, but is still in its infancy. Gaps in our knowledge are easily revealed by analysis of requirements for detailed scenarios. For example, requirements for a robot to see its hand grasping and moving a complex object in the proximity of other complex objects include representing "multi-strand processes", in which different relationships between parts of different objects change concurrently, some continuously (e.g., getting closer) and some discretely (e.g., coming into contact, and changing affordances).

8.2. *The Need to Survey Spaces of Possibilities*

Meta-level analysis of a space of possibilities (e.g., for forms of representation, for

mechanisms, for architectures) should help to end fruitless debates over such questions as to whether representations are needed in intelligent systems, or which sorts of representations are best. Some debates are inherently muddled because what one faction offers as an *alternative* to using representations another will describe as merely using a different *sort* of representation. If we have a deep understanding of the structure of the space of possibilities containing the proposed alternatives, and their trade-offs, then how we *label* the options is of lesser consequence. Agreeing on labels may sometimes arise from agreement on what variety of things we are labelling. (Compare the importance of the periodic table of the elements in the history of the physical sciences.)

The current state of teaching regarding whether to use symbolic forms of representation, or artificial neural nets and numerical/statistical formalisms and methods causes harm. Learners often simply pick up the prejudices of their teachers, and, in some cases, do not even learn about the existence of alternatives to the approach they are taught. This became very clear when we were attempting to select candidates for a robotics research position: several applicants with MSc or PhD degrees in AI/Robotics had never encountered a symbolic parser, problem solver, or planning system. (An excellent introduction to AI planning mechanisms is Ghallab, Nau, and Traverso [2004].) Similarly, although there have been many proposed architectures, some of them surveyed in Langley and Laird (2006), students who learn about a particular sort of architecture may never learn about very different alternatives. A generation of researchers trained with blinkered vision will not achieve the major advances in such a difficult field, even if different subgroups have different blinkers. To summarize:

- Before choosing the best X, try to understand the space of possible Xs.
- Often there is no best X, but a collection of trade-offs.

- Instead of trying to determine precise boundaries between Xs and non-Xs, it is often more fruitful to investigate varieties of X-like things, the dimensions in which they vary, and the trade-offs: often the X/non-X distinction evaporates and is replaced by a rich taxonomy of cases.

8.3. *Toward an Ontology for Types of Architectures*

Over the last two decades, there has been a shift of emphasis in research on computational models from investigations of *algorithms* and *representations* for specific tasks, to the study of *architectures* combining many components performing different tasks. Various specific architectures have been proposed, some of them surveyed in Langley and Laird (2006). That survey illustrates how unfortunate definitions can blinker vision, for it *defines* an architecture as something that cannot change, thereby excluding research into whether infants start with a limited architecture extended under the influence of the environment (Chappell & Sloman, 2007; Petters, 2006).

The research community has so far not developed an agreed analysis of requirements for different sorts of architectures nor an adequate ontology for describing and comparing alternatives. Moreover, the existing terminology that is widely used for labelling components, for example as "reactive", "deliberative", "reflective", "affective", "symbolic", "sub-symbolic", is not based on well-defined, clearly specified categories. For example, some will label as *deliberative* any system in which sensory inputs can activate rival responses, one of which is selected by a competitive process; whereas Sloman (2006b) calls that *proto-deliberative*, following AI tradition in reserving the label *deliberative* for mechanisms that search for and manipulate representations of variable structure and complexity, using compositional semantics. A richer meta-level ontology for types of architectures would allow a variety of intermediate cases. Some researchers use the label "reactive" to exclude internal state change, whereas others allow reactive systems to learn and have changing goals, as long as they lack deliberative mechanisms for constructing and comparing hypothetical alternatives. As indicated in Section 6.2, the word "reflective" is also used with different meanings when describing architectures or components of architectures. Papers in the Cognition and Affect project (http://www.cs.bham.ac.uk/research/cogaff/) present the *CogAff schema* as a first draft attempt to provide a more principled ontology for possible architectures, which will need to be related to *niche space*, the space of possible sets of requirements.

Researchers wishing to move beyond the present terminological mess can assume that biological evolution produced many intermediate cases not yet understood, some occurring during early stages of human infant and child development, although observing processes in virtual machines that bootstrap themselves is a task fraught with difficulties (Sloman & Chappell, 2005). We need to understand intermediate cases that occurred in nature if we are to match designs for working models to the variety produced by evolution, whether for scientific or for practical purposes. A better ontology for architectures may also help us develop better tools to support cognitive modeling (cf. Ritter, 2002; Kramer & Scheutz, 2007).

9. Assessing Scientific Progress

A psychologist once commented that whenever he heard researchers giving seminars on computational models, they talked about what they were going to do, and occasionally what they had done, but rarely about what they had *discovered*. Can the cognitive modeling research community map out intended *advances in knowledge* – as opposed to merely forming plans for *doing things*, however worthwhile? A partial answer was given in Sections 7 and 8: There is scientific work to be done producing systematic meta-level theories about varieties of forms of representation, mechanisms, architectures, functions, and requirements that define the spaces from which we can choose components of designs and explanatory theories. That can provide a framework for further work on substantive questions about how human vision works, or how crows build nests, or how children learn language, or how capabilities found in nature may be replicated or improved on in artificial systems. For scientific purposes, merely building systems that work is of limited value, if we do not understand how they work and why they are better or worse than other possible designs, etc., or better in some contexts and worse in others.

Much funded applied research is defined in terms of specific practical goals, for example, producing a system that will do something that no machine has done before, whether it be attending a conference and giving a talk (Simmons et al., 2003), performing well at soccer (http://www.robocup.org), helping with rescue operations after a disaster (http://www.rescuesystem.org), helping with domestic chores (http://www.ai.rug.nl/robocupathome), or identifying potential terrorists at airports. In addition to identifying specific, somewhat arbitrary, target systems, however interesting and important, we should attempt to identify a structured set of scientific goals that advance our *knowledge and understanding*, as opposed to merely advancing our *practical capabilities* (however important that may be). We cannot expect there to be anything as simple and clear as Hilbert's list of unsolved mathematical problems in a field as complex and diverse as the study of intelligence, which will probably never have the clarity and rigour of mathematics at the start of the twentieth century, because cognitive science encompasses the study of all forms of cognition, including future products of evolution and human-machine integration. But we can attempt to identify important questions that need to be answered.

9.1. *Organizing Questions*

Just as mathematicians showed that answering some questions will enable others to be answered, or at least simplified, so should cognitive modelers try to identify relations between unsolved problems. For example, if we can describe in detail some of the competences displayed by young children at different stages of development in different cultures, and if we analyze in detail the architectural and representational requirements for those competences, that will give us insight into the variety of developmental paths available to humans. That in turn may give us clues regarding the mechanisms that are capable of generating such patterns of learning and development. In particular, instead of doing only research with a narrow focus, such as language learning, visual learning, or development of motor control, we can look at typical interactions between these kinds of learning and other things such as varieties of play, growth of ontologies, kinds of enjoyment, kinds of social interaction, and kinds of self-understanding.

This may help us overcome the difficulty of identifying what needs to be explained, referred to as "ontological blindness" in Section 3. It can also address a further difficulty, namely that different subcommunities disagree as to what is important or interesting, partly because they are in competition for limited funds, or simply because of limitations in what they have learned. So instead of trying only to propose specific scientific goals, over which there is likely to be strong disagreement regarding priorities, perhaps researchers can agree on a principled methodology for generating and analyzing *relations* between structured collections of goals that can provide milestones and criteria for success, allowing new goals to be set as we continue to apply the method. One such method is based on the use of detailed scenarios described in Section 7.

9.2. *Scenario-Based Backward Chaining Research*

Suppose we describe *in great detail* a variety of scenarios involving various kinds of human-like or animal-like behavior whose achievement is far beyond the current state of the art. The dishwasher-loading, and picture-puzzle scenarios in Section 7 are examples, but we could produce hundreds more, relating to everyday competences of humans of different ages and sorts as well as other animals. If we then analyze requirements for producing the detailed behaviors, this may enable us to generate "precursor scenarios" for those scenarios, and precursors for the precursors, where a precursor to a distant scenario at least prima facie involves competences that are likely to play a role in that scenario.

9.3. *Assessing (Measuring?) Progress*

By carefully analyzing long-term and intermediate goals, and working backward from them, we can expect to identify a *partially* ordered set of scenarios. Those scenarios can be annotated with hypotheses to be tested regarding kinds of knowledge, kinds of learning, forms of representation, mechanisms, and architectures that may enable the scenarios to be achieved. That will define milestones for measuring progress. The "measure" will not be a number, but a location in a partially ordered collection of initially unexplained capabilities. Of course, as the research proceeds, the collection of scenarios, the presupposition/precursor links, and the hypothesized components of adequate models and explanations will change.

Sometimes rival hypotheses will be proposed, and that will help to sharpen some of the research goals associated with the scenarios, by suggesting variants of the scenarios, or constraints on implementation. That should lead to tests that can show which hypothesis is better, or whether each is better only for a subset of cases. Sometimes one hypothesis will eventually turn out to be better at defining a long-term "progressive" research program in the sense of Lakatos (1980).

We can also work forwards from the current state of the art, identifying new competences selected on the basis of their apparent relevance to the more remote scenarios, but we are likely to make better short-term choices after we have sketched at least some of the terrain a long way ahead: otherwise

more attractive short term goals will be selected.

9.4. *Replacing Rivalry with Collaboration*

We can separate two kinds of meta-level tasks involved in planning research:

- the task of *describing* and *analyzing* research problems, their relationships to other problems, the evidence required to determine whether they have been solved, the methods that might be relevant to solving them, and the possible consequences of solving them; and
- the *prioritizing, justification*, or *selection* of research problems: deciding what is important and should be funded.

People can collaborate and reach agreement on the former while disagreeing about the latter. The process of collaborating on the first should lead researchers to be less intensely committed to answers to the second question: Questions about what is important are not usually themselves important in the grand scheme of advancing knowledge. (The philosopher J. L. Austin is rumored to have silenced an objector by saying "Truth is more important than importance".)

Understanding the science better will enable us to discuss the benefits of different ways of allocating scarce research resources. Work on clarifying and analyzing a problem can contribute to a decision to postpone research on the problem, by revealing a hard prior problem, or by clarifying the relative costs and benefits of different options. Meta-level theoretical work revealing good routes to intermediate goals can be a significant contribution to knowledge about a hard problem, especially analysis of which mechanisms, formalisms, architectures, or knowledge systems, will or will not be sufficient to support particular types of scenarios (compare the role of complexity theory in software engineering).

By making construction, analysis and ordering of possible scenarios, along with analysis of corresponding design options and trade-offs, an explicit community-wide task (like the Human Genome project), we separate the task of identifying research problems and their relationships, a task that can be done collaboratively, from projects aiming to solve the problems or aiming to test specific rival hypotheses, which may be done competitively. This can also reduce the tendency for research groups or subcommunities to specify their own evaluation criteria independently of what others are doing, a symptom of an immature and fragmented science. This can also provide a means of evaluating research *proposals*. Computational modeling researchers often propose to do what previous researchers had proposed to do, but failed to do, provoking the question: Why should the new proposals be taken seriously? New proposals are too often "forward-chaining" proposals regarding how known techniques, formalisms, and architectures, will be used to solve hard problems: a well-tried recipe for failure. Perhaps, if more research is selected on the basis of detailed "backward-chaining" analysis of long-term task requirements for integrated systems, a major change in the fortunes of research projects will follow.

10. Conclusion

Previous chapters have mainly focused on achievements. This one has reviewed some gaps that still need to be filled, outlining some ways of accelerating progress toward the development of models that are more human-like, using deeper and more comprehensive theories of human and animal cognitive competences and their development. There are many gaps and much work still to be done. For instance, most of what can be done by one to two-year-old toddlers is far beyond anything we can now model. We also cannot yet model finding something *funny* or *aesthetically pleasing,* neither of which is a matter of producing any behavior.

Perhaps this partial overview will help provoke researchers to address new prob-

lems, such as how scaling out happens, and new ways of thinking about the long-term challenge of integrating multiple competences. Perhaps documents like this will provoke some very bright young researchers to strike out in new directions that in future years will be seen to have transformed the research landscape, leading to deep new scientific understanding and many new applications that are now far beyond the state of the art. This will require overcoming serious institutional impediments to such developments. It may also require the invention of new forms of computation.[1]

Acknowledgments

Some of this work was inspired by participation in the EU-Funded project *CoSy: Cognitive Systems for Cognitive Assistants,* described at http://www.cognitivesystems. org, and owes much to discussions with members of the CoSy project and also interactions with, or publications of, Margaret Boden, Jackie Chappell, Ron Chrisley, John McCarthy, Marvin Minsky, Matthias Scheutz, and the late Push Singh. Ron Sun and anonymous referees made useful editorial suggestions. Peggy Rote very kindly took great trouble to provide help at the copy-editing stage. The copy-editor cannot be blamed for the author's intransigence in rejecting most proposed changes of wording or punctuation.

References

Anderson, M., Meyer, B., & Olivier, P. (Eds.). (2001). *Diagrammatic representation and reasoning.* Berlin: Springer-Verlag.

1 The references that follow should not be treated as a comprehensive bibliography. They are merely samples of what is available. Increasingly, the important up-to-date literature is not in printed documents but in Web pages, including draft books and papers, online reviews, and the like, so several Web sites have been listed as sources of further information. There are many more. The author accepts responsibility for refusal to provide retrieval dates for URLs.

Arbib, M., & Fellous, J.-M. (Eds.). (2005). *Who needs emotions? The brain meets the robot*. New York: Oxford University Press.

Barrow, H., & Tenenbaum, J. (1978). Recovering intrinsic scene characteristics from images. In A. Hanson & E. Riseman (Eds.), *Computer vision systems*. New York: Academic Press.

Beaudoin, L. (1994). *Goal processing in autonomous agents*. Unpublished doctoral dissertation, School of Computer Science, The University of Birmingham, Birmingham, UK. (http://www.cs.bham.ac.uk/research/projects/cogaff/81-95.html#38)

Berthoz, A. (2000). *The brain's sense of movement*. London, UK: Harvard University Press.

Boden, M. A. (1990). *The creative mind: Myths and mechanisms*. London: Weidenfeld & Nicolson.

Boden, M. A. (2006). *Mind As Machine: A history of Cognitive Science (Vols 1–2)*. Oxford: Oxford University Press.

Boyer, P., & Lienard, P. (2006). Why ritualized behavior? Precaution Systems and action parsing in developmental, pathological and cultural rituals. *Behavioral and Brain Sciences*, 29(6), 595–650. (http://www.bbsonline.org/Preprints/Boyer-04042005/)

Brooks, R. A. (1991). Intelligence without representation. *Artificial Intelligence*, 47, 139–159.

Chappell, J., & Kacelnik, A. (2002). Tool selectivity in a non-mammal, the New Caledonian crow (Corvus moneduloides). *Animal Cognition*, 5, 71–78.

Chappell, J., & Kacelnik, A. (2004). New Caledonian crows manufacture tools with a suitable diameter for a novel task. *Animal Cognition*, 7, 121–127.

Chappell, J., & Sloman, A. (2007). Natural and artificial meta-configured altricial information-processing systems. *International Journal of Unconventional Computing*. (http://www.cs.bham.ac.uk/research/projects/cosy/papers/#tr0609)

Chomsky, N. (1965). *Aspects of the theory of syntax*. Cambridge, MA: MIT Press.

Colton, S., Bundy, A., & Walsh, T. (2000). On the notion of interestingness in automated mathematical discovery. *International Journal of Human-Computer Studies*, 53(3), 351–375.

Csibra, G., & Gergely, G. (2006). Social learning and social cognition: The case for pedagogy. In M. H. Johnson & Y. Munakata (Eds.), *Processes of change in brain and cognitive development: Attention and performance XXI* (pp. 249–274). Oxford: Oxford University Press. (http://www.cbcd.bbk.ac.uk/people/gergo/a&p_pedagogy.pdf)

Cummins, D., & Cummins, R. (2005). Innate modules vs innate learning biases. *Cognitive Processing: International Quarterly Journal of Cognitive Science*, 3(3–4), 19–30.

Fodor, J. (1975). *The language of thought*. Cambridge, MA: Harvard University Press.

Fodor, J. (1983). *The modularity of mind*. Cambridge, MA: MIT Press.

Ghallab, M., Nau, D., & Traverso, P. (2004). *Automated planning, theory and practice*. San Francisco, CA: Elsevier, Morgan Kaufmann Publishers.

Gibson, J. (1979). *The ecological approach to visual perception*. Hillsdale, NJ: Lawrence Erlbaum Associates. (Revised edition 1986)

Goodale, M., & Milner, A. (1992). Separate visual pathways for perception and action. *Trends in Neurosciences*, 15(1), 20–25.

Grice, H. (1975). Logic and Conversation. In D. Davidson & G. Harman (Eds.), *The logic of grammar* (pp. 64–75). Encino, CA: Dickenson.

Grush, R. (2004). The emulation theory of representation: Motor control, imagery, and perception. *Behavioral and Brain Sciences*, 27, 377–442.

Halliday, M. (1975). *Learning how to mean: Explorations in the development of language*. London: Edward Arnold.

Hayes, P. J. (1984). Some problems and non-problems in representation theory. In R. Brachman & H. Levesque (Eds.), *Readings in knowledge representation* (pp. 3–22). Los Altos, California: Morgan Kaufmann.

Hayworth, K. J., & Biederman, I. (2006). Neural evidence for intermediate representations in object recognition. *Vision Research*, 46(23), 4024–4031. (doi:10.1016/j.visres.2006.07.015)

Hendler, J. (2005, March/April). A Letter from the Editor: Fathoming Funding. *IEEE Intelligent Systems*, 20(2), 2–3. (http://ieeexplore.icee.org/iel5/9670/30619/01413163.pdf?arnumber=1413163)

Karmiloff-Smith, A. (1994). Precis of: Beyond modularity: A developmental perspective on cognitive science. *Behavioral and Brain Sciences*, 17(4), 693–706. (http://www.bbsonline.org/documents/a/00/00/05/33/index.html)

Kramer, J., & Scheutz, M. (2007). Development environments for autonomous mobile robots:

A survey. *Autonomous Robots*, 22(2), 101–132. (DOI 10.1007/s10514-006-9013-8)

Lakatos, I. (1980). The methodology of scientific research programmes. In J. Worrall & G. Currie (Eds.), *Philosophical papers Vol I*. Cambridge, UK: Cambridge University Press.

Langley, P., & Laird, J. (2006). *Cognitive architectures: Research issues and challenges* (Tech. Rep.). Palo Alto, CA.: Institute for the Study of Learning and Expertise. (http://cll.stanford.edu/ langley/papers/final.arch.pdf)

Lungarella, M., & Sporns, O. (2006). Mapping information flow in sensorimotor networks. *PLoS Computational Biolology*, 2(10:e144). (DOI: 10.1371/journal.pcbi.0020144)

Marr, D. (1982). *Vision*. San Francisco: Freeman.

McCarthy, J. (1995). Making robots conscious of their mental states. In *AAAI spring symposium on representing mental states and mechanisms*. Palo Alto, CA: AAAI. (http://www-formal.stanford.edu/jmc/consciousness.html)

McCarthy, J. (2004). *What is Artificial Intelligence?* Stanford University. (http://www-formal.stanford.edu/jmc/whatisai/whatisai.html)

McCarthy, J., & Hayes, P. (1969). Some philosophical problems from the standpoint of AI. In B. Meltzer & D. Michie (Eds.), *Machine Intelligence 4* (pp. 463–502). Edinburgh, Scotland: Edinburgh University Press. (http://www-formal.stanford.edu/jmc/mcchay69/mcchay69.html)

McGurk, H., & MacDonald, J. (1976). Hearing lips and seeing voices. *Nature*, 264, 746–748.

Michie, D. (1991). Machine intelligence and the human window. *Applied Artificial Intelligence*, 5(1), 1–10.

Miller, G., Galanter, E., & Pribram, K. (1960). *Plans and the structure of behaviour*. New York: Holt.

Minsky, M. L. (1963). Steps towards artificial intelligence. In E. Feigenbaum & J. Feldman (Eds.), *Computers and thought* (pp. 406–450). New York: McGraw-Hill.

Minsky, M. L. (1992). Future of AI Technology. *Toshiba Review*, 47(7). (http://web.media.mit.edu/~minsky/papers/CausalDiversity.html)

Minsky, M. L. (2006). *The emotion machine*. New York: Pantheon.

Newell, A. (1990). *Unified theories of cognition*. Cambridge, MA: Harvard University Press.

Petters, D. (2006). *Designing agents to understand infants*. Unpublished doctoral dissertation, School of Computer Science, University of Birmingham, Birmingham, UK. (http://

www.cs.bham.ac.uk/research/projects/cogaff/06.html#0605)

Philipona, D., O'Regan, J. K., & Nadal, J.-P. (2003). Is there something out there? Inferring space from sensorimotor dependencies. *Neural Computation*, 15(9). (http://nivea.psycho.univ-paris5.fr/Philipona/space.pdf)

Piaget, J. (1954). *The construction of reality in the child*. New York: Ballantine Books. (Last chapter online http://www.marxists.org/reference/subject/philosophy/works/fr/piaget2.htm)

Ritter, F. (Ed.). (2002). *Techniques for modeling human performance in synthetic environments: A supplementary review*. Ft. Belvoir, VA: Defense Technical Information Center. (http://ritter.ist.psu.edu/papers/SOAR-Jun03.pdf)

Saxena, A., Driemeyer, J., Kearns, J., Osondu, C., & Ng, A. Y. (2006). Learning to Grasp Novel Objects using Vision. In *10th International Symposium of Experimental Robotics, ISER 2006*.

Scheutz, M. (Ed.). (2002). *Computationalism: New directions*. Cambridge, MA: MIT Press.

Simmons, R. G., Goldberg, D., Goode, A., Montemerlo, M., Roy, N., et al. (2003). Grace: An autonomous robot for the aaai robot challenge. *AI Magazine*, 24(2), 51–72.

Simon, H. A. (1967). Motivational and emotional controls of cognition. In H. A. Simon (Ed.), *Models of thought* (pp. 29–38). Newhaven, CT: Yale University Press.

Simon, H. A. (1997). *Allen Newell (1927–1992) (Biographical Memoir)*. National Academy of Sciences. (http://stills.nap.edu/readingroom/books/biomems/anewell.html)

Singh, P. (2005). *EM-ONE: An architecture for reflective commonsense thinking*. Unpublished doctoral dissertation, MIT, Cambridge, MA. (http://web.media.mit.edu/~push/push-thesis.html)

Sloman, A. (1971). Interactions between philosophy and AI: The role of intuition and non-logical reasoning in intelligence. In *Proceedings 2nd international joint conference on ai* (pp. 209–226). London: William Kaufmann. (http://www.cs.bham.ac.uk/research/cogaff/04.html#200407)

Sloman, A. (1978). *The computer revolution in philosophy*. Hassocks, Sussex, UK: Harvester Press. (http://www.cs.bham.ac.uk/research/cogaff/ crp)

Sloman, A. (1979). The primacy of non-communicative language. In M. MacCafferty & K. Gray (Eds.), *The analysis of meaning:*

Informatics 5 Proceedings ASLIB/BCS Conference, Oxford, March 1979 (pp. 1–15). London: Aslib. (http://www.cs.bham.ac.uk/research/projects/cogaff/81-95.html)

Sloman, A. (1982). Image interpretation: The way ahead? In O. Braddick & A. Sleigh. (Eds.), *Physical and biological processing of images (Proceedings of an international symposium organised by The Rank Prize Funds, London, 1982.)* (pp. 380–401). Berlin: Springer-Verlag. (http://www.cs.bham.ac.uk/research/projects/cogaff/06.html#0604)

Sloman, A. (1989). On designing a visual system (towards a gibsonian computational model of vision). *Journal of Experimental and Theoretical AI, 1*(4), 289–337. (http://www.cs.bham.ac.uk/research/projects/cogaff/81-95.html#7)

Sloman, A. (1993). Varieties of formalisms for knowledge representation. *Computational Intelligence, 9*(4), 413–423.

Sloman, A. (1996). Towards a general theory of representations. In D. M. Peterson (Ed.), *Forms of representation: An interdisciplinary theme for cognitive science* (pp. 118–140). Exeter, UK: Intellect Books.

Sloman, A. (2002). The irrelevance of Turing machines to AI. In M. Scheutz (Ed.), *Computationalism: New directions* (pp. 87–127). Cambridge, MA: MIT Press. (http://www.cs.bham.ac.uk/research/cogaff/00-02.html#77)

Sloman, A. (2006a). Polyflaps as a domain for perceiving, acting and learning in a 3-D world. In *Online Position Papers for 2006 AAAI Fellows Symposium.* Menlo Park, CA: AAAI. (http://www.aaai.org/Fellows/fellows.php and http://www.aaai.org/Fellows/Papers/Fellows16.pdf)

Sloman, A. (2006b, May). *Requirements for a fully deliberative architecture (or component of an architecture)* (Research Note No. COSY-DP-0604). Birmingham, UK: School of Computer Science, University of Birmingham. (http://www.cs.bham.ac.uk/research/projects/cosy/papers/#dp0604)

Sloman, A., & Chappell, J. (2005). The Altricial-Precocial Spectrum for Robots. In *Proceedings IJCAI'05* (pp. 1187–1192). Edinburgh: IJCAI. (http://www.cs.bham.ac.uk/research/cogaff/05.html#200502)

Sloman, A., & Chappell, J. (2007). Computational Cognitive Epigenetics. *Behavioral and Brain Sciences.* (http://www.cs.bham.ac.uk/research/projects/cosy/papers/#tr0703; Commentary on Jablonka, E. and Lamb, M. J.

(2005). *Evolution in Four Dimensions: Genetic, Epigenetic, Behavioral, and Symbolic Variation in the History of Life* MIT Press, 2005).

Sloman, A., Chappell, J., & CoSyTeam, T. (2006, June). How an animal or robot with 3-D manipulation skills experiences the world. In *The tenth annual meeting of the Association for the Scientific Study of Consciousness.* Oxford, UK: ASSC. (http://www.cs.bham.ac.uk/research/projects/cosy/papers/#pr0602)

Sloman, A., Chrisley, R., & Scheutz, M. (2005). The architectural basis of affective states and processes. In M. Arbib & J.-M. Fellous (Eds.), *Who needs emotions? The brain meets the robot* (pp. 203–244). New York: Oxford University Press. (http://www.cs.bham.ac.uk/research/cogaff/03.html#200305)

Sloman, A., & Chrisley, R. L. (2003). Virtual machines and consciousness. *Journal of Consciousness Studies, 10*(4-5), 113–172.

Sloman, A., & Chrisley, R. L. (2005, June). More things than are dreamt of in your biology: Information-processing in biologically-inspired robots. *Cognitive Systems Research, 6*(2), 145–174.

Sloman, A., & Croucher, M. (1981). Why robots will have emotions. In *Proceedings 7th international joint conference on AI* (pp. 197–202). Vancouver: IJCAI.

Tomasello, M., Carpenter, M., Call, J., Behne, T., & Moll, H. (2005). Understanding and sharing intentions: The origins of cultural cognition. *Behavioral and Brain Sciences, 28*(5), 675–735.

Trehub, A. (1991). *The cognitive brain.* Cambridge, MA: MIT Press. (http://www.people.umass.edu/trehub/)

Turing, A. (1950). Computing machinery and intelligence. *Mind, 59,* 433–460.

Várady, T., Martin, R. R., & Cox, J. (1997). Reverse engineering of geometric models – An introduction. *Computer Aided Design, 29*(4), 255–268. (http://ralph.cs.cf.ac.uk/papers/Geometry/RE.pdf)

Winograd, T. (1972). Procedures as a representation for data in a computer program for understanding natural language. *Cognitive Psychology, 3*(1).

Winterstein, D. (2005). *Using diagrammatic reasoning for theorem proving in a continuous domain.* Unpublished doctoral dissertation, University of Edinburgh, School of Informatics. (http://www.era.lib.ed.ac.uk/handle/1842/642)

Author Index

Abbott, L. F., 480
ABC Research Group, 302
Abelson, R., 5, 506, 512, 524, 671, 677
Abrahamsen, A., 25, 561
Accornero, N., 635
Ackerman, P. L., 361, 575
Ackley, D. H., 31, 70, 200
Acosta, S., 643, 644
Adams, D., 364
Adams, J. A., 387
Adams, J. K., 204
Adelman, L., 577
Adelson, E. H., 617
Aggleton, J. P., 189, 190
Agre, P. E., 668
Ahlert, M., 542
Ahn, W., 245, 333
Aho, A. V., 344, 478
Ainsworth, L. K., 567, 568, 574
Aitken, M. R. F., 593, 595, 600, 605
Aizawa, K., 24
Ajjanagadde, V., 354
Akhavan, A. C., 119
Akshoomoff, N., 468
Albrecht, D. G., 618, 619
Albus, J., 636, 649
Aleksander, I., 676
Alexander, J., 532
Alfonso-Reese, L. A., 62, 272

Algom, D., 437
Allais, M., 304
Allan, L. G., 592, 605
Allemang, D., 551
Allen, J., 128, 485, 486, 489
Allopenna, P. D., 486
Alloy, L. B., 601
Allport, A., 422, 440
Almaraz, J., 592, 596, 605
Alonso, A. A., 213
Alonso, J. M., 615
Althaus, P., 118
Altmann, E., 383, 533
Altmann, G., 406, 407, 410, 414, 461,
    462
Alvarez, P., 215
Amaral, D. G., 191, 213
Amari, S., 118, 121
Ameel, E., 277, 282
Amir, E., 161, 364
Amirikian, B., 460
Amit, D., 112, 658
Ammann, F., 515
Andersen, E., 49, 261, 468
Andersen, H., 533
Andersen, S., 533
Anderson, C. H., 427, 557
Anderson, J., 24, 45, 128, 133, 134, 270, 492,
    530, 532, 534, 535, 541, 543

Anderson, J. R., 5, 7, 8, 13, 14, 61, 128, 172, 173, 176, 177, 178, 180, 181, 182, 183, 207, 215, 234, 277, 283, 285, 286, 287, 289, 290, 292, 323, 362, 365, 366, 367, 368, 370, 372, 375, 377, 378, 379, 381, 382, 383, 384, 387, 410, 411, 413, 416, 423, 441, 442, 443, 452, 456, 457, 470, 505, 551, 565, 566, 568, 571, 575, 576, 577, 675
Anderson, M., 206, 690
Anderson, N., 534
Andre, A. D., 576
Andreoletti, C., 512
Angstadt, P., 207
Ans, B., 46
Ansorge, U., 444
Anzai, A., 618
Anzai, Y., 362
Araya, R., 376
Arbib, M., 701
Arbib, M. A., 675, 676
Arcediano, F., 599, 601, 605
Arkoudas, K., 134, 154, 158, 160, 161
Arndt, J., 207
Aron, A. R., 438
Aronson, E., 506, 512
Arthur, A. E., 461, 463, 465
Asch, S. E., 524
Ashby, F. G., 62, 271, 272, 273, 293, 311
Ashcraft, M., 133, 135, 140
Ashe, J., 119
Ashkenazi, A., 211, 212
Aslin, R. N., 40, 249, 418
Aston-Jones, G., 437
Atick, J. J., 615
Atkeson, C., 658
Atkins, P., 487
Atkinson, J. W., 517
Atran, S., 85, 326, 533
Attias, H., 656
Attneave, F., 615
Atwood, M. E., 569, 577
Aubie, B., 556, 561
Austin, G., 229, 272, 669
Axelrod, J., 543
Axelrod, R., 531, 541
Axtell, R., 531, 543
Aydelott, J., 43
Ayers, M. S., 207
Azmi, A., 596

Baars, B. J., 399
Baayen, H., 482
Bach, E., 488
Bacon, F., 325
Baddeley, A. D., 387

Baddeley, R. J., 615
Baillargeon, R., 458, 459, 561
Bain, J. D., 201
Baker, A. G., 592, 597
Baker, C. L., 59, 491
Baldi, P., 425
Bale, A. C., 453, 461, 462
Ball, J. T., 566, 572, 582
Ballard, D. H., 570, 571, 581
Balleine, B. W., 593
Balota, D. A., 487
Baluja, S., 452
Banaji, M. R., 519
Bandelow, S., 49
Bandura, A., 369
Banich, M. T., 436
Bara, B., 344
Baraduc, P., 655
Baraff, E. R., 78
Barch, D. M., 436, 437, 438, 441
Barense, M. D., 196
Bargh, J. A., 509
Barkai, E., 194
Barkema, G. T., 87, 88–89
Barker, P., 533
Barlow, H. B., 615
Barnes, J. M., 205
Barnet, R. C., 592, 599
Barrow, H., 690, 692
Barsalou, L., 232, 671
Barto, A., 329, 407, 592
Barton, C., 318
Barwise, J., 136, 141, 143, 343, 466
Basso, G., 445
Bastian, A., 119, 120
Bates, E., 42, 43, 44, 47, 50, 468, 480, 672
Baxter, G., 15
Baxter, R. A., 190
Bayes, T., 63
Bearse, M. A., 618
Beasley, C. M., 362, 372, 377
Beatty, J., 59
Beaudoin, L., 674, 675, 698
Bechtel, W., 4, 25, 561
Beck, J. M., 656
Becker, S., 190, 191, 193, 194, 213, 215
Beckers, T., 593, 599, 603, 605
Been, S. L., 602
Beenhakker, M. P., 119
Behne, T., 701
Belavkin, R. V., 310
Bell, A. J., 615
Bell, B. G., 380
Bell, D. E., 302
Bem, S., 423

Benbasat, I., 577
Bergener, T., 117
Berger, J. O., 70
Berglan, L. R., 595
Berko, J., 34
Bermejo, R., 107
Bernardo, J. M., 67
Bernstein, N., 641, 642
Berry, D. C., 181, 396, 397, 403
Bertenthal, B., 233
Berthouze, L., 452
Berthoz, A., 650, 687
Berwick, R., 478, 488
Besner, D., 486
Best, B., 545
Beth, E. W., 340
Bettman, J. R., 302, 308, 576
Bever, T. G., 479
Bharadwaj, K. K., 375
Bhatnagar, N., 371, 375, 377
Bicho, E., 111, 117
Biederman, I., 617, 689
Bileschi, S., 618
Billman, D., 244
Birch, D., 517
Birnbaum, M. H., 305, 306
Biro, S., 233
Bishop, C., 86, 95, 658
Bishop, D. V. M., 50, 51
Bizzi, E., 635, 636, 645, 646, 649, 650, 658
Bjork, E. L., 206
Bjork, R. A., 206, 209
Black, P. K., 577
Blackmon, M. H., 567, 581, 582
Blair, N. J., 276, 597, 598
Blaisdell, A. P., 593, 599–600
Blake, D. V., 668
Blanchard-Fields, F., 404
Blei, D., 68, 90, 92, 93, 94, 95, 497
Blessing, S. B., 367, 378
Block, N., 399, 470
Blok, S. V., 327
Blum, B., 59, 74, 78, 290
Boakes, R. A., 603
Boas, M. L., 80
Bobrow, R., 581
Bod, R., 482, 489
Bodelon, C., 194
Boden, M., 4, 667, 668, 669, 670, 672, 673, 676, 677, 679, 685, 690
Bodner, G. E., 234
Boehm-Davis, D. A., 383, 565, 570
Bogacz, R., 197, 198, 199, 200
Bolles, R. C., 593
Bongiolatti, S. R., 445

Bookheimer, S. Y., 189
Bookman, L., 5, 10, 670
Boolos, G. S., 151, 163
Borenstein, E., 626
Borkowski, W., 519
Bostic, R., 306
Bothell, D., 172, 176, 180, 183, 423, 534, 535, 542, 544, 565, 571, 576
Bott, L., 271, 325, 335
Botvinick, M., 43, 210, 211, 436, 438, 441
Boucher, L., 406, 411, 418
Bourbaki, N., 128
Bourgeois, M. J., 520
Bourne, L. E., 272
Bouton, M. E., 596, 602
Bouvrie, J. V., 626
Bovair, S., 366, 571
Bower, G. H., 270, 382
Boyer, M., 397, 414
Boyer, P., 11, 533, 701
Boyle, J., 151
Bozeat, S., 257, 259, 260, 261
Brachman, R. J., 127
Bradley, A. L., 294
Bradley, L., 487
Bradley, M. M., 209
Brady, M., 641
Brainard, D. H., 60
Braine, M., 136, 340, 341, 343
Brainerd, C. J., 195
Braitenberg, V., 119
Brandstätter, E., 308
Bransford, J. D., 671
Brashers-Krug, T., 650
Braun, J., 423, 424, 425
Braver, T. S., 47, 436, 437, 438, 441, 444, 445
Brayton, R. K., 352
Breazeal, C., 130
Brenner, L., 318
Bresnick, T., 577
Brewer, M. B., 508
Bridle, J. S., 293
Briggs, J., 271, 335
Bringsjord, E., 135, 136, 143, 158
Bringsjord, S., 131, 133, 134, 135, 136, 143, 150, 154, 157, 158, 160, 161, 164
Brinkman, U., 481, 493
Broadbent, D. E., 181, 397, 403, 669
Broadbent, E. D., 423
Brockbank, M., 233
Brockmole, J. R., 581
Brodsky, B., 534, 539, 540, 541, 542, 543, 544
Brooks, L. R., 403, 414
Brooks, R., 102, 130, 668, 694
Brown, C., 488

Brown, G. D. A., 318, 487, 488
Brown, J. S., 367, 373
Brown, J. W., 437, 438, 441
Brown, M. W., 189, 190, 195, 197, 198, 199, 200
Browne, M. W., 68
Brownstein, A. L., 515, 516
Brozinsky, C. J., 189
Bruce, V., 33
Bruckhoff, C., 117
Brumbaugh, C. C., 517
Brunel, N., 437
Bruner, J. S., 229, 272, 669, 670
Bruno, R., 436
Bryant, P., 487
Brysbaert, M., 489
Bucciarelli, M., 128, 344, 352
Buckingham, D., 455, 461, 462, 467
Budescu, D. V., 318
Buehner, M., 75, 76, 78, 333
Bugajska, M., 128
Bukowski, L., 107
Bullemer, P., 398
Bullock, T. H., 118
Bumby, D., 135
Bundesen, C., 433
Bundy, A., 698
Burgess, C., 90, 495
Burgess, N., 190, 213, 215
Burgess, P. W., 445
Burke, J., 593, 594, 595, 600
Burnett, R., 334
Burns, B. D., 383
Burns, T., 542, 544
Burton, A. M., 33
Buschke, H., 387
Busemeyer, J. R., 272, 304, 311, 313, 314, 315, 316, 317, 318
Buss, R. R., 404
Bussey, T. J., 196
Butner, J., 521, 544
Butterfield, E. C., 455
Butterworth, B., 485, 487
Bybee, J., 30
Bylander, T., 551
Byrne, M. D., 172, 176, 178, 180, 183, 423, 442, 565, 566, 567, 571, 572, 573, 574, 576, 582, 583
Byrne, R. M. J., 343, 344, 346, 348, 349, 352, 355

Cacioppo, J. T., 515
Cai, D., 618
Cairns, P., 484
Call, J., 701

Caltagirone, C., 212
Camerer, C., 533
Canny, J. F., 630, 631
Caño, A., 592, 604, 605
Capitani, E., 256
Caramazza, A., 256
Carbonell, J. G., 367, 370
Card, S. K., 176, 565, 566, 567, 568, 569, 571, 576, 577, 580
Carey, S., 45, 78, 245, 465
Carlesimo, G. A., 212
Carley, K., 531, 536, 537, 538, 542, 544
Carlin, J. B., 79, 80, 81
Carlson, R. A., 399
Carpenter, G. A., 44, 270
Carpenter, M., 701
Carpenter, P. A., 177, 444, 489
Carper, R., 468
Carreiras, M., 346, 354
Carroll, J., 359, 506, 512, 524
Carswell, C. M., 578
Carter, C., 436, 215, 436, 437, 438, 441
Cassimatis, N., 128, 130
Castelfranchi, C., 532
Castelhano, M. S., 581
Castilo, M., 11
Castro, L., 594, 595
Cavanagh, P., 626
Cave, K. R., 424
Caverni, J. P., 334, 344, 352
Cecconi, F., 532, 544
Centola, D., 520
Cezayirli, E., 196
Chaiken, S., 515
Chalkley, M., 494
Chang, L., 423
Changeux, J. P., 400, 415, 436, 672
Chao, L. L., 260
Chapman, D., 668
Chapman, G. B., 592
Chappell, J., 687, 688, 689, 690, 694, 698, 703
Chappell, M., 203
Chapple, W., 635
Charles, D., 596
Charness, N., 380
Charney, R., 466
Charniak, E., 72, 133, 164, 489, 492, 498
Chase, C., 140
Chater, N., 42, 45, 59, 60, 61, 183, 318, 334, 352, 354, 383, 414, 480, 481, 482, 484, 487, 488, 490, 491, 492, 494, 495, 496, 498
Chatlosh, D. L., 592
Chein, J. M., 365, 380, 382, 443
Chen, S., 533
Chen, X., 533

Cheng, P., 75, 567, 578, 579, 582
Cheng, P. W., 75, 76, 78, 333, 592
Chi, M. T. H., 368, 373, 566
Chiat, S., 466
Chipman, S. F., 565
Chisholm, R., 133, 154
Cho, J. R., 404
Choi, D., 373
Choi, I., 11, 533
Chomsky, A. N., 668, 671
Chomsky, N., 60, 477, 479, 481, 490, 491, 492, 493, 694
Chong, R. S., 176
Chopra, G., 515, 516
Chrisley, R., 15, 678, 692, 696, 698
Christensen, H. I., 118
Christiansen, M., 42, 47, 486, 488, 492, 493, 494, 495, 498
Cisek, P., 120
Claessen, K., 158
Clahsen, H., 481, 493
Clancey, W., 534, 539, 540, 541, 542, 543, 544
Clark, A., 406, 411, 412, 668, 671
Clark, E. V., 466
Clark, M., 154, 158, 160
Clark, S. E., 202, 203
Cleeremans, A., 397, 398, 400, 401, 402, 404, 405, 406, 408, 414, 415, 445
Clegg, B. A., 398
Clifford, D., 75
Clifton, C. J. R., 479
Clippinger, J. H., 674
Clore, G. L., 511
Coats, S., 519
Cobos, P. L., 592, 604, 605
Cohen, A. L., 295
Cohen, G., 49
Cohen, J., 436
Cohen, J. D., 25, 47, 210, 211, 212, 213, 424, 434, 435, 436, 437, 438, 439, 440, 441, 443, 444
Cohen, L. B., 461, 462, 463, 465
Cohen, M., 105, 543
Cohen, M. X., 189
Cohen, N., 182, 190, 411
Cohen, P. R., 671, 677
Cohen, Y., 427
Colby, K. M., 506, 515, 518, 524, 669, 674
Cole, R. P., 599
Coley, J. D., 326, 327
Collins, A., 89, 155, 227, 228, 229, 237, 323, 327, 334, 382, 511
Collins, D., 135
Collins, M., 489, 492
Coltheart, M., 481, 485, 487

Colton, S., 698
Colunga, E., 465, 466
Conditt, M. A., 650, 652
Condoleon, M., 603
Conklin, J., 557
Conrad, F. G., 566
Conrey, F., 521, 522, 533
Conte, R., 531
Conway, F., 362
Cook, K. A., 567, 576
Cook, S. A., 342
Cooke, A. D. J., 306
Cooke, N. J., 572
Coombs, C., 7
Cooper, G., 74
Cooper, R., 171
Copeland, B. J., 678
Corbett, A. T., 566
Corlett, P. R., 605
Corley, M. M. B., 489
Corrigan-Halpern, A., 371, 374
CoSyTeam, T., 694, 698
Cottrell, G., 43, 44
Courchesne, E., 468
Courville, A. C., 59, 290
Cowan, J. D., 111, 118
Cowan, N., 444
Coward, A., 5, 6, 7, 8, 9, 11, 14, 533, 537
Coward, L., 11, 554, 555
Cox, J., 685
Crain, S., 478, 480
Crestani, F., 234
Crevier, D., 362
Criss, A. H., 195, 205
Crocker, M., 43, 479, 488, 490
Crossman, E., 376
Croucher, M., 687
Crowder, R. G., 589
Cruse, P., 674
Crutch, S. J., 256
Csibra, G., 233, 698
Cuetos, F., 489
Culhane, M. S., 424
Cummins, D., 698
Cummins, R., 698
Curran, T., 206, 413
Curtis, B., 487
Cutler, A., 484
Czyzewska, M., 397, 414

Daelemans, W., 482
Dahm, P., 117
Daigle, M., 161
Dailey, M. N., 44
Dallaway, R., 296

Damasio, A., 11, 260, 674
Damasio, H., 260
Damer, B., 534, 539, 540, 541, 542, 543, 544
Danks, D., 45, 78, 290, 333, 555
Darby, R. J., 592, 596, 604, 605
Daston, L., 59
Datey, A. V., 213
Daugherty, K., 457
Davachi, L., 189
Davelaar, E. J., 47, 211, 212
Davidsson, P., 531
Davies, M., 29
Davies, R. R., 196
Davis, J. H., 522
Davis, L. J., 424
Davis, N., 424
Davis, R., 362
Daw, N. D., 59, 290
Dawes, R., 7
Dawson, M., 8
Dayan, P., 8, 10, 11, 290, 437, 480
DeAngelis, G. C., 618
De Baecke, C., 489
Deco, G., 215, 424, 425, 428, 429, 430, 431, 432, 433
DeCoster, J., 510
DeGroot, M., 656
Dehaene, S., 400, 415, 436
De Houwer, J., 593, 599, 603, 605
De Jong, K., 363
Dell, G. S., 234
Denève, S., 120
Denhiére, G., 580, 581
Dennett, D., 133, 676
Dennis, S., 59, 205, 250
Denniston, J. C., 593, 599, 600
De Pisapia, N., 438, 445
Depue, R. A., 517
Derevensky, J. L., 467, 468
Desimone, R., 189, 195, 423, 428
Desmet, T., 489
D'Esposito, M., 189
Destefano, M., 161
Destrebecqz, A., 397, 400, 414, 415
Detre, G. J., 198, 200, 201, 206
Devlin, J., 49, 261
De Vooght, G., 346
Dewey, G. I., 272, 399
Dhar, R., 317
Dick, F., 43
Dickinson, A., 592, 593, 594, 595, 600, 602, 605
Dickinson, D. K., 465
Dickmann, M. A., 147
Diederich, A., 311, 312, 313, 316

Dienes, Z., 396, 398, 403, 404, 406, 407, 409, 410, 411, 414, 418, 461, 462, 672
Dierckx, V., 346
Dietrich, E., 106
DiGirolamo, G. J., 398
Dineva, E., 113, 115, 121
Dingwell, J. B., 652, 653, 654
Dinse, H. R., 119
Di Paolo, E. A., 677, 678
Discenna, P., 190
Doane, S. M., 364, 370
Dobbins, I. G., 189
Domangue, T., 413
Dominey, P. F., 406
Donald, M., 369
Doran, J., 531, 532
Dorris, M. C., 113, 581
Dose, M., 117
Dougherty, M. R. P., 318
Douglas, R. J., 119
Douglas, S., 565, 571, 576
Douglass, S., 172, 176, 180, 183, 423
Downes, J. J., 196
Doya, K., 95
Dreyfus, H. L., 668
Drieghe, D., 489
Dronkers, N., 43
Druhan, B., 404
Duda, R. O., 62
Duff, S., 366
Dulany, D. E., 399, 400
Dumais, S. T., 89, 90, 91, 95, 227, 250, 251, 255, 495, 580
Dunbar, K., 25, 47, 434, 436, 437, 439, 440, 443
Duncan, J., 423, 428
Dunlea, A., 468
Dunn, J. C., 401
Durkheim, W., 9
Durrant-Peatfield, M. R., 261
Durstewitz, D., 211, 437, 438
Dwyer, D. M., 595
Dy, C. J., 189
d'Ydewalle, G., 346, 354

Eagley, A. H., 515
Ebbinghaus, H., 139, 146, 148, 361
Eberhard, K. M., 490
Edelman, G. M., 399
Edelman, S., 273
Edwards, W., 289, 303
Egbers, E., 135
Egeth, H., 427
Eggermont, J. J., 113
Egorov, A. V., 213

Ehret, B. D., 566
Eichenbaum, H., 190, 189, 190
Eisenstadt, S., 150, 151
Eiser, J. R., 515
Eldridge, L. L., 189
Elek, S. M., 592
Eliasmith, C., 556, 557, 558
Elio, R., 367, 378, 381
Elkind, J. I., 565
Elliman, D., 15
Ellis, E., 259
Elman, J., 43, 24, 25, 33, 38, 39, 40, 41, 42, 43,
    44, 47, 50, 51, 182, 211, 227, 247, 248, 249,
    250, 251, 254. 255, 402, 405, 457, 461, 462,
    468, 480, 481, 482, 483, 484, 488, 492, 495,
    659, 670, 672
Emery, L., 444
Engel, S. A., 189
Engelberg, S., 387
Engels, C., 117
Engle, R. W., 444
Epstein, J., 531
Erev, I., 318
Erickson, M. A., 272
Ericsson, K. A., 131, 380
Erlhagen, W., 107, 117, 119
Ernst, A. M., 365, 374
Ervin, S. M., 34
Escobar, M., 599
Espinet, A., 593
Espino, O., 354
Espinoza, J., 112, 113
Estes, W., 208, 268, 291, 382, 401, 404, 534,
    598
Etchemendy, J., 136, 141, 143
Evans, D., 674
Evans, J. S. T., 130
Evenden, J. L., 602
Everling, S., 582

Fagin, R., 147
Fahey, R., 398
Fahlman, S., 25, 43, 452, 453
Falkenhainer, B., 366, 370, 554
Farah, M., 256, 257, 258, 260, 424, 436
Farahat, A., 581
Faubel, C., 117
Fauconnier, G., 387, 671
Favilla, M., 107
Fayol, M., 414
Fazio, R. H., 515
Feeney, A., 324, 325, 327
Fehlau, B. P., 194
Feigenbaum, E. A., 668
Feinstein, M., 140

Feldman, A., 635
Feldman, J., 25, 352, 353, 668
Fellous, J., 211, 512, 617, 701
Feltovich, P. J., 380, 566
Fencsik, D. E., 178
Fennema, M. G., 577
Ferino, F., 213
Fernandez, P., 592, 596
Ferreira, F., 479
Ferretti, R. P., 455
Ferrucci, D., 131
Festinger, L., 512, 523
Fichman, M., 398
Fiedler, K., 509, 510, 511
Field, C., 164
Field, D. J., 615, 616
Fiez, J. A., 48
Fikes, R. E., 387
Finch, S., 492, 494, 496
Fiorito, G., 638
Fischer, B., 582
Fischer, G. W., 510
Fischer, K. W., 375, 387
Fisher, A. V., 327, 335
Fisher, D. L., 569
Fisher, J., 207
Fiske, S. T., 508
Fitts, P., 363
Fitts, P. M., 674–575
Flanagan, J., 387, 650
Flannery, B. P., 289
Flash, T., 636, 638, 650
Fletcher, P. C., 189
Flum, J., 139, 146, 148
Fodor, J., 30, 182, 479, 480, 483, 667, 673,
    679, 694, 695
Fodor, J. D., 479
Foltz, P. W., 251
Forbus, K. D., 366, 370, 554
Forde, E. M., 261
Forgy, C. L., 178
Forrester, N. A., 36
Forster, K. I., 482
Forster, M. R., 68
Fortin, N. J., 189
Fotedar, M. S., 213
Foulsham, T., 581
Fox, J., 171
Fraley, R. C., 517
Frank, M. J., 211, 214
Fransen, E., 213
Frazier, L., 479, 489
Freed, M., 565
Freeman, R. D., 618
Freeman, R. P. J., 295

Freeman, W. T., 60, 617
French, R., 46, 510
Frensch, P. A., 396
Freud, S., 24
Friedman, N., 87
Frith, C. D., 445
Frohardt, R., 602
Fu, W. T., 378, 580, 582
Fuchs, N. E., 164
Furmanski, C. S., 189
Fuster, J. M., 118

Gabbay, D., 139
Gagné, R. M., 384
Galanter, E., 4, 362, 668, 672, 696
Gallego, G., 410
Gallistel, C. R., 365, 387
Gandolfo, F., 650, 652
Ganong, W. F. I., 483
Gao, S. J., 406, 407, 410, 414
Gärdenfors, P., 387
Gardner, H., 361
Gardner, M. K., 380
Garfield, J., 140
Garrard, P., 257, 259, 260, 261
Garrett, M. F., 479
Gaskell, M. G., 485, 486
Gasser, L., 531
Gati, I., 276
Gazdar, G. J. M., 671
Gazzaniga, M., 534
Gelade, G., 423, 424
Gelman, A., 79, 80, 81
Gelman, R., 232, 244, 365, 465
Gelman, S. A., 78, 478
Geman, D., 88
Geman, S., 88
Genesereth, M., 148
Gentner, D., 287, 323, 366, 370, 465, 554
Georgopoulos, A. P., 107, 119, 460
Gerbino, W., 582
Gergely, G., 233, 698
Gernsbacher, M. A., 43, 363
Gettys, C. F., 318
Ghahramani, Z., 68, 70, 387, 657, 658
Ghallab, M., 702
Ghez, C., 107
Ghilardi, M. F., 107
Ghirlanda, S., 593
Gibson, E., 479, 489, 490, 493
Gibson, F., 398
Gibson, J., 688
Gielen, S., 427
Giese, M., 107, 113, 119
Giesen, B., 532

Gigerenzer, G., 59, 302, 308, 670
Gilbert, N., 531, 532, 543
Gilbert, S. J., 439, 440, 441
Gilks, W., 88
Gillan, D. J., 578
Gillund, G., 201
Gilovich, T., 555
Gilroy, L., 108
Girotto, V., 131, 334, 344, 352, 356
Giszter, S., 635, 645, 646, 658
Giunchiglia, E., 364
Glanzer, M., 204
Glaser, R., 566
Glass, J. M., 178
Glauthier, P., 270, 286
Glautier, S., 603
Glenberg, A., 209, 251
Glowinski, J., 213
Gluck, K. A., 566, 572, 582
Gluck, M., 198, 199, 215, 231, 270, 286
Glymour, C., 45, 74, 130, 150, 290, 333, 554, 555
Gobet, F., 15
Goble, L., 147
Goddard, N. H., 193
Godijn, R., 581, 582
Goebel, R., 37
Goedert, K. M., 605
Gold, E. M., 491
Gold, K., 467
Goldberg, A. E., 482, 498
Goldberg, D., 670, 678, 694, 704
Goldin-Meadow, S., 468
Goldman-Rakic, P. S., 213
Goldspink, C., 542
Goldstein, D. G., 670
Goldstein, E. B., 133
Goldstein, H., 80, 640
Goldstone, R., 267, 268, 287, 543
Goldvarg, Y., 352
Gonnerman, L., 49, 261, 494
González, F., 593
González-Vallejo, C., 318
Good, I. J., 79
Goodale, M., 107, 671, 689
Goodale, N., 11
Goode, A., 215, 694, 704
Goodman, N., 465
Goodnow, J., 229, 272, 669
Goodwin, G., 346, 353
Goodz, E., 467, 468
Gopnik, A., 45, 78–79, 95, 245, 290, 333, 555
Gordon, G. J., 290
Gordon, J., 107
Gordon, R. D., 441

Gortler, J. R., 597
Goshen-Gottstein, Y., 211, 212
Gott, R. E., 271, 273
Gottman, J. M., 555
Gotts, S. J., 30
Grafman, J., 445
Graham, G., 4
Graham, K., 259
Graham, N., 259
Grahame, N. J., 592
Gratch, J., 544
Gray, B., 366
Gray, J. A., 516
Gray, W., 378, 383, 533, 565, 566, 567, 569, 570, 577, 581, 582
Green, D. C., 28
Green, P. A., 572
Greene, G., 11
Greeno, J. G., 365
Greenwald, A. G., 519
Gregory, R. L., 670
Grether, D. M., 306
Gretz, A. L., 209
Grice, H., 695
Griffin, D., 318, 555
Griffiths, T., 45, 59, 68, 75, 76, 77, 78, 79, 80, 86, 87, 90, 93, 95, 250, 274, 287, 290, 327, 330, 495, 497
Grill, W., 645
Grillner, S., 635
Grimson, E., 625
Grimwood, P. D., 388
Grinnell, A., 118
Grodner, D., 490
Gronlund, S. D., 202, 203
Grossberg, S., 5, 24, 25, 44, 105, 118, 190, 191, 195, 217, 270, 309
Grosz, B., 671, 677
Gruppuso, V., 197
Grush, R., 690
Guarraci, F. A., 597
Guidry, C., 413
Gullahorn, J., 506
Gunturkun, O., 211, 437
Gunzelmann, G., 572
Guo, F. Y., 309
Gureckis, T. M., 44, 267, 277, 282, 283, 288, 291, 292, 462, 463, 566
Gutfreund, Y., 638
Gutowski, W. E., 309
Gutscher, H., 515

Haarmann, H., 47, 211, 212, 489
Habekost, T., 433
Hachtel, G. D., 352

Hacking, I., 59
Hadley, R. F., 461
Hadley, W. H., 13
Hagmayer, Y., 603
Hahn, U., 324, 325, 481, 493
Haken, H., 105
Hale, J., 490
Halford, G. S., 366
Hall, G., 593, 597
Haller, M., 487
Halliday, M., 693
Halpern, J., 134, 147
Hamam, B. N., 213
Hamilton, D. B., 618, 619
Hamilton, T. E., 521, 522
Hamker, F. H., 424
Hancock, P. J. B., 615
Haralick, R. M., 629
Hare, M., 457
Harm, M., 469, 487
Harman, D., 580
Harman, G., 553
Harnett, G., 108
Harper, R., 134
Harris, C. M., 655
Harris, P., 458, 471
Hart, P. E., 62
Hasselmo, M. E., 190, 191, 193, 194, 198, 213, 219
Hasson, U., 344
Hastie, R., 289, 335, 509, 522
Hatfield, G., 643
Haugeland, J., 667, 668
Haxby, J. V., 260
Hay, J., 482, 489
Hayes, B. K., 324, 326, 327, 335
Hayes, P., 687, 702
Hayes-Roth, F., 362, 364
Hayhoe, M. M., 570, 571
Hayworth, K. J., 689
Heath, R. A., 311
Hebb, D. O., 27, 669
Heckerman, D., 74
Hegselmann, R., 531
Heibeck, T., 82
Heider, F., 523
Heinke, D., 424, 427, 431
Heisenberg, M., 104
Heit, E., 271, 323, 324, 325, 326, 327, 328, 330, 331, 332, 334, 335
Helmhout, M., 533
Hempel, C. G., 551
Henderson, J. M., 581
Hendler, J., 686
Henson, R. N., 189

Henthorn, T., 207
Herd, S. A., 436
Herrnstein, R. J., 306
Hertwig, R., 308, 383
Heskes, T., 427
Hesse, M. B., 675, 676
Hiebert, J., 366
Higgins, E. T., 509
Higham, P. A., 400
Hildreth, E., 629, 670
Hilgard, E. R., 382
Hill, A. V., 645
Hill, T., 397
Hindton, G. E., 29
Hintikka, J., 147
Hinton, G. E., 24, 25, 26, 27, 30, 31, 44, 70, 200, 227, 234, 235, 237, 239, 270, 606, 658
Hintzman, D., 6, 196, 201, 206, 273, 291, 509, 510, 566
Hintzmann, D., 401, 404
Hiraki, K. A., 207
Hirschfeld, L. A., 478
Hirshman, E., 207
Hitch, G., 213
Hochberg, J., 565
Hochner, B., 638
Hock, H. S., 107, 108, 112, 113
Hockema, S. A., 486
Hockley, W. E., 207
Hodges, J., 257, 259, 260, 261
Hodson, G., 518
Hoeffner, J. H., 37, 469
Hoff, M. E., 506
Hoffman, H., 414
Hoffman, R. R., 380
Hofmann, T., 90
Hofstadter, D. R., 667
Hogan, N., 635, 636, 638, 641, 645, 650, 658
Hogg, D. C., 671
Hogg, T., 385
Holdefer, R. N., 638
Holden, J. E., 205, 206
Holdstock, J., 196
Holland, J. H., 363, 551
Hollander, J., 34, 36
Hollands, J. G., 578
Hollerbach, J., 641
Hollis, M., 677
Holyoak, K., 309, 310, 323, 366, 367, 370, 513, 551, 592, 595, 603
Honavar, V., 14
Honey, G. D., 605
Honey, R. A. E., 605
Hopcroft, J. E., 478
Hopfield, J. J., 25

Hopkins, R. O., 189
Hore, J., 650
Horning, J. J., 491
Hornof, A. J., 179, 567, 581, 582
Horwitz, B., 215, 433
Houghton, G., 23, 427, 438, 485, 487
Hovland, C. I., 566
Hovland, C. L., 353
Howard, M. W., 190, 203, 208, 209, 210, 211, 212, 213, 214, 251
Hoyer, P. O., 616
Hsieh, S., 440
Hubel, D., 615, 616, 618
Huber, D. E., 195
Huber, J., 307
Huberman, B. A., 385
Hudson, P. T., 424, 428, 436
Huey, B. M., 565
Huffman, S. B., 180, 364, 370
Huisman, A., 107
Hull, C. L., 397
Hume, D., 333
Hummel, J. E., 367
Humphreys, G., 261, 424, 427, 431
Humphreys, M. S., 201, 205
Hund, A. M., 116
Hunkin, N. M., 196
Hurwitz, J. B., 273
Husbands, P., 675
Huston, T. A., 435, 436, 439
Hutchins, E., 11, 677
Huxley, A. F., 645
Hyvaarinen, A., 616

Iba, W., 128
Imai, M., 465
Immerman, N., 134
Indefrey, P., 37
Inhelder, B., 130, 136
Irwin, J. M., 205
Isaac, C. L., 196
Ishii, S., 95
Itti, L., 423, 424, 425, 426, 427, 428, 433, 581
Ivanoiu, A., 259
Iverson, G. J., 204

Jackendoff, R., 387
Jackson, E. M., 195
Jackson, S., 43
Jacobs, R., 44, 407, 658
Jacoby, L. L., 197, 400
Jahn, G., 346
Jain, N. K., 375
James, W., 24, 361, 443
Jami, L., 637

Jancke, D., 119
Jannedy, S., 482, 489
Janssen, H., 117
Janssen, M., 543
Jay, T. M., 213
Jazayeri, M., 656
Jeffrey, R., 151, 163, 341
Jeffreys, W. H., 70
Jenkins, H. M., 75, 353, 566
Jennings, J. M., 197
Jensen, O., 215
Jepson, C., 82, 326
Jewett, J., 11, 385, 386
Jiménez, L., 400
Joanisse, M. F., 37, 49
Johansen, M. K., 273, 276
John, B. E., 565, 569, 575, 577
Johnson, E. J., 302, 308, 576, 577
Johnson, J. G., 311, 313, 314, 315, 316, 318
Johnson, M., 29, 42, 44, 47, 48, 49, 50, 458, 672
Johnson, M. K., 671
Johnson, S., 233
Johnson, T., 641
Johnson-Laird, P., 128, 131, 136, 137, 334, 340, 343, 344, 346, 348, 349, 350, 352, 355, 356, 387, 566, 671
Johnston, R. A., 33
Johnstone, R. A., 49
Johnstone, T., 399
Jolicoeur, P., 231
Jones, C. R., 509
Jones, G., 368
Jones, J. P., 615
Jones, M., 626, 627, 628, 629, 631, 632
Jones, R., 367, 368, 371, 373, 374, 375, 376, 377
Jones, R. S., 270
Jones, S., 232, 465
Joordens, S., 207
Jordan, M., 25, 38, 44, 68, 90, 92, 93, 94, 95, 407, 635, 650, 655, 658, 659
Jordens, K., 513, 514
Jose, J. V., 640, 658
Josephson, J., 551, 553
Josephson, S. G., 553
Joublin, F., 117
Jovicich, J., 423
Juang, B. H., 482
Juarrero, A., 103
Juliano, C., 488
Jung, K. J., 215
Juola, P., 49
Jurafsky, D., 72, 490
Juslin, P., 293, 294, 604, 605

Just, M. A., 177, 444, 489
Juvina, I., 581

Kacelnik, A., 698
Kahan, J., 533
Kahana, M. J., 190, 201, 202, 203, 208, 209, 210, 211, 212, 214, 251
Kahneman, D., 131, 303, 304, 309, 332, 354, 555
Kakade, S., 290
Kalaska, J. F., 120
Kalick, S. M., 521, 522
Kalish, M. L., 272
Kamin, L. J., 590
Kane, M. J., 444
Kanfer, R., 575
Kara, P., 615
Karbor, P., 581
Karmiloff-Smith, A., 37, 42, 44, 47, 49, 50, 406, 411, 412, 468, 469, 671, 672, 673, 701
Karniel, A., 652
Kashima, E. S., 511
Kashima, Y., 511
Kass, R. E., 68
Kaufman, M. A., 593
Kaur, I., 567, 581, 582
Kawamoto, A. H., 485, 492
Kawato, M., 635, 650
Keane, M. T., 366
Keele, S. W., 398, 413
Keijzer, F. A., 103
Keil, F., 233, 245
Keim, D. A., 576
Kekelis, L. S., 468
Kelc, M., 211, 437
Keller, T. A., 444
Kelley, C. M., 197
Kello, C. T., 33
Kelso, J. A. S., 105, 106, 107, 120, 635
Kemp, C., 45, 59, 79, 80, 81, 82, 83, 85, 86, 327, 332, 466
Kendler, T. S., 464
Kenny, D. A., 517
Kenrick, D., 521, 544
Kersten, A., 267, 268
Kersten, D., 59
Kettner, R. E., 119
Khemlani, S., 161
Kieras, D., 13, 173, 176, 178, 179, 366, 442, 565, 567, 569, 570, 571
Kieras, O. E., 176
Kikuchi, M., 512
Kim, K., 204
Kim, S., 533
Kinder, A., 406, 415

King, D., 511
King, J., 215, 362
Kintsch, W., 364, 387
Kirlik, A., 566, 567, 572, 573, 574, 582
Kirschenbaum, S. S., 566
Kirsh, D., 403, 668
Kirsner, K., 401
Kirwan, B., 567, 568, 574
Kitajima, M., 567, 581, 582
Kitchener, E. G., 189
Kitcher, P., 551, 553
Klahr, D., 362, 452
Klahr, P., 364
Klein, D., 492, 494
Klein, E., 671
Klein, R. M., 113, 581
Kleinmuntz, D. N., 577
Kline, P., 362, 372, 377
Klitz, T. S., 488
Kloeden, P. E., 123
Klutch, R., 135
Kluver, J., 544
Knauff, M., 346
Knoeferle, P., 43
Knowlton, B. J., 189, 414
Knutson, J., 244
Kobayashi, H., 465
Koch, C., 423, 424, 425, 426, 427, 432, 581
Koechlin, E., 445
Koedinger, K., 13, 378
Koehler, D. J., 318
Kogan, K., 112
Köhler, W., 103
Kohonen, T., 24, 25, 288
Kokinov, B., 323, 367
Kolaitis, P., 134
Kolen, J. F., 492, 495
Koller, D., 87
Konolige, K., 551
Koos, O., 233
Kopecz, K., 113
Korb, K., 73
Kording, K. P., 59
Kosslyn, S. M., 231
Kotaleski, J. H., 635
Kotovsky, L., 561
Koutstaal, W., 195
Krackhardt, D., 533
Kraljic, T., 484
Kramer, J., 703
Krampe, R. Th., 380
Krantz, D. H., 82, 326
Kraus, T. A., 209
Krawczyk, D. C., 310
Krebs, J. R., 580

Krems, J. F., 377
Kroll, N. E., 189
Kroon, F. W., 544
Kruger, L., 59
Kruger, N., 617
Krupa-Kwiatkowski, M., 43
Kruschke, J. K., 234, 267, 268, 272, 273, 275, 276, 277, 278, 290, 291, 292, 293, 294, 597, 598
Kruskal, J. B., 269
Krusmark, M. A., 566, 572, 582
Kuczaj, S. A., 34
Kugler, P. N., 635
Kuhn, G., 409, 411, 414
Kunda, Z., 82, 326, 508, 511
Kurtzman, H., 488
Kushnir, T., 45, 290, 333
Kushur, T., 555
Kwak, H. W., 427
Kyllingsbaek, S., 433

Labiouse, C., 508, 510
Labov, W., 481
Lachnit, H., 593, 595, 596, 599, 600
Lacquaniti, F., 638, 650
Lafferty, J., 94
Lagnado, D., 74
Laham, D., 251
Lai, Y., 424
Laiacona, M., 256
Laird, J., 128, 171, 172, 180, 364, 368, 370, 372, 373, 382, 675, 702, 703
Lakatos, I., 705
Lakoff, G., 387
Lallement, Y., 575
Lamberts, K., 277, 280, 281, 294, 295
Lambon Ralph, M. A., 257, 259, 260, 261
Laming, D. R., 311
Landau, B., 232, 465
Landauer, T. K., 89, 90, 91, 95, 227, 250, 251, 255, 495, 580
Langdon, R., 481, 485
Langer, J., 459, 472
Langley, P., 11, 128, 362, 367, 368, 371, 373, 374, 375, 377, 455, 702, 703
Lansner, A., 635
Lari, K., 492
Larkin, J. H., 372, 378, 578
Larkin, M. J. W., 593, 595, 600
Larson, J. R. J., 523
Lashley, K. S., 24
Lassaline, M. E., 323
Latané, B., 520
Latash, M., 118, 635
Latham, P., 120, 656

Lauber, E. J., 178
Lave, J., 9, 539
Law, K., 366, 424, 427
Lazarus, R. S., 511
Leake, D. B., 553, 554
Lebiere, C., 5, 7, 8, 13, 14, 25, 43, 45, 128, 133, 134, 172, 176, 177, 180, 182, 183, 207, 383, 398, 413, 423, 453, 470, 505, 530, 532, 534, 535, 541, 542, 543, 544, 545, 565, 571, 576
Ledgeway, T., 366
LeDoux, J., 11
Lee, A. C., 196
Lee, A. K., 215
Lee, D. K., 424, 425
Lee, F. J., 180, 379, 574, 575
Lee, J., 364
Lee, M. D., 80, 277, 278, 279, 280
Lee, T. S., 428, 430, 431
Leeser, K., 641
Lee-Tiernan, S., 518
Legate, J. A., 492
Legendre, G., 481, 488, 498
Legge, G. E., 488
Legrenzi, M., 334, 344, 352
Legrenzi, M. S., 131
Legrenzi, P., 131, 334, 344, 352, 356
Lemaire, B., 580, 581
Lemay, M., 645
Lenat, D. B., 372
Le Pelley, M. E., 595, 597, 598, 605
Lepper, M. R., 513
Léveillé, E., 513
Levesque, H. J., 127
Levine, M., 270
Levitt, J. B., 211
Levow, G., 581
Levy, B. A., 387
Levy, J., 261, 484
Levy, W. B., 190, 217
Lewandowsky, S., 272, 596
Lewicki, P., 397, 400, 414
Lewin, K., 524
Lewis, C., 372, 379
Lewis, D. A., 211
Lewis, J. D., 468
Lewis, R. L., 175, 176, 177
Lewis, S., 410
Li, L., 189, 195
Li, N., 521, 544
Li, S. C., 596
Lichtenstein, S., 306
Lienard, P., 701
Lifschitz, V., 364
Lightfoot, D., 478

Lim, J., 213
Lin, L., 11
Lin, Z., 536, 537, 538, 542, 544
Lindman, H. R., 306
Lindsay, D. S., 197
Linebarger, M. C., 489
Ling, C., 4, 14, 15, 455, 456, 457
Link, S. W., 311
Linster, C., 194
Linville, P. W., 510
Lipson, P., 625
Lipton, P., 553
Lisman, J. E., 211, 215
Liu, J. H., 520
Livesey, E. J., 603
Ljung, L., 653
Loasses, A., 212
Lodge, M., 533
Loehlin, J. C., 506, 515, 517, 524
Loftus, E. F., 89, 228, 382
Logan, G. D., 273, 379, 384, 441, 442, 443
Lohmiller, W., 647
Lohse, G. L., 577, 578
Lombardi, W., 509
Lombardo, V., 344
Lopes, L. L., 303
López, A., 83, 323, 324, 325, 326, 329, 330, 332, 334, 335, 327–328
López, F. J., 592, 596, 604, 605
Loughry, B., 211
Love, B. C., 44, 267, 277, 282, 283, 288, 291, 292, 462, 463, 566
Lovett, A., 459
Lovett, M. C., 176, 177, 437, 568
Lovibond, P. F., 602, 603, 605
Lovick, T. A., 675
Lowe, C., 257, 260, 261
Lozano Perez, T., 641
Luce, R. D., 7, 275, 302, 305, 306
Luchins, A. S., 380
Luchins, E. H., 380
Luhmann, C. C., 333
Lukashin, A., 119
Lund, J. S., 211
Lund, K., 90, 495
Lupyan, G., 492
Lurito, J. T., 107
Lusk, E., 151
Lyon, D. R., 572

Ma, W. J., 656
Macario, J. F., 245
MacDonald, J., 685, 699, 701
MacDonald, M. C., 47, 480, 488, 489
Mack, M., 581

MacKay, D. J., 30
Mackay, D. J. C., 67, 70, 73, 86, 88
Mackinlay, J. D., 577
Mackintosh, N. J., 597
Mackworth, A. K., 670
Macuga, K. L., 183, 574
MacWhinney, B., 43, 491, 494, 496
Macy, M., 520
Maddox, W. T., 271, 272, 293
Magnuson, J. S., 486
Mahon, B. Z., 256
Maia, T. V., 30, 445
Malecki, R., 544
Mallet, P., 111, 117
Malmberg, K. J., 197, 203, 205, 206
Mandler, J. M., 233, 244, 561
Mann, V. A., 484
Manning, C., 59, 60, 72, 481, 492, 494
Manns, J. R., 189
Mansinghka, V. K., 79, 80, 86
Mao, W., 544
Maratsos, M., 479, 494
Marchman, V., 35, 37, 457, 672
Marcus, G., 34, 36
Marcus, G. F., 30, 406, 461, 480, 481, 493
Marcus, M., 479, 671
Marcus-Newhall, A., 507, 508, 560
Mareschal, D., 29, 43, 47, 48, 49, 455, 458,
    462, 463, 470, 471
Marfia, G. A., 212
Marinelli, K., 195
Marinier, R. P., 172
Marinov, M., 455, 456, 457
Marjanovic, M., 130
Mark, M., 13
Markman, A. B., 106, 387
Markman, E., 82
Marr, D., 8, 9, 25, 29, 45, 61, 66, 131, 139,
    157, 190, 470, 599, 612, 617, 629, 636, 649,
    670, 702
Marsella, S., 544
Marslen-Wilson, W., 482, 485, 486, 488
Martin, A., 256, 260
Martin, J. H., 72
Martin, K. A. C., 119
Martin, R. R., 685
Martin, S. J., 388
Marvin, F. F., 577
Mason, M., 641
Mason, W., 533
Massaro, D., 5
Massey, J. T., 107
Masson, M. E., 234
Mataric, M., 544, 670, 678

Matessa, M., 177, 565, 571
Mathews, R. C., 404, 413
Mathis, W. D., 415
Matsuka, T., 289
Matthews, P. B., 655
Matute, H., 593, 599, 605
Matveeva, I., 581
Matzel, L. D., 599
Mavor, A., 4, 13, 15, 543, 565
Mayberry, M. R., 43
Mayes, A., 196
Maynard-Reid, P., 161
Maynard-Zhang, P., 364
McCain, N., 364
McCandliss, B. D., 48, 487
McCann, R. S., 486
McCarthy, J., 364, 491, 687
McCarthy, R., 256
McClelland, J., 3, 5, 12, 24, 25, 26, 27, 29, 30,
    31, 32, 33, 34, 35, 36, 37, 38, 45, 46, 47, 48,
    50, 51, 182, 190, 193, 197, 203, 227, 238,
    239, 240, 242, 243, 244, 245, 246, 250, 252,
    253, 254, 255, 256, 257, 258, 259, 260, 261,
    270, 294, 295, 296, 310, 311, 398, 402, 403,
    404, 405, 406, 434, 435, 436, 437, 439, 440,
    443, 455, 458, 469, 482, 483, 484, 486, 487,
    492, 507, 509–510, 511, 514, 519, 524, 606,
    667, 671
McCloskey, M., 182, 411
McCulloch, W. S., 24, 25
McDermott, D., 133, 164
McDonald, J., 327
McDonald, R. J., 597
McDonald, S. A., 490
McDowell, J., 668
McEvoy, C., 95, 161
McGuffin, P., 51
McGuire, W. J., 506, 512
McGurk, H., 685, 699, 701
McIntyre, J., 650
McKee, S. P., 581
McKeon, R., 129, 147
McKinley, S. C., 270, 286, 291, 293
McKusick, K. B., 128
McLaren, I. P., 294, 595, 597, 598, 605
McLeod, P., 25
McLin, D., 113
McMullen, C. T., 352
McNamara, D. S., 364
McNaughton, B. L., 45, 46, 182, 190
McNeill, D., 468
McPhee, J. E., 596, 603
McQueen, J. M., 484
McRae, K., 489

Mead, G. H., 677
Medin, D. L., 44, 62, 232, 234, 267, 271, 272, 273, 277, 282, 283, 287, 288, 291, 326, 327, 335, 401, 404, 566, 592, 595
Meehl, P. E., 679
Meeter, M., 191, 194, 198, 199, 215
Mehta, M. R., 215
Meir, R., 632
Melara, R. D., 437
Melchers, K. G., 593, 595, 596, 599, 600
Mellars, P., 532
Mellers, B. A., 304, 306
Melton, A. W., 205
Meltzoff, A. N., 78–79
Mendez, C., 400
Mensink, G., 201, 205, 208
Menzner, R., 117
Merrill, E., 174, 371, 372, 374, 377, 382, 675
Merton, P., 636
Mervis, C. B., 227, 230, 244, 273, 324
Meseguer, E., 354
Messick, S., 506, 515, 517, 524, 669
Mesulam, M. M., 196
Metropolis, A. W., 87, 88
Metzler, J., 136, 343
Meyer, B., 690
Meyer, D., 13, 173, 176, 179, 442, 565, 570, 571
Meynert, T., 24
Miall, R., 650
Michalski, R., 155, 323, 327, 334
Michie, D., 695
Mignault, A., 512
Miikkulainen, R., 43, 190, 488
Miller, E. K., 189, 195, 434, 436
Miller, E. N., 423
Miller, G., 4, 175, 362, 387, 410, 479, 668, 671, 672, 696
Miller, L. C., 507, 513, 515, 516, 523
Miller, L. E., 638
Miller, R. R., 592, 593, 597, 599, 600, 601, 603, 605
Miller, R. S., 230
Millgram, E., 309
Milner, A., 671, 689
Milner, B., 190
Milner, D., 11
Minai, A. A., 217
Minda, J. P., 272
Minka, T., 94
Minsky, M., 5, 7, 24, 364, 667, 668, 675, 676, 695, 701
Mischel, W., 515, 517, 518
Mitchell, C. J., 602, 603

Mitchell, D. C., 489
Mitchell, J. P., 189
Mithen, S., 533
Miyata, Y., 488
Molenaar, P. C. M., 464
Moll, H., 701
Moll, M., 190
Monaghan, P., 492, 495
Monroe, B. M., 515, 516
Montague, P. R., 290
Montague, R., 344
Montaldi, D., 196
Montemerlo, M., 694, 704
Montoya, J. A., 507, 508
Moran, T. P., 176, 565, 567, 568, 569, 576
Morasso, P., 638, 639
Moravec, H., 164
Morgan, J., 671
Morgenstern, O., 303, 534
Morris, R., 213, 190, 213, 388
Morris, W., 43
Morrison, J. B., 580
Morrone-Strupinsky, J. V., 517
Morton, J., 25, 31, 46, 482
Moscovitch, M., 676
Moses, Y., 147
Mosier, K. M., 643, 644
Mosler, H., 515
Moss, H. E., 261
Moss, S., 531, 543
Mostow, D., 364
Mostow, J., 371, 375, 377
Motwani, R., 478
Movellan, J. R., 30, 31, 200
Movshon, J. A., 656
Mozer, M. C., 415, 423, 424, 425, 427
Mukherjee, S., 618
Muller, H. J., 424
Mumford, D., 626
Munakata, Y., 25, 28, 46, 50, 182, 190, 191, 216, 217, 403, 423, 427, 435, 439, 458, 459, 460, 510, 515, 556
Munch, R., 532
Munoz, D. P., 113, 581
Murdock, B. B., 201
Murnane, K., 205
Murphy, G. L., 232, 267, 271, 326, 335
Murphy, R. A., 597
Murray, E. A., 196
Murray, J. D., 555
Murre, J., 191, 194, 215
Mussa-Ivaldi, F., 635, 636, 641, 643, 644, 645, 647, 649, 650, 651, 652, 653, 654, 658
Myers, C. E., 198, 199, 215

Myers, C. W., 565
Mysore, S. P., 471
Myung, I. J., 68, 318

Naber, P. A., 192
Nadel, L., 190
Nakisa, R., 37, 481, 493
Narayanan, S., 490
Nason, R., 365
Nason, S., 172, 382
Nau, D., 702
Navalpakkam, V., 428, 433
Navarrete, J. B., 305
Navarro, D. J., 277, 278, 279, 280
Naveh, I., 11, 16, 533, 534, 535, 538, 539, 542, 544
Neal, R. M., 68, 87, 88, 290
Neapolitan, R., 554
Neches, R., 362, 376, 381
Needham, A., 561
Negishi, M., 461, 462
Neimark, E. D., 382
Nelson, D. L., 95
Nelson, T. H., 334
Nerb, J., 377, 511
Neuberg, S. L., 508
Neves, D. M., 365, 370, 379
Newcomb, T. M., 506, 512
Newell, A., 3, 4, 5, 6, 7, 8, 9, 14, 128, 132, 165, 171, 172, 176, 178, 182, 183, 340, 344, 361, 362, 364, 367, 368, 372, 373, 378, 381, 384, 410, 452, 455, 530, 542, 543, 544, 551, 565, 566, 567, 568, 569, 571, 576, 669, 670, 673, 675, 685, 698, 699
Newman, E. L., 198, 200, 201, 206
Newman, M. E. J., 87, 88–89
Newport, E. L., 40, 249, 418
Newsome, W. T., 120
Newstead, S. E., 130
Ng, A. Y., 90, 92, 93, 94
Nhouyvanisvong, A., 207
Nichols, D. F., 107, 113
Nichols, T. R., 637
Nicholson, A., 73
Niebur, E., 424, 425, 426, 427
Nilsson, N., 130, 131, 148, 161, 387
Nisbett, R., 11, 82, 326, 397, 551, 553
Nissen, M. J., 398
Niyogi, P., 488, 493
Niyogi, S., 79
Noel, R., 135, 136, 143, 158
Noelle, D., 444
Noll, D., 436
Norenzayan, A., 11, 533
Norman, D. A., 435, 670

Norman, K. A., 190, 191, 193, 195, 196, 197, 198, 199, 200, 201, 206, 211, 212, 213, 216
Norris, D., 483, 484
Norris, J. R., 71
Norvig, P., 72, 73, 95, 130, 140, 150, 160, 161, 364, 551, 670
Nosofsky, R., 62, 234, 270, 272, 273, 275, 277, 283, 286, 287, 291, 293, 294, 295, 311, 566
Novick, L. R., 333
Nowak, A., 518, 520
Nowalk, A., 519
Nowlan, S. J., 44, 658
Nowlis, S. M., 317
Nuflo, F., 424
Nusbaum, M. P., 119
Nute, D., 144

Oakeshott, S. M., 597, 605
Oaksford, M., 59, 61, 334, 354, 383, 481
Oberauer, K., 345
O'Brien, D., 136, 340, 343
Oden, G., 14, 303
Ogata, K., 636
Ogden, E. E., 318
Ohlsson, S., 11, 365, 366, 368, 371, 374, 375, 377, 378, 381, 384–385, 386
Ohzawa, I., 618
O'Keefe, J., 190, 215
Oliver, W. L., 365, 382
Olivier, P., 690
Olshausen, B. A., 427, 615, 616
Onnis, L., 494
Oppy, B., 206
O'Reilly, R. C., 25, 28, 29, 45, 46, 47, 50, 182, 190, 191, 193, 195, 196, 197, 198, 199, 201, 211, 214, 215, 216, 217, 219, 403, 423, 427, 435, 436, 437, 438, 439, 444, 510, 515, 556, 597
Oren, M., 625
Orkand, R., 118
Ortony, A., 511
O'Shea, M., 675
Osherson, D., 83, 323, 324, 325, 327–328, 329, 330, 332, 334, 335, 340, 347
Oshima-Takane, Y., 455, 466, 467, 468
Osuna, E., 625
Ott, S. R., 675
Ottes, F. P., 113
Otto, P. E., 318
Otto, T., 190
Overbeek, R., 151
Owen, M. J., 51

Pacteau, C., 399, 414
Pacton, S., 411, 414

Paller, K. A., 196
Palmer, L. A., 615
Palmer, M., 532
Palmeri, T. J., 270, 286, 293, 294, 311, 566
Pandya, D. N., 213
Panksepp, J., 517
Panzer, S., 445
Papageorgiou, C., 625
Papert, S., 24, 667, 668
Parisi, D., 42, 44, 47, 50, 459, 472, 532, 544, 672
Parkhurst, D., 424, 427
Pashler, H., 15, 171, 178, 423, 441
Passannante, A., 207
Patterson, K., 37, 48, 259, 487
Pauen, S., 245
Pauw, B., 581
Payne, J. W., 302, 307, 308, 576
PDP Research Group, 3, 5, 12, 25, 27, 667
Pearce, J. M., 277, 280, 281, 286, 595, 596, 597, 604
Pearl, J., 70, 71, 73, 74, 76, 333, 490, 554
Pearlmutter, N. J., 480
Peebles, D., 567, 578, 579, 582
Peereman, R., 417
Pélisson, D., 107
Pelletier, F. J., 352
Pelz, J. B., 570
Peng, K., 11, 533
Penrod, S., 522
Penrose, R., 177
Perales, J. C., 594
Pereira, F. C. N., 481
Perfors, A., 80, 81, 82, 85, 466
Perkins, D. N., 380
Perko, L., 102
Perner, J., 415, 672
Perotte, A. J., 198, 200, 201
Perrault, C. R., 671, 677
Perruchet, P., 399, 402, 410, 411, 414, 416, 417
Perry, C., 481, 485
Perry, J., 466
Peterson, L. R., 213
Peterson, M. R., 213
Peterson, T., 45, 174, 371, 372, 374, 377, 382, 675
Petrides, M., 107, 213
Petrov, A. A., 367, 383
Petters, D., 685, 703
Petty, R. E., 515
Pew, R., 4, 13, 15, 543, 565, 566, 567
Pezaris, J. S., 615
Phaf, R. H., 424, 428, 436
Philippides, A., 675
Phillips, S., 366

Piaget, J., 113, 130, 136, 340, 375, 454, 457, 459, 698
Picard, R. W., 674
Pickering, M. J., 490
Pietrini, P., 445
Pike, R., 201
Pillon, A., 256
Pineno, O., 603
Pinker, S., 34, 36, 37, 412, 456, 478, 480, 481, 493, 672
Pirolli, P., 366, 367, 368, 373, 382, 567, 577, 580
Pitman, J., 66
Pitt, M. A., 68, 484
Pitts, W., 24, 25
Plate, T., 557, 558
Platen, E., 123
Plaut, D., 25
Plaut, D. C., 30, 33, 37, 42, 43, 48, 210, 211, 261, 398, 401, 486, 487, 491, 494
Ploeger, A., 107, 108
Plomin, R., 51
Plott, C. R., 306
Plunkett, K., 25, 35, 37, 42, 44, 47, 49, 50, 457, 458, 471, 672
Poggio, T., 25, 103, 104, 617, 618, 625, 626, 627, 628, 629, 631, 632
Poldrack, R. A., 438
Polk, T. A., 344
Pollack, M. E., 671
Pollatos, O., 428, 431
Pollock, J., 149, 154
Polson, P. G., 567, 571, 581, 582
Polyn, S. M., 198, 200, 201, 211, 212, 213
Pomplun, M., 581
Pook, P. K., 570, 571
Popper, K., 408
Popper, K. R., 178, 677
Port, R. F., 104, 106
Porter, T., 59
Posner, M. I., 427, 443, 674–675
Pouget, A., 95, 120, 656
Prablanc, C., 107
Prasada, S., 493
Prescott, T. J., 515
Press, W. H., 289
Pribe, C., 105
Pribram, K., 4, 362, 668, 672, 696
Price, J. L., 213
Price, P. C., 605
Prietula, M., 531, 536, 537, 538, 542, 544
Prince, A., 36, 480, 672
Proctor, R. W., 569
Proffitt, J. B., 326
Pucak, M. L., 211

Pullman, S., 107
Pullum, G., 492, 671
Pustejovsky, J., 387
Puto, C., 307
Pylyshyn, Z., 30, 131, 139, 157, 182, 387, 480, 667

Qi, D., 678
Qin, Y., 172, 176, 180, 183, 423
Quaife, A., 164
Quartz, S. R., 43, 471
Queller, S., 510
Quiggin, J., 304
Quillian, M. R., 89, 227, 228, 229, 237
Quin, Y., 565, 571, 576
Quine, W. V. O., 352
Quinlan, J. R., 452, 454, 457

Raaijmakers, J. G., 201, 203, 204, 205, 208, 215
Rabiner, L. R., 482
Rack, P. M. H., 645
Rafal, R. D., 427
Raftery, A. E., 68
Raiffa, H., 302
Raijmakers, M. E. J., 464
Ramble, C., 11, 533
Ramus, S. J., 414
Ranganath, C., 189
Ranney, M., 560
Rao, R. P. N., 95, 570, 571, 581
Rapaport, W., 128
Rapoport, A., 533
Rasmussen, J., 11
Rastle, K., 481, 485, 487
Ratcliff, R., 311
Rätsch, G., 632
Rayner, K., 626
Read, S., 507, 508, 511, 513, 515, 516, 523, 560
Reali, F., 492, 493
Reason, J., 380
Reber, A., 396, 397, 398, 400, 406, 410, 413, 537
Recker, M., 366
Reder, L. M., 176, 177, 207, 575, 582
Redington, M., 43, 414, 480, 492, 494, 496
Reed, J. M., 189
Reed, S. K., 62, 270, 273
Reeder, R. W., 580
Rees, E., 365, 366, 371, 374
Regier, T., 5, 14, 273, 497
Rehder, B., 271, 326, 327, 334, 335
Reichardt, W., 103, 104
Reicher, G. M., 31
Reid, R. C., 615

Reimann, P., 368
Reimers, S., 294
Reiter, R., 162
Remington, R. W., 565
Repp, B. H., 484
Rescorla, R. A., 333, 506, 590–592, 598, 601
Restle, R., 375
Reyna, V. F., 195
Reynolds, J. R., 441
Reynolds, R., 532
Rholes, W. S., 509
Rice, H. J., 189
Rice, J. A., 65
Richardson, F., 36, 44
Richardson, S., 88
Riehle, A., 119, 120
Riesenhuber, M., 617, 618
Rieskamp, J., 304, 318
Rigutti, S., 582
Riley, M. S., 365
Rinella, K., 143, 157, 158
Ringach, D. L., 616
Rips, L., 83, 128, 136, 141, 153, 228, 323, 324, 325, 327, 330, 335, 340, 341, 342, 343, 354, 566
Rispoli, J., 327
Rissland, E., 140
Ritchi, R., 650
Ritter, F., 15, 368, 377, 692, 698, 703
Ritz, S. A., 270
Rivera, M., 107
Rizzello, S., 533
Robbins, S. J., 592
Roberts, B. W., 517
Roberts, N., 196
Roberts, S., 15, 171
Robertson, D. A., 251
Robertson, G. G., 576, 577
Roe, R. M., 311, 316, 317
Roelofs, A., 436
Rogers, T. T., 196, 227, 238, 239, 240, 242, 243, 244, 245, 246, 257, 259, 260, 261, 606
Rohde, D. L. T., 42, 43, 491
Rolls, E. T., 25, 190, 191, 215, 424, 428, 431, 432, 433
Romero, R. D., 424, 436
Roney, C. J. R., 518
Rosch, E., 227, 230, 273, 324
Rose, J. M., 577
Roseman, J. J., 511
Rosen, R., 121
Rosen, T., 34, 36
Rosenbaum, D. A., 659
Rosenberg, M. J., 506, 512
Rosenblatt, F., 24, 25, 667

Rosenbloom, P., 128, 171, 178, 361, 368, 372, 373, 384, 675
Rosenbluth, A. W., 87, 88
Rosenbluth, M. N., 87, 88
Rosenholtz, R., 574, 581
Rosenthal, D., 400
Ross, B. H., 326
Roszkowska, E., 542, 544
Rotello, C. M., 334
Rougier, N. P., 444
Roussel, L. G., 413
Rousset, S., 46
Roy, D., 497
Roy, N., 694, 704
Royer, C., 581
Rubin, D. B., 79, 80, 81
Rubinstein, J., 326, 328, 332
Rudy, J. W., 190, 215, 219, 596, 597
Ruiz, D., 378, 381
Rumelhart, D., 3, 5, 12, 24, 25, 26, 27, 29, 31, 32, 33, 34, 35, 36, 51, 217, 237, 238, 258, 270, 296, 435, 440, 507, 509–510, 511, 514, 519, 524, 650, 667, 671
Russchen, F. T., 213
Russell, D. M., 577
Russell, S., 72, 73, 95, 130, 140, 150, 160, 161, 364, 551, 670
Rychener, M. D., 364
Ryle, G., 359

Sabb, F. W., 436
Sabes, P., 650
Sadr, J., 618
Saffran, E. M., 489
Saffran, J. R., 40, 249, 418
Sag, I. A., 671
Sagness, K. E., 596, 603
Sahdra, B., 511
Sahota, M., 670
Sak, S. G., 577
Saksida, L. M., 196
Salakhutdinov, R. R., 31
Saletan, E. J., 640, 658
Salmon, W., 551, 554
Salomon, G., 380
Salovey, P., 510
Salthouse, T. A., 376
Saltzman, E., 635
Salvucci, D. D., 183, 367, 442, 567, 574
Samson, D. S., 256
Samuel, A. C., 484
Samuel, A. G., 484
Samuels, M., 327
Samuelson, L., 465, 466
Sangiovanni-Vincentelli, A. L., 352

Santamaría, C., 346, 354
Sarnecka, B. W., 45
Sattath, S., 306
Savage, L. J., 303
Savary, F., 137, 352
Savastano, H. I., 593, 599, 600, 601
Sawyer, R., 532
Saxe, R. R., 59
Scassellati, B., 130, 459, 467
Sceidt, R. A., 643, 644
Schaal, S., 658
Schacter, D. L., 189, 190, 195, 397
Schaeken, W., 346, 354
Schaffer, M. M., 62, 273, 401, 404
Schall, J. D., 120
Schank, P., 560
Schank, R., 5, 512, 553, 671
Schapire, R. E., 632
Scharf, P. B., 367, 378, 381
Scheidt, R. A., 652, 653, 654
Scheier, C., 113, 121, 459, 460
Scheines, R., 333
Scherer, K. R., 511
Scheutz, M., 678, 692, 693, 703
Schiff-Meyers, N., 466
Schimanski, B., 154, 158, 160
Schkade, D. A., 577
Schlesinger, M., 459, 472
Schmidt, J., 544
Schmidt, W. C., 455, 457
Schneider, D. W., 441
Schneider, S., 107, 113
Schneider, W., 365, 380, 382, 443, 444
Schnell, E., 194
Schoelles, M. J., 383, 565
Schoener, G., 459, 460
Scholz, B., 492
Scholz, J. P., 106
Schöner, G., 105, 106, 107, 109, 111, 112, 113, 115, 116, 117, 118, 119, 120, 121, 123
Schooler, L. J., 383, 566
Schraedley, P. K., 580
Schreiber, D., 542
Schreiber, T. A., 95
Schroyens, W., 354
Schult, T. J., 368
Schultz, A., 128
Schultz, L. E., 555
Schulz, L., 45, 29, 330
Schumacher, E. H., 178
Schunn, C. D., 207, 575
Schutte, A. R., 112, 115, 116
Schütze, H., 72, 492, 495
Schützenberger, M. P., 477
Schüz, A., 119

Schwartz, A., 107, 119, 306
Schwartz, M. F., 489
Schwartz, M. L., 213
Schwarz, K., 515
Schweickert, R., 569
Schwertel, U., 164
Schwitter, R., 164
Sciavicco, L., 641
Scott, S. H., 107
Scott, S. K., 445
Scott Kelso, J. A., 635
Scoville, W. B., 190
Seamans, J. K., 211, 438
Sedivy, J. E., 490
Seergobin, K., 486
Seger, C., 537
Seidenberg, M. S., 37, 48, 49, 261, 457, 469, 480, 481, 485, 486, 487, 489
Sejnowski, T., 25, 30, 31, 43, 70, 200, 211, 438, 468, 615
Sekuler, R., 201, 202
Selemon, L. D., 213
Selfridge, O. G., 25, 31, 677
Sergent, C., 400, 415
Serre, T., 618
Servan-Schreiber, D., 47, 405, 424, 436, 437
Servan-Schreiber, E., 410, 411, 416
Seung, H. S., 27, 29, 120
Seymour, T. L., 178
Shadbolt, N., 15, 578
Shadlen, M. N., 120
Shadmehr, R., 649, 650, 651, 652, 653, 654
Shaffer, M. M., 232, 234
Shafir, E., 83, 323, 324, 325, 327–328, 329, 330, 332, 334, 335
Shafto, P., 326, 327, 332
Shallice, T., 48, 256, 435, 439, 440, 441, 670
Shang, J., 582
Shankar, N., 165
Shanks, D. R., 333, 399, 400, 406, 415, 506, 592, 593, 594, 595, 596, 599, 600, 602, 603, 604, 605
Shapiro, S., 128
Sharkey, A., 43
Sharkey, N., 43
Shastri, L., 354
Shaw, J. C., 362, 669
Shell, D., 544
Shepard, R., 136, 269, 274, 275, 343, 353, 566, 643
Shepherd, A., 568, 574
Sherman, S. J., 317
Sherrington, C., 636, 638
Sherry, D. F., 190
Shevill, I., 593

Shiffrin, R., 195, 201, 203, 204, 205, 206, 215, 443, 444
Shillcock, R. C., 484, 490
Shilliday, A., 154, 158, 160
Shimamura, A. P., 189, 191, 213
Shipley, C., 379, 381
Shipp, S., 432
Shneiderman, B., 577
Shoben, E. J., 228
Shoda, Y., 515, 517, 518
Shrager, J., 376, 379, 381, 385
Shultz, T. R., 25, 43, 48, 453, 455, 461, 462, 463, 464, 467, 470, 471, 513
Siciliano, B., 641
Siebler, F., 513, 514
Sieg, W., 164
Siegelman, J., 362
Siegler, R., 376, 379, 381, 452, 454, 455, 458
Sierhuis, M., 534, 539, 540, 541, 542, 543, 544
Silverstein, J. W., 270
Simmering, V. R., 112
Simmons, R. G., 694, 704
Simon, D., 309, 310
Simon, H., 171, 131, 150, 151, 362, 364, 367, 380, 383, 551, 567, 576, 578, 668, 669, 673, 701
Simons, H. A., 670, 673
Simons, J. S., 189
Simonson, I., 307, 317
Simpson, C., 230
Sims, C. R., 383
Singh, P., 685
Singley, M. K., 366, 370, 566
Sinha, P., 618, 625, 626, 627, 628, 629, 631, 632
Sirios, S., 29, 47, 48, 49, 461, 462, 464, 470
Sitton, M., 48, 423, 424, 425, 427
Skinner, B. F., 477
Skyrms, B., 150
Sloman, A., 15, 671, 674, 675, 676, 678, 679, 687, 688, 689, 690, 692, 693, 694, 695, 696, 698, 701, 702, 703
Sloman, S., 74, 154, 323, 326, 327, 328–330, 332, 333, 335, 602
Slotine, J. J. E., 647
Sloutsky, V. M., 327, 335
Slovic, P., 306, 555
Slusarz, P., 12, 13, 174, 176, 181, 368, 371, 372, 374, 382, 413, 454, 505, 602
Smallman, H. S., 576
Smelser, N., 532
Smith, A. F. M., 67
Smith, B. C., 678
Smith, D. A., 365

Smith, E., 83, 228, 323, 324, 325, 326, 327–328, 329, 330, 332, 334, 335, 509, 510, 511, 519, 521, 522, 533

Smith, J. D., 234, 272

Smith, L., 103, 113, 115, 121, 232, 460, 465, 466, 615

Smith, P. L., 311

Smithson, M., 518

Smolensky, P., 25, 29, 182, 270, 411, 481, 488, 498

Smyrnis, N., 119

Snow, C., 494, 496

Snyder, C. R. R., 443

Sobel, D., 333

Sobel, D. M., 45, 245, 290, 555

Soechting, J. F., 638

Sohal, V. S., 198

Sohn, M. H., 215, 441

Sohn, Y. W., 364, 370

Soja, N. N., 465

Sompolinsky, H., 120

Sorensson, N., 158

Sorrentino, R. M., 518

Spada, H., 511

Speck, O., 423

Spelke, E., 465

Spellman, B. A., 366, 513, 605

Spence, K. W., 463

Spencer, H., 24

Spencer, J. P., 109, 112, 115, 116, 118

Sperber, D., 672

Spiegelhalter, D. J., 88

Spieler, D. H., 487

Spiers, H. J., 189

Spirtes, P., 333

Spivey-Knowlton, M. J., 489, 490

Sprague, N., 570, 571

Spratling, M., 29, 47, 48, 49

Squire, L. R., 189, 190, 191, 215, 414

Srull, T. K., 509

St. John, M., 250, 252, 253, 254, 255, 400, 492, 576

Stafford, T., 515

Stanley, W. B., 404

Stanovich, K. E., 134

Stanton, R. D., 294

Starmer, C., 303, 304

Stasser, G., 318, 522, 523

Steedman, M., 480, 481

Steele, G., 151

Stefik, M. J., 577

Steinhage, A., 118, 119, 123

Stenger, V. A., 215

Stephens, D. W., 580

Stern, H. S., 79, 80, 81

Stevenson, J. A., 209

Stevenson, S., 492

Stewart, N., 294, 318

Steyvers, M., 59, 74, 78, 90, 93, 95, 201, 203, 204, 250, 290, 495, 497

Stigchel, S., 441

Stillings, N., 140

Stoica, C., 544

Stone, G., 195

Stork, D. G., 62

Storms, G., 277, 282, 326, 327

Stout, S. C., 599, 601

Stroop, J. R., 434

Styles, E. A., 440

Subrahmanyam, K., 465

Suchman, L., 539

Sun, R., 3, 4, 5, 6, 7, 8, 9, 10, 11, 12, 13, 14, 15, 16, 45, 128, 132, 134, 136, 138, 154, 155, 156, 174, 176, 178, 181, 182, 323, 328, 329, 335, 368, 371, 372, 374, 377, 382, 398, 401, 402, 413, 415, 454, 505, 530, 532, 533, 534, 535, 537, 538, 539, 540, 541, 542, 543, 544, 545, 554, 555, 602, 670, 675, 677, 678

Suret, M., 294

Sutherland, R. J., 190, 596

Sutton, R., 329, 592

Suzuki, R., 635

Swanson, C. C., 555

Swanson, K. R., 555

Swier, R., 492

Swijtink, Z., 59

Szamrej, J., 520

Taatgen, N. A., 173, 178, 180, 181, 183, 364, 379, 381, 398, 413, 456, 457, 574, 575

Tabachnik, N., 601

Tabor, C., 533

Tabor, W., 488

Taira, M., 119

Takane, Y., 467

Talamini, L. M., 191, 194

Tambe, M., 178

Tanenhaus, M. K., 480, 486, 488, 490

Tanenhaus, M. T., 489

Tangen, J. M., 605

Tannenbaum, P. H., 506, 512

Tanner, M., 551

Taraban, R., 250, 252, 253

Taylor, J., 154, 158, 160

Taylor, L. A., 523

Teller, A. H., 87, 88

Teller, E., 87, 88

Tenenbaum, J., 45, 59, 68, 74, 75, 76, 77, 78, 79, 80, 81, 82, 83, 85, 86, 87, 90, 95, 274,

287, 290, 327, 330, 332, 464, 466, 482, 497, 690, 692
Terna, P., 531
Terry, C., 12, 13, 174, 176, 181, 368, 371, 372, 374, 382, 413, 454, 505, 602
TeschRomer, C., 380
Tesser, A., 519
Teukolsky, S. A., 289
Teyler, T. J., 190
Thagard, P., 309, 323, 366, 367, 370, 507, 508, 511, 532, 544, 551, 552, 553, 554, 555, 556, 557, 560, 561
Theeuwes, J., 581, 582
Thelen, E., 103, 113, 115, 121, 459, 460
Thierry, A. M., 213
Thomas, A. G., 48
Thomas, J., 567, 576
Thomas, M. S. C., 29, 33, 36, 37, 43, 44, 47, 48, 49, 50, 468, 469
Thomas, W., 139, 146, 148
Thompson, E., 676
Thompson, K., 128
Thompson, R., 45, 50, 367
Thoresz, K., 618
Thorndike, E. L., 361, 366, 371, 375
Thoroughman, K. A., 652, 653
Thulborn, K. R., 444
Tipper, S. P., 427, 438
Titus, W., 523
Titzer, R., 113
Tjan, B. S., 488
Tkachuk, M. J., 209
Todd, P., 237, 238, 302, 577
Todorov, E., 635, 655
Tom, S., 189
Tomasello, M., 482, 701
Tomkins, S. S., 506, 515, 517, 524, 669
Tononi, G., 399, 400
Touretzky, D. S., 30, 44, 59, 290
Townsend, J. T., 311, 313, 316, 317
Townsend, W. T., 641
Trafton, J., 128
Trappenberg, T. P., 113, 581
Traverso, P., 702
Traxler, M. J., 490
Trehub, A., 698
Treisman, A., 423, 424
Tresch, M. C., 645
Treves, A., 190
Trueswell, J. C., 480
Tsapogas, J., 566
Tsotsos, K. J., 424
Tufte, E. R., 578
Tuholski, S. W., 444
Tulving, E., 227

Tuner, H., 364
Tunney, R. J., 400
Turing, A., 3, 163, 170, 692
Turken, A. U., 272
Turner, M., 387, 533, 671
Turney, P., 580
Turvani, M., 533
Turvey, M. T., 635
Tversky, A., 7, 131, 276, 302, 303, 304, 306, 307, 309, 332, 354, 555
Twilley, L., 486
Tyler, L., 261
Tyson, R., 555

Ullman, J. B., 513
Ullman, J. D., 344, 478
Ullman, M., 34, 36
Ullman, S., 424, 425, 426, 432, 626
Underwood, B. J., 205
Underwood, G., 581
Ungor, M., 596
Uno, Y., 635
Urada, D. I., 511
Usher, M., 47, 197, 210, 211, 212, 294, 310, 311, 437, 444
Usrey, W. M., 615
Uttley, A. M., 668

Vallacher, R. R., 518, 519
van Beers, R. J., 655
van de Laar, P., 427
Van den Bosch, A., 482
Van der Heijden, A. H., 423, 424, 428, 436
Van der Henst, J. B., 343
van der Maas, H., 455
Van Der Wege, M., 580
Vandierendonck, A., 346
Vandorpe, S., 605
Van Essen, D. C., 427
van Fraasen, B., 7, 543, 544
van Gelder, T., 30, 103, 104, 106, 470
van Gisbergen, J. A. M., 113
Van Haeften, T., 192
van Hamme, L. J., 594, 595, 600
van Heuven, W., 33
Vanhoomissen, T., 510
van Koten, S., 464
VanLehn, K., 365, 367, 368, 370, 371, 372, 373, 374, 375, 376
Vanman, E. J., 523
van Oostendorp, H., 581
Van Overwalle, F., 506, 507, 508, 510, 513, 514
van Rijn, D. H., 183
van Rijn, H., 455

Van Rooy, D., 506, 510
van Someren, M., 455
Van Wallendael, L. R., 289
van Wijk, J. J., 576
Vanyukov, P. M., 582
Várady, T., 685
Vardi, M., 134, 147
Vaughan, S. I., 523
Veksler, V. D., 581
Velleman, P. F., 576
Veloso, M. M., 367, 370
Vera, A., 565, 668
Verghese, P., 581
Verguts, T., 277, 282
Vetter, T., 626, 627, 628, 629, 631, 632
Vetterling, W. T., 289
Vianu, V., 134
Vicente, K., 4, 11
Vijayan, S., 461
Vilcu, M., 461
Vinter, A., 402, 411, 416
Vishton, P. M., 461
Vitányi, P., 183, 352, 491
Vitolo, T. M., 365
Vokey, J. R., 400
von der Malsburg, C., 617
Vonk, W., 489
von Neumann, J., 303, 534
Vorberg, D., 106
Vygotsky, L., 533

Wagenaar, W., 534
Wagenmakers, E. J., 59, 74, 78, 290
Wagner, A. D., 189
Wagner, A. R., 333, 506, 590–592, 594, 601
Wai, K. W. Y., 424
Wainer, H., 576
Wald, M. L., 572
Waldmann, M. R., 333, 603, 605
Waldron, E. M., 272
Walker, A. M., 518
Walker, J. M., 603, 605
Wallace, J. G., 452
Wallach, D., 181, 398, 413
Wallenstein, G. V., 193, 194
Walling, D., 519
Wallsten, T. S., 318
Walsh, C., 352
Walsh, T., 698
Wang, J., 4, 11
Wang, X. J., 211, 437
Wanner, E., 479
Ward, L., 534
Ward, R., 428, 432
Ward, W. C., 75

Ware, C., 581
Warren, D. H. D., 481
Warren, P., 485, 486
Warren, T., 626
Warrington, E. K., 256
Wason, P., 130, 135
Wasserman, E. A., 280, 592, 594, 595, 597, 600
Waterman, D., 362
Watson, J. B., 361
Watts, S., 650
Weber, K., 582
Weckerly, J., 42
Weekes, B. S., 487
Weinberg, A., 488
Weinshall, D., 273
Weintraub, S., 196
Weise, R., 481, 493
Weisler, S., 140
Welford, A. T., 362
Wellman, H. M., 78
Welsh, A., 482
Wenger, E., 540
Wennerholm, P., 293, 294, 604, 605
West, R., 134, 534, 535, 542, 544
Westbury, D. R., 645
Westerberg, C. E., 196
Westermann, G., 29, 43, 44, 47, 48, 49, 457, 462, 463, 470
Wexler, K., 493
Wheeler, M. W., 668
White, N. M., 597
White, P. A., 333
Whitten, W. B., 209
Wichmann, S., 368
Wickelgren, W. A., 387, 596
Wickens, C. D., 576, 578
Widrow, G., 506
Wiesel, T., 615, 616, 618
Wiesel, T. N., 615
Wigner, E., 163
Wilhelm, O., 345
Wilimzig, C., 107, 113
Wilkie, O., 83, 323, 324, 325, 327–328, 329, 330, 332, 334, 335
Wilkinson, F., 11
Willer, R., 520
Williams, D. A., 593, 596, 603
Williams, E. M., 232
Williams, K. E., 565
Williams, R. J., 24, 28, 237, 485
Williamson, M. M., 130
Wills, A. J., 294
Wilson, D., 672
Wilson, H., 11, 111, 118
Wilson, M., 570

Wilson, M. A., 215
Wilson, R. A., 233
Wilson, T. D., 397
Wilson, W. H., 366
Wing, A., 106, 650
Wingfield, A., 203, 208
Winman, A., 293, 294, 604, 605
Winograd, T., 359, 479, 671, 690
Winston, P. H., 375
Winterstein, D., 695
Wiskott, L., 617
Witter, M. P., 192, 213
Wittgenstein, L., 230
Wolf, L., 618
Wolf, R., 104
Wolfe, C. J., 577
Wolfe, J., 424, 425, 428, 581
Wolpert, D., 59, 387, 650, 655, 657, 658
Woltz, D. J., 380
Wong, P. C., 567, 576
Wood, D. J., 368
Woods, W. A., 671
Woodworth, R. S., 361, 363
Woolcock, J., 511
Wos, L., 151
Wouterlood, F. G., 192
Wright, I. P., 674, 675
Wright, S. P., 189
Wu, M., 323
Wu, X., 190
Wulfeck, B., 43
Wyble, B., 190, 191, 193, 194, 219
Wyer, R. S., 509

Xiang, J. Z., 189, 195
Xie, X., 27, 29
Xu, F., 34, 36, 59, 464
Xu, J., 197, 203, 206

Yang, C. D., 492
Yang, L. X., 272
Yang, Y., 134, 136, 143, 157, 158, 343, 352, 515, 516
Yates, J. F., 605
Yeh, W., 232
Yngve, V. H., 488
Yonelinas, A. P., 189, 190, 191, 197
Yoshioka, T., 211
Young, M. E., 280
Young, R., 15, 175, 176, 672
Young, S. Y., 492
Younger, B. A., 462
Yu, A. J., 437
Yuille, A., 45, 59, 482
Yurgenson, S., 615

Zajac, H., 444
Zaki, S., 134, 286, 293
Zaki, S. R., 286
Zanone, P. G., 106
Zautra, A., 517
Zebrowitz, L. A., 512
Zeelenberg, R., 203
Zelazo, P. D., 676
Zenzen, M., 5, 6, 7, 8, 9, 11, 14, 160, 533, 537, 554, 555
Zerubavel, E., 16, 533
Zettlemoyer, L. S., 492
Zhang, K., 468
Zhang, X., 154, 176, 323, 329
Ziegler, J., 481, 485
Ziemke, T., 452
Zihl, J., 424, 428, 431
Zimmermann, J. M., 306
Zipser, D., 28, 217, 270, 485
Zochowski, M., 518
Zorzi, M., 485, 487

Subject Index

AA. *See* auto-association (AA)

AARON program, 690

ABLE model, 378

abstraction, 416

   multiple levels of, 31–34

abstract models and dual process theories,
      206–207

ACC. *See* anterior cingulate cortex (ACC)

acceptance probability, 88

acetylcholine, 194

ACME, learning mechanisms, 370*t*

ACSM, learning mechanisms, 381*t*

activation confusion model, 207

ACT model, 362, 372

   learning mechanisms, 370*t*, 377*t*, 381*t*

   optimization mechanism, 379

ACT-R (Adaptive Control of Thought, Rational
      theory), 5, 12, 13, 45, 128, 150, 364,
      413, 442–443, 452, 455*t*, 457*t*, 505,
      534–535, 542, 565, 573, 575–576,
      675. *See also* cognitive engineering,
      cognitive modeling

   bottleneck in human cognition, 178

   capacity limitations, 177

   cognitive performance, 176*t*, 178

   implicit to explicit learning, 181–182

interpretation of instructions stored in
      memory, 180–181

   learning, 176*t*

   learning mechanism, 381*t*

   neuroscience and, 176*t*

   overview, 172–173

   perceptual and motor systems, 176*t*

   subsymbolic and symbolic computation in,
      31

   working memory capacity, 176*t*, 177

actuator coordinates, 638–639

ADAPT, learning mechanisms, 370*t*

adaptive learning, computational approach,
      648–649

Adaptive Strategy Choice Model (ASCM),
      379–380

ADAPT-PILOT, 364–365

ADDCOVE model, 291

Additive ALCOVE (ADDCOVE), 282

ADIT model, 597–598

affective balance theory, 309

AGL. *See* artificial grammar learning (AGL)

AI. *See* artificial intelligence (AI)

air traffic control (ATC) issues, 567

ALCOVE (Attentional Learning Covering
      map), 267, 273, 274*f*, 275–276,

ALCOVE (*cont.*)
        277–278, 279–280, 287–288, 290,
        293, 294, 463
    characteristics, 277*t*
Allais paradox, 304–305
alphabet, 141, 147. *See also* language
Amari formulation, 111
analogy rule, 457
animals, models of animal learning and their
        relations to human learning, 589–611
    altricial and precocial skills, 697–698
    associative accounts of predictive learning,
        601–604
        rule learning, 604
        use of prior knowledge about the structure
            of causal relationships, 602–604
    associative models of predictive learning,
        590–601
        late computation models, 598–601
        predictive values of absent cues, 592–595
        predictive values of configurations of cues,
            595–597
        relevance of cues, 597–598
        Rescorla-Wagner model, 590–592, 591*t*
    boundary conditions for different processes,
        604–606
    new directions in associative models of
        predictive learning, 606
    overview, 589–590
ANN. *See* artificial neural network (ANN);
        connectionist models of cognition
A-not-B error, 459, 460, 460*t*, 472
ANOVA (analysis of variance), 538
anterior cingulate cortex (ACC), 438
anti-Hebbian model, 198–199
anxiety, 674
aphasia, grammaticality ratings in, 489
APPLE model, characteristics, 277*t*
application symbols, 139
approach-avoidance model, 516
argument semantics, 140, 162
argument theory, 146. *See also* proof theory
Aristotle, 128, 129–130, 129*n*2
artificial grammar learning (AGL), 397, 398*f*,
        400, 402–403, 402*f*
artificial intelligence (AI), 17, 127, 130–131,
        164, 359, 667, 676, 684–685. *See also*
        GOFAI (good old-fashioned artificial
        intelligence)
    machine translation, 671
artificial neural network (ANN), 23, 28. *See also*
        connectionist models of cognition
artificial syntax, 461–462, 462*t*
ASCM. *See* Adaptive Strategy Choice Model
        (ASCM)

associative recognition, 202
ATC. *See* air traffic control (ATC) issues
ATNs. *See* augmented transition networks
attention and cognitive control, 422–450
    models of goal-driven attentional control,
        433–445
        automaticity and actions without attention,
            443–444
        base model, 434–436, 434*f*
        dual-task coordination, 441–443
        extensions and alternatives to the base
            model, 436–438
        multi-tasking, 438–441, 439*f*
        unresolved issues and future directions,
            444–445
    object attention, 431, 432*f*
    overview, 422–423
    task switching, 439–440, 439*f*
    visual attention, 423–433
        base model, 424–425, 424*f*
        explicit computation and representation of
            attention, 425–428, 426*f*
        interactive emergence of attention,
            428–431, 429*f*
        key issues in models of, 431–433, 432*f*
attention switching mechanism, 313
attitudes, 512–515
attractor neural network, 658
Augmented Transition Networks (ATNs), 479,
        671
autism, 468, 469*f*
auto-association (AA), 452

background knowledge effects, 325–327
background relative luminance contrast
        (BRLC), 107–109, 108*f*, 113
back-propagation (BP), 27, 452, 464
balance scale model, 454–456
    characteristics, 455*t*
Bayesian models of cognition, 59–100, 330–
        332, 332*t*, 452–453, 466, 555,
        555*f*
    basics of Bayesian inference, 62–70
        Bayes' rule, 63–64
        comparison of hypotheses, 64–65
        model selection, 68–70, 69*f*
        parameter estimation, 65–68
    framework for motor learning, 656–657
    graphical models, 45, 70–79, 71*f*
        Bayesian networks, 70–72, 71*f*
        causal graphical models, 73–74
        causal induction from contingency data
            example, 74–79, 74*t*, 76*f*, 77*f*
        representation of probability distributions
            over propositions, 72–73, 73*f*

hierarchical Bayesian models, 79–86, 80*f*, 81*f*
    learning about feature variability example, 82–83
    property induction example, 83–86, 84*f*
inductive reasoning, 330–332, 331*t*
inference of connectionist models and, 30–31
Markov Chain Monte Carlo (MCMC) example, 86–95, 89*f*
    inferring topics from text example, 89–95, 91*f*, 92*f*, 93*f*, 94*f*
overview, 59–62
probability theory, 50, 62
properties, 289–290
psycholinguistics and, 481–482, 497, 497*f*
Bayes' rule, 63–64
behavior
    dynamical systems thinking and, 103
    forward and inverse models as a basis for adaptive behavior, 649–650
    patterns of, 105
    planning of desired, 645
    scenarios to sharpen vision, 701
    serial, 182
    understanding, 5–6
behaviorist learning theories, 380–381
Bernoulli, Daniel, 303
Bernoulli likelihood, 66
beta distribution, 80, 80*f*
biased competition model, 428–430, 429*f*
binding problem, 182
blackbox theories, 4
body kinematics, 641. *See also* motor control, models of
Boltzmann machine learning algorithm, 30–31
Boolean concepts, 352–353, 353*t*
boundary models, 271
BP. *See* back-propagation (BP)
brain. *See also* neuroscience
    abstraction and, 120
    anterior cingulate cortex, 438
    constraints at the level of individual brain cells, 182
    cortical activation dynamics, 118
    entorhinal cortex, 191
    hippocampus, 189
    imaging constraints at the global brain architecture level, 183
    inferotemporal cortex, 425
    mechanisms, 692
    medial temporal lobe structures, 215
    perirhinal cortex, 189
    posterior parietal cortex, 425
    prefrontal cortex, 189, 425
    processing systems, 47
    structures, 213
    TCM in, 210–213
    temporal context model, 210–213
brain degradation, 24
    neural plausibility, 28–30
BRLC. *See* background relative luminance contrast (BRLC)

C4.5, 452, 454, 455*t*, 462*t*
CAP2 model, 365
CAPS. *See* Cognitive-Affective Processing System (CAPS)
cascade-correlation algorithm, 43–44, 452, 453–454
Cascade model, 368, 373
    learning mechanisms, 370*t*
catastrophic interference, 182
categorization
    everyday, 268
    in the laboratory, 268
category coherence, 244
category learning, 462–463, 463*t*
category prototypes, 230
CAUs. *See* cognitive-affective units (CAUs)
causal induction, 74–79, 74*t*, 76*f*, 77*f*, 560–562
    Bayesian approach and, 78–79
causality, 560–562
causal learning, 333–334, 506–507
causal reasoning, 507–508
CC. *See* cascade-correlation algorithm; Competitive Chunking (CC)
CELEX, 493
child development, computational models, 12
CHILDES, 494–495
    word clusters and, 496*f*
chunking, 372, 373
    implicit learning and, 416–417
circular convolution, 557
circular correlation, 557
CLARION (Connectionist Learning with Adaptive Rule Induction ONline), 5, 12–13, 45, 128, 153–156, 371, 372, 374–375, 382, 413, 454, 505, 535–536, 537–538, 537*t*, 539, 542, 544, 675. *See also* implicit learning
cognitive performance, 176*t*, 178–179
constraints at the level of individual brain cells, 182
hidden computational power, 178–179
implicit to explicit learning, 181–182
learning from direct instruction, 176*t*, 180
learning mechanism, 377*t*
neuroscience and, 176*t*
overview, 174–175

CLARION (*cont.*)
  perceptual and motor systems, 176*t*
  working memory, 176*t*
Classical Computational Theory of Mind, 23
closed world assumption (CWA), 149*n*9
CLS. *See* Complementary Learning Systems
        (CLS) model
cognition. *See also* connectionist models of
        cognition; visual information
        processing, computational modeling of
  cognitive mechanisms, 10
  competences, 691
  connectionist models and, 23–58, 45–46
  constraints at the level of individual brain
        cells, 182
  control of, 422–450, 433
  dynamical systems approaches to, 101–126
  forgetting, 535*n*3
  higher-level, 60–63
  influences on cognitive theory, 45–51
    cognitive development, 47–48
    knowledge versus processing, 46–47
    origins of individual variability and
        developmental disorders, 49–50
    study of acquired disorders in cognitive
        neuropsychology, 48–49
  language and, 102
  link to sensory and motor surfaces, 101–102
  processes of, 397
  subsymbolic theories, 29–30
  understanding with computational cognitive
        modeling, 4–5
  via comprehensive theoretical language,
        138–139
Cognition and Affect project, 703
Cognitive-Affective Processing System (CAPS),
        382, 515, 517
cognitive-affective units (CAUs), 515
cognitive architecture, 7, 7*n*2, 170–185, 530*n*1.
        See also ACT-R; CLARION; EPIC
  challenges, 132
  constraints on modeling, 175–183, 176*t*
    cognitive performance, 177–179
    learning, 179–182
    from neuroscience, 182–183
    perceptual and motor systems, 179
    working memory capacity, 175–177
  future directions, 14–15
  overview, 170–171
cognitive engineering, cognitive modeling,
        565–588, 566–567*n*2. *See also*
        cognitive science
  approaches, 567–571, 567*n*5
    legacy of Card, Moran, and Newell,
        569–571

  unit task as control construct, 568
  from unit tasks through interactive routines
        to embodiment, 568–569, 569*t*, 570*f*
  issues and applications, 571–582
    complex systems, 571–576
      driving, 574
      predator uninhabited air vehicle, 572
      predicting skilled performance from
        analyses of novices, 574–575
      runway incursions, 572–574, 573*f*
    visual analytics, 576–582
      history, 576–578, 577*f*
      informational displays, 579–582, 581*f*
      reasoning from graphs, 578–579, 579*f*
  overview, 565–567
cognitive science, 533, 566–567*n*2. *See also*
        cognitive engineering, cognitive
        modeling; cognitive social simulation;
        psychology
  assessment of scientific progress, 703–706
    measurement, 705
  computational cognitive modeling and, 17,
        667–683
    cognitive aspects, 669–673
    emotions and motivation, 673–675
    humanity and, 675–676
    overview, 667–669
    social interaction, 676–678
  epigenesis, 672–673
  future directions, 13–14
  history, 4, 4*n*1
  language and, 671
  linguistics and, 672
  models, 4
    causality, 560–562
    deductive, 551–553
    of explanation, 562, 562*t*
    neural network, 556–560, 556*f*, 559*f*
    overview, 549–551
    probabilistic, 554–556, 555*f*
    schema and analogy models, 553–554
    of scientific explanation, 549–564
  scenario-based backward chaining research,
        704–705
  theory, 4
Cognitive Science, 5, 532
Cognitive Science Society, 5, 532
cognitive social simulation, 530–548. *See also*
        cognitive science
  conferences, 532
  deductive versus inductive approach to, 531
  dimensions, 541–543
  directions, 544–545
  equation-based approach, 541
  examples, 534–540

simulation of games, 534–535, 535*n*1
simulation of group interaction, 539–541
simulation of organizations, 535–539, 536*t*, 537*t*
intelligence level, 537
issues, 543–544
overview, 530–534
Cognitive Systems Research, 5, 530*n*2, 532
communication, 133. *See also* cognitive social simulation
with other fields studying learning and inference, 61
person-level mechanization, 164
Competitive Chunking (CC), 410–411, 412*f*, 416–417
Complementary Learning Systems (CLS) model, 190–197, 192*f*
application to CLS to episodic memory, 191
cortical and hippocampal model details, 218–219, 218*t*, 219*t*
cortical familiarity, 194–196, 195*f*
Hebbian learning, 217–218
of hippocampal recall, 191–194, 192*f*
memory decision-making, 196–197
point neuron activation function, 216–217
pseudocode, 216
representative prediction from, 196
weight contrast enhancement, 218
Winners-Take-All inhibition, 217
complex information processing, 362. *See also* artificial intelligence (AI)
Computational and Mathematical Organization Theory, 532
computational cognitive modeling. *See also* episodic memory, computational models; logic-based computational cognitive modeling (LCCM)
analysis, 8
assessment of scientific progress, 703–706
measurement, 705
organizing questions, 704
rivalry versus collaboration, 705–706
scenario-based backward chaining research, 704–705
of attention and cognitive control, 422–450
challenges, 132
for cognitive engineering, 565–588
in cognitive science, 667–683
description, 3–5
of developmental psychology, 451–476
examples, 4–5
functions of vision, 687–692
developmental routes to related cognitive competences, 691
importance of mobile hands, 688–689

processes, affordances, and empty spaces, 689–690
role of perception in ontology extension, 691–692
seeing without recognizing objects, 690–691
future directions, 13–16
humanity, 696–699
altricial and precocial skills in animals and robots, 697–698
meta-semantic competence, 698–699
of implicit learning, 396–421
description, 396–399, 398*f*
models, 401–413, 402*f*
connectionist, 403–410, 405*f*, 407*f*, 408*f*, 409*f*
fragment-based, 410–411, 412*f*
hybrid, 411–413
overview, 396
theoretical and conceptual implications, 413–415
conscious versus unconscious knowledge, 401, 415
rules versus statistics, 413–414
separable systems, 414–415
verification, 399–401
institutional obstacles, 686
intrinsic difficulties in making progress, 686–687
in judgment, 318
language for communication, 693–694
levels of, 8–12, 8*t*, 9*t*
componential, 10
cross-level analysis, 10–11
knowledge level, 8–9
mixed-level analysis, 11
physical level, 9
physiological level, 10
psychological, 10
sociological, 9–10
symbol level, 9
levels of analysis and explanation, 685–686
models of animal learning and their relations to human learning, 589–611
models of motor control, 635–663
ontological blindness, 687
overview, 16–17
in personality and social psychology, 505–529
as process-based theories, 4
of psycholinguistics, 477–504
purpose, 5–8
of reasoning, 134–138
representational capabilities, 692–696
resolving disputes, 701–703
analyze before choosing, 701–702

Computational (*cont.*)
    ontology for types of architectures, 703
    spaces of possibilities, 702–703
    scenarios to sharpen vision, 699–701
      behavior specifications, 701
      fine-grained scenarios, 700
      sample competences, 699–700
    scope, 684–685
    of skill acquisition, 359–395
    social stimulation and, 15–16
    three-level theory, 8–9
    understanding cognition and, 4–5
    varieties of complexity, 694–696
    of visual information processing, 612–634
    Web sites, 5
computational psychology
  as a discipline, 16
  future research, 17
computational theory, 8, 8*t*
computer programming, logic-based,
    156
concept learning, 464–468, 466*f*
conditional elimination, 136
Conditional Principal Components Analysis
    (CPCA) Hebbian Learning, 191, 193,
    198
conditional probability, 63
conditioned inhibition, 506
conditioned stimulus (CS), 589
conjugate priors, 67
connectionist models of cognition, 23–58, 452,
    667. *See also* cognition
  architectures for cognitive models, 485*f*
  auto-associator network, 403–404
  background, 23–31
    historical context, 24–26, 25*f*
    key properties, 26–28
    neural plausibility, 28–30
    relationship between Bayesian inference
      and connectionist models, 30–31
  bottom-up models to top-down effects, 484,
    485*f*
  connectionist/symbolist divide, 668
  criticisms, 29–30
  future directions, 50–51
  human cognition and, 45–46
  HU unit, 39, 39*f*
  illustrative models, 31–43
    interactive activation model (IA), 31–33,
      32*f*
  of implicit learning, 403–410, 405*f*, 407*f*,
    408*f*, 409*f*
  influences on cognitive theory, 45–51
    cognitive development, 47–48
    knowledge versus processing, 46–47

    origins of individual variability and
      developmental disorders, 49–50
    study of acquired disorders in cognitive
      neuropsychology, 48–49
  model of English past tense formation, 34–38,
    35*f*
  overview, 23
  PDP, 677
  psycholinguistics and, 480–481
  related models, 43–45
    Bayesian graphic models, 45
    cascade-correlation and incremental neural
      network algorithms, 43–44
    hybrid models, 44–45
    mixture-of-experts models, 44
  relationship to symbolic models, 29–30
  simple recurrent network, 405–408, 405*f*,
    407*f*, 408*f*, 409*f*
  structure in time, 38–43, 39*f*, 41*f*
  subsymbolic cognitive theories, 29–30
  superpositional memory, 36
  TRACE model, 33–34
conscientiousness, 516
consciousness, 445
consequence, 145
constraint-based rule specialization, 374
constraint satisfaction model, 514–515
constructive dilemma, 142
CONSYDERR architecture model, 45, 155
content/boundary quality and on-the-fly
    equivalence, 271
context, free recall, and active maintenance
  TCM in the brain, 210–213
    architectures for active maintenance,
      210–211
    integrating active maintenance and
      long-term memory, 211–213
    O'Reilly and Frank Prefrontal Network,
      211
    relevant brain structures, 213
    Usher and Cohen Localist Attractor
      Network, 211
context-dependent preferences, 306–308
contingencies, table representation used in
    elemental causal induction, 74–75, 74*t*
convergence theory of semantic memory, 256,
    257*f*, 259–261
coordinate systems, 637–641
  actuator coordinates, 638–639
  endpoint coordinates, 638, 639*f*
  generalized coordinates, 639–641
coordination patterns, 105–106
CORP-ELM, 536, 536*n*4
CORP-P-ELM, 536, 536*n*4
CORP-SOP, 536, 536*n*4

correspondence bias, 507
COUNTPLAN model, 365–366
COVIS model, 272
CPCA. *See* Conditional Principal Components Analysis (CPCA) Hebbian Learning
CPM-GOMS, 565, 569, 570–571, 570*f*
CPT. *See* cumulative prospect theory (CPT)
cross-level analysis, 10–11
CS. *See* conditioned stimulus (CS)
cues
    predictive values of absent cues, 592–595
    predictive values of configurations of cues, 595–597
    relevance, 597–598
cumulative prospect theory (CPT), 303–304, 304*n*1
CWA. *See* closed world assumption (CWA)
cybernetics, 361–362

Davelaar et al Free Recall Model, 212–213
décalage, 459
decision field theory (DFT), 311–313, 311*f*, 312*f*, 317
    probabilities, 316–317, 316*t*
decision-making, 196–197. *See also* micro-process models of decision-making
    accounting for paradoxes in, 314–317
    computational models, 308–314
    heuristic rule-based systems, 308–309
    micro-process models, 302–321
    paradoxes with utility models in, 304–308
    state-of-the-art decision models, 303–308
declarative/logic-based cognitive modeling, 127–169. *See also* logic-based computational cognitive modeling (LCCM)
    in conformity to LCCM, 150–156
    Johnson-Laird models, 153
    production rule-based modeling, 150–152
    PSYCOP modeling, 152–153
deductive reasoning, 61
    simulations of human, 339–358
        concepts, models, and minimization, 352–354, 353*t*
        formal theories of reasoning, 340–343, 341*t*
        nature of human deductive reasoning, 354–356
        overview, 339–340
        sentential reasoning using mental models, 347–352, 347*t*, 349*t*, 351*t*
        spatial reasoning using mental models, 343–347, 345*t*
deictic words, 466

Delta Rule, 403–404
    learning algorithm, 236
DeMorgan's Laws, 143, 143*f*
derivational analogy, 367
developmental disorders
    genetic, 50
    individual variability, 49–50
developmental psychology, computational models of, 451–476
    abnormal development, 468–469, 469*f*
    artificial syntax, 461–462, 462*t*
    balance scale, 454–456, 455*t*
    C4.5, 454
    cascade-correlation, 453–454
    computational techniques, 451–453
        complementary computation, 470
        computational bakeoffs, 470–472
        computational diversity, 469–470
        development via parameter settings, 472
        qualitative versus quantitative changes, 471
    concept and word learning, 464–468, 466*f*
    developmental issues, 451
    discrimination shift learning, 463–464
    object permanence, 457–461, 458*f*, 460*t*
    overview, 451
    past tense, 456–457, 457*t*
    similarity-to-correlation shift in category learning, 462–463, 463*t*
DFT. *See* decision field theory (DFT); Dynamical Field Theory (DFT)
DICE model, 522
direction, dynamics of, 103, 104*f*
Dirichlet Allocation, 92, 93*f*
discrimination shift learning, 463–464
DISCUSS model, 522–523
diversity effects, 325
dopamine, 436, 437
double dissociation, 49
drift, in children, 116
driving, 574
Dynamical Field Theory (DFT), 111*f*, 112–116, 114*f*, 115*f*, 116*f*
    dynamic neuronal field, 119
    multifunctional, 121
    simulation models, 123
dynamical systems approaches to cognition, 101–126
    account of dynamical systems thinking, 120–121
    dynamical field theory, 109–116
        activation fields, 109–110, 109*f*
        behavioral signatures of dynamic fields, 112–116, 114*f*, 115*f*, 116*f*
        field dynamics, 110–112, 110*f*, 111*f*, 112*f*

Dynamical Field Theory (DFT) (*cont.*)
  dynamical systems thinking, 103–109, 104*f*, 108*f*
  embodied and situated approach, 116–118
  embodiment, situatedness, and dynamical systems, 102–103
  neurally-based, 118–120
  overview, 101–102
  of perseverative reaching, 121–123
  stability and, 117
dyslexias, acquired, 486–487

EBA. *See* elimination by aspects (EBA) model
Ebbinghaus, Hermann, 361
EBRW. *See* Exemplar-Based Random Walk model (EBRW)
ECHO, 309–310, 507, 508, 513, 553, 560
EGCM. *See* Extended Generalized Context Model (EGCM)
EGCM Response Time (EGCM-RT), 295–296
EGCM-RT. *See* EGCM Response Time (EGCM-RT)
EIPs. *See* elementary information processes (EIPs)
elementary information processes (EIPs), 576–577
Elements (Aristotle), 130
elimination by aspects (EBA) model, 307
ELM model, 515
emergence, 120
emotions, 445
  cognitive science and, 673–675
  coherence, 511
encoding mode, 194
endpoint coordinates, 638, 639*f*
energy function, 658
entorhinal cortex (EC), 191
EPAM, 150
EPIC (Executive-Process Interactive Control), 442, 565. *See also* cognitive engineering, cognitive modeling
  bottleneck in human cognition, 178
  cognitive performance, 176*t*
  overview, 173–174
  perceptual and motor systems, 176*t*, 179
episodic memory, computational models, 189–225
  abstract models of recognition and recall, 201–207
    REM model of recognition and recall, 203–207
      abstract models and dual-process theories, 206–207
      differences in how models explain interference, 205–206

representative REM results, 204–205
source of activation confusion model, 207
alternative models of perirhinal familiarity, 197–201
  anti-Hebbian model, 198–199
  Meeter, Myers, and Gluck model, 199–200
  oscillating learning algorithm, 200–201, 201*n*3
biologically based models, 190–201, 192*f*, 195*f*
  CLS model, 190–197
    applying CLS to episodic memory, 191
    of cortical familiarity, 194–196, 195*f*
    of hippocampal recall, 191–194, 192*f*
    memory decision-making, 196–197
    representative prediction from, 196
context, free recall, and active maintenance, 207–213
  TCM in the brain, 210–213
    architectures for active maintenance, 210–211
    integrating active maintenance and long-term memory, 211–213
    O'Reilly and Frank Prefrontal Network, 211
    relevant brain structures, 213
    Usher and Cohen Localist Attractor Network, 211
  temporal context model, 208–210, 210*f*
    in the brain, 210–213
    how TCM accounts for recall data, 209–210, 210*f*
definition, 189
overview, 189–190
weight-based versus activation-based memory mechanisms, 190
Euclidean distance, 243*f*, 638
  motor planning and representation, 643, 644*f*
EUREKA system, 367, 371, 378
  learning mechanism, 377*t*, 381*t*
European Social Simulation Association, 532
exclusive disjunction, 144
Executive-Process Interactive Control (EPIC), 442
Exemplar-Based Random Walk model (EBRW), 294
exemplar models, 272–296. *See also* models of categorization
  exemplary, 273–276, 274*f*
  similarity, 276–287
    continuous scale
      sensitive to differences only, 277–278, 277*t*

sensitive to matches, 278, 279*f*
nominal scale
    sensitive to differences only, 279–280
    sensitive to matches, 280–286, 285*f*
    summary of similarity formalizations,
        286–287
exemplary recruitment, 290–293
  incessant recruitment, 291
  no recruitment/pre-loaded exemplars,
    290–291
  novelty-driven recruitment, 291
  performance-driven recruitment, 291–293
expected utility, 303
explicit models, 353*t*, 354, 355*t*
Extended Generalized Context Model
    (EGCM), 294–295
external perception/action challenge, 160–163,
    160*n*14
extroversion, 516, 517

face perceptions, 511–512
  prosopagnosia, 691
  visual information processing and, 618, 619*f*,
    620*f*, 621*f*, 624*f*, 627–632, 627*f*,
    628*f*, 630*f*, 631*f*
FAIL-SAFE-2, learning mechanism, 377*t*
Farah-McClelland model, 256, 257*f*, 260
feature variability, 82–83
feedback circles, 361–362
Fermat, Pierre, 303
field theory, dynamical, 109–116
  activation fields, 109–110, 109*f*
  behavioral signatures of dynamic fields,
    112–116, 114*f*, 115*f*
  field dynamics, 110–112, 110*f*, 111*f*, 112*f*
  perseverative reading of dynamical field
    theory, 121–123
fixed dimensionality, 557
Flashline Mars Arctic Research Station, 539–541
fMRI. *See* functional magnetic resonance
    imaging (fMRI)
FOA. *See* focus of attention (FOA)
focus of attention (FOA), 427
force fields, 645, 646–647, 646*f*, 648*f*, 649
  adaptation experiment, 650, 651*f*
  random, 653, 654*f*
  vectors, 658
forgetting, 535*n*3
formation rules, 145–146
formula semantics, 140
fragment-based model, of implicit learning,
    410–411, 412*f*
free recall, 208
functional brain imaging techniques, 50–51,
    433, 605

functional magnetic resonance imaging (fMRI),
    171
functional specialization, 401
fundamental attribution error, 507

GABA. *See* gamma-aminotrityric acid (GABA)
gambling theories, 303–304
games, cognitive social simulation and,
    534–535, 535*n*1
gamma-aminotrityric acid (GABA), 194
Gardner, Rea, 268
GCM. *See* Generalized Context Model (GCM)
Generalized Context Model (GCM), 273–275,
    274*f*, 277–278
  characteristics, 277*t*
generalized coordinates, 639–641
generalized force, 640–641
General Problem Solver (GPS), 171–172
genetics
  behavioral research and, 51
  developmental disorders and, 50
Gestalt psychology, 102, 524
Gibbs sampling, 88–89
GIPS model, 371, 376
GOFAI (good old-fashioned artificial
    intelligence), 667, 668, 670, 675. *See*
    also artificial intelligence (AI)
"Goldwater Machine," 512
GOMS, 567, 567*n*4, 568–569, 569*t*
GosNets, 675
GPS. *See* General Problem Solver (GPS)
grammar, 141, 147. *See also* language;
    psycholinguistics, computational
    models of
  cognitive science and, 671
  implicit learning and, 397
  overgeneral, 490*f*
  word clusters, 496*f*
Graph-Based Reasoning model, 578–579, 579*f*
graphical models, 70–79, 71*f*, 623, 623*f*
  causal graphical models, 73–74
  causal induction from contingency data
    example, 74–79, 74*t*, 76*f*, 77*f*
  directed, 70
  representation of probability distributions
    over propositions, 72–73, 73*f*
  undirected, 70
group interaction, cognitive social simulation
    and, 539–541

HAM model, 5
hand movements, 638, 639*f*, 643, 644*f*. *See*
    also motor control, models of
  experiments, 650, 651*f*
hardware implementational level, 8

Hebbian algorithms, 2, 191, 194, 272
Hebbian learning, 47, 217–218, 430
Hebb Rule, 403–404
Heit model, 331*t*
heuristics, 103, 362
higher-order thoughts (HOTs), 672
Hinton's distributed model, 234–237, 235*f*
Hippocampal model, 189, 193–194
  pattern-separated representations, 190
holographic reduced representations (HRRs),
        557–558
HOTCO, 511
HOTs. *See* higher-order thoughts (HOTs)
HPM model, learning mechanism, 381*t*
HRRs. *See* holographic reduced representations
        (HRRs)
HS, learning mechanism, 377*t*
humanity, cognitive science and, 675–676,
        696–699
  altricial and precocial skills in animals and
        robots, 697–698
  meta-semantic competence, 698–699
human level artificial intelligence, 130–131
humans. *See also* communication; language;
        reasoning
  self-consciousness, 133
  will to make choices, 133
HU unit, 39, 39*f*
hybrid models, 44–45, 271–272, 454
  of implicit learning, 411–413
hyperproofs, 143, 143*n*6
hypothesis, 63. *See also* probability theory
hypothesis space, 64

IA. *See* interactive activation model (IA)
ICARUS, 128
ID3, 456–457, 457*t*
IMP. *See* IMPression formation model
implicit learning. *See also* CLARION
        (Connectionist Learning with
        Adaptive Rule Induction ONline)
  computational models, 396–421
  conscious versus unconscious knowledge, 415
  exemplar-based models, 404*n*1
  fragment-based model, 410–411, 412*f*
  rules versus statistics, 413–414
  separable systems, 414–415
IMPression formation model, 508
impressions, formation of, 508–509
incremental neural network algorithms, 43–44
independence axiom, 305
inductive reasoning, models of, 322–338
  causal learning and causal reasoning, 333–334
  computational models of humans, 327–332
    Osherson et al., 327–328
    Sloman, 328–330

human inductive reasoning, 323–327
  background knowledge effects, 325–327
  Bayesian model, 330–332, 331*t*
  diversity effects, 325
  Heit model, 331*t*
  similarity effects, 324
  typicality effects, 324–325
  knowledge and, 335–336
  overview, 322
infants. *See also* toddlers
  abnormal development, 468–469, 469*f*
  age in developmental psychology, 459
  cognitive development, 47–48
  dynamical systems and, 115–116, 115*f*,
        116*f*
  me-you game, 467
  object concept and, 458
  reaching, 459
inferences, 80–81, 81*f*, 85
  abductive, 552–553, 556, 556*f*, 558–559,
        559*f*
  probabilistic, 150
inferotemporal cortex (IT), 425
informal/formal models, 270
information, theory of, 580. *See also* World
        Wide Web
information processing, visual, computational
        modeling of, 612–634
Information Speificity Principle, 360,
        361*f*
inhibition of return (IOR), 427
inhibitions, conditioned, 506
input-output theories, 4
instar learning, 191
interaction kernel, 110
Interactive Activation and Competition model,
        519
interactive activation model (IA), 31–33, 32*f*,
        483*f*
interference
  how models explain, 205–206
  structural, 214
International Conferences on Cognitive
        Modeling, 5
IOR. *See* inhibition of return (IOR)
IT. *See* inferotemporal cortex (IT)

James, William, 361
Johnson-Laird model, 153
joint probability, 63
Journal of Artificial Society and Social Simulation,
        532

kernels
  interaction, 110, 110*f*
  transition, 88, 89

kinematic redundancy, 641–643, 642*f*. *See also* motor control, models of
knowledge level, 8–9
  abstract declarative, 365–366
  active and latent representations, 46
  compilation, 379
  conscious versus unconscious, 401, 415
  definition, 172
  inductive reasoning and, 335–336
  knowledge-driven factors in visual search, 52
  lexical-semantic, 37
  optimization, 376, 378
  practical, 359
  prior, 83–84, 602–603
  procedural, 359
  versus processing, 46–47
  transfer of prior, 366–368
    analogy, 366–367
    identity, 366
    subsumption, 367–368
  use of prior knowledge about the structure of causal relationships, 602–604

lag-recency effect, 209–210
language, 133. *See also* psycholinguistics, computational models of; semantics; verbs; word recognition
  acquisition, 490–497
  challenges, 132
  cognition unification, 138–139
  cognitive science and, 671
  for communication, 693–694
  competence, 481
  fragments of natural, 164
  inflectional morphology, 37
  knowledge of, 60
  natural, 144
  past tense, 456–457, 457*t*
  phonological representations, 35*f*
  probabilistic models of, 481–482
  scaling-out, 695
  scientific theory of cognition and, 102
  sentence structure, 40
  syntax, 38
Latent Dirichlet Allocation, 92, 93*f*
latent semantic analysis (LSA), 91*f*, 95, 227, 250–252
Law of Effect, 361, 375–376
LCCM. *See* logic-based computational cognitive modeling (LCCM)
LEABRA algorithms, 28
leaky competing accumulator model, 310
learning, 160, 160*n*15
  of associations, 287–290
    Bayesian learning, 289–290

co-occurrence counting, 287
  gradient descent on error, 287–288
  systematic or random hill-climbing, 288–289
biases, 106
categories, 272, 462–463, 463*t*
causal, 333–334, 506–507
computational approach to adaptive learning, 648–649
computational models of language learning, 492
concept and word learning, 464–468, 466*f*
as constraint in cognitive architecture, 179–182
delta-rule learning algorithm, 236
from direct instruction, 180
discrimination shift learning, 463–464
explanation-based, 364, 364*n*2
Gibbs sampling algorithm, 93–94, 94*f*
Hebbian, 47
history, 361–363
at impasses, 372–373
implicit, 382, 396–421. *See also* computational cognitive modeling
from implicit to explicit, 181–182
instructive, 363–364
mechanisms, 36, 369, 370*t*, 377*t*
modeling, 78–79
models of animal learning and their relations to human learning, 589–611
model versus task, 403
new directions in associative models of predictive learning, 606
oscillating algorithm, 200–201
predictive, 590–601
principles, 36
rules, 604
shift in sources of information, 385*f*
similarity-to-correlation shift in category learning, 462–463, 463*t*
state space models of motor learning, 652–654, 653*f*, 654*f*
subsymbolic, 382
unlearning effects, 653, 653*f*
without awareness, 397
letter perception. *See* interactive activation model (IA)
letter recognition, 31–32, 32*f*
LEX. *See* lexicographic (LEX)
lexicographic (LEX), 307–308
likelihood, 63. *See also* probability theory
likelihood ratio, 65
linguistics, 17. *See also* motor primitives cognitive science and, 672

linguistics (*cont.*)
  competence, 479
  performance, 479
locus classicus, 148–149
logical systems, 139–150, 143*n*6, 147–148,
      147*n*7
  nonmonotonic, 148–150
  probabilistic, 150
logic-based computational cognitive modeling
      (LCCM), 127–169. *See also*
      computational cognitive modeling
  algorithmic level, 131
  ancient roots of, 129–130
  challenges facing, 134–139, 156–163
    cognition unification via comprehensive
        theoretical language, 138–139
    data from psychology of reasoning,
        134–138
    lack of mathematical maturity, 139
    mechanizing human reasoning, 156–160,
        159*f*
    meeting the challenge, 160–163, 161*f*,
        162*f*
  declarative modeling in conformity, 150–156
  description, 127–129
    levels of, 131–132
  goals, 133–134
  limitations and the future, 163–165
  logical systems, 139–150
  logic-based computer programming, 156
  logic-based human-level AI and, 130–131
  overview, 127–133
  rule-based, similarity-based, and
      commonsense reasoning, 153–156
  symbolic level, 131
logic-based computer programming, 156
LSA. *See* latent sampling analysis (LSA); latent
      semantic analysis; latent semantic
      analysis (LSA)

MAP. *See* maximum a posteriori (MAP)
marginalization, 64
marginal probability, 63–64
Markov Chair Monte Carlo (MCMC), 86–95,
      89*f*
Markov condition, 71, 71*f*
  hidden Markov model, 72
Marr's Principle of Least Commitment, 599
material conditionals, 144
mathematics
  computational cognitive modeling with lack
      of maturity, 39
  meta-theory for attributes, 140–141
mating, 520–522
Matrix model, 201

maximum a posteriori (MAP), 66–68
maximum likeihood, 65
MCMC. *See* Markov Chair Monte Carlo
      example (MCMC)
Meeter, Myers, and GLuck model, 199–200
memory. *See also* episodic memory,
        computational models; semantic
        memory, computational models of
  decision-making, 196–197
  drift in children, 116
  interpreting instructions stored, 180–181
  limitations, 356
  reach, 460
  solutions from, 379–380, 381*t*
  superpositional, 36
  targeting, 189
  temporal context, 190
memory buffer model, 408–410, 408*f*, 409*f*
memory targeting, 189
mental logic, 136, 152
mental meta-logic, 136–137
mental models, 136
  mechanisms for forming conjunctions of pairs
      of models, 350–351, 351*t*
  sentential reasoning and, 347–352, 347*t*,
      349*t*, 351*t*
  spatial reasoning and, 343–347, 345*t*
meta-theories, 145
Metropolis-Hastings algorithm, 88, 89*f*
me-you game, 467
micro-process models of decision-making,
      302–321
  accounting for paradoxes in decision-making,
      314–317
    accounting for context dependent
        preferences, 316–317, 316*t*
    accounting for preference reversals,
        315–316
    accounting for violations of independence
        and stochastic dominance, 314–315,
        315*t*
  comparison among models, 317–318
  computational models of decision-making
      example, 311–314
    attention switching mechanism, 313
    connectionist network interpretation,
        312–313, 312*f*
    model parameters, 314
    response mechanism, 313–314
    sequential sampling deliberation process,
        311–312, 311*f*
  computational models of decision-making
      survey, 308–310
    dynamic systems/connectionist networks,
        309–310

affective balance theory, 309
ECHO, 309–310
leaky competing accumulator model, 310
heuristic rule-based systems, 308–309
models cast in cognitive architectures, 310
connections to computational modeling in judgment, 318
overview, 302–303
state-of-the-art decision models, 303–308
evolution of utility-based models, 303–304
paradoxes with utility models in decision-making, 304–308
Allais paradox, 304–305
context-dependent preferences, 306–308
preference reversals, 305–306
stochastic dominance, 305
MINERVA 2 model, 201, 202
mixture-of-experts models, 44, 658
model of English past tense formation, 34–38, 35*f*
models. *See also* individual models
explicit, 353*t*, 354, 355*t*
generative, 72
hidden Markov model, 72
selection, 68–70, 69*f*
models of categorization, 267–301
exemplar models, 272–296
exemplary models, 273–276, 274*f*
exemplary recruitment, 290–293
incessant recruitment, 291
no recruitment/pre-loaded exemplars, 290–291
novelty-driven recruitment, 291
performance-driven recruitment, 291–293
learning of associations, 287–290
Bayesian learning, 289–290
co-occurrence counting, 287
gradient descent on error, 287–288
systematic or random hill-climbing, 288–289
response probability, 293–294
similarity, 276–287
attention in similarity, 286
continuous scale
sensitive to differences only, 277–278, 277*t*
sensitive to matches, 278, 279*f*
nominal scale
sensitive to differences only, 279–280
sensitive to matches, 280–286, 285*f*
summary of similarity formalizations, 286–287

overview, 267–272
categorization in the laboratory, 268
everyday categorization, 268
informal and formal models, 268–269
learning of categories, 272
types of representation and processes, 269–272, 269*nn*1–2
boundary models, 271
content/boundary quality and on-the-fly equivalence, 271
exemplar models, 270
hybrid models, 271–272
prototype models, 270
rule models, 270
theory models, 271
response time and choice as a function of time, 294–296
model-tracing process, 13
modus ponens, 152, 552
modus tollens, 143, 143*f*
motion, 107–108, 108*f*
dynamics, 640
modification of, 649
state of, 640
motor control, models of, 106–107, 635–663
adaptation to state- and time-dependent forces, 650–654, 651*f*
state space models of motor learning, 652–654, 653*f*, 654*f*
architectures for neural computation, 657–659
Bayesian framework for motor learning, 656–657
computational approach to adaptive learning, 648–649
coordinate systems, 637–641
actuator coordinates, 638–639
endpoint coordinates, 638, 639*f*
generalized coordinates, 639–641
forward and inverse models as a basis for adaptive behavior, 649–650
kinematic redundancy, 641–643, 642*f*
modification of motion, 649
motor planning and representation of Euclidean space, 643, 644*f*
motor primitives and field approximation, 647–648, 648*f*
noise and uncertainty, 654–656
organization of muscle synergies in the spinal cord, 645–647, 646*f*
overview, 635–637
plans into actions, 643, 645
velocity, 650
motor primitives, 647–648, 648*f*. *See also* linguistics

motor surfaces, 109
  cognition and, 101–102
multicausality, 121
multinomial distributions, 92

NASA. *See* National Aeronautics & Space
    Administration (NASA)
National Aeronautics & Space Administration
    (NASA), 572
National Research Council, 15
NEF. *See* Neural Engineering Framework (NEF)
NEMO. *See* Noisy Exemplar model (NEMO)
NESim, 556–557
NETtalk, 408
neural computation, 657–659
Neural Engineering Framework (NEF),
    556–557, 560
neural learning algorithms, 452, 468. *See also*
    developmental psychology,
    computational models of
neural network models, 5, 556–560, 556*f*,
    559*f*
  architecture schematic, 25*f*
  attractor, 658
  layered, 658
  neural plausibility, 28–30
  stochastic, 30–31
neurocognitive models, 255–262
  category-specific semantic impairment,
    255–258, 257*f*
  convergence model, 259–261
neuropsychology
  study of acquired disorders in cognitive
    neuropsychology, 48–49
  traditional cognitive, 48–49
neuroscience, 50. *See also* brain
  constraints at the global brain architecture
    level, 183
  constraints at the level of brain cells, 182
  information processing and, 176*t*
neuroticism, 516
"Newell's Program" 133–134
New Yorker Magazine, 268
NGOMSL format, 569, 569*t*
noise, 641
  external environment, 655
  uncertainty and, 654–656
Noisy Exemplar model (NEMO), 201, 202
nonenthymematic argument, 155
North American Association for Computational
    Social and Organizational Science,
    532
No-Vision (NV) protocol, 644*f*
null space, 642–643
NV. *See* No-Vision (NV) protocol

object attention, 431, 432*f*. *See also* attention
    and cognitive control
object permanence, 457–461, 458*f*, 460*t*
OHE. *See* outgroup homogeneity effect (OHE)
O'Reilly and Frank Prefrontal Network, 211
Organon (Aristotle), 129*n2*
oscillating learning algorithm, 200–201
outgroup homogeneity effect (OHE), 510–511
overshadowing, 506, 591*t*

Parallel Distributed Processing (PDP) model,
    23, 227
Parallel Distributed Processing Research Group,
    24
parameter estimation, 65–68
parameterization, 75–76
PARC, 580
PARSER, 411, 417–418
Pascal, Blaise, 303
past tense, 456–457, 457*t*
pattern completion, 193
PCA. *See* principal components analysis (PCA)
PDP. *See* artificial neural network (ANN);
    connectionist models of cognition;
    Parallel Distributed Processing (PDP)
    model
PDP++, 510, 515–516
PEIRCE tool, 553
perceptions, 107
  facial, 511–512
  group, 509–511
  learned high-level influences in early,
    627–632, 628*f*, 630*f*, 631*f*, 6327*f*
  in ontology extension, 691–692
  perception/action challenge, 160–163,
    160*n16*, 161*f*, 162*f*
perceptron convergence rule, 24
perirhinal cortex, 189
personality, computational models in, 505–529
  attitudes and attitude change, 512–515
  causal learning, 506–507
  causal reasoning, 507–508
  dyadic interactions and, 518
  dynamics of human mating strategies,
    520–522
  emotional coherence, 511
  face perceptions, 511–512
  group perception and stereotyping, 509–511
  impression formation, 508–509
  overview, 505–506
  the self, 518–519
  social influence, 519–520
PFC. *See* prefrontal cortex (PFC)
philosophy, 17, 668
PHINEAS program, 554

physical level, 9
Piaget, Jean, 113, 114*f*, 458, 672
planning, 61
Polyn, Norman, and Cohen model, 211–212
Polyscheme, 128
posterior mean, 66
posterior parietal cortex (PPC), 425
posterior predictive distribution, 66
posterior probability, 63
postulates, 345
PPC. *See* posterior parietal cortex (PPC)
preference reversals, 305–306
prefrontal cortex (PFC), 189, 425
primitive, 647
principal components analysis (PCA), 41, 41*f*
Principle of Maximally Efficient Learning,
    386
prior odds, 65
probabilistic model, 554–556, 555*f*, 573*f*
probability
    densities, 66
    matching, 382
    models of language learning, 492
    prior, 63
    theory, 63. *See also* Bayes' rule
problem solving, 61
process dissociation procedure, 400
Prodigy, learning mechanisms, 370*t*
production compilation, 379
product theories, 4
pronoun acquisition, 472
proof theory, 139–140
    argument theory, 146
    by contradiction, 142
    indirect, 142
proposal distribution, 88
prosopagnosia, 691
prospect theory, 303
prototype models, 270
PRP. *See* psychological refractory period (PRP)
    paradigm
PSS3, learning mechanism, 381*t*
psycholinguistics, computational models of,
    477–504. *See also* language
    computational frameworks, 478–482
        Chomsky and the symbolic tradition,
            478–480
        connectionist psycholinguistics, 480–481
        probabilistic models of language, 481–482
    future directions, 497–498
    language acquisition, 490–497
        computational models of language learning,
            492
        lexical semantics acquisition, 495–497,
            496*f*, 497*f*

        morphological structure acquisition,
            493–494
        stimulus, 491–492, 491*f*, 492–493
        syntactic categories acquisition, 494–495,
            496*f*
    overview, 477–478
    sentence processing, 488–490
        complexity judgment and reading time
            data, 488–489
        grammaticality ratings in aphasia, 489
        parse favoritism, 490
        plausibility and statistics, 489–490
        probabilistic approaches to sentence
            processing, 489
    from signal to word, 482–488, 483*f*
        acquired dyslexias, 486–487
        bottom-up connectionist models capture
            top-down effects, 484, 485*f*
        distributed representations, 484–486
        probabilistic approaches, 487–488
        psycholinguistic data capture, 487
        reading aloud, 486
        speech segmentation, 486
psychological refractory period (PRP) paradigm,
    441–442
Psychological Review, 362
psychologists, developmental, 12
psychology. *See also* cognitive science;
        developmental psychology,
        computational models of
    computational, 16–17
    experimental, 17
    faculty, 673
psychology of reasoning, 134–138
PSYCOP, 128
    modeling, 152–153

Radar-Soar, 536, 536*n*4
rank dependent utility (RDU), 304, 304*n*1
RASCALS robot, 161, 162*f*
RASHNL (Rapid Attention Shifts 'N' Learning
    model), 273, 288
rational analysis, 383–384
rational model of categorization, 234
    characteristics, 277*t*
ratio-template, 621–622, 621*f*
RBC. *See* recognition by components
    (RBC)
RDU. *See* rank dependent utility (RDU)
reach memory, 460
reaction time (RT), 398
reading
    aloud, 486
    models, 48–49
    sentence processing and, 488–489

reasoning, 131*n*3, 134–138
  causal, 333–334, 507–508
  challenges, 132
  computational cognitive modeling data from
        psychology of reasoning, 134–138
  correct, 130
  deductive. *See* deductive reasoning
  from graphs, 57*f*, 578–579
  inductive, 322–338
  mechanizing, 156–160, 157*f*, 159*f*
  modeling mental logic-based, mental
        models-based, and mental
        metalogic-based, 136–137
  models of inductive, 322–338
  procedures for using models, 345, 345*t*
  psychology of, 134–138
  sentential, 347–352, 347*t*, 349*t*, 351*t*
  simulations of human deductive reasoning,
        339–358
  spatial, using mental models, 343–347, 345*t*
recognition
  abstract models, 203–207
  learned high-level influences in early
        perception, 627–632, 627*f*, 628*f*,
        630*f*, 631*f*
  qualitative model, 618–626, 619*f*, 620*f*,
        621*f*
    first-order analysis, 622–623, 623*f*
    implementation issues, 623–624
    match metric, 622
    tests, 624–626, 624*f*, 625*f*
recognition by components (RBC), 617
REM. *See* Retrieving Efficiently from Memory
        (REM) model
  representative results, 204
Repair Theory, 373
RePast, 532
representation and algorithm level, 8, 8*t*
Rescorla-Wagner (RW) model, 590–592, 591*t*
resolution, 152
response mechanism, 313–314
response probability, 293–294
response time and choice as a function of time,
        294–296
retrieval mode, 194
retrieval rule, 457
retrieved-induced forgetting, 206
Retrieving Efficiently from Memory (REM)
        model, 2–3, 201, 207*n*7
  dual-process theories, 206–207
  interference and, 205–206
  recognition and recall, 203–207
  results, 204–205
rhythmic movement, 105
Rip's theory and system, 341, 342*t*, 343

robotics
  altricvial and precocial skills, 697–698
  cognitive science and, 672
  process model, 102
RT. *See* reaction time (RT)
rule composition, 379, 604
rule learning, 604
rule models, 270
RULEX moel, 270
Rumelhard model, 237–247, 238*f*, 239*n*1,
        240*f*, 243*f*, 246*f*
RW. *See* Rescorla-Wagner (RW) model

SAGE, 375, 455*t*
  learning mechanism, 377*t*
SAIM. *See* Selective Attention for Identification
        Model (SAIM)
SAM. *See* Search of Associative Memory (SAM)
        model
"sausage machine," 479
SCADS. *See* Strategy Choice and Discovery
        Simulation (SCADS)
schizophrenia, 436
science. *See* cognitive science
SCODEL model, 289
SD. *See* semantic dementia (SD)
SDCC. *See* sibling-descendant
        cascade-correlation (SDCC)
SDM model. *See* Sparse Distributed Memory
        (SDM)
  characteristics, 277*t*
Search of Associative Memory (SAM) model,
        201, 202–203
  interference and, 205–206
Selective Attention for Identification Model
        (SAIM), 427
selective feature weighting, 245
self, 518–519
semantic dementia (SD), 259
semantic memory, computational models of,
        226–266
  definition, 226–227
  distributed semantic models, 234–247
    context sensitivity, 245–247, 246*f*
    feature weighting and category coherence,
        239–245, 240*f*, 243*f*
    Hinton's distributed model, 234–237,
        235*f*
    Rumelhart model, 237–239, 238*f*
  hierarchies and prototypes, 227–234
    challenges for current theories, 231–233
      abstract concepts, 233
      category coherence, 231
      context sensitivity, 232
      feature selection, 232

representing multiple objects, relationships, and events, 233
prototype and similarity-based approaches, 229–231
neurocognitive models, 255–262
category-specific semantic impairment, 255–258, 257*f*
convergence model, 259–261
open issues, 262–263
overview, 226–227
temporal structure, events, and abstract concepts, 247–255
latent semantic analysis, 250–252
sentence Gestalt model, 252–255, 253*f*
simple recurrent networks, 247–250, 248*f*
semantics, 90, 91*f*, 132, 147. *See also* language
argument, 140, 162
consistency, 145
formal, 143–144
formula, 140
lexical acquisition, 47*f*, 495–497, 496*f*
meta-semantic competence, 698–699
relatedness measures, 580–581
relations between lexical items, 497, 497*f*
sense-think-act model, 695
sensory surfaces, cognition and, 101–102
sentence Gestalt model, 252–255
architecture, 253*f*
sentences. *See also* language
processing, 488–490
sentential reasoning, using mental models, 347–352, 347*t*, 349*t*, 351*t*
sequence learning (SL), 397–398
serial behavior, 182
serial reaction time (SRT), 398
shapes, 465, 466*f*
sibling-descendant cascade-correlation (SDCC), 453–454
Sierra model, 368
similarity effects, 324
simple recurrent network (SRN), 39–42, 41*f*, 211*n*8, 247–250, 248*f*, 402, 452
implicit learning and, 405–408, 405*f*, 407*f*, 408*f*, 409*f*, 412*f*
psycholinguistics and, 484, 485*f*
reading time data and, 488–489
SIS model, 522
skill acquisition, computational models of, 359–395
history, 361–363
improving beyond mastery, 376–380, 377*t*, 381*t*
optimization at the computational level, 378–379

optimization at the knowledge level, 376, 378
solutions from memory, 379–380, 381*t*
improving partially mastered skills, 369–376
learning at impasses, 372–373
negative feedback, 374–375
discrimination, 375
reduce strength, 374
specialization, 374–375
positive feedback and subgoal satisfaction, 369, 371–372
create a new rule, 371–372
generalize rules, 372
increase rule strength, 371
obstacles and paths to further progress, 384–388, 385*f*
overview, 359–360, 361*f*
skill practice, 363–369
interpretation of exhortations, 363–365
learning mechanisms, 369, 370*t*
reasons for abstract declarative knowledge, 365–366
study someone else's solution, 368–369
transfer prior knowledge, 366–368
analogy, 366–367
identity, 366
subsumption, 367–368
statistical structure of the environment, 380–384
SL. *See* sequence learning (SL)
Sloman model, 328–330
SME, learning mechanisms, 370*t*
SNPS, 128
Soar (States, Operators, And Reasoning), 5, 128, 150, 151*n*10, 373, 455*t*, 675
cognitive performance, 176*t*
learning, 176*t*
learning mechanisms, 370*t*, 377*t*, 381*t*
overview, 171–172
perceptual and motor systems, 176*t*
working memory capacity, 175, 176*t*, 177
social influence, 519–520
social interaction, cognitive science and, 676–678
social psychology, computational models in, 505–529
attitudes and attitude change, 512–515
causal learning, 506–507
causal reasoning, 507–508
dyadic interactions and, 518
dynamics of human mating strategies, 520–522
emotional coherence, 511
face perception, 511–512
group perception and stereotyping, 509–511

social psychology (*cont.*)
  impression formation, 508–509
  overview, 505–506
  the self, 518–519
  social influence, 519–520
Sparse Distributed Memory (SDM), 281
spatial reasoning, using mental models,
    343–347, 345*t*
SPEAK model, 523
speech, 486. *See also* language; psycholinguistics,
    computational models of
  segmentation, 486
spinal cord, organization of muscle synergies,
    645–647, 646*f*
spreading activation theories, 227, 229
SRN. *See* simple recurrent network (SRN)
SRT. *See* serial reaction time (SRT)
stationary distribution, 88
stereotyping, 509–511
stochastic neural networks, 30–31
Strategy Choice and Discovery Simulation
    (SCADS), 376, 379–380
  learning mechanism, 381*t*
String Theory, 14
STRIPS operator, 387
Stroop test model, 434–435, 434*f*, 436,
    437–438, 440
structure-function correspondences, 44, 49
structure in time, 38–43, 39*f*, 41*f*
suppositions, 142
SUSTAIN (Supervised and Unsupervised
    Stratified Adaptive Incremental
    Network), 267, 282–283, 288,
    291–292
  characteristics, 277*t*
SWALE project, 553–554
Swarm, 532
switch costs, 439
syllogisms, 130, 228
symbol level, 9
syntax, 38, 132. *See also* language
  artificial, 461–462, 462*t*
  categories acquisition, 494–495, 496*f*

TASA. *See* Touchstone Applied Science
    Associates (TASA) corpus
task switching, 439–440, 439*f*
tectonic model, 437
temperature, influence on networks, 30–31
temporal context memory, 190
temporal context model, 208–210, 210*f*
  in the brain, 210–213
  how TCM accounts for recall data, 209–210,
    210*f*
tensor product model (TPM), 511

theorems, 139*n*5
theory models, 271
Theory of Distributed Associated Memory
    (TODAM) model, 201
Theory of Visual Attention (TVA), 433
thinking
  dynamical systems, 103–109, 104*f*, 108*f*,
    120–121
  timing and, 117
Thorndike, Edward, 361
timing, dynamical thinking and, 117
TODAM. *See* Theory of Distributed Associated
    Memory (TODAM) model
toddlers. *See also* infants
  dynamical fields and, 115–116, 115*f*, 116*f*
top-down processing, 31. *See also* interactive
    activation model (IA)
TOTE-units (test, operate, test, exit), 668, 695
Touchstore Applied Science Associates (TASA)
    corpus, 90, 92, 92*f*
TPM. *See* tensor product model (TPM)
TRACE model, 31–43
  psycholinguistics and, 482–484, 483*f*
transduction, 161, 161*n*17
transition kernel, 88, 89*f*
truth tables, 144
  for exclusive disjunction, 347, 347*t*
tutoring systems, 13
TVA. *See* Theory of Visual Attention (TVA)
typicality effects, 324–325

UAV. *See* uninhabited air vehicle (UAV)
uncertainty orientation, 518
unconditioned stimulus (US), 589
UNICOM, 364
uniform, 66
uninhabited air vehicle (UAV), 566, 572
US. *See* unconditioned stimulus (US)
Usher and Cohen Localist Attractor Network,
    211

validities, 144
verbs. *See also* language
  learning the past tense of English verbs,
    34–38, 35*f*
Virtual Personality model, 517
visual attention, 423–433
  base model, 424–425, 424*f*
  biased competition model, 428–430, 429*f*
  explicit computation and representation of
    attention, 425–428, 426*f*
  interactive emergence of attention, 428–431,
    429*f*
  key issues in models of, 431–433, 432*f*
  stimulus-driven factors, 581, 581*f*

visual information processing, computational
modeling of, 612–634. *See also*
cognition
capabilities, 693
conceptualizing, 613
modeling early visual processing, 615–617,
616*f*
modeling recognition based on outputs of
early visual stages, 617–626
overview, 617–618
qualitative model of recognition, 618–626,
619*f*, 620*f*, 621*f*
first-order analysis, 622–623, 623*f*
implementation issues, 623–624
match metric, 622
tests, 624–626, 624*f*, 625*f*
modeling the influence of recognition on early
vision, 626–632
learned high-level influences in early
perception, 627–632, 627*f*, 628*f*,
630*f*, 631*f*
overview, 626
overview, 612–615, 615*f*
three-dimensional objects, 619–622, 619*f*,
620*f*, 621*f*

WADD. *See* weighted additive (WADD)
rule
Watson, J. B., 361

Watson Selection Task, 135
Web sites, 576, 579–582, 581*f*
for computational cognitive modeling, 5
weight contract enhancement, 218
weighted additive (WADD) rule, 308, 317
Weiner, Norbert, 361–362
"Wickelfeature" representation, 35*f*
willingness to accept (WTA), 306
willingness to pay (WTP), 306
Winners-Take-All inhibition (WTA), 216,
427
word recognition, 31, 90, 91*f*, 464–468, 466*f*.
See also interactive activation model
(IA); language
clusters, 496*f*
deictic words, 466
letter strings, 32–33
pronoun acquisition, 472
from signal to word, 482–488, 483*f*
WRM model
characteristics, 277*t*
WTA. *See* willingness to accept (WTA);
Winners-Take-All inhibition (WTA)
WTP. *See* willingness to pay (WTP)

X-outcome associations, 599–600
X system, 368, 373

zero rule, 457

Printed in Great Britain
by Amazon.co.uk, Ltd.,
Marston Gate.